ESSAYS IN HONOR OF BERNARD LEWIS

THE ISLAMIC WORLD

From Classical to Modern Times

C. E. Bosworth, Charles Issawi,
Roger Savory, and A. L. Udovitch,
Editors

THE DARWIN PRESS, INC.
PRINCETON, NEW JERSEY

Library of Congress Cataloging in Publication Data
The Islamic world from classical to modern times.

"Bibliography of Bernard Lewis' works": p. xiii
1. Middle East. 2. Civilization, Islamic.
3. Lewis, Bernard—bibliography. I. Bosworth, Clifford Edmund.
II. Lewis, Bernard.
DS42.4.I82 1988 909'.097671 88–30034
ISBN 0–87850–066–9

The paper in this book is acid-free neutral pH stock and meets the guidelines for permanence and durability of the Committee on Production Guidelines for Book Longevity of the Council on Library Resources.

∞

Third Printing, 1991

Printed in the United States of America

CONTENTS

CONTRIBUTORS

(and affiliation at the time article was written)

THE CLASSICAL AND MEDIEVAL ISLAMIC WORLD

SYED BARAKAT AHMAD
Former Ambassador of India

HANEDA AKIRA
University of Kyoto

MOHAMMED ARKOUN
Université de la Sorbonne Nouvelle, Paris

WILLIAM M. BRINNER
University of California, Berkeley

JOHN BURTON-PAGE
School of Oriental and African Studies

CLAUDE CAHEN
Académie des Belles Lettres

PATRICIA CRONE
The University of Oxford

E. VAN DONZEL
The Netherlands Institute for the Near East, Leiden

ANDREW S. EHRENKREUTZ
University of Michigan

G. R. HAWTING
School of Oriental and African Studies, University of London

P. M. HOLT
School of Oriental and African Studies, University of London

R. STEPHEN HUMPHREYS
University of Wisconsin

A. K. S. LAMBTON
School of Oriental and African Studies, University of London

GEORGE MAKDISI
University of Pennsylvania

FEDWA MALTI-DOUGLAS
University of Texas, Austin

ANDRÉ MIQUEL
Collège de France

F. OMAR
University of Baghdad

HERBERT H. PAPER
Hebrew Union College

CHARLES PELLAT
Université de Paris, Sorbonne

HASSANEIN RABIE
University of Cairo

FRANZ ROSENTHAL
Yale University

KAMAL SALIBI
American University of Beirut

PAULA SANDERS
Rice University

IRFAN SHAHÎD
Georgetown University

DENIS SINOR
Indiana University

A.L. UDOVITCH
Princeton University

G. M. WICKENS
University of Toronto

OTTOMAN STUDIES

NURHAN ATASOY
Istanbul University

DAVID AYALON
The Hebrew University of Jerusalem

ELEAZAR BIRNBAUM
University of Toronto

C. E. BOSWORTH
The University of Manchester

AMNON COHEN
The Hebrew University of Jerusalem

CARTER VAUGHN FINDLEY
Ohio State University

HALIL INALCIK
The University of Chicago

KEMAL H. KARPAT
University of Wisconsin

G. M. MEREDITH-OWENS
University of Toronto

MYRIAM ROSEN-AYALON
The Hebrew University of Jerusalem

ANDREAS TIETZE
Institut für Orientalistik der Universität Wien

JOHN R. WALSH
University of Edinburgh

THE MODERN MIDDLE EAST

GEORGES C. ANAWATI
Institut Dominicain D'Études Orientales, Cairo

BENJAMIN BRAUDE
Boston College

MICHAEL COOK
Princeton University

J. B. KELLY
London, England

C. MAX KORTEPETER
New York University

MARTIN KRAMER
University of Tel-Aviv

DANKWART A. RUSTOW
City University of New York

ITAMAR RABINOVICH
University of Tel-Aviv

ROGER M. SAVORY
Trinity College, Toronto

NORMAN A. STILLMAN
State University of New York at Binghamton

YEDIDA K. STILLMAN
State University of New York at Binghamton

C. A. O. van NIEUWEN-HUIJZE
Institute of Social Studies, The Hague

P. J. VATIKIOTIS
School of Oriental and African Studies, University of London

M. E. YAPP
School of Oriental and African Studies, University of London

INTRODUCTION

Adapting Johnson's eulogy of Goldsmith, one can say that there is no period of Middle Eastern history that Bernard Lewis has not touched, and none he touched that he has not adorned. And covering all those periods have been two enterprises on which he has been engaged for most of his active life. First, the editorship of *The Encyclopaedia of Islam*: he has been on it from its early days, in the 1950s, and has been one of the most active and versatile members of the Board. Second, his teaching: in the course of more than four decades in Britain and in this country he has guided hundreds of students, from dozens of countries, representing the widest varieties of ethnic and religious backgrounds. Some of them, as well as many colleagues and friends, are represented in this collection of essays written in his honor. Many others have testified to the help he gave them, the interest he took in their work, and the soundness with which he directed their research.

Bernard Lewis was born in London, on 31 May 1916. He was educated at the University of London, obtaining a BA in History (First Class Honours) in 1936 and a Ph.D. in 1939: in the interim, he spent a year at the University of Paris, where he was granted a Diplôme des Études Sémitiques, in 1937. He also traveled in the Middle East on a Research Fellowship. He was appointed an Assistant Lecturer in Islamic History at the School of Oriental and African Studies in 1938 and promoted to Lecturer in 1940. The War interrupted his academic career—he served in the British Army but spent most of the war years, as he euphemistically states, "attached to a Department of the Foreign Office"; it called on his already considerable linguistic ability and powers of analysis, and took him to the Middle East, where he deepened his knowledge of the area and became aware of its current problems.

As soon as the War was over, he returned to SOAS and speedily rose to become Professor of the History of the Near and Middle East in 1949, at the exceptionally early age of thirty-three. On leave from London, he was a Visiting Professor at Columbia University, Indiana University, Princeton University, and the University of California at Los Angeles and spent a year as a Visiting Member at the Institute for Advanced Study, Princeton. In 1974 he left London for Princeton University, serving as Cleveland E. Dodge Professor of Near Eastern

Studies until his retirement in 1986. Concurrently, he was a long-term member of the Institute for Advanced Study at Princeton.

Bernard Lewis' work has received widespread recognition. He was elected a Fellow of the British Academy in 1963, a Corresponding Member of the Institut d'Égypte in 1969, an Honorary Member of the Turkish Historical Society in 1972, a Member of the American Philosophical Society in 1973, a Fellow of University College, London in 1976, a Member of the American Academy of Arts and Sciences in 1983, an Honorary Fellow of the School of Asiatic and African Studies in London and an Honorary Member of the Société Asiatique in Paris. He was awarded a Citation of Honor by the Turkish Ministry of Culture in 1973. He was awarded Honorary Doctorates by the Hebrew University of Jerusalem, Tel-Aviv University, The State University of New York, Binghamton, The University of Pennsylvania, and Hebrew Union College, Cincinnati. In 1978 he obtained the Harvey Prize. He has been active in several learned societies in Britain, the United States, and elsewhere. At the moment, he is a Member of the Board of Governors of the Institute for Turkish Studies and serves on the Editorial Board of *The American Scholar* and as Director of the Annenberg Research Institute in Philadelphia.

The attached bibliography bears witness to the depth of his knowledge, his far-ranging erudition, the scope of his interests, and the fertility of his pen. However, one has to read extensively in it in order to appreciate Lewis' outstanding qualities—the exceptionally wide range of his languages, his great knowledge of so many aspects of Middle Eastern history and culture, his capacity for apprehending the essence of a problem and understanding the interrelationships of its parts, and the felicity of his terse, subtle, and precise style. It is these qualities that make him the outstanding historian of the region.

Charles Issawi

BIBLIOGRAPHY OF BERNARD LEWIS' WORKS

BOOKS

The Origins of Ismailism. Cambridge: W. Heffer & Sons, 1940; reprinted New York: AMS Press, 1975.

British Contributions to Arabic Studies. London: Longmans, Green & Co., 1941.

A Handbook of Diplomatic and Political Arabic. London: Luzac & Co., 1947; reprinted 1956.

The Arabs in History. London: Hutchinson & Co., 1950; reprinted 1954, 1956. 2d ed. 1958; reprinted 1960, 1962. 3d ed. 1964. 4th ed. 1966; reprinted 1968. 5th ed. 1970; reprinted New York: Harper & Row, 1975.

Notes and Documents from the Turkish Archives. Jerusalem: Israel Oriental Society, 1952.

The Emergence of Modern Turkey. London and New York: Oxford University Press, 1961. Revised ed. 1968; reprinted 1969, 1987.

The Kingly Crown (translation of Solomon Ibn Gabirol). London, Vallentine, Mitchell, 1961.

[Coauthored with others.] *Constantine Porphyrogenitus, De administrando imperio*, volume 2: *Commentary*. London: Athlone Press, 1962.

[Coeditor with P. M. Holt.] *Historians of the Middle East*. London and New York: Oxford University Press, 1962; reprinted 1972.

Istanbul and the Civilization of the Ottoman Empire. Norman: University of Oklahoma Press, 1963; reprinted 1968, 1972.

The Middle East and the West. Bloomington: Indiana University Press, and London: Weidenfeld & Nicolson, 1964; reprinted (paperback) New York: Harper & Row, 1966, 1968.

The Assassins: A Radical Sect in Islam. London: Weidenfeld & Nicolson, 1967. New York: Basic Books, 1968; reprinted 1972, 1980. New York: Oxford University Press, 1987.

[Coeditor with others.] *The Cambridge History of Islam*. 2 vols. in 4. Cambridge: Cambridge University Press, 1970.

Race and Color in Islam. New York: Harper & Row, 1971; reprinted New York: Octagon Books, 1979. Expanded version in progress.

Islam in History. London: Alcove Press, 1973.

Islam from the Prophet Muhammad to the Capture of Constantinople. 2 vols. New York: Walker, 1974; reprinted (paperback) New York: Harper & Row, 1974; Oxford University Press, 1987.

History—Remembered, Recovered, Invented. Princeton: Princeton University Press, 1975; reprinted New York: Simon & Schuster, 1987.

[Editor.] *The World of Islam: Faith, People, Culture.* London: Thames & Hudson, 1976. Simultaneously published in the United States as *Islam and the Arab World.* New York: Knopf, 1976.

Studies in Classical and Ottoman Islam, 7th–16th Centuries. London: Variorum Reprints, 1976.

[Coauthor with Amnon Cohen.] *Population and Revenue in the Towns of Palestine in the Sixteenth Century.* Princeton: Princeton University Press, 1978.

The Muslim Discovery of Europe. New York: W. W. Norton, 1982; reprinted (paperback) 1985, 1988.

Introduction and additional notes to Ignaz Goldziher, *Introduction to Islamic Theology and Law,* translated by Andras Hamori and Ruth Hamori. Princeton: Princeton University Press, 1981.

[Coeditor with Benjamin Braude.] *Christians and Jews in the Ottoman Empire.* 2 vols. New York: Holmes & Meier Publications, 1982.

The Jews of Islam. Princeton: Princeton University Press, 1984; reprinted (paperback) 1987.

Le Retour de l'Islam. Paris: Gallimard, 1985.

[Coeditor with Edmund Leites and Margaret Case.] *As Others See Us: Mutual Perceptions East and West.* New York: International Society for the Comparative Study of Civilizations, 1985 (= *Comparative Civilizations Review* 13 [Autumn 1985] and 14 [Spring 1986]).

Semites and Anti-Semites. New York: W. W. Norton, 1986; reprinted (paperback) 1987.

The Political Language of Islam. Chicago: University of Chicago Press, 1988.

BOOKS in TRANSLATION

ARABIC

The Arabs in History. Beirut: Dar al-Ilm li'l-Malayin, 1954; later reprints.

The Assassins. Beirut and Damascus: Dar al-Fikr, 1971. A second translation Cairo: Madbouli, 1986.

British Contributions to Arabic Studies. N.p., n.d.

Istanbul and the Civilization of the Ottoman Empire. Benghazi and Beirut: Benghazi University Press, 1974; reprinted Al-Dar al-Su'udiyya li'l-Nashr, 1982.

The Middle East and the West. N.p.: Muslim Brothers, n.d.

The Origins of Ismailism. Baghdad: Muthanna, 1947.

DUTCH

The World of Islam. Antwerp: Fonds Mercator, 1976.

FRENCH

The Arabs in History. Brussels: Office de Publicité and Neuchâtel: La Baconnière, 1958.

The Assassins. Paris: Berger Levrault, 1982; reprinted Brussels: Éditions Complexe, 1984.

The Jews of Islam. Paris: Calmann Lévy, 1986.

The Muslim Discovery of Europe. Paris: La Découverte, 1984.

Race and Color in Islam (expanded version). Paris: Payot, 1982.

Semites and Anti-Semites. Paris: Fayard, 1987.

The World of Islam. Antwerp: Fonds Mercator, 1976; reprinted Paris: Bordas, 1981.

GERMAN

Islam from the Prophet Muhammad to the Capture of Constantinople. Zurich and Munich: Artemis, 1981.

The Jews of Islam. Munich: Beck, 1987.

The Muslim Discovery of Europe. Berlin: Propyläen-Ullstein Verlag, 1983.

Semites and Anti-Semites. Berlin: Ullstein Verlag, 1987.

The World of Islam. Brunswick: Georg Westermann Verlag, 1976.

GREEK

The Middle East and the West. Athens: Papazini, 1970.

HEBREW

The Arabs in History. Tel Aviv: Ketavim, 1955.

The Emergence of Modern Turkey. Jerusalem: Magnes Press, 1976.

Islam in History. Tel Aviv: Zmora Bitan, 1973.

The Middle East and the West. Tel Aviv: Maarakhot (Israel Ministry of Defense), 1970.

Semites and Anti-Semites. (in progress)

HUNGARIAN

Istanbul and the Civilization of the Ottoman Empire. Budapest: Gondolat Konyviado, 1981.

ITALIAN

The Muslim Discovery of Europe. Milan: Mondadori, 1983.

Race and Color in Islam. Milan: Longanesi, 1975.

JAPANESE

The Arabs in History. Tokyo: Misuzu Shoboh Co., 1967.

The Assassins. Tokyo: Shinsen-sha Co., 1973.

MALAY

The Arabs in History. Kuala Lumpur: Dewan Bahasa Dan Pustaka, Kementerian Pelajaran Malaysia, 1977.

PERSIAN

The Assassins. Tehran: Bunyad-i Farhang-i Iran, 1970; reprinted Tehran: Intisharat-i Tus, 1983.

Istanbul and the Civilization of the Ottoman Empire. Tehran: B.T.N.K., 1971; reprinted Tehran: Shirkat-i Intisharat-i Elmi ve Farhangi, 1986.

The Origins of Ismailism. Tehran: Intisharat-i Tus, 1983.

POLISH

The Emergence of Modern Turkey. Warsaw: Panstowowe Wydawnictwo Naukowe, 1972.

PORTUGUESE

The Arabs in History. Lisbon: Editorial Estampa, 1982.

SERBO-CROAT

The Arabs in History. Zagreb: IIK, 1956.

The World of Islam. Belgrade: Jugoslovenska Revija Vuk Karadzic, 1979.

SPANISH

The Arabs in History. Madrid: Espasa-Calpe, 1956.

History—Remembered, Recovered, Invented. Mexico City: Fondo de Cultura Economica, Mexico, 1979.

TURKISH

The Arabs in History. Istanbul: Istanbul University, Faculty of Arts Press, 1979.

The Emergence of Modern Turkey. Ankara: Turk Tarik Kurumu, 1970; reprinted 1984.

Istanbul and the Civilization of the Ottoman Empire. Istanbul: Varlik, 1975.

URDU

British Contributions to Arabic Studies. New Delhi: Government of India, Information Department, n.d.

TRANSLATIONS of POETRY

TURKISH

Encounter 38.3 (March 1972): 31.

Literature East and West 7.1 (March 1973): 26–28, 58–60 (= *Modern Turkish Literature*, edited by Talat Sait Halman [Austin, Tex.: Jenkins Publishing Company, 1973]).

Edebiyat: A Journal of Middle Eastern Literature 1 (1976): 151–52.

The Penguin Book of Turkish Verse, edited by Nermin Menemencioglu and Fahir Iz, pp. 176, 181–82, 188, 192, 194, 217, 222–23, 261–64. Harmondsworth: Penguin, 1978.

The Worlds of Muslim Imagination, edited by Alamgir Hashmi, pp. 139–45. Islamabad: Gulmohar, 1986.

ARABIC

TR, edited by Abdullah al-Udhari, 1 (1974): 52–53; 2 (1975): 46–47; 3 (1976): 71.

ARTICLES

"The Islamic Guilds." *Economic History Review* 8 (1937): 20–37.

"An Isma'ili Interpretation of the Fall of Adam." *Bulletin of the School of Oriental and African Studies* (hereafter *BSOAS*) 4 (1938): 179–84.

"An Arabic Account of a Byzantine Palace Revolution." *Byzantion* 14 (1939): 383–86.

"A Jewish Source on Damascus just After the Ottoman Conquest." *BSOAS* 10 (1939): 179–84.

"Jewish Science According to an Arabic Author of the Eleventh Century." *Sinai* 4 (1940): 25–29.

"An Epistle on Manual Crafts." *Islamic Culture* 17 (1943): 142–51.

"Arabic Sources on Maimonides." In *Metsuda*, edited by S. Rawidowicz, vol. 3/4, pp. 171–80. London: Ararat Publishing Society, 1945.

"Some Modern Turkish Poems." *Islamic Culture* 20 (1946): 41–48.

"Isma'ili Notes." *BSOAS* 12 (1948): 597–600.

"Specimens of Modern Turkish Poetry." In *Islamic Research Association Miscellany* (Bombay) 1 (1948): 87–91.

"An Apocalyptic Vision of Islamic History." *BSOAS* 13 (1950): 308–38.

"The Legend of the Jewish Origin of the Fatimid Caliphs." *Melilah* 3–4 (1950): 185–87.

"The Danish East India and Asiatic Company Records in the State Archives (Rigsarkiv) in Copenhagen." *Indian Archives* (New Delhi) 5 (1951): 138–40.

"The Near and Middle East." In *Handbook of Oriental History*, edited by C. H. Philips. London: Offices of the Royal Historical Society, 1951.

"The Ottoman Archives as a Source for the History of the Arab Lands." *Journal of the Royal Asiatic Society* (1951): 139–55.

"Recent Developments in Turkey." *International Affairs* 27 (1951): 320–31.

"The Impact of the French Revolution on Turkey." *Journal of World History* 1 (1952): 105–25. Revised version in *The New Asia: Readings in the History of Mankind*, edited by G. S. Métraux and F. Crouzet, 31–59. New York: New American Library, 1965.

"Islamic Revival in Turkey." *International Affairs* 18 (1952): 38–48.

"Population and Revenue in Palestine in the Sixteenth Century, According to Turkish Documents." *Jerusalem* 4 (1952): 133–37.

"The Privilege Granted by Mehmed II to His Physician." *BSOAS* 14 (1952): 550–63.

"Saladin and the Assassins." *BSOAS* 15 (1952): 239–45.

"Some Observations on the Significance of Heresy in the History of Islam." *Studia Islamica* 1 (1952): 43–63.

"The Sources for the History of the Syrian Assassins." *Speculum* 17 (1952): 475–89.

"An Arabic Account of the Province of Safed." *BSOAS* 11 (1953): 477–88.

"Europe and the Turks" (trans. Turkish). *History To-Day* (October 1953): 673–80.

"The Fatimids and the Route to India" (trans. Turkish). *Review of the Faculty of Economics* (Istanbul) 11 (1950–53): 1–5.

"History Writing and National Revival in Turkey." *Middle Eastern Affairs* 4 (1953): 218–27.

"Izlanda'da Turkler." *Turkiyat Mecmuasi* 10 (1953): 277–84.

"Three Biographies from Kamal ad-Din." In *Mélanges Fuad Köprülü*, 325–44. Istanbul: Osman Yalçın Matbaası, 1953.

"Ägypten von der Eroberung durch die Araber bis zur Besetzung durch die Osmanen." In *Handbuch der Weltgeschichte*, edited by A. Randa, vol. 1, pp. 1011–16. Olten: Walter, 1954.

"Communism and Islam." *International Affairs* 30 (1954): 1–12.

"Early Educational Reforms by Middle Eastern Government." *Yearbook of Education* (1954): 446–51.

"Islam." In *Orientalism and History*, edited by D. Sinor, 16–33. Cambridge: Cambridge University Press, 1954; reprinted Bloomington: Indiana University Press, 1970.

"Nationalism and Patriotism in the Middle East." *World Affairs Interpreter* (1954): 208–12.

"Studies in the Ottoman Archives I" (trans. Hebrew). *BSOAS* 16 (1954): 469–501.

"The Concept of an Islamic Republic." *Die Welt des Islam* n.s. 4 (1955): 1–9.

"Constantinople and the Arabs" (trans. Turkish). In *The Fall of Constantinople: A Symposium*, 12–17. London: London University School of Oriental and African Studies, 1955.

"Democracy in the Middle East." *Middle Eastern Affairs* 6 (1955): 101–8.

"An Historical Document in the Responsa of R. Samuel de Medina." *Melilah* 5 (1955): 169–76.

"The Isma'ilites and the Assassins." In *A History of the Crusades*, general editor K. M. Setton, vol. 1: *The First Hundred Years*, edited by M. W. Baldwin, 98–132. Philadelphia: University of Pennsylvania Press, 1955. 2d ed. Madison: University of Wisconsin Press, 1969.

"Jerusalem in the XVIth Century." *Jerusalem* 5 (1955): 117–27.

"A Note on Some Danish Material in the Turkish Archives in Istanbul." *Acta Orientalia* 22 (1955): 75–76.

"Some Danish–Tatar Exchanges in the 17th Century." In *Symbolae in honorem Z. V. Togan*, 137–46. Istanbul: Maarif Press, 1955.

"The Middle Eastern Reaction to Soviet Pressures." *Middle East Journal* 10 (1956): 125–37.

"Turkey: Westernization." In *Unity and Variety in Muslim Civilization*, edited by G. E. von Grunebaum, 311–31. Chicago: University of Chicago Press, 1956.

"A Karaite Itinerary Through Turkey in 1641–42." *Vakiflar Dergisi* (Ankara) 3 (1957): 97–106 and 315–25.

"The Muslim Discovery of Europe." *BSOAS* 20 (1957): 409–16.

"The Ottoman Archives, a Source for European History." In *Supplement to Research Bibliography*. Middle East Institute, Washington, D.C.

"Der Islam im Osten: Vorderasien, Ägypten, Balkan." In *Historia mundi*, edited by Fritz Valjavec *et al.*, vol. 6, pp. 474–510. Bern: Francke, 1958.

"The Islamic Middle East." In *Democratic Institutions in the World Today*, edited by W. Burmeister, 45–61. London: Stevens, 1958.

"An Islamic Mosque." In *Temples and Faiths*, edited by Arthur Walter James, 47–50. London: Skeffington, 1958.

"The Middle East in World Affairs." In *Tensions in the Middle East*, edited by P. W. Thayer, 50–60. Baltimore: The Johns Hopkins University Press, 1958.

"On Writing the Modern History of the Middle East." *Middle East Forum* (Beirut) (June 1958): 15–17.

"The Mughals and the Ottomans." *Pakistan Quarterly* (Summer 1958): 4–9.

"Some Reflections on the Decline of the Ottoman Empire." *Studia Islamica* 9 (1958): 111–27.

"Men, Women and Traditions in Turkey." *The Geographical Magazine* (December 1959): 346–54.

"Ibn Dihya's Account of the Embassy of al-Ghazal." In *The Poet and the Spae-wife*, edited by W. E. D. Allen, 19–25. Dublin: A. Figgis, 1960.

"Mas'udi on the Kings of the Franks." In *Al-Mas'udi Millenary Commemoration Volume*, 7–10. Aligarh: Indian Society for the History of Science and the Institute of Islamic Studies, Aligarh Muslim University, 1960.

"The Near and Middle East and North Africa." In *The New Cambridge*

Modern History, vol. 12, pp. 207–12. Cambridge: Cambridge University Press, 1960.

"The Ottoman Archives, a Source for European History." *Archives* 4 (1960): 226–30.

"The Political Ideas of the Young Ottomans." In *International Islamic Colloquium Papers, December 29, 1957–January 8, 1958*, 97–99. Lahore: Panjab University Press, 1960.

"The Invading Crescent" (trans. Swedish). In *The Dawn of African History*, edited by R. A. Oliver, 30–36. Oxford: Oxford University Press, 1961.

"Approaches to Islamic History in Europe and America." In *Colloque sur la sociologie musulmane, 11–14 septembre 1961: Correspondance d'Orient* 5 (Brussels, 1962): 103–17.

Contribution to Constantine Porphyrogenitus, *De administrando imperio*, vol. 2: *Commentary*, edited by R. J. H. Jenkins. London: University of London, Athlone Press, 1962.

"Islam Devlet Muessese ve telakkileri üzerinde bozkir ahalisinin tesiri." *Review of the Institute of Islamic Studies* (Istanbul) 2 (1962): 209–30.

"Ottoman Observers of Ottoman Decline." *Islamic Studies* (Karachi) 1 (1962): 71–87.

"Quelques Thèmes andalous de la littérature turque au xixe siècle." In *Études d'orientalisme dédiées à la mémoire de Lévi-Provençal*, 185–90. Paris: Maisonneuve et Larose, 1962.

"The Use by Muslim Historians of Non-Muslim Sources." In *Historians of the Middle East*, edited by Bernard Lewis and P. M. Holt, 180–91. London and New York: Oxford University Press, 1962.

"Maimonides, Lionheart, and Saladin." *Eretz-Israel* (Jerusalem) 7 (*L. A. Mayer Memorial Volume*) (1963): 70–75.

"Registers on Iran and Adharbayjan in the Ottoman *Defter-i Khaqani*. In *Mélanges Massé*, 259–63. Tehran: Tehran University Press, 1963.

"Islah al-anzima al-baladiyya fi 'ahd al-imbaraturiyya al-'uthmaniyya." In *Takhtit al-mudun fi'l-'alam al-'arabi*, 99–108. Cairo: Egyptian Society of Engineers and Congress for Cultural Freedom, 1964.

"Orta Şarkin Tarihi Huviyeti." *Ankara Universitesi Ilahiyat Fakültesi Dergisi* 7 (1964): 75–81.

"Problems as the Outcome of Changing Social Values in Developing Countries." In *Social Aspects of Economic Development*, 109–24. Istanbul: Economic and Social Studies Conference Board, 1964.

"Nazareth in the Sixteenth Century According to the Ottoman Tapu Registers." In *Arabic and Islamic Studies in Honor of Hamilton A. R. Gibb*, edited by George Makdisi, 416–23. Cambridge, Mass.: Harvard University Press, 1965.

"The Ottoman Empire in the Mid-nineteenth Century: A Review." *Middle Eastern Studies* 1 (1965): 283–95.

[Coauthored with S. M. Stern.] "Arabic Dawn Poetry." In *Eos*, edited by A. T. Hatto, 215–43. The Hague: Mouton, 1965.

"Government, Society and Economic Life Under the Abbasids and Fatimids." In *The Cambridge Medieval History* (new edition), vol. 4, pp. 638–61. Cambridge: Cambridge University Press, 1966.

"Kamal al-Din's Biography of Raşid al-Din Sinan." *Arabica* 13 (1966): 225–67.

"Turkey." In *Dustūr: A Survey of the Constitutions of the Arab and Muslim States*, 6–24. Leiden: Brill, 1966.

"Paltiel: A Note." *BSOAS* 30 (1967): 177–81.

"The Sources for the History of Iran." *Rahnema-ye Ketab* (1967): 228–32.

"The Consequences of Defeat." *Foreign Affairs* (1968): 321–35.

"Friends and Enemies: Reflections After a War." *Encounter* (February 1968): 3–7.

"Jaffa in the Sixteenth Century, According to the Ottoman Tahrir Registers." In *Necati Lugal Armağanı*, 435–45. Ankara: Türk Tarih Kurumu Basımevi, 1968.

"The Mongols, the Turks and the Muslim Polity." *Transactions of the Royal Historical Society* 5th ser. 18 (1968): 49–68.

"The Pro-Islamic Jews." *Judaism* (New York) 17 (1968): 391–404.

"The Regnal Titles of the First Abbasid Caliphs." In *Dr. Zakir Husain Presentatiaon Volume*, 13–22. New Delhi: Maktaba Jamia, 1968.

"Some English Travellers in the East." *Middle Eastern Studies* 4 (1968): 296–315.

"The Great Powers, the Arabs and the Israelis." *Foreign Affairs* (1969): 642–52.

"Joseph Schacht." *BSOAS* 33 (1970): 378–81.

"On the Revolutions in Early Islam." *Studia Islamica* 32 (1970): 215–331.

"Race and Colour in Islam" (trans. Spanish). *Encounter* 35 (1970): 18–36.

"Russia in the Middle East." *The Round Table* (1970): 257–63.

"Sources for the Economic History of the Middle East." In *Studies in the Economic History of the Middle East from the Rise of Islam to the Present Day*, edited by M. A. Cook, 78–92. London and New York: Oxford University Press, 1970.

"Assassins of Syria and Isma'ilis of Persia." In *La Persia nel Medioevo*, 573–80. Rome: Accademia nazionale dei Lincei, 1971.

"The Contribution to Islam." In *The Legacy of Egypt*, edited by J. R. Harris (2d ed.), 456–77. Oxford: Clarendon Press, 1971.

"Semites and Anti-Semites." *Survey* (2) 79 (1971): 169–84.

"An Interpretation of Fatimid History." In *Colloque international sur l'histoire du Caire*, 287–97. Cairo: Ministère de la Culture, 1972.

"Islamic Concepts of Revolution." In *Revolution in the Middle East*, edited by P. J. Vatikiotis, 30–40. Totowa, N.J.: Rowman and Littlefield, 1972.

"The Study of Islam." *Encounter* (1972): 31–41.

"Corsairs in Iceland." *Revue de l'Occident musulman et de la Méditerranée* (1973): 139–44.

"Ali Pasha on Nationalism." *Middle Eastern Studies* 10 (January 1974): 77–79.

"Fatimids." *Encyclopaedia Britannica*, 15th ed. (1974), vol. 7, pp. 193–94.

"On Some Modern Arabic Political Terms." In *Orientalia hispanica*, edited by J. M. Barral, vol. 1: *Arabica–Islamica*, 465–71. Leiden: Brill, 1974.

"On That Day, a Jewish Apocalyptic Poem on the Arab Conquests." In *Mélanges d'islamologie, volume dédié à la mémoire d'Armand Abel*, edited by Pierre Salmon, 197–200. Leiden: Brill, 1974.

"Politics and War (in Islam)" (trans. German). In *The Legacy of Islam*, edited by Joseph Schacht and C. E. Bosworth, 156–208. 2d ed. Oxford: Oxford University Press, 1974.

"An Anti-Jewish Ode: The *Qasida* of Abu Ishaq Against Joseph Ibn Nagrella." In *Salo Wittmayer Baron Jubilee Volume*, 657–68. Jerusalem: American Academy for Jewish Research, 1975.

"The Palestinians and the PLO" (trans. Dutch, Hebrew, Portuguese). *Commentary* 59 (January 1975): 32–48.

"The African Diaspora and the Civilization of Islam." In *The African Diaspora: Interpretive Essays*, edited by M. L. Kilson and Robert I. Rotberg. Cambridge, Mass.: Harvard University Press, 1976.

"The Anti-Zionist Resolution." *Foreign Affairs* 55 (October 1976): 54–64.

"Cold War and Detente in the 16th Century." *Survey* 3/4 (100/101) (Summer/Autumn 1976): 95–96.

"Gibbon on Muhammad" (trans. Italian and Spanish). *Daedalus* 105 (Summer 1976): 89–101.

"Return of Islam" (trans. French and Spanish). *Commentary* 62 (January 1976): 39–49.

"Right and Left in Lebanon." *The New Republic* 177 (10 September 1977): 20–23.

"Settling the Arab-Israeli Conflict." *Commentary* 63 (June 1977): 50–56.

"The Egyptian Perspective." *Commentary* 66 (July 1978): 37–45.

"Turkey." *The Washington Review* 1 (January 1978): 103–6.

"Turkey: A Loyal United States and NATO Ally." In *NATO, Turkey and United States Interests*, 22–27. Washington, D.C.: American Foreign Policy Institute, 1978.

"Turkey Turns Away." *The New Republic* 178 (18 February 1978): 18–21.

"Ottoman Land Tenure and Taxation in Syria." *Studia Islamica* 50 (1979): 109–24.

"The State of Middle Eastern Studies." *The American Scholar* 48 (Summer 1979): 365–81.

"Acre in the Sixteenth Century According to the Ottoman Tapu Registers." In *Bibliothèque de l'Institut français d'études anatoliennes d'Istanbul* (Paris) 28 (*Memorial Omer Lutfi Barkan*) (1980): 135–39.

"The Bases of Political Power and Perceptions in the Middle East." In

The Political Economy of the Middle East: 1973–78, a Compendium of Papers Submitted to the Joint Economic Committee Congress of the United States, 503–20. Washington, D.C.: Government Printing Office, 21 April 1980.

"L'Islam et les non-musulmans." *Annales: Économies, Sociétés, Civilisations* 35 (May–August 1980): 784–800.

"The Ottoman Empire and Its Aftermath." *Journal of Contemporary History* 15 (1980): 27–36.

"Palestine: On the History and Geography of a Name" (trans. French and Hebrew). *International History Review* 11 (January 1980): 1–12.

"Slade on Turkey." In *Turkiye'nin Sosyal ve Ekonomik Tarihi (1071–1920): Social and Economic History of Turkey (1071–1920)*, edited by Osman Okyar and Halil Inalcik, 215–26. Ankara: Meteksan Sirketi, 1980.

"Some Statistical Surveys of 16th Century Palestine." In *Middle East Studies and Libraries: A Felicitation Volume for Professor J. D. Pearson*, edited by B. C. Bloomfield, 115–22. London: Mansell, 1980.

"Translation from Arabic." *Proceedings of the American Philosophical Society* 124 (February 1980): 41–47.

"The United States, Turkey and Iran" (trans. Hebrew). In *The Middle East and the United States: Perceptions and Policies*, edited by Haim Shaked and Itamar Rabinovitch, 165–80. New Brunswick, N.J.: Transaction Books, 1980.

"Assassins." *Dictionary of the Middle Ages*, vol. 1, pp. 589–93. New York: Charles Scribner's Sons, 1981.

"A Letter from Little Menahem." In *Studies in Judaism and Islam in Honor of Professor S. D. Goitein's 80th Birthday*, 181–84. Jerusalem: Magnes Press, 1981.

"Loyalties to Community, Nation and State" (trans. Turkish). In *Middle East Perspectives: The Next Twenty Years*, edited by George S. Wise and Charles Issawi, 13–33. Princeton: Darwin, 1981.

"Panarabismo." *Enciclopedia del Novecento*, vol. 5, pp. 67–78. Rome, 1981.

"Hukûmet and Devlet." *Belleten* (Ankara) 46 (1982): 415–21.

"Kimlik ve Politika." In *Türkiye ve Müttefiklerinin Güvenliği*, 19–33. Ankara: Foreign Policy Institute, 1982.

"Meşveret." *Tarih Enstitusu Dergisi* 12 (1981–82): 775–82.

"Orientalism: An Exchange." *New York Review of Books* (12 August 1982): 44–48.

"The Question of Orientalism." *New York Review of Books* (24 June 1982): 49–56.

"Comment l'Islam regardait l'Occident." *L'Histoire* 56 (May 1983): 44–55.

"Judaeo-Osmanica." In *Hayut u-maaseh: Sefer Zikaron le-Shimon Ravidovits bi-meleat esrim ve-hamesh shanim le-moto*, edited by A. Grinboim and A. Ivri, i–viii. Tel Aviv: Tserikover avur Universitata Hefah, ha-Fakultah le-madaei ha-ruah, 1983.

"The Revolt of Islam." *New York Review of Books* (30 June 1983): 35–38.

"The Tanzimat and Social Equality." In *Économie et sociétés dans l'empire ottoman,* edted by Jean-Louis Bacque-Grammont and Paul Dumont, 47–54. Paris: Éditions du Centre national de la recherche scientifique, 1983.

"The Egyptian Murder Case" (review of *Autumn of Fury: The Assassination of Sadat,* by Mohamed Heikal). *New York Review of Books* (31 May 1984): 21–25.

"Histoire d'un mot: Palestine." *L'Histoire* 72 (1984): 84–88.

"The Impact of the Exotic" (review of *The Oriental Renaissance* by Raymond Schwab). *New York Times Book Review* (23 December1984): 15–16.

"Islamic Political Movements." *Middle East Insight* 3 (April 1984): 12–17.

"The Judaeo-Islamic Tradition." *Pe'amim* 26 (1984): 3–13.

"The Ottoman Obsession." *Franco Maria Ricci* 5 (1984): 89–99.

"Poems from the Arabic." In *La Sapienza: Studi in onore de Francesco Gabrieli,* 443–45. Rome: University of Rome, 1984.

"Usurpers and Tyrants: Notes on Some Islamic Political Terms." In *Logos Islamikos: Studia islamica in honorem Georgii Michaelis Wickens*, edited by Roger M. Savory and Dionisius A. Agius, 259–67. Papers in Mediaeval Studies 6. Toronto: Pontifical Institute of Mediaeval Studies, 1984.

"The Crows of the Arabs." *Critical Inquiry* 12 (Autumn 1985): 88–97.

"How Khomeini Made It" (review of *The Reign of the Ayatollahs: Iran and the Islamic Revolution,* by Shaul Bakhash). *New York Review of Books* (17 January 1985): 10–13.

"The Search for Symmetry" (review of *The Blood of Abraham,* by Jimmy Carter). *New York Times Book Review* (28 April 1985): 10.

"Serbestiyet." *Journal of the Faculty of Economics of the University of Istanbul* 41 (*Omer Lufti Barkan Memorial Volume*) (1985): 47–52.

"The Shi'a." *New York Review of Books* (15 August 1985): 7–10.

"Siyasa." In *In Quest of an Islamic Humanism: Arabic and Islamic Studies in Memory of Mohamed al-Nowaihi,* edited by A. H. Green, 3–14. Cairo: The American University in Cairo Press, 1985.

"The Arab World Discovers Anti-Semitism." *Commentary* 81 (May 1986): 30–34.

"Ibn Khaldun in Turkey." In *Studies in Islamic History and Civilization in Honour of Professor David Ayalon,* edited by M. Sharon, pp. 527–30. Jerusalem: Cana, and Leiden: E. J. Brill, 1986.

"Islam and the West." In *National and International Politics in the Middle East: Essays in Honour of Elie Kedourie,* edited by Edward Ingram, pp. 16–30. London: Frank Cass, 1986.

"The New Anti-Semitism." *New York Review of Books* (10 April 1986): 28.

"On the Quietist and Activist Traditions in Islamic Political Writing." *Bulletin of the School of Oriental and African Studies* 49 (1986): 141–47.

"The Ras Burqa Affair." *The New Republic* 194 (24 March 1986): 18.

"State, Nation and Religion in Islam." In *Nationalism and Modernity: A Mediterranean Perspective*, edited by Joseph Alpher, pp. 30–46. New York and London: Praeger, 1986.

"The Shi'a in Islamic History." In *Shi'ism, Resistance, and Revolution*, edited by Martin Kramer, 21–30. Boulder, Colo.: Westview Press, and London: Mansell Publishing, 1987.

"Some Notes on Land, Money and Power in Medieval Islam." In *Varia Turcica IX: Turkische Miszellen, Robert Anhegger Festschrift*, edited by Jean-Louis Bacque-Grammont, Barbara Flemming, Macit Gokberk, and Ilber Ortayli, 237–42. Istanbul: Editions Divit, 1987.

I

THE CLASSICAL AND MEDIEVAL ISLAMIC WORLD

1
Conversion from Islam

Syed Barakat Ahmad

A NEW PENAL code was promulgated in the Ottoman Empire during the *Tanẓimāt* reforms (1858). Under this code, all *ḥadd* punishments were abolished. However, the death penalty for conversion from Islam was retained.[1] The genesis of this law and its necessity as a deterrent need re-examination.

Religious liberty is not an exclusively modern concept. Every prophet, religious leader, and reformer needs it; his own mission depends on it, and it is not in his interest to stifle freedom of conscience. St. Paul warned the Corinthians, "When you sin against the brethren and wound their weak conscience, you sin against Christ."[2] The Prophet of Islam was not an innovator. He did what the earlier Christians and the biblical prophets had done before him. The *Sūrat al-Kāfirūn,* revealed in the early period of the Prophet's ministry, is a most forthright statement of policy on the subject of freedom of conscience. The Prophet was asked to tell the unbelievers: there is absolutely no meeting ground between your way of life and mine, and as we are in complete disagreement, not only with regard to the basic concepts of religion, but also with regard to its details and other aspects, there can be no possible compromise between us. Hence, "for you your religion and for me my religion."[3]

The Prophet was also repeatedly told not to worry if the unbelievers were not ready to accept his message, since after all, he was not their *wakīl. Wakīl* means "guardian, warder, or watchman." God says: "Thy people have rejected the message that we have sent through thee, though it is the truth. Say: I am not appointed a *wakīl* over you."[4] This statement was made in the Meccan period, when the Prophet and his followers were being persecuted. But on the Prophet's arrival in Medina and his assumption of power, this statement was not modified. Indeed, it was made more explicit. The first Medinan sūra in which we find a discussion of the subject of freedom of conscience is *al-Baqarah.* Verse 256 of this sūra contains the clearest pronouncement on the subject:

> There shall be no compulsion in religion. Surely, guidance has become distinct from error, whosoever refuses to be led by those who transgress, and believes in Allah has surely grasped a strong handle which knows no breaking. And Allah is All-Hearing, All-Knowing.

In this verse we find a confident declaration on the part of a prophet who has organized an umma in a town where his power is supreme. Lest the subject of *jihād* be misunderstood, Muslims are told that true virtue lies in practical deeds of kindness and good faith (2:168–242), and the majesty of God is called to mind in the Throne Verse (2:255). The commandment of "no compulsion in religion" comes immediately after the Throne Verse. The injunction to make special sacrifices in the cause of Allah and to fight those enemies who had transgressed against the umma was likely to create the misunderstanding that God wished the Muslims to use force in propagating their religion. The verse therefore enjoins Muslims in very clear and strong words not to resort to force in converting non-Muslims to Islam. The importance of this verse can be gauged from a ḥadīth quoted in the *Jāmi'* of Tirmidhī, which says that the summit of the Qur'ān is *al-Baqarah,* and that Satan will not enter the house of anyone who recites ten verses from this chapter, namely, the first four verses, the Throne Verse, the two verses which follow it (256 and 257), and the last three verses.

This principle of "no compulsion" was reiterated after the victory of Badr,[5] and again in *al-Mā'ida,* which is the last sūra. Now that Muḥammad's authority had become fully established, not only in Medina but also in Mecca, it was necessary to emphasize that the only responsibility which the Prophet bore was that of conveying the message. "Obey Allah and obey the Messenger, and be on your guard; but if you turn away, then remember that the duty of our Messenger is only to convey our message clearly."[6] And finally: "The Messenger's duty is only to convey the message. *And Allah knows what you reveal and what you hide.*"[7] Religious belief is a personal matter and it is God alone—not the state or the religious authorities—who knows what one reveals and what one hides. This verse leads to the subject of the *munāfiqūn,* or "hypocrites." The term *munāfiqūn* describes those inhabitants of Medina who had outwardly accepted Islam, but were considered suspect for various reasons.

There are numerous references to the *munāfiqūn* in the Qur'ān, but in four passages they have been defined as *murtaddūn* ("recanters"). The first of these is in *Sūrat Muḥammad.* This is a Medinan sūra which briefly mentions the aims and objects of war according to Islam, and says that while the believers welcome a revelation enjoining them to fight in the way of Allah, the *munāfiqūn* feel that they are being driven to death. Thus, true believers are separated and sifted from those who are insincere or false in their profession of faith. The sūra continues:

> Surely those who turn their backs (*artaddū*) after guidance has become manifest to them, Satan has seduced them, and holds out false hopes to them.
> That is because they said to those who hate what Allah has revealed, "We will obey you in some matters" and Allah knows their secret talk.[8]

These verses mention no punishment for these people.

The next reference to the *munāfiqūn,* who first believed and then disbelieved, is in *Sūrat al-Munāfiqūn,* which was revealed toward the end of 6/628. This sūra exposes the infidelity and dishonesty of the *munāfiqūn,* and condemns their loud professions of faith as false and treacherous. This was a public reprimand:

> Allah bears witness that the *munāfiqūn* are liars. They have made their oaths a cloak that they may thereby turn people away from the way of Allah. Evil is that which they practice. That is because they believed and thereafter disbelieved; so a seal was set upon their hearts and they have no understanding. . . . They are the enemy, so beware! . . . It is the same for them whether thou ask for forgiveness for them or not, Allah will never forgive them. Surely, Allah guides not a rebellious people.[9]

The last two references to the *munāfiqūn* are in one of the last sūras, *al-Tawba*: "Offer no excuse, you have certainly disbelieved after having believed. If we forgive a party from among you, a party shall we punish, for they have been guilty."[10] The party to be forgiven is obviously those *munāfiqūn* who repented and became sincere Muslims. As for those who are to be punished, the subsequent verse says: "Allah promises the *munāfiqūn,* both men and women, and the unbelievers the fire of Hell, wherein they shall abide. It will suffice them. And they shall have a lasting punishment."[11] And finally:

> They swear by Allah that they said nothing, but they did say the word of disbelief *and did disbelieve after they had embraced Islam*. . . . So if they repent, it will be better for them, but if they turn away, Allah will punish them with a grievous punishment in this world and the Hereafter, and they shall have neither friend nor helper in the earth.[12]

The Prophet knew that 'Abdallāh ibn Ubayy ibn Salūl was the leader of the *munāfiqūn,* but he took no action against him. On the contrary, the Prophet prayed for him when he died. 'Umar ibn al-Khaṭṭāb is reported to have said:

> When the Prophet went and stood by the dead body of 'Abdallāh ibn Ubayy and was about to pray, I asked him: "Are you going to pray over God's enemy?" The Prophet smiled and said, "Get behind me 'Umar. I have been given a choice and I have chosen. It was said to me, 'Ask pardon for them or ask it not. If you ask pardon for them seventy times God will not pardon them.' If I knew that, if I were to add to the seventy, he would be forgiven, I would add thereto." Then he prayed over him and walked with his dead body, and stayed at his grave until he had been buried.[13]

Freedom of conversion is the acid test of the principle "no compulsion in religion." It cannot be a one-way freedom to enter Islam, but not to recant from it, if one so chooses. There are ten direct references to recantation in the Qur'ān. One is in the Meccan sūra of *al-Naḥl*; the remaining nine are to be found in the Medinan sūras. In none of these verses is there the slightest hint of capital punishment.

One of the most explicit statements on recantation in the Qur'ān is Verse 143 of *al-Baqarah.* The *qibla* was changed from Jerusalem to Mecca in the second year of the Hijra. Ibn Isḥāq reports:

> And when the *qibla* was changed from Syria to the Ka'ba, Rifā'a ibn Qays, Qardam ibn 'Amr, Ka'b ibn al-Ashraf, Rāfi' ibn Abī Rāfi', al-Ḥajjāj ibn 'Amr, and an ally of Ka'b's, al-Rabī' ibn al-Rabī' ibn Abū' l-Huqayq came to the Prophet and asked: "Why have you turned your back on the *qibla* you used to face when you claimed to follow the religion of Abraham? If you would return to the *qibla* in Jerusalem we would follow you and declare you to be true." Their sole intention was to seduce him from his religion, so God sent down concerning them. . . . "And We appointed the *qibla* which you formerly observed only that We might know him who will follow the messenger from him who turns upon his heels," that is, to test and to find them out. "In truth it was a hard test except for those whom Allah has guided." [2.143][14]

The Qur'ān prescribes no penalty for these recanters, nor does history record anyone who was punished for recantion after the *qibla* had been changed.

Sūrat Āl 'Imrān, which was revealed after the victory of Badr (2/624), contains the following two verses, which pointedly mention the recantation of some of the Jews of Medina:

> 72. O People of the Scripture: Why do you confound the truth with falsehood and knowingly conceal the truth?
>
> 73. And a party of the People of the Scripture say: Believe in that which had been revealed unto those who believe at the opening of the day and disbelieve at the end thereof, in order that they may return.

Ibn Isḥāq has given the names of those who hatched this plot:

> 'Abdallāh ibn Ṣayf and 'Adiy ibn Zayd and Al-Ḥārith ibn 'Awf agreed among themselves that they should affect to believe in what had been sent down to Muḥammad and his companions at one time, and to deny it at another time so as to confuse them, with the object of getting them to follow their example and give up Muḥammad's religion. Therefore, God sent down concerning them.[15]

None of these three Jews was punished.

Another reference is to be found in *al-Nisā'*. It says: Those who believe, and then disbelieve, then again believe, and then disbelieve, and then increase in disbelief, Allah will never forgive them, nor will He guide them to the way."[16] A recanter cannot enjoy the repeated luxury of believing and disbelieving if the recantation is punished by death. A dead man has no further opportunity to "again believe and then disbelieve."

The sunna, "the divinely inspired behavior of Muḥammad,"[17] is the second source of the *sharī'a.* There is also no penalty for conversion from Islam in the sunna. The names of those persons who were given capital punishment by the Prophet are preserved in the sīra and the ḥadīth, and the names of persons who recanted, and rejected Islam in his life are also preserved.

A bedouin Arab accepted Islam at the hand of the Prophet, and a little later suffered from fever while he was still in Medina. He asked the Prophet to release him from his pledge. He made this request three times, and was refused three times. He left Medina unmolested. The Prophet, on hearing of his departure, observed: "Medina is like a furnace which separates the dross from what is pure."[18]

Ibn Isḥāq reports that the Prophet had instructed his commanders when they entered Mecca only to fight those who resisted them, except the following criminals who were to be executed even if they were found beneath the curtains of the Ka'ba:[19]

1. 'Abdallāh ibn Sa'd ibn Abī Sarah,
2. 'Abdallāh ibn Khaṭal of Banū Tayam ibn Ghālib, and his two dancing girls, who used to sing satirical songs about the Prophet. One of them was Fartanā, the name of the other girl is not given by Ibn Isḥāq.[20]
3. Al-Ḥuwayrith ibn Nuqaydh ibn Wahb ibn 'Abd ibn Quṣayy,
4. Miqyas ibn Ṣubāba,
5. Sarāḥ, freed slave of one of the Banū 'Abd al-Muṭṭalib,
6. 'Ikrima ibn Abī Jahl.[21]

'Abdallāh ibn Sa'd was one of the scribes of the Prophet in Medina. He recanted, and defected to the Meccan unbelievers. Since he had written down revelations at the Prophet's dictation, and had enjoyed a position of trust, his defection was bound to create confusion among the Muslims, as well as doubt among the Quraysh of Mecca concerning the authenticity of the revelation itself. After the situation in Mecca had become tranquil, his foster-brother, 'Uthmān ibn 'Affān, interceded with the Prophet on his behalf, and 'Abdallāh was pardoned.[22] Had there been a Qur'ānic penalty for recantation, the Prophet could not have done so. The Prophet's policy on intercession in respect to *ḥadd* punishment is well illustrated by the incident of the Makhzūmī woman who was found guilty of theft. When Usāma ibn Zayd tried to intercede on her behalf, the Prophet rebuked him and said, "Do you intercede in respect to a punishment prescribed by Allah? I call to witness that if Fāṭima, daughter of Muḥammad, were found guilty of theft, I would certainly cut off her hand."

'Abdallāh ibn Khaṭal was sent by the Prophet to collect *zakāt*, in the company of an Anṣārī who served him. When they made a halt, he ordered his companion to kill a goat for him, and to prepare some food. He then went to sleep. When he woke up, the man had done nothing, and 'Abdallāh ibn Khaṭal killed him in anger. He then recanted, and defected to the Quraysh of Mecca.[23] He was executed for the murder of this Anṣārī Muslim by Sa'īd ibn Ḥurayth al-Makhzūmī and Abū Barza al-Aslamī acting together.[24]

One of Ibn Khaṭal's two singing-girls was put to death for creating disorder with her satirical songs, while the other one was pardoned.[25]

Al-Ḥuwayrith ibn Nuqaydh was in the party of Habbār ibn al-Aswad ibn al-Muṭṭalib ibn Asad when the latter overtook the Prophet's daughter, Zaynab, while she was going from Mecca to Medina. Al-Ḥuwayrith goaded Zaynab's camel. Zaynab, who was pregnant at the time, had a miscarriage as a result of the attack, and had to return to

Mecca. The Prophet sent out a number of people, ordering them that if they should be able to seize Habbār ibn al-Aswad or al-Ḥuwayrith, they should kill them.[26] Al-Ḥuwayrith, however, escaped. 'Alī killed him afterward in Mecca.[27]

Miqyas ibn Ṣubāba came to Medina from Mecca and said, "I come to you as a Muslim seeking the bloodwit for my brother who was killed in error." The Prophet ordered that he should be paid the bloodwit for his brother Hishām. After receiving the bloodwit, Miqyas stayed with the Prophet for a while. But as soon as he found an opportunity, he killed his brother's slayer. He then recanted and defected to Mecca.[28] Miqyas was executed by Numayla ibn 'Abdallāh for killing the Anṣārī, on whose behalf the bloodwit had already been paid.[29]

Sarāḥ, who was accused of insulting the Prophet, was not killed during the Prophet's lifetime.

'Ikrīma ibn Abī Jahl fled to the Yemen. His wife, Umm Ḥakīm, became a Muslim. She requested immunity for him, and it was granted by the Prophet.[30]

Thus, there seems to be no evidence to show that the Prophet punished anyone for recantation from Islam.

With the death of the Prophet in 11/632, the young Muslim administration faced a dangerous crisis. Disorders broke out in various parts of the Arabian peninsula, and many tribes detached themselves from Medina, through their refusal to pay *zakāt.* This movement is known by the name of *al-ridda.* The suppression of this movement was the principal task of the Prophet's successor, Abū Bakr. His first duty, however, was to send on to its destination an expedition which the Prophet had ordered before his death. Accordingly, an army under the command of Usāma ibn Zayd ibn Ḥārith was sent to the Syrian border two days after the proclamation of Abū Bakr's caliphate.

After the departure of Usāma and his army, most of the Arab tribes fell away from Medina. Only Mecca, Medina, and their surroundings remained loyal to the central administration. The Muslim agents whom the Prophet had appointed over these rebel tribes before his death were now forced to flee their posts, and to return to Medina. It was a full-fledged revolt.

Having decided to fight the rebels, Abū Bakr sent messengers to some tribes which remained loyal, summoning them to his aid. While Abū Bakr was waiting for these reinforcements, Kharja ibn Ḥiṣn, led by 'Unayna ibn Ḥiṣn al-Fazārī and al-Aqra' ibn Ḥābis al-Tamīmī staged a surprise attack on the Muslims. The Muslims dispersed in confusion, but then reassembled and counterattacked Kharja's men, who were defeated.

Before the skirmish at Dhū 'l-Qaṣṣa, a delegation of Arab tribes went to Medina to negotiate with Abū Bakr on the question of *zakāt*. However, Abū Bakr refused to parley. Several prominent *muhājirūn* disagreed with Abū Bakr's decision to fight the withholders of the *zakāt*. The fact that these tribes were anxious to negotiate indicates that they had not recanted, and did not want to sever their relations with Medina, but that at the same time they were not prepared to accept Medina's control over them. The issue was not belief in Allah and His Prophet, but rather the tax imposed on them (*zakāt*). A group of prominent Companions, led by 'Umar, objected to Abū Bakr's decision to fight the rebels. 'Umar is reported to have said to Abū Bakr, "What right do you have to fight these people, when the Prophet said, 'I was ordered to fight people until they say, "there is no God but Allah." If they say this, they safeguard themselves and their property from me."[31]

After the delegation left Medina, Abū Bakr gathered the Muslims of Medina and addressed them as follows:

> The delegation has observed the smallness of your numbers in Medina. You do not know if they will attack you by night or by day. Their vanguard is only one day's journey from Medina. They wished for us to accept their proposals, and to make an agreement with them, but we have rejected their requests. So make ready for their attack. [Within three days they attacked Medina.][32]

The war of *al-ridda* caused much bloodshed, and "it was inexplicable to the subsequent historians of the Arabian State that after the death of Mahomet so many wars were necessary on Arabian soil; they accounted for this fact by a *Ridda*,"[33] a religious movement against Islam. The jurists of later generations, who failed to find a precedent in the Qur'ān or the sunna for capital punishment in the case of a Muslim accused of *kufr*, or of waging war against a Muslim power, accepted this assumption without further examination.

Discussing the legality of Abū Bakr's war against Muslim rebels, al-Shāfi'ī says: "*Ridda* is falling back from a previously adopted religion into disbelief, and refusing to fulfill previously accepted obligations."[34] This means that mere recantation is not enough; it must be aggravated by breach of agreement. Ibn Abī 'l-Ḥadīd, a scholar of a very different school, in his commentary on the *Nahj al-Balāgha*, clarifies the entire situation with the following comment: those tribes which refused to pay the *zakāt* "were not recanters, but were so called by the Companions of the Prophet by way of metaphor."[35]

According to Wellhausen, the *ridda* was a break with the leadership in Medina, and not with Islam *qua* religion. The majority of the tribes wished to continue to worship Allah, but without paying any tax. Caetani agreed with Wellhausen, remarking that the *ridda* was not a movement of recantation, and that these wars had political causes. Becker followed Wellhausen and Caetani, and concluded:

> The sudden death of Mahomet gave new support to the centrifugal tendencies. The character of the whole movement, as it forces itself on the notice of the historian, was of course hidden from contemporaries. Arabia would have sunk into particularism if the necessity caused by the secession of *al-Ridda* had not developed in the State of Medina an energy which carried all before it. The fight against the *Ridda* was not a fight against apostates; the objection was not to Islam *per se* but to the tribute which had to be paid to Medina; the fight was for the political supremacy over Arabia.[36]

Bernard Lewis makes it quite clear that the *ridda* "represents a distortion of the real significance of events by the theologically coloured outlook of later historians." He goes on to say:

> The refusal of the tribes to recognize the succession of Abū Bakr was in effect not a relapse by converted Muslims to their previous paganism, but the simple and automatic termination of a political contract by the death of one of the parties. The tribes nearest to Medina had in fact been converted and their interests were so closely identified with those of the Umma that their separate history has not been recorded. For the rest, the death of Muḥammad automatically severed their bonds with Medina, and the parties resumed their liberty of action. They felt in no way bound by the election of Abū Bakr in which they had taken no part, and at once suspended both tribute and treaty relations. In order to re-establish the hegemony of Medina, Abū Bakr had to make new treaties.[37]

'Alī was assassinated in 661, and with him ended the true concept of a Muslim ruler combining the functions of head of state and of religion. With Mu'āwiya began the rule of the Umayyad dynasty (661–750), the political rulers of Islam. They had none of the religious aura of the Pious Caliphs, and were regarded more or less as secular kings. As guardians of the *sharī'a*, the *'ulāmā'* came to occupy a position which may be compared in some respects to that of the clergy after the conversion of Constantine. Like the medieval European clergy, they were respected for their learning and piety, and their support was sought to legitimize the power of a despot or of an unpopular ruler. They also acted as opposition leaders, and tried to influence political power rather than assume it themselves.

Political and social revolts now became justified in religious terms, and dynastic struggles soon hardened into deep schisms of religious doctrine. Khārijism and Shī'ism, the two main movements which split off from the Muslim community after the assassination in 644 of 'Uthmān, the third Caliph, had their origin in a succession struggle. The Khārijites were the first Muslims who maintained that a grave sinner no longer remains a Muslim, and they were also the first to proclaim *jihād* against those Muslims who, according to them, were not true believers. They originally belonged to the party of 'Alī, but left him on the question of arbitration to settle the quarrel between 'Alī and Mu'āwiya arising out of the murder of 'Uthmān. They said, "judgment belongs to Allah alone," and not to a human tribunal. Their importance lies in the development of dogma. They were particular about the qualifications of a Muslim and about his attitude toward his fellow men, Muslim and non-Muslim. They were the first distinct sect to appear in Islam. They were also the first to reject the principle of justification by faith. They maintained that a grave sinner no longer remains a Muslim, and cannot re-enter the faith. He should be killed, together with his wives and children. They considered all non-Khārijites outlaws and non-Muslims. As we have seen earlier, the Prophet knew the *munāfiqūn* of Medina and their leader 'Abdallāh ibn Ubayy, and yet took no action against them. He did not judge the quality of a Muslim's faith. On the contrary, he said: Whoever prays as we pray, and turns to our *qibla*, and eats what we ritually kill, is a Muslim; he is *dhimmat Allah* and *dhimmat al-rasūl*. So do not put Allah in contravention of his *dhimmah*.[38]

The Khārijites were in direct conflict with the teaching of the Qur'ān and the sunna of the Prophet. Their declaration that "judgment belongs to God alone" (*lā ḥukma illā lillāh*) was in total contradiction to the sunna. The Prophet appointed Sa'd ibn Mu'ādh as *ḥakam* to decide the fate of the Jewish tribe of Banū Qurayẓa, and his sentence was carried out.[39] Commenting on the *Ṣaḥīh Muslim* report of Sa'd's judgment, al-Nawawī (d. 676/1272) said, "In their disputes Muslims are allowed to resort to *taḥkīm*."[40] In fact, if two Muslim parties are at war, it is incumbent on Muslims to make peace between them. The Qur'ān says, "All believers are brothers, and be mindful of your duty to Allah that you may be shown mercy."[41]

The Khārijites were the initiators of that rigid and intolerant dogmatism which has always gripped the Islamic world in times of crisis. Ibn Taymīya (1263–1326), a respected jurist, a fearless fighter, and an outspoken Ḥanbalī scholar, who justified and defined this Khārijite dogmatism in theological and juridical terms, was born at a time of crisis. Baghdad was sacked by Hülagü five years before Ibn Taymīya's birth. At the age of six, he had to flee Damascus with his family, when the Mongols conquered northern Syria. He was thirty-six years old when the Mongols defeated the Mamlūks. But the times had changed between his childhood and youth. The Mongols, who had utterly destroyed the rich civilization of the Abbasid empire, were in turn conquered by Islam. The new Ilkhān Ghazān Maḥmūd (r. 1295–1304), who in 1299 defeated the Mamlūks near Ḥimṣ, was a Muslim.

Ibn Taymīya and his disciple Ibn Kathīr (1300–1372/3) knew of Mamlūk transgressions in matters of taxes and the use of alcohol, but also knew that Sultan Baybars (1260–1277), who fought the Mongols at 'Ayn Jālūt (1260) was, at the same time, organizing yearly expeditions against the Christian principalities: the Order of the Knights of the Temple and the Order of the Hospitallers. Ibn Taymīya did, however, not know or fully comprehend that the Ilkhanid capital, Tabriz, was shaping into a great center of Islamic civilization, and that in its eastern suburb alone, there were 200 reciters of the Qur'ān, and that another 400 scholars, theologians, jurists, and traditionalists also resided there. He was faced with a dilemma: could war against the Ilkhanids still be *jihād*, or had it become a mere clash between two Sunni powers? Ibn Taymīya and Ibn Kathīr saw safety in the *status quo*. Commenting on verses 33 to 50 of *Sūrat al-Mā'ida*, Ibn Kathīr says that these verses refer to people who follow laws and regulations set by men, to fill their own misguided desires and whims. The Mongols who follow the *Yasa* code of Genghis Khan are infidels, and should be fought until they comply with the laws of God.[42]

Referring to Muslim Mongols, Ibn Taymīya states:

> It has been established from the Book, from the sunna and from the *ijmā'* (the general unanimity) of the umma that he who forsakes the Law of Islam should be fought, though he may have pronounced the two formulas of Faith.[43]

The way in which Ibn Kathīr wrested the fiftieth verse of *al-Mā'ida* from its context, so as to make it read as a command to fight the

Muslim Mongol rulers, together with Ibn Taymīya's approval (in a *fatwa*) of this interpretation, opened the way for religious sanction of internecine wars between Muslim rulers and repression of Muslim minority groups. This interpretation of the Qur'ān by Ibn Kathīr and Ibn Taymīya is very similar to that of St. Augustine when he wrested the phrase *compelle intrare* from its context in the parable of the supper (Luke 14:23), and interpreted it as an injunction to enforce the submission of heretics and believers. According to St. Augustine, the parable of the tares meant that tares should be uprooted, if it could be done in such a manner that no wheat would be uprooted with them. The basis of intolerance in medieval Christianity was the alliance between Church and State. In medieval Islam, it was a concord between the *'ulāmā'* and the Muslim rulers, which facilitated the application of religious argument to settle problems that were essentially political.

The Qur'ānic verse which Ibn Taymīya quoted and upon which Ibn Kathīr commented, so as to declare the Muslim Mongols heretics and *kāfirs*, is from a sūra which deals mainly with Christians, and in particular denounces the Christian doctrine that the Law is a curse. This verse could not provide a basis for describing the Muslim Mongols as *kuffār*.

The concept of *takfīr*, declaring Muslims unbelievers, and then punishing them on the basis of their differences from a certain standard prescribed by a religious authority, is alien to Islam. The Prophet himself defined a Muslim as one who declares faith in the unity of Allah and the prophethood of Muḥammad.[44] This is the only definition by which a Muslim can be judged. Discussing the subject of *takfīr*, Bernard Lewis says:

> Even open rebellion did not automatically involve *takfīr*. In 923 the chief *Qādī* Ibn Buhlul refused to denounce the Carmathian rebels as unbelievers, since they began their letters with invocations to God and the Prophet, and were therefore *prima facie* Muslims. The Shāfi'ī law insists that the sectarian, even in revolt, is entitled to be treated as a Muslim; that is to say, that his family and property are respected, and that he cannot be summarily despatched or sold into slavery once he becomes a prisoner.[45]

The institution of *takfīr*[46] was not, however, founded by jurists. As we have seen earlier, it was a Khārijite excuse for denouncing 'Alī. But having adopted this Khārijite innovation, the jurists could not arrive at an agreed definition of a Muslim. They tried to add various qualifications to the Prophet's simple definition, and thus, in the words of al-Ghazālī (450/1058–505/1111), constricted "the vast mercy of God to make Paradise the preserve of a small clique of theologians."[47] The result of their efforts has been summed up by the former Chief Justice of Pakistan, Muhammad Munir, who presided over the Court of Inquiry to investigate the Punjab (Pakistan) Disturbances of 1953. He said:

> Keeping in view the several definitions given by the *ulama*, need we make any comment except that no two learned divines are agreed on this fundamental. If we attempt our own definition as each learned divine has done and that definition differs from that given by all others, we unanimously go out of the fold of Islam. And if we adopt the definition given by any one of the *ulama*, we remain Muslims according to the view of that *alim* but *kafirs* according to the definition of everyone else.[48]

An attempt to comb thirteen hundred years of Islamic history to find the number of Muslims who were put to death because of their conversion from Islam would prove futile. There were unsuccessful attempts to execute Maimonides in Cairo,[49] the Maronite emir Yūnus in Lebanon,[50] or to persecute Rashīd al-Dīn in Tabriz,[51] but such instances are very rare. In Moghul India there is only one instance of a Portuguese friar who embraced Islam and then reverted to his former faith. He was executed at Aurangabad.[52] The reasons for his execution were political, not religious. The friar was under heavy suspicion of spying for the Portuguese under cover of Islam.

Ja'd ibn Dirham was put to death on the orders of Hishām ibn 'Abd al-Malik in Kufa or Wāsiṭ in 124/742 or 125/743. He was accused of having advanced the Mu'tazilite doctrines of the Created Qur'ān and the free will. In 167 or 168/784, the Iraqi poet Bashār ibn Burd was accused of *zandaqa*, and beaten and thrown into the swamp of Baṭīha. Al-Ḥusayn ibn Manṣūr al-Ḥallāj was executed in 309/922 for blasphemy, because he claimed to have achieved *ḥulūl* (substantial union with God). Shihāb al-Dīn Yaḥya al-Suhrawardī was put to death at the order of al-Malik al-Ẓāhir (119/578). His crime was that he regarded all that lives, or moves, or has its being as light, and even based his proof of God upon the symbol of light. The martyr of the seventeenth century was Muḥammad Sa'īd Sarmad. Born of Jewish parents at Kāshān, Sarmad was a rabbi before embracing Islam. A great Persian poet, he was a monist, and denied the existence of matter. He was executed in the reign of Aurangzīb (r. 1658–1707). His *mazār*, tomb, which is opposite the Jāmi' Masjid in Delhi, daily attracts hundreds of Muslims, who offer flowers and the *Fātiḥa*. It is also reported that the Ismā'īlī *dā'ī* of the Bohra sect, Sayyid Quṭb al-Dīn of Ahmadabad, was put to death by the order of Aurangzīb.[53]

In Afghanistan, two Aḥmadīs were executed for accepting the claim of Mirzā Ghulām Aḥmad of Qādiyān as the Promised Messiah. Ṣaḥibzādah 'Abd al-Laṭīf, who performed the coronation ceremony of Amīr Ḥabib Allāh Khān, was stoned to death in 1903, and Maulawī Ni'mat Allāh was stoned to death in 1924. Both of them were given the option of renouncing the claim of Mirzā Ghulām Aḥmad, but they refused to do so.

In the Sudan, Muḥammad Maḥmūd Ṭāhā was executed in 1985. He considered that the Medinan part of the Qur'ānic legislation was no longer applicable.

The death penalty for conversion from Islam to another religion, sanctioned neither by the Qur'ān nor by the sunna, was retained, but not because it had any practical value. It was more a symbol of dominance than an instrument for preventing a Muslim from converting to the faith of his choice. It was a scarecrow in a desert.

The nineteenth century brought doom and disgrace to the Muslim world. While the Moghul Empire had disintegrated, the Ottoman Empire was in the process of dissolution. Java and Sumatra had become a part of the Dutch Empire. It was during this period that Christian missionaries undertook the evangelization of the Mulsim world. In 1906, the "First Missionary Conference on behalf of the Mohammedan World" was held in Cairo. The papers read at this conference, and "the discussion thereon, which by order of the Conference were not to be issued to the public, but were to be privately printed for the use of missionaries and the friends of missions,"[54] throw some light on the work undertaken by the Church. The Reverend E. M. Wherry, in his introduction to these papers, said:

> The reason of this conference is that the work of evangelization of the Moslems should be advanced all along the ordinary lines of missionary effort, and that a definite work for the evangelization of the Moslems should be undertaken by all societies. Men and women, especially fitted for this work, should be sent forth into every Moslem land without delay, who by tactful effort should seek especially to win the Moslems back to the allegiance of Christ the Saviour of the world.[55]

Voluminous literature was produced to prove the superiority of Christianity to Islam. The Reverend S. Lee[56] and the Reverend Charles

Foster[57] wrote a large number of tracts against Islam. It will be instructive to assess the result of the missionary work in one area of India, Bengal, where the evangelization of Muslims had started as early as 1793. It was in that year that the Reverend William Carey, chief of the Baptist Missionary Society, landed in Bengal and established his mission, which is known as the Serāmpur Mission. It was followed by many other missions.[58] Hafeez Malik provides the following background:

> In 1837 there was a famine in India. A great many people died of hunger and pestilence and their orphans were taken over by the government. They were brought up in orphanages by English missionaries in the Christian faith. This was construed as indication of the government's wish to convert the entire population. In 1850, Act XXI designed to encourage conversion to Christianity, was passed in the legislative council in Calcutta. It provided that a person who was converted to Islam could not inherit the property of his parents. If, however, he embraced the Christian faith he would not be subject to this penalty.[59]

The way was thus prepared to facilitate the evangelization of Indians, and especially Indian Muslims. The Reverend D. C. G. Pfander wrote two books, one in Persian, *Mīzān al-Haqq*, and the other in Urdu, *Miftāḥ al-asrār*, to prove that Muḥammad is not the Apostle of God, and that the Qur'ān is not the word of God. Rev. Pfander also persuaded Sir William Muir, a civil servant of the government of India, to write a biography of the Prophet, *The Life of Mahomet*,[60] which proved to be a turning point in the history of Islam-Christianity controversy in India. In this biography, Sir William attacked the fundamental principles of Islam as being incompatible with piety or morality.

In 1911, the "Second Missionary Conference on behalf of the Mohammedan World" was held in Lucknow, which, along with Delhi, was the center of Muslim culture and religious activity in India.[61] In an "Introductory Survey" at the conference, the Reverend Samuel M. Zwemer said:

> India leads the list with 62,458,077 Moslems, and it is a startling fact that there are now under British rule more Mohammedans than under any other government in modern or in medieval days. Counting her possessions and dependencies, at least 95,000,000 followers of the prophet of Mecca are to-day enjoying the blessings of the British Empire.[62]

Concluding his survey, Rev. Zwemer said:

As our eyes sweep the horizon of all these lands dominated or imperiled by this great rival faith, each seems to stand out as typical of one of the factors in the great problem. . . . Each of these typical conditions is itself an appeal. The supreme need of the Moslem world is Jesus Christ.[63]

The Reverend John Takle, who was working in Bengal, referring to the slow work of the Mission, said that sometimes Europeans in an outburst of impatience have urged force in converting to Christianity:

A German Jesuit named Hounder, says, "Clovis and Charlemagne (who drove the heathen Saxons in masses into the Elbe for baptism) have been more effective pioneers of Christianity than thousands of native and foreign missionaries. . . . God closely binds the use of the sword to the religious development of a people." [Quotation from *Record of Christian Work* for October, 1910.][64]

Rev. Takle, however, rejected force, and said, "Compulsion and Christianity are incompatible." But some sort of compulsion was used. Some proselytizing officers of the East India Company used their influence. During the inquiry by the Governor of Bengal and Council, Col. Wheeler of the 34th Bengal Native Infantry, who prided himself on being a Christian missionary, said:

During the last twenty years I have been in the habit of speaking to natives of all classes, sepoys [soldiers] and others, making no distinction, since there is no respect of persons with God, on the subject of our religion, in the highways, cities, bazaars and villages. I have done this from a conviction that every converted Christian is expected or rather commanded by the Scriptures to make known the glad tidings of Salvation to his lost fellow creatures.[65]

Under Moghul rule, the Muslims occupied almost all government posts, but under the British they were gradually excluded from government service. Their *maktabs* (high schools) and *madrasas* (colleges) began to disappear for want of financial support from the state, and western-style educational institutions or mission schools took their place. In 1871, among the judges of the High Court of Judicature there were two Hindus but no Muslims. Quoting a daily Persian-language newspaper of Calcutta, *Dūrbīn*, William Wilson Hunter said:

All sorts of employment, great and small, are being gradually snatched away from the Moslems, and are bestowed on men of other races, particularly the Hindus . . . yet the time has come when it [the government] publicly singles out the Moslems in its Gazettes for exclusion from official posts. . . .

Moslems have now sunk so low, that even when qualified for government employ, they are studiously kept out of it by government notifications.[66]

In spite of this heavy economic pressure, the Muslims of Bengal could not be converted, either to Hinduism or to Christianity. When British officers first came in contact with the people of Bengal, they estimated that roughly only about one percent were Muslims. But in 1830, when the first census of the city of Dacca was taken, there were 35,238 Muslims and 31,429 Hindus. In another census, taken in 1872 in Lower Bengal, Muslims were found to constitute forty-five percent of the population. In the Dacca district, the Hindus numbered only 793,798, or 43.3 percent, of the whole population. Since Muslims no longer had political control, and as there was no longer a migration of Muslims from northern India, the increase in the population of Muslims in East Bengal must have been due to peaceful conversion to Islam.[67]

In 1871, there were seventeen million Hindus and sixteen and a half million Muslims in Bengal. But in 1901, there were eighteen million Hindus and a little over nineteen and a half million Muslims. During the space of thirty years, the Muslims, who were in the minority of half a million, had not only gained on the Hindus, but came out with a lead of a million and a half. Since polygamy could be one of the contributing factors, it was found that only twenty-nine in every thousand of the Bengali Muslims had more than one wife. Commenting on these figures, Lt. Col. U. N. Mukerjhee of the Indian Medical Service, in a booklet entitled "A Dying Race," said "in Bengal, the future was with the Muslims," while the Hindus were "waiting for extinction."[68]

Islam was not under attack by Christians alone. The Hindus were also trying to reclaim those Muslims whose ancestors were originally Hindus and who were, according to them, forced to accept Islam. Swami Dyananda Saraswati (1824–1883), a Hindu reformer, founded the *Arya Samaj* movement in 1875, to revitalize Hinduism by transforming it into an Aryan religion, and to destroy false beliefs which had impeded the progress of Hinduism and the regeneration of religion and society.

In the fourteenth chapter of his work *Satyarath Prakash,* Swami Dyananda closely examined the Qur'ān, and declared that God was present in the Qur'ān in inappropriate, anthropomorphic terms and He was depicted as acting in a manner which would suggest that He is unjust and encourages sin. . . . The Swami questioned the character of the Prophet, giving special attention to the personal relationships of Muhammad with women and in particular to his marriage to Zainab bint Djahsh who had been formerly the wife of an adopted son. Dayanand charged that Muhammad was not entitled to the designation of a Prophet and that the Quran did not merit being considered revealed scripture but rather was a book which was made in order to serve selfish human ends. . . . The world would be better off without them. Wise men would do well to discard a religion so absurd and accept the *Vedic* faith which is absolutely free from error.[69]

Taking his cue from Lt. Col. Mukherjee, another *Arya Samaj* leader, Swami Shraddhanand made an appeal for the *Shuddhi* movement. Its aim was to reconvert those Hindus who had become Muslim under the Turco-Afghan and Moghul rulers. Writing under the heading "Save the Dying Race,"[70] Sharaddhanand said that the contemporary descendants of the ancient Aryans in India were a dying race, because of internal divisions and narrow, selfish interests. Referring to an announcement by the Rajput Mahasabha, that 450,000 Muslim Rajputs were ready to return to the Hindu fold, Sharaddhanand appealed for funds and volunteers to work for the reconversion of these Muslim Rajputs.

By the summer of 1923, it was clear that the work of reconverting half a million Rajputs would not be easy. G. R. Thursby, who studied "the Hindu side of Hindu-Muslim relations, and more particularly on the role of the *Arya Samaj* movement," describes the failure of this movement in the following words:

Some of the major leaders in the Hindu coalition effort were either worn down or drawn toward other pursuits. . . . Sharaddhanand, with Bright's disease but zeal unflagging, spent much of his time on speaking tours in order to spread the movement and to raise funds. When he went to Bihar, a *maulvi* from the Punjab was imported to counteract his effect, and in Bengal "Ulema Sanghas" were formed and communal boycott was discussed.[71]

Hindus and Christians both thought that the Qur'ān, if translated into local languages, would expose Islam. "The Moslem advance might be further checked by using the Koran more in our work" said Rev. Takle. He went on to say: "We should turn their own work, Islam's supreme weapon, against her for her complete unending. We must show the people that in the Koran 'what is true is not new, and what is new is not true.' "[72]

সুরা আল্-এনাম।

وَلَوْ اَنَّنَا نَزَّلْنَا اِلَيْهِمُ الْمَلٰئِكَةَ وَكَلَّمَهُمُ الْمَوْتٰى

১১১ আর আমরা যদি তাহাদিগের উপর ফেরেস্তাগণকে নাজেল করিতাম, এবং মৃতেরা তাহাদিগকে কথা

وَحَشَرْنَا عَلَيْهِمْ كُلَّ شَيْءٍ قُبُلًا مَا كَانُوا

বলিত, এবং আমরা তাহাদিগের নিকট সমস্ত বস্তু দলে দলে একত্র করিতাম, তথাপি খোদা ইচ্ছা না

لِيُؤْمِنُوا اِلَّا اَنْ يَشَاءَ اللّٰهُ وَلٰكِنَّ اَكْثَرَهُمْ يَجْهَلُوْنَ ۝

করিলে, তাহারা যে ইমান আনে, এইরূপ হইত না[১], কিন্তু তাহাদিগের অধিকাংশ লোক অজ্ঞাত আছে।

وَكَذٰلِكَ جَعَلْنَا لِكُلِّ نَبِيٍّ عَدُوًّا شَيٰطِيْنَ الْاِنْسِ وَالْجِنِّ

১১২ আর এইরূপে আমরা প্রত্যেক নবীর জন্য এক একটী শত্রু করিয়াছি—মনুষ্য ও জীনদের শয়তান সকল[২];

টীকা।

১ কাফেরগণ মহম্মদ সাহেবকে বলিয়াছিল, তুমি যদি খোদার রসুল হও, তাহা হইলে আসমান হইতে এক জন ফেরেস্তাকে আনয়ন কর; কিন্তু তিনি তাহা করিতে অপারগ হইয়া এই আয়েৎ প্রচার করিয়াছিলেন, যেন খোদা স্বয়ং বলিতেছেন 'আমরা তাহাদের বাক্যমত এক ফেরেস্তাকে প্রেরণ করিলেও তাহারা ইমান আনিবে না'। কোরাণের অনেক স্থানে কাফেরগণের এইরূপ বাক্যের উল্লেখ দেখিতে পাওয়া যায়, কিন্তু মহম্মদ সর্ব্বদাই একরূপ উত্তর দান করিয়া বলিতেন, 'মাজেজা (অর্থাৎ আশ্চর্য্য কার্য্য) খোদার হস্তে, আর আমি এক জন প্রচারক মাত্র।' পাঠক এই বিষয়ে এই সুরার ৩৫, ৩৭ এবং ১০৯ আয়েৎ ও সুরা আল্-ইমরাণের (৩) ১৮৩ আয়েৎ পাঠ করিবেন।

খলাসাৎ-উল্-তফাসীরের ২ খণ্ডের ২ পৃষ্ঠায় লিখিত আছে যে, قبلا میں کئی قراءتیں اور معانی مختلف ہیں অর্থাৎ, "কুবুলা (দলে দলে) শব্দের ভিন্ন ভিন্ন ভাব-প্রকাশক ভিন্ন ভিন্ন পাঠ দেখিতে পাওয়া যায়।" অর্থাৎ, কোরাণের এই বাক্য তহরীফ হইয়াছে।

২ এই আয়েতে লিখিত আছে যে, খোদা প্রত্যেক নবীর জন্য এক শত্রু, অর্থাৎ শয়তান, নিযুক্ত করিয়াছেন, যেন সে ঐ নবীকে ভ্রান্ত করিতে পারে। কোরাণের অন্য এক স্থানেও ঠিক এইরূপ শিক্ষা পাওয়া যায়, যথা:—

وَمَا اَرْسَلْنَا مِنْ قَبْلِكَ مِنْ رَسُوْلٍ وَلَا نَبِيٍّ اِلَّا اِذَا تَمَنّٰى اَلْقَى الشَّيْطٰنُ فِيْ اُمْنِيَّتِهٖ ٭

অর্থাৎ, "আমরা তোমার পূর্ব্বে (হে মহম্মদ) এমন কোন রসুল ও নবী প্রেরণ করি নাই যে, সে যখন পাঠ করিত, তখন শয়তান তাহার পাঠের মধ্যে (কিছু) নিক্ষেপ করে নাই।" (সুরা আল্-হজ (২২) আয়েৎ ৫১।) কথিত আছে যে, এক সময়ে মহম্মদ সাহেব আরব কাফের-গণকে লাভ করিবার ইচ্ছায় তাহাদিগের দেবতাদিগের নাম উল্লেখ করিয়া বলিলেন, উঁহাদের শফায়ৎ বাঞ্ছনীয়; কিন্তু তিনি পরে সেই উক্তির জন্য দুঃখিত ও লজ্জিত হইয়া বলিলেন যে, শয়তান ঐ সমস্ত কথা আমাকে বলিতে শিখাইয়াছিল। ঘটনাটী মৱাহিব-আল্-লুদুনিয়া নামক মুসলমান কেতাবে এইরূপে বিবৃত হইয়াছে,

قرأ رسول الله صلعم بمكة و النجم فلما بلغ افرأيتم اللات و العزي و مناة الثالثة الاخري القي الشيطان
على لسانه تلك الغرانيق العلى و ان شفاعتهم لترتجى فقال المشركون ما ذكر الهتنا بخير قبل اليوم
فسجد و سجدوا فنزلت هذا الاية و ما ارسلنا من قبلك من رسول ولا نبي الا اذا تمنى القى الشيطان
في امنيته ٭

অর্থাৎ, "রসুল-আল্লা (তাঁহার উপর খোদার শান্তি ও আশীর্ব্বাদ বর্ত্তুক) মক্কাতে সুরা আল্-নজম পাঠ করিতেছিলেন, আর যখন তিনি এই বাক্য প্রাপ্ত হইলেন, 'অনন্তর তোমরা কি আল্-লাৎ, আল্-আজ্জা ও অপর তৃতীয় মনাৎকে দেখিয়াছ?' তখন শয়তান তাঁহার ওষ্ঠাধরে এই বাক্যগুলি নিক্ষেপ করিয়াছিল, 'ইঁহারা গৌরব ও মর্য্যাদা সম্পন্না কুমারী ও তাঁহাদের শফায়ৎ আশা করা যায়।' তাহাতে কাফেরগণ বলিল, 'তিনি আমাদের দেবতা সম্বন্ধে উত্তম বলিয়াছেন।' অনন্তর তিনি সেজ্দা করিলেন ও তাহারা সেজ্দা করিল, এবং তৎপরে এই আয়েৎ নাজেল হইল, 'আমরা তোমার পূর্ব্বে (হে মহম্মদ) এমন কোন রসুল বা নবী প্রেরণ করি নাই যে, সে যখন পাঠ করিত, তখন শয়তান তাহার পাঠের মধ্যে (কিছু) নিক্ষেপ করে নাই।'" পাঠক সুরা আল্-হজের (২২) ৫১ আয়েৎ ও উহার টীকা পাঠ করিলে এই ঘটনার বিস্তারিত বিবরণ প্রাপ্ত হইবেন।

Figure 1.1 A page from the Reverend William Goldsack's Bengali translation of the Qur'ān: the translation is given below each line of text, followed by a short commentary in Bengali.

The earliest Bengali translation of the Qur'ān was made by a Hindu Brahmin, Bhai Givish Chandra Sen (1835–1910), on the initiative of Keshab Chandra Sen, a leader of the *Brahmo Samaj* founded by Raja Ram Mohan Roy (1776–1833). Ram Mohan Roy was the outstanding leader of the Hindu reform movement and the father of modern India. The translation was published in three parts, in 1881, 1882, and 1886.[73]

In 1908, the Reverend William Goldsack also made a translation of the Qur'ān, which was published by the Christian Literary Society for India (Calcutta). Rev. Takle found this translation very useful for his work in Bengal:

> So important have I felt the use of the Koran to be, that when intelligent Hindus have been inclined to praise Mohammedanism, I have given them the Rev. W. Goldsacks's Bengali translation of the Koran to read. In this way the eyes of many have been opened to see the absurdities of the book. My belief is that if only we can get the Hindus and Mohammedans to understand what the Koran really teaches, we shall be able to check the advance.[74]

The British ruled India for almost two hundred years. It fell to the East India Company in 1757, when Sirāj-al-Dawla was defeated at the Battle of Palassy. The British left India in 1947 after dividing it into India and Pakistan. Islam in India was a militarily defeated culture, and the Bengali Muslims were caught in a pincer by Christian evangelists and Hindu revivalists who were determined to convert them to Christianity or to reconvert them to Hinduism, the religion of their forefathers. The British government had insured religious freedom to preach and convert. But when the British relinquished the Raj in 1947, Christians formed only 2.5 percent of the total population of India, and they were neither converts from Islam nor did they live in East Bengal (now Bangladesh),[75] which is the most populous Muslim region in the world.

The law prohibiting conversion from Islam to other religions is not only against the express teachings of the Qur'ān and in direct contravention of the Prophet's sunna, but is also unnecessary. As we have seen in the case study of Bengal, there were no conversions among the Muslims under two centuries of British rule. North Africa under French rule and Indonesia under the Dutch crown present the same picture.

Threatened by foreign aggression and internal strife, the medieval jurist found in "the Book and the sunna" his own fears and the remedies which he could devise within his own limited perspective. Anyone who seemed to endanger the *status quo* was an infidel, and any ḥadīth, irrespective of its authority and context,[76] became his argument. "And ultimately these accretions of juristic interpretation had all come to be artificially expressed, particularly through the growth of Traditions, as manifestations of the divine command."[77]

NOTES

1. N. J. Coulson, *A History of Islamic Law* (Edinburgh, 1969), p. 151.
2. 1 Cor. 8:12.
3. Qur'ān 109:6.
4. Ibid., 6:66. See also 6:108, 10:108, 17:54, 39:41, and 42:6. The word *wakīl* has been explained by Imām Fakhr al-Dīn Rāzī in *Tafsīr Kabīr* (Cairo, A.H. 1308), IV, 62–63, and also by Muḥammad 'Abduh in *Tafsīr al-Qur'ān al-shahīr bi-tafsīr al-manār*, ed. Muḥammad Rashīd Riḍā (Beirut, A.H. 1337), VII, 501–03, 662–63.
5. Qur'ān 3:20.
6. Ibid., 5:93.
7. Ibid., 5:99.
8. Ibid., 47:25–26.
9. Ibid., 63:1–6.
10. Ibid., 9:66.
11. Ibid., 9:68.
12. Ibid., 9:74 (emphasis added).
13. Ibn Hishām, *Kitāb sīrat Rasūl Allāh*, ed. F. Wüstenfeld (Göttingen, 1860), p. 927.
14. Ibid., p. 381.
15. Ibid., p. 384.
16. Qur'ān 4:137.
17. Coulson, op. cit., p. 56.
18. *Ṣaḥīḥ al-Bukhārī* (Cairo, n.d.), I, iii, 28.
19. Ibn Hishām, p. 818.
20. Ibid., p. 819.
21. Ibid., p. 819.
22. Ibid., p. 818–19.
23. Ibid., p. 819.
24. Ibid., p. 819.
25. Ibid., p. 820.
26. Ibid., pp. 468–69.
27. Ibn Hishām, p. 820. Al-Zurqānī, *Sharḥ al-mawāhib al-ladunīyah* (Cairo, A.H. 1325), II, 315; see Shair 'Alī, *Qatl-i Murtadd awr Islām* (Amritsar, 1925), p. 119.

28. Ibn Hishām, p. 728.

29. Ibid., p. 819.

30. Ibid., p. 819.

31. Muḥammad Idrīs al-Shāfi'ī, *Kitāb al-Umm*, ed. Muḥammad Zahrī al-Najjār (Cairo, n.d.), VIII, 256.

32. Al-Ṭabarī, *Ta'rīkh al-rusul wa'l-mulūk*, ed. M. J. de Goeje (Leiden, 1964), IV, 1874.

33. C. H. Becker, "The Expansion of the Saracens," in *The Cambridge Medieval History* (New York, 1913), II, 335.

34. Shāfi'ī, *Al-Umm*, VIII, 255–56.

35. 'Abd al-Ḥamīd Hibat Allāh ibn al-Ḥadīd, *Sharḥ nahj al-balaghah*, ed. Muḥammad Abū 'l-Faḍl Ibrāhīm (Cairo, 1956–64), XIII, 187.

36. Becker, op. cit., p. 335.

37. Bernard Lewis, *The Arabs in History* (London, 1958), pp. 51–52.

38. Bukhārī, "Kitāb al-Ṣalāt," "Bāb faḍl istiqbāl al-qibla."

39. Ibn Hishām, pp. 688–89.

40. *Ṣaḥīḥ Muslim with Sharaḥ al-Nawawī* (Lahore, 1958–62), II, 112–13.

41. Qur'ān 49:10.

42. Ibn Kathīr, *Tafsīr* (Beirut, n.d.), II, 590.

43. Ibn Taymīya, *Al-Siyasa al-shar'iya*, ed. Muḥammad 'Abdallāh al-Samān (Cairo, 1961), p. 128. See Emmanuel Sivan, *Radical Islam* (New Haven, 1985), for Ibn Taymīya's influence on modern politics.

44. See *Ṣaḥiḥ al-Bukhārī*, and *Ṣaḥīḥ Muslim*, "Kitāb al-Īmān" for various reports with slightly different wording.

45. Bernard Lewis, *Islam in History: Ideas, Men and Events in the Middle East* (London, 1973), p. 233.

46. See Bernard Lewis' detailed analysis of the genesis and evolution of this institution in Islamic history in *Islam in History*, pp. 217–36, and also *The Jews of Islam* (Princeton, 1984), pp. 53–54.

47. Al-Ghazālī, *Fayṣal al-Tafriqa bayna al-Islām wa'l-zandaqa* (Cairo, 1901), p. 68; see Bernard Lewis, *Islam in History*, p. 232.

48. *Report of the Court of Inquiry Constituted Under Punjab Act, II of 1954 to Enquire into the Punjab Disturbances of 1953* (Lahore, 1954), p. 218.

49. Bernard Lewis, *The Jews of Islam*, p. 100.

50. Ignaz Goldziher, *Mohammed and Islam*, trans. Kate Chambers Seelye (New Haven, 1917), p. 74 n. 3.

51. Bernard Lewis, *The Jews of Islam*, p. 101.

52. Sir Jadanath Sarkar, *Short History of Aurangzīb* (Calcutta, 1954), pp. 105–06.

53. Ibid., pp. 105–06.

54. *Methods of Mission Work Among Moslems.* For Private Circulation Only (London and Edinburgh, 1906).

55. Ibid., p. 11.

56. Rev. S. Lee, *Controversial Tracts on Christianity and Muhammedanism* (Cambridge, 1824).

57. Rev. Charles Foster, *Mohommedanism Unveiled* (London, 1829).

58. James Long has given details of these missions in his *Handbook of Bengal Missions, in connexion with the Church of England Together with an account of general educational efforts in north India* (London, 1848).

59. Hafeez Malik, *Moslem Nationalism in India and Pakistan* (Washington, D.C., 1963), p. 205.

60. London, 1859.

61. The papers presented at the conference have been published in *Islam and Missions*, eds. E. M. Wherry, S. M. Zwemer, and C. G. Mylrea (New York, 1911).

62. Ibid., p. 14.

63. Ibid., pp. 41–42.

64. Ibid., p. 214.

65. Hafeez Malik, op. cit., p. 204.

66. William Wilson Hunter, *The Indian Musalmans* (London, 1871), p. 156.

67. Hafeez Malik, op. cit., p. 27.

68. *Islam and Missions*, p. 213.

69. G. R. Thursby, *Hindu-Muslim Relations in British India* (Leiden, 1975), p. 13. Swami Dayanand's quotation from *Satyarath Prakash* has been translated by Chiranjiva Bharadwaja, as *Light of Truth*, 3d ed. (Lahore, 1927), p. 63.

70. *Leader*, Allahabad, 23 February 1923; see G. R. Thursby, op. cit., p. 151.

71. G. R. Thursby, op. cit., pp. 155–56.

72. *Islam and Missions*, pp. 217–18.

73. Mofakhkhar Hussain Khan, "A History of Bengali Translation of the Holy Ḳur'ān," *The Muslim World*, LXXII, ii, pp. 132–33.

74. *Islam and Missions*, p. 218.

75. Indian Christians are mostly the descendants of those Hindus who were converted to Christianity before the advent of Islam. The Syrian Church of Kerela, in South India, is believed to have been founded in A.D. 52 by St. Thomas, one of the Disciples. Later, two waves of Christian immigrants from the Middle East, one in 345 and the other about 800, settled in Kerela.

76. Heffening has mentioned all of these traditions without any criticism in his article on *Murtadd* in *EI*[1], including rhyming adages or epigrams such as "Slay him, who changes his religion."

77. N. J. Coulson, *A History of Islamic Law*, p. 224.

2
On Chinese Rhubarb

Haneda Akira

RHUBARB IS A general term for some twenty-five species of perennial herbs of large form, often two meters high, assigned to the genus *Rheum*, family *Polygenaceae*. The distribution of this plant is so vast that it is said to grow all over Asia, except for the tropical and Arctic regions. However, the world-famous species taken by the Chinese since ancient times as a laxative and a stomachic were products of China, especially of the mountainous area in the west from Gansu and Qinghai to Sichuan and Yunnan.

Today, exported Chinese rhubarb is represented by the product of Sichuan, *Rheum officinale*, commonly named "Ox tongue rhubarb," because of its shape. But the most appreciated species was *Rheum palmatum* and its var. *tanguticum* (on this name see below).

In any case, we must note the fact that the Taoist physician Tao Hongjing of the sixth century stated that some Sichuan rhubarb rootstocks have purple veins (as those of Gansu and Qinghai) and that blackish ones are sometimes better in quality (than those of Gansu and Qinghai). This statement proves that, even before the Tang period (616–907), the Sichuan rhubarb had become more or less widely known. It is true that Chinese foreign trade by sea developed in the course of time after the mid-Tang period, particularly during the Sung period (960–1279). If the geographically favored rhubarb of Sichuan was increasingly exported by sea, there is no cause for wonder. The problem of quantity and that of quality are not the same. The article on rhubarb in the *Chinese Encyclopedic Dictionary (Chung-wen da-ci-dian)* is probably misled by the trend of Chinese sea trade. Li Shi-zhen, the last great editor, at the end of the sixteenth century, of Chinese traditional medico-botanical *(bencao)* literature, seems to have made the same mistake.

Originally, insofar as the name "ox tongue" comes from the shape of the product, when it has been dried in the shade or in the sun after having been pressed, no veins can be seen, unless it has been sliced. On the other hand, the root stocks of the species *Rheum palmatum*, or its var. *tanguticum*, once they have been dug out, sliced, and dried over a fire, show their fine veins, literally "brocade patterns" (*jin-wen*). Consequently, the traditionally famous "*jin-wen* rhubarb" must be *Rheum palmatum*, or *tanguticum*.

We have no evidence about when the Chinese began to take rhubarb as medicine. On a certain number of the wooden tablets (about 1,000 pieces in all) from the end of the Former Han (second and first centuries B.C.), discovered by Sir Aurel Stein in the ruins of the Great Wall near Dunhuang, we find records of distribution of rhubarb as a drug to the soldiers of the frontier garrison. It is certain that at that time the medicinal properties of rhubarb were already sufficiently well known. Westerners, who had begun to frequent China via the Silk Road, acquainted themselves with Chinese rhubarb, and then wished to acquire it. The Chinese rhubarb trade may have begun in this fashion.

However, there is no reason to think that even the rhubarb known by the ancient Greeks and Romans originally came from China. The name "rhubarb," familiar to the modern European languages, is derived from the Greek *rheon barbaron* and Latin *rheum barbarum*. But it is not certain what foreign countries were signified by the words *barbaron* and *barbarum*. In *De materia medica* by Dioscorides (circa A.D. 60), military physician to the Emperor Nero, the name *rha* occurs, and according to the fourth-century historian Ammianus Marcellinus, the plant received its name from the River Rha, that is, the modern Volga. But we have no evidence either for the statement that rhubarb grows on the banks of the Volga, or that Rha was the ancient name of the Volga. B. Laufer thus assumes that *barbar* meant the highlands of Iran, where there grows a species known as *Rheum undulatum*, and that *rheon* and *rheum* were derived from the ancient Persian *rewon*. For the time being, we will accept his opinion without objection.

It should be mentioned that *Rheum undulatum* is a ubiquitous species found not only in Iran, but also in Siberia and Mongolia. In the eastern part of China, it is called native rhubarb (*tudahuang*). Though inferior in efficacy, it still has its active function as a laxative and a stomachic. Tōdaiō (Chinese rhubarb) and Wadaiō (Japanese rhubarb), introduced and cultivated in Japan in the Edo period, may be cited as examples.

During the Middle Ages, when Muslim merchants (Arabs, Persians, and Turks) played an active part in East-West trade, by land and by sea, the Chinese rhubarb (*riwandi čini*) trade was given into their hands. It is quite natural for Laufer to infer that the mountains of Buthink were the region from Gansu to Qinghai, which the Arab geographer Idrīsī (1100–1165) mentioned as the habitat of Chinese rhubarb, on his map of the world in silver made for the Norman king of Sicily. In fact, the Chinese geographical work of the ninth century, *Yuan-he jun-xian tu-zhi*, mentions Kuo-su as a growing district or distribution center of Chinese rhubarb. Kuo-su was a city near Xining, capital of the Qinghai province, and famous as a market of rhubarb of good quality until recent times.

The Chinese rhubarb transported initially via the Silk Road, and then gradually also by sea, by Muslim merchants was appreciated in the Near East, and finally as far as Europe. The Europeans, who did not know exactly where it came from, vaguely considered Turkey as its country of provenance—whence the name "Turkish rhubarb."

From the thirteenth to the fifteenth centuries, during the reigns of the Mongols and the Timurids, many European travelers visited Central Asia, Mongolia, and China with a variety of purposes. Some of them furnished new information on Chinese rhubarb. Of these, Europeans owe their first authentic account of the rhubarb to Marco Polo. According to him, "All over the mountains of the *Tangut* province (the northwestern part of China around Gansu particularly near Susu) we may find rhubarb in great abundance. Numerous buyers from all parts of the world come there. They bring the precious product back with them." Many later writers gave information that echoed Marco Polo's report. In Behaim's globe (1492), the name Succus is indicated on the location of Tangut, as the district of the provenance of rhubarb. On the map of Tartary in the work of Ortelius, *Theatrum orbis terrarum* (1570), it is also noted that rhubarb grows in the mountainous region of Succuir.

Under the Chinese Ming dynasty (1368–1644), which replaced the Mongolian Yuan (1271–1368), the importance of Susu as the trading center of rhubarb remained intact. This is confirmed by the Venetian geographer B. G. Ramusio, who learned about it in the middle of the sixteenth century from an Iranian merchant. This merchant went to China, but could go no further than Susu, because of the so-called tributary trade system (i.e., controlled trading system) of the Ming. Therefore, he bought rhubarb in quantity at Susu, and returned to Venice to sell it at a good price. According to the hearsay reported by this geographer, superior rhubarb is produced in the rugged mountains with their many springs, numerous gigantic trees, and loamy soil, in the neighborhood of Susu. Evidently, this points to the Qilian range which divides the Gansu and Qinghai provinces.

Moreover, according to the information available to this merchant, rhubarb grows abundantly in various parts of China, but the plant used for internal medicine is very limited. It is used largely as incense, fuel, and as an external remedy for horses. These uses are still carried on, probably with native rhubarb, namely, *Rheum undulatum*. Otherwise, the rhubarb of Yunnan, similar to that of Sichuan, seems to be used mainly as a yellow dye.

In any case, down to early modern times, to say nothing of the Middle Ages, the Europeans, except for Marco Polo and a few other travelers, owed their knowledge of Chinese rhubarb to the Muslims, and above all to Muslim merchants. It was Gracia da Orta, a Portuguese physician, who, based upon his own experience during his stay in East India for thirty years in the first half of the sixteenth century, confirmed that rhubarb of high quality was a native product of China, and that it was transported to the Western countries via the Silk Road and then imported to Europe from the Near East, mainly from Turkey. He attributed this preference for the land route to the deteriorating conditions along the sea route. It seems to me that he did not distinguish the difference in quality between *Rheum palmatum* (or var. *tanguticum*) and *Rheum officinale*.

From the end of the Ming to the beginning of the Qing, the Europeans, especially the Jesuit missionaries, progressed with their own field surveys and research, and gave good descriptions of Chinese rhubarb, of the main producing districts, of the plant's properties, when to collect it and how to dry it, how to prepare it, and its uses. *Flora sinensis* (1656) by Michael Boym is the first monumental work of this kind.

It is well known that in the market established at the border of Russia and Mongolia by the Kiakhta treaty (1727) between the Russians and the Qing (Man-chu), Chinese rhubarb became a major item of export, ranking with tea. In any case, it is to be noted that the Chinese rhubarb trade proceeded in the traditional way. It was Muslim Turkish merchants of Xinjan (i.e., modern Uighurs) of several distinct families, who went to buy rhubarb at Xinig, and who then transported it to Kiakhta (more precisely, to Russian chemical officers staying there).

3

The Concept of Authority in Islamic Thought: Lā ḥukma illā lillāh*

Mohammed Arkoun

MY MAIN CONCERN in this essay is not to describe once again the historical genesis of different doctrinal developments on the concept of authority in Islam; this has been done in several books and articles.[1] But most recent studies are more focused on *power* in its political expression on the level of the state. The Orientalist approach remains more narrative than critical, while the Islamic presentation is still dominated by the ideological need for legitimating the present regimes in the so-called Muslim societies. For these reasons, it becomes urgent to initiate a critical evaluation of authority in Islamic thought in the perspectives I proposed in my *Critique de la Raison islamique* (Maisonneuve-Larose, 1984).

Before we start our analysis, it is necessary to remind ourselves of some basic facts. Are there authors, texts, or periods which could be considered as more relevant than others to a critical, decisive evaluation? Is it possible to discover a hierarchy or a solid articulation among levels of authority as it has been represented in Islamic thought during its classical and contemporary periods? We shall try to answer these difficult questions and, beyond that, to propose some personal developments on authority and powers.

I. Methodological Issues

The first obstacle to be identified is the vocabulary used by ancient, as well as by contemporary thinkers or writers in dealing with any

*This text has been presented in a symposium held at the University of Aarhus on *Islam: State and Society*, 30 August–1 September 1984.

religious phenomenon. Much has been said on authority, the sacred, rite, belief, faith—to build an ideal theology or to apply an ideological system of explanation! From this point of view, the theorizing of al-Māwardī or al-Ghazālī does not differ from the essays of E. Durkheim or of Marxist sociologists of religion.[2] The only possibility of clarifying the situation is to show, for each text, the ideological frame in which it was written. This we cannot do entirely here; we shall only point to the aspects which necessitate a new analysis to prepare a comprehensive and objective theory of authority. For this purpose, we need not only to reconstruct the historical background of each text, or period; we must also have a philosophical scale for the modern evaluation of all problems related to authority. The philosophical reference is particularly important and relevant to our subject for the following reasons:

1) It has been eliminated by all the jurists who contributed to the theory of authority in Islam; a competition developed between jurists and *falāsifa* until the triumph of so-called orthodoxy.
2) Philosophical criticism has been equally eliminated by Orientalists as irrelevant to their narrative and philological approach.
3) Only philosophical questioning allows the possibility of going beyond the purely technical description of doctrines and the ideological assurance implicit in all Western scholars' discourse when they compare Islam and the West on the confusion or separation of religious and temporal authority. This point has a particular importance in the debate taking place for some years on the revival of Islamic law and modern procedures of legislation.

The comparative method raises many objections. There is no significance, for example, in saying that Arabic has no word for the concept of authority as it has been developed in Roman Law, opposing *auctoritas* to *potestas*. But this remark becomes important if the entire historical process leading to Roman and Islamic conceptions is carefully presented. Let us go further in this critical research for a new approach based on a text quoted in the introduction to *State and Government in Medieval Islam* by Ann K. S. Lambton.[3]

We can make the following observations about this excerpt:

1) "Islam" is used here according to the ideological construction of the concept by Orientalist discourse: it is a substantial, stable, definite space (*in* Islam) where all kinds of categoric definitions,

answers, rules, practices are to be found in any time and any society; at the same time, "Islam" is a sovereign subject: he *knows*, he decides, he confuses morality and legality. In spite of all these confusions, this complex, obscure, and active entity is compared to Europe, a precisely known historical, social, cultural space; one would expect a comparison with the Church, which was also identified with all of organized society in the Middle Ages; all comparisons traced are related more to Europe after the sixteenth and even eighteenth centuries than to the Middle Ages.

2) "The clear-cut boundary between morality and legality," "the separation between the spiritual and the temporal" are, as usual, presented as ideal solutions found very early in Europe, and ignored until today by so-called Islam. It is unobjectionable that there should be no formal doctrine of separation proposed by a Muslim thinker; but this fact is less important than discovering the historical and cultural reasons for both situations and their respective philosophical consequences. The social and political struggle between the bourgeoisie and the Church has been more decisive than the formal doctrine which is still used today to legitimate ideological positions, such as we saw recently in France on the issue of public and private schools.[4] The philosophical approach of so-called *laicité* has to be renewed.

3) The common anthropological issues, implicit to all the points touched on in the comparison between Islam and Europe, are not stressed as basic and prior to any narration of events or doctrines developed in both historical experiences: I mean historicity, the societal, the polity, the state, the individual and the person, meaning, the rational, the imaginary,[5] consciousness, unconsciousness, ideation, ideology, myth, etc. Islam is given, as A. K. S. Lambton says, "State is given." One then has only to read, to listen, and to report formally the *given speech* of Muslims, showing the ideological genesis and functions of such speech produced by social groups in competition for power and, consequently, the epistemological distance between ideation and ideology, critical knowledge, and controlled, offensive-defensive speech—all this is out of the "scientific" perspectives of classical Orientalism.

4) If one aims any objective, critical, comparative understanding of the concept of authority in the cultural space of "Societies

of the Book,"[6] three modalities of historical development are to be considered: Islam, Christianity, and the West. The West is a new model, which emerged in Europe against the common *vision du monde* related to the phenomena of revelation. The theological differences which developed on revelation by the Judaic, Christian, and Islamic traditions, must be ranged under the ideological productions of communities using various cultural material; on the contrary, revelation and secularism (I prefer the concept of *laicité*) are axial, basic, structural forces commanding the movements of the human mind toward knowledge and all related behaviors of social agents. *Laicité* is an alternative which developed in the West since the thirteenth and fourteenth centuries more successfully than in classical Islam (second to fifth centuries of the Hijra) for social, economic, and cultural determinants which have not yet been studied comparatively, out of the ideological pressure of each cultural tradition. The success—with different degrees in European countries—of *laicité* is more a *de facto* relation of social forces (bourgeoisie and, with Marxist-Leninist revolution, proletariat against peasantry and so-called religious communities) than a philosophical attitude unanimously accepted in any country (just as a *de facto* separation between the spiritual and the temporal existed in Islam without any intellectual attempt to give it cognitive foundations).[7]

These propositions are more of a program for a new exploration of our subject than definite explanations.[8] I want to put an end to the ethnographic approach of so-called "Islam"; it is urgent that we initiate an applied anthropology answering to the requirements of our contemporary societies. I have told how the relevant debate which has taken place in France since the Left came to power is illuminating for our issues. Even the relation between authority attached to the Constitution Law and political power, with its strategies and tactical trickeries, is revealed these days by the initiatives of President F. Mitterand and the reactions of the opposing forces.

How to approach, then, the concept of authority in Islamic thought? Would it be sufficient to start again with authority of sacred texts, the Qur'ān and the ḥadīth, and to continue with the "orthodox" sources claimed by each great tradition as being Islam (Sunnis, Shīʿis, Khārijites)? Certainly we need to read these texts, but we must do so with a *progressive-regressive* method: We need to go back to the past not to project onto fundamental texts the demands and the needs of present-day Muslim societies—as the *iṣlāḥī 'ulamā'* do—but to reach the historical mechanisms and factors which produced these texts and assigned them such functions (i.e., regressive procedure); but at the same time, we cannot neglect the fact that these texts are still alive and active as ideological systems of beliefs and knowledge shaping the future; we need, then, to look to the process of the transformation of initial contents and functions into new ones (i.e., progressive procedure). The role played in contemporary Islamic discourse[9] by the substantive, essentialist, mythical "Islam" is so dominant that it imposes on all scholars the progressive-regressive method with all required references to traditional as well as to modern knowledge.

Let us see how all these methodological remarks could be applied.

II. Authority in Classical Thought

We shall consider five points in this section:

A. The Emergence of the Concept: The Qur'ān and the Medinan Experience;
B. The Formative Period;
C. The Role of *ijtihād: 'Aqīda* and Intellectual Authority;
D. Tradition and Authority; and
E. Ideologies and Authority.

A. The Emergence of the Concept

According to our previous definition of the progressive-regressive method, we cannot read the Qur'ān and the historical experience of Muḥammad with all the vocabulary used by Muslim tradition after the triumph of the Islamic state. At the stage of Muḥammad's preaching and struggle, the authority of the revelation itself had to be defined, explained, and exercised in daily initiatives to overcome the opposition of the *Jāhilīya* (pagan Arab society) and the People of the Book. I have examined the conditions of this opposition and the linguistic tools used in the Qur'ān to assert the authority of the Messenger through the constant intervention of God.[10]

The originality of the process lies in the exceptional combination of a successful political, social, cultural action and its sublimation in a specific religious discourse using a large, organized system of metaphors. The Prophet's followers were engaged in creative movements and raised by the rich symbolization of the ends assigned to each initiative. The impact of any civilization is proportional to its ability to symbolize human ways of existence; the Qur'ān achieved a great deal in this direction; its permanent influence on contemporaries as well as on later generations can be traced to its symbolic expression of profane, contingent history. In spite of all this, there were groups of bedouins (*a'rāb*) who continued to refuse any obedience to the Prophet, avoiding participation in the *jihād* and paying the *ṣadaqa*.[11]

This means that symbolized authority needs time, repetition, ritualization, and a long process of literarization in order to become interiorized as transcendent norms by all the members of the community produced by and producing the tradition. We have to insist on this point: originally, the authority of the Prophet was directly attested and perceived through his charismatic historical action and the semantic, syntactic, and rhetorical structure of Qur'ānic discourse; after his death, this integrated representation of lived authority broke up in two processes of development: the Qur'ān and the ḥadīth were collected, transmitted, registered, and interpreted, resulting in a large corpus of scriptural tradition; the state, on its side, used this face of authority to exercise a concrete political, cultural power controlling more and more the first process which resulted in the scriptural tradition. We shall return to this double mechanism (not perceived by modern scholarship) submitted to the ideological version on the authority attached to the caliphate-imamate.

There is another significant point to emphasize in the phase of the emergence of authority in the perspective of God's revealed Speech. We have paid much attention to the texts as material documents to be used by historians; but very few considerations have been given to the aesthetic of reception:[12] how discourse—oral or written—is received by listeners or readers. This question refers to the conditions of perception fixed by each culture, or, more precisely, each level of culture corresponding to each social group in each phase of its historical development. The successive and various exegesis and interpretations of the Qur'ān are a good example for studying the development of the aesthetic of reception of religious discourse. One could say that these are very trivial remarks; everybody knows that it is almost impossible to read any text—and especially symbolic religious texts—totally free from the specific postulates of the currently dominant culture. But even if this psychological linguistic mechanism is now recognized, we have to confess that the *history of perception* in a given culture is still an unknown discipline. I tried to raise the problem when I studied the marvelous in Qur'ānic discourse.[13] The respective dimensions and mechanisms of mythical and historical knowledge in Islamic thought have not yet been considered, by either Muslim or Orientalist, in spite of the fact that this historical chapter must precede any attempt to explore the basic cognitive organization of a given culture.

These considerations will receive their true significance when we deal with *ijtihād*: a methodical, intellectual activity of transferring the authority based on the symbolic sublimation of history to the constraining legal power of the *sharī'a*. The same discursive transformation will affect the charismatic authority of the Prophet as expressed and perceived by his contemporaries, when it becomes narrated in the *sīra* with the procedures and ideological trends of all Muslim historiography. The psychological forces at work in the evolution from the state of emergence to the official centralizing state are the social imagination and the search for pragmatic rationalization. Imagination and reason already appear interacting in the Qur'ān; the consolidation of the state after 661 favored a specialization of the imagination in all kinds of *akhbār*, *āthār* and literary productions of reason in speculative disciplines. But the separation will never be total and irreversible. The contents and functions of authority will depend on this psychological cultural evolution.

B. The Formative Period

W. M. Watt and J. van Ess have traced the main lines of this period. For our purpose, we need to concentrate on the new conditions of perception and thinking created by the Umayyad and Abbasid state. The relevant point here is the inversion of the process described for the Qur'ān and the charismatic presence of Muḥammad: priority was given to the definition, expansion, and interiorization of authority as coming from God and Guiding, legitimating decisions and implementations of the Prophet; authority was chronologically and ontologically preceding any exercise of power (the preaching in Mecca focused on the authority of divine Commandments and teachings). In the period of so-called Rightly guided Caliphs, the collective memory of the *Ṣaḥāba* and the cultural climate of Medina helped to preserve—at least in part—the hierarchy of values which prevailed in the time of the prophet. But the struggle between traditional conceptions and mechanisms of Arabic society and the new vision set by the Qur'ān had already shown the power of profane history on efforts to transcend human existence. The fact that 'Umar, 'Uthmān, and 'Alī have been assassinated is suffficient to confirm the radical violence prevailing in all societies, and consequently the true and limited function of authority as revealed religions try to impose it; the purpose is to control the natural violence of human beings through ethical and spiritual sublimation of their urges. This way of controlling violence had some success, but seems ultimately to be inadequate, since societies remain basically systems of inequalities imposed by bloody or structural violence.

The state established by the Umayyads and, after them, by the 'Abbasids was a product of bloody violence, which means the inversion of the hierarchy ethical-spiritual authority/power using violence to impose a political social order fixed and run by the victorious group. A state, as a constraining and controlling power, will use authority as a necessary reference in order to legitimate a temporal power originally lacking any intrinsic authority of its own. We can then speak of official ideology imposing an *image* of legitimate power by misrepresenting the actual genesis of the state. This is the main characteristic of ideology: misrepresenting the true process of history to maintain the adhesion of people to an idealized image of legitimacy. We can see now why ideological constructions differ from Prophetic discourse aiming at symbolization, and from rational discourse aiming at objective knowledge; and we can understand the responsibility of a violent state transforming, for its own advantage, the open symbols of a religion into a constraining system of so-called *orthodox* religion. Orthodoxy—in its Sunni or Shī'i version—is no more than the official religion resulting from the collaboration of a majority of the so-called *'ulāmā'* with the state. This is very obvious with the Umayyads and 'Abbasids; but we depend more on the historians and jurists who worked under the 'Abbasids. This is why the term *mulūk* is applied to the Umayyads but not to the 'Abbasids, who developed the conception of the caliph as a sacred representative of divine authority.[14]

All the theories elaborated by the jurists to meet official demands must be described under the heading of ideological activity in Islamic thought. Nevertheless, it is correct to detect in these theories the impact of the Model of authority as it has been represented and interiorized through the main corpus claimed by the tradition: Qur'ān, *ḥadīth*, *Nahj al-Balāgha*, and various speeches collected in anthologies. All these texts are full of existential experiences expressed in genuine, concise, lyrical language. And through this literature we can reach three faces of authority: 1) the ideological face used to strengthen the legitimate image of the official state, or to remind the princes of the ideal rules, which have always to be imitated; 2) the mythical and mythologizing face consisting of literary construction of ideal-typical figures of authority by projecting all desirable virtues and abilities on historical personalities such as Muḥammad, 'Alī, 'Umar I and 'Umar II, and Abū Bakr[15]; and 3) the original authority of the personality used to build an ideal-type, such as Muḥammad, 'Alī, and Ja'far al-Ṣādiq. This third face is the deepest in the stratified construction of the collective memory awakened and worked up by historiographers, *muḥaddithūn, 'ulāmā', udaba'*, the modern historian can reach some aspects of this level after a critical evaluation of ideological and mythological elements which are, of course, relevant to the knowledge of all faces of authority.

In the formative period, we must not look only to the state and its evolution; before the state could control all fields of social and cultural activities, authority was emerging and expanding in the study of Arabic language, history (*akhbār, āthār*), poetry, exegesis, theological discussions, and elaboration of the Law. In the first century of the Hijra, many lines of development were still possible; this was clearly expressed by Ibn al-Muqaffa' when he wrote his famous *Risālat al-Ṣaḥāba*;[16] but all the ideological movements which were fighting for power or independence from the new state had to refer to the same sources of authority: The Qur'ān and the Model represented by Muḥammad, known through the *ḥadīth* and the *sīra*. To make this authority explicit, the technical authority of the *akhbāri*, the philologist, the grammarian, the theologian, and the jurist were needed. The virtues assembled under the concept of *'adāla* were the conditions usually required of the transmitter, the *qāḍī*, the *mujtahid*, the imām, or the caliph. Here we meet a significant convergence of qualities, behavior and functions in the concept of authority: the ideal Muslim acting in the ideal city had to reproduce the perfect Model actualized by Muḥammad (and 'Alī for the Shī'is) who concentrated in his person all the attributes of authority. This Model will actually be endlessly imitated in many different ways: the Mahdī—like Ibn Tūmart in the Maghrib—the saints or *murābiṭūn*, the *Ṣūfī*, the *qāḍī*, the *'ālim*, the *walī* and the more humble believer have each striven to reach some degree of authority by walking in the steps of the Prophet, or of 'Alī, or of other imāms and saints who represent more concretely and immediately the desired ideal.

This aspect of authority is collective and independent of the State, which is seen, for this reason, as the manipulator of power, especially when the sultanate and the emirate took the place of the caliphate. One could say that in the popularized Model of authority, through the sermons and the various narrations about the prophets, *Ṣaḥāba*, and imāms by the popular story-tellers (*quṣṣas*), authority as an articulated system of ideal desired images of ethical-spiritual thinking and acting circulated more widely and durably than did the power reserved to the State and its servants. But we must add that this type of authority has been and still is interiorized by social *imaginaire*[17] more than it is formulated by critical, theoretical thought. That is why in present-day Islamic discourse, social *imaginaire* is so easily mobilized for an Islamic revolution restoring the central themes of a Model rooted for centuries in the collective soul, or a common Islamic *imaginaire*. The more authority is reduced to a combination of ideal Images, structuring the social *imaginaire*, the more it works as a powerful collective force which is easily engaged in revolutionary movements by militant leaders (see the cases of the Mahdīs in the Sudan, Senegal, and the Maghrib, the Ismā'īlī missionaries, and recently Khomeini).

To complete these brief observations, we must mention the authority of the poet and poetry, especially in the time of the Umayyads and the first 'Abbasids. The new State needed the help of the poet as much as it wanted the support of high religious-minded personalities like Ḥasan al-Baṣrī. We know the role played by great poets like Jarīr, Farazdaq, al-Akhṭal, Kuthayyir, Bashshār, etc. The authority of literary aesthetics is used for ideological support, together with the authority of religious texts and personalities; the pressure of official demands can help the creativity of the poet, and did so in some cases; but it can also transform the best talent into a vulgar propagandist. The significant point in all this is the historical dynamism introduced by the State in all levels of social and cultural existence; authority and power, interacting continuously in all fields, reflect, finally, the whole movement of the societies penetrated by Islamic phenomena.

C. *'Aqīda* and Intellectual Authority

'Aqīda means all beliefs and propositions accepted without questioning as matters of faith. Muslim *'aqīda* is basically the same for all Muslims in its main principles; when the core is accepted, each *mujtahid* can develop his own *'aqīda*, including or excluding some irrational beliefs.[18]

In the high intellectual context of Islamic cities during the classical age, Islamic thought had to rationalize many elements of the *'aqīda*. The most important exercise developed in this direction is represented by two disciplines: *uṣūl al-dīn* and *uṣūl al-fiqh*: the first corresponds to theology, the second to a methodology and at some extent, an epistemology of the Law. We shall pay more attention to *uṣūl al-fiqh* because we can discuss the significance and the role of *ijtihād* as the intellectual foundation of authority.

Let us here again point to the inadequacy of the Orientalist method. Ann K. S. Lambton gives a simple description of the *uṣūl* as they have been used by the representative Sunni authors; nothing is said on the validity of the postulates used by this discipline, which claims precisely to practice a rigorous intellectual control. More than that: we know how several Islamic states, today, enforce the *sharī'a* on the basis of the intellectual authority of the classical *mujtahidūn* who elaborated the *corpus juris* and *uṣūl*. This means that the authority of the *uṣūl* is not a mere historical one for learned scholars; it is a burning issue on intellectual authority for all contemporary Islamic societies. We have to be then, in the same movement of research, learned historians and solid thinkers.

Uṣūl al-dīn and *uṣūl al-fiqh* are interdependent; both are built on the following postulate:

God has delivered his revelation to Muḥammad in a clear Arabic language, understandable by all Arabic-speaking people; Arabic has thus been transcendentalized and confirmed, at the same time, in its human dimension.

This postulate has many consequences which must be made explicit:

1) To be reliable, the *ijtihād* of the jurist must be based on a perfect knowledge of Arabic grammar, lexicography, semantics, and rhetoric; that is why all treatises on *uṣūl al-fiqh* open with an introduction on linguistic problems.
2) Since *uṣūl al-fiqh* is accepted as an authoritative discipline, the authors have reached the required perfect knowledge of Arabic, so that there is no cause for any revision of their work.
3) The methodology defined and used by jurists trained in Arabic is so reliable that all the *aḥkām* correctly derived from the sacred texts express the authentic *ḥukm* of God Himself; that is why all the *sharī'a* is the Law given by God, sacred and transcendent, not subject to revision by any human legislator.
4) *Ijmā'* and *qiyās* depend, for their correct use, on the Qur'ān and

the *ḥadīth*; they again refer to competence in reading Arabic texts.

In practice, *ijmāʿ* and *qiyās* have been always a subject of divergence; Qur'ān and *ḥadīth* are accepted as stable, objective sources of the Law; but if the entire Qur'ān is received in one version by all Muslims, the *ḥadīth* is presented in two very different *corpora*: the Sunni (Bukhari, Muslim, and others) and the Shīʿī (Kulaynī, Ibn Bābūya). Add to this, divergent readings and interpretations which make the *uṣūl* less authoritative than it claims to be. If we raise problems of reading according to modern linguistics and semiotics—as I have done—we may start a task heretofore never undertaken in Islamic thought: the critique of Islamic reason. Obviously, the Shīʿī theory of *ijtihād*, which relies on the authority of the imāms and *marjiʿ al-taqlīd*, falls within the scope of the same critique.[19]

D. Tradition and Authority

We have alluded to the tradition as a source of authority and a field for its expansion. We do not mean only the technical concept of prophetic traditions, or sunna; but all the practical knowledge, beliefs, habits, and values which assure the order, the security, the identity of a group, or a community. Sunna or *ḥadīth* is a selection of elements in wider and diversified traditions under the authority of the Prophet. We do not have to discuss here the problem of authenticity: the point relevant to our subject is that all traditions collected in the received corpus give authority to thoughts or behaviors of Muslims. Scriptural tradition, assuming valuable elements of local traditions, is the consciousness of the Community of its historical emergence. The process of this concentration of history in the tradition and control of history by the tradition started with the death of the Prophet. In this process, there is a constant conflict between tradition and innovation (*bidʿa*); through this conflict, we find manifested also a tension between the authority of interiorized traditional values and the power of as yet unintegrated ideas, discoveries, and events (which we call now modernity). Let us try to clarify such a dialectic with some answers to three questions:

1) What type of authority is perpetuated by the tradition?
2) How is tradition authoritative?
3) What is the value of authority as expressed by the tradition?

1) The authority of scriptural, as well as oral, tradition is related to the memory of the group as it is perpetuated by its wisest and more learned members. The difference between scriptural and oral tradition is linked to writing, which is a cultural phenomenon related to the triumph of a powerful, centralizing state. Linguistic analysis of written and oral discourse shows significant differences in the procedures of reason to articulate thoughts; but these differences do not necessarily refer to an intrinsic superiority of written tradition: we have to pay special attention to the so-called theological theory of tradition in order to discover the ideological biases imposed by the ruling class and its intellectual servants.[20] This too is a new intellectual task for "the people of the Book" who have developed, separately and with constant polemics, three conflicting scriptural traditions on the basis of the same anthropological oppositions between authority and power, plurality of power centers and a single centralizing state, poetic and logocentrist expression, paganism (as a philosophical attitude) and monotheism monopolized by theological speculation with the unavoidable trend toward orthodoxy.[21]

The authority of scriptural tradition is conditioned by the value of each testimony. Only the generation of the *ṣaḥāba* have *seen* and *heard* the circumstances and the words which are reported as the Qur'ān, the *ḥadīth*, and the *sīra*. Historically, it is difficult, if not impossible, to assert how each reporter saw and heard the object of his report. In spite of this fact, the so-called theological theory imposed the dogma that all the *ṣaḥāba* are infallible (*ma'ṣūm*) in their testimony.[22]

It is recognized by the tradition[23] that after the *ṣaḥāba*, there is a degradation of the information and its authenticity; the transmitters had more and more to rely on stories made by memory, which means a *literarized*[24] narration of the original wording appraised in a unique existential situation. Many difficult problems are aimed at through my formulation: historical, literary, psychological, sociological, linguistic, and semiotic. A radical critique of the entire tradition must be done in the lines traced, for example, by P. Ricoeur in *La Narrativité* (CNRS 1980) and *Temps et récit* (Seuil 1982). Tradition—with or without a capital—is alive and authoritative as long as it protects itself from the changing scientific environment. I shall give below a very recent and significant example of this socio-cultural mechanism. This protection has been assured until now by the following postulates (*musullamāt*):

- *Ṣaḥāba* were infallible and carefully transmitted in their entirety the authentic texts and "historical" facts related to the mission of Muḥammad.
- The following generations continued the same transmission of the Tradition learned—with due control and critical mind—from the *ṣaḥāba.*
- The results of this transmission were registered in the *muṣḥaf* and the authentic corpus of the *ḥadīth.*
- All historiographical literature completed and consolidated this Tradition as far as it was conceived and elaborated with the same critical criteria used for the sacred Tradition.
- The *'ulāmā' mujtahidūn* added to the sacred corpus, the *corpus juris*—the sacred Law—elaborated according to the principles and methods given in the *uṣūl al-fiqh.*
- The totality of the reliable corpus thus constituted gives us the possibility of producing a world history entirely integrated, controlled in and by the Tradition: this history is then oriented to the eschatological end.
- The Caliph-Imām is legitimate as far as he protects and applies the Tradition which, in return, is used to establish the legitimacy of a Muslim government.

2) We see better how tradition is authoritative: the group, or the community recognizes and respects in it what it selects of his own history and integrates into its mythical-historical memory. The secret of such authority is in the process and the criteria of the selection made; it is also in the variable combination, in all traditions, of mythical ways of knowledge and historical elements.

The concepts of selection and mythical-historical memory are totally excluded by the structure and the ends aimed at by the tradition; they are unthinkable (*impensables*) in the tradition itself because they lead us to discover that the tradition did everything to cover up. Here we understand why Orientalist scholarship applied to the *ḥadīth*, the *sīra*, and Qur'ān is still rejected by Muslims: it disqualifies the mythical knowledge with the postulates of positivist historicism, without any intellectual attempt to deepen anthropologically and philosophically the concept of mythical-historical memory which is also basic for the Christian and Western traditions. This is why we insist on the question: how is tradition authoritative? It is necessary to know the right chronology, the genuine facts, the historical individuals; but it is misleading to cut this positive history off from the support of the mythical *imag-*

inaire which is at work in all social-cultural traditions. This approach is an achievement of recent studies on history, considered under the rubric of the anthropology of the past.

The tension between historicism and myth reached a high degree when the Mu'tazilite movement imposed its rationalism as an official ideology. But neither the so-called rationalism of the Mu'tazila nor the traditionalism of the religious opposition has been analyzed in the perspective of the tension between *muthos* and *logos*, the rational and the social *imaginaire*. Then, we can know that the issues are not in the manifested arguments exchanged by the two parties, but more essentially related to the cognitive systems represented by the *'ulūm 'aqliyya* (called *dakhīla* by its opponents) and *'ulūm dīniyya*, or *naqliyya*.[25] Why and how did the authoritative tradition ultimately become the winner? The answer will be found in historical psychology and sociology.

3) What is the value, then, of authority as expressed and exercised by the tradition? In other words, what are the respective roles of rationality and *imaginaire* in the genesis and the functioning of the tradition? At what levels and to what degree did rationality emerge in a socio-cultural space completely dominated by mythical knowledge? If we succeed in answering these questions *historically*, we shall have to face the philosophical problem of mythical and rational knowledge.

Even concerning our modern societies, sociologists can still speak of their "*imaginaire* institution";[26] what is to be said, *a fortiori*, of medieval societies? We use an inadequate vocabulary elaborated in the positivist climate of nineteenth-century Europe to describe religions, and especially so-called "popular religion": the marvelous, the supernatural, the sacred, the profane, the secular, the miraculous, the charismatic, superstitions, survivals, all this conceptual apparatus refers to a negative *imaginaire* as opposed to a positive rationality.[27] The *imaginaire* is structured by fables, illusionary representations, popular tales, mythological beliefs; reason is the critical, analytical faculty, in charge of the scientific control which leads to true knowledge. Islamic thought, highly influenced by strong trends of Aristotelianism, developed this false opposition, in spite of the impact of the other philosophical trend: Platonism and Neoplatonism.[28]

Historically, we have first to underline the nonexistence, in medieval societies, of the principal media of our modern rationality: no paper, few written documents, no generalized teaching in public schools (see the later role of the official *madārīs* in strengthening the orthodoxy which is a narrowing, degrading use of rationality), no or few and weak technical tools, weak and limited administration. On the contrary, oral cultural tradition, with its code of honor, pragmatic ways of learning and working (peasants, craftsmen), "symbolic capital,"[29] collective consciousness merged in a common cosmic vision were sociologically and structurally dominant. Consequently, social *imaginaire* had to play a positive, constant, and determinant role at all levels of social and cultural existence. The so-called Islamic tradition cannot be separated from this context; but, since the Qur'ān itself,[30] it aimed a kind of rationalization integrating convictions, beliefs, representations considered as matters of faith, but psychologically related to the social *imaginaire*. The authority of this type of rationality is expressed in so-called "Oriental wisdom" (*ḥikma*) by positivist reason. *Ḥikma* is a psychological attitude, a behavior, a style of knowledge, thought, and perception; it is a collective *ethos* integrated, enlarged, and expanded by the Qur'ān and the tradition. In and with this ethical-spiritual *ethos*, *imaginaire* and rationality are combined at a deep level (see the psychology defined by the Qur'ān through the concept of heart = *qalb*) that a typical harmony, an internal distance are the characteristics of the truly wise man, representative of the living tradition.

This positive aspect of the authority of the living tradition cannot be separated from the negative one represented by the dogmatic, conservative control of emancipating history (scientific, economic, social, and political innovations). The wise attitude is marginal, reserved to a minority; ideological use of the tradition has a larger and stronger impact on the society; we have to clarify, then, the problem of ideologies and authority.[31]

E. Ideologies and Authority

The concept of ideology has been developed by modern critical thought; it was used in a very impressive way by K. Marx, who influenced subsequent practice of the social sciences. Islamic thought has not yet discovered the importance of this concept; it produced conquering ideologies which misrepresented even its own past and values, without free access to contemporary scientific research. Islamic discourse claims to be scientific, at the same time as the human and social sciences are rejected as pure products of Western societies and tools for cultural aggression (*al-ghazw al-fikrī*). It is difficult to explain to Muslim militants, or to *'ulāmā'* trained in the traditional sciences, that human and social sciences are the vital counterpart of the ideologies produced in industrialized as well as in developing countries.

The ideologies of developing countries are mostly negative and inadequate; they are obliged to accept Western models of political, social, and economic organization in order to meet the massive needs of a growing population; but they give the illusion of going back to the tradition, so as to protect and to restore Islamic ways of life and thinking. Who is able to take over such a historical project? Official ideologies, people say; *min al-sha'b ilā 'l-sha'b* ("from the people to the people") claims a well-known slogan written everywhere in many "revolutionary" countries. The implications of this sentence are exactly opposed to the constant principle adopted by classical theology: The masses (*al-'awamm*) must be kept away from any participation in *ijtihād*, which means the exercise of authority (sce *Iljām al-'awamm 'an 'ilm al-kalām* by Ghazālī). Actually, the decision-makers are very few in the new regimes; they all depend on the leader: king or general secretary of the unique party. The *'ulāmā'* have less independence than in the past; they are officers of the state, and must maintain the fiction of a spiritual authority illuminating and assuring legitimacy to the political power.

In the past, ideologies existed, but were eliminated or criticized under the name of sects, heresies, or religious errors. The hard and suggestive polemic between Sunnis and Shī'is is an excellent example, illustrating the ideological basis of theological reason. Only the modern critic of ideologies can show that each orthodoxy is ultimately founded on ideological postulates. We face, then, a general crisis of authority: not merely the authority of political institutions, of the established tradition, of the cultural legacy, but of reason as the source and instrument of any knowledge used by men. Today, the problem of authority does not depend on any religious or secular institution; as far as reason has won its autonomy from outside authorities (revelation, church, *sharī'a*, state), it has the responsibility to constitute knowledge as a region of authority accepted and respected unanimously: knowledge independent of ideologies, effficient enough to explain their formation and to survive their impact.

Let us enlarge these remarks by looking at authority and power in the present-day world.

III. Authority and Power Today

Under this title, we shall mainly consider two points:

A. The Problem of Secularism *(laïcité).*

B. The Reappraisal of Islam.

A. The Problem of Secularism Today

The commonly received view is that Islam did not allow any secularism. This is true if we accept the traditional definitions of the Law as enforced by all types of government in Islamic societies. But we have shown how ideological systems can be presented and accepted as the orthodox truth revealed by God. Accordingly, the concept of religion cannot be approached as a system of knowledge and beliefs manipulated by various social forces to transform initial spiritual aims into ideological principles so as to enforce a special social and political order.

The French Revolution imposed secularism as a political and philosophical alternative to the regime controlled by the Church. Universal suffrage became the source of authority, in the place of a Revelation interpreted and applied by the authorized spiritual authorities. Louis XVI was executed to symbolize the death of the sacred monarchy and the rise of secular authority. On the other hand, when Khomeini came to power, he wanted to judge and execute the Shah as a symbol of the death of the secular *Ṭāghūt* and the reappearance of the sacred Imām.

Secularism is much more than a simple distinction between spiritual and temporal affairs. Such a distinction exists *de facto* in all societies, even when it is negated and hidden by a religious vocabulary. When it is recognized by law and enforced in several institutions, it does not lead to the division of each person into a religious and a secular part! These radical oppositions translated into political parties, as in France, show the necessity, today, of finding a new language going beyond the polemical definitions used in social and political competition. The intellectual attitude underlying such new language exists already on both sides: secularists able to integrate a critical acceptance of traditional religions, religious minds working to consolidate secularism as a decisive step toward the emancipation of human reason from all forms of wrong consciousness. But the appropriate concepts for expressing this new attitude of mind confronting the problem of knowledge and its proper communication do not as yet exist.

How can we speak adequately about secularism when we do not have an acceptable theory of the sacred, and how can we deal with the sacred, the spiritual, the transcendent, and with the ontology, when we are obliged to recognize that all this vocabulary, which is supposed to refer to stable, immaterial values, is subject to the impact of historicity? One could say that these values have been eliminated, or misinterpreted by triumphant material powers; but, on the other side, who could object to the wrong consciousness, the religious dogmatism and fanaticism developed during centuries by a religiously controlled state?

One could also speak of secular religions: the new widespread, dominating ideologies (communism/liberalism; socialism/capitalism) are used and practiced as religions with their respective institutions, economic organizations, celebrations, rites, systems of knowledge, and beliefs. Here is proof that our so-called modern culture is not yet emancipated from the mythological and ideological constraints which conditioned traditional cultures.

In the light of these observations, we can revise our ideas on the place of secularism in Islam and the position of official Islam concerning secularism. Islamic societies are more engaged than ever in a secular history; since the impact of colonialism enlarged by the ideology of development, they have all adopted the attributes of material modernity; this total engagement is precisely the reason for the success of so-called fundamentalist movements which claim an integral application of Islamic law and teachings. These movements are themselves secular in their daily life, their professions, their basic needs; the majority of the militants come from low classes, cut off from the traditional culture, unable to reach the modern urban culture; they rightly ask for more justice, less brutal oppression, possibilities of participating in the new history; but to express this basically secular project and hopes, they use elements of religious language, the only one at their disposal.

The future of secularism in Islam depends essentially on the large diffusion of what I called intellectual modernity.[32] I do not minimize the importance of political and economic changes in creating new possibilities for the circulation of emancipating culture; but I maintain that intellectual modernity is the more needed and efficient means of undertaking a whole reappraisal of Islam. This may be ascertained by the attitude of the middle classes and the new bourgeoisie about the issue of Islam and its role in the present phase of history. Those who enjoy all economic and social privileges are ready to share conformist and very conservative views on Islam, because they do not have access to intellectual modernity! We also know that many students in the technical sciences adhere to the fundamentalist movements: they have no idea about the critical views developed in the human and social sciences, especially history.

In such a context, dominated by a cultural vacuum, secularism cannot be developed in its positive virtualities. There is no political and cultural possibility for an enriching confrontation between a secular and a religious world vision: two ways of perception, thinking, acting, creating, and knowing. Western thought has explored new fields through this confrontation since the sixteenth century. For the time being, secularism is, in the Muslim societies, an ideological theme for criticizing the atheism and materialism of the West; a process of materialization with machines, cars, and gadgets imported from this same criticized West. Thus, all obstacles are accumulated to prevent any serious thinking to discover *laicité* as a dimension of thought, a way and a space to constitute a new concept and a new subsequent practice of authority. This is not the place to develop correctly this decisive point: it requires a special essay; but I can summarize the main lines of a deconstructive history of Islamic thought:[33]

1) Secularism is included in the Qur'ān and the Medinan experience.
2) The Umayyad-'Abbasid state is secularist; the ideological theorization by the jurists is a circumstantial production covering the historical and political reality; with conventional and credulous arguments this theorizing, in any case, is built on an outdated theory of knowledge.
3) Military power played very early a preeminent role in the caliphate, the sultanate, and all later so-called Islamic forms of government.
4) Attempts to rationalize this *de facto* secularism and to develop a secular attitude were made by the *falāsifa*; that is why a new history of Islamic thought has to devote a chapter to the *sociology of the failure* of philosophy: it is one of the conditions for again including the philosophical attitude in Islamic thought.
5) So-called "orthodox" expressions of Islam (Sunnī, Shī'ī, and Khārijī equally claim the monopoly on orthodoxy) are arbitrary selections and ideological use of beliefs and ideas and practices given to be perceived as authentically religious.
6) The whole status of the religious, of the sacred, and of revelation has to be reexamined in the light of a modern theory of knowledge.
7) All political regimes which appeared in Islamic societies after their liberation from colonialism are *de facto* secular, dominated by Western models, cut off from the classical theory of authority as well as from intellectual modernity.

8) From the point of view adopted in this essay, *laicité*, as a source and a space of intellectual freedom to initiate a new theory and practice of authority, is a work also to be undertaken in Western societies today.

B. The Reappraisal of Islam

The eight points which have just been mentioned are an important part of a large program for the reappraisal of Islam. I have developed many other points of this program in my *Lectures du Coran* and *Pour une Critique de la Raison islamique*: it is a task for future generations. But we already see very clearly the lines and the methods to be followed, the themes to be emphasized, the intellectual conditions to be fulfilled.

The reappraisal of Islam is not only an urgent answer to the demands of Islamic societies. This is certainly a vital task, but Islam has three other dimensions highly significant for two present purposes: pursuing the elaboration of a continuing critical theory of knowledge, and contributing to or improvement of peaceful cooperation in the world. These three dimensions are:

*the religious perspective and its place in human existence, and the calling of the absolute;

*the historical perspective on the cultural space particular to the societies of the Book, with special attention paid to the Mediterranean dimension;

*international cooperation today for a new cultural, political, and economic order based on a new theory and practice of authority.

With such exciting perspectives, one may easily see how scholarship on Islam remains intellectualy inadequate and absent from our burning history! Is it not disappointing to read cold, distant, narrative or militantly apologetic presentations of classical Muslim so-called theories of authority? Scholars teaching and publishing at the highest level are still prisoners of the image of a provincial, ethnographically defined Islam partially closed in by its classical formulations, poorly reused in contemporary ideological slogans. The living core of Islam in the perspectives mentioned is more and more covered both by classical Orientalist discourse and by so-called revolutionary Islamic discourse. A growing number of silent voices await the possibility of expressing a rich experience rooted in the core of Islam; when this political possibility arises, will learned scholars begin to write new views in a new spirit? But the only scholars engaged in a continuous fight to create new spaces of freedom, to give new intellectual articulations to the silent voices, are those who harmonize their thought to their concrete engagement and their engagement to their thought (*al-'ilm bi'-l-'amal wa'l-'amal bi'l-'ilm*). This is the ultimate source of Authority, symbolized by the prophets; and with this Authority, we can actualize the philosophy of the person summarized in this sentence:

"La personne, tout en faisant partie de l'Etat, transcende l'Etat par le mystère inviolable de la liberté spirituelle et par sa vocation aux biens absolus" (J. Maritain, *Christianisme et Démocratie*, 1932).[34]

NOTES

1. Ann K. S. Lambton, *State and Government in Medieval Islam* (Oxford University Press, 1981), *La Notion d'autorité au Moyen-Âge, Islam, Byzance, Occident* (ed. P.U.F., 1982); Pouvours, *Les Régimes Islamiques* (P.U.F., 1980); *L'Islam et l'etat dans le monde d'aujourd'hui*, sous la direction d'O. Carré (P.U.F., 1982). M. Arkoun, "Autorité et pouvoir en Islam," in *Critique*, pp. 155–92.

2. For a critical approach to recent theories, cf. Paul Ladrière, "Le Sens du sacré et le métier de sociologue," *Archives des sciences sociales des religions* lvii, i (1984), pp. 115–39.

3. Here is the text from p. XV–XVI:

In Islam the antithesis between the individual and the state or the government is not recognised, and no need is therefore felt to reconcile and abolish this antithesis. Islam knows no distinction between state and church.[4] The parallel between Islam and Europe in the Middle Ages when church and society were one is, perhaps, close.[5] In Islam there is no doctrine of the temporal end which alone belongs to the state and the eternal end which belongs to, and is the prerogative of, the church; no balance between the two; each equal to the other when acting in its own sphere; each equally dependent on the other when acting in the sphere of the other and no tension between the historic community and the church as custodian of the universal common elements in human existence. The state is "given", and it is not limited by the existence of an association claiming to be its equal or superior, to which it can leave the preaching of morality and the finding of sanctions for its truth. It has itself to repress evil and show the way to righteousness; there is no clear-cut boundary between morality and legality.[6] In practice, temporal power was often usurped and there was a *de facto* separation between the spiritual and the temporal but there was no ideological separation; no ruler, however much he may have violated the law, challenged the principle of its universal application.[7] The lack of any formal doctrine of a separation of such powers had important consequences in the field of individual freedom. It contributed to, if it was not actually responsible for, the creation of a situation in which power was arbitrary and exercised by the last despot who had usurped it. It also had important consequences for the attitude towards civil war and internal disturbances.

4. See the debate carried on in *Le Monde* from October 1983 to August 1984.

5. Which is different from the French concept of *imaginaire* to which I refer in my presentation, "Imaginaire Social et leaders dans le Monde Musulman Contemporain," in *ARABICA*, 1988/1.

6. On this concept, see my *Critique*, pp. 162–75; and "The Concept of Revelation: from *Ahlal-Kitāb* to the Societies of the Book," in *Die Welt des Islam, Festschrift* (F. Steppat, Brill), 1988.

7. Since I wrote this paragraph I have developed the same ideas in my book: *L'islam, morale et politique*, UNESCO-Desclée-De-Brouwer, 1986.

8. *Critique*, pp. 43–64.

9. I have given a description of this concept in "L'Islam dans l'histoire," *Maghreb-Machreq*.

10. Cf. M. Arkoun, *Lectures du Coran*, 2e éd. (Paris, 1988), pp. 145–56.

11. Cf. Sūrat *al-tawba* and my analysis in "Les Sciences de l'homme et de la société appliquées a l'étude de l'Islam" in *Les Sciences sociales in Algérie*, OPU, Alger 1986.

12. On this concept, cf. Hans R. Jauss, *Pour une Esthétique de la réception* (Gallimard, 1978).

13. See my *Lectures du Coran*, p. 87–144.

14. A. Abel, "Le Calife, presence sacrée," in *Studia Islamica* 1957/VII; and Ann K. S. Lambton, op. cit., p. 264 s.v.

15. An ideal-Type of Islamic Authority can be described with the portraits of these mythical Figures, or transfigured historical personalities; this ideal-Type can then be distinguished from that given by the literature of Mirrors for princes.

16. Edited and translated by Ch. Pellat, Maisonneuve-Larose, 1976.

17. I use the French word for this concept which has no exact equivalent in English. See my "Imaginaire Social et leaders dans le Monde Musulman Contemporain," in *ARABICA* 1988/1.

18. Cf. H. Laoust, *La Profession de foi d'Ibn Baṭṭa* (Damas, 1958).

19. For a more developed critic on *uṣūl*, cf. M. Arkoun, *Critique*, op. cit., pp. 65–100, and for a Shī'ī position, ibid., pp. 129–54. We must notice that *uṣūl* literature came after the elaboration of the *corpus juris*, mainly on a pragmatic basis; this fact underlines the ideological function—*aprés coup*—of the *uṣūl*.

20. On the anthropological opposition oral/written, cf. J. Goody, *La Raison graphique* (Gallimard, 1980).

21. Cf. M. Arkoun, "Pour une Autre Pensée religieuse," in *Islamo-christiana* 1978/4.

22. Ibn Taymīya has given a clear definition of this concept, in *Naqḍ al-Manṭiq*, ed. M. H. al-Fiqqī (Cairo, 1951), p. 79.

23. I write Tradition with capital T to refer to the idealized sacred legacy of texts used by each community.

24. Literarization is a general phenomenon which all historians have to master, but the modern historian is supposed to be more conscious of the difficulty and to pay great attention to the critic of each concept used to describe the past.

25. This opposition has not yet been well analyzed as a sociological and ideological issue.

26. C. Castoriadis, *L'Institution imaginaire de la société*, Seuil, 19.

27. Cf. P. Ladrière, op. cit. and the books of F. A. Isambert analyzed in this article, *Le Sens du sacré*, ed. Minuit, 1982.

28. Cf. M. Arkoun, "Logocentrisme et vérité reliqieuse dans la pensée *islamique," in Essais sur la pensée islamique,* Maisonneuve-Larose, 3e éd., 1984, pp. 185–232.

29. Expression used by P. Bourdieu.

30. Cf. my *Lectures*, op. cit., pp. 87–144.

31. For more explanations about Tradition, see my "Current Islam faces its Tradition," in *Architecture Education in the Islamic World*, The Aga Khan Award for Architecture, 1986.

32. On this concept, cf. M. Arkoun, *L'Islam, hier, demain*, 2e éd. (Buchet-Chastel, 1982).

33. The concept of deconstruction is related to the concepts of systems of thought and episteme well developed by J. Derrida and M. Foucault.

34. See my "Actualité du problème de la personne dans la pensée islamique," in *Revue internationale des sciences sociales*, UNESCO, 1988/14.

4
Karaites of Christendom—Karaites of Islam

William M. Brinner

IN A RECENT book, Bernard Lewis, using the terms "Jews of Christendom" as contrasted with the "Jews of Islam,"[1] seems to have done so primarily to contrast the experiences of Jews living in these two different religious civilizations. It might also be useful to say, however, that the widely divergent experiences of these two Jewish communities have given rise to varying Jewish responses—in essence, to different Jewish civilizations. Thus, Christianity and Islam have left profound and lasting impressions on the Jews who lived in their respective realms and, more importantly, on their Judaism. One of the most neglected by-paths of Jewish and, indeed, Middle Eastern history is the story of the rise, flourishing, and decline, as well as the near disappearance, of the once widespread and intellectually creative sect of Judaism known as Karaism.[2] The issue addressed by this paper is whether and how the concept outlined above, of the different forms that Judaism takes under the influence of the dominant civilization (a concept which seems to hold true for what has been called "normative," Talmudic, or Rabbinic Judaism), is realized in Karaism, the only major sectarian movement in Jewish history, as well.

With the notable exception of one period, Jewish history has not favored sectarian development. During the latter part of the period of the Second Temple and its aftermath (170 BCE–135 CE), and certainly after the full impact of Hellenism had been felt by the Jews in the land of Israel, sects with widely diverging views on a variety of major aspects of Jewish belief and practice did arise. This, at least, is the picture we receive from the writings of the great contemporary Jewish historian Flavius Josephus. What we read in his works has been confirmed, by and large, in the texts of the Qumran communities, discovered and published during the past half century.[3]

Due in part, no doubt, to the political powerlessness of the Jews after the fall of the Second Temple and the failure of rebellions against Roman rule, the need to draw together in the face of powerful enemies—the direct opposite of Jewish political and religious behavior during the Hasmonaean and Herodian periods—seems to have been a dominant theme. Another factor, however, was possibly the lack of strong dogmatic demands made upon post-Second Temple Jews, so long as they followed the emerging way, or *halakhah*, of the community. By contrast, Christianity's insistence on dogmatic purity has given rise to tens, even hundreds, of diverging sectarian groups, some vainly seeking reunion today after centuries of separation. Although Islam, like Judaism, has not raised dogmatic barriers such as those which exist in Christianity, conflict over the proper repository of the succession to leadership of the community after the death of the Prophet Muḥammad, later reinforced by differences in dogma and ritual, has left the community of Islam split between Sunnis and Shīʿis, as well as the least numerous of the three divisions, the Ibāḍī Khārijites of North Africa and Oman.

In Judaism, on the other hand, with the exception of the very early and relatively insignificant Samaritan schism, only a few major themes have tended to give rise to sectarian development. This was true in late antiquity, in medieval, and in modern times. Among those themes, which include mysticism and messianism, the most important and lasting is, without a doubt, the question of the sources, authority, and interpretation of the Law. One need only mention three such instances, and one virtually exhausts the list of major Jewish sectarian development based on this question: Sadducean versus Pharisaic Judaism; Karaism versus Rabbinism; and Reform versus Orthodoxy. Although it is perhaps too early to evaluate the historical significance of the third of these, each of the previous two has had a profound effect on Jewish unity and Jewish thought. This was so, if only because of the re-thinking and reformulation of positions by the majority which the opposition of the minority group inspired.[4]

Historically, Karaism is said by some scholars to have influenced the development of Rabbanite Judaism, by serving as the adversarial focus around which the scholarly study of the Hebrew language, the interpretation of the biblical text,[5] and the concept of the centrality of the Land of Israel and the return to it received significant impetus and inspiration in the medieval period.

The question of Karaite origins can not have a definitive answer as yet, but there exist several possible responses, each based on a different ideological perspective, rather than firm historical evidence. Some Rabbanite Jewish scholars have accepted the Karaite claim of descent from the Sadducees, thus placing the former group squarely in the camp of heresy. Others accept the possibly apocryphal story of Anan ben David, the defeated and embittered candidate for the exilarchate in Baghdad in the eighth century, claiming to have created a new religion in order to save his life. Still others, while accepting the eighth-century date, reject the Anan story, reserving for him the lesser role of founder of the Ananite sect of Karaism. Modern Karaite scholars, as we shall see, are divided on the subject of their origin.[6] Some leading intellectuals of the Reform movement in the early post-Emancipation period supported the theory of Sadducean origin of the Karaites, and saw certain similarities of attitude, if not of practice, between Sadducean, Karaite, and Reform Judaism.[7] Karaite practice itself, both legal and ritual, can be seen either as a continuation or revival of non-Pharisaic practice, or as being profoundly influenced by the Islamic environment in which Karaism seems to have emerged, or at least developed.

Whatever the truth of its origin-story, and whether it is connected with the figure of Anan ben David or not, Karaism seems to have found a ready response among certain elements within Babylonian and Iranian Jewish society of the eighth and ninth centuries. The preceding centuries had already witnessed many conflicts over leadership of the Jewish community: whether between the schools of Palestine and those of Babylonia/Mesopotamia, or, within the latter, between the exilarchs and the *gaonim*, or heads of the great academies. The disputes were usually extremely bitter, ending often in dismissals from office, demotions, or even excommunication. There was, therefore, fertile ground for any movement that rejected the authority of the Talmud and, more significantly, one which rejected the authority of the rabbis and the entire scholarly caste, an authority based on the study and interpretation of the body of Talmudic literature and the enforcement of the legal system, or more properly: way of behavior, *halakhah*, that developed from it. According to some views, Karaism seems to have found its first major response among the poor and miserable elements of society, and only later to have attracted some intellectuals and wealthier members of the community. Whatever the process, in developing a vigorous response to the virulent attacks upon it by the great Rabbanite intellectual figure Saadiah Gaon (870–935), Karaism launched a counter-offensive and missionary effort.[8] In fact, it probably reached the height of its intellectual importance during the ninth and tenth centuries, suffering a steady decline thereafter. For example, it enjoyed a new lease on life in Constantinople and the Balkans during the twelfth and thirteenth centuries, and later too, in newly-rising Eastern European centers, all of which have now virtually disappeared. Even in its area of origin and early spread, however, an especially gifted figure might appear during the long ages of decline.

Scholars are generally agreed that Karaism first spread among Jewish communities close to its point of origin in Baghdad, namely Mesopotamia and Iran. But with the rise within it of the movement of *Avelei Zion*, or mourners for Zion, and the doctrine of the need to return to Jerusalem, significant Karaite settlement took place there during the tenth century, creating an important and, for a time, powerful center.[9] The Karaite movement spread through the lands of Islam in North Africa, reaching as far as Spain, eventually giving rise to three main regional centers in the world of Islam: Iraq and Iran in the east; Palestine, with its offshoots in Syria and Egypt, in the central areas; and Spain in the west. During the tenth century, however, a movement northward from Muslim Iraq and Iran into Christian Byzantium took place. The history of the subsequent spread northward and eastward from there becomes somewhat obscure. What is clear, however, is that Karaism spread into Byzantine areas around the Black Sea which controlled or adjoined various Mongol and Tatar states, such as the Khanates of the Golden Horde and of Crimea. Just how it spread from there through Khazar territory, and northward to the then vast lands of Poland and Lithuania, is also not very clear. Modern Karaite scholars, at any rate, connect the northward spread to the conversion of migrating Turkic groups, especially the Khazars, and their eventual settlement in the territories in which they were found until the nineteenth century at least. These Karaite historians link the migration to Poland and Lithuania with the period of Vytautas (Witold, 1350–1430), who served as vice-regent of the Grand Duchy of Lithuania from 1382 to 1430.[10] In 1397, after conquests in the Crimea and the Ukraine, he is said to have brought Tatars and Karaites to settle areas bordering on the territories of the Teutonic Knights.[11]

From its height, when it represented a considerable demographic element, with some influence on Jewish intellectual concerns, Karaism declined to its present state of a total of perhaps 15,000–20,000 adherents, mostly in the State of Israel.[12] At its zenith, however, as mentioned above, Karaism inspired Rabbanite apologetic polemics, as well as competing Hebrew grammatical studies, to support the newly developing field of biblical exegesis.

Before World War II, Karaite communities were found in two major geographical areas. In the Middle East there were communities, in declining order of magnitude, in Egypt, Palestine, Istanbul, and Hīt in Iraq. The European communities were to be found in historical Poland—Troki (Trakai)[13] and Wilno (Vilna) in Lithuania; Luck (Lutsk) in Volhynia; Halicz in Galicia—and in Soviet Russia—Yevpatoria (Goslov)[14] in the Crimea, as well as nearby Odessa.[15] These two widely separated centers, one in lands of Islam in the Middle East, and the other in Christian (or Marxist) Eastern Europe,[16] preserved communal contacts and loyalties in spite of great cultural, linguistic, and ethnic differences. In 1830 and 1840, for example, the great Russian Karaite scholar Abraham Firkovich visited the Karaites of the Middle East. A century later, in 1934, a Karaite rabbi from Russia, Tuvyah Babovich (Bobowicz), became the communal leader and Chief Hakham of the Karaites of Egypt, a position which he held until his death in 1956. This appointment was not unusual, because for a considerable period Egyptian Karaites had been importing communal leaders from Constantinople or the Crimea. During his term, the Egyptian Karaites, at first numerically the largest Karaite community in the world, began the decline in numbers which now seems to have reached its nadir.[17]

By the end of the nineteenth century, whatever Karaite scholarship remained alive was largely centered among the Karaites of the Russian Empire—then numbering some 10,000. Even their co-religionists in the Middle East, as we have seen, received their leadership, inspiration, and texts from the schools and printing presses of Eastern Europe. A peculiar remnant of this relationship is to be found in the daily and Sabbath prayerbook (*Siddur ha-tefillot*) of the Egyptian Karaites, published as late as 1948. Here the full-page traditional prayer for the ruler, printed in Russian, still contains the name of Alexander III (1881–94), the czar during whose reign the infamous anti-Jewish pogroms began. The Egyptian Karaites, not knowing Russian, simply reprinted this as part of the religious heritage they had traditionally received from Eastern Europe.

Rabbanite Jewish responses to Karaism and Karaites varied over the centuries from neglect to active opposition. When Maimonides came to Cairo, where the Karaites had succeeded in using their superior numbers to influence Rabbanite practice, he used an approach which mixed severity and kindness, and succeeded in reasserting Rabbanite independence and supremacy. In his legal and philosophical works, he never ceased to argue against the views of the Karaite authorities, whom he often refers to as "the fools."[18]

Whatever the attitude of the rabbis toward them, and however weak or strong the contacts between Middle Eastern and European Karaites, the two latter groups developed strongly divergent views toward Jews, Judaism, and the land of Israel, especially during the past century and a half. This can be traced, in fact, with greater precision to the second quarter of the nineteenth century.

One chief factor that seems to have triggered this split during those years was the completion of the process of the spread of Russian rule over all the territories inhabited by the European Karaites.[19] Perhaps more significantly, there was a change in Russian government policy toward the very large and territorially concentrated Jewish population that had become absorbed into the Russian Empire as a result of its expansion. As part of his program of consolidation, centralization, and modernization, Czar Nicholas I (1825–55) effected drastic changes in the status of Jews in the Russian Empire.[20] Over ninety percent of these Jews, descendants of subjects of two great states of Eastern Europe, the Kingdom of Poland and the Grand Duchy of Lithuania, had become Russian subjects as a result of the successive partitions of Poland in 1772, 1793, and 1795.

The policy of Nicholas was dictated by two aims: to change the relationship of the Jews to the state, and to speed up the conversion of Jews to Russian Orthodox Christianity. In part, at least, this was to be effected by the policies set forth in the Recruitment Statute of the Jews issued on 26 August 1827.[21] It is therefore not surprising that the leaders of the Crimean Karaites, who since the Russian conquest in 1795 had been recognized as legally separate from their Rabbanite Jewish compatriots, should have reacted strongly to this new statute, with two important moves. In 1827, the year of the introduction of Jewish military recruitment, the Crimean Karaites drafted a statute for recognition as a separate religious grouping or church, and moved to persuade the government to exempt the Karaites from the military service imposed on the Jews.[22] Successfully led by two *hakhamim* of the Crimean Karaites, Simhah Babovich and Joseph Solomon Lucki, the delegation that petitioned the government for this exemption later succeeded in gaining the same privileges for the Karaites of Lithuania as well.[23]

Shortly thereafter, there emerged the leading scholarly (and political) figure of modern Karaism—one who almost single-handedly played a central role for almost half a century, and who wrote a history that effectively traced the separation between Karaism and Judaism to earliest times. This important figure is the aforementioned Abraham Firkovich, who used the pen-name Even Reshef (1786–1874). Born in the Polish Karaite community of Luck (Lutsk), and broadly educated in traditional Karaite exegesis and, it is said, in Talmudic studies as well, Firkovich embarked on his scholarly mission of establishing the independence of Karaism from Talmudic Judaism. In 1825, he wrote a memorandum to the Russian government "suggesting the removal of Jews from areas contiguous to the western border in order to prevent smuggling and urged the desirability of encouraging Jews to enter agriculture . . . which would, he felt, limit the opportunity for fraudulent commercial practices of the Jews."[24] Firkovich accompanied the Hakham Babovich to Palestine in 1830, and after writing two anti-Hasidic and anti-Rabbanite books,[25] he carried on extensive travel in the Middle East, during which he bought and brought back to Russia a large collection of manuscripts, documents, and books bearing on Karaite history.[26] He also engaged in archaeological work in the Crimean Peninsula, in an attempt to prove that Karaites had entered Crimea from Byzantium and that it was they, and not the Rabbanites, who had converted the Khazars to Judaism—or the Mosaic religion, as contemporary European Karaite writers would have it.

The major aim of Firkovich's industrious efforts seems, however, to have been what proved to be a successful attempt to dissociate the Karaites from Judaism. By proving, through documents and tombstone inscriptions, that Karaites had entered what was to become Russian territory from the East at a very early date, Firkovich hoped to distance them from any possible accusation of involvement in the Crucifixion.[27] In 1840, Karaites in the Russian Empire were placed on an equal footing with Muslims, and in 1863, they were granted equal rights with Russian Christians. In the course of this legal development, the official name by which the community was known changed, from Jews-Karaites, to Russian Karaites of the Old Testament Faith, to simply Karaites or Karaims.[28] This newly enfranchised community was officially divided into two separate segments, each headed by a *hakham* or communal leader: one in Feodosiya in the Crimea, and the other in Troki in Lithuania.[29]

The political efforts of Babovich and Firkovich, and the latter's scholarly work as well—marred though it was, at times, by forgeries in his zeal to prove the Karaite case[30]—bore significant results, as we have seen, for the status of Karaites in the Polish, Lithuanian, and Crimean regions of the Russian Empire, and led to their total estrangement from Russian Jewry. Added to the political factors that brought this about was an important linguistic/cultural one. The vast majority of their Jewish neighbors spoke Yiddish. The Karaites, or Karaims, however, used their own Turkic language, identified by Soviet scholars as a medieval form of Kipchak, a language of an area north of the Caucasus. This "Jewish language,"[31] containing the usual admixture of Hebrew words, and written in the Hebrew script, has been variously known as Karaimic, Karay (in Lithuania), and Chaltay (in the Crimea).[32]

For a variety of reasons, the period between the two world wars saw a rapid decline in the European Karaite population, as well as its dispersion, largely to scattered communities in Western Europe. The story of the fate of the remaining European Karaites under the Nazi invaders of Poland, Lithuania, and Russia is much less well documented and certainly less well known, and deserves further study. What is clear, however, is that once again, and in sharper and more fateful form, the question of Karaite identity—whether they were Jews or not—had to be addressed. This time the question had stronger racial than religious overtones. Once again the answer—but this time from both Jewish rabbis and Karaite leaders—was the same: the Karaites were not Jews but a separate and distinct people. In the words of Karaite scholars, they were of Turkish or, at any rate, of Asiatic origin.[33]

Middle Eastern Karaites, however, held a somewhat different view. Living side by side with Rabbanite Jews in Cairo, albeit in separate quarters (*Ḥarat al-Yahūd* [Quarter of the Jews] for the Rabbanites, and *Ḥarat al-Yahūd al-qarā'īyīn* [Quarter of the Karaite Jews] for the Karaites), they considered themselves, and were certainly considered by other Egyptians, Muslim and Christian alike, to be Jews. Under Mamlūk rule in Egypt and Syria (1260–1517), for example, for purposes of representation before the Sultan, the Jewish community was officially seen as divided into three sub-groups: Rabbanite Jews,

Karaite Jews, and Samaritan Jews.[34] This convenient grouping made easier the application of the Muslim concept of *dhimma*, or protection of non-Muslims belonging to "Peoples of the Book."[35] Clearly, to have gone through the efforts of Firkovich and the leaders of the Russian Karaites in a Muslim context, to prove that Karaites were not Jews, would not only have been disadvantageous, but might have proved dangerous, by depriving the Karaites of the "protection" of their Jewish identity.

Nowhere is the difference of attitude among Karaites themselves toward this question more clearly displayed than in three recent books by Karaite authors: two Europeans, and the other of Egyptian origin, but now residing in Israel.

The oldest of these works is by the Polish Karaite scholar Ananiasz Zajączkowski, *Karaims in Poland*, published in 1961.[36] The other work by a European Karaite is *Le Karaïsme: Ses Doctrines et son histoire* by Simon Szyszman, published in 1980.[37] The third one, written by a leader of the formerly Egyptian Karaite community in Israel, Yosef al-Gamil, is a two-volume work entitled *Toledot ha-yahadut ha-qara'it*, published in 1979.[38]

In examining the differences in attitude between these two European Karaites and the Egyptian/Israeli one, their responses to only three issues will be examined: 1) the origin of Karaism and its spread; 2) the relationship of Karaism to Rabbanite Judaism; and 3) their attitude toward the land of Israel. In addition, their very different responses to the Holocaust and the fate of the European Karaites will be instructive.

Very striking, indeed, is the emphasis placed both by Zajączkowski and Szyszman on the ethnic distinctiveness of the European Karaites, their Turkic origin, and their almost accidental connection with Jewish history through the origins, but not subsequent development, of their religious beliefs and practices. Zajączkowski, for example, makes the statement:

> . . . all Karaims are of Karaim religion, which is sometimes the only link of the Karaim community connecting the particular ethnical groups, e.g. Polish and Egyptian Karaims. The feeling of community is sometimes much weaker than, for instance, among the Roman Catholics of different countries, as France, Poland, etc.[39]

As to origins, this author takes a two-fold approach: in Chapter I, entitled "Karaims: Origin and History (Ethnogenesis)," he deals solely with the "Kipchak-Turkic character of Karaim culture."[40] Chapter II, on the other hand, entitled "The Karaim Faith," begins with the bald statement:

> The Karaim religion arose in the beginnings of the 8th century in the Eastern province of the Muslim califate in Iraq. The first Karaim legislator and teacher was Anan ben Dawud [*sic!*] of Basra. . . .[41]

In this second chapter on religion, no mention at all occurs of Jews or Judaism. Karaites "do not allow any additions or commentaries to the Holy Scripture,"[42] and frequent mention is made of similarities to Christian teaching in this regard, even to the point of stressing that "the Karaim religion played a part similar to that of the Reformation,"[43] and that "it allows a perfectly free investigation, similar to that of the Protestant religion."[44] Zajączkowski mentions that "some orientalists compare the Karaim principle of rejecting the oral tradition to the Shiism in Islam," and criticizes this view, because "the early Karaim religion borrowed very much of the dogmatically-ritual school, and particularly of Abu Hanifa. . . ."[45] He concludes the paragraph with the statement:

> From the Muslims also the Karaim religion adopted the belief that Mohammed had been the prophet of Islam, and similarly Anan believed in Christ as in a prophet and teacher sent to the Christians (according to the testimony of an Arabian writer Makrizi).[46]

Other evidence is adduced to show the tremendous influence of Islam not only on the religion, but also on the language and culture of the European Karaites. He ends the second sub-division of the chapter entitled "Articles of the Karaim Creed (Faith)" with a summary of the biblical sources of the Karaite faith and liturgy, and with the statement:

> They [the Psalms] provide a considerable part of the Karaim divine service, just as in the Roman Catholic Church and other Christian religions.[47]

In no place is Judaism mentioned, either as a point of origin or as a factor for comparison. When it comes to Jerusalem and the land of Israel, two sentences are devoted to what has traditionally been seen as a central feature of Karaite doctrine and practice:

> The chief center of Karaism was transferred by Anan ha-Nasi from his former homeland Iraq to Jerusalem. The Holy Land enshrouded in the glamour of

Messianism, the land of prophets and patriarchs, has always attracted the hearts of the believers of monotheistic religions, Mosaism, Christianity or Islam.[48]

After devoting Chapter III to the Karaite language, in Chapter IV Zajączkowski turns to anthropology, consisting largely of physical measurements and bloodtypes, to prove the Turkic/asiatic origin of the Karaites, and to ethnography, mostly dealing with Kipchak folklore among the Karaites. The next chapter, "Karaim Settlements and Demography," traces the history of Karaim settlement in Poland and follows the changes in their legal status until 1936. The next sentence begins "After the liberation of Poland from the Nazi occupation," with no mention of what happened during that horrible period. The only reference to the great demographic changes brought about by the two world wars is the bald statement:

The chief difficulty of treating this subject [Karaite ethnography] lies in the altered economic and social conditions in which the Karaims have lived for the past scores of years.[49]

Szyszman's work is very different in nature and attitudes from this work by Zajączkowski, although similar in the stress placed on the Turkic, non-Jewish character of the European Karaites. In regard to the question of origins, Szyszman begins the book with the following sentences:

L'histoire du karaïsme est souvent écrite d'une manière fantaisiste et donne de ce mouvement une image fort éloignée de la réalité. Un récit largement diffusé dans la littérature peut en servir d'exemple.[50]

The story he tells is the traditional tale of Anan ben David related above, and apparently accepted, at least in part, by our previous Karaite author. Asking how such an origin could explain the spread and strength of a new religion, Szyszman goes on in his opening chapter, "Origines du karaïsme au sein des religions monothéistes," to paint a picture of the two different tendencies in biblical Israelite religion, the particularist and the prophetic: the first giving rise to Pharisaic religion, and the second to the Sadducean and Essene forms. Pharisaic religion evolved into Talmudic Judaism, while the Sadducees and Essenes, instead of disappearing, combined in the Diaspora with Hellenistic groups close to the ideas of Philo of Alexandria. Weakened by the spread of Christianity, which absorbed many adherents of this religious view, they remained strong enough to influence the nascent Islam:

Mahomet a connu surtout les *ébionites* judéo-chrétiens qui représentait une symbiose des doctrines chrétiennes et sadocites.[51]

In the environment of the new Islamic Empire, in which the abolition of many political and cultural boundaries favored spiritual life, the semi-underground movement of "Fils de Sadok" (Zadokites, not Sadducees) resurfaced to become the Karaite religion:

Déjà le fait que les auteurs anciens parlent des "ananites parmi les karaites" suffit à prouver qu'Anan et ses plus proches et actifs collaborateurs n'étaient qu'un groupe dans le grand ensemble du karaïsme qui existait bien avant eux et auquel ils ont donné une impulsion nouvelle au VIIIe siècle.[52]

While paying considerable attention to the influence on Karaism of forces as diverse as Philo of Alexandria and the Mu'tazilite movement in Islam, Szyszman, unlike Zajączkowski (who may have been unaware of their existence or importance when he wrote), devotes an entire chapter to the influence of the Essenes on Karaism. By "Essenes" he means, of course, the Jewish sectarians of Qumran, the writers of the Dead Sea Scrolls, the significance of which in Karaism has been the subject of considerable debate and discussion.[53] Going even further than that, he traces "Sadocite" tendencies in Yemen and Abyssinia and states:

Depuis longtemps on a, par ailleurs, remarqué dans les croyances des falachas de nombreux traits communs avec celles des karaïtes, des samaritains et celles de la communauté de Qumrân.[54]

In other words, Szyszman sees Karaite religious ideas as being much more general and widespread than does Zajączkowski, and finds them in most early Jewish sectarian developments, which he labels "Sadocite." While placing great emphasis on the Polish-Lithuanian-Russian centers of European Karaism, he does not insist on the ethnic separatism of the Karaims. He speaks of the gradual decline and decadence of the European centers, and of the loss of the largest center surviving into the twentieth century, that of Egypt, specifically Cairo. This loss he attributes, with a mixture of anger and hatred, both to the unsuitability and inactivity of the leader of the Cairo Karaites, the aforementioned Tuvyah Babovich, and, above all, to the

State of Israel and its insistence that the Karaites be Zionists. He writes about both these factors:

L'activité ou plutôt l'inactivité de cet homme accéléra la désagrégation de la communauté et facilita la tâche de ceux qui sans cesse cherchaient à détruire le karaïsme. . . . Pour eux, l'existence de ce dernier foyer karaïte vivant était comme du sel sur une plaie. Toute sortes de provocations, jusqu'aux plus viles, ont été alors mises en oeuvre, entrainant la mort de plusieurs hommes.[55]

He goes on to relate the events which led to the execution of the young Karaite, Dr. Moshe Marzouk, by the Egyptians in 1955 and states:

Cette mort fut largement exploitée, tant contre l'Egypte, pour la discréditer aux yeux des karaïtes, que contre les karaïtes eux-mêmes, les présentant comme des alliés de la politique sioniste.[56]

This section, which neglects to mention that a Rabbanite Jew was executed along with Marzouk, is followed by an even more bitter attack against the state of Israel and its policies and actions toward the Karaites. As for the Holocaust and its effect on European Karaites, or their role in it, there is complete silence, strangely followed by the words:

Avec la deuxième guerre mondiale la liberté des cultes est devenue possible en Crimée et dans les territoires situés au nord de la mer Noire.[57]

One receives a very different picture of almost all these issues from the book by al-Gamil. The origins of Karaism are presented in a simple fashion:

Those who followed Shimon ben Shetach were called Pharisees, and from them descends the religion of the Rabbanite Jews, while those who folowed Rabbi Judah ben Tabbai, who accepted only the Written Law, were called Sadducees, and from them descends the religion of the Karaite Jews.[58]

What is significant here is not the oversimplification of history, but the use of the term "Karaite Jews," which marks him off from his European co-religionists. In speaking of the latter, he is interested in their common religion, and not in their differing ethnicity. He contrasts the differing attitudes toward Jewish identity in describing the problems of the Hakham Babovich in Egypt:

> Hakham Babovich symbolized the conservative school, but the reality of Egypt differed in essence from what he knew in his own land. Here he found a community which identified itself with and belonged to the people of Israel, which maintained close social ties with Rabbanites. . . . This feeling was strengthened further when his contacts with the Russian Karaites were cut off at the outbreak of World War II.[59]

Al-Gamil pays much attention to the importance of the Karaite presence in Jerusalem from the days of Anan's supposed settlement there, to various efforts at re-settlement, down to the present mass immigration of the Karaites of Egypt to Israel, and the establishment of their religious center there. As for the Holocaust,

> . . . the Nazis discriminated between (Rabbanite and Karaite) blood. . . . after the Nazi conquest (in Russia) in 1942, Dr. Lev Landau was asked by the Nazis to prepare a memorandum on the origins of the Karaites. . . . similar memoranda were demanded from the Karaites of Warsaw and Vilna. . . . The Karaites were permitted to live. At the beginning, indeed, the Germans believed that the Karaites were not Jews. But in the end, they rejected that argument, and slaughtered them as they did the rest of the Jews. The Karaites preferred to die courageously with their Jewish brothers.[60]

This is, of course, a very different presentation from that of the two European Karaites. How are we to explain the difference? One might attribute it cynically to al-Gamil's wishing to see his community legally recognized as Jews in Israel—although one cannot deny that this may be one out of many factors. What is most important, however, is the consistency of the vastly different approaches of these spokesmen to some basic questions.

In the Christian world, and especially in the area of eastern Europe to which European Karaites were almost totally confined before recent individual migrations to the west, to be a Jew was a curse, a tragedy, a cause for the annihilation of a group. Small wonder, then, that with the spread of the Enlightenment and of western learning into the Russian Empire, a Karaite scholar like Firkovich, with a modicum of modern training, should have put his knowledge to use in proving historically the very ancient dissociation of Karaism from Judaism. Since Karaism was connected with Sadducean ideas and practices, and was clearly non-Pharisaic in outlook, Karaites could not be accused of complicity in the death of Christ and, being exculpated from that charge, should not be subjected to anti-Jewish measures. Under the Nazis, the Turkish, non-Semitic ethnic origin of the

Karaites, supported by their use of the Turkic Karaimic language, was used to show conclusively that they were not Jewish in an ethnic or racial sense, no matter what religious similarities might exist with Judaism. Did not Christianity itself share some religious features with Judaism?

As has been intimated above, in the world of Islam the situation was quite different. To be recognized as *ahl al-kitāb* ("people of the book," or "scriptuary"), if only as a sect within one such group, was clearly more desirable than to be outside that category as a *mushrik* ("one who joins partners to God"—a polytheist). The scriptuary, Jew or Christian, was guaranteed *dhimma* ("protection") under specific circumstances in the Islamic polity, a condition greatly to be preferred over being outside that sphere. Since Christianity clearly had several different sects, all of which claimed to be Christian, and equally deserving of *dhimma* with all others, so Judaism could have a number of sects as well. That this was formally recognized in the Islamic realm is most clearly shown in the aforementioned account of al-Qalqashandī on the Islamic chancery, where he describes the non-Muslim religious groups recognized by the Mamlūk state.[61]

It becomes clear, then, that the differing presentation of Karaite identity and loyalty is due more to the attitudes and values of the surrounding majority religion to which Karaism was forced to adapt itself, than to indigenous Karaite religious beliefs and principles. Salo Baron wrote what was probably meant as an epitaph:

> Ultimately excluded more rigidly than Gentiles from the connubium with Jews, unable and unwilling to establish far-reaching contacts with the non-Jewish world, the Karaites gradually sank to a position of minor significance in the history of their people.[62]

This harsh statement cannot be applied to all of Karaite history. In some ways, it does apply to the "Karaites of Christendom," who have almost entirely vanished due, in no small measure (as we have tried to demonstrate), to their efforts at accommodating themselves to the demands of their environment, precisely in order to ensure their survival. The remnants of the "Karaites of Islam," on the other hand, perhaps because of their stubbornness in clinging to their Jewish identity and ties, are now creating a new community in Israel, one which will test both their powers of survival in a Jewish—rather than Christian or Muslim—context, and the religious toleration of Rabbanite Judaism and the State of Israel as well.

NOTES

1. Bernard Lewis, *The Jews of Islam* (Princeton, 1984), p. xi.

2. Some rather recent works by Karaite authors are dealt with below. These are not, however, based on new research, nor are most other recent historical works on Karaism. Important exceptions are Z. Ankori, *Karaites in Byzantium: The Formative Years, 970–1100* (New York, 1959), and H. H. Ben-Sasson, "The First of the Karaites: The Trend of Their Social Conception" [in Hebrew, with English summary], *Zion* XV (1950), pp. 42–55. Some new material on the Karaites from the Cairo Geniza may be found in S. D. Goitein, *A Mediterranean Society* (Berkeley and Los Angeles, 1967–88), Vols. I-V. The standard scholarly expositions are still those of Leon Nemoy, *Karaite Anthology* (New Haven, 1952), pp. xiii-xxvi; and J. Heller and L. Nemoy, "Karaites," in *Encyclopaedia Judaica* (Jerusalem, 1971), X, 761–82 (henceforth Nemoy, "Karaites"). See also Salo Baron, *A Social and Religious History of the Jews* (Philadelphia, 1957), V, 209–85, "Karaite Schism."

3. See some of the many works on this subject, especially those that connect the Qumran sectarians with the Karaites; e.g., Norman Golb, "The Dietary Laws of the Damascus Covenant in Relation to Those of the Karaites," *Journal of Jewish Studies*, VIII (1957), pp. 51–69, or N. Wieder, "The Qumran Sectaries and the Karaites," *The Jewish Quarterly Review*, XL (1956), pp. 97–113. See also Nemoy's skeptical view of Karaite–Qumran connections, "Karaites," pp. 762–63.

4. Nemoy argues, for example, that Saadiah's attack on Karaism forced "the consolidation of the quarreling schismatic groups into a more or less organized sect, and it forced Karaism . . . to purge itself . . . of the excessive rigorism and pedantry inspired by Anan. . . ." At the same time, it "showed that Rabbanism had the seed of reform within itself. . . ." Nemoy, *Anthology*, p. xxi.

5. The scholarly argument over this, and a presentation of his own negative views, may be found in Baron, *Social and Religious History*, V, 275–84. A different view is found in W. Chomsky, *Hebrew: The Eternal Language* (Philadelphia, 1957), p. 120.

6. See the citations below from the books of three recent Karaite writers: Zajączkowski, Szyszman, and al-Gamil.

7. Abraham Geiger, for example, who also edited the text of an important Karaite scholar, Isaac ben Abraham Troki. Most early European proponents of reform differed from the Karaites in their use of rabbinic as well as biblical sources for their changes. J. J. Petuchowski, in the article "Reform Judaism," *Encyclopaedia Judaica*, XIV, 24, speaks of the "quasi-Karaite" early leaders of British and American Reform who rejected the Talmud, and accepted only the Bible as a basis for Judaism.

8. See the description by Nemoy, "Karaites," p. 768; and Baron, op. cit., "Karaite Propaganda," pp. 267–75; "Rabbanite Reactions," pp. 275–84.

9. Nemoy, "Karaites," p. 769.

10. Lithuania and Poland were merged under one king, Jagaila (Jagiello, 1377–1434), at this time, but Vytautas was able to maintain some sort of autonomous rule.

11. There is no documentary evidence for this action by Vytautas, as these historians note, but later mention in Polish sources seems to support this account. See A. Zajączkowski, *Karaims in Poland* (The Hague, 1961), pp. 64–65; S. Szyszman, *Le Karaïsme: Ses Doctrines et son histoire* (Lausanne, 1980), pp. 87–90.

12. See the figures given by Nemoy, "Karaites," p. 777: 7,000 Karaites in Israel in 1970, as contrasted with those of Yosef al-Gamil, *Toledot ha-yahadut ha-qara'it* [The History of Karaite Judaism] (Ramleh, 1979), I, 219: 18,000 (3,600 families) in 1979. The rapid decline of the European Karaite population can be seen from Szyszman's maps of Karaite centers in Europe (op. cit., pp. 118–19): twenty-two centers are shown for 1914, and five for 1937. Most of the latter disappeared during World War II.

13. This important medieval center, located near the historic capital of Lithuania, Vilna, is today the home of probably the last remnant of European Karaism. See al-Gamil, pp. 187–90.

14. Also known as Eupatoria and Kiseliev.

15. Vilna and Odessa were the two large nearby cities to which many of the Karaites migrated from the ancient centers of Troki and the Crimea, respectively.

16. Although there have been indications that some Karaites, and perhaps even Karaite communities, still exist in the Soviet Union, there are no factual data on this subject. See al-Gamil, p. 200. Szyszman, on the other hand, states (p.127) that Troki is the sole surviving community. The Karaite synagogue in Luck, for example, is now a warehouse, according to him.

17. Today literally only a handful remain, largely in order to keep watch over community property, such as synagogues, school buildings, and manuscript treasures.

18. See his statement in Book XIV, Chapter 3 of *Mishneh Torah:* ". . . their children and grandchildren who, misguided by their parents, were raised among the Karaites and trained in their views, are like a child taken captive by them and raised in their religion. . . . Efforts should be made to bring them back to repentance, to draw them near by friendly relations, so that they may return to the strength-giving source, *i.e.*, the Torah." I. Twersky, ed., *A Maimonides Reader* (Philadelphia, 1972). See also L. I. Rabinowitz, "Maimonides, Moses," in *Encyclopaedia Judaica*, XI, 759–60: ". . . they were to be regarded as Jews . . . their dead buried, and their children circumcised, their wine permitted; they were however not to be included in a religious quorum. . . . Only when they flouted rabbinic Judaism was a barrier to be maintained."

19. This resulted from Russian conquests in the East, especially the an-

nexation of the Crimea in 1783, as well as the acquisition of parts of Poland after the successive partitions of the eighteenth century.

20. See the study of this period, and its effect on the Jews in general, in M. Stanislawski, *Tsar Nicholas I and the Jews: The Transformation of Jewish Society in Russia, 1825–1855* (Philadelphia, 1983).

21. Stanislawski, pp. 13–34, "Conscription of the Jews."

22. See Nemoy, "Karaites," p. 774.

23. Nemoy, loc. cit.

24. S. Berkowitz, "Firkovich, Avraham," in *Encyclopaedia Judaica*, VI, 1305. Zajączkowski uses the Polish form of the name, Firkowicz, and gives a brief biographical sketch, pp. 84–85.

25. *Sela ha-Mahaloket* in 1834, and *Massah u-Merivah* in 1838.

26. These works, in two collections, now make up an important part of the Hebrew manuscript holdings of the State Public Library of Leningrad.

27. Bernard D. Weinryb, *The Jews of Poland* (Philadelphia, 1973), p. 21.

28. This name, using the Hebrew plural form *Kara'im* as a singular, is common only among the European Karaites. Thus the Yiddish title of the work by R. Mahler, *Karaites*, is *Karayimer*, adding the Yiddish plural *-er* to the Hebrew plural.

29. Nemoy, "Karaites," p. 774. Zajączkowski uses *hakhan* (possibly considering it of Turkic origin?) instead of the Hebrew *hakham*, e.g., p. 71, for the title of the communal leader.

30. The argument over the forgeries began almost immediately after publication of his findings. See Nemoy, "Karaites," p. 775. See also Weinryb, p. 22. Zajączkowski, defending Firkovich, states ". . . the vague insinuations of 'forgery,' highly injuring to the memory of the investigator, have rendered an ill service to the cause of science," p. 86.

31. Vernaculars used by Jews for oral and written communication, usually containing Hebrew vocabulary elements and, in the past, invariably written in Hebrew script. Yiddish, Ladino (or Spanyolit), Judeo-Arabic, and Judeo-Persian are some examples among many. See S. A. Birnbaum, "Jewish Languages," in *Encyclopaedia Judaica*, X, 66–69: see also David L. Gold, "Recent American Studies in Jewish Languages," *Jewish Language Review* (Haifa), I (1981), pp. 32–45.

32. See Birnbaum, "Jewish Languages," p. 68.

33. See n. 60 below. For the presentation of the Turkic origins, see the aforementioned chapters by Zajączkowski: "Ethnogenesis of Karaims" and "Results of Anthropologic Researches" in his *Karaims in Poland*, pp. 12–13, 49–52. He states, for example, that (p. 52) ". . . the Khazars entered the Karaim formation in such a considerable degree that this may be treated as an anthropologic foundation . . . of equal importance with the other basic ethnico-anthropologic component," p. 52.

34. This is discussed at some length by al-Qalqashandī in his important work *Ṣubḥ al-Aʿshā* (Cairo, 1913–20), XI, 385–92, where he describes the po-

sition of *ra'īs al-yahūd* ("head, or chief, of the Jews"), and gives the distinguishing characteristics of each of the groups.

35. For the best explanation of these concepts and this institution, see the work by Bernard Lewis mentioned in n. 1 above, *Jews of Islam*, especially Chapter I, "Islam and the Other Religions," pp. 3–66.

36. Printed in the Hague, but published by Panstwowe Wydawnictwo Naukowe of Warsaw. See n. 11 above.

37. See n. 11 above.

38. See n. 12 above.

39. Zajączkowski, p. 9.

40. Ibid., p. 12.

41. Ibid., p. 24. Note his use of the Arabic "Dawud."

42. Ibid., p. 25.

43. Ibid., p. 25.

44. Ibid., p. 26.

45. Ibid., p. 26.

46. Ibid., p. 26.

47. Ibid., p. 29.

48. Ibid., p. 32.

49. Ibid., p. 53.

50. Szyszman, p. 17.

51. Ibid., p. 24.

52. Ibid., p. 25.

53. See n. 3 above.

54. Szyszman, p. 58.

55. Ibid., pp. 128–29.

56. Ibid., pp. 128–29.

57. Ibid., p. 117.

58. Al-Gamil, p. 43.

59. Ibid., p. 157.

60. Ibid., p. 198. Nemoy, "Karaites," p. 776, states that the Rabbanite authorities questioned by the Nazis were Zelig Kalmanovitch, Meir S. Balaban, and Itzhak Schipper. "In order to save them, all three gave the opinion that the Karaites were not of Jewish origin."

61. See n. 34 above.

62. Baron, p. 285.

5
The *Sitāra-i Sulaymān* in Indian Muslim Art

John Burton-Page

THERE ARE MANY instances of the use of the *sitāra-i Sulaymān*, the six-pointed star formed by interlacing two opposed equilateral triangles around a common center, in Indian Muslim art: some on buildings (in a group to which I pay particular attention below, prominently and on major building works), many shown as a decorative device on buildings in Moghul painting, others depicted on dress, a few on coins and on items of Kleinkunst. The star in outline also occurs commonly as a part of one pattern of stone screen or surface geometrical decoration. The latter may occur in most ages; but the other instances occur only at irregular intervals in the history of Muslim building. Indian Muslims call it *sitāra-i Sulaymān*, "Solomon's star"; it is the device known also as the "shield of David," *magen David*, or as the hexagram (sometimes, by confusion, as the pentagram).

The device itself is certainly ancient: it occurs in India as early as some punch-marked coins from Patna, which may be Mauryan and of the third or second century B.C.,[1] although the device is not continued on other early Indian coinages; it is known as a decoration in pre-Roman times on a few European Bronze Age and Iron Age artifacts; in the early Middle Ages it is commonly used as a magical sign, in both early Christian and Judeo-Christian magic, and widely used in Arabic magic works from the tenth to the fourteenth centuries, the Jewish and Arabic traditions later diverging. Its use has speculatively been connected with the representation of Saturn; in alchemy it may represent a harmony between the antagonistic elements of water and fire. Not until the seventeenth century onward does it start to be used as a messianic sign, the "shield of the son of David."[2]

Figure 5.1. Hexagons in contact at their points: screens in the 'Alā'ī darwāza, Delhi.

The hexagram finds a use in Indian tantric works, particularly those of the Hatha-yoga school, to signify one of the mystical *čakras*, probably a hypostatization of nerve-plexuses within the spinal column, together with other more complicated representations of *čakras*; it may occasionally be found in tantric painting, and as an ornament on the person and on begging-bowls. It was never of widespread currency, however, and its place in a general Indian corpus of design which might be taken into Muslim art seems improbable. There was certainly from time to time a rapprochement between Ṣūfīs and Hindū mystics, but I find no trace of the device having been carried over into the decoration of any Ṣūfī *dargāhs*. Its tantric connections therefore seem to be coincidental and irrelevant.

The repertory of occurrences presented here has been compiled through an interest awakened by a phrase in the writings of Hermann Goetz, discussed below, as a result of which I have deliberately kept my eyes open for the device on my visits to the sub-continent over the last twenty-odd years; it is therefore as complete as I can conveniently make it, although I make no claim that it is exhaustive. A familiarity with almost the entire corpus of Indian Muslim building allows me to make what is perhaps a significant observation of where

Figure 5.2. *Sitāra-i Sulaymān* on the soffit of an arch of the 'Alā'ī darwāza.

the device does *not* occur: I have sought it in the provincial building styles of India,[3] entirely in vain except for a couple of instances in the Panjāb, and there only as a casual constituent of a tilework pattern. The repertory which follows is as far as possible in chronological order.

The earliest occurrences in Indian Muslim art or craftsmanship I can trace are on a copper coin of Muḥammad ibn Sām[4] (where the sultan's name occurs on the obverse within a "hexagon within two intersecting triangles," with a word which seems to be *'nwl'*, possibly the town of Ānwalā near Badā'ōn, in a similar device on the reverse), and on coppers of Iltutmish (*Iltutmish* within a hexagram on obverse, *sulṭān* similarly on reverse;[5] reverse of two coins with the inscription, صرب ملىان *ḍarb banyān/multān?*[6] with similarly set *'adl* on obverse and *dihlī* on reverse,[7] or with *al-sulṭān* and *'adl*).[8] The device is not found on gold, silver, or billon coins of these rulers.

The *jālī*, stone screen of geometrical pattern, is of such frequent occurrence in Indian Muslim building that it would be pointless to give copious examples; but the pattern based on the hexagon is both common and simple. Regular hexagons in contact at their angles generate, of course, the six-pointed star.[9] The first monumental occurrence of this, naturally the six-pointed star rather than the interlaced triangles, is in the time of Iltutmish in small pieces of *jālī* work above the entrance doorways on the north, east, and south of his tomb, ca. 632/1235;[10] however, the hexagram occurs nowhere else in his tomb, nor in buildings of this sultan elsewhere, in Ajmēr or Nāgawr.

The great gateway ('Alā'ī darwāza) constructed by 'Alā' al-Dīn Khaljī in 711/1311 as part of his extension of the Masjid Quwwat al-Islām shows the *sitāra-i Sulaymān* quite explicitly as a device on each side of the soffit of each of the three arched doorways, contained within a circle within a square, and filled with low-relief floral designs. The larger of the paired window openings on each face are filled with the hexagon-and-star *jālī*, and all the interior wall surfaces are covered with the same pattern in low-relief. But apart from the *jālī* infills to the openings of the courtyard intended as an extension to the mosque, and similar *jālīs* in two small windows of the so-called Jamā'at-Khāna mosque in Nizamuddin, there is no other occurrence of the hexagram in 'Alā' al-Dīn's building works, nor on any of his coins.

The Tughluq, "Sayyid," and Lōdī periods yield no examples in Delhi, except for a few *jālī* openings not listed here (and once only as a mint-mark on a coin of Muḥammad ibn Tughluq, Wright 724a); elsewhere there are only the two examples of tilework from the Panjāb: one in the tomb of Rukn-i 'Ālam at Mūltān (originally built for the tomb of Tughluq Shāh before his translation to Delhi, and hence before 720/1320), where it occurs casually in a hexagon pattern of raised tilework in the tympana of the lower openings, and as a low-relief carving pattern, based again on the hexagon *jālī*, within; and in the tomb of Jahāniyān Jahān-gasht in Uččh, where large star-shaped blue tile patterns relieve the brick walls.

We thus come to the tenth/sixteenth century with only a handful of occurrences of the hexagram in the corpus so far. The picture changes dramatically in tenth/sixteenth century Delhi, with a plethora of examples starting with the Old Fort, known as Purānā Qil'a (hereafter abbreviated PQ). Here the *sitāra-i Sulaymān* appears conspicuously in the spandrels over the arch of the western (main) gateway, the lines of the constituent triangles inlaid in blue-black stone on a fawn sandstone background, their central hexagon enclosing the stone boss which represents a stylized lotus flower; the device recurs within two of the three buildings which stand within the fort walls. One is a ruined *ḥammām* with no decoration remaining; one is the two-storied octagonal kiosk identified as Humāyūn's library, from which the ruler fell to his death (*Humāyūn bādshāh az bām uftād* is its chronogram!), but which goes generally by the name of Shēr mandal; and the third is an exquisite mosque whose common name of "Shēr Shāh's mosque" has brought confusion to several generations of art historians. Here the hexagram occurs in relief in the stonework of the spandrels of the great arches which support the central dome, where Goetz refers to "medaglioni pieni di fiori di loto o del sigillo di Salomone, lo stemma di Šēr Šāh."[11]

Now, my old friend Hermann Goetz was a brilliant art historian, who on many occasions had illuminated many an obscure problem with a flash of insight. His suggestion had therefore to be treated with respect. Alas, I can only report, after the expenditure of much time and shoe-leather, and after many miles pursuing the confirmation of his assertion, that he was on this occasion demonstrably mistaken. Visits to the tomb of Shēr Shāh's grandfather Ibrāhīm Khān in Nārnawl, which Shēr Shāh caused to be built only after his arrival as sultan in Delhi in 1540, and to the buildings of the Sūr family in Sasarām, including Shēr Shāh's own monumental tomb, and Shēr's buildings at Rohtāsgaṛh in Bihār, revealed no more than a couple of trivial examples of the hexagram; not sufficient evidence, in my opinion, to interpret it as the *stemma* of either Shēr Shāh or his house.[12] The attribution must therefore be sought elsewhere.

It is the name of "Shēr Shāh's mosque" which begs the question.

The PQ, on a mound beside an old course of the Jamnā which, as recent excavations have shown, has a fair claim to represent the Indraprastha of the *Mahābhārata*, has an accumulated tell certainly in Muslim occupation before the tenth/sixteenth century, and was the site which Humāyūn selected as his capital in 937/1530. Humāyūn built the walls (possibly on the trace of a mud fort of Lōdī times), and occupied the site both before and after the Sūr interregnum, as did Akbar after him, before his escape from the *atga khayl* and the establishment of his court in Āgrā and Fatḥpur Sikrī. A citadel mosque would have been a necessity. Shēr Shāh's chroniclers certainly record the building of a mosque within the PQ by Shēr Shāh, with full (and fulsome) detail; but the textual descriptions are not reconcilable with the design and decorations of the mosque which now occupies the site; furthermore, much of its internal decoration in inlay, and the inlaid stone decoration of the central bays of the facade, is compatible rather with the datable decoration of Akbar's early years (for instance, of the Masjid Khayr al-Manāzil [the name is a chronogram, = 969/1561–62], and the mosque of 'Abd al-Nabī, both in Delhi, and his first buildings in Āgrā and Fatḥpur Sikrī). Indeed, on the evidence of Shēr Shāh's known building projects in Nārnawl, Sasarām, Rohtās (Panjāb), Rohtāsgaṙh (Bihār), and odd Shērgaṙhs elsewhere, and even of what remains of Shēr Shāh's Delhi (a monumental gateway and a couple of short stretches of town wall), there seems little which might connect him with the PQ building.[13] It therefore seems more secure to suggest that the PQ mosque was begun by Humāyūn, and then possibly modified; or perhaps that the building in train was merely continued by Shēr Shāh, and the building brought to its finished state by Akbar.[14] The hexagrams in the mosque, conspicuous though they are, are outnumbered by those in the "Shēr mandal," which seems certainly to have belonged to Humāyūn's first regnal period; here they appear as white marble inlay in the spandrels of the red sandstone arches of the upper floor, in a coarse *opus sectile*; the soffits of all the arches bear a white marble inlay of five- and six-pointed stars also. The western gateway of the PQ also seems to be more compatible with the period of Akbar.

I am not trying to suggest that the *sitāra-i Sulaymān* may be rather the *stemma* of Humāyūn, although one might jump to that conclusion on seeing the profuse use of hexagrams at Humāyūn's tomb. They are everywhere, like the cats in the song. The facade of the mausoleum shows it in the spandrels of the four great *aywān*-like arches, enclosing a central lotus boss; in the spandrels of the two arches, one atop the other, which are set back from those main arches on three sides, in these cases black stone inlaid on white marble; in those of the five upper arches of each of the enjoined corner octagons, here in slate-blue stone inlaid on fawn or red sandstone; in the spandrels of the arches of the entrance gate, and in those of the northern gate of the 'Arab sarā'ī, in white marble on red sandstone. Furthermore, the tall drum at the base of the dome shows a crude *opus sectile* design of six-pointed stars alternating with hexagons, in fawn sandstone inlaid on red sandstone. There are also several *jālīs* showing the six-pointed star shape within patterns based on the hexagon; and the floor of the inner court is of white marble hexagons and six-pointed stars in a *jālī* design of red sandstone. The tomb itself was founded in the fourteenth *jālūsī* year of Akbar's reign (976/1569),[15] and the 'Arab sarā'ī some nine years earlier, so there is no likelihood of Humāyūn himself having been involved in the design. The architect, one Mīrza Ghiyāth, is believed to have been of Persian origin, working with imported as well as local craftsmen, but there is no immediate Persian prototype for this sudden lavish use of the hexagram.

Figure 5.3. *Sitāra-i Sulaymān* enclosing a lotus boss: Humāyūn's tomb, Delhi.

Humāyūn's tomb was thus erected well into the reign of Akbar, and it is to this ruler that we must proceed to find further profuse examples. Of his other buildings in Delhi, only the tomb of Adham Khān (executed 969/1562; he and his mother Māham Anaga were buried "in a tomb which Akbar had built for them"[16]) shows the *sitāra-i Sulaymān* in the spandrels of the *inner* entrance arches within the octagonal veranda, in white marble, enclosing the lotus boss, on red sandstone. The so-called Jahāngīrī maḥall in Āgrā fort (which is of Akbar's time, ca. 973/1565, rather than Jahāngīr's) does not reveal the device on the external façade of the *aywān* entrance, but the tympanum of the inner opening has three great *sitāra-i Sulaymān* in white marble inlaid on red sandstone, two flanking the upper doorway architrave, the third above it. It occurs, together with other geometric and floral designs, filling in part of the blind arches on the outer walls of the building, in low-relief carving; and it recurs, again in white marble, several times in the spandrels of arches underneath balconies in the riverside court of this maḥall. I have not noted it elsewhere in Āgrā fort, but it may be remembered that most of the Akbarī red sandstone buildings were replaced by others in white marble in Shāhja-

Figure 5.4. Three *sitāra-i Sulaymān* within the gateway of the so-called Jahāngīrī maḥall, Agra fort.

Figure 5.5. Decorative niche on an outer wall of Jahāngīrī maḥall, with *sitāra-i Sulaymān* in low-relief carving on sandstone.

hān's reign. The *sitāra-i Sulaymān* does, however, appear at Fatḥpur Sikrī, conspicuously in the spandrels of the arched entrance gateway to the principal palace of the *zanāna*, known as "Jōdh Bāī's palace," the constituent triangles not here inlaid but carved, standing proud of the sandstone background and enclosing the lotus boss; also, almost apologetically, in spandrels in a small water pavilion at the lakeside in the southwest corner of the city; and heavy sandstone six-pointed stars, in *opus sectile* similar to that of the drum on Humāyūn's tomb, on the tower called Hiran mīnār, a stylized "tusk" projecting from the center of each.[17]

Figure 5.6. *Sitāra-i Sulaymān* in spandrels of arch in river court of Jahāngīrī maḥall; white marble inlay on red sandstone.

This seems to close the repertory of the hexagram on Akbarī building. The device does not occur on any coins of Akbar, except in one doubtful instance as a mint-mark on an Ujjain rupee.[18] As *sitāra-i Sulaymān*, it is incised on what is usually known as "Akbar's shield," and it not infrequently occurs casually in Moghul painting, usually as nothing more than a device in a clothing border. In the well-known "Jahāngīr holding a portrait of his father," it is Jahāngīr's collar, rather than Akbar's, which is enhanced by the *sitāra-i Sulaymān*.

The device does not seem to have been used in the time of any later Moghul rulers, except only in the tomb of 'Abd al-Raḥīm Khān-khānān in Delhi. 'Abd al-Rahīm died at the age of seventy-two in 1036/1626–27, but it is likely that his tomb was constructed long before, possibly even in the reign of Akbar. Here the *sitāra-i Sulaymān* occurs conspicuously, but only in the spandrels of the four great *aywān* arches, enclosing a lotus boss, and not in the subordinate arches.

It will be seen from the above that the period of high-frequency use of the *sitāra-i Sulaymān* runs from about 967/1560 to 1008/1600, and mostly in the earlier part of this period. Consequently, it must be associated most closely with the reign of Akbar. Many of the examples occur before there is any report of his being unconvinced of the sufficiency of Islam, and in consequence hobnobbing with Hindu mystics, so any assimilation of the *sitāra-i Sulaymān* to the tantric *čakra* seems unlikely. There is no reference of which I am aware in the chronicles of the period which might explain its sudden flourishing and decline. Nor does there seem to be any precedent in the Islamic architecture of Central Asia or Afghanistan, where we find interlaced triangles as one design among many in the soffit of an arch in Ghiyāth al-Dīn's mausoleum at Qal'a-i Bust, but otherwise just the *jālī* design in

Figure 5.7. *Sitāra-i Sulaymān* in spandrel of arch leading to ḥaram (the so-called Jōdh Bā'ī's palace), Fatḥpur Sikrī.

brickwork at the palace at Shahr-i Sabz, a similar pattern in the tilework of the Blue Mosque at Tabrīz, and one or two other instances where the star is engendered as a result of a network based on the hexagon. The star shape appears, certainly, on the gates of the tomb of Maḥmūd of Ghaznī;[19] but there is nothing from the tomb of Tīmūr, nor from the buildings of Qazwīn, which might have been expected to have a special appeal to the Indian Moghuls. Nor can I detect any connection between the various buildings or other works of art which bear this design. The best I can do is offer both the repertory and the problem.

NOTES

1. E. H. C. Walsh, "Indian punch-marked coins," *JRAS Centenary supplement* (October 1924), pp. 175–89.

2. The information here is summarized from G. Scholem's article "Magen David," in *Encyclopaedia Judaica*, XI (1972), pp. 687 f. It may be added that in E. Goodenough's *Jewish Symbols in the Graeco-Roman Period*, neither the hexagram nor the pentagram is represented.

3. As set out in my article "Hind. vii—Architecture," in *EI*², III, 440 f.: Panjāb; Bengal; Jawnpur sultanate; Gujarāt; Mālwā; the Bahmanī sultanate; the Barīd Shāhī, 'Imād Shāhī and Niẓām Shāhī sultanates; 'Ādil Shāhī sultanate; Quṭb Shāhī sultanate; Kashmīr; Sind.

4. H. N. Wright, *The Coinage and Metrology of the Sultans of Delhi* (Delhi, 1936), catalog no. 35a.

5. Wright, nos. 124–28.

6. Wright, nos. 138–39, and note to 138, with reference to a discussion of this disputed reading. No. 138 is illustrated on Wright's Plate II.

7. Wright, nos. 140–41; this is the commonest type among early Delhi coppers which bear the hexagram, and occurs in my own collection.

8. Wright, no. 153a.

9. For the analysis of this and other geometrical patterns see E. H. Hankin, *The Drawing of Geometric Patterns in Saracenic Art* [=*MASI* 15] (Calcutta, 1925).

10. The tomb, standing to the west of the Masjid Quwwat al-Islām in Old Delhi (plan in art. "Dihlī" in *EI*², II, 259), is identified by presumption; there is no identificatory or dating inscription, but the style is thoroughly consistent with what is certainly known to be the work of Iltutmish elsewhere, and there seems to be no reason to doubt the traditional ascription.

11. Hermann Goetz, "Arte dell'India musulmana e correnti moderne," *Le Civiltà dell'Oriente* (Rome, 1962), IV, 780–882.

12. The hexagram does not occur in the designs of Sūrī coins either, but is known as a sporadic mint-mark on coins of Shēr Shāh (Wright nos. 1074

[note], 1098–1100, of A.H. 951 and 952); Islām Shāh (nos. 1318–26, dates between 952 and 960); and Muḥammad ʿĀdil Shāh (no. 1438, of 961).

13. Hence the assertions of the art historians Fergusson (1876), Havell (1913), and Percy Brown (1937, in *CHI*, IV) of *two* distinct Sūrī styles, those of Sasarām and Delhi, necessarily founder, since there is not sufficient proved Sūrī Delhi from which to argue. (Percy Brown decides that the mosque bears the name "Qilʿa-i Kuhna Masjid," apparently not realizing that *qilʿa-i kuhna* is the exact Persian translation of *purānā qilʿa.*)

14. I have heard it suggested that the unusual form of the *kalima* carved in the southernmost *mihrāb, lā ilāh ilā 'llāh, Ibrāhīm khalīl Allāh,* reflects the liberal ideas of Humāyūn's *dīn-panāh,* of which the PQ was the citadel; but I am not sure whose *panāh* is thereby being secured.

15. Dating following Sangīn Bēg, *Siyar al-manāzil,* MS Delhi Fort Mus., of the late eighteenth century, rather than Sayyid Aḥmad Khān's 973/1565 (in *Āthār al-Ṣanādīd,* 1846), followed by most later writers.

16. According to Blochmann's note in his translation of *Āʾīn-i Akbarī* (Calcutta, 1873), I, 324.

17. Possibly on which to display animal heads as trophies? Cf. the Nīm sarāʾī mīnār, between Gawŕ and Pāndu'ā in Bengal, described in Catherine B. Asher, "Inventory of Key Monuments," in G. Michell (ed.), *The Islamic Heritage of Bengal* (UNESCO/Paris, 1984), p. 108.

18. *Panjab Museum Catalogue,* no. 160.

19. The "Ghaznī gate," brought to Agra by British troops as booty after the 1842 Afghanistan campaign.

6
Continuité et discontinuité: L'Asie Mineure des Seldjuqides aux Ottomans

Claude Cahen

L'HISTOIRE DE l'Asie Mineure pendant la période qui s'étend de la dislocation de l'empire Ilkhanide au développement de l'État Ottoman est difficile à écrire en raison de la maigreur, de la dispersion et de l'hétérogénéité des sources et du relativement faible intérêt que lui ont porté les savants modernes tant européens que turcs. Elle serait cependant essentielle de deux points de vue différents. Comme on s'est surtout intéressé à l'histoire d'une part de la Turquie seldjuqide, d'autre part à celle de l'État ottoman—c'est-à-dire des deux États structurés et puissants qui encadrent la période, on a méprisé celle des Principautés morcelées qui occupent la période intermédiaire, comme si leur seul rôle devait être de servir de préface à l'histoire ottomane sans aucun caractère spécifique; mais réciproquement dans la mesure où forcément cet État à commencé au milieu d'elles, on ne peut arriver à préciser ce qui leur était commun ou au contraire ce qui les séparait, et l'on saute des Seldjuqides aux Ottomans comme s'il n'y avait rien entre les deux ou qu'il était évident que ces principautés étaient simplement les prémisses de l'histoire ottomane postérieure. Il va de soi que nous ne pouvons ici en quelques pages revoir toutes ces questions, mais il peut n'être pas inutile de dire tout de même quelques réflexions de manière à orienter le travail de nos jeunes successeurs. Continuité? Discontinuité? Tel sera notre fil conducteur.

Jusqu'au milieu du quatorzième siècle, rien de fondamental ne pouvait distinguer la principauté ottomane de celles qui l'entourent. Le saut se produit, plus pour raison géographique que de volonté humaine, lorsque les circonstances ont amené les Ottomans à franchir les Dardanelles et à pénétrer en Europe, c'est-à-dire à intervenir dans l'histoire de l'empire Byzantin (des Turcs avaient déjà depuis deux siècles pris part aux querelles byzantines en Europe, mais à quelques exceptions près n'y étaient pas restés). La différence entre la principauté ottomane et les autres n'est pas seulement dès lors de divisions géographiques mais d'organisation intérieure, du moins faut-il se poser la question.

C'est, on le sait, dans la deuxième moitié du quatorzième siècle, que sont inaugurés le *devşirmeh* et la troupe nouvelle des *Janissaires* fantassins à côté des cavaliers traditionnels. Les forces militaires des autres principautés consistaient surtout en cavaliers recrutés parmi les pasteurs nomades turcomans. Cela ne signifiait certes pas qu'il n'y eût aucun fantassin, aucun indigène incorporé à ce titre; mais cela restait relativement faible et inorganique, le cadre la cavalerie turque. Dans l'armée ottomane nouvelle les proportions tendaient, peu à peu, à s'inverser. Dans les autres principautés il n'y eut pas vraiment d'«armée nouvelle.»

Il est bien connu que dans l'État ottoman l'organisation politico-militaire repose pour une bonne part sur l'institution du *timar*, c'est-à-dire que l'État délègue à des officiers, cavaliers et administrateurs, des domaines appelés de ce nom et dont il leur alloue les revenus. Quelque chose de grosso modo analogue avait existé ou existait encore dans les États musulmans antérieurs ou voisins, en général sous le nom d'*iqṭā'*. Il n'y a guère de doute, sauf nuance ou détail, que dans un pays donné passé d'une administration antérieure à l'administration ottomane, le domaine alloué en *iqṭā'* et plus tard en *timar* est le même: les limites terriennes imposés par la géographie et la tradition ne peuvent pas changer brusquement, il serait difficile de le faire, et on ne voit guère le profit qu'en tirerait le nouveau système. En ce qui concerne spécialement les Ottomans, il est bien connu, d'après les cas où, en Europe ou en Asie, nous avons moyen de suivre les réalités, ils n'ont cherché qu'exceptionnellement et secondairement à opérer des transformations véritables. Cependant les mots ne sont pas les mêmes: *timar* et *iqṭā'* ou autre.

Divers documents ottomans parlent de domaines qui avaient été constitués tels longtemps auparavant, ou sous les Seldjuqides. En admettant leur authenticité et l'authenticité des renseignements fournis sur le passé, cela signifie que le domaine continue tel qu'il était à tel ou tel point de vue, mais non que le nom de *timar* existait auparavant ou du moins faudrait-il, là encore, le trouver attesté dans les principautés turcomanes ou ailleurs, ce qui jusqu'à présent n'a jamais été le cas. Si le mot *timar* et le mot *iqṭā'* ont pratiquement désigné des choses voisines, leur sens de base est tout à fait différent. *Iqṭā'*, mot arabe, signifie un découpage du domaine public, *timar*, persan, une bienfaisance, sollicitude du prince envers ses officiers. En ce sens vague, le mot *timar* est attesté depuis longtemps dans le domaine irano-mongol, voire antérieurement, comme en grec byzantin *pronoia*, en latin *beneficium*, mais jamais, que je sache, avant et hors les Ottomans, pour signifier le bien concret qu'à Byzance ou en pays latin avait fini par s'appliquer à la *pronoia* et au *beneficium*. Il semblerait donc que le *timar* ottoman ait été dérivé du terme iranien vague, par contanimation du synonyme byzantin *pronoia*. Dans les régions où avait prévalu le terme *iqṭā'*, l'administration ottomane n'en introduira pas moins le terme *timar*. Peut-être uniquement pour l'uniformisation du vocabulaire administratif, mais peut-être tout de même aussi parce que le *timar*, héritier dans certaines régions de la *pronoia* byzantine, n'était pas ressenti comme juste équivalent à l'*iqṭā'*. Cette hypothèse, si elle était confirmée, signifierait que malgré la continuité géographique et une certaine parenté institutionnelle, le *timar* n'était pas ressenti comme l'exact héritier d'une institution de la période turcomane.

Quelques questions peuvent se poser dans d'autres conditions.

Il a été consacré il y a quelques années une grosse étude sur le régime fiscal dit *mālikāne dīwānī*, qui concernait une partie de l'Asie Mineure au début de l'empire ottoman.[1] Étude qui abonde en précisions détaillées qui, en elles-mêmes, ne prêtent guère à discussion, mais qui nécessitent peut-être quelque mise au point dans leur interprétation globale. Pour l'auteur, le régime continue le régime seldjuqide de la période seldjuqido-mongole en Asie Mineure. Entre autres raisons, le régime *mālikāne-dīwānī* est approximativement limité à la région proprement seldjuqide du territoire anatolien; d'autre part, le mot *mālīkāne* seul, ou associé à *dīwānī*, se rencontre dans l'État ilkhānide, quelque fois, bien que rarement, en Asie mineure. Il y aurait donc une continuité du régime seldjuqide au régime ottoman, si bien que, vu l'insuffisance de la documentation pour les temps anciens, on pourrait la compenser par l'abondance relative de la documentation ottomane. Loin de nous l'idée qu'il ne puisse y avoir, du treizième au seizième siècle, aucune continuité. Mais laquelle et comment? Le régime *mālikāne-dīwānī*, si l'on y regarde de près, n'est, ni pour l'assiette ni pour la perception de l'impôt, très original. Les deux mots signifient possesseurs privés et fisc public, ce qui veut dire que le caractère du régime réside dans la répartition du produit de l'impôt entre les possesseurs particuliers et l'État ou ses délégués. À ce compte, le régime a, de façon ou autre, sous un nom ou un autre, éxisté presque depuis le début de l'Islam en Iran ou en tout cas depuis le début l'organisation irano-turque.

Depuis longtemps, on distingue les impôts sur la terre d'après les définitions de la Loi *(sharī'a)* et les impôts d'usage *('urf)* sur les personnes ou les opérations sans rapport avec la terre. Les détails ont pu varier, non le principe. L'ensemble a pu être plus ou moins réglementé, plus ou moins contrôlé, non fondamentalement transformé. Le vocabulaire a pu changer, beaucoup moins les réalités. Il s'agit donc moins d'un régime modifié que de modifications verbales.

Par suite, ce qu'il en a été entre le treizième siècle et la fin du quinzième, dans la période turcomane, serait essentiel à connaître. Malheureusement, nous manquons de textes capables de nous renseigner à cet égard, qu'il s'agisse des réalités ou des mots. Il faut donc insister sur l'effort à faire pour cette période dans les deux directions.

La régime, tel qu'il nous est décrit, concerne les domaines agricoles. Il y a évidemment à côté d'eux les domaines pastoraux. La combinaison des deux se rencontre aussi bien dans les régions ex-seldjuqides que dans les régions ex-byzantines sans que la réglementation soit forcément identique, ni par conséquent le vocabulaire qui s'y applique. L'empire ottoman ayant finalement englobé l'un et l'autre, il peut y avoir dans ce cas continuité remontant à l'origine des principautés et aux régimes fiscaux antérieurs.

Il est connu que les noms des vingt-quatre tribus entre lesquelles se divise le peuple oghuz avant sa migration en Asie occidentale se recontrent encore constamment à l'époque ottomane bien que dans une structure sociale bien différente. Il a cependant été insisté sur ce que dans les faits ces divisions en Asie Mineure ne correspondent pas à de grandes réalités, et que d'ailleurs à l'époque seldjuqide les noms se rencontrent fort peu. On a montré[2] que c'est au quinzième siècle qu'ils réapparaissent dans l'empire ottoman, et on pourrait le montrer aussi bien ailleurs, comme élément de stabilisation d'éléments nomades. S'en suit-il qu'il y ait là une véritable organisation? On ne semble guère pouvoir le constater, et, de toute façon, il faudrait certainement distinguer entre les grandes confédérations tribales de l'Anatolie orientale et environs et les petites principautés de l'Occident anatolien. Les premières portent des noms de confédérations, et précisent souvent leurs composantes tribales, ou la tribu dominante; celles de l'ouest au contraire portent simplement le nom du fondateur ou de sa famille (sauf les Germyān). Les noms tribaux introduits dans l'histoire seldjuqide de Yazidji-Oghlu ne sont pas dans l'original d'Ibn Bībī et ne portent donc témoignage que de la politique ottomane ou du mouvement des idées au quinzième siècle. Il serait donc difficile de voir une véritable continuité entre Seldjuqides et Ottomans par l'intermédiaire des principautés turcomanes.

Nous n'avons pas l'intention d'énumérer toutes les questions qui pourraient être posées. Rappelons seulement que selon les régions il s'agit surtout de principautés turcomanes, ailleurs de survivances turco-mongoles (la principauté d'Eretna et de son successeur indigène le cadi poète Burhān al-Dīn de Sīwās). D'autre part les annexions ottomanes ne se sont pas faites toutes au même moment ni dans les mêmes conditions. Les principautés turcomanes de l'ouest n'ont guère ou pas du tout survécu au quatorzième siècle; celles de l'est ont parfois dépassé le quinzième. Tout cela signifie que les héritages recueillis par les Ottomans ne peuvent avoir été tous analogues même si l'on admet un certain nombre de points communs. Le conservatisme même de l'administration ottomane l'amenait, là où il y avait des différences, à les conserver largement. Le problème des continuités existe donc, mais il ne peut être étudié en bloc comme dans une société qui aurait été indifférenciée.

NOTES

1. Irène Beldiceanu, «Fiscalité et formes de possession de la terre arable dans l'Anatolie préottomane,» *JESHO* XIX (1976).
2. Paul Lindner, *Nomads and Ottomans in Medieval Anatolia* (1983).

7
On the Meaning of the 'Abbasid Call to *al-Riḍā*

Patricia Crone

IT IS WELL known that the recruiting officers of the Hāshimīya in Khurāsān called to *kitāb Allāh wa-sunnat nabīyihi wa'l-bay'a lil-riḍā min āl/ahl bayt Muḥammad/rasūl Allāh.*[1] What did contemporaries take this to mean? Apparently they took the first half of the slogan to mean that the movement involved principles. Whoever called to the book of God and the sunna of his Prophet in early Islam proclaimed himself to be acting "out of anger on behalf of God" (*ghaḍaban lillāh*), as opposed to out of anger on his own behalf.[2] The principles involved would be specified after the call to book and sunna, and the second half of the Hāshimite slogan duly identified the Hāshimīya as a movement committed to *ahl-bayt*ism. But what did the word *al-riḍā* mean? That is the question to which this birthday offering is devoted.

The sources tell us that *al-riḍā* was a cover name. Muḥammad ibn 'Alī, the first 'Abbasid imām, instructed the leaders of the Hāshimīya not to mention his name to ordinary recruits, but rather to refer to him as the *riḍā*; if asked to identify him, they should say, "we are in *taqīya*, and have been ordered to keep the name of our imām secret."[3] Ibrāhīm ibn Muḥammad, the second imām, likewise preferred to keep his identity secret.[4] Modern scholars generally accept this explanation, though they tend to see it in a somewhat Machiavellian light: the cover name did not merely serve to hide the 'Abbasids from the authorities, but also, and perhaps more importantly, from adherents of the 'Alids, whom they thus contrived to recruit for their own cause.[5] But there is reason to believe that this explanation should be rejected: the 'Abbasid use of *al-riḍā* would appear to have been neither precautionary nor Machiavellian in intent.

The word *riḍā* means "satisfaction" and "agreement," or, when applied to a person, "someone with whom one is satisfied, to whom one has given one's consent." If this meaning is taken seriously, a person who claims to be *al-riḍā* claims to owe his position to communal choice: in some sense or other he claims to have been elected. The literal meaning is of course somewhat lost on the modern reader, who generally assumes the 'Abbasids to have meant very little by their choice of this particular word: insofar as the cover name had any significance, it amounted to no more than a vague promise of future satisfaction with whatever ruler they might in due course produce. But in texts relating to the Umayyad period, the literal meaning of the word is very much alive. Here *al-riḍā* is precisely someone who owes his position to communal agreement; more specifically he is someone elected by *shūrā*, "consultation," as the following passages show.

1. In 77/696, Muṭarrif ibn al-Mughīra ibn Shu'ba and the Khārijites of Mesopotamia entered into negotiations with a view to an alliance. When asked to declare his stance, Muṭarrif announced, "I call you to . . . making this matter [sc. the caliphate] a *shūrā* among the Muslims, so that they can set up as their imām over themselves the person of whom they approve for themselves (*man yarḍawna li-anfusihim*), in the same way in which 'Umar ibn al-Khaṭṭāb left them to do it. The Arabs will agree when they know that by a *shūrā* one simply means *al-riḍā* of Quraysh" (*fa-inna al-'arab idhā 'alimat annamā yurādu bi'l-shūrā al-riḍā min Quraysh raḍū*). The Khārijites responded to this by declaring that Quraysh did not in their view have any better right to the caliphate than other Arabs [*sic*], that the Muslims should choose whoever was best, and that they themselves had already chosen "the person of whom we approve most and who is the strongest among us" (*qad ikhtarnā li-anfusinā arḍānā fīnā wa-ashaddanā*). Both sides thus took *al-riḍā* to mean somebody chosen by the community; they merely disagreed as to whether the choice should be made from within Quraysh or, on the contrary, from within the entire community of Arabs/Muslims.[6]

2. 'Abdallāh ibn 'Umar is said to have voiced an opinion similar to Muṭarrif's on an earlier occasion. When Mu'āwiya put pressure on the Medinese to accept his son Yazīd as his successor, Ibn 'Umar objected that the caliphate was not hereditary, and that 'Umar had set up the *shūrā* on the assumption that within Quraysh it belonged to whoever was most fit for it, and of whom the Muslims approved

as the most God-fearing and satisfactory person (*wa-innamā hiya fī Quraysh khāṣṣatan liman kāna lahā ahlan mimman irtaḍāhu al-muslimūn li-anfusihim man kāna atqā wa-arḍā*). Ibn 'Umar's *man irtaḍāhu al-muslimun* is clearly synonymous with *al-riḍā*.[7]

3. When Ibn al-Zubayr had allegiance sworn to himself, Abū Ḥurra, the *mawlā* of Khuzā'a, is said to have exclaimed, "Is this what we helped you for? You used to call for *al-riḍā wa'l-shūrā*. Why did you not wait and consult (*a-fa-lā ṣabarta wa-shāwarta*)? We would have chosen you and given allegiance to you."[8]

4. Mu'āwiya is said to have argued against the Banū Hāshim along the following lines: "As for the caliphate, it has passed from one group of Quraysh to another by the consent of the masses and consultation of the elite (*bi-riḍā al-'āmma wa-bi-shūrā al-khāṣṣa*). . . . For what reason should you have it? By consent and agreement on you regardless of kinship, or by kinship regardless of agreement and consent, or by both together?" (*a-bi'l-riḍā wa'l-jamā'a 'alaykum dūna al-qarāba am lil-qarāba dūna al-jamā'a wa'l-riḍā am bihimā jamī'an?*). Here *riḍā, shūrā,* and *jamā'a* are enumerated as so many titles to power arising from communal agreement, in contradistinction to titles arising from descent.[9]

5. In 116/734–35, the Khurāsānī rebel al-Ḥārith ibn Surayj called his opponents to "the book of God and the sunna, and to allegiance to *al-riḍā*."[10] He frequently clamored for a *shūrā (ij'al al-amr shūrā)*.[11] The contexts in which he clamored for a *shūrā* show that he had the governorship and subgovernorships of Khurāsān in mind,[12] but one assumes that he also wanted the caliphate to be a matter of *shūrā*. (It is, after all, to the caliphate that the slogan *al-amr shūrā* normally refers.) His call for *al-riḍā* is thus likely to have been a call for a caliph to be elected by *shūrā*; at all events, it was obviously a call for "someone acceptable," and not for a specific person.

6. The earlier rebel Yazīd ibn al-Muhallab is likewise said to have favored the principle *al-amr shūrā* on his capture of Basra in 102/720, and to have called to *al-riḍā*, more specifically *al-riḍā min Banī Hāshim*, shortly thereafter.[13] That Yazīd meant the same thing by these two slogans seems likely, though it cannot be proved:[14] he proceeded to call to al-Faḍl (or al-Mufaḍḍal) ibn 'Abd al-Raḥmān ibn al-'Abbās ibn Rabī'a ibn al-Ḥārith ibn 'Abd al-Muṭṭalib without a *shūrā fī Banī Hāshim* having been enacted.[15] But however this may be, his call for *al-riḍā min Banī Hāshim* was clearly a call for "whatever Hāshimite will turn out to be acceptable," not for a specific member of that

family whom he did not dare to name: *al-riḍā* was somebody who remained to be chosen.

7. ʿAbdallāh ibn Muʿāwiya, the ʿAlid who staged a revolt in Kufa and western Persia in 127–29/744–47, is said to have called either to *al-riḍā min āl Muḥammad* or else to himself.[16] The import of this information is evidently not that he called either to a Hāshimite whose name he did not dare to divulge or to himself, but rather that he called either to the Hāshimites in general (more precisely, to "whatever Hāshimite will be acceptable"), or else to himself in particular. This suggests that Ibn Muʿāwiya's *daʿwa* underwent the same evolution as that of Ibn al-Zubayr; in other words, that he began by calling to *al-riḍā wa'l-shūrā* (this time within the Prophet's family), but proceeded to dispense with the *shūrā* in the belief that the choice was a foregone conclusion.

8. Judayʿ ibn ʿAlī al-Kirmānī, the leader of the Yamanīya in Khurāsān, is said to have called to *al-kitāb wa'l-sunna wa'l-riḍā min āl Muḥammad* upon his escape from Naṣr ibn Sayyār's prison, that is, before his alliance with Abū Muslim.[17] This may well be wrong. Whether it is right or wrong, however, al-Kirmānī is clearly envisaged as calling to *al-riḍā* in the sense of "someone acceptable to all," not a specific person, let alone someone whose name he did not wish to divulge; for he explained his call with reference to the fact that "he could not accept Naṣr and his governors as rulers of the Muslims" (*lā yarḍā bi-Naṣr wa-ʿummālihi wulātan ʿalā al-muslimīn*). Moreover, an alternative account of his wishes at that time states that he wanted the Khurāsānīs to choose "a man from Bakr ibn Wā'il on whom we can all agree (*narḍāhu jamīʿan*) and who can govern all of us until a caliphal command arrives."[18] Al-Kirmānī was thus remembered as having wanted a *riḍā*, whether from Bakr ibn Wā'il or from the Prophet's family; a *riḍā* in the sense of someone acceptable to all and who still remained to be chosen.

9. Adherents of al-Mukhtār are said to have called followers of Muṣʿab ibn al-Zubayr to "the book of God and the sunna of His messenger, and to allegiance to the *amīr* al-Mukhtār, and to making this matter a *shūrā* in the family of the messenger."[19] The idea of a *shūrā* in the *ahl al-bayt* was thus a familiar one in Shīʿī circles, or more specifically, those circles with which the leaders of the ʿAbbasid revolution are generally believed to have been connected.

In sum, the word *al-riḍā* is associated with *shūrā* in passages relating to persons as diverse as Muʿāwiya, Ibn al-Zubayr, Muṭarrif ibn al-

Mughīra, and the Khārijites of Mesopotamia. The association is also attested for Khurāsān at the time of al-Ḥārith ibn Surayj, when ʿAbbasid missionaries were active there. The call for *al-riḍā* recurs in other contexts, two of them contemporary with the revolution, in which it must have been a call for a person yet to be elected or approved; and finally, the call for a *shūrā* in the Prophet's house is documented for the revolt of al-Mukhtār, a revolt with which the ʿAbbasid revolution was connected. In short, the Hāshimite call to *al-riḍā* can hardly have been intended or understood as anything other than a call for a caliph elected by *shūrā fī ahl al-bayt*; the movement called to *al-riḍā* because it had no specific candidate for the throne.

This conclusion is corroborated by the fact that a *shūrā fī ahl al-bayt* was in fact attempted after the revolution. Indeed, it is possible that such a *shūrā* was also attempted before the revolution. As regards the pre-revolutionary attempt, we are told by Abū 'l-Faraj al-Iṣbahānī, a Shīʿī author, that a number of ʿAlid and ʿAbbasid members of the Hāshimite house (including Ibrāhīm and the future al-Manṣūr) met at al-Abwāʾ near Mecca shortly after the murder of al-Walīd II; with the exception of Jaʿfar al-Ṣādiq, all agreed to acknowledge Muḥammad ibn ʿAbdallāh (al-Nafs al-Zakīya) as the *mahdī*.[20] They met again in the reign of Marwān II, but on this occasion Ibrāhīm was informed by a messenger that the Khurāsānīs were gathering troops for his cause, whereupon the ʿAlids dissociated themselves from him.[21] The story of the second meeting is also found in *Akhbār al-ʿAbbās*, a pro-ʿAbbasid work, in a slightly different form. A number of Hāshimites met at Mecca in 129/746–47 in order to pay homage to Muḥammad ibn ʿAbdallāh as the *mahdī*. Ibrāhīm heard of this and joined them, but a messenger informed him of the activities of the Khurāsānīs on his behalf, whereupon he managed to have the meeting postponed. When ʿAbdallāh ibn al-Ḥasan, the *mahdī's* father, despaired of winning Ibrāhīm for his son's cause (or alternatively, when Marwān II got wind of the movement in Khurāsān, and suspected ʿAbdallāh ibn al-Ḥasan of being its leader), the latter denounced Ibrāhīm and dissociated himself from his deeds.[22] The ʿAbbasid version thus stresses that Ibrāhīm's presence at the meeting was accidental, that he avoided paying allegiance to the ʿAlid, and that the ʿAlids publicly renounced such rights as they might have to the fruits of the revolution; but it does not deny that ʿAlids and ʿAbbasids had in fact come together on the eve of the revolution to elect a leader from among themselves. Quite different sources also inform us that the caliph al-Manṣūr had paid allegiance to Muḥammad ibn ʿAbdallāh at Mecca.[23]

Even so, however, the story may not be true. Muḥammad ibn ʿAbdallāh does not refer to his supposed election by the Hāshimite house in his correspondence with al-Manṣūr regarding their respective rights to the caliphate, though he would certainly have mentioned it there if it had actually taken place (and if the correspondence is authentic)[24]; and the story of the second *shūrā* makes no reference to the first.[25] Moreover, even if we accept the reality of these meetings, the fact that ʿAbbasids participated in them is no guarantee that they were arranged by the Hāshimīya movement.[26] Further, they are not explicitly called *shūrās*; and though they could obviously be qualified as such in the general sense of "consultation," they were not electoral bodies nominated by the community and/or its representatives; that is, they were not *shūrās* in the technical sense of the word.[27] All in all, then, they will have to be discounted.

The *shūrā* which was attempted after the revolution presents a different case. As regards this episode, we are told that the death of Ibrāhīm al-Imām shortly before the arrival of the Khurāsānī troops in Iraq prompted Abū Salama, the leader of the Kufan organization, to contact three senior ʿAlids, either because he wished to transfer the caliphate to one of them,[28] or else because he intended to "make it [the caliphate] a *shūrā* between the sons of ʿAlī and al-ʿAbbās."[29] Either way, his plans came to nothing,[30] but his behavior has always been something of a puzzle. It is not very likely that Abū Salama should have been a secret adherent of the ʿAlids all along: if his heart had never been in the Hāshimīya movement, then why would he have invested his life and fortune in it? Nor does it seem likely that Ibrāhīm's death should have caused him radically to reconsider the objective to which his life had been devoted. The chances are that he was acting out of loyalty to the movement as he had always known it, and the oddity of his behavior disappears if we assume it to have stood for *al-riḍā min ahl al-bayt* in the sense of "Hāshimite singled out by *shūrā*": if Abū Salama took Ibrāhīm to have been the *riḍā* in this sense, the latter's death evidently meant that another *shūrā fī ahl al-bayt* had to be staged.[31] That this is how he reasoned cannot be proved, but he plainly did not regard Ibrāhīm's rights, however acquired, as hereditary; and what is more, many other members of the movement apparently did not do so either. The sources are, of course, at pains to assure us that the imamate had been hereditary within the ʿAbbasid family since Muḥammad ibn ʿAlī acquired it from Abū Hāshim, but there are three good reasons for rejecting their claim.

First, Ibrāhīm's death caused too many members of the Hāshimīya to look for candidates among the 'Alids. According to *Akhbār al-'Abbās*, Ibrāhīm's death caused a schism in the 'Abbasid movement, as some argued that the imamate now reverted to the 'Alids[32]; according to Ibn A'tham, Kufa at the time of the arrival of the Khurāsānīs was divided between people who expected an 'Alid to be enthroned and others who expected the enthronement of an 'Abbasid;[33] and according to all, the senior leader of the revolution was one of those who wanted an 'Alid, or who wanted a *shūrā* between 'Alids and 'Abbasids (possibly meaning that he hoped and/or expected a *shūrā fī ahl al-bayt* to produce an 'Alid candidate). What we are confronted with here are not naive philo-'Alids duped by the use of labels such as *al-riḍā*, *ahl al-bayt*, or *āl Muḥammad* into supporting a cause which they now wished to abandon, but on the contrary, members of the leadership aware of and satisfied with the candidature of the 'Abbasid Ibrāhīm. If a whole section of the Hāshimīya loyal to Ibrāhīm could turn to the 'Alids on Ibrāhīm's death, Ibrāhīm's rights to the imamate cannot have been widely regarded as hereditary.

Second, the sources are too obsessed with the idea of *shūrā*. Thus, one version of the events surrounding Ibrāhīm's death has it that Qaḥṭaba approved of Ibrāhīm's *waṣīya* to Abū 'l-'Abbās on the ground that without it "the matter would become a *shūrā* within his family."[34] Another story has it that, as already mentioned, Abū Salama attempted to convoke such a *shūrā*. A third story reassures us that some sort of *shūrā* was indeed enacted: the result was the election of Abū 'l-'Abbās.[35] How can this obsession with elective procedures be squared with the assertion that Ibrāhīm had acquired hereditary rights which he passed on by bequest to his brother?

Finally, there is a conspicuous absence in all this of people who held that the imamate had passed to Ibrāhīm's sons. If Ibrāhīm had inherited the imamate from his father, he would indeed have been able to bequeath it to his brother; however, given that the circumstances in which Ibrāhīm was alleged to have made the bequest (that is, on his deathbed in prison) were such that the reality of the bequest was disputed, one would have expected some to have advocated the cause of his sons. Yet nobody did so: the choice was between Abū 'l-'Abbās and the 'Alids. It is true that both of his best-known sons were too young to qualify for the caliphate at the time,[36] but one does not get the impression that it was their age which disqualified them: nobody seems to have displayed the slightest interest in the fact that they even existed.[37] How can this be reconciled with the claim that the imamate was hereditary within the 'Abbasid line?

In short, it would seem that the revolutionaries called to *al-riḍā min ahl al-bayt* in the same spirit in which Muṭarrif ibn al-Mughīra called to *al-riḍā min Quraysh*: they happened to believe that the caliphate belonged to whoever was chosen as the most suitable person from within the groups in question. Given that the revolution resulted in the establishment of a new dynasty, rather than a succession of caliphs elected by *shūrā*, it must soon have come to appear obvious that the revolutionaries had called to *al-riḍā* in the loose sense of "acceptable person," with reference to the imām from among themselves; by the time Abū 'l-Sarāyā had oaths of allegiance taken *'alā al-riḍā min āl Muḥammad*, the word had come to mean little more than "legitimate imām"[38]; and though al-Ma'mūn emphasized that his al-Riḍā had been chosen from among 'Alids and 'Abbasids as the most suitable candidate,[39] the very fact that he called him al-Riḍā transformed the programmatic word into a personal name.[40] But it was evidently not as a meaningless word that the revolutionaries had first adopted it.

If this is accepted, three points follow automatically. First, the story of Abū Hāshim's testament is spurious. According to this story, Abū Hāshim ibn Muḥammad ibn al-Ḥanafīya bequeathed his imamate to Muḥammad ibn 'Alī ibn 'Abdallāh ibn 'Abbās, from whom it passed to Ibrāhīm ibn Muḥammad, and therafter to the 'Abbasid caliphs: it was precisely because Muḥammad ibn Alī had acquired rights which he hoped to encash that he organized (or took over) the mission in Khurāsān.[41] Now if the 'Abbasids had regarded themselves as legitimate imāms by hereditary right since the mid-Umayyad period, then their call to *al-riḍā* would indeed have to be explained on the assumption that *al-riḍā* was a cover-name; but if their call to *al-riḍā* was a call for a *shūrā*, it follows that they cannot have regarded themselves as such imāms after all: the story must be false. This is not to deny that there are links between the revolt of al-Mukhtār and the 'Abbasid revolution: it was presumably thanks to these links that the 'Abbasids seized on Ibn al-Ḥanafīya when they decided to claim the caliphate by hereditary right.[42] But the story of Abū Hāshim's testament cannot have made its appearance before the *shūrā* ideal had broken down.[43]

Second, the Hāshimīya movement owed its name to Hāshim, the eponymous ancestor of the Prophet's house, not to Abū Hāshim, the supposed bequeather of 'Alid rights to the 'Abbasids.[44] In fact, one scarcely needs the *riḍā*/*shūrā* theory to see this point. If members of a clan called Hāshim led a movement called Hāshimīya devoted to the rights of the clan in question, it would be very odd if the reference were not to Hāshim, the eponymous ancestor of the Hāshimite clan, but rather to an obscure member of it remembered or invented only for his supposed transfer of the imamate from one branch of this clan to another. Differently put, in a culture in which poetry about the *ahl al-bayt* was known as *Hāshimīyāt* with reference to the founder of the family in question, a movement sponsoring the rights of the *ahl al-bayt* could scarcely call itself, or come to be known as, *Hāshimīya* with reference to someone else. Both the missionaries and their opponents are frequently made to single out Banū Hāshim as central to the concerns of the *da'wa*, whereas Abū Hāshim never figures.[45] Given that the story of Abū Hāshim's testament came to be invented, we should not be surprised that some heresiographers assumed the term Hāshimīya to be derived from his name;[46] but it is, in fact, more likely that Abū Hāshim owes his name to the revolutionary movement than the other way round.

Finally, the relationship between the 'Abbasids and the revolution customarily named after them is nothing if not problematic. Why did the organizers of this revolution choose to stage it on behalf of a member of the Prophet's family still to be chosen? If we accept that the organizers were 'Abbasids, a plausible answer would be that their own membership in this family was too marginal for them to claim the imamate on the basis of descent alone, or indeed to claim it at all: to contemporaries of the revolution, the term *ahl al-bayt* conjured up descendants of 'Alī.[47] If their membership in the *ahl al-bayt* was so marginal as to count for nothing, we must envisage them as laymen hankering for a Hāshimite ruler, without having a Hāshimite candidate to hand: they called for an acceptable member of the Hāshimite house in the same spirit in which al-Kirmānī is supposed to have done so, that is, with a view to handing over to an 'Alid as soon as one had been chosen. Alternatively, their membership in the *ahl al-bayt* was sufficiently real for them to qualify for election by *shūrā*, a procedure which had the advantage of placing strong emphasis on personal merit: as organizers of the revolution, they were demonstrably superior to the 'Alids in terms of political talent. This seems more likely, especially in view of the parallel with Ibn Mu'āwiya; but in either case, things were unlikely to turn out as calculated. If the 'Abbasids succeeded in acquiring power, they were going to think twice about handing over to an 'Alid figurehead. At the same time, the

'Alids were unlikely to renounce such power by consenting to the election of an 'Abbasid; sooner or later, the 'Abbasids would thus have to justify their possession of power with reference to hereditary rights. Since it was the 'Alids rather than the 'Abbasids who were regarded as kinsmen of the Prophet, this meant postulating that the 'Alids had bequeathed their rights to the 'Abbasids, or in other words, it meant inventing the story of Abū Hāshim.

If this is so, the shift from an ideology of *shūrā* to one of *waṣīya* may well have been initiated by Ibrāhīm. A Shī'ī author such as Abū 'l-Faraj has no doubt that the story of the testament was invented about this time;[48] and it would seem difficult to deny that the Hāshimīya expected Ibrāhīm al-Imām to succeed, for all that no *shūrā* appears to have elected him. But Ibrāhīm can hardly have claimed more than that Abū Hāshim had designated him as his successor:[49] the fully developed story in which Abū Hāshim makes a permanent transfer of rights to the imamate from one branch of the Hāshimite house to another must reflect the establishment of the new dynasty, for all that this dynasty was soon to reject it.[50]

We must, however, also consider the possibility that, contrary to what is usually claimed, the 'Abbasids were not the organizers of the revolution which enthroned them. Thus, a passage in *Kitāb al-'uyūn wa'l-ḥadā'iq* has it that it was the Khurāsānīs who chose the 'Abbasids, rather than the other way round: when the Khurāsānīs wanted to set up a mission in favor of the Prophet's family, they looked for a candidate who could be described as the noblest, the most generous, and the most meritorious in respect of religion; they decided on 'Abdallāh ibn al-Ḥasan ibn al-Ḥasan, whom they approached without revealing their true intentions; but 'Abdallāh ibn al-Ḥasan led them to Muḥammad ibn 'Alī ibn 'Abdallāh ibn 'Abbās.[51] If the Khurāsānīs began by working for the Prophet's family in general, as this story implies, then *al-riḍā min āl al-rasūl* was indeed the obvious slogan for them to adopt.

The same source also tells another story in which the 'Abbasids make their appearance in the *da'wa* at a late stage. According to this story, the Prophet himself predicted that the 'Abbasids would rule, and the 'Abbasids were eagerly awaiting their appointed time. Meanwhile there were Shī'ī missionaries in Khurāsān who were calling to Banū Hāshim in general, and others who were calling to Abū Hāshim in particular, the leaders of the former [*sic*] being Ibn Kathīr and Abū Salama. When Abū Hāshim was poisoned, he transferred his rights to the 'Abbasids and wrote to his missionaries informing them of this fact; they accepted it, even though Abū Salama was secretly in favor of Ja'far al-Ṣādiq. Abū Hāshim was poisoned by al-Walīd II (d. 125/743), and the transfer took place *fī awwal riyāsat Abī Muslim.*[52] Now there is obviously something wrong with this story. If Ibn Kathīr and Abū Salama were missionaries on behalf of the Hāshimites in general (as indeed they would seem to have been), then they were not the missionaries over whom Abū Hāshim had control;[53] and if we emend the story to say that they were missionaries on behalf of Abū Hāshim, then the reference to the others working on behalf of the Hāshimites in general becomes pointless. This suggests that the story had an earlier version in which the Shī'ī missionaries in Khurāsān begin by working for Banū Hāshim in general, whereupon the leadership of the Hāshimite family passes to Abū Hāshim, whereupon Abū Hāshim dies bequeathing the leadership to the 'Abbasids. In other words, what we have here seems to be an alternative account of how Khurāsānīs working for Hāshimites in general ended up by sponsoring 'Abbasids in particular. Even if this interpretation is rejected, the story explicitly dates the 'Abbasid connection with the *da'wa* to the 740s, and more precisely, to *after* Abū Muslim's arrival in Khurāsān in 128/745–46. However the story is understood, the Khurāsānīs must thus have adopted the call to *al-riḍā* before they committed themselves to the 'Abbasids, as the first story also implies.

This is not the only information in the tradition which suggests that Khurāsānīs and 'Abbasids only came together late.[54] Thus, the story of the meetings at al-Abwā' and Mecca present Ibrāhīm as unaware that the Khurāsānīs were preparing a revolution on his behalf,[55] and several members of the 'Abbasid house, including the future al-Manṣūr, joined the revolt of 'Abdallāh ibn Mu'āwiya on the eve of the Khurāsānī revolution, in apparent ignorance of the fact that this revolution was being prepared.[56] Admittedly, if Ibn Mu'āwiya had called to *al-riḍā min āl Muḥammad*, the 'Abbasids could have joined him in an effort to further the common aim (instructing Abū Muslim to liquidate him as soon as he ceased to be useful, as he proceeded to do in 129/746–47). But one would have expected at least one 'Abbasid to have gone to Khurāsān to assist matters there. Why was the future al-Manṣūr happy to administer a minor district in al-Ahwāz on behalf of Ibn Mu'āwiya, when he could have participated in the raising of black banners among his own followers in Khurāsān?[57] Why was neither he nor any other 'Abbasid instructed to move on when the Khurāsānī missionaries asked for a member of the *ahl al-bayt* and got Abū Muslim instead?[58] Why, in short, was there no ʿAbbasid involvement with the Khurāsānī war effort until the Khurāsānīs arrived in Iraq? It must be added that other participants in Ibn Muʿāwiya's revolt seem to have been equally ignorant of the supposed ʿAbbasid involvement with Khurāsān. Thus, Sulaymān ibn Ḥabīb ibn al-Muhallab, Ibn Muʿāwiya's governor of al-Ahwāz, belonged to a family which was both well connected with Khurāsān and favorable to the revolution once it was underway;[59] indeed, he himself is said to have called to Abū Salama [*sic*] on the arrival of the Khurāsānī troops in Iraq.[60] But that the future al-Manṣūr was more than an ordinary subgovernor had not apparently come to his knowledge: he would scarcely have been so foolhardy as to beat and extort money from a member of the ʿAbbasid family if he had known that the ʿAbbasids were preparing a bid for the caliphate on their own.[61]

The relationship between the dynasty and the movement which enthroned it is evidently a problem which takes us far away from the meaning of *al-riḍā*, but it should be clear that the history of this movement has been subject to more ideological rewriting than is normally assumed: if *al-riḍā* meant what it appears to have meant, we must confess that we do not yet (or any longer) know how or why the ʿAbbasid revolution came to be ʿAbbasid.

POSTSCRIPT

T. Nagel, *Untersuchungen zur Entstehung des Abbasidischen Kalifates* (Bonn, 1972) also argues that *al-riḍā* was a person chosen by *shūrā*.

NOTES

1. *Akhbār al-dawla al-ʿabbāsīya wa-fīhi akhbār al-ʿAbbās wa-waladihi*, ed. ʿA. ʿA. al-Dūrī and ʿA. J. al-Muṭṭalibī (Beirut, 1971), pp. 200, 204, 282 f., 287, 291, 323, 329, 335, 340, 365, 389, 391; Ṭabarī, *Taʾrīkh al-rusul waʾl-mulūk*, ed. M. J. de Goeje *et al.* (Leiden, 1879–1901), II, 1957, 1988 f., 1993, 2003; III, 24; Balādhurī, *Ansāb al-ashrāf*, Vol. III, ed. ʿA. ʿA. al-Dūrī (Beirut and Wiesbaden, 1978), pp. 115, 130 f., 136; *Kitāb al-ʿuyūn waʾl-ḥadāʾiq*, ed. M. J. de Goeje (Leiden, 1871), p. 192; cf. also Balādhurī, *Ansāb*, III, 183; G. van Vloten, "Zur Abbasidengeschichte," *Zeitschrift der Deutschen Morgenländischen*

Gesellschaft LII (1898), p. 225, on al-Manṣūr in Basra. Needless to say, some sources present the missionaries as having called to Banū 'l-'Abbaās right away, see for example Dīnawarī, *al-Akhbār al-ṭiwāl,* ed. V. Guirgass (Leiden, 1888), p. 335; Ibn Kathīr, *al-Bidāya wa'l-nihāya fī 'l-ta'rīkh* (Cairo, 1351–58), x, 30, 32.

2. P. Crone and M. Hinds, *God's Caliph, Religious Authority in the First Centuries of Islam* (Cambridge, 1986), pp. 61 f.

3. *Akhbār al-'Abbās,* p. 204. Cf. p. 194; Ṭabarī, II, 1988; III, 24.

4. *Akhbār al-'Abbās,* p. 391.

5. Cf. most recently, M. Sharon, *Black Banners from the East* (Jerusalem and Leiden, 1983), pp. 147, 157 f.

6. Ṭabarī, II, 984 ff. The edition by M. A. F. Ibrāhīm (*Ta'rīkh al-Ṭabarī* [Cairo, 1960–69], VI, 287) reads *anna mā,* which makes nonsense of the passage unless an *illā* is inserted before *al-riḍā.* The meaning of Muṭarrif's message is quite clear from the Khārijite counter-argument (note especially . . . *mā dhakarta lanā min al-shūrā ḥīna qulta inna al-'arab idhā 'alimat annakum innamā turīdūna bi-hādha al-amr Qurayshan.* . . .). It follows that we must here have the word *annamā* in the same sense as in Qur'ān 21:108; cf. E. W. Lane, *An Arabic-English Lexicon* (London, 1863–93), I, col. 109a, s.v. *anna.*

7. Ibn Qutayba (attrib.), *Kitāb al-imāma wa'l-siyāsa* (Cairo, 1909), p. 162. Cf. Ṭabarī, II, 446 f., on the Basrans in the second civil war: at first they disagreed about whom they should make their emir, "then they agreed that two men were to make the choice for them: when the two had agreed, they would give their consent" (*thumma tarāḍaw bi-rajulayn yakhtārān lahum khīratan fa-yarḍawna bihā idhā ijtama'ā 'alayhā*). "They agreed on . . . [X and Y] to choose whomever they might find acceptable for them" (*fa-tarāḍaw bi . . . an yakhtārā man yarḍayān lahum*). "[X] made people promise that they would accept whomever he might choose" (*la-yarḍawna bimā yakhtāru*). "He said, 'I have chosen this one on your behalf'; so they cried, 'we accept'" (*qāla a-lā innī qad raḍītu lakum bihi, fanāḍaw qad raḍīnā*). The person chosen by this form of *shūrā* could clearly also be described as *al-riḍā.*

8. Balādhurī, *Ansāb al-ashrāf,* Vol. V, ed. S. D. F. Goitein (Jerusalem, 1936), p. 188.

9. *Akhbār al-'Abbās,* pp. 51, 74 (the reply is unilluminating). Cf. Ṭabarī, II, 488 f., where the Khurasānīs in the second civil war are invited to pay homage to Salm ibn Ziyād *'alā al-riḍā ḥattā yastaqīma amr al-khilāfa,* "on the basis of agreement on him until the caliphate should be put in order," that is, on the basis of popular choice as opposed to caliphal appointment.

10. Ṭabarī, II, 1567.

11. Ṭabarī, II, 1918–19, 1931.

12. Cf. Ṭabarī, II, 1919, where Naṣr ibn Sayyār, the governor of Khurāsān, has to step down so that "the matter" can be resolved by *shūrā*; and II, 1918, where a *shūrā* for the selection of subgovernors is actually set up.

13. F. Gabrieli, "La Rivolta dei Muhallabiti nel 'Irāq e il nuovo Balāḏurī," *Rendiconti della Accademia Nazionale dei Lincei,* classe di scienze morali, storiche

e filologiche, 6th ser., XIV (1938), pp. 214 f., with reference to al-Balādhurī (unpublished) and *'Uyūn*, pp. 58, 65 (I owe this reference to Martin Hinds).

14. Balādhurī would seem to have found the two programs contradictory: cf. his *za'ama*, discussed by Gabrieli, "Rivolta," p. 214 n.

15. Gabrieli, "Rivolta," p. 215 n; *'Uyūn*, p. 66.

16. Abū 'l-Faraj al-Iṣbahānī, *Kitāb maqātil al-Ṭālibīyīn* (Najaf, 1353), pp. 121 f. idem, *Kitāb al-aghānī* (Cairo, 1927–74), XII, 228.

17. Al-Maqdisī, *Le Livre de la création et de l'histoire*, ed. and trans. C. Huart, Vol. VI, (Paris, 1919), p. 62.

18. Ṭabarī, II, 1866.

19. Ṭabarī, II, 722.

20. *Maqātil*, pp. 161, 178.

21. Ibid., p. 178.

22. *Akhbār al-'Abbās*, pp. 385 f., 389. The date of this meeting is given as "while 'Abd al-Wāḥid ibn Sulaymān ibn 'Abd al-Malik was *amīr* of the *ḥajj*."

23. Ṭabarī, III, 152 (cf. III, 264); van Vloten, "Zur Abbasidengeschichte," citing a Zaydī manuscript (cf. *Maqātil*, p. 145).

24. A point noted by van Vloten, "Zur Abbasidengeschichte," p. 215. R. Traini, "La Corrispondenza tra al-Manṣūr e Muḥammad 'an-Nafs az-zakiyyah,' " *Annali del Istituto Orientale di Napoli*, n.s. XIV (1964), defends the authenticity of the correspondence (pp. 785 ff.), and holds that it once did refer to Muḥammad's election (pp. 795 ff.); T. Nagel, "Ein früher Bericht über den Aufstand des Muḥammad b. 'Abdallāh im Jahre 145 h," *Der Islam* XLVI (1970), pp. 247 ff., is more skeptical without reaching any firm conclusions regarding either the correspondence or the meetings in question.

25. Abū Salama seems to have been unaware of the election of Muḥammad ibn 'Abdallāh, cf. below.

26. They could have taken place before the 'Abbasids became involved with the Khurāsānī *da'wa*, cf. below; indeed, the story of the second meeting implies that Ibrāhīm knew nothing of the activities of the Khurāsānīs on his behalf before the messenger informed him.

27. The paradigmatic *shūrā* is the one appointed by 'Umar, who designated six men in his capacity of leader (in the sense of representative) of the community; 'Umar's example is said to have been strictly imitated by Sa'īd ibn Baḥdal al-Khārijī in the Jazīra in 127 (Khalīfa ibn Khayyāṭ, *Ta'rīkh*, ed. S. Zakkār [Damascus, 1967–68], pp. 568 f.). However, another version has it that he asked his *quwwād* to designate ten men, from among whom he selected four; these four chose two from among themselves, who were then asked to agree between themselves who was to be the leader (ibid.). In late Umayyad Khurāsān, Naṣr ibn Sayyār and al-Ḥārith ibn Surayj each designated two men, who were to choose the governors of Transoxania (clearly not from among themselves), and who were also to draw up the rules which these governors had to follow (Ṭabarī, II, 1918). In mid-Umayyad Basra, the community itself designated two men to make the choice for it (above, n. 7; this procedure is not, however, explicitly called a *shūrā*).

28. Thus the majority of the sources, see F. Omar, *The 'Abbāsid Caliphate* (Baghdad, 1969), pp. 139 ff.

29. *Arabskii anonim XI veka,* ed. P. A. Gryaznevich (Moscow, 1960), fol. 290a; *'Uyun,* p. 196; cf. p. 191.

30. The response of the 'Alids was unencouraging, while in the meantime, impatient Khurāsānīs elevated Abū 'l-'Abbās to the throne. Cf. Omar, *Caliphate,* pp. 143 ff.

31. If so, he can scarcely be said to have made a "bewildered" convocation for a "prosaic" *shūrā* (P. Crone, *Slaves on Horses, the Evolution of the Islamic Polity* [Cambridge, 1980], p. 65).

32. *Akhbār al-'Abbās,* p. 403.

33. Ibn A'tham, *Kitāb al-futūḥ,* Vol. VIII (Hyderabad, 1975), p. 177.

34. *'Uyūn,* p. 191.

35. Cf. Ibn A'tham, *Futūḥ,* VIII, 178, where Abū Salama makes the choice on behalf of the community: "O people, will you accept what I do?" (*hal antum rāḍūna bimā aṣna'u*). They said, "we accept your command" (*raḍīnā bi-amrika*), "do what you like." He said, ". . . Abū Muslim . . . wrote to me ordering me to set up a Hāshimite caliph for the people . . . we have considered the best (*akhyār*) of Banū Hāshim . . . and have accepted 'Abdallāh ibn [Muḥammad ibn] 'Alī ibn 'Abdallāh ibn 'Abbās on your behalf . . . do you agree?" (*qad irtaḍaytu lakum . . . fa-hal raḍītum?*). They answered, "Yes, we agree" (*raḍīnā*). Normally, Abū 'l-'Abbās is said to have been Ibrāhīm's legatee; here he is *al-riḍā,* chosen in open competition with other Hāshimites.

36. Both were minors at the time according to Ibn Ḥazm, *Jamharat ansāb al-'arab,* ed. 'A. S. M. Hārūn (Cairo, 1962), p. 31. Muḥammad ibn Ibrāhīm was born in 122, and was thus only ten years old at the time of the elevation of Abū 'l-'Abbās (Ṭabarī, II, 1716). His brother 'Abd al-Wahhāb seems to have been granted his first public office in 139 or 140, seven or eight years after Abū 'l-'Abbās' accession, when he was put in charge of a summer campaign and/or appointed governor of the Jazīra (Balādhurī, *Futūḥ al-buldān,* ed. M. J. de Goeje [Leiden, 1868], p. 187; Ṭabarī, III, 125; Kalīfa, p. 641; cf. *Akhbār al-'Abbās,* p. 404). Ibrāhīm's other sons are rarely mentioned; they died without issue (Balādhurī, *Ansāb,* III, 127), which could be taken to mean that they died in childhood.

37. Both were present in Kufa along with the rest of the 'Abbasids (Ṭabarī, III, 27; Ya'qūbī, *Ta'rīkh,* II, 419), and their existence could thus have been expected to elicit some comment.

38. *Maqātil,* p. 343; the word comes alive at pp. 349 f., where Abū 'l-Sarāyā's imām has testated in favor of another 'Alid: *wa-in raḍītum bihi fa-huwa al-riḍā wa-illā fa'khtārū li-anfusikum.* They end up by choosing another.

39. "His choice . . . from the two families as a whole has been 'Alī ibn Mūsā . . . on account of . . . his perfect excellence, his clear knowledge, his manifest godliness, his genuine abstinence, his leaving off of this world, and his assertion of freedom from the people," as al-Ma'mūn put it in the document of succession (Crone and Hinds, *God's Caliph,* p. 138). Compare Ibn Khallikān, *Wafāyāt al-a'yān,* ed. I. 'Abbās (Beirut, 1970–72), III, 270 (no. 423), where we

are told that al-Ma'mūn gathered the *khawāṣṣ al-awliyā'*, and told them that of all the descendants of al-'Abbās and 'Alī he had found no one more meritorious and deserving of the caliphate than 'Alī al-Riḍā.

40. The choice of the epithet was al-Ma'mūn's. Cf. Crone and Hinds, *God's Caliph*, p. 138; *Maqātil*, p. 369.

41. Cf. S. Moscati, "Il Testamento di Abū Hāšim, *Rivista degli Studi Orientali* XXVII (1952); Sharon, *Black Banners*, ch. 5.

42. Cf. Crone, *Slaves on Horses*, n. 456.

43. It is reassuring to see that Islamicists of the late nineteenth and early twentieth centuries generally regarded this story as apocryphal (J. Wellhausen, *The Arab Kingdom and Its Fall*, trans. M. G. Weir [Calcutta, 1927], p. 503; Nöldeke and others in Moscati, "Testamento," p. 35).

44. *Pace* a number of scholars of whom Wellhausen seems to be the earliest (*Kingdom*, pp. 503 f.), and Sharon the most recent (*Black Banners, passim*).

45. Thus a certain *naqīb* acted as story-teller, *fa-yadhkuru maḥāsin Banī Hāshim wa-yadhummu Banī Umayya* (Ibn Kathīr, *Bidāya*, x, 32). Yūsuf ibn 'Umar al-Thaqafī would imprison anyone known for *muwālāt Banī Hāshim wa-mawaddat ahl al-bayt* (Dīnawarī, *Akhbār*, p. 339). Qaḥṭaba called the Syrians to *mā fī hādhā al-muṣḥaf min tafḍīl Muḥammad ṣl'm wa-tafḍīl Banī Hāshim* (Ibn A'tham, *Futūḥ*, VIII, 172). The missionaries called to *imāmat Banī Hāshim* (Maqdisī, *Création*, VI, 59). The mission was a *da'wa li-Banī Hāshim* (Ya'qūbī, *Ta'rīkh*, II, 408–409 and *passim*). Abū Salama was ordered to enthrone a *khalīfatan Hāshimīyan*, and chose Abū 'l-'Abbās as the best of Banū Hāshim (Ibn A'tham, *Futūḥ*, VIII, 178). And so on.

46. But as Sharon notes, we have to await al-Shahrastānī before we see them do it (*Black Banners*, p. 84 n.).

47. Cf. Sharon, *Black Banners*, ch. 4.

48. *Maqātil*, p. 161: the missionaries of Banū Hāshim went out to preach in favor of the 'Alids on the death of al-Walīd II; when things began to go well for them, each *farīq* would adduce a *waṣīya* in favor of its own candidate.

49. If so, the transition from an ideology of *shūrā* to one of *waṣīya* may have been less drastic than it sounds. In Umayyad court poetry, 'Uthmān's position rests on both *shūrā* and *waṣīya*, in the sense that he was elected by a *shūrā* set up by 'Umar on his deathbed, sc. by *waṣīya* (Crone and Hinds, *God's Caliph*, p. 32, n. 41). By the time we reach Abū 'l-Sarāyā, the person chosen directly by the imām on his deathbed was the *riḍā* if the community would accept him (*Maqātil*, p. 349).

50. There is surprisingly little reference to it in the historical (as opposed to heresiographical) literature. Neither Abū 'l-'Abbās nor Dāwūd ibn 'Alī refers to it in the accession speeches of 132; they also do not say anything incompatible with it (Ṭabarī, III, 29 f.). It must be with reference to the alleged testament that Muḥammad al-Nafs al-Zakīya asks al-Manṣūr how the 'Abbasids can claim to have inherited 'Alī's power, given the fact that 'Alī's descendants are still alive (ibid., p. 209); but al-Manṣūr himself does not invoke it, being well on the way to adopting the position which his son al-Mahdī

was later to make official, namely, that the 'Abbasids had not inherited the imamate from an 'Alid, but rather from al-'Abbās himself (especially ibid., p. 215; cf. Traini, "Corrispondenza," p. 794). Muḥammad al-Nafs al-Zakīya's question demonstrates the polemical weakness of Abū Hāshim's testament vis-à-vis 'Alid claims.

51. *'Uyūn*, pp. 179 f.

52. *'Uyūn*, pp. 180 f.

53. The text is explicit: *qad intashara bi-Khurāsān du'āt min al-shī'a wa-qad inqasamū qismayn, qism minhum yad'ū ilā āl Muḥammad 'alā al-iṭlāq wa'l-qism al-thānī yad'ū ilā Abī Hāshim ibn Muḥammad ibn al-Ḥanafīya, wa-kāna al-mutawallī li-hādhihi al-da'wa ilā āl rasūl Allāh ṣl'm Ibn Kathīr wa-kāna al-du'āt yarji'ūna fī 'l-ra'y wa'l-fiqh ilā Abī Salama.* And it is quite true that Ibn Kathīr and others called to *āl Muḥammad*, Abū Salama himself being known as *wazīr āl Muḥammad* and Abū Muslim as *amīn āl Muḥammad.* None of them breathed a word about Abū Hāshim.

54. Similarly Sharon, *Black Banners*, but in a quite different vein.

55. Cf. above, n. 26.

56. Ya'qūbī, *Ta'rīkh*, II, 468; Balādhurī, *Ansāb*, III, 182; Jahshiyārī, *Kitāb al-wuzarā' wa'l-kuttāb*, ed. M. al-Saqqā *et al.* (Cairo, 1938), p. 98; Ibn Ḥazm, *Jamhara*, p. 369 (I owe these references to Martin Hinds); Ibn Khallikān, *Wafāyāt*, II, 410 (no. 276); Dhahabī, *Siyar a'lām al-nubalā'*, ed. Sh. al-Arna'ut *et al.* (Beirut, 1981–), VII, 23, 83; van Vloten, "Zur Abbasidengeschichte," pp. 214, 226. According to Jahshiyārī, *all* Hāshimites joined Ibn Mu'āwiya, whether they were of 'Alid, 'Abbasid, or other descent.

57. He was governor of Īdhaj (thus Jahshiyārī, Balādhurī, and van Vloten in the preceding note) on behalf of Sulaymān ibn Ḥabīb ibn al-Muhallab, Ibn Mu'āwiya's governor of al-Ahwāz (thus all except Jahshiyārī).

58. Ṭabarī, II, 1949.

59. Cf. Crone, *Slaves on Horses*, pp. 133 f. One Muhallabid was in charge of Abū Muslim's vanguard in 131 (namely, Abū Sa'īd ibn Mu'āwiya ibn Yazīd ibn al-Muhallab; cf. *Akhbār al-'Abbās*, p. 337); two Muhallabids appear as members of Qaḥṭaba's army at Isfahan and Nihāwand in the same year (namely, 'Umar ibn Ḥafṣ al-'Atakī and Yazīd ibn Ḥātim; cf. ibid., pp. 338 f. (corrupt), 352 f.; Ṭabarī, III, 4, 139); another one appears as a member of this army in Iraq ('Abd al-Raḥmān ibn Yazīd ibn al-Muhallab, *Akhbār al-'Abbās*, p. 378; but cf. Balādhurī, *Ansāb*, III, 138); and two of them rebelled in Basra on behalf of the approaching armies (Sufyān ibn Mu'āwiya and Rawḥ ibn Ḥātim, *Akhbār al-'Abbās*, pp. 355 f.; M. Hinds, *An Early Islamic Family from Oman: al-'Awtabi's Account of the Muhallabids* (forthcoming), pars. 102–105 and the notes thereto).

60. Hinds, *Early Islamic Family*, par. 106.

61. Cf. the references given above, n. 56. Some of the sources (especially Jahshiyārī) credit Abū Ayyūb al-Mūryānī, Sulaymān ibn Ḥabīb's secretary, with the foresight which Sulaymān lacked. His rough treatment of Abū Ja'far was to cost him his life.

8
Ibn al-Jawzī on Ethiopians in Baghdad

E. van Donzel

IN *Race and Color in Islam,*[1] Professor Bernard Lewis draws attention to the *Tanwīr al-ghabash fī faḍl al-sūdān wa'l-ḥabash* of Abū 'l-Faraj 'Abd al-Raḥmān ibn 'Alī Ibn al-Jawzī.[2] The *Tanwīr* has been used by M. Weisweiler,[3] and above all by G. Rotter in his fundamental study *Die Stellung des Negers in der islamisch-arabischen Gesellschaft bis zum XVI. Jahrhundert.*[4]

Ibn al-Jawzī's reason for writing this *Lighting the Morning Twilight, On the Excellent Qualities of the Blacks and the Ethiophians*[5] is found in the Introduction:[6] "I have seen a number of outstanding Ethiopians whose hearts were breaking[7] because of their black color. So I let them know that respect is based on the performance of good deeds, and not on beautiful forms. I therefore composed for them this book, which deals with a good number of Ethiopians and blacks." Apparently, black was not beautiful in Baghdad in the twelfth century.

This contribution in honor of Professor Lewis is an endeavor to show that it is not improbable that there were indeed Ethiopians in Baghdad in the twelfth century. A positive proof on the basis of one or more texts cannot be given, since such texts, to my knowledge, are so far unknown. If, however, the terms *Sūdān* and *Ḥabash* can be taken to be identical with "slaves"—and this seems quite obvious—then it may be worthwhile to try to answer the question of whether slave-trade existed between Ethiopia and Baghdad, at least until the end of the twelfth century.

For the time being, it does not seem useful to try to distinguish between *Ḥabash* and *Sūdān*. As Rotter has already pointed out,[8] *Ḥabash* only very rarely indicates a real Ethiopian. They were usually included in the general term *Sūdān*. Although the difference in color and physiognomy between blacks and Ethiopians, especially those originating from the traditional heartlands like Tigre and Amḥara, is quite evident, it may well have been that the inhabitants of Baghdad, and the Arabs in general for that matter, did not distinguish, or care to distinguish, between the many different African races living among them. If Ibn al-Jawzī did see real Ethiopians, who are rather *sumr* (sing. *asmar*), or "brown," he must have noticed the difference with the *Sūdān*, even though he never makes any distinction so far as color is concerned. In Chapter II of the *Tanwīr*, entitled "On the cause of their (i.e., of the *Sūdān*) color being black," he writes:[9]

"As for colors, it is evident that they were created such as they are, without ostensible reason [*al-ẓāhir fī 'l-alwān annahā khuliqat 'alā mā hiya 'alayhi bilā sabab ẓāhir*],[10] except what we have already transmitted,[11] namely that the sons of Nūḥ—peace be upon him—divided the earth among themselves after the death of Nūḥ. The one who divided the earth among them was Fāligh ibn 'Ābir. The sons of Sām went [*nazzala*] to the center [*surra*] of the earth; they were tawny and white [*fa-kānat fihim al-adama wa'l-bayāḍ*]. The sons of Yāfith went in the direction [*majrā*] of North and East [*al-shamāl wa'l-ṣabā*]; they were red and blond [*al-ḥumra wa'l-shuqra*]. The sons of Ḥām went in the direction of South and West [*al-janūb wa'l-dabūr*], while their color changed. As for the story that Nūḥ's pudenda were uncovered, that Ḥām did not cover them up, that Nūḥ then cursed him, and that Ḥām then became black, that is something which is neither established nor authentic *[fa-shay' lā yathbutu wa-lā yaṣiḥḥu]*."

When treating early Islam (Chapters VIII–XIV), Ibn al-Jawzī usually uses the term *Ḥabash*, as may be expected from an author who was so well versed in Muslim tradition (e.g., on the contacts between the Prophet and the *Najāshī*). But even the latter is occasionally included in the term *Sūdān*, as on fol. 40a of the Gotha manuscript, where the author says that there are four black chiefs (*sādat al-Sūdān arba'a*): Luqmān, Mahja', Bilāl, and the Najāshī. Although we are not well informed about the color of the Ethiopian kings, it may well be surmised that they generally must have been of a rather light-brown color. It should, however, be remarked that the kings of the Zagwē dynasty, who ruled during the twelfth century, may have been somewhat more dark-colored.

The practice of trading Ethiopians as slaves is much older than Islam. Already around A.D. 50, the *Periplus Maris Erythraei*[12] mentions Berberā (Malao), Bandar Ḥais (Munos), Ras Ḥafūn (Opone), and Adulis, the port of Aksum,[13] all on the African coast and, at least in part, directly linked with Ethiopia, as places from which slaves were exported.

At the time of the Prophet, there were numerous Ethiopian slaves in Mecca.[14] According to tradition, the Ethiopians were known for their dexterity with spears. In Chapter XI of his *Tanwīr*, Ibn al-Jawzī speaks of the arrival of the Ethiopians before the Prophet and their play with spears (*ḥirāb*) and shields (*daraq*) in his presence. At Uḥud, Ḥamza ibn 'Abd al-Muṭṭalib, the paternal uncle of the Prophet, was slain by the Ethiopian slave Waḥshī,[15] an expert at throwing the Ethiopian spear,[16] perhaps one of those fine-shaped, long weapons (described by Labīd[17]), which came from Samḥar in Ethiopia.[18]

In the early ninth century, under the caliph al-Amīn (193/809–198/813), there was in Baghdad a military corps of Ethiopians, known as *ghurābīya* ("crows").[19] In A.D. 976, half of the thousand slaves who were sent every year from Dahlak to Yemen consisted of Ethiopian and Nubian women.[20] This information is confirmed by Ibn Khaldūn,[21] who adds that the kings of Ethiopia used to offer presents to the ruler of the Yemen, and to seek his friendship.

During the reign of al-Muqtadir (289/902–295/908), there were 20,000 *ghilmān al-dār*, palace servants—not necessarily blacks—and 11,000 male servants, including 4,000 white Slavs and 7,000 blacks. Of the 7,000 eunuchs, 3,000 were black, while the black pages other than eunuchs totaled 4,000.[22] Also in the tenth century, Ibn Ḥawqal relates that Abū 'l-Jaysh ibn Ziyād, the governor of Zabīd, received slaves from the ruler of Dahlak.[23] At about the same time, al-Muqaddasī[24] remarks that the Ethiopians and eunuchs were the most important among the slaves arriving at Aden.

The Banū Najāḥ, a dynasty of Ethiopian slaves in Zabīd between 1022 and 1159, maintained a brisk trade in slaves from Ethiopia.[25]

In the thirteenth century, Ibn Sa'īd al-Maghribī (1213–1286) mentions Hadiya, a region in South Ethiopia, as an important center of the slave-trade. In a nearby village, the slaves were castrated.[26] The same author[27] remarks that the Karla (=Galla?) occupy a prominent place among the Ethiopian slaves and that they are sought after for their beauty. "One might say that the Ethiopians, generally speaking, are the most beautiful group among the Negroes; it is they who provide eunuchs for kings and notables [in the Muslim world]."

Information from sources which are dated after Ibn al-Jawzī's days cannot be used to corroborate his remark on the presence of Ethiopian slaves at Baghdad in his time. But these sources confirm the impression that there may have been a more or less direct slave-trade between Ethiopia and Baghdad. It would be surprising indeed if a considerable number of the highly valued Ethiopian slaves had not been transported to the ʿAbbasid capital, at least until the capture of the city by the Mongols in 1258. The slave-trade may even have profited from the temporary revival of ʿAbbasid power under the caliph al-Nāṣir li-dīn Allāh (1180–1225),[28] during whose reign the *Tanwīr* was composed.[29]

During the fourteenth century, the Muslim slave-traders were given the opportunity to continue their traffic, notwithstanding the victories of the Ethiopian kings over their Muslim adversaries. In the name of King ʿAmda Ṣyon (1314–1344), and to his profit, the Muslim merchants in Ethiopia carried on their commercial relations with Egypt, Yemen, and Iraq—and thus, by implication, Baghdad. Besides ivory and cereals, slaves were among the most important export articles.[30] During the reign of this conqueror-king, the Ethiopian saint Ewosṭātēwos is said to have reproached the inhabitants of Sarā'e in northern Ethiopia for selling Christians as slaves.[31] Raids organized by Muslims of the Red Sea coast provided the merchants with new slaves,[32] while the very high number of prisoners of war during the reign of ʿAmda Ṣyon constituted another important means of supply.[33] Taddesse Tamrat remarks[34] that "some hagiographical traditions tend to rule out Christian participation in the slave-trade, which is considered to have been an exclusively Muslim affair," and that monastic circles apparently had some reservations about slavery in general. On the other hand, the Christian families themselves had many slaves, and the latter were occasionally even presented to prominent monks.

In the same fourteenth century, Ibn Faḍl Allāh al-ʿUmarī[35] repeats that Hadiya, which he calls one of the *mamālik bilād Zaylaʿ*, was a well-known center for the castration of slaves, a practice which had been forbidden by the Ethiopian king, but without much success.[36] They were taken from every non-Muslim region in Ethiopia, even from the Christian heartlands of Saḥart (Tigre) and Amḥara.[37] Zaylaʿ (Zāligh), in Ibn Ḥawqal's time still a Christian town,[38] became the most important port for the slave-trade in that part of the African coast,[39] followed by Masawwaʿ and Dahlak.

A trace of the way in which the slave-trade was carried out may be found in the Ethiopian term *naggādi* ("merchant, slave-trader, Muslim"), while the word *ḥabshī* is a reminder of the slave-trade from Ethiopia to far-away countries. It was used in India to designate African communities whose ancestors had originally come into the country as slaves, in most cases from the Horn of Africa.[40]

In the fifteenth and sixteenth centuries, Arabic, Ethiopian, and European sources yield a few more details about the slave-trade in Ethiopia. According to al-Maqrīzī (1364–1442),[41] Jamāl al-Dīn of Awfāt (Ifāt, 1425–1432) "killed and captured [*asara*] innumerable [*mā lā yadkhulu taḥta ḥaṣr*] infidel Amḥaras [*Amḥara akfara*], so that Hind, the Yemen, Hormuz, the Ḥijāz, Egypt, Syria, Rūm, Iraq, and Persia were filled with Ethiopian slaves [*raqīq al-ḥabasha*] whom he had captured and taken prisoner [*sabāhum*] during his incursions [*ghazawāt*]." During the reign of King Eskender (1478–1494), an Ethiopian was taken prisoner by the Muslims, and sold as a slave to an inhabitant of the Yemen.[42] Francisco Alvares relates that the Muslims recruited slaves in Damot, who were then sold at high prices as far away as India and Greece,[43] and that every year the king of Adal sent great numbers of Abyssinian slaves to Mecca, making presents of those slaves to the king of Arabia and to other princes; in return he received horses and weapons.[44] Finally, the great number of Ethiopian slaves brought to Zayla‘ and beyond increased dramatically during the devastating wars of Aḥmad Grāñ.[45]

Bilād al-Sūdān, the "land of the blacks," i.e., non-Muslim Africa, in particular the Horn, was probably by far the most important of the three reservoirs from which the Arab-Muslim world was provided with slaves, the other two being *Bilād al-Saqāliba*, the "land of the Slavs" (Central and Eastern Europe), and *Bilād al-Atrāk* , the "land of the Turks" (Central Asia). Slave caravans followed various routes which led from interior Africa to the Islamic heartlands. One went to Zayla‘, while another brought the so-called Berberine slaves to the Aswan region.[46] From there, the slaves were directed to Cairo, Damascus, and Baghdad. From Zayla‘, two routes led to the Gulf and Baghdad, one via Zabīd, the other via Socotra.[47]

Thus, slave-trade from Ethiopia, as well as routes for slave caravans leading from Ethiopia to Baghdad, certainly did exist, most probably also in Ibn al-Jawzī's time, even though no direct and concrete details on either of these can as yet be given. There were many mamlūks (white slaves)[48] in Baghdad in his days, some of them highly placed,[49] but the presence of Ethiopian slaves in the ‘Abbasid capital in the twelfth century, and any form of discrimination against them, cannot be proved from elsewhere. However, on the basis of the data collected above, there is no reason not to accept Ibn al-Jawzī's short remark as referring to reality.

NOTES

1. *Race and Color in Islam* (New York, 1971), p. 37; expanded French translation, *Race et couleur en pays d'Islam* (Paris, 1982), p. 38.

2. Recent studies on this well-known Ḥanbalite of Baghdad (1116–1201) are: Henri Laoust, "Ibn al-Jawzī," with bibliography, in *EI*²; Daniel Reig, "Le Ṣayd al-Ḥāṭir d'Abū 'l-Farağ ibn al-Ğawzī," *Studia Islamica* XXXIV (1971), pp. 89–123; Merlin L. Swartz, *Ibn al-Jawzī's Kitāb al-Quṣṣāṣ wa'l-mudhakkirīn*, (Beirut, 1969); Qāsim al-Sāmarrā'ī, *Kitāb al-quṣṣāṣ wa'l-mudhakkirīn* (Riyāḍ, 1403/1983); Stefan Leder, *Ibn al-Ğauzī und seine Kompilation wider die Leidenschaft. Der Traditionalist in gelehrter Überlieferung und originärer Lehre*, Beiruter Texte und Studien XXXII (Beirut, 1984). Cf. also Joseph Norman Bell, *Love Theory in Later Hanbalite Islam* (Albany, 1979), pp. 11–45; Angelika Hartmann, *An-Nāṣir li-Dīn Allāh (1180–1225)* (Berlin-New York, 1975), index *s.v.*

3. Max Weisweiler, ed. and trans., *Buntes Prachtgewand: Über die guten Eigenschaften der Abessinier von Muḥammad ibn 'Abdalbâqî al-Buḫârî al-Makkî* (Hanover, 1924), I, 3–7.

4. Diss. Bonn, 1967. Cf. B. Lewis, *Race*, p. 24; French trans. p. 12.

5. On this title, see E. van Donzel, "Quelques Remarques sur le *Tanwīr al-ghabash*," in *Actas del XII Congreso de la U.E.A.I.* (Malaga, 1984) (Madrid, 1986), pp. 243–55.

6. Wilhelm Pertsch, *Die arabischen Handschriften der Herzoglichen Bibliothek zu Gotha* (Gotha, 1881), III, no. 1692, pp. 288–290. Other manuscripts of the same work are kept in the Escorial, no. 1757, and in Istanbul, Şehid Ali Paşa 2803/4, fols. 88–107. Since the Gotha MS, which only lacks the first folio, has 100 folios, the Istanbul MS must be an abridgment. A Turkish translation is to be found in Istanbul, Hacī Mahmud Effendi 4958. According to Muḥammad Bāqir 'Alwān ("Al-Mustadrak 'alā mu'allafāt Ibn al-Jawzī," *Al-Mawrid* I [1971], p. 184), Yale University (Catalog p. 127, no. 1571) keeps another manuscript, entitled *Nūr al-ghabash fī faḍl al-Ṣūdān wa'l-Ḥabash.* In the same catalog (p. 127, no. 1570) is listed an abridgment (*mukhtaṣar*) under the title *Īwān al-ghabash fī faḍā'il al-Ṣūdān wa'l-Ḥabash*, which, according to Muḥammad Bāqir, is in deplorable condition. The same author adds that he is in possession of an illustrated (*muṣawwara*) copy of these two manuscripts. Pertsch's remark (op. cit., p. 288) that the manuscript "handelt über Abbessinien and seine Bewohner" is only partly true, as can be seen from the Arabic titles (Pertsch, pp. 288–89) and their German translation in Weisweiler, *Buntes Prachtgewand*, pp. 4–5 and Rotter, *Die Stellung*, p. 14.

7. Cp. B. Lewis, *Race*, pp. 11–15, French trans. pp. 28–34.

8. *Die Stellung*, p. 91, n. 3; p. 115.

9. Fol. 5a of the Gotha manuscript. On colors, see B. Lewis, *Race*, p. 7, f; French trans., pp. 18ff., and bibliography given there.

10. Cf. Qur'ān 30:22, and B. Lewis, *Race*, p. 6, French trans., p. 17.

11. In Chapter I.

12. Wilfred H. Schoff, ed. and trans., *The Periplus of the Erythraean Sea. Travel and Trade in the Indian Ocean by a Merchant of the First Century* (London-Bombay, 1912), index *s.v.* slaves.

13. Schoff, op. cit., index *s.vv.*; EI[2] *s.vv.*, and *s.v.* Guardafui. Cf. also Carlo Conti Rossini, *Storia d'Etiopia* (Bergamo, 1928), I, 117 (Ras Hafun), I, 104–106, 121 (Adulis). For the latter, see also Taddesse Tamrat, *Church and State in Ethiopia, 1279–1570* (Oxford, 1972), p. 14, n. 4; Joseph Cuoq, *L'Islam en Éthiopie des origines au XVIe siècle* (Paris, 1981), pp. 36–37.

14. Cf. EI[2] *s.v.* 'Abd. On the Aḥābīsh mentioned there, see ibid., *s.v.* Ḥabash, Ḥabasha. Cf. also EI[2] *s.v.* 'Abd Allāh b. Djud'ān; Conti Rossini, *Storia*, pp. 296–97.

15. See EI[2] *s.v.* Ḥamza b. 'Abd al-Muṭṭalib.

16. *The Life of Muhammad. A Translation of Ibn Isḥāq's Sīrat rasūl Allāh*, ed. and trans. A. Guillaume (Oxford, 1955), pp. 371, 375–77.

17. Theodor Nöldeke, *Fünf Mo'allaqât*, in *Sitzungsberichte der Philos.-Hist. Classe der kais. Akad. der Wissenschaften*, Vol. 142 (Vienna, 1900), V. Abhandlung: *Die Mo'allaqa Labīds*, verse 50 (p. 61); cf. ibid., Vol. 140, VII. Abhandlung, verse 36 (p. 27) and p. 36.

18. Ibn Sa'īd al-Maghribī, in Abū 'l-Fidā, *Taqwīm al-buldān*, trans. J. T. Reinaud, *Géographie d'Aboulféda* (Paris, 1848), II, i, pp. 227–28; Yāqūt, *Mu'jam al-buldān*, ed. Wüstenfeld (Leipzig, 1866–73), III, 146. For the spears, Reinaud (p. 210 n. 3) refers to "les Séances de Hariri, éd. de Sacy, p. 195."

19. Ṭabarī, *Ta'rīkh al-rusul wa'l-mulūk*, ed. M. J. de Goeje *et al.*, III, 950, quoted in Daniel Pipes, *Slave Soldiers and Islam. The Genesis of a Military System* (New Haven-London, 1981).

20. H. C. Kay, *Yaman, its Early Medieval History* (London, 1892), pp. 8, 143.

21. Kay, *Yaman*, p. 106 (Arabic text), p. 143; cf. Cuoq, *L'Islam*, p. 46.

22. Jacob Lassner, *The Topography of Baghdad in the Early Middle Ages. Text and Studies* (Detroit, 1970), p. 267, n. 7. See also Guy Le Strange, *Baghdad during the Abbasid Caliphate from Contemporary Arabic and Persian Sources* (Oxford, 1900), pp. 123–24.

23. *Configuration de la terre (Kitāb ṣūrat al-arḍ)*, ed. and trans. J. H. Kramers and G. Wiet (Beirut-Paris, 1964), I, 22.

24. *Aḥsan al-taqāsīm*, ed. M. J. de Goeje, BGA IIIa (Leiden, 1877), p. 242.

25. See EI[1] *s.v.*; Conti Rossini, *Storia*, p. 299; Kay, *Yaman*, pp. 81–123.

26. Cf. Abū 'l-Fidā, *Taqwīm*, trans. Reinaud, *Géographie*, II, i, 229; Tamrat, *Church*, pp. 86–87.

27. Reinaud, *Géographie*, II, i, 226; cf. al-'Umarī, *Masālik* (= Gaudefroy-Demombynes, *L'Afrique*, pp. 30–31); B. Lewis, *Race*, French trans., pp. 143, 145.

28. Angelika Hartmann, *an-Nāṣir*.

29. Fol. 2a, cf. Pertsch, op. cit., p. 290.

30. Tamrat, *Church*, pp. 85–86.

31. Tamrat, *Church*, p. 86, n. 4.

32. Tamrat, *Church,* p. 86, n. 4.

33. Jules Perruchon, "Histoire des guerres d'Amda Seyon, roi d'Éthiopie," *Journal Asiatique,* Sér. 3, Vol. XIV (1889), pp. 287, 294, 434–38, quoted by Tamrat, *Church,* p. 87, n. 6.

34. *Church,* p. 87.

35. *Masālik al-abṣār fī mamālik al-amṣār* (= Maurice Gaudefroy-Demombynes, *L'Afrique moins l'Égypte* [Paris, 1927], pp. 16–17; cf. al-Maqrīzī, *Historia regum islamiticorum in Abyssinia,* ed. and trans. F. T. Rinck (Leiden, 1790), pp. 14–15.

36. On Hadiya, see now Ulrich Braukämper, *Geschichte der Hadiya Süd-Äthiopiens. Von den Anfängen bis zur Revolution 1974* (Wiesbaden, 1980).

37. Kay, *Yaman,* pp. 104, 117.

38. *Configuration,* I, 54.

39. Idrīsī, *Description de l'Afrique et de l'Espagne,* ed. R. Dozy and M. J. de Goeje (Leiden, 1866), p. 30; cf. Cuoq, *L'Islam,* pp. 55–56.

40. See EI[2] *s.v.*

41. *Historia,* p. 32 (Arabic text); p. 36 (trans.).

42. Lanfranco Ricci, "Le Vite di Ĕnbāqom e di Yoḥannĕs, Abbati di Dabra Libanos di Scioa," in *Rassegna di Studi Etiopici,* XIII (1955), p. 100; cf. p. 113, n. 33.

43. Charles F. Beckingham and G. W. B. Huntingford, *The Prester John of the Indies. A true Relation of the Lands of the Prester John. Being the narrative of the Portuguese Embassy to Ethiopia in 1520, written by Father Francisco Alvares,* Hakluyt Society, 2d Series (Cambridge, 1961), Vols, CXIV, CXV; Chapter 134 (p. 455).

44. Ibid., Chapter 113 (p. 408).

45. René Basset, ed. and trans., *Histoire de la conquête de l'Abyssinie (XVIe siècle) par Chihab eddin Aḥmed ben 'Abd el Qâder* (Paris, 1879–1901).

46. Maurice Lombard, *L'Islam dans sa première grandeur (VIIIe–XIe siècles)* (Paris, 1971), p. 194. On the "Berberine" slaves, see EI[2] *s.v.* Barābra, and E. van Donzel, *Foreign Relations of Ethiopia, 1642–1700* (Leiden, 1979), pp. 16, 193 (n. 20).

47. On the trade routes to Masawwa' and Dahlak, see Cuoq, *L'Islam,* p. 53.

48. Cf. B. Lewis, *Race,* pp. 38, 64 (French trans. p. 63).

49. Angelika Hartmann, *An-Nāṣir,* pp. 273–282.

9
The Silent Force Behind the Rise of Medieval Islamic Civilization

Andrew S. Ehrenkreutz

I

THIS IS NOT a "professional" article but rather a set of impressionistic reflections on an aspect of medieval Near Eastern history, a subject to which I was initiated in the fall of 1947 at the School of Oriental and African Studies (University of London) by the very scholar to whom the present volume is dedicated. During the subsequent forty years I have witnessed a remarkable heuristic progress and didactic expansion of that academic specialty. It would hardly be an exaggeration to state that to no small degree this was achieved thanks to the prolific and diversified contributions of *Ustādh al-asātidha* Bernard Lewis—a rigorous, indefatigable scholar, stimulating teacher and author, and a delightful, friendly colleague.

Particularly impressive advances have been accomplished in the study of the economic aspects of the Near East in the Middle Ages, which at the time of my undergraduate beginnings constituted an underdeveloped academic area. It was thanks to the influence of Lewis that I quickly became attracted to this field—not so much because of his "The Fāṭimids and the Route to India"[1] (which I came to appreciate at a later stage of my studies), but because of the frequent "economica" in his basic lectures on the Caliphate, and specifically his citation of Ya'qūbī's account of the materialistic motives behind al-Manṣūr's selection of the site of the new 'Abbāsid capital.[2]

This interest was stimulated by my doctoral research in the field of medieval Near Eastern monetary history, pursued under the inspirational and instructive direction of D. Storm Rice; and in the following decades this study has been rewarded by a dramatic progress in research and literary output covering the economic life of the *Dār al-Islām.* The medieval Egyptian economy alone has absorbed the attention of a good number of historians, e.g., E. Ashtor, J. L. Bacharach, Cl. Cahen, R. S. Cooper, S. D. Goitein, Hassanein Rabie, G. Hennequin, Subhi Y. Labib, Bernard Lewis, R. A. Messier, Rāshid al-Barrāwī, and A. L. Udovitch. A great number of articles, studies, and monographs have appeared since the appearance of Claude Cahen's postulative article, "L'Histoire économique et sociale de l'Orient musulman médiéval" (*Studia Islamica* III [1955], pp. 93–115), to mention only such collective publications as *Studies in the Economic History of the Middle East* (1970); *Islam and the Trade of Asia* (1970); *Wirtschaftsgeschichte des Vorderen Orients in islamischer Zeit* (Handbuch der Orientalistik, Erste Abteilung, Sechster Band, Sechster Abschnitt, 1977); *The Islamic Middle East, 700–1900; Studies in Economic and Social History* (1981); and the *Journal of the Economic and Social History of the Orient* (1957–).

In spite of such voluminous literature, I do not think that this subject has received *adequate* recognition in our *teaching* of Islamic history. As mentioned above, it has gained recognition as a subject deserving heuristic and hermeneutic attention. The presence and the relationships between the economic and political ingredients in the behavior of individual rulers or dynastic regimes has been ingeniously examined. However, *the economic factor has not been understood as a powerful catalyst and means bringing about the spectacular phenomenon in human history, which is usually referred to as Islamic civilization.*

In my opinion one cannot divorce the success of the *Dār al-Islām* in the sphere of culture, including its ruling religion, from its success in the area of economics. I would even go further by questioning whether the expansion and efflorescence of Islamic civilization could have been possible without the regeneration of the Near Eastern economy achieved by or under the victorious Muslim regime. Let me digress for a moment from the Islamic Middle East to twentieth-century Central and Eastern Europe. I suggest that the Marxist ideology and system installed in those regions by the Soviet conquerors would not have been so detested by the subjugated peoples had the Communist masters succeeded in generating favorable economic trends and in raising the standards of living. Neither would there be any need for the doctrinally deviationist experiments in which some of the Communist regimes have indulged to prop up their stagnant or declining economies.

In the same sense one may hypothesize that if the behavior and policies of the early Muslim regimes had adversely affected the economic status of the conquered peoples of the Near East, the expansion of Islam—as a new religion and as a new socio-economic system—would have weakened.

The fact remains, however, that far from hurting the material situation of the subjugated peoples, the Arab conquerors reversed the catastrophic economic trends prevailing in the Near East at the time of the rise of Islam. Next to the new religious doctrine this reversal of the economic trends—from precipitous decline to progressively expanding market economy—constituted the most dramatic and fundamental contribution of the Arabs to medieval Near Eastern and Mediterranean history.

II

Fifteen years ago I outlined the initial stages of this regeneration of Near Eastern economy by the Arabs.[3] I stressed the non-destructive character of the great Islamic conquest, which meant that the dramatic political takeover was accomplished without substantial losses by the tax-paying civilian population or by revenue-yielding establishments. In sociological terms the Arab invasion amounted to the mass migration of the surplus population of the Arabian peninsula to the sedentarized zone of the Near East. Except for a small minority, the mass of the Arab immigrants represented unskilled labor which under normal conditions might have caused a major economic and social upheaval. As it was, far from encumbering the ailing local economies the new settlers stimulated their recovery. This happened because of the introduction by the Caliphate of an innovative system of fiscal benefits, according to which all full-fledged members of the victorious Arab people were entitled to regular cash stipends, the *'aṭā'*, in addition to their lower taxation rates. The ingenious system was financed by taxes paid by the conquered peoples. Although not immune to abuses, the system of *'aṭā'* remained in operation for a century and brought it about that the early Arab immigrants, far from being an economic liability, constituted a strongly subsidized social and ethnic group enjoying cash stipends to be invested or otherwise used to consequent benefit of the Near Eastern economy. Obviously, Arab settlers, whether ruling elite or members of the rank and file, constituted a potent consumer class which generated a substantial increase of economic productivity. The expansion of old towns and proliferation of new urban settlements created a boom in the housing industry. And this growth of the urban population stimulated diverse manufacturing activities; it generated a strong demand for food supplies, giving rise to speculative agriculture and interest in acquisition of landed property. Likewise, internal trade benefited from the new situation by performing vital economic functions between the urban and rural populations.

Equally dynamic developments characterized Near Eastern participation in intercontinental commerce. As it happened, the political consequences of the great Arab victory had contributed to a major change in this sector. With the expulsion of the Byzantines and the destruction of the Sasanids, the political barrier which had hitherto divided the Near East into two separate blocs ceased to exist. The transformation of the vast western and eastern regions into a "common market" under the same political and ideological regime meant that the *Dār al-Islām*, enjoying relative internal stability and expanding economy, became the most lucrative area to serve the needs of investors and merchants engaged in long distance trade linking the Far East with Western Europe, the Indian Ocean with the Atlantic, and the Baltic regions with Africa.

These favorable economic trends were reflected in the concurrent monetary developments culminating in the epoch-making coinage reform of Caliph ʿAbd al-Malik. This decision of the Arab administration to release vast quantities of gold (*dīnār*), silver (*dirham*), and copper (*fals*) coins—its alleged religious or ideological background notwithstanding—must have been made in response to expanding market conditions. Although the supply of new coins gradually attained tremendous proportions, no inflationary developments were set off by such a monetary policy. General stability of prices or, to be more precise, lack of evidence pointing to drastic rise in the prices of commodities, seems to suggest that the sustained intensive output of coins in the early Caliphate bore witness to the great vitality of the Near Eastern economy regenerated by the Muslim regime. Certainly, before the masses of the conquered Near Eastern population adopted the religion of the Arab conquerors they had readily and profitably welcomed the new coinage—a powerful instrument and symbol of an expanding economy.

III

For several centuries after this victory of the Arabs, Near Eastern society generally enjoyed higher standards of living than those that had prevailed under the Byzantine and Sasanid domination. The socio-economic system evolved by the Arab conquerors and their multi-ethnic successors proved its viability: it reduced psychological, religious animosity or indifference which the conquered people might originally have felt toward Islam, and induced mass conversion. One should stress, however, that opportunities to partake in and to benefit from the economic expansion were not limited to Muslim believers. Although the non-Muslim communities (the *ahl al-dhimma*) did not enjoy their legally prescribed but not rigidly enforced inferior social status, and although they were fiscally discriminated against, their output was integrated with the rest of the Near Eastern economy. In some sectors, such as intercontinental trade or banking, they proved to be very active and successful.

Without the creation of conditions conducive to economic regeneration, without a proper exploitation of human and physical resources, and without the ensuing profit-oriented social climate, the spectacular expansion of Islamic civilization might not have taken place at all. It was because of the accumulation of wealth that the *Dār al-Islām* experienced such impressive progress in different spheres of its societal endeavors. It was that wealth which allowed the revitalization and extension of the flow of trade along a widespread network of land, sea, and river routes, and which provided itinerant merchants and peripatetic scholars with such facilities as caravanserais, hostels, bazaars, and harbor amenities. Thanks to this wealth Islamic towns were famous not only for their resplendent mosques, lavish palaces, and scholarly libraries and hospitals, but also for public utilities such as baths, aqueducts, and sewage systems. Such wealth promoted technological inventiveness and innovations. Could the production of paper, several centuries before its introduction to Europe, and its rapid spread—from Central Asia to Islamic Spain—have taken place without adequate investment capital and sufficient market demand? Without that basic commodity of a truly revolutionary character, the widespread dissemination of texts, the popularizing and preserving of the scholarly legacy of the classical and medieval past would not have been possible. Commercial transactions and correspondence would have also been inhibited.

Could a society without the "social overhead capital" have reached such high educational standards involving elementary schools, colleges, libraries, observatories, and "medical academies"? Can one imagine that the diversified sophistication of the Islamic world of learning—be it in theology, philosophy, literature and literary criticism, medicine, psychology, agriculture, or zoology—could have taken place without sufficient economic resources sustaining such pursuits by successive generations of Near Eastern savants? Would the jurists of medieval Islam have exerted themselves to study and codify complicated legal problems, financial and commercial, in the absence of an intensive banking and commercial life?

The brilliance of medieval Islamic civilization has long been recognized. It is time to make clearer and to acknowledge the *silent* force which made that civilization possible.

NOTES

1. *Revue de la Faculté des Sciences Économiques de l'Université d'Istanbul*, XI (1949–50).

2. Cf. Bernard Lewis, *The Arabs In History* (London, 1956), p. 82.

3. "Another Orientalist's Remarks Concerning the Pirenne Thesis," *Journal of the Economic and Social History of the Orient*, XV (1972), pp. 94–104.

10
The Development of the Biography of al-Ḥārith ibn Kalada and the Relationship Between Medicine and Islam

G. R. Hawting

[Al-Ḥārith ibn Kalada] was the doctor of the Arabs in his time. In origin he was one of Thaqīf of the people of Ṭā'if. He travelled to Persia and acquired knowledge of medicine from the people of those parts—the people of Jundishapur and others—in the *jāhilīya* and before Islam.[1] He excelled in this craft, and he practised medicine and healing in Persia. As a result, he became wealthy there, and those Persians who saw him witnessed his knowledge. He had treated one of their great men, who had recovered and given him wealth and a slave girl in payment. This slave girl al-Ḥārith named Sumayya. Then his soul yearned for his own country, and he returned to Ṭā'if, where his medicine became renowned among the Arabs.[2]

THE BIOGRAPHY OF al-Ḥārith ibn Kalada[3] contained in the biographical dictionary of doctors, scientists, and philosophers of Ibn al-Qifṭī (d. 624/1227), of which the above is the start, is typical of the genre. Much of Ibn al-Qifṭī's material on him overlaps with that contained in the works of the same type by Ibn Juljul (d. after 384/994) and Ibn Abī Uṣaybi'a (d. 669/1270).[4] Following the above introduction, Ibn al-Qifṭī supplies us with information about the offspring of Sumayya, notably the famous governor of Iraq and the East for the Umayyads, Ziyād ibn Abīhi. He then goes on to tell us that the Prophet used to send sick people to consult al-Ḥārith, illustrating this with two reports of how, on the Prophet's orders, al-Ḥārith treated the sick

Sa'd ibn Abī Waqqāṣ. The treatment described, which involved the use of dates, underlines for us the character of al-Ḥārith as an *Arab* doctor, and further reported dicta and opinions of his increase the impression of a doctor whose medicine was uncomplicated, common-sensical, and self-sufficient, both in the sense that its *materia medica* were locally available simples, and in that it placed an onus on the individual to look after himself by sensible diet and habits. All of these are characteristics too, I think, of the so-called prophetic medicine. The biography thus establishes an ambiguity in the image of the type of medicine which al-Ḥārith practised: on the one hand, he is linked with the Hellenistic tradition of Persia and Jundishapur, on the other his character as an Arab and the simplicity of his remedies are emphasized.

A doubt about the authenticity of al-Ḥārith's acceptance of Islam is then mentioned, and the point is made that the Prophet's willingness to refer invalids to him shows that it is legitimate for sick Muslims to consult doctors from among the *ahl al-kufr* (Ibn Ḥajar, *Iṣāba: ahl al-dhimma*[5]). Finally, having noted that al-Ḥārith had learned to play the lute while in Persia, Ibn al-Qifṭī cites another alleged dictum of his, also reported by Ibn Juljul and Ibn Abī Uṣaybi'a: asked by the caliph Mu'āwiya, "What is medicine?", al-Ḥārith replied, *al-azm*, a word which is glossed as "abstention from, or frugality with, food."[6]

The main significant addition to Ibn al-Qifṭī's biography to be found in Ibn Abī Uṣaybi'a is a long conversation on medical matters between al-Ḥārith and the famous Sasanid shah Khusraw Anushırwan (d. 579). Whatever the provenance of the text of this discussion, it is sufficient to note here that it reinforces the ambiguity about the nature of al-Ḥārith's medicine which is to be seen in Ibn al-Qifṭī's text: al-Ḥārith is both a doctor in the "scientific," Hellenistic tradition, and an Arab whose art is free from scientific obscurities and complications. While the bulk of his discussion with the shah consists of saws which may be considered typical of folk or popular medicine ("do not go to the bath with a full stomach, do not come to your wife while drunk, do not remain naked at night, and do not sit down to a meal while angry"), and while the text emphasizes the shah's amazement that a primitive people like the Arabs could produce a man of such learning, the setting of the discussion again emphasizes the Persian connection, and in the course of it al-Ḥārith shows himself to be fully conversant with the doctrine of the four humors, even proving himself capable of clearing up some of the shah's puzzlement over it.[7]

If we now compare the information on al-Ḥārith to be found in this genre of doctors' biographies, mainly concerned, of course, with the Hellenistic tradition and its continuation in Islamic times, with the information on him in what might be termed our "usual" sources for the Arabian origins of Islam—chiefly *sīra* (including *maghāzī*) and *ta'rīkh,* we cannot fail to be struck by a contrast. In these latter sources the information about al-Ḥārith is fragmentary, references to his profession as a doctor are not consistent and, where they occur, tend to be incidental, and there seems to be little information about the nature of his medicine or detail about his life. Relevant material in these sources seems to fall naturally into three groups, and it is only in one of them that attention really focuses on al-Ḥārith as a doctor.

The first group consists of references to al-Ḥārith in connection with the Prophet's freeing of the slaves of Ṭā'if. When the Prophet was besieging the town, a number of the slaves of its people accepted his offer of freedom if they would leave the town, join the Muslims and accept Islam. Several of those who accepted this offer are named, and one or two of them are linked with al-Ḥārith—we are told that they were slaves of his. Furthermore, when the town finally submitted to the Prophet a number of its citizens complained to him about the loss they had suffered in the emancipation of their slaves, and asked for them to be returned. He refused. Al-Ḥārith ibn Kalada is mentioned as one of those who spoke to the Prophet in this vein. In none of this is al-Ḥārith mentioned as a doctor; he is simply a prominent man of Ṭā'if, who can be presumed to be known to the audience—at least there seems to be no need to provide any explanatory details about him.[8]

Second, there are references to al-Ḥārith in a group of reports which appear to center around the person of Sumayya. This woman sometimes appears to be the mother not only of Ziyād ibn Abīhi, but also of the Companion 'Ammār ibn Yāsir, and various other named individuals. Evidently the traditions are confused; Pellat suggests that there has been a conflation of two originally independent Sumayyas, one the mother of Ziyād, the other, Sumayya bint Khubāṭ, the mother of 'Ammār. In both cases the Sumayya in question is associated in the sources with al-Ḥārith. With reference to the mother of Ziyād ibn Abīhi, we are told that Sumayya was a Persian slave girl in the possession of al-Ḥārith ibn Kalada, and that she was also the mother of others who were called sons of al-Ḥārith, even though he was not their real father. According to some, he was infertile and had no real offspring. It is in connection with the story of how Suymayya came into his possession that mention is made of him as a doctor. Again, there are variant traditions, but the gist of them is that Sumayya was a Persian girl who was given to al-Ḥārith by a notable personage—a Persian, a Yemeni returning from Persia, or a Gulf pirate who had abducted her from Persia—in exchange for medical services which al-Ḥārith provided.[9] Ibn al-Qifṭī's report summarizes one of these variants. There is also a tradition, cited by Pellat from al-Mas'ūdī, according to which the mother of the other great Thaqafī governor of Iraq and the East for the Umayyads, al-Ḥajjāj, had once belonged to al-Ḥārith ibn Kalada. This may be a variant of, or derived from, the traditions associating Ziyād with al-Ḥārith.

Compared with the stories about Ziyād's mother, which seem to give a fairly central place to al-Ḥārith, in those concerned with the descent of 'Ammār ibn Yāsir, al-Ḥārith's part is more marginal, and his role as a doctor is not remarked upon. In these we are told that Sumayya was a slave girl belonging to 'Ammār ibn Yāsir's father, who had acquired her from the man in Mecca who was his patron following his own migration to Mecca from the Yemen. After Sumayya had borne 'Ammār for him, she passed into the hands of a certain al-Azraq, a Greek (*Rūmī*) blacksmith belonging to al-Ḥārith ibn Kalada. This al-Azraq was one of the slaves of Ṭā'if who accepted the Prophet's offer of freedom and Islam. Subsequently, the descendants of al-Azraq and Sumayya claimed descent from al-Ḥārith ibn Abī Shamar al-Ghassānī, so as to be *ḥulafā'* of the Umayyad family, and *ashrāf* in Mecca. One of them married into the Umayyad family. This does not seem to be the place to attempt to sort out this tangled web. Pellat is inclined to explain the traditions partly by reference to anti-Umayyad motives, and partly by the desires of *mawālī* to provide themselves with an Arab genealogy.[10] My concern here is with the role of al-Ḥārith as a doctor.

It is in the third group that attention seems to focus more on al-Ḥārith's role as a doctor, for in it he is associated with various sick- or deathbed scenes of early Islam. By far the most common association is that already noted—with the sickbed of Sa'd ibn Abī Waqqāṣ—a tradition which is used in a variety of ways. When it is cited in works of various types concerned with medicine, the point of the tradition sometimes seems to be to show that the Prophet himself recommended the use of medicine and doctors,[11] but elsewhere it is used as material in the legal debate about the rights of a dying man to bequeath his estate,[12] or to show the Prophet's concern that a *muhājir* like Sa'd should not die in Mecca.[13] In some traditions al-Ḥārith is also connected with the final illness of Abū Bakr,[14] and even with that of 'Umar.[15]

The report about Abū Bakr's illness is especially interesting, because there is some ambiguity in it about the function of al-Ḥārith. We are told that the first caliph was poisoned by the Jews, and that al-Ḥārith also ingested some of the poison, which was in some rice, but that he stopped before the dose was fatal. He recognized the poison, and told Abū Bakr that he had a year left to live; a year later the caliph died after a fortnight's illness. While he was ill, someone suggested to him that he should call *the* doctor (*al-ṭabīb*), but he answered that he had been seen by the doctor, who had told him that he was doing what he wanted. The significance of this is somewhat obscure but, in his *Iḥyā'*, Ghazālī used the report in support of his argument that, upon occasion, refusal to use medicine is a praiseworthy thing, for example, if it has been revealed to the sick man, in one of a number of ways, that his life is at an end, and that recourse to medicine is pointless. This was exactly the case with Abū Bakr, since he would not otherwise have refused to see a doctor, having seen that the Prophet himself had recourse to doctors and medicine. Ghazālī seems to be understanding Abū Bakr's reference to "the doctor" who had seen him as a reference to God.[16] In other traditions, the Prophet also indicates that God is the only true doctor.[17] But however we understand the last part of the story about Abū Bakr's illness, what interests me here is the role of al-Ḥārith. Does the story tell us that he was a doctor? Possibly, I think, but I am not sure.

It is easy to see that some of the seeds of the image of al-Ḥārith which appears in the genre of biographies of doctors are present in the *sīra* and *ta'rīkh* material. There is the connection with Ṭā'if, and it may be that the connection with Persia which appears in some of the reports about Sumayya lies behind the much more elaborate accounts of al-Ḥārith's medical and musical studies in Persia which we find in Ibn al-Qifṭī's work, and in others of a similar sort. It is certainly striking that the Yemen is associated with Persian influence (as it often is in Muslim historical tradition about the *jāhilīya*), both in some of the traditions about how al-Ḥārith came to possess Sumayya, and in the accounts of his medical training in the collections of doctors' biographies. Equally clearly, however, the latter type of accounts of al-Ḥārith's life are much more cohesive, and contain more detail about his career as a doctor and the nature of his medicine. Given that the *sīra* tradition can be traced back considerably earlier than the biographies of doctors type of literature, it seems clear that generally, the biography of al-Ḥārith in the latter genre is the result of the gradual elaboration of material, only some of which was available when the biography of the Prophet was taking on its earliest form. In spite of this, historians of medicine have tended to be fairly credulous about the biographies of al-Ḥārith given by Ibn al-Qifṭī, Ibn Abī Uṣaybiʿa, and others,[18] some going so far as to credit the Prophet's own knowledge of medicine (as witnessed in the "prophetic medicine" literature!) to the influence of al-Ḥārith ibn Kalada.[19] Manfred Ullmann and Franz Rosenthal are notable for a more skeptical approach to the material, both going as far as referring to al-Ḥārith as to some extent a "legendary" figure.[20] Detailed textual criticism of the material has not been done, and may not prove very fruitful. I do not propose to undertake such a criticism here, but, starting from the position that the more or less elaborate biographies of al-Ḥārith are not likely to be based on much solid historical information (note that, if all the material is accepted, he lived long enough to enjoy a scholarly discussion with Khusraw Anushirwan who died in 579, and to be consulted by the caliph Muʿāwiya who died in 680), I should like to draw attention to two ways in which al-Ḥārith is used by Muslim writers on medicine, and which might help to explain why the taking up and elaboration of this, in the *sīra* rather obscure and minor figure, may have occurred.

First, al-Ḥārith is sometimes used by those who need to justify the use of medicine and doctors by Muslims. Given the great achievements of Islamic culture in the medical field, it might, at first, seem surprising that such a justification or defense of medicine was considered necessary at all; but it is clear that there was a certain uneasiness about the practice of medicine, even an outright opposition to it, on the part of many Muslims, and consequently the defense of medicine is a frequent theme in the literature. This is not the place to explore in detail the nature of the ambiguous relationship to medicine of medieval Islam, to which I. Goldziher, B. Reinert, and F. Rosenthal have been prominent in drawing attention,[21] but it seems important to underline certain of its features, in order to show that it was indeed strong enough to serve as a possible motive for the taking up of the figure of al-Ḥārith by those who wished to argue the legitimacy of the practice of medicine.

Unease about medicine on religious grounds is not uncommon

in Semitic monotheism generally. In Judaism and Christianity, as well as in Islam, examples of it are not difficult to find alongside, of course, evidence of respect for medicine and of flourishing medical practice. Evidently, the relationship between religion and medicine differed from circle to circle, and from time to time. The Jewish and early Christian material showing the anxiety felt by some has recently been surveyed by Vivian Nutton, and one might also refer to relevant articles by Leopold Löw and H. Schadewaldt.[22] The fundamental reason for the anxiety seems to be the feeling that medicine may attempt to thwart God's purposes. Since He creates everything for His own purposes, including illness and disease, and since He uses sickness and other tribulations to punish, to test and to purify His creatures, the practice of medicine or the seeking of cures may be thought illegitimate by some. The same sort of attitudes to sickness and disease may be seen in some Muslim traditions, for example, that which describes the plague (*al-ṭāʿūn*) as a punishment sent down by God on Banū Isrā'īl or "those who were before you,"[23] or that in which the Prophet points out that to die without any preliminary illness is not the blessing it may seem, since God uses illness to wipe out our offenses, and consequently, to diminish the pains we must suffer after death.[24] In Islam these considerations may have been intensified by the relatively greater emphasis which is placed on God's predetermining power, and we certainly find defenders of medicine insisting that to seek cures does not in any way imply lack of acceptance of the divine *qadar* and *qaḍā'*: if God does not wish the cure to be successful, a man's seeking it will not make any difference.[25]

It sometimes seems to be thought that, although uneasiness about recourse to doctors and medicine may have existed in Islam, it was limited to ascetic circles and was a secondary development, associated with the Ṣūfī elaboration of the doctrine of *tawakkul*. Concentration on the flourishing medical tradition of medieval Islam has sometimes led to underestimation of the force of the feelings against medicine. However, Goldziher drew attention to the report that as early as the end of the second century of the Islamic era, al-Ḥasan ibn Ziyād al-Lu'lu'ī (d. 209/819), a companion of Abū Ḥanīfa and not especially known as an ascetic, upheld the doctrine that "the seeking of cures is not legitimate, since it is an obstacle to *tawakkul*," while even so central a figure as Ibn Ḥanbal is said by Ghazālī to have approved of *tark al-tadāwī*.[26] Perhaps the strongest indication that uneasiness about medicine in Islam was not merely marginal, however, is the fact that the need to justify the use of medicine is evident in our earliest Muslim literature. The classic defense of medicine in Islam is probably the *ḥadīth* in which the Prophet declares, "He who sent down the disease also sent down the remedy" (*alladhī anzala al-dā' anzala al-dawā'*), or variants of this phrase. This *ḥadīth* is found in Mālik's *Muwaṭṭa'* and in the classical *ḥadīth* collections, and it is constantly cited in the more elaborate defenses of medicine to be found in literature of various types.[27] It sometimes comes with a tag which seems to confirm that it was fear of appearing to limit God's omnipotence which lay behind the anxiety about the legitimacy of medicine: "He teaches it [the remedy] to whomever He teaches it, and He makes ignorant of it whomever He makes ignorant [?]" (*'Allamahu man 'allamahu wa-jahhalahu man jahhalahu [?])*.[28] If there was not a strong and early unease about medicine in Islam, it is difficult to see why this tradition would have come into existence and become so widespread. It is striking, too, that the Prophet's affirmation that the remedy, like the disease, comes from God is sometimes reported in response to a questioner who expresses doubts about the validity of medicine, or surprise that the Prophet should approve of it.[29]

It is this background which helps to explain the defenses of medicine which sometimes feature in the works of writers on medicine and others. One of the most obvious ways of justifying the use of medicine in Islam was to show that the Prophet himself and the pious ancestors used it. Ghazālī, wishing to show that rejection of medicine, although not always right, is praiseworthy under certain circumstances, begins by admitting that many of the *salaf* sought cures; he then goes on to list some of those who, in specific circumstances, rejected it. His aim is to isolate their reasons for so doing. In considering the case of Abū Bakr, already noted, Ghazālī indicates that he would not have abandoned medicine lightly, since he knew that the Prophet had used it.[30] Ibn Qayyim al-Jawzīya (d. 751/1350) begins his book of prophetic medicine, after a brief description of what is meant by the word *ṭabīb*, by calling on the example of the Prophet: "Of the Prophet's guidance there are his deeds in treating himself medically, and his ordering of it to those of his family and companions who were afflicted by illness."[31]

Now, it seems possible that the association of al-Ḥārith ibn Kalada with the illnesses of some of the Prophet's companions may have resulted from the need to show that the Prophet himself did indeed have recourse to medicine and doctors. This is exactly how the tradition about Sa'd ibn Abī Waqqāṣ's illness is used in the *Ṭibb al-nabī* of Abū Nu'aym al-Iṣfahānī (d. 430/1038). After beginning by citing a whole series of versions of the "He who sent down the disease also sent down the remedy" tradition, Abū Nu'aym then adduces various reports about the Prophet using doctors for the treatment of the sick, and concludes with two about the illness of Sa'd.[32] I am not suggesting that the tradition of Sa'd's illness originated for this purpose—I am inclined to agree that the debate about the testamentary rights of a dying man may be the original focus of the tradition—but once the tradition existed, it could be adapted for a variety of purposes, and to introduce al-Ḥārith into it and to make the focus of it the Prophet's using a doctor to treat his sick companion would seem obvious, given the requirement of providing examples of the Prophet's dealings with doctors and medicine. The association of al-Ḥārith with the sicknesses of Abū Bakr and 'Umar could be further examples of the same tendency.

All this assumes, of course, that al-Ḥārith was already, at an early stage, firmly identified as a doctor, something which is not obvious in all of the material referring to him in the *sīra*; but it is clear that the fact of his being a doctor became the most salient point regarding him quite early on.[33] Why this should have happened, I am not sure. It may be a reflection of historical fact, but equally it could have resulted from the need to provide some explanation of the background of Sumayya—we have seen that one of the versions of her origins says that she was given to al-Ḥārith as a reward for medical services, but that this is only one version, another saying that she was given to 'Ammār ibn Yāsir's father in Mecca. At any rate, against the background of the uneasiness about medicine which at least some Muslims felt, it seems clear that the defenders of medicine would find it useful to be able to point to a doctor who had links with the Prophet, and who was involved in the treatment of some of the leading early Muslims. This, I suggest, is one of the reasons why al-Ḥārith was taken up, and his biography elaborated in the way it was.

The second aspect of medicine in Islam which I think may help to explain the elaborated biography of al-Ḥārith in the medical-biographical type of literature is the opposition between the tradition of scientific medicine and that of prophetic medicine. By "prophetic medicine," I am referring to that body of literature which reports medical ideas and treatments allegedly followed by the Prophet, prominent examples of which are the works devoted to it by Abū Nu'aym,

Ibn Qayyim al-Jawzīya, al-Suyūṭī,[34] and others, but which evidently already existed at an earlier date, since traditions about the Prophet's medicine occur also in our early collections of *ḥadīth*. As I have already said, this type of medicine is characterized by a commonsensical and self-reliant attitude to health, with emphasis on the notion of moderation in all things, especially diet. It is perhaps not difficult to envisage why such a tradition of medicine came into existence in Islam. To the need felt for prophetic guidance in all spheres of life, there might be added the need felt by nascent Islam to provide its adherents with an autonomous medical system as a defense against medical or magical ideas from foreign and non-Muslim sources. The connection between medical and religious success is now a commonplace.

It might be difficult, on chronological grounds, to argue that prophetic medicine was consciously and from the start opposed to the tradition of scientific medicine. The very nature of prophetic medicine, however, would seem to make it inevitable that it would see the scientific Hellenistic tradition as a rival:[35] its insistence on self-sufficiency and common sense seems designed to keep its followers out of the hands of wise men or experts of all sorts, and its frequent recommendations of cauterization and cupping seem aggressively primitive. Furthermore, it is evident from some of the discussions which we find in works of prophetic medicine that some of the medicaments and methods used by the scientific tradition were suspect to pious Muslims—we may note the discussions about the permissibility of the use of religiously prohibited articles such as wine, answered negatively, and the apparent uneasiness about medical treatment being administered by a person of the opposite sex.[36] On top of this was the non-Muslim origin, not only of the scientific tradition of medicine, but also of many of its practitioners.

As an example of the possible hostility between the two traditions one may compare the general discussions of medicine by, in the scientific tradition, Ibn Abī Uṣaybiʿa and, in the prophetic, Ibn Qayyim al-Jawzīya. The former praises the value and usefulness of medicine, and stresses the primary importance of health as a prerequisite for both worldly and religious endeavor. He says that *ʿilm al-abdān* and *ʿilm al-adyān* are associated. The *ḥukamāʾ* have distinguished between the delights of this world and those of the next, but "he who seeks them can only attain them so long as his health and physical strength last, and that is only achieved by the art of medicine, which preserves existing health and restores that which has been lost." In other words, the historian of scientific medicine seems to be placing that science above all others, even the religious ones. Ibn Qayyim al-Jawzīya, in contrast, argues that medicine is inferior to revelation: "the relationship between what they have of *ṭibb* and this revelation (*waḥy*) is like the relationship between their sciences (*'ulūm*) and that which the prophets brought. Indeed, the Prophet has brought the healing of hearts and spirits, something which the minds of the greatest of the *aṭibbā'* could not do, nor their sciences, nor their empiricism, nor their analogies." He then launches into a statement of the superiority of "simples," typical of nomadic peoples like the Arabs and others, over "composites," associated with town dwellers, and particularly with the Romans and Greeks.[37]

The achievements of the scientific tradition in the Golden Age of Islamic culture meant, of course, that the prophetic tradition could not but be impressed by it, and there appears a tendency in books about *al-ṭibb al-nabawī* to discuss things in scientific terms—as witness Ibn Qayyim al-Jawzīya's discussion of the relative merits of "simples" and "composites."[38] But it seems clear that the two systems of medicine were fundamentally incompatible. In this context it seems to me that a motive for the elaboration of the links of al-Ḥārith ibn Kalada with Persia and its Hellenistic tradition may possibly be found. It was not enough for the partisans of scientific medicine to show that the Prophet used doctors and medicine; they had to show that he used a doctor who was familiar with scientific medicine. Thus, possibly building on the links with Persia already present in the stories about Sumayya, there grew up the details about al-Ḥārith's education in Persia and (Persian) Yemen (specific mention of Jundishapur does not seem to occur until Ibn al-Qifṭī), and his discussion of medical matters with Khusraw Anushirwan.

Naturally, I do not suggest that this is the whole story. The disputes of the period of the Shu'ūbīya perhaps also have something to do with the elaboration of al-Ḥārith's biography, with those wishing to oppose the Shu'ūbīs finding it useful to be able to cite the example of this *jāhilī* Arab who was able to amaze the shah with his learning, and in a general way, one can see the utility of the doctor associated with the Prophet for both the scientific and the religious traditions in Islamic medicine. The origin of the material about al-Ḥārith in the *sīra* literature also remains to be explained. I hope, however, that these general considerations about aspects of the relationship between religion and medicine in Islam help to make some sense of the way in which al-Ḥārith's biography came to be elaborated.

NOTES

1. Lippert read . . . *fī 'l-jāhilīya wa-qabila al-islām*, ". . . in the *jāhilīya*, and he accepted Islam."

2. Ibn al-Qifṭī, *Ta'rīkh al-ḥukamā'*, ed. J. Lippert (Leipzig, 1903), p. 121.

3. See the article on him by Ch. Pellat in EI², *Supplement, s.v.*; I am grateful to Professor C. E. Bosworth for drawing my attention to this.

4. Ibn Juljul, *Ṭabaqāt al-aṭibbā' wa'l-ḥukamā'*, ed. Fu'ād Sayyid (Cairo, 1955), pp. 54 f.; Ibn Abī Uṣaybi'a, *'Uyūn al-anbā' fī ṭabaqāt al-aṭibbā'* (Beirut n.d.), II, 13 f.

5. Ibn Ḥajar, *Iṣāba,* with Ibn 'Abd al-Barr's *Istī'āb* on the margin (Tangiers, 1328), no. 1475.

6. Ibn al-Qifṭī, pp. 121–22.

7. Ibn Abī Uṣaybi'a, pp. 13–17; F. Sezgin, *Geschichte des arabischen Schrifttums* (Leiden, 1967–), III, 203–04.

8. Ibn Hishām, *Sīra*, ed. Muṣṭafā al-Saqā *et al.* (Cairo, 1375/1955), II, 485; al-Wāqidī, *Maghāzī*, ed. Marsden Jones (Oxford, 1966), pp. 931–32; Balādhurī, *Ansāb al-ashraf*, Vol. I, ed. Muḥammad Ḥamīd Allāh (Cairo, 1959), p. 367; Ibn Qutayba, *Ma'ārif*, ed. Tharwat 'Ukāsha (Cairo, 1969), p. 288.

9. Balādhurī, *Ansāb*, I, 489; Ibn Qutayba, *Ma'ārif*, p. 288.

10. Balādhurī, *Ansāb*, I, 157; Ibn Qutayba, *Ma'ārif*, p. 256; Pellat, loc. cit., pp. 354b–355a.

11. Abū Da'ūd, *Ṭibb*, 12; Abū Nu'aym, *Ṭibb al-nabī, apud* Omer Recep, *Tibb an-nabi* (Marburg/Lahn, 1969), Arabic text pp. 14–15; Ibn Juljul, p. 55.

12. See the sources used by R. Marston Speight, "The Will of Sa'd ibn Abī Waqqāṣ: The Growth of a Tradition," *Der Islam*, I (1973), 249–67 and David S. Powers, "The Will of Sa'd ibn Abī Waqqāṣ: A Reassessment," *Studia Islamica*, LVIII (1983), pp. 33–53.

13. Wāqidī, *Maghāzī*, p. 1116.

14. Ṭabarī, *Ta'rīkh al-rusul wa'l-mulūk*, ed. M. J. de Goeje *et al.* (Leiden, 1879–1901), I, 2127–28; Pellat, p. 355a.

15. Ibn Juljul, p. 56.

16. Al-Ghazālī, *Iḥyā' 'ulūm al-dīn, Kitāb al-tawḥīd wa'l-tawakkul* (Beirut, n.d.), IV, 264; Richard Gramlich, *Muḥammad al-Ġazzālīs Lehre von den Stufen zur Gottesliebe* (Wiesbaden, 1984), pp. 611 f.

17. Cf. the versions of the tradition in which an Arab claims to be a doctor, and offers to cure the Prophet by operating on him to remove the mark on his back, which we know as the seal of prophecy, and in which the Prophet replies that the doctor was He who put it there: Abū Nu'aym, p. 17; and cf. also the version of Abū Bakr's response to the suggestion that a doctor be called, given by 'Alī al-Qārī (see n. 26 below): *al-ṭabību amraḍanī.*

18. Lucien Leclerc, *Histoire de la médecine arabe* (Paris, 1876), I, 28; E. G. Browne, *Arabian Medicine*, pp. 10–11.

19. Leclerc, loc. cit.

20. M. Ullmann, *Die Medizin im Islam* (Leiden and Cologne, 1970), pp. 19–20; F. Rosenthal, *apud* his translation of Ibn Khaldun's *Muqaddima*, II, 373; Sezgin, III, 4 is non-committal; Pellat does not doubt the historicity of this "physician of the Arabs," but describes his personality as "surrounded by a host of legends."

21. I. Goldziher, "Materialien zur Entwicklungsgeschichte des Sufismus," *Wiener Zeitschrift für die Kunde des Morgenlandes* XIII (1899), pp. 52–54; B. Reinert, *Die Lehre vom tawakkul in der klassischen Sufik* (Berlin, 1968), pp. 207 f.; F. Rosenthal, "The Defense of Medicine in the Medieval Muslim World," *Bulletin of the History of Medicine*, XLIII (1969), pp. 519 f.; cf. also G. E. von Grunebaum, "Der Einfluß des Islam auf die Entwicklung der Medizin," *Bustan*, IV (1963), pp. 19—22, esp. p. 22: "Alles in allem genommen, täte man dem klassischen Islam sicher unrecht, wollte man sagen, daß er mit dem Fortschritt der medizinischen Wissenschaft unvereinbar gewesen sei; . . . Anderseits täte man der islamischen medizinischen Wissenschaft unrecht, wenn man die theologischen Hemmnisse außer acht ließe, unter denen sie sich entwickeln mußte."

22. L. Löw, "Über Ärzte," in his *Gesammelte Schriften* (Szegedin, 1893), III, 370–75; H. Schadewaldt, "Die Apologie der Heilkunst bei den Kirchenvätern," *Veröffentlichungen der internationalen Gesellschaft für Geschichte der Pharmazie*, XXVI (1965), pp. 115 f.; V. Nutton, "Murders and Miracles: Lay Attitudes towards Medicine in Classical Antiquity," in Roy Porter (ed.), *Patients and Practitioners* (Cambridge, 1985), esp. pp. 45 f.

23. Mālik, *Muwaṭṭa', K. al-Jāmi', bāb: mā jā'a fī 'l-ṭā'ūn*, no. 2.

24. Ibid., *bāb: mā jā'a fī ajr al-marīḍ*, nos. 1–4; Ghazālī, *Iḥyā', K. al-tawḥīd wa'l-tawakkul, Bayān anna tark al-tadāwī qad yuḥmadu fī ba'ḍ al-aḥwāl, Al-sabab al-rābi'.*

25. E.g., al-Zurqānī, *Sharḥ 'ala al-mawāhib al-ladūniyya* (Cairo, 1907–10), VII, 59 f., esp. 62.

26. Goldziher, "Materialien," p. 53; 'Alī al-Qārī, *Sharḥ musnad Abī Ḥanīfa* (Beirut, 1985), p. 595: *dhahaba (al-Ḥasan ibn Ziyād) ilā anna al-tadāwī lā yajūzu li-annahu yamna'u al-tawakkul;* Ghazālī, loc. cit.: *wa-kāna Aḥmad ibn Ḥanbal yaqūlu: uḥibbu li-man i'taqada al-tawakkul wa-salaka hādha al-ṭarīq tark al-tadāwī min sharb al-dawā' wa-ghayrihi.* On al-Lu'lu'ī see Ibn Abī 'l-Wafā', *Al-Jawāhir al-muḍī'a* (Hyderabad, 1332/1914), no. 449; Ibn Quṭlubughā, *Tāj al-tarājim*, ed. G. Flügel (Leipzig, 1862), no. 55; perhaps the report that he insisted on dressing his slaves to the same standard as he dressed himself, in accordance with the *ḥadīth*, indicates a tendency to asceticism, but I have not seen a reference to his alleged dislike of medicine in a source earlier than that used by Goldziher, 'Alī al-Qārī's commentary on the so-called *Musnad* of Abū Ḥanīfa; the authenticity of the report may be open to question.

27. Mālik, *Muwaṭṭa', K. al-Jāmi', bāb: fī ta'āluj al-marīḍ;* A. J. Wensinck, *Concordance, s.vv dā', dawā';* Abū Nu'aym, *Ṭibb*, pp. 2–11.

28. E.g., Ibn Ḥanbal, *Musnad*, I, 377, 413, 443, 446, 453.

29. E.g., the Prophet uttered the *ḥadīth* when two doctors whom he had asked to treat one of his companions, surprised at his request, asked him, "Is there good then in medicine, o Prophet?" (Mālik, loc. cit.); the Prophet's remark is cited by Abū 'Abd al-Raḥmān al-Sulamī, when 'Aṭā' ibn al-Sā'ib tried to prevent him from seeking medical treatment (Abū Nu'aym, *Ṭibb*, p. 2).

30. See n. 15.

31. Ibn Qayyim al-Jawzīya, *Al-Ṭibb al-nabawī* (Beirut, 1957), p. 5.

32. Abū Nu'aym, *Ṭibb*, pp. 14–15.

33. Ibn Sa'd's short notice of him clearly centers on the fact that he was a doctor—*kāna ṭabīb al-'arab* (*Ṭabaqāt*, v, 371–72).

34. Suyūṭī's work has been translated into English: C. Elgood (trans.), "Tibb-ul-Nabbi or medicine of the Prophet," *Osiris* (Bruges), XIV (1962), pp. 33–192.

35. Cf. J. Christoph Bürgel, "Die wissenschaftliche medizin im Kräftefeld der islamischen Kultur," *Bustan* (1967), pp. 9–19, arguing that the tradition of prophetic medicine was extremely deleterious so far as the scientific tradition in Islam was concerned.

36. Abū Nu'aym, *Ṭibb*, pp. 19–20, 22–24.

37. Ibn Abī Uṣaybi'a, I, 7; Ibn Qayyim al-Jawzīya, p. 5.

38. Ibn Qayyim al-Jawzīya, pp. 5–6; Bürgel, p. 16 on the work of al-Surramarrī (d. 1374), which sets out to present prophetic medicine in scientific terms.

11
The Presentation of Qalāwūn by Shāfiʿ ibn ʿAlī

P. M. Holt

NĀṢIR AL-DĪN SHĀFIʿ ibn ʿAlī al-Asqalānī was born in 649/1251–52, and died on 27 Shaʿbān 750/15 June 1330. He came from a family of clerks in the royal chancery in Caior; his maternal uncle was Muḥyī al-Dīn Ibn ʿAbd al-Ẓāhir, whose son Fatḥ al-Dīn was the first in the long succession of secretaries (*kuttāb al-sirr*) to the Mamlūk sultans. Shāfiʿ ibn ʿAlī's own service as a chancery clerk ended after the battle of Ḥimṣ against the Mongols in 680/1281, when he was struck by an arrow and blinded. After this accident he settled down, not uncomfortably, to half a century of life as a literary man and a bibliophile. He left, we are told, eighteen presses of valuable books, which his wife (who knew the price of every one) sold in the nine years following his death. He is the subject of a respectful notice by his acquaintance, al-Ṣafadī,[1] and a somewhat different picture of his personality emerges from his own writings.[2]

Among his works were two biographies of contemporary Mamlūk sultans. That of al-Ẓāhir Baybars (658–76/1260–77), *Ḥusn al-manāqib al-sirrīya al-muntazaʿa min al-sīra al-Ẓāhirīya*,[3] completed in 716/1316, is ostensibly an abridgment of the official biography by Muḥyī al-Dīn Ibn ʿAbd al-Ẓāhir, *Al-Rawḍ al-zāhir fī sīrat al-Malik al-Ẓāhir*.[4] The second biography, and the principal concern of this essay, deals with al-Manṣūr Qalāwūn (678–89/1279–90), and is entitled *Al-Faḍl al-ma'thūr min sīrat al-sulṭān al-Malik al-Manṣūr*.[5] Unlike *Ḥusn al-manāqib*, the text of this work, extant in a unique MS in the Bodleian Library, has not been published apart from a single document, which was edited and translated into German seventy years ago by Axel Moberg, who in his introductory pages gives a brief account of the contents of the whole work.[6] As with *Ḥusn al-manāqib,* Shāfiʿ ibn ʿAlī is here paralleling and, as it were, competing with the work of his uncle, since Muḥyī al-Dīn also wrote a biography of Qalāwūn, *Tashrīf al-ayyām wa'l-ʿuṣūr fī sīrat al-Malik al-Manṣūr.*[7] The two works are very different in contents and style. Shāfiʿ does not here claim to be basing his biography on that by Ibn ʿAbd al-Ẓāhir, whose covering of the reign (so far as can be judged from the extant part) is fuller and more systematic, and whose sober prose contrasts with his nephew's propensity to parallelism and the employment of *sajʿ*. There is, however, one passage describing the Hospitaller castle of al-Marqab which is quoted verbatim from *Tashrīf al-ayyām wa'l-ʿuṣūr*, but ascribed by Shāfiʿ to Fatḥ al-Dīn.[8]

The date of *Al-Faḍl* is something of a puzzle. Throughout the first 125 of the work's 126 folios, mention of Qalāwūn is fairly frequently followed by the benediction on a living ruler, *khallada 'llāhu sulṭānahu/mulkahu*. That it also reports Qalāwūn's death and burial might mean no more than that it was completed after the event, as was the case with Ibn ʿAbd al-Ẓāhir's *Al-Rawḍ*. But there are indications that the history of the work's composition is more complex than this. There is, for example, a short chapter (fols. 118a–119a) describing the installation of al-Ṣāliḥ ʿAlī, Qalāwūn's son, as joint sultan with his father, which on the evidence of the benediction must have been written during their lifetimes, i.e., before the death of al-Ṣāliḥ ʿAlī (who predeceased his father) on 4 Shaʿbān 687/3 September 1288. The sickness and death of the young sultan are in fact described in the following section (fols. 119a–121b), which terminates with an elegy composed by Shāfiʿ. Other anomalies appear in the account of the campaign which culminated in Qalāwūn's victory at Ḥimṣ (fols. 39b–58a). This was originally written as a separate report, in effect (to use an anachronistic term) a *fetḥnāme*, since Shāfiʿ concludes it with the words "I have devoted to it an independent part by order of the Royal Library" (*bi-rasm al-khizāna al-ʿālīya al-mawlawīya al-sulṭānīya*).[9] The separate origin of this account is further indicated by the inclusion in it of a summary of the earlier history of the Mongols (fols. 54b–55b), which is substantially repeated in fols. 66a–67a. The latter passage comes at the end of an account of the negotiations between the *ilkhan* Aḥmad Tegüder and Qalāwūn, suggesting that this also is an originally independent report incorporated in the biography.

Al-Faḍl al-maʾthūr, then, appears to be a compilation both in the sense that it incorporates reports written at different times during Qalāwūn's reign, and also in the sense that Shāfiʿ includes, often *in extenso* or nearly so, state papers drafted by himself, his uncle, and his cousin, Fatḥ al-Dīn. One of these, that published by Moberg, is a memorandum of instructions drafted by Muḥyī al-Dīn for al-Ṣāliḥ ʿAlī when Qalāwūn set out on the Ḥimṣ campaign. This forms one of a group of three such memoranda, the other two being drafted by Fatḥ al-Dīn and Shāfiʿ respectively (fols. 82b–99b). Ibn ʿAbd al-Ẓāhir also gives documents in *Tashrīf al-ayyām*, but with the exception of the correspondence exchanged with Aḥmad Tegüder, they are different from those transmitted by Shāfiʿ, and are of greater historical value, since Shāfiʿ was primarily anxious to display the rhetorical skill of himself and his kinsmen.

There remains the problem of establishing the date when Shāfiʿ finished his compilation. This cannot be earlier than 1293. On two occasions (fols. 6a, 107b) he mentions Muḥyī al-Dīn's name with the benediction for the dead. He must therefore have completed the work after Muḥyī al-Dīn's death on 3 Rajab 692/9 June 1293. A slightly later date is suggested by a reference (fol. 129a) to al-Ashraf Khalīl ibn Qalāwūn as *al-shahīd*, a term customarily applied at this date to a deceased sultan. This would push the *terminus post quem* to 12 Muḥarram 693/14 December 1293, the date of al-Ashraf Khalīl's murder. There is no direct evidence as to how long after this the work was completed, but one may surmise that it appeared at much the same time as *Ḥusn al-manāqib*, to which it is in some respects a companion-piece.[10] During the years following the murder of al-Ashraf Khalīl, the future of the Qalāwūnid dynasty was precarious. Al-Nāṣir Muḥammad, the younger brother of al-Ashraf Khalīl, was twice installed as a puppet sultan, first in 693/1293 (when he was eight years old) and again in 698/1298, and twice deposed by usurpers before he regained the throne for his third and highly successful reign in 709/1310. It is unlikely that Shāfiʿ would have risked producing a eulogistic biography of the founder of the dynasty at any time after 1293 until al-Nāṣir Muḥammad was firmly in control.

Al-Faḍl al-maʾthūr is indeed essentially an encomium of Qalāwūn. In presenting him as a paragon among Muslim rulers, Shāfiʿ had two principal difficulties to overcome. In the first place, Qalāwūn had usurped the sultanate from the sons of Baybars, and Baybars had been his former comrade (*khushdāsh*) in the military household of al-Ṣāliḥ Ayyūb, and subsequently his sovereign lord. In the second place, in his military achievements, impressive as they were, Qalāwūn was following in the footsteps of Baybars, whose earlier victories had safeguarded Syria from the Mongols, and initiated the reconquest of Frankish-held territory. The greater part of *Al-Faḍl* is therefore devoted to an implicit justification of Qalāwūn on these two issues, denigrating his opponents, and even slighting the reputation of Baybars himself.

The need to provide an apologia for Qalāwūn's usurpation explains the very considerable proportion of the work (fols. 3a–26b) describing his career before he became sultan, and the attention given both in this section and subsequently (fols. 30b–33b) to his relations with Baraka Khān,[11] Baybars's son and successor, and his brother, Khaḍir (fols. 99b–103a). The implicit argument of these passages is twofold: that Qalāwūn was the best fitted to rule, and that the unworthy behavior of Baraka Khān cost him the throne, as that of Khaḍir lost him the autonomous kingdom of al-Karak.

The record of Qalāwūn's early career opens (fol. 3) with the assertion that his Mamlūk contemporaries unanimously agreed that no finer recruit had ever arrived in the country. He was then fourteen years old, and in the competition to obtain him, thousands of gold pieces were spent on him. This refers to Qalāwūn's nickname of *al-Alfī*, but reference to his slave status is delicately avoided. His first master, the amir Aqsunqur al-Kāmilī, is not mentioned, but we are told that Qalāwūn escheated to al-Ṣāliḥ Ayyūb, who particularly favored him; and rightly surmised that he would inherit the kingdom! After al-Ṣāliḥ Ayyūb's death, Qalāwūn became the leader and model of his khushdāshīya. This passage parallels in miniature Ibn 'Abd al-Ẓāhir's account of the early career of Baybars, who is also presented as the rightful successor to al-Ṣāliḥ Ayyūb by reason of his worth, and as the leader of his comrades, the Ṣāliḥīya, after their master's death.[12] There may also be a point of propaganda in the assertion that Qalāwūn was fourteen years old when he became a Mamlūk: another contemporary, al-Dhahabī (673–748/1274–1348), cites his own father as saying, "He [Qalāwūn] talked like a foreigner; he could hardly make himself clear in Arabic, and that was because he was full-grown [*kabīr*] when he was brought from the land of the Turks."[13]

Shāfi' goes on (fols 3b–4a) to speak briefly of Qalāwūn's continued high standing with the successive rulers of Egypt, Shajar al-Durr, Fāris al-Dīn Aqṭāy [*sic*], Aybak and his son Qāqān (i.e., al-Manṣūr 'Alī), and

Quṭuz, while all his khushdāshīya fell into disgrace. This is simply untrue, if we are to believe Ibn 'Abd al-Ẓāhir, who mentions Qalāwūn as one of Baybars's companions in exile after the breach between the Ṣāliḥīya and Aybak.[14] Shāfi' then approaches the sensitive topic of Qalāwūn's relations with Baybars as sultan, who (he says) made him his chief counselor, and treated him as no king ever treated an amir nor any sultan an adviser. Baybars personally selected a suitable bride for him, the daughter of Sayf al-Dīn Karmūn, one of Hülagü's commanders, who had defected to the Mamlūk sultan (fol. 4b). Another state marriage was that of Baraka Khān, the heir apparent, to Qalāwūn's daughter, by which Baybars hoped to secure his son's succession (fols. 5b–6a).

Baybars died on the return from his expedition to Anatolia, which is described in fols. 12a–13a, and from this point Shāfi' gives a very detailed account of the crisis in Baraka Khān's reign, and the developments by which Qalāwūn came to the throne. Shāfi' was well placed to report these matters: he was a clerk in the royal chancery, first serving Baraka Khān, then, at the height of the crisis, changing sides, and fleeing to Qalāwūn (fol. 24). Such changes of masters were an occupational hazard for royal clerks of the period, and the literary devotion which Shāfi' lavished on his new lord is reminiscent of the tributes which those earlier distinguished turncoats, Bahā' al-Dīn Ibn Shaddād and 'Imād al-Dīn al-Iṣfahānī, had paid to Saladin a century before.

Two themes are emphasized in the account of Baraka Khān's brief and disastrous reign (676–78/1277–79): Qalāwūn's fatherly attitude to the young sultan, and Baraka Khān's incorrigible frivolity under the influence of evil advisers. But this conflict of personalities across a generation gap was symptomatic of a more fundamental phenomenon, which was recurrent throughout the Mamlūk period, viz. the mutual factional hostility of the households of Royal Mamlūks. In this instance, Qalāwūn and his comrades, the veteran Ṣāliḥīya, were struggling to secure their political ascendancy (which Baybars had sworn on his accession to maintain) against their younger rivals, the Ẓāhirīya, whom Baybars had recruited, as well as Baraka Khān's own inner circle of Mamlūks, his *khāṣṣakīya*.

The crisis broke at Damascus, where Baraka Khān had gone reluctantly, and on Qalāwūn's insistence, as a Mongol invasion of Syria was expected (fols. 13b–14a). At this point the sultan's evil advisers were the Ẓāhirīya, but when Baraka Khān reached Damascus, the

Mongol threat had vanished. His own Mamlūks then came to the fore, and he gave himself up to pleasure and amusement. An ugly situation developed when Baraka Khān refused admittance to the Ṣāliḥīya amirs, who attended daily to serve in his court. Ultimately they forced him to give them audience, and Qalāwūn reproached him for his unkingly behavior. At Qalāwūn's own request, he and his comrade, Baysarī, were put in command of an expedition against Lesser Armenia (fols. 14b–16a). While they were absent, a further factional split developed, this time among the Ẓāhirīya who had stayed with the young sultan in Damascus, and a group of Mongol origin fled to Qalāwūn. They were headed by Kawndak, previously viceregent of Egypt, and himself a Mongol (fols. 16b–17a).[15] Meanwhile, Qalāwūn's suspicions of Baraka Khān's intentions toward him were growing, and another critical episode occurred when the sultan refused to come out of Damascus to greet the returning army (fol. 19a). A race for Cairo then ensued. Baraka Khān's mother endeavored to mediate between Qalāwūn and her son. The terms offered by Qalāwūn illuminate the power struggle between the factions. Baraka Khān's partisans were to be received on an equal footing with the corresponding ranks under Qalāwūn, but Qalāwūn's supporters (in effect the Ṣāliḥīya) were to hold the great offices at court *together with their sons*. In the words of the text: *wa-naḥnu natawallā waẓā'if khidmatihi bi-nufūsinā wa-awlādinā*. This attempt to establish an hereditary Mamlūk aristocracy is interesting, but the scheme failed. Baraka Khān would have accepted the terms, but he was overruled by the Ẓāhirīya around him (fols. 20a–21a). Events proceeded on their way until Baraka Khān found himself besieged in the Citadel of Cairo. He was deposed, and allowed to retire to al-Karak, where his father had left a hoard of treasure (fol. 25a). It was during the siege of the Citadel that Shāfi' joined the entourage of Qalāwūn.

Qalāwūn is then shown as demonstrating his loyalty to the memory of Baybars by installing the ten-year-old Salāmish as sultan, albeit with himself as *atabeg*.[16] Only under pressure from the great amirs, who were afraid that the Ẓāhirīya would regain their ascendancy, did he consent to take the sultanate—or so we are told (fols. 25b–26a)! The continued residence of Baraka Khān at al-Karak with considerable financial resources was a standing threat, and Qalāwūn sent an army to besiege him. At this juncture, Baraka Khān died, and Shāfi' expatiates on the propriety of Qalāwūn's behavior on the occasion (fol. 33). He sat in state to receive condolences, and when in Damascus, he acceded to the request of Baraka Khān's mother that her son should lie in Baybars's tomb. The emirs of all ranks were ordered to go out at night carrying candles to meet the coffin, and accompany it to the Ẓāhirīya mosque. Qalāwūn awaited its coming and rose at its entry, holding back his tears in accordance with royal protocol. Finally, he provided the dead sultan's mother with a residence in Damascus and an appropriate maintenance allowance.

However, he had not yet done with the family of Baybars. Al-Karak passed to another of Baraka Khān's brothers, Khaḍir, who (according to Shāfiʿ) used the fortress as a base from which to launch predatory attacks on the neighborhood and its routes. A punitive expedition sent by Qalāwūn produced submission, and an amnesty, drafted by Shāfiʿ, formalized the status of al-Karak in the sultanate. Further disagreement and raiding occurred, and ultimately Qalāwūn sent an expedition to bring Khaḍir and Salāmish, who was with him, to Cairo, tactfully alleging that this was done to relieve the poverty which had led to intolerable behavior. They were honorably received by the sultan, and lodged in the Citadel of Cairo (fols. 99b–103a). This occurred early in 685/1286, although here, as so often, Shāfiʿ does not provide a date.[17]

The account which Shāfiʿ gives of Baraka Khān, by demonstrating his unfitness to rule, provides, so to speak, a negative justification of Qalāwūn's usurpation of the sultanate. The positive justification comes with the presentation of Qalāwūn as the great *mujāhid*, an unrivaled captain in the Holy War against the enemies of Islam, the Mongols and the Franks. Here the long report already mentioned above of the Ḥimṣ campaign is of central importance. Although it is, for the most part, a detailed narrative of events, the concluding folios indicate its purpose. Shāfiʿ speaks of the campaign as one unparalleled in Islam. There are two verse eulogies of the sultan's victory, composed by Fatḥ al-Dīn and Shāfiʿ himself (fols. 56a–58a), preceded by an account of the earlier history of the Mongols (fols. 54b–55b). This is significant in that it does not mention Baybars in connection with the battle of ʿAyn Jālūt (fol. 55a). The parallel passage in the other account of the history of the Mongols (fol. 66b) explicitly ascribes the victory at ʿAyn Jālūt to Qalāwūn, who is represented as urging the novice sultan, Quṭuz, to go out and fight the Mongols, and then as himself clearing them out of Syria after the battle—roles ascribed by Ibn ʿAbd al-Ẓāhir to Baybars. Baybars's campaigns against the Mongols are indeed mentioned in fol. 67a, but Qalāwūn, it is implied, was chiefly responsible for their success. Not only in war but also in peace, Qalāwūn is shown as standing in a unique position in regard to the Mongols. The section which deals with the diplomatic contacts between the sultan and the ilkhan is entitled "What befell our lord the sultan uniquely among kings: the abasement of the Mongols and their king's request for peace." Throughout these negotiations, Qalāwūn is represented as being both cautious and disdainful of the ilkhan's overtures.[18] The overthrow of Tegüder ended an episode in which Qalāwūn had given little encouragement to his brother in Islam.

Qalāwūn's dealings with the Franks were clearly of less importance to Shāfi' than his dealings with the Mongols. They become prominent only in the latter part of the biography, where an account is given of relations with the Hospitaller castle of al-Marqab and its capture (fols. 103b–106b), the negotiations for a truce with Tripoli (fols. 106b–117a) and for a truce with Acre (fol. 117). A later passage, in what would seem to be an appendix to the biography (since it is placed after an excursus on the sultan's merits and good works in fols. 121b–127a), describes the events which were the *casus belli* for Qalāwūn's intended campaign against Acre, and goes on to deal with the sultan's death and burial, followed by al-Ashraf Khalīl's capture of the city. On this victorious note, Shāfi' ends *Al-Faḍl al-ma'thūr.*

Largely composed as an encomium of Qalāwūn in his lifetime, *Al-Faḍl* fulfilled a further function as a defense of the legitimacy of his rule, and hence of the rule of his sons. This may account for its final compilation during and after the reign of al-Ashraf Khalīl from diverse materials written earlier. The theme of legitimacy, which is implied in the account of Qalāwūn's rise to the sultanate, and in the presentation of him as the supreme *mujāhid,* is stated explicitly in one of the documents transcribed by Shāfi', a letter sent by Qalāwūn to his refractory *khushdāsh,* Sunqur al-Ashqar, who, when Qalāwūn usurped the throne, declared himself sultan in Syria. The letter contrasts (at fol. 37b) Sunqur's vain pretensions with Qalāwūn's legitimate sovereignty, resting as it did on consensus and appointment by the caliph:

Where is he upon whom there was consensus in Egypt and Syria, for whom those who loose and bind pronounced the *khuṭba* of deposition and appointment, whom the Commander of the Faithful made his delegate, to whom he extended his hand in the *bay'a,* . . . and upon whom he conferred his 'Abbāsid livery?

The passage aptly sums up the constitutional basis of the Mamlūk sultanate, which came to be symbolized in the accession ceremonies.[19]

NOTES

1. Al-Ṣafadī, *Al-Wāfī bi'l-wafayāt,* Vol. XVI (Wiesbaden, 1982), p. 77 f. (no. 97).

2. P. M. Holt, "A Chancery Clerk in Medieval Egypt," *The English Historical Review,* CI, 400, 1986, 671–79.

3. 'Abd al-'Azīz ibn 'Abdallāh al-Khuwayṭir (ed.), *Kitāb ḥusn al-manāqib al-sirrīya al-muntaza'a min al-sīra al-Ẓāhirīya* [Riyad, 1396/1976]. See n. 10 below.

4. 'Abd al-'Azīz al-Khuwayṭir (ed.), *Al-Rawḍ al-zāhir fī sīrat al-Malik al-Ẓāhir* (Riyad [1396/1976]).

5. Bodleian Library, Oxford, MS Marsh 424.

6. Axel Moberg, "Regierungspromemoria eines ägyptischen Sultans," *Festschrift Eduard Sachau zum siebzigsten Geburtstage gewidmet von Freunden und Schülern* (Berlin, 1915), pp. 406–21.

7. Murād Kāmil (ed.), *Tashrīf al-ayyām wa'l-'uṣūr fī sīrat al-Malik al-Manṣūr* [Cairo, 1961]. Only the final second part is extant.

8. *Al-Faḍl,* fols. 104b–105a; *Tashrīf,* p. 85.

9. Moberg, op. cit., p. 406, translates an almost identical formula by "als Eigentum der Bibliothek des Sultans."

10. On *Ḥusn al-manāqib,* see further P. M. Holt, "Three Biographies of al-Ẓāhir Baybars," in D. O. Morgan (ed.), *Medieval Historical Writing in the Christian and Islamic Worlds* (London, 1982), pp. 26–27. The point is there made that Shāfi' is implicitly and explicitly critical of both Ibn 'Abd al-Ẓāhir and Baybars. *Ḥusn al-manāqib* is also given a pro-Qalāwūnid twist by the insertion of material about Qalāwūn which is not strictly relevant to the ostensible subject of the work. These passages are largely identical in subject with passages in *Al-Faḍl,* and are chiefly concerned with Qalāwūn's conquest of Tripoli and intended campaign against Acre.

11. The form of the name used throughout is Baraka (so vocalized) Qān.

12. It is ironic that Shāfi', who in *Al-Faḍl* suppresses reference to Qalāwūn's first master, at *Ḥusn al-manāqib,* p. 27, criticizes Ibn 'Abd al-Ẓāhir for a similar suppression of mention of Baybars's first master "in order to glorify him."

13. Cited by Ibn Taghrībirdī, *Al-Nujūm al-zāhira* (Cairo ed.), VII, 325.

14. *Al-Rawḍ al-zāhir,* 56.

15. Kawndak's Mongol origin appears from Ibn al-Dawādārī's account of this episode: *Fa-rakiba Kawndak fī jamā'a min jinsihi al-Tatār.* Ibn al-Dawādārī, *Kanz al-durar*, ed. Ulrich Haarmann, Vol. VIII (Freiburg/Cairo, 1971), p. 227.

16. Moberg, op. cit., p. 407, erroneously states that "Das Scheinsultanat des Salāmiš wird nicht erwähnt."

17. During the reign of al-Ashraf Khalīl, the two brothers were banished to Constantinople, where Salāmish died in 690/1291 (Ibn Taghrībirdī, *Nujūm*, VII, 238). His remains were brought back when Khaḍir and his family were recalled from exile by his brother-in-law, al-Manṣūr Lāchīn in 696/1296–97 (al-Maqrīzī, *Sulūk*, I/3, 827–28, 831). Khaḍir died in 708/1308–09 (Abu'l-Fidā', *Al-Mukhtaṣar, sub anno*).

18. On this episode, see further P. M. Holt, "The Ilkhān Aḥmad's Embassies to Qalāwūn: Two Contemporary Accounts, " *BSOAS*, XLIX, i (1986), pp. 128–32.

19. On the accession ceremonies, see further P. M. Holt, "The Position and Power of the Mamlūk Sultan," *BSOAS*, XXXVIII, ii (1975), pp. 241–45.

12
Politics and Architectural Patronage in Ayyubid Damascus

R. Stephen Humphreys

NIKITA ELISSÉEFF SIMPLY reaffirms the general conclusion of modern scholarship when he declares that "the 7th/13th century was one of Dimashq's most brilliant epochs . . . most of the monuments which still adorn the city date from this period."[1] Heretofore such conclusions have been reached chiefly on the basis of the visual evidence yielded by the contemporary city's traditional quarters, but it is possible to put them on more rigorous foundations as well, by comparing the construction activity of the Ayyubid period (589/1193–658/1260) with that of the two flanking periods: the seventy-seven years from 490/1097 to 570/1174, when the city was governed by Saljuqid and Zangid princes, and the eight decades from 658/1260 to 741/1341, which constituted the first and most flourishing epoch of the Baḥrī Mamlūk regime.[2]

The superiority of the Ayyubid epoch is in fact even greater than it first appears, simply because the Ayyubid period is shorter than either of the others (67 years, versus 80 for each of them). Even the years of greatest activity in the two non-Ayyubid periods, represented respectively by the reign of Nūr al-Dīn (549/1154–569/1174) and the governorship of Sayf al-Dīn Tankiz (712/1312–740/1340), could not maintain the overall pace of Ayyubid times. The easiest way to establish this point is to give a set of equalized figures, with the data for these periods calculated to show the average number of acts of patronage per annum. (The differences between these figures cannot be shown

TABLE 1
ACTIVITY IN TWO CATEGORIES OF CONSTRUCTION FOR THE SALJUQID–ZANGID, AYYUBID, AND EARLY MAMLŪK PERIODS

Period	*Monumental Categories*	
	Educational Foundations	*Religious, Charitable Educational Foundations*
Saljuqid-Zangid[(a)]	24	—
Ayyubid	63	135
Mamlūk[(b)]	39	83

[(a)] Nikita Elisséeff, *Nur ad-Din: un grand prince musulman de Syrie au temps des Croisades* (Damascus, 1967), III, 757–59, 762–64, 914, 919–30.

[(b)] I. M. Lapidus, *Muslim Cities in the Later Middle Ages* (Cambridge, MA, 1967), pp. 199–202.

TABLE 1-A
AVERAGE CONSTRUCTION PER ANNUM IN TWO CATEGORIES FOR THE SALJUQID–ZANGID, AYYUBID, AND EARLY MAMLŪK PERIODS

Period	*Monumental Types*	
	Educational Foundations (original & conversion)	*Religious, Charitable, Educational (including restorations)*
Saljuqid-Zangid	0.31	—
Nūr al-Dīn[3]	0.60	—
Ayyubid	0.94	2.02
Mamlūk	0.48	1.03
Tankiz[3]	0.54	1.39

to be statistically significant, but in any case they have descriptive and heuristic value.)

If the intense architectural activity of Ayyubid times in Damascus is easy to establish, the same is certainly not true of the causes for it. Again, Elisséeff presents the generally accepted interpretation of this matter:

> Progress began again under the Ayyubids when Dimashq became the seat of a princely court. The growth in population and new resources which such a promotion implies had repercussions on its economic life, all the more appreciable since the calm reigns of al-ʿĀdil and his successor brought a peaceful atmosphere. This improvement in economic activity went side by side with the development of commercial relations. From that time on, Italian merchants began to come regularly to Dimashq. Industry took an upward trend. . . .[4]

The key element in this interpretation of the rise in architectural activity during the first half of the thirteenth century is clearly the presence of a resident princely court. It is, of course, natural to assume that such a court would always be a center of patronage of architecture, the arts and literature, but the way in which courts exerted their influence has been only superficially analyzed. Moreover, the presence of a court *per se* need not imply anything like the degree of architectural activity exhibited in Ayyubid times; after all, Damascus had been an independent principality for nearly a century when Saladin occupied the city in the autumn of 570/1174.

Can the members of the Ayyubid house, then, be given the credit for the architectural efflorescence of their capital during the sixty-seven years of their reign? Our data on the occupational backgrounds of the patrons appears to contradict this hypothesis, at least in its crude form.

TABLE 2
OCCUPATIONAL BACKGROUNDS OF PATRONS,
BASED ON NET CENSUS

Occupation	*Number of Patrons*
Royal Family	24
Non-Ayyubid Rulers	2
Military	38
Religious Establishment	23
Ṣūfīs	15
Civil Bureaucracy	9
Courtiers & Retainers	7
Merchants	2
Unknown	21
TOTAL	141

It is clearly not the ruling house which supplied the largest number of patrons of architecture, but rather the men and women of the military class (i.e., the emirs, the household officers such as *ustādh al-dār* or *khāzindār*, and their wives, daughters, and sisters). Moreover, if we adjust our data by looking at these groups, not merely in terms of their career patterns, but in terms of their broader social backgrounds, the royal family is not even the second largest of the groups of patrons. From this adjusted perspective, it makes sense to consider the civil bureaucracy as akin to the religious establishment (the *'ulamā'*, *qāḍīs*, etc.); this combined group then numbers 32 persons. The ruling family *per se* clearly did not constitute a majority, or even a plurality, of the patrons of architecture.

But this level of presentation leaves the matter even less certain than it was to begin with; it simply tells us how many patrons from each group are known, without suggesting from which groups the most prominent patrons came, or how many acts of patronage are due to each group. Let us then examine an additional set of data, on the number of acts of patronage actually contributed by each occupational group:

TABLE 3
NUMBER OF ACTS OF CONSTRUCTION SPONSORED BY EACH OCCUPATIONAL GROUP AMONG THE PATRONS, BASED ON NET CENSUS

	Type of Construction			
Occupational Group	*Original*	*Conversion*	*Restoration*	*Totals*
Ayyubid Family	23	10	24	57
Non-Ayyubid Princes	2	0	0	2
Military	39	5	6	50
Religious Establishment	20	7	2	29
Ṣūfīs	12	2	1	15
Civil Bureaucracy	8	0	2	10
Courtiers & Retainers	5	5	0	10
Merchants	2	0	0	2
Unknown	13	1	8	22
TOTALS	124	30	43	197

Out of 197 acts of patronage in the net census, we know the occupational backgrounds of the sponsors of 175. Out of these 175, 146 acts of patronage can be attributed to members of the same three groups—i.e., 74% of the total net census (146/197), and 83% of the cases with patrons of known occupation (146/175). On a base of 197, the Ayyubid family supplied 29% (57/197) of the total, the military supplied 25% (50/197), and the combined religious establishment–civil bureaucracy supplied 20% (39/197). (On a base of 175, the percentages are as follows: Ayyubid family—33%; military—29%; religious establishment–civil bureaucracy—22%.) The two tables both give us a rough proportion of thirds, then, with the Ayyubid house leading the other two groups, but not by any overwhelming degree; it is rather a matter of a gradual stepping down.

Moreover, if we make one further adjustment to the data, the relative equality of the three groups becomes even more striking. Both by right and in fact, only the ruling prince of the city or the sultan of the dynasty could undertake military construction. Repairs and additions to the citadel and walls of Damascus total 17 items in our catalog of acts of construction; remove these, and it appears that the Ayyubid house's contribution to Damascus was no greater than that of the combined religious establishment and civil bureaucracy, and rather smaller than that of the military.

In brief, architectural patronage in Ayyubid Damascus was the work of a tripartite elite, in which no one of the component elements really dominated either of the others. The patronage of the Ayyubid family was, of course, of high importance. But in order to maintain the thesis that the presence of a princely court was the decisive element in the architectural efflorescence of Ayyubid Damascus, we would have to establish at least one of the following propositions: 1) that the Ayyubid princes and their households somehow provided vital seed money for the construction of the period; or 2) that the Ayyubid court constituted a powerful pole of attraction for members of the military, religious, and bureaucratic elites of Egypt, Syria, and the Jazīra to come and contribute their interest and wealth to the development of Damascus; or 3) that the presence of the Ayyubid court simply ensured local political control, so that the surplus resources of the city and its hinterland would not be drained off for the greater glory of Baghdad or Cairo, but would rather be expended locally.

The first of these seems beyond our capacity to establish or refute, given our tenuous knowledge of the economic structures of Damascus during this period. The third, though it is attractive and plausible, involves proving a counter-factual proposition; moreover, it is clear from the history of Aleppo under the Mirdasids (eleventh century), or of Damascus under the Saljuqids (up to 459/1154), that local political control in and of itself did not ensure a high level of architectural patronage. Nevertheless, the themes of local political control, of autonomy, of long-term commitment to Damascus by the socio-political elite, will inevitably recur in our argument in the following pages, even though the precise quantitative effect of these things cannot be established. Finally, then, we might think of the Ayyubids as a "pole of attraction." To develop the implications of this proposition a bit further, let us suppose that the military, the religious establishment, and the bureaucracy were chiefly made up of long-established residents of Damascus, and drew their wealth from local sources directly controlled by them for some time past. In this case, we could argue that they were financially independent of the Ayyubid court, and would have been in Damascus in any case. In such a situation, surely the city would have flourished, perhaps not mightily but at least decently, without the Ayyubids.

All this implies three lines of questioning. First, we should determine how many of the members of the three groups in question were *originaires* of Damascus, and how many were immigrants who had been born and had received at least their basic education elsewhere. Second, we should try to determine the sources of their wealth, and to what degree they were really dependent on the favor and largesse of the ruling dynasty. Finally, we want to know what kinds of ties bound them to Damascus, and specifically how far their presence there was dependent on the court, and how far it was independent of the particular political configuration of the time. Perhaps it is needless to say that we should keep our analysis of the three groups as distinct as possible, so as not to obscure possibly significant differences in their behavior.

Since the military forms the most numerous body of patrons, we begin with them. It is natural to suppose that the military must have been more closely tied to the court, and more dependent for its resources on the ruling dynasty, than any other class of patrons. First, a large number of soldiers were recruited as *mamlūks* by the princes, to form at least the core of the standing royal regiments (*'askar*, pl. *'asākir*). Even more critical, the *iqṭā'*s, governorships, etc., which were the whole basis of their position in Ayyubid society, were in principle matters entirely within the discretion of the princes. These things would imply very direct, personal ties between the military class and the court, and would suggest that the emirs would be a stable element of patronage just so long as the dynasty was able to maintain itself—in short, that the commitment of the emirs to Damascus was ultimately fragile and contingent. But a close scrutiny of the evidence, both textual and quantitative, will suggest that this a priori view somewhat distorts the real relationship between the dynasty, the military, and Damascene society.

Was there in fact a close personal bond between the emirs and the the Ayyubid princes? If we assume that the bulk of them had been *mamlūks*, we should certainly be inclined to argue so, because of the close personal bond between the slave, uprooted from his original environment and alienated from any local identity, and his master, his only focus of identity and status in local society. On the other hand, even for *mamlūks* this view of things rather drastically oversimplifies. However strong a *mamlūk's* attachment to his *ustādh* might be, that loyalty hardly outlived the latter; it was by no means automatically transferred to the master's sons, let alone to any descendants of further generations, or collaterals.[5] This is in fact exactly what happened in Ayyubid Damascus. Saladin had in general obtained loyal service from the *mamlūks* of his father and uncle (for instance, Bahā' al-Dīn Karakush al-Asadī, Kiymaz al-Najmī). His successors, however, did not have the same good fortune with the chiefs of his own Ṣalāḥī corps, several of whom were at the very center of the ten-years' turbulence that followed their master's death. In fact, Saladin had established many of his emirs as hereditary *muqṭa*'s in the reconquered lands and fortresses of Palestine and Lebanon, and these men acted very much as free agents, bound only by their own direct interests, in the period after his death. It took Saladin's brother al-'Ādil most of his reign to re-establish direct royal control over these districts.[6] In later generations, the same process repeated itself in a more limited way: al-Mu'aẓẓam 'Īsā (615/1218–624/1227) established his able *ustādh al-dār* 'Izz al-Dīn Aybeg as *muqṭa'* of Ṣalkhad in the Jabal al-Durūz, a position which the latter maintained until 646/1248; in effect he was an independent ruler, though his interest dictated that he support the princes of Damascus in their recurrent struggles with the sultans in Egypt.[7] Even among the *mamlūk* emirs, then, we are often dealing with men who considered themselves free agents, not bound by personal ties to any one Ayyubid prince or local dynasty, although they never rebelled against the House of Ayyub generally.

The hypothesis that the emirs would be closely bound to the court which they served—here, to the princes of Damascus—is further weakened by the fact that many, probably a substantial majority, of the Ayyubid emirs had never been *mamlūks*, but were men of free birth and hereditary status. Minorsky long ago drew attention to the important Kurdish element in Saladin's forces, and my own studies have suggested that the free-born element in the Ayyubid armies was far more important than it was to become among the Mamlūks.[8] The data we have collected on patrons of architecture only serves to reinforce this view of things. However, this prominence of free-born emirs cannot be attributed to any high proportion of Arabs or Kurds among the military chiefs. Among our patrons, at least, the data reveal no Arabs and only four Kurds, as opposed to twenty Turks and four blacks (two of whom may in fact be *Rūmīs*).

TABLE 4

PERSONAL STATUS OF MEMBERS OF THE MILITARY ESTABLISHMENT OF AYYUBID DAMASCUS, BASED ON THE NET CENSUS

Career

Personal Status	*Emir*	*Household Officer*	*Women*	*Totals*
Free-born	15	1	3	19
Mamlūk	6	5	0	11
Unknown	6	1	1	8
TOTALS	27	7	4	38

Even if we assume that all persons of unidentified personal status were *mamlūks* (which is most unlikely), no less than 50% of the military patrons were persons of free birth. Even more than the *mamlūks*, these emirs were free agents, men who could go wherever the best opportunities led them.

Just as we cannot maintain the notion that the emirs of Ayyubid Damascus were bound to their princes by the close ties of servitude or clientship, so we should not overestimate the importance of the princes' right to assign *iqṭā*'s and governorships. It is indeed true that after al-'Ādil, a hereditary landed caste never succeeded in establishing itself in the domains of the princes of Damascus. On the other hand, this situation may not have been an element of strength for the court. On the contrary, we could argue that this combined with certain other features of the politics of Ayyubid Damascus to put the emirs in a relatively strong position vis-à-vis the dynasty. First, there were the complex political divisions of the Ayyubid Empire, in which Egypt and every major town in Syria and the Jazīra were ruled by an autonomous house. Second, within this general context, Damascus was generally the focus of the power struggles within the family, and after the fall of al-Nāṣir Dāwūd (626/1229), a hereditary succession was never again established there. In this context, Damascus' lack of an ensconced local military aristocracy might well have meant that she could maintain an adequate level of military power *only* if immigrant adventurers and soldiers of fortune could be attracted there. If this is true, it would mean that we are dealing with men who, in fact, did not depend on the largesse of the dynasty, but were rather able to demand high consideration from it. Certainly during the troubled quarter-century following the death of al-Ashraf Mūsā in 635/1237, the Damascene emirs were powerful figures indeed, often able to overawe the princes whom they served. (This stands in considerable contrast to the reigns of al-'Ādil, al-Mu'aẓẓam 'Īsā, and al-Ashraf, when the court plainly dominated the situation.)

If the above analysis is correct, then we should expect to find a substantial number of immigrants among the military men included among our patrons, and that in fact is the case. There are 13 members of this group (out of 38) whose regional origins are known to us; of these 13, only two were Damascene by birth. The others came almost equally from Egypt (3), North Syria (3), and the Jazīra (4), with one apparently from Iran. (Of these 13, 11 were free-born; the only two of *mamlūk* origin were black household officers who had begun their careers in the last years of the Fatimid Caliphate.) The results of so small and haphazard a sample cannot constitute proof, of course, but they still give us at least a strong indication. Ultimately, then, we cannot argue that the presence of the Ayyubid court in Damascus imposed any close and permanent personal or political ties on the military establishment to the city and dynasty. Rather, we would conclude that the emirs of Damascus were there because of free choice exercised within a system where the princes of the city were obliged to compete for their services. In some ways, to be sure, their commitment to local society was deeper than it would have been had their position been altogether subject to the favors of the princes. Precisely because the emirs were at least partially an independent body (and had been so since the death of Nūr al-Dīn), they were free to carve out a body of local interests for themselves wherever circumstances seemed favorable. Precisely because of its need for enough trained soldiers, and precisely because the court was often in a rather weak position, Damascus offered them such circumstances. On the other hand, the emirs' ability to make their own way in Damascus, as well as its attractiveness to them, were things strongly dependent on a particular, specific political configuration or conjuncture. When this disappeared, the commitment of the emirs to Damascus was bound to wither away as well.

We can reinforce this point by comparing the architectural patronage of the Ayyubid military with that of its counterparts in the Saljuqid-Zangid and Mamlūk periods.

TABLE 5

MILITARY PATRONAGE OF EDUCATIONAL INSTITUTIONS IN EACH OF THREE PERIODS (EXCLUDING RESTORATIONS)

Period	*Saljuqid-Zangid*	*Ayyubid*	*Mamlūk (to 741/1341)*
Monuments (original & conversion)	12	24	9

N.B.: the figures include *zāwiyas* as educational foundations, in spite of the evolution in meaning of this term over the 250 years in question.

On one level, it is no mystery that the Ayyubid emirs sponsored far more buildings than did their Saljuqid-Zangid counterparts, for they were far more numerous. According to Gibb, the regular garrison of Damascus around 1178 was about 1,000 heavy cavalry; if we estimate the size of a single company *(ṭulb)* at 70—the minimum number—that would mean an officer corps numbering 14 emirs. The regular forces of the city in later Ayyubid times were about 3,000 cavalry (until the last decade of Ayyubid rule); applying the same ratio (3,000/70), we would get an officer corps of 43 emirs at any given time. Both figures are probably slightly underestimated, since they would not include household officers, emirs technically posted elsewhere but with residences and family in Damascus, and so on, but they should give a reasonable order of magnitude.[9]

On the other hand, the Mamlūks probably maintained far larger forces in the city. This should have provided a broader basis for architectural patronage, and yet the Mamlūk emirs did not do as much even as the Saljuqid-Zangid amirs. This difference between the Mamlūks on the one hand, and the Saljuqids and Zangids on the other, may be explainable by the differences in their terms of service. Under the Mamlūks, the senior emirs at least—precisely those persons most likely to be patrons of architecture—were posted in Damascus only temporarily. All the more important emirs expected to be rotated to several different posts and ranks; most, it is fair to say, ultimately had their ambitions fixed on a high post in Cairo. For such men, Damascus was only a way-station. Moreover, the leading figures in the Mamlūk army were usually men of slave origins, reared and trained in the royal barracks-schools in Cairo. It was natural that such men would feel no real attachment to a provincial city, where their careers would be hindered and where they had never had much opportunity to develop long-term local ties. A number of the emirs of lower rank, or the chiefs of the *ḥalqa* troops, may well have been permanently stationed in Damascus, but they would have had far fewer resources to expend on religious and charitable foundations.[10]

These points can be illustrated by reviewing the patronage of four Ayyubid emirs in the context of their political careers. One of the most prominent men of early Ayyubid times was ʻIzz al-Dīn Ibrāhīm ibn Shams al-Dīn Muḥammad ibn ʻAbd al-Malik, a member of the famous and long-prominent Banū al-Muqaddam. This family had gotten its start in the service of the Saljuqids of Iraq, and had then passed over to the Zangids. ʻIzz al-Dīn's father rose to great eminence under Saladin; he was governor-*muqṭa*ʻ of Baalbek, then viceroy of Damascus from 579/1182 until his death in 584/1188, and more than once emir of the Syrian *ḥajj*. It was Shams al-Dīn who created his family's ties to Damascus; before his death near Mecca, he had built a *madrasa* within the walls, near the Bāb al-Farādīs, and beside it a large residence. In addition, his foundations in Damascus included a *masjid*, a *turba*, and a *khān*. Upon his death, his eldest son Ibrāhīm was confirmed in his father's *iqṭā*ʻ (granted by Saladin 574/1178 to replace Baalbek), consisting chiefly of Bārīn, Apamea, and Kafarṭāb. Ibrāhīm was able to maintain his possessions until the long civil war which followed the death of Saladin. Then, by aligning himself with al-ʻĀdil, he drew on himself the wrath of al-Ẓāhir Ghāzī of Aleppo. In 595/1199 he was in Damascus to assist al-ʻĀdil in the defense of that city against a coalition of al-Ẓāhir and al-Afḍal ʻAlī; while he was there, his key possession of Bārīn was seized, and he was forced to remain in Damascus until his death two years later (597/1200). It was probably during this time that ʻIzz al-Dīn Ibrāhīm built a *madrasa* (generally called the Turbat Ibn al-Muqaddam) north of the Bāb al-Farādīs. We have here an emir whose landed possessions were located in northern Syria, but whose father's political career and property interests had been centered in Damascus. Even though 'Izz al-Dīn Ibrāhīm was normally compelled to reside in his northern Syrian lands, he retained his family's property and house in Damascus. In the end, it was not only political vicissitudes which brought him to Damascus, but also the property interests established by his father in that town during the reigns of Nūr al-Dīn and Saladin.[11]

In many ways, both the career and the patronage of Fakhr al-Dīn Istār Jahārkas al-Ṣalāḥī might stand as a paradigm for Saladin's *mamlūk* emirs in the first generation after that ruler's death. So far as we know, Jahārkas had had no long-standing or regular connection with Damascus before his master's passing. He was from the outset at the very center of the political struggles surrounding the succession to Saladin, and his ambitions took him variously to Cairo and Syria. As commandant (*muqaddam*) of the Ṣalāḥīya regiment in Cairo at the time of al-'Azīz 'Uthmān's death in 595/1198, he was a key factor in the complicated intrigues which eventually brought al-'Ādil to the head of the Ayyubid confederation. In reward for his rather inconstant services, he was assigned in *iqṭā'* Bānyās and the vital castle of Toron, in addition to the castles of Beaufort and Tyron (bilād al-Shaqīf) previously given him by Saladin. He had become an extraordinarily powerful figure, in short. Precisely because his holdings were administrative dependencies of Damascus, he found it necessary to go there from time to time, though we are not certain that he maintained a regular residence in the city. (His military and administrative responsibilities would surely have required him to spend most of his time on his *iqṭā'*s.) His patronage was not limited to Damascus; almost certainly his major monument must have been a reputedly splendid *qaysārīya* which he built in Cairo (now disappeared). In Damascus itself, he set aside the endowment of a *turba* in al-Ṣāliḥīya for himself; the *turba* is joined to a small oratory, which was, according to our texts, intended to serve not only as a place of prayer but also as a *madrasa*. The texts tell us also, however, that it was not Jahārkas himself who saw to the foundation of his funerary *madrasa*, but his *mamlūk* Ṣārim al-Dīn Khuṭlubā, who added to the endowment established by his master. Khuṭlubā later built a second tomb-chamber immediately abutting on the first, probably to hold the body of Jahārkas' son and heir who died in 615/1218. Khuṭlubā himself died in 635/1238, and was interred in this latter structure. Here we have the case of a patron whose direct ties to Damascus were somewhat marginal, but whose career stemmed from the politics of that city, and was necessarily tied to it. Clearly, he had established some property interests in Damascus and the immediate vicinity, and it was the logical place for the chief lord of southern Lebanon to be buried. Quite as interesting is the fact that his son and his *mamlūk* continued and extended these interests in the city. After the death of Jahārkas' son, his *iqṭā*'s were rescinded by al-Mu'aẓẓam 'Īsā, who reassigned at least Bānyās to one of his own brothers; but Khuṭlubā continued to find service with the princes of Damascus, and remained there till his own death twenty years later. Again, it is a general context of freely established interests and a particular political structure which prove decisive, rather than any direct personal bonds.[12]

'Izz al-Dīn Aybeg al-Mu'aẓẓamī represents the middle generation of Ayyubid emirs, those attached to princes like al-Kāmil Muḥammad, al-Mu'ẓẓam 'Īsā, or al-'Azīz Muḥammad. Originally a *mamlūk* of al-Mu'ẓẓam 'Īsā's, he became his *ustādh al-dār* and then was assigned the important fortress of Ṣalkhad in *iqṭā*' in 611/1214. He held this district for nearly forty years, immune to all the incredible changes and confusions in Damascene politics, until 644/1247, when he was compelled to resign it by the Sultan al-Ṣāliḥ Ayyūb; during his long tenure there, he made intensive investments in the area—irrigation works, caravanserais, fortifications, mosques. But he never cut his ties with Damascus, where he was responsible for founding three *madrasas* (one in 621—still extant; a second after 626; and a third at an undetermined date). Again we have a man who was promoted to power by the favor of his prince and *ustādh*. But once he had obtained high standing, he was able to maintain himself quite independently of any prince's favor, and his interests in Damascus and its hinterland were directly tied to his place within a decentralized political structure.[13]

Finally, we can look at a Kurdish emir of the last Ayyubid period, Nāṣir al-Dīn al-Ḥusayn ibn Abī 'l-Fawāris al-Qaymarī, who retained his status and much of his power into the reign of Baybars, for in 661/1263 he was made *nā'ib al-salṭana* (literally, "viceroy") for the reconquered districts of the Sāhil, and he died in 665/1266, probably in the course of skirmishes before Acre. He had risen to prominence with his Qaymarīya in the time of al-Ṣāliḥ Ayyūb, and after the murder of Tūrānshāh he was instrumental in the successful conspiracy to turn Damascus over to the last major Ayyubid prince, al-Nāṣir Yūsuf II of Aleppo. Kurdish elements were of great importance in the army of al-Nāṣir Yūsuf, perhaps more important than they had been since the time of Saladin himself, partly because of an influx of new tribal elements, replenishing the old groups recruited in Zangid times. In this context, Nāṣir al-Dīn al-Qaymarī became extremely powerful and influential, commanding higher respect and obedience than the Sultan himself among the Kurdish contingents of the army. He held from al-Nāṣir the largest non-royal *iqṭā'* known to us in Ayyubid times—250 horsemen. His patronage in Damascus seems in accord with all this: two *madrasas* within the walls (and possibly a third in al-Ṣāliḥīya), and a *suwayqa* to provide endowment income for the larger of these. The lavishness of his larger foundation is suggested by the 40,000 *dirhams* which he spent on the clocks placed over its portal. It is striking that Nāṣir al-Dīn's position in southern and central Syria was so solid that it could survive the revolutions of the Mongol invasion and the Mamlūk re-occupation. Quite as significant is the political situation in which he had been able to build his power and wealth—a situation where he was in fact more powerful than his prince, but in which his political power depended on the order of things enshrined and guaranteed by that prince.[14]

In summary, then, we can suggest that *as a group*, the emirs of Damascus originated outside that city and were immigrants to it; that a very substantial proportion, probably a majority, were free-born and held their rank by hereditary right; that their rank, status, and influence in Damascus were largely independent of the dynasty which they served. To serve in the army of Damascus was for them largely a voluntary choice, which they were free to revoke. On the other hand, the presence of a wealthy emirate in Damascus, and its capacity to endure through so many troubles and crises, was dependent on a specifically Ayyubid political structure—and in particular, the political decentralization of Syria and the focal position of Damascus within the Ayyubid confederation.

The position of the third major cluster of patrons, the *'ulāmā'* and the civil bureaucracy (collectively termed "men of the turban," *muta'ammimūn*), is not nearly so different from the military as we might suppose from the disparity of their ideal social roles, or from our usual notion that Turks or Kurds were foreigners in a "native," Arabic-speaking environment.

It is beyond dispute that a substantial majority of these people were immigrants to Damascus—to be precise, 18 out of 28 (64%) among those whose regional origins can be identified; and 18 out of the 32 total members (56%) of these occupational groups:

TABLE 6

REGIONAL ORIGINS OF PATRONS AMONG THE 'ULAMĀ' AND CIVIL BUREAUCRACY IN AYYUBID DAMASCUS, BASED ON NET CENSUS

Occupation

Region of origin	*'ulama*	*civil bureaucracy*	*Total*
Damascus-Ghuta	9	1	10
South-central Syria	1	1	2
North Syria	2	1	3
Jazīra	2	0	2
Iraq	3	0	3
Iran	0	0	0
Maghrib	1	0	1
Egypt	3	4	7
Unknown	2	2	4
TOTALS	23	9	32

In view of our ordinary conceptions about the way wealth and influence were acquired by the "native" (e.g., Arabic-speaking) elites of Syria, such figures seem remarkable. Among these people, status was (we suppose) earned slowly, even over generations, by marriage ties with the established local notables of the city, or by earning a position of high prestige in one of the recognized *madhāhib*. And yet in Ayyubid Damascus, the immigrant *'ulāmā'* and bureaucrats were quickly able to command the resources of wealth and influence to play a major role in the city's architectural development. Indeed, their role far surpassed that of the city's "old" families (i.e., those which had resided in Damascus for three or more generations). The established notables of Damascus contributed only nine patrons of architecture (out of 141), and eleven acts of patronage (out of 197). Of these nine, seven belonged to the religious establishment, which would mean that less than one-third of the known patrons from that group (30%) belonged to any sort of long-established religious aristocracy in Damascus.

It is not in the regional origins of the *muta'ammimūn*, nor in their supposed "nativeness," that we shall find the true differences between them and the military patrons, but rather in the role of the Ayyubid court in attracting them to Damascus. If the role of the court seems somewhat passive in the case of the military, it was certainly not so with regard to the *'ulāmā'* and the civil bureaucracy. Rather, we find here the fruits of a positive and conscious policy first developed in Syria by Nūr al-Dīn (admittedly on an already existing Saljuqid model), to establish an alliance between the dynasty and the men of religion. This was to be achieved in several ways: (1) close consultation between the ruler and the *'ulāmā'*, even in matters of state such as taxation and foreign policy; (2) by drawing the state bureaucracy from among persons with a solid Sunni education; (3) providing a network of *madrasas* which would ensure a solid education in Shāfi'ī or Ḥanafī *fiqh*, under the supervision of the prince and his close associates, for all potential *'ulāmā'* or bureaucrats. In this way, the schism between state and religion, between a Sunni religious elite and a bureaucracy staffed by Shī'is or *dhimmīs*, could be healed. Likewise, the dynasty could evolve the rapport with the subject populace necessary to suppress Shī'i or even Ismā'īlī sympathies and elements within that populace.[15]

The establishment of *madrasas* naturally demanded the appointment of professors of great eminence, if they were to achieve their intended purpose. To some extent, such men could be found among the native Sunni *'ulāmā'* of Syria—e.g., the Banū al-'Ajamī or the Banū al-'Adīm of Aleppo, the Banū 'Asākir, the Qurashīs or the Shīrāzīs of Damascus. Indeed, most of these families attached themselves to the new *madrasa* movement by establishing such foundations on their own behalf. Nevertheless, given the number of *madrasas* that were founded, and the astounding rapidity of their emergence as the monuments of prestige in the area, the native *'ulāmā'* could not begin to staff them. By necessity, therefore, Nūr al-Dīn had to look farther afield. Naturally enough, two sources were especially prominent: the Jazīra and Iran. For this choice, Professor Sourdel advances two reasons: "one, purely political, is connected with the fact that the Atabegs of Mosul quite naturally chose their collaborators in the Jazira and the Kurdish mountains—a tradition which was maintained under their Ayyubid successors; the other, cultural in character but also linked to the historical evolution of the times, is attached to the renown of the Iranian professors, who had been champions of the Sunni restoration in the country where the first *madrasas* had been founded under Turkish domination." As Sourdel shows, in the century between

1150 and 1250, no less than 57 out of the 113 known Shāfiʿī and Ḥanafī professors in Aleppo (i.e., 50%) were first- or second-generation immigrants from Iran and the Jazīra.[16]

What Nūr al-Dīn had begun, the Ayyubids most energetically continued. The Ayyubids surrounded themselves with scholars and litterateurs, and several of them were personally skilled in rhetoric, poetry, and the religious sciences. In the case of the Ayyubids of Damascus, al-Muʿaẓẓam ʿĪsā and his brother and rival al-Ashraf Mūsā were especially committed to inviting scholars to the city, to making places for them within the religious establishment, and to including them within their circles of advisers and intimates. But specifically invited or not, any well-known or talented scholar who found his way to Damascus could be quite sure that the Ayyubid princes would make a place for him in the local religious establishment—a professorship in a *madrasa*, or a post as *khaṭīb* or imām in a major mosque. At least two newcomers—the Egyptian Jamāl al-Dīn al-Miṣrī and the Azerbayjani Shams al-Dīn al-Khuwayī—attained the eminence of Chief Qāḍī of the city. With such a degree of royal patronage, even a newly arrived scholar might hope to be in a position to establish some pious work in his own name.[17]

In the case of the *ʿulāmā'*, then, we are dealing with active royal patronage; in a very real way, this group was more directly dependent on royal or princely favor for its high status and its capacity to sponsor construction than was the military. As newcomers without the direct access to state revenues enjoyed by the emirs, the *ʿulāmā'* could acquire the means to sponsor architecture only through royal favor. Indirectly, they also profited, though certainly less lavishly, from the general political situation which had attracted the emirs, for the presence of the emirs created a second (and secondary) source of patronage and influence for the *ʿulāmā'*. On the other hand, a scholar's career, once it was well launched, was not so vulnerable to political changes as was that of a soldier. A *madrasa*, once it had been founded, would always have its endowment to furnish his salary; a big city like Damascus, whatever its exact administrative status, would always need imāms, professors, preachers, and *qāḍīs*. Nevertheless, when a city was no longer a political center, its intellectual and religious life would begin to atrophy; its most famous scholars were tempted by new centers of patronage such as Cairo, while the flow of new immigrants, bringing a new outlook, a different set of social contacts, even fresh ideas, would tend to dry up.[18] Over time, too, institutional endowments would fall in value, and were less likely to be replaced. Not only directly, but in the general ambience which it promoted, the presence of a wealthy and sympathetic court was a vital factor in the capacity of the *'ulāmā'* to sponsor a significant amount of religious and charitable architecture.

The situation of the civil bureaucracy was somewhat different, because of the very direct ties by which bureaucrats were typically bound to the princes. Men who had reached the higher echelons of the bureaucracy, at least, seem normally to have attached themselves to the entourage of some one prince; they made their career in his service, and whither he went, so went they. (In a very real way, though they shared the ethnic, cultural, and educational background of the *'ulāmā'*, the bureaucracy were like a prince's household retainers.) Precisely because a stable hereditary regime never took root in Damascus, its princes were normally men who had previously governed some other part of the empire (usually Egypt or the Jazīra), and had acquired a bureaucratic entourage there. When Damascus fell into the possession of these new princes, they brought with them the men whom they intended to put in charge of the civil administration. Of all the groups we have studied, then, we should expect the bureaucrats to be the least stable, the most closely tied to even minor political ripples, for they had no institutional structure between them and the prince whom they served. Both the numerical data (eight out of nine were immigrants) and our information about individuals conform to this hypothesis.[19]

In our discussion of the roles of the military, the *'ulāmā'*, and the civil bureaucracy, we have laid much stress on the role of immigrants within these three groups. It is time to sum up the contribution made to architectural patronage by immigrants during this period. We can identify the regional origins of 60 patrons (excluding members of the Ayyubid family, who cannot be classified by regional origin). Of these 60, only 13 were natives of Damascus; that is, of those patrons whose place of birth and upbringing is known, 78% were immigrants. The significance of these numbers becomes all the greater if one adds to them the patrons of the Ayyubid house—24 persons. Our net census contains 141 patrons altogether, and 71 were either immigrants or members of the ruling family—i.e., 50%. From a different perspective, out of the 197 acts of construction included in the net census, immigrants to Damascus were responsible for 58 items, and members of the royal family for 57: that is, 115 acts of patronage out of 197, or 58%—a minimum figure, since the regional origins of so many patrons cannot be identified.

In the end, then, our appreciation of the role of the Ayyubid princes in the patronage process must be sharply altered. We cannot simply say of them that they sponsored a very substantial body of work, but were in this regard really no more than the equals of the military chiefs or the religious establishment. Instead, we have come to identify this tiny group of men and women—only two dozen in all—as the hub of the whole mechanism. They were so, not because they personally did so much, but because they alone were in a position to attract the immigrants—emirs, *'ulāmā'*, and bureaucrats—who did.

The foundations of the architectural efflorescence of Ayyubid Damascus were thus very frail, because so much depended on the continuance of an intricate and inherently unstable system of politics. In a very real sense, the Mongol conquest of 658/1260 and the Mamlūk reoccupation which followed did not simply mean a change of masters for the people of Damascus. When Hülegü's armies obliterated the Ayyubid regime in Syria, they also shattered the fragile political structure which had underwritten the city's growth and development during the previous century.

APPENDIX

The tables in this paper are derived from a census of architectural activity in the walled city of Damascus, its immediate suburbs, and the outlying settlement of al-Ṣāliḥīya during the period from 589/1193 to 658/1260—i.e., during the years between the death of Saladin and the Mongol occupation, when Damascus was the political and administrative center of an autonomous principality within the Ayyubid confederation.

The census aims first of all to register every *act of construction* in Damascus during the sixty-seven years in question. Such acts of construction may represent a new building, the restoration and repair of an old one, or the conversion of an existing structure from one use to another (most commonly, the conversion of a private mansion to a *madrasa*). Monuments have been registered both under the Arabic terms by which they were identified in the sources (e.g., *masjid, turba, dār al-ḥadīth*), and under broad functional categories (e.g., "educational institutions," "places of worship," "shrines"). There are ambiguities, of course: every *madrasa* contains a mosque, and a building called *masjid* in our texts may sometimes be a saint's tomb rather than a place for the ritual *ṣalāt*. I have made every effort to be consistent and to avoid double-counting, however, and on the whole I believe I have succeeded. For the purposes of this survey, differences of cost and scale between one act of construction and another have been ignored, since it is seldom possible to obtain any concrete data on such matters.

Second, the census tries to identify every *patron* of architecture in the city during this period—i.e., every person at whose behest an act of construction, restoration, or conversion was carried out, and who provided the funds for it. For each patron, we have tried to obtain as much social background information as possible: (1) his or her *madhhab* or sect; (2) personal status (slave or free origin); (3) ethnic identity; (4) dates and places of birth, upbringing, principal residence, and death; (5) social/occupational role (e.g., member of the Ayyubid family, emir, *qāḍī*, *Ṣūfī*, merchant). Although there are gaps in our data, especially in regard to more obscure persons, enough can be obtained to construct a meaningful overall profile of the patrons. In general, data based on surmise and mere likelihood have been kept to a minimum throughout. In particular, the *nisbas* in personal names are often very misleading—a man may be called al-Shīrāzī because his great-grandfather had come from that city—and I have used these as a source of biographical data only when I could corroborate them independently.

Certain types of buildings are far more consistently cited in our sources than others. We can be confident that we have a nearly complete record of the *madrasas* (both new constructions and conversion) and their patrons, for example, while for such crucial organs of urban life as *sūqs* and *khāns* we find only sporadic notices in the chronicles and biographical dictionaries. For this reason, I have based my discussion in this paper strictly on a *net census*—i.e., a census which includes only those types of monuments (mostly educational and religious institutions) which were consistently and systematically surveyed in our sources. Thus our data are partial—they exclude by design such vital sectors as residential and commercial construction—but they should be highly reliable for the classes of construction which they do contain. These classes of construction, because of their great social and cultural prestige, should be broad indicators of the role in architectural patronage played by each of the various groups in Damascene society.

The following figures may give a general sense of the difference between the "gross" and "net" census. The gross census records 241 acts of construction of all types, sponsored by 174 different patrons. The net census records 197 acts of construction (for *madrasas* and other educational institutions, congregational mosques [*jāmi*'s], Ṣūfī convents [*khānqāhs, zāwiyas, ribāṭs*], mausolea [*turba*s] and military structures), by 141 patrons.

The sources used for this census are both textual and archaeological. The former consist chiefly of an important series of historical topographies composed by Damascene scholars between the mid-6th/12th and mid-10th/16th centuries. Some of these are really biographical dictionaries, arranged by institution rather than by persons, and the data in them can be collected and quantified in a manner now familiar from studies by Richard Bulliet, Carl Petry, and Dominique Urvoy. The textual tradition represented by the topographical works is discussed in Nikita Elisséeff's introduction to his invaluable translation of Ibn 'Asākir. The archaeological evidence has never been adequately published, but we have a few useful (albeit very terse) general inventories of the city's monuments, together with a number of short monographs dealing with individual structures. I tried to confirm the information in these studies, so far as possible, by personal inspections of the extant monuments in 1972–73. The principal sources used to construct the census are as follows:

I. Textual Sources

Ibn 'Asākir, *Ta'rīkh Dimashq*, ed. S. D. al-Munajjid (Damascus, 1954), Vol. I, part 2. French translation by N. Elisséeff, *La Description de Damas d'Ibn 'Asākir* (Damascus, 1959).

'Izz al-Dīn ibn Shaddād, *Al-A'lāq al-khaṭīra fī dhikr umarā' al-Shām wa'l-Jazīra. Ta'rīkh Dimashq*, ed. Sāmī al-Dahhān (Damascus, 1956).

'Abd al-Qādir al-Nu'aymī, *Tanbīh al-ṭālib wa-irshād al-dāris fī mā fī Dimashq min al-jawāmi' wa'l-madāris*, ed. Ja'far al-Ḥasanī, as *Al-Dāris fī ta'rīkh al-madāris* (Damascus, 1948–51).

Shams al-Dīn ibn Ṭūlūn, *Al-Qalā'id al-jawharīya fī ta'rīkh al-Ṣāliḥīya*, ed. M. A. Duhmān (Damascus, 1949–56).

'Abd al-Basīṭ al-'Ilmāwī (abridgment of al-Nu'aymī), trans. Henri Sauvaire, *Description de Damas, Journal Asiatique*, sér. IX, nos. 3–7 (1894–96).

II. Archaeological and Epigraphic Sources

Alfred Freiherr von Kremer, *Topographie von Damaskus*, Denkschriften der Kaiserlichen Akademie der Wissenschaften, Wien: Phil-Hist. Classe, Vols. v/2 (1855), vi/2 (1856).

Karl Wulzinger and Carl Watzinger, *Damaskus: Die islamische Stadt* (Leipzig and Berlin, 1924).

Jean Sauvaget, *Les Monuments historiques de Damas* (Beirut, 1932).

Jean Sauvaget and Claude Écochard, *Les Monuments ayyoubides de Damas*, fascicles 1–3 (Paris, 1938–48).

Ernst Herzfeld, "Damascus: Studies in Architecture," *Ars Islamica*, IX–XIV (1942–48). Notes collected by Herzfeld before World War I for the Damascus volume of the *Matériaux pour un corpus inscriptionum arabicarum*, which was never published. Cf. the critical review by Jean Sauvaget, "Notes sur quelques monuments musulmans de Syrie: À propos d'une étude récente," *Syria*, XXIV–XXV (1944–48).

Répertoire chronologique d'épigraphie arabe, ed. Étienne Combe, Jean Sauvaget, Gaston Wiet, *et al.* (Cairo, 1931–).

A further discussion of some of the methodological issues sketched here can be found in Chapter Eight, "Urban Topography and Urban Society," of my *Islamic History: A Framework for Inquiry*.

NOTES

1. N. Elisséeff, "Dimashḳ," *EI*², II, 284.

2. The data on Ayyubid patronage in Table 1 and the rest of the paper are derived from a systematic survey of monuments built or restored, and of the persons connected with their construction, repair, and funding, during the period from the death of Saladin (589/1193) to the Mongol invasion of Syria (658/1260). The survey, based on both texts and archaeological information, was carried out by me between 1968 and 1974, with occasional revisions and corrections in the years since. A sketch of the methodology used in this survey is given in the Appendix.

3. When Nūr al-Dīn occupied Damascus (549/1254) there were already twelve Sunni educational institutions (*madrasas* and *zāwiyas*) there; during his twenty-year reign in the city, twelve more were established, eight of these at his behest. During the twenty-eight years of Tankiz' regime as viceroy of Damascus, fifteen new educational institutions were established, in addition to twenty-four other religious and charitable foundations—i.e., thirty-nine overall, or almost half the total from the early Mamlūk period.

4. Elisséeff, loc. cit.

5. The most influential and best documented statements on the social identity and personal loyalties of the mamlūk are by David Ayalon. See "L'Esclavage du mamelouk," *Oriental Notes and Studies*, I (Jerusalem, 1951), pp. 25–37; and more concisely, "Mamlūkiyyāt," *Jerusalem Studies in Arabic and Islam*, II (1980), pp. 327–28.

6. R. S. Humphreys, *From Saladin to the Mongols* (Albany, 1977), pp. 91–123, on the succession struggle after Saladin's death; ibid., pp. 141–45, on al-'Ādil's reorganization of the *iqṭā*'s in central Syria.

7. On the career of 'Izz al-Dīn Aybeg al-Mu'aẓẓamī, see ibid., index.

8. V. Minorsky, *Studies in Caucasian History* (London, 1953), pp. 139–46; R. S. Humphreys, "The Emergence of the Mamluk Army," *Studia Islamica*, XLV (1977), pp. 92–93; XLVI (1977), pp.149–50. Prof. Ayalon's conclusions (in "Aspects of the Mamluk Phenomenon: Ayyubids, Kurds, and Turks," *Islam*, LIV [1977], pp. 1–32) may appear to contradict this statement, but two points should be noted: (1) both of us agree that the Kurds had only a modest and occasional role in the Ayyubid armies, though I believe that Prof. Ayalon discounts them too sharply (cf. "Aspects," pp. 29–31); (2) I am more concerned with the officer corps, Prof. Ayalon with the ordinary trooper. In addition, Prof. Ayalon seems to argue that every passage referring to *mamālīk* is in fact describing soldiers of slave origin. In Ayyubid times, however, the term *mamlūk* is often simply an expression of deference. Prof. Ayalon has himself noted one example of this in an earlier article: "Studies on the Structure of the Mamluk Army," *BSOAS*, XV (1953), p. 466, in reference to a line in Ṣāliḥ ibn Yaḥyā's *Ta'rīkh Bayrūt*.

9. H. A. R. Gibb, "The Armies of Saladin," in Gibb, *Studies in Islamic History and Civilization* (London, 1962), p. 76; N. Elisséeff, *Nur ad-Din*, III, 723–24 (where he corrects the number of *aṭlāb* cited by Gibb from 174 to 147; Humphreys, *From Saladin to the Mongols*, pp. 176, 443; Humphreys, "The Emergence of the Mamluk Army," *Studia Islamica*, XLV (1977), pp. 74, 78–80.

10. Humphreys, "The Emergence of the Mamluk Army," pp. 161–62.

11. On 'Abd al-Malik: Elisséeff, *Nur ad-Din*, II, 439–40, 767. On Shams al-Dīn Muḥammad: ibid., II, 439–40, 695–98; A. S. Ehrenkreutz, *Saladin*, and M. J. Lyons and D. P. Jackson, *Saladin*, index (under "Ibn al-Muqaddam"). On 'Izz al-Dīn Ibrāhīm: Humphreys, *From Saladin to the Mongols*, pp. 82, 99, 105, 112–14, 119. On the patronage of the Banū al-Muqaddam in Damascus: Ibn Shaddād, *Al-A'lāq al-khaṭīra*, p. 226; al-Nu'aymī, *Dāris*, I, 594 f., 599 f.; Sauvaire, *Description de Damas*, IV, 284–86; Sauvaget, *Monuments historiques de Damas*, pp. 59–60; Khalid Moaz, "La Mausolée d'Ibn al-Muqaddam," *Mélanges de l'Institut Français de Damas* (1929), I, 67–74. (Both Ibn Shaddād and al-Nu'aymī give the *laqab* of Ibrāhīm as Fakhr al-Dīn, but Sibṭ ibn al-Jawzī and Ibn Wāṣil, who are usually more reliable, consistently use 'Izz al-Dīn.)

12. On the career of Fakhr al-Dīn Jahārkas: Humphreys, *From Saladin to the Mongols*, index. On his patronage: Sibṭ ibn al-Jawzī, *Mir'āt al-zamān*, pp. 364–65, 466; Ibn Khallikān, *Wafayāt al-a'yān*, I, 381; al-Nu'aymī, *Dāris*, I,

496–97; Ibn Ṭūlūn, *Al-Qalā'id al-jawharīya*, pp. 135 f.; Sauvaire, *Description de Damas*, IV, 249 f.; Sauvaget, *Les Monuments ayyoubides de Damas*, fasc. I, pp. 41–50.

13. On the career of 'Izz al-Dīn Aybeg al-Mu'aẓẓamī, see above, n. 7. On his patronage: Ibn Shaddād, *al-A'lāq al-khaṭīra*, pp. 215–16, 221; al-Nu'aymī, *Dāris*, I, 550, 555–58; Sauvaire, *Description de Damas*, IV, 269–70; Sauvaget, *Monuments historiques de Damas*, p. 64; Sauvaget, *Monuments ayyoubides de Damas*, fasc. II, pp. 65–75.

14. On the career of Nāṣir al-Dīn al-Qaymarī: Humphreys, *From Saladin to the Mongols*, pp. 252, 305–6, 373, 463. On his patronage: Ibn Shaddād, *Al-A'lāq al-khaṭīra*, p. 245; al-Nu'aymī, *Dāris*, pp. 441 f.; Sauvaire, *Description de Damas*, III, 438; Ibn 'Abd al-Hādī, *Thimār al-Maqāṣid*, ed. A. Talass (Damascus, 1943), pp. 148, 244. The careers of some other emirs are sketched in Humphreys, "Emergence," pp. 70–72.

15. Elisséeff, *Nur ad-Din*, III, 749–50, 779; Emmanuel Sivan, *L'Islam et la Croisade* (Paris, 1968), pp. 70–73.

16. D. Sourdel, "Les Professeurs de madrasa à Alep aux XIIe–XIIIe siècles d'après Ibn Shaddad," *Bulletin d'Études Orientales de l'Institut Français de Damas*, XIII (1949–51), pp. 111–115. Quotation: p. 113. None of this means that the local *'ulāmā'* or notable families were not important elements of the religious establishment in Ayyubid Damascus. Obviously they were, but as professors rather than as founders of *madrasas*. On these families, see Joan E. Gilbert, "The Ulama of Medieval Damascus and the International World of Islamic Scholarship" (Ph.D. diss., Univ. of California-Berkeley, 1977), pp. 152–94. She summarizes her general argument in "Institutionalization of Muslim Scholarship and Professionalization of the *'Ulama'* in Medieval Damascus," *Studia Islamica*, LII (1980); on the proportions of native-born to immigrant scholars among the *'ulāmā'* as a whole, see pp. 122–24.

17. Humphreys, *From Saladin to the Mongols*, pp. 186–87.

18. This is precisely what seems to have happened in Damascus by the late 8th/14th century. The city remained a significant center of learning, to be sure, but we no longer find scholars of the caliber of Ibn Taymīya, al-Dhahabī, and Ibn Kathīr making their careers there. The leading scholars of the 9th/15th century established their reputations in Cairo.

19. Some comments on this point can be found in Humphreys, *From Saladin to the Mongols*, pp. 250–51, 313–14, 377–80. Cf. the conclusions of Carl Petry, *The Civilian Elite of Cairo in the Fifteenth Century* (Princeton, 1981), pp. 312–25.

13
Personal Service and the Element of Concession in the Theory of the Vizierate in Medieval Persia

A. K. S. Lambton

THOSE WHO WROTE on the vizierate in Saljuq times regarded the vizier as the pivot of the administration. This broadly coincided with the situation as it was in the reign of Malikshāh (465–85/1072–92), when the Saljuq empire was at its height. The vizier was the head of the supreme *dīwān*, the *dīwān-i a'lā*. He was directly appointed by the sultan, whose servant he was. When the sultan who appointed him died or was replaced, the vizier (with his followers) normally fell from office. Niẓām al-Mulk, who was vizier first to Alp Arslan (455–65/1063–72), and then to his son and successor Malikshāh, is an exception to the general rule. Broadly, the duty of the vizier was to supervise the general conduct of affairs on behalf of the sultan, and in particular to foster agriculture and the prosperity of the country, in order to increase the revenue. In addition, he sometimes presided over the *dīwān-i maẓālim*, the court for the redress of grievances, even though *'urf* jurisdiction was mainly delegated to military officials. He also had general supervision of the religious institution—this because of the connection between religious dissent and political opposition, and also because of the considerable revenues belonging to *awqāf*. Lastly, as the personal servant of the sultan, he conducted the relations of the sultan with other rulers and with the caliph. There is no record in Saljuq times of any formal charge (*muwāḍa'a*) laying down the terms of the vizier's appointment, other than his diploma of appointment, such as was apparently given to Aḥmad ibn Ḥasan al-Maymandī when he became vizier to the Ghaznavid Mas'ūd ibn Maḥmūd in 422/1031.[1]

Niẓām al-Mulk, under Malikshāh, presided over a great empire, and his office was one of prestige. He was held in great respect by his contemporaries, including the military. Al-Ghazālī compared him to the Barmakids,[2] and the Imām al-Ḥaramayn al-Juwaynī held him in high esteem.[3] The caliph al-Muqtadī also treated him with honor. On the occasion of the betrothal of Malikshāh's daughter to the caliph in 474/1081–82, he was allowed to be seated in the caliph's audience, and given a robe of honor with a border (*ṭirāz*) inscribed with the words "in the name of the just and perfect vizier Niẓām al-Mulk, *raḍī amīr al-mu'minīn.*"[4] After the death of Niẓām al-Mulk, few viziers held office for long, apart from Fakhr al-Mulk ibn Niẓām al-Mulk, who was vizier to Sanjar from 490/1096–97 to 500/1106–07, and his son Ṣadr al-Dīn Muḥammad, who succeeded him and held office until 511/1117–18. In the late Saljuq period, few viziers escaped murder, imprisonment, or the confiscation of their wealth. The emirs encroached upon their power, and no *dīwān* official after Niẓām al-Mulk succeeded in imposing control over the emirs; those who tried came to an untimely end. With the fragmentation of the empire after the death of Muḥammad ibn Malikshāh in 511/1118, the viziers no longer presided over a large and expanding empire. In the western provinces ruled by the Saljuqs of Iraq, they were viziers not to independent sultans, but to subordinate rulers, and were sometimes appointed and dismissed by Sanjar, who kept Marv as his capital and allowed his nephews to rule in the western provinces. Under the Khwārazmshāhs the vizierate perhaps regained some of its former influence, in measure as the Khwārazmshāh became the most important ruler in the eastern provinces of the Muslim world. But in view of the widespread disorders which prevailed in the empire of the Khwārazmshāhs, it is unlikely that the vizier was able to wield effective power.

The main sources for the theory of the vizierate are mirrors for princes. These were written by men of letters, bureaucrats, and sometimes by *'ulamā'*, and are colored by the prejudices of the "men of the pen." Their authors were not intellectual innovators, and they looked to the wisdom of the past. Their expositions are mainly in ethical terms, rather than in terms of the functions of the vizier. We know nothing of the ruler's conception of the vizierate, or of that held by the "men of the sword," except so far as we can judge from their actions. Al-Māwardī's discussion of the two vizierates, the "vizierate of delegation" (*wizārat tafwīḍ*) and the "vizierate of execution" (*wizārat tanfīdh*), was, no doubt, known to writers of the Saljuq period, but it does not seem to have influenced their expositions. This may be because their purposes were different. Al-Māwardī's concern was to bring, or keep, the holders of power and their officials within the framework of Islamic government, while that of the writers of *adab* works was to restate the wisdom of the past, and to give an idealized version of the vizierate. Perhaps they hoped thereby to strengthen the bureaucracy against the growing militarization of the state. It is also probably true that they were able to bring precepts to the attention of their patrons by putting them in the mouth of some venerable figure of the past, when a more direct approach would have met with rebuff. It must also be remembered that the viziers exercised considerable powers of patronage, and that those who enjoyed, or hoped to enjoy, their patronage were likely to exaggerate the importance of the vizierate.

Some of those who wrote on the vizierate were, or had been, employed in the bureaucracy. But even Niẓām al-Mulk, who had long experience in the vizierate, does not lay down detailed guidance for Malikshāh on the duties of the vizier in his manual on government, the *Siyāsat-nāma*. This may have been, as Bowen suggests, because the vizierate was in his own hands and functioning satisfactorily, making it unnecessary for him to lay down rules for its conduct.[5] More probably, he did not do so because he wished to retain a degree of flexibility. Be that as it may, Niẓām al-Mulk discusses the vizierate only in very general terms. He appears to have been under no illusion as to the integrity of those who held office. While he makes clear the paramount importance of the vizier's office, he emphasizes at the same time the need for personal supervision by the sultan of every branch of the administration, including the vizierate. He states, "The condition of viziers and the way they exercise office must be enquired into, because the wellbeing of both the ruler and the kingdom depends upon the vizier."[6]

But behind this injunction there also lay the element of concession. All power was delegated by the ruler, who was responsible for the actions of those to whom he delegated power, and would be called to account for their actions at the final reckoning in the next world. Niẓām al-Mulk continues, "When the vizier is of good conduct and possesses good judgment, the kingdom flourishes and the army and the subjects are contented, peaceable, and wealthy, and the ruler happy at heart. But when the vizier is of evil conduct, indescribable confusion appears in the kingdom, and the ruler is always distressed and afflicted in mind, and the kingdom disturbed."[7] A good vizier gave the king a good name, and made his conduct good. "All kings," he states, "who have been great and who will be held in renown until the end of time, are kings who have had good viziers."[8]

The qualifications which Niẓām al-Mulk demands of a vizier are that he should be of right religion—a Ḥanafī or a Shāfi'ī—and that he should be capable, well-versed in financial transactions (*mu'āmalat-dān*), generous, and loyal to the king. If he came from a family of viziers, so much the better. If a vizier was extortionate, corrupt, and tyrannical, the tax-collectors, whose offices depended upon him, would be the same or even worse.[9]

The late Professor Goitein in his article "The Origins of the Vizierate and Its True Character,"[10] and Professor Dominique Sourdel in *Le Vizirat 'abbaside*,[11] have discussed the vizierate in the early centuries of Islam. By Saljuq times, if not before, the early theories of the vizierate had been largely replaced by an idealized conception of the Sasanian vizierate. Just as Anūshīrwān is considered the prototype of the just king, his minister Buzurgmihr is regarded as the prototype of the just vizier. He is seen as the helper (*yār*) of the ruler, a concept which looks back to the meaning of the Arabic term *wazīr*. Al-Ghazālī puts these words into the mouth of Ardashīr ibn Bābakān: "The most fitting helper (*yār*) of the king is a good, wise, kind, and honest vizier, with whom he can consult and to whom he can tell his secrets."[12]

Al-Ghazālī, like Niẓām al-Mulk, stresses the importance of the vizier. He states that kingship is made perfect only by a worthy, just, and capable vizier. Like many other writers, he seeks sanction for the office of vizier in Mūsā's appointment of Hārūn as his vizier, a Quranic reference which will have been familiar to his audience, both to the literate and to the illiterate. Further, by recalling that the prophet had said "consult them in affairs," al-Ghazālī would seem to imply that the ruler was to consult the vizier.[13] The duty of counsel, so far as it refers to the vizier (or others of the ruler's officials), is, however, muted. So far as counsel is mentioned, it is in terms of the king consulting his officials, rather than of the vizier offering counsel, even though Najm al-Dīn Rāzī and the anonymous author of the *Tārīkh-i shāhī-i Qara-Khitā'iyān* appear to take a different view (see below).

"In every age," al-Ghazālī states, "God singles out certain of His servants, such as kings, viziers and wise men (*'ālimān*) for the manifestation of His power and the prosperity of the world."[14] It is possible that al-Ghazālī intended to imply by these words that the vizier was appointed directly by God and not by the sultan, but this is not clear from his words. Discussing the functions of the vizier, he states that "the good minister is the guardian of the king's secrets and on him depends the orderly handling of business, the revenue and the prosperity of the realm and the treasury. Through him the monarchy acquires adornment, prestige and power. Suggesting (courses of action) and answering questions are his constant tasks. He gladdens the king's friends and confounds the king's enemies. No man is more deserving of encouragement and esteem than such a minister."[15]

Al-Ghazālī lays down three principles for the guidance of the ruler in his treatment of the vizier. First, he should not be hasty in punishing him; secondly, he should not covet the wealth of the vizier should the latter become wealthy; and thirdly, if the vizier has some request of the ruler, he should grant it. The ruler must always be accessible to the vizier; he must not listen to those who speak evil against him—a necessary admonition, since false accusations and calumny were one of the curses of public life—and he must have no secrets from the vizier—the good vizier was the keeper of the king's secrets.[16]

Al-Ghazālī conceives of the vizier not only as the "helper" of the king, but also as his guide and mentor. He attributes this aspect of the vizierate also to a Sasanian model, but, as Goitein has shown, in actual practice it was derived from Arab tribal custom.[17] Al-Ghazālī alleges that Anūshīrwān said to his son, "treat well the vizier who, when he sees you indulging in something unseemly, does not join you in this." If the king is disposed toward the good and was kind to his subjects, the vizier should encourage him, but if he is not, the vizier should gently bring him back to the right course. The stability of the king's rule depends on the vizier and the stability of the world on the king.[18]

As for the qualities which al-Ghazālī demands of the vizier, these are learning, wisdom, and the experience which came from age. But if his affairs are to proceed satisfactorily, he also requires prudence, that he may know the outcome of anything he embarks upon, knowledge, courage, uprightness, and the ability to keep the king's secrets at all times.[19]

Al-Ghazālī no doubt knew from experience the tension which existed between the bureaucracy and the military classes. Perhaps it was with this in mind that he enjoins the vizier to speak with kindness to the military and to treat them with courtesy, "because many viziers have been killed at their hands in ancient times."[20] The viziers and stewards (*kadkhudāyān*) of the king must keep to the customs of the ancients, and when they demand taxes from the subjects they must have in mind the welfare of the kingdom. They must demand the taxes at the proper time, and impose only such burdens upon the subjects as are within their capacity to pay.[21]

The *Naṣīḥat al-mulūk* of al-Ghazālī was known to and often quoted by later writers; and it is perhaps not fanciful to see an echo of al-Ghazālī's theory in a document for the vizierate dated 544/1149–50. The preamble of this document states that the interests and affairs of the people, the good order and adornment of the kingdom depend on the vizier, and points to the need for a pious, learned, capable, experienced, and upright vizier, a man of good conduct and well-versed in the laws of the kingdom, who will truthfully report the condition of the subjects to the king. He is the king's helper, and sanction for his office is to be found in the appointment of Hārūn as vizier to Mūsā.[22] A diploma issued by the Khwārazmshāh Tekish (568–96/1172–99) for the office of vizier to his son Malikshāh, then governor of Jand, also declares that the good order of the kingdom is dependent upon the vizier and the "men of the pen," and that the sword requires for its effectiveness the support of the pen.[23]

Afḍal al-Dīn Abū Ḥāmid Aḥmad ibn Ḥāmid Kirmānī, who wrote in the late sixth/twelfth century in Kirmān, was also convinced of the importance of the vizierate. He recalls that "wise men have said that a king who gives his vizierate to an incompetent man places his kingdom in jeopardy."[24]

Those who wrote on the theory of rule frequently enjoin the ruler to regard the subjects as a trust from God. However, it is noteworthy that they seldom mention that the vizier had a duty to care for the subjects, except in terms of refraining from extortion, and of collecting taxes justly. The expositions of Najm al-Dīn Rāzī and Sirāj al-Dīn Urmawī are exceptions in this respect (see below). Behind this attitude toward the duties of the vizier lay the element of personal service in the vizierate. The vizier's duties are seen mainly in relation to the ruler, and his primary duty as the servant of the ruler was to provide his master with revenue to enable him to maintain internal order, and to prevent external aggression. A full treasury could only be ensured on a long-term basis by an orderly and just tax administration, and it was the vizier's duty to establish this.

However much writers may have emphasized the importance of the vizier, the crucial fact remains that his office originated in the personal service of the ruler. As Goitein points out, it was because this aspect dominated the vizierate that its functions were never clearly defined, but were expanded and restricted according to the inclinations and power of the ruler and the character of the vizier.[25] And it is here that the principle of concession, which runs through most governmental institutions in medieval Persia, comes in. By the fifth/eleventh century, the theory that the holder of governmental power had been singled out by God to wield power was growing. Niẓām al-Mulk expresses this view in the following words: "God most High chooses in every age someone from among the people, and adorns him with kingly virtues, and relegates to him the affairs of the world and the peace of His servants."[26] The power thus given by God was not something to which the recipient had any right, or which he could claim by right. "God," in the oft-quoted Quranic phrase, "gives the kingdom to whom He wills." He not only gave the kingdom, but He also took it away. The conferment of rule on the king was the exercise of God's will and pleasure, and so also it was the ruler's will and pleasure to distribute favors to others, and to appoint them to office. Just as divine power descended to the king, so the king's power descended to his officers, and from the vizier to his subordinates. An essential attribute of the vizier was, therefore, that he should be a good judge of character. Niẓām al-Mulk, according to Bundārī, had this gift. He states that Niẓām al-Mulk selected each man for the work for which he was best suited, and gave him office accordingly.[27] The subject had no right to any function, unless it was conceded to him. Appointment to office by the ruler was an effluence of his grace; and similarly the withdrawal of office was the exercise of the self-same powers by which the ruler had himself been appointed. The vizier was entirely dependent upon the good will of the ruler. He had no right to the vizierate, and no security; and there was no room for discussion or debate. It was, no doubt, at least partly because of this element of personal service and concession in the vizierate that it was regarded as an office of difficulty and danger—as indeed it was. This view is to be found in the work of Ibn al-Muqaffaʿ already in early ʿAbbasid times. Naṣīr al-Dīn Ṭūsī, quoting Ibn al-Muqaffaʿ, states, "No task is harder than the vizierate, because it is subject to much competition; those who envy the vizier are the friends of the ruler, his companions on his journeys, and partners in his revenues, and they continually covet the vizier's office and watch for opportunities to lay snares for him."[28]

Najm al-Dīn Rāzī, who fled from Hamadān before the Mongols in 618/1221, and was for a time in the service of Kay Qubād, the Saljuq of Rūm, discusses the ideal conduct of the vizier in a work entitled *Mirṣād al-ʿibād min al-mabdaʾ ilā al-maʿād*. He emphasizes the need to appoint to office persons worthy of such an appointment and asserts that all disturbances in religious and temporal affairs come from a contrary practice. He alleges that offices are not given to those who are worthy and able; neither the ruler nor the vizier looks carefully into the suitability of those whom they appoint. Those who are worthy of office, out of concern for their own honor and for the honor of religion, do not permit themselves to go to the court of kings in order to pay service to worthy or unworthy persons and to sing their own praises. "Kings and viziers," he continues, "seldom have the zeal or steadfastness to summon those who are worthy of a particular office and to give them office accordingly. Consequently, most religious and temporal offices fall into the hands of the unworthy and ignorant. Whatever in these matters does not follow its proper course is the fault of the viziers, the notables, the *ashrāf*, and the *nuwwāb* of the court because they do not investigate affairs, and do not summon people of learning and religion [to take office], and leave the learned to go to waste. Filled by corrupt desires, they give office to the unworthy."[29]

Whereas many writers on the vizierate considered wisdom to be in the past, and saw the duty of the present to be a recapitulation and restatement of the wisdom of the ancients, Najm al-Dīn, who wrote from the standpoint of a *Ṣūfī*, introduced certain novel features. He bases the sultan's need for a vizier on the division of labor. If the ruler occupies himself with affairs which properly belong to the vizierate, he will be held back from the tasks which pertain to kingship, and as a result the affairs of the kingdom and the subjects will fall into disorder. Like Niẓām al-Mulk, he considers that a good vizier gives stability and order to religious and temporal affairs, and to the affairs of the kingdom and the subjects. Through him the latter will always be at ease, and their desires fulfilled. Conversely, if the kingdom is without a vizier who commands respect and authority, the kingdom will not have power or adornment (*shukūh wa zīnat*). If the vizier is worthy, the king must show him respect and honor, and consider his authority to extend throughout the kingdom, because the respect and honor shown to the vizier "brings strength to the arm of the greatness and dominion of the king." Continuing, Najm al-Dīn states: "As God said when He appointed Hārūn vizier to Mūsā, 'We will certainly strengthen thy arm through thy brother, and invest you both with authority.' "[30] Thus, Najm al-Dīn implies (in clearer words than those used by al-Ghazālī) that the vizier derives his power not from the ruler, but directly from God. Perhaps because of this, Najm al-Dīn has rather more to say on the vizier's duty toward the subjects than do those writers who see the vizier's power as deriving from the ruler, whose servant he is.

Najm al-Dīn likens the ruler to the body, and the vizier to the intelligence which guides the body in its actions.[31] Therefore, no ruler could dispense with a good vizier; Najm al-Dīn insists on the need for full consultation between the ruler and the vizier. The latter he sees as a paragon of virtue. He must be learned, just, endowed with common sense, capable, honest, well-informed, experienced, zealous, generous, possessing good judgment, good-tempered, and pious; he must hold the right religion, be compassionate and competent, and know what is right and what is advisable.[32]

Using a rather unusual simile, Najm al-Dīn likens the kingdom to a tent, and the central tent-pole to the vizier. The various ropes, large and small, are the *umarā'*, the *ashrāf*, and the notables. The ropes around the skirt of the tent are the *nuwwāb* and the "men of the pen." The ropes which go into the loops of the tent are the soldiers (*ajnād*) and the *umarā'* of the army, while the tent pegs are justice, equity, and generosity (*muruwwat*). As the tent is made steady only by tent pegs, so the kingdom is given stability and durability only by justice, equity, and generosity. As the central tent-pole needs to be upright, tall, steady, and able to bear weight, so the vizier needs four similar qualities. First, he requires uprightness. This will result in his being true and sincere toward the ruler, so that, while observing due respect and civility toward him, he will tell him, in the most delicate way when opportunity offers, what the exigency of the moment and good judgment demand. Uprightness will also result in his showing compassion and care toward the *umarā'*, the notables, the subjects in general, and the soldiers; he will make available the equipment they need, see that their followers are well provided for, and not place heavy burdens upon them. Such a satisfactory state of affairs, however, can only be brought about if the vizier exerts himself in the agricultural development of the country, and is not greedy in amassing taxes. He must not exercise tyranny or violence (*bid'a*), because this will result in the ruin of the subjects; nor must he decrease the wages (*jāma wa waẓīfa*) of the soldiers, because this will result in their being without equipment. The ruin of the subjects will bring ruin to the country, and the ruin of the country will result in commotion (*tazalzul*), the expectation of calamity, sedition, and great confusion. The vizier must therefore be sincerely concerned for the prosperity of the country and of the subjects, the *ashrāf*, the notables, the soldiers and their followers. Najm al-Dīn thus accepts the traditional view that revenue derives principally from agriculture, that it is to be expended primarily on the army, and that a failure to provide for the needs of the army will result in sedition.

Secondly, just as the tent-pole needs height, so the vizier requires high-mindedness, so that he will not allow himself to be deceived by the world, and will not expect presents or bribes from the subjects. Thirdly, like the tent-pole, he needs steadiness, to make him steadfast in the affairs of religion, doing whatever he does to please God, and not the people, while fearing no one. Steadfastness in the service of the king results in loyalty, while steadfastness toward the notables and *ashrāf* of the kingdom, and toward the subjects and the entourage of the king (*khadam wa ḥasham*) means that when he gives office to an emir or tax-collector, or anyone else, he will not remove him on account of idle accusations, or listen to the vain words of those who had ulterior motives. However, once the commission of an act of corruption has been confirmed, the vizier must not show any negligence in punishing its perpetrator. He must show compassion toward the subjects, and prevent injustice and oppression against them. It is incumbent upon a wise vizier to exercise care in the appointment of officials, and to ensure that those appointed be worthy of their appointments.

Fourthly, like the tent-pole which has to carry a load, the vizier must be able to bear the burden of loyalty involved in the performance of duties imposed by the *sharī'a*, and, in relation to the king, he must show patience and endurance in whatever the king does or says in anger toward him or anyone else, and be ready to pour oil on troubled waters; and if enmity arises between the king and other rulers, he must use his good judgment to put the matter right, and not involve the king in danger through war. However, if the matter cannot be settled by agreement, and war comes, he must encourage the king; and if there should be war with infidels, he must embolden the king and make him eager to undertake such war, and help him. It is the vizier's burden to place before the king whatever the interests of religion, the kingdom, and the subjects demand; and it is his burden to carry the weight of the subjects and the kingdom on the shoulders of uprightness, highmindedness, steadfastness, and endurance, and to look upon the subjects with mercy. Small failures on their part were to be forgiven, unless they were of such a nature as to lead to disturbances in the kingdom. The vizier must not allow himself to be apathetic, because the interests of the kingdom and the subjects are destroyed by apathy. He must shoulder his burden, and inform himself of the conditions of the kingdom and the subjects, of friends and foes, and of other kings and countries, so that he may be forewarned and prevent the occurrence of disorder of any kind.[33]

Sirāj al-Dīn Urmawī (594–682/1198–1283), who also spent much of his life in Qonya, has a somewhat similar view to Najm al-Dīn. He describes the vizier as the one who bears the burdens of the subjects' afflictions, and states that the vizier is in charge of affairs in order to fulfill the needs of the people. The word vizier means "the one who bears." In support of this, he quotes the Quranic phrase "no bearer of burdens can bear the burden of another," and interprets this to mean that the true vizier is the one who alleviates the afflictions of the subjects, and not the one who imposes his own afflictions on the subjects. In early times, he states, the vizier was called the *'amīd*, i.e., the one whose intention was to provide what was needed. And so he concludes that anyone who fails to provide the wants of the subjects is not a true vizier or *'amīd*. This is a rather different perspective from the traditional view of the vizier as primarily the servant of the ruler.[34]

The anonymous *Tārīkh-i shāhī-i Qara-khitā'iyān*, written in Kirmān in the late seventh/thirteenth century, belongs in time to the Ilkhanate, but nonetheless belongs in character to the preceding period, and is remarkable for its familiarity with the works of earlier writers. The author of this work also bases the ruler's need for a wise and competent vizier on the division of labor. He states that, however wise and perceptive the ruler may be, he requires a vizier to give him advice. If the kingdom lacks a capable vizier, the king will have no support, and no one on whom he can rely. Serious kings are concerned with the sword, with conquest, and with the subjugation of enemies; but frivolous kings give themselves up to hunting, amusement (*tamāshā*), and pleasure. Consequently, a wise vizier is needed to preserve the interests of the kingdom, to order its affairs, to exact the claims of the *dīwān*, to collect royal funds, to keep the accounts of the kingdom, and to provide the food of the soldiers. To bring home his point, he quotes the well-known story of Malikshāh, who, one day toward the end of his reign, sent a message to Niẓām al-Mulk asking him whether he was his partner (*sharīk*) in the throne, since he did whatever he wished without consulting him, and gave provinces and *iqṭā'*s to his sons, and warning him that he might order the turban of the vizierate to be removed from his head. Niẓām al-Mulk replied, "He who gave thee the crown placed on my head the turban, and these two are inseparably connected and bound together."[35] Fine words, if they are not apocryphal. But the reality was otherwise. The vizier may have been the center of the administration, but whatever his strength, he remained subject to disgrace and dismissal at the whim of the ruler.

The period of Mongol ascendancy brought major—if temporary—changes in the position of the vizier. Whereas the acceptance of the concept of the sultan as the Shadow of God upon earth, and the anchoring of his power in God had enabled the Saljuq sultan (and his ministers) to break the fetters which bound him as a tribal leader to his people, under the Mongols the relationship of the ruling family with their tribal followers remained crucial to their rule. Sovereignty was held to belong by hereditary right to the Chingizid family. The authority of the Īlkhān was that of a military commander, and the support which he received from his followers was in proportion to his ability to allocate booty and pasture to them. There was no room here for a bureaucracy, with a vizier at its head to whom oversight of the affairs of the empire could be delegated. The vizier, sometimes known as the *ṣāḥib dīwān*, no longer supervised the whole range of the administration. Acting alongside Mongol officials, his duties were confined to the field of finance, and in particular, to taxation. In the early years of Mongol rule, it was apparently the usual practice to place the local "civil" official under the actual or nominal supervision of a Mongol emir. Sa'd al-Dawla, who was appointed *mushrif* of the *dīwān* of 'Irāq in 688/1289 in the reign of Arghun (683–90/1284–91), had beside him the emir Arduqiya as governor, and later, when he became *ṣāḥib dīwān* in Tabrīz, Arduqiya continued beside him.[36] Apart from this contraction in the range of the vizier's authority, joint viziers were appointed from time to time, a practice which fostered intrigue and faction. The vizierate in the early period of Mongol rule was thus a very different system from the vizierate of earlier times. The Mongols were the ruling people, with their own customs and laws, and following a religion different from that of the subject population. They despised towndwellers and agriculturalists, and believed that they should be exploited as vigorously as possible for the benefit of the Mongols. In such a situation, a vizier charged with the well-being of the countryside clearly had no place; and the office tended accordingly to be conferred on those who would undertake to extort the largest possible amount from the taxpayers in the shortest possible time. The viziers (and others who held high office) were often subjected to the most humiliating treatment by their masters, including the infliction of the bastinado. Few held office for long, though there are exceptions.[37] Execution was frequently the consequence of dismissal, not only of the vizier but often of his subordinates also, while his family and followers were mulcted of their fortunes. Ḥamd Allāh Mustawfī states that Tāj al-Dīn 'Alī Shāh was the only vizier during the Mongol period to die a natural death.[38] None of this, however, is reflected in writings on the theory of the vizierate. The great viziers of the Ilkhanate, Shams al-Dīn Juwaynī and Rashīd al-Dīn Faḍl Allāh, have left no account of their conception of the vizierate, even though the latter wrote copiously on a variety of subjects. Those who wrote on the theory of government felt, perhaps even more strongly than before, that it was their duty to hand down the wisdom of the past.

By the time Waṣṣāf came to write, the vizier had in some measure regained his former position as the central figure in the administration, though joint viziers were still appointed. Rashīd al-Dīn, vizier to Ghazan and then joint vizier to Öljeitü, exercised great influence. Waṣṣāf, who enjoyed the patronage of Rashīd al-Dīn, addressed his mirror, entitled *Akhlāq al-salṭana*, to Öljeitü. While admitting that the king is perfect, just and capable of conducting the affairs of the kingdom himself, Waṣṣāf, like Najm al-Dīn and the author of the *Tārīkh-i shāhī*, considers it improper for the king personally to undertake the affairs of the vizierate: if he did so, he would be a vizier and not a king. In Waṣṣāf's view, the affairs of the kingdom cannot be properly conducted without capable and competent viziers, and the subjects would not be blessed without such. The vizier is the hands, heart, eyes, tongue, and ears of the king, who must rely upon him in all the affairs of the kingdom, the finances, the army, and in secret matters, just as he relies upon the members of his own body. The king must not permit intrigues against the vizier from any quarter.[39] This warning was especially necessary, since intrigue in public life was particularly rife in the Ilkhanate. To revile the vizier was to revile the king. No office after the sultanate was more exalted than the vizierate, and no work more difficult and exacting. Innumerable persons were envious of him, and sought to supplant him in the favor of the king.[40]

Among the qualities which Waṣṣāf demands of the vizier, in keeping with the traditional requirements of his office, are a knowledge of finance and agriculture.[41] There had been, at the end of the reign of Ghazan, Öljeitü's predecessor, an attempt to revive agriculture, but in Fārs, Waṣṣāf's home province, Ghazan's agricultural reforms had had little permanent effect, and when Waṣṣāf was writing, agriculture in the province was in a state of near-disaster because of maladministration and extortion.[42] Like Najm al-Dīn, Waṣṣāf was under no illusions as to the qualities of those who aspired to office, and he remarks that wise and intelligent viziers were not found every day.[43]

The theoretical reassertion of the traditional functions of the vizierate, including the duty of the vizier to make the country prosperous and populous, is also to be seen in three undated documents for the vizierate in the *Dastūr al-kātib fī ta'yīn al-marātib* of Muḥammad ibn Hindūshāh ibn Sanjar Nakhchīwānī. The author was employed in the *dīwān al-inshā'* in the reign of Abū Sa'īd, the last Īlkhān, and was closely associated with Ghiyāth al-Dīn Muḥammad ibn Rashīd al-Dīn. He did not, however, write the *Dastūr al-kātib* until after the collapse of the Ilkhanate, and it is dedicated to Shaykh Uways ibn Shaykh Ḥasan-i Buzurg. In these documents, the vizier is given full powers over the administration generally, including the payment of the military. His paramount duty is to make the country prosperous and populous. Taxes are to be levied according to the ability of the taxpayer to pay. He is also entrusted with the supervision of the religious classes and the appointment of religious officials. He is to appoint over the provinces and districts of the empire honest, reliable men, well-versed in financial transactions,[44] capable, just, and wealthy persons, and to take from them undertakings that they would levy the taxes as laid down, and bonds that they would not commit extortion.[45] The injunction to appoint wealthy officials is perhaps an echo of the warning given by Kay Kā'ūs ibn Iskandar to his son, some two centuries earlier, that in the event of his becoming vizier he should not grant office to impecunious or impoverished men, because they would first provide for themselves before busying themselves with the affairs of the vizierate.[46] Ideally, Muḥammad ibn Hindūshāh regards the vizier as the link between the ruler and his people, and in this he follows his father, the author of the *Tajārib al-salaf*, who states that the vizier is an intermediary (*wāsiṭa*) between the king and his subjects, and must therefore be temperamentally at ease with both.[47] The aspect of personal service is, however, not entirely absent from the documents in the *Dastūr al-kātib*. In one of them, the vizier is enjoined to give his attention to what is necessary for the royal court (*wājibāt-i khāṣṣa-i ḥaḍrat-i mā*), because what is required for the support of the army (*gerekyaraq*) and other affairs depends thereon; and the vizier must give precedence to these things over other matters.[48]

As it began, so it continued. During some three centuries, from the coming of the Saljuqs to the end of the Ilkhanate, there was very little change in the theory of the vizierate, and this in spite of the changes in practice which resulted from the Mongol invasions. Writers looked back to the golden age of the past, and saw the "good" vizier as the pivot of the administration. No new theory was produced. Different writers merely expounded their view of what the vizier was and what he should do—how he should strike a balance and achieve a reconciliation between the interests of the ruler and the taxpayers, and between the rival groups of society, the military, the *'ulāmā'*, the merchants and the rest. Behind their expositions lay the fact that the vizier was the servant of the ruler, and that power was conceded to him. There was no law behind him, and he therefore had no security. Hence, in practice, a balance was seldom achieved. Nevertheless, the great viziers of the period, Niẓām al-Mulk, Shams al-Dīn Juwaynī, and Rashīd al-Dīn Faḍl Allāh, were remembered as "reconcilers," as men who cared for the interests not only of the ruler, but also of the subjects. So far as this was true, the theory of the vizierate, as set forth in Mirrors for Princes and other literary works, was not at all times wholly at variance with practice.

NOTES

1. Fasīḥī, *Mujmal-i fasīḥī*, ed. Maḥmūd Farrukh (Mashhad, 1339–41/1958–61), II, 151–55.

2. *Naṣīḥat al-mulūk*, ed. Jalāl Humā'ī (Tehran, 1351/1972–73), pp. 183–84.

3. See Wael B. Hallaq, "The Political Thought of Juwaynī," *The Muslim World*, LXXIV (1984), pp. 26–41.

4. Ibn Khallikān, *Wafāyāt al-a'yān*, trans. G. de Slane (Paris and London, 1842–71), I, 413.

5. "Niẓām al-Mulk," *EI*[1] s.v.

6. *Siyāsat-nāma*, ed. Ch. Schefer (Paris, 1891), p. 18.

7. Ibid., pp. 18–19.

8. Ibid., p. 150.

9. Ibid., p. 151. It may be that Niẓām al-Mulk is using the term *mu'āmalat-dān* in a technical sense. *Mu'āmalat* is also a tax term, synonymous with *muqāsama*, the assessment of taxation by way of a proportion of the crop, and it may be that it is knowledge of this that Niẓām al-Mulk demands.

10. *Islamic Culture*, XVI (1942), pp. 255–62, 380–92, Appendix; *Journal of the American Oriental Society* (1961), pp. 425–26; also in S. D. Goitein, *Studies in Islamic History and Institutions* (Leiden, 1968), pp. 168–96.

11. Damascus 1959–60.

12. *Naṣīḥat al-mulūk*, p. 176.

13. Ibid., p. 175.

14. Ibid., p. 183.

15. Ibid., p. 176. Translation as in F. R. C. Bagley, *Ghazālī's Book of Counsel for Kings* (London, 1964), p. 107.

16. Ibid.

17. Goitein, op. cit., p. 180.

18. *Naṣīḥat al-mulūk*, p. 177.

19. Ibid., p. 180.

20. Ibid., p. 183.

21. Ibid., p. 184.

22. 'Abbās Iqbāl, *Wizārat dar 'ahd-i salāṭīn-i buzurg-i saljuqī* (Tehran, 1338/1957–58), pp. 25–26.

23. Bahā' al-Dīn Baghdādī, *al-Tawassul ilā al-tarassul*, ed. Aḥmad Bahmanyār (Tehran, 1315/1936–37), p. 29.

24. *'Iqd al-'ulā*, ed. 'Alī Muḥammad 'Āmirī Nā'īnī (Tehran, 1311/1932–33), p. 81.

25. Goitein, op. cit., p. 192.

26. *Siyāsat-nāma*, p. 5. See further A. K. S. Lambton, "The Dilemma of Government in Islamic Persia: The *Siyāsat-nāma* of Niẓām al-Mulk," *Iran*, XXII (1984), pp. 55–66.

27. *Dawlat al-saljuq* (Cairo, 1318/1900–1), p. 54.

28. *The Nasirean Ethics*, trans. G. M. Wickens (London, 1964), pp. 240–41 (slightly adapted). Muḥammad ibn Maḥmūd Āmulī repeats this statement and also attributes it to Ibn al-Muqaffa' (*Nafā'is al-funūn*, vol. I, ed. Abu'l-Ḥasan Shi'rānī [Tehran, 1377/1958], vol. II, ed. Ibrāhīm Miyānjī [Tehran, 1379/1959], p. 440).

29. Ed. Ḥusayn al-Ḥusaynī al-Ni'matallāhī (Tehran, 1312/1933), p. 271. Najm al-Dīn finished the *Mirṣād al-'ibād* in Sīvās in 620/1223–24.

30. Qur'ān, XXVIII, 35; *Mirṣād al-'ibād*, p. 257.

31. *Mirṣād al-'ibād*, p. 257.

32. Ibid., pp. 256–57.

33. Ibid., pp. 266–73.

34. *Laṭā'if al-ḥikma*, ed. Ghulām Ḥusayn Yūsufī (Tehran, 1351/1972), p. 274.

35. Ed. Muḥammad Ibrāhīm Bāstānī Pārīzī (Tehran, Shāhinshāhī 2535/ 1976–77), 76–77. See also E. G. Browne, *Literary History of Persia*, II, 185. According to Ibn al-Athīr, Qodun, the *shaḥna* of Marv, toward the end of Malikshāh's reign, complained to him that he had been seized by Shams al-Dīn 'Uthmān, Niẓām al-Mulk's son, then *ra'īs* of Marv. So Malikshāh wrote to Niẓām al-Mulk, reproaching him in the following words: "These your children have each gained mastery over a large district, and govern a large province. But this does not satisfy them, and they exceed what is politic and demand to do this and that" (*al-Kāmil fī'l-ta'rīkh*, ed. C. J. Tornberg (Leiden, 1851–76), X, 138–39. Cf. also Bundārī, op. cit., pp. 59–60, and Iqbāl, *Wizārat*, p. 186).

36. When Sa'd al-Dawla fell at the end of Arghun's reign in 690/1291 and was executed, Arduqiya shared his fate.

37. See B. Spuler, *Die Mongolen in Iran*, 4th ed. (Berlin, 1985), pp. 238–40, for a list of those who held the office of vizier in the Ilkanate.

38. *Tārīkh-i guzīda*, ed. 'Abd al-Ḥusayn Nawā'ī (Tehran, 1336–39/1958–61), p. 616.

39. *Tajziyat al-amṣār wa tazjiyat al-a'ṣār* (also known as *Tārīkh-i Waṣṣāf*), ed. M. M. Iṣfahānī, lith. (Bombay, 1269/1852–53), p. 492.

40. Ibid.

41. Ibid.

42. See further A. K. S. Lambton, "Mongol Fiscal Administration in Persia," *Studia Islamica*, fasc. LXV, 117 ff.

43. *Tārīkh-i Waṣṣāf*, p. 493.

44. See above, n. 9.

45. Ed. A. A. Alizade (Moscow, 1964–76), II, 73–91.

46. *Qābūs-nāma*, ed. Ghulām Ḥusayn Yūsufī (Tehran, 1345/1967), p. 220.

47. Persian text in facsimile with introduction and notes by Amīr Sayyid Ḥasan Rawḍātī (Iṣfahān, 1361/1982–83), p. 85.

48. *Dastūr al-kātib*, II, 88; cf. II, 83–84.

14
La Corporation à l'époque classique de l'Islam

George Makdisi

La Thèse de Louis Massignon

LOUIS MASSIGNON, en 1920, pendant ses premières années au Collège de France, publia un article sur les corporations intitulé, «Les Corps de métiers et la cité islamique.»[1] Cet article avait été le sujet d'une leçon faite au collège le 4 février 1920, dans son cours de sociologie et sociographie musulmanes. Le sujet traité suscita et continue à susciter de longues discussions. La thèse de Massignon, telle qu'on peut la dégager à partir de cet article ainsi que d'autres qui lui succédèrent,[2] et qui fut l'objet de controverse, est que la corporation existait en Islam classique et qu'elle influa sur la corporation en Occident au Moyen-Âge. Certains savants acceptèrent cette thèse; d'autres la contestèrent; et l'une et l'autre des deux thèses sont soutenues par des savants de grande réputation.[3]

La controverse porte sur une question: à savoir si, à l'époque classique de l'Islam, il existait des corporations, ce qu'on appela en anglais *guilds*. On en admet généralement l'existence à partir de la fin du Moyen-Âge et à l'époque moderne; mais on la nie en ce qui concerne l'ère de l'Islam classique. A cet égard, on fait remarquer que, si la corporation existait déjà à cette époque-là, les documents susceptibles d'en prouver l'existence ne sont pas encore mis à jour.

Dans les pages qui suivent, j'espère pouvoir montrer que la corporation existait à l'époque classique de l'Islam. Dans son article de 1920, Massignon voyait son existence dans ce qu'il appelait le centre universitaire, qu'il considérait comme un corps de métier parmi d'autres. Par «centre universitaire» il faut comprendre l'institution musulmane d'enseignement appelée *madrasa*. C'est bien ce centre qui nous intéresse ici, à notre tour, puisqu'il fait partie de l'association qui fut, à mon sens, une corporation musulmane à l'époque classique. Par le mot «corporation,» j'entends une association de personnes professionnelles, groupées dans le but de réglementer leur profession et de défendre leurs intérêts. Une telle corporation existait dans le *madhhab* juridique, terme arabe diversement traduit comme «rite,» «secte,» ou «école juridique.»

Objections à cette thèse

Quelles sont les objections essentielles soulevées contre la thèse de Louis Massignon? C'est dans l'article sobre et équilibré de Claude Cahen[4] qu'on trouve les précisions nécessaires. Il s'agit de trois points essentiels. L'un de ces points concerne l'époque qu'il s'agit d'étudier, et les deux autres se rapportent à la forme de l'organisation: à sa forme professionnelle et à sa forme juridique.

L'époque qu'il importe d'étudier, ce n'est pas, dit M. Cahen, «la fin de ce que nous appelons le Moyen-Age, et les temps modernes,» mais plutôt l'époque qui précède. Car on admet qu'«il existe dans la plupart des pays musulmans une certaine organisation professionnelle corporative . . . la tendance n'en est pas contestable.» Pour ce qui est de la forme professionnelle, «la question est de savoir si . . . c'est la profession qui définit et constitue les cadres de certaines d'entre elles, ou si elles son bâties sur d'autres bases.» Quant à la forme juridique, la question est de savoir «s'il s'agit d'organisation corporative, c'est-à-dire, consistant en organisations spontanées encadrant plus ou moins largement la vie de leurs adhérents, ou si nous avons affaire à des organismes émanant de l'appareil administratif étatique.»

M. Cahen achève ses précisions de la façon suivante:

> Je résume donc: existe-t-il dans les âges dits classiques de l'Islam des associations privées à base et à rôle professionnels, ou réciproquement, l'organisation professionnelle est-elle à base d'associations privées spontanées?

Madhhab, masjid et madrasa

Pour aborder ces points précis, je voudrais prendre pour exemple les *madhhab*s juridiques et leur organisation institutionnelle de l'enseignement du droit à partir du troisième siècle de l'Islam, le neuvième de notre ère, à Baghdad, centre culturel du monde musulman à l'époque. Cet enseignement fit ses premiers pas vers l'organisation professionnelle après l'inquisition dite *al-miḥna*, vers le milieu du neuvième siècle. C'est aux dixième et onzième siècles que l'on peut discerner cette organisation de l'enseignement du droit; d'abord, dans le collège-mosquée appelé *masjid*, avec, à côté, le *khān*, qui servait de logement pour les étudiants de droit venant d'autres villes; et ensuite, dans le collège appelé *madrasa*. Ce collège réunit le lieu de l'enseignement (*masjid*) et le lieu du logement (*khān*) dans une seule fondation. Ces institutions représentaient ce que Massignon appelle «le centre universitaire» dans son article de 1920; et la *madrasa* revient dans les articles de deux de ses critiques, S. M. Stern et Claude Cahen.

La Madrasa d'après Stern

Lorsque Stern en vient à parler des institutions d'enseignement supérieur, il cite les écoles de l'Occident latin au douzième siècle qui furent constituées en corporations ou *universitates*, ce qui donna les universités, avec leurs officiers élus, tout comme auparavant dans les cathédrales, les chapitres furent organisés dans le but d'élire leurs évêques. Stern voyait un contraste frappant entre la civilisation occidentale et celle de l'Islam; et pout l'illustrer il cite la *madrasa* comme exemple.

> A partir du XIe siècle, [dit-il], les écoles étaient florissantes et la nouvelle institution de la *madrasa* conquit une province après l'autre. L'innovation dans la *madrasa* fut précisément qu'elle substitua à l'enseignement individuel et privé des maîtres un collège organisé avec des chaires à fondation (*endowed chairs*). S'il y avait dans la civilisation islamique une tendance aux corporations ç'aurait été le bon moment pour quelque chose comme l'université contemporaine de l'occident latin. Pourtant, aucun développement de ce genre n'eut lieu, et la *madrasa* demeura une institution qui est typiquement apparentée aux écoles de l'Antiquité et de Byzance dotées par l'Etat.[5]

Dans ce passage il y a certains points à rectifier: (1) l'enseignement dans la *madrasa* du dixième-onzième siècles resta ce qu'il était auparavant dans le collège-mosquée, c'est-à-dire, individuel et privé. Dans la *madrasa*, comme dans le *masjid*, il n'y avait qu'un seul professeur de droit (*mudarris*), un seul «maître,» les autres enseignants, de moindre niveau, s'occupaient de la grammaire, du Qur'ān, du *ḥadīth*, c'est-à-dire des sciences auxiliaires, accessoires à l'étude du droit, l'objet principal de ces collèges de droit. Un professeur de droit pouvait plus tard être nommé à plus d'une seule chaire, d'une seule *madrasa*; il enseignait dans une de ces *madrasa*s et embauchait des députés ou substituts (*nā'ib mudarris*) pour enseigner à sa place dans les autres *madrasas* où il avait ses chaires. Encore plus tard, la chaire professorale d'une *madrasa* se partageait entre deux, trois ou quatre titulaires, chacun recevant la moitié, le tiers ou le quart des revenus destinés à cette chaire qui resta unique, bien que divisée. Pour l'étudiant de la *madrasa*, il pouvait avoir, au cours de ses études, plusieurs professeurs de plusieurs *madhhabs* (ḥanafite, mālikite, etc.) mais son appartenance à l'un de ces *madhhabs* était déterminée par celle de son professeur de droit (*fiqh*). (2) Ces collèges-mosquées, dits *masjid*, étaient à fondation (en anglais: *endowed*), tout comme les *madrasas* qui s'y joignirent vers la fin du dixième siècle. (3) La *madrasa* n'était pas fondée par l'État, mais par des particuliers; et quand le fondateur était un homme d'Etat, il accomplissait son acte de fondation en tant que particulier musulman.[6]

Un peu plus loin dans son article, Stern pousuit son argumentation:

> Si on se réfère au meilleur manuel que nous ayons sur le droit musulman [celui de D. Santillana] pour découvrir ce qu'il a à dire sur le statut légal des corporations, on trouvera en effet un chapitre sur les personnes morales, à savoir la succession d'un défunt, la fondation pieuse (*waqf*), le trésor public—mais cela représentait toutes les personnes morales dont l'Islam eût connaissance. En effet, après avoir énuméré les personnes morales reconnues par le droit romain . . . [Santillana dit] expressément: «Les juristes musulmans ne connaissent . . . ni la personne morale des municipalités, ni celle des collectivités de personnes telles que les corporations (*guilds*).»[7]

Ici, j'irai même plus loin que Stern en affirmant que l'Islam ne reconnaissait pas du tout de personnalité morale à une quelconque de ces institutions: y compris le *waqf*, la succession et le trésor public. A vrai dire, l'Islam des temps classiques n'avait pas conscience de la personnalité morale; il ne la reconnaissait que pour la personne physique.[8] J'imagine que cette déclaration aurait plu à Stern, qui n'admet qu'à contre-coeur ce qu'il cite comme les trois personnes morales de l'Islam, puisque cette affirmation semble apporter de l'eau à son moulin; mais il n'en est rien, car les corporations au début de leur existence en Europe n'étaient pas douées de personnalité morale.

De plus, Stern suivait l'opinion générale de son époque selon laquelle la *madrasa* se présentait comme une institution étatique. La *madrasa* du dixième-onzième siècle fut sans doute une innovation; mais ce qu'elle apporta de nouveau ne changea en rien son statut tout à fait privé. Elle était aussi privée que le collège-mosquée qui l'avait devancée, où l'enseignement du droit était à l'honneur, où le professeur titulaire de droit siégeait sur une chaire à fondation, constituée par un particulier. L'innovation de la *madrasa* consistait en ce que le fondateur, un particulier musulman, pouvait contrôler le destin de sa *madrasa* en se nommant l'administrateur de la fondation, aussi bien que son professeur titulaire et en se payant un salaire pour chacun de ces deux postes; ceci n'était pas possible pour le fondateur d'un collège-mosquée dont le statut était assimilé à l'esclave affranchi, d'où la désignation du *waqf* comme étant un *waqf taḥīr*,[9] *waqf* d'émancipation; c'est-à-dire que le fondateur d'un collège-mosquée (*masjid*) ne pouvait se nommer lui-même ni administrateur ni professeur. L'État en tant que tel, n'a jamais fondé une *madrasa*. D'après la loi du *waqf*, ne peut être fondateur qu'un particulier musulman. Ce fait est illustré par la déclaration du prince zankide Nūr al-Dīn, gouverneur de Damas. Celui-ci se faisait gloire d'avoir utilisé son propre argent pour fonder ses *madrasa*s et autres institutions d'enseignement à base de *waqf*. Il agissait comme tout autre particulier musulman. Il ne touchait pas au trésor public,[10] chose que d'autres hommes d'État se permettaient de faire, en détournant ces fonds pour constituer des fondations pieuses à leur avantage. Sans bourse délier, elles leur valaient un grand gain de prestige pour leur régime.

Waqf et madrasa d'après Cahen

Dans son article, M. Cahen traite de la fondation-*waqf*, et ce qu'il en dit là, à mon sens, doit être nuancé. Je le cite:

> Le fiqh (droit musulman) interdit toute fondation *waqf* au bénéfice d'une catégorie professionnelle, celle-ci ne devant être constituée qu'au bénéfice des pauvres de cette catégorie (cela même se fait rarement); par le biais des fondations au bénéfice d'une mosquée, d'une *madrasa*, d'un hôpital, etc., on peut constituer un *waqf* au bénéfice de tous ceux qui y sont inclus professionnellement, mais non pas de la profession plus largement.[11]

En réalité, les *madrasa*s, et les collèges-mosquées de l'époque précédente, étaient fondés au bénéfice d'une catégorie professionnelle, à savoir les jurisconsultes, *fuqahā'*. De plus, on constituait le *waqf* d'une de ces institutions d'enseignement pour la profession du droit au bénéfice d'une ou de plusieurs écoles ou *madhhab*s parmi les quatre écoles sunnites de droit musulman, réservé à leurs membres, non pas seulement aux pauvres parmi eux, mais bien à «la profession plus largement.»

Plus loin dans son article, M. Cahen affirme que non seulement le chef des médecins est nommé par le gouvernement et contrôlé par le *muḥtasib*, mais aussi «les instituteurs» (c'est-à-dire, les professeurs de *madrasas*).

Ici aussi il y a une modification à apporter. En ce qui concerne les *madrasas*, ce n'était pas le gouvernement qui nommait les professeurs, de quelque rang qu'ils fussent; et le *muḥtasib* ne les contrôlait pas. Seul le fondateur avait le droit en premier de choisir le professeur titulaire et il pouvait, s'il voulait, assigner le professorat aux descendants de ce professeur jusqu'à la fin de sa lignée, et même déterminer le mode de nomination par la suite. Le *qāḍī* n'était impliqué qu'exceptionnellement: lorsque le fondateur avait négligé de nommer l'administrateur de la fondation, selon le principe séculaire du *waqf*; car la fondation ne doit pas échouer faute d'un administrateur. Comme autre exemple, on peut citer le cas de Abū Muḥammad Di'lij ibn Aḥmad ibn Di'lij al-Sijistānī al-Baghdādī (m. 351/962). C'était un marchand, traditionniste et jurisconsulte,[12] l'un des hommes le plus riches de son époque et réputé pour sa philanthropie. Il constitua des *waqf*s au bénéfice de deux professions en tant que telles: (1) au bénéfice de la profession du droit shāfi'ite, en fondant un *khān* destiné au logement des étudiants de ce droit et un collége-mosquée destiné aux professeurs et étudiants de cette même école; et (2) au bénéfice de la profession de la science du *ḥadīth* à Baghdad, à la Mecque et dans la province de Sijistān (*lahū . . . wuqūfun 'ālā ahl al-ḥadīth fī Baghdād wa-Makka wa-Sijistān*).[13] C'est-à-dire que ne bénéficiaient de ces *waqf*s que ceux qui s'adonnaient à la science du *ḥadīth*, à l'exclusion de toute autre science. D'ailleurs il n'y a rien de surprenant à cela, car les *madrasas*, dès leur apparition, étaient destinées aux seuls jurisconsultes et même comme nous venons de le dire, aux jurisconsultes d'une seule école juridique, selon le choix du fondateur. La loi de *waqf* confère au fondateur une liberté complète à cet égard.[14] Et ce furent les jurisconsultes qui façonnèrent cette loi.

En parlant de corporations dans son article, M. Cahen dit que personne ne conteste que le monde musulman, dès l'époque envisagée, c'est-à-dire vers le neuvième ou dixième siècles, a connu quelque forme d'organisation professionnelle. «La question est de savoir jusqu'à quel point, et surtout s'il s'agit d'*organisation corporative* . . . ou si nous avons affaire à des *organismes émanant de l'appareil administratif étatique*,»[15] ou encore «s'il existait dans les âges dits classiques de l'Islam des *associations privées à base et à rôle professionnels*.»[16] Il s'agit donc de déterminer le caractère de l'organisation professionnelle en Islam classique: était-elle une émanation de l'appareil administratif étatique ou bien une organisation corporative, privée et indépendante de l'État?

Les Madhhabs juridiques

Les *madhhabs* juridiques, représentant les quatre écoles de droit de l'Islam sunnite, étaient, dès leurs débuts, des associations spontanées, de caractère foncièrement privé, échappant à l'appareil administratif de l'État. En plus, leurs «ateliers,» les collèges, c'est-à-dire les *masjid*s et les *madrasa*s, étaient privés aussi, à base de *waqf*.

À mon sens, ce qui distingue les associations professionnelles musulmanes de celles de l'Occident chrétien au Moyen-Âge c'est ce que leur droit permettait comme forme de perpétuité juridique. Pour l'Islam il n'y avait que le *waqf* comme forme juridique de perpétuité, alors que pour l'Occident chrétien il y en avait deux: (1) ce qui correspondait au *waqf*, par exemple: la *fondation* en France et le *charitable trust* en Angleterre; et (2) la corporation à base de personnalité morale. Le *waqf*, comme la *fondation* ou le *charitable trust*, permettait la jouissance d'un bien à perpétuité, tout comme la corporation ou ce qu'on appelle en France «société anonyme» douée de personnalité morale. Une association basée juridiquement sur la corporation-personne morale est caractérisée par la souplesse d'organisation administrative, par l'adaptabilité; au contraire, quand elle se base sur le *waqf* ou le *trust* pur et simple, l'association est figée, stagnante, sans changement d'organisation possible. La corporation-personne morale est douée d'un principe de gouvernement qui lui est particulier, lui permettant de modifier les règles qui la régissent pour être toujours de son temps, ce que la loi régissant le *waqf-trust* ne permettait pas, car il fallait régir le *waqf* selon l'acte du fondateur. Celui-ci, une fois l'acte signé, ne pouvait plus le modifier en quoi que ce fût. C'est pour cela que Merton, le fondateur de Merton College à Oxford, changea le statut juridique de son *College* en 1274, jusqu'alors un simple *trust* ou fondation charitable, en le doublant d'une corporation, dotant ainsi son *College* de deux formes juridiques de perpétuité: une fondation charitable coiffée d'une corporation-personne morale. Avant l'avènement du collège médiéval du type Merton, nombreux étaient les collèges basés sur un *trust simple*, qui finirent par disparaître, ce genre de fondation n'ayant pas la capacité d'avancer avec le temps.

M. Cahen avait raison de dire qu'«une corporation professionelle musulmane, même si on en admet l'existence, ne peut correspondre pleinement à ce qu'ont été les corporations de l'Europe chrétienne à leur belle époque.»[17] Les corporations-personnes morales étaient dynamiques, à côté des fondations charitables dont la forme était figée à tout jamais. Ce n'est donc pas l'Islam qui influa sur *cet aspect juridique* de la corporation européenne.

Mais si les associations corporatives occidentales du Moyen-Âge ne doivent rien à l'Islam pour ce qui est de leur *forme* juridique, il n'en est pas de même pour leur *contenu* social, c'est-à-dire leurs autres éléments constitutifs. Car la structure du personnel professionnel dans la *madrasa* musulmane à l'époque classique se retrouve plus tard dans celle du collège médiéval anglais et dans les corps de métiers en Angleterre et en France, comme on va le voir par la suite.

Louis Massignon désigna comme quatrième centre de la cité islamique, le centre de l'enseignement supérieur: «C'est le commerce de la science qui s'établit entre les étudiants et les maîtres et c'est par l'exercice, d'ailleurs, de la concurrence que l'étudiant devient un maître.» Ce sont les *madhhab*s sunnites qui firent de l'enseignement une profession: celle de l'*enseignement du droit*; elles aussi qui développèrent la méthode scolastique médiévale dont les éléments composants étaient le *khilāf*, le *jadal* et la *munāẓara*, qu'on retrouve plus tard dans le *sic et non*, la dialectique et la *disputatio* de l'Occident latin. Cet enseignement en Islam, comme plus tard en Occident, demandait de longues années d'études et d'entraînement pour obtenir le doctorat, l'autorité d'enseigner, *ijāzat al-tadrīs*, en latin médiéval, la *licentia docendi*. C'est de cette profession que Massignon parlait quand il disait que c'était par l'exercice de la concurrence que l'étudiant devenait un maître. Pour ceux qui désirent plus de détails, je me permets de leur signaler mon ouvrage récent sur l'essor de collèges médiévaux.[18] C'est après l'expérience islamique qu'une expérience presque identique eut lieu à Bologne, où le doctorat était un doctorat de droit et où la méthode scolastique débuta en Europe.

L'Enquête d'Elia Koudsī

Dans son article sur les corporations, Massignon cita une enquête faite par Elia Koudsî sur les corporations de Damas. Elle fut publiée dans les actes du VIe Congrès International des Orientalistes tenu à Leyde en 1883. Selon cette enquête, rédigée en arabe moderne, les métiers à Damas, vers cette fin du dix-neuvième siècle, se composaient du personnel suivant:

(1) Un chef suprême, dénommé «Maître des Maîtres» (*ra'īs a'ẓam wa-huwa Shaykh al-Mashāyikh*)

(2) Des chefs secondaires, dénommés «Maîtres des Métiers» (*ru'asā' thānawīyūn wa-hum Mashāyikh al-Ḥiraf*)

(3) Des «maîtres enseignants,» dénommées *mu'allimūn*
(4) Des «compagnons des métiers,» dénommés *ṣunnā'*
(5) Des «apprentis» ou des «valets,» dénommés *mubtadi'ūn* ou *khuddām.*

Cette organisation, dit Koudsī, correspond d'une façon générale à celle des francs-maçons, *al-fa'ala al-aḥrār.*[19]

M. Cahen avait sans doute raison de dire que si ce type d'organisation de métiers existait bien à Damas au dix-neuvième siècle, il ne doit pas «nécessairement dériver d'un précédent»; son existence à une époque reculée, à l'époque classique de l'Islam, aura besoin d'être prouvée. Massignon de son côté, avait eu la conviction profonde—une conviction partagée par Carlo Landberg[20]—que cette organisation devait venir de loin, tout en admettant que les documents n'étaient pas encore réunis pour le prouver.

L'Atelier artisanal bagdadien au onzième siècle

Nous croyons pouvoir dire à présent que le type d'association professionnelle, qu'Elia Koudsī décrit comme existant à Damas au dix-neuvième siècle, avait son correspondant à Bagdad à l'époque classique de l'Islam. En ce qui concerne la corporation artisanale et maçonnique, il y a un texte conservé dans un chronique du Moyen-Âge où une partie essentielle de la division tripartite de l'atelier du métier, c'est-à-dire les numéros 3, 4, et 5, dans le schéma ci-dessus, existait déjà au onzième siècle. Voici le schéma que l'on peut tirer de ce texte:

(3) un «maître artisan,» dénommé *'arīf*
(4) des «compagnons-artisans,» dénommés *ṣunnā'*
des «compagnons-maçons,» dénommés *fa'ala»*
(5) des «apprentis» ou «valets,» dénommés *mubtadi'ūn* ou *khuddām*: il nous est permis de supposer qu'ils ont existé dans les métiers; ils existaient bien dans les *madrasas*.][21]

Voici le texte dont il s'agit, cité dans le *Muntaẓam* d'Ibn al-Jawzī et dans le *Mir'āt al-zamān* de Sibṭ, son petit-fils; le texte de ce dernier, moins développé que celui du grand-père, ne parle que de *ṣunnā'*. Il est à remarquer que le maître s'addressait au Calife, non pas au *muḥtasib*, pour se plaindre et qu'à ces occasions ses «Compagnons» étaient avec lui.

> Au mois de Ṣafar [de l'an 479/mai–juin 1086] le maître-artisan (*'arīf*) des «compagnons-artisans» (*ṣunnā'*) et des «compagnons-maçons (*fa'ala*) entra dans le Palais Califal accompagné, *comme d'habitude*, des compagnons. Le Calife

al-Muqtadī sortait pour se promener dans le cour du Palais. Trois hommes s'approchèrent de lui, touchèrent la terre puis leurs lèvres et leur front [en signe de soumission] et dirent: «nous sommes des chefs (*ru'asā*) [22] du quartier du canal de Faḍl, nous avons été dépouillés et malmenés; et nous avons attendu en vain d'être admis chez le Calife. Nous avons finalement réussi à le faire en passant par la porte des ouvriers.» Le Calife leur demanda: «qui vous a fait cela?» Ils répondirent: «Ibn Zurayq, le *nāẓir* (gouverneur) de Wāsiṭ.» Le Calife promit de s'occuper de l'affaire. Alors, ils partirent. Le Calife donna aussitôt des ordres pour être éclairé à ce sujet. S'ils disaient vrai, Ibn Zurayq devait renoncer à percevoir les taxes de Wāsiṭ, et être conduit à Baghdad enchaîné.

Le Calife ordonna donc, à l'officier des Maẓālim de veiller à lui transmettre toute plainte de ses sujets. Il envoya avec ceux qui se rendirent a Wāsiṭ un de ses agents pour veiller à ce que le bien confisqué par Ibn Zurayq fût restitué à ses propriétaires et que ses ordres en ce qui concerne Ibn Zurayq fussent exécutés.[23]

L'Organisation professionnelle des madhhabs juridiques

Ce texte montre qu'une partie essentielle de l'organisation *dans l'atelier du métier* était déjà connue à l'époque classique. Mais l'organisation des métiers dans l'enquête de Koudsī en rappelle une autre à Bagdad, à l'époque classique, une autre qui lui ressemble plus étroitement encore. Il s'agit des associations dites *madhhab*, organisées par les intellectuels religieux qui se consacraient à la science du droit (*fiqh*), à savoir, les jurisconsultes (*fuqahā'*; singulier: *faqīh*).

Les islamisants, avons-nous dit, traduisent différemment ce mot *madhhab*: «rite,» «secte,» ou «école juridique.» Au deuxième siècle de l'Islam (huitième de notre ère), les anciennes écoles juridiques avaient des désignations locales ou régionales: par exemple, l'école de Kufa et de Basra en Iraq, de Médine et de la Mecque au Ḥijāz, l'école de Syrie. Après le début du troisième siècle, peu après la mort de Shāfi'ī (m. 204/820), les écoles désignées géographiquement finirent par disparaître alors qu'émergeaient les écoles «personnelles,» désignées par le nom d'un grand maître autour duquel les membres se groupaient: l'école shāfi'ite, nommée d'après le grand *imām* al-Shāfi'ī; l'école ḥanbalite d'après Aḥmad ibn Ḥanbal; la ḥanafite, d'après Abū Ḥanīfa; la mālikite, d'après Mālik; et ainsi de suite.[24] Ces grands hommes n'étaient pas des fondateurs, comme on a encore l'habitude de le dire, mais simplement des éponymes.

Pourquoi cette transition d'une désignation locale ou régionale à une autre, personnelle? C'est avec les deux dernières des quatre écoles qui survécurent que l'on peut voir clairement la raison pour laquelle ces intellectuels s'étaient constitués en groupes organisés. Les raisons en étaient principalement religieuses. Les deux écoles, shāfi'ite et ḥanbalite, s'opposèrent l'une après l'autre au mouvement rationaliste: le mu'tazilisme. Ce mouvement avait réussi à se faire soutenir par le pouvoir central. La lutte qui commença à l'époque de Shāfi'ī aboutit à l'inquisition, la *miḥna*, sous le califat d'al-Ma'mūn (198–218/813–833). L'inquisition dura quinze ans, de 833 à 848, menée par les théologiens mu'tazilites rationalistes contre les jurisconsultes traditionalistes, aboutissant pourtant au triomphe de ces derniers. À partir de cette époque, au milieu du neuvième siècle, les écoles juridiques, les *madhhab*s, se mirent à parfaire leur organisation professionnelle.

La profession qu'ils entendaient parfaire était celle du droit, en opposition avec le mouvement de théologie philosophique, dite *kalām*. La logique de leur position religieuse était nette: *l'Islam du Prophète est un système de droit, de droit positif divin, une nomocracie; sa théologie est juridique, non pas philosophique.* C'est là l'essentiel du message de Shāfi'ī, message qui sous-tend sa *Risāla*.[25] Y adhérat religieusement le grand *imām* Aḥmad ibn Ḥanbal. Traditionaliste, ce message préconisait la primauté de la révélation, *shar'*, contre le mu'tazilisme qui préconisait la primauté de la raison, *'aql*. L'histoire du développement ultérieur de l'enseignement institutionnel en Islam montre, de la façon la plus claire, la victoire des écoles juridiques sur les mouvements rationalistes de la théologie philosophique, le *kalām*, fût-il mu'tazilite ou ash'arite.[26]

Ce n'est qu'après Shāfi'ī et Ibn Ḥanbal et à l'instar de ces derniers avec leurs «compagnons» (*ṣāḥib*, pl. *aṣḥāb*), que les écoles locales ou régionales de l'Iraq et de Médine commencèrent à s'identifier d'après deux de leurs grands *imāms*, Abū Ḥanīfa et Mālik, en signe de ralliement à l'idée traditionaliste. Celle-ci consistait à suivre la «voie» (*madhab*, cf. *ṭarīqa*) du Prophète, le grand maître, le chef suprême, avec ses «Compagnons,» ses *aṣḥāb*. Ces écoles «personnelles» s'appelaient *madhhab*, la «voie» à suivre, la «méthode» de vie, le «mode» d'agir, de tel *imām*, chef, maître. On dit que vers l'an 300/912–13, cinq cents *madhhab*s avaient disparu, tant il y avait de ces «écoles juridiques.» Mais de tous ces *madhhabs* il restait une dizaine environ au quatrième/dixième siècle, qui ne tardèrent à se réduire à quatre à Bagdad, au siècle suivant, ceux-là même qui sont parvenus jusqu'à nos jours. Le mouvement traditionaliste se rendait compte, semble-t-il, que la prolifération des *madhhabs* tendait à les diviser, C'est donc à partir de cette époque, vers la fin du troisième/neuvième siècle—début du quatrième/dixième siècle, que les *madhhabs* commencèrent à se professionnaliser dans leur organisation, surtout pour l'enseignement du droit, depuis l'*apprentissage* jusqu'à la *maîtrise* de leur profession juridique.

Voici le schéma de l'organisation des *madhhab*s et de leurs «ateliers,» c'est-à-dire les collèges, où l'enseignement du droit était organisé professionnellement. Ce schéma, avec ses cinq degrés, correspond au schéma d'Elia Koudsī pour les métiers de Damas au dix-neuvième siècle.

(1) Un «chef suprême,» éponyme du *madhhab* (Abū Ḥanīfa, Mālik, Shāfi'ī, Aḥmad ibn Ḥanbal), dénommé *imām al-madhhab*
(2) Des «chefs» secondaires, des *ra'īs* locaux, dénommés *ra'īs al-madhhab*
(3) Des «maîtres-enseignants» du «métier» du droit, dénommés *faqīh-mudarris*
(4) Des «compagnons» du «métier» du droit, dénommés *faqīh-ṣāḥib*
(5) Des «apprentis» ou des «valets,» dénommés *faqīh-mutafaqqih*, et dont les pauvres parmi eux étaient des valets (*khādim*) des professeurs ou des étudiants riches

Le mot *faqīh* signifiait «celui qui possède une connaissance du droit»; aussi ce terme embrassait-il tous ceux qui se vouaient à ce domaine de science, qu'il fussent «sous-gradués» ou «gradués» ou professeurs. Le «sous-gradué» s'appelait *mutafaqqih*, «celui qui se consacre à l'étude du droit.» Une fois choisi par le professeur de droit (*mudarris*) pour poursuivre ses études sous sa direction en tant que «gradué,» l'étudiant faisait la transition de *mutafaqqih* à *ṣāḥib*, et ainsi devenait le compagnon (*ṣāḥib*) du professeur. Le troisième degré de l'échelle professionnelle était atteint quand le *ṣāḥib* recevait de son professeur la «licence d'enseigner le droit» (*ijāzat al-tadrīs*), qui lui donnait le *droit* de donner des avis légaux (*fatwā*) aux croyants qui les sollicitaient, et les *titres* le qualifiant comme apte à occuper une chaire de professeur de droit, *mudarris*.

C'étaient là donc les trois étapes que l'étudiant de droit devait parcourir. La première étape, celle de *mutafaqqih*, durait généralement quatre ans. La deuxième pouvait durer jusqu'à vingt ans ou plus. Durant cette période le *ṣāḥib* se consacrait à l'étude de la dialectique (*jadal*) pour se parfaire dans la pratique de la *disputatio* (*munāẓara*) et passait la plus grande partie de son temps à mémoriser les questions disputées (*al-masā'il al-khilāfīya*) avec leurs solutions. C'était pendant cette période qu'il était apte à travailler comme répétiteur (*mu'īd*; Latin: *repetitor*) des leçons du professeur aux étudiants *mutafaqqih*. Il était possible qu'un *mu'īd* ne devînt jamais professeur, *mudarris*. La troisième étape était celle où le gradué-*ṣāḥib*, ayant souvent réussi à défendre ses thèses contre ses adversaires, recevait de son professeur la licence d'enseigner le droit et de formuler des avis légaux, *ijāzat al-tadrīs wa'l-iftā'*.

Il est intéressant de noter que le terme arabe, *ṣāḥib*, représentant le deuxième degré de l'étudiant de droit, le «gradué,» se retrouve dans le système des collèges médiévaux anglais, traduit par le mot *fellow*, du Latin médiéval *socius*, et représentait le même degré d'étudiant: au dessus du «sous-gradué» appelé *scholar*, et au dessous du niveau de doctorat, *magister, doctor*. Il se retrouve aussi, en français, dans l'ordre corporatif et maçonnique, appelé *compagnon*, représentant aussi le deuxième degré de la distinction tripartite.

Ce mot arabe, *ṣāḥib*, remonte à la haute antiquité musulmane. Lorsque les écoles anciennes de droit, désignées géographiquement, passèrent de cette désignation à la désignation «personnelle,» ce passage symbolisait l'adoption, par les jurisconsultes traditionalistes, de la voie du Prophète, de sa méthode. Suivant ce modèle, chacune des écoles de droit «personnelles» avait son chef religieux, *imām*, le «saint patron» pour ainsi dire, et les membres se ralliant à son nom étaient ses compagnons, ses *ṣāḥib*s. Le parallèle correspondant à cette voie ou *madhhab* se retrouve ches les premières associations ouvrières connues dans l'Occident médiéval, les confréries religieuses rassemblant maîtres et compagnons du même métier. Chacune avait son saint patron; par exemple, St. Dominique pour les tailleurs; Ste. Anne pour les menuisiers; St. Joseph pour les charpentiers; etc.

Ainsi les corporations des jurisconsultes existaient déjà en Islam à partir du milieu du neuvième siècle de notre ère. Les degrés dans l'atelier du métier de droit correspondaient à ceux de l'ordre corporatif et maçonnique. Et il est probable que les écoles de droit «personnelles» dites *madhhab*, qui se manifestèrent peu après la mort du grand *imām* Shāfi'ī, en 204/820, influèrent sur l'organisation corporative telle qu'elle se présente dans le texte du *Muntaẓam* cité plus haut, datant de l'an 479/1086, et impliquant une origine remontant à une date lointaine. Dans le schéma suivant on peut noter la division tripartite particulière aux ordres «universitaire,» corporatif et maçonnique.

Schéma comparatif de la division tripartite des ordres
(1) l'ordre «universitaire»

madrasa	*collège médiéval/université*	
Islam	*Angleterre*	*France*
1. mutafaqqih	scholar	escolâtre
2. ṣāḥib	fellow	bachelier
3. muftī/mudarris	magister/master	magister/maître

(2,3) l'ordre corporatif et maçonnique

Islam		*Occident*	
époque classique	*Damas 19ᵉs.*	*Angleterre*	*France*
1. mubtadi'/ khādim	mubtadi'/ khādim	apprentice	apprenti/valet
2. ṣāni'/fā'il	ṣāni'/fā'il	journeyman	compagnon
3. 'arīf/amīn (etc.)	mu'allim	master	maître

Les écoles de droit «personnelles,» avec leurs «ateliers» (mosquées-collèges et *madrasa*), étaient des associations professionnelles spontanées et autonomes, échappant au contrôle de l'appareil administratif étatique. Leurs institutions d'enseignement se fondaient au bénéfice d'une des *madhhab*s juridiques; elles étaient donc ou ḥanafites, ou mālikites, ou shāfi'ites, ou ḥanbalites, au gré du fondateur (*waqif*). Celui-ci fondait l'institution, agissant en qualité de particulier musulman offrant sa donation moyennant un acte charitable (*waqf*) dont le but religieux était de se rapprocher de Dieu (*qurba*). C'était dans ces mosquées-collèges et *madrasa*s que la licence d'enseigner *ijazāt al-tadris* (Latin: *licentia docendi*) était conférée. *Cette licence ou autorisation ne se conférait que pour le domaine du droit*; et c'était le professeur de droit qui *seul* pouvait la conférer à l'aspirant. Ni le calife, ni le sultan, ni leurs vizirs, ni personne d'autre ne pouvait conférer cette licence, ou obliger le professeur de droit à la confèrer. Celui-ci la conférait librement en qualité de professeur de droit attitré (*mudarris*) d'une des écoles de droit. Les collèges étaient des fondations charitables (*waqf*), consistant en un ensemble architectural et en propriétés (terres cultivables, marchés, caravansérails, etc.) qui produisaient des revenus pour subvenir aux besoins de l'institution à perpétuité. Le *waqf* était la seule forme juridique de perpétuité en Islam.

Conclusion

Dans les pages qui précèdent je crois avoir fourni les éléments nécessaires pour répondre aux questions soulevées par M. Cahen:

(1) L'époque à laquelle existait la corporation musulmane était bien l'époque dite classique; c'est-à-dire, à partir du neuvième siècle, période durant laquelle les écoles «personnelles» émergent en associations privées, groupant les jurisconsultes traditionalistes dans leur lutte contre le rationalisme rampant des Mu'tazilites.

(2) C'est bien la profession, en l'occurrence celle de droit, qui définissait et constituait ses propres cadres, fondés à base de *waqf* dont la profession de droit elle-même fut et l'auteur, et l'interprète, et le conservateur.

(3) Il s'agissait bien d'une organisation corporative, consistant en associations spontanées encadrant plus ou moins largement la vie de leurs adhérents; il ne s'agissait pas d'organismes émanant de l'appareil administratif étatique.

Il est tout à fait vrai que la corporation des métiers islamique avait une forme juridique dépourvue de personnalité morale, personnalité que la corporation européenne ne possédait pas non plus dès le début, mais seulement plus tard, surtout à partir du treizième siècle. Ces deux types de corporation se ressemblaient en ce qui concerne leurs membres, leur hiérarchie sociale, mais non pas toujours en ce qui concerne leur statut juridique.[27] Le type islamique se basait sur le *waqf*; celui de l'Occident, sur la corporation-personnalité morale, non pas à l'origine, mais au treizième siècle. Le *waqf* était statique; la corporation, dynamique. L'acte du *waqf*, une fois fixé et signé par le fondateur, ne pouvait plus être modifié, même par le fondateur; au contraire, la corporation-personne morale pouvait subir toute modification provenant de son conseil d'administration (les *trustees*). C'est dire que l'organisation occidentale pouvait évoluer au gré des besoins, pouvait se parfaire; mais cela ne veut pas dire qu'elle n'ait pas eu ses origines dans l'Islam, avant d'être reconnue comme personne morale. Massignon, lui, l'avait bien pressenti; et pourtant, à son époque, manquaient les documents et les études susceptibles d'apporter des éclaircissements sur ce sujet. Ce n'est là qu'un exemple, parmi tant d'autres, de ces percées de Louis Massignon. Il sut nous montrer le chemin.

NOTES

1. Dans la *Revue internationale de sociologie* (Septembre 1920), pp. 473–89. Cette étude a été donnée en conférence à l'occasion du Centenaire Louis Massignon célébré à Paris en 1983.

2. Voir notamment «Guilds,» dans *Encyclopedia of the Social Sciences*, s.v.; «Sinf,» dans *EI*^{1}, s.v.; «La 'futuwwa' ou 'pacte d'honneur artisanal' entre les travailleurs musulmans au Moyen Age,» dans *La Nouvelle Clio* (1952).

3. Les idées de Massignon furent reprises par Bernard Lewis, dans un article intitulé «The Islamic Guilds» (*Economic History Review* [1937], pp. 20–37). Lewis avait étudié sous la direction du grand maître. D'autres savants souscrirent également à la thèse de Massignon; tels, H. A. R. Gibb et H. Bowen, *Islamic Society and the West* (London, 1950–57), I, 283; A. von Kremer, *Kulturgeschichte des Orients unter den Chalifen* (Vienna, 1875–77), II, 186; et J. Sauvaget, *Introduction à l'histoire de l'orient musulman* (Paris, 1961), p. 98, traduction anglaise (Berkeley et Los Angeles, 1965), p. 92. Les orientalistes suivants s'inscrirent en faux contre sa thèse: C. C. Nallino, *Encyclopedia Italiana*, art. «Corporazione,» p. 463a; S. D. Goitein, *Studies in Islamic History and Institutions* (Leiden, 1966), pp. 267–70; et, récemment, S. M. Stern, «The Constitution of the Islamic City,» dans *The Islamic City*, ed. A. H. Hourani et S. M. Stern (Oxford et Philadelphie, 1969), pp. 25–50, surtout pp. 36 et ss.; et Cl. Cahen, «Y a-t-il des corporations professionnelles dans le monde musulman classique?» dans *The Islamic City*, pp. 51–63.

4. Voir la fin de la note précédente.

5. Stern, *op. cit.*, p. 48.

6. Voir mon *The Rise of Colleges: Institutions of Learning in Islam and the West* (Edinburgh, 1981).

7. Stern, *op. cit.*, pp. 48–49.

8. Cf. J. Schacht, *Introduction to Islamic Law* (Oxford, 1964), p. 125.

9. Voir *Rise of Colleges*, pp. 28–33.

10. Al-Nu'aymī, *Ad-Dāris fī tārīkh al-madāris* (Damaṣ 1367–70/1948–51), I, 614, ll. 8–10; *Rise of Colleges*, pp. 42–43.

11. Cahen, *op. cit.*, p. 58 n. 20.

12. Voir sa notice dans *Shadharāt adh-dhahab fī akhbār man dhahab* (Le Caire 1350/1931), III, 8.

13. Voir *Al-Muntaẓam fī tārīkh al-mulūk wa'l-umam*, ed. Krenkow (Hyderabad, 1367–69/1938–40), VII, 10.

14. Voir *Rise of Colleges*, p. 35, «Founder's Freedom of Choice.»

15. Cahen, *op. cit.*, p. 52 (italisation ajoutée).

16. *Ibid.* (italisation ajoutée).

17. Cahen, *op. cit.*, p. 62.

18. *Rise of Colleges*, surtout pp. 35 et ss. sur la loi du *waqf*, et pp. 99 et ss.

19. Elia Koudsī [=Ilyās 'Abduh Qudsī], «Notice sur les corporations de Damas,» dans *Actes du Sixième Congrès International des Orientalistes* (Leide, 1885), pp. 1–34, voir p. 9.

20. Voir E. Koudsī, *op. cit.*, dans la Préface de Carlo Landberg p. 5; «L'histoire des corporations de Damas remonte à une haute antiquité; les pratiques encore conservées en font foi.»

21. Voir *Rise of Colleges*, pp. 171, 173, 256.

22. Il est à noter que le *'arīf* était considéré comme le chef, *ra'īs*, du métier; ce qui pourrait signifier que les numéros 2 et 3 de la hiérarchie corporative à Damas au dix-neuvième siècle ne faisaient qu'un au onzième siècle à Bagdad.

23. *Muntaẓam*, IX, 27. Ce texte se trouve aussi dans le *Mi'rāt az-zamān* de Sibṭ ibn al-Jawzī, Paris MS arabe 1506, *sub anno* 479, fol. 195a, mais en abrégé et avec quelques modifications, en général sans importance, sauf là où Sibṭ ne mentionne que les *ṣunnā'*, mot qui, tout seul, signifie «ouvriers» et perd ainsi son sens technique. Sibṭ passe sous silence les termes pour le maître artisan, *'arīf*, et les maçons, *fa'ala*.

24. Voir J. Schacht, *Origins of Muhammadan Jurisprudence* (Oxford, 1950), p. 10: «Soon after the time of Shāfi'ī the geographical character of the ancient schools of law disappeared more and more, and the personal allegiance to a master became preponderant.»

25. Voir notre étude «The Juridical Theology of Shāfi'ī: Origins and Significance of *Uṣūl al-Fiqh*,» dans *Studia Islamica*, LIX (1984), pp. 5–47.

26. Voir *Rise of Colleges, passim.*

27. Ils se ressemblaient dans leur statut juridique quand on se réfère aux *Inns of Court* anglais qui, depuis le Moyen-Âge, sont dépourvus, eux aussi, de personnalité morale, à l'instar de leurs analogues, les *madrasas*. Nous aurons à en parler dans une autre étude en préparation; l'espace nous manque ici. (Voir maintenant cette étude intitulée «The Guilds of Law in Medieval Legal History: An Inquiry into the Origins of the Inns of Court,» dans *Zeitschrift für Geschichte der arabisch-islamischen Wissenschaften* [Frankfurt], I (1984), pp. 233–52.

15
Mentalités and Marginality: Blindness and Mamlūk Civilization*

Fedwa Malti-Douglas

IN *Illness as Metaphor,* Susan Sontag has shown that diseases can transcend their biological realities and become the focus for other cultural concerns, and that they can become part of a language through which a given society articulates social and cultural values.[1] One can then agree with the cultural historian of medicine, Marcel Sendrail, that each epoch has "its own pathological style," consisting not so much of the specific maladies of any time and place as of the manner in which a society defines its relationship to disease, its concepts of illness and of health.[2]

But what is true of different epochs is certainly even more true of different civilizations. And what is true of disease is clearly also true of pathological conditions and physical handicaps, like blindness. Indeed, it will be the purpose of this study to show that the physical handicap of blindness serves as a kind of metaphor for a significant group of concepts, values, and ideals in medieval Islamic civilization. The conceptions that medieval Islamic civilization, and specifically Mamlūk civilization, held of the blind formed an important part of the *mentalités* of that civilization.

But what are *mentalités*? The term has been rendered into English as mentalities, mind sets, or, less frequently, mental structures. *Men-*

*I would like to thank the NEH, the SSRC/ACLS, and the ARCE, whose generosity made this work possible. An earlier version of this study was delivered as a public lecture at the University of Chicago on May 3, 1984, and in its present form is a contribution to the work of the Equipe de Recherche 06 0302 of the C.N.R.S. in Paris.

talités history can be understood as a school whose goal is the explanation of popular social attitudes and forms, and whose chief method is the exploration of the networks of structures through which social conceptions are conveyed. Structure, according to Patrick Hutton, "refers to all of the forms which regularize mental activity, whether these be aesthetic images, linguistic codes, expressive gestures, religious rituals, or social customs."[3]

For Jacques Le Goff, perhaps the foremost historian of medieval European *mentalités,* the first appeal of *mentalités* history resides precisely in its "imprecision," in its ability to designate that "je ne sais quoi" of history.[4]

But Le Goff does elaborate a more detailed, if not precise, definition of *mentalités* history: the blending of traditional history with other branches of the human sciences, notably ethnology and sociology. In this connection, Le Goff also emphasizes the special relationship that the history of *mentalités* enjoys with social psychology, noting the development of studies on criminality, marginals, and deviants. Le Goff adds that this type of history can be located at the juncture of the individual and the collective, the unconscious and the intentional, and the marginal and the general. Linked to this for the French medievalist is the additional area which distinguishes the historian of *mentalités,* the types of sources which he exploits, including literary and artistic documents. The latter sources remove the emphasis of the historical activity from the presentation of "objective" phenomena to the representation of these phenomena. The important element in a historical source is no longer the facts which it presents, but rather the manner in which the source presents them.[5]

But the history of *mentalités* is also associated with the work of Michel Foucault. His studies on insanity, the birth of the prison, and so on, have, to use Paul Veyne's expression, "revolutionized" history.[6] Foucault aims at the isolation of epistemes and their mutation in the course of Western history. Hayden White has characterized the Foucaultian episteme as the " 'total set of relations that unite, at a given period, the discursive practices that give rise to epistemological figures, sciences, and possibly formalized systems' of knowledge."[7] Hutton has pointed out that what makes Foucault's approach similar to that of earlier *mentalités* historians, such as Norbert Elias, is that he bases the search for common attitudes in the "common codes of knowledge through which the world is perceived." These codes, his "discourses," are "the verbal expression of the mental structures . . .

through which man organizes his activities and classifies his perceptions of the world."[8]

In fact, whatever the area of inquiry (madness for Foucault or the civilizing process for Elias), most historians dealing with Western mental structures have tended to follow the developmental mode. This, of course, must be seen in relation to the larger school from which *mentalités* history emerged, the *Annales* school. The *Annales* school is well-known for its emphasis on what Braudel called "social time," as opposed to "political time." For Braudel, the level of social time lies beneath that of political time. "Deeper still" for him is "geographical time, where change is barely perceptible."[9]

But the fact that political events may be set aside as markers of change has not meant an abandonment of diachrony. Historians like Philippe Ariès, in his studies of death, and Michel Foucault adhere to a diachronic framework. It is simply a framework which englobes greater periods of chronological time. When Foucault, for example, discusses the "carceral" mode in Western society, in his study of insanity or that of the penal system, he associates this with the development of new attitudes in the West, and development implies diachrony. As Hutton demonstrates, the emphasis in Foucault, as in Norbert Elias, is on a diachronic shift from external to internal codes of behavior.[10]

The developmental tendency of most, though not all,[11] *mentalités* historians is not logically necessary to the study of the history of mentalities. Such approaches have arisen to a considerable degree in response to preexisting historical problematics, like the rise of the modern West for Elias and Foucault or the sea-change from early medieval to late medieval culture for Radding.[12] Since such problematics are foreign to our study of Mamlūk civilization, we shall adopt a completely synchronic approach. Logically, synchronic examinations of Arabo-Islamic mentalities must precede diachronic comparisons. A synchronic examination of Mamlūk civilization does not, therefore, in any way imply an eternal Islamic cultural essence. Nor does it imply that nothing important changed in the two and a half centuries during which the Mamlūks ruled much of the Arab world. It merely seeks to delineate those cultural elements which remained constant during this period. Since all that can be attempted in the present study is the identification of the principal roles of blindness and the blind in Mamlūk mentalities, little scope is left for diachronic comparisons.

The synchronic bias of this study means that it draws as much from literary critical (especially structuralist) approaches as it does from purely historical ones. It is the text which provides the starting point for the analysis of mental structures, and it is the subsequent comparison between structures present in various texts which will then permit us to speak of mental structures in general.

A mental structure concerning blindness does not generally exist in isolation from the totality of a society's mentalities. Mental structures are usually articulated as part of discourses, that is, a specific language (or, to be more precise, semiotic system) which the society uses to articulate its values. Hence, we have moral discourses, discourses of the body, etc. In addition, blindness is integrated into these discourses under the sign of a particular mental operation or mode, that is, the relationship or conception impressed upon blindness to integrate it into that particular discourse.

This conception of social consciousness as articulated through discourses owes much, of course, to that of Foucault. So too does our understanding of the relationship between the facts of social life (institutions, social roles, etc.) and the ideas or values consciously articulated by a society. As Foucault has shown, it makes little sense to see ideas as either the causes of, or after-the-fact generalizations from, social institutions. Thus, institutional frameworks and social roles, just like literary images or proverbs, are direct reflections of basic mental structures. Social reality is just as much the seat of discourse and the articulator of values as are purely literary or textual phenomena.[13]

The nature of the textual sources for this study raises another issue evoked by historians of mentalities. Hutton makes it clear that in his view, history of mentalities "considers the attitudes of ordinary people toward everyday life."[14] And this point of view would be shared by many a *mentalités* historian. Insofar as "ordinary" here means "anonymous," or "collectively held," Hutton's proposition is implicit in the history of mentalities. But if "ordinary" means "non-elite," it is not. Our approach, based upon written sources, will, of necessity, tend to reflect elite positions. However, there is no reason to assume that the mental structures present in them are not shared by lower social strata. On the contrary, it is in the nature of many classical sources, like *adab* works, to include materials whose origins may be popular, or at least traditional, like proverbs. In addition, Arab scholars were alive to popular sayings and practices, and felt free to comment upon them.

Le Goff has mentioned the study of marginal groups as falling within the history of mentalities.[15] And here again, of course, the definition of marginality is important. In *Aspects de la marginalité au Moyen-Age*, several scholars of the medieval West have attempted to define marginality for that society. One can speak, for example, of statistical marginality; or one can speak of structural marginality, in which the marginal is someone outside the norm, someone who is not well integrated, or who is excluded from society. Thus, the study of a society's discourse on marginality can help us to understand the way this society conceives of the normal and of its relationship to the marginal, or to a plurality of marginalities.[16]

We have repeatedly spoken of historians of the medieval West and how they perceive that society. Yet, the problems posed for the historian of Islamic mentalities need not necessarily be the same. Although the methodologies exploited by historians of the West can shed light on the path to be followed, the area to which the path is leading need not be identical. We should not necessarily be led into the study of a concept or an area, simply because that concept has been studied in the West. Foucault's problematics need not be our own. Nor should we await a study by a Western historian before deciding that a given topic is worthy of scholarly investigation.

When we speak of a society's mentalities, we are talking not just about the attitudes that this society brings to different social facts. We are speaking also of the relative importance that the society in question gives to different components or concepts. Hence, automatically to shift categories from one civilization to another is, in a way, to prejudge the morphology of that society's mentalities.

Each society articulates its own concerns through concepts or issues that are central to it. And we must extract the key concepts and issues from within the society itself. Blindness is such a concept for Islamic society, one which acts as the focus for the articulation of a large range of social values.

Why blindness specifically for a study of Mamlūk mental structures? The question of blindness is an important one in Islamic civilization, and appears in virtually all of the major types of sources in the medieval period: from the theological and the legal through the historical to the literary and the philological.

This importance becomes more clearly visible under the Mamlūks, the slave soldiers who ruled Egypt and Syria from about 1250 until 1517. There is no question but that the visually handicapped formed part of the background of social life in the Mamlūk domains. Eye disease leading to blindness has been prevalent in the Nile Valley since antiquity.[17] While the physical presence of the blind is not sufficient to explain their ubiquity in texts, it is probably a condition of it.

In addition, the question of blindness transcends the mere problem of a physical handicap, to touch on the important area of vision, both physical and spiritual. Blindness also plays a central role in crucial debates in Islamic culture, as it touches on the problems of vision vs. hearing, and written vs. oral culture.

The Mamlūk period is distinguished by the richness of its sources. The most important for our purposes is the biographical compendium and general study on blindness and the blind, the *Nakt al-himyān fī nukat al-ʿumyān*, by the Mamlūk official Khalīl ibn Aybak al-Ṣafadī (d. 764/1361).[18] In addition, this period represents the culmination of a long tradition of learning in the Arabic and Islamic disciplines. As such, it includes within it sources from earlier periods, such as ḥadīths, the Qur'ān, proverbs, etc. Thus, the fact that a source may have been written before our period does not eliminate it from the texture of Mamlūk mental structures. To take an extreme case, even though the Qur'ān was revealed long before the Mamlūk period, it was still considered a normative document by most representatives of Mamlūk society, and had to be integrated into their mental structures. It is merely necessary in this case that we have some indication of how particular verses were understood at that time. Since medieval Islamic civilization had a considerable reverence for traditional materials of both a religious and a secular nature, a similar situation obtains with a large variety of written sources, provided that we have some reason to believe that these texts were still important in Mamlūk times. Hence, the historical or intellectual conjunctures which may have presided over the birth of a given text are no longer relevant to us. What is important is the place that this text, or any of its ideas, occupies in the systems of Mamlūk mentalities.

Despite the variety of literary sources, multiplied in turn by the composite nature of these sources, there are a limited number of ways in which blind individuals appear. These types of categories should be understood as being at once textual and social. They are social in that they do represent different social levels in Mamlūk society. But they are also textual because they represent the social types isolated textually, and not necessarily all those existing in the society at large. Nor, as we shall see, are they the result of a systematic attempt to paint blindness in different social classes. Each comes from a different kind of text and reflects different kinds of concerns with blindness.

The first, and most numerous, category is that of the individuals who inhabit the biographical dictionaries. A biographical dictionary can be organized around different principles, geographical, chronological, or occupational. The genre reached its apex in the Mamlūk period.[19] The *Nakt al-himyān* of al-Ṣafadī, our most comprehensive source on blindness, presents over three hundred biographical notices of blind individuals. Since this dictionary is organized around a specific physical characteristic, absence of vision, it covers a large range of individuals, from scholars to poets, Qur'ān reciters, ḥadīth transmitters, rulers, etc. But the visually handicapped appear in other types of biographical dictionaries, when they fit within the parameters of the work in question.

The personages who inhabit the biographical dictionaries are the individuals whose blindness is most often specified. In these works, we are normally told the cause of blindness: was it congenital, was it acquired through a disease or through blinding, was it a result of old age? It is also in this category that we find the famous blind personages of medieval Islam, the 'Abbasid poets Bashshār ibn Burd (d. 167 or 168/784–785) and al-Ma'arrī (d. 449/1057), the Andalusian lexicographer Ibn Sīda (d. 458/1066), and others.[20] Blind poets are represented not only in biographical literature but also through their poetry, and thus may appear in *adab* works, poetic compendia, etc.

Socially, the subjects of biographical notices, whether sighted or blind, are members of the elite, though an elite understood in the broadest sense. Hence, biographical literature presents us with the view of the elite blind: who they were, how they lived, etc. There are, however, other social/textual types of the blind; and the clearest of these, after the "elite," is its social opposite, the beggars. There is no doubt that blind beggars were prevalent in medieval Islam. Yet, we do not expect to find accounts of beggars in the biographical literature. Instead, this category has a tendency to appear in the literary sources: in *adab* works and in the *maqāmāt*. What is particularly interesting in this literature is that alongside the relatively small number of genuine blind beggars, we find a large number of falsely blind beggars, that is, beggars who feign blindness.[21] It is clear from this literature that blindness is considered not only an exemplary physical defect for a beggar but also one likely to be mimicked.

Of course, when we speak of the elite and of beggars, we are speaking of two categories which are reasonably easy to distinguish. They are at opposite ends of the social spectrum and rarely appear together in the sources. But, the literary world of late medieval Islamic civilization does not restrict itself to these two categories. What about the average blind individual, that common man of *mentalités* history? That category most often surfaces in the literary sources, specifically in the anecdotal material. These common individuals are not famous personages. The onomastic information pertaining to them is often absent, or restricted to a first name. In other words, their identity remains unknown. It is clear, however, that these individuals who inhabit the anecdotes are not beggars. We may be told their occupation: in one case, we know that the subject of the anecdote is a water carrier. We get glimpses at times of their marital situations. It is in this context that we find the anecdotes which relate the extraordinary feats of the blind; these extraordinary acts are most often attached to what we have called "common individuals." Here we read, for example, about a blind individual who, despite his handicap, could thread a needle and sew.[22]

Though blind individuals are represented through three social/textual types, the blind as a unified social group also have a place in medieval *adab* works. First and foremost, the blind are placed among the other handicapped, usually referred to as *ahl al-ʿāhāt*, those possessing a physical infirmity or defect. This category includes those whom we would consider handicapped, like the blind and the lame, but also many who are physically abnormal. Ibn Qutayba (d. 276/889), for example, included the blue-eyed, and those with bad breath, among others,[23] while the Damascene scholar Yūsuf ibn ʿAbd al-Hādī (d. 909/1517) combined the blind with the hemiplegic, the wall-eyed, the flat-nosed, and the large-mouthed.[24] Al-Nuwayrī (d. 732/1332), in his *Nihāyat al-arab*, places the blind between women and beggars, and shortly after idiots.[25] Hence, the blind form part of a larger group, which is, at first sight, not easy to define. This group does, however, consist of the marginal. But how is this marginality defined? In fact, there are two discourses of marginality, one of which is purely physical. But this physical marginality is not that of a handicap, but merely one of physical difference, of a variation from the normal, and not one which excludes from society as a whole. Hence, in this schema, a blind individual is physically different but not necessarily handicapped. One could almost, in these cases, speak of a merely statistical marginality.

The other discourse of marginality is a social one. And here we see the blind placed with other social categories in Mamlūk society whose status could be defined as relatively unfavored, like beggars and women. The relationship between blindness and beggary has already been alluded to above, while that between the blind and women will be discussed later. Suffice it to say that the discourse of the blind as one among many marginal groups suggests the conception of blindness as a relative and not an absolute handicap. And by extension, blindness forms part of an integrated marginality.

Perhaps one of the best ways of seeing the mental structures of a given civilization on a given concept is to examine the terms which the civilization uses to express that concept. And for the visually handicapped, there is thus no better indication than the philological tradition itself. As Pierre Henri has shown, the terminology for blindness and the blind in the West is linked to the notions of darkness (for example, in the French word *cécité*), of being mixed-up or troubled (the German and English *blind*), to the notion of being hidden or closed (the Slavic languages), and to the concept of smoke, with the Greek *tuphlos*, from which we derive "typhlology," knowledge relating to blindness.[26]

Unlike the Western languages, where the available vocabulary for the concept of blindness is actually quite restricted, Arabic has a multiplicity of words. For the blind, the most common usages are *aʿmā, kafīf, makfūf,* and *ḍarīr*. There is also a word applied to the congenitally blind, *akmah*. But, what do these words tell us? *Aʿmā* comes from the verbal root *ʿ-m-y*, and according to the lexicographical sources, including the *Tāj al-ʿarūs* of al-Zabīdī (d. 817/1415) and *al-Muḥkam* of Ibn Sīda, the verb expresses the disappearance of vision altogether.[27] But al-Ṣafadī, who is something of a *mentalités* historian himself, delves into the question of this verb in one of his introductions to the *Nakt al-himyān*. Al-Ṣafadī explores many verbs whose roots have the radicals *ʿayn* and *mīm* in the first two positions, but whose third radical may be another consonant. This enables him to show that, in fact, these verbs all express the idea of covering and hiding or disappearance. He thus links them to the concept of *ʿamā*, or blindness.[28]

Interestingly enough, al-Ṣafadī limits himself to this one verb in his philological discussion. And this despite the fact that he does exploit the other synonyms in the rest of the work, be it in the remaining introductions or in the biographical notices themselves.

Although the word *aʿmā* could be considered the generic term for a blind man, the appellation *al-ḍarīr* is the one which is most common in the onomastic chains, or lists of names, in the biographical notices themselves. This commonness is also attested in specialized works on names, such as the *Tabṣīr al-muntabih* of Ibn Ḥajar al-ʿAsqalānī (d. 852/1449).[29] *Al-ḍarīr* appears to have been the most polite way of designating a visually handicapped individual. *Ḍarīr* comes from the root *ḍ-r-r* whose basic meaning is "to harm" or "to injure." And, again, according to the lexicographical sources, it is used to signify one whose vision has gone, or one who has been injured by an illness.[30]

As for the two words *al-kafīf* and *al-makfūf*, they are both derived from the same verbal root, *k-f-f*, whose basic meaning has the sense of "filling" or "wrapping." The verb is used in the passive with the word *baṣar, kuffa baṣaruhu*, to signify that someone has been blinded or lost his sight.[31]

To these terms, we can add *akmah*, which refers to one who is born blind, as when it is said, *kamiha baṣaruhu*, which the lexicographers relate to darkness obliterating someone's sight.[32] There is yet one more term, and rare at that, used to refer to a blind individual, and that is *maḥjūb*. This word, whose basic meaning is "covered," is thus used with reference to someone who is blind.[33]

The term *baṣīr*, or "sighted," is also sometimes presented as referring to the blind. However, as I have shown elsewhere,[34] even though *baṣīr* is generally listed in the *aḍdād* works as possessing the meaning "blind," it did not really have this usage in the Mamlūk period, and was only used with specific individuals when referring to an aspect in which they could be said to be sighted.

It is clear that there are tendencies in the lexicographical tradition which relate to blindness. *Akmah*, used for the congenitally blind, is not exploited nearly to the same extent as the words derived from the other verbal roots. In fact, al-Ṣafadī, when he provides information about congenital blindness, almost always writes *wulida aʿmā* (he was born blind) rather than *akmah*.[35] Furthermore, in the appellations used for blind personages, al-Akmah does not appear at all. And yet, as we have seen, this term is, in the philological tradition, the only one with a clear connection to darkness. The three other terms, which are also the more common ones, provide a connection between blindness and the physiological problem of the loss of sight: that the sight may be covered or that it may disappear, without any overt connection between this loss of sight and darkness. It would seem that the connection of blindness with darkness, a connection which clearly exists in the West,[36] is shunned in the medieval Islamic tradition.

The terms for blind and blindness carry two general associations: one, the most common, with the idea of covering, and one with the idea of injury or defect. The notion of defect is already familiar to us. But when we compare both these ideas with the Western philological associations with darkness or confusion, we perceive that the Arabic concepts remain more closely attached to the physical reality of the absence of sight. They do not expand the idea of blindness into a larger world of darkness or the even more general notion of confusion. The relatively down-to-earth aspects of the Arabic terminology, therefore, reduce the separation between the blind and the sighted. The blind are injured or defective, to be sure, but their injury is not projected outward into a more general state. This is a mental structure which we shall see again and again: blindness remains in the physical realm and does not escape into mental or spiritual differences.

Blindness thus plays a role in philology, in the discourse of words and their ultimate meanings. But, how the blind actually lived also reflected itself in the consciousness of Mamlūk civilization. The living patterns of the blind were taken up as part of a larger discourse of daily life.

The aspect of the daily life of the visually handicapped which receives the greatest attention in the written sources is that of mobility. This vital aspect of daily life appears in virtually all the sources, from the legal to the anecdotal. Most of the anecdotes relating extraordinary feats by blind individuals involve mobility. We are told, for example, about al-Faḍl Abū ʻAlī, who in the midst of a gathering would get up to fulfill a need and would navigate a room full of people without ever falling. Al-Ṣafadī tells us that he once saw a blind man walking with his wife. He was guiding her by the hand and warning her about pitfalls in the road.[37]

But these stories are clearly meant to be extraordinary. They are included because they run counter to the norm. The texts make it clear that blind individuals were quite commonly led by guides. The question of guiding a blind individual receives attention in the various types of sources. The legist Anas ibn Mālik said that he who guides a blind man for forty steps will not be touched by Hellfire, obviously an injunction which encourages the guiding of the blind. The issue of a guide also enters into the question of the religious duties of a blind individual. Is the Friday prayer, for example, incumbent upon him? The advice in this area is that if he has a guide or can afford one, then he should attend. Other questions arose from this as well. In one case, for example, a man was guiding a blind individual, and they both fell into a well. The blind man fell on top of his sighted guide and killed him. Who was responsible? In fact, there was a well-developed jurisprudence to deal with legal questions arising from the interdependence of the blind man and his guide.[38]

That the guide was the preferred mode of mobility for the visually handicapped is also attested to, for example, by the fact that the eighth-century caliph, al-Walīd I, ordered that a companion be provided to guide every blind individual in the kingdom.[39]

The role of the guide can be seen as more than simply one of facilitating the mobility of the blind individual. More importantly, he played a mediating role between the visually handicapped and his physical and social environment. The blind poet al-Khuraymī mentions in one of his poems that his guide would also tell him whom to greet.[40]

But of course, the visually handicapped moved about on their own, be it with the help of a stick or otherwise.[41] This seems, however, to have been much less the preferred technique, and receives far less attention in the sources.

Hence, the mobility of the blind seems to be one of the central concerns in the texts at hand, with emphasis placed on the guidance of the blind. However, how does this help us to understand the mental structures about the visually handicapped? On the one hand, one can construe the information on mobility as deemphasizing the independence of the visually handicapped. But concomitant with this is the more significant fact that the blind are encouraged to circulate, when necessary, with another individual, a guide. This, of course, places the stress on the communal aspect, the visually handicapped individual being conceived as part of the social system. Hence, this emphasis on the mobility of the blind person and his relationship with his guide is integrative. But the mode of integration is that of dependence. Dependence, in this context, could be defined as inferiority plus integration.

That this association of the blind with their guides along the mode of dependence reflects a basic mental structure can be seen in the way it is exploited in the onirocritical literature. We are told, for example, that one who dreams that someone is blinding him will be led astray by that person.[42] Even more interesting is the interpretation provided for the individual who dreams that his two eyes are someone else's eyes. This indicates that the dreamer will become blind and that someone will show him the way.[43] Hence, blindness represents a dependence on someone else's eyes—not darkness, but dependent vision.

The other area of the daily life of the blind which is noted by the medieval sources is that of eating. The Qur'ānic verse from Sūrat al-Nūr: "There is no fault in the blind, and there is no fault in the lame, and there is no fault in the sick, neither in yourselves, that you eat of your houses, etc.," is interpreted by al-Qurṭubī (d. 671/1273) in his commentary as an injunction to eat with the blind, the lame, and the sick. Al-Qurṭubī further noted that people had an aversion to eating with the blind. In this period, people usually ate from a common dish, which explains al-Qurṭubī's remark that the sighted were disturbed by the blind whose hands had a tendency to roam over the food.[44] The difficulty which the visually handicapped normally encountered while eating can be seen from another perspective. Al-Tha'ālibī (d. 429/1038) notes that after Ḥassān ibn Thābit became blind, he would ask if the food before him was "of one hand" or "of two hands" before reaching out to it.[45] Though this anecdote is positive rather than negative, it testifies, as much as al-Qurṭubī's commentary, to the difficulties experienced by the blind when eating. Yet, in both cases, the emphasis is on the blind and the sighted eating together, which activity is presented as a laudable one. Partaking of a common meal was, and remains, one of the most important social activities of Islamic civilization. Thus, the problems encountered with eating, like the linked notions of mobility and dependence, must be seen in the context of social integration. And in the consciousness of Islamic society, the two greatest problems to be overcome in this quest for integration were mobility and table manners.

Perhaps one of the most fascinating areas for the understanding of the mental structures about the blind in medieval Islam is what we can call a discourse on the body. In his extremely interesting study, "En Marge du monde connu: Les Races des monstres," Bruno Roy isolates conceptions about unusual physical types in the medieval West. According to Roy, these classifications represent an attempt on the part of Western European man to confirm his own normality.[46] By extension from Roy's analysis, we can argue that the discussions of the physically unusual in the Mamlūk sources also help to define what society considered normal. When society discusses the physically unusual, it is, in effect, articulating values about the physically normal and its significations, that is, a discourse on the body.

We have already noted in the philological discussion that blindness was treated as an essentially physical state. But what kind of physicality are we dealing with? There is no doubt that one of the most significant aspects of this physicality is its link to the notion of physical imperfection. Part of this, of course, can be seen in one of the terms used for the visually handicapped individual, *al-ḍarīr*, someone who has been injured, and hence someone whose physical integrity has been called into question.

But this mental structure of physical imperfection is present on a deeper level. It is well known that one of the practices used to dethrone a ruler in Islam was to blind him. This procedure, which began in the tenth century, was accomplished in order to make the individual physically imperfect, and hence improper for holding office.[47] This practice, of course, testifies to the connection between blindness and physical imperfection.

If physical perfection or integrity was a qualification for the status of ruler, how much more might it be so for that of prophet. The concern with the physical integrity of prophets lies at the root of the debate on whether or not a prophet could be blind. For the medieval Muslims, the problem was provoked by the "fact" of the blindness of the prophet Jacob, attested in the Qur'ān (Sūrat Yūsuf, verse 84). The controversy manifests the difficulty of integrating the Qur'ānic story with the conception of the physical integrity of prophets. The fact that some Muslim scholars attempted to deny the blindness of Jacob,[48] thus flying in the face of the more obvious meaning of the Qur'ānic story, testifies to the importance of the idea that a prophet could not be blind, and its attendant mental structure that blindness represents a serious physical imperfection.

The question of whether a visually handicapped individual was fit for other legal and theological functions receives a great deal of attention in the sources. Most of these issues are quite complicated and arguments were, as a rule, adduced for both sides. The legists, for example, discuss the issue of whether a blind individual could be an appropriate witness. Another controversial area is the ability of the visually handicapped to be reliable transmitters. In both issues, the problem can be seen to be linked to the possibility of confusion arising from the hearing process.[49] But it is the argument in favor of acceptability which is striking in this context. It is noted that when the wife of the Prophet, 'Ā'isha, and other holy women in early Islam transmitted, they did so from behind a curtain. Their hearers would then transmit on their authority. It is well known, al-Ṣafadī adds, that, in this case, the state of the sighted woman is the same as that of the blind man.[50] What this example points to is a relationship between blind men and sighted women. In fact, in legal works, one can also observe this close relationship between the blind and women. In cases where the visually handicapped are not treated like the sighted, their status is sometimes specified as being similar to that of women. We can see this, for example, in the discussion which al-Suyūṭī (d. 919/1505) devotes to the blind in his compendium of Shāfi'ī *fiqh, al-Ashbāh wa'l-naẓā'ir*.[51]

That this relationship between women and blind men is not accidental and that it forms in fact an integral part of the mental structure of physical imperfection, can be seen when we examine other types of texts. I have shown in other studies the significance of the arrangement of medieval encyclopedic *adab* works.[52] The arrangement of topics in these multi-subject works reflects a social arrangement presented in descending order, with the most important topics preceding the less important ones. Women are usually discussed toward the end of the text, and have a tendency to appear along with children and the insane, among others. For our purposes, it is what this arrangement tells us about the blind that is significant. The visually handicapped in these encyclopedic *adab* works invariably find themselves allied to the women. This is the case in the prototypical encyclopedic *adab* work, the *'Uyūn al-akhbār* of Ibn Qutayba, as well as in the fourteenth-century encyclopedia, the *Nihāyat al-arab* of al-Nuwayrī.[53] And insofar as the women are also most often linked to the notions of physicality and sexuality, the blind, by extension, are also associated with these notions.

But the placement of the visually defective alongside women can also tell us about the attitude to this defect in general. Women are, of course, an integral part of Islamic society, whether or not one approves of the mode of integration. Mentally associating the blind with women is an integrative attitude to the visual defect. One could argue from this comparison that the blind are not even being treated as abnormal. Theirs is a state of physical inferiority that is as much a normal part of society as is the state of womanhood. And, as we shall see shortly, the blind also share with women associations with physicality and sexuality.

A defect, of course, can be conceived as a loss or a lack. But a lack poses the question of compensation, the idea that this unusual absence may be balanced by an unusual presence. It is, therefore, no surprise that we find the mode of compensation associated with the blind. We are familiar with one form of compensation: spiritual vision replacing physical vision. In the West, examples of this abound: Oedipus, the blind seer Teiresias, the poet Homer, and so on.[54] It is noteworthy that this particular form of compensation does not exist in the Islamic tradition. In fact, it is so alien to the mental structures governing blindness in Islam that we find the sources fleeing from it, as in the discussions centering around the blindness of Jacob. After his vision is restored, Jacob says to his doubting sons: "Did I not tell you I know from God that you know not?" referring to knowledge he gained while he was blind.[55] And, yet, no attempt is made to connect physical blindness with spiritual vision. In effect, the absence of an argument in this direction, along with the attempt to deny Jacob his visual handicap, attests to the fact that this mode of compensation did not form part of the mental structures of blindness.

An area where compensation is developed, however, is the sexual, the blind man being given special qualifications in this sphere. A proverb states *ankaḥ min aʿmā*, "more virile than a blind man."[56] This is, of course, meant to indicate that the blind individual possesses that characteristic to such a degree that he becomes the model against which other individuals are measured. The geographer and cosmographer al-Qazwīnī (d. 682/1283), in his *ʿAjāʾib al-makhlūqāt*, notes that the blind individual is the most virile of people, just as the eunuch is the one whose vision is the most correct. And that is because, in fact, the two functions, vision and sexuality, represent two opposite but complementary poles: what is missing from one is increased in the other.[57] Al-Qazwīnī, by setting the blind individual against the eunuch, makes the mode of compensation even clearer. But what is equally significant in this application of the mode of compensation is its socially integrative conclusion.

Here, of course, it is the blind man who is in question. The sexuality of the blind woman is another matter altogether. In fact, blind women receive scant attention in the sources. A discussion of the blind means a discussion of blind men.[58] The principal reason for this would seem to be that women are, themselves, already a specialized category of humanity. Thus, we do not find, for example, *adab* sections on handicapped women. This entire problem of the degree to which women can take on the properties associated with specific groups in Mamlūk civilization lies beyond the scope of this study.

But the relationship between blindness and sexuality is not peculiar to medieval Islamic civilization. The mental structures governing blindness in the West exploit it as well, but with a crucial difference.

Blindness in the West is linked to sexual transgression: Oedipus plucks out his eyes because of his incestuous relationship with his mother. Concomitant in the Western tradition is the notion of castration: blindness being seen as castration and the blind individual as one whose sexual abilities have been called into question. First of all, blinding, when used as a punishment for a sexual offense, can be, as with Oedipus, understood as a symbolic castration. Second, there seems to be in the modern West, as shown by Kirtley and Henri, a general association of blindness with castration and a general perception that the blind are desexualized or lacking in sexual interest or abilities.[59] Thus, in the West, blindness has an adverse relationship with sexuality.

In the Islamic tradition, on the other hand, the opposite is the case. Al-Qazwīnī expressed this well when he paired off blindness and sexuality and contrasted them with castration and vision.

The medieval Islamic position on the sexuality of the blind is thus the opposite of the Western one. Where the West uses equivalence, the East uses compensation. This should lay to rest the notion that such conceptions derive in any direct manner from the physical realities of blindness. It should also call into question the Freudian variant of this position, that such notions are based upon universal psychological laws.

This idea of compensation, when it is carried to the sexual sphere, is, of course, related to the notion of the physicality of the blind, mentioned above. Thus, the physicality which flows from the nature of the blind as defective also influences the mode of compensation.

Blindness in the West forms part of the moral discourse of crime and punishment, the crime being some form of sexual transgression. This moral discourse is also present in Islam, but free of the sexual connection. Blindness represents a punishment, and its removal a mercy. This is clear in the oniric material present in the biographies of blind individuals in the *Nakt al-himyān*. The removal of the defect invariably takes on religious significance, as when Simāk ibn Ḥarb, who lost his vision, saw Abraham in a dream. Simāk said that his vision had gone, whereupon Abraham told him to go down to the Euphrates and open his eyes with his head under the water, and that God would return his sight to him. Simāk did this and his sight was restored.[60]

Perhaps even more significant for our purposes are the examples in which the Prophet restored sight to blind individuals. These accounts of miracles include, for example, the case of a believer who came to the Prophet with his sight gone. The Prophet asked him what had befallen him, to which he replied that he had been feeding one of his camels and inadvertently put his foot on a snake egg, so his eyes became white, a euphemism for the onset of blindness. The Prophet breathed on his eyes and he was able to see again.[61] These cases show the removal of blindness as a mercy.

When blindness appears as a punishment, the punishment is often connected to theological or religious issues. For example, Qur'ānic verses in Sūrat Ṭāhā (verses 124–126) state that on the resurrection day, the individual will be raised blind because he did not heed God's signs. The dream interpreters adduced this verse to show that he who dreams that he is blind will forget the Qur'ān.[62] There is also the case of Hārūn ibn Ma'rūf, a famous ḥadīth transmitter, who lost his sight and was told in a dream that he who preferred the ḥadīth over the Qur'ān would be punished. Hārūn understood this as an explanation for his having lost his sight.[63]

Clearly, we are dealing with a spiritual transgression which is punished by physical blindness. Hence, blindness can, though it need not always, have a moral significance. When it does, it is as a punishment for a particularly Islamic type of religious fault.

We have seen that blindness can play a role in discourses on the body and physicality as well as in moral ones of crime and punishment. But it is perhaps blindness as a discourse on society which is the most provocative. The blind played a number of visible roles in Mamlūk society. We are speaking here, of course, not necessarily of the actual living conditions of the majority of blind individuals, but of the social roles set out for them by the society, and associated with them by that society. These form as much a part of the *mentalités* of blindness as do religious-legal prescriptions or textual treatments.

The principal professions of the blind were Qur'ān reciter, *mu'adhdhin*, scholar, and poet.[64] What is important for understanding the relationship between these professions and the role of the blind is that these careers were neither specifically reserved for the blind nor exceptional for them. The visually handicapped represented a minority in all these roles, though this minority could become very large, as, for example, with Qur'ān reciters.[65] This means that the blind poet or scholar worked alongside his sighted colleague. It was not generally assumed that a blind man made a better Qur'ān reciter or poet than a sighted individual.

What role do these blind personages then play? If a blind individual can recite the Qur'ān, it means that Qur'ānic recitation is an essentially oral activity, that an oral rendering of the Qur'ān is a full and correct rendering. The same can be said of the blind poet: he testifies to the essential orality of poetry.

Thus, the blind functioned as constant reminders that some of the most central aspects of Islamic culture contained an irreducible oral component. This extends even to scholarship. And it should be remembered in this context that since classical Arabic was rarely written with vocalization, the oral transmission of a text could be vital to its proper understanding. To say the least, an individual's seeing and reading a written Arabic text does not have the decisive advantages over an individual's hearing it, such as he would have, for example, in English.

This problem of oral vs. written forms of cultural transmission and their respective reliance on hearing and vision did not go unnoticed in the Mamlūk sources. We have already alluded to the problems raised by a visually handicapped transmitter; arguments in favor of such a transmitter were linked to the fact that early pious women such as 'Ā'isha transmitted from behind a curtain, and hence without seeing the source of a given statement. This controversy, however, went beyond the specific question of transmission, and provoked a lively debate over the questions of the superiority of sight vs. hearing, deafness vs. blindness.[66] Al-Ṣafadī, in his usual balanced way, presents both sides of the argument. But he includes an argument which demonstrates very well the selectivity that could be employed in the citation of Qur'ānic evidence. In Sūrat al-Baqara, the Qur'ān lists handicaps in the following order: deaf, dumb, blind. Al-Ṣafadī adduces this as evidence of the superiority of hearing, since "deaf" precedes "blind."[67] Yet, in Sūrat al-Isrā' (verse 97), the order is blind, dumb, deaf.

Perhaps the strongest evidence adduced in this argument is that relating to the question of whether a prophet can be blind or deaf. No prophet, al-Ṣafadī argues, was ever deaf; but the blindness of certain prophets was a known fact. In addition, deafness brings along muteness: the mute individual cannot speak because he cannot hear. But if sight disappears, it does not obliterate the faculty of speech. All of this permits our Mamlūk author to conclude that the evidence for the superiority of hearing is stronger than that for the superiority of vision.[68]

It is clear from al-Ṣafadī's discussion that his position did not command universal assent. But it is the very presence of this debate in the tradition which testifies to the role of blindness as a central concern in medieval Islamic civilization; and that because blindness and the blind articulate the values of oral vs. written culture.

When we speak of "oral" and "written," we should keep in mind that in the context of Islamic civilization, this distinction does not have the associations often linked to it of "low" vs. "high" culture. The oral component in classical Islamic civilization is intimately linked to high culture, and forms part and parcel of that civilization. In effect, Islamic culture balances between written and oral concepts of culture and cultural transmission. The division between high and low culture in medieval Islam which forms an equivalent to the Western dichotomy of written and oral culture lies in the diglossia between proper classical Arabic and more dialectical forms of language. Oral high culture is classical Arabic culture. And it remains an elite culture, even if some of its elements may ultimately have had a popular origin.

The oral component was clearly dominant in Islamic civilization at its inception. The backbone of early Arabic secular culture was *jāhilī*, or pre-Islamic, poetry; and even if this poetry was occasionally written down, it was conceived of as having been orally composed and transmitted.[69] Likewise with the Qur'ān: the revelation was a quintessentially oral one, and was only codified in writing at a later stage.

After the conquests, and subsequent greater contact with the older civilizations of the region, written culture became more important. But cultural values of the earlier period survived, and with them the importance of oral culture. It is well known, for example, that the philological tradition relied heavily on oral transmission, and that the oral authority of the bedouin continued long after the rise of urban centers.[70] It is the sanctity of this oral philological tradition which permits someone like the great Mamlūk scholar al-Suyūṭī to discuss the question of the oral transmission of language in his philological compendium *al-Muzhir*.[71]

Hence, we can speak of at least two highly valorized cultural traditions: a secular one based on poetry, and a religious one based on the Qur'ān. Both center on the oral component. It is no accident, therefore, that the blind play a major role in both traditions, as poets and Qur'ān reciters. Nor is it accidental that the proverbial literature gives us *aḥfaẓ min al-'umyān*, or "more capable of retaining in memory than the blind,"[72] on the one hand; while a word from the same verbal root, *ḥāfiẓ*, is employed for someone who has memorized the Qur'ān in its entirety. Memorization is a sacred activity.

This discussion also shows that the distinction between the nature of the oral and the written, as explored in the West from Plato to Paul Ricoeur (and recently "deconstructed" by Jacques Derrida)[73] cannot automatically be applied directly to Islamic civilization. Oral discourse in Islam is not necessarily more contextual than written. It partakes, for example, of the textual property of "autonomy" associated by Ricoeur with the written.[74]

We have seen that blindness and the blind appear in a variety of discourses, and through a variety of modes. There is one final area through which Mamlūk civilization took a global view of its relations with its blind members. This area is humor. Blindness was a fit subject for humor, and we find humorous anecdotes about blind individuals in a variety of medieval Arabic sources. These anecdotes, almost without exception, conform to a general literary model and reflect the same mental structures.

For us, however, two anecdotes will have to suffice. The first concerns the famous eighth-century blind poet, Bashshār ibn Burd. The anecdote was popular and appeared in sources from the ʿAbbasid biographical compendium, the *Ṭabaqāt al-shuʿarāʾ* of Ibn al-Muʿtazz, to Mamlūk texts like the *Nihāyat al-arab* of al-Nuwayrī and the *Nakt* of al-Ṣafadī.

Someone said to Bashshār ibn Burd: "God has never removed the two eyes of a believer without substituting some good for them. So with what did He compensate you?" So Bashshār replied: "With not having to see disagreeable people like you."[75]

The second anecdote has an anonymous hero:

Someone relates that he alighted at a village and went out at night to answer a call of nature. And, behold, there was a blind man on whose shoulder was a jar and who was carrying a lamp. So the sighted man said to him: "You there! As far as you are concerned, night and day are the same. So what is the meaning of the lamp?" The blind man replied: "O busybody! I carry it with me for the blind at heart like you to be guided by it so they do not stumble upon me and make me fall and break my jar."[76]

These anecdotes are superficially different: the protagonist in one is well known, the poet Bashshār ibn Burd; in the other, he is an anonymous blind individual. The anecdote with Bashshār is brief, being composed of a question and an answer. The second anecdote, on the other hand, is more complicated. But both anecdotes display the same functions (understanding a function in the Proppian/Bremondian sense[77]) and, hence, the two anecdotes display the same structure. In both, we have a question posed to a blind individual which puts him on the spot, and in both this blind individual provides a clever reply, ending the anecdote.

It might seem that we are dealing with the cleverness of blind individuals, as opposed to their sighted colleagues. And we might subsequently wish to interpret these actions as indicators of compensation.

But these anecdotes must be seen in the context that generates such stories in the Arabic literary tradition: that of *adab*. *Adab* works abound in anecdotes which display cleverness, and whose protagonists range from misers to party crashers, from thieves to the insane, etc. Verbal cleverness is one of the leitmotifs of medieval Arabic *adab* literature.[78]

If the message of these two anecdotes is thus not primarily that of cleverness, then what is it? To answer this question, we must examine the anecdotes from the point of view of blindness. In both anecdotes, the questions posed to the blind individuals call attention to their state of being different. They are both attempts to set blind individuals apart, to segregate them. However, the two replies, which literally leave the questioners speechless, confound this attempt at segregation. They effectively invert the situation created by the question, by directly involving the questioner and making him the butt of the joke. In one case, he becomes the disagreeable person whom God has spared the blind individual from seeing; in the other, he is the busybody who could conceivably cause the blind man to fall and break his jar. By inverting the situation, both replies call attention to the outlandish nature of the attempt to set the blind individual apart. The anecdotes, in fact, argue for an integrative attitude toward the visually handicapped.

In these anecdotes, and in many others in the literary sources, the sighted person is trying to call attention to, and hence to strengthen, the marginality of the blind individual. Associated with this on the part of the sighted person is a feeling of superiority. The blind man reverses this relationship of normality/marginality and superiority/inferiority by casting the sighted person into the marginal, inferior category. He is disagreeable or blind at heart. This role reversal is, of course, a familiar literary humoristic technique.[79] It is being used here to encapsule a dialogue between the sighted and the blind. And this dialogue represents Mamlūk society's overview of the problem of blindness and the blind. This is a view which recognizes the fundamental difference of the blind, along with their marginality, as seen in the reaction of the "normal" sighted individual. At the same time, this view cautions against the drawing of segregative conclusions from this difference. Finally, it is clearly no accident that this integrating, or in this case we had better say desegregating, message is placed not in the mouth of some benevolent sighted authority but in that of the blind individual himself.

NOTES

1. Susan Sontag, *Illness as Metaphor* (New York, 1978).

2. Marcel Sendrail, *Histoire culturelle de la maladie* (Toulouse, 1980), p. XIII.

3. Patrick H. Hutton, "The History of Mentalities: The New Map of Cultural History," *History and Theory*, XX, 3 (1981), p. 238.

4. Jacques Le Goff, "Les Mentalités: Une Histoire ambigüe," in Jacques Le Goff and Pierre Nora, eds., *Faire de l'histoire*, vol. III, *Nouveaux Objets* (Paris, 1974), p. 76.

5. Le Goff, "Les Mentalités," pp. 77–86.

6. Paul Veyne, "Foucault révolutionne l'histoire,'" in Paul Veyne, *Comment on écrit l'histoire* (Paris, 1978), pp. 201–42.

7. Hayden White, "Michel Foucault," in *Structuralism and Since: From Lévi-Strauss to Derrida*, ed. John Sturrock (Oxford, 1979), p. 92.

8. Hutton, "History of Mentalities," p. 252. Norbert Elias' most important works in this context are: *The History of Manners, Power & Civility*, and *The Court Society*, both translated by Edmund Jephcott (New York, 1982 and 1984).

9. Hutton, "History of Mentalities," p. 240. On the *Annales* school, see, also, Traian Stoianovich, *French Historical Method: The Annales Paradigm* (Ithaca, 1976).

10. Hutton, "History of Mentalities," p. 256. See, also, Philippe Ariès, *L'Homme devant la mort* (Paris, 1977); Michel Foucault, *Histoire de la folie à l'âge classique* (Paris, 1972); idem, *Surveiller et punir: Naissance de la prison* (Paris, 1975).

11. Jean Delumeau would be an exception. See, for example, Jean Delumeau, *La Peur en Occident* (Paris, 1978).

12. Charles M. Radding, "Superstition to Science: Nature, Fortune, and the Passing of the Medieval Ordeal," *American Historical Review*, LXXXIV (1979), pp. 945–69.

13. Veyne, "Foucault révolutionne l'histoire."

14. Hutton, "History of Mentalities," p. 237.

15. Le Goff, "Les Mentalités," p. 78.

16. Guy-H. Allard et al., *Aspects de la marginalité au Moyen-Age* (Montreal, 1975).

17. Ronald Hare, "The Antiquity of Diseases Caused by Bacteria and Viruses, A Review of the Problem from a Bacteriologist's Point of View," p. 128, and A. T. Sandison, "Diseases of the Eye," p. 457, both in Don Brothwell and A. T. Sandison, eds., *Diseases in Antiquity: A Survey of the Diseases, Injuries and Surgery of Early Populations* (Springfield, 1967); Folke Henschen, *The History and Geography of Diseases*, trans. Joan Tate (New York, 1966), p. 270.

18. Al-Ṣafadī, *Nakt al-himyān fī nukat al-'umyān*, ed. Aḥmad Zakī Bāshā (Cairo, 1911).

19. On the medieval Islamic biographical dictionary, see, for example, Fedwa Malti-Douglas, "Biography, Islamic," in the *Dictionary of the Middle Ages*, ed. Joseph R. Strayer, vol. II (New York, 1983), pp. 237–39; Ibrahim Hafsi, "Recherches sur le genre *'Ṭabaqāt'* dans la littérature arabe," *Arabica* XXIII (1976), pp. 227–65 and XXIV (1977), pp. 150–86.

20. See, for example, al-Ṣafadī, *Nakt*, pp. 125–30, 101–10, 204–5. Ibn al-Mu'tazz, *Ṭabaqāt al-Shu'arā'*, ed. 'Abd al-Sattār Aḥmad Farrāj (Cairo, 1968), pp. 21–31; Ibn Qutayba, *Al-Shi'r wa'l-shu'arā'* (Beirut, 1969), pp. 643–46; Ibn Khallikān, *Wafayāt al-a'yān*, ed. Iḥsān 'Abbās (Beirut, n.d.), III, 17–18; Yāqūt, *Mu'jam al-udabā'*, ed. D. S. Margoliouth (London, 1923–31), V, 84–86. For the numerous notices on al-Ma'arrī, see Moustapha Saleh, "Abū'l-'Alā' al-Ma'arrī, bibliographie critique," *Bulletin d'Etudes Orientales*, XXII (1969), pp. 133–204 and XXIII (1970), pp. 197–274.

21. See, for example, al-Jāḥiẓ, *al-Bukhalā'*, ed. Ṭāhā al-Ḥājirī (Cairo, 1971), p. 53; al-Bayhaqī, *al-Maḥāsin wa'l-masāwī*, ed. Muḥammad Abū l-Faḍl Ibrāhīm (Cairo, n.d.), II, 415–16; Al-Tanūkhī, *Nishwār al-Muḥāḍara*, ed. 'Abbūd al-Shālijī (Beirut, 1971–73), II, 358; al-Hamadhānī, *al-Maqāmāt*, ed. Muḥammad 'Abduh (Beirut, 1968 pp. 78–81. See also the excellent study by C. E. Bosworth, *The Medieval Islamic Underworld: The Banū Sāsān in Arabic Society and Literature* (Leiden, 1976), vol. I, especially p. 39 f.

22. Al-Ṣafadī, *Nakt*, pp. 86, 85; al-Nuwayrī, *Nihāyat al-arab fī funūn al-adab* (Cairo, n.d.), IV, 22.

23. Ibn Qutayba, *al-Ma'ārif*, ed. Tharwat 'Ukāsha (Cairo, 1969), pp. 578–79.

24. Yūsuf ibn 'Abd al-Hādī, *Kitāb al-ḍabṭ wa'l-tabyīn li-dhawī al-'ilal wa'l-'āhāt min al-muḥaddithīn*, MS. Ẓāhirīya. For similar mildly abnormal categories, see al-Jāḥiẓ, *Kitāb al-burṣān wa'l-'urjān wa'l-'umyān al-ḥūlān*, ed. 'Abd al-Salām Muḥammad Hārūn (Baghdad, 1982).

25. An-Nuwayrī, *Nihāya*, IV, 16–23.

26. Pierre Henri, *Les Aveugles et la société* (Paris, 1958), pp. 7–15.

27. See, for example, al-Zabīdī, *Tāj al-'arūs* (Beirut, n.d.), X, 255; Ibn Sīda, *al-Muḥkam wa'l-muḥīṭ al-a'ẓam fī al-lugha* (Cairo, 1958), II, 190; Ibn Manẓūr, *Lisān al-'arab* (Cairo, n.d.), XIX, 329. On the appellations of the blind

in al-Ṣafadī, see Fedwa Malti-Douglas, "Pour une Rhétorique onomastique: Les Noms des aveugles chez aṣ-Ṣafadī," *Cahiers d'Onomastique Arabe*, I (1979), pp. 7–19.

28. Al-Ṣafadī, *Nakt*, pp. 6–12.

29. Ibn Ḥajar al-ʿAsqalānī, *Tabṣīr al-muntabih bi-taḥrīr al-mushtabih*, eds. ʿAlī Muḥammad al-Bijāwī and Muḥammad ʿAlī al-Najjār (Cairo, 1966), III, 856; Malti-Douglas, "Pour une Rhétorique," p. 6.

30. See, for example, al-Zabīdī, *Tāj*, III, 348–49; Ibn Manẓūr, *Lisān*, VI, 153–54.

31. See, for example, al-Zabīdī, *Tāj*, VI, 234–36; Ibn Manẓūr, *Lisān*, XI, 211–14.

32. See, for example, al-Zabīdī, *Tāj*, IX, 409; Ibn Manẓūr, *Lisān*, XVII, 433.

33. See, for example, al-Zabīdī, *Tāj*, I, 203; Ibn Manẓūr, *Lisān*, I, 290.

34. Malti-Douglas, "Pour une Rhétorique," pp. 7–19.

35. Al-Ṣafadī, *Nakt*, pp. 114, 127, 145, 209, 212, 312.

36. Donald D. Kirtley, *The Psychology of Blindness* (Chicago, 1975), pp. 20–21; Henri, *Les Aveugles*, pp. 7, 37–38.

37. Al-Ṣafadī, *Nakt*, pp. 225, 86. See also al-Tanūkhī, *Nishwār*, III, 49.

38. See, for example, al-Ṣafadī, *Nakt*, pp. 39, 48, 58–59, 138, 305; al-Suyūtī, *al-Ashbāh wa'l-naẓā'ir fī qawāʿid wa-furūʿ fiqh al-shāfiʿīya* (Cairo, n.d.), p. 274. Cf. *Kitāb Kalīla wa-Dimna*, ed. Louis Cheikho (Beirut, 1969), p. 54.

39. See, for example, Ibn al-Ṭiqṭaqā, *Ta'rīkh al-duwal al-islāmīya (al-Fakhrī)* (Beirut, 1960), p. 127. See also Michael Dols, "The Leper in Medieval Islamic Society," *Speculum*, 58 (1983), p. 899.

40. Al-Ṣafadī, *Nakt*, p. 71; Ibn Qutayba, *ʿUyūn al-akhbār* (Cairo, 1963), IV, 57.

41. See, for example, al-Tanūkhī, *Nishwār*, III, 49.

42. Al-Ṣafadī, *Nakt*, p. 19; Ibn Sīrīn, *Muntakhab al-kalām fī tafsīr al-aḥlām*, printed on the margins of al-Nābulusī's *Taʿṭīr al-anām fi taʿbīr al-manām* (Cairo, n.d.), I, 86; al-Nābulusī, *Taʿṭīr*, II, 85.

43. Al-Ṣafadī, *Nakt*, p. 21. Cf. Artemidorus, *Kitāb taʿbīr al-ru'yā*, trans. Ḥunayn ibn Isḥāq, ed. Tawfīq Fahd (Damascus, 1964), p. 66.

44. The verse is from Sūrat al-Nūr, verse 61. A. J. Arberry, *The Koran Interpreted* (New York, 1974), II, 54; al-Qurṭubī, *al-Jāmiʿ li-aḥkām al-qur'ān* (Cairo, 1967), XII, 313. The same denial of fault can be found in Sūrat al-Fatḥ, verse 17, but without the reference to eating.

45. Al-Thaʿālibī, *Thimār al-qulūb fī 'l-muḍāf wa'l-mansūb*, ed. Muḥammad Abū 'l-Faḍl Ibrāhīm (Cairo, 1965), pp. 608–9.

46. Bruno Roy, "En Marge du monde connu: Les Races des monstres," in Allard et al., *Aspects de la marginalité*, pp. 71–80, and especially p. 76.

47. Adam Mez, *The Renaissance of Islam*, trans. Salahuddin Khuda Bukhsh and D. S. Margoliouth (London, 1937), p. 9. Cf. al-Ṣafadī, *Nakt*, p. 56.

48. Al-Ṣafadī, *Nakt*, pp. 42–44; al-Qurṭubī, *al-Jāmiʿ*, IX, 248. Cf. the arguments over whether an *imām* could be blind, al-Ṣafadī, *Nakt*, pp. 43–44; al-Suyūṭī, *al-Ashbāh*, p. 275; al-Shāfiʿī, *al-Umm* (Beirut, 1973), I, 165.

49. Al-Ṣafadī, *Nakt*, pp. 44–62; al-Suyūṭī, *al-Ashbāh*, pp. 274–75; al-Shāfi'ī, *al-Umm*, I, 165, VII, 46.

50. Al-Ṣafadī, *Nakt*, p. 62.

51. Al-Suyūṭī, *al-Ashbāh*, pp. 273–76.

52. Fedwa Malti-Douglas, *Structures of Avarice: The Bukhalā' in Medieval Arabic Literature* (Leiden, 1985), pp. 12–16.

53. Ibn Qutayba, *'Uyūn*, IV, 1–147; al-Nuwayrī, *Nihāya*, IV, pp. 18–22.

54. See, for example, Kirtley, *Psychology*, pp. 20, 53.

55. Arberry, *Koran*, I, 265.

56. Al-Ṣafadī, *Nakt*, pp. 21–22; al-Maydānī, *Majma' al-amthāl* (Beirut, n.d.), II, 412.

57. Al-Qazwīnī, *'Ajā'ib al-makhlūqāt wa-gharā'ib al-mawjūdāt*, ed. Fārūq Sa'd (Beirut, 1981), p. 348. Cf. al-Ṣafadī, *Nakt*, p. 54.

58. The principal exception would be the discussion over whether a nurse-maid can be blind. See al-Ṣafadī, *Nakt*, pp. 54–55; al-Suyūṭī, *al-Ashbāh*, p. 274.

59. Kirtley, *Psychology*, pp. 21, 27–30, 39, for example; Henri, *Les Aveugles*, pp. 36–37, 56, 61, for example.

60. Al-Ṣafadī, *Nakt*, p. 161. On the dreams of the blind in the *Nakt*, see Fedwa Malti-Douglas, "Dreams, the Blind, and the Semiotics of the Biographical Notice," *Studia Islamica*, LI (1980), pp. 137–62.

61. Al-Ṣafadī, *Nakt*, pp. 227–28.

62. Al-Ṣafadī, *Nakt*, p. 19. Cf. Ibn Sīrīn, *Muntakhab*, I, 86; al-Nābulusī, *Ta'ṭīr*, II, 85.

63. Al-Ṣafadī, *Nakt*, p. 302.

64. This can be seen not only in the *Nakt* but also in biographical compendia devoted to Qur'ān reciters, scholars, etc.

65. See, for example, the notices in Ibn al-Jazarī, *Ghāyat al-nihāya fī ṭabaqāt al-qurrā'*, ed. G. Bergsträsser (Beirut, 1980).

66. Al-Ṣafadī, *Nakt*, pp. 17–18. Cf. André Roman, "À Propos des Vers des yeux et du regard dans l'oeuvre du poète aveugle Baššār b. Burd," *Mélanges de l'Université Saint-Joseph*, XLVI (1970–71), p. 481.

67. Sūrat al-Baqara, verse 18; al-Ṣafadī, *Nakt*, p. 17.

68. Al-Ṣafadī, *Nakt*, pp. 17–18.

69. Of course, modern scholars have debated the authenticity and orality of pre-Islamic poetry, but for the medieval Arabs, neither was really in question. See, for example, Gaudefroy-Demombynes, "Introduction" to Ibn Qutayba, *Introduction au livre de la poésie et des poètes*, trans. Gaudefroy-Demombynes (Paris, 1947), p. XXXI.

70. See, for example, Anwar G. Chejne, *The Arabic Language: Its Role in History* (Minneapolis, 1969), pp. 48, 150.

71. Al-Suyūṭī, *al-Muzhir fī 'ulūm al-lugha wa-anwā'ihā*, eds. Muḥammad Aḥmad Jād al-Mawlā et al. (Cairo, n.d.), I, 137 f.

72. Al-Ṣafadī, *Nakt*, p. 83; al-Maydānī, *Majma'*, I, 318. Here also we find the mode of compensation, but it is not developed to the same degree that sexual compensation is. In addition, memorization is not spiritual vision. It is an intellectual activity of the most mechanical sort.

73. Paul Ricoeur, *Hermeneutics & the Human Sciences*, ed. and trans. John B. Thompson (Cambridge, 1981), pp. 139–40, 199–201; Jonathan Culler, "Jacques Derrida," in Sturrock, ed., *Structuralism*, pp. 166–73.

74. Ricoeur, *Hermeneutics*, pp. 139–40.

75. Al-Ṣafadī, *Nakt*, p. 66. With slight variants in Ibn al-Mu'tazz, *Ṭabaqāt*, p. 22; Abū 'l-Faraj al-Iṣbahānī, *Kitāb al-aghānī* (Beirut, 1970), III, 34; al-Nuwayrī, *Nihāya*, IV, 420–21.

76. Al-Ṣafadī, *Nakt*, p. 67. With slight variants in al-Nuwayrī, *Nihāya*, IV 22; Ibn al-Jawzī, *Akhbār al-adhkiyā'*, ed. Muḥammad Mursī al-Khawlī (Cairo, 1970), p. 154.

77. Vladimir Propp, *Morphologie du conte*, trans. Marguerite Derrida (Paris, 1970); Claude Bremond, *Logique du récit* (Paris, 1973).

78. See, for example, Malti-Douglas, *Structures of Avarice*; idem, "Structure and Organization in a Monographic *Adab* Work: *al-Taṭfīl* of al-Khaṭīb al-Baghdādī," *Journal of Near Eastern Studies*, 40 (1981), pp. 227–45; idem, "Classical Arabic Crime Narratives: Thieves and Thievery in *Adab* Literature," *Journal of Arabic Literature*, forthcoming.

79. See, for example, Henri Bergson, *Le Rire: Essai sur la signification du comique* (Paris, 1972), p. 73; Malti-Douglas, *Structures of Avarice*, pp. 108–37.

16
Sur un Poème d'Abū Nuwās

André Miquel

ON SE PROPOSE ICI, en hommage à ce parfait connaisseur de la langue français qu'est Bernard Lewis, la traduction de l'un des poèmes les plus célèbres d'Abū Nuwās. On la fera suivre de quelques commentaires qui, sans prétendre apporter quoi que ce soit de neuf à notre connaissance de cet auteur, traitent d'une problème important: le statut du poète et de son oeuvre.

1 Ne pense plus au souvenir des campements,
Lorsque le vent du sud les noie dans la poussière,
Lieux vivants hier encore, et rongés par le temps!
2 Laisse au fier animal, à son maître, une terre
Où vont trottant chameaux et chamelles de race!
3 Pour plantes, ces pays ont le *ṭalḥ*, le *‘ushar*;
À part l'hyène et le loup, on y fait maigre chasse.
4 Avec ceux du désert, renonce à tout espoir
De plaisir et de vie, car leur vie est misère!
5 Laisse-les donc boire leur lait, puisqu'ils sont gens
À ne connaître rien des douceurs de la terre,
6 Et si le lait se caille, alors, pisse dedans,
Tu le peux: il n'est pas de péché en l'affaire.
7 Mieux vaut un vin bien clair, rafraîchi sous le vent,
Qu'un courtois échanson présente dans un verre,
8 À la ronde; la jarre, au secret, l'a vieilli,
Bouillant, mais de la flamme ignorant la brûlure,
9 Et son bruit, dans la jarre, imitait le murmure
Du prêtre en oraison devant son crucifix.
10 Il te vient présenté par la main d'un garçon
Aux inflexions fluettes: un vrai faon de gazelle.
11 Ses nourrices ont su lui faire la leçon:
En lui, grâces, parfum et beauté, tout se mêle.

12 Si peu qu'il boive, il va se débrider pour toi,
Et le vin, insidieux, dénouer sa ceinture.
13 Caresse-le et, pris à d'étranges appas,
Ton coeur en oubliera les vieilles meurtrissures.
14 Sa hanche ploie; s'il marche, on voit se dessiner
Une verge cachée aux plis de sa tunique.
15 Il se penche sur toi, t'agace à ses mimiques,
Laisse croire qu'il tombe: à fondre il est tout prêt.
16 Vois les femmes, nigaud: quand le mari s'absente,
Leur oeillade est reçue d'un drôle, à point nommé.
17 Eh! vous, femmes! Cessez un peu de me blâmer!
Vais-je me repentir, croyez-vous? Vaine attente!
18 Vous flétrissez le vice, et après? Quel courage
Et quelle liberté n'auraient pas de travers?
19 C'est cela, vivre, et non la tente, le désert!
C'est cela, vivre, et non se nourrir de laitages!
20 Que pèse le désert face à l'arc de Kisrā,
Et l'enclos aux bestiaux face à un hippodrome?
21 Tant pis pour vos efforts: je ne suis point votre homme.
C'est jour de deuil pour vous. Se repentir? Pas moi.

NOTES

Le poème est bâti sur le mètre *wāfir*.

v. 2: *wajnā'*: robuste ou mafflue (chamelle), en fait: animal de bât. J'ai traduit par: "fier animal."

v. 3: respectivement *acacia gummifera* et *calotropis procera*.

v. 4: "ceux du désert" (*A'rāb*): les Arabes bédouins.

v. 20: l'arc de Kisrā (Īwān Kisrā): restes du palais des souverains sassanides (dont Chosroès, Kisrā, est le symbole), en bordure du Tigre, dans la région de Bagdad, à Ctésiphon (al-Madā'in). "Hippodrome," *mayādīn*, plur. de *maydān*: les fastes de la ville opposés aux chétivités du désert.

COMMENTAIRE

Ce poème (pp. 35–37 de l'edition Dār Ṣādir—Dār Bayrūt, Beyrouth, 1382/1962; début: *Da'i 'l-aṭlāla tasfīhā 'l-janūbu . . .*; rime en *-bu*) est l'une des pièces bachiques (*khamrīyāt*) d'Abū Nuwās, qui vécut de 145 à 199 de l'Hégire (762–814 ap. J.C.), soit à l'époque où le jeune califat abbasside de Bagdad donne un cadre nouveau au débat entre anciens et modernes, entre Arabes rivés aux mythes du désert et Persans soucieux de se tailler leur juste place dans une civilisation ouverte à toutes les cultures. Le poème est exemplaire à plus d'un titre. Il propose, en effet, le poème nouveau, le poète nouveau et, pour l'un et l'autre, un nouveau statut.

Poème nouveau, disais-je. À la vieille ode (*qaṣīda*), Abū Nuwās substitue, derrière l'apparente spontanéité du propos, une composition nouvelle, nette et même brutale. Composition qui, en fait, n'est qu'une opposition: entre deux modèles de vie, confrontés l'un à l'autre sans transition aucune (vv. 1–6 et 7–16), à quoi fait suite la conclusion (vv. 17–21). En d'autres termes: thèse, antithèse, choix. Les finesses de l'organisation de détail confirment la rigueur de la présentation, le travail poétique doublant régulièrement les trouvailles de l'inspiration. Pour le modèle récusé, la condamnation est immédiate et insistante: "ne pense plus . . .", "laisse . . .", "laisse-les donc . . .". Elle se double de l'affirmation péremptoire du v. 6 et de mots (*ṭalḥ, 'ushar,* "maigre chère," "misère) qui sont autant de critiques d'une vie résumée par un mot: l'indigence, économique et culturelle. Variation brutale avec le modèle proposé: ici, un seul mot d'approbation ("mieux vaut"), la défense du modèle étant laissée au tableau lui-même et aux mots du plaisir. Quant à la conclusion, elle répond aux lois d'une rhétorique parfaite. Elle élargit en effet le débat, dont elle reprend les termes, mais en les transformant: le modèle récusé est maintenant réduit à un terme unique, la pauvreté économique ("tente," "laitages," "enclos aux bestiaux"); à l'inverse, le modèle approuvé se développe sous trois traits impliqués, certes, dans sa description concrète des vv. 7–16, mais qui ne sont explicités qu'ici: la vraie vie, la grandeur ("arc de Kisrā," "hippodrome"), le conflit entre péché et liberté.

Nouveauté de la forme, sans doute, mais plus encore du fond, qui suscite et sous-tend la première. La révolution—car c'en est une—réside dans le propos choisi, à savoir la critique de la vie bédouine, et dans la violence même de cette critique. Les moyens en sont variés. Voyez d'abord comment débute le poème: ni plus ni moins qu'à la manière d'une *qaṣīda* classique; rien ne permet, en ces deux premiers vers, de penser que nous allons nous installer dans un autre registre. D'où la violence de l'attaque du v. 3, dérobée jusqu'ici, et qui éclate. La noblesse étalée aux vv. 1–2 révèle ici, comme derrière un rideau brusquement déchiré, ses coulisses, ses pauvres coulisses: à la "terre," la mère noble, succèdent des pays, sous le pluriel de l'anonymat; aux animaux de race, les prédateurs et deux plantes dont l'une est un épineux et l'autre (employée surtout comme médicament) un trompe-l'oeil, une imposture: les dictionnaires et glossateurs nous disent en effet que les fruits du *'ushar*, en grappes violettes, sont splendides d'apparence, mais cendre au dedans. La critique conclut par la redondance: par trois fois, le poète dénie à la vie bédouine l'appellation même de vie (vv. 4–5, où j'ai traduit, la troisième fois, par "douceurs de la terre" le *raqīqu 'l-'ayshi* de l'original); redondance qui met en cause et une ethnie (les Arabes, sous leur modèle du désert, au v. 4) et un code (ces prétendus "vrais hommes," *rijāl*, les "gens" du v. 5, pratiquent une vertu à la fois sans mérite—puisque imposée par la frugalité elle-même imposée par la misère—et trop chèrement payée). Dès lors, la critique féroce et crue peut se donner libre cours au v. 6, autour du mot-clé de péché (*ḥūb*): celui-ci ne réside pas dans la contestation, fût-elle outrancière, d'une fausse vie, mais dans cette vie même.

Après la critique, l'éloge. Il consiste, en évitant les mots abstraits, à proposer un certain nombre de termes et tableaux concrets du plaisir. Mais en même temps, à travers ceux-ci, sont posées trois catégories générales qui contrastent, terme à terme, avec celles du modèle récusé. À l'espace du strict nécessaire est substitué celui du superflu, au liquide qui tient lieu de tout, le lait, celui qui vient après tout, le vin, au vent dévastateur du sud celui, vivifiant, du nord sur le vin rafraîchi (v. 7, avec *shamūl*). Le désert était l'espace d'une vertu, trop chèrement payée on l'a dit; lui succède ici l'espace du dévoiement, les "hommes" étant relayés par les femmes (les nourrices-maquerelles, *dāyāt*, et les femmes adultères) et surtout les êtres ambigus (les éphèbes). Le tout avec un renversement notable des connotations: la croupe (*ridf*, "hanche" du v. 14) est celle non plus de la femme aimée selon les canons de la vieille poésie, mais de l'éphèbe; la bride (*'inān*, v. 14) celle non plus de l'animal noble, dans l'esprit de la chevalerie (*furūsīya*), mais de l'amour interdit; enfin, on notera le *rasha'* du v. 10, ce "faon" égaré des puretés du désert aux compromissions de la ville. Troisième et dernier contraste, qui résume le tout: si le désert est le lieu de la nature, la culture prend tous ses droits avec la ville, ses bonnes manières (*adīb*, "courtois," au v. 7) et ses abords célèbres (v. 9 où l'évocation du prêtre rappelle, d'une part, le rôle connu des chrétiens dans ce commerce du vin, avec les tavernes près des couvents, et, d'autre part, que le terrain "interdit" du vin rejoint un autre domaine des marges, celui des sujets protégés, des *dhimmī*).

Le poète, on le voit, est déjà engagé dans ce programme: la revendication d'une poésie nouvelle lui impose, à lui aussi, de changer de peau. Partant, la poésie et lui changent de statut. La fonction du poète ne se réduit pas à un simple métier (*ṣinā'a*) dont il suffirait de changer les règles. Elle vise plus haut: à un rang et à un rôle sociaux. Le poète est plus qu'un artiste: une voix. Comme jadis dans la tribu sans doute, mais la tribu n'existe plus. C'est désormais à l'échelle d'une société plus vaste, quasi universelle, que se délivre le message. Face aux Arabes, face à l'Islam, face à la vie.

Vis-à-vis des Arabes, le message consiste à récuser non pas la *'arūba,* mais les formes périmées de celle-ci. La vertu? Mais qu'est-ce que la vertu sans la tentation? Liberté? Mais qu'est-ce que la liberté dans la misère et dans la crainte, cette crainte qui s'exprime si bien au v. 20, où l'enclos, la *zarība,* devient symboliquement l'antithèse de l'espace tant vanté, illimité, du désert? Le plaidoyer pour la ville et la nouvelle histoire dont elle est à la fois la cause et l'effet n'est pas dirigé contre les Arabes et leur langue. Il tend, au contraire—et dans cette langue même, avec les prestiges de sa plus haute expression possible, la poésie—à réintégrer l'arabe dans l'histoire, à l'arracher à une vie dépassée pour lui faire parler le langage de son siècle. Fût-ce, à chaque fois que c'est possible, en respectant les formes—celles du langage, encore une fois, appuyées à une *formation* sans faille en cette matière, comme ce fut le cas pour Abū Nuwās—et le ton: ce poème n'est, après tout, que l'expression évoluée d'un genre très en honneur dans l'ancienne poésie, la satire (*hijā'*).

Face à l'Islam, le message est plus subtil, comme on peut le voir dans la conclusion (vv. 17–21). On a dit que, pour ce qui est de la vie bédouine, le péché n'existe pas par cela même qu'il n'a rien où s'alimenter. Ou, alors, que le péché était de vivre cette vie misérable. Pour la vie urbaine et le poète qui l'incarne, la situation est tout autre car, ici, la tentation est permanente. Pire: le péché n'est pas seulement une nécessité de l'ordre de l'existence, il paraît aussi revendiqué sur le plan des valeurs; le refus du repentir (*tawba*) s'exprime fortement aux vv. 17–18, et davantage: c'est sur lui que se clôt le poème. Provocation? Oui et non. Je dirais que, si le péché est ainsi posé comme allant de soi, il n'est pas revendiqué cependant comme une devise, valable pour tous et pour toujours; affirmé, plutôt, comme un mal nécessaire et passager. Nécessaire: il est l'expression marginale d'un mode de vie, celui du luxe citadin, envers du monde nomade réintégré pour la circonstance dans la conclusion, avec ses tentes et son lait; il est aussi, ce péché, le mal d'une classe d'hommes, non plus les *rijāl* et les *A'rāb* du désert, mais les *fityān* et les *aḥrār* (v. 18), représentants de communautés mâles sans doute, mais de communautés urbaines et qui en ont les caractéristiques, bonnes et mauvaises. Mal passager: le "jour" du dernier vers laisse entendre que le péché est une chute, indéfiniment passagère et renouvelée, inhérente à la condition humaine, mais ne remettant pas en cause la référence suprême qui permet de le qualifier, précisément, de péché; c'est le lieu de se souvenir qu'Abū Nuwās se vantait d'avoir fait tout ce qui déplaît à Dieu, hormis de verser dans le polythéisme. Le principe (*aṣl*), on le voit, est sauf, et tout se joue au niveau des applications (*furūʿ*).

Mais Abū Nuwās ne se définit pas que dans une histoire et une société. Les Arabes et l'Islam lui permettent, en fait, de revendiquer le statut essentiel, éternel, du poète face à toutes les histoires, à toutes les sociétés possibles: dans son être même, en un mot. La violence du propos, sa crudité qui culmine avec la désignation de l'intimité de l'éphèbe, au v. 14, ont valeur emblématique. De quoi s'agit-il finalement? Ni plus ni moins que de liberté. À condition d'en préciser les modes. Et d'abord, dans les faits, liberté absolue? Voire. Quelques-uns des poètes du temps ont payé de leur vie un langage trop franc, dans la mesure où cette franchise heurtait trop brutalement la politique, le dogme religieux ou, simplement, ces bonnes moeurs dont les limites, on le sait, varient de société à société et d'époque à époque. Malgré l'indulgence reconnue et affichée pour les poètes—et les fous—un homme comme Bashshār ibn Burd sut ce qu'il en coûtait d'aller trop loin, et quant à Abū Nuwās lui-même, est-il mort au cabaret, en scène dirais-je, ou en prison?

Ces questions, en réalité, en masquent ou en appellent d'autres, les vraies, qui me semblent toucher au coeur du débat. Mon sentiment est que la liberté poétique est essentiellement une liberté de forme, qui vise, tout ensemble, le registre, le champ d'exercice et la finalité du discours du poète. Le registre, d'abord. Il tient en un mot, un seul: le scandale, conçu comme langage libéré et envers de la morale codifiée. Une des formes de la liberté consiste en effet à admettre, implicitement ou non, que la violence du discours poétique est directement proportionnelle à l'hypocrisie des réalités sociales. Prenons par exemple le péché. Le langage théologique pose qu'il est dans la nature du pauvre d'être tenté puisqu'il n'a rien, et dans celle du riche d'être blasé puisqu'il a tout. Le poète, lui, brouille les termes: le pauvre, ici l'Arabe du désert, est heureux du peu qu'il a—et il n'a donc aucun mérite puisque ignorant la tentation—le riche, celui des villes d'Iraq, est parfaitement heureux du superflu qu'il possède, et il faut lui pardonner de vivre dans une tentation perpétuellement victorieuse. Autre exemple: l'homosexualité. L'ordre social l'admet, hypocritement, tant qu'elle se cache et n'est pas attentatoire à l'ordre public, tandis que le scandale poétique consiste dans la revendication de cette déviance, revendication qui est, de fait, scandaleuse en ce que, justement, elle se veut publique.

Quelle est donc la fonction du poète? La réforme de la société? Certainement pas, non plus que celle de la religion. Il peut s'y vouer, mais c'est un autre problème. Le véritable exercice de la poésie consiste à réclamer, pour son auteur, la liberté au sein d'une société codifiée par et pour d'autres. En faveur du poète et des hommes nouveaux, nouveaux héros (*fityān*), nouveaux libres, libérés ou libertins (*aḥrār*), on plaidera donc pour un comportement élitiste; un comportement que la société, à condition de n'être pas poussée à bout, ici comme ailleurs finalement concède.

Ainsi, le but de la poésie ne réside pas, en dernière analyse, dans la quête d'une vérité, mais dans la proclamation de ce que l'on croit qu'elle est, et dans la revendication de la liberté et des moyens nécessaires à ce message. Elle est donc, doublement, une manière de dire: dire les choses telles qu'elles sont (ou telles qu'on les voit), et le dire autrement. Quant à dire autre chose, cela, décidément, est encore une autre affaire. Et un autre débat pour la poésie.

17
The Islamization of the Gulf

F. Omar

Introduction

THIS ARTICLE IS an attempt to study the conditions of the Arab Gulf region at the advent of Islam, and how the new religion was accepted in that region. Although the Arab Gulf region comprises many provinces, the present research is limited to the only two provinces known during the early Islamic period, Bahrain and Oman.[1]

Bahrain is a province which extends along the western coast of the Arab Gulf between Basra in Iraq and Jurfar in Oman.[2] Muslim geographers[3] considered it a part of the Arabian peninsula, but the information they provide about its boundaries are scanty and of a general nature. This is probably to be attributed, among other reasons, to the fact that Bahrain is geographically a part of the Arab homeland on the one hand, and because of the integration of the Arab population of Bahrain with their Arab neighbors in Yamāma, Oman, and Iraq, on the other hand.

According to Yāqūt,[4] Bahrain consisted of many regions: al-Khat, al-Qaṭīf, al-Āra, Hajar, Baynūna, al-Zāra, Juwātha, al-Sābūr, Dārīn, al-Ghāba, Hajar al-Ṣafa, and al-Mashqar. Yāqūt adds that Hajar was the center of Bahrain, and its most important city.

As for the province of Oman, it lies in the southeastern part of the Arabian peninsula, overlooking both the Arabian Gulf and the Arabian Sea. Its geographical location, therefore, had great commercial and military importance during the early Islamic period. Oman's ports became at that time the greatest centers for maritime trade, as well as military bases to insure the security and stability of the Gulf.

Although the geographical location of Oman is strategically far more important than that of Bahrain, no clear or full description of its boundaries is found in Islamic sources.[5] However, it can be deduced from many traditions[6] that Oman extended between Jurfar in the north, and al-Ashfa, which is part of Shaḥar on the southern coast of the Arabian peninsula. These Omani boundaries were subject to variation according to political and administrative conditions.

These two provinces, as the sources indicate, seem to have been thickly populated at the advent of Islam. The majority of the tribes of 'Abd al-Qays, and part of the tribes of Tamīm, Bakr ibn Wā'il, and Azd dwelled in Bahrain.[7] As for Oman, it can be observed that Azd was its biggest and most powerful tribe, a fact which led early historians to describe Oman as "the homeland of the Azd." Other tribes which inhabited Oman were Sāma ibn Lu'ay, 'Abd al-Qays, Tamīm, and Bakr ibn Wā'il.[8] Minority elements of alien races, such as Persians, Zuṭṭ, and Sayābija, were also to be found in these regions. The metropolitan character of Oman and Bahrain accounts for the existence there of a variety of religions,[9] such as paganism, Judaism, and Christianity. Christianity found more fertile ground in the Gulf regions than did Judaism, partly because of the isolated nature of Judaism. Many Christian missionaries sent by the Roman Empire played roles in converting the people to this religion. Christianity also spread through the Nestorian Lakhmids of Iraq, who enjoyed political influence over the Arab Gulf region before Islam. However, the influence of Christianity remained limited in the Gulf region, as it was associated with the political and military activities of Rome and Abyssinia.

As for Judaism, it is difficult to estimate the exact period of its spread into the Gulf area. It seems, however, that the Jews came as traders and immigrants mainly from Iraq, and distinguished themselves in commerce, finance, and agriculture, although they remained a small minority.

The teachings and complicated rituals of Magianism held no appeal for the Arabs. This religion was, in addition, associated with the expansionist policy of the Sasanians. The hegemony of Islam put an end to it, and fire worship ceased in the Gulf.

The Spread of Islam In Bahrain

Bahrain is one of the regions in the Arab Gulf which accepted the Islamic *da'wa* peacefully.[10] Early Islamic sources, as well as local Gulf historians, describe how Islam spread in Bahrain, the "delegations" (*wufūd*) of the tribes to Muḥammad, and the many letters exchanged between the Prophet and a number of distinguished personalities in Bahrain.

Many differently phrased and presumably independent accounts agree that the people of Bahrain were prepared for a new *da'wa*, and ready to accept a new religion.[11] Early historians agree that the Prophet himself took the initiative, by sending a letter with al-'Alā ibn al-Ḥaḍramī to al-Mundhir ibn Sāwa al-Tamīmī in Hajar, calling upon him to accept Islam.[12] Historical accounts differ on the date of this letter, but it is only natural to assume that it was sent after the year 8/629, when the Islamic *da'wa* became stronger and the fame of the Prophet spread all over Arabia. Al-Mundhir al-Tamīmī accepted Islam together with his Arab followers and some non-Arabs.[13] As for the rest of the inhabitants, such as the Christians, Jews, and Magians, they held on to their faith, and agreed to pay land tax (*kharāj*), especially on dates, and poll tax (*jizya*).

However, although these events are well established facts, they bear an element of exaggeration. It was not possible to speak of a wholesale spread of Islam among the Arabs. The Muslim state was still new in comparison with the old Sasanian Empire, whose influence was still felt in some regions of the Gulf, especially in the coastal area. At any rate, accounts of the Prophet's early contacts with Bahrain, and of his sending a delegation to it are all authentic. The early acceptance by al-Mundhir ibn Sāwa of Islam can be explained because of the additional strength and political influence which it gave him against the Persian Sasanian strongholds in Bahrain. This accounts for his survival as ruler of Bahrain until his death in A.H. 11/A.D. 632.

Caetani[14] rejects all these historical accounts, assuming that they were later fabrications, and that the spread of Islam in Bahrain was weak and limited. In addition, he states that the ruler of Bahrain forced some groups of Arabs to accept Islam.

Caetani gives two reasons for his claim: first, because Bahrain was distant from the Hijaz, and its contacts with the new *da'wa* were weak. Second, the wars of *al-ridda* (apostasy) in Bahrain after the Prophet's death were fierce, which means that Islam must have met with strong resistance.

However, Caetani's claim has no foundation, because he does not depend on historical accounts. Different early historians agree that commercial contacts between Bahrain and the Hijaz had already existed previously.[15] As for the wars of *al-ridda*, they were, in fact, not as Caetani tries to describe them: the Muslim forces under the command of al-'Alā ibn al-Ḥaḍramī crushed the apostates before they had gained much ground in Bahrain.

As for the Prophet's letters to Bahrain, our early sources, both chronicles[16] and local histories,[17] agree neither on the number of letters nor on the names of those who received them. There are about eight letters, some of them to individuals, others to Arab tribes or Magians of Hajar, and others to the "people of Bahrain" or the "people of Hajar" in general.[18]

Historical accounts also differ on when these letters were sent, especially as there are no dates on the letters themselves. It seems, however, that most of them were sent after the conquest of Mecca in 8/629, since by that time the new Islamic state had become stronger and better established in the Hijaz. Upon examining these letters, we find that they can be divided into two groups: the first group contained only the instructions and information on Islam given to the delegations which visited Medina, while the second group called upon the people of Bahrain to join Islam, and promised them help.

On the other hand, these letters reflect the fact that Islam faced some resistance from tribal factions in Bahrain. Another important phenomenon reflected by these letters is that the people of Bahrain were divided into many sections before the advent of Islam. These tribal and regional groups, which valued their freedom, did not pay much attention to any central authority; this accounts for the large number of letters sent by the Prophet to each section of the population.

It is worth citing an example of one of these letters from the Prophet to Bahrain:

> The Messenger of God, God bless and preserve him, wrote to al-Mundhir ibn Sāwa: "Furthermore, my messengers have praised you. Insofar as you act well, I shall act well towards you, and reward you for your work; and you shall deal uprightly with God and His Messenger. Peace be upon you." He sent it by al-'Alā ibn al-Ḥaḍramī.
>
> . . . al-Mundhir wrote to the Messenger of God, announcing his acceptance of Islam and his belief in it: "I have read your letter to the people of Hajar. Some of them like Islam and admire it, and have entered it; and some dislike it. In my country there are Magians and Jews. Tell me what you command about that." The Messenger of God wrote to him: "Insofar as you act well, we shall not remove you from your position as ruler. He who remains a Jew or a Magian is obliged to pay the tax. . . ."[19]

The people of Bahrain also sent delegations (*wufūd*) to Muḥammad. Sources give many different accounts on these delegations. It is most probable that these were two delegations of the tribe of 'Abd al-Qays to Medina. The first took place in 9/630, and was led by al-Ashaj al-Mundhir ibn 'Āidh al-'Abī. The delegation consisted of about twenty men including al-Jārūd Bishr ibn Ḥanash al-'Abdī. The latter was Christian, and accepted Islam on this occasion at the hands of the Prophet.[20] Ibn Hishām relates the story of the meeting as follows:

> . . . when he [al-Jārūd] came to the apostle he spoke to him, and the apostle explained Islam to him and invited him to enter it with kindly words. He replied: Muhammad, I owe a debt. If I leave my religion for yours, will you guarantee my debt? The apostle said, 'Yes I guarantee that what God has guided you to is better than that,' so he and his Companions accepted Islam.[21]

It seems, however, that al-Ashaj al-'Abdī was not a chief among his people, and therefore had no great influence on them. At his meeting with the Prophet, he did not promise to work for the spread of Islam in Bahrain, but rather asked the Prophet to write a letter to the people of Bahrain. The Prophet agreed, and the letter was sent with al-'Alā ibn al-Ḥaḍramī, who returned with the delegation to Bahrain. The letter was delivered to al-Mundhir ibn Sāwa al-Tamīmī, who was the ruler of Bahrain at that time, and exercised great influence. Ṭabarī calls al-Mundhir al-Tamīmī *ṣāḥib al-Bahrain*. Other sources call him king or governor (*'āmil*) of Bahrain.[22] He probably had some ties with the Sasanians, whose authority was only nominal, and limited to some coastal parts of Bahrain. It is noticeable that our historical traditions do not speak of the role played by al-Ashaj al-'Abdī and his delegation in spreading the Islamic *da'wa*. This substantiates the theory that they were of no influence in the region. Al-Ashaj himself, together with some members of the delegation, immigrated to Basra in Iraq shortly after his return to Bahrain. It is known that most of the tribe of 'Abd al-Qays immigrated to Basra when this new city became the center of the Islamic conquests extending eastward into southwestern Persia.

The second delegation from Bahrain was headed by al-Jārūd Bishr ibn Ḥanash al-'Abdī, who was an influential chief among 'Abd al-Qays. This delegation took place in 10/631. Al-Jārūd became a real Muslim, and his role in spreading Islam among his people was great.[23]

Al-Jārūd's influential position was instrumental during the Ridda wars. He succeeded in deterring his tribe from apostasy, and backed the governor of Bahrain, al-'Alā ibn al-Ḥaḍramī, against the apostates from Banū Bakr and other tribes, who were led by al-Ḥātam ibn Ḍubay'a. Al-Jārūd not only backed Islam against the apostates, but also succeeded in winning over a section of Bakr led by al-Muthannā al-Shaybānī, who joined the Muslim armies, and helped al-ʿAlā to achieve final victory.

Before the advent of Islam, Bahrain was semi-independent. One should not exaggerate the connections between the Sasanians and the people of Bahrain, which were not strong at all. Sasanian rule over Bahrain was only nominal and limited to certain coastal areas where the Sasanian ships put into harbor. It seems that their aim was merely to prevent the Arabs from carrying out hostile actions against Persian interests, especially mercantile ones. It is also probable that the Sasanians were trying in vain to stop Arab immigration to the eastern coast of the Arab Gulf,[24] and to control contacts between the Arabs of the eastern and western coasts.

Before the advent of Islam, Sibīkhit, the Sasanian Marzuban, resided in Hajar with a small garrison. There took place an exchange of letters between him and Muḥammad, in which the Prophet invited him to visit Medina, the capital of the new Islamic state: however, it seems that he did not accept Islam. At the same time, Sibīkhit did not ally himself with the enemies of Islam, or with the apostates in Bahrain. This non-aligned stand taken by the Marzuban did not satisfy the Sasanians, who dismissed him, and appointed a new Marzuban named al-Mukaʿbar Fayrūz, who was the commander of the Persian garrison in Bahrain. Al-Mukaʿbar transferred his residence from Hajar to the coastal port of al-Zāra, to be near the Persian fleet, and prepared to meet an attack. Al-Mukaʿbar's resistance to Islam did not last long, since he was defeated and killed in 13/634, during the caliphate of Abū Bakr al-Ṣiddīq.[25]

After the defeat of the apostates, Bahrain became part of the Muslim state, and al-Mundhir al-Tamīmī stayed as the real ruler of Bahrain, helped by other tribal chiefs. We do have a list of the governors (*wulāt*) of Bahrain sent by the caliphs of Medina, but the real power was still in the hands of tribal heads in Bahrain. It is true that the Muslim governor was responsible for maintaining peace and order, and for spreading Islam, as well as for collecting taxes from the people. Apart from that, his influence was only minor.

Bahrain was at first connected administratively with Medina, but was later assigned to the governor of Basra in Iraq during the caliphate of ʿUthmān (23–35/644–656).[26] This helped to increase tribal migration from Bahrain to Iraq.

The Islamization of Oman

Historical accounts[27] agree that Oman had peacefully accepted Islam by the end of the Prophet's life. It is related that Muḥammad sent 'Amr ibn al-'Āṣ to Jayfar and 'Abd, the two sons of al-Julunda, to deliver a letter calling them to Islam. They responded along with their tribes. However, accounts differ on whether this took place in A.H. 6, 8, or 11. In our opinion these different accounts are not necessarily contradictory, for it is possible that the Prophet began his initiative in 6/627 after the Ḥudaybīya pact with Quraysh, and then reestablished contacts in 8/629, after the conquest of Mecca, when the new Islamic state acquired strength and fame all over Arabia. It is worth mentioning that the ties between Oman and the Hijaz were deeply rooted.[28] Arab tribes such as Banū Sāma ibn Lu'ay had immigrated to Oman centuries before Islam and settled there.

Commercial contacts between Oman and Hijaz, especially the export of Omani and Ṣuḥārī textiles, were strong. The geographic, strategic, and commercial position of Oman must have caught the Prophet's attention, a fact which might account for the early contacts of the Islamic state with the people of Oman.

Caetani,[29] on the contrary, presumes that the initiative came from the Julunda rulers of Oman, who were facing strong tribal opposition and needed help from the Islamic state in Medina. This assumption is groundless, as it is not based on authentic historical accounts. It is true that their acceptance of Islam gave the rulers of Oman a stronger position and many political advantages, but it did not put an end to tribal and regional opposition to the rule of al-Julunda. This indicates that tribal factionalism was not altogether abolished with the advent of Islam.

The central government in Medina did not impose heavy duties on the people of Oman. The Arab 'Omānīs were, of course, expected to pay taxes, such as *zakāt* and *kharāj*, to Medina. As for the Magians, Jews, and others, they paid the *jizya*. Many historical accounts speak of different 'Omānī delegations to meet the Prophet in Medina.[30] Most of them represented the Azd of Oman. It must be said, however, that some of these accounts are fabrications of a later period, when the struggle for power fostered competition among the tribes over primacy in accepting Islam and meeting the Prophet. What is notable is that these delegations reflect dissensions among tribal factions in Oman, and the lack of a central authority exercising power over all Oman. It is also noticeable that these delegations did not play a major and active part in spreading Islam in Oman, which indicates that they had no political or social influence over their tribes. The prophet Muḥammad also sent letters to Oman probably after the conquest of Mecca in A.H. 8/A.D. 629. The sources describe three different letters:[31] one to Jayfar and ʻAbd, the Julunda rulers of Oman; another went to the delegation of the tribes Thumāla and Ḥadān; and a third letter was sent to the people of Oman in general. These letters are brief and to the point. In them, the Prophet calls upon the Omanis to accept Islam, and promises to back them if they do so. On the other hand, if they do not accept Islam, the letter threatens to destroy their authority. It seems, however, that these letters show the early stages of contacts between the Islamic state and the people of Oman. From a historical point of view, nothing substantial can be analyzed on the basis of these letters, as they mention no important political events.

Al-Azkawī relates[32] that Jayfar ibn al-Julunda contacted the Persians of Oman, calling on them to become Muslims, and that when their refusal was received, a tribal army marched against them. The Persians were defeated, and their commander killed in the battle. The triumphant Arabs marched on the main Persian center at Ṣuḥār, and laid siege to the fortified garrison quarters of Damstajird. Eventually, the Persians sued for peace, and accepted safe conduct to their ships, on condition that they and their families never attempt to return to Oman.

The power of al-Julunda increased with the advent of Islam, but at the same time opposition to them also grew. It must be mentioned that this opposition was political, and had nothing to do with Islam as a faith or with the new measures introduced by the Islamic administration in Oman. The oppostion was gathered round Laqīṭ ibn Mālik al-Azdī in Diba. He was an influential figure, and enjoyed power which equaled that of al-Julunda. Historians relate that one of his epithets was "the one with the crown." He was supported by his tribe and by sections of other tribes. From Diba he extended his authority toward the rich coastal plains, and forced the Julunda to flee to the mountains. Meanwhile, the Prophet died in 11/632, and Jayfar ibn al-Julunda sent a letter to the new caliph Abū Bakr al-Ṣiddīq, asking him for help.[33]

The "Diba affair," as Professor Wilkinson calls it, was described by some accounts as an apostasy war fitting in with the general political picture of the time. But other historical accounts, supported by local

Omani sources, agree that what happened was a minor misunderstanding over the *zakāt* due from a woman of Banī 'l-Ḥārith, which developed into a conflict between Laqīṭ's forces and those of al-Julunda. The caliph Abū Bakr acted quickly, sending two contingents: one led by Ḥudhayfa al-Ghalfanī from northern Oman, the other led by 'Arfaja al-Bāriqī from Mahra in southern Oman. He also ordered 'Ikrima ibn Abī Jahal to move from Yamāma to Oman to help them if need be. Al-Julunda's position was strengthened, and they advanced and re-occupied Ṣuḥār. From Ṣuḥār they sent many letters to those Arab chiefs who were with Laqīṭ al-Azdī, and succeeded in winning them over. The Julunda forces backed by Banū Nājiya and 'Abd al-Qays suppressed the rest of Laqīṭ's supporters, and sent some of them as hostages to Medina.

At the advent of Islam, the Julundites, as we have already mentioned, were the rulers of Oman. Dr. Wilkinson asserts that before Islam, Oman was under Persian rule; while Dr. Al-'Ānī says that there is nothing in the authentic sources to substantiate this point of view. However, Ibn Ḥabīb[34] relates that the kings of Persia used the Julundites "as rulers" of Oman. It could be said, as in the case of Bahrain, that at the advent of Islam Persian rule was only nominal and limited to coastal regions, especially the rich plains and some ports, while the rest of Oman was independent and ruled by the Julundites and other Arab chiefs.

During the caliphate of 'Uthmān, Oman, like Bahrain, was administratively associated with the governor of Basra in Iraq. This encouraged the substantial migration of the Azd of Oman to Basra to join the Muslim armies in the conquest of Persia.

Conclusion

Although Persian control of the Arab Gulf region during the late Sasanian period was nominal and limited to certain coastal ports and plains, it is important to observe that one of the greatest appeals of Islam to the Arabs of the Gulf was the fact that they saw in it a power capable of casting away the hated Persian yoke. This was beyond mere political freedom, but rather represented an opportunity to regain rich land and to extend their settlements, to increase maritime trade with the outside world, and to make direct contact with their Arab brothers who had settled in large numbers on the eastern coast of the Arab Gulf many centuries before Islam, as historical sources indicate.[35]

The advent of Islam was indeed to reestablish Arab sovereignty over both sides of the Gulf, at least during the first three centuries of Islam, thereby fixing the Arab identity of the Gulf. It was as early as 15/636 that al-ʻAlā ibn al-Ḥadramī, then governor of Bahrain, started his abortive attempt to conquer the eastern coast of the Gulf.[36] The second attempt was made in 16/637, when caliph ʻUmar ibn al-Khaṭṭāb ordered the governor of Bahrain, ʻUthmān ibn Abī 'l-ʻĀṣ, to conquer the eastern coast.[37] Three thousand Arabs from Azd, Rāsib, Nājiya, and ʻAbd al-Qays crossed the Gulf from Jurfar, and captured Kawān Island. The Persian governor of Kirman met them at Qasam Island, and a new battle ensued in which the Arabs were victorious. This battle put an end to Persian Sasanian sovereignty over the Gulf.

However, Islamic central authority over the Arab Gulf region during the early decades of Islam had to face trouble from the Khārijite movement, a dissident Arab sect which spread through the region, establishing a somewhat revolutionary republic in Bahrain, and a moderate imamate in Oman, a matter which lies outside the scope of this study.

NOTES

1. For a general history of the Gulf, see F. Omar, *History of the Arab Gulf During the Early Islamic Period* [in Arabic], 2d ed. (Bahgdad, 1985).

2. Al-Zamakhsharī, *Al-Jibal wa'l amkina* (Najaf), p. 20.

3. Ibn Rusta, *Al-Aʻlāq al-nāfisa* (Leiden, 1891), p. 182. Yāqūt, *Muʻjam* (Leipzig, 1868), I, 506.

4. Ibid. See also Ibn Khurdadhaba, *Al-Masālik* (Leiden, 1889), p. 152.

5. Al-Isfahānī, *Aghānī* (Cairo, A.H. 1322), XVI, 259. Yāqūt, op. cit., I, 507.

6. See al-Bakrī, *Al-Masālik*, MS at the College of Arts, Baghdad, fol. 215b; Yāqūt, op. cit., I, 507.

7. Ibn Ḥazim, *Jamharat ansāb al-ʻArab* (Cairo, 1962), p. 299; Al-Bakrī, *Muʻjam ma'lstʻjam* (Cairo, 1364), pp. 80–81.

8. Balādhurī, *Futūḥ* (Leiden, 1866), p. 76; al-Zubayrī, *Nasab Quraysh* (Cairo, 1951), p. 13. See also al-ʻAnī, *ʻUmān* (Baghdad, 1977), pp. 43–52.

9. On this subject see J. Ali, *Tārīkh al-ʻArab* (Baghdad, 1954), VI, 59; Fiey, "Le Ber Qatraye" in *Mémorial Mgr. Gabriel Khouri-Sarkis, 1898–1968* (Belgium, Imprimerie orientaliste, 1969).

10. Balādhurī, *Futūḥ*, p. 80; Ṭabarī, *Tārīkh* (Leiden), I, 1559 f.

11. Masʻūdī, *Murūj al-Dhahab* (Cairo, 1958), I, 68. Iḥsā'ī, *Tuḥfa* (Riyad, 1960), I, 60.

12. Ibn Sa'd, *Tabaqāt* (Leiden, 1324), I, ii, 12. Balādhurī, *Futūḥ*, p. 78. Ṭabarī, op. cit., III, 1559.

13. Ṭabarī, I, 1600.

14. Caetani, *Annali dell' Islam* [Turkish trans.] (Istanbul, 1925), VI, 121–23.

15. See al-'Anī, *Bahrain During the Early Islamic Period* (Baghdad, 1971), pp. 85–86.

16. Ibn Sa'd, op. cit., II, ii, 19; Balādhurī, *Futūḥ*, p. 80; Ṭabarī, op. cit., I, 1600; Abū Yūsuf, *Al-Kharāj* (Cairo, 1382), p. 31.

17. Azkawī, *Kashf al-ghumma*, ed. Qaysī (1980), pp. 37–38; anon., *Tārīkh ahl 'Umān* (Oman, 1980), pp. 40–41; Ma'wulī, *Qiṣaṣ wa Akhbār* (Oman, 1979), pp. 36–37.

18. See M. Watt, *Muhammad at Medina* (London, 1966), pp. 360–61.

19. Ibid.

20. Ibn Sa'd, op. cit., I, ii, 54.

21. See A. Guillaume, *The Life of Muhammad* (London, 1955), pp. 635–36.

22. Ṭabarī, I, 1561; Ibn Hishām, *Sīra*, IV, 72; Ibn Ḥajar, *Al-Iṣāba* (Cairo, 1939), III, 439.

23. Ibn Hishām, *Sīra*, IV, 221–22; Ibn Sa'd, op. cit., V, 407–8; Ṭabarī, I, 1736.

24. On this issue see al-'Anī, *'Umān*, Chapter VI.

25. Ibn Sa'd, op. cit., I, 7; Balādhurī, *Futūḥ*, pp. 78–85; Ṭabarī, I, 985.

26. Ṭabarī, I, 2832.

27. Ṭabarī, I, 1560–61, 1894; Ibn Hishām, op. cit., IV, 254; Ibn Sa'd, op. cit., I, 18; Balādhurī, *Futūḥ*, p. 276.

28. See al-'Anī, *'Umān*, pp. 49–50, 37–40.

29. Caetani, op. cit., VI, 122–30.

30. Ibn Sa'd, op. cit., I, 19–82; Balādhurī, *Futūḥ*, p. 78; Ya'qūbi, *Tārīkh* (Leiden), II, 82–84; Ṭabarī, I, 1559 f.

31. Ibn Sa'd, op. cit., I, 35, 82; Ibn Ḥajar, *Al-Iṣāba*, IV, 105; Qalqashandī, *Ṣubh al-a'shā* (Cairo, 1913), VI, 380. See also al-Azkawī, op. cit., p. 37; anon., *Tārīkh ahl 'Umān*, p. 40; al-Ma'walī, *Qiṣaṣ*, pp. 37–38.

32. Azkawī, op. cit., p. 38. See also Ma'wulī, op. cit., p. 39; Wilkinson, "The Julunda of Oman," *J.O.S.*, I (1975), p. 99.

33. Balādhurī, *Futūḥ*, pp. 76–77; Ṭabarī, I, 1977–79. Cf. al-Sālimī, *Tuḥfa al-a'yān* (Cairo, 1350), I, 51–57.

34. Ibn Ḥabīb, *Al-Muḥabbar* (Hyderabad, 1942), p. 265. Many local historians agree with Ibn Ḥabīb in one way or another.

35. See, for example, al-Aṣma'ī, *Tārīkh al-'Arab* (Baghdad, 1959), p. 88; al-Hamdanī, *Ṣifat Jazīrat al-'Arab* (Cairo, 1953), p. 211; Ṭabarī, I, 836. See also al-'Ānī, op. cit., pp. 95–106.

36. Ṭabarī, I, 2546–50.

37. Ṭabarī, I, 2698; al-Sālimī, op. cit., I, 52.

18
Joel in Judeo-Persian

Herbert H. Paper

TRANSLATIONS INTO JUDEO-PERSIAN of the biblical books of the Minor Prophets are rather rare. The text of Joel presented here is the only one known to me. It is found in a large manuscript book that belongs to the Ben-Zvi Institute in Jerusalem—No. 4559—that was acquired in Iran in 1973 by Professor Amnon Netzer of the Hebrew University. It is with their kind permission that this particular section of the text may be given at this time.

The manuscript contains all of the Pentateuch in Judeo-Persian, together with all of Isaiah and the Minor Prophets—an unusual combination to be found in one collection of biblical books. The Pentateuch alone consists of some 680 pages of text. It is our good fortune that a colophon is to be found in the middle of the book, and there we find the date of the manuscript as the third day of Tishri, 5549 (1788 C.E.). This date is also confirmed on the same line with a *hijra* date written in Hebrew. This colophon appears immediately after the non-biblical text entitled *Seder nevuat hayyeled*, which comes at the end of the book of Isaiah.

The entire manuscript was written by a single scribe. His handwriting is quite typical for the date of composition. In some instances the scribe himself has crossed out his own errors and made his own corrections, either in the body of the text or in one of the margins. But there are also numerous interventions by a later hand. These are characterized by a line drawn through the original word or phrase and a "corrected" or "alternative" translation written in above the line. The identity of this later scribe is not determinable. However, it is clear that the script and the ink differ and are much later than those of the original.

It is by now well known that the Judeo-Persian Bible translations are always extremely literal and follow very closely the word order of the Hebrew original. This is a common practice in all "Holy Book" translations of other religious cultures as well.

We now present the text of Joel. Where a word or phrase is lined through in the manuscript, it is given here as underlined, and the inserted correction or addition is in a different font immediately thereafter.

[This small contribution is offered here in friendship and gratitude to an outstanding scholar and dear friend, Bernard Lewis.]

יואל 1.1- 1.12 — מב״ץ 4559

/1/ 1.1 כלאם כ̇ודא כה בוד בא יואל פסר פתואל:

1.2 בשנויד אינך פיראן וגוש גיריד כול נשסתגאן און זמין אי́א
בודסת אינך דר אייאם שומא ואגר דר אייאם פדראן שומא:

1.3 אינך בפסראן שומא חכאיית כוניד ופסראן שומ̇א בפסראן אישאן
ופסראן אישאן בדוראן דיגר:

1.4 באקי́את בורנדה מַלַך̇ בכ̇ורד בסיאר מַלַך̇ ובאקי́את בסיאר מַלַך̇ בכ̇ורד
ליסנדה מַלַך̇ ובאקי́את ליסנדה מלך̇ בכ̇ורד סבז מלך̇:

1.5 בידאר שו́יד מסתאן וגרייה כוניד ומוייה גויד כול תנג̇איון זָ̇יָן
אַבַר שִׁירַה כה ניסת שוד אז דהן שומא:

1.6 כה קאם ביומד בזמין מן קויסת וניסת שומארה דנדאן או דנדאן
שיר וארו́ארה מאדה שיר באוסת:

1.7 בגזאשת מוו מן ביראנה ואנג̇יר מן בקזב זאהר כרדן זאחר כרד
וביאנדאכ̇ת ספ̇יד שודן שאכ̇א הא או:

1.8 ג̇מאעת מן מסל באכרה בסתה פלאס בסאחב כודכי או:

1.9 ניסת שוד מנחה וגוסתאר אז כ̇אנה כ̇ודא בכ̇ורדן און כהנים צ̇אכרון
כ̇ודא⟨:⟩

1.10 קארת שוד סהרע עזא דאר שוד זמין או כה קארת שוד קלה או כ̇ושג
שוד שִׁירַה או בוג̇מורדה שוד צ̇רבי או:

1.11 כ̇ושג שרמנדה שונד באקבון הא מוייה גויינד רַזְבּון הא וגנדום
וג̇וו כה גום שוד דרוו סהרא:

1.12 און מוו כ̇ושג שוד ואנג̇יר בוג̇מורדה̇ שוד נאר ניז כ̇ורמא וסיב
וכול דרכ̇ת הא סהרא כ̇ושג שודן כה ו́אבור שוד שאדי אז בני אדם:

יואל 2.2-1.13   מב״יץ 4559

<u>1.13</u> פלאס פושיד ותעזיית גיריד אי כוהנים מויה גויד צׄאכרון קורבאן גאה ביאיד מנזל גיריד דר כוצׄהא צׄאכרון כׄאלק מן כה מנע שוד אז כׄאנה כׄאלק שומא מנחה וגוסתאר:

<u>1.14</u> מוהיא כוניד רוזה בכׄאניד גׄעמיית גׄמע כוניד פיראן כול נשסתגאן און זמין כׄאנה כׄודא כׄאלק שומא ובנאליד בכׄודא:

<u>1.15</u> ו׳אי באון רוז כה <u>נזכיסת</u> נזדיכסת רוז כׄודא מסל קארת אז כאפׄי כׄנדאיי ביאייד:

<u>1.16</u> אינך /2/ מוקאבל צׄשמאן מא כׄוראכי ניסת שוד אז כׄאנה כׄאלק מא שאדי ונשאט:

<u>1.17</u> גנדידה שודן דאנהא זיר כולוק הא אישאן ו׳יראנה שודן כׄזינהא כׄראב שודן אמבאר הא כה כׄושג שוד קלה:

<u>1.18</u> צׄה ג׳מגין שוד בהאיים ברהם כׄורדה שודן גלהא גאב כה ניסת צׄרה גאה באישאן ניז גלהא גוספנד פרישאן שודן:

<u>1.19</u> בתו כׄודא בר מי כׄאנם כה אתש בסואזניד מעוא ביאבון ושועלה בליסיד כול דרכׄת הא סהרא:

<u>1.20</u> ניז חייואן הא סהרא שְיהַה כשן בתו כה כׄושג שודן גׄוב האי אב ואתש בסוזאניד מעוא און ביאבון:

<u>2.1</u> דר זניד שופר דר ציון וקלבגי כוניד דר כוה כׄאץ מן בלרזנד כול נשסתגאן און זמין כה ביומד רוז כׄודא כה נזדיכסת:

<u>2.2</u> רוז תאריכי וזולמאת רוז עַבְר וערפׄאל מסל סובח פהן שודה בר כוהא קאם בסיאר וקו׳י מסל או נבודים[1] אזאן עאלם ועקב או ⟨בסיאר⟩ נכׄאהד שוד תא סאל הא דווראן ודוראן:

2.3 בפיש או בסוזד אתש ועקב או דר גירד שועלה מסל בוסתאן עדן און זמין בפיש או ועקב או ביאבון וׄיראנה וניז רסתה נבאשד בר או:

2.4 מסל מנזר אסב מנזר או ובכותל הא צ̇נין בדונד:

2.5 מסל אוואז מרכב הא בסר הא כוה רכ̇ץ כונן צ̇ון אוואז שועלה אתש בסוזונד סופ̇אר צ̇ון קאם קו̇י תרתיב גוזאשתה מסאף̇:

2.6 אז פיש או בתרסן קאם הא וכול רו הא ג̇מע שודן סיאהי:

2.7 מסל שוג̇איון בדונד מסל מרדמון מסאף̇ ברוונד בארו וניסת בראה או ברוונד ונה כג̇ כונן ג̇עדהא אישאן:

2.8 ומרדי בראדר או נה דור שוונד מרדי בג̇עדהא ברוונד ודר סהרא ביופ̇תנד נה זכ̇ם כ̇ורדה שוונד:

2.9 דר שהר באזאר גירן דר בארו בדונד דר כ̇אנה ביאיינד דר פס פנג̇רה ביאיינד מסל דוזד⟨:⟩

2.10 בפיש או בלרזד זמין בצ̇נדן אסמאן ואפ̇תאב ומחתאב סייאה שודן וסתארהא אכ̇ר כרדן רושנאי אישאן:

2.11 וכ̇ודא בדאד אוואז או /3/ בפיש לשגר או כה בסיארסת בקאיית לשכר או כה קויסת כונא סוכ̇ן או כה בזורגסת רוז כ̇ודא וסהממנד קאיית וכה מיגונגונד מי תואנד אורא:

2.12 וניז אל חאל מי פ̇רמאייד כ̇ודא באז גרדיד ג̇מאעתון מן ב⟨כול⟩ דל[1] שומא ⟨ו⟩דר רוזה וגרייה ותעזיית⟨:⟩

2.13 בשכאפ̇יד דל שומא ונה ג̇אמה שומא ותוובה כוניד בכ̇ודא כ̇אלק שומא כה שפ̇קת כוננד⟨ה⟩ ורחם כוננדהסת או ותחמול באר בסיאר פ̇זל ואנסראב פ̇רמאייא דר בדי:

2.14 כה מי דאנד תובה כונד ופשימאן שוד ובאקי גוזארד עקב או אפרין פישכשי וגוסתאר בכ֗ודא כ֗אלק שומא:

2.15 בזניד שופר דר ציון מוהיא כוניד רוזה בר כ֗אניד געמיית:

2.16 גמע כוניד קאם מוהיא כוניד גמאעת גמע כוניד פיראן וגמע כוניד טפלאן ושיר כ֗ארגון פסתאן ביראן אייד דומאד אז חֲדַרוֹ או ועֲרוס בְהֲגַלָה או:

2.17 מיאן און סופה וקורבאן גאה גרייה כוננד און כהנים צ֗אכרון כ֗ודא ובגויינד שפקת כון כ֗ודא בר קאם תו ונדהי אחסן תו בעאר במוסלט שודן באישאן קאם הא צ֗רא בגויינד דר קאם כוגאס כ֗אלק אישאן:

2.18 קייז גרפת כ֗ודא בראי זמין או ושפקת כרד בר קאם או:

2.19 וגואב גופת כ֗ודא ואמר כרד בר קאם או אינך מן מי פרסתם בראי שומא און קלה ואון שִׁירָה ואון צ֗רבי וסיר שויד אורא ונדהם שומארא דיגר באז עאר דר קאמון:

2.20 ואון שייטאן מלך דור כונם אז באלא שומא וביאנדא⟨ז⟩ם אורא בזמין תשנה זאר וויראנה מר רוי או בדריא משרקי ואכ֗ר או בדריא אכ֗רין ובר שוד גנד או ובראייד בוכ֗אר או כה בסיאר סד בכרד:

2.21 נתרסי און זמין שאד שויד ונשאט כוני כה בסיאר כרד כ֗ודא בכרדן:

2.22 נתרסי חייואן הא סהרא *מז* /4/ כה כ֗ורם שודן מעוא ביאבון כה דרכ֗ת בר דאשת סמר או אנגיר ומוו בדאדן קוות אישאן:

2.23 אהל ציון כ֗ורם שויד ושאד שויד בכ֗ודא כ֗אלק שומא כה בדאד בשומא און דורושת בארון בעדאלת ופורוד בארד בשומא בארון דורושת וריזה בארון דר אוול:

2.24 ופור שונד און כ̇רמן הא קלה ורואן שונד און קדוו כוריש
הא שירה וצ̇רבי:

2.25 ⟨ו⟩עווז דהם בשומא און סאל הא אונצ̇ה או בכ̇ורד און בסיאר
מלך וליסנדה מלך ואון סבז מלך ובורנדה מלך קוות מן בזורג אונצ̇ה
בפ̇רסאדם בשומא:

2.26 ובכ̇וריד[1] כ̇ורדן וסיר שודן וחילול כרדיד מר אסם כ̇ודא כ̇אלק
שומא אונצ̇ה בכרד בא שומא בעג̇איב נמודן ונה שרמנדה שונד קאם מן
בעאלם:

2.27 ובדאניד כה אשכארם מן במי́אן ישראל ומנם כ̇ודא כ̇אלק שומא
וניסת דיגרי ונה שרמנדה שונד קאם מן בעאלם:

3.1 ובאשד בעדזין בריזם רוח קא כ̇אץ מן בכול בשר ונבאוות כוננד
פסראן שומא ודוכ̇תראן שומא פיראן שומא כ̇אב הא ביננד ג̇ו́אנאן שומא
מנזר הא בביננד⟨:⟩

3.2 וניז באון קולאם הא וכניז הא דר און רוזגארון אישאן בריזם
מר רוח מן:

3.3 ובדהם מר מועג̇ז הא דר אסמאן וזמין כ̇ון ואתש ונכ̇ל דוד:

3.4 אפ̇תאב גשתה שוד בתאריכ̇י ומחתאב בכ̇ון פיש אז אומדן רוז כ̇ודא
בזורג וסהממנד:

3.5 ובאשד הרכה בכ̇אנד אסם כ̇ודא כ̇לאץ שוד כה דר כוה ציון ודר
ירושלים באשד כ̇לאסי צ̇ניך כה פ̇רמוד כ̇ודא ובזורגאן כה כ̇ודא בר כ̇אניד:

4.1 כה אינך דר רוזגארון אישאן ודראן וכ̇ת אונצ̇ה בר גרדאנם מר
ו́רדהי יהודא וירושלים:

4.2 וגׄמע כונם מר כול און קאם הא ופׄרוד ברם אישאן רא בְּדַרַה
יהושפט ושרע כונם בא אישאן רא בא קאם מן ואחסן מן ישראל אונצׄה
פׄראכׄנדה שודן דר קאם הא ומר זמין מן בכׄש כרדן:

4.3 ובקאם מן ביאנדאכׄתן קורה ובדאדן און בצׄה רא דר /5/[1] בד
ראהע ואון בצׄה רא בפׄרוכׄתן דר יין ובתנגׄידן:

4.4 וניז צׄיסת שומא[1] במן צׄין ומאצׄין וכול אולכהא פׄרנג הא מוכאפׄאת
שומא עווז מי דהיד שומא במן ויא מוכאפׄאת שומא מן סבוך תעגׄיל באז
גרדאנם מוכאפׄאת שומא בסר שומא:

4.5 אונצׄה[1] נוקרהי מן וטלא מן בר דאשתיד וארזומנדון ניכויאׄן
ביאוורדיד במהראב שומא:

4.6 ואהל יאודא ואהל ירושלים בפׄרוכׄתיד באהל יָוָן בסבב דור בורדן
אישאן אז באלא חד אישאן⟨:⟩

4.7 ⟨אינך⟩ אז שהר אישאן אזאן מקאם כה בפׄרוכׄתיד אישאן רא אונגׄא
ובר גרדאנם מוכאפׄאת שומא בסר שומא:

4.8 ובפׄרושם מר פסראן שומא ודוכׄתראן שומא בדסת אהל יאודא ובפׄרושנם
אישאן רא ⟨לִשְׁבָאִים⟩ בקאם דור כה כׄודא כלאם פׄרמוד:

4.9 בר כׄאניד אינך בקאם הא מוהיא כוניד מסאׄף אגאה כוניד שוגׄאעון
נזדיך שוונד וביאיינד כול מרדמאן מסאׄף:

4.10 בכוניד כולנג הא שומא בשמשיר הא ומוובור הא שומא בניזהא און
סוסת בגוייד כה שוגׄאעם מן:

4.11 בכוביד וביאיד וביאווריד כול און קאם הא אז חואלי וגׄמע שוונד
אונגׄא ⟨הַנְחַת ה' גִּבּוֹרֶיךָ⟩:

4.12 ⟨יֵעוֹרוּ וְיֵעָלוּ הַגּוֹיִם אֶל עֵמֶק יְהוֹשָׁפָט כִּי שָׁם⟩ בנשינם בשרע
פורסידן מר כול און קאם הא אז חואלי הא:

4.13 בפ̇רסתיד דאס כה ברהם כ̇ורדה שוד דרוו ביאיד דראן דבה ופ̇רוד
שויד כה פור שוד כוריש כ̇רמן רו̇אן שודן כוריש הא כה בסיאר שוד
בדי הא אישאן:

4.14 לשגר לשגר[1] דראן דרה בלרזן כה נזדיכסת רוז כ̇ודא דראן דרה
מכ̇תע שווד:

4.15 אפ̇תאב ומחתאב סי́אה כ̇אהן שודן וסתארהא אכ̇ר כ̇אהן כרדן רושנאי
אישאן:

4.16 וכ̇ודא אז ציון שיה כונד ואז ירושלים בדהד אוואז או ובצ̇נדן
אסמאן וזמין וכ̇ודא פנאה הסת בקאם או ויאוור בפסראן ישראל:

4.17 ובדאניד כה מנם כ̇ודא כ̇אלק שומא סאכן דר ציון כוה כ̇אץ מן
ובאשד ירושלים כ̇אץ וביגאנה נגזרד בר או דיגר:

4.18 ובאשד דראן רוז בצכ̇ן כוהא שִׁירה וכמר הא /6/ רוואן כוננד
שיר וכול גוב הא יהודא ברוונד אב וצ̇שמהי אז כ̇אנה כ̇ודא ביראן איד
ובתנגּונד מר רוד כ̇אנה שיטים:

4.19 מצרים בויראנה באשד ואדום ביאבון כ̇ראבה באשד אז זולם פסראן
יאודא כה בריכ̇תן כ̇ון אישאן נאחק בזמין אישאן:

4.20 ויהודא בעאלם מעמור באשד וירושלים בדווראן ודווראן:

4.21 ועאזאד ⟨כונם⟩ ואלא כ̇ון אישאן נה עאזאד כונם וכ̇ודא סאכן דר
ציון:

תם

19
Le Témoignage d'al-Jāḥiẓ sur les Manichéens

Charles Pellat

ABŪ 'UTHMĀN serait probablement resté interdit si quelque devin lui avait annoncé qu'en Europe, au début du quinzième siècle de l'hégire, non seulement on parlerait de lui, mais encore on le compterait au nombre des hérésiographes.[1] Et pourtant, sans être à cet égard comparable à un Ash'arī, un Ibn Ḥazm, un Baghdādī ou un Shahrastānī, n'est-il pas, selon ses propres dires dans l'introduction du *Kitāb al-Ḥayawān*, l'auteur d'exposés (*ḥikāya*) sur différentes sectes musulmanes,[2] ce qui implique, de sa part, une certaine aptitude à l'objectivité requise? Ne lui a-t-on pas attribué un *Kitāb fī 'l-firaq al-islāmīya?*[3] N'a-t-il pas adopté, en revanche, une attitude polémique dans son *Radd 'alā 'l-Naṣārā?*[4] Aussi, après avoir offert au comité chargé de préparer les *Mélanges Tadeusz Lewicki* un article sur «Djāḥiẓ et les Khāridjites»[5] et donné le titre de *Christologie ǧāḥizienne*[6] à l'hommage que j'ai rendu à la mémoire de Joseph Schacht, ai-je pris la liberté d'intituler «Ǧāḥiẓ hérésiographe»[7] la brève étude rédigée pour les *Mélanges Henri Laoust*. Pour boucler la boucle, il faudrait encore examiner son témoignage sur les Shī'ites et reprendre ce qu'il dit des Juifs, auxquels il n'a pas ménagé critiques et attaques, mais la perte d'importants textes relatifs à ces deux dernières communautés risque de fausser la perspective. Outre les Sabéens de Ḥarrān, les Mandéens, les Mughtasila et les Mazdakites, dont il ne parle guère, ou les Hindous,[8] qu'il met à contribution pour célébrer les mérites des Noirs, les seuls adeptes d'autres religions étrangères à l'Islam qu'il cite assez fréquemment sont les Mazdéens et les Manichéens.

J'aurais aimé manifester autrement l'amitié que je porte depuis de longues années à Bernard Lewis, mais comme je me sens pris de court, qu'il me soit permis, pour participer à ce nouveau *Festschrift*, de me borner à ajouter un faible maillon à la chaîne en formation et à consacrer un exposé succinct aux sectateurs de la dernière de ces religions dualistes, aux Manichéens tels qu'al-Jāḥiẓ avait pu les observer tant à Bagdad qu'à Baṣra.

Alors que les Mazdéens étaient tolérés, les adeptes de Manès avaient été sévèrement pourchassés au temps de la jeunesse de notre auteur[9] et, s'ils semblent avoir joui un peu plus tard d'assez de liberté pour pouvoir discuter non seulement avec des théologiens mu'tazilites, mais encore, comme on le verra bientôt, avec le calife en personne, il n'en demeure pas moins qu'ils étaient généralement contraints de se cacher. Pourtant, les Manichéens authentiques n'étaient pas, pour l'Islam, de redoutables adversaires, et s'il est vrai que «les princes du *kalām* et les maîtres du *jadal* ont fait aux impies [= aux Manichéens] une guerre acharnée,»[10] Abū 'Uthmān n'a probablement pas été tenté de se livrer à une réfutation systématique, d'autant que, des fidèles de toutes les religions connues de lui, ils étaient, dit-il,[11] les seuls à n'avoir jamais eu «ni royaume ni rois» et à être «tués ou obligés soit de fuir, soit de dissimuler leur croyance.» Cette question faisait sans doute l'objet de débats puisqu'al-Jāḥiẓ rappelle[12] l'argument supposé d'un interlocuteur selon lequel cette situation serait due au fait que «les gens auxquels leur religion interdit de combattre et qui, d'instinct, refusent de faire du mal, sont pillés et réduits en esclavage»; «mais alors, lui rétorque-t-on, pourquoi les Byzantins se défendent-ils, bien que leur religion n'admette ni combat ni résistance?» Ce rapprochement avec le Christianisme n'est pas fortuit, car le Manichéisme en est considéré comme dérivé, puisque Manès, qui serait le Paraclet,[13] est né et a vécu parmi les Mughtasila de Dast-i Maysān,[14] eux-mêmes assimilés aux Mandéens, qui sont parfois regardés comme chrétiens. Sans entrer dans les détails, on rappellera qu'une source arabe primordiale sur le Manichéisme, le *Fihrist* d'Ibn al-Nadīm,[15] affirme que Mānī tire sa doctrine du Mazdéisme et du Christianisme.

Al-Jāḥiẓ, quant à lui, ne s'exprime nulle part sur ce point. De temps en autre, il appelle les Manichéens Manāwīya[16] ou Mānīya,[17] mais le plus souvent Zanādiqa, et l'on sait que, sous cette appellation péjorative, se cachent toutes sortes d'hérétiques[18] et de Musulmans impies contre lesquels la lutte avait été engagée, mais qui n'ont guère de rapport avec Mānī et sa doctrine. G. Vajda, qui a étudié avec soin les listes de *zindīq*s[19] que l'on rencontre dans la littérature arabe et notamment dans le *Kitāb al-Ḥayawān*,[20] n'a découvert qu'un seul crypto-

Manichéen, 'Abd al-Karīm ibn Abī 'l-'Awjā',[21] et l'on a déjà constaté que la *zandaqa* était souvent une attitude de snobs[22] qui voulaient simplement se distinguer, à une époque où une partie de la haute société et des milieux intellectuels visait à paraître blasée et affichait un détachement calculé.

Cela ne veut pas dire que la doctrine était ignorée, et il est bien possible que le mauvais état de conservation de la littérature archaïque soit responsable de l'absence de sources vraiment exploitables avant la fin du troisième/neuvième siècle; et encore les plus anciennes sont-elles peu explicites, ainsi qu'il ressort de l'étude effectuée par G. Vajda sur al-Māturīdī[23] et des textes arabes et persans commodément rassemblés par Aḥmad Afshār Shīrāzī.[24] En fait, les renseignements commencent à être détaillés vers la fin du quatrième/dixième siècle, et c'est précisément le *Fihrist* qui a fourni pendant longtemps les informations les plus circonstanciées sur la vie et la doctrine de Manès. Parmi les sources réunies par Shīrāzī, al-Jāḥiẓ vient après l'auteur le plus ancien, al-Qāsim ibn Ibrāhīm (246/860), mais occupe une place fort modeste.[25] G. Vajda, qui commente les principales références sur le Manichéisme,[26] ne consacre que quelques lignes à son témoignage[27] et juge que, «dans la "description" méprisante et peu compréhensive qu'il fait des "livres des zindīqs,"[28] [il] se borne à nommer *al-hum(m)āma* parmi d'autres vocables mythiques usités par les Manichéens.» Notre regretté collègue paraît encore influencé par la légende toujours aussi tenace d'un Jāḥiẓ plaisantin; s'il est bien évident, en effet, que ce dernier ne s'étend pas outre mesure sur les doctrines manichéennes qu'il connaît certainement très mal, son témoignage n'en demeure pas moins intéressant, car il permet, avec la prudence d'usage, de mesurer ou tout au moins de faire ressortir les lacunes qui subsistent, volontairement ou non, dans la culture d'un homme aussi intelligent et curieux que notre Abū 'Uthmān. Même si ses premières références sont indirectes, en ce sens qu'il rapporte des conversations qui se sont déroulées entre, d'une part, un *zindīq* et Abū Isḥāq [al-Naẓẓām],[29] puis, d'autre part, entre un autre Manichéen et al-Ma'mūn[30] lui-même, les passages que l'on peut relever sont instructifs. Malheureusement, le texte en est très altéré, comme souvent lorsqu'il s'agit de notions étrangères à l'Islam, et 'Abd al-Salām Hārūn, malgré tout son savoir, n'a pas réussi à l'établir d'une façon satisfaisante.

La primière question, simple selon al-Jāḥiẓ, concerne les éléments ou genres (*ajnās*) qui constituent le monde:

Les Manichéens disent que le monde, avec tout ce qu'il contient, est constitué de dix genres, dont cinq sont de Bien (*khayr*) et de Lumière (*nūr*) et cinq de Mal (*sharr*) et d'Obscurité (*ẓulma*).[31] Tous sont doués de sensation et [. . .] chauds.[32] L'homme est composé de tous les *ajnās*, mais, dans chaque individu, ceux du Bien peuvent l'emporter (*rujḥān*) sur ceux du Mal et inversement. [D'autre part,] l'homme est doué de cinq sens, et il y a dans chacun d'eux des principes [de chacun] des cinq genres et de son contraire.[33] Quand il jette un regard bienveillant, ce regard vient de la Lumière et du Bien; quand il est menaçant, il vient des Ténèbres. Il en est de même pour tous les organes des sens.

L'ouïe est un genre à part. Le Bien et la Lumière qui se trouvent dans le sens de la vue ne viennent pas soutenir le Bien qui existe dans celui de l'ouïe, mais ils ne s'y opposent pas, ne lui nuisent pas et ne l'empêchent pas [de fonctionner]; s'ils ne le soutiennent pas, c'est à cause de la différence de genre,[34] mais ils ne se dressent pas contre lui parce que ce ne sont pas des antagonistes.

Les genres du Mal sont différents entre eux et adversaires de ceux du Bien. Ces derniers sont différents entre eux, mais pas adversaires [les uns des autres]. L'entraide et le soutien ne se produisent pas entre genres différents ou opposés, mais seulement entre ceux qui concordent.

Viennent ensuite un passage sur les organes des sens et une question[35]

posée au *zindīq* qui portait la *kunya* d'Abū 'Alī par le Commandeur des Croyants [al-Ma'mūn] qu'agaçaient la prolixité de Muḥammad ibn al-Jahm [al-Barmakī],[36] l'incapacité d'al-'Utbī,[37] l'incompréhension d'al-Qāsim ibn Sayyār.[38] «Je te questionnerai, lui dit-il, sur deux points seulement. Dis-moi, est-ce que l'auteur d'un méfait s'en est jamais repenti, ou bien est-ce nous qui ne nous sommes jamais repentis?—Non, beaucoup se sont repentis de leurs méfaits.—Dis-moi si ce repentir d'une mauvaise action est une mauvaise ou une bonne action.—Bonne.—Le repentant est-il celui qui a fait le mal ou quelqu'un d'autre?—C'est celui qui a fait le mal.—Donc, celui qui a fait le bien [en se repentant] n'est autre que celui qui a fait le mal, et ainsi est rejeté votre point de doctrine selon lequel celui qui jette un regard menaçant n'est pas le même que celui qui regarde avec bienveillance.—Je prétends que celui qui a fait le mal est différent de celui qui se repent.—Se repent-il d'une faute qu'il a commise lui-même ou qui l'a été par un autre?» Cette question a laissé le *zindīq* tout interdit, mais il ne s'est pas converti et n'est pas revenu de sa croyance jusqu'à sa mort et au jour où Dieu l'a chauffé au feu de la Géhenne.

Une fois de plus, al-Jāḥiẓ rapproche les Manichéens des Chrétiens à propos de la violence, de la chasse et des mauvais traitements infligés aux animaux lorsqu'il écrit[39]:

Il ne convient pas de se désintéresser de ce qui peut conduire un jour ou l'autre à la violence (*qaswa*). J'ai surtout entendu parler de cette question par des Ṣūfīs et des Chrétiens, parce que ces derniers ressemblent aux Zanādiqa, en ce sens qu'ils rejettent les sacrifices, détestent de verser du sang et s'abstiennent de consommer de la viande.[40]

Les *zindīqs* ne devraient pas suivre ce principe quand il s'agit des oiseaux prédateurs et des quadrupèdes féroces. Quant aux serpents et aux scorpions, il ne devraient pas hésiter un instant à les tuer. En effet, ces "choses" ne peuvent manquer soit d'être un pur Mal, soit d'avoir le Bien qu'elles contiennent noyé dans le Mal qu'elles recèlent. Le Mal, c'est Satan; l'Obscurité, c'est l'ennemi de la Lumière. Laisser vivre les Ténèbres, alors que tu as la capacité de les faire mourir, n'est pas l'œuvre de la Lumière; au contraire, il faut que la bienveillance de la Lumière, qui s'étend à toutes les créatures [animales] et humaines, aille jusqu'à les sauver des maux des Ténèbres.

De même qu'il faut [considérer] qu'il est bon, selon la raison, de laisser la vie à la Lumière et d'agir en vue de sa sauvegarde et de sa défense, de même, il convient [de juger] qu'il est bon de tuer l'Obscurité, de la faire mourir et d'aider à son affaiblissement et à sa perte.

L'animal qu'ils jugent à propos de défendre aussi est un mélange [de Bien et de Mal], mais la [proportion du] Mal y est plus faible. Donc, quand ils lui laissent la vie, ils laissent en vie les maux qui sont mêlés à sa [constitution]. S'ils disent que cette [attitude] leur est permise parce que la partie dominante de la nature de cet animal est la Lumière, alors, qu'ils pardonnent donc le rôle nuisible qu'il peut jouer parce qu'il contient peu d'éléments du Mal, comme ils tiennent compte,[41] pour le défendre, du Bien et de la joie qu'il procure, malgré les éléments des Ténèbres qu'il contient, puisque la plupart de ses composantes sont de Lumière.

J'ai fait état de ce qui précéde uniquement parce qu'ils disent: «La preuve que consommer chaque jour de la chair d'animaux égorgés est répréhensible aux yeux de Dieu, c'est que vous n'avez jamais vu les gens qui égorgent des bêtes ou qui tuent des hommes ou ceux qui ne se nourrissent que de viande réussir et s'enrichir.»

Ce dernier argument est assez longuement développé, mais l'auteur pense alors beaucoup plus aux Chrétiens qu'aux Manichéens.

Dans un autre passage[42] tout aussi important, al-Jāḥiẓ remarque que chaque groupe humain a une prédilection pour un lexique spécial:

Tout prosateur, tout poète de talent emploie nécessairement des termes qu'il affectionne particulièrement et il s'efforce de les utiliser, même s'il possède un vaste savoir, beaucoup d'idées et un riche vocabulaire. Pour les Zanādiqa, les mots qui se présentent à leur esprit conviennent à leur nature et constituent en quelque sorte ce que l'on a tendance aujourd'hui à qualifier de «langue de bois,» sont *tanākuḥ* [«relations sexuelles»],[43] *natā'ij* [«produits» des précédentes], *mizāj* [«mélange»], *nūr* [«Lumière»], *ẓulma* [«Obscurité»], *daffā'* [«défenseur»], *mannā'* [«empêcheur»], *sātir* [«protecteur»], *ghāmir* [«inculte»], *munḥall* [«décomposé»], *buṭlān* [«nullité»], *wijdān* [«conscience, sentiment»], *ṣiddīq* [«croyant sincère»], *'amūd al-subḥ* [«colonne de louange (ou de gloire)»[44]].

Quelques-uns de ces termes techniques figurent dans un autre passage[45] consacré à la critique des livres des Manichéens par al-Jāḥiẓ, qui n'en cite d'ailleurs aucun[46]; il les connaissait probablement par ouï-dire.

Il n'y a dans leurs livres, écrit-il, ni proverbe courant, ni histoire intéressante, ni règle de conduite, ni adage original, ni philosophie, ni question de théologie, ni enseignement d'un métier artisanal ou agricole, ni façon de fabriquer un outil, ni manière de conduire la guerre, ni défense d'une religion, d'une secte. L'essentiel de leur contenu concerne la Lumière et les Ténèbres, les rapports sexuels des diables et des *'ifrīts*, la mention du Ṣindīd,[47] la menace du *'amūd al-subḥ*,[48] des renseignements sur Shaqlūn[49] et sur la Hummāma,[50] et tout cela est bavardage, manque de talent, légende, facétie et mensonge. On ne voit dans ces livres ni homélies, ni discours élégants, ni moyens d'organiser sa vie matérielle, ni façon de conduire le peuple ou de fixer la hiérarchie de l'élite. Quel écrit plus ignorant, quelle méthode plus mauvaise qu'un livre qui impose d'obéir, de s'incliner devant [les obligations d'une] religion à laquelle on ne réfléchit pas et que l'on n'aime pas, qu'un livre dans lequel on n'enseigne la bonne façon ni de vivre ici-bas, ni de préparer l'Au-delà!

Même s'il n'a jamais eu l'occasion de prendre directement connaissance du *Shābuhraghān* ou d'un autre écrit de Mānī, al-Jāḥiẓ a entendu un jugement très élogieux sur l'aspect extérieur de ces livres que ses contemporains admiraient, notamment Ibrāhīm ibn al-Sindī,[51] qui lui dit un jour[52]:

Je serais heureux que les Zanādiqa ne soient pas aussi enclins à dépenser de fortes sommes pour se procurer un beau papier blanc, à choisir une encre d'un brillant éclatant, à écrire parfaitement et à intéresser les calligraphes, car je n'ai jamais vu de papier aussi beau que celui de leurs livres, ni d'écriture aussi parfaite. Lorsque je dépense beaucoup—bien que j'aime l'argent et déteste la dépense—pour me procurer des livres, ma générosité est une preuve de respect à l'égard du savoir, et le respect du savoir dénote de la noblesse d'âme et prouve que l'on est à l'abri de l'ivresse de. . . .[53]

Je lui répondis: les dépenses que les Zanādiqa supportent pour leurs livres ressemblent à celles des Chrétiens pour leurs couvents. Si leurs livres étaient des livres de sagesse et de philosophie, des livres sur les *maqāyīs*[54] et les traditions, sur la rhétorique et le bien-dire, ou s'il s'agissait de manuels destinés à l'enseignement des divers métiers et des moyens de faire du commerce et de gagner de l'argent, ou encore des livres sur les usages et les ascèses, la réflexion ou les belles-lettres—même si tout cela ne rapproche pas de la richese et n'éloigne pas de la misère—on pourrait accorder aux Zanādiqa du respect pour le talent littéraire et le désir de bien s'exprimer, mais il s'agit là de doctrine religieuse, de glorification de leur régime, et les dépenses qu'ils engagent à cette fin ressemblent à celles que consentent les Mazdéens pour leurs pyrées, les Chrétiens pour leurs croix d'or et les Hindous pour le service des idoles. Si c'était le savoir qu'ils recherchent, [ils le trouveraient], car il leur est offert, les livres de philosophie sont à leur disposition, et les voies pour parvenir à se les procurer, aisées et connues. Pourquoi donc n'agissent-ils ainsi qu'en ce qui a trait aux livres de leur religion, comme les Chrétiens qui ornent [richement] leurs lieux de culte? Si pareille attitude était appréciable aux yeux des Musulmans ou s'ils y voyaient une invitation à la piété, une incitation à l'humilité, ils obtiendraient sans peine des résultats auxquels n'atteignent pas les Chrétiens en déployant les plus grands efforts.

Une dizaine de pages sont encore consacrées aux Zanādiqa dans le *Kitāb al-Ḥayawān*, et c'est là qu'en figure une liste[55] complétée par une épigramme d'Abū Nuwās[56] contre Abān ibn 'Abd al-Ḥamīd al-Lāḥiqī[57] qu'al-Jāḥiẓ commente en affirmant en particulier que dans le vers où le poète prête à Abān ces paroles: «Louange à Mānī,» il honore grandement Jésus, et ne peut par conséquent pas répondre dans le vers suivant que le fondateur du Manichéisme est «un envoyé de Satan.» On a déjà dit que ces personnages, qui étaient débauchés et certainement peu respectueux de l'Islam et de ses devoirs, ne pouvaient nullement être considérés comme d'authentiques Manichéens.

Le témoignage de Jāḥiẓ ne saurait donc, en fin de compte, être considéré comme vraiment enrichissant, et il apparaît clairement qu'à la différence de celui d'Ibn al-Nadīm, les spécialistes de cette religion peuvent parfaitement s'en passer. A première vue, il conviendrait par conséquent de dresser un procès-verbal de carence et de s'en tenir là, mais il serait peut-être imprudent d'émettre un jugement trop hâtif.

En premier lieu, al-Jāḥiẓ apporte la preuve d'un changement d'attitude à l'égard des sectateurs de Manès de la part des autorités qui, après les avoir persécutés, en sont arrivées à une tolérance qui se traduit même par des discussions avec le calife en personne. Il n'en a probablement pas tenu lui-même et il s'abstient de commenter les réponses faites par l'interlocuteur d'al-Ma'mūn aux questions posées par ce dernier, et c'est tout juste s'il donne son avis sur les animaux qui méritent d'être soit tués soit laissés en vie, non sans aller cependant jusqu'à suggérer aux Zanādiqa de développer leur doctrine relativement à ceux qui sont nuisibles.

D'une façon générale, il ne cherche nullement à exposer les croyances des Manichéens, mais tout en négligeant d'énumérer les «genres» du Bien et du Mal qui constituent le monde et représentent un point capital de leur doctrine, il sait du moins qu'ils sont au total au nombre de dix.

Un aspect intéressant de son témoignage concerne leurs livres, d'une présentation particulièrement soignée, qui circulaient apparemment dans le public; comme il en critique sévèrement le contenu, sans en citer nommément aucun, on peut se demander s'il en vu personnellement des spécimens et s'il a pu en prendre connaissance; en effet, à moins que certains d'entre eux aient été traduits en arabe, ce qui semble peu vraisemblable d'après le témoignage d'Ibn al-Nadīm, il ne pouvait pas en comprendre la langue, qu'il ne précise d'ailleurs point. Les remarques négatives qu'il fait sur leur contenu ne manquent cependant pas d'intérêt, car elles acquièrent finalement une valeur positive, en ce sens qu'elles permettent de se faire une idée de la façon dont il concevait un livre religieux dû non pas à une inspiration divine, mais au génie des humains seuls. Il leur reproche en somme d'être consacrés à la doctrine—ce qui est après tout assez légitime!—et quand il énumère les qualités qu'ils devraient posséder, il montre que, loin de songer à une comparaison avec le Qur'ān—car une telle démarche serait impie—il pense plutôt aux livres d'*adab* ou mieux d'*ādāb*, qui lui paraissent convenir aux religions non-révélées.

NOTES

1. Il se trouve que G. Monnot, qui a recensé *Les Écrits musulmans sur les religions non-bibliques* (dans *MIDEO*, XI [1972], pp. 5–48), fait sa place à notre auteur (p. 21).

2. Voir mon «Nouvel essai d'inventaire de l'œuvre ǧāḥiẓienne,» *Arabica*, XXX/2 (1984), n°s 1, 83, 195, 199, 244 au moins.

3. «Nouvel essai,» n° 60.

4. «Nouvel essai,» n° 165.

5. Dans *Folia orientalia*, XII (1970), pp. 195–209.

6. Dans *Studia islamica*, XXXI (1970), pp. 219–32.

7. Dans *BÉO*, XXX (1978), pp. 147–58.

8. Voir «Al-Ǧāḥiẓ et les peuples du sous-continent,» dans *Orientalia hispanica . . . F. M. Pareja . . . dicata* (Leyde 1974), pp. 542–50.

9. Voir en particulier: M. Guidi, *La Lotta tra l'Islam e il manicheismo* (Rome, 1927). Les poursuites engagées donnent à al-Jāḥiẓ l'occasion de faire de l'humour noir à propos des longues oreilles qui sont censées présager une longue vie (*Bayān*, I, 355). On verra aussi l'anecdote plaisante racontée par al-Mas'ūdī dans les *Murūj* (VII, 12–16 = §§ 2705–7) à propos d'un pique-assiette qui se mêle à des Zanādiqa conduits devant al-Ma'mūn et condamnés à mort.

10. G. Monnot, «Māturīdī et le manichéisme,» *MIDEO*, XIII (1977), p. 50.

11. *Ḥayawān*, IV, 432.

12. *Tarbī'*, §138.

13. Voir H. Ch. Puech, *Le Manichéisme* (Paris, 1949), p. 67.

14. *Ibid.*, p. 40.

15. Éd. du Caire, p. 458.

16. Par ex., *Ḥayawān*, IV, 441.

17. Par ex., *Ḥayawān*, IV, 81.

18. Voir *EI*[1], s.v. *zindīḳ*.

19. «Les zindīqs en pays d'Islam au début de la période abbaside,» *RSO*, XVII (1937), pp. 173–229.

20. Voir *infra*, p. 275; Vajda, *op. cit.*, pp. 203 sqq.

21. Voir *EI*[2], s.v. Ibn Abī l-'Awdjā'; Vajda, *op. cit.*, p. 221; Pellat, *Milieu*, p. 21.

22. Voir Pellat, *Milieu*, p. 258.

23. «Le témoignage d'al-Māturīdī sur la doctrine des Manichéens, des Dayṣānites et des Marcionites,» *Arabica*, XIII/1 (1966), pp. 1–38.

24. Sous le titre de *Mutūn-i 'arabī wa fārisī dar barā-yi Mānī wa Mānawīya*, appendice (71–536) à S. Ḥ. Taqīzāda, *Mānī wa dīn-i ū* (Téhéran, 1335/1956).

25. *Op. cit.*, pp. 84–100.

26. Dans son art. sur le témoignage de Māturīdī.

27. *Op. cit.*, pp. 14, 19.

28. Voir *infra*, p. 274.

29. *Ḥayawān*, IV, 441–42. On trouvera également un réfutation du Manichéisme par al-Naẓẓām dans le *Kitāb al-Intiṣār* d'Ibn al-Khayyāt, éd.-trad. A. Nader (Beyrouth, 1957), §§ 17–19.

30. *Ḥayawān*, IV, 442–3.

31. Les cinq éléments du Bien sont: l'Air, le Vent, la Lumière, l'Eau et le Feu; les cinq éléments du Mal: le Fumée, le Feu dévorant, l'Obscurité, le Vent empoisonné et le Brouillard (voir *Fihrist*, éd. Caire, p. 459; Puech, *op. cit.*, pp. 75, 77). Al-Jāḥiẓ ne fournit à cet égard aucun détail.

32. *Ḥārra*. On ne voit pas très bien ce que vient faire cet adjectif; étant donné qu'il est précédé de la copule *wa-*, alors qu'il n'est pas incompatible avec *ḥāssa*, il est probable qu'il y a là une lacune et que *ḥārra* s'applique à un membre de phrase relatif au monde des Ténèbres, qui est chaud (cf. *Fihrist*, p. 464).

33. Le mot *mutūn*, traduit par «principes,» est embarrassant. D'autre part, dans la phrase *fa-inna fī kull ḥāssa mutūn*[an] *min ḍiddih min al-ajnās al-khamsa*, le pronom de *ḍiddih* ne se rapporte à rien; on peut donc proposer de faire précéder ce mot de [*kull jins wa-min*].

34. On a lu *fī 'l-jins* au lieu de *wa'-l-jins*. Il faut sans doute comprendre que les *ajnās* de la vue, de l'ouïe, etc. se soutiennent quand ils sont identiques dans deux organes des sens différents, comme par ex. le Feu et l'Eau, mais que le Feu de l'un ne soutient pas l'Eau de l'autre.

35. *Ḥayawān*, IV, 442–43.

36. Contemporain d'al-Jāḥiẓ qui occupa des fonctions administratives sous al-Ma'mūn. Notre auteur fait de lui un portrait peu flatteur (éd. Ṭ. al-Ḥājirī dans *al-Kātib al-miṣrī*, février 1947, pp. 55–68; trad. partielle Pellat, dans *Arabische Geisteswelt* et *The Life and Works of Jāḥiẓ*, texte XXV); voir aussi G. Lecomte, dans *Arabica*, V/3 (1958), 263–71.

37. Muḥammad ibn 'Abd Allāh al-'Utbī, lettré originaire de Baṣra qui fréquenta la cour de Bagdad et laissa plusieurs ouvrages d'*adab*. Il mourut en 228/843. Voir Sam'ānī, f. 383; Ibn Qutayba, *Ma'ārif*, p. 538.

38. Courtisan d'al-Ma'mūn, qui semble avoir participé à diverses réunions. Voir *Rasā'il* (éd. Hārūn), I, 39, 43, 44 = III, 198, 202.

39. *Ḥayawān*, IV, 428–30.

40. Voir H.-Ch. Puech, *Sur le Manichéisme* (Paris, 1979), pp. 71 ssq.

41. Le mot *ightafara* paraît fautif, et la traduction est conjecturale.

42. *Ḥayawān*, III, 366.

43. Entre divers éléments pour la création des humains (voir *infra*, p. 274).

44. Colonne de lumière qui relie la terre au firmament et par laquelle passent les âmes des défunts montant vers le royaume céleste. Voir Puech, *Le Manichéisme*, pp. 79–80; idem, *Sur le Manichéisme*, pp. 191–92, 274–75.

45. *Ḥayawān*, I, 57–58. G. Monnot (*Māturīdī*, pp. 49–50) met en relief le fait que, dans ce passage, al-Jāḥiẓ relève «la faiblesse des livres manichéens quant aux discussions serrées auxquelles étaient rompus les gens du *kalām*.»

46. Le *Fihrist* (éd. du Caire, p. 470) énumère sept ouvrages de Mānī, dont un en pehlevi et six en syriaque, et donne ensuite (470–71) une liste de ses épîtres. Cf. Puech, *Le Manichéisme*, pp. 62, 67. Le premier de ces ouvrages, le *Shābuhraghān*, devait être le plus connu, car il est reproduit en partie par al-Bīrūnī (voir Puech, *Sur le Manichéisme*, index, s.v.).

47. Le Ṣindīd est le plus haut de archontes (voir *infra*); il est cité dans le *Fihrist* (Caire, p. 463), où il est mis en rapport avec Ève et Adam et empêche ce dernier d'élever un enfant qu'Ève vient de lui donner. Quant aux archontes, ils ne sont pas cités dans le *Kitāb al-Ḥayawān*, mais *al-Arkūn al-muntaẓar* est mentionné dans le *Tarbī'* (§ 65), ce qui provient probablement d'une confusion avec le Mazdéisme, ainsi qu'entre l'Arkūn et Saoshyant. Les archontes démoniaques sont au nombre de cinq; ils ont tous une forme animale, et chacun d'eux règne sur un monde des démons: le roi des bipèdes, sur celui de la Fumée; le roi des quadrupèdes, sur celui du Feu dévorant; le roi des volailles, sur celui de l'Air; le roi des poissons, sur celui de l'Eau, et le roi des reptiles, sur celui des Ténèbres. Voir Puech, *Sur le Manichéisme*, p. 128 et index.

48. Lire ainsi, comme en III, 366 (voir *supra*) et non *al-ṣubḥ*.

49. On trouvera dans le *Tarbī'* (p. 37) une longue note sur Shaqlūn=Ashaqlūn=Saklas, qui est un démon mâle, père, avec le démon femelle Namrā'īl, des deux premiers humains, qui sont Gēhmurd et Murdyānagh. Voir aussi Puech, *Sur le Manichéisme*, pp. 44, 137.

50. Le texte portait *al-hāma*, que l'éditeur a jugé bon de conserver en ajoutant [*wa-l-h.māma*], mais il faut simplement corriger la leçon des manuscrits et lire *al-Hummāma*. Ce nom, qui ne se rencontre que chez les auteurs arabes, représente pour Ibn al-Nadīm l'Esprit des Ténèbres; c'est la «reine du principe Est du monde de la ténèbre» (Puech, *Sur le Manichéisme*, p. 134; voir aussi G. Monnot, *Penseurs musulmans et religions iraniennes, 'Abd al-Jabbār et ses devanciers* [Paris, 1974], 121–25).

51. Fonctionnaire au service des 'Abbāsides, qui était aussi un ami d'al-Jāḥiẓ. Voir *EI*², s.v.

52. *Ḥayawān*, I, 55–56.

53. Je ne comprends pas l'expression qui figure dans le texte: *sukr al-āfāt* «l'ivresse des calamités.»

54. Je ne vois pas davantage ce que ce terme désigne ici.

55. IV, 447–8.

56. IV, 448–50.

57. Sur ce poète, voir *EI*², s.v.

20
Mamlūk Campaigns Against Rhodes (A.D. 1440–1444)

Hassanein Rabie

THE PURPOSE OF this paper is to elucidate the role of Rhodes in the history of the Crusades in the later Middle Ages. It is worth mentioning in brief the earliest Muslim campaign against the island. This campaign goes back to the year A.D. 653, four years after the Muslim conquest of Cyprus. The Muslims plundered the island and attacked it many times later on. In A.D. 672, the Umayyad caliph Mu'āwiya sent Muslim settlers to Rhodes; this took place before the first Muslim siege of Constantinople in 673. The Muslim settlers returned to Syria at the command of the caliph Yazīd ibn Mu'āwiya (680–83). Later on, when the Muslims threatened Constantinople for the second time in 717 during the caliphate of Sulaymān ibn 'Abd al-Malik, their fleet captured Rhodes on the way. The failure of the Muslims to capture Constantinople and the accession of the caliph 'Umar ibn Abd al-'Azīz compelled the Muslims to evacuate Rhodes, which then reverted to the Byzantine Empire. In 807, the 'Abbasid caliph Hārūn al-Rashīd sent his fleet to conquer the island, but the Muslims were unable to establish themselves there.

In the later Middle Ages, the island of Rhodes, like Cyprus, played an important role in the history of the Crusades. By the end of the thirteenth century, the Mamlūks of Egypt and Syria had mopped up the Crusaders' principalities on the Syrian coast, and acquired great prestige in the Islamic world. In May 1291, Acre succumbed to the Mamlūk sultan Khalīl ibn Qalāwūn. The remaining Crusader towns surrendered within a few months; this was the end of one chapter and the beginning of another in the history of the Crusades.

Knights of the Order of St. John of Jerusalem (the Hospitallers) came to Rhodes in 1306 after the fall of the Crusader kingdom in the East. They succeeded in capturing the city of Rhodes in 1309, and extended their power over some surrounding islands including Castelorizo, Boodron, and Smyrna. Under the Hospitallers, Rhodes, like Cyprus, became one of the most important Crusader castles in the Mediterranean. The two islands had to face the danger of the two Muslim powers, the Mamlūks of Egypt and Syria and the growing Ottoman Turks in Asia Minor. The Knights of Rhodes and the Kings of Lusignan of Cyprus therefore had an identity of purpose, and it was in the interest of both islands to work together.

The Mamlūk sultans did not forget the Cypriot sudden attack upon Alexandria in 1365 by Peter I of Lusignan. Peter, who was the most adventurous of the Lusignan kings, led a combined fleet, in which he was supported by the Knights of Rhodes. He seized the port of Alexandria, plundered it, and sailed away with boats and prisoners. We have a full, contemporary account of the Cypriot attack written by an Alexandrian eyewitness, that is, al-Nuwayrī in his book *Kitāb al-imām*. The Lusignan King Peter II tried again in 1369 to attack Alexandria for the second time. The Cypriot fleet appeared off Alexandria after it had attacked Tripoli in Syria. The campaign failed, and the Mamlūk sultans had to wait for a chance to retaliate.

In 1422 Barsbay, the strongest of the Circassian Mamlūk sultans, obtained the seat of the Sultanate. He wanted to gain popularity in his first years by waging a holy war. He sent three expeditions against Cyprus, in 1424, 1425, and 1426. In the last of these campaigns the Island of Cyprus was captured by the Mamlūks, and the Cypriot king Janus was taken to Cairo as a prisoner. Janus was released after he had agreed to pay ransom and annual tribute to the Mamlūk sultans. He signed a treaty with Sultan Barsbay who undertook, on his part, to defend his "viceroy in Cyprus" against the Venetians and the Catalans.

King Janus sailed to Cyprus with the Rhodian ambassadors who had come to Cairo to make a treaty with Sultan Barsbay. The Rhodians were afraid that the Mamlūk sultan might be incited to extend his ambitions toward Rhodes, since the Mamlūks' relations with Rhodes were not better than their relations with Cyprus. In Cyprus, the Hospitallers had private estates and settlements, especially at Kolos near Limassol. It was the responsibility of each Grand Master to defend and to help the kings of Cyprus against any attack, and to work together. This explains why the Cypriot fleet which surprised Alexandria in 1365 consisted of Rhodian as well as of Cypriot warriors, and why Anthony Fluvian or De la Rivière, the Grand Master of Rhodes, helped Cyprus during the Mamlūk Campaigns of 1424–26. Fluvian and Rhodes surmised that the victory of the Mamlūks in Cyprus might encourage them to attack Rhodes. His fears were confirmed when Sultan Barsbay threatened to carry out an expedition against Rhodes during the negotiations for the ransom of King Janus of Cyprus. Fluvian sent a gift, together with an envoy who was instructed to make a new treaty with the Sultan, and to extract from him a promise not to wage war upon Rhodes. It seems that the Rhodian envoy obtained a favorable response from the Sultan, and left Egypt with the ransomed Cypriot King Janus.

However, Fluvian armed Rhodes and its possessions, so as to be prepared to counter any Mamlūk campaign. Barsbay made no attempt to invade Rhodes before his death in 1438. He was preoccupied with both Shah Rukh, son of Tamerlane, and Kara-Yelet, chief of the Aq-Qoyunlu Turkomans. In Egypt he had also to face the consequences of plague, famine, and Mamlūk riots.

Yūsuf succeeded his father Barsbay, but only for about three months, after which he was replaced by Jaqmaq in 1438. Although the new sultan was known for his piety, he had Barsbay's triumph in mind, and wanted to gain fame as had his predecessor. The new sultan also wanted to keep the Mamlūks busy with the *jihād*, and to put an end to their disputes and riots. He hoped to terminate the piracy which prevailed in the Eastern Mediterranean, and which threatened the trade routes to Egypt and Syria. The contemporary historian al-Maqrīzī states that Sultan Jaqmaq swore to demolish the centers of piracy in Rhodes.

One might add that there was contact with the Ottoman Sultan Murād II. Murād—according to Vertot—was anxious to keep the Knights of Rhodes busy defending their island, instead of joining the league of Christian powers that was about to attack the Ottomans. Murād II also wanted, in his own interest, to weaken the Mamlūks of both Egypt and Syria, as well as the Rhodians. Grand Master Lastic, who succeeded Fluvian, tried in vain to renew a peace treaty with the Ottomans. Lastic became more suspected for Ottoman-Mamlūk understanding. He sent his nephew William Lastic, the seneschal of the Order, with two vessels to approach the Egyptian coasts and collect information. William received sufficient information of Mamlūk preparations through a spy in Damietta. He arrived at Rhodes to warn the Knights of a Mamlūk attack, and to urge them to prepare without delay.

The Mamlūk fleet left Būlāq, near Cairo, on Monday, 8 August 1440, setting out for Rhodes. It consisted of 15 grabs (vessels) under the command of two high-ranking emirs, Taghrī Barmush and Yūnus al-Maḥmūdī. The Egyptian fleet sailed later on from Damietta on the Mediterranean toward Cyprus, with about a thousand warriors. From Cyprus they proceeded to al-'Alāyā on the coast of Asia Minor, whose prince reinforced them with a number of troops; they then set sail for the city of Rhodes, which they reached on 25 September 1440. The island was ready and fully prepared. The Mamlūk fleet was attacked by ten Rhodian vessels in an engagement "which did no justice to either side." On the following morning another indecisive encounter took place off the mainland. The Mamlūks decided to return home after attacking a Rhodian hamlet, plundering a sugar-mill, and capturing some workers and farmers. At last the Mamlūk fleet arrived in Cairo on 18 October 1440 with no gains.

Sultan Jaqmaq decided to send a greater expedition, since the first one had proved no match for the Rhodians. He ordered that new vessels should be built, and old ones reconditioned. The sultan tried at the same time to secure the neutrality of certain Mediterranean powers in the future war. He concluded treaties with Fantin Quitini of Venice, John II of Cyprus, and others.

In Rhodes, Grand Master Lastic put the island in fighting trim, as news came to him of the Mamlūk preparations. He tried to contact the Sultan for peace, and sent envoys who arrived in Cairo in April 1443 with gifts and a number of Muslim prisoners. The Mamlūk sultan thought wrongly that they had come to mislead him, and the Rhodian envoys were arrested and imprisoned.

On Sunday, 11 August 1443, the Mamlūk ships and warriors under the command of 'Inal al-'Alā'ī set out from Damietta accompanied by some jurists and preachers. Facing stormy weather, some ships arrived at Beirut, and the rest at Tripoli. The Egyptian and Syrian fleets met at Paphos in Cyprus, from where they sailed for Adalia. They then proceeded to Fineka, thence to Kashtil al-Rūj (*Châteauroux*, modern Castel Lorizo) on 7 October 1443. Although commander 'Inal was of the opinion that the fleet should sail directly to Rhodes, the troops urged him to lay siege to the fort of Châteauroux, since its garrisons had stirred up the Mamlūk soldiers. The Mamlūks attacked the fort and demolished its castle on 12 October 1443. The campaigning season was over, winter was near, and there was no possibility of an attack on Rhodes. After they had decided to spend the winter at Makri in Asia Minor, bad weather compelled them to think first of Cyprus, and finally of returning to Egypt. They reached Būlāq harbor on Wednesday 21 December with about 200 prisoners, "old men and women," and pieces of furniture from the castle of Châteauroux. Sultan Jaqmaq was disappointed that his second expedition, like the first, had not fulfilled its original task, the conquest of Rhodes, because of unfavorable winds and stormy seas. The Mamlūks thought that "it had at all events done better than the first expedition," and the Sultan was encouraged to prepare another attempt.

The forces of the third expedition were much greater in number (more than 1,500, in addition to the volunteers) and better equipped than those of its two predecessors. The Sultan separated the sea from the land commands, appointing the former to Tamur Bey and the latter to 'Inal al-'Alā'ī of the second expedition.

The third expedition left Būlāq on 3 July 1444, and sailed from Damietta to Tripoli, where it was reinforced by Syrian forces. The Mamlūk fleet reached the city of Rhodes in mid-August, and landed at once. The Mamlūks pitched their tents, and built a camp on the two promontories to the southeast of the church of Saint Anthony, and a group of Mamlūks penetrated the island. Following a heavy fight, in which many men from both sides were killed, the Rhodian fleet surprised the Mamlūk ships; however, the emir Yelkhoja answered their fire, and succeeded in repulsing the Rhodians after losing 3 ships. Afterward, a company of Rhodians attacked the Mamlūk soldiers camped around the church of Saint Anthony. The Mamlūks were defeated and discouraged. For several days the battle went on, until at last the Rhodian knights and mercenaries rushed the Mamlūk camp. A great number of Mamlūks were killed or taken prisoner, as the rest managed to escape to their galleys.

The news reached Sultan Jaqmaq in Cairo, before he knew that his fleet had decided to return home. He dispatched reinforcements, which soon returned with the news that Taghrī Barmush had been killed, together with about 300 men, and that a similar number had been wounded, with many more captured. A contemporary Mamlūk historian comments: "And in short, the aims of the troops were not realized, nor did they come back with any result; and for that reason their former zeal for holy war in that quarter was dampened for a long time to come. And to God alone is the ultimate end of all things."

Despite their victory, the Rhodian knights had been greatly

weakened by the three successive Mamlūk campaigns. They appealed to Pope Eugenius IV and to the kings and princes of Europe for help in the event of further Mamlūk attacks. The Europeans at that time were preoccupied with their own quarrels, and the Pope advised the Grand Master to terminate his war with the Mamlūk Sultan. The Rhodians chose the great French merchant Jacques Coeur, and entrusted their affairs to him. Jacques Coeur, whose reputation inspired confidence both in the East and in the West, enjoyed very good relations with the Mamlūk sultans. With the consent of King Charles VII, Jacques Coeur undertook a peace mission by sending one of his agents to Egypt. Peace was concluded, and a decree of the Grand Master's office, dated 8 February 1446, acknowledged the services of Jacques Coeur, and instructed the Order's representatives in Provence to reimburse Coeur for the amount of his expenses.

The Rhodians then became more concerned with their other enemy, the Ottoman Turks.

21
Abū Zayd al-Balkhī on Politics

Franz Rosenthal

OUR KNOWLEDGE OF the early Muslim literature on politics shows many important gaps which prevent us from gaining an accurate picture of the development of political thought in the formative years of Islamic civilization. A small fragment of a political work by Abū Zayd al-Balkhī, preserved by the great *littérateur* Abū Ḥayyān al-Tawḥīdī, therefore deserves some attention. It is a rather rare example of a concise, scholarly definition of *siyāsa*, in the sense of political leadership and political theory, attempting to encompass in a few words the essence of a vast subject.

Al-Tawḥīdī indicates that he derived the passage from the *Kitāb al-siyāsa* of Abū Zayd al-Balkhī. Al-Balkhī was born around 236/850, and he died in 322/934. Dates of birth are, of course, very often uncertain, but for tracing the course of intellectual developments, they are by and large more significant than the better-established dates of death. Even if they are usually only approximations, they are close enough for all practical purposes and can be relied upon to provide suitable signposts here.

Not much information on al-Balkhī's political treatises appears to have been preserved. More quotations are very likely to be recovered, and there is always the hope that the treatises themselves will show up in the future. It may be noted that al-Balkhī wrote a good deal on philosophy, medicine, geography, astrology, and cultural history, apparently in the fertile tradition of al-Kindī whose student he is said to have been (even though this is unlikely in any literal sense). He is credited with two works on *siyāsa*, distinguished as the large work and the small work on the subject (*Fihrist*, ed. Flügel, p. 138, l. 15). We have no express statement as to which *Kitāb al-siyāsa* was the source of the definition of politics.

There is another reference to al-Balkhī's *Kitāb al-siyāsa*, again without further qualification. It is stated to be a work composed for Yānis al-Khādim, who at the time was governor of Balkh. He remains to be identified. There were a number of rather prominent individuals named Eunuch John at around that time. The best known of them is Yānis al-Muwaffaqī, who died in 311/923–24. He cannot, however, be placed securely at Balkh during any time of his busy military career; but since soldiers and officials were speedily whisked from one part of the realm to another on a moment's notice, it is not entirely inconceivable that he did a brief stint of duty at Balkh at some time. The reference is to be found in the biography of Abu 'l-Qāsim al-Ka'bī (also al-Balkhī) in al-Ṣafadī's *Wāfī*.[1] Al-Ka'bī and al-Balkhī were engaged from time to time in written disputations and exchanges of views; in scholarly literature, they were occasionally mixed up. The passage in the *Wāfī* mentions al-Ka'bī's criticism of al-Balkhī's efforts in the area of political science. He is said to have attacked al-Balkhī's work on politics as a waste of time and labor. In his view, all political wisdom that one needs to know is contained in Qur'ān 8:45 f. These Qur'ānic verses praise readiness for and steadfastness in fighting, the avoidance of internal strife, and the constant awareness of God under all conceivable circumstances. They are generally interpreted to show that nothing, not even the pressures of battle, should divert Muslims from *dhikr Allāh*. This has little to do with the kind of political theory and practice that al-Balkhī appears to have had in mind. Presumably, it was an attack on his philosophical stance and on his reputed doubtful orthodoxy from the point of view of a rival *mutakallim*. The *Kitāb al-siyāsa* criticized by al-Ka'bī may have been the small work. It is unclear, in any case, whether or not it was the same work from which the definition of politics is derived.

The small work is presumably meant by *al-Siyāsa al-mukhtaṣara*, which is quoted in a work entitled *Kitāb rusul al-mulūk* by a certain Ibn al-Farrā' who supposedly lived in the late tenth century.[2] The quotation concerns al-Balkhī's views on what makes a good ambassador. This problem is dear to the hearts of the authors of *Fürstenspiegel* works, but does little to illuminate al-Balkhī's particular political thought.

These are all the references to his *siyāsa* treatises known to me at this time. It may be added that a quotation from al-Balkhī in the tenth-century *Kitāb al-sa'āda wa'l-is'ād* may possibly go back to one of his political writings, since the *Kitāb al-sa'āda* is our main witness to the Muslim approach to political science exclusively by way of the Greek tradition. This quotation, however, has nothing to do with politics as such, but concerns al-Balkhī's views on *ra'y* ("opinion"), and thus could go back to any one of his numerous works.[3] If the author of the *Kitāb al-sa'āda* was indeed Abu 'l-Ḥasan al-'Āmirī, we would be dealing here with a putative student of al-Balkhī, but that relationship is very much open to doubt.

The text of the quotation in al-Tawḥīdī's *Kitāb al-baṣā'ir wa'l-dhakhā'ir*, brief as it is, is marred by small mistakes, at least in the edition of Ibrahim Keilani published in Damascus.[4] A new edition now being prepared in Beirut may possibly prove them to be the editor's fault. If they are found in the manuscript tradition, they could be due to al-Tawḥīdī in some cases, but the original author cannot be held accountable for them. It seems certain that what we have here is Abū Zayd al-Balkhī's *ipsissima verba*. A translation as literal as possible and, it is hoped, as correct as possible reads as follows:

> *Siyāsa* is a craft (*ṣinā'a*), in fact, one of the most important and highest-ranking crafts. For it is a craft that allows the cultivation (*'imāra*) of a country and the protection of the human beings in it to take shape.
>
> In order to bring forth his product, every human craftsman cannot do without five things that are the causes of the craft in question.[5] One is a matter [that is a tool] for the craftsman [and a matter][6] with which he works. The second is a form toward which he aspires with his activity. The third is a motion which he uses for support in uniting (*tawḥīd*) that form with the matter. The fourth is a purpose conceived by him in his imagination on account of which he does what he does. And the fifth is a tool for him to employ for setting the matter in motion.
>
> Take as an example the craft of building: the matter from which the building is built is earth, clay, stones, and wood. The form toward which the builder aspires in his imagination is the form of the house. The agent is the builder. The purpose on account of which he makes an inhabitable house is to give shelter wherever needed. And the tool with which he works is the building tools.
>
> Or take as another example the craft of medicine: the matter with which the physician works ⟨is the human body. The form toward which he aspires⟩[7] in his imagination is precisely (*innamā*) health. The agent is the physician engaged in treatment. The purpose that causes the physician to act is for the body of the person under treatment to last the length of time it is prepared to last. And the thing which the physician uses as a tool for treatment and for procuring health is, for instance, bloodletting or medicinal drafts.
>
> Now, applying this example to the craft of politics, we say:
>
> The matter here is the affairs of the subjects which the ruler is charged to execute.

The form here is precisely the general welfare (*maṣlaḥa*) toward which he aspires. It is the counterpart of health, because the general welfare is a kind of health, and health is a kind of general welfare. Correspondingly, corruption is a kind of sickness, and sickness is a kind of corruption.

The agent is the ruler's concern (*'ināya*) with the affairs of the subjects he deals with.

The purpose for which he works is for the general welfare to last permanently.

The thing which for him is like the tool of his craft is precisely causing desire (*targhīb*) and intimidation (*tarhīb*).

The activity of the politician (*sā'is*), which is the counterpart of the physician's treatment, falls altogether into two parts. One of them is "care" (*ta'ahhud*), and the other "improvement" (*istiṣlāḥ*). "Care" is the preservation of the subjects' affairs[8] that are in good shape (*mustaqīm/istiqāma*), and orderly quiet and tranquillity, so that they do not deviate from the best (*fāḍila*) form. "Improvement" is the restoration of well-being (*ṣalāḥ*) and harmony wherever the good shape of the affairs of the subjects[9] is affected by corruption and confusion contrary to it. Such care and improvement in the craft of politics are the counterparts of the preservation and restoration of health in the craft of medicine, which is *siyāsa* as it affected human bodies. Just as all of medicine is comprised in these two chapters, thus all of politics is comprised in their counterparts, namely, care and improvement.

For al-Balkhī, *siyāsa*—at least, the form of it with which he was dealing in his work—is not *'ilm* ("theoretical knowledge"), but a craft. It is, in fact, one of the most important of crafts. This statement is hardly surprising, since he could have gotten it from the beginning of the *Nicomachean Ethics* (1094a27), and no doubt, this was his direct or indirect source. According to Aristotle, the leading science (*epistēmē*) is *hē politikē*. Aristotle used "science," and not "craft." However, in this particular passage, he did not intend to make a sharp distinction between *praxeis, technai,* and *epistēmai*. Significantly, the Arabic translation of the *Nicomachean Ethics* speaks of *ṣinā'at tadbīr al-mudun*, if this is the reading of the manuscript.[10] Al-Balkhī's justification for the assumption that politics ranks highest among the crafts, because it shapes (*hayya'a*) civilization and protects the population of a country, somehow reminds us of the political wisdom that had long been known to the Muslims as being of Persian origin, rather than owed to Greek philosophy.

Now, al-Balkhī argues that *siyāsa* being a craft, it must be considered in the same light as any other craft—needless to say, a very dubious assumption that is likely to lead to trouble. Like any other craft, *siyāsa* must follow a rigorous scheme of classification, as does everything in the world according to Aristotelian tradition. It is classifiable by means of a circumscribed number of criteria which together define and exhaust the concept of "craft." Such schemes were eagerly pursued in Muslim scholarship. Thus we hear, for instance, about the ten basic principles which have always to be followed in the study of philosophy and of the works of Aristotle, and which were derived from the Greek introductory writings on Aristotle,[11] or the seven conditions determining authorship put together by Ibn Khaldūn,[12] or the seven *muqaddamāt* for commentaries mentioned in connection with Euclid.[13] The list of five points for defining the concept of "craft" seems noteworthy, and may possibly be original with al-Balkhī. The points themselves are, of course, common in Aristotelianism. That the "agent" should be called "mover" is not incompatible with Aristotelian usage in connection with the crafts. While the "matter" is something given, the "form" is of the craftsman's choosing. The "purpose" also requires an initiative coming from the artisan's imagination, in order to enable him to chart the course of his activity.

Before applying the general definition of "craft" to the craft of politics, al-Balkhī explains what he has in mind by means of two other crafts, building and medicine. It so happens that in late antiquity, medicine and architecture were considered together as potential candidates for inclusion among the Liberal Arts, but eventually did not make the grade, being seen as too practically oriented.[14] The Muslims were not privy to this discussion. As a matter of fact, while Greek literature quite commonly linked medicine together with politics, the combination with building was much less common. Aristotle mentions medicine and building together in the *Metaphysics* (1070b33, 39) but in a context that has nothing to do with politics. Later, al-Fārābī speaks of the political man as the physician of the soul, and of the craft of politics as compared to all the other crafts as that of master architects in comparison to ordinary construction workers,[15] apparently following the same tradition as al-Balkhī and distorting it. If building is discussed by al-Balkhī first, this would seem to be for the simple reason that his scheme works well in connection with it; but it could also be due to the fact that in al-Balkhī's view, medicine is conceptually so very close to politics. It may be noted that in the case of building, it is the "form" that is described as resulting from the builder's imagination, and not the "purpose" which is a given here.

Medicine does not fit quite so easily into the scheme. The human body can possibly be assumed to constitute its "matter," but it seems strained to consider health as the "form" to be shaped by the physician. If the text translated here has been reconstituted correctly, health as the form of medicine is to be shaped according to the physician's imagination—allowing us to conclude that, just as the house of the builder may be given various shapes, health may also vary in appearance, presumably according to the constitution of individual human beings. The stated "purpose" of medicine, as seeing to it that the patient lives as long as possible, seems in a way to run afoul of the common Muslim view that the length of an individual's lifespan is predetermined, and that medicine can do nothing to change it.[16]

The discussion of building and medicine is assumed to have paved the way for understanding and defining the essence of *siyāsa*. Al-Balkhī seems hardly aware that in reality, this requires a quantum leap. The "craft" of politics does not deal with anything concrete in the sense that building and, to some degree, medicine do, at least within the consensus of the tradition to which al-Balkhī belonged. This forced him to try to turn abstract ideas into material data, and to claim general validity where no basic agreement could possibly be expected. The affairs of the subjects become the "matter" of politics, and the general welfare of the ruled (and, of course, the rulers) its "form," suggesting that there is a manageable concrete entity that has to be molded into the best possible shape.

In Muslim political thought, politics continued to be viewed as being based on matter and form wherever the influence of Greek philosophy predominated, as, for instance, in the *Fuṣūl* of al-Fārābī.[17] The author of the *Kitāb al-sa'āda* quotes a recent philosopher, presumably al-Fārābī, for this elaboration of the matter-form complex in politics: "The matter of *siyāsa* is the conditions of the people in their various shapes and ethical outlooks (*fī hay'ātihim wa-akhlāqihim*), and its form is virtue (*faḍīla*), which is also the intended object of causing desire and intimidation."[18] This remark calls forth an extremely thoughtful comment by the author of the *Kitāb al-sa'āda* himself, to the effect that *siyāsa* does not move in a single direction, but rather in several directions, and that consequently, neither its matter nor its form can be a single one; the author then goes on to describe the physical and moral training of human beings in a way reminiscent of al-Balkhī's conception of the crafts. Several centuries later, Ibn Khaldūn declared civilization (*'umrān*) and the world in its entirety to be the "matter" of politics with which political leaders have to work, while kingship or royal authority is the "form" to be imposed upon civilization as the "matter" of politics. This is a rather different point of view. However, the consequence drawn by Ibn Khaldūn, that the two are inseparable, of course is not different.[19]

The "agent" in the craft of politics who accomplishes the marriage of human affairs and general welfare seems to be not the ruler as such, but rather, as al-Balkhī puts it, "the ruler's *concern* with the affairs of his subjects." The difference appears to be meaningful and should not be overlooked. It seems to point to an abstract rather than personal element as determining political affairs on top of the social pyramid. This is not necessarily contradicted by the fact that elsewhere, al-Balkhī speaks of kings as being personally in charge of the political guidance of human beings and the civilization of the country (*siyāsat al-'ibād wa-'imārat al-bilād*).[20]

Permanence of the general welfare is the "purpose" of politics. Thus the craft of politics, if properly designed and executed, must not be concerned merely with achieving quick solutions to ephemeral political problems. It should aspire to the establishment of a well-functioning society which can last a long time.

While other crafts are at their most concrete with respect to their tools, the political tool is pleasing people ("causing desire," *targhīb*) on the one hand, and intimidating them (*tarhīb*), on the other. In the context of politics, it is often debated what form this carrot-and-stick approach should take.[21]

Since, according to al-Balkhī, the "form" of politics, the general welfare, can be compared to the "form" of medicine, which is health, the political leader's activity can be compared to the treatment administered by the physician. The task of medicine was generally seen as consisting of the preservation of health, and its restoration through the curing of disease. The equivalents in politics are, in al-Balkhī's terms, *ta'ahhud* and *istiṣlāḥ*.[22] His work on medicine, to which attention has been called by H. H. Biesterfeldt,[23] and which has been made available in a fine reproduction of one of the two Aya Sofya manuscripts of the work,[24] is instructive for the use of these terms. The unusual fifth conjugation of the root *'-h-d* occurs in a seemingly political context in the famous *'Ahd Ardashīr*.[25] It is a key term in al-Balkhī's medical treatise which defines medicine as *ta'ahhud* of the body in two ways, the preservation of the body's existing health and the restoration of its lost health.[26] The closeness in meaning of *ta'ahhud* to "preservation," with "care" covering its more general range of meaning, is underlined by its frequent pairing with *ṣiyāna* "protection." *Ta'ahhud* and *ṣiyāna* are also once joined by *istiṣlāḥ*.[27] *Istiṣlāḥ*, in contrast to *ta'ahhud*, is a common word in the language, but its earlier history remains to be investigated.[28] According to the *Kitāb al-sa'āda*, the participle *mustaṣliḥ* occurs in the correspondence of Aristotle and Alexander,[29] and Plato used *istiṣlāḥ* in speaking about improving conditions threatened by internal quarrels and dissension.[30] For al-Balkhī, its meaning would seem to be "seeking well-being (*ṣalāḥ*)," or more precisely, "seeking to restore the political entity's *ṣalāḥ*," rather than aiming at *maṣlaḥa* ("general welfare"). Still, considering the genius of Arabic as a Semitic language, the use of *istiṣlāḥ* here is probably the most idiomatic way of expressing the idea that the constitutional task of government is to "promote the general welfare."

The situation with respect to al-Balkhī's use of *targhīb* and *tarhīb* as the tool of politics is even more complicated, even though, or perhaps because, the two terms are very well known and much attested. Their roots appear paired in Qur'ān 21:90, as well as in the old ḥadīth, but they are not associated there in any manner with political concerns. Their occurrence there in combination, however, indicates solid Arabic and Islamic roots. Hellenistic influence may have been at work in connection with their application to political thought, but the Greek origin of a quotation ascribed to Plato in the *Kitāb al-sa'āda* requires more precise determination: "The technique (*ḥīla*) to be used for making people comply with what the law commands them to do is *targhīb* by means of pleasurable things. The technique to be used for keeping people from what the law forbids them to do is *tarhīb* by means of harmful unpleasant things."[31] It may, however, be more significant that the combination of the two terms appears to have been at home in the old political literature supposedly of Persian origin, as witnessed by the often repeated statement attributed to Anūsharwān or other Persian authorities: "Exercise political leadership over good people by means of love, and over low-class people by means of intimidation. For the general run of people, mix desire with fear (*al-raghba bi'l-rahba*)!"[32]

As a whole, al-Balkhī's definition of politics, brief as it is, reveals itself as a skilful blend of the three major components of his contemporary civilization which were in conflict with one another. In the first place, there are some traditional Muslim echoes, as reflected in the use of terms such as *maṣlaḥa* and, possibly, *istiṣlāḥ*. It is not surprising that they are as weak as they are, since al-Balkhī had no intention of competing with Muslim theology and jurisprudence and their particular views of political theory. Next, there are a few elements recalling supposedly Persian ideas, such as the explanation of what makes the craft of politics so important, or the *targhīb/tarhīb* complex. They are meant to constitute a nod to the large earlier "Persian" political literature, long familiar in Islam, and until the ninth century totally dominating political thinking (and, of course, living on through the centuries). The third, and most notable, component is Greek philosophical ideas, Aristotelian in origin.[33] This clearly was al-Balkhī's inspiration, and it gave shape to the whole. Notwithstanding its overpowering influence, al-Balkhī attempted to incorporate it into a traditional framework, while preserving its main characteristic, the trend toward rational systematizing.

At first glance, al-Balkhī's definition gives the impression of being commonplace. However, considering the very careful manner in which it has been worked out, it cannot be dismissed as negligible. It appears to be a noteworthy accomplishment and one quite in keeping with what we know about al-Balkhī's stature as a scholar. If it does not succeed in doing what it sets out to do, and does not describe the true meaning of politics exhaustively to everybody's satisfaction, this is to be expected. Given the enormous complexity of the subject, it cannot be done. It had rarely been attempted in a serious manner in earlier times.

Beyond its intrinsic interest, this short text deserves attention because of its position in Muslim political writing during the crucial ninth century. Most of the relevant literature has not yet been recovered and may be lost, leaving us very poorly informed. We can, however, gain a certain idea of what went on in the field in the course of that century from bibliographical references to works having *siyāsa* in their titles. Little can be done about works that may have dealt with politics without indicating it expressly.

Works on *siyāsa* are credited to Sahl ibn Hārūn (*Fihrist*, p. 120, ll. 11f.) and Abū Dulaf (*Fihrist*, p. 116, l. 21), both born in the late eighth century, although no more precise birthdates are available. These works can safely be assumed to belong to the empirical political writing of the *Fürstenspiegel* genre. It would be interesting to know whether it was of the Persian variety or according to the Hellenistic model known from the correspondence between Aristotle and Alexander.

Al-Kindī comes first in the ninth century, since his birth is usually placed in 801, although in fact it may be that he was already born in the nineties of the eighth century.[34] He was followed in the next generation by his student al-Sarakhsī (b. ca. 835). Both al-Kindī and al-Sarakhsī wrote at least two works on *siyāsa* (*Fihrist*, p. 260, ll. 2 f., and p. 262, ll. 13 f.), just as al-Balkhī did later on. It may be that this is not a coincidence, but rather indicates some sort of relationship. One might speculate that the difference between the two works was not merely a difference in size; it may be that one of them was more theoretically oriented, while the other relied more on the traditional *Fürstenspiegel* material. It must also be left open whether there is some connection here with the fact that Ibn al-Muqaffaʿ wrote *two* works on political *adab*, a large and a small one. Not much younger than al-Kindī was Ḥunayn ibn Isḥaq (b. 808) who commented (*fassara*) on Plato's *Politeia* (*Fihrist*, p. 246, l. 5). Presumably, he offered nothing that led directly to al-Balkhī.[35]

Between al-Kindī and al-Sarakhsī, the historian of Baghdad Aḥmad ibn Abī Ṭāhir Ṭayfūr (b. 819–20) and the scientist Qusṭā ibn Lūqā (b. ca. 820) figure as *siyāsa* authors (*Fihrist*, p. 146, ll. 21 ff., and p. 295, l. 13). The historian is likely to have approached the subject in the *Fürstenspiegel* manner. Qusṭā, on the other hand, may have continued the role of non-Muslims in the development of Muslim political thought; thus, his work would seem to be of obvious importance to our quest. Like Qusṭā, the historian and scientist Thābit ibn Qurra (b. ca. 836), a close contemporary of al-Sarakhsī, also came from a non-Muslim environment, and may have introduced new ideas on *siyāsa*, if indeed he did write on the subject.[36] Another contemporary, the Ṭāhirid ʿUbaydallāh ibn ʿAbdallāh ibn Ṭāhir (b. 838), in his *Risāla fī 'l-siyāsa al-mulūkīya* (*Fihrist*, p. 117, l. 17), can be assumed to have followed the *Fürstenspiegel* tradition of his family; his father ʿAbdallāh was the recipient of the famous letter of ʿUbaydallāh's grandfather on how a statesman should act.

Al-Balkhī follows here in the chronological sequence, since he was born ca. 850.[37] His birth preceded that of the great innovator in Muslim political thought, al-Fārābī, by about twenty years. Al-Fārābī's close contemporary was Qudāma ibn Jaʿfar, born in 873. Qudāma is the only one of the pre-Fārābian authors mentioned here whose writing on *siyāsa* appears to be preserved. As suggested by S. A. Bonebakker,[38] his *Kitāb al-siyāsa*, known through bibliographical reference (*Fihrist*, p. 130, l. 25), may be identical with the eighth and last chapter of his *Kitāb al-kharāj*, which deals with politics. This chapter has now been edited and studied by Muṣṭafā Ḥiyārī, who has also provided a German résumé.[39] Ḥiyārī's conclusion is generally the same as the one presented here in connection with al-Balkhī: Qudāma tried to combine the three strains of political thought, Islamic, Persian, and Greek. Qudāma's definition of politics, however, is totally different from that of al-Balkhī. According to him, "politics . . . is the guidance by kings and *imāms* of their subjects, who let themselves be guided and who assume obedience to them, to praiseworthy and acceptable actions and to straight and strong ways."[40] This is again in the earlier political tradition, combined with the Greek view of politics as a part of ethics. There is nothing in Qudāma's work that might constitute a link between him and al-Balkhī.

With al-Fārābī (born ca. 870), we finally escape from the shadows of bibliographical reference into the light of direct information from preserved writings. It is a strange and very changed light, at least as it emanates from al-Fārābī's *Best City*.[41] His *Fuṣūl*, however, harken back to what were his and al-Balkhī's common sources. The *Best City* attempts a synthesis of theological and philosophical views of the world. In the philosophical view, politics had by now become a branch of ethics. Already when al-Kindī spoke of Aristotle's ethico-political works, he described the *Nicomachean Ethics* as a work dealing with ethics and *siyāsa* of the (individual) soul; Aristotle's other book on the subject of politics, the *Politika*, deals with the same subject as the *Nicomachean Ethics*, but in it, al-Kindī says, Aristotle discusses principally political leadership (*al-siyāsa al-madanīya*).[42] For better or worse, this approach to politics continued to predominate in both East and West, and al-Fārābī's variation of it remained influential in Islam.

If al-Balkhī's definition is indicative of his political thought in general, he holds a middle ground, as he is also chronologically right in the middle between al-Kindī as the first developer of Greek philosophical and political thought, and al-Fārābī with his grand and bold innovative theory. He attempted to achieve some sort of solid, down-to-earth synthesis of the possibilities known to him. He apparently had no use for and paid no attention to "virtue" as the central governing force of politics, and "happiness" as the overarching goal of man individually and politically. Even less was he inclined to elaborate on some metaphysical foundation of all human societal life. This, at least, is what comes through in his definition. Whatever other ideas his political writings may have contained, his general view as expressed here describes the political process in concrete and rational terms, firmly set in and holding the balance between the intellectual currents of his time. It represents something that to some degree seems to have been lost in the grander efforts undertaken in later centuries.

It is not known at this time how much al-Balkhī depended in his definition and thought on his predecessors, in particular, al-Kindī and al-Sarakhsī. They may have done better than he did. He may even have purloined his definition from them. This, however, may be strongly doubted. No matter how much inspiration he may have drawn from his predecessors, the ultimate product is likely to be his own creation, and to reflect his proven scholarship and independent spirit. However this may be, al-Balkhī is a rare witness to a ninth-century concern that was shared by many of the outstanding thinkers of the age. The goal was to produce a political philosophy that did not do violence either to accepted earlier Muslim thought on politics or to the powerful Greek ideas then becoming generally known, but that would do justice to both.

NOTES

1. Ed. D. Krawulsky (Wiesbaden, 1982 [*Bibliotheca Islamica* 6q]), XVII, 26.

2. 2d ed., ed. Ṣalāḥ al-dīn al-Munajjid (Beirut, 1972), pp. 34 f.

3. *Kitāb al-sa'āda*, ed. Mojtaba Minovi (Wiesbaden, 1957–58), pp. 407, 419.

4. (Damascus, n.d.), II, 2, 763–65.

5. The only possible antecedent for *lahā* seems to be an implied *ṣinā'a*.

6. "Craftsman" seems to be the only possible referent for *lahū*. The mention of "tool" is out of place here. The indicated deletion is probably necessary.

7. Supply *hiya jism al-insān wa'l-ṣūra allatī yanḥūhā al-ṭabīb*.

8. The translation is based upon the assumption that the object pronoun in *'āraḍahū* refers to *mustaqīm* ("good shape"), and that the suffix in *minhā* refers to the *umūr* of the subjects, and that there is a possible omission of *min* after *minhā*. Other combinations are possible but would not greatly affect the intended meaning.

9. Possibly, *wa-umūr* should be corrected to *min umūr*.

10. Cf. 'Abd al-Raḥmān Badawī (ed.), *Al-Akhlāq ta'līf Arisṭūṭālīs*, p. 55, l. 3 (Kuwait, 1979). Although references from later Muslim literature are not mentioned here as a rule, one later statement regarding the paramount position of the craft of politics vis-à-vis the other crafts may be permissible. The chapter on *siyāsa* from Ibn Ḥamdūn's *Tadhkira* (Cairo, 1345/1927 [*Al-Rasā'il*

al-nādira 3]), p. 37, thus speaks of *siyāsa* as the craft producing harmony (*ta'līf*), social unity (*ijtimā'*), and cooperation and effectiveness in all other activities. The same work (p. 44), incidentally, offers one of the traditional descriptions of politics, which it may be useful to hold against al-Balkhī's definition. It is ascribed to the caliph 'Abd al-Malik speaking to his son al-Walīd: "[Politics involves] respect of the elite combined with their true love, guidance of the hearts of the common people by fairness to them, and tolerance of the mistakes (*hafawāt*) of the crafts (*al-ṣanā'i'*[?], or "the men working for the government"[?])."

11. Cf., for instance, al-Fārābī's *Fīmā yanbaghī an yuqaddama qabla ta'allum al-falsafa*, or 'Abdallāh ibn al-Ṭayyib's commentary on the *Categories*.

12. *Muqaddima*, trans. F. Rosenthal (New York, 1958 [*Bollingen Series* 43]), III, 284 ff.; al-Maqqarī, *Azhār al-riyāḍ* (Cairo, 1358–61), III, 33 f.

13. As found in a note on fol. 1a of the Euclid manuscript in the Royal Library in Rabat, no. 1101.

14. See Pauly-Wissowa, *Realencyclopaedie*, XIV, 2, 2008, *s.v.* Martianus Capella; H. H. Biesterfeldt, "Some Opinions on the Physician's Remuneration in Medieval Islam," *Bulletin of the History of Medicine*, LVIII (1984), p. 26, n. 57.

15. Cf. al-Fārābī, *Fuṣūl al-madanī*, ed. D. M. Dunlop (Cambridge, 1961), text p. 104, trans. p. 28, corresponding to *Fuṣūl muntaza'a*, ed. Fauzi M. Najjar (Beirut, 1971), p. 25. It is not totally excluded that there is some connection here with the Aristotelian usage of *architektōn* in the meaning of "skilled" (in any craft), with no restriction to building.

16. Al-Balkhī evades verbs meaning "to create" or the like, but uses *tahayya'a* ("is prepared").

17. Ed. Dunlop, text p. 105, trans. p. 29; ed. Najjar, p. 26.

18. See *Kitāb al-sa'āda*, pp. 211 f.

19. See *Muqaddima*, II, 291, 300.

20. See al-Balkhī, *Maṣāliḥ al-abdān*, p. 149 (below, notes 23 and 24).

21. A rare equation with hope and fear appears in *Kitāb al-sa'āda*, p. 217.

22. Ibn Farīghūn, *Jawāmi' al-'ulūm*, p. 86, shows dependence on al-Balkhī in his choice of words: "The activity of the politician falls into care for what is in good shape and restoration to harmony of what is corrupt." See the manuscript facsimile published by Fuat Sezgin (Frankfurt am Main, 1985).

23. "Notes on Abū Zayd al-Balḫī's Medico-ethical Treatise *Maṣāliḥ al-abdān wa-l-anfus*," in *Actes du 8me Congrès de l'Union Européenne des Arabisants et Islamisants, Aix-en-Provence, 1976* (Aix-en-Provence, 1978), pp. 29–34.

24. Published by Fuat Sezgin (Frankfurt am Main, 1984). A note at the end of the manuscript mentions the *Kitāb al-siyāsa* among the very few of al-Balkhī's works listed there.

25. Ed. Iḥsān 'Abbās (Beirut, 1387/1967), p. 54. There too, *ta'ahhud* is used with reference to the human body. [I have meanwhile noted quite a few usages of *'-h-d* V, making *ta'ahhud* less "uncommon" than I originally thought.]

26. *Maṣāliḥ al-abdān*, pp. 3–11, also pp. 129, 223, 231.

27. *Maṣāliḥ al-abdān*, p. 10. See also above, n. 22.

28. Wael B. Hallaq thus assumes comparatively late origin for the technical use of the term in jurisprudence, see "Considerations on the Function and Character of Sunnī Legal Theory," in *JAOS*, CIV (1984), p. 686.

29. See *Kitāb al-sa'āda*, p. 215.

30. See *Kitāb al-sa'āda*, p. 274.

31. See *Kitāb al-sa'āda*, p. 217. Solon defined the law as *tōn men deilōn phobos, tōn de tolmērōn kolasis*, and Cicero quotes him as having said that the state is held together by reward and punishment, see *Gnomologium Vaticanum*, ed. L. Sternbach (reprint Berlin, 1963), p. 187, no. 507; Cicero, *Epistola ad Brutum*, I, 15, 3, as quoted by Sternbach, p. 128, in connection with no. 322. Similar statements are, as to be expected, quite common in Greek literature, but so far I have found nothing that would qualify as the direct source of the statement attributed to Plato.

32. The wording rendered here is that of *Kitāb al-sa'āda*, pp. 218, 301 f. Cf. also, for instance, Ibn Qutayba, *'Uyūn al-akhbār* (reprint Cairo, 1963–64), I, 8; Usāma b. Munqidh, *Lubāb al-ādāb* (Cairo, 1354/1935), 39. For a Hellenized form ascribed to Plato, cf. al-Mubashshir, *Mukhtār al-ḥikam*, ed. 'Abd al-Raḥmān Badawī (Madrid, 1958), p. 150, ll. 4–6.

33. For the problem of identifying Platonic references with respect to political theory in Arabic sources, see R. Walzer, *Al-Fārābī on the Perfect State* (Oxford, 1985), pp. 425 ff.

34. Cf. F. Rosenthal, "Al-Kindī als Literat," in *Orientalia*, n.s. XI (1942), p. 283.

35. Another Greek work on politics, by Themistius, was translated into Arabic, it seems, only during the tenth century, and probably could not have been known to al-Balkhī; see Irfan Shahid, in *Themistii Orationes*, ed. G. Downey and A. F. Norman (Leipzig, 1974), III, 73–119. It yields little for the present investigation.

36. His work is not listed in the *Fihrist*. Al-Qifṭī, ed. J. Lippert (Leipzig, 1903), p. 120, ll. 4 f., speaks of "a discussion (*kalām*) on *siyāsa* of (Thābit's) own composition, which was then translated into Arabic." Ibn Abī Uṣaybi'a, *'Uyūn al-anbā'*, ed. A. Müller (Cairo-Königsberg, 1882–84), I, 220, ll. 22 f., refers to it as *kalām fī 'l-siyāsa*.

37. The work by al-Balkhī's close contemporary, the famous vizier 'Alī ibn 'Īsā (b. 859), entitled *Kitāb al-kuttāb wa-siyāsat al-mamlaka wa-sīrat al-khulafā'* (*Fihrist*, p. 129, l. 6), was probably a handbook for government officials and may have contained little or no discussion of political theory.

The *Kitāb al-Siyāsa wa'l-khulafā' wa'l-umarā'* of the celebrated mystic al-Ḥallāj (b. 858) (*Fihrist*, p. 192, l. 7) may possibly have had some connection with political theory, since it was dedicated to a military/political figure (see Massignon, III, 292, no. A 38), but this is by no means certain or even likely. See L. Massignon, *La Passion de Husayn Ibn Mansūr Hallāj*, 2d ed. (Paris, 1975), I, 188, n. 2; II, 430–31; III, 290, 292.

38. See *EI*², V, 320b, *s.v.* Ḳudāma b. Dja'far.

39. "Qudāma b. Ǧaʿfar's Behandlung der Politik," in *Der Islam*, LX (1983), pp. 91–103. Al-Ḥiyārī's edition of the Arabic text was not available to me. I had to be satisfied with the edition of Qudāma's *Kitāb al-kharāj* by Muḥammad Ḥusayn al-Zabīdī, which appeared in Baghdad in 1981.

40. Ed. al-Zabīdī, p. 427. See Hiyari's article, p. 97.

41. See now R. Walzer's treatment of the work (above, n. 33).

The allegedly contemporary treatise, entitled *Al-Siyāsa wa'l-balāgh al-akbar wa'l-nāmūs al-aʿẓam*, and supposedly written by the first Fāṭimid ʿUbaydallāh al-Mahdī to the son of Abū Saʿīd al-Jannābī, has nothing to do with *siyāsa* as understood here, but is intended to show how the sectarians tried to convert people to heretical beliefs. See ʿAbd al-Qāhir al-Baghdādī, *al-Farq bayn al-firaq*, ed. Muḥammad Badr (Cairo, 1328/1910), pp. 278 ff.; trans. A. Halkin, *Muslims Schisms and Sects* (Tel-Aviv, 1935), II, 131 f.

The date of the *Risālat al-siyāsa wa'l-riʾāsa*, listed in I. K. Poonawala, *Biobibliography of Ismāʿīlī Literature* (Malibu, 1977), p. 341, is unknown and may be comparatively recent. It is the only *siyāsa* title listed by Poonawala.

42. Cf. M. Guidi and R. Walzer, "Uno Scritto introduttivo allo studio di Aristotele," in *Memorie della R. Accademia Nazionale dei Lincei, Cl. di Scienze mor., stor. e filol.*, Serie V, Vol. VI, Fasc. 5, 403, 418 f. (Rome, 1940); M. ʿAbd al-Hādī Abū Rīda (ed.), *Rasāʾil al-Kindī al-falsafīya* (Cairo, 1950–53), I, 384. For the knowledge of Aristotle's *Politika*, which was apparently not translated into Arabic, see S. Pines, "Aristotle's Politics in Arabic Philosophy," in *Israel Oriental Studies*, V (1975), pp. 150–60.

22
The West Arabian Topography of Genesis 14

Kamal Salibi

AMONG THE PATRIARCHAL stories of the Bible, Genesis 14 has so far been regarded as standing in a category by itself, because it alone appears to relate the career of Abraham to "international political events" of his time. On the surface, the text does seem to speak of a "foreign invasion" of territories close to where Abraham lived, by the joint forces of "four kings" setting out from their respective realms on a punitive expedition. Traditionally, it has been taken for granted that the invaded territories—Sodom (*śdm*), Gomorrah (*'mrh*), Admah (*'dmh*), Zeboiim (*ṣbyym*), and Bela (*bl'*), also called Zoar (*ṣ'r*)—were a "pentapolis" comprising five ancient cities of the valley of the Jordan and the Dead Sea in Palestine, where none of these place names has been found in historical times. The invaders, it has been assumed, must have been the rulers of powerful kingdoms, coming all the way from Mesopotamia and northern Syria. Some scholars, tantalized by some of the details given in the biblical account of the invasion, have endeavored to decipher the names of the four invading kings and their respective kingdoms, hoping thereby to clarify the much-needed synchronism that would establish the historicity of the patriarchal narratives. Others, noting the paucity or dubiousness of the extra-biblical and archaeological evidence regarding this assumed "foreign invasion" of the Jordan valley in the Middle Bronze age (the time conventionally assigned to the patriarchal period of biblical history) have treated Genesis 14 more skeptically, even to the extent of discounting its historicity altogether.[1]

On reading Genesis 14, however, one is struck by its ring of authenticity. The four invading kings are fully identified by name and territory; so are the names of the peoples or kings of the invaded territories. The motive for the invasion is also specified: the punishment of five kings of the invaded regions, who were vassals to one of the invaders (and not to all four of them), for their rebellion. The course of the invasion is described in detail, and the site of the decisive battle specified. The topography of the invaded area is also vividly depicted, consisting of rugged valleys (one of them full of *b'rwt ḥmr*, or "hiding pits")[2] and mountains. One can hardly imagine such historical and geographical detail to be pure invention, or a garbled concoction of bits and pieces of history confused with dimly remembered lore. Granted, the story of the seemingly historical invasion, as related in Genesis 14:1–11, could have been confused by some folk tradition with the legend of Abraham and his nephew Lot (Genesis 14:12 f.). But this is altogether a different matter. The invasion itself must have been a historical event, though perhaps not of "international" moment. Moreover, the setting in which the event took place need not have been Mesopotamia and Syria. Judging by the place names cited, it is my belief that it could only have been West Arabia.

In an earlier study of biblical geography,[3] I contended that the biblical Sodom, Gomorrah, Admah, and Zeboiim could not have been cities of the Jordan and Dead Sea in Palestine, but were rather ancient towns of the fertile valleys of the coastal lowlands of the Jīzān region, in West Arabia. As place names, Bela (*bl'*) and Zoar (*z'r*) have proved so difficult to identify in terms of the Jordan valley that the first name has been dismissed by no less than three scholars as a "pejorative epithet" meaning "destroyed," while the second has been classified as "ambiguous."[4] Actually, both Bela and Zoar still exist by their unchanged biblical names in the same vicinity of Wādī Najrān in West Arabia, across the hills from the coastal Jīzān region. The first survives there as Bālū'a (*bl'*), the second as Ṣāghir (*ṣġr*, cf. Hebrew *ṣ'r*).

The valley of Wādī Najrān, no less than the wadis of the Jīzān region to the west, is an area of great fertility. In both areas, industrious peasants have cultivated the land since times immemorial.[5] Traditionally, mountain tribes have always tended to dominate the peoples of the valleys, and ancient West Arabia is unlikely to have been an exception. Here it seems that at some period of remote antiquity, the highland tribes of the Ṭā'if, Zahrān, and Ghamid regions in the southern Hijaz had gained political dominance over peasant communities inhabiting the fertile valleys of the Najrān and Jīzān regions, close by the present borders of the Yemen. The "kings," or chiefs, of these peasant communities became the vassals of the "kings" or chiefs of the highland tribes of the southern Hijaz. On one occasion, it seems, the peasant vassals rebelled against their tribal lords, and these lords or "kings"—four in all—advanced against them to suppress the insurrection. Along the way, they raided three other peasant communities in the valleys of the southern Hijaz; further south, they made attacks on the tribes of the 'Asīr and Jīzān highlands, who probably competed with them for control of the adjacent valleys. A topographical analysis of the narrative of Genesis 14, in the context of West Arabia, bears this out in almost every detail:

The four leaders of the punitive expedition, according to the text, were the kings of Shinar (*šn'r*), Ellasar (*'lśr*, or *'l śr*), Elam (*'ylm*), and Goiim (*gwym*). The territories in question were those of Sharā'in (*šr'n*), in Wādī Kalākh, of the Ṭā'if highlands; Āl Siyār (*'l syr*), in the Ghamid highlands; Jabal 'Almā' (*'lm'*) in the Zahrān highlands; and Jabal Qaym (*qym*), also in the Zahrān highlands. Setting out from their respective territories, the four invading chiefs first go down the valley of Wādī Aḍam, by way of the Buqrān mountain pass, south of Ṭā'if. Here, and in the valleys nearby, they subdue "the Rephaim (*rp'ym*, singular *rp'y*) in Ashteroth-qarnaim, the Zuzim (*zwzym*, singular *zwzy*, from *zwz*) in Ham (*hm*), and the Emim (*'ymym*, singular *'ymy*, from *'ym*) in Shaveh-kiriathaim (*šwh qrytym*)." The Rephaim in question could have been the historically attested Yarfā (*yrp̄'*) tribe of West Arabia; the place where they were subdued, in any case, was the village of 'Ashāriyāt (*'šrt*), near Dhā al-Qarnayn (*qrnyn*), in the vicinity of Ghumayqah, west of Wādī Aḍam. The Zuzim were definitely the people of Zayzā' (*zyz'*), in Wādī Aḍam, who were defeated in Dhāt al-Hām (*hm*), in the same vicinity.[6] From the same valley came the Emim, whose home territory was Far' Ayām (*'ym*), which is still there today. Those were defeated in Shaveh-kiriathaim, today Shawī (*šwy*), in the same Wādī Aḍam, close by Qāratān (*qrtn*), cited in the Arabic geographical literature as a village of the same area.[7]

Next, the invaders proceeded southward into the 'Āsir highlands (*hr s'yr*, cf. the present name *'syr*). Here they subdued the Horites (*ḥry*)—apparently the inhabitants of what is today Ḥarāy (*ḥry*), in the region of Rijal Alma'—and pursued them to El Paran (*'yl p'rn*), which is Āl Farwān (*'l p̄rwn*), at the southernmost end of these highlands, between the Jīzān and Najrān regions. This El Paran was *'l h-mdbr*: not "by the desert," as it is described in the standing translations, but "above *h-mdbr*," which is today the village of Mabradah (*mbrd*), below

Āl Farwān, on the slopes of Jabal Harūb, in the hill country of the Jīzān region.

From El Paran, or Āl Farwān, the invaders "turned back" (*yšwbw*) to reach a "holy place" (*qdš*) called *špt*, which is today Ṭafashah (*ṭpš*), in the Rayth highlands of the Jīzān hinterland; then they proceeded from there in the direction of the southeast, around the foothills of the Jīzān ridges, to reach *'yn*, which is 'Ayn (*'yn*), in Jabal Banī Mālik.[8] From the strategic heights of this ridge, which today lies along the international frontier between the Yemen and Saudi Arabia, the invaders now descended into the heartlands of the Jīzān region to subdue the Amalekites (*'mlqy*, from *'mlq*), whose homeland there was the vicinity of *Ma'ālīq (m'lq)*, in the 'Āriḍah hills bordering the coastal plain. Next they turned eastward and crossed the mountains inland to reach Hazazon-tamar (*ḥṣṣn tmr*): the village of Ḥazāzīn (*ḥzzn*), in the vicinity of Ibn Thāmir (*ṯmr*), in Wādī Najrān. There they defeated the local Amorite (*'mry*, from *'mr*) settlers, whose original home, further inland, was the oasis of Amār (*'mr*), in the region of Yamāma.

The chiefs of the peasant communities of the Jīzān and Najrān regions must have been gravely alarmed by this tremendous show of force. Rather than wait to be attacked, they "went out" (*w-yṣ'w*) to meet the invaders in the valley of Siddim (*'mq sdym*, Hebrew plural of *sd*), where they were routed and put to flight. The place where the battle was fought today is called Sudūd (Arabic plural of *sd*), and it is located in Wādī Ḥabūnā, not far north of Wādī Najrān. This Siddim (or Sudūd) is described as being *ym h-mlḥ*, usually taken to mean the "sea of salt," as a reference to the Dead Sea in Palestine. It is largely for this reason that the biblical Sodom, Gomorrah, Admah, Zeboiim, and Bela-Zoar came to be thought of as a "pentapolis" of that area. Actually, *ym* happens to be attested in Hebrew in the sense of "west," and *mlḥ* (as *milḥ*) in the Arabic dialect of the Najrān and Ḥabūnā regions means "sand, sands," as well as "salt." Where Genesis 14, speaking of the valley of Siddim (or Wādī Ḥabūnā) says *hw' ym h-mlḥ*, I would translate the Hebrew as meaning "it is west of the sands." Wādī Ḥabūnā is in fact located to the west of the largest single expanse of sand in the world—that of the desolate Empty Quarter of South Arabia. The strip of pastoral desert into which Wādī Ḥabūnā drains froms part of what is called to this day Bilād Yām (*ym*)—perhaps meaning originally the country "west" of the sands.

Traveling through Wādī Ḥabūnā, H. St. J. B. Philby noted "a sandstone frieze pitted with caves" on one side of the valley.[9] According to Genesis 14, it was the valley of Siddim that was full of "hiding pits" (*b'rwt ḥmwr*, see above). As they fled the battlefield in defeat, the kings of Sodom and Gomorrah reportedly "lay there" for temporary safety (*w-yplw šmh*, the verb being *npl*, "fall, lie"). According to the usual translations, these two kings "fell" by accident into the "bitumen pits" of the Dead Sea valley. So far, it has not been really established that "pits" of bitumen in that area ever existed, although some claims to the effect have been made.

For those willing to concede that accepted notions of biblical geography can be wrong, the evidence presented in this paper, to interpret Genesis 14 as the record of desert warfare in West Arabia rather than an imperial invasion of Palestine, would be enough. All the place names cited in the text survive virtually unchanged in West Arabia, and none survive in Palestine. Between the southern Hijaz and the Jīzān and Najrān regions bordering the Yemen, one can follow the movement of the invading forces step by step, from start to end. For those unwilling to make the concession, no further belaboring of the point would help. There would always be those who would insist that the invaders of the story were the kings of a *'ylm* which was "Elam" on the northeast of the Persian Gulf; of a *šn'r* which "certainly stands for the region of Babylonia"; of an *'lsr* which is "plausibly . . . a phonetic reading of the ideograms A-LA-SAR," which could have stood for *'šwr*, the usual biblical name for Assyria; of a *gyym* which was not the name of a country or locality, but the Hebrew word for "nations," referring to the Hittites, who had several kings called Tudhalias (identified as the biblical Tidal, or *td'l*).[10]

The fact remains, however, that Genesis 14, when set in West Arabia, loses its enigma and acquires a new significance as the earliest coherent record of the sort of tribal politics that must have marked the history of West Arabia—and of other tribal regions of the Near East—at all times. Moreover, a word-by-word translation of the original Hebrew, keeping in mind the observations that have been made in this chapter, captures the subtle lilt of the epic verse in which this West Arabian desert story was most probably originally sung:

It was in the days of Amnaphel, king of Shinar;
    Arioch, king of Ellasar;
Chedarlaomer, king of Elam;
    And Tidal king of Goiim:
They made battle with Bera, king of Sodom;
    With Birsha, king of Gomorrah;

Shinab, king of Admah;
    Shemeber, king of Zeboiim;
And the king of Bela—it is Zoar.

All those marched united to the valley of Siddim:
    It is west of the sands.
Two years, ten years they served Chedarlaomer,
    And thirteen years they rebelled.

Within fourteen years came Chedarlaomer
    And the kings who were with him:
They smote the Rephaim in Ashteroth-karnaim;
    The Zuzim in Ham;
The Emim in Shaveh-kirathaim;
    And the Horites in their mountain Seir
All the way to El Paran—which is above Midbar.

They turned back and came to En from Shaphat—
    It is a holy place—
And they smote all the country of the Amalekites—
    Also the Amorites who dwelt in Hazazon-tamar.
And out came the king of Sodom,
    The king of Gomorrah,
    The king of Admah,
    The king of Zeboiim,
    The king of Bela—it is Zoar—

And they fought with them a battle in the valley of Siddim:
    With Chedarlaomer, king of Elam,
    Tidal, king of Goiim,
    Amraphel, king of Shinar,
    And Arioch, king of Ellasar—four kings against five.

The valley of Siddim had many hiding pits:
    The kings of Sodom and Gomorrah lay there,
    And the rest fled to the mountain.
They took all the herds of Sodom and Gomorrah,
    And all their food stocks,
    And went away.

NOTES

1. For the different views on Genesis 14, see the text and notes in John Van Seters, *Abraham in History and Tradition* (New Haven, 1975), pp. 112–20.

2. The Hebrew *ḥmr* here is usually taken to mean "bitumen," the word being attested in this sense in Genesis 11:3 and Exodus 2:3. Here, however, *ḥmr* is the verbal noun from the same root meaning "cover" (also attested in Exodus 2:3, cf. Arabic *ḫmr*, "cover, hide, keep away from sight"). See below for the context.

3. Kamal Salibi, *The Bible Came from Arabia* (London, 1985), pp. 30, 57–60, 90–92.

4. John Van Seters, op. cit., pp. 116–17.

5. See Kamal Abdulfattah, *Mountain Farmer and Fellah in 'Asīr, Southwest Saudi Arabia: The Conditions of Agriculture in a Traditional Society* (Erlangen, 1981).

6. Dhāt al-Hām does not appear to exist any more today there, but it is cited by name as a village of that neighborhood in Hamdānī, *Ṣifat jazīrat al-'Arab* (San'ā', 1983), p. 236.

7. Ibid.

8. The Hebrew here reads, *w-yb'w 'l 'yn mšpt* (my reading *'l 'yn m-špt*) *hw' qdš*; the conventional translation of it understands, "And they came to En-mishpat, which is Kadesh"; I understand, "And they came to *'yn ('Ayn)* from *špṭ* (Ṭafashah)—it is a holy place."

9. H. St. J. B. Philby, *Arabian Highlands* (Ithaca, N.Y., 1952).

10. John Van Seters, op. cit., pp. 113–14. Actually, *td'l* can be readily interpreted as a Semitic tribal name meaning "ruse, stratagem" (archaic feminine substantive of *d'l*, Arabic "set a trap, waylay, ensnare, deceive"). In Biblical Hebrew, as in Arabic, men's names are frequently feminine substantives of this type: *e.g.*, Tibni (*tbny*, 1 Kings 16:21 f., possibly from *bnh*, "build"); Tolad (*twld*, 1 Chronicles 4:29, from *yld*, "bear, bring forth children"); Tola (*twl'*, Genesis 46:13, etc., from *l'*, "lick, sip"); Terah (*trḥ*, Genesis 11:24–26, etc., probably from *'rḥ*, "be on the road, wander"). In Arabic, names of this structure are equally numerous (Tabī', Tamīm, Talīd, etc.).

23
From Court Ceremony to Urban Language: Ceremonial in Fatimid Cairo and Fusṭāṭ

Paula Sanders

THE CEREMONIES OF Islamic dynasties have been studied primarily as expressions of political legitimacy. Ritual and ceremony have been regarded as expressions of ideology and as reflections of changes in the political fortunes of dynasties. Studies have focused on insignia of sovereignty, administrative structure, and the personnel of the court in order to provide a context for interpreting the ceremonies. This emphasis on political and religious ideology has meant that other, equally significant, meanings have been overlooked.

I am going to argue that Fatimid "court" ceremonies were an expression of a particular urban experience, and were as deeply imbedded in the social and religious life of Cairo and Fusṭāṭ in the eleventh and twelfth centuries as they were in more narrowly conceived concerns for political legitimacy. These ceremonies responded as much to the changing urban landscape of Cairo and Fusṭāṭ as they did to dramatic political and religious changes in the Egyptian history of the dynasty. In the process, they developed into a complex urban language.[1] As an urban language, they helped to define an evolving relationship between the two cities; they also helped to mark dramatic changes within one of those cities—Cairo. No change was so dramatic as the transformation of Cairo from a palace complex into an urban center. This transformation did not come easily, and was fraught with tension. For these were two cities of remarkably different complexion and character.

Cairo was the Fatimid city. Like the North African capitals al-Mahdīya and al-Manṣūrīya, Cairo was a palace complex built on the outskirts of an existing commercial center. In Ifrīqiya, that center was Qayrawān; in Egypt, it was Fusṭāṭ. Long after the foundation of Cairo, Fusṭāṭ remained a separate city with its own distinctive character. In spite of Cairo's proximity to Fusṭāṭ (it was only about two miles away) and the prestige associated with the Fatimid court, Fusṭāṭ's inhabitants clearly preferred the commercial city. Well into the thirteenth century, travelers in Egypt continued to express their preference for the congenial residents of Fusṭāṭ over their neighbors in Cairo.[2]

Cairo was Ismā'īlī. It was, in some respects, a reflection of the "spiritual topography" of Ismā'īlism, which placed the imām at the center of the faith. In Cairo, the traditional linked mosque-and-palace complex was replaced by a separate palace at the center of the walled city and a mosque that was very close, but not joined, to the palace.[3] Fusṭāṭ, on the other hand, was not only Sunni, but Christian and Jewish as well. In Fatimid times, as in the early Islamic period, it was still home to sizable Christian and Jewish populations, with their churches and synagogues. By the late eleventh century, Fusṭāṭ had become the seat of both the Coptic patriarchate and the office of Head of the Jews.[4] Its heart was the Mosque of 'Amr in the old al-Rāya quarter. If there was any single area of the city where Jews, Christians, and Muslims were likely to cross each other's paths—and they often did so—it was here. Long before the Fatimid period, the Mosque of 'Amr had become a center of urban life, responding to the rhythms of the Coptic calendar as well as to those of the Muslim calendar: it was the terminal point for parades on Nawrūz, the Coptic New Year.[5] It was also the site of disorder and dissension, as well as of peacemaking and reconciliation.[6] Fusṭāṭ never became an Ismā'īlī city; it remained a stronghold of Sunnism throughout the Fatimid period.

Cairo was a closed city. It was the seat not only of an imperial power, but also of a spiritual authority. The caliph was separated from the general population by walls and gates, by bodyguards, and by protocol. Even entering the city gates (let alone the palace itself) was a difficult and potentially dangerous procedure, which could be accomplished only through adherence to a rigidly prescribed and carefully controlled protocol. With the exception of highly honored officials, no one was permitted to enter the city mounted; during processions, the qāḍī and the vizier would dismount and salute the caliph as soon as they had passed through the city gate; and on some occasions, the qāḍī would even parade around the perimeters of Cairo, dismounting to kiss each gate through which the caliph passed.[7]

By contrast, Fusṭāṭ—the center of economic and commercial life—was open. Its location on the banks of the Nile made it a major emporium. Fusṭāṭ was the inland port for goods imported from both the Mediterranean Sea and the Indian Ocean.[8] Its markets, mosques, and residences were all clustered together. But in Fusṭāṭ, the familiar unit of the mosque-marketplace was joined by synagogues and churches that also bordered on these same markets, and on each other.

Fusṭāṭ was open in another sense: people moved in and out of the city as easily as did goods. It was a cosmopolitan city, with a diverse population connected with its active international trade. Numerous foreigners dwelled among the local inhabitants. In the port city of Alexandria, foreign traders came and went without establishing any permanent ties in the city, and were often at odds with the volatile local population; whereas in Fusṭāṭ, traders were likely to put down stakes by marrying local girls and buying property.[9] They were easily and readily integrated into the local society. Networks revolved around relationships of formal friendship and informal cooperation. In a different sense, Cairo was also filled with foreigners. The Fatimids had come from North Africa and established a palace complex; their armies had consisted primarily of Kutama Berbers, and later, of Turkish, Armenian, and Sudanese slave troops. But these men had a direct connection with the court. The determining factor in their relationships with each other was not the complex networks of familial ties and formal friendship that characterized the society of Fusṭāṭ, but the ties that each of them had with the Fatimid caliph himself.

These two cities in close proximity to one another had remarkably different characters. Cairo's public life was organized around the rhythms of the court. These rhythms were both regular and sporadic: the Islamic calendar and its festivals (reckoned in the Ismā'īlī fashion)[10] came with predictable regularity, and the rest of the year was punctuated unevenly by the arrival of embassies or the departure of armies. But the rhythms of Fusṭāṭ's public life were different and equally complicated: the rise of the Nile, the coming and going of ships that swelled its population at certain times, the Coptic ritual calendar, the celebration of local festivals (often of local Egyptian saints, whether Islamic or Christian).[11] Over the course of time, Fatimid ceremonies began to respond to the rhythms of Fusṭāṭ. They also responded to changes within Cairo, as it developed in the twelfth century into an urban center in its own right.

How did Fatimid ceremonies link the two very different cities without compromising their integrity, how did they express the characters of the two cities and mitigate tensions between them, and how did they respond to the very real changes within Cairo itself? The extraordinary capacity of Fatimid court ceremonies to express urban meanings is nowhere more evident than in the processions and banquets that celebrated Ramadan and the Two Festivals, *ʿīd al-fiṭr* and *ʿīd al-aḍḥā*.[12] From the beginning to the end of the Fatimid period, caliphs went in procession to lead prayer on Fridays during Ramadan and on the Festivals. During Ramadan, these processions took them to mosques, during the Two Festivals, to the *muṣallā* outside the northern gates of Cairo. As Cairo expanded, and as additional mosques were built, they had to be linked to the palace. The caliph al-ʿAzīz rode in procession in 380/990 to the Mosque of Cairo (more commonly known as the Azhar)—the only mosque within the walls of the city—accompanied by 5,000 soldiers. After establishing a new mosque outside of Bāb al-Futūḥ,[13] he led prayer there, as well as at the Azhar. But the practice was not, at first, consistent. Leading prayer in more than one place during Ramadan was introduced as new Friday mosques were built in Cairo, and as they were successively integrated into the ritual life of the court.[14] The processions from palace to mosque expressed symbolically the Ismāʿīlī system in which the imām stood at the center of all devotions (as the palace stood at the center of the city).[15]

This specifically Ismāʿīlī ritual unity, with palace at center, is even more striking in the processions to the *muṣallā* on the Two Festivals. The caliph al-ʿAzīz introduced an important addition to these celebrations when he ordered the construction of benches (*maṣṭabas*) from the palace to the *muṣallā* in 380/990, the year in which he laid the foundation for his new mosque outside of Bāb al-Futūḥ. He ordered the Ismāʿīlīs to sit on the *maṣṭabas* and recite the *takbīr* as soon as he mounted his horse at the palace gate "so that it would be continuous from the palace to the *muṣallā*."[16] These activities in 990—founding a new mosque, building the *maṣṭabas*, staging elaborate processions—point to a different conception of the role of ritual in the capital city. From this year on, processions during Ramadan and on the Festivals were not merely a means of getting from one point to another; they were meant to connect the points as well.

One might argue that the procession to the *muṣallā* could be read as an assertion of political and military unity, of loyalty to the caliph in the face of external threats to the empire's stability, whereby the urban map became a kind of symbolic map for the caliph's political and military aspirations. The *maṣṭabas* established a physical link between the palace and the *muṣallā*; the continuous recitation of the *takbīr* constituted a liturgical link that actually incorporated the procession into the prayer. These physical, liturgical, and processional links between palace and *muṣallā* on the one hand, and between palace and mosque, on the other, asserted the ritual unity of Cairo itself and the continuing centrality of the palace. Moreover, it asserted it as a specifically Ismā'īlī unity with a powerful ideological message integrated into it.

Al-Ḥākim, the son of al-'Azīz, was faced with a more daunting task, that of integrating the city of Fusṭāṭ into the ritual life of the court. In addition to building two mosques in Fusṭāṭ, and completing the mosque which his father had begun, al-Ḥākim also patronized both the Mosque of Ibn Ṭūlūn and the Mosque of 'Amr, the two venerable old congregational mosques of Fusṭāṭ. In the year 403/1012–13, al-Ḥākim led the Friday prayer during Ramadan at three mosques: the newly completed mosque outside of Bāb al-Futūḥ, the mosque at Rāshida, and the Mosque of 'Amr. Both of these mosques were in Fusṭāṭ, and this was the first year in which a Fatimid caliph had ever led the prayer there. Al-Ḥākim was integrating Fusṭāṭ into the ritual and ceremonial life of the court, forty years after the Fatimid conquest of Egypt.[17]

But the processions to the Fusṭāṭ mosques were of a different character from the procession in Cairo. When al-Ḥākim went to the Rāshida and 'Amr mosques, the chroniclers relate, the common people walked at his stirrup, "coming between him and his entourage (*mawkib*)."[18] There is no report of al-Ḥākim accepting petitions in Cairo, as he did in Fusṭāṭ. With the addition of the Mosque of 'Amr—the center of ritual life for the Muslims of Fusṭāṭ—and the mosque at Rāshida to his itinerary during Ramadan, al-Ḥākim integrated Cairo and Fusṭāṭ into a single ritual city.

From the reign of the caliph al-Mustanṣir, Fatimid ceremonies began to change in noticeable ways. Over the course of a century, the Fatimids had become increasingly aware not only of the power of ceremonial, but also of the need to effect social unity in the changing environment of Cairo and Fusṭāṭ in the twelfth century. Fatimid efforts to convert the local population had failed. Ritual unity could no longer be Ismāʿīlī. If official ceremonies were now to work as an urban language, they would have to be divested of their explicitly Ismāʿīlī content.

The viziers Badr al-Jamālī and his son al-Afḍal rescued the Fatimids from serious disorder. They restructured the armies and the administration, establishing the vizier as the primary political power of the state. Al-Afḍal arrogated enormous powers to himself during the reigns of al-Mustaʿlī (whom he had raised to the caliphate over Nizār, the eldest son of al-Mustanṣir, thus provoking the Nizārī schism) and of al-Āmir. He was so bold as to move his residence from Cairo to Fusṭāṭ—a blatant assertion of his independence from the caliph. This move was so presumptuous that even his own sons refused to accompany him to his Fusṭāṭ residence. Finally, he abandoned the celebration of festivals.

It was the vizier al-Ma'mūn who "restored glory to the dynasty" by reviving the ceremonies that had been abandoned by al-Afḍal. But he did this under very different circumstances. The Fatimid empire was now a different empire. The bases of power in the state had been transformed; and equally significant changes had taken place in the capital city. Al-Ma'mūn, more than either Badr or al-Afḍal, seems to have sensed the importance of governing the cities of Cairo and Fusṭāṭ as much as he did the importance of governing the whole empire—in essence, perhaps, because these two cities constituted the only truly stable area at the core of a withered empire. Al-Afḍal had failed in his attempt to establish Fusṭāṭ as a viable rival to Cairo even for temporal administration. Cairo was still the seat of the Fatimid caliphate, and her symbolic value was too powerful to ignore.

The intense construction within Cairo during the period from 1074 to 1125 was accompanied by marked changes in the character of the population of the city.[19] Cairo was, from this period onward, less a royal enclave than an emerging urban center in its own right. Badr al-Jamālī rebuilt the walls of an expanded Cairo in cut stone, and allowed the Armenian Christian regiments who had accompanied him to establish their own quarters within the city: construction in the city of Cairo.[20] Other regiments were given permission to establish their own quarters in the twelfth century. The Maṣāmida, a regiment formed during the reign of al-Mustanṣir, built their own quarter outside of Bāb Zuwayla only during the vizierate of al-Ma'mūn. Jewish and Christian notables now lived in Cairo. In a word, Cairo could no longer be an unequivocally closed city.[21] It now had something it had not had before: a civilian population.

Al-Ma'mūn's energetic building program reflected this change in the character of its population. He conceived of Cairo as both an official administrative center and as a potential economic center. Fusṭāṭ, even when it had been the administrative center of the 'Abbasids, had never derived its primary income from state revenue: its economy had been based on commerce. Al-Ma'mūn tried to capture some of this economic activity for the caliph's city. He built a new mint within Cairo, and a *dār al-wakāla* (warehouse for merchants' representatives) for merchants coming from Syria and Iraq.[22] Al-Ma'mūn pulled the general population closer to Cairo in another way: he rebuilt and repopulated the largely abandoned district of al-Qaṭā'i', reconstructing the ruins between the Mausoleum of al-Sayyida al-Nafīsa and Bāb Zuwayla.[23] He established five new parks in Fusṭāṭ, renovated the pavilions along the Nile, and sponsored the construction of a number of mausolea for 'Alid saints, thus marking the beginning of an official cult of 'Alid saints in Cairo.[24]

Al-Ma'mūn's transformations of the urban landscape were not superficial. They were accompanied by the creation of a powerful ritual language that was both broad enough to appeal to the diverse populations of Cairo and Fusṭāṭ, and rich enough to be invested with meaning on many different levels. He did not simply restore "the customs that had existed before the days of Badr and al-Afḍal." He created out of the court ceremonies and the popular religious practices of the population of Fusṭāṭ a ritual *lingua franca* that served to link Cairo and Fusṭāṭ, to link the caliph to his non-Ismā'īlī (and even non-Muslim) local population.

Fatimid ceremonies now seemed to obscure boundaries rather than to mark them. On the urban map, the boundary between Cairo and Fusṭāṭ became obscured—perhaps even obliterated—by processions to Fusṭāṭ mosques during Ramadan. The streets, we are told, were decorated by the merchants and residents, and the *wālīs* of the cities took charge of the decoration. The *wālī* of Cairo supervised these activities from the palace to the Mosque of Ibn Ṭūlūn; the *wālī* of Fusṭāṭ from the Mosque of Ibn Ṭūlūn to the Mosque of 'Amr (or wherever the terminus of the procession might be). This is precisely the area that was undergoing a profound demographic change in the 1120s, as al-Ma'mūn pursued his vigorous policy of construction and repopulation.

Just as the boundary between the cities became obscured, the boundary between Ismā'īlī and Sunni was also being obscured. The Fatimid state was still Ismā'īlī, but it had already been rent by one serious schism and would soon face another. In the twelfth century, many of the caliph's staunchest allies and supporters were Sunnis. The Fatimid imām was Ismā'īlī, but neither his capital city of Cairo, nor the neighboring city of Fusṭāṭ, were of that faith. If ritual unity were to be achieved, it had to be in a broadly Islamic—and not specifically Ismā'īlī, or even Shī'ī—context. The celebrations of the Two Festivals in the period of the caliph al-Āmir and his vizier al-Ma'mūn illustrate the ways in which a ritual *lingua franca* was created and how this might mitigate urban religious tensions.

'Īd al-fiṭr in 1122 was celebrated at the palace with two banquets, one before the procession to the *muṣallā*, and the other on returning from prayer. But at these banquets, the guests did not actually break their fast. Rather, they accepted food from the caliph, kissed it, and placed it in their sleeves. "No one," the historian tells us, "was compelled to break his fast." The significant act was receiving the food, making the symbolic gesture of kissing it, and placing it in the sleeve—not actually ingesting it. This gesture was now the central activity of the banquet. This was an elegant solution to the tension created by the presence of large numbers of officials who did not adhere to the Ismā'īlī calendar, and who observed the end of the fast on a different day.

But the importance of this ritual activity was not confined to the palace. People were encouraged to take food from the caliph's banquet and redistribute it outside the palace. There are even reports that some of this food was sold in the marketplace. In addition, staggering quantities of clothing were distributed. These robes of honor were so abundant during the reign of al-Āmir that the festival came to be known as *'īd al-ḥulal*, the festival of gala costumes.

The distributions of such large quantities of food and clothing and their redistribution among the population were part of the creation of a ritual *lingua franca* that deliberately emphasized those aspects of ritual that could be conceived of as broadly Islamic, of a language that was, in fact, urban. Although banquets had always been a feature of Fatimid festival celebrations, they had never been conceived as a way of transmitting the *baraka* of the caliph to the general population. Nor had the Fatimids ever so explicitly borrowed from popular religious practices as they did now. The cult of saints was deeply imbedded in the religious consciousness of Egyptians of all religious affiliations. What sorts of things did people—ordinary people—do at saints' tombs? They went there on festivals, they donned new clothing, they prayed there, they held banquets there. These were not only pious acts: they also had a powerful communal aspect.

The vizier al-Ma'mūn responded by integrating the ritual life of the court into this existing and flourishing local religious tradition. He accomplished this in part by sponsoring an official cult of 'Alid saints, in part by increasing the material aspects of the celebrations to allow for redistribution, and finally by deemphasizing the explicitly Ismā'īlī aspects of particular ceremonies and rituals. Even the official celebration of the Day of Ghādir Khumm—the Shī'ī festival that commemorates the Prophet's designation of 'Alī as his heir apparent (*waṣī*)—was in the period of al-Ma'mūn divested of its ideological content and celebrated in the same fashion as the Two Festivals. This does not mean that such ceremonies no longer had a message for the Ismā'īlī minority. Rather, they were restructured in subtle ways, so that they could be invested with a greater number of meanings by diverse groups of people, while the Ismā'īlīs, with their penchant for allegorical interpretation and insistence on the priority of esoteric meaning could invest them with the same meaning they had always had.

We should not be surprised at how easy it was to accomplish this. Fusṭāṭ had a long tradition of festival celebrations transcending the boundaries of religion: the Christian festivals of Epiphany, the Festival of the Cross, and Nawrūz were celebrated by the entire population. Some festivals, most notably the celebration of the inundation of the Nile, had always been urban and communal events. In the environment of Fusṭāṭ—the open city—the development of a common ceremonial culture was a natural occurrence. Differences in religion, the integrity of religious communities, were not necessarily compromised by the common public celebration of festivals. Certainly, there was some official resistance in the early days of the Fatimid caliphate. Periodically, caliphs would publish proclamations prohibiting the common celebration of festivals. But they were never successful at halting the practice. It was too tightly woven into the social fabric of Fusṭāṭ. By the late Fatimid period, Cairo itself emerged as an urban center, and the ceremonies of the court had to be stretched to accommodate the new character of the capital city. As the social implications of these changes and the growing need for a comprehensive urban language became clear, the Fatimids looked to Fusṭāṭ's common ceremonial culture. In the twelfth century, Fatimid court ceremonies became a part of that shared culture.

NOTES

1. I would like to acknowledge my intellectual debt to the work of Natalie Zemon Davis in formulating this argument. Her article, "The Sacred and the Body Social in Sixteenth-Century Lyon" (*Past and Present*, XC (1981), pp. 40–70) has particularly influenced my thinking and the language I have chosen to discuss the problem in the remarkably different context of medieval Egypt.

2. Numerous references are provided by S. D. Goitein, *A Mediterranean Society*, IV, 11, n. 39 and Ayman Fu'ad Sayyid, in his unpublished thesis, "Al-Qāhira et al-Fusṭāṭ: Essai de reconstitution topographique," III, 647–50.

3. On mosque-palace complexes, see *EI*[1] s.v. "Masdjid" (III, 318b, 346b–347a) and *EI*[2] s.v. "Architecture" (I, 616–18).

4. See Mark R. Cohen, *Jewish Self-Government in Medieval Egypt* (Princeton, 1980) for a complete analysis of the internal conditions within the Jewish community that contributed to the origins and rise of the office of Head of the Jews in Cairo. Cohen's book has the great merit also of providing the only scholarly reconstruction of the history of the Coptic patriarchate in the context of Fatimid social and political realities that has yet been undertaken.

5. Kindi, *Kitāb al-wulāt*, ed. R. Guest (Beirut, 1908), p. 269.

6. Ibid., pp. 134, 274–75.

7. On the protocol for entering the palace city, see my unpublished Ph.D. thesis, "The Court Ceremonial of the Fatimid Caliphate in Egypt" (Princeton, 1984), Chapter I.

8. On the economic and commercial life of Fusṭāṭ, and on international trade, see S. D. Goitein, *A Mediterranean Society*, vol. I, *Economic Foundations* (Berkeley and Los Angeles, 1967).

9. Goitein, *A Mediterranean Society*, vol. IV, *Daily Life*, p. 8.

10. The Ismāʿīlīs reckon their calendar by astronomical calculation; Sunnis use the sighting of the moon.

11. On shipping seasons, see Goitein, *A Mediterranean Society*, I, 303–17. The Coptic calendar regulated seafaring even though the local Christian population played almost no role in the shipping business (I, 311).

12. I have discussed the development of these ceremonies in detail in my thesis, Chapter III.

13. The mosque was completed by his son, the caliph al-Ḥākim, and came to be known as the Mosque of al-Ḥākim. On the history of the structure, see Jonathan Bloom, "The Mosque of al-Ḥākim in Cairo," *Muqarnas*, I (1982).

14. See al-Maqrīzī, *al-Khiṭaṭ* (Bulaq edition), II, 277–80, and *Ittiʿāẓ al-ḥunafā*, I, 272, 276, 279, 283.

15. For a discussion of the Ismā'īlī interpretation of mosque and prayer, and its relationship to ceremonial, see my thesis, pp. 68–70 and 109.

16. al-Maqrīzī, *al-Khiṭaṭ*, I, 451, II, 277, and *Itti'āẓ al-ḥunafā*, I, 267.

17. Although the Shī'i call to prayer had been introduced into the mosques of Fusṭāṭ early in the Fatimid period, these mosques had not been visited by the caliphs and clearly still served a largely Sunni population. On the introduction of the Shī'i *adhān* at the Mosque of Ibn Ṭūlūn in 359/970, see al-Maqrīzī, *Itti'āẓ*, I, 120–21.

18. *al-Khiṭaṭ*, II, 28, and *Ittai'āẓ*, II, 96–97.

19. For a discussion of the changes in Cairo and Fusṭāṭ, see Ayman Fu'ād Sayyid's thesis, vol. III.

20. Materials were taken from ruins in al-Qaṭā'i' to build houses in Cairo. Ayman Fu'ād Sayyid, p. 509. On Armenians in army, see William Hamblin's unpublished Ph.D. thesis, "The Fāṭimid Army During the Early Crusades" (University of Michigan, 1984), pp. 19–27.

21. See S. D. Goitein, "Cairo: An Islamic City in the Era of the Geniza Documents" in *Middle Eastern Cities*, ed. Ira Lapidus (Berkeley and Los Angeles, 1969), pp. 80–96.

22. Goitein, *A Mediterranean Society*, I, 186–96.

23. Ayman Fu'ad Sayyid, p. 511.

24. On the cult of 'Alid saints, see Caroline Williams, "The Cult of 'Alid Saints in the Fatimid Monuments of Cairo," *Muqarnas*, I (1983), pp. 37–52; III (1985), pp. 39–60.

24
Ghassān *Post* Ghassān

Irfan Shahîd

Al-nāsu bi-azmānihim ashbahu
minhum bi-ābā'ihim

THE ARAB MUSLIM victory at Yarmūk in A.D. 636 and the subsequent fall of the Diocese of Oriens (*Bilād al-Shām*) to Islam made a dramatic change in the fortunes of the Ghassānids. They had returned to Bilād al-Shām from Anatolia after Heraclius' victory over the Persians at Nineveh in A.D. 628. The emperor had specifically singled them out for honorable mention in the victory bulletin which he sent to the Senate, and consequently they could now look forward to a privileged position in Oriens as Byzantium's shield against the Arabian Peninsula. But the annihilating defeat of the Yarmūk completely threw their plans into disarray and dimmed their prospects; and it confronted them with a crisis of identity. Their previous search for identity had ended when they were Christianized and became Byzantium's allies throughout the sixth century, during which time they lived in Oriens both as Arabs in former Nabataean Arab territory, and as Christians in the new Christian Roman Empire. Now after Yarmūk they were confronted with a dilemma: they could (1) either stay on in the shadow of the New Order in *Dār al-Islām* as Arabs but *dhimmīs* ("covenanters"); or (2) emigrate to *Dār al-Ḥarb*, the Christian realm of Byzantium, and live in a new non-Arab environment. It was not easy to escape between the horns of the dilemma; so some of the Ghassānids stayed on in Bilād al-Shām and *Dār al-Islām*, the land of the Islamic Caliphate, while others emigrated across the Taurus and settled in Anatolia in *Dār al-Ḥarb*, in the realm of the Christian Roman Empire. And they prospered in the service of the two Orders to which they now belonged. To trace the fortunes of each of these two groups of Ghassānids in the two empires which divided between them the Greater Near East in the Middle Ages is the object of this study.[1]

I

In the history of those Ghassānids who crossed the Taurus Mountains and settled in Anatolia, the figure of Jabala, the last Ghassānid king, is of paramount importance. It was his decision to emigrate finally to Anatolia, and to cut off his relations with the new Muslim Arab order that created that nucleus of Ghassānid Arabs who lived in *Dār al-Ḥarb*, and played a relatively unknown role in the history of Byzantium, especially in the ninth century.[2]

A. Jabala is the greatest Ghassānid historical figure of the seventh century, one who had already played an important role in the history of Arab-Byzantine relations for at least a quarter-century at the time of the battle of Yarmūk in A.D. 636. The detailed episode of his encounter with Caliph ʻUmar in the period following Yarmūk is one of the best constructed stories in the whole corpus of Arabic letters.[3] It is not easy to disentangle the web of fact and fiction of which the story is composed. It does not seem very probable that the Ghassānid chief, after a long association with Christian Byzantium, would have adopted Islam; but this possibility cannot be entirely ruled out.[4] After a tumultuous military career which had involved him in furious battles with the Persians, his will could have been broken after the disastrous defeat of Yarmūk, and it is thus just possible that he decided to adopt Islam, the religion of the victors. However that may be, the certain fact of the story is that he emigrated to Anatolia, whether or not after disagreement with ʻUmar,

The Arabic sources are informative on where he settled in Bilād al-Rūm. The beautiful story referred to above finds him in Constantinople, living comfortably. Although the details of the story may be rejected, it is possible that he lived in Constantinople for a short time immediately following his withdrawal from Bilād al-Shām, and echoes from the Arab historians could confirm what the story says.[5] But it is unlikely that his sojourn in Constantinople lasted long. Al-Iṣṭakhrī says that he settled in Kharshana (Charsianon) in central Anatolia, where his descendants were later also to be found.[6] It is practically certain that this was the case. For Byzantium would have stationed him near the new Muslim border where he and his descendants, because of their knowledge of Arabic and of conditions in the lands of the Islamic Caliphate, would be very helpful in the long struggle between Byzantium and Islam.

Although little is known of Jabala's activities after his emigration to Anatolia, his place in the history of the Ghassānids in the Middle Byzantine period is important, since it was he who established a strong Ghassānid presence in Byzantine Anatolia, one which lasted for many centuries. The climax of this presence was the elevation of one of his descendants to the purple and his establishment of a short-lived dynasty which might be described as the House of Nicephorus.

B. Nicephorus (A.D. 802–11) was a descendant of the Ghassānid Jabala.[7] He had been a high official in the previous reign (logothete, or minister of finance), and yet, in spite of his background in imperial finance, he played an important and vigorous role in the military and ecclesiastical history of Byzantium throughout the nine years of his reign. Byzantine historiography was not very kind to him, in view of his ecclesiastical policy, but modern historians have recognized his worth as a strong and capable ruler who instituted reforms necessary for the national interest, even though he was fully aware that these would not make him popular.[8] His role in the economic, ecclesiastical, and military history of Byzantium has been examined and studied by Byzantinists, but in the context of an article on "Ghassān *post* Ghassān," something may be said about his role in the military history of the Empire, because of its relevance to the Arabs.

Nicephorus was the contemporary of none other than the 'Abbasid ruler Hārūn al-Rashīd (A.D. 786–809). A well-known exchange of letters between the two rulers has been preserved in the sources with colorful details.[9] In spite of Nicephorus' vigorous administration and watchful efforts, his empire was no match for the Caliphate in its heyday under its most powerful ruler, Hārūn al-Rashīd, who won the upper hand in the struggle. But Nicephorus' gaze was fixed elsewhere than on the eastern frontier, and he was thus prepared to buy peace with Hārūn in order not to have to fight on two fronts. Nicephorus correctly judged that the rising power of the Bulgars constituted the real threat to Byzantium. Hence his determination to destroy the empire of the Bulgarian khan, Krum; but despite his initial successes, he allowed himself to be trapped by the Bulgarians. His army was annihilated and he himself was killed. Thus ended in a second Trasimene the promising reign of the first Arab emperor to rule in Constantinople.[10]

His reign presents the curious spectacle of two Arabs presiding over the destinies of the two imperia of the *oikoumene*—the Christian Roman Empire of Byzantium and the Muslim Arab Empire of the 'Abbasids—Nicephorus in Constantinople and Hārūn in Baghdad. Nicephorus had to deal not only with Hārūn al-Rashīd but also with the illustrious Carolingian in Western Europe, Charlemagne, who also had relations with the Arabs in Spain and in the East. The strong and obstinate Nicephorus rebuffed Charlemagne and refused to recognize his claim to the imperial title, which the latter had assumed in A.D. 800.[11]

C. The defeat of Nicephorus by the Bulgarian Krum not only brought to a disastrous end the promising reign of a capable ruler, but also prevented the rise of a long-lived Ghassānid dynasty such as the Heraclian or the Isaurian. For his son and successor, Stauracius, was so severely wounded in the battle that he reigned for only some two months, at the end of which he had to abdicate in favor of his brother-in-law, Michael Rangabe, or Michael I (A.D. 811–13). But at the time of his death in A.D. 811, he had reigned with his father Nicephorus for some eight years since A.D. 803, when he had been crowned Augustus and coemperor.[12]

Although his son Stauracius ruled for only two months, Nicephorus lived on in the purple through his daughter Procopia, who was the wife of the emperor Michael I, in whose favor Stauracius abdicated.[13] She was crowned Augusta ten days after the coronation of her husband. Michael was a feeble ruler, and during his short reign of two years, it was Procopia who guided him and controlled him, and she may thus be said to have ruled as well as reigned in this biennium in the history of ninth-century Byzantium. Just as the Bulgarian Krum put an end to the reign of her father Nicephorus in A.D. 811, he also ended that of her husband, Michael I, at the battle of Versinicia in A.D. 813. This defeat elevated Leo the Armenian to the purple, and the empress ended her life in the monastery of her namesake St. Procopia.[14]

Not only did Nicephorus' daughter become Augusta; his grandson Theophylactus, Procopia's eldest son, also became Augustus, being crowned coemperor with his father Michael I on Christmas day, A.D. 811, and then reigning with him for two years. On the elevation of Leo the Armenian after the fall of his father, Theophylactus, like his father, took monastic garb, and assumed the name Eustratios.[15]

The House of Nicephorus in the ninth century was represented both in the *imperium* and in the *ecclesia*. Another grandson of Nicephorus through Procopia, Nicetas, finally became Patriarch of Constantinople. As Ignatius, he twice became Patriarch, the first time from 847 until he was deposed in 858, and the second time, after his being reinstated, for the period 867–77. The famous Photius was his adversary, succeeding him twice, first on his deposition in A.D. 858, and then upon his death in 877. It was thus given to a grandson of Nicephorus to reach the highest rank in the Byzantine *ecclesia*, to run it for some twenty years, and to take part in the important ecclesiastical controversies of the period.[16]

The Patriarchate of Ignatius raises the question of the doctrinal persuasion of the Ghassānids. They had been staunch Monophysites as *foederati* in Oriens in pre-Islamic times, but some two centuries later they appear as Orthodox Christians, with one of them occupying the seat of Orthodoxy itself by his incumbency of the Patriarchate of Constantinople. The loss of Oriens to the Arabs had rid Byzantium of the Monophysites, and after the sixth Ecumenical Council of 680–81, with its strict return to Chalcedonian Orthodoxy, a Monophysite Ghassānid colony in Anatolia would not have been tolerated. It is therefore natural that the Monophysite refugees from Oriens should have adopted the doctrinal persuasion of the Byzantine State, and should have become Chalcedonians.

D. The ninth century thus represents the period that witnessed the rise of the Ghassānids to the pinnacle of power in Byzantium, when one of them became Emperor Nicephorus and another, his grandson Nicetas, became Patriarch Ignatius. After the ninth century their shadow naturally diminished, but it did not entirely disappear from the Byzantine scene, and the name "Jabala" appears intermittently in the annals of Byzantium. Instead of following up the fortunes of these individual Ghassānids,[17] it is proposed in this article to trace the last phase of the Ghassānid presence in Anatolia.

Although there was obviously a Ghassānid presence in western Anatolia and in Constantinople itself, their strongest presence must have been in central Anatolia in this middle period after the Arab Conquests. According to the Arabic sources it was in the military districts of Charsianon and Cappadocia.[18] And it was natural that they should have been stationed there along the frontier that divided Byzantium from the lands of the 'Abbasid Caliphate. But just as the history of Byzantium was fatally and dramatically changed by the appearance of a new virile Muslim people, the Saljuq Turks, in eastern Anatolia, so was the history of the Ghassānids. The Ghassānids now lived in the new Anatolia created by the Battle of Manzikert (A.D. 1071), which had set the stage for the turkification and islamization of the Byzantine heartland. Their isolation in the new world of the Saljuq Turks was intensified by the fall of Constantinople to the Crusaders in 1204. This must be the background for the few precious data on the Ghassānids in the Arabic sources.

1. According to the historian al-Khazrajī,[19] the Ghassānids of Anatolia emigrated to the land of the Turkomans and lived with one of the noblest Turkoman tribes, called Majik.

2. According to Ibn Khaldūn,[20] quoting other sources such as Ibn Sa'īd, some of them emigrated to Jabal Sharkas, the "Mountain of the Čerkes," where they mingled with these Christian tribes and allied themselves with them, and many of the Čerkes claim that they are descended from Ghassān. Ibn Khaldūn adds that this happened after the decay of the dominion of the *Qayṣars* (the Caesars).[21]

Both statements are consonant with the historical background outlined in the preceding paragraph. The Ghassānids referred to by al-Khazrajī linked their fortunes to the Saljuq Turkomans in the Sultanate of Iconium, and must have become Muslim. The Ghassānids of Ibn Khaldūn, isolated after the fall of Constantinople to the Latins in 1204 and wishing to remain Christian, emigrated to the easternmost part of Anatolia, the eastern Caucasus near the Caspian,[22] where they lived with the Christian communities of the region. Both Ghassānid communities finally crossed over to *Dār al-Islām*; those of al-Khazrajī (who lived with the Turkomans) emigrated to Iraq, where the 'Abbasid caliph in Baghdad made use of their services; those of Ibn Khaldūn, together with the Čerkes with whom they had lived, moved to Egypt. Both communities were to play an important role in late medieval Islamic history: one of them became the Rasūlids of Yemen, while the other formed an important element among the Burjī Mamlūks who, even in Egypt, continued to claim descent from the Ghassānids. Both Ghassānid groups thus received a new lease on life when they went over to *Dār al-Islām*, where they became a factor in the making of history in Yemen and Egypt in late medieval times.

II

Those Ghassānids who stayed on in Bilād al-Shām also distinguished themselves. And it could not have been otherwise. For more than a century, the Ghassānids, the *foederati* of Byzantium, had lived and worked in the shadow of the most advanced civilization of the world, and naturally they had acquired skills which the new order could not ignore. It was in their "capital," al-Jābiya in the Jawlān, that the "Covenant of 'Umar" was drawn up immediately after the Conquest. Muslim Arabs who had known them in their glorious pre-Islamic times respected them and admired them. In the words of that *fāris* (knight) of early Islamic times, 'Amr ibn Ma'dīkarib, "They were lords in the *jahilīya* and stars in Islam."

A. It was, however, the enlightened rule of Mu'āwiya in Bilād al-Shām, first as governor and then as caliph, that provided the framework which enabled the Ghassānids to find a niche for themselves in the new order. Throughout the twenty years of his governorship of Bilād al-Shām during the period of the Orthodox Caliphs, Mu'āwiya drew heavily on the talents of those Christian Arabs who had been allies of Byzantium in the course of the last three centuries, the Tanūkhids, the Salīḥids, and the Ghassānids, the dominant federate groups of Byzantium in the fourth, fifth, and sixth centuries respectively. The tribal politics that Mu'āwiya played in supporting the South Arabian tribes also contributed to their prosperity, and the Ghassānids derived their descent from the large tribal group of al-Azd, who had originally come from South Arabia. The Battle of Ṣiffīn in A.D. 657 decided the fate of Bilād al-Shām and the Caliphate for the next ninety years or so—that Mu'āwiya would be the caliph, and that Bilād al-Shām would become the metropolitan province of the Umayyad Empire. This ensured the continuance of Mu'āwiya's tolerant rule, and even gave him a freer hand in carrying out his policy in Bilād al-Shām, a policy in which the Christian Arabs were privileged. Mu'āwiya understood that he needed the talents of the officials of the previous Byzantine administration for effectively ruling the region, and both of these facts were important pillars of his successful administration of Bilād al-Shām. The caliph reflected his adherence to these principles in his family life, when he married none other than Maysūn[23] the daughter of Baḥdal, the chief of the Christian Arab tribe of Kalb, which had also been an ally of the Byzantines just as the Ghassānids had been, and who were the main prop of the new dynasty in both its Sufyānid and its Marwānid branches. His own son Yazīd took a leaf out of Mu'āwiya's book when he, too, married a Ghassānid wife, who gave birth to his daughter, Ramla.[24]

The star of the Ghassānids rose even higher with the establishment of the Marwānid branch of the Umayyads. The founder of that branch employed troops from Ghassān and Kalb in order to win the battle of Marj Rāhiṭ, a battle which gave him the Caliphate. He reflected this in one of his verses:

> lammā ra'aytu 'l-amra amran ṣa'bā
> yassartu Ghassānan lahum wa-Kalbā.

But it was in the reign of 'Abd al-Malik that Ghassānid figures appear most prominently in the making of Umayyad history. And this was consonant with the policy of 'Abd al-Malik, who inherited that of Mu'āwiya in relying on Christian South Arabian tribes such as Kalb and Ghassān. Perhaps the most significant fact of the reign which reflects this policy is the laureateship of the poet al-Akhtal, a Christian from the (Christian) tribe of Taghlib. The sources for this Umayyad period have many references to Ghassānid figures, but prominence among them could be given to one great historical figure, Ḥassān ibn al-Nu'mān al-Ghassānī. It is practically certain that this general of 'Abd al-Malik must have adopted Islam; this may have been true of other Ghassānids who rose high in the Marwānid administration, such as those who rose to the rank of chief of police (*ṣāḥib al-shurṭa*).[25]

As the most prominent Ghassānid of Umayyad times who fought for *Dār al-Islām*, Ḥassān deserves a brief notice. After the loss of Ifrīqiya to the Byzantines and the death of the Umayyad general Zubayr ibn Qays al-Balawī, Ḥassān was dispatched to lead the struggle against the Byzantines and to reconquer Ifrīqiya. He succeeded in capturing Carthage and in routing the Byzantine army and its Berber allies, and marched against the famous al-Kāhina. A sharp reverse put an end to his victorious march, and he had to evacuate Ifrīqiya and retreat to Quṣūr Ḥassān (named after him), located to the east of Tripoli. After a period of three years of hibernation in Tripolitania, Ḥassān resumed the offensive, reinforced by a new strong army. He succeeded in recapturing Carthage. Thus, the final consolidation of Ifrīqiya was due to the generalship of this Ghassānid. He constructed the *dār al-ṣinā'a* (the arsenal) at Tunis, and rebuilt the famous mosque of Qayrawān. His contributions to the welfare of the Marwānids were poorly rewarded, since he was dismissed by 'Abd al-Malik's brother 'Abd al-'Azīz, the governor of Egypt. But this did not discourage the old warrior from rejoining the Umayyad army in Bilād al-Shām. He died in the campaign of A.D. 699–700, fighting against the former overlords and patrons of his house of pre-Islamic times.[26]

Ḥassān ibn al-Nuʿmān was not the only or the last Ghassānid to reach the Islamic West. Other Ghassānids penetrated farther than he did and installed themselves across the Straits of Gibraltar in Andalusia. They came with other tribal groups from Umayyad Syria for the consolidation of the newly conquered province Andalusia, and some of them, apparently from Jund Dimashq, settled in a *qarya* near Granada in the *kūra* of Elvira, which they nostalgically called Ghassān.[27]

B. With the advent of the ʿAbbasids, the fortunes of both Bilād al-Shām and the Ghassānids experienced considerable change. The *translatio imperii* brought with it the ʿAbbasid cultural revolution, one of whose manifestations was an acceleration of the islamization of the Empire. Most references to the important Ghassānids of the ʿAbbasid period are not to Christian but to Muslim Ghassānids; among them the most important group are the Rasūlids of Yemen, who deserve a brief notice.[28]

This Ghassānid family reached Yemen with the Ayyubid Tūrānshāh in the thirteenth century. Its eponym Rasūl acquired this title after the ʿAbbasid caliph had sent him on many diplomatic missions in which he distinguished himself. One of his sons, ʿUmar, asserted his independence after the departure from Yemen of the last Ayyubid, Masʿūd. He made Zabīd his capital whence he extended his power, which at its fullest extent reached from Mecca in the north to Hadramawt in the southeast. In addition to being a capable ruler, he was also a prince of peace—builder of mosques and *madrasas*, and a patron of learning. And such were his descendants and successors who ruled Yemen for two centuries after his assassination in A.D. 1249–50. The last Rasūlid sultan abdicated in 1454, and spent the rest of his life as an exile in Mecca. It was remarkable that they lasted as long as they did, in view of the difficult people and terrain they had to control, the opposition of the Zaydī Sharīfs, and the intrigues and insubordination of the *mamālīk*.

Although Yemenite historians are unanimous on their Ghassānid origin, other historians expressed some doubts. But as the editor of *al-ʿAsjad al-masbūk* has pointed out, their Ghassānid origin, vouched for by those who should know, has to be accepted.[29] He based his conclusion on the argument of Khazrajī, but the question of their Ghassānid origin may be restated as follows:

1. Khazrajī states that after the Ghassānids went over to the Byzantines and lived in Anatolia, they moved again to the east and lived with one of the noblest of the Turkoman tribes, Majik; hence, some

thought they were Turkoman, but they were not, and they remained aware of their Ghassānid origin. Later they moved southward to Iraq and entered the service of the ʿAbbasid caliphs.[30] This is consonant, as has already been pointed out in this article, with the historical situation created by the Battle of Manzikert in 1071, while Ibn Khaldūn's statement on the movement of another group of Ghassānids to the Caucasus after 1204 suggests a parallel case.

2. Khazrajī is unaware that this was not the first time that the Ghassānids returned to their original country, which they had left as part of the great *Völkerwanderung* in Arabia called *tafarruq al-Azd*. Late in the sixth century, and after Emperor Maurice had broken their power as the dominant *foederati* (allies of Byzantium), the Ghassānids left the service of Byzantium and went to various places, one of which was Yemen.[31] The Ghassānids did not forget their past, and no doubt when they returned to Yemen in the thirteenth century, they could have remembered the previous return of some seven centuries before.[32] There is thus a precedent for the return of the Ghassānids, this time as Rasūlids, to Yemen.

3. Finally, the Rasūlids themselves were aware of their Ghassānid descent, and were proud of it.[33] The natural question arises: why would they have concocted such a lineage, if they had not truly been descended from the Ghassānids of old? Furthermore, why would they, as Muslims, have chosen a descent from those Christian Ghassānids, whose last king had had that well-known encounter with Caliph ʿUmar, and who had gone over to ally himself with the chief enemy of Islam, the Byzantine Empire? It is, therefore, practically certain that the Rasūlids were Ghassānids.

The Rasūlids represent the strongest Ghassānid presence in Islamic times, since it was that of a dynasty that endured for two centuries, and not of individuals, important as these were, such as the conqueror of Ifrīqiya, Ḥassān ibn al-Nuʿmān. Thus the Ghassānid Rasūlids in Islamic times[34] balance in their historic role as a dynasty the Ghassānid Jafnids, the allies of Byzantium in Oriens in pre-Islamic times.

If the Rasūlids as a dynasty represented the strongest Ghassānid political presence in late Islamic times, al-Azraqī must be adjudged the most important Ghassānid author in the field of letters in the early Islamic period; and that fundamental work on the history of Mecca, *Akhbār Makka*, is his work. Unfortunately, the Ghassānid origin of this author of early ʿAbbasid times is controversial. So his inclusion in this account of "Ghassān *post* Ghassān" is only tentative, until such time as his Ghassānid affiliation is settled one way or the other.[35]

III

The Rasūlids of Yemen represented not only the strongest Ghassānid presence in the late Islamic Middle Ages, but also the last. In Ottoman times, the Ghassānid presence became restricted to those who chose to remain in Bilād al-Shām, and who through the tolerant rule of the Umayyads in that region had remained Christian, and who have survived in the Ḥawrān region of Syria, in Lebanon, and in Jordan until the present day. Many of the Christian families[36] of this region trace their descent to the last group of Arab allies which Byzantium had in Bilād al-Shām in pre-Islamic times, the Ghassānids.[37]

Before they went over to the Byzantines after the battle of the Yarmūk, the Ghassānids had been for more than a century the recipients of panegyrics from some of the foremost poets of pre-Islamic Arabia, including al-Nābigha, one of the poets of the Seven Suspended Odes. In Islamic times, they continued to receive tributes from poets. It is therefore not altogether inappropriate to bring this article on the Ghassānids in Islamic times to a close with a short fragment composed by the early 'Abbasid poet Salm al-Khāsir, on the Ghassānid 'Āṣim ibn 'Utba.[38] It is not an unworthy pendant to the necklace of splendid odes composed by al-Nābigha on the Ghassānids of pre-Islamic times.

li-'āṣimin samā'u 'āriḍuhā hattānu
amṭāruhā 'l-ibrīzu wa'l- lujaynu wa'l-'iqyānu
wa-nāruhū tunādī idh khabati 'l-nīrānu
al-jūdū fī qaḥṭāni mā baqiyat ghassānu
islam wa-la tubālī mā fa'ala 'l-ikhwānu
ṣallat lahu 'l-ma'ālī wa'l-sayfu wa'l-sinānu
mā ḍarra murtajīhi ma fa'ala 'l-zamānu
man ghālahu makhūfun fa-hwa lahū amānu.

NOTES

1. The history of the Ghassānids in Islamic times has never been written; hence the present attempt. Their history in medieval times is full of many problems of a technical nature, which cannot be discussed in this short article, but they will be in a future publication, probably in the present writer's volume, titled *Byzantium and the Arabs in the Sixth Century*. For bibliographical orientation on the fortunes of the Ghassānids in Byzantine Anatolia, the

Arabist and Islamist is referred to the following three works: J.B. Bury, *History of the Eastern Roman Empire* (London, 1912); *The Cambridge Ancient History* (Cambridge, 1966), Vol. IV, *The Byzantine Empire*; and G. Ostrogorsky, *History of the Byzantine State* (New Brunswick, 1969). The first is the most detailed.

2. Principally to the Arabist and Islamist, but also to the Byzantinist, since the identity of some of the Ghassānids who figure in the history of Byzantium in the Middle Period is not often pointed out or remembered.

3. For this truly beautiful and often touching story, see Ibn 'Abd Rabbihi, *Al-'Iqd al-farīd* (Beirut, 1982), II, 56–62. Some parts of the story did not fail to move even the dour Nöldeke: see following footnote.

4. The principal elements in the story were accepted by Nöldeke as historical. See his *Die Ghassânischen Fürsten aus dem Hause Gafna's* (Berlin, 1887), pp. 45–46.

5. Ibn Khaldūn, *Kitāb al-'Ibar* (Beirut, 1956), II, 588.

6. Al-Iṣṭakhrī, *Masālik al-mamālik, BGA* (Leiden, 1870) II, 45.

7. This valuable information comes from Ṭabarī; see *Tārīkh* (Cairo, 1966), VIII, 307 where he speaks of Jafna, the eponym of the Ghassānids, rather than Jabala. The passage was brought to the attention of Byzantinists by E. W. Brooks in "Byzantines and Arabs in the Time of the Early Abbasids," *English Historical Review*, XV (1910), p. 743. It has been accepted by Byzantinists such as Bury and Anastos; for the first, see op. cit., p. 8; for the second, see his article in the *Cambridge Medieval History*, IV, Part One, p. 91. The Arab origin of Nicephorus is also vouched for by Michael the Syrian; see his *Chronique*, ed. J. B. Chabot (Paris, 1899–1924), III, 15. Nicephorus' Arabness is reflected in his dislike of the term "Saracen" as applied to the Arabs because of the perjorative tone that it carried; see Ibn al-Athīr, *al-Kāmil*, ed. C. J. Tornberg (Beirut, 1965), I, 336.

8. See the sober and favorable evaluations of Bury, op. cit., pp. 8–9 and Ostrogorsky, op. cit., pp. 186–87.

9. Ṭabarī, op. cit., VIII, 307–08. For an English translation of this exchange, see E. Gibbon, *The Decline and Fall of the Roman Empire*, ed. J. B. Bury (London, 1902), VI, 35. The authenticity of the letters was accepted by Gibbon, and I am inclined to think he was right.

10. A comparison is often drawn between this disaster and that of Adrianople in A.D. 378, in which Emperor Valens fell fighting; see Bury, op. cit., p. 345. Ammianus Marcellinus, the primary source for the battle of Adrianople, invoked the memory of the second Punic War and called that disaster a second Cannae. This battle also can with much justification be called the second Trasimene, since the two battles witnessed the complete and perfect entrapment of two Roman armies. No name is given to the battle in which Nicephorus lost his life. But the "Battle of the Greek Hollow" may not be inappropriate; see ibid. p. 344 and n. 1.

11. For the reign of Nicephorus, the fullest account may be found in Bury's *Eastern Roman Empire*; but it is scattered in various chapters of the book. For a short, competent, and continuous account, see Ostrogorsky, op. cit., pp. 186–200.

12. For Stauracius, see Bury, op. cit., pp. 16–21.

13. His family name was Rangabe and this has been considered a Greek family; see Bury, op. cit., p. 22 and Ostrogorsky, op. cit., p. 197 n. 2. This family name will be examined in a future publication; see supra, n. 1.

14. On Procopia, see Bury, op. cit., index.

15. On Theophylactus, see Bury, op. cit., pp. 14, 23, 29, 30.

16. For the career of this son of Procopia, Patriarch Ignatius, see the detailed account of Bury, op. cit., index.

17. This will be taken up in a future publication. See supra, n. 1.

18. On what Iṣṭakhrī says, see supra, n. 6; for Ibn al-Kalbī, see Nöldeke, op. cit., p. 46 n. 1.

19. See *Al-ʿUqūd al-luʾluʾiyya*, I, 27; on al-Khazrajī and his work, see infra, n. 28.

20. Ibn Khaldūn, op. cit., pp. 588–89.

21. Ibn Khaldūn must have had in mind the fall of Constantinople to the Latins in 1204, and not its fall to the Ottoman Turks in 1453, since he died in 1406.

22. This geographical precision is possible because Ibn Khaldūn also speaks of Bāb al-Abwāb, the port on the Caspian, in connection with the Ghassānids in the Caucasus.

23. On Maysūn and the Christian Arab officials around Muʿāwiya, see Philip K. Hitti, *History of Syria* (London, 1951), pp. 425, 438–39.

24. See al-Balādhuri, *Ansāb al-Ashrāf*, ed. Iḥsān ʿAbbās (Wiesbaden, 1979), IV.1, 290.

25. Three of these Ghassānids are attested: (1) Yaḥyā ibn Qays for Marwān ibn al-Ḥakam; (2) Abū Nātil Riyāḥ ibn ʿAbduh for ʿAbd al-Malik; and (3) Riyāḥ ibn ʿAbduh for al-Walīd ibn ʿAbd al-Malik. See Sāliḥ al-ʿAlī, "Muwaẓẓafū Bilād al-Shām fī ʾl-ʿahd al-umawī," *al-Abḥāth* (Beirut, 1966), pp. 52–53.

26. For a succinct account of Ḥassān ibn al-Nuʿmān, see the article in the new *Encyclopaedia of Islam*, s.v., with its good bibliography.

27. See Lisān al-Dīn ibn al-Khatīb, *Al-Iḥāṭa fī akhbār Garnāṭa*, ed. M. A. ʿInan (Cairo), I, 128. The name of the present-day *qarya* in Spain is Cacin.

28. A primary source for the history of the Rasūlids, at least until the reign of al-Malik al-Ashraf Ismāʿīl who died in A.D. 803, is al-Khazrajī's *Al-ʿUqūd al-luʾluʾīya fī tārīkh al-dawla al-rasūlīya*, ed. M. B. ʿAsal, *Gibb Memorial Series*, III, 4 (Leiden, 1913), Vols. I–II; the article in the first edition of the *Encyclopaedia of Islam* will give an outline of the history of the dynasty; of late, the Rasūlids have been treated succinctly by J. Chelhod in *L'Arabie du Sud: Histoire et civilisation* (Paris, 1984), pp. 42–47. One of the works of al-Malik al-Ashraf has been published, namely, *Al-ʿAsjad al-masbūk waʾl-jawhar al-maḥkūk fī ṭabaqāt al-khulafāʾ waʾl-mulūk*, ed. Sh. ʿAbd al-Munʿim (Baghdad, 1975). This volume has a good introduction on *Al-ʿAsjad*, on its author, and on al-Khazrajī.

29. See the valuable discussion of the problem by Sh. ʿAbd al-Munʿim in *Al-ʿAsjad*, pp. 50–52.

30. *Al-'Uqūd al-lu'lu'īya*, I, 26–28.

31. This and other aspects of Ghassānid history will be treated in detail in my volume on the Ghassānids, entitled *Byzantium and the Arabs in the Sixth Century*.

32. The Rasūlids remembered their descent from Jabala (*'Asjad*, p. 51), whose *floruit* goes back to the first half of the seventh century. The return of some of the Ghassānids to Yemen in the reign of Maurice took place only some fifty years before the time of Jabala.

33. And poets remembered their Ghassānid lineage in their panegyrics on the Rasūlid rulers; see, for instance, the poem of Khazrajī on al-Malik al-Afḍal in *Al-'Uqūd al-lu'lu'īya*, II, 160–63, especially p. 162.

34. I have not included the rule of the Burjī Mamlūks as an example of a Ghassānid presence in Egypt in the late Middle Ages. I am inclined to think that these were mainly Circassians with a sprinkling of Ghassānids among them. In addition to what Ibn Khaldūn said of their Ghassānid origin, see the references to them in the article "Čerkes," in the *Encyclopaedia of Islam*, sec. II, on the Mamlūk period with references to their Ghassānid origin in Ibn Iyās; also P. Holt, "The Exalted Lineage of Ridwan Bey," *BSOAS* (1959), pp. 221–30. Noteworthy in this connection is the fact that the Burjī Mamlūks were not Arabophone, unlike the Rasūlids who were, and in this context this is significant.

35. J. W. Fück thinks he was not a Ghassānid; see his "Der Ahn des Azraqī," in *Studi Orientalistici in onore di G. Levi Della Vida* (Rome, 1956), I, 336–40. On the other hand, the more recent editor of Azraqī is convinced that he was a Ghassānid; see R. Malḥas in *Akhbār Makka* (Mecca, 1965), pp. 12–13; see also the section on the quarter of the House of Azraq in Mecca, ibid., I, 247–48, which suggests that the family was an Arab one, and not descended from a Rūmī, who was a slave of al-Ḥārith ibn Kalada.

36. For these, see 'Īsā Iskandar al-Ma'lūf, *Dawāni al-quṭūf fī tārīkh Banī Ma'lūf* (B'abda, 1908).

37. It is noteworthy that an earlier group of *foederati* (allies of Byzantium), the Tanūkhids, had become entirely Muslim; see Philip K. Hitti, op. cit., p. 545.

38. See 'Abd al-Rahim al-'Abbāsī, *Ma'āhid al-tanṣiṣ 'alā shawahid al-talkhīs*, ed. M. 'Abdul-Hamid (Beirut, 1947), IV, 45.

25
Diplomatic Practices in Medieval Inner Asia

Denis Sinor

IN THE TANGLED web of international relations, ambassadors have always played an important role. Even nowadays, in an age of "hot lines" between heads of state, of "summit meetings," of a constant flow of information provided by the media, no sovereign state that I know of has dispensed with the services of diplomats. Traditionally, the conduct of foreign affairs has always been the privilege of the head of state, since the very existence of the country or nation over which he ruled would depend in a large measure not on its internal situation, but rather on the balance of forces prevailing between it and other nations over which the ruler had no control. There have always been two prerequisites for the conduct of foreign affairs: information on the conditions in countries other than one's own, and communication with them. At a time when telecommunications were nonexistent, the only way to satisfy either or both of these requirements was to send appropriate persons charged with the tasks of obtaining first-hand information and of delivering oral or written messages in both directions. The gathering of information could be open, done with the consent or at least the knowledge of the officials of the foreign state, or clandestine. The first type of activity was entrusted to what we may loosely call ambassadors, whereas spies were sent to obtain information intended to be kept secret.

The triteness of these remarks will, I hope, not be taken amiss; I felt it necessary to recall the basic justification of diplomatic intercourse which, it is safe to say, has universal validity. Although diplomatic practice may vary in time and space, it does seem to follow patterns which, because they derive from the imperatives of the aims to be accomplished, show a certain uniformity. Privileges and immunities accorded to diplomats do not find their justification in some abstract, artificial rule of etiquette, but rather in enlightened self-interest, in the necessity of receiving the message, however unpleasant, brought by the ambassador who on a minimal level was little else but a carrier of messages; the German word for ambassador, *Botschafter*, still carries this same meaning.

For a long time, historians have been aware of the existence of diplomatic missions sent into or coming from medieval Inner Asia. However, perhaps because such activities were considered "normal" by those familiar with them, few attempts have been made, beside those of Bertold Spuler,[1] to examine them in some detail. Hundreds of such embassies are mentioned in Chinese sources, and abundant material can also be found in other texts. Unfortunately most of the information provided concerns diplomatic practice obtaining in the receiving country, such as China or Byzantium, and at best sheds only indirect light on the Inner Asian handling of foreign relations. Also, because of the desperate scarcity of written material originating in Inner Asia, we know next to nothing about diplomacy as practiced within that area. In what follows, for lack of space, only a few aspects of diplomatic usage will be mentioned, and only some select illustrations given. I have avoided considering philological or interpretational problems presented by the texts—I have mostly relied on translations made by others—for my aim in this short article is limited to assembling some data on the subject, and also to showing that it is one which might deserve further, more comprehensive examination.

In the period and the region with which we are concerned, diplomatic missions were often dangerous, and almost always adventurous. Often the ambassador was in fact an explorer, with desires and methods akin to those that propelled the conquistadors. As in our days, abuse of diplomatic privileges allowed quick and easy profits to be made. When Monsieur de Callières wrote his *De la Manière de négocier avec les Souverains* in 1716, he proffered the following advice, since then often ignored:

> A wise minister may well be content to enjoy the large privileges to which he is entitled in every foreign country without attempting to abuse them for his own private profit, or by countenancing any fraud which is committed under the protection of his name.[2]

This lofty principle had little appeal to would-be Chinese diplomats recruited to penetrate into the largely unknown parts of Inner Asia. In the words of the *Han Shu*:

The Son of Heaven thought that because they were cut off by great distances, these were not places where people would go for pleasure. . . . Calling for officials and men to volunteer, and quite regardless of their origins, he provided [envoys] with large retinues, and sent them out in order to extend [the use of] the roads. On the outward and return journeys there could not fail to be cases where valuable goods were stolen or where the envoys ignored [imperial] instructions. . . . The Son of Heaven always had the cases investigated and construed as being worthy of capital punishment, in this way goading the men to seek remission from punishment by offering to go out on further journeys. The means of serving as an envoy were thus unrestricted, and infringement of the laws was regarded as a light matter.[3]

More than a thousand years after these opinions were expressed, the *Kutadgu Bilig*, a "mirror for princes" written in Kashgar, in a Middle Turkic language, drew a more flattering picture of the, admittedly ideal, ambassador.

The envoy [in Turkic, here, *yalavach*] ought to be the choicest of mankind, wise, intelligent and courageous. For God chose the very best of his servants to be his envoys. And by means of an envoy many fine things may be accomplished. So the envoy must be intelligent, steady, and wise, and a good interpreter of words. Words are his business: he has to know them inside and out. . . . He should be loyal, content in eye and heart, reliable, sincere, and upright. . . . As for the greedy-eyed man: he has no self control and so is unfit for the office of envoy.[4]

The enumeration of the qualifications of the ideal envoy are continued over seventy-some lines, and one might wonder whether such a paragon of virtue was ever in the service of any Inner Asian prince. But at least it is clear that, in the view of the writer, reflecting the opinions of his milieu, ambassadors were expected to be men of great qualities.

It is safe to say that the immunity of the ambassador's person—which in its simplest form ensures that he not be put to death—is certainly the key element of all diplomatic practices. As Harold Nicolson put it in his much used book *Diplomacy:*

Even in prehistory there must have come moments when one group of savages wished to negotiate with another group of savages. . . . From the very first, even to our Cromagnon and Neanderthal ancestors, it must have become apparent that such negotiations would be severely hampered if the emissary from one side were killed and eaten by the other side before he had time to deliver his message.[5]

This most practical and essential of all diplomatic conventions was scrupulously adhered to by Inner Asian rulers. Probably the most telling example of abiding by this practice is provided by the rather astonishing story of an assassination plot hatched in Constantinople, and aimed at eliminating Attila, ruler of the Huns.

In 448 the eunuch Chrysapius, powerful chamberlain of Emperor Theodosius, noticing the deep impression the richness and splendor of the imperial court made on the Hun ambassador Edeco, thought that he might be amenable to a bribe. At a feast at his residence, through the good offices of the interpreter Bigilas, Chrysapius proposed nothing less to Edeco than that he murder Attila, to whom he had free access. Once the deed was accomplished, Edeco could return to Constantinople to lead a life of plenty. The Hun seemed interested in the proposal but asked for some money—not much, a mere fifty pounds of gold—which would allow him to obtain the cooperation of some people in Attila's entourage. A Byzantine counter-embassy which, besides the ambassador Maximinus included also Bigilas and, to our good fortune, the historian Priscus (who later was to give a detailed description of the events), was to accompany Edeco on his return journey. As it turned out, Edeco revealed the plot to his master, who feigned ignorance, invited Maximinus and his entourage to a banquet, and continued to treat them in the customary manner until such time when Bigilas—who had to go back to Roman territory to fetch the fifty pounds of gold—returned to Attila's camp. He was then seized and ordered to explain why he had this important sum in his possession. Reluctant at first to reveal the truth, Bigilas broke down when Attila threatened to have his young son cut down unless he spoke up. When thus the truth was revealed, Attila merely ordered him to be put in chains until another fifty pounds of gold would be paid as a ransom. Neither Bigilas nor any other member of the Byzantine embassy was harmed, a truly telling example of the Huns' respect for diplomatic immunity. The special treatment given to these diplomats contrasts sharply with that given to a "Scythian" spy sent to the Huns by the Romans who, having been caught, was summarily impaled.[6]

Another, perhaps less clear-cut and less impressive example of the same attitude antedates Attila's rule. In 412 or 413 an East Roman embassy led by the historian Olympiodorus visited the Hun ruler Karaton, in whose entourage there lived a man called Donatus. Modern historians tend to see in the latter a Hun "king," perhaps a co-ruler of Karaton, an opinion to which the texts lend no support and which, in view of the Christian name of Donatus, is *a priori* unlikely. Be that as it may, the Greeks murdered Donatus—and got away with their deed. Though very angry, Karaton allowed himself to be pacified by presents, and did not harm members of Olympiodorus' embassy.[7] In my view, the whole scenario is one often enacted in the times in which we now live; most probably Donatus was a political refugee who sought and found asylum among the Huns, where he became a trusted man of the Hun ruler. He was murdered by his own compatriots, to whom his very existence was an irritant, and who abused their diplomatic privileges, clearly respected by the "barbarian" Hun.

Of course there are instances in which we encounter temporary infringements of the unwritten law protecting diplomats. Thus for instance, in 568 Bayan, kaghan of the Avars, had two Byzantine diplomats put in chains, as Priscus indignantly remarked "in disregard of generally accepted principles."[8] Of these principles the Avars themselves were certainly not ignorant, as appears from their attitude when, in the 70s of the sixth century, one of their diplomatic missions fell victim to an attack by robbers. The Avars claimed compensation for their losses and their demand was met by Emperor Tiberius.[9]

In the middle of the sixth century, the foundation of the Türk empire created a hitherto unprecedented situation in Inner Asia. For the first time in recorded history, a more or less unified nomad empire extended from the borders of China to that of Byzantium and Iran, necessitating diplomatic contacts between the Türks on the one hand, and the three major sedentary civilizations on the other. Some fragmentary information on their diplomatic intercourse has been preserved, and it shows with great clarity the respect shown by the Türks for the principle of diplomatic immunity.

Diplomatic relations between Constantinople and the Türks were quite frequent: between 568 and 576 we know of five Roman embassies to Türk rulers. The last of these, led by an experienced diplomat called Valentine, then on his second mission to the Türks, was sent to inform them of the accession of Tiberius II to the dignity of coemperor with Justin II, and also to strengthen the anti-Persian alliance which, for some time, had been at the center of Turko-Byzantine foreign policy. The Türk ruler Silziboulos had just died, and his son and successor Turxath received the Roman emissaries, who expected a friendly reception, with an outburst of rage which bode ill not only for the success of the mission but for the very lives of the diplomats. Reproaching them with their alleged duplicity, as manifested by the Romans' offering asylum to the Avars whom Turxath considered his fugitive slaves, he vowed to put them all to death without further ado. The Türks, so he said, were not accustomed to dealing with liars. Valentine had a difficult time extricating himself and his companions from this dangerous situation. He argued that Turxath, who had inherited his father's land, had also become heir to his foreign policy, and should not jeopardize in a fit of ill-temper the alliance freely entered upon by Silziboulos. But—and this was the brunt of his speech as recorded by Menander—it was even more important that he abide by the rule which guarantees the personal safety of the ambassadors. Though he, Valentine, would rather die than hear his emperor called a liar, he could not but be horrified at the thought of how Turxath would be judged by the whole world, were he to lay hands on the Roman emissaries. Valentine lived to tell the tale, so it is clear that his arguments carried considerable weight with the irate Turxath.[10]

The distinction between diplomatic and commercial envoys (who may have been simple tradesmen) was not always easy to perceive, but it is safe to assume that those who sent them on their perilous missions were quite aware of the purpose they were to serve. The latter were not protected by the immunity accorded to the former. Around 568 a Türk mission led by the Sogdian Maniakh, and consisting mainly of Sogdian tradesmen, traveled to Persia with a view to establishing there a basis for the silk trade. The Persians disliked this idea, but were reluctant to harm the emissaries, whose status was probably not clear to them. They bought the merchandise from the Sogdians and burnt it in a public place, a not very subtle, yet harmless indication of the Persians' reluctance to take up trade with the Türks. Undaunted, possibly egged on by the Sogdians, the Türks sent a second mission whose members, however, succumbed to the rigors—or so the Persians claimed—of the hot climate to which they were not accustomed. No retaliatory actions seem to have followed; clearly the second mission, composed of merchants, was not considered diplomatic.

The distinction between a commercial and a political mission was not always easy to make, and merchants tended to play the role of diplomats, so as to take advantage of the privileges to which these were entitled. In the first century B.C. the country of Chi-pin (approximately the northwestern provinces of Pakistan) sent a mission to the Chinese, but it was observed that "there are no members of the royal family or noblemen among those who bring the gifts; the latter are all merchants and men of low origins."[11] There are instances of true metamorphosis from merchant to diplomat. The Sogdian Maniakh, whose main interest lay in the silk trade, became the head of the Türk delegation which, sent by the aforementioned Silziboulos, arrived in Constantinople in 568, carrying written credentials.

A mistake as to the identity of a mission may well have caused one of the great cultural disasters of late medieval history. The execution in 1217 of some "merchants" sent by Chinggis khan to Muhammad II, shah of Khwārazm precipitated the Mongol attack on Khwārazm, and ultimately led to the great Mongol campaigns against the West. Juvainī tells us that when news of the murder of the merchants reached the ear of Chinggis khan, "The fire of wrath so set him upon the hurricane of violence that with the water of destruction and perdition he annihilated the very soil of the Sultan's empire."[12]

The Mongols were extremely strict in demanding immunity for their envoys. The Franciscan John of Plano Carpini—about whom much will be said later in this paper—was quite clear on this point: "it is the custom of the Tartars never to make peace with men who kill their envoys, until they have taken vengeance on them."[13] He feared to be accompanied on his return journey from Mongolia by Mongols lest they be killed in Europe, "for our people are for the most part arrogant and proud."[14] The Mongols' willingness to receive and to respect foreign envoys was perhaps first stated publicly in the testimony given in France in 1244 by the so-called "Archbishop Peter of Russia," according to whom the Mongols "*nuntios benigne admittunt, expediunt, et remittunt.*"[15] The fact deserved mention because in Western tradition, as it was later summarized and codified by Grotius, "The law of nations, in fact, does not enjoin that all [ambassadors] be admitted."[16]

Interesting information on the Mongols' diplomatic activity and on the treatment their messengers received from the hands of East and Central European rulers is contained in a letter report sent to the bishop of Perugia by the Hungarian Dominican Julian. Julian had been sent by Béla IV, king of Hungary, partly in search of the Hungarians who had remained in central Russia, in the land known as Magna Hungaria, partly also, one must presume, to bring information on the Mongols. According to Julian, who had visited Suzdal,

> [the Mongols] sent envoys to the king of Hungary who were captured by the prince of Suzdal as they came through his territory and he took from them the letter sent to the king [of Hungary]; and I myself, as well as the companions assigned to me, saw the envoys, and this letter was given to me by the prince of Suzdal and I took it to the king of Hungary.[17]

Although there is no evidence that the Mongol envoys seen by Julian were in any way mistreated by the prince of Suzdal, it is nevertheless clear that they were prevented from continuing their journey, and that the letter they were carrying was taken away from them. Fortunately, in Julian's report there is a Latin translation of this Mongol ultimatum which, together with some other valuable information, provides a glimpse at the Mongols' preoccupation with the fate of their ambassadors. Written by an unidentified Mongol chief and addressed to Béla IV, the text runs as follows:

> I, Chayn, messenger of the Heavenly King, to whom he has given the power on earth to exalt those who submit to him and to cast down his adversaries, I wonder at you, King of Hungary, that although I have sent you messengers thirty times, you have sent none of them back to me, nor did you send me messengers of your own or letters. I know that you are a rich and powerful king, and that you have many soldiers under you, and that by yourself you govern a great kingdom. It is therefore difficult for you to submit to me voluntarily. I have further learned that you keep the Cumans, my slaves, under your protection. Whence I charge you that henceforward you not keep them with you, and that you not make me your enemy on their account. For it is easier for them to escape than for you, since they, having no houses and continually on the move with their tents, may possibly escape. But as for you, living in houses and possessing fortresses and cities, how can you flee from my grasp?

This is not the place to comment on this little-known and highly interesting document. Only the passage complaining about the disappearance of the Mongol envoys sent to the king of Hungary is of direct relevance to our present subject. There is no way of knowing whether this breach of the rule of immunity was one of the causes for the subsequent invasion of Hungary.

The Mongols not only expected their ambassadors to be treated properly; they were ready to respect, even in trying circumstances, the immunity of foreign envoys. A good case in point is that of the Dominican Ascelinus, one of four envoys dispatched to the Mongols by Pope Innocent IV in the spring of 1245. Ascelinus was a singularly undiplomatic diplomat who, on arrival in the camp of Baiju, commander of the Mongol forces in Transcaucasia, not only refused to perform the treble genuflexion due to Baiju as a representative of the Great Khan, but thought it his duty to tell him that the Pope was greater than any other man, and that the Mongols should do penance for all the crimes they had committed. Baiju, who himself was a man of exceedingly short temper, wanted to have Ascelinus and his companions put to death.[18] Suggestions were made to flay Ascelinus and return his skin stuffed with straw to the Pope. But moderation prevailed. Baiju's principal wife intervened in favor of the envoys, pointing out the disastrous impression such an execution would create abroad, and the possible danger that could well arise out of it for Baiju's own ambassadors. The dignitary in charge of receiving embassies threatened to refuse to execute any order endangering the life of the papal envoys, and told Baiju that he would rather flee to the Great Khan, where he would denounce Baiju. Most appropriately this official recalled another occasion when, on Baiju's order, he had killed an envoy and carried across the camp his torn-out heart attached to the breast-strap of his horse, so as to frighten other ambassadors; a case which had upset the Great Khan considerably when it came to his knowledge. Although the story—as recorded by Simon de Saint-Quentin—does relate an instance in which the law of the inviolabilty of an ambassador's person was broken, it shows at the same time that the validity of this law was fully accepted by the Great Khan Güyük.

The *Kutadgu Bilig* gives a good summation of the respect prevailing in Inner Asia for the person of an ambassador. It puts the following saying in the mouth of an imaginary khan of the Turks:

> Do not punish the messenger for the message; he deserves neither punishment nor death so long as he truly reports what he heard; rather a messenger, as the ambassador of peace, is inviolable, and if he transmits the message that was entrusted him, then praise and reward are his due.[19]

Baiju's displeasure with Ascelinus' mission was justified by the latter's tactless behavior, and also by the tone of the papal letter which, at least implicitly, claimed jurisdiction over the whole world. A Chinese embassy sent to Timur in 1395 found itself in an analogous situation. In the letter presented by the ambassador, the Chinese emperor referred to Timur as his vassal, an involuntary insult but one which the recipient greatly resented. The refusal of the Chinese envoys to kowtow to Timur did not improve their popularity; nonetheless, their lives were spared, even though they were compelled to undertake a "conducted tour" over Timur's vast domains, and were not allowed to return to China. A second embassy, sent in 1397 to inquire about the fate of the first, was similarly detained and a third embassy, sent in 1403, received, as we shall see, a rather insulting reception.[20]

Although the inviolability of the ambassador was generally accepted and respected, the same special protection was not always fully accorded to other members of the mission. Although Hugo Grotius maintained that "The right of ambassadors is also extended to the suite of an ambassador," even the learned Dutchman did not consider this an absolute rule, since he added: "only so far as seems good to the ambassador."[21] We have seen that while diplomatic immunity saved Bigilas' life, it did not fully protect him, whereas no harm at all was done to his ambassador Maximinus. The following example shows clearly the important distinction made between the chief of a mission and the members of his entourage.

In 762 a Chinese embassy led by the prince of Yung visited the Uighur kaghan. Upon arriving at the audience, the prince failed to perform the ceremonial dance demanded by etiquette. His action was defended by a certain Tzu-ang of his party, on the grounds that the prince was in mourning and that the rite would therefore be improper; moreover, since he was the heir apparent of the Middle Kingdom, how could he possibly perform a ceremonial dance in front of a foreign kaghan? The two parties argued for a long time. Finally, the Uighur courtiers lost their patience, and had four of their Chinese counterparts, including Tzu-ang, given a hundred strokes of the rod each. Two of them died after this beating, but the prince was not harmed, and was allowed to return to his camp.[22]

If, at least in theory, and usually also in practice, the lives of ambassadors were safe, these ambassadors could be harassed in many ways, and had on occasion to endure considerable verbal abuse. I have already mentioned the insults hurled at Valentine by the Türk Turxath. On a previous occasion, in 569, at a banquet at which the Byzantine ambassador was entertained by Silziboulos, the Türk ruler vented his anger at the Persian ambassador who was also present. In such circumstances it was apparently possible for the diplomat to put up a spirited defense and, in the case here mentioned, something of a shouting match took place between Silziboulos and his Persian guest. How far such an altercation could go depended on the circumstances and, let us face it, also on the courage or temper of the ambassador. On occasion the diplomat could go beyond what was acceptable to his host. Probably in 560 a certain Mezamiros, a "garrulous blockhead" and ambassador of the Antae to the Avars, went beyond what seemed tolerable behavior. A Kutrigur who lived among the Avars, and who hated the Antae, took advantage of the kaghan's irritation with Mezamiros' behavior by suggesting that he be killed, and that the country of the Antae then be invaded. The ambassador was put to death; the historian Menander recorded with great disapproval this flagrant violation of the law of nations.[23] There were ways and means of punishing impertinent envoys without openly breaking the law of nations. When Han envoys spoke "without restraint" to the king of Ta Yüan (Ferghana), and went so far as to smash the golden horse they had brought him as a present, he let them depart but ordered his vassal, the king of Yü-ch'eng, to attack and kill them on their way. Even so, Chinese retaliation followed, and the inhabitants of Ta Yüan were quite aware of what had caused the Chinese to attack.[24] Clearly, gross abuse of diplomatic privilege by the ambassador could induce a ruler to disregard his personal inviolability, but normally the ambassador was free to speak out.

In the year 1255 on the day of Pentecost, the Franciscan William of Rubruck had his last audience with the Great Khan Möngke. Although many modern scholars speak of Rubruck as an ambassador of Louis IX of France, he was in fact nothing but a humble, single-minded missionary, as will appear from what follows. In the long, and in many respects moving description of their conversation Rubruck remarks:

> From then onwards I had neither the opportunity nor the time to put the Catholic faith before him, *for a man may not say more in his presence than he desires, unless he be an envoy; an envoy can say whatever he will,* and they always enquire whether he wishes to say still more. I, however, was not allowed to continue speaking, but had to listen to him and reply to the questions he put.[25]

While he enjoyed special protection, the ambassador was not free to disregard local customs, and was expected to submit to the not always pleasant rules of etiquette as practiced in the host country. In the view of Monsieur de Callières, "Genius is no substitute for good manners," and diplomatic agents were certainly expected by their hosts to behave "properly." Particularly painful were the obligations of those attending the funerals of a defunct prince. Valentine and members of his party, who reached the Türks shortly after Silziboulos' death, were required to lacerate their faces, a general Inner Asian sign of mourning. The same gesture was expected from the Chinese ambassador attending the funeral in 572 of another Türk ruler, Muhan. He obstinately refused to submit himself to this rite and the Türks, in deference to his diplomatic privileges, finally acquiesced.[26]

John of Plano Carpini, the most successful of the papal envoys of 1245, gave detailed descriptions of the reception ceremonials in the camp of Batu (commander of the Mongols' western forces and quasi co-ruler), and also in the court of the Great Khan himself. Before being received by Batu, Plano Carpini's party was told that

> we would have to pass between two fires, a thing we were on no account willing to do. But they said to us: "Go without fear, for we are making you pass between two fires for no other reason than this that, if you are planning to do any evil to our lord or if you happen to be carrying poison, the fire may remove all that is harmful." . . . they led us into the dwelling after we had first made a bow and received the warning about not treading on the threshold. . . .[27]

The obligation for ambassadors to pass between fires is recorded by Menander in his description of Zemarkhos' reception by Silziboulos. The existence of this custom is thus attested over a period of at least eight centuries and shows the remarkable continuity of Inner Asian diplomatic ceremonial through time and space.

To enter into the presence of Güyük was not an easy task. The envoys' names were taken and noted down, as were the names of those who sent them; they had to genuflect four times, and were thoroughly searched for knives. Obvious reasons of security justified such a search, but diplomats less adaptable, and more interested in their own dignity than in the task to be accomplished were not always willing to submit to this procedure. Thus, for example, Zemarkhos on his return journey paid a visit to the ruler of the Alans, who insisted that the Türks in whose company he was traveling should lay down their arms before entering into his presence. It took Zemarkhos three days to persuade his Türk companions to do so. Their reasonableness was rewarded: the Alan ruler gave them valuable advice on how to avoid a trap set by the Persians to seize the whole party.[28] Plano Carpini and his companions entered the khan's tent by a door on the east side, for "no one dare enter from the west with the sole exception of the emperor." However Plano Carpini remarked that "those of lower rank do not pay much attention to such things."[29] He also noted that

> It is the custom for the Emperor of the Tatars never to speak to a foreigner, however important he may be, except through an intermediary [*per interpositam personam*], and he listens and gives his answer, also through the intermediary.[30]

The custom is confirmed by a certain Al-Ṣārim Uzbek, a Mamlūk who defected to the Mongols.

> When I stood before Hülegü [he was to report] he spoke with me through the intermediary of four chamberlains and said to me, "You are a mamluk of al-Malik al-Ashraf, the Lord of Ḥims, the bahadur of the Muslims?" I said, "Yes." Then he began to talk to me through one chamberlain after another, the fourth chamberlain addressing me in the Turkish language. When Hülegü saw that I had an eloquent tongue, a good mind, and a quick answer, he brought me near to him and ordered that there should only be one chamberlain between him and me.[31]

It is impossible to know whether this custom was due to linguistic difficulties or whether it would have applied also to a "foreigner" speaking Mongol. Clearly, in most cases, such as that of Plano Carpini, the intermediary was in fact an interpreter.

According to the *Kutadgu Bilig*, it was the grand chamberlain who was in charge of the court ceremonial, and whose duty it was to deal with foreign ambassadors, "arranging their comings and goings, the exchange of gifts and the permission to depart, seeing to their food and lodging, and treating both those with gifts and those without."[32]

The rules of protocol governed not only the behavior of the envoy and the receiving ruler but also, as in the modern world, the not always friendly relationships among diplomats meeting in a foreign land. Set rules of precedence were nonexistent, and much depended on the whim of the ruler receiving the diplomats and on the degree of inflation of the latter's ego. The seating arrangements at a banquet would give clear indications of the relative importance of the envoys in the eyes of the ruler, and of the feelings he had toward them. In the first century B.C., the Chinese complained that the ruler of K'ang-chü (probably the Samarkand region) behaved arrogantly, "refusing to treat our envoys with the respect that is their due," as shown by the fact that they were seated below the envoys of Wu-sun and various other states.[33] In Attila's court the place of honor was to the sovereign's right, but the Byzantine embassy to which Priscus was attached was assigned the seats to his left. As reported by Ibn Faḍlān, the same custom prevailed in the court of the ruler of the Bulgars in the middle of the tenth century, with the foreign envoys being assigned seats to the left of their host.[34] It may be noted here that in Batu's court, emissaries on their way to the Great Khan were seated on his left. On their return from Mongolia, perhaps as a symbolic recognition of the honor they had achieved by having been received by the Great Khan, Batu asigned them seats on his right. In 1403 the Spanish ambassador Ruy Gonzalez de Clavijo and the emissary of the Chinese Yung-lo emperor were both present at a banquet given by Timur. Precedence had been given to the latter, but at Timur's orders the seating had to be changed in favor of Clavijo. Timur went so far as to explain the action by pointing out that he felt that the ambassador of the king of Spain, "the good friend of Timur and his son, must indeed take place above him who was the envoy of a robber and a bad man, the enemy of Timur."[35]

Unwillingness on the part of an ambassador to yield precedence to the representative of another country—the annals of western diplomacy are replete with anecdotes illustrating such an attitude—can be met with also in Inner Asia. The *Chiu T'ang Shu* relates the following as having taken place in 758:

> . . . eighty Uighur envoys . . . and six Abbasid Arab chiefs . . . came simultaneously to [the Chinese] court to have audience. When they arrived at the pavilion gate, they argued over who should go in first. The visitors' and audience officials separated them into right and left and they entered at the same time through the east and west gates.[36]

William of Rubruck noted differences in the way ambassadors were received in the respective courts of Batu and Möngke. In Batu's camp they were lodged separately, care being taken that they should not meet except at court, whereas in Möngke's camp they were lodged together and were free to see one another. This was also the practice in Attila's court. Generally speaking, no efforts were made to prevent contacts between ambassadors and the local population, and in this way much valuable information could be obtained. Priskos had many interesting encounters while strolling freely in Attila's camp. These included one with a Greek defector who assured him that among the Huns "men are accustomed to live at ease after a war, each enjoying what he has, causing very little or no trouble and not being troubled."[37] More astonishingly he could also pay an informal visit to Attila's wife. "I gained entrance," he was to report, "through the barbarian at the door and came upon her lying on a soft spread. . . . Approaching, I greeted her and presented our gifts and then went out."[38] Some eight hundred years later, in Mongolia, John of Plano Carpini took advantage of this same liberality:

> We picked up many other bits of private information about the emperor from men who had come with other chiefs, a number of Russians and Hungarians knowing Latin and French, and Russian clerics and others, who had been among the Tartars, some for thirty years, through wars and other happenings, and who knew all about them, for they knew the language and had lived with them continually some twenty years, others ten, some more, some less. With the help of these men we were able to gain a thorough knowledge of everything. They told us about everything willingly and sometimes without being asked, for they knew what we wanted.[39]

The Mongols' easy-going way contrasts sharply with the European attitude shown, at least on one documented occasion, toward Mongol envoys. In the summer of 1248 two of these, Aybeg and Sargis by name, attached to the returning embassy of Ascelinus, arrived in Lyons. They carried with them a letter of Baiju, and also one written by Güyük himself. Matthew Paris reported that, although these messengers were treated well by the Pope, who gave them valuable gifts, they were kept in sequestration.[40] It could be that the restrictions imposed on them were motivated by the feelings of John of Plano Carpini who, when faced with Güyük's offer to send with him some Mongols to France, was "afraid lest [the Mongols] seeing the dissensions and wars which are rife among us . . . might be all the more encouraged to attack us."

Altogether, the Franciscan gives six reasons why it did not seem expedient to him that Mongol emissaries should accompany him on his return journey. Beyond the one just given, I will cite two more of his arguments against the coming of Mongols with him: he feared that "their real purpose might be to spy out the land," and he thought "that no good purpose would be served by their coming, since they would have no other mandate or authority than that of taking to the Lord Pope and to the other princes the letters which we had."[41]

Plano Carpini's concerns were justified, yet the Mongol request was in no way unusual, and conformed to Inner Asian diplomatic tradition which favored the practice that any embassy on its way home should be accompanied by a counter-embassy. There are scores of examples showing that this indeed was the favored procedure, and it does have a practical justification: it clearly alleviated the problems inevitably faced by a group of foreigners traveling through difficult, often uncharted terrain. We have seen an example in the case of the Hun Edeco accompanied on his return to Attila's camp by the ill-fated embassy of Maximinus. On his return from Constantinople the aforementioned Türk delegation led by Maniakh was accompanied by a Byzantine delegation headed by Zemarkhos who—because of Maniakh's death—traveled in the company of Tagma, head of the new Türk mission to Constantinople. When in 576 Valentine set out to meet Turxath, he was accompanied by more than a hundred Türks returning to their country. I have mentioned Aybeg and Sargis who accompanied Ascelinus on his return journey to Baiju; in 1248 the two "Mongol" envoys, David and Mark, who presented themselves to Louis IX of France, took with them on their journey home the French king's embassy headed by Andrew of Longjumeau. The Nestorian monk Rabban Sauma sent to the West by the ilkhan Arghun returned from his mission in 1288 accompanied by Gobert de Helleville, ambassador of Philip IV the Fair. Many more similar examples could be given.

This system presented the undeniable advantage of facilitating the progress of the foreign embassy but, at the same time, it also reduced its freedom of movement and its possibility of acquiring information which the host country was unwilling to provide. In the torrent of reproaches heaped on Valentine by Turxath, one concerned the Romans' habit of leading the Türk embassies across the Caucasus by pretending that there was no other, easier road to Byzantium.

In the foregoing rather sketchy presentation, only a few aspects of Inner Asian diplomatic practices could be touched upon. Among those left unmentioned, that of written accreditations, and that of the nationality of the envoys are particularly challenging. It would appear almost as if a body of "international civil servants" (to use a modern term) had existed, at least in the Mongol period. In a recent article I dealt at some length with the role of the interpreters.[42] Yet even this fragmentary documentation shows that had Inner Asian data been available to Hugo Grotius, they would not have altered substantially the thrust of his work. At least within the Eurasian continent the validity of the "law of nations" seems to have been universal.

NOTES

1. In *Die Mongolen in Iran*, 2d ed. (Wiesbaden, 1965); *Die Goldene Horde*, 2d ed. (Wiesbaden, 1965). Each work has a special section devoted to *Das Gesandtenwesen.*

2. *On the Manner of Negotiating with Princes,* trans. A. F. Whyte (Notre Dame, Ind., 1963), p. 81.

3. A. F. P. Hulsewé, *China in Central Asia. The Early Stage: 125 B.C.–A.D. 23. An Annotated Translation of Chapters 61 and 96 of the History of the Former Han Dynasty.* With an Introduction by M. A. N. Loewe. *Sinica Leidensia* XIV (Leiden, 1979), pp. 221–22.

4. Robert Dankoff, ed. and trans., *Yūsuf Khāṣṣ Ḥājib, Wisdom of Royal Glory (Kutadgu Bilig). A Turko-Islamic Mirror for Princes* (Chicago, 1983), pp. 125–26. For the Turkic original of this and the other passages cited, see Reşid Rahmeti Arat, *Kutadgu Bilig,* I (Istanbul, 1947).

5. 3d ed. (Oxford, 1963), p. 171.

6. The story is told in considerable detail by Priscus. The relevant passages are found translated in C. D. Gordon, *The Age of Attila* (Ann Arbor, 1966), pp. 70–102.

7. Cf. L. Dindorf, *Historici Graeci minores* I (Leipzig, 1870), fr. 18, p. 457.

8. Reported by Menander Protector, *Excerpta de legationibus*, ed. C. de Boor (Berlin, 1903), p. 456. I take this opportunity to call attention to the very useful collection of Byzantine data concerning the Avars, assembled and translated into Hungarian by Samu Szádeczky-Kardoss, "Az avar történelem forrásai," in *Archeologiai Értesitő*, CV–CVIII (1978–81).

9. Menander, p. 460.

10. Reported by Menander Protector, trans. Ernst Doblhofer, *Byzantinische Diplomaten und östliche Barbaren*, Byzantinische Geschichtsschreiber IV (Verlag Styria, 1955), pp. 169–74.

11. Hulsewé, op. cit., p. 109.

12. John Andrew Boyle, *'Ata-Malik Juvaini, The History of the World-Conqueror* (Manchester, 1958), II, 368.

13. The best editions of the original Latin texts of John of Plano Carpini and William of Rubruck are by A. van den Wyngaert, *Sinica Franciscana,* I (Florence, 1929). In this article, I follow with minimal changes the translation of both texts made by a nun of Stanbrook Abbey, as published in Christopher Dawson, *Mission to Asia* (New York, 1966).

14. Dawson, *Mission*, p. 68.

15. Matthew Paris, *Chronica majora*, ed. Luard, IV, 389.

16. Hugo Grotius, *De jure belli ac pacis libri tres*, trans. Francis W. Kelsey (repr. New York, 1964), II, 440 (II.XVIII.iii, of the original).

17. The best edition of the text is by Heinrich Dörrie, *Drei Texte zur Geschichte der Ungarn und Mongolen: Die Missionsreisen des fr. Julianus O.P. ins Uralgebiet (1234/5) und nach Russland (1237) und der Bericht des Erzbischofs Peter über die Tartaren*, Nachrichten der Ak. d. Wiss. in Göttingen, I. Phil.-Hist. Kl. 1956, No. 6. I find the dates suggested by Dörrie unacceptable. See Denis Sinor, "Un Voyageur de treizième siècle: Le Dominicain Julien de Hongrie," *BSOAS*, XIV (1952), pp. 589–602.

18. Jean Richard, in *Simon de Saint-Quentin, Histoire des Tartares*, Documents relatifs à l'histoire des Croisades VIII (Paris, 1965), assembled the passages embedded in the *Speculum historiale* of Vincent de Beauvais. The events here related are on p. 101, where it is said of Baiju that he, "innocentem eorum sanguinem effundere non abhorrens nec omnium gentium consuetudinem approbatam metuens infringereque permittit ubique nuncios progredi et regredi libere et secure."

19. Dankoff p. 164, Turk text 3818–20 (ed. Arat p. 384).

20. Cf. Morris Rossabi, "Cheng Ho and Timur: Any Relation?" *Oriens Extremus*, XX (1973), pp. 129–36; on other, later embassies between China and the Timurids, see also Morris Rossabi, "Two Ming Envoys to Inner Asia," *T'oung Pao*, LXII (1976), pp. 1–34, especially pp. 15–34.

21. Op. cit., II.XVIII.viii.

22. Colin Mackerras, *The Uighur Empire According to the T'ang Dynastic Histories* (Canberra, 1972), pp. 72–75.

23. Doblhofer, op. cit., p. 92. The translation, closely following the original, considers Kotrageros an individual.

24. Hulsewé, op. cit., p. 232.

25. Dawson, op. cit., p. 195.

26. Edouard Chavannes, *Documents sur les Tou-kiue (Turcs) Occidentaux* (St. Petersburg, 1903), p. 240.

27. Dawson, op. cit., p. 56.

28. Doblhofer, op. cit.

29. Dawson, op. cit., p. 64.

30. Dawson, op. cit., p. 95.

31. Bernard Lewis, *Islam from the Prophet Muhammad to the Capture of Constantinople* (New York, 1974), I, 90.

32. Dankoff, op. cit., pp. 121–22.

33. Hulsewé, op. cit., p. 127.

34. A. Zeki Validi Togan, *Ibn Faḍlān's Reisebericht*, in *Abhandlungen für die Kunde des Morgenlandes*, XXIV.2 (1939).

35. Guy Le Strange, *Clavijo. Embassy to Tamerlane 1403–1406* (London, 1928), p. 233. Francisco Lopez Estrada, *Embajada a Tamorlán* (Madrid, 1943), pp. 159–60.

36. Mackerras, op. cit., p. 62.

37. Gordon, op. cit., p. 86.

38. Gordon, op. cit., p. 90.

39. Dawson, op. cit., p. 68.

40. *Chronica majora*, ed. Luard, V, 37.

41. Dawson, op. cit., p. 69.

42. Denis Sinor, "Interpreters in Medieval Inner Asia," in Marcel Erdal, ed., *Studies in the History and Culture of Central Eurasia = Asian and African Studies. Journal of the Israel Oriental Society*, XIV, 3 (1982), pp. 293–320.

26
Scenes From Eleventh-Century Family Life: Cousins and Partners—Nahray ben Nissim and Israel ben Natan

A. L. Udovitch

FAMILIES IN TRADITIONAL Middle Eastern societies are not easily accessible to outsiders. Notions of honor and propriety have, like the facade of a traditional Middle Eastern house, blocked the gaze of external observers. Private life was intended to remain private. Through their field work, ethnographers have succeeded in collecting the kind of data which permits a description and analysis of many facets of recent and contemporary family life. For the historian, however, field work is excluded; and the task of uncovering the workings of the Middle Eastern family in past centuries remains formidable. Classical literary sources are most reticent with respect to family matters, and documentary sources are scarce, and have not yet been fully (or even adequately) exploited for the purposes of family history.[1] A major exception is the documents of the Cairo Geniza which, during the past decade, have already served as a basis for several major studies on the family in the medieval Mediterranean world.[2]

The individuals—mostly males—whose lives and activities the Geniza documents record were obviously subject to all the cultural biases of their time and place. One of the most pervasive of these biases was a profound reticence with respect to the women in their lives—be they mothers, wives, sisters, or daughters. Although the documents are not completely silent in this regard, direct references to womenfolk are uncommon. In other areas, however, where there was no such cultural barrier, these documents offer us an unmediated and unobstructed view of family relations.

The two protagonists of the following tale were first cousins whose lives spanned the last three quarters of the eleventh century. Both were born in Qayrawan roughly between 1020 and 1025. In their youth, both embarked upon careers as merchants, and both moved eastward with the flow of international Mediterranean trade, one settling permanently in Egypt and the other moving on from Egypt to Byzantium and ending his days as an impoverished scribe in Jerusalem. Both are known to us solely through the documents of the Cairo Geniza.

The younger of the two, Nahray ben Nissim, has the distinction of being represented in the Geniza by more items than any other single individual—over four hundred letters, contracts, and other miscellaneous documents. His first paternal cousin, Israel ben Natan (in some letters the father's name is rendered as Sahlun, one of the Arabic equivalents of the Hebrew Natan) was one of his frequent correspondents, and it is through their exchange and that of some of their common acquaintances that we can perceive some of the realities of family life in the eleventh century and, more particularly, the way in which family and other ties intersected in the "middle class" society of the time.

Nahray and Israel shared a common grandfather and were related in the following way:

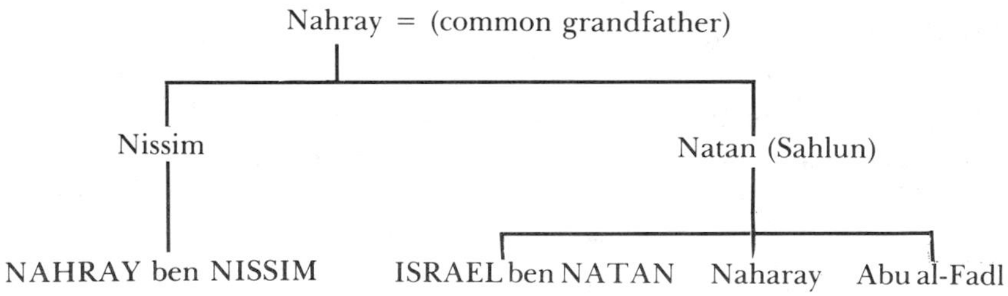

Israel ben Natan was certainly the most colorful of all Nahray's relatives. He led a rather adventurous life, much more so than the average young man issuing forth from Qayrawan in the early eleventh century. Nahray and Israel were roughly contemporaries. Israel was probably about ten years Nahray's senior. Sometime in the mid-1030s, he left Qayrawan to seek his fortune as a trader in the flourishing Mediterranean commerce between Egypt and Tunisia. By 1040 he was already a moderately successful merchant established, at least temporarily, in Alexandria. For reasons unknown and unexplained in any of his letters, he departed shortly thereafter for a prolonged and eventful sojourn in Byzantium. We hear nothing further from him or of him for the next ten years. About 1049 or 1050, he reappeared in Jerusalem and from there resumed a lively and frequent exchange of letters with his cousin Nahray.[3]

His earliest letter, sent from Alexandria to Nahray in Qayrawan in the early summer of 1039 or 1040, sheds interesting light on some of the economic consequences—or at least possibilities—of kinship.[4]

My brother and lord who is very dear to me, may God prolong your life and preserve your happiness. I am writing from Alexandria on the 3d day of Sivan (May/June), may God bestow upon you its blessing as well as that of the months that follow. I am well and happy, but longing for you, may God bring close the time of our meeting in the best circumstances, for He is the master of such events. Your letters arrived containing news of your good health and well-being. May God preserve these for you.

In your letter you asked that I purchase on your behalf the very same goods which I acquire for myself. By the time your letter arrived, I had already wound up most of my work. However, I was able to buy two bales of indigo from the firm of my lord, Abu Nasr, may God preserve his exalted status. One-third of this is for Ibn al-Ashqar, and a third for Abu Sulayman Da'ud ibn 'Ammar ibn 'Azrun who bought it on behalf of Abu Ishaq Barhun and one-third is in partnership between yourself and myself. This indigo is of better quality than that bought by others; may God see to its safe arrival. The cost of this indigo, including all expenses until its delivery to the ship came to seventy and one-half dinars. Half of this sum—thirty-five and one-quarter dinars—is on your account.[5]

I have also bought, in partnership with 'Abd al-Rahman, a quantity of loose and strung pearls, of which one-quarter is for you, and one-quarter for me and one-half for 'Abd al-Rahman. These are being transported with great care by Abu Sulayman Da'ud ibn 'Ammar ibn 'Azrun. The price of our share was fifty and one-half and one-eighth dinars, half of which, that is twenty-five dinars and one-sixth and one-eighth of a dinar and one-half *qirat*, are on your personal account.

I also purchased ten flasks of musk at a price of fifty-three and one-quarter plus one-third dinars, of which you owe twenty-six and two-thirds and one-eighth dinars.

Together with the indigo, I also acquired a small bale of cinnamon in which you have a half interest. It is being sent in the ship of Ibn al-Iskandar as part of the bale of pepper in which we have a half interest at the rate of twelve and one-half dinars per *qintar*. To date, the accounting for this bale has not been completed. . . .[6]

As for al-Andalusi, he says that he does not owe you anything. Get hold of the document written by Braya, and I will make a claim against him on your behalf. He is remaining in Fustat, and he took delivery of the goods that belonged to him in your package in the place at which it was unpacked. I, however, have not received anything . . . and if anything does reach me, I will hand nothing over to him until I recover what belongs to you.

I sold the [. . .] to Yusuf and with its price I bought a fur(?) that, together with all my other goods, is in the ship of Ibn al-Hawaniti. They are being cared for on the ship by Surur, the servant [*ghulam*] of Yehuda. He is traveling with Abu al-Fadl ibn Sa'ada ibn Salih. You owe Yusuf the outstanding balance of the account for one-eighth dinar's worth of rhubarb [*rawand*] which is in possession of Abu Sulayman Da'ud ibn 'Ammar ibn 'Azrun, and it amounts to one-quarter of an *'uqiyya*.

As he requested, I bought a pair of sandals of good quality for Abu Yusuf ibn Khalfun, and I sent them with Abu al-Bishr Sulayman ibn Farah al-Qabisi. Likewise, I sent you a string of pearls for your personal account in the ship of Ibn al-Hawaniti, as well as two additional strings of pearls. The price of all of these came to six dinars less one-eighth.

I am unable to give a detailed report on the sales and on the amount of money they brought in because of other tasks that I have to accomplish and because the work on the account for the expenses of the beads given to Abu Nasr is not yet completed. When I get to Fustat, I will draw up the account. Perhaps there will be an opportunity to sell the furs.

The miscellaneous spices were sent in the ship of Ibn Sandalayn. It has already set sail, may God see to its safe arrival.

I have bought a basket of "pomegranate seeds" containing ten thousand strings at a unit price of five and one-quarter dinars per thousand.[7] Five thousand of these are for you, and the other five thousand are for Abu Ishaq and Yehuda. The basket is in the *ilawa*[8] in the ship of al-'Arud, may God see to its safe arrival.

I am writing in haste, so please excuse me. I send you my regards. Regards to all who ask after me. Greetings to your mother and sister. Convey my regards also to Harun, to Abu al-Khayr, and to Shmuel. Please let me know how they are all doing, and how Shmuel and my brother Abu al-Fadl are faring. Please do not keep anything from me.

News has reached me that the European merchants have made large purchases of beads from you, and I hope that you fared well in these transactions.

May your well-being increase.

[Address] To my brother and master Abu Yahya Nahray ben Nissim
From Israel ben Natan, his paternal cousin.
To be delivered to Qayrawan, God willing.

At the time this letter was written, Nahray was under twenty years old. He was still resident in Qayrawan, living there with his mother and sister. While his older cousin Israel ben Natan was spending the summer in Egypt and may have even just settled there, he still had a brother, Abu al-Fadl, left behind in Qayrawan. In any case, both Nahray and his cousin were beginners in international Mediterranean commerce and thus the degree of their investment in this trade is quite noteworthy. More than one hundred fifteen dinars worth of Egyptian goods are mentioned in this letter alone as having been dispatched or acquired for Nahray.

Nahray ben Nissim and Israel ben Natan were not only first cousins, they were also close business associates. Cousinship and partnership do not necessarily and automatically go together, although kinship ties do make economic ties more likely.

Israel ben Natan was both the agent and the partner of Nahray. He had left Tunisia in the spring of the same year (i.e., several months before the writing of this letter) carrying with him, among others, goods belonging to Nahray. Most of these were sold, although, as he writes to Nahray, the pressure of events and other tasks did not permit him to draw up a final accounting. With the money realized from these sales he acquired for Nahray Egyptian or eastern goods to be sold in the markets of Qayrawan at the end of the summer or the autumn. This was standard operating procedure between colleagues in the East-West trade of the period. What is noteworthy here is the fact that Nahray and Israel ben Natan are full and equal partners in almost all the goods being shipped to Tunisia.

According to our letters, this partnership came about at Nahray's express request when he wrote asking that Israel ben Natan acquire for him the same commodities as Israel intended to acquire for himself. It is very likely that these two were also partners in the Maghribi goods that Natan sold. Although in theory associations of this kind covered specific goods on a single voyage, it seems likely that Nahray and his cousin had an ongoing partnership; one which, while not exclusive, was nevertheless quite comprehensive. In the letter translated above, only one or two items of comparatively small value are not "between you and me"—that is, jointly owned.

Partnership, of course, was a widely practiced form of commercial association between merchants for which no kinship relationship was necessary. Its forms, comprehensiveness, and duration were open to great variations. In this particular case, the open-ended and comprehensive character of their association was certainly connected to the fact of their being cousins. It is precisely this kind of inclusive partnership which in the Geniza documents is most frequently encountered between brothers. Abu Ishaq Barhun ibn Ishaq Taherti, Nahray's senior associate, maintained this kind of encompassing joint arrangement with his younger brother Nissim, as did Barhun ibn Musa Taherti, another Qayrawanese mentor of Nahray's, with his younger brother Yusuf. Although we have numerous examples in the Geniza records of partnerships between cousins, the all-embracing nature of the business ties between Nahray and his cousin Israel is more characteristic of that between brothers than that between cousins.

However, it should be emphasized once again that long-standing, inclusive partnerships could exist between two merchants who were not related except by friendship and trust. Nahray's own career contains numerous examples of these kinds of association. In his mature career, Nahray had close and extensive commercial ties, including partnerships of various kinds, with a number of colleagues in Alexandria and Fustat to whom he was not related. In Nahray's case, nonkinship commercial associations were the dominant pattern.

While kinship certainly offered the natural occasion for the pooling of commercial resources and efforts (especially close kinship ties like that of father and son or of brothers), it was neither a prerequisite nor the most common occasion for business associations. Pooling capital and sharing risks took place between people who knew and trusted each other and this was a condition which frequently, although by no means always, pertained between close relatives.

Israel ben Natan's career in commerce did not last very long. He may have spent the following winter in Fustat, for we have a letter from him sent from Fustat in early Shevat (January/February) to Qayrawan. The recipient was Abu Ishaq Barhun ibn Ishaq Taherti, a relative on the maternal side of Nahray ibn Nissim, and the man who subsequently became Nahray's chief commercial mentor.[9] The letter contains the normal kind of business information and mentions many of the same people who are named in the letter translated above (e.g. Ibn al-Ashqar, Abu Nasr, Ibn al-Hawaniti) proving once again that much of the international commerce of the first half of the eleventh century was transacted within stable and fairly small networks of merchants. After this letter Israel ben Natan drops out of sight for approximately a decade, to reappear in Jerusalem about the year 1050 with a tale of fascination and woe.

For reasons which he never explains and does not even allude to, Israel ben Natan abandoned this promising mercantile career in Egypt and settled in Byzantium, probably Constantinople. In this respect, Israel ben Natan's behavior was certainly unusual. While there were travelers back and forth between Byzantium and Egypt—especially Byzantine merchants coming to trade in Alexandria and Fustat—Israel ben Natan's is the only case known to me in the Geniza of a Jewish resident of the *Dār al-Islām* actually settling in Byzantium. In any case, the very fact that this could take place at all says something about the porousness of political frontiers in the eastern Mediterranean of the eleventh century.

It may have been an affair of the heart which drew Israel ben Natan to Constantinople or it may have been business and trade. Whatever it was that led him there, his sojourn in the Byzantine capital was for him an ill-starred adventure from every point of view. Writing from Jerusalem in the autumn of 1049 or 1050, he says:

> . . . I am sending this letter from Jerusalem on the eve of the festival of Sukkot after having arrived here from the land of the Rum [in this case Byzantium], may God lay its territory to waste. God showed His kindness toward me, and redeemed me from there. So great were my tribulations that, were I to detail them, even two loads of paper would not suffice.
>
> God set me free from imprisonment [*habus*] in Constantinople. While I was in the land of the Rum, I vowed to myself that if God redeems me, I will settle in Jerusalem.[10]

The personal debacle of Israel ben Natan's stay in Constantinople is fully detailed in a subsequent letter. His son died in Constantinople. His wife, who was almost certainly from a local family, apparently refused to follow him after he decided to leave Byzantium for Palestine. He was therefore obliged to divorce her and leave behind an infant daughter.[11]

After leaving Constantinople, he spent twenty months at some unnamed location where he earned his livelihood as a copyist of Hebrew religious works. It was only by reducing his expenses to a subsistence level that he was able to accumulate enough money to continue his journey to Jerusalem. Israel ben Natan reached Jerusalem penniless and destitute. He immediately wrote to his former friends, associates, and relatives. From Abu Ishaq Barhun Taherti he requested a loan of eight dinars. From Nahray, he requested a loan of four or five dinars, a sum sufficient for Nahray to procure some warm clothes for him.

And now, my lord, please do not neglect all the matters about which I have written to you, for I am perishing from cold here. I have neither a cloak [*jibba*] nor any other [garment]. I had some Byzantine clothes, but I sold these in Tyre, and I am in great straits.[12]

The contents of this letter set the tone for his letters to Nahray for the subsequent decade. The once prosperous, promising merchant was reduced to a semidependent existence. He spent most of his time in Jerusalem. He dabbled in trade in a modest way but without much apparent success. He earned part of his livelihood as a scribe and bookseller. He was constantly badgering Nahray to find him customers for his scribal work, to send him paper and other materials necessary for his scribal activities. He was passionately interested in news arriving in Fustat from "the West," that is, Tunisia, where he had left behind two brothers and other relatives and where he had also left some objects of value, especially books, which he was now anxious to retrieve.

During the following years, roughly 1050 to 1060, Israel ben Natan's livelihood became more precarious and his behavior increasingly abrasive and idiosyncratic. He became involved in the political intrigues of the Jersusalem Jewish community and of the Jerusalem Academy, in which Nahray ibn Nissim's star was rising and, as we shall see presently, he may even have harbored some dangerously heretical notions. During the same years, Nahray's life and career were flourishing. In 1051 Nahray married into a prominent Fustat Jewish family. He was establishing himself as a merchant in his own right, increasingly independent of his early mentors of the Taherti family, and was gaining in stature as a trusted and able businessman, community leader, and religious scholar.

In a long and interesting letter to Nahray written in early October 1063 or 1064, Nahray's friend and associate Abun ibn Sadaqa writes from Jerusalem:

. . . It is now four years that I have been writing, detailing in my letters to you how I and my family have been taking care of R. Israel, in overseeing his affairs, in visiting him, in showing him generosity and giving him a helping hand. I owe this to him, not on account of anything he has done, but for the sake of preserving your friendship and because of the ties that exist between us and the generosity and kindnesses that I owe to you. I also do all of this because of his loneliness and his being a stranger.

. . . I have informed you how R. Israel acted toward me. I cannot discern any reason for this behavior except lack of intelligence, lack of self-respect, and envy. And he continued to behave in a manner which is well known to you and not only persisted but even went further in this behavior.

Previously this affair was known to hardly anyone—only a few people knew. Now it has become a matter of public knowledge, known even to strangers here. His behavior has evolved in such a manner that he now expresses opinions on matters such as the revivification of the dead, on astrology and similar subjects—opinions which, because of the "pitfalls of letters," should not even be set down in writing.

He carries on in this manner and everywhere he goes, people are prepared to bring testimony against him. Our late master, may God sanctify his soul, was a man of unblemished spirit and when some of this information would come to his attention, he would not believe it and would chide the person who reported it. But now, this matter has become well known and circumstances have taken their course. . . .

By your life, my lord, I am quite worried about him (i.e., R. Israel). Any time I hear anything of the sort, I do reproach him; but he acts as if "he does not hear the voice of the whisperers."

And the reason I do not add details about these events in my letter is that I do not wish to upset you any further, may God protect you. You are surely able "to understand one thing from another and for a wise man a hint suffices, and he will act according to his wisdom."

A few days ago, I found him in the synagogue proclaiming publicly: "My cousin (i.e., Nahray) is involved with our Master the Rabbi (i.e., Yehuda ben Yosef, rabbi in Fustat); he is trying to restore his former prestige and to speak on his behalf."

He also pronounces other things which cannot be mentioned or imagined. May God restore his good sense! I have informed you of this and I am sure you will take the necessary steps.

I will try to put this matter out of my mind and will not reprimand him, but will continue to protect him out of my respect for you and because of what I owe to you.[13]

One can only regret Abun ibn Sadaqa's reticence to set down in writing more details concerning Israel ben Natan's behavior and views. What exactly were his deviant and shocking opinions on "the revivification of the dead, on astrology and similar subjects"? More than a century later, the troubling question of the quickening of the dead was the subject of a treatise—one might even call it an encyclical—from the pen of Maimonides. As for astrology, the powers it attributed to the stars and signs in controlling human destiny always posed problems for monotheistic believers. As far as I know neither of these questions was a hotly debated issue in Jerusalem at this time, but these were problems on which it was not difficult to hold nonconformist and shocking views.

Whatever Israel ben Natan's views on these sensitive topics, these were only one manifestation of his bizarre, socially unacceptable comportment, a comportment which was not only beginning to raise eyebrows in Jerusalem Jewish society, but also inciting some to consider taking action to curb his verbal and other excesses. Abun ibn Sadaqa was distressed at the prospect of a public scandal and was doing what he could to control Israel ben Natan and to protect him. He felt impelled to do so not because of any special concern for Israel ben Natan himself but, as he reiterates several times, on account of his relationship with Nahray. Although he was some years younger than his paternal cousin, Nahray was clearly perceived—and probably considered himself—responsible for his welfare and behavior. The cousin relationship in this case seemed to imply connections and responsibilities resembling those between brothers with Nahray, not by virtue of his age but by virtue of his attainments in the spheres of commerce, learning, and community service, assuming the role of the head of the family and responsible for its well-being and its honor. This being the case, it becomes easier to understand how Abun ibn Sadaqa's feelings of obligation toward Nahray ben Nissim in Fustat is translated, in Jerusalem, in his efforts to help and protect Israel ben Natan. Abun ibn Sadaqa was connected to Nahray by ties of trade and of friendship; Nahray was an important link in Abun's contacts with Egypt, North Africa, and Sicily, and he admired his growing status and authority in the affairs of the Jerusalem academy. Israel ben Natan was, thus, the beneficiary of the intersection of ties and bonds of which he was not directly a part.

NOTES

1. The bibliography on the family in the pre-modern—and especially the medieval—Arab Middle East is surprisingly meager. As an example, see the very slight bibliographic indications in the entry *'a'ilah* in the new edition of the *Encyclopaedia of Islam*, or in the very recent article by Thierry Bianquis, "La Famille en Islam arabe," in André Burguière *et al.*, eds., *Histoire de la famille*, 2 vols. (Paris, 1986), I, 557–601. Much of the literature in European languages on the Islamic family consists of summaries of the chapters on marriage, divorce, and inheritance from Islamic law books. See for example M. Gaudefroy Demombynes, *Muslim Institutions* (London, 1954), pp. 159–76, and Reuben Levy, *The Social Structure of Islam* (Cambridge, 1965), pp. 91–149. Legal sources do indeed constitute a potentially rich source for the social history of the family in the medieval Islamic world, but to date they have not been exploited from this point of view. The same applies to the data on family matters dispersed in other genres of medieval Arabic and Islamic writings, and even to documentary sources such as the papyri and *waqf* deeds. With the growth of interest in the social history of Islamic societies, such research will probably not be very long delayed.

2. The entire third volume of S. D. Goitein's *A Mediterranean Society: The Jewish Communities of the Arab World as Portrayed in the Documents of the Cairo Geniza* (Los Angeles, 1978), is devoted to a reconstruction of the social, economic, and psychological aspects of the Jewish family in the eleventh through thirteenth centuries based on Geniza material emanating from Egypt, North Africa, and Syria-Palestine. An interesting combination of both the legal and the social history of the family based on Geniza materials is the studies of Mordechai A. Friedman, *Jewish Marriage in Palestine*, 2 vols. (Tel Aviv and New York, 1980), and his recent book on the Jewish practice of polygyny, *Jewish Polygyny in the Middle Ages* (Hebrew) (Tel Aviv, 1986).

3. Israel ben Natan sent a total of twenty letters to his cousin Nahray ibn Nissim. Of these nineteen were sent from the Levant (mostly Jerusalem) to Nahray in Fustat, and all date from the period after Israel ben Natan's "occultation" in Byzantium. The only surviving letter to Nahray from the pre-Byzantine period is the one translated below. Another early letter from Israel ben Natan, addressed not to Nahray but to Nahray's mentor Abu Ishaq Barhun ibn Ishaq Taherti in Qayrawan, is Cambridge University Library, T.S. 12.362.

The texts of all of Israel ben Natan's letters from Palestine have been published together with Hebrew translations and notes by M. Gil, *Palestine During the First Muslim Period (634–1099)*, 3 vols.(Hebrew) (Tel-Aviv, 1983).

4. The original of this document is in the Bodleian Library of Oxford University, MS Heb. a2, folio 18. A transcription and Hebrew translation were published by Joshua Starr, "*Le-toldot Nahray ben Nissim*" (Toward a history of Nahray ben Nissim), *Zion*, I, 439–41. The translation presented here differs in a number of significant details from the one published by Starr.

5. Neither the space available nor the purpose of this article permits a full, detailed commentary on all the commercial and personal matters mentioned in this letter. However, some orientation might contribute to a fuller appreciation of its contents.

Most of the individuals mentioned here belonged to an informal, but stable, network of North African and Egyptian merchants who maintained long-term ties of collaboration in their commercial activities.

Abu Nasr, whose exalted status God is asked to preserve, is Abu Nasr al-Fadl ibn Sahl al-Tustari, one of the richest and most powerful Cairene Jewish merchants in the 1030s and 1040s. Some years after the date of this letter, he was very helpful to Nahray during one of his earliest expeditions to Egypt; he was also a close business associate of Nahray's relative and mentor Abu Ishaq Barhun ibn Ishaq Taherti (see S. D. Goitein, *Letters of Medieval Jewish Traders* [Princeton, 1975], pp. 145–57). Abu Nasr was the brother of Abu Sa'd al-Tustari, who had important connections at the Fatimid court and who fell victim to court intrigues in October 1047. In spite of our writer's prayers, Abu Nasr's "exalted status" did not very long survive his brother's downfall and murder.

Abu Sulayman Da'ud ibn 'Ammar ibn 'Azrun is mentioned frequently in Nahray's correspondence. At the end of 1052, Nahray prepared a detailed account for him covering the shipment of bales of flax and other goods (see Bodleian, MS Heb. d.75, folio 12).

Ibn al-Ashqar did not exchange any letters with either Nahray or Israel ben Natan, but is frequently mentioned as an associate in numerous business ventures.

Abu Ishaq Barhun ibn Ishaq was a member of the commercially powerful Taherti clan from Qayrawan. He was a relative of Nahray's and his early business mentor. They remained closely associated until Abu Ishaq's death by drowning in 1051 or 1052.

Most—but not all—of the members of this commercial network were Jews. The 'Abd al-Rahman mentioned in the following paragraph (usually called Abu al-Qasim 'Abd al-Rahman) was a partner of the Taherti family, and was one of a number of Muslim merchants with whom Nahray maintained a close and ongoing business connection.

6. The translation of the following five lines (recto, 19–24) has been omitted here. The passage deals with Israel ben Natan's acquisition of some furs, and its exact meaning is not clear.

7. The "pomegranate seeds" mentioned here refer to some type of bead or other inexpensive component used in the fabrication of costume jewelry.

8. An *'ilawa* was a small package fastened to the top of a larger container or bale. It was used as a means of sending small items from one port to another. See Goitein, *A Mediterranean Society*, I, 337.

9. Cambridge University, T.S. 12, folio 36; this document is unpublished.

10. Cambridge, T.S. 13J 16, folio 4; text and Hebrew translation in M. Gil, *Palestine During the First Muslim Period*, II, 120–23.

11. Cambridge, T.S. 13J 16, folio 7; text and translation in Gil, op. cit., II, 127–32. See also Goitein, *Mediterranean Society*, III, 177 and 200.

12. T.S. 13J 16, folio 4, lines 23–25.

13. The full text of this fascinating letter has been reconstituted from two fragments in the Cambridge University library: T.S. 10J 5, folio 10 and 10J 11, folio 13. It has been published and translated into Hebrew in Gil, op. cit., II, 233–42, see especially 239–40.

27
Notional Significance in Conventional Arabic "Book" Titles: Some Unregarded Potentialities

G. M. Wickens

IT IS NO doubt obvious that the following article does not fit neatly into any of the categories suggested by the editors, though from the general standpoint of time and culture it might well belong better in the first than elsewhere. In any case, it is offered to Bernard Lewis as a very inadequate tribute to his own lifelong penchant for scrutinizing all manner of taken-for-granted phenomena in Middle Eastern studies with a fresh, ironic, and insightful gaze.

The titles of Arabic writings—whether these be *risālas*, individual books proper, or multivolume *magna opera*—have nearly always received rather casual, not to say cavalier, treatment by scholars and bibliographers in East and West alike. In the Arabic-using world itself, the same work will sometimes be found with both long and short titles; with several titles that vary somewhat, occasionally quite substantially; or with nominal titles that are little more than an identification of general content (*Tārīkh* is a very common instance here). Neither is it always clear what title the author may himself have given the work, either initially or on later reflection. Attention to an exordium or preface could sometimes clarify such uncertainties, but those very sections themselves—some of supreme interest and even value—tend also to be neglected, while the researcher's eye remains alert for the *ammā ba'd* or similar markers where (it is traditionally felt) the "real statement" begins. In Western scholarship, such original problems are often confounded still further by a pragmatic inclination to ignore the title as such in favor of the author's (for the West) conventional name-form (Ibn al-Athīr's chronicle is a case in point, and one which ignores the fact that he had two eminent brothers likewise named Ibn al-Athīr); or of that name with a word or two of the title appended as deemed necessary (e.g., "Ghazālī's *Tahāfut*" or "Ghazālī's *Iḥyā'* "). Again, where it is decided to accord the title the dignity of translation, this tends to be done so stiffly or literally as usually to achieve only inanity, if not downright inaccuracy. One absurd literalism is the regular, automatic rendering of the original prefatory words *kitāb, risāla,* etc., where these, in most instances, merely serve to signal a title in a writing system inherently devoid of quotation marks or of any simple equivalent for italics. (On title pages themselves, this same purpose is commonly achieved by the use of special, often elegant script, retaining or dropping the signaling term at will.) Of late, some of these Western idiosyncrasies have also begun to affect indigenous practice, though not uniformly so.

All this would not in itself be a matter of major significance (though it has created much confusion, especially in Western, nonexpertly cataloged collections). The more important fact, however, is that Arabic titles do in most cases convey substantive or allusive information of various kinds; and in some instances a fuller appreciation of such information might help to do better justice to the author's purpose, and even lead to a clearer understanding of the work's essential character.

Of course, one cannot ignore the reality that just as there are bad or mediocre books, so there are (as much in Arabic as elsewhere) titles that are ill-chosen, foolish, obscurely allusive, or just obscure, pretentious, cynically titillating, and even virtually meaningless. However, the majority still deserve to be taken seriously, and can often point us to interesting apprehensions of what we may expect from the text itself—as well, at times, as apprehensions of what we should *not* expect.[1]

It is proposed here to examine a number of titles of Arabic works in different genres, many of them in the front rank, to see in each case what can be gleaned from a closer study of their wording and—where applicable—any recognized variations thereof, especially the "known as" variants. While the titles are arranged in no particular order, the phenomena discussed will be briefly classified at the conclusion.

1. *Iḥyā' 'ulūm al-dīn* by al-Ghazālī, often known (as indicated above) simply as "Ghazālī's *Iḥyā'*," or even "the *Iḥyā'* " pure and simple. A common rendering of this title (which is regularly translated because of its perceived cultural significance) gives the key word as "revival/re-vivification." This seems to suggest that the author's main concern was to enliven a body of learning that had once been vital but had become moribund or comatose. Not only does the Arabic term used not properly correspond to this view, but the whole tenor of the work (as one might expect from Ghazālī) is to the effect that these sciences, however well-purposed, remain inert until informed by the spirit, whether in Ghazālī's own day or at any time in the history of Islam. Bousquet's *Analyse* appears to recognize this by rendering the term as *vivification* (the form in *re-* exists in French as well, if he had cared to use it). The Persian work sometimes regarded, with limited justice, as an abridgment of this text is even more significantly named: *Kīmiyā' al-sa'āda,* properly "The Alchemy of Felicity," namely, something which, by its virtually magical effect, will confer on the individual soul the blessings of destiny—a title with a general humanistic ring, even perhaps a note of superstition, but with no specifically Islamic connotation at all.[2] It goes without saying that Ghazālī was in fact ultimately concerned with spiritual well-being, and not with happiness in any ephemeral sense.

2. *Al-Munqidh min al-ḍalāl,* also by al-Ghazālī, and again often known simply as "Ghazālī's *Munqidh.*" Once more, this is a title often rendered for its essential importance, but practically all such renderings (where they do not lapse into fantasies like "confessions") agree with Watt in translating the first term abstractly as "deliverance," a word which might open doors to several paths of inappropriate speculation. What the original "deliverer" rather suggests is a powerful, living agent of such deliverance. In other words, the work is not a mere record of the author's own spiritual pilgrimage or of his meditations, but a sort of instrument or exercise intended to set others on a sure path of salvation. As with the case of the *Iḥyā',* the usual rendering loses both the typical personal touch of this author and, more importantly, an "inwardness" of purpose as well.[3]

3. *Al-Akhbār al-ṭiwāl,* of al-Dīnawarī, the somewhat anomalous third/ninth-century history written from an Iranian "nationalist" standpoint. This title is usually jejunely rendered by something like "Long Histories" or "Long Narratives."[4] What has to be remarked upon is the presence of the word "long" as such: when Greek literature

conventionally speaks, for example, of the length or massiveness of the walls of Tiryns, there is no suggestion that virtually all cities of the time were not similarly fortified, but rather that Tiryns was a quite special case. Similarly here, Dīnawarī's own special method is to develop his accounts (many of them rare) without the usual frequent interruptions for the inclusion of the supporting *impedimenta* still carried by most such works in his day (though progressively abandoned in later centuries—at least until Western footnoting was adopted in modern times). What seems to be needed, then, is a title along the lines of "Continuous Reports," or "Reports *in extenso*," some formula that will at least not suggest that Dīnawarī's accounts are necessarily fuller than any other historian's in sheer volume, but are rather framed in a different manner.

4. *Al-Ḥamāsa* (of Abū Tammām). Charles Pellat's *Encyclopedia of Islam* contribution reasserts the commonsense view that this is merely a case of a book being named after its first section or topic, "On Valor."[5] (One might point to a parallel with many modern collections of short stories—in both East and West—which tend to be named for the first, or the best known, or what is perceived as the most important story in the group.) Perhaps more significant is the fact that the author himself appears to have opted, at least initially, for the flatly prosaic, if minimally informative, title *Al-Ikhtiyārāt min shi'r al-shu'arā'*, "Selections from the Poetry of the Poets"—a title which it would surely be more than difficult to undertranslate or, indeed, to overdress! (Few, if any, professional bibliographers—with their cultivated concern for exactitude and uniformity, even at any practical cost—seem to have become aware of this original title, so that the usual inconveniences and diversions of catalog searching do not often beset the academic user in this case.) Once the name *Ḥamāsa* gained currency for Abū Tammām's work, it of course went on to be applied to al-Buḥturī's similar (if perceivedly inferior) collection and to other analogous productions, besides being used at various times and places to denote, and that not always clearly or consistently, such genres as the heroic epic.[6] Finally, the title itself is sometimes amplified as *Dīwān/Ash'ār al-ḥamāsa*, but this is of no great help, and here there is surely one good case for referring to the work quite simply as *The Ḥamāsa of*—— and extending this to the other instances.

5. *Irshād al-arīb* by Yāqūt, often referred to as "Yāqūt's Biographical Dictionary." Title-wise, this is a somewhat complex case. The full, rhyming, two-part title, as originally assigned, seems to have been

Irshād al-arīb ilā ma'rifat al-adīb, that is, "The Intelligent Man's (authoritative) Guide to Acquaintance with the Man-of-Letters." Few writers in succeeding generations, whether in East or West, have given any serious attention to the first half of this title (which is certainly in part a piece of self-recommendation), and little enough interest has been evinced in the second as it stands. In the Arabic-using world, this has become a classic example of the prevalent "known as" variation. Two main alternatives exist: *(al-ma'rūf bi-) Mu'jam al-udabā'*, or *Ṭabaqāt al-udabā'*. The first, "Alphabetical Dictionary of Men-of-Letters," correctly indicates the work's sometimes rather inexact and confused technical arrangement; the second, "Classes of Men-of-Letters," is misleading, since this is not really a classified biographical work in the genre sense of the term. Even within its own single declared classification, it includes a wide variety of writers, many quite *non*-literary in their output. Brockelmann consistently cites the title in reverse of the normal practice, as *Mu'jam al-udabā' al musammā bi-* (= "named/called": it is not clear exactly how this should be taken) *Irshād. . . .*[7]

In their references to the work, Western scholars have handled the situation variously. Nicholson opts for "Dictionary of Littérateurs," a not unacceptable version of the *Mu'jam* variation. Gibb does something the same, but concludes awkwardly with "Men of Letters" (*Irshād*), while Hitti prefers "literati."[8] Margoliouth's (not very rigorous) edition[9] rings virtually all the changes as between cover, title page, and English reference-designations. In the latter he even includes the author's name in two different forms ("Yāqūt's/of Yāqūt"); and his English rendering as "Learned Men," while corresponding fairly well to much of the actual content of the work, represents what might be termed in translation theory an "implicit improvement" of the author's own choice.

Perhaps, all in all, this might be summarized as a situation in which natural and contrived complications have not seriously affected the essential relation between work and title. However, no comment seems to have been made at any time on the semipopular, unpedantic note struck from the outset by the word *ma'rifa* and the singular forms of *arīb* and *adīb* in the original title: it seems almost as though Yāqūt were proposing to introduce socially a typical smart fellow to a representative *adab*-writer! Unquestionably (though this has not been much remarked, and the work is constantly, perhaps necessarily, treated as something of a standard authority), Yāqūt's biographies do tend to reveal an impromptu, unpredictable character of their own: some of the entries are very short and dry, even skeletal; others are lengthy, but insubstantial, albeit often entertainingly anecdotal; still others offer a skillful amalgam of learned detail (e.g., much discussion of precise days and dates) and artistic craftsmanship. Nor would the treatment always seem to correspond to the subject figure's essential importance: indeed, we are offered, it appears, very much what Yāqūt had available and/or felt in a mood to give: it is a gathering of mammoth proportions, and one can always move on to other guests. His original title, if not the variations, might be taken to promise just that much.

6. *Al-Mustaṭraf* (the work sometimes referred to as "The *Mustaṭraf* of al-Abshīhī/Ibshīhī," 790/1388–850/1446). The full title is *Al-Mustaṭraf fī kull fann mustaẓraf*, which yields something like "The Gleanings/Croppings/Reconditioned Items from Every/Any Area of Interest." While, as usual, the mnemonic rhyme (or, perhaps more properly, the alliteration-assonance) may constrain the expression, and hence the idea in some degree, this is a fair enough statement of the author's purpose: in it he makes claim to little more than compilation, but suggests that he has searched widely to gather all manner of material having some entertainment value from the works and mouths of others, reworking it somewhat to present it in a fresh and engaging form. There are, of course, a vast number of such compilations in the main Islamic languages—some, like the graphically named and frequently published *Kashkūl*, "Beggar's Bowl" (of Bahā' al-Dīn al-'Āmilī, d. 1030/1621), transcending linguistic barriers in quasi-macaronic fashion. Most such works, like the present one, purport to offer some measure of moralistic edification or life-guidance to their readers, a mixed bag containing anything from stoical reflection on life's inevitable troubles, to a fragmented mirror-for-princes, or tips for aspiring ascetics.

The *Mustaṭraf* has been copied, lithographed, or printed many times in the Middle East, and was translated into French by the infelicitously named G. Rat (Paris 1899–1902); but despite its great popularity in the Arabic-using lands over the past five centuries, it has received little other serious attention in the West. Gibb refers to it as "The Literary Delectus,"[10] and very curtly praises its material and "style" (singular). This imposed title, however, is open to grave objection: first, Abshīhī does not offer his work so much as an anthology of all that is finest in "literature" (whatever application one may make of such a concept to Arabic in premodern times), but primarily as a work of entertainment culled from the broadest variety of sources; second, the term *delectus* carries a clear school-primer or workbook association, which was hardly in the author's own mind, however well the text might lend itself later to practice in diversified Arabic styles. (Indeed, as with its fringe benefit of casting fresh light on many traditionally neglected topics and situations, one of its other incidental values for the Western scholar might be seen to lie in the very variety of its styles and linguistic levels.[11]) As it happens, all of this—so neatly presaged in the title, as here suggested—is brought out quite explicitly in both the author's and the translator's own introductions, while Rat's personal version of the title (when he does not simply refer to the work as "le/*al-Mostatraf*" is overwhelmingly clear: *Recueuil de Morceaux choisis çà et là dans toutes les branches de Connaissances réputées attrayantes.*

7. *Shadharāt al-dhahab fī akhbār man dhahab*, the millennial annalistic-biographical compendium of Ibn al-ʿImād (al-ʿAkarī). The author, a true representative of later encyclopedic activity (1032/1623–1089/1679), apparently proposed to produce a major, but handy, general reference-work for those unable to afford a wide variety of such publications; but his book has proved so valuable in itself (if not always acknowledged to be so) that it is often one of the few sources, and sometimes the sole source, for the subjects concerned, particularly where these are too late to come within the purview of such major predecessors as Ibn al-Athīr, Yāqūt, and Ibn Khallikān. His ostensible *terminus ad quem* is, nevertheless, somewhat before his own lifetime, namely, 1000/1591.

For all the work's merit, Franz Rosenthal[12] justly complains that the Cairo edition usually available (8 vols., 1350–51/1931–32) is not sufficiently scholarly even to include the basic index indispensable to a text of this kind (though one might in fairness point out that each volume does contain a moderately detailed contents-list, while the annalistic arrangement makes it possible, with some little trouble, to locate figures whose death dates are reliably known). Again, if the work has not been translated—though, apart from its research value, much of it would translate very agreeably—its very title seems never to be rendered either. The latter no doubt strikes many serious scholars as a typical example of frivolous irrelevance, but it could equally well be seen as particularly suggestive and even precise: "The Parings of Gold, Being the Accounts of Those Who Have Departed/Gone Before." Unlike the case of Ibn Khallikān's title, for example, here we are clearly dealing with a necrology, but one declared to be of modest and derivative scope in this case; at the same time, the material itself is, by definition, of the highest quality, as coming from the most precious sources. The first part of the title is not wholly unique in its wording, but its neat, punning marriage with the second, to give an original and pointed indication of what we may expect to find in the text, deserves perhaps more serious consideration than it has ever received. As always, the extent to which the text itself fulfills the promise is another matter, but there are in fact few disappointments here.

8. *Ṣubḥ al-aʿshā fī ṣināʾat al-inshāʾ*, the magisterial (and surely over-elaborately classified) compendium for "secretaries" by al-Qalqashandī (d. 821/1418). Again, this title is virtually never translated or taken seriously, the work normally being referred to by the author's name, or as his "manual," with or without the addition of the first word or phrase in the Arabic. It might be rendered: "Clear Morning Light[13] for the Weak-sighted, on the Craft of Chancellery Correspondence." As usual, the "meat" of the statement undoubtedly lies in the second half of the rhyming formula, the first part being in fact a somewhat vaunting self-advertisement: that is, the veriest tyro, or even an incompetent, can hardly go wrong with this splendid work at his service. In this last respect, it might be contrasted with another work (one of very many) using the motif of light, in one guise (or implication) or another, in its title: Ghazālī's *Mishkāt al-anwār* (see next item).

9. *Mishkāt al-anwār*, generally considered to be a late work, dating from Ghazālī's final period of mature, sober mysticism or quietism. Whether Ghazālī did in fact write a quite different work with an identical or similar name, and whatever the definitive title of the one here intended, the most likely full version seems to have been *Mishkāt al-anwār wa-miṣfāt al-asrār*, "The Niche for the (Divine) Lights and the Filter of the (Ineffable) Mysteries."[14] W. H. T. Gairdner's translation bears the bald title "The Niche for Lights," which is at best meaningless or at worst reminiscent of a home-furnishing advertisement; Roger Deladrière does considerably better with "Le Tabernacle des lumières."[15] In any event, however the title may be rendered in translation, notwithstanding its explicit relation to the "Light" Verse, the heart of the *sūra* so named,[16] what cannot but be of interest here (as suggested in the previous item) is the essential modesty of Ghazālī's "promise": he seems to be saying that his little *risāla* aspires to be, first, a mere receptacle or resting place for the divine refulgences; and, second, a humble sieve to catch some of the mysteries of the Unknown, and of

those—as in the nature of sieves—by no means the most subtle, for these will elude all meshes of human contrivance. Ghazālī's titles are always serious in intent, and this one can hardly be an exception.

10. *Man lā yaḥḍuruhu al-faqīh*, specifically the do-it-yourself (if you have to!) Shī'ī legal manual of Ibn Bābūya (Bābawaih, d. 381/991). This might be characterized as an example of the uncontrived, explicit title *as statement*, and one from which a prefatory word or two is commonly omitted as being clearly understood; the full sense is therefore "(A book/brochure/digest/etc. for) anyone who has no lawyer at hand." (Such a formula was also used in relation to similar works on medical problems, calendrical calculation [no easy matter for the layman in premodern times], and so forth.) An obvious, and perhaps necessary, rendering of such a title in translation might be something like "Everyone his own . . . ." (Historically and culturally, of course, it would be inappropriate to strive for a neuter or bisexual translation.)

11. *Al-maḍnūn bihi 'an ghayri ahlihi*, yet another treatise by Ghazālī, exemplifying essentially the same case as the foregoing instance, and also displaying Ghazālī's unambiguous "elitism" in matters theological and intellectual. Once more, one could "understand" some prefatory words to the title as given, such as *risāla fī*, and render the whole as: "(An Essay on Matters) not Suitable for/to be Withheld from the Unworthy/Unqualified." In this case, moreover, the title is not simply a statement, but virtually a prescriptive injunction. It seems difficult, accordingly, to justify a total ignoring of its import, as is done in the customary reference to the work by part or all of its Arabic title as a mere label of identification.

12. *Al-Tanbīh wa'l-ishrāf*, probably the shortest of all the size-ranged "historical" compilations of the semipopular polymath al-Mas'ūdī (d. 345/956). This is a title more or less devoid of artifice, clearly designating the work's ostensibly essential purpose: to serve as a sort of index, or reasoned catalog, or reference list, to his other, more massive publications, and it might be rendered as "The Reminder/Memory-Jogger and Summary Overview." Nevertheless, in practice the various translations of this title into Western languages (and, for some reason, this is one that nearly always tends to be translated) offer a good example of scholarly fascination, among a former generation of Arabists, with the Arabic lexical record rather than with real usage or context; in consequence, the results are usually literal and wooden, sometimes to the point of inanity. Carra de Vaux, the work's French translator, offers *Le Livre de l'avertissement et de la révision*,"[17]

of which it can at least be said that the second part makes clearer sense than the first. Gibb's rendering seems as though it came from this French version rather than directly from the original: "The Book of Indication and Revision."[18] Nicholson chooses "Book of Admonition and Recension," but betrays some uneasiness by a footnote in which he balances de Sacy's *Le Livre de l'indication et de l'admonition ou l'indicateur et le moniteur* against de Goeje's glossary entry on *ishrāf* ("textual correction"), on p. xxvii of his edition of the Arabic text.[19] Hitti avoids translation altogether (op. cit., p. 391), while J. de Somogyi (in his English version of Goldziher's *Short History of Arabic Literature*)[20] merely mystifies with "Intimation and Scrutiny." Despite all this curious preoccupation with what sound obscurely like hints and warnings, checkings-out and dressings-down (as though the work were in some way threatening and apocalyptic), the author's own introduction—as Carra de Vaux points out[21]—makes clear enough his purpose in choosing the title he does, no matter whether *ishrāf* be taken to contain an element of "correction," together with its "review," or not.

It might be worth adding that Mas'ūdī has caused a good deal of difficulty to Western scholars with others of his apparently straightforward titles. For example, Charles Pellat, in his updated version of the old Meynard-Courteille translation of the *Murūj al-dhahab*, briefly discusses the problem of calibrating this first half of the title with the second, *ma'ādin al-jawhar*.[22] Quite clearly, "*meadows* of gold" pairs somewhat awkwardly with "*mines* of jewels"—awkwardly enough to suggest that Mas'ūdī could easily have produced something more felicitous if he had meant to do so. Most scholars in the West, however, seem simply to have felt that such a fanciful title only too often leads to illogical and irrelevant nonsense, however valuable the work in itself may be. Pellat, who decides to abide by the traditional rendering for the sake of convenience, plausibly dismisses an earlier proposed tinkering with the clear plural *murūj* which might give the notion of "gold panning." But a whole false trail may start from our seeing the essential anomaly as residing in the word *murūj* at all. In a society in which the primary sources of raw materials, and ultimately of all levels of wealth, were crops and minerals, "fields" and "mines" may accord perfectly well, so that attention should perhaps be paid rather to the "gold" and the "jewels": a pun of sorts undoubtedly links the two in one respect, but is it not also conceivable that *dhahab* here might be an unattested technical or (so to speak) jargonic term for the best type of wheat or some other grain? This would give the possibility of something like "Fields of Fine (Golden) Corn and Mines of Precious Jewels."

13. *Fuṣūṣ al-ḥikam fī/wa-khuṣūṣ al-kilam*, one of the two best-known works of Ibn 'Arabī (d. 638/1240), this one embodying the encapsulated teaching of more or less the usual recognized prophets—with, of course, a mystical coloration. In the West, the title tends to be referred to simply as "The/Ibn 'Arabī's *Fuṣūṣ*," or translated so loosely as to give various misleading impressions. Surprisingly, that great expert on mystical literature R. A. Nicholson renders it as "The Bezels of Philosophy,"[23] leading one to wonder what exactly he thought "bezels" might be, and why the term would be used here; also whether he really believed that the work treated of philosophy in any real sense, rather than with the sorts of ethical precepts and inspired utterances that lend themselves to embodiment in aphoristic form (the sense normally carried by the plural *ḥikam*). Hitti does somewhat better with "the bezels of wise precepts"—not capitalized, perhaps as being regarded as a sort of paraphrase.[24] Gibb does not refer to the work at all in his brief notice on Ibn 'Arabī.[25] Titus Burckhardt, for his French abridgment of the work, chooses *La Sagesse des prophètes*, that is, having recourse to a sensible paraphrase or interpretation of the work's general purport.[26] Somogyi provides the infelicitous version, "The Seal-Stones of Wisdoms" [sic].[27]

This is undoubtedly a cryptic case. To start with, the term "bezel" may well have been misapplied, in the belief that here we had yet another title incorporating a reference to precious stones. In fact, a bezel is a particular way of trimming a stone or a carefully crafted piece of glass, or even metal, to insure effect as well as fit and retention. In the case of jewels, it might be best termed "setting." What the Arabic term *faṣṣ* normally connotes, as Somogyi undoubtedly realized, is "signet-stone," namely, a marker lending authenticity and hence authority to a documentary statement. (The *faṣṣ* need not be, and perhaps seldom is, precious in itself.) Accordingly, we have something to the effect of "Impressed Authentications of the Wise *Dicta*." The second half of the title is no less problematic: presumably, *khuṣūṣ* should be taken as a plural (of *khuṣṣ*?), to offset *fuṣūṣ*; and *kilam* as the plural of *kilama*, a somewhat rare doublet of *kalima*. Thus the whole might give: "The Choicest Parts[28] of the Aphoristic Utterances." As to the link between the two halves, Brockelmann has *fī*, and the *EI*[2] article gives *wa-*. While the former might be plausible enough in most two-part titles, the latter alternative seems more likely in the present instance, since the two parts are here fully complementary and do not stand in any apparent posture of relative subordination or qualification.

A brief additional remark may be in order on the subject of Ibn ʿArabī's other major work, of which the first (and most common) half-title is *Al-Futūḥāt al-makkīya*, almost universally rendered as "The Meccan Revelations."[29] In practice, one might not easily apprehend from such a version that *futūḥāt*—a somewhat unusual double plural—here connotes the various divine aids or favors conferred upon a true mystic, an opening-up for him personally of the ineffable mysteries themselves, rather than the sort of "revelations" mediated to humanity by a (so to speak) traditional prophet. (Some, of course, would say that Muḥammad filled both roles and more.) There is also undoubtedly an evocation here of the Prophet's own message as received in Meccan territory, as well as of his "conquest" of that city in his ultimate political and spiritual triumph.[30] In this sense, Ibn ʿArabī may here be seen as repeatedly renewing this conquest in something of the same way that the Christian Eucharist is felt to renew the Messianic sacrifice, that is, without substantially changing it, or adding to it or multiplying it, but rather by making it continuously meaningful and effective until the end of the world. If such an interpretation might seem outrageous, it has to be remembered what sort of a figure Ibn ʿArabī was on any showing, and also that other mystics have claimed even more—almost to the point of implying that their grand experience would have been the same with or without Muḥammad's mission to pave the way for them, or to provide their operational ambiance.

As to the second half of the title (which is virtually never translated), so much confusion and discrepancy prevails in almost every respect—at least, as to detail—that little useful speculation can be made on what might be taken as its "authentic" or "definitive" purport. However, what—in any version—it seems to *suggest* is something like: ". . . concerning (acquaintance with) the secrets of the lordly/angelic realm."[31]

14. *Al-Milal wa'l-niḥal*, specifically the *Kitāb al-fiṣal fī 'l-milal wa'l-ahwā' wa'l-niḥal* of Ibn Ḥazm (384/994–456/1064), though the title is rarely given thus fully; and the first substantial word seems to be an ongoing source of trouble, with some reading *faṣl and others fiṣāl*. (Both alternatives would seem to be unlikely in consideration of sense and/or the requirements—however tolerant—of assonance, but it is difficult to invest *fiṣal* itself with any special sense distinct from, say, *fuṣūl*, i.e.,

"categorizations/definitive conclusions.") This is a title of special importance, not only because of the work's intrinsic significance (for its originality and long-term influence), but inasmuch as it became the eponymous ancestor of other such titles, and indeed of almost the whole genre of comparative religious writing as carried on from within the faith or culture of Islam itself. A fair rendering might read as follows, disregarding the later technical crystallization of the key terms: "The Methodical/Definitive Study on Communal Denominations, Odd Persuasions, and Religious Groupings (generally)." As is well known, Ibn Ḥazm (like Shahristānī after him) is remarkably comprehensive, at least of everything he is able to find out; and he is often harder on Muslim deviants (as he, somewhat ubiquitously, sees them) than on non-Muslims, particularly if the latter are fairly traditional and well-behaved. Virtually anything from Ibn Ḥazm's pen is certain to be original and powerfully presented: what makes the present work particularly unusual is his readiness (conscious or not) to "distance" himself in the sense of treating religion as a virtually universal phenomenon, not just as ordained to be so by God in His cosmic purpose, but as one having its own psychological, social, organic, and organizational processes at the human level, which enable it to be treated in many respects across the boundaries of faith. Little of this, however, is apparent in the title as usually presented or translated. The very interesting middle term (which essentially connotes something like "idle fancies") tends to be simply omitted in both East and West; and when one or other of the residues is rendered into another language, we end up in nearly all cases with "The Book of Religions and Sects," which would seem to promise little more than the sort of dry list that is all too common in such "literature." Sometimes, whatever was in the translator's mind, we find terms that are even more misleading.[32]

15. *Nishwār al-muḥāḍara wa-akhbār al-mudhākara*, the eight-volume collection of interesting (and frequently valuable) "real-life" anecdotes, often recounted with great economy, manipulative skill, and dramatic effect by Abū 'Alī al-Muḥassin ibn 'Alī al-Tanūkhī (329/940–384/994). This title tends to be avoided, abbreviated, or paraphrased in both East and West, though it very clearly sets forth the author's perceived context of mood. The reason for this may be deliberate, a stylistic or aesthetic choice: it may equally well arise from bafflement at the linguistic level or at that of the referential point—or both. The first word is a fairly typical Arabic "corruption" of the Persian *nishkhwār* ("cud/predigested or partly digested fodder"). The title as a whole may

accordingly be rendered: "Something to chew on in discussion, and anecdotes for (social) conversation." In other words, though the work is precious enough to justify the serious textual and historiographical editing lavished on it in a recent production,[33] it was originally intended for oral presentation in fairly relaxed circumstances. (Tanūkhī's contemporaries would naturally have appreciated the "inwardness" of most of this material, as well as its circumstantial incidentals, very much more readily than do we.) Margoliouth established a precedent by choosing as a title for his edition/translation of two limited excerpts "Table-Talk of a Mesopotamian Judge."[34] For once, this is a paraphrase so apt as to excite only admiration. Nevertheless, Gibb goes along with a "known-as" variant, *Jāmiʿ al-tawārīkh*, and misleadingly refers to the work as "The Collection of Histories," though he redeems himself somewhat by placing his mention of it in the more or less appropriate context of cheering and exhortatory entertainment.[35] The other literary histories referred to throughout this article do not touch it at all.

16. The *Tahāfut al-tahāfut* of Ibn Rushd, a work of inestimable importance over time and in geographical and cultural extent, not only for its forceful attempt to rehabilitate the *classical philosophical* position within Islam, but also because of the personal, wide-ranging power and originality of mind it displayed to an eagerly receptive world outside Islam. Nevertheless, its title has suffered uniformly clumsy and insensitive treatment in translation, pointed and witty though it may be in the original. In some important instances, it is not rendered at all.[36] (Most of what will be said here, of course, takes in also the title of Ghazālī's primary "seed"-work, the *Tahāfut al-falāsifa*.) The standard translation (though, for all its learning, particularly on the "Greek" side, it is one open to many objections, and could well stand thoroughgoing revision) uses "The Incoherence of the Incoherence."[37] Gibb agrees exactly with this, and Hitti also parallels it, albeit with lowercase initials, as though to suggest an informal, tentative paraphrase.[38] Somogyi offers another, though not original, version: "The Destruction of 'The Destruction.' "[39] Nicholson refers in passing to Ghazālī's *Tahāfut*, but surprisingly fails to do more than mention Ibn Rushd's "rejoinder," let alone to translate its title.[40]

All of these versions (and others too), not to overstate the case, mystify at worst, while suggesting at best some profound philosophical concept which is here totally inappropriate. No analogy was intended, and none should be even adumbrated, with such propositions as *ex nihilo nihil*, or "zero times x = zero," or "the product of two minus quantities is a positive," and so forth. The word *tahāfut* connotes basically a reciprocal, accelerating fall or an inner collapse, originally of physical objects (such as buildings) and, by extension, of internally contradictory lines of argument. We have to do here, in fact, with something akin to the Kantian "antinomies of reason," the notion that virtually any line of rational argument can without great difficulty be taken to opposite conclusions. It is true that "incoherence" may, etymologically and even in archaic usage, be invested with this sense, but it is more commonly used to connote, rather loosely, a general idea of "muddle/illogicality." In the case of Ghazālī's original title, an appropriate rendering might be "The Inconsistency/Contradictions/Ambiguity of the (Arguments of the) Philosophers." Moreover, Ibn Rushd's title in its turn must take account of Ghazālī's title *qua* title, as only Somogyi (to judge by his punctuation) seems to realize. Accordingly, a minimally intelligible rendering for the title here principally discussed might be: "The Inconsistency of 'The Inconsistency' (of al-Ghazālī)." Severe though Ibn Rushd is in his treatment of the latter, he is hardly suggesting that his work is "utter confusion" from end to end. As for "destruction," such a notion is superfluous, since the work is represented to be "*self*-destructing," as current espionage jargon would have it.

The foregoing review of a total of some twenty, mostly well-known, titles will suffice to afford scope for some conclusions and classifications relating to Arabic publication-titles in general, though—as with most problems centering on translation in any rigorous and considered sense—the ultimate address to any individual instance must inevitably be somewhat ad hoc and inconsistent, heavily dependent on subjective and aesthetic reaction. None of the categories suggested below is clearcut, and some pass beyond contiguity to a degree of overlapping. Needless to add, they are also far from exhaustive, and no attempt has been made to take account of the *bizarre*, as often favored by, for instance, al-Ma'arrī.

1. *The short, plain, straightforward title,* usually from a fairly early period and relating to a serious topic. Examples are the biographies (*sīra*) of the Prophet, accounts of his or his successors' campaigns (*futūḥ, maghāzī*), and "literature" on practical but fundamental matters like taxation (*kharāj*). These normally present no problems of understanding or rendering, and they have not been discussed here as such.

2. *The simple, but mildly pretentious title.* These are applied to similar

works (histories, manuals of "disciplinary" skills, etc.), but these are usually somewhat less portentous and also later in period. Their mark is a small prefatory boost for the author in the use of such terms as *al-kāmil* ("the acme"), *al-nihāya* ("the ultimate/the last word"), or *al-kāfī* ("the comprehensive/everything you need"). Such terms are normally followed by the word *fī* ("on/about"), which introduces the general reference to the topic itself: history, medicine, geometry, etc.[41] Again, these have not been discussed here, any decision to include or omit the "puff " being more or less optional and arbitrary. (It can, in practice, sometimes be a useful distinguisher in cases of otherwise identical titles.)

3. *The come-by-chance title.* This is a case where the title, while not simply plucked out of the air, has no essential relation to the work as a whole. An obvious example is *Al-Ḥamāsa*, discussed above as item 4. Such titles nearly always present difficulties; however, attempts to substitute something simpler or more informative rarely succeed, and custom eventually reduces the title to a mere label, doubtless on the principle that, in language, repeated use can sanction almost anything.

4. *The title as statement.* These are clearly not titles in the normal sense at all, that is, they are not catchy and convenient, however clearly they state the purport of the document in question. For this reason, they tend to be applied to pamphlets or useful manuals (see the discussion under items 10 and 11 above), rather than to full-length, discursive books intended to entertain and/or edify, and to become the subject of frequent, allusive citation.

5. *The title with character and "challenge."* This is usually fully informative, if sometimes rather subtly so, but it invites the prospective reader to reflect carefully before he opens the work, and the prospective translator (or commentator in another language) to do likewise before entering upon his self-appointed task. Characteristic of this category are the Ghazālī titles discussed here (and in general), and also Dīnawarī's history (item 3).

6. *The more elaborate, two-part title,* linked by *fī* or *wa-*, and with an approach to rhyme and/or assonance, for mnemonic purposes or even for sheer effect. Overall, these are perhaps the majority. They are the ones in which the element felt to be fanciful (normally the first) is ignored or deliberately dropped in favor of the significant kernel; or where, alternatively, an outright paraphrase or rewrite is adopted. Most of the examples discussed above are of this category, and various

ways of looking at (and more adequately dealing with) them have been suggested.

Perhaps the simplest conclusion is that all titles should be taken seriously until found wanting, and that careful consideration should be given to the reasons for the checkered and protean history of some of them. Furthermore, in rendering them into other languages, some lightness and freedom should be striven after (see what I have suggested for items 10, 11, and 15 in the above discussion). This is more than a benevolent ideal: as more and more works are translated (and, despite growing obstacles, an astonishing number are still appearing), they will be used—whether in general cultural activities or within non-Arabist disciplines—by those who have no acquaintance with the originals but need an appropriate and acceptable title for reference purposes. It is not easy to put confidence in a foreign cultural statement when its titles are totally incomprehensible, or when they seem meaningless or ludicrous.

The subject offers fascinating vistas of speculation, and it can hardly be soon exhausted. What, for example, did a writer of the stature of al-Māwardī really have in mind when he called one of his works by the ostensibly ill-assorted title of *Adab al-dunyā wa'l-dīn*? Why did Ibn Sīnā call his work on medicine *Al-Qānūn*, and one of those on "philosophy" *Al-Shifā'*? It is true, of course, that he was presenting the classical subphilosophical branch of medicine in an authoritative and standard form; and that an overall grasp of philosophy as such was felt to set, and to keep, mind and body wholesomely to rights. But is this all that was involved?

NOTES

Since the names or titles discussed are usually easily traceable in such standard reference works as Carl Brockelmann's *GAL* or the *EI*[1] or *EI*[2], no indication is made to these except where necessary or particularly significant.

1. Such considerations are rarely raised for their own sake in Islamic scholarship generally, not even in studies on related topics, e.g., *The Arabic Book* by Johannes Pedersen (Princeton, 1984 [original Danish text, 1946]); or *Islamic Bindings and Bookmaking* by Gulnar Bosch, John Carswell, and Guy Petherbridge (Chicago, 1981); or *Islamic Bookbindings* by Duncan Haldane, World of Islam Festival Trust (London, 1983). However, in quite another, and more general, cultural connection Wilfred Cantwell Smith has an interest-

ing article *On Mistranslated Booktitles* (*Religious Studies,* XX [1984], pp. 27–42), in which he argues the fundamental importance of trying to understand a title properly; and even the fruitful, if unintended, consequences of misunderstanding it occasionally! (I am indebted for this last reference to my friend Dr. Jane D. McAuliffe of Emory University, Atlanta.)

2. The general situation can perhaps be most typically surveyed in W. M. Watt's *Muslim Intellectual: A Study of al-Ghazālī* (Edinburgh, 1963), bibliography and *passim*. This work, incidentally, follows the usual "Arabist" practice of virtually ignoring Ghazālī's writings in his mother tongue of Persian, where the personal note I have alluded to here is struck with particular clarity.

3. Cf. the previous note.

4. Cf. R. A. Nicholson, *Literary History of the Arabs*, any printing, p. 349; and Philip Hitti, *History of the Arabs*, 5th ed., p. 389.

5. See *EI*², III, 110 b.

6. The *EI*² article on *ḥamāsa,* of which the item referred to in the previous note forms part, in fact extends over some nine or ten pages, a tribute to the intrinsic importance of the term and to its widespread adoption throughout Islamic culture generally. It may also be noted that while the modern Arabic term for "heroic epic" is *malḥama, ḥamāsa* is still used in that sense in Persian, where, of course, the concept plays a much more fundamental cultural and literary role.

7. *GAL* I, 481, SI, 880.

8. Nicholson, op. cit., p. 357; H. A. R. Gibb, *Arabic Literature: An Introduction* (Oxford, 1963), pp. 127–28. Hitti, op. cit., p. 386.

9. Published by Luzac and Co., London, but printed in Cairo and at the Cambridge University Press, 1923–31. The seven volumes of this edition belong to the Gibb Memorial Series, New Series, VI, 1–7.

10. Gibb, op. cit., 97.

11. Cf. *EI*², III, 1005 a–b, where the work is more or less decisively asigned to the category of ethical *adab*. Such a judgment seems to overlook the originality by which it very often transcends its allegiance to such a category, however broadly interpreted the latter may be.

12. In his brief notice in *EI*², III, 807 b.

13. Cf. Lane's *Lexicon* under *ṣubḥ*, p. 1642, col. I.

14. On both points, see various references in *GAL*, where Brockelmann consistently cites the final word as *anwār*. This would, of course, not only be more or less meaningless in the context, but also constitute a very rare example of a "rhyming" two-part title merely repeating the original term. The issues (particularly the second) are succinctly discussed in Abū 'l-'Alā' 'Afīfī's edition (Cairo, 1383/1964), pp. iii–iv of the editor's introduction (in Arabic).

15. Gairdner: Royal Asiatic Society Monographs XIX (London, 1924); Deladrière: Paris, 1981.

16. *Qur'ān*, 24:35. See Ghazālī's own brief introductory remarks for a ritual explanation of the circumstances of composition.

17. Paris, 1897.

18. Gibb, op. cit., p. 82.

19. Nicholson, op. cit., p. 354 and note. De Goeje's edition: Leiden, 1894, in the series *Bibliotheca geographorum arabicorum.*

20. (Hyderabad-Deccan, n.d. [but post-1958]), p. 92; a reprint from articles in *Islamic Culture* (1957–58), with altered (and sometimes confused) pagination.

21. See n. 17 above: in the author's preface, p. iii.

22. "Jewels/precious stones," in the plural, is (apart from necessary sense) presumably based on taking *jawhar* as a rare collective form. Somogyi (see n. 20 above) gives the plural form *jawāhir,* as occasionally do others—possibly as a slip, possibly as a conscious but undeclared emendation. If symmetry is to be preserved, the singular form seems required, to balance the undivided, unquantified singular-of-substance *dhahab,* just as *murūj* only offsets *ma'ādin* if taken as a plural (the latter point noted by Pellat).

23. Nicholson, op. cit., p. 400.

24. Hitti, op. cit., p. 586.

25. Gibb, op. cit., p. 129.

26. Paris, 1955.

27. Somogyi, op. cit., p. 43.

28. One of several meanings apparently attaching to *khuṣṣ*; "fine wine" (permissible in a mystical writer) might be another. These are not attested in the standard lexicons, but occur in texts in such plausible meanings, and both Freytag (*Lexicon Arabico-Latinum*) and Steingass (*Persian-English Dictionary*) cite "fine wine." If *khuṣūṣ* still be taken as a singular, the meaning is not affected, though the symmetry obviously is.

29. Nicholson, op. cit., p. 400 may serve as just one example of the general practice here.

30. Cf. Lane, op. cit., p. 2328, col. III, *fatḥ,* for both senses.

31. For a fairly complete overview of the muddle, contrast, for instance, *EI*², III, 708 b with Brockelmann's entries. Somogyi, op. cit., p. 43 more or less agrees with my rendering of the essential gist of the second half: ". . . on the knowledge of the Angelic (= *malakīya* as the only one of several possibilities) Secrets."

32. Nicholson, op. cit., p. 427. (In a note on p. 341, however, Nicholson admits to problems with the *original* title.) Gibb, op. cit., p. 114, identifies the nature of the content as "Comparative Religion," but renders the title as "The Book of Religious *and Philosophical* Sects." Hitti, op. cit., p. 558 opts for an uncapitalized paraphrase: "the decisive word on sects, heterodoxies and denominations." Somogyi, op. cit., p. 97 offers "A Book on Denominations and Parties." Finally, the study by M. Asín Palacios, with its partial translation (Madrid, 1927–32), carries a special title of its own, which includes the well-chosen words: *su historia crítica de las ideas religiosas.*

33. By 'Abūd Shālijī (Abood Shalchy) (Beirut, 1391–93/1971–73).

34. For full details, see *GAL*, SI, 253.

35. Gibb, op. cit., p. 97.

36. The *EI*² article on Ibn Rushd by R. Arnaldez, which extends to over ten pages (III, 909–20), avoids rendering the titles altogether, or even paraphrasing them in relation to content.

37. Simon van den Bergh, *Averroes' Tahāfut al-Tahāfut (The Incoherence of the Incoherence)* (London, 1954).

38. Gibb, op. cit., p. 137; Hitti, op. cit., p. 583.

39. Somogyi, op. cit., pp. 44, 74.

40. Nicholson, op. cit., p. 341.

41. For an absurdly literal rendering of the third term (as "the sufficient"/ "the sufficient work"), see Hitti, op. cit., pp. 379, 686.

POSTSCRIPT: *Additional Notes to Text*

Re: *futūḥāt*, p. 380, l. 8: For further light on the sort of connotations suggested, see "The Story of Junaid and the Barber," in A. J. Arberry's selected translations from Farīd al-Din 'Aṭṭar's *Tadhkirat-al-auliya': Muslim Saints and Mystics* (London 1965, Chicago 1966), p. 207. The story also appears in other sources.

Re: item 5. on p. 384: A classic simple title with character and challenge is undoubtedly Ṭabari's *Tārīkh al-rusul wa'l-mulūk*, which makes clear from the outset an intention to review not only the histories of the people with an accepted scripture but also of those with merely secular claims to significance.

II

OTTOMAN STUDIES

28
Introduction to Genre Scenes in Turkish Miniatures

Nurhan Atasoy

ONE OF THE most important characteristics of Turkish miniatures is their documentary value. In this context, it is possible to obtain information on various subjects from miniatures, as well as from written sources.[1] Miniatures can tell us more about daily life than can be learned from the written sources alone; and close scrutiny of them may enable us to follow the development of Turkish miniature art. If we look at Turkish miniatures from this point of view, the earliest examples which have survived are from central Asia and the Turfan region. In these fragments are found scenes of religious ceremonies. These miniatures are similar to the frescoes of the period in terms of style and subject, and show scenes arranged in a row of figures in formal style.[2]

Unfortunately, the works which could have shown the continuous development of Turkish miniatures, covering the period of the Turkish migration toward the West and Anatolia, have not survived.

Of the miniatures of the Seljuk period which are relevant to our topic, we should mention the Konya manuscript, illustrated by Muḥammad ibn ʻAbd al-Mu'min of Khoy showing the marketplace scene from a Persian translation of an Arabic love story, Varka and Gulshah (see Figure 28.1).[3] This might be considered the earliest illustration of daily life. The initial scenes showing the marketplace (with a butcher and a few shops with their shopkeepers) are not directly related to the story itself; but perhaps they are included because of the painter's wish to provide information to the reader about the place where the love story occurred.

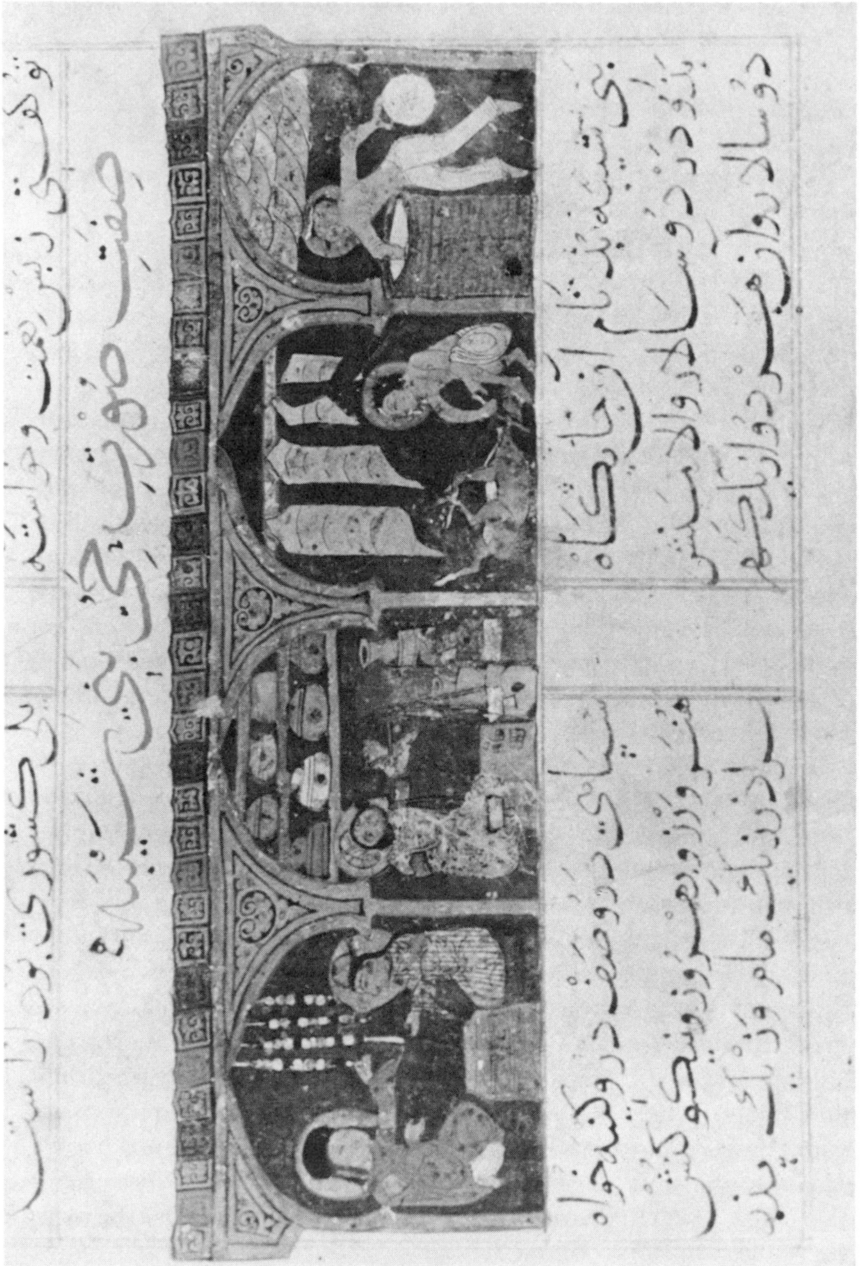

Figure 28.1. Muhammad ibn 'Abd al-Mu'min's depiction of the marketplace in the Konya manuscript, Topkapı Palace Museum H. 841.

Early Ottoman manuscripts are mostly literary, for example: the *Iskandar-namah* of Ahmedī, painted in Edirne in 819/1416 (Bibliothèque Nationale, turc 309); Bādī al-Dīn Minucehr al-Tacirī al-Tebrizī's *Dilsuz-namah*, painted in Edirne in 860/1455 (Oxford, Bodleian Library, Ouseley 133); Hatifī's *Khosrau va Shirin*, 904/1498–99 (New York, Metropolitan Museum of Art, 69.27);[4] Ahmedī's *Iskandar-namah*, first introduced by Ernst Grube at the Congress of Turkish Art in Munich, and now at the Library of San Marco in Venice; and finally, Katibī's *Külliyat*.[5] If one looks at the miniatures of these manuscripts from the point of view of daily life, one can obtain some information, especially from the scenes of social gatherings (*meclis*) which show musical instruments and entertainment of the period; but since they are presented in a ceremonial atmosphere, it is not possible to consider them scenes of daily life.

These miniatures reflect the influence of the Aq Qoyunlu school of Shiraz. Another style which also survives from the period developed under the influence of the Italian artists who were invited to the Ottoman court in Istanbul by Sultan Mehmet II, because of his interest in Western art. In the Ottoman miniatures, portraiture developed as a special branch. The first example is a portrait of Sultan Mehmet II (Topkapı Palace Museum H.2153) painted by Sinan Bey[6] who, according to the archives, worked with an Italian painter. Sinan not only combined Eastern and Western styles, but also brought a new approach to the subject. Mehmet is portrayed neither as the great conqueror of the Byzantines and of the great city of Istanbul, nor as the ruler of an empire; instead, he is represented as a private individual lost in thought, sitting cross-legged, and smelling a rose in a graceful manner. The archer's ring on his thumb is no doubt in recognition of his skill in archery. There is no ceremonial attitude or formality in his appearance, or in the way he sits.

This style of portraiture in Turkish miniature art existed as a continuing tradition until photography took its place in the nineteenth century. One of Sinan Bey's successors was Haydar Reis, known as Nigarī, originally an admiral in the Ottoman Navy. In his portrait of Barbarossa Hayreddin, he used the same style as did Sinan Bey in his portrait of Mehmet the Conqueror. This famous admiral, who had threatened the entire Mediterranean Sea, is represented as an elderly man smelling a flower.[7] Nigarī usually leaves the background solid dark green in his illustrations; however, in his portrait of Süleyman I[8] in his old age, strolling with his sword bearers behind him, Nigarī merely painted the trunk of a tree with a small branch with one leaf at the bottom right corner of the miniature, to show that the scene takes place outdoors. Süleyman I is represented as a humble old man, rather than as a great emperor who had enjoyed tremendous military success. (See Figure 28.2.)

Another portrait painted by Nigarī, which is in the Prince Sadruddin Aga Khan Collection (env. no. 6),[9] shows Sultan Selim II with a cup in one hand and a handkerchief in the other. Nigarī is successful in representing the physiognomic characteristics of his subject. By presenting Selim II with cup in hand, he wishes to emphasize the sultan's addiction to drink, of which we also know from the historical sources. In this context, Nigarī preferred to represent him in his daily life. One should also mention another painting of Nigarī's showing Sultan Selim II.[10] Here the sultan wears an archer's ring on his finger. An arrow has just sped from the bow held in his left hand; his right hand has just let the arrow loose. His chief falconer is holding a target, and the chief sword bearer is behind him. In this miniature, the sultan can again be seen in an aspect of his daily life, rather than his formal life, as he takes exercise and shows his skill in archery (Topkapı Palace Museum H. 2134/3).

While Nigarī painted the sultans and Barbarossa in a manner far from formal, showing aspects of their daily lives, he also painted a Turkish pasha[11] (Binney Collection, 11) with his attendants, together with musicians, in a more formal atmosphere. But even in this scene he softens the atmosphere, by portraying the musicians with sheepskins over their shoulders. Nigarī's method of portraying the sultans in their private daily lives influenced one later type of portraiture of the sultans. This type of portrait of the sultans is to be found in the six copies of *Qiyāfat al-insānīya fī shamā'il al-'Uthmānīya*, written by Seyyid Loqman and illustrated by Nakkaş Osman, in Istanbul University Library (T. 60870, 987/1579); British Library (Add. 7880, 887/1588); Topkapı Palace Museum (R. 1265, 1113/1595); three additional copies lacking colophons are found in the Istanbul University Library (T. 6088), Topkapı Palace Museum (A. 3632 and H. 1563). The twelve portraits of the sultans in these manuscripts, as is explained in the introduction, are painted from information collected about the physiognomic features of the sultans from local and foreign sources. The sultans in these portraits, usually represented in a space through an arch, are seated cross-legged or on their knees, on a cushion with another cushion behind their backs, and they hold either a handker-

Figure 28.2. Nigarī's portrait of Süleyman I, followed by his sword bearers, Topkapı Palace Museum H. 2134/8.

chief, a fruit, or a flower which they smell. The fact that their qualities as statesmen or commanders are not represented results from the tradition of portraiture which developed during the period of Mehmet I.

There are also other works in which the sultans are portrayed in this manner. In *silsile-namahs* ("genealogies"), the prophets, beginning with Adam, are shown in small circles. Here it is stressed that the Ottoman sultans were the descendants of these prophets, whose portraits are similar to those in the *qiyafat-namahs*, but are smaller in size. There are five copies of genealogies at the Topkapı Palace Museum (H. 1592, H. 1324, H. 1624, H. 3100, H. 3109). Of these five, three lack colophons, but two are dated 1006/1597. The portraits in these express more or less the same characteristics. In the H. 3109 copy, there are twenty-nine instead of twelve, while the last seventeen portraits are painted by Levnī in the same manner, having been added later in the 1720s. There are more copies, one in Dublin at Chester Beatty Library (T. 423) and another in Vienna, the *Ṣubḥat al-akhbar* (Nationalbibliothek, cod. A.F. 50) painted by Nakkaş Hasan.[12] This type of portrait of sultans is to be found in other works, such as *Zübdet üt-Tawarikh*, which is a kind of genealogy, and *Tasawir-i salatin-i othmaniya* (Topkapı Palace Museum, H. 1321, 991/1583);[13] Turkish and Islamic Museum, 1973, 991/1583 (the part up to the time of Ahmet I was added later); Dublin, Chester Beatty Library (T. 414, 991/1583); Paris, Bibliothèque Nationale (suppl. turc 126, an addition was made to the manuscript in the eighteenth century); *Tasawir-i salatin-i othmaniya* (ca. 1865), containing thirty-two portraits of sultans, in the Turkish and Islamic Art Museum (env. no. 1976). In fact, these portraits of sultans result from distinct features of Turkish miniatures and from the concept of realism. The starting point for this type of portraiture is to search for the subject's physiognomic characteristics, and to capture them in the painting. It is not possible to separate the portraits from the aspect of the genre scene, because the sultans are represented in an informal manner, in their daily lives.

Miniatures of historical subjects developed as a new branch of painting in the period of Süleyman I. However, we again find here realistic details and representations of daily life.

In the *Süleyman-namah*, which is dated 987/1579 (env. no. 413)[14] at the Chester Beatty Library in Dublin, the sultan is shown taking a rest on the terrace of one of his courts; this scene is included among the events of historical importance during his rule. He sits on a cushion with his *silahtar* ("sword bearer") and *ibriktar* ("ewer bearer") in back of him, with a water jet in front. A pleasant garden is there, consisting of flowering trees and cypresses. Some of the falconers hold the falcons which are to be used during his stroll through the garden, while others bring food to the sultan. In front of him, there is a pier and the side of a boat decorated with a dragon motif.[15]

In the *Hüner-namah* (Topkapı Palace Museum H. 1523), the miniature which shows the incident of Murad I's falcon taking flight as the sultan arrives at Kaplıca Imareti comes closer to representing a genre scene than it does to representing a ceremonial scene. In the same manuscript, there is a representation of the Topkapı Palace which includes the Sarayburnu and the city walls near the Alay Kiosk. Here the sultan sits on a chair in front of a pool with a water jet, as he watches the exercise of a falcon which is tied to the end of a rope, and which flies in the air (see Figure 28.3). The sultan is represented in his daily life, far from all his formal duties.[16] This genre scene is a small detail in a stylistic representation of the palace. In the *Nusrat-namah* (Topkapı Palace Museum, H. 1365), which represents the Persian campaign of 1478, which had Lala Mustafa Pasha as its commander, we see the commander in chief giving a feast for the Janissaries.[17] This miniature illustrates eating customs. Another illustration shows food being sold to the soldiers in a time of scarcity, and is a livelier genre scene. The scene[18] which shows the interior of the Mawlana Mausoleum at Konya with the whirling dervishes is also a good example of a genre scene.[19]

The astronomers are seen in their daily routines in the first volume of the *Shahan Shah-namah* dated 989/1581 (Istanbul University Library, F. 1404). This reflects important events of the time of Murad III, and tells about the observatory which that ruler established.[20]

The *Surnamah* (Topkapı Palace Museum H. 1344) shows the circumcision ceremony and festivities for Sultan Murad III's son, the Crown Prince Mehmet, which lasted fifty-two days and nights in 1582. All the guilds participated, carrying their goods either by hand or in portable workshops, to the At Meydanı, the Hippodrome, in procession before the sultan.[21] In these scenes, we witness how baths are taken in the public baths, how slippers, boots, swords, bookbindings, threads, turbans, mats, locks, and arrows are made in workshops, how archery exercises are performed in exercise halls, how silver and copper are wrought, how glass is blown, how caftans and baggy trousers are sewn, how the tent is set up, and many other activities. All these

Figure 28.3. The Topkapı Palace, miniature in the *Hüner-namah*, Topkapı Palace Museum H. 1523.

Figure 28.4. Bakers in procession on the occasion of Crown Prince Mehmet's circumcision, 1582, from the *Surnamah*, Topkapı Palace Museum H. 1344.

details from the *Book of Festivities* constitute only a part of the compositions, but are still perfect examples of genre scenes. (See Figure 28.4.)

The butcher's shop (Edwin Binney Collection, 13) is represented in a full-page miniature in the *Rawḍat al-'ushshāq*, where the details of a butcher shop of the sixteenth century, including the interaction of the butcher and his customers, are reflected.[22] Since this butcher shop is very much like the portable shop in the Murad III *Surnamah*, one might suppose it to be an enlargement from the *Surnamah*. The writer of the Binney Collection Catalog emphasizes that this miniature is "the earliest genre scene in Turkish painting."[23] In another miniature in the Binney Collection, Murad III is represented sitting on a thronelike armchair in his library, surrounded by the books which he enjoys, in an aspect of his daily life.[24] There is a fountain surrounded by vases of flowers in front of him, and in the bottom corners of the scene there are filled bowls, ewers, and vessels, all completing the court scene. This scene of Murad III has the same compositional style as the court scene of Murad IV (Topkapı Palace Museum, H. 2148).[25] In the center of this picture, we see vases of flowers and a round tray laden with fruits and vessels. Two candles in holders are burning, indicating that the scene takes place at night. At the very bottom of the scene, there is a flowered area indicating a garden. In the miniature of Mehmet IV we see the sultan depicted as a young man seated on his throne with a book in his hand, as attendants stand nearby (Paris, Bibliothèque Nationale, suppl. turc 326, ca. 1650).[26] In the *Shah-namah-i Ta'līq-i Zāda*, Süleyman I is represented together with his son.[27] The sultan sits on a cushion. His writing chest, with one drawer open, is in front of him. At his back may be seen a book cupboard with one door opened, with books on its shelves. In the background on the sultan's left, there is a small table with books. On his right, there is a tablelike chest with an inkpot and other things. The sultan has turned toward his son, his sword bearers are behind him, and there is a pool with a water jet in front of him. Around the pool, there are five tiny figures, which are either dwarfs of the court, or else unimportant figures; they are drawn smaller in size, in order not to detract from the importance of the sultan and his son. In the 1620s, Nakşī painted Mehmet III (*Divan-ı Nadirī*, Topkapı Palace Museum, H. 889)[28] together with his son. The throne is here placed on the right, and the Şehzade is in the middle of the top in front of the balcony door. At the lower part of the scene, there is a pool drawn from a bird's-eye view, with musicians on one side, while two wrestlers have a match on the other side. At the bottom and in the middle are vases of flowers, such as always appear in court scenes. The way the wrestlers are portrayed gives a feeling of daily life to the scene.[29]

Mustafa III, shown talking with his son, without any figure around them, is an example of scenes of sons in the presence of sultans. The room and the objects around them are given in detail, but without diverting attention from the figures (Istanbul University Library T. 9366).[30] In *Shah-namah-i Selim Khan* (Topkapı Palace Museum A. 3595, 1581), the illustration and the text work together, like the scene at the end of *Shah-namah-i Mehmet III* (ca. 1596) in which all the artists are represented working at their desks (Topkapı Palace Museum H. 1609; see Figure 28.5).[31] Nakşī, in a scene similar to these, in *Tārcūma-i shaqāyiq-i nu'mānīya* (Topkapı Palace Museum H. 1263, ca. 1619) represented himself together with Sadrazam Mehmet Pasha.[32] In this scene the two oversized figures are Nakşī and the grand vizier, who is carrying prayer beads in one hand. The grand vizier, seen in profile, is talking cordially to Nakşī. Behind the door to the room where they are conversing, a man—made more noticeable by being drawn smaller than the seated figures—stands concealed.

It was at this time that scenes from the daily life of ordinary people began to be depicted in books on pages by themselves, not as inserts in text.

The album of Ahmet I includes genre scenes from the beginning of the seventeenth century, as well as the miniatures of single figures which were not book illustrations. Among them, we find one depicting entertainment in the harem, with a pool in the center in which two ducks are swimming, with women musicians on one side and two lovers seated on the other. There are women around the lovers serving them drinks and fanning them. In the background is the garden where the entertainment is taking place, with trees in full blossom and cypresses in a row (Topkapı Palace Museum, B. 408). On the same page at the bottom there is an entertainment scene which includes only men. In the center, men with funny-looking masks and hats are dancing. Surrounding the exuberant dancing men are musicians and male spectators. Burning candles indicate that the entertainment is taking place at night. (See Figure 28.6).[33]

In the albums with paintings of single figures, there are also appealing scenes of the countryside and picnics. The album Topkapı Palace Museum H. 2148, cited above, includes illustrations of court scenes, including miniatures which are dated, according to stylistic

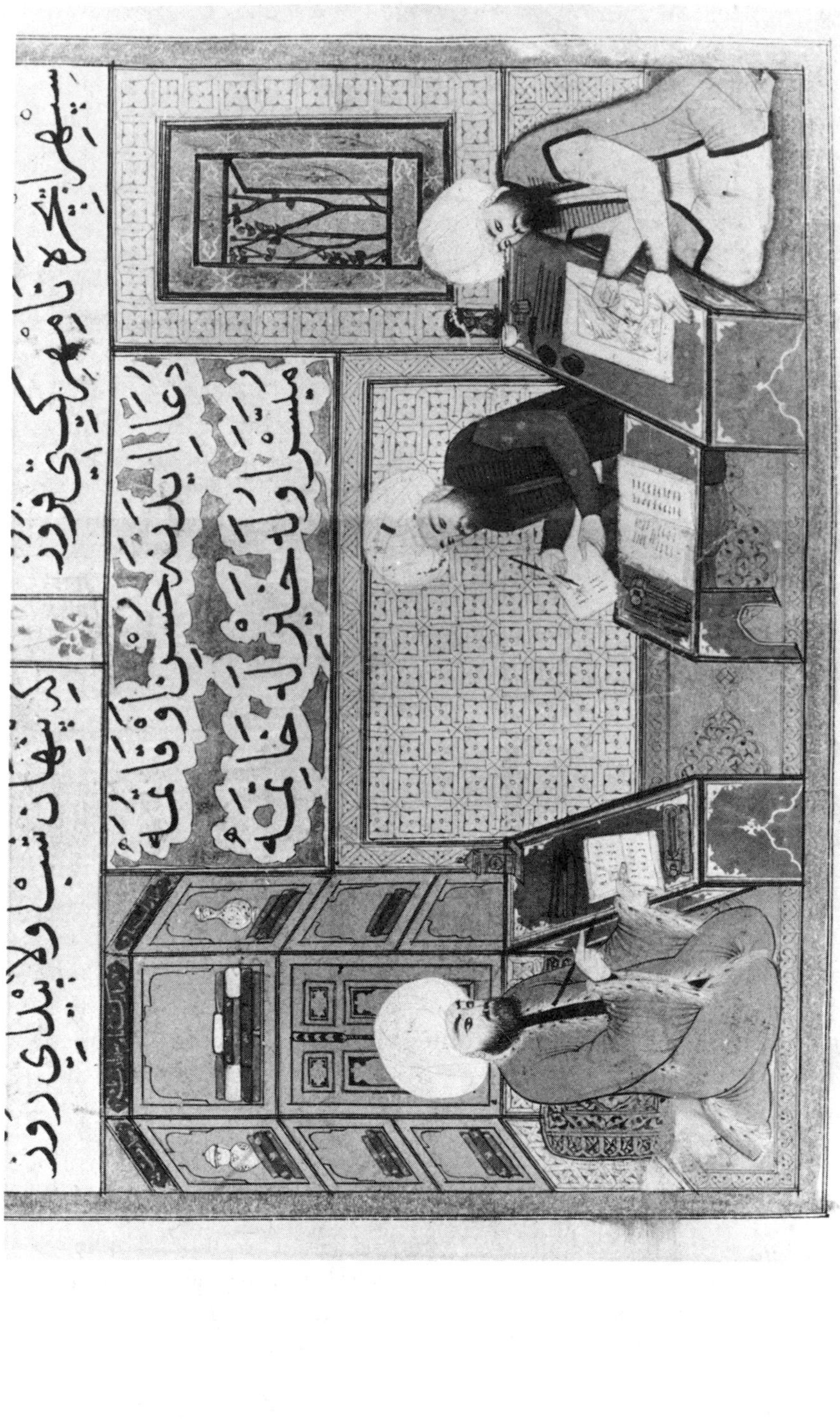

Figure 28.5. Artists working at their desks, from *Shah-namah-i Mehmet III* (ca. 1596), Topkapı Palace Museum H. 1609.

Figure 28.6. A scene of merrymaking, from the album of Ahmet I, Topkapı Palace Museum B. 408.

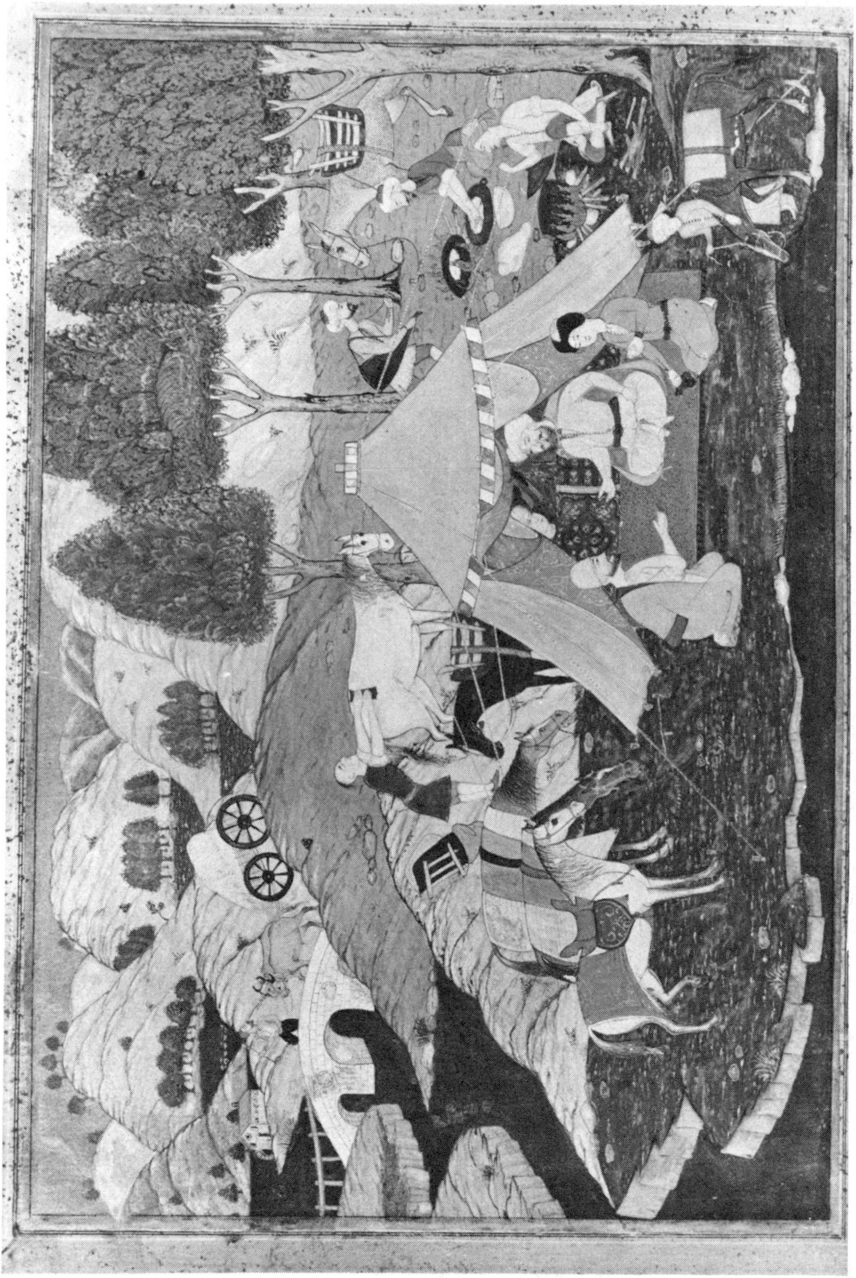

Figure 28.7. Travelers encamped, from an album of the seventeenth century, Topkapı Palace Museum H. 2148.

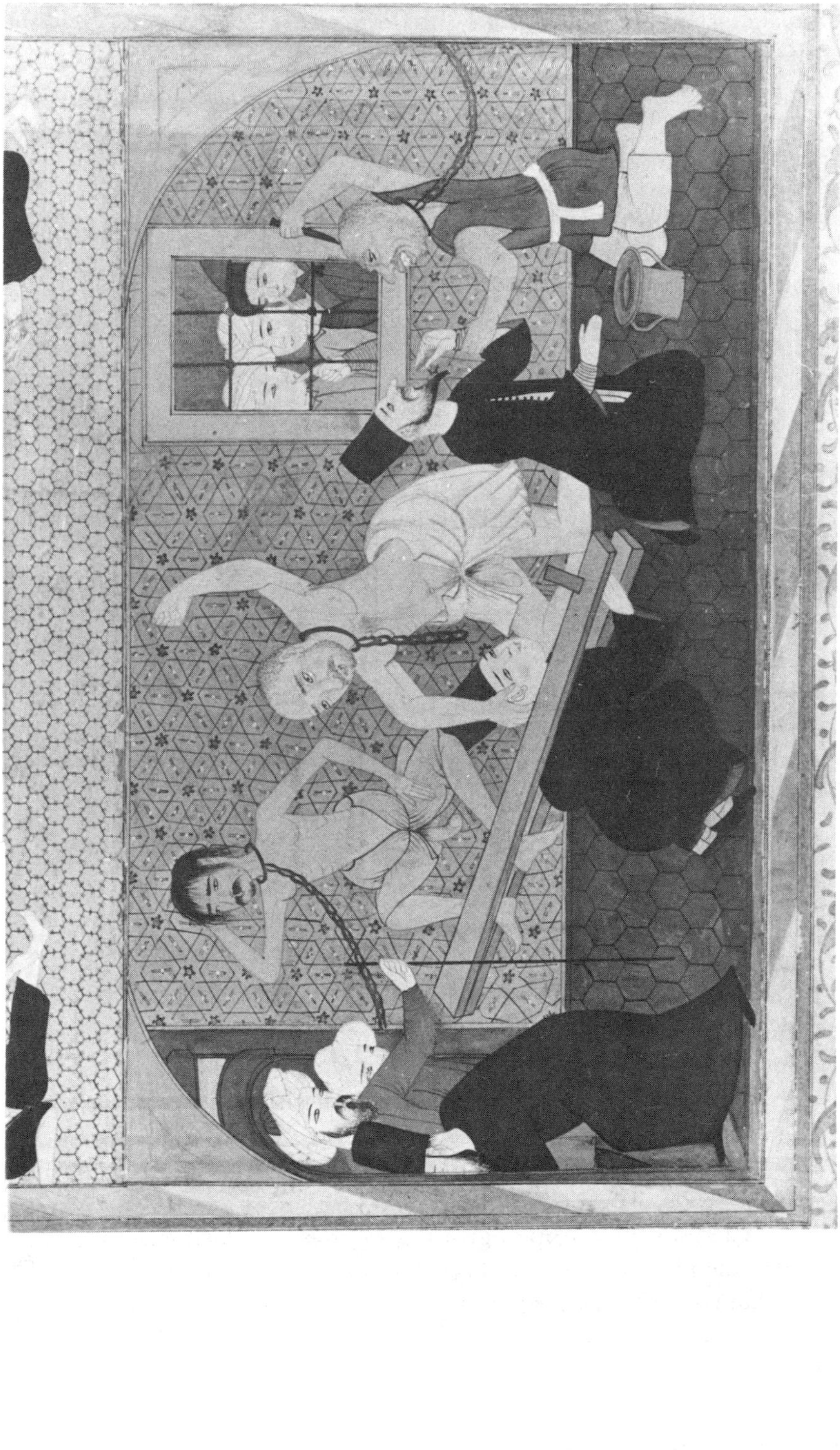

Figure 28.8. A lunatic asylum, from an album of the seventeenth century, Topkapı Palace Museum H. 2148.

features, to the seventeenth century. The camping scene[34] and the lunatic asylum scenes indicate the desire for new subject-matter for illustration. The travelers are represented at a camp by a river during their journey. They have unloaded their animals, set up their tents, and started a fire. Someone is preparing dough for bread, the food is being cooked on the fire, and the animals are being taken care of, while in the tent the travelers are talking to two seated men. A bridge, a carriage, and other details in the background, together with the trees complete the landscape. Although the proportions are not free from error, the artist is clearly concerned with application of the principles of linear perspective. (See Figure 28.7.)

One can also find the use of perspective in the lunatic asylum scenes. But most amazing is this departure from standard subject-matter to depict such an unusual scene, with the expressive faces of the inmates and the fear of their warders. (See Figure 28.8.)

This new development in Ottoman miniatures is not only influenced by the political situation and by military losses, but also from a new interest in styles of art developing in both East and West. The album of Ahmet I (Dublin, Chester Beatty Library, 459) is another example of this new choice of subject matter. The artist, instead of representing a sultan or a high-ranking person, preferred to show common people involved in quotidian activities. In a coffee-house scene, men are sitting, chatting, drinking coffee, while being entertained by a dancer. In this scene, men are also shown playing *tavla* (backgammon), as one of them puts his headgear on the floor in an expressive gesture which probably signifies that he has just lost the game. Here the flowers in the windings of the men's turbans are similar to the headgear ornamented with flowers carved in relief on tombstones in cemeteries. This indicates that wearing flowers on turbans is a custom, stemming from the widespread love for flowers.

In the Album Amicorum in the Victoria and Albert Museum in London there is another scene representing common people's entertainment. This one shows a festival in Istanbul in 1614–16, with merry-go-rounds, ferris wheels, and swings, and with men, children, and women enjoying themselves together. Strangely dressed men showering water onto a group of women reflect a joyful atmosphere with pranks.

As a result of Europe's growing interest, Turkish customs, religious practices, costumes and appearance were introduced. There is an album which was prepared for use in Europe by a local artist.

Figure 28.9. A street barber, from the Täschner Album (Hanover, 1925).

Although it was damaged during the Second World War, a book has been published about it, which gives us some information about the original. It is called the Täschner Album after its publisher's name.[35] It reflects the common life of the Turkish people in the seventeenth century (see Figures 28.9, 28.10). There is another album similar to

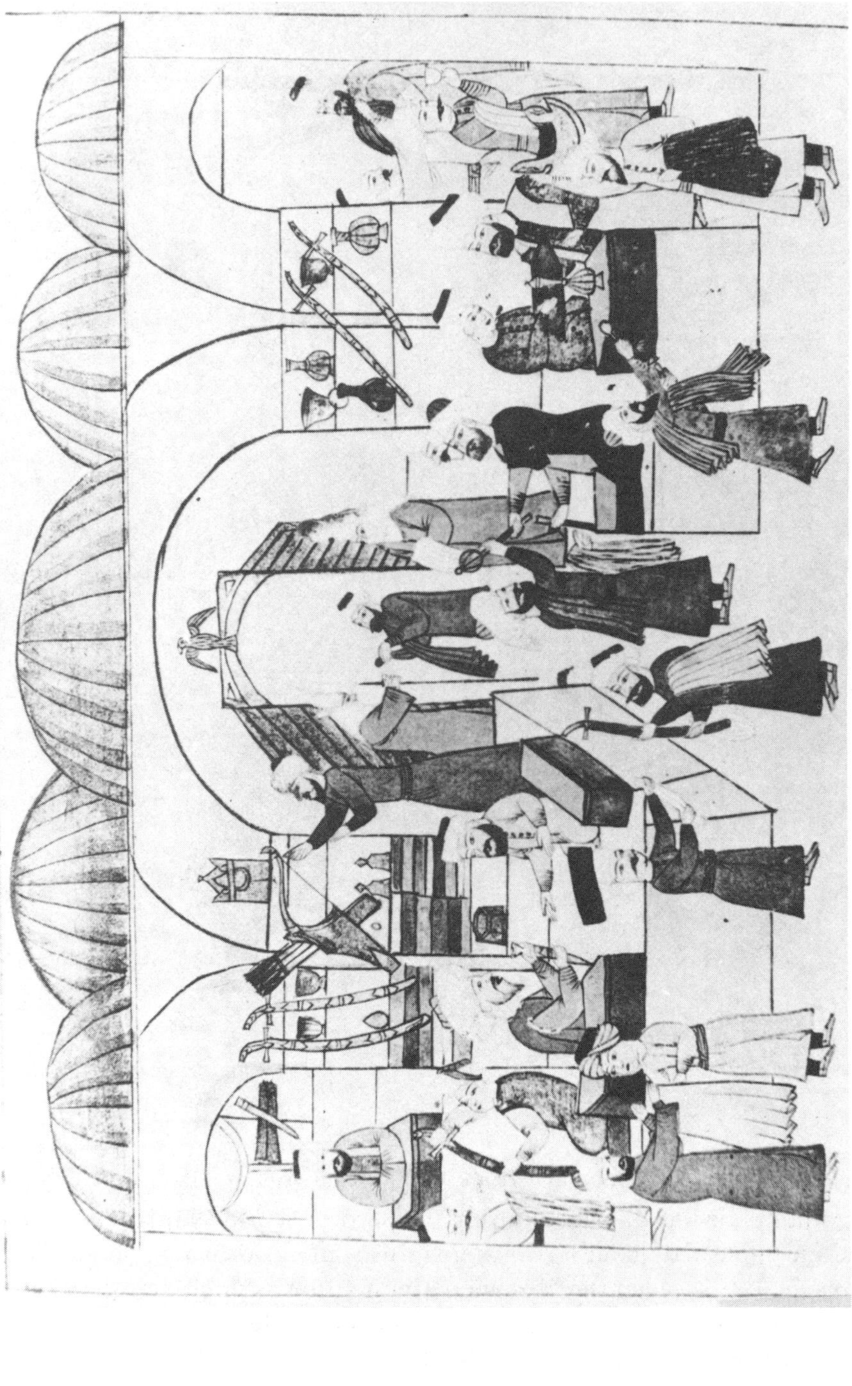

Figure 28.10. Market (*bezistan*) in Istanbul, from the Täschner Album (Hanover, 1925).

it in the Museo Corer, in Venice. In it are depicted some very lively scenes of city life in Istanbul: various shops and shopkeepers in the marketplace; people having coffee at home in front of the fireplace; pipe-smoking; fires in Istanbul destroying a section of the city; and men and women shopping at the Avrat Pazarı near the Column of Arcadius, where fresh fruits and flowers were sold.

In the seventeenth century, among the new subjects depicted in Turkish miniatures were representations of common people, by themselves or together with high-ranking people, shown in various aspects of their daily lives. In these miniatures, the influence of Western art becomes stylistically more noticeable. Levnī from Edirne and Abdullah Buharī are the most prominent artists of the time, and their works could be a topic for further research. The most famous works of this period are *Hamseī Ataī*, copies of which are to be found in the Topkapı Palace Museum (R. 816), the Turkish and Islamic Museum in Istanbul (no. 1969), and Baltimore, Walters Art Gallery (666); and the *Zenennamah*, of which there are copies in the British Library in London (Or. 7094), in the Edwin Binney Collection (no. 80), and in the Istanbul University Library (T. 5502).[36]

Scenes of daily life increased in number during the eighteenth century, but in the nineteenth century miniature paintings were replaced by Western European-style large-scale works, and the subject-matter of European painting was adopted.

NOTES

1. N. Atasoy, "Türk Minyatüründe Tarihi Gerçekçilik," *Sanat Tarihi Yıllığı*, I (1965), pp. 103–09; and "The Documentary Value of Turkish Miniatures," *Quatrième congrès international d'art turc (Aix-en-Provence, 10–15 septembre 1971)* (1976), pp. 11–17.

2. A. Grünwedel, *Altbuddhische Kultstaetten in Chinesisch-Turkistan (3. Expedition)* (Berlin, 1912); A. von Le Loq, *Chotscho, Königlich-Preussische Turfan-Expedition (2. Expedition)* (Berlin, 1913); A. von Le Loq, *Bilderatlas zur Kunst und Kulturgeschichte Mittelasiens* (Berlin, 1925); Sir A. Stein, *Innermost Asia* (Oxford, 1928); M. Bussagli, *Die Malerei in Zentralasien* (Geneva, 1963); E. Esin, "Central Asian Turkish Painting Before Islam," *Studies on Pre-Islamic Turkish Art* (Istanbul, 1972), pp. 186–311.

3. A. Ateş, "Un Vieux Poème romanesque persan: Recit de Warkah et Gulshah," *Ars Orientalis* IV (1961), pp. 143–52; A. S. Melikian-Chirvani, "Le Roman de Varqe et Gulsah," *Ars Asiatique* XXII (1970); M. K. Özergin, "Sel-

çuklu Sanatçısı Nakkaş Abdülmü'min el Hoyi Hakkında," *Belleten* XXXIV, no. 134 (April 1970), pp. 119–230.

4. I. Stchoukine, *La Peinture turque d'après les manuscrits illustrés* (Paris, 1966), I, 13–21, 45–50; E. Atıl, "Ottoman Miniature Painting Under Sultan Mehmet II," *Ars Orientalis*, IX (1973), pp. 103–20; E. Atıl, *Turkish Art* (Washington, D.C., 1980), pp. 137–239.

5. Filiz Çağman, "Sultan Mehmet II Dönemine ait bir Minyatürlü Yazma: Külliyat-ı Kâtibî," *Sanat Tarihi Yıllığı* (Istanbul, 1976), VI, 333–47.

6. N. Atasoy and F. Çağman, *Turkish Miniature Painting* (Istanbul, 1974), Plate I; F. Çağman, "Türk Minyatüründen Örnekler," *The Turkish Contribution to Islamic Arts* (Istanbul, 1976), pp. 84–88; F. Çağman, *Anatolian Civilizations III (Catalogue of the Council of Europe XVIIIth European Art Exhibition May 22–October 30, 1983)* (Istanbul, 1983), p. 110.

7. Atasoy and Çağman, *Turkish Miniature Painting*, Plate 20; Atıl, *Turkish Art*, Illustration no. 86.

8. S. Ünver, *Ressam Nigari, Hayatı, Eserleri* (Istanbul, 1949); F. Çağman, "Türk Minyatüründen Örnekler," Plate 16; Atıl, *Turkish Art*, Illustration 85; Çağman, *Anatolian Civilizations* III, p. 110.

9. A. Welch and C. Welch, *Arts of the Islamic Book: The Collection of Prince Sadruddin Aga Khan* (Ithaca and London, 1982), Illustration 6, and Plate II.

10. Atıl, *Turkish Art*, Illustration 97; Çağman, *Anatolian Civilizations* III, pp. 175–76.

11. E. Binney, *Turkish Treasures from the Collection of Edwin Binney*, 3d ed. (Portland, 1979), p. 23.

12. N. Anafarta, *Topkapı Sarayı Padişah Portreleri* (Istanbul, 1966); N. Atasoy, "Nakkaş Osman'ın Padişah Portreleri Albümü," *Türkiyemiz*, VI (1972), pp. 2–4.

13. Ş. Rado, Y. Öztuna, and K. Holter, facsimile from Vienna, *Österr. National-bibl. Cod., A.F. 50* (Istanbul, 1968); T. al-Samman and D. Duda, *Kultur des Islam, Ausstellung der Handschriften- und Inkunabelsammlung der österreichischen Nationalbibliothek* (Vienna, 1980), pp. 248–50; G. Renda, "New Light on the Painters of the *Zübdet-al Tawarikh* in the Museum of Turkish and Islamic Arts in Istanbul," in *Quatrième Congrès international d'art turc* (1976), pp. 183–200; G. Renda, "Istanbul Türk ve Islam Eserleri Müzesindeki Zübdet-üt Tevarih'in Minyatürleri," *Sanat* (June 1977), pp. 58–67.

14. Stchoukine, *La Peinture turque d'après les manuscrits illustrés*, I, Plate XXXI.

15. N. Anafarta, *Hünername Minyatürleri ve Sanatçıları* (Istanbul, 1966), Plate V.

16. Ibid., Plate XL; Atasoy and Çağman, *Turkish Miniature Painting*, Plate XXIV.

17. Atasoy and Çağman, *Turkish Miniature Painting*, Plate XXVII.

18. Stchoukine, *La Peinture turque*, I, Plate LX; Atasoy and Çağman, *Turkish Miniature Painting*, PL. XXVIII.

19. Stchoukine, *La Peinture turque*, Plate LXI.

20. Atasoy and Çağman, *Turkish MIniature Painting*, Plate XVI; A. I. Sabra, "The Scientific Enterprise," *The World of Islam*, ed. B. Lewis (London, 1976), pp. 193, 200; Atıl, *Turkish Art*, Illustration 94.

21. Stchoukine, *La Peinture turque*; R. Ettinghausen, *Turkish Miniatures from the 13th to the 18th Century* (New York, 1965), Plates XVIII–XXI; Atasoy and Çağman, *Turkish Miniature Painting*, Plate XXI; M. Ş. Ipşiroğlu, *Masterpieces from the Topkapı Museum: Paintings and Miniatures* (London, 1980), Plates XLIII–XLV.

22. Binney, *Turkish Treasures*, Illustration 27.

23. Ibid., p. 26.

24. Ibid., Illustration 36.

25. Stchoukine, *La Peinture turque*, II, Plate I.

26. Ibid., II, Plate XXXII.

27. Atıl, *Turkish Art*, Illustration 97, p. 203.

28. Stchoukine, *La Peinture turque*, I, Plate CI.

29. Ibid., II, Plate XCV.

30. Atıl, *Turkish Art*, Illustration 93.

31. Ibid., Illustration 99.

32. Ibid., Plate XXX.

33. Stchoukine, *La Peinture turque*, II, Plate LIX; Atasoy and Çağman, *Turkish Miniature Painting*, Plate XLII; F. Çağman and Z. Akalın, *Topkapı Saray Museum Islamic Miniature Painting* (Istanbul, 1979), Figure 63.

34. G. Renda, *Batılılaşma Döneminde Türk Resim Sanatı, 1700–1850* (Ankara, 1977), pp. 30–31; Çağman and Akalın, *Topkapı Saray Museum Islamic Miniature Painting*, Figure 64.

35. F. Täschner, *Alt Stambuler Hof- und Volksleben, ein türkisches Miniaturalben aus dem 17. Jahrhundert* (Hanover, 1925).

36. F. Gabrieli, *Mohammed in Europa, 1300 Jahre Geschichte, Kunst, Kultur* (Munich, 1982), pp. 120, 121, 122, 130.

29

Mamlūk Military Aristocracy During the First Years of the Ottoman Occupation of Egypt

David Ayalon

THE EXPANSION OF the Ottomans into the lands of Islam in the second decade of the sixteenth century brought about one of the most profound changes which ever took place within the boundaries of those lands. A major victim of that expansion was the Mamlūk Sultanate, which was wiped out as its territories were incorporated into the Ottoman Empire. Reconstructing the process of transition from Mamlūk to Ottoman rule is essential for various reasons, not the least of them being the fact that the Mamlūk Sultanate was the leading Muslim power until the time of its extinction.

As far as Egypt, the main country of that Sultanate, is concerned, we are lucky to have the superb chronicle of Ibn Iyās, which continues six years into the Ottoman conquest. It is a mine of first-class information on various subjects. For drawing a full picture of that process of transition, all the available sources have, of course, to be consulted. None of them, however, can match that of Ibn Iyās. Furthermore, until now that source has not been sufficiently used, while its data have not been examined and interpreted against the background of the pre-Ottoman period in Egypt.

The following lines will deal with the policy of the Ottomans toward the Mamlūks of Egypt in the period covered by our source.[1]

The Ottoman conquest of Egypt was, on the whole, quite orderly and lenient; barring a few exceptions, it was not accompanied by persecution and plundering of the civilian population. The life and property of civilians were safeguarded, so long as they did not cooperate with the Mamlūks.[2] Ottoman policy toward the Mamlūks and their collaborators was, however, completely different, particularly during the period immediately following the conquest. On the eve of the battle of al-Raydānīya, in the approaches of Cairo (Dhū 'l-Ḥijja 922/January 1517), Sultan Selīm I (918–926/1512–1520), who headed the conquering Ottoman army, declared that he would not return to his capital before having conquered Egypt and annihilated all its Circassian Mamlūks.[3] As soon as the Ottomans entered Cairo, they embarked on a large-scale search and hunt for the Mamlūks, and whenever they caught one, they immediately cut off his head.[4] At the same time, they announced that any civilian who hid a Circassian Mamlūk would be hanged over his own doorstep.[5] Most of the captured Mamlūks were transported to the Ottoman sultan's camp in al-Raydānīya, and beheaded. After having executed a very great number of Mamlūks in this way, the Ottomans erected poles, and connected them with ropes, from which they dangled the cut-off heads. The number of those executed by the Ottomans from among the Mamlūks, the bedouins (*'urbān*), and the Mamlūks' manservants (*ghilmān*)[6] in the first few days after their victory was about 4,000.[7] In the next few days, they executed another 800 Mamlūks of all ranks.[8] They also executed in the Alexandria prison[9] the former sultan al-Ẓāhir Qānṣūh (904–05/1498–99), fearing that the Mamlūks might proclaim him their king.[10] Mamlūks of all ranks who did not try to go into hiding, and who gave themselves up voluntarily, were chained and dispatched to Alexandria, and thence to Constantinople. Their number was 700 or more.[11] On Rabī' I 923/April 1517, a group of fifty-four Mamlūk commanders (emirs) of various ranks was transported to al-Raydānīya, where all of them were beheaded.[12] After the battle of Wardān[13] (Rabī' I 923/April 1517), in which the last Mamlūk sultan Ṭūmānbāy[14] was defeated and captured (and later executed), the Ottomans once again carried out a great slaughter of the Circassian Mamlūks and their allies. Eight hundred cut-off heads of these Mamlūks and bedouins were dispatched to Cairo. The rest were thrown into the Nile near the field of battle.[15] Ottoman soldiers married the wives of the executed Mamlūks, despite the explicit prohibition of the Ottoman *qāḍī*, and with the full assistance of the local *qāḍīs*.[16]

There is no way to estimate the number or proportion of the Mamlūks killed by Sultan Selīm, for we do not know the total number of the Mamlūks at that time.[17] That the proportion was very high can be learned from the fact that Ibn Iyās, in his summing up of the life of Sultan Selīm, on the occasion of the death of that monarch several years *after* the massacre, states that he killed most of the Circassian Mamlūks (*qatala ghālib ʿaskar Miṣr min al-mamālīk al-jarākisa*).[18] It should also be remembered, in this connection, that just before these massacres the Mamlūks must have suffered very heavy casualties at Marj Dābiq (August 1516) and al-Raydānīya (January 1517), two of the bloodiest battles in their entire history.

In this period of an all-out war of extermination and expulsion which the Ottomans waged on the Circassian Mamlūks, the sons of those Mamlūks (*awlād al-nās*) fared much better than their fathers. The Ottomans wanted at first to kill them off as well, but after having been told that these were not Mamlūks, they contented themselves with a money ransom.[19] Out of fear that they would be mistaken for Mamlūks, the *awlād al-nās* discarded the typical Mamlūk headgear of the time, the *takhfīfa* hats (pl. *takhāfīf*) and the *zamṭ* hats (pl. *zumūṭ*),[20] and wore, instead, the *ʿimāma*, the headgear typical of ecclesiastics, that is, the educated Muslims of nonmilitary class.[21] This practice of changing from the headgear which until very recently had been the most prestigious, to a headgear worn by a class which was lower in the social ladder was adopted not only by the sons of the simple Mamlūks, but also by the sons of the Mamlūk commanders (emirs) and even by the sons of the Mamlūk sultans. Henceforth the use of *takhāfīf* and *zumuṭ* ceased completely in Egypt.[22]

Simultaneously with the destruction of the Mamlūk army and the physical annihilation of a very substantial portion of its elite units, Sultan Selīm dismantled the country's armaments. He confiscated the arsenals of Alexandria,[23] and transferred the heavy artillery of the Cairo citadel to Istanbul.[24]

The first change for the better in the Ottoman policy toward the Circassians took place on 21 Shaʿbān 923/9 September 1517, on the very eve of Sultan Selīm's departure from Egypt (23 Shaʿbān/11 September), for Istanbul. Khāyrbak, the newly appointed viceroy of Egypt, released fifty-four Mamlūk emirs who had been incarcerated in the Daylam prison of Cairo.[25] At the end of the same month, immediately after the departure of Sultan Selīm (who left behind him an Ottoman garrison of 5,000 horsemen and 500 arquebusiers),[26] Khāyrbak proclaimed a general amnesty to those Circassians who were in hiding. These men emerged from their hiding places in pitiable condition, wearing tattered *fellah* clothing.[27] A greater shame and disgrace, according to their own standards, could hardly have been inflicted upon them.

In mid-Ramaḍān of the same year (early October 1517), the viceroy permitted them to ride horses and to buy arms, shortly after he himself had forbidden them to do so.[28] This far-reaching measure of reinstating the Mamlūks as a military power in Egypt was taken by Khāyrbak in spite of the stiff opposition of the Ottoman soldiers, who tried to derive advantage from this dispute with the viceroy by demanding from him feudal fiefs (*iqṭā'āt*), and all the other kinds of payments which the Mamlūks were accustomed to receive during the Mamlūk Sultanate. Khāyrbak refused to meet their request, on the ground that only the Ottoman sultan had the authority to do so.[29] On 23 Dhū 'l-Qa'da of the same year (7 November 1517), when pay for the Circassian Mamlūks was proclaimed, they appeared from all directions, their number exceeding 5,000![30] It would appear that the greatest, and perhaps also final, emergence of the Mamlūks from their hiding took place around this last-mentioned date. In the six weeks separating the general amnesty from the pay announcement, many of the Mamlūks seem to have remained wary and hesitant. However, their inclusion in the payroll must have removed any remaining doubts in their minds about the seriousness and durability of the amnesty. In Rabī' I 924/February 1518, Khāyrbak received an order from Sultan Selīm to pay a monthly salary (*jāmakīya*), "according to the old custom" (*'alā al-'āda*) to the Circassian Mamlūks and the *awlād al-nās*.[31] In the same month the viceroy appointed over every twenty Mamlūks one of their own commanders (*aghawāt*) of previous times[32] as their supervisor. A main duty of those *aghawāt* was to insure that all the Mamlūks under their supervision should report for duty when called upon to take part in military campaigns.[33] In Jumādā I of the same year (May 1518), the Circassian Mamlūks were already taking part in quelling the mutiny of the Ottoman Sipahi and Janissary regiments.[34] There is no doubt that the unruliness and quarrels of the Ottoman units stationed in Egypt greatly facilitated the task of the reestablishment of the Mamlūks. During the years 924–26/1518–20, the Circassian Mamlūks and *awlād al-nās* took part in three military campaigns: two to Red Sea destinations (Jidda;[35] Ayla and Aznam[36]), and one to a Mediterranean destination (Alexandria[37]). The purpose of all three of these expeditions was defense against the Franks.

With the death of Sultan Selīm, and the accession of his son, Sultan Suleyman the Magnificent (926–74/1520–66) to the throne,[38] the position of the Circassian Mamlūks improved greatly. Khāyrbak tried to please and conciliate them much more than he had done before. He paid them two months' *jāmakīya* all at once. The general attitude toward them had also changed completely. Whereas until then people would call them "O dogs! O [inferior type of] shoes!" (*yā kilāb yā zarābīl*) they now began to address them saying "O masters!" (*yā aghawāt*). Our source concludes: "Once the Circassian Mamlūks heard of the death of Sultan Selīm, their [fallen] crests became erect" (*wa-qad aqāmat al-mamālīk al-Jarākisa ṣudūrahā min ḥīn sami'ū bi-mawt Salīm Shāh ibn 'Uthmān*).[39] Sultan Suleyman did, indeed, firmly refuse to allow those Circassian emirs and Mamlūks who had been exiled to Istanbul to return to Egypt together with the other exiles, who were permitted to do so.[40] But on the other hand, he informed the viceroy through a personal emissary (who arrived in Cairo in Rajab 928/June 1522) that he would like to include a special contingent of Circassian Mamlūks, with their emirs, in the campaign which he was planning for the reconquest of the island of Rhodes.[41] The Egyptian expeditionary force to Rhodes numbered 1,500 men, of whom 500 or 800 were Circassians. The rest were Ottoman units of the Sipahis, Janissaries, and the Gönüllü. The Circassians had their own commander, while all the other Ottoman units were under another commander.[42] In Rhodes, Sultan Suleyman, who was personally in command of the besieging army, welcomed the Circassians warmly, and praised them highly. He deplored his father's policy toward them, describing it as unwise, and declared: "Is it possible that Mamlūks such as these would be killed?" (*istaqalla 'aql wālidihi Salīm Shāh alladhī qatala al-mamālīk al-Jarākisa wa-qāla mithla hādhihi al-mamālīk tuqtal*).[43]

Payments

One of the most reliable yardsticks for examing the attitude of the Ottoman authorities toward the defeated Mamlūks is their policy of payment to them in comparison with other units. This requires us to list these units. Our author mentions seven "bodies" or "groups" (*ṭawā'if*, sing. *ṭā'ifa*), which he gives in the following order: (a) Ottoman emirs; (b) *Sipahis* (cavalry); (c) Janissaries (infantry); (d) Gönüllü (volunteer cavalry); (e) Circassian emirs; (f) Circassian Mamlūks; (g) the Mamlūks of the viceroy.[44] The commanders of the Sipahis, Janissaries, Gönüllü (in Ibn Iyās's transcription, *Kamūlīya*) were called *aghawāt*.[45]

Whatever was left of the Mamlūk army after its defeat and decimation was divided into two categories: the Circassian Mamlūks and the *awlād al-nās*. The latter are not mentioned among the groups enumerated in the above list, and it would appear that for purposes of payment they and the Circassian Mamlūks were considered as one group,[46] even though the pay of the *awlād al-nās* was much less (see below).

According to the list provided by our author, the Circasians occupied only the fifth and sixth places among the units of the Ottoman army stationed in Egypt. The *awlād al-nās*, who were passed over in silence in that list, fared even worse. They gradually lost their feudal fiefs through a series of decrees and of arbitrary acts of injustice.[47] Once the Mamlūks had been granted amnesty and partially restored, the only thing which could befall the *awlād al-nās* was a more rapid decline. It is true that Sultan Selīm, on his return to his capital, ordered that they be paid a monthly salary (*jāmakīya*), but this was an extremely small one, ranging from two-thirds of a dinar to one dinar to two dinars.[48] This means that even the highest-paid among them received a salary three and a half times smaller than that of an ordinary Circassian Mamlūk, whereas the salary of lowest-paid among them was ten and a half times smaller.[49] As for the Circassians, the Ottomans continued to pay them exactly the same *jāmakīya* which they used to receive in the latter part of the Mamlūk Sultanate, namely, 2,000 dirhams, or seven dinars.[50] But neither they nor the other Ottoman units are said by our source to have received, in addition to the *jāmakīya*, the entire wide range of payments which they used to receive before the Ottoman conquest.[51] It is true that in Shawwāl 926/September 1520, a letter from Sultan Selīm arrived in Cairo, ordering the viceroy to pay the Circassian Mamlūks not only the *jāmakīya*, but other payments as well, such as their meat and fodder allowances "in accordance with the old usage" (*'alā al-'āda al-qadīma*).[52] Ibn Iyās, however, informs us on a later occasion that the Mamlūk's *jāmakīya* also included the pay for the meat ration,[53] which might imply that the sultan's order was not strictly observed.[54]

The monthly salaries of the Mamlūk emirs were: emir *ṭablkhāna*, forty dinars; "emir of ten," twenty-five dinars. In the case of these officers, it is specifically stated that they were granted this salary in lieu of their fiefs and their meat and fodder rations.[55] It is significant that the top rank of Mamlūk emīrs, the "emir of a hundred," completely disappears under the Ottomans in the period covered by Ibn Iyās (in the Mamlūk Sultanate the official number of emirs of that rank was twenty-four, but in fact it underwent considerable fluctuation).[56]

As for the various Ottoman units stationed in Egypt, their monthly salaries were as follows: (a) Sipahis. These were divided into several groups according to the amount of their pay. The salary of a soldier belonging to the group in the highest income bracket was sixty dinars. That of a soldier in the lowest income bracket was twenty dinars. (b) Janissaries. Most of them received fifteen dinars, and the rest only twelve dinars. (c) The *Ṣūbāshīya*, who, according to Ibn Iyās, were the heads (*aghawāt*) of the Janissaries,[57] received thirty dinars. (d) The Gönüllü. The majority of them received twelve dinars, and the rest, ten or eight dinars. (e) Circassian Mamlūks: seven dinars.[58]

The total monthly payment to each of those groups was: Sipahis, 11,000 dinars; Janissaries, 13,000 dinars; Gönüllü, 11,000 dinars; Circassian Mamlūks and *awlād al-nās*, 11,000 dinars; the Mamlūks of the viceroy and his retinue, 13,000.[59]

The above figures are very instructive in several ways. First of all, they make it abundantly clear that the Circassian Mamlūks at this stage occupied the bottom of the pay scale. Not less significant is the fact that some of the Ottoman horsemen received salaries which were 50 percent higher than the salaries of the highest-ranking Mamlūk emirs. Unfortunately, we know practically nothing about the salaries of the Ottoman commanders. It is also interesting that the total sums received by the various units were so similar in size. The above figures also indicate the already strong position of the Mamlūks of the viceroy, who received a total sum greater than that received by the rest of the Circassian Mamlūks and the *awlād al-nās*. There is no indication, however, that the monthly salary of a single Mamlūk of the viceroy was higher than that of another Mamlūk.

These payments to the army weighed very heavily on the depleted economic resources of the country, according to our source.[60] Payments were not made regularly; the accumulation of debts to the army increased steadily, and became a chronic phenomenon.[61] Under such conditions, the Mamlūks, and in particular the *awlād al-nās*, were the first to suffer. In Muḥarram 928/December 1521, during a pay parade to the Circassians, the viceroy declared that only those who intended to take part in the military expedition would be paid. He then summoned the Circassians one by one to his presence, and chose the youngest and strongest out of every ten, to join the military expedition.

In the same parade, he struck off the payroll 1,000 Circassian Mamlūks and *awlād al-nās*, among whom there were respected veteran Mamlūks of Sultan Qāytbāy (873–901/1468–95).[62] In Jumādā II of the same year (May 1522), he cut in half the salaries of numerous Circassians and *awlād al-nās*, and pensioned them off. The number of those pensioned off included young, vigorous men, capable of taking part in a campaign.[63] In Rajab (June) of the same year, he cut in half the salary of twenty emirs of *ṭablkhāna* and emirs of ten.[64]

The Ottomanization of the Mamlūk Aristocracy

The incorporation of the Mamlūks into the Ottoman army, described above, served as the basis of the Ottomanization of that aristocracy, within the framework of the Ottomanization of the entire military, administrative, and judicial apparatus. Ibn Iyās gives a detailed description of that process (especially if one takes into account the short period involved), and, on the whole, a very reliable one. But whereas one can find no reason to contest his facts, so far as they are restricted to his own time, his evaluation of those facts is quite often, though by no means always, open to criticism. There were, in my view, two principal, closely connected, reasons for Ibn Iyās's weakness in this respect. First of all, as a man who had been brought up in, and who had lived in the Mamlūk Sultanate, which was so fundamentally different from the Ottoman Empire, he, like so many of his compatriots, could not understand some of the basic, positive aspects of that empire. Second, he was a partisan of the defunct Sultanate, and a bitter antagonist of the new rulers.

Ibn Iyās was by no means a panegyrist of the Mamlūk aristocracy and of Mamlūk rule in general. Indeed, the very opposite is true. Like most of the historians of the Circassian period (784–922/1382–1517), he depicts a very gloomy picture of the Sultanate, and does not mince words in severely criticizing it.[65] However, as soon as the Mamlūks have been overpowered by the Ottomans, he almost completely forgets all the evils of the *ancien régime*, which he himself had so frequently exposed and castigated, and embarks on an idealization of that regime, turning all his fury against the newcomers. But for all Ibn Iyās's subjectiveness, one cannot say that he lacks insight into some of the fundamental differences between the two regimes.

In comparison with the pomp and the complicated ceremonial of the Mamlūk court, and the lavish way of life of the Mamlūks, the

Ottomans of that time seem still to have been lacking in polish and refinement. The urban population of Egypt, and particularly that of Cairo, which was not accustomed to such simplicity, was very adversely affected by the crudeness of its new rulers. Ibn Iyās epitomizes that prevalent feeling in the following, most revealing, short statement: "Sultan Selīm did not follow in Egypt the rules and patterns of the previous sultans of that country. Neither he, nor his high-ranking officials, nor his commanders, nor his army, had an acknowledged order. They were [all] barbarians and savages. One could not distinguish among them between the master and his servant" (*wa-lā mashā Salīm Shāh fī Miṣr 'alā qawā'id al-salāṭīn al-sālifa bi-Miṣr wa-lam yakun lahu niẓām yu'rafu lā huwa wa-lā wuzarāyihi* [sic!] *wa-lā umarāyihi* [sic!] *wa-lā 'askarihi bal kānū hamaj lā yu'rafu al-ghulām min al-ustādh*).[66] The degree of shock and aversion caused by the unfamiliar Ottoman way of government and way of life is demonstrated by Ibn Iyās's frequent repetitions of this same derogatory statement in similar words.[67]

Among the things which particularly antagonized the local population were the Ottomans' being clean-shaven (*ḥalq al-dhuqūn*), or, at most, wearing short beards; their wearing the *ṭarṭūr* headgear;[68] their habit of eating on horseback in the streets of the capital; and, above all, their public disregard of some of the basic ordinances of the Muslim religion (especially their drinking wine, their eating during the fast of Ramaḍān—both perpetrated publicly—and their refraining from participation in prayers in the mosques).[69] A longing for the splendor and stateliness of the regime which had so recently expired is reflected in almost every page of our chronicle.[70]

As far as military matters (including matters connected with military ceremony) were concerned, the population felt particular sorrow and nostalgia at the abolition of the *furūsīya* exercises and games, which had constituted the foundation of Mamlūk military training,[71] and which had included polo (*kura*), and exercises with the lance (*rumḥ*) and mace (*dabbūs*), etc.;[72] the abolition of the orchestras (*kūsāt*) which used to play in front of the gates of the Mamlūk emirs' houses;[73] and the disappearance of the sumptuous Mamlūk costume, such as the *kalafta* hat, the *qabā'* coat, the *takhfīfa* headgear, the beaver (*qundus*) fur, the red *zamṭ* hat, the robes of honor (*al-tashārīf wa'l-muthammar*), the spurs (*mihmāz*), and the *khuff* boots.[74]

As for the dress of the Circassian Mamlūks in the years under study, it was subjected to the following developments (or, more exactly, changes) in the Ottomans' attitude toward the Mamlūks. In Ramaḍān

923/September–October 1517, that is, immediately after the announcement of a general amnesty for the Circassians, they were ordered to wear *zamṭ* hats and *mallūṭa* (pl. *malālīṭ*) coats,[75] exactly as they used to do under their own sultans. The reason for this order was that numerous Circassians, like the soldiers of the Ottoman army, wore caftans (*qafṭānāt*) and turbans (*'amā'im*), and enjoyed, like them, the privilege of robbing the merchandise and snatching off the headgear of passers-by.[76] It would appear, however, that this order was not strictly observed. For as early as Dhū 'l-Qa'da of that year (November–December 1517), we are informed that the Circassian Mamlūks and emirs wore velvet (*mukhmal*) and woollen (*jūkh*) caftans, woollen *ṭarṭūrs*, round turbans (*'amā'im*) and leather *suqmān* shoes, as did the Ottomans. As a result, the Mamlūks became confused with the Ottomans to such a degree as to make it impossible to distinguish between them. They could only be distinguished by the Mamlūks' having beards and the Ottomans' being beardless (*wa-ṣārat al-mamālīk tu'rafu bi-dhuqūnihim wa'l-'Uthmānīya bi-ghayr dhuqūn*).[77] This shows how difficult it was for the Mamlūks to part with their beards, despite the great incentive they had for doing so (see also below). In Shawwāl 927/September 1521, the viceroy issued an order rescinding that of October 1517. According to this order, Mamlūks, Ottomans, and *awlād al-nās* were forbidden to wear the red *zamṭ* hat (which, as mentioned earlier in this paper, was the typical headgear of the Mamlūks in the final decades of their reign). Those who would not obey that order were warned that they would be sent to the gallows without the right of appeal. At the same time, the viceroy prohibited the Circassian emirs from wearing the Mamlūk *sarmūja* shoe, especially on their visits to the seat of government in the Citadel. Our author's comment on this order is that it was issued because of the viceroy's deep-seated hatred of all the Circassians (*wa-hādhā kulluhu 'ayn al-maqt lil-Jarākisa wa-bughḍan lahum qāṭibatan*).[78] In the following month, the Circassian amirs and *khāṣṣakīya* were forbidden to have their servant (*ghulām*) ride behind them on a mule when they rode their horses (as had been the Mamlūk custom), and ordered them to have him walk on foot in front of his master, in accordance with the Ottoman custom.[79] In Muḥarram 928/December 1521, during the same parade in which the viceroy struck 1,000 Mamlūks and *awlād al-nās* out of the payroll, he stepped toward each long-bearded Mamlūk, cut off about half his beard with his own hand, handed it over to the Mamlūk, and said to him: "Follow the Ottoman rules in cutting your beards, in making the sleeves of your dresses narrow, *and in everything which the Ottomans do*" (*imshū 'alā al-qānūn al-'uthmānī fī qaṣṣ al-liḥā wa-taḍyīq al-akmām wa-kullamā yaf'alūnahu al-'Uthmānīya*).[80]

Khāyrbak's persecution of the Circassian Mamlūks[81] and *awlād al-nās*, together with his deliberate policy of Ottomanization, should not be interpreted as an attempt on his part to exterminate the Mamlūks as such. What he really intended to do was to foster, strengthen, and increase the number of *his own* freedmen (i.e., Mamlūks purchased and manumitted by himself), at the expense of other Mamlūks who owed allegiance to other patrons. In this respect, he had only to follow the old established custom of the Mamlūk sultans, each of whom, on acceding to the throne, used to weaken the Mamlūks of his predecessor by various means, including expelling them from the barracks (*ṭibāq*, sing. *ṭabaqa*) of the Cairo citadel, and stationing his own Mamlūks in those barracks, while attempting to increase the number of his own Mamlūks by all means available to him.[82] We have already seen how strong Khāyrbak's Mamlūks and retinue had become, and how substantial was their portion of the monthly payments. On the occasion of his death we learn that he, like all the Mamlūk sultans, kept his Mamlūks near his person in the *ṭibāq* of the citadel. All of them were removed from there a fortnight after his death, even *before* the arrival of his successor Muṣṭafā Pasha. Ottoman units replaced Khāyrbak's Mamlūks in the citadel.[83] In all probability, Khāyrbak kept the citadel to himself and to his own Mamlūks throughout his viceroyalty. There is no mention of Mamlūks of other patrons, nor of any kind of Ottoman soldiery being stationed there during that period.

Khāyrbak's determination to strengthen his own and his Mamlūks' position can be gauged from the immense fortune which he accumulated, in spite of the very short period of his reign (*fī hādhihi al-mudda al-yasīra*). More than 600,000 dinars were found in his private possession, in addition to the unspecified amount found in the coffers of the Treasury (*bayt al-māl*). On top of this, he left immense quantities of movable property, which exceeded those left by his patron the great Sultan Qāytbāy, who had ruled almost thirty years (873–901/1468–95), as compared to the rule of his Mamlūk Khāyrbak, which lasted little more than five years.[84] Khāyrbak succeeded in accumulating this fabulous fortune in a time of severe economic crisis by, among other means, his refusal to pay the money due to those Mamlūks who were not his own freedmen, and to those Ottoman units which he disliked.[85]

Whereas Jānbirdī al-Ghazālī tried to obstruct and curb the Ottomanization of his Syrian province as best he could throughout the greater part of his short reign,[86] Khāyrbak went out of his way to accelerate this process in Egypt in various areas. There seems, however, to have been one focal point which he protected from radical Ottomanization, and this was the Cairo Citadel. It would appear that he wanted to have around his person as much as possible of the atmosphere and people formerly surrounding the Mamlūk sultan, and with which he had grown very familiar both as a Royal Mamlūk in the *ṭabaqa* and as Grand Emir. However, his attempt to preserve the Mamlūk character of the Citadel was crushed soon after his death, in two swift stages. In the first stage his own Mamlūks were replaced there by Ottoman units, as has just been mentioned. About a month later, as we are informed by Ibn Iyās,

> The viceroy [Muṣṭafā Pasha] took the keys of all the storehouses and depots (*ḥawāṣil*) from the doorkeepers (*bawwābūn*), and handed them over to a group of Ottomans (*Arwām*) of his own retinue, and drove away all the doormen, servants, grooms, jockeys, attendants, and others. He even dismissed the cooks of the Royal Kitchen and the water carriers, and replaced all these by Ottomans (*Arwām*). He also fired all the Qur'ān readers in the Citadel, as well as all the muezzins, and appointed just one muezzin to the mosque of al-Ḥawsh. In short, *he abolished the entire old system of the Citadel, and introduced* [in its stead] *the order of the Ottomans, which is the most evil of all orders (abṭala jamī' niẓām al-qal'a alladhī kānat 'alayhi qadīman wa-mashā 'alā al-qānūn al-'uthmānī alladhī huwa ashyam* [sic!] *qānūn).*[87]

The Ottomanization of the Cairo Citadel was thus accomplished within six weeks of Khāyrbak's death. The importance of this measure can hardly be overestimated, for the Citadel constituted the focal point of the entire Mamlūk Sultanate, as well as of the capital, from which it was dominated, and contributed much more than any other structure to the shaping of Mamlūk aristocracy. In order to uproot the old system, the Ottomans had to wipe out all its traces in the place which constituted its very heart. But the Citadel did not lose its focal position under the new rulers. The unfolding of the internal relations of the Mamlūks, as well as their relations with the Ottomans stationed in Cairo, against the background of the Citadel, will always remain one of the major subjects of the study of Ottoman Egypt.

We do not know what happened to the Mamlūks of Khāyrbak after they had been removed from the Citadel. What is absolutely certain is that this did not bring about the end of the Mamlūks in

Egypt. In the short period under discussion there is no reference, in the sources upon which this paper is based, to the importation of new Mamlūks to Egypt. Yet one cannot see how Khāyrbak could strengthen his position without such importation. The attitude of the Ottomans to the bringing over of Mamlūks to Egypt, particularly in the first decades of their rule, is another major subject which awaits systematic study.

To sum up: Mamlūk military aristocracy in Egypt, during the first years of Ottoman occupation, managed, on the one hand, to survive, but underwent a quite thorough process of Ottomanization, on the other. That process was accelerated immediately after Khāyrbak's death, especially by the transformation of the Cairo Citadel into an Ottoman bastion. It is unknown, however, how long the acceleration lasted. What is known for certain is that that aristocracy was relegated to the bottom of the Ottoman socio-military pyramid, and that it rose very little, if at all, from that level in the period covered by Ibn Iyās. In view of the scarcity and the poor quality of most of the historical sources in the period stretching between the end of the chronicle of Ibn Iyās and the beginning of the chronicle of al-Jabartī, any full reconstruction of the growth of Mamlūk power during that period will be very conjectural.[88] Under existing conditions, however, the more thoroughly the chronicle of Ibn Iyās is studied, the better are the chances for making more plausible conjectures, at least about the immediately following years.

NOTES

1. Ibn Iyās, *Badā'i' al-Zuhūr fī waqā'i' al-Duhūr*, ed. P. Kahle, M. Mostafa, and M. Sobernheim (Istanbul, 1931), vol. v. The present paper is a completely revised and enlarged version of a brief survey in Hebrew called "The Mamlūk Army at the Beginning of the Ottoman Conquest," published in *Tarbitz* (Jerusalem, 1952), pp. 221–26. My original intention was to deal with Ottoman policy toward the Mamlūks of Egypt *and* Syria simultaneously, but because of limitations of space, this could not be done. An article that compliments the present one, and which was published in *Studia Islamica*, fascicle 65 (1987), pp. 125–48 under the title "The End of the Mamlūk Sultanate," has the subtitle "Why Did the Ottomans Spare the Mamlūks of Egypt and Wipe out the Mamlūks of Syria?"

2. Upon entering Gaza the Ottoman army did not at first harm the population in any way. Only after the local garrison attacked the Ottomans,

killing 400 of their men, did a great slaughter of the townspeople take place (Ibn Iyās, v, 129, l. 15–130, l. 12). When Sultan Selīm arrived in Bilbays, on his way to Cairo from the Sinai, he issued strict orders not to molest the population. All the people of Bilbays, and the peasants of the neighborhood, welcomed him warmly (Ibn Iyās, v, 138, l. 22–139, l. 1). Upon occupying Cairo, the Ottoman army looted it for three days, but the looting was abruptly stopped by the sultan's order (ibid., v, 144, l. 20–145, l. 16). Although some of the peasants cooperated with the Mamlūks (ibid., v, 139, ll. 14–16; 140, ll. 2–4), most of them were indifferent to the change of government. On the eve of the battle of al-Raydānīya, they refused to pay the rent on cultivated lands (*kharāj*) to their Mamlūk masters, claiming that they had first to know to whom the country was going to belong, to the Mamlūks or to the Ottomans, so that they would not have to pay the rent twice (ibid., v, 130, ll. 20–22).

3. Ibid., v, 121, ll. 18–19. At that period the Ottomans are called *'Uthmānīya, Rūm* (or *Arwām*), and quite frequently *Tarākima* or *Turkmān* (see, for instance, ibid., v, 75, ll. 3–9; 184, ll. 13–17; 206, ll. 20–21; 207, l. 22; 208, l. 2; 231, l. 16; 244, l. 5; 252, ll. 13–14; 254, ll. 15–21; 298, ll. 1–10; 304, ll. 1, 9; 309, l. 13; 310, l. 5; 328, l. 2; 374, ll. 8–14; 481, ll. 20–22). The Mamlūks in this period are usually called *Jarākisa,* but the names *Atrāk* and *Turk* are by no means extinct (see, for instance, ibid., pp. 164, l. 5; 193, l. 2; 272, ll. 3–4). The name *Dawlat al-Turk* or *Dawlat al-Atrāk* is the usual name of the Mamlūk Sultanate, also in the period of Circassian predominance. The name *Turk* as designating the Ottomans or the "Turks" is extremely rare in the Mamlūk reign.

4. Ibn Iyās, v, 145, ll. 18–20; 146, ll. 9–10.

5. Ibid., v, 144, l. 22–145, l. 1.

6. Every Mamlūk usually had two servants, one white-skinned, called *ghulām* (pl. *ghilmān*), the other black, called *'abd* (pl. *'abīd*). The *ghulām* had to perform the less menial tasks.

7. Ibn Iyās, v, 146, ll. 1–16.

8. Ibid., v, 153, ll. 12–17. The executioner (*mashā'ilī*) was, according to our source, a Frank or a Jew from Anatolia (ibid., v, 153, l. 18).

9. The prison of Alexandria was the most important prison of the Mamlūk aristocracy throughout the reign of the Mamlūks.

10. Ibn Iyās, v, 160, ll. 6–17.

11. Ibid., v, 161, ll. 14–22.

12. Ibid., v, 165, l. 16–166, l. 11.

13. Wardān is situated on the western arm of the Nile, to the north of Cairo.

14. Ṭūmānbāy became sultan after Sultan Qānṣūh al-Ghawrī (906–22/1500–1516) was defeated and killed in the battle of Marj Dābiq (August 1516).

15. Ibn Iyās, v, 169, ll. 1–3.

16. Ibid., v, 180, ll. 11–20.

17. On the numbers of the Mamlūks in the Mamlūk Sultanate see my

"Studies on the Structure of the Mamlūk Army," *BSOAS*, xv (1953), pp. 222–28.

18. Ibn Iyās, v, 356, ll. 11–12. According to information arriving in Damascus in Rabīʿ ii 923/May 1517, Sultan Selīm "annihilated the Circassians" (*afnā al-Jarākisa*) (Ibn Ṭūlūn, *Mufākahat al-khillān fī ḥawādith al-zamān* [Cairo, 1964], ii, 60). Such information might, of course, be too much influenced by these still very recent and very exciting events, and would therefore tend to be exaggerated. However, together with Ibn Iyās's detailed account and his summing up in 1520 (just cited), it reflects the very great dimensions of the massacre of the Mamlūks.

19. Ibn Iyās, v, 148, ll. 4–7. The Mamlūk forces stationed in Egypt during the lifetime of the Mamlūk Sultanate were divided into three main parts:

i. The Royal Mamlūks (*al-mamālīk al-sulṭanīya*, very rarely: *mamālīk al-sulṭān*). These were of two categories:

a. The Mamlūks of the ruling sultan (*mushtarawāt, ajlāb*, or *julbān*).

b. Mamlūks who passed from the service of the ruling sultan to the service of other sultans (*mustakhdamūn*). These were divided into two:

1. Mamlūks who passed into the service of the reigning sultan from that of former sultans (*mamālīk al-salāṭin al-mutaqaddima, qarānīṣ* or *qaraniṣa*);

2. Mamlūks who passed into the service of the reigning sultan from that of the emirs, because of the death or dismissal of their masters (*sayfīya*).

ii. The Emirs' Mamlūks (*mamālīk al-umarā', ajnād al-umarā'*).

iii. The troops of the *ḥalqa* (*ajnād al-ḥalqa*), a corps of free, i.e., non-Mamlūk cavalry. There was within the *ḥalqa* a special unit, composed of the sons of the emirs and of the Mamlūks, called *awlād al-nās*. The commanders (*umarā'*, sing. *amīr*) of the Mamlūk army were divided into three basic ranks: (a) Emirs of a hundred; (b) Emirs of forty (also called emirs of (*ṭablkhāna*); (c) Emirs of ten. The overwhelming majority of the emirs rose to their various ranks from a special bodyguard of the sultan, called *khāṣṣakīya*, whose members were chosen mainly from among his own mamlūks. The *ḥalqa* had commanders of its own, called *muqaddamū al-ḥalqa*.

For a detailed discussion of this subject, see my "Studies on the Structure of the Mamlūk Army," *BSOAS*, xv (1953), pp. 203–28, 248–76; xvi (1954), pp. 57–90.

20. L. A. Mayer, *Mamlūk Costume* (Geneva, 1952), index s.v.

21. Ibid.

22. Ibn Iyās, v, 147, ll. 6–9. This is evidence which requires further proof, considering the very short period covered by Ibn Iyās's chronicle.

23. Ibid., v, 183, ll. 13–15.

24. Ibid., v, 186, l. 23–186, l. 5.

25. Ibid., v, 200, l. 21–202, l. 1.

26. Ibid., v, 202, ll. 20–22.

27. Ibid., v, 204, ll. 15–19. According to the historian al-Isḥāqī, Sultan

Selīm allowed the inclusion of the Circassians as a separate unit in the Ottoman garrison, on the eve of his return to his capital, in response to Khāyrbak's request (*Akhbār al-Uwal,* p. 130, ll. 8–17).

28. Ibn Iyās, v, 208, l. 22–209, l. 3.

29. Ibid., v, 209, ll. 3–14.

30. Ibid., v, 220, ll. 1–8.

31. Ibid., v, 240, ll. 3–10.

32. On the *aghawāt* and *aghawāt al-ṭibāq* in the Mamlūk Sultanate, see *L'Esclavage du Mamelouk,* Oriental Notes and Studies, no. 1 (Jerusalem, 1951), index s.v.

33. Ibn Iyās, v, 240, ll. 14–17.

34. Ibid., 251, l. 3–252, l. 14.

35. Ibid., 257, ll. 17–21, 307–9.

36. Ibid., 273, ll. 2–5.

37. Ibid., 325, ll. 14–16.

38. The death of Sultan Selīm caused great rejoicing among the Circassian Mamlūks (ibid., v, 358, ll. 2–6).

39. Ibid., v, 361, l. 12–362, l. 3.

40. Ibid., 358, ll. 13–21.

41. Ibid., 458, ll. 15–17.

42. Ibid., 459, ll. 3–12.

43. Ibid., 470, ll. 7–12.

44. Ibid., 425, ll. 7–20. Cf. references in the following notes, and A. N. Poliak, *Feudalism in Egypt, Syria, Palestine and the Lebanon, 1250–1900* (London, 1939), p. 53 and notes. For information on the units of the Ottoman army see: H. A. R. Gibb and H. Bowen, *Islamic Society and the West* (London, 1950), I, i, and Stanford J. Shaw, *The Financial and Administrative Organization of Ottoman Egypt, 1517–1798* (Princeton, 1962). Khāyrbak, the viceroy (*nā'ib*) of Egypt, also held the title "King of the Emirs" (*malik al-umarā'*). This title was bestowed, in the Mamlūk Sultanate, on some important viceroys of the Syrian provinces. He already had that title as Viceroy of Aleppo under the Mamlūks, and he kept it under the Ottomans, undoubtedly in order to enhance his prestige.

45. Ibn Iyās, v, 313, l. 22; 314, ll. 4–5; 325, l. 4; 329, l. 11; 351, l. 18; 361, ll. 16–17; 427, ll. 1–2; 428, l. 23; 431, l. 22; 481, l. 12; 484, l. 24.

46. Ibid., 425, ll. 22–23.

47. Ibid., 158, l. 22–159, l. 1; 189, ll. 19–20; 249, l. 22–250, l. 3; 287, ll. 16–19.

48. Ibid., 240, ll. 4–10; 305, ll. 7–10.

49. See the immediately following lines.

50. Ibid., 240, ll. 4–10; 242, ll. 16–19; 250, ll. 19–23.

51. In the Mamlūk Sultanate, a Mamlūk who held the rank of simple soldier received, in addition to the income from his feudal fief (*iqṭā'*) the

following payments: (a) the *jāmakīya*, or monthly pay; (b) the *nafaqa*, a payment made irregularly, and especially shortly before a campaign, in order to cover its particular expenses; (c) *nafaqat al-bay'a*, a payment which the mamlūk received upon the accession of a new sultan to the throne; (d) the *kiswa*, or payment for the mamlūk's clothing (given once a year, but possibly twice a year in the early part of Mamlūk rule); (e) the *laḥm*, or meat (given in kind or in money; a daily payment); (f) *aḍḥiya* or *ḍaḥāyā*, sheep for sacrifice (given in kind or in money, once a year, in the month of Dhū al-Ḥijja, on the eve of 'Īd al-Aḍḥā, the Feast of Immolation); (g) *'alīq*, fodder (given in kind or in money, twice a week); (h) *khayl wa-jimāl*, horses and camels (given once or twice a year). The full value of the *nafaqa* (including *nafaqat al-bay'a*) was 100 dinars; that of the *jāmakīya* was seven dinars. All the other payments amounted to several tens of dinars. The income of a Mamlūk emir was, of course, much higher. For a detailed study of this subject, see my "The System of Payment in Mamlūk Military Society," *Journal of Economic and Social History of the Orient*, I (1958), pp. 37–65, 257–96.

52. Ibn Iyās, v, 348, ll. 21–23.

53. Ibid., 404, l. 22–405, l. 1.

54. See, however, ibid., v, 403, ll. 3–5, where the payment for fodder is mentioned in addition to the *jāmakīya*.

55. Ibid., v, 242, ll. 16–19; 250, ll. 9–23.

56. See "Studies on the Structure of the Mamlūk Army," pp. 468–69.

57. Ibn Iyās, v, 362, l. 10. On them see also Gibb and Bowen, op. cit., and Shaw, op. cit., indexes.

58. Ibn Iyās, v, 404, l. 15–405, l. 1. For an important piece of information on the daily pay of the Ottoman army in Egypt see ibid., 486, ll. 9–22.

59. Ibid., v, 425, l. 20–426, l. 1.

60. Ibid., v, 403–5, 424–26.

61. Ibid., v, 251, 273, ll. 13–14; 298, ll. 15–16; 305, l. 7; 448, ll. 16–17; 455, ll. 16–19. It should, however, be remembered that a quite similar situation existed during the greater part of the Circassian period in the Mamlūk Sultanate.

62. Ibid., v, 424, l. 20–425, l. 11.

63. Ibid., v, 448, ll. 17–21.

64. Ibid., v, 453, ll. 13–17.

65. Out of numerous instances, see, for instance, *Gunpowder and Firearms*, p. 107.

66. Ibn Iyās, v, 159, ll. 7–14.

67. E.g., ibid., v, 194, ll. 1–2; 204, ll. 4–5, 9–10; 488, ll. 14–15. Ibn Iyās even goes so far as to state that the reputation of the Ottomans as exceedingly just rulers, which they enjoyed before the conquest of the Mamlūk Sultanate, did not show itself at all in Egypt under the occupation (*fa-in kāna yushā' al-'adl al-zā'id 'an awlād Ibn 'Uthmān wa-hum fī bilādihim qabla an yadkhula Salīm Shāh ilā Miṣr fa-lam yaẓhar li-hādhā al-kalām natīja* [ibid., v, 159, ll. 11–12]).

This is decisive unconscious evidence for the good name which Ottoman justice enjoyed far beyond the boundaries of the Ottoman Sultanate. Such a good name cannot be earned without justification. Whether Ibn Iyās was blinded by his hatred of the new rulers, or whether the Ottomans did not observe, at that stage of their occupation, their reputed justice to the full, is beyond the scope of this paper, and should be studied separately. Whatever low opinion the people of the Mamlūk Sultanate formed of Ottoman refinement, their view of the newly established Safavid state was even lower. Commenting on the poor dress and shabby appearance of the envoys of the Safavids, who arrived in Cairo in Sha'bān 913/December 1507, our author says: "They do not have any splendor [*rawnaq*], *in contrast to the envoys of the Ottoman Sultan*[!]" (Ibn Iyās, IV, 123, ll. 14–18). At a later period such a comment could not be made, for the Safavid court developed into one of the most splendid and most refined in Muslim history.

68. Ibid., v, 194, ll. 1–2. When Sultan Selīm and his retinue went to a public bath in Damascus "they washed and shaved" (*ightasalū wa-ḥalaqū*), Ibn Ṭūlūn, II, 82, l. 12). Muṣṭafā Bāshā, who succeeded Khāyrbak as the viceroy of Egypt, is described as "clean shaven (*ḥalīq al-liḥya*) wearing only a yellow mustache" (Ibn Iyās, v, 485, ll. 11–12). For Ottoman small beards see below. For the *ṭarṭūr* headgear, see Mayer, *Mamlūk Costume*, p. 71 and Dozy's *Supplément aux dictionnaires arabes*, s.v.

69. Ibn Iyās, v, 204, ll. 5–9. It is noteworthy that even as late as the eighteenth century, the historian al-Jabartī frequently criticizes the irreligious behavior and lax morals of the Ottoman soldiers newly arriving in Egypt from other parts of the Empire.

70. In addition to references cited in other notes, see also ibid., v, 194, ll. 6–8.

71. See my "Notes on the Furūsiyya Exercises and Games in the Mamlūk Sultanate," *Studies in Islamic History and Civilization*, ed. Uriel Heyd, *Scripta Hierosolymitana*, vol. IX (Jerusalem, 1961), pp. 31–62.

72. Ibn Iyās, v, 194, ll. 9–10.

73. Ibid., 195, l. 7.

74. Ibid., 195, ll. 2, 3–5, 11. For all the terms mentioned above see Mayer, op. cit., indexes.

75. For the red *zamṭ* hats and the *mallūṭa* coats as a typical dress of the Circassians toward the end of their rule, see Mayer, op. cit., p. 24.

76. Ibn Iyās, v, 209, ll. 14–21.

77. Ibid., 216, ll. 1–12.

78. Ibid., 402, ll. 8–14.

79. Ibid., 402, l. 22–403, l. 2.

80. Ibid., 425, ll. 11–14.

81. In addition to earlier references see also: Ibn Iyās, v, 480, ll. 13–15.

82. See "Studies on the Structure of the Mamlūk Army," *BSOAS*, XV (1953), pp. 208 ff.

83. The tragic irony of the entire event was that it was Sinān Bak who ousted Khāyrbak's Mamlūks from the Citadel. The same Sinān was the person whom Khāyrbak appointed as his successor and to whom he entrusted, beside the State Treasury, his sons, his family, his retinue, and his Mamlūks (Ibn Iyās, v, 476, l. 23–477, l. 3; ll. 15–20).

84. Ibn Iyās, v, 478, ll. 14–16; 482, ll. 7–8; 487, ll. 8–12; 488, ll. 15–16.

85. See also ibid., v, 362, ll. 3–8, 8–11; 368, l. 23–369, l. 1.

86. Jānbirdī al-Ghazālī's policy is discussed in the paper mentioned in note 1.

87. Ibn Iyās, v, 488, ll. 8–15.

88. I include, of course, in this category, my article dealing with the transformation of Mamlūk society in Egypt under the Ottomans (*JESHO*, III [1960], pp. 148–74, 275–325), although I believe that some of the analogies with the Mamlūk Sultanate will prove to be correct.

Postscript

The article that complements the present one, and which was published in *Studia Islamica*, fascicle 65 (1987), pp. 125–48 under the title "The End of the Mamlūk Sultanate" has the subtitle "Why did the Ottomans spare the Mamlūks of Egypt and wipe-out the Mamlūks of Syria?" Here the "wiping out" does not mean the physical annihilation of every single Mamlūk, but the destruction of the Mamlūks as a sociomilitary and political entity.

30
An Ottoman Printing Puzzle:
The *Ḥilye-i Khāqānī* of 1264/1848*

Eleazar Birnbaum**

IN 1264/1848, the Ottoman Imperial Press in Istanbul (*Ṭab'khāne-i 'Āmire*) issued the first printed edition of the *Ḥilye-i Khāqānī (Ḥākānī)*, a beautiful production in a newly designed *ta'līq* typeface. I will demonstrate below that this was not a single edition, as has been assumed, but in fact five bibliographically quite distinct productions which, surprisingly, all bore the identical date of publication, 7 Ṣafar 1264/14 January 1848.

The beginnings of Ottoman Islamic printing have engaged the attention of scholars, both professional and amateur, for many years, and a fair amount is known about the establishment of Ibrāhīm Müteferriqa's press in Istanbul, and the books printed in it from 1141/1729 onward. In 1727 he had addressed a petition to the Grand Vizier Ibrāhīm Pasha, who was Sultan Aḥmed III's son-in-law, requesting the Pasha's influence in obtaining both an imperial *fermān* (order) authorizing the establishment of a press to print books on useful secular sciences, and a *fetwā* (legal opinion) from the Shaikh al-Islām attesting to the legality of such a press.

In his petition, Ibrāhīm Müteferriqa expressed the intention of printing in "*nesikh (naskh)* and *ta'līq* and other styles of script."[1] However, he never printed anything in *ta'līq*.

From the fifteenth century and even earlier, Turkish calligraphers had increasingly adopted the practice of using *ta'līq* as the preferred style for copying books of poetry. Since most of the works printed by Müteferriqa were in the "useful sciences," such as history, language, geography, and applied sciences, the first printing type which he cast was in the *nesikh* style commonly used by calligraphers for such subjects. Although this type was difficult to design, it was relatively simpler than would have been the case with *ta'līq*. The design of a suitable type for the latter involved much greater technical problems, in particular because of the larger number of levels at which different letters must be linked to those preceding and following, and the greater differences in shape that each letter takes according to these same circumstances. In addition, the printer in *ta'līq* would be likely to have a readership which was aesthetically very demanding: sophisticated connoisseurs of *dīwān* (court) poetry, accustomed to the beauty of poetic manuscripts in elegant *ta'līq* calligraphy. It is perhaps not surprising, then, that Müteferriqa never did cast the *ta'līq* type fount which he had once intended.

Early European efforts to design *ta'līq* printing type produced artistically very unsatisfactory results, as is evident from a glance at works printed in the large, ugly, clumsy-looking type cast by Vincent Figgins and printed in Calcutta from 1801.[2] The smaller *ta'līq* type used in Vienna in 1838 is no less of an eyesore.[3]

In the Islamic world, the design of movable *ta'līq* types was taken up in Egypt. In the early 1830s, a number of books using them were issued from the press established at Būlāq near Cairo by the governor of Egypt, Meḥmed (Muḥammed) 'Alī about 1237/1821.[4] Most of these *ta'līq* editions were in Turkish, though a few were in Persian.[5] In Istanbul, *ta'līq* printing seems to have begun a little later. The first items were two separate editions of a fifteen-page booklet on the Sunni Muslim creed, written by Ibrāhīm Qaṣṣābbaşızāde under the title *Risāle-i i'tiqādīye*. The texts were the same, except for the very different contents of their colophons, the first dated in the middle decade (*ewāsiṭ*) of Ramaḍān 1258/16–25 October 1842, and the second in the final decade (*ewākhır*) of Ramaḍān 1258/26 October–4 November 1842. They were printed at the Ṭab'khāne-i 'Āmire, the Imperial Press, in a fine 18 point type, cut from calligraphy specially drawn, as the colophons tell us, by the great calligrapher Yesārīzāde Muṣṭafā 'Izzet (d. 1265/1849).[6]

Some five years later, the same press issued a 55-page book printed in a different style of *ta'līq*, which was also rather larger (24 point): the *Ḥilye-i Khāqānī*, a pious religious work in Turkish *mesnewī* verse (couplets), describing the physical features and qualities (*shemā'il*) of the Prophet of Islam. The poem had been composed by Meḥmed Khāqānī in 1007/1598–99. The prose colophon of the Istanbul print (pp. 53–55) is dated 7 Ṣafar 1264/14 January 1848. It tells how the work came to be printed. Sultan 'Abd al-Majīd ('Abdülmecīd), being a connoisseur of the arts, requested that a more beautiful *ta'līq* type fount be produced at the Imperial Press. The sultan having personally approved the appearance of a specimen line of verse submitted to him, the whole type fount was designed and cut. A short work, some forty to fifty pages in length, was sought in order to test the new type in practice, and in particular to see whether the difficult problem of achieving harmonious joins between the individual letters had been successfully resolved. The *Ḥilye* was the text chosen for the trial edition, since it was both the right length and a "blessed work"—a poem in honor of the Prophet. The new *ta'līq* typeface was designed by a certain Rājiḥ (Rāciḥ) Efendi to resemble *muraqqa*'s (decorative pages of calligraphy) which had been written by 'Imād al-Ḥasanī (d. 1024/1615), one of the most famous Persian masters of *ta'līq*. The book's long colophon, giving all the details mentioned in this paragraph, was composed by the press's director Meḥmed Sa'īd in rather ornate Ottoman Turkish prose.[7]

The major bibliographies and catalogs of Turkish printed books record the 1264 edition of the *Ḥilye*; none of them indicates any awareness that there was not just one issue bearing this date, but at least five different ones.

In my own collection of early Islamic books, I have two copies of the *Ḥilye* dated 1264, one with a narrow border frame 4.5mm wide around each page of text; the other has the same frame surrounded by a second and much more elaborate broad frame 13mm wide made up of type ornaments. An illustration of the colophon of the 1264 edition of the *Ḥilye* in an article published in 1980 surprised me when I noticed that it showed yet another variation in the layout of the final page.[8] It became clear to me then that the printing history of this work was complicated. This led me to look at as many copies as possible. Until now I have been able to examine fifteen copies of the *Ḥilye*, in original or in partial photocopy.[9] These divide into no less than five separate groups. I have tried to see a logic in the differences, so that the sequence in which the editions were issued may be determined.

The textual variation between editions is insignificant. I found only one word changed between the first edition and the rest: on page 55, line 14, the word *ḥażretleriniñ* (with genitive suffix) of the first edition has become *ḥażretlerini* (with definite direct object suffix) in the others. The various editions are distinguished from one another otherwise only by changes in the layout of the last few lines, and in the use or position of type ornaments decorating the pages. I provide here reproductions of the final page (p. 55) in each of the five editions, and list the differences, so that my interpretation of the edition sequence becomes clear. (Needless to say, the edition numbers used below do not appear on the books, and are my own numbering.)

First Edition

Copies in Libraries: a. Toronto, E. Birnbaum's collection, Haqani I
b. Istanbul, Süleymaniye, Tahir Ağa 494
c. Toronto, University of Toronto Library, PL248 H24 H7 1847

Characteristics:

Line 13: Begins *bī-minnetimiz*; long ligature in *'Abd*; ends *Khān.*

Line 14: Begins *Efendimiz ḥażretleriniñ*; ends *mażhariyyetle.*

Line 15: Begins *ilā*; ends *shān.*

Line 16: Text *buyursun Āmīn*, flanked by date elements at left and right.

Type ornaments: 1. Text surrounded by narrow frame. Page number immediately outside frame.

Second Edition

Copy in Library: a. Istanbul, Turgut Kut's private collection, Hakani A

Characteristics:

As first edition except:

Line 14: *ḥażretlerini* (instead of *ḥażretleriniñ* of first edition).

Third Edition

Copy in Library: a. Istanbul, Süleymaniye, Nafiz Paşa 155

Characteristics:

As second edition except:

1. A large outer frame of type ornaments 13 mm wide has been added outside the inner frame around the text on all four sides, giving the page an air of luxury and elegance.
2. The page number has been moved to the outer edge of the new ornamental frame.

Fourth Edition

Copies in Libraries:

a. Istanbul, Süleymaniye, Ḥafid Ef. 289
b. Istanbul, Süleymaniye, Ihsan Mahvi 92
c. Istanbul, Süleymaniye, M. Arif-M. Murad 211
d. Istanbul, Turgut Kut's private collection, Hakani B
e. Unidentified copy, reproduced in M. Uğur Derman's article (p. 11), in work cited in note 6
f. Cairo, University Library, 7491 T

Characteristics:

Lines 13–16 reset, as compared with previous editions.

Line 13: *'Abd* ligature shortened and *Efendimiz* transferred from line 14.

Line 14: Begins *hażretlerini*; ends *ilā ākhır*, the latter two words having been moved up from the beginning of line 15 of previous editions.

Line 15: Begins *il-ezmān;* ends *buyursun*, the latter word having been moved up from line 16.

Line 16: Contains only *Āmīn*, flanked by date elements on either side.

Type ornaments:

1. Added at inner corners of inner frame.
2. No *outer* frame of type ornaments.

Fifth Edition

Copies in Libraries:

a. Toronto, E. Birnbaum's collection, Haqani II
b. Istanbul, Süleymaniye, Düğümlü Baba 64 M
c. Istanbul, Süleymaniye, Hacı Mahmud 4494
d. Istanbul, Turgut Kut's private collection, Hakani C

Characteristics, as compared with fourth edition:

1. Addition of outer frame of type ornaments 13 mm wide on all four sides, of the same design as in third edition. Nevertheless, the outer frame type elements show different areas of damage, and more of them, than in the third edition. A different casting of border frame would account for this.

2. Page number moved outside large frame, as in third edition.

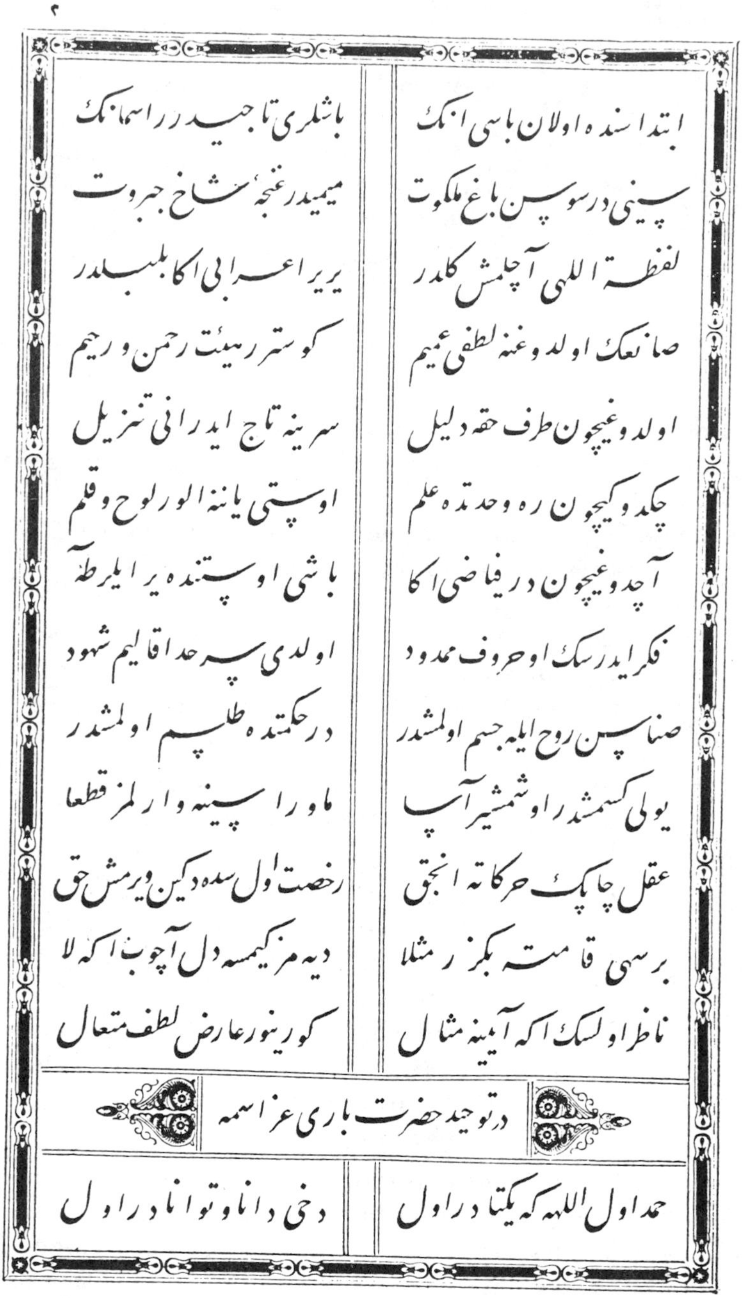

٢

ابتداسنده اولان باسی انک — باشلری تاجیدر راسمانک

سینی درسوسن باغ ملکوت — میمیدر غنچهٔ شاخ جبروت

لفظة اللهی آچلمش کلدر — یریراعرابی اکا بلبلدر

صانعک اولدوغنه لطفی عمیم — کوسترر هیئت رحمن و رحیم

اولدوغیچون طرف حقه دلیل — سرینه تاج ایدرانی تنزیل

چکدوکیچون ره وحدتده علم — اوستی یانینه الور لوح وقلم

آچدوغیچون در فیاضی اکا — باشی اوستنده یرایلر طهٰ

فکرایدرسک اوحروف ممدود — اولدی سپر حداقالیم شهود

صناسن روح ایله جسم اولمشدر — درحکمتده طلسم اولمشدر

یولی کسمشدر او شمشیر آب — ماورا سینه وارلمز قطعا

عقل چاپک حرکاته انجق — رخصت اول سده دکین ویرمش حق

برسهی قامته بکزر مثلا — دیه مزکیمسه دل آچوب اکه لا

ناظر اولسک اکه آیینه مثال — کورینور عارض لطف متعال

در توحید حضرت باری عز اسمه

حمد اول اللهه که یکتادر اول — دخی داناو توانادر اول

Figure 30.1. First edition of the *Ḥilye-i Khāqānī* (Istanbul, 1264/1848): first opening, pp. 2–3.

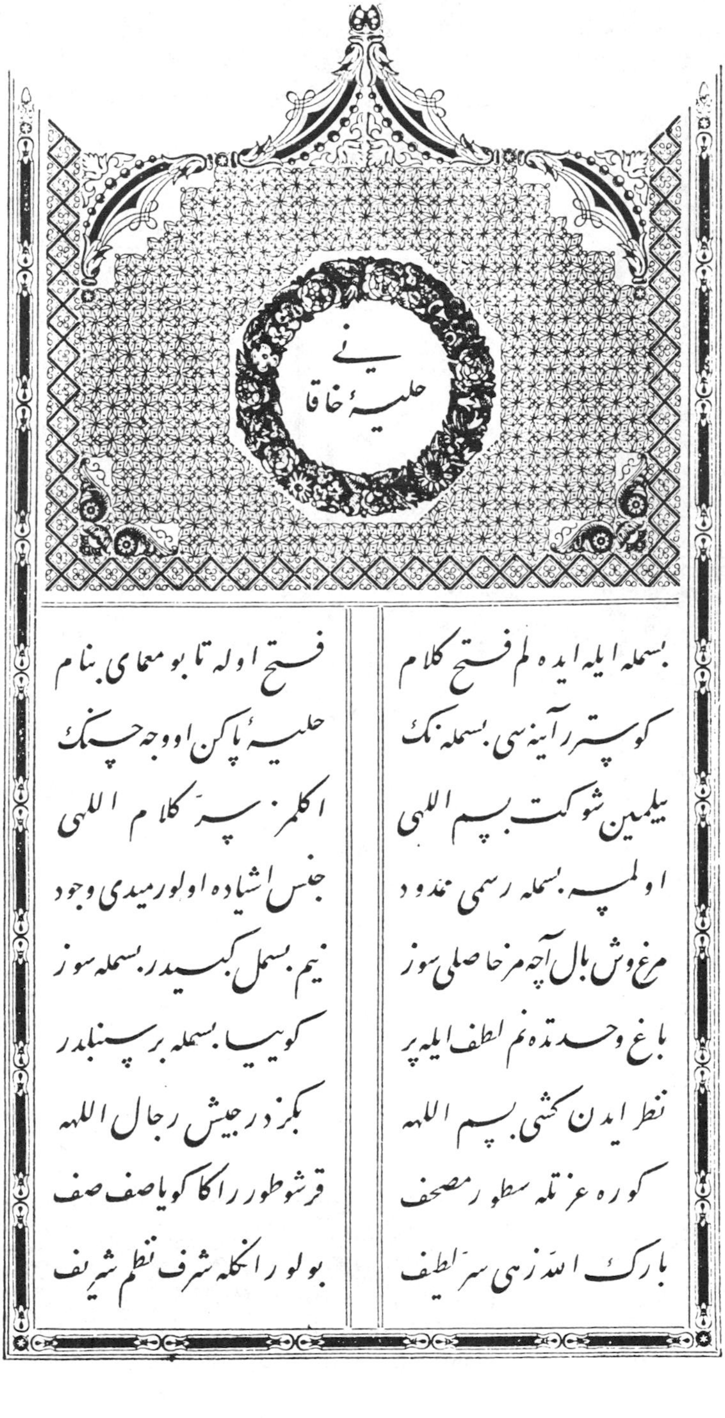

حلیهٔ خاقانی

بسمله ایله ایده لم فتح کلام — فتح اوله تا بو معمای بنام

کوستر آیینه سی بسمله نک — حلیهٔ پاکن اووجه چنک

بیلمیین شوکت بسم اللهی — اکلمز سر کلام اللهی

اولمیه بسمله رسمی ممدود — جنس اشیاده اولورمیدی وجود

مرغ وش بال آچه مزحاصلی سوز — نیم بسمل کبیدر بسمله سوز

باغ وحدتده نم لطف ایله پر — کوییا بسمله بر سنبلدر

نظر ایدن کشی بسم اللهه — بکزر در جیش رجال اللهه

کوره عزتله سطور مصحف — قرشو طورراکا کویا صف صف

بارک الله زهی سر لطیف — بولوراکله شرف نظم شریف

ابتدا سنده اولان باسی انک | باشلری تاجیدر زر اسمانک
سینی درویشن باغ ملکوت | میمیدر غنچهٔ شاخ جبروت
لفظهٔ اللهی آچلمش کلدر | یریر اعرابی اکا بلبلدر
صانعک اولدی وغنهٔ لطفی عمیم | کوستر ربیتی رحمن ورحیم
اولدوغیچون طرف حقه دلیل | سرینه تاج ایدرانی تنزیل
چکدوکیچون ره وحدتده علم | اوستی یاننه اکور لوح وقلم
آچدوغیچون در فیاضی اکا | باشی اوستنده یر ایلرطه
فکر ایدرسنک او حروف ممدود | اولدی سرحد اقالیم شهود
صناسن روح ایله جسم اولمشدر | درحکمتده طلسم اولمشدر
یولی کسمشدر او شمشیر آسا | ماورا سینه وارلمز قطعا
عقل چاپک حرکاته انجق | رخصت اولمسده دکین ویرمش حق
بر سهی قامته بکزر مثلا | دیه مز کیمسه دل آچوب اکه لا
ناظر اولسک اکه آینه مثال | کورینور عارض لطف متعال

در توحید حضرت جناب باری عز اسمه

حمد اول اللهه که یکتادر اول | دخی داناو توانادر اول

Figure 30.2. Fifth edition of the *Ḥilye-i Khāqānī* (Istanbul, 1264–1848): first opening, pp. 2–3.

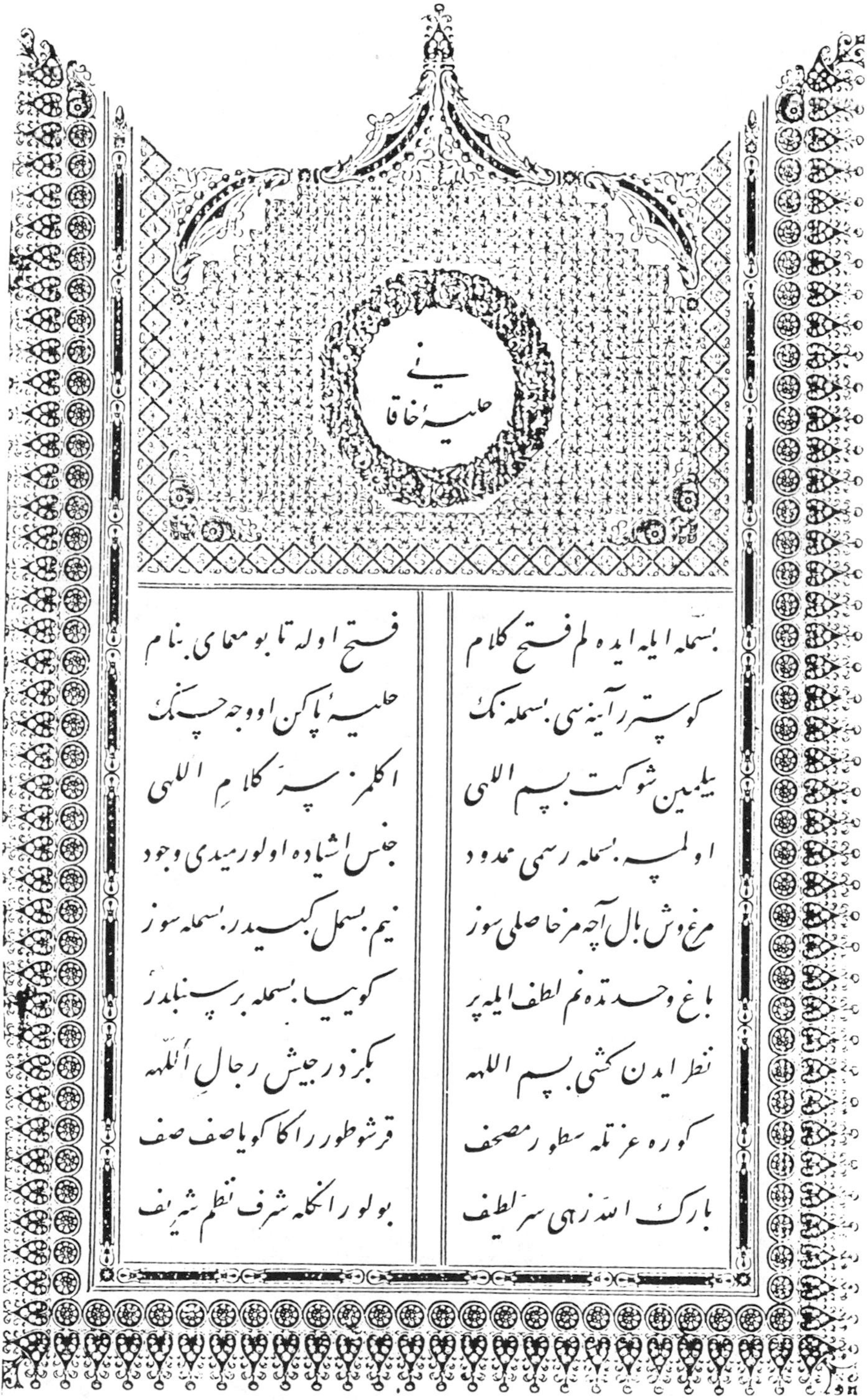

حلیهٔ خاقانی
بسمله ایله ایده لم فتح کلام
فتح اوله تا بو معمای بنام
کوستر آیینه سی بسمله نک
حلیهٔ پاکن او وجه حسنک
بیلمین شوکت بسم اللهی
اکلمز سر کلام اللهی
اولمیه بسمله رسمی ممدود
جنس اشیاده اولورمیدی وجود
مرغ وش بال آچه مز حاصلی سوز
نیم بسمل کبیدر بسمله سوز
باغ وحدتده نم لطف ایله پر
کویا بسمله بر سنبلدر
نظر ایدن کشی بسم الله
بکزدر جیش رجال الله
کوره عزتله سطور مصحف
قرشو طورر اکا کویا صف صف
بارک الله زهی سر لطیف
بولور انکله شرف نظم شریف

٥٥

بنی آدم صلی الله تعالی علیه وسلم افندمز حضرتلرینک اصح روایات اوزره
منقول اولان حلیهٔ شریفهٔ نبویه لرینک مفهوم ونظمنده اثبات مدعای بلاغت
ایدن واصل رحمت سبحانی مشهور خاقانی مرحومک منظومهٔ شریفه سی
آثار جلیلهٔ متیمنه دن بولنمش اولدیغنه مبنی تیمنا وتبرکا حروفات جدیدهٔ
مذکوره نک ترتیب وطبعنه اشبو حلیهٔ خاقانی ایله شروع ومباشرت قلنمشدر
حقا که مانند حروفات مرقعات عماد هردرلو کلمه نک قواعد خط تعلیق اوزره
ترتیب وجمعیله بر نقطه سی نقصان اولمیه رق لوحهٔ اکماله ایرادینه طالب
الطاف رب مجید محمد سعیدک نظارت عاجزانه سیله صرف مقدرت ایدن
راجح افندی طوغریسی اثبات مدعای خدمت ولیاقت ایتمش وسایهٔ
معالیوایهٔ جناب شاهانه ده بوندن بویله حروفات مذکوره ایله هرنوع
کتب نفیسه ودواوین سلیسه طبع اولنه جغی درکار بولنمش اولمغله همان
جناب خالق النون والقلم پادشاه معارف علم وشهنشاه عدالت شیم ولی نعمت
بیمنتمز السلطان ابن السلطان السلطان عبدالمجید خان
افندمز حضرتلرینک نیجه نیجه آثار نافعه یه مظهریتله
الی آخر الازمان اریکه پیرای شوکت وشان
ص ٧ فی بیورسون آمین سنه ١٢٦٤

Figure 30.3. First edition of the *Ḥilye-i Khāqānī*, p. 55. At the upper left margin, the page number is outside the narrow frame; on line 13, *'Abd* has a long ligature; on line 14, *Ḥażretlerinin̄* (with genitive suffix); and on line 16, *buyursun Āmīn*, flanked by the date at the left and right.

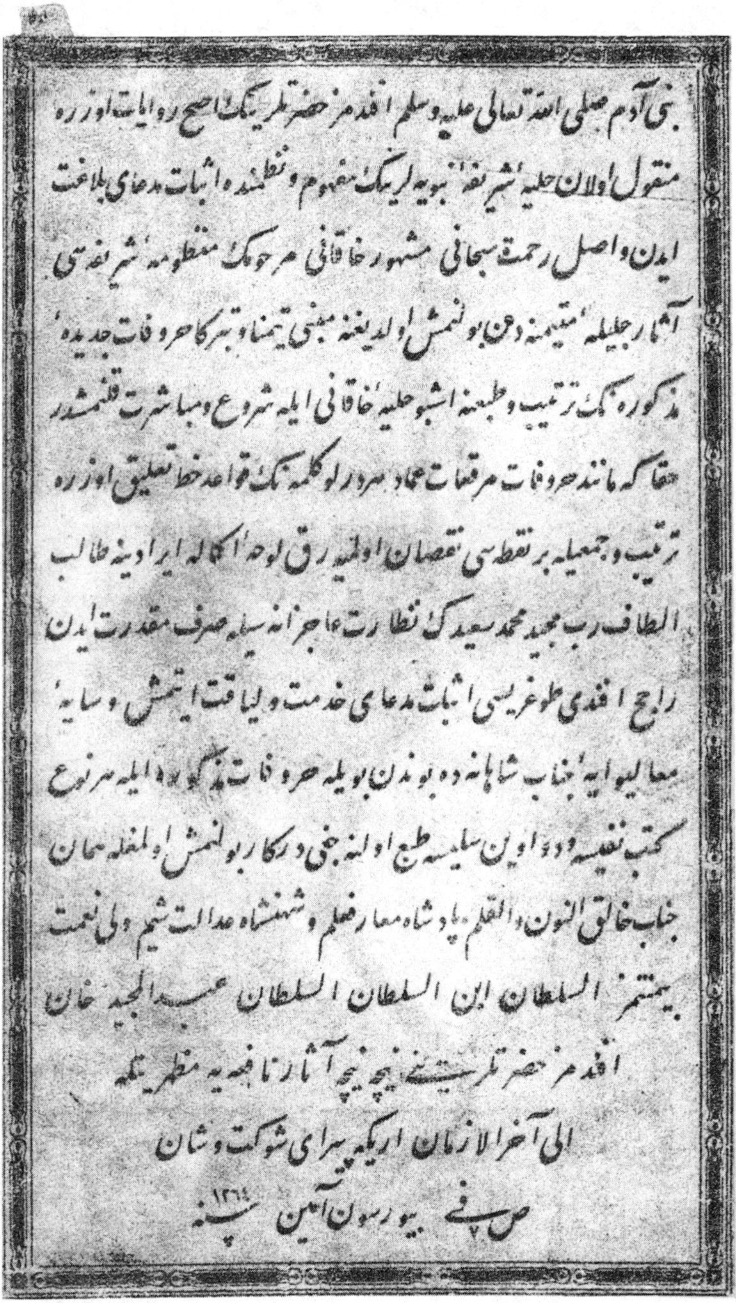
نبی آدم صلی الله تعالی علیه وسلم افندمز حضرتلرینک اصح روایات اوزره
منقول اولان حلیهٔ شریفهٔ نبویه لرینک مفهوم و نظمنده اثبات مدعای بلاغت
ایدن واصل رحمت سبحانی مشهور خاقانی مرحومک منظومهٔ شریفه سی
آثار جلیله مقیمه دعن بولنمش اولدیغنه مبنی تیمنا و تبرکا حروفات جدیدهٔ
مذکوره نک ترتیب و طبعنه اشبو حلیهٔ خاقانی ایله شروع ومباشرت قلنمشدر
حقا که مانند حروفات مرقعات عادة صورلو کلمه نک قواعد خط تعلیق اوزره
ترتیب و جمعیله بر نقطه سی نقصان اولمیه رق لوحه اکاله ایرادینه طالب
الطاف رب مجید محمد سعیدک نظارت عاجزانه سیله صرف مقدرت ایدن
راجح افندی طوغریسی اثبات مدعای خدمت ولیاقت ایتمش وسایهٔ
معالیوایهٔ جناب شاهانه ده بوندن بویله حروفات مذکوره ایله هر نوع
کتب نفیسه ودواوین سلیسه طبع اولنه جغی درکار بولنمش اولمغله سبحان
جناب خالق النون والقلم پادشاه معارف علم وشهنشاه عدالت شیم ولی نعمت
بیمنتمز السلطان ابن السلطان السلطان عبد المجید خان
افندمز حضرتلرینی نیجه نیجه آثار نافعه یه مظهر ایلیه
الی آخر الزمان اریکه پیرای شوکت وشان
ص ٥٥ فی بیورسون آمین سنه ١٢٦٤

Figure 30.4. Second edition of the *Ḥilye-i Khāqānī*, p. 55. This edition is the same as the first, except for line 14, which has *Ḥażretlerini* (with definite direct object suffix).

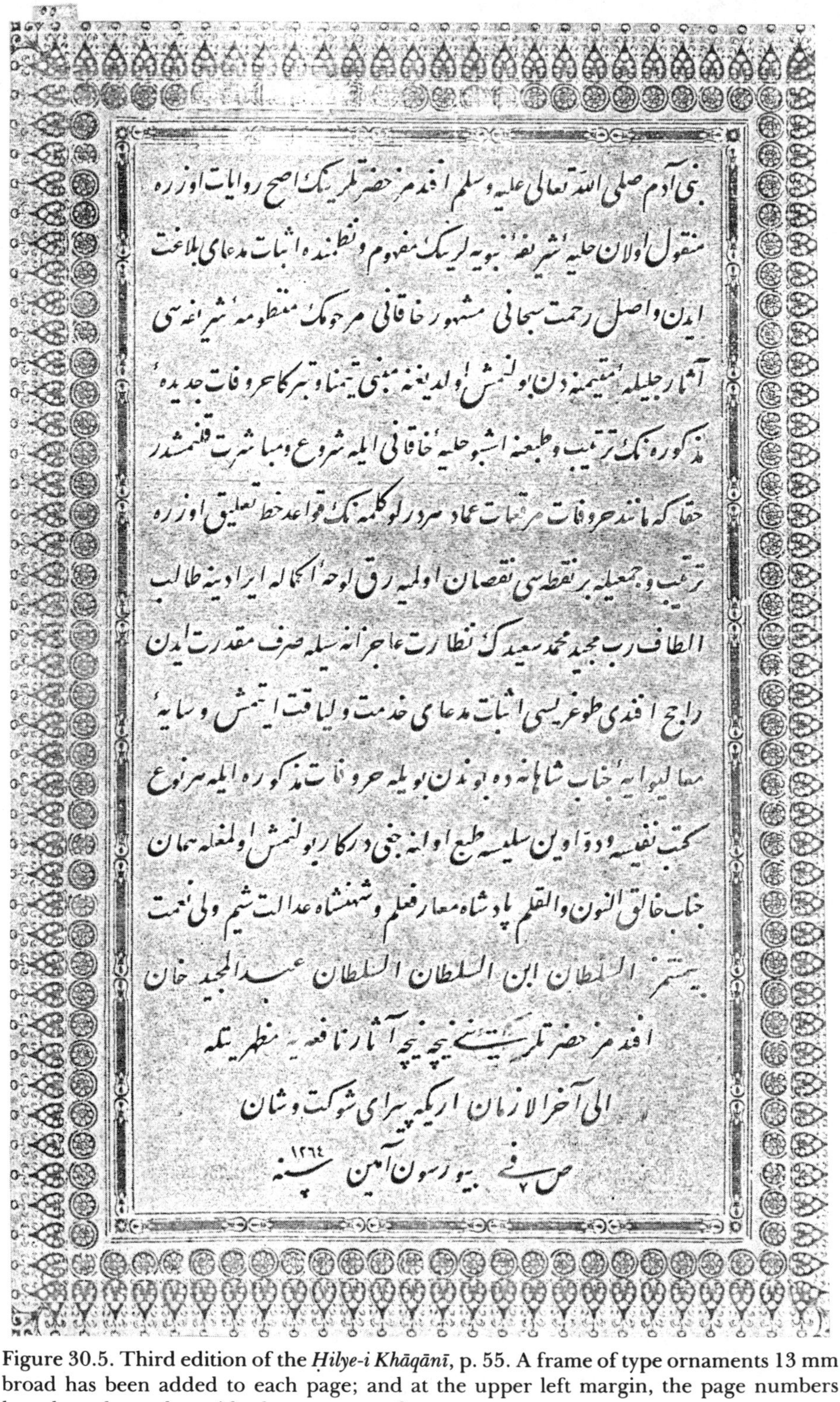

نبی آدم صلی الله تعالی علیه وسلم افندمز حضرتلرینک اصح روایات اوزره
منقول اولان حلیهٔ شریفهٔ نبویه لرینک مفهوم و نظمنده اثبات مدعای بلاغت
ایدن واصل رحمت سبحانی مشهور خاقانی مرحومک منظومهٔ شریفه سی
آثار جلیلهٔ مقیمنه دن اولنمش اولدیغنه مبنی تیمنا و تبرکا حروفات جدیدهٔ
مذکوره نک ترتیب و طبعنه اشبو حلیهٔ خاقانی ایله شروع و مباشرت قلنمشدر
حقا که مانند حروفات مرقعات عماد صردرلو کلمه نک قواعد خط تعلیق اوزره
ترتیب و جمعیله بر نقطه سی نقصان اولمیه رق لوحهٔ اکماله ایرادینه طالب
الطاف رب مجید محمد سعید ک نظارت عاجزانه سیله صرف مقدرت ایدن
راجح افندی طوغریسی اثبات مدعای خدمت و لیاقت ایتمش و سایهٔ
معالیوایهٔ جناب شاهانه ده بوندن بویله حروفات مذکوره ایله سر نوع
کتب نفیسه ودواوین سلیسه طبع اولنه جغی درکار بولنمش اولمغله همان
جناب خالق النون والقلم پادشاه معارف علم و شهنشاه عدالت شیم ولی نعمت
بیهمتز السلطان ابن السلطان السلطان عبد المجید خان
افندمز حضرتلرینی نیجه نیجه آثار نافعه یه مظهر ایلیه
الی آخر الازمان اریکه پیرای شوکت و شان
ص ۲ فی بیوررسون آمین سنه ۱۲۶۴

Figure 30.5. Third edition of the *Ḥilye-i Khāqānī*, p. 55. A frame of type ornaments 13 mm broad has been added to each page; and at the upper left margin, the page numbers have been located outside the new outer frame.

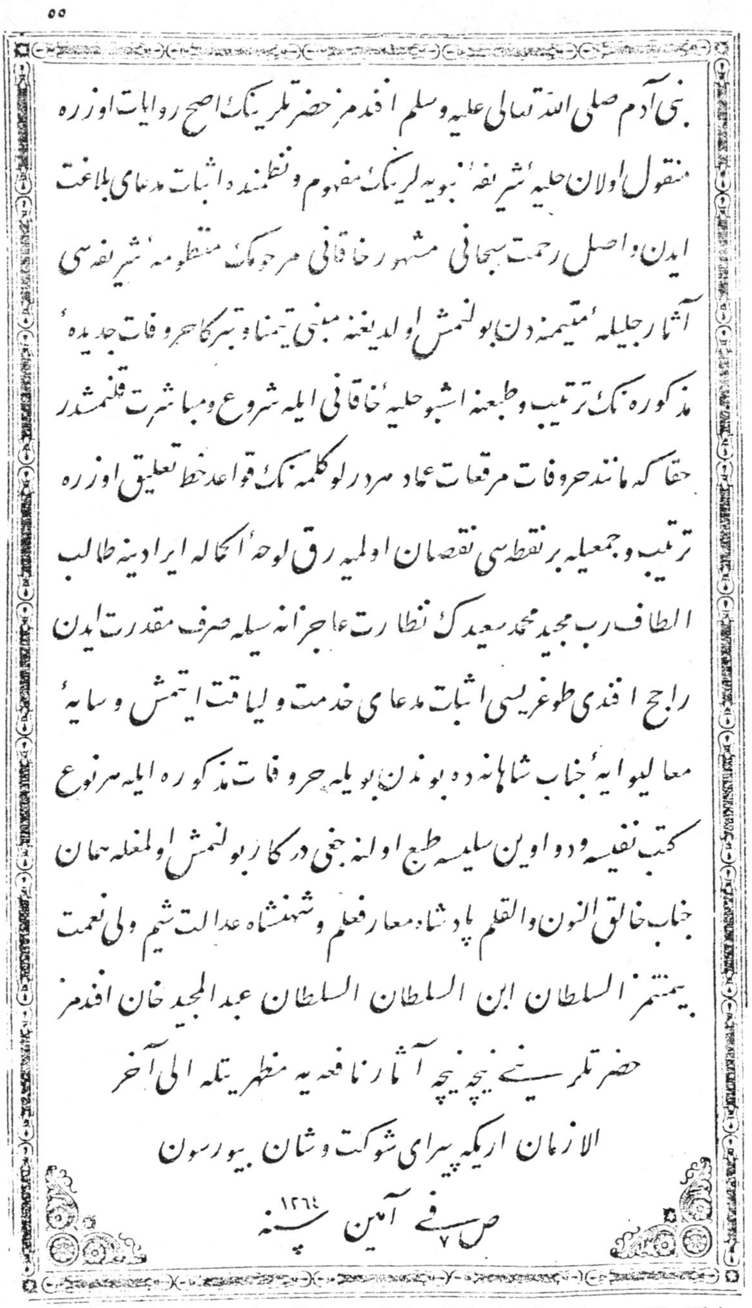
٥٥

بنی آدم صلی الله تعالی علیه وسلم افندمز حضرتلرینک اصح روایات اوزره
منقول اولان حلیهٔ شریفهٔ نبویه لرینک مفهوم ونظمنده اثبات مدعای بلاغت
ایدن واصل رحمت سبحانی مشهور خاقانی مرحومک منظومهٔ شریفه سی
آثار جلیلهٔ متیمنه دن بولنمش اولدیغنه مبنی تیمنا وتبرکا حروفات جدیدهٔ
مذکوره نک ترتیب وطبعنه اشبو حلیهٔ خاقانی ایله شروع ومباشرت قلنمشدر
حقا که مانند حروفات مرقعات عماد مفردرلو کلمه نک قواعد خط تعلیق اوزره
ترتیب وجمعیله بر نقطه سی نقصان اولمیه رق لوحهٔ اکماله ایرادینه طالب
الطاف رب مجید محمد سعیدک نظارت عاجزانه سیله صرف مقدرت ایدن
راجح افندی طوغریسی اثبات مدعای خدمت ولیاقت ایتمش وسایهٔ
معالیوایهٔ جناب شاهانه ده بوندن بویله حروفات مذکوره ایله هر نوع
کتب نفیسه ودواوین سلیسه طبع اولنه جغی درکار بولنمش اولمغله تمامن
جناب خالق النون والقلم پادشاه معارفعلم وشهنشاه عدالتشیم ولی نعمت
بیمنتمز السلطان ابن السلطان السلطان عبد المجید خان افندمز
حضرتلری سینه نیچه نیچه آثار نافعه یه مظهریتله الی آخر
الازمان اریکه پیرای شوکت وشان بیورسون
ص ۷ فی آمین سنه ۱۲٦٤

Figure 30.6. Fourth edition of the *Ḥilye-i Khāqānī*, p. 55. This edition has no outer frame; lines 13–16 are reset with different spacing from the first through third editions. Line 13 shows a shortened ligature for *'Abd*; in line 15, the verb *buyursun* is no longer surrounded by date elements; and in line 16, type ornaments have been added in the inner corners of the frame, and only the word *Āmīn* is left, flanked by the date elements.

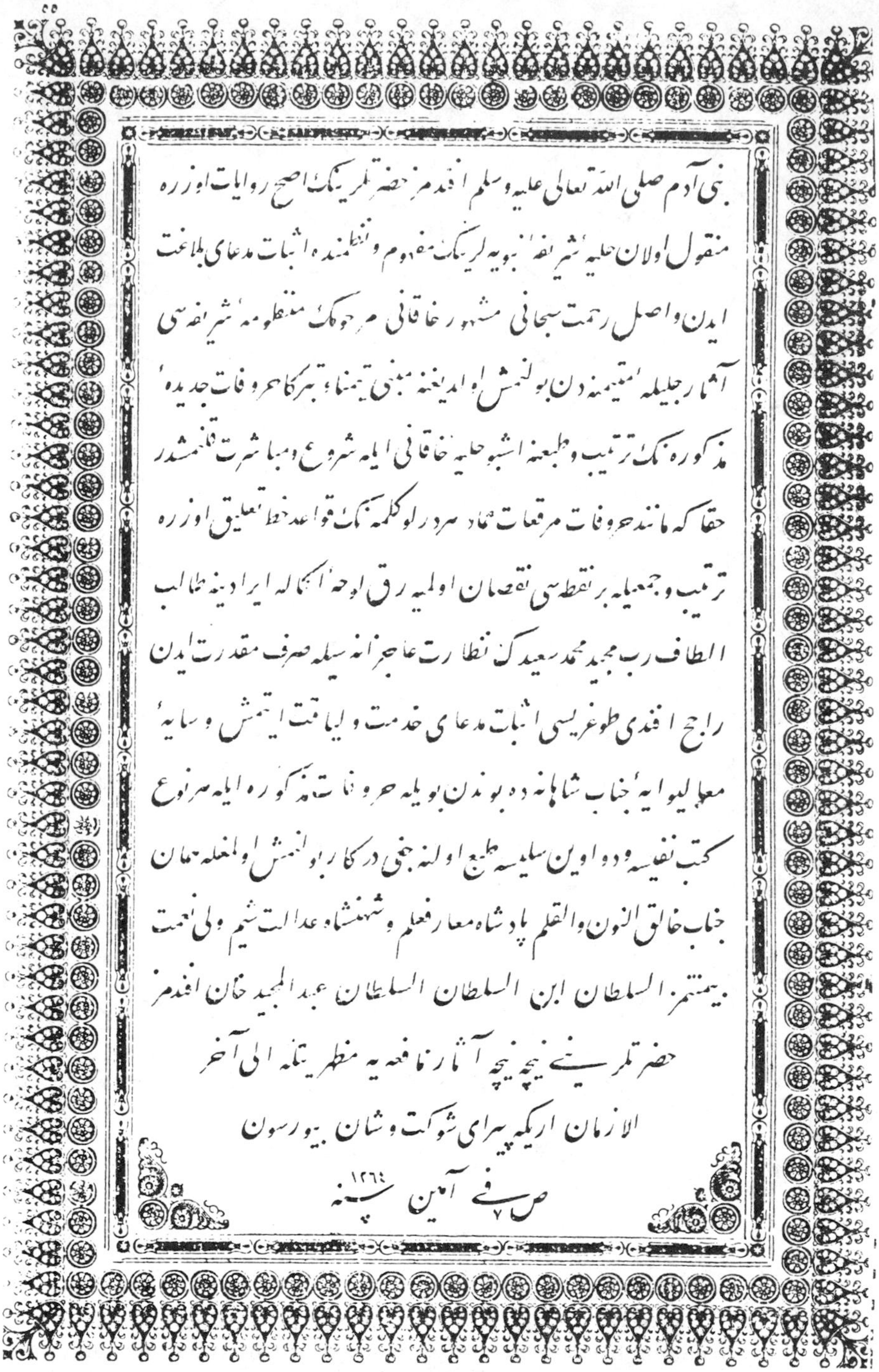

٥٥

نبی آدم صلی الله تعالی علیه وسلم افندمز حضرتلرینک اصح روایات اوزره

منقول اولان حلیهٔ شریفهٔ نبویه لرینک مفهوم ونظمنده اثبات مدعای بلاغت

ایدن واصل رحمت سبحانی مشهور خاقانی مرحومک منظومهٔ شریفه سی

آثار جلیلهٔ متیمنه دن بولنمش اولدیغنه مبنی تیمناً وتبرکاً حروفات جدیدهٔ

مذکوره نک ترتیب وطبعنه اشبو حلیه خاقانی ایله شروع ومباشرت قلنمشدر

حقا که مانند حروفات مرقعات عماد سردرلو کلمه نک قواعد خط تعلیق اوزره

ترتیب وجمیله بر نقطه سی نقصان اولمیه رق اوحهٔ اکماله ایرادینه طالب

الطاف رب مجید محمد سعیدک نظارت عاجزانه سیله صرف مقدرت ایدن

راجح افندی طوغریسی اثبات مدعای خدمت ولیاقت ایتمش وسایهٔ

معدلتوایهٔ جناب شاهانه ده بونده بویله حروفات مذکوره ایله صنوع

کتب نفیسه ودواوین سلیسه طبع اولنه جغی درکار بولنمش اولمغله تمان

جناب خالق النون والقلم پادشاه معارفعلم وشهنشاه عدالت شیم ولی نعمت

بیمنتمز السلطان ابن السلطان السلطان عبد المجید خان افندمز

حضرتلرینک نیچه نیچه آثار نافعه یه مظهریتلری الی آخر

الازمان اریکه پیرای شوکت وشان بیورسون

آمین فی ص ۷ سنه ۱۲٦٤

Figure 30.7. Fifth edition of the *Ḥilye-i Khāqānī*, p. 55. Within the inner frame, the text, type layouts, and ornaments are identical with the fourth edition not the third. An outer frame, 13 mm broad, has been added on all sides; it is made of the same elements as the outer frame in the third edition, but parts of it show different damage, which indicates that it has been reset. The page numbers have been moved outside the frame, as in the third edition.

From the details given in the colophon, it is evident that the printing of the *Ḥilye* in *ta'līq* type was experimental in several ways, and the multiplicity of editions dated 1264 can all be explained as parts of this experiment. I suggest the following scenario.

The first edition turned out to be a great visual success, proving that the excellent design of its type had overcome the many difficulties inherent in reproducing the calligraphic variations of letter shapes and levels according to letter sequence. The appearance was enhanced by framing each page in a multiple-ruled narrow frame 4.5 mm wide. The second edition was the same, except for the correction of a typographical error (page 55, line 14). The third edition was apparently designed for a luxury market, possibly for presentation to, or purchase by, high officials, or sophisticated members of the wealthy and educated classes. While the text and layout of the second edition was retained unchanged, each page was enhanced by the addition, outside the original narrow frame, of a broad new frame, 13 mm wide, made up of type ornaments. The page numbers of the first two editions had been outside the small frame, but in the third edition they had to be moved to the outer edge of the new large frame. Each page of the third edition bore an air of elegance such as had perhaps never been seen in an Islamic *printed* book. The fourth edition, surprisingly, does not have the beautiful ornamental outer frame. It differs from the three previous editions in having the type of the last four lines of page 55 entirely reset. Although the wording of the text is unchanged, the verb *buyursun* has been shifted up one line (to line 15) and is no longer uncomfortably wedged between the two halves of the date statement on line 16. The contents of lines 13 to 16 have consequently been rearranged. The final line has become shorter. The typesetter therefore balanced it by adding corner ornaments within the corner angles of the inner frame. The fifth edition is the luxury counterpart to the fourth, using its modified text and central layout of page 55 unchanged (including the *buyursun* in line 15), but adding the same large outer frame which was first tried out in the third edition. However, the frame used in the third edition is not absolutely identical with that in the fifth; for example, on page 55, the damaged type "flowers" found in various parts of the outer frame of the third edition are not in the same locations as damaged "flowers" in the fifth. It seems that the two editions used different castings of the same basic type ornament fount.

One puzzle remains in this interpretation of the sequence of editions. Why is there a luxury outer frame border in the third and fifth editions, but not in the fourth? If the frame had already been set up for the third edition, it would surely have been absurd to remove it from all fifty-five pages before printing the fourth edition, only to replace the frame laboriously again on all these pages to print the fifth edition.

The definitive answer is probably to be found in the papers of the Ṭab'khāne-i 'Āmire—if they are still extant. In the meantime, I suggest that the technique of stereotype printing may resolve the puzzle.[10] In preparing a more elegant edition, a stereotype of the second edition may have been taken (since the text and layout of page 55 are identical in both), and to each stereotype page a new broad ornamental outer frame border was affixed. The result was printed as the third edition: a trial run to test a luxury version. While this was being prepared, the continuing demand for the *Ḥilye* led to the issue of the fourth edition. The decision was apparently made to move the main verb of the final sentence from its anomalous position, wedged between date elements on the bottom line, to a place of greater clarity at the end of line 15. This necessitated rearranging and therefore resetting the last four lines of page 55 in the second edition. Since the final line of text thus became shorter, it was now filled up by the addition of corner ornaments at each end of the line. This fourth edition was to become the main regular edition of the *Ḥilye*. A decision was then made to issue a definitive luxury edition, but since page 55 of the fourth edition was an improvement in clarity and appearance over the third, the elegant wide border tested in the third edition was added to a stereotype of the fourth edition; this constituted the fifth edition.

The fifteen *Ḥilyes* which I have examined (in original prints or partial photocopies) divide into the following editions:

Edition number	*Number of copies examined*
1	3
2	1
3	1
4	6
5	4

While the limited size of the sample makes firm statistical deductions unsafe, it might tentatively support the following interpretation: the second and third editions (and perhaps the first also) were experimental, and for limited circulation only. The fourth was intended as the definitive regular edition for the general market, and the fifth the definitive special or luxury edition.

Further research may yet determine whether all five editions were indeed all printed in the year 1264/1848, or whether some were issued later to meet the demand for copies.

NOTES

* As a student of Bernard Lewis (formally from 1947 until 1950 at SOAS, and informally through his books and articles ever since), I take great pleasure in dedicating this small contribution to him on his seventieth birthday.

** Acknowledgements and sources of the illustrations:
Fig. 30.1 (Hakani I) Collection of E. Birnbaum, Toronto.
Fig. 30.2 (Hakani II) Collection of E. Birnbaum, Toronto.
Fig. 30.3 (Hakani I) Collection of E. Birnbaum, Toronto.
Fig. 30.4 (Hakani A), Courtesy of the owner, A. Turgut Kut, Istanbul.
Fig. 30.5 (Nafiz Paşa 155) Courtesy of the Süleymaniye Library, Istanbul.
Fig. 30.6 (Hafid Ef. 289) Courtesy of the Süleymaniye Library, Istanbul.
Fig. 30.7 (Hakani II) Collection of E. Birnbaum, Toronto.

1. *Nesikh we ta'līq we sā'ir . . . khuṭūṭ envā'ı*, in the penultimate paragraph of the manuscript of his petition, which is reproduced fully but reduced to eye-destroying size among the unnumbered illustrations at the back of Selim Nüzhet Gerçek, *Türk Maṭba'acılığı* (Istanbul, 1928). *Nesikh* is the commonest form of Arabic script used in printing. *Ta'līq* is the Turkish name of the form called *nasta'līq* in Persian and *fārisī* in Arabic.

2. Used in Francis Gladwin's *The Persian Moonshee* (Calcutta and London, 1801). The same type is used in *The Tooti Nameh or Tales of a Parrot* (Calcutta and London, 1801). The publisher was enthusiastic about the new fount. His advertisement for Gladwin's book (printed at the back of the *Tooti Nameh*) describes it as "elegantly printed in the new *Talîk* type cast by Figgins for Wilson and Co. of the Oriental Press."

3. See, e.g., Ghazzālī's *O Kind! [Ayyuhā 'l-walad,* ed. and trans. into German] Joseph von Hammer-Purgstall (Vienna, 1838).

4. See Richard N. Verdery, "The Publications of the Būlāq Press Under Muḥammad 'Alī of Egypt," JAOS, XCI (1971), pp. 129–32, and the works cited there.

5. The earliest which I have seen is Sa'dī's *Gulistān* in Persian dated *ghurrat Ṣafar* 1249/end of June 1833 (colophon, p. 275); 279 pp., in a large *ta'līq* type. (It is not listed in Abū'l Futūḥ Riḍwān, *Ta'rīkh Maṭba'at Būlāq,* Cairo, 1953, but I possess a copy). The same large *ta'līq* is used for the Persian poetry citations in the Turkish *Hümāyūnnāme* printed in Būlāq, Jumādā I 1251/September 1835. Within two years the Būlāq press was printing beautiful books in a smaller and much more graceful *ta'līq* typeface: the Turkish poems of Sāmī (separately numbered sequences of his *Dīwān* [=Qaṣā'id], *Tevārīkh, Ghazelī'yāt*), the final colophon being dated *ewākhir* Rebī' II 1253/July 1837.

The poetical works of Nedīm in Turkish are printed in identical form, and with the same type ornaments; although the book is undated, it was obviouisly printed at almost the same time as *Dīwān-i Sāmī.*

The Persian texts printed at Būlāq all belong to a small group of medieval Persian literary classics which for several centuries served as textbooks throughout the Ottoman Empire and were used to impart a broader and more sophisticated Ottoman Turkish vocabulary and literary style, particularly to young men destined for public service in the religious or administrative establishments.

6. See reproductions of the colophons in the valuable article by M. Uğur Derman, "Yazı san'atının eski matbaacılığımıza akisleri," in *Türk Kütüphaneciler Derneği Basım ve Yayıncılığımızın 250. Yılı Bilimsel Toplantısı, 10–11 Aralık, 1979. Ankara. Bildiriler* (Ankara, 1980), p. 110; discussion, pp. 98–100.

7. *Meḥmed Sa'īd' iñ neẓāret-i 'ādjizānesiyle ṣarf-ı maqderet eden Rādjiḥ Efendi.* . . . Only the composer of the colophon would have used the term "humble" (*'ādjizāne*).

8. Cited in note 6 above.

9. I wish to express warmest gratitude to Turgut and Günay Kut for kindly sending me photocopies of nine copies of various 1264 editions of the *Ḥilye,* three of them from Turgut Bey's own collection and six from the Süleymaniye.

10. A page of type is covered by papier mâché (paper pulp) which takes the shape of the type. Into the resulting mold (matrix), metal is cast. This becomes the plate or stereotype from which the page may be printed. When the stereotype becomes worn or damaged a new one can easily be made from the same matrix.

31
A Janissary Poet of Sixteenth-Century Damascus: Māmayya al-Rūmī

C. E. Bosworth

I

IN EARLY PRE-MODERN Islam, the "people of the sword" and the "people of the pen" were normally two sharply distinguished social and ethnic groups, and each rarely crossed over into the other's sphere. With the gradual takeover, from the third/ninth century onward, of so much of the Islamic world by Turkish military slaves or Turkish tribal elements, the Turkish military had been at first inevitably cut off, by its ignorance of the Arab-Persian cultural heritage, from the Arab and Persian civilian elements who administered the Turks' patrimonies and who continued almost exclusively to man the Islamic religious institution. By the time of the great empires of the post-Mongol period, the divide was, however, less sharp. The Qipchaq and Circassian slaves who made up the Mamlūk ruling class received instruction in the Islamic religious and literary sciences as part of their training, and their non-Mamlūk sons often carved out considerable reputations for themselves as scholars, theologians, and littérateurs, as such names as Ibn Taghrībirdī, Ibn Iyās, Ibn Ṭūlūn, and the like attest.[1] In the Ottoman Empire, the Janissaries, originally in the main Christian children from Rumelia who were brought into Islam at an early age, were given a thorough Islamic education, especially those who were selected as Inner Service pages (*ich oghlans*) in the *Enderūn* or Inner Section of the Palace.[2]

II

The personage whom we shall consider in this paper, Māmayya, began his adult career as a Janissary, apparently through local recruitment in Syria (see below), but subsequently abandoned his military career for the life of a literary man and civil servant in Damascus, attaining in this second phase of his career a considerable contemporary reputation in Syria.

Our sources for Māmayya's life and works are the Arabic biographical dictionaries of the late tenth/sixteenth and eleventh/seventeenth centuries. The most important of these is the Damascene writer Sharaf al-Dīn Mūsā ibn Yūsuf, called Ibn Ayyūb (948–1000/1541–92), member of a line of distinguished Shāfi'ī *qāḍīs*, and author of a collection of biographies of 367 notables of Damascus—emirs, judges, scholars, merchants, etc.—whose lives covered a time span from 745/1344–45 to the end of 998/1590. Ibn Ayyūb was conscious that he was following in such distinguished footsteps as those of Ibn 'Asākir, Ibn Khallikān, Ibn Kathīr, Ibn Shākir al-Kutubī, al-Ṣafadī, Ibn Ḥajar al-'Asqalānī, and so on, but his own *Kitāb al-rawḍ al-'āṭir* is especially valuable because of his comments on the scholars and literary men of his own time, most of whom he knew personally, as was indeed the case with Māmayya.[3] The compilers of biographical works of the next three or four generations seem to have derived their information on Māmayya from Ibn Ayyūb, usually condensing it to a lesser or greater extent and quoting a smaller amount of his poetry, although they do not acknowledge any debt to Ibn Ayyūb concerning this, and only Najm al-Dīn al-Ghazzī seems ostensibly to be aware of his existence.[4] Moreover, only al-Khafājī makes any attempt, sketchy and impressionistic though it is, at a critical estimate of Māmayya's literary abilities (see below, end of section II).[5]

The exact form of the curious name Māmayya(h) and its origin remain uncertain. The spelling of the biographical sources *Mām.y.h* points to a vocalization like Māmayya(h) or Māmiyya(h), but when the author himself inserts his name into one of his poems, as he frequently does, he normally renders it Māmāya (*Māmā.y*). Martin Hartmann cited the poetry of Māmayya in his book on the poetic form of the *muwashshaḥ*, and later speculated on its etymology, citing parallels in, amongst other things, Mandaean, and suggesting an Aramaic origin from a diminutive of *emmā* ("mother"), yielding a meaning like "Mummy."[6] Māmayya/Māmāya does indeed sound as if it had a hypocoristic meaning like this, but beyond the fact of the geographical proximity of Damascus to pockets of surviving Neo-Aramaic speech in the Anti-Lebanon to the west of Damascus, it is hard to see how a resident of Damascus with a Turkish background should acquire such a name. Māmayya's full *nasab*, as given in the biographical sources, Muḥammad ibn Aḥmad ibn ʿAbdallāh al-Rūmī, makes one think of an originally non-Turkish, convert background for him, possibly from the Anatolian or Balkan Christian communities. Al-Khafājī gives an additional nominal element, that of Ibn Ukht al-Khayyālī (referring to descent from a shadow player, a practitioner of the *khayāl al-ẓill*?[7]), otherwise unexplained.[8]

Secondary sources like Kaḥḥāla, al-Ziriklī, Hartmann, and Brockelmann give a birthdate for Māmayya of 930/1524, but the present writer has not been able to find evidence for this in the primary sources. These last state that he was born and lived as a child in Istanbul, but then moved to Damascus, and on attaining manhood, enrolled in the Janissary corps (*min jumlat al-n.k.shārīya, zumrat al-y.n.k.j.rīya*[9]); Ibn Ayyūb states that he put on the Janissary cap and drew a stipend of five *ʿuthmānīs* per day.[10] By this time—about 1540 or 1550—the original concept of a single-stream entry into the Janissary corps of *Qapı Qulları*, via the *devshirme*, or collection of Christian (and Bosnian Muslim) children from the Balkans, had broken down. The demands for manpower of the middle and later tenth/sixteenth century wars led to the *devshirme* levies being extended to the Christian populations of southern and eastern Anatolia (e.g., to Sis and Kayseri in the 1560s, and to Marʿash and Diyarbakir in 981/1573). For such a provincial garrison of Janissaries as that of Damascus (which seems to have been maintained, in the middle decades of this century, at a strength of about a thousand[11]), the State was either itself recruiting locally in order to supplement the troops sent out from Istanbul, or else local people were being insinuated, by methods more or less corrupt, into the Janissary ranks so that these interlopers might enjoy the pay and privileges of membership; service in Damascus at this time cannot have been very hazardous or demanding.[12] The trend toward an influx of locals was sufficiently noticeable for the Sublime Porte itself to show concern, but not, apparently, to halt the trend. In 979/1571 Selīm II had commanded the governor of Damascus and the Agha of the Janissaries to dismiss local intruders; a new firman of Murād III in 985/1579 again ordered the *beglerbeg* to give vacant places in the Janissary garrison to Rūmīs (here, it seems, those from the old Ottoman lands of Anatolia and Rumelia), brave young men (*yigitler*), and not to rich locals (*yerlü*), foreigners (*tāt*, sc. Kurds, Persians, etc.), and bedouin (*'Arab*). Coming as he did from Istanbul, Māmayya would, however, obviously fulfill the desideratum of Rūmī birth laid down in such decrees.[13]

A firm date emerges in Māmayya's life, that of 960/late 1553, when he and a group of other Janissaries stationed in Damascus joined the Syrian pilgrimage caravan and visited the Holy Places. This seems to have been the turning point of his career. His literary interests were already apparent, and he now threw over the military profession and became a student in Damascus, first at the feet of the scholar Shams al-Dīn Abū 'l-Fatḥ Muḥammad ibn Muḥammad ibn 'Abd al-Salām al-Tūnisī al-Mālikī (901–75/1495–1567) for *adab*,[14] and then of Shihāb al-Dīn ibn Badr al-Dīn Muḥammad al-Ghazzī,[15] with whom he studied the *Ājurrūmīya*. The purist views which this grammatical training engendered led him (unfortunately for modern students of this interesting genre of literature) to tear up the greater part of a *dīwān* which he had written in dialect poetry (*malḥūn*)—deprecatingly described by Ibn Ayyūb as *sakhīf* ("lightweight, frivolous")—and to correct the rest in accordance with the norms of classical Arabic grammar.[16]

Māmayya secured a job as a translator (presumably between Turkish and Arabic) at the *maḥkama* or *sharī'a* court at al-Ṣāliḥīya just outside Damascus, and then at the chief one of the six courts in Damascus itself, *al-maḥkama al-kubrā*. At the same time, he plunged into a busy life of poetic activity, acquiring a reputation as the foremost local poet in the popular genres of *zajal, mawwāl*, and *muwashshaḥ*. Ibn Ayyūb mentions his role as protagonist in two poetic contests with Egyptian rivals, held in the north porch of the mosque of al-Sayfī Yalbughā in Damascus, in the second of which, taking place in 972/1564–65, Māmayya overwhelmed the Egyptian *zajjāl* and aroused the audience to dancing and to transports of emotion and joy.[17] In addition to his expertise here, his skill as a satirist is also mentioned, this being often of a scabrous nature—he is described as *khabīth al-lisān* ("foul-mouthed")—so that people feared his tongue as "the venom of vipers." Not surprisingly, he also wrote in the vein of *mujūn*; much married and divorced himself, he wrote verses on the themes of sexual indulgence (including that in pederasty, cited specifically by Ibn Ayyūb), wine drinking, and hashish eating (for this last, see below, section IV).[18]

For some unknown reason, but perhaps because of a loss of official favor, his over-sharp tongue, or his matrimonial entanglements, he fell into poverty and hunger. But his fortunes revived when he praised in an ode (Ibn Ayyūb says that he was personally present when Māmayya recited this *dālīya*) the new Chief *Qāḍī* of Damascus, Shams al-Dīn Muḥammad ibn Muḥyī al-Dīn Muḥammad al-Ḥanafī, called Ibn Chiwī-zāde (in the Arabic sources, Jawī-zāda).[19] On learning of his indigence, Muḥammad Efendi Ibn Chiwī-zāde asked him to choose his own office, so Māmayya asked him for a post as translator again at the *maḥkama* in the Jawzīya *madrasa,* a job he had already held before at some point in the past. Further ups and downs followed for him, and after he lost this job, he was once more active as a panegyrist of the great and good in Damascus, living off their gifts, and becoming a protégé of the Shaykh al-Islām ʿImād al-Dīn Ismāʿīl ibn Aḥmad al-Nābulusī, the most noted Shāfiʿī legal scholar in the city after the death of Badr al-Dīn al-Ghazzī.[20] Possibly it was this patronage which secured him a further post as translator, this time in the tribunal concerned with the division of inheritances (*qisma*).[21] He now seems to have entered the final phase of his life, one of prosperity, fathering many children, and living in style as a popular literary figure whose verses were much recited and sung at parties and assemblies. He died eventually in Dhu 'l-Ḥijja 987/January–February 1580, or Muḥarram 998, according to the biographical sources,[22] although inferences from a poem connected with his death, appearing in the Manchester manuscript of his *dīwān* (see below), and dates in the colophon of the British Library manuscript provide a death date of 985/1577–78.[23] He was buried at the Bāb al-Farādīs of Damascus by the graves of Ibn Mulayk[24] and his teacher Abū 'l-Fatḥ al-Mālikī.[25]

In this final period of an easier existence, Māmayya's attitudes to life and literature appear to have mellowed. When he had gathered his poetry into two volumes—in 971/1563–64 according to a chronogram in the exordium giving the date of its composition—he had already omitted the satires. He continued to compose verse, acquiring a special reputation for his skill in inserting into his verses riddles and enigmas (*lughz, muʿammā*) and chronograms (*ta'rīkh*)—Ibn Ayyūb describes him as "the sultan of that art" in an age when many of the contemporary literary men lacked the skill, so he says, to produce chronograms and could make up only contrived and inferior ones—and also from his felicitous use of quotation (*iqtibās*). He thought enough of himself to style himself "the second Ibn al-Rūmī" (*Ibn al-Rūmī al-muta'akhkhir*), successor of the famous 'Abbasid poet.[26]

Māmayya thus surmounted the handicap of being originally a non-native speaker of Arabic, and Ibn Ayyūb praises him as a poet of spontaneous and unforced expression, *maṭbū'*;[27] clearly, he had become by the end of his life a popular and much-appreciated figure in Ottoman Damascus. The only note of criticism to be found amongst his biographers emanates from al-Khafājī. He concedes that Māmayya did well to write so successfully in what was for him originally an alien tongue: "How excellent an eloquent one he was, for a person who had not had repeated drinks from the water of the roots of the fragrant [desert] *qayṣūm* plant and the *shīḥ* wormwood shrub, who had not been nourished by the suckling of the Arabic language, and who had not received an education by the freshly gathered fruits of the sciences, since he came from the Pale Ones (*Banū 'l-Aṣfar*[28]), had suffered catastrophic [literally, 'black'] deprivation, and faced violent death." But gradually, the beneficent influence of the region of Damascus had pervaded his nature, so that "his faculty of poetic improvization became polished, and his natural qualities became more refined and pleasanter than the northerly breeze." Notwithstanding, al-Khafājī found something to reprehend: "I have studied closely his *Dīwān*, and have noted that it contains faults and weaknesses, and that inadequacy enters into the frameworks of its ideas and its structures."[29]

III

The main *dīwān* of Māmayya survives in several manuscripts in Egypt and in several Western European libraries, though one might have expected rather more copies to have survived from a writer so well known in his own city and age; one or two other minor poetic works survive also.[30] This main *dīwān* bears the title *Rawḍat al-mushtāq wa-bahjat al-'ushshāq* ("Garden of the Yearning One and Delight of the Lovers"). Good descriptions of it may be found in the British Library, Gotha, Berlin, and Manchester catalogs;[31] in the second of these, Ahlwardt noted that, although the biographical sources state that Māmayya collected his *dīwān* together in 971/1563–64 (see above), the manuscripts actually contain poems of a later date than that, going up to at least 983/1575–76, on the evidence of chronograms in these poems.

The present writer has examined the Manchester manuscript, which dates from 1028/1619, some forty years after the author's death. Its 175 closely written folios comprise *qaṣīdas, zajals, mawwāls, muwashshaḥs*, and a large number of *dū-bayts* or quatrains. Many of the poems are addressed to friends of his in Damascus or to the emirs and judges of that city, and contain references to various local events, such as the building of the mosque and baths by the governor Dervīsh Pasha (fols. 161a, 170b),[32] on the appointment of the *defterdār* Muḥammad (fol. 170b) and on the fountain erected by Shaykh Shihāb al-Dīn Aḥmad ibn Sulaymān (fol. 174b).[33] Māmayya's great fondness for chronograms is much in evidence here, as is also his liking for the poetic form of the *takhmīs* or *mukhammas* (sc. that of five hemistichs, usually comprising a verse of some well-known poem by another author appended to three original hemistichs, in the same rhyme throughout the first stanza, but with a varying rhyme scheme for subsequent ones[34]). Māmayya's *takhmīsāt* include one on the *Qaṣīda nūnīya* of the great Ottoman Shaykh al-Islām Abū 'l-Su'ūd Efendi (d. 982/1574),[35] called *al-Mashāhid al-'aynīya* (fols. 66a–70b); one of those innumerable ones composed on the *Qaṣīdat al-burda* of al-Būṣīrī (d. between 694 and 696/1294–97)[36] which, Māmayya says, was the forty-first *takhmīs* on this to be written, so that he had named it the *Quṭb al-arba'īn* ("The Pole of the Forty") (fols. 82a–91b);[37] and on the famous wine poem of Ibn al-Fāriḍ (d. 632/1235),[38] which Māmayya called *al-Nash'a al-azalīya fī takhmīs al-Khamrīya* (fols. 47a–48a). On fol. 171b appear ten lines of poetry in Turkish, with the marginal heading of *mulaḥ bi'l-turkī* ("facetiae in Turkish").

No critical examination of the various manuscripts of the *dīwān* has, to the present writer's knowledge, been made, hence it is unclear whether the contents of the manuscripts vary significantly.

IV

Finally, translations of two *dū-bayts* and of two more extensive *qaṣīdas* from the *dīwān*, made from the Manchester manuscript alone, hence not to be considered as based upon a firmly established text are appended.

The quatrains are interesting as being further material to that collected by Professor Franz Rosenthal in his book, at once fascinating and erudite, *The Herb, Hashish Versus Medieval Muslim Society.*[39] The Arabic poetry examined by Rosenthal as the basis for much of his book extends chronologically broadly from the Ayyubid through the Mamlūk to the early Ottoman periods. It illustrates, *inter alia,* the attitude of those who condemned hashish as a narcotic, a drug whose legal position was to be assimilated to the prohibited grape wine, and the attitude of those who defended the use of hashish as not specifically condemned by the Qur'ān, hence with no defined *ḥadd* punishment.[40] In these two quatrains of Māmayya, the poet whimsically takes up two viewpoints, but not including the one advocating prohibition of all stimulants and narcotics. Instead, the first one praises the benefits of wine over hashish, whereas the second one praises the benefits of hashish over wine; what the poet's own views were does not specifically emerge. Since the Arabic text appears straightforward and virtually free from ambiguity, it is given here in transliteration as providing a fleeting taste of Māmayya's actual style.[41]

Quatrain 1 (meter: *kāmil*) (fol. 172a)

(a) Text
1. *laysa l-ḥashīshatu ka'l-mudāmati ṭab'uha* *inna l-ḥashīshata āfatun yā nāsu*
2. *wa'l-rāḥu lil-arwāḥi fīhā nashwatun* [text, *nashā'*] *wa-shifā l-ḍanā wa-manāfi' lil-nāsi*

(b) Translation
1. Hashish is not like wine in its essential nature: indeed, hashish is a disastrous thing, O people!
2. Whereas wine is good for souls, and contains an intoxicating headiness, a cure for languor and beneficial qualities for mankind.

Quatrain 2 (meter: *kāmil*) (fol. 172a)

(a) Text
1. *kun qāni'an bi-ḥashīshatin fī rawḍatin* *wa-da'i l-khumūra fa-bābuhu matbū'u*
2. *fīhi l-ta'arbudu wa'l-ṣudā'u maḥalluhu* *fa-hwa l-muḥarramu wa'l-ḥashīshu rabī'u*

(b) Translation

1. Be contented with hashish in a garden, and leave aside wine,
   for its usage and effects are well known and
   oft followed.
2. It contains quarrelsomeness and inevitably brings along
   headaches; wine is forbidden, whereas hashish is like
   the spring.[42]

The second two poems are in form *qaṣīdas*, the first one of seven verses in the meter *kāmil* and the rhyme *-adu*, and the second one of twenty-eight verses in the meter *basīṭ* and the rhyme *-īn*. Both were written by Māmayya to celebrate the capture in 1570–71 of Cyprus from the Venetians by the Ottoman fifth vizier Lāla Muṣṭafā Pasha, who had been transferred from the governorship of Syria (and who was to return afterward to Damascus as governor[43]) to be *serdār*, or commander-in-chief, of the land forces dispatched from the southern coasts of Anatolia against the island. The Ottoman conquest began more than three centuries of Turkish rule in Cyprus, and the achievement justly merited Māmayya's encomia, an achievement which balanced the naval disaster for the Turks at Aynabakhtı (Lepanto) which took place at this same time.[44] The state of the text of the *dīwān* here does not allow of the providing of a firm Arabic text in transliteration, but a translation is here given of the two odes, although this itself must obviously be regarded as in certain parts a provisional one only.

Ode 1 on the conquest of Cyprus (fol. 53b)

Translation

1. Indeed, the one who is secure in his exalted position (*salīm al-sha'n*, sc. Sultan Selīm II), the most noble, the just, the victorious, the one whose power is perpetually established,
2. When he raided the land of unbelief with a conquering army, and led them into battle as their leader, the one led by God on the right course,
3. He pressed them hard, until they complained volubly of being driven into a tight corner by him, and the hard, open plain became narrow with his army.
4. They sought victory from God, and every overbearing tyrant fell into disappointment;[45] they [the Muslim warriors] fell as martyrs in battle on the day of attack at which they were present.

5. They shouted *takbīrs*, with al-Muṣṭafā as their leader (*imām*),[46] with the sword like a *miḥrāb* for heads which bowed down in prostration.
6. They handed down from mouth to mouth the story of the capture of Cyprus amongst all other creation, and a fully authenticated report of the victory has been spread abroad.[47]
7. The sultan was told, in a chronogram composed of the phrase, "The troops conquering Cyprus are to be highly praised!"[48]

Ode 2 on the conquest of Cyprus (fols. 53b–54a)

Translation

1. God's victory and the clear conquest came along; Cyprus was conquered in the noblest of years.
2. It was taken by the sword, with violence and force; the great ones of the believers raised their *takbīrs* there.
3. The Merciful One gave aid to al-Muṣṭafā's army,[49] and it took captive the hosts of the heretical ones' army.
4. They inflicted grief upon the unbelievers when they shouted the *tahlīl* and raised their voices with their cries, rejoicing.
5. They threw open the gates of Cyprus, and recited, "Enter it, in peace and security!"[50]
6. The minds of the infidels were thrown into confusion when they came face to face with horses of noble breed, [rushing forward] like birds flying through the air.
7. In Cyprus, like lions of the Turks, they left behind, for the sake of God, families and children.
8. They exerted themselves to the utmost in battle when their souls pledged their allegiance in carrying war against the heretics and infidels.
9. They bore witness with their hearts that, if they should be killed, they would be martyrs, securing a heavenly reward.
10. They left behind their wealth and their progeny, and preferred as their consorts houris and wide-eyed maidens [i.e., in Paradise].
11. They set upon them [the enemy] with the points of their spear-shafts, and set upon them in battle encounters which laid them [the enemy] low.
12. They displayed grim faces (*qaṭ[ṭ]abū*) when they went forth, [and] when there came to them the succor of the pole (*quṭb*) of the forty saints.[51]

13. The bishop, the ignobly born one (*al-usquf al-aqfas*)[52] lamented, and wept on account of the Turks, with a grieving heart.
14. They established firmly the might of an everlasting faith [sc. Islam] when they pulled down the supporting column of the lofty state of the ignorant ones.
15. They rendered black [i.e., reduced to a state of shame and humiliation] the faces of the Pale Ones (*Banū 'l-Aṣfar*) with their gleaming sword blades, even though they were made to resemble ignorant barbarians (*ḥumr jāhilīn*) [because covered with blood from the battle].[53]
16. They girded on their swords, slung around [?] their necks [lacuna][54], as the essence of their souls and like a precious necklace.
17. Rain clouds of blood sent down their showers when the lightning gleam of the warriors' swords shone forth.
18. How often did they assault them with a gleaming meteor-shaft, and hit the target of every accursed devil!
19. They [the Muslims] attacked them; all those engaged in the battle clashed together, and blood flowed like the sea, so that they were drowned.
20. How many drownings, how many times did they drown everyone who plunged in [into the fight] and every disgraced devil!
21. Whilst the warriors of Syria in their battle assault were hardening their hearts,[55] and some of them never relented at all.
22. And the one who is secure in his exalted position [Sultan Selīm II], the sultan of the community of the Muslims, the one who renders victorious the Holy Law, the destroyer of the evildoers,
23. And who is, I hold fast in my memory, the personification of good fortune seated on his throne (*al-bakht fī 'l-takht*), possessing an awesomeness which has made India and China quake with fear.
24. The pavilion of victoriousness has been erected over him, the one who unites all deeds of pride, the *Imām* of the just ones.
25. If any person in any assembly of people invokes God's blessing on him in prayer, the whole of creation will add "Amen!"
26. From the progeny of 'Uthmān, exalted (*'alī*) in faithfulness, the devoted follower of the divine law, the one attesting the truth (*ṣiddīq*) of the certain faith.[56]
27. He is an explicit focus of spirituality (*quṭb ẓāhir*) in a concealed guise, the one who ordains justice, the ruler of the Muslims.

28. O God of the Divine Throne, be his helper perpetually, and keep him safe through the faithful guide [through the guidance of the Prophet Muḥammad]!

NOTES

1. As D. Ayalon has noted, "many sons of Mamlūks became men of religion and letters, and a large part of the history of the Mamlūk Sultanate was written by Mamlūk descendants" ("The Muslim City and the Mamlūk Military Aristocracy," *Proceedings of the Israel Academy of Sciences and Humanities* [Jerusalem, 1968], II, 327, reprinted in *Studies on the Mamlūks of Egypt (1250–1517)* [London, 1977], no. VII).

2. See B. Miller, *The Palace School of Muhammad the Conqueror* (Cambridge, Mass., 1941), pp. 79 f.; H. A. R. Gibb and H. Bowen, *Islamic Society and the West, I: Islamic Society in the Eighteenth Century* (London, 1950), I, 56–57.

3. The credit for rescuing Ibn Ayyūb from almost total obscurity goes to Dr. Ahmet Halil Güneş, whose study and edition of forty-two of the biographies has been used here: *Das Kitāb ar-rauḍ al-'āṭir des Ibn Aiyūb. Damaszener Biographien des 10./16. Jahrhundert. Beschreibung und Edition* (Berlin, 1981). The biography devoted to Māmayya is on pp. 83–93 of the Arabic text, no. 280 in the editor's own numbering, no. 281 in that of the original MS. Cf. Güneş's epitomized biography of the poet, German section, p. 64.

4. See Güneş, German section, pp. 5, 10.

5. These subsequent sources on Māmayya are as follows: Aḥmad ibn Muḥammad, called Ibn al-Qāḍī (d. 1025/1616), *Durrat al-ḥijāl fī ghurrat asmā' al-rijāl*, ed. I. S. Allouche ('Allūsh) (Rabat, 1934–36), II, 320, no. 883 (very brief); Najm al-Dīn Muḥammad ibn Muḥammad al-Ghazzī (d. 1061/1651), *al-Kawākib al-sā'ira bi-a'yān al-mi'a al-'āshira*, ed. Jibrā'īl Sulaymān Jabbūr (Beirut-Jūniya-Ḥarīṣā, 1945–58), III, 50–51; Shihāb al-Dīn Aḥmad ibn Muḥammad al-Khafājī (d. 1069/1659), *Rayḥānat al-alibbā' wa-zahrat al-ḥayāt al-dunyā*, ed. 'Abd al-Fattāḥ Muḥammad al-Ḥilū (Cairo, 1386/1967), I, 158–64; 'Abd al-Ḥayy ibn Aḥmad al-Ḥanbalī, called Ibn al-'Imād, *Shadharāt al-dhahab fī akhbār man dhahab* (Cairo, 1350–51/1931–32), VIII, 413–14. The brief mentions on Māmayya in 'Umar Riḍā Kaḥḥāla, *Mu'jam al-mu'allifīn* (Damascus, 1376–81/1957–61), VIII, 280–81, and in Khayr al-Dīn al-Ziriklī, *al-A'lām* (Damascus, 1373–78/1954–59), VI, 235, are based on the above sources, as are the biographical details in Brockelmann, *GAL*, II^2, 350, S II, 382.

6. *Das arabische Strophengedichte, I: Das Muwaššaḥ* (Weimar, 1897), pp. 66–67; review of Lidzbarski's *Ephemeris für semitische Epigraphik*, in *Deutsche Litteraturzeitung*, XVII (1901), cols. 1045–47. I am grateful to Professor Manfred Ullmann of Tübingen University for making a copy of this last available to me.

7. *Khayyālī* is found in Damascus as a doublet of *Karakūzātī*, i.e., Karagöz player; see Jamāl al-Dīn al-Qāsimī and Khalīl al-'Aẓm, *Qāmūs al-ṣinā'at al-shāmiyya. Dictionnaire des métiers damascains* (Paris and The Hague, 1960), II,

384–85, no. 311. However, since putting forward this suggestion, my student Dr. Taysīr al-Zawāhira has pointed out to me the existence in the first part of the tenth/sixteenth century of at least two Turkish scholars of Istanbul with the name Khayyālī/Khayālī, sc. an al-Khayyālī who was a student of 'Alā' al-Dīn 'Alī ibn Yūsuf al-Fanārī (d. 903/1497–98; see on him *EI*² art. "Fenārī-zāde" [J. R. Walsh]) and al-Mawlā al-Fāḍil al-Khayyālī, with whom various noted scholars studied (see al-Ghazzī, *al-Kawākib al-sā'ira*, I, 162, 278–79, 292). Māmayyā's mother could certainly have been, on both chronological and geographical grounds, a sister of one of these scholars.

8. *al-Kawākib al-sā'ira*, I, 158.

9. Rendering the Turkish term *Yeñi cheri* caused difficulties for non-Turkish-speaking Arab writers; from the efforts of the biographers derive the deformations in the *nisbas* for Māmayya "al-Anğisārī (Anqišārī)" given by Brockelmann, *GAL*, S II, 382.

10. *al-Rawḍ al-'āṭir*, ed. Güneş, Arabic text, p. 83. *'Uthmānī* was the term used in Damascus for the standard Ottoman silver coin, the *aqche* or asper; see J.-P. Pascual, *Damas à la fin du XVI*ᵉ *siècle d'après trois actes de waqf ottomans* (Damascus, 1983), I, 121–22, "Annexe. La monnaie."

11. Muhammad Adnan Bakhit, *The Ottoman Province of Damascus in the Sixteenth Century* (Beirut, 1982), p. 96, quoting Ibn Ṭūlūn for the position in the 1520s.

12. I am grateful to Professor V. L. Ménage for useful information about Janissary recruitment at this time; see further his article in *EI*² s.v. "Dev-shirme." Specific information on the Janissary element in the military forces in Damascus during these years can be found in Nawfān Rajā al-Ḥumūd, *al-'Askar fī bilād al-Shām fī 'l-qarnayn al-sādis 'ashar wa'l-sābi' 'ashar al-milādīyayn* (Beirut, 1401/1981), pp. 42–43. See also Bakhit, op. cit., 96–97.

13. U. Heyd, *Ottoman Documents on Palestine 1552–1615: A Study of the Firmans According to the Mühimme Defteri* (Oxford, 1960), pp. 68–69.

14. Güneş, op. cit., German section, pp. 68–69, with further references. Ibn Ayyūb's biography of this scholar is not included in the part edited by Güneş.

15. For the father, Badr al-Dīn Muḥammad al-Ghazzī, see Güneş, op. cit., German section, p. 71, with further references; again, Ibn Ayyūb's biography is not included in the part edited by Güneş.

16. Ibid., Arabic text, p. 83; al-Ghazzī, *Al-Kawākib al-sā'ira*, III, 50.

17. Ibn Ayyūb, loc. cit.

18. Ibn Ayyūb, Arabic text, pp. 83–84, 87.

19. Died 995/1587. Ibn Ayyūb has a biography, not in the part edited by Güneş, but see the latter's German section, p. 70, giving further biographical references, notably Ibn al-'Imād, *Shadharāt*, VIII, 436–37. The date of Māmayya's reciting of his ode must have been Ṣafar 977/July–August 1569, for this is the date given by Ibn al-'Imād for Ibn Chiwī-zāde's brief assumption of office in Damascus before going on to become Chief *Qāḍī* in Egypt during this same year. See further, *IA*, art. "Çivi-zâde" (M. Cavid Baysun), and *EI*² art. "Čiwi-zāde" (V. L. Ménage).

20. Died 993/1582. Ibn Ayyūb has a biography, not in the part edited by Güneş, but see the latter's German section, p. 61; al-Ghazzī, op. cit., III, 130–35; Ibn al-'Imād, op. cit., VIII, 429–30.

21. For this office in Ottoman times, see *EI*² art. "Ḳassām" (Cengiz Orhonlu).

22. To which should be added Ḥājjī Khalīfa, *Kashf al-ẓunūn*, ed. Flügel, III, 313, no. 5661, and Ismā'īl Bāshā al-Baghdādī, *al-Īḍāḥ al-maknūn, dhayl Kashf al-ẓunūn* (Istanbul, 1943), I, 491.

23. A. Mingana, *Catalogue of the Arabic Manuscripts in the John Rylands Library at Manchester* (Manchester, 1934), cols. 799–800, no. 478.

24. Scholar and poet of Ḥamāt and then of Damascus, 'Alā' al-Dīn 'Alī ibn Muḥammad al-Fuqqā'ī, called Ibn Mulayk, d. 917/1512; see Brockelmann, *GAL*, II², 23, S II, 13.

25. Ibn Ayyūb, Arabic text, p. 93; al-Ghazzī, op. cit., III, 51.

26. Ibn Ayyūb, Arabic text, pp. 84, 91, 93.

27. Ibid., p. 91.

28. See below, p. 461.

29. *Rayḥānat al-alibbā'*, I, 158–59.

30. See Brockelmann, *GAL*, loc. cit. The other *dīwān* of Māmayya—presumably the second of the two volumes which he is said to have collected together in 971/1563–64—is called the *Burhān al-burhān*, written to illustrate the various rhetorical figures of *badī'* in Arabic, according to Brockelmann, *GAL*, II², 350, who records only one manuscript of it.

31. W. Cureton and C. Rieu, *Catalogus codicum manuscriptorum orientalium qui in Museo Britannico asservantur. Pars secunda, codices arabicos complectens* (London, 1846–71), cols. 298–99, no. 631; W. Pertsch, *Die arabischen Handschriften der Herzoglichen Bibliothek zu Gotha* (Gotha, 1878–92), IV, 311, no. 2320; W. Ahlwardt, *Verzeichnis der arabischen Handschriften der Königlichen Bibliothek zu Berlin* (Berlin, 1887–99), III, 115–17, nos. 7945–47; Mingana, *Catalogue of the Arabic Manuscripts in the John Rylands Library*, cols. 799–800, no. 478.

32. Governor in Damascus from 979/1571 until his death in 981/1573–74; see H. Laoust, *Les Gouverneurs de Damas sous les Mamlouks et les premiers Ottomans (658–1156/1260–1744), traduction des annales d'Ibn Ṭūlūn et d'Ibn Ǧum'a* (Damascus, 1952), pp. 187–88.

33. Ibn Ayyūb has a biography of this Qādirī Ṣūfī shaykh, not, however, in the part edited by Güneş; but see his German section, p. 45, and also al-Muḥibbī, *Khulāṣat al-athar fī a'yān al-qarn al-ḥādī 'ashar* (Cairo, 1284/1867), I, 207–8. The items of topographical information which can be gleaned from Māmayya's *dīwān* have been utilized by Pascual in his *Damas à la fin du XVI*ᵉ *siècle*, vol. I.

34. For a clear exposition of the structure of the *takhmīs* and of other multiple poems, see E. G. Browne, *A Literary History of Persia* (London, 1906), I, 42–43; also Tâhir-ül Mevlevī, *Edebiyat lügatı* (Istanbul, 1973), pp. 101–2, 141–42.

35. See on him, *EI*² art. s.v. (J. Schacht).

36. See on him, *EI*[2] Suppl., art. s.v. (Ed.). This *takhmīs al-Burda* of Māmayya exists also in separate manuscripts; see Brocklemann, *GAL*, S I, 469.

37. With allusion to the belief in the *quṭb*'s headship in a saintly hierarchy, with a body of forty saints permanently pervading the world with their sanctity.

38. See on him, *EI*[2] art. s.v. (R. A. Nicholson and J. Pedersen).

39. Leiden, 1971.

40. Cf. Rosenthal, op. cit., pp. 101 ff.

41. The two quatrains accordingly form a brief addition to Rosenthal's translations in his Appendix A, "Some Hashish Poems Translated," in op. cit., pp. 163–74.

42. There seems to be a *tawriya*, a secondary and hidden meaning, here, alluding to the month of Muḥarram, ill-omened from the death of al-Ḥusayn in it, whereas Rabīʿ is blessed, from the birth in it of the Prophet, traditionally placed in 12 Rabīʿ I.

43. From 971/1563–64 until 975/1567–68; see Laoust, op. cit., pp. 186–87.

44. For the historical background of the conquest of Cyprus, see Sir George Hill, *A History of Cyprus, III: The Frankish Period 1432–1571* (Cambridge, 1948), pp. 878 f. (from Western sources); Ismail Hami Danişmend, *Izahlı osmanlı tarihi kronolojisi* (Istanbul, 1947–61), II, 388–94; I. H. Uzunçarşili, *Osmanlı tarihi, III/1: Selim'in tahta çıkışından 1699 Karlofça andlaşmasına kadar* (Ankara, 1951), pp. 9–15 (from Turkish sources also). See further *IA* art. "Mustafa Paşa, Lala, Kara" (Bekir Kütükoğlu).

45. Qur'ān 14:18(15).

46. The surface reference being to the commander of the Turkish forces, Lāla Muṣṭafā Pasha, but with an allusion, however, to the spiritual leadership of the Chosen One, al-Muṣṭafā, the Prophet Muḥammad.

47. This verse uses the technical language of Muslim tradition, *'anʿanū* ("they handed down from mouth to mouth") and *ḥadīth musnad* ("a fully authenticated report").

48. The second hemistich, *ahl fatḥ Qubruṣ muḥammad*, yields 36 + 488 + 362 + 92 = 978 (1570–71).

49. The same *tawriya* as in v. 5 of the previous ode.

50. Qur'ān 15:46.

51. Here the *quṭb* ("pole, axis") as the head of a hierarchy of saints is identified with the Prophet, as being the Perfect Man; see *EI*[2] art. "Ḳuṭb" (F. de Jong), and also n. 37 above.

52. *Aqfas*, literally "born of a slave father, the son of a slave girl" (*Lisān al-ʿArab*[1], VIII, 62). Cyprus had at the time of the Ottoman assault two parallel Christian ecclesiastical hierarchies, one of the Latins and one of the Orthodox; the three Latin bishops were all killed or enslaved by the Turks, only the Archbishop of Nicosia, Philip Mocenigo, being fortunately away in Venice at the time. See Hill, op. cit., III, 1098–1104; vol. IV, *The Ottoman Province and the British Colony* (Cambridge, 1952), pp. 305 f.

53. This verse is rich in the symbolism in Arabic of colors, with mention

of "blackening of the face," the "Pale Ones" [the Greeks], the "white" sword blades (*al-bīḍ*) and the "Red Ones," i.e., the light-skinned non-Arabs, and especially the Persians. See I. Goldziher, *Muhammedanische Studien* (Halle, 1889–90), I, Excursus 5, "Schwarze und Weisse," pp. 268–69, trans. C. R. Barber and S. M. Stern, *Muslim Studies* (London, 1967–71), I, 243–44; *EI*² arts. "Aṣfar" (Goldziher) and "Lawn" (A. Morabbia).

54. The word *naḥrihim* supplied here as the basis for translation fits both the sense and the meter.

55. *Qāsiyūn al-qalb*, but with a hidden allusion—since Syrian troops are mentioned here—to the Jabal Qāsiyūn which overlooks Damascus, here regarded as a symbol of solidity; Mount Qāsiyūn was further regarded as particularly sacred because of the number of saints' caves and grottoes on it (see *EI*² art. "Ḳāsiyūn" [N. Elisséeff]).

56. This verse has allusions to three of the Patriarchal Caliphs, namely 'Uthmān, 'Alī, and Abū Bakr al-Ṣiddīq.

32
The Walls of Jerusalem

Amnon Cohen

THE MYRIAD SITES and monuments of historical importance in Jerusalem may seem to contradict the commonly held image of the city as essentially spiritual. The fact that the sites are concentrated in a relatively small area, circumscribed by the walls of the old city, highlights this contradiction even further. The monuments vary in external size as well as intrinsic nature and functional aim, and whether buried in the ground or conspicuous on the surface, they constitute separate entities linked in many cases only by their physical proximity. The walls surrounding the old city, almost intact until today, are by definition among the few bonds joining together all they encompass. But they are more than that: they well deserve to be regarded as a most impressive relic of Jerusalem's past. Often referred to by European travelers over the past five hundred years, sketched by cartographers in a somewhat general and inaccurate fashion, appearing in all the famous nineteenth-century paintings of the city and, of course, almost regularly being filmed and televised in color by present-day tourists and media, the old city's walls have left the Holy Sepulchre and the Wailing Wall in relative obscurity. Second only to the Dome of the Rock they became, in the eyes both of the peoples of the Middle East (for complex political reasons) and of the international community (for elementary artistic considerations, or merely simplistic ones), a symbol of Jerusalem. Bearing in mind the basic fact that this is an Ottoman monument (much better preserved than similar relics such as the walls of Istanbul), it is appropriate to shed some light on a few historical aspects of the construction of the walls.

When observed at close range, the Ottoman nature of these walls emerges clearly and even precisely. The inscriptions over most of the gates ascribe the construction of "this blessed wall" to Suleiman the

Magnificent. The dates of these inscriptions are given in Hijri years and months, so that the project can easily be placed in its precise historical time setting, and the stages of its completion can be traced. Max Van Berchem summed it up as follows:

> En 944 on construit les fronts nord et nord-ouest, les plus exposés, parce qu'ils sont dominés par le terrain d'approche. L'année suivante on élève le front est, de l'angle nord-est à la porte Sainte Etienne, peut-être au delà, et parallèlement, le front ouest jusque vers la citadelle. L'année suivante, qui n'est marquée par aucune date, voit sans doute s'achever ces deux fronts; enfin l'année 947 est consacrée à la réfection du front sud.[1]

The entire project seems to have been completed in the course of the years 1538–41. Three to four years is a remarkably short period for such an immense undertaking, and one may safely assume that overall construction took substantially longer: preparatory stages were most probably initiated earlier than mid-1538, whereas final touches were very likely applied long after the winter of 1540. Careful preparations and efficient execution only partially account for the impressive pace at which these walls were erected. Another important element to be borne in mind is that not all of the old walls were dilapidated; parts were still in reasonable condition and could either be used as a source for building materials or actually be incorporated into the new line.

The Ottoman initiative thus became part of a long historical chain of similar activities inspired by geographical reality as much as by political wisdom. The city's being located in a hilly area (in local terms referred to as mountainous) made it incumbent upon its rulers to surround it with a substantial defense system consisting of strong walls studded with turrets—and such was the reality of Jerusalem as recorded ever since biblical times. The Latin defense system was repaired by Saladin, but the decline of the Mamlūk state witnessed a steady deterioration and collapse of the walls during the fourteenth and fifteenth centuries.[2]

When Jerusalem was incorporated into the Ottoman Empire in the early sixteenth century, it became part of the strongest military power in the entire area bounded by Vienna, Baghdad, and Cairo, as well as one of the great political powers on the European scene. A relatively small town in the Ottoman and Syrian context, Jerusalem proved to be of very marginal importance both militarily and politically. The initiative taken to build a defense system around the town, and the efforts and means invested in carrying out this project should, however, be seen in a wider perspective than the above scenario would seem to imply. In their overall approach to the newly acquired territories, it was important for the new rulers to assert their presence in a way that would indicate to the local population the basic differences between the defunct Mamlūk state and that of the victorious Ottomans. But behind the Ottomans' building activity in Palestine during the two or three decades[3] following their conquest lay other considerations of a substantive, rather than an image-building nature.

To overcome the economic and demographic decline which Jerusalem had undergone during the late Mamlūk period, an element of stability, buttressed by the enforcement of law and order, had to be introduced. The reconstruction of the walls was intended to provide the town and its inhabitants with all of these, thus directly affecting the immediate conditions of life as well as the ongoing historical processes of economic development and social progress. Defense considerations were the most important: situated as it was on the verge of the desert, Jerusalem had for some time been exposed to threats and actual incursions by bedouin tribes. As already noted by Van Berchem and others, this provided the authorities with one incentive to build the walls. On the other hand, the distance of thirty to forty miles separating Jerusalem from the undefended Mediterranean coast made it a potential target for covetous Christian enemies, both pirates active in those waters and European navies that might renew their attempts on the Holy Land. The religious importance of the town thus had a two-faceted relevance. It had a positive element, inasmuch as safeguarding the town would be regarded as an expression of religious fervor on the part of the new rulers toward this "first *qibla* and third *ḥaram*." On the other hand, providing Jerusalem with a proper defense system would serve as a barrier to possible hidden Christian schemes, or to actual attempts on the part of the Christians to renew their grip on the holy places.[4]

The benefits which might accrue from the plan to erect a defensive wall all around the town and the Temple Mount seemed clear. Now the idea and the project had to be translated into action, and until recently we thought we knew just how this was done. A Jewish source written in late seventeenth-century Cairo, the famous *Sefer divrei Yoseph* by Sambary, refers to it in what seemed to be a clear, dependable manner: "He [Suleiman the Magnificent] had the walls of Jerusalem built by the [Jewish] Nagid, Rabbi Abraham Castro."[5] Flattering as this reference was to the Jewish people, in that it attributed such a momentous enterprise to one of its sons, a famous leader of his community, more than one eyebrow might have been raised over its reliability. For although the rabbi had previously been entrusted with other official assignments in Egypt (governor of the Royal Mint), and had moved to Jerusalem in the wake of the Ottoman occupation, would it not be somewhat presumptuous to expect a *dhimmī* like Castro to be charged with such a major undertaking? Affluent as he may have been, and perhaps even versed in the conduct of public affairs on a large scale, is it not somewhat farfetched to think of him as responsible for such a tremendous and highly sensitive security project?

The *sijill* archives of the Shar'i court of Jerusalem, recently made available to students of history, provide us with a very clear and definitive answer to this question. Abraham Castro's name recurs in these volumes on several different dates, and in connection with various matters. He indeed moved to Jerusalem, acquired several pieces of property, and became involved in community affairs.[6] The scattered references to his name and activities make no mention of his involvement in, let alone responsibility for, the construction of the walls. Another name, however, emerges as the one and only official in charge of the entire operation. This person, an Ottoman by the name of Muḥammad Çelebi al-Naqqāsh, was sent to Jerusalem to collect the *mīrī* taxes due to the sultan (*al-amīn* or *al-nāẓir 'alā al-amwāl al-sulṭānīya*). The honorific titles preceding his name make it clear that he was not only a Muslim, but a high-ranking official at that (*mawlānā mafkhar al-akābir wa'l-amāthil wa'l-amājid*). In the course of the year 1536, a few references in the court proceedings[7] allude to him, but only in reference to tax collection. Then, at the end of the same year, al-Naqqāsh appears bearing another title: "the superintendent of the wall" (*al-amīn 'alā al-sūr*).[8] From then on, his name is usually followed by either of the two titles or, more accurately, by both.[9] This combination seems very natural, since the construction involved exorbitant expenses which could easily be funneled through the chief tax collector.

Before taking a closer look at some of the financial aspects of the project, the man's name seems to merit further consideration. The term *çelebi*,[10] then usually applied to members of the upper classes and to men of letters, is linked not only with the title *mawlānā*, mentioned above, but also with his surname (*laqab*) *al-naqqāsh*, which literally means "the sculptor," "the engraver." This title, rather bizarre and irrelevant in the context of tax collection, becomes very appropriate when collecting taxes is coupled with a major building project involving the recurrent use of the chisel for commemorative inscriptions engraved in stone over gates and elsewhere.

In the course of the late 1530s and early 1540s, Muḥammad Çelebi al-Naqqāsh was involved in several other projects in Jerusalem. When the Franciscan monks of the Mount Zion monastery were apprehended by the authorities, during the winter of 1538, he was entrusted with the money seized from them, and was then instructed to spend part of it on their most basic needs. The following year, he forwarded a substantial amount of money for the upkeep of the Janissary units stationed in the Citadel.[11] In the year 1541–42, he attended a public meeting on the Temple Mount, where he reported on another project he had just completed, that of supplying Jerusalem with fresh water through the repaired and reconstructed aqueduct running from Solomon's pools.[12] All of these indicate a high degree of public activity and, under different headings, they fall into the general pattern of providing Jerusalem and its inhabitants with better and safer standards of living. By the same token, only in a much more meaningful manner and on a much larger scale, al-Naqqāsh undertook his major assignment, that of building the walls of Jerusalem.

The main function of Muḥammad al-Naqqāsh was to provide the funds for the entire project. Since the sums involved were very large, financing could not be on a local or voluntary basis; it had to be taken care of by the central administration. Naqqāsh's prior responsibility, the collection of the taxes due to Istanbul, technically referred to as those of the Imperial Domains (*khāṣṣ-i shāhī*), must have taken the lion's share of his time and energy. He could not rely on Istanbul to provide him with sufficient funds for the wall. This is the overall impression acquired from reading the *sijill*. Moreover, no documentation is preserved in Jerusalem as to the financial aspects of building the wall.[13] Nor have we come across any relevant data in the central archives of Istanbul, where detailed account books for such expenditures were kept. Certain insights, however, can be gleaned from scattered references, and one detailed document, in the *sijill* of Jerusalem. Five pages found at the end of one of the earliest volumes of the *sijill* (vol. VI) provide us with concise information on some aspects of the system used to finance the project. During the years 1536 to 1538, large sums of money collected in various parts of Palestine and Syria were diverted from their regular channels to meet the immediate expenses incurred in the building of the walls. The combined sum was 791,435 *pāra*, levied in good silver coins struck several years earlier by Suleiman the Magnificent.[14]

Upon looking more closely at a breakdown of the figures, we see that all other districts (*sancak*) of Palestine, not only Jerusalem, contributed toward the project from their annual tax contributions. Gaza's share was about 70,000 *pāra*, that of Nablus just over 122,000 *pāra*; Jerusalem and Ramle contributed about 10 percent of the entire sum. It is hard to compare these figures with the amounts due annually from the various administrative and fiscal units, since the entries do not always specify whether they include the entire *sancak* revenues or just those of the main town from which the *sancak* got its name. In one case, however, that of Nablus, there is specific reference to "the town." The sum sent to Jerusalem at the end of 1536 was 35,350 *pāra*, i.e., 70,700 *akçe*, and another 11,000 *pāra*, i.e., 22,000 *akçe*.[15] Two years later, in the *taḥrīr* of 1538–39, we can easily calculate all that was due from the imperial domains of Nablus: 110,160 *akçe*.[16] In other words, even making allowances for the fact that "the *khāṣṣ* income of Nablus" mentioned in the other entries refers only to the district, the general conclusion remains valid: all of the annual imperial domain income from the town of Nablus, and a very substantial part of the income of the district, were channeled to the special budget for the walls. To a lesser degree, this also emerges from the figures pertaining to the other districts of Palestine; hence, one may generalize and conclude that during the years in which the walls were built a high percentage, perhaps most, of the fiscal income due from Palestine was earmarked for the financing of this project.

This was by no means true only for Palestine. After all, these *sancaks* were parts of the *eyalet* of Damascus. More than half of the total sum mentioned above actually came from Damascus itself. A military contingent of Janissaries headed by their *bölük başı* (commanding officer) was sent to secure the transport of three large installments (338,230; 10,000; 185,000 *pāra* respectively) dispatched in May, August, and October 1537. Unlike the sums arriving from Palestine, these were not reallocated annual taxes, but rather came directly from the treasury of Damascus on the explicit orders of the *defterdar* of the *eyalet (al-daftardār bi'l-mamālik sl-'arabīya wa-ma ma'aha)*. The *fiscus* of Damascus was itself not a source; it served as a clearing house, so these sums, like the Palestinian ones, might have been received from the *mīrī* income of other *sancaks* in Syria. There is, however, a note written in the margin of the first of these entries: "The rest of the money received in gold [coins] is left in the exalted treasury [of Damascus]."[17] This could not refer to any tax income: taxes were usually not levied in gold coins, and the use of the verb *wāṣil* ("arrived," "received") could not mean "collected." It may be concluded from this rather innocuous remark that the money sent from Damascus to Jerusalem was part of a larger sum that had been received in Damascus from a superior source, namely, Istanbul. In other words, substantial funds for the execution of the plan were sent from Istanbul to Damascus as a major contribution on the part of the central treasury. The gold coins thus received were deposited in the *hazine* of Damascus and released incrementally in coins of much smaller denomination, that is, silver aspers.

Military escort for the transport of these funds was provided not only by the Damascus garrison: *Mustaḥfiẓān* soldiers stationed in the citadel of Jerusalem and their commanding officer were employed for this task as well. Several entries relating to Jerusalem, Nablus, and Safed make this point very clearly. The Safed entry has a rider, added later in different ink: "This was spent for the construction of the water-conduit." In his capacity as superintendent of tax collection in Jerusalem, al-Naqqāsh did not limit himself to the project of the walls. In his view, the adequate supply of water to the town was an element of its defense system, and he very likely also had instructions to that effect. He therefore diverted part of the funds received (18,166 *pāra* from Safed; 20,205 *pāra* from Gaza) to the reconstruction of the dilapidated water supply system leading from Solomon's Pools to Jerusalem.

The *jizya* (poll tax), calculated according to classical Islamic tradition on a gold coin basis, could have been levied (at least partially) in gold. This income was also put at al-Naqqāsh's disposal as part of his overall budget. He opted, however, to spend it not on the building of the walls, but toward a more direct and immediate religious goal. Three hundred *qubrusi* gold coins (= 12,000 *pāra*) were thus earmarked "for the gilding of the banner of the Dome of the Rock," and another 100 gold coins for the mosque of al-Aqṣā. Moreover, another sum of 9,300 *pāra* was allotted "for the construction of [the complex of the tomb of the prophet] *sayyidunā* Mūsā."[18] This, too, was a religious cause related, although remotely, to Jerusalem.[19]

At this point it is appropriate to return to the question raised in the first part of this article: was Abraham Castro involved in this project at all? It is clear by now that he was not—nor could he have been—put in charge of this major security project, not only because of its sensitive nature, but also because it involved various elements imbuing it with Islamic religious implications. Muḥammad al-Naqqāsh was the person held responsible for the entire operation, and actually directed it. Might he nevertheless have been somehow linked to Castro in the context of Jerusalem, or was Sambari's contention a pure and simple fabrication? The answer to this question can also be found in the *sijill*. In March 1538, an important deal was struck in Jerusalem between Jews and Arabs: a large tract of land was leased for one hundred years, with specific authorization to build additional rooms on it.[20] This piece of property, part of the *waqf* of the Dome of the Rock, was leased by a certain Jew acting as deputy of another Jew, "*al-mu'allim* Ibrāhīm ibn Yūsif, alias Castro." The procedure the court followed in this case indicated special caution: the technical data were provided by the chief builder of Jerusalem (*mu'allim al-bannā'īn*), the Ḥanbalī *qāḍī* attested to the validity of the deal, and it was then reconfirmed by the Ḥanafī *qāḍī* of the town. Among those present in court was Muḥammad al-Naqqāsh, who would not have attended unless he were somehow involved. Since neither the location of the land nor the nature of the deal indicated any connection with the building of the walls or the collection of taxes, Naqqāsh must have been there out of curiosity, or because of his acquaintance with Castro.

Most of the above-mentioned individuals reappear in another *sijill*, issued some two years later.[21] At an earlier unspecified date, a messenger had been sent from Jerusalem to Cairo, in an attempt to enlist the services of an expert builder for the project of the walls. Meeting with the governor of Cairo, he complained of the lack of cash reserves for the immediate expenses of the project, whereupon Ibrāhīm Castro handed over 10,000 *'uthmānī* to the governor who in turn gave them to the messenger. This sum of money was to be forwarded as a loan to Muḥammad al-Naqqāsh, who was expected eventually to pay it back to Castro's deputy in Jerusalem. By the end of July 1540, the last installment was paid, according to the understanding reached between Cairo and Jerusalem. Hence, whatever the exact nature of the transaction may have been, the acquaintance between Naqqāsh and Castro was closely linked to the financing of the project.

A more positive statement of the exact nature of the relationship between these two emerges from a remark made in a totally different context. Toward the end of 1540, a complaint against the Jewish community was brought to the attention of the governor of Jerusalem.

To ward off the allegation that they had acted unlawfully by making unauthorized alterations in their synagogue, the leaders of the community claimed that they had been given official permission. They stated in court that the entire project was carried out by Ibrāhīm Castro who served as *al-ʿāmil ʿalā al-amwāl al-sulṭānīya.*[22] Entrusting Jewish people with high-ranking positions in the financial bureaucracy of Palestine was not at all exceptional[23] at that time. There were even two Jewish *ʿāmils* in charge of the *kafar* (road tax) of Gaza; they contributed a substantial share of their collection to the walls project (in October 1537). The question that should be addressed is how this title bestowed on Castro relates to the very similar one (*al-amīn ʿalā al-amwāl al-sulṭānīya*) conferred upon al-Naqqāsh. The answer is simple, and it also resolves the ambiguity as to their relationship. Every *amīn*, "reliable" high-ranking tax collector, was assisted by an *ʿāmil*, a commissioner subordinate to him. Thus al-Naqqāsh, aware of Castro's wealth and administrative experience, appointed him as one of his aides, to help with tax collection in Jerusalem.

Rabbi Abraham Castro, a Jewish public figure highly respected by his contemporaries, was not the builder of the walls of Jerusalem. This monumental building project and impressive administrative achievement was carried out by a Muslim for his Muslim ruler as part of an overall scheme both to protect and glorify the Muslim character of Jerusalem. Castro also played a certain role in it: he personally helped finance it, and officially participated in providing adequate funds, following the instructions of Istanbul and Damascus. This he did as an important member of the bureaucratic apparatus of Jerusalem, perhaps even a major one. Unlike Naqqāsh, who was in charge of the project through all its stages, Castro's official involvement was limited only to certain parts of it. In the detailed accounts of 1536–38, where the names of many functionaries are recorded, his name was not even mentioned; he probably joined the team toward the end of the 1530s. In 1540, however, he was formally referred to as being deeply involved. Indeed, the proceedings of the *sharʿi* court of those days belittle his role in terms of duration and of actual participation. They put him in a more realistic—and much more solid—perspective within the wider context of Ottoman building and development activity in Palestine in the early sixteenth century.

NOTES

1. Max Van Berchem, *Matériaux pour un Corpus Inscriptionum Arabicarum* (Cairo, 1922), II, i, 443–44.

2. Van Berchem, pp. 445–49. For travelers' descriptions of the walls in earlier periods, see II, i, 444, nn. 1, 2.

3. For an elaboration of this argument, see my article "Local Trade, International Trade and Government Involvement in Jerusalem During the Early Ottoman Period," *Asian and African Studies*, XII (March 1978), pp. 5–12.

4. For the contemporary Christian approach to a possible comeback to the Holy Land sent by Emperor Charles V, see A. di Arande, *Verdadera Información de Terra Sancta* (Toledo, 1537), pp. xxi–xxii, as cited by A. Arce, "Restrictions upon the Freedom of Movement of Jews in Jerusalem (15th–16th Centuries)," in B. Z. Kedar, *Jerusalem in the Middle Ages, Selected Papers* (Jerusalem, 1979), pp. 216–17 [in Hebrew]. For the relevance of Christian pirates' activity near Jaffa to the precautionary defensive steps taken in Jerusalem, see *sijill* of the court of Jerusalem, VI, 67.

5. Y. Sambari, *Sefer divrei Yoseph*, MS Paris AIU H130A (Jerusalem, 1981), p. 163 [in Hebrew].

6. For a detailed discussion of his activity see my "Were the Walls of Jerusalem Built by Abraham Castro?" [in Hebrew], *Zion* (Jerusalem, 1982), XLVII, pp. 407–18. See also E. Shohatman's article on Castro [in Hebrew], *Zion*, XLVIII, pp. 387–403.

7. *Sijill*, V, 386; VI, 68.

8. Ibid., VI, 713.

9. *Al-nāẓir ʿalā al-amwāl al-sulṭānīya wa-ghayrihā* (VII, 260); for the two titles of the tax collector and the superintendent of construction combined, see X, 16.

10. For this term see *EI*² (Barthold-Spuler) and M. Z. Pakalın, *Osmanlı Tarih Deyimleri ve Terimleri Sözlüğu* (Istanbul, 1946), pp. 342–45.

11. VII, 259, 260, 279; X, 546. For the more far-reaching repercussions of this episode, see my article, "On the Expulsion of the Franciscans from Mount Zion" in *Turcica*, XVIII (1986), pp. 147–57.

12. A summary of the relevant *waqfīya* as reproduced in Muḥammad Asʿad al-Imām al-Ḥusaynī, *Al-Manhal al-ṣāfī fī 'l-waqf wa-aḥkāmihi* (Jerusalem, 1982), pp. 109–110.

13. Even though detailed books were kept there, both on income and on expenses related to the project. There were several scribes in charge of these accounts (*Yāzijī, kātib ʿalā ʿimarat al-sūr*), and when one of them had to leave Jerusalem for the *ḥajj* via Cairo, he deposited all these books with a colleague (XII, 905).

14. These were not only referred to by the regular term *darāhim fiḍḍa* or *qiṭaʿ sulaymānīya*, but also described as *qiṭaʿ muḥallaqa* ("round, circular"), still

keeping their original shape and full value, unlike other coins which by this time were trimmed, defective, and thereby reduced in value.

15. In the first case the term used was simply *al-madīna*; the latter refers to Nablus *al-ma'mūr*.

16. A. Cohen and B. Lewis, *Population and Revenue in the Towns of Palestine in the Sixteenth Century* (Princeton, 1978), pp. 150–53.

17. *wa-ziyādat al-māl al-wāṣil min al-dhahab bāqī bi'l-khazā'in al-sharīfa.*

18. Located about fifteen miles east of Jerusalem. For a detailed description of its architectural and constructional elements, see Sh. Tamari, "Maqām Nabī Mūsā" in *Assaph, Studies in Art History* (Tel Aviv, 1980), I, 167–90. See also Y. Sadan, "The Tomb of Moses (*Maqām Nabī Mūsā*), Rivalry Between Regions as to Their Respective Holy Places," in *Hamizraḥ Heḥadash*, XXVIII (1979), pp. 22–38, 220–38 [in Hebrew].

19. In reality, there seems to have existed a closer relationship between Jerusalem and *Maqām* Nabī Mūsā than may be inferred from the distance separating the two. An entry of the *sijill* (XIV, 303), written on 20 Dhū 'l-Ḥijja 948, refers to the closing down of the court and suspension of all its routine activity during the preceding three days, due to the seasonal visit (*ziyāra*) of Nabī Mūsā.

20. VII, 411.

21. XII, 360.

22. XII, 502. For further details on this as well as related episodes see my *Jewish Life Under Islam* (Cambridge, Mass., 1984), pp. 76–86. See also " 'Āmil" in *EI*².

23. For an elaboration of this point, see my *Jewish Life Under Islam*, pp. 140–45.

33
A Muslim Pilgrim's Progress: Aşçı Dede İbrāhīm Halīl on the Ḥajj, 1898*

Carter Vaughn Findley

WHAT FOLLOWS IS a pilgrimage narrative by the *dervīş* memoirist, Aşçı Dede İbrāhīm Halīl (1828–ca. 1910).[1] In several respects, this is not an ideal account of the *ḥacc*. The passage shows signs—including omission of all reference to some of the most important rites—of being an unrevised first draft. The orthography is error-prone, and the text suffers from the prolixity that seemed to overtake the author as his age and piety advanced. (Some of the underbrush has accordingly been thinned in the translation.) Not an advanced mystic, the author sometimes overextended himself in trying to discuss abstruse religious concepts. While his accounts of the most important events in his life always have vivid moments and a winning spontaneity, in general, the later parts of the autobiography lack the clarity of line or brilliance of color that distinguish his childhood memories. Yet despite these flaws, the account merits notice as an illustration both of the conditions in which pilgrims then traveled and of the author's mentality.

Aşçı Dede made his pilgrimage just a decade before the Ḥicāz railway reached Medina.[2] As if in keeping with this fact, his pilgrimage was a "modern" one in some respects, but not in others. His account illustrates the significance for the pilgrims of such nineteenth-century innovations as the quarantine, the telegraph, and the railroad. These had improved the pilgrim's lot in many ways—however uncertain the

*This article uses an adaptation of modern Turkish spelling.

steamer connections. Yet the journey was still taxing. At least one of his traveling companions died en route, and Aşçı Dede—then aged seventy, or more by the *hicrī* calendar—found the journey difficult. The most serious problem was that the pilgrimage route was not yet secure. His caravan sustained casualties in an encounter with the bedouin between Medina and Mecca. This was a problem with which the Ḥicāz railway project would help.

Aşçı Dede's narrative illustrates not just a moment in the history of the pilgrimage, but more than that a particular outlook which also had both "modern" and "traditional" traits. One of the most "modern" traits was a disturbing one: the nationalist exclusivism that intruded into his view of his Arab fellow-Muslims. His anti-Arab feelings, sharpened during difficult years of bureaucratic service in Damascus, come through very strongly here in his strictures against the behavior of the Alexandrians in the shrines of that city and in his comment—actually made in reaction against abuses by the camel-drivers with his caravan on the Yanbū'–Medina road—that "such places [the Ḥicāz] are not necessary to us [the Ottomans!]."

Far more prominent in Aşçı Dede's thinking, however, are old-fashioned traits of an ecstatic *ṣūfī* mentality more interested in spiritual love relationships (the *'işḳ-i mecāzī* and *'işḳ-i ḥaqīqi*),[3] in saints and miracles, in ecstatic experiences of union with God, perhaps even in the day-to-day human contacts that an experience like the pilgrimage made possible, than in the forms of religious expression dictated by the *sharī'a*. Hence, we may argue, comes the "functionality," in the literary context of his narrative, of what might otherwise appear to be its defects as an account of the pilgrimage. If he dwells on an encounter with a *dervīş* who happens to live in the house where he grew up more than on some of the key rites of the pilgrimage, this fact highlights a dimension of human interaction that had always been one of the driving forces of his religious life, especially given his absorption in the mystical love philosophy. If his account omits some of the important *ḥacc* rites, it may be the result of an unintended elision that he would have caught and corrected, had he gone back over his account to polish it. The omission certainly cannot be due to ignorance; for Aşçı Dede had close connections with the official leadership of the Ottoman pilgrimage caravan, in which there must have been a number of people minutely acquainted with the prescriptions of Ḥanafī jurisprudence for the *ḥacc* rites, even if Aşçı Dede personally was not. What the omission of these rites from the narrative does, in any case, is to highlight one of the climactic moments of the pilgrimage for Aşçı Dede: the ecstasy that he experienced at his first approach to the Ka'ba. This and the miracle that he believed occurred on his last visit to the Prophet's Tomb in Medina are certainly the emotional highspots of his account; and if he described the rites of the visitation in Medina fully, the difference may be due to the fact that they are much shorter and simpler than those to be performed in and near Mecca.

Tomb-worship, ecstasy, and miracles—Aşçı Dede's religious outlook was exactly that which the Wahhābīs would attempt, a quarter-century later, to expunge once and for all from the two Holy Cities. Indeed, they had attempted to do so already before—not that Aşçı Dede shows any awareness whatsoever of them or the religious mentality they represent. For him, Islam was still that of the *ṣūfī* orders as known in the latitudinarian synthesis prevalent during the Ottoman centuries. Considering his failure to mention some of the essential rites, a strictly *sharī'a*-oriented Muslim could not be sure from his account that Aşçı Dede had an honest claim to the title of *ḥāccī*, of which he—like most returning pilgrims—seems so self-consciously proud. For him, however, it probably would not have seemed right in his narrative to allow details of rites and obligations to obscure the experiences of ecstasy and union. It is certainly this subjective and experiential emphasis that appears in the account's final tableau: the "*ḥāccī* party," in which the returned Aşçı Dede held open house for his friends.

This is not a normative account of how the *ḥacc* should be performed. With appropriate allowance for that fact, however, what follows has a certain appeal as an illustration of what the pilgrimage meant to a pious Muslim with an outlook that was very widespread over long centuries, however much it may have been reproved by *sharī'a*-minded activists then and since.

This Section Recounts What Came to Pass from My Intention to Direct Myself Humbly to the Ḥicāz . . .

[T79, 505:] . . . In order that I might prostrate myself, with face coal-black from the smoke of sin, before the Lord of Prophecy . . . and at the great House of God, the noble Ka'ba, exalted in degree as the heavenly spheres and covered with divine black light, in hopes that my spiritual supplications and entreaties would bear fruit, and in order that I might late in life take the warrant of a small light from the fire of estrangement (?—*nār-ı bu'diyetden çırağiyet berātını almak üzere*), in the year 1315 [1897–98], the saints (*erenler*) gave permission for me to set out for the Ḥicāz, whose adornment is forgiveness (*Ḥicāz-i mağfiret-ṭirāz*). . . .

As explained in detail in the earlier section on the *ḥacc* in our treatise, although it was divinely ordained in dreams I had . . . that I should prostrate myself in the Ḥicāz, it had remained unknown when that would occur. Indeed, when our Master, Şeyh Fehmī,[4] returned to Erzincan from his first pilgrimage and was telling about that region, he deigned to address me, saying "If it pleases the Almighty, you will go there and see it." Later I formed the intention [of going] to the Ḥicāz; and while I was making preparations, in my dreams (*'ālem-i ma'nāda*) . . . I found myself in Mecca. It seemed that I was in the presence of Şeyh Fehmī. He deigned to address me in reproachful terms: "Why have you come?" I answered: "Sir, you were going to recite the *hatm-i hvācegān*.[5] I came for that. . . ." [506:] He responded: "When a *hatm-i hvācegān* is to be recited, we shall call you," and I woke up.

For this reason, I had not been able to succeed until now in this matter. But glory and thanks be to Him, the time must finally have come; for two years ago, when I was in Istanbul, the noble Trusteeship of the Treasure to be sent to Mecca and Medina (*ṣürre emānet-i şerīfesi*)[6] for the year 1315 was entrusted to His Excellency, our soul and spirit, Muhtār Efendi; and this shameless sinner. . . had firm intentions from that date on, setting by a sum from my salary each month for necessary expenses (*tertībāt-i ḥicāzīye*). . . . [Aşçı Dede continues for more than a page about his preparations to depart, the spiritual signs that it was permissible for him to go, and his arrangements for his household during his absence. He set out from his home in Edirne for Istanbul on 18 Şa'bān 1315/12 January 1898.]

[508:] As soon as I got off the train, I went straight to the mansion of His Excellency, the corresponding secretary (*mektūbī* [of the Ministry of War, Aḥmed Muhtār Efendi])[7] and paid my respects to him in the presence of the brethren there. He displayed extraordinary pleasure and said: "The office of steward (*kethüdā*) was to have been entrusted to you,[8] but what could be done when another was recommended by order from the palace? . . . Now there is a duty for you greater and nobler than the stewardship or anything else; and that is the sacred office of transporting twenty-five chests of white (or camphorated?) wax candles (*şem'-i 'asel-i kāfūrī*) specially prepared and embellished for the Prophet's Garden (*ravża-i muṭahhara*) in Medina.[9] So, then, I have entrusted this office to you. Ten men will accompany you. Take them, see to the safeguarding of the money that will be given you to cover necessary expenses en route, and take care that [the candles] reach Medina."

At that, weeping and unable to control myself on account of a state of rapture that came over me from the fullness of love and longing, I threw myself down before him and kissed his foot. Then I withdrew, weeping as I went. Immediately, his son Ṣubḥī Bey Efendi ran after me, grasped my hand, and kissed it. Thus, he too, sought to gain blessing from this state of rapture. From there, still weeping, I went home. And, praise God, at my kissing his foot, a strange and wonderful state appeared in the corresponding secretary, such that he was unable to move from his place; rather, without moving his foot, he stood there as if frozen. . . .

The next day [509:], to give thanks properly, I went to Eyyūb Sulṭān,[10] paid my respects in reverence at the exalted, blessed shrine, and praised God extraordinarily. Then I began my preparations for the journey. For provisions for the Ḥicāz (*tertībāt-ı ḥicāziye*), I had eighty Ottoman liras.[11] Of these, I spent twenty in Istanbul, partly for the marriage of my [step-] son İsmā'īl Efendi's betrothed [daughter], partly for my [step-] brother, Lieutenant (*mülāzım*) Bahā el-Dīn. Having been transferred from the Third Army to the Fourth, he had come to Istanbul with his family en route to the headquarters of his unit, when, thanks to the collision of two vessels, they fell into the sea. Glory and thanks to Him, God and the saints came to their aid; they were pulled from the sea stark naked (*çırıl çıplak*), with their clothes and everything lost. A room was rented for them in our neighborhood, but then the birth of a daughter a week later reduced them to empty-handed beggary. Seeing to their needs, and giving them money to subsist on during Ramażān, I made both them and the saints happy.

With the remaining sixty liras, we set out, calling on God and the saints (*hū erenlerim diyerek*), on Wednesday, 11 Ramażān [?—Thursday, 4 February 1898?] with the postboat for Egypt. Its name was the "Divine Guidance" (*Tevfīḳ-i Rabbānī*). . . . [When] I saw this name, I was greatly pleased and gave thanks and praise to God. Thus, with the ten noble gentlemen who were to accompany me and the twenty-five cases of wax candles, I set out for Medina the Radiant (*Medīne-i Münevvere*) by way of Egypt. . . . [A. D. digresses about signs that he would visit first Medina, then Mecca, and about a dream he had.]

[511:] One of the noble gentlemen going to the Ḥicāz in the retinue of His Excellency Muhtār Efendi was ʿĀdil Efendi, employed in the customs department as an appraiser (*istimator*). If we start to talk about this gentleman, we shall again depart from our theme; but to be brief, this gentleman was one of the disciples of His Excellency's spiritual master, that is, of El-Ḥācc Şeyh İsmāʿīl Efendi.[12] This man was a preceptor in the school of gnosis, a master teacher of mysticism (*mekteb-i ʿirfānın kalfası ve tasavvufātın dersiʿām hocası*), adept at every language, a righteous man, straight as the *elif* of *elif-lām*, a truly just (*ʿādil*) man on the way of justice, the point of revelation of the secret meaning of the names sent down from the heavens, and a wise man. His brother-in-law (*enişte*) Tevfīḳ Efendi occupied a postion superior even to ʿĀdil's; for he was a deputy (*halīfe*) of His Excellency, İsmāʿīl Efendi. With this Tevfīk Efendi, there was much talk en route. Thanks to this, many noble gentlemen became acquainted with me and learned what an unworthy sinner I am. Well, this ʿĀdil Efendi was in charge of all the provisions of our benefactor (*velī niʿmet bey efendimiz ḥażretleri*) for the journey; and all purchasing was done through him; for on account of the languages he knew, all the tradesmen were obedient and tractable to him. Something that another person could get for ten *kuruş*, he could no doubt get for six or seven, and the seller would be happy at that price, too. In one so young, such wisdom and such mastery of languages are [512:] truly a gift from God; there is no other word for it.

All the necessities for the trip, and the steamer tickets, for our group were bought by this man. For eight liras from my own pocket, I got the second cabin. As mentioned before, all of us, together saying *bismillāh* and asking leave of the saints (*destūr erenler deyüb*), then boarded the steamer, departed from Istanbul with proper farewells, and came to Piraeus. . . . We departed from there toward evening. Although we got caught that night in a memorable storm, arriving—praise be—safe and sound at Alexandria toward morning on Saturday 14 Ramażān, we went to the hotel of Giridli Ḥasan Ağa. Staying there one night, the group went on the morrow by train to Suez. To get the candles off the steamer and forward them to Suez, I and the police agent, İsmāʿīl Efendi, remained at the hotel. Then, the following day, I went to Suez with the candles. Of the sacred sites (*maḳāmāt-ı ḳudsīye*) I visited while at Alexandria, the foremost was the mosque of Imām Muḥammad Būṣirī [sic, for Būṣīrī], may God sanctify his innermost heart, the author of the "Ode on the Mantle" (*bürīde*, for *bürde*), where he himself lies buried in the perfumed earth (*medfūn-i ḥāk-ı 'ıṭırnāk*). I am quite unable to describe the outward ornamentation and beauty of this mosque and mausoleum; it is known to those who have seen it.[13]

On the evening (*akşam*) of Sunday, 15 Ramażān, which is the night (*gece*) of Monday the sixteenth,[14] the "Ode on the Nativity of the Prophet" was to be recited there in honor of the aforementioned (Būṣīrī). Praise and thanks be to Him, I went together with İsmā'īl Efendi, and after the evening prayer, the ode was recited. But since İsmā'īl Efendi could not understand it, on account of its being recited entirely in Arabic, we took that as a pretext to retire to the mausoleum, where it seemed appropriate to concentrate our thoughts on Būṣīrī himself (*kendülerine teveccüh ve rābıṭada bulunmak*). So it was; but the mausoleum was brimful with Arabs and such vermin (*evlād-ı 'arab ve ba'ẓı haşarāt* [sic, for *ḥaşarāt*] *ile malāmal*). We took refuge in a corner; but a moment later I saw a coffeeseller approaching with his pot and a lot of cups in his hands. Seeing that he was trying to get us to drink coffee, and that the people—excepting only that they did not have [513:] cigarettes in their hands—were sitting around, just as in a coffeehouse, raising their voices to the skies in vain talk, we could neither concentrate nor even remain in peace; so I decided to get our shoes and flee immediately. I was astounded. I went outside, and there were so many tradesmen and hawkers that it was like the last judgment. I got through with difficulty and returned to the hotel. But we had made our visit, whatever was given was given, and may God add his blessing, my friend! Since there were also separate sites (*maḳāmlar*) for Alexander the Two-Horned, Dānyāl the Prophet, and Loḳmān the Physician, those were also visited. . . .[15]

On Monday, 16 Ramażān, toward morning, we boarded the train, reached Suez at two in the evening, and met the group. We intended to go by steamer to Yanbū' the next day, but having gotten to Alexandria by divine guidance, by the decree of Providence we wound up going to Jidda instead of Yanbū'. That is, we pulled out a ways from the port at Suez, then it became apparent that we were going to Jidda and afterward to Yanbū'. Although we protested, they answered: "There's no use protesting; this week the ship goes first to Jidda, from there to Suwākin, then to Yanbū'. If you give fifty liras [?—number illegible], then first to Yanbū'."[16] I smiled and said, "The saints, through the corresponding secretary [Muhtār Efendi], gave fifty Ottoman liras as travel expenses for the men who are accompanying me and the candles, and part of this has been spent. So we have no choice but to submit to events." Giving praise to God, and with no trouble at sea (*deniz meniz olmıyarak*), we arrived safe and sound at Jidda on Friday 20 Ramażān at seven o'clock. [514:] Then we stopped at the inn (*konak*) of Seyyid Aḥmed Efendi, the agent in Jidda of Revvāşīnzāde Şeyh 'Abbās Efendi the Meccan, whom we had in fact met with in Istanbul and engaged as a guide (*delīl*). The boat went on to Suwākin with the candles still on it. The next day, with the aid of the guide, we went to the cemetery to visit [the shrine of] Our Mother Eve.[17] After paying our respects to Mother Eve, we also went to the mausoleum of the late governor of the Ḥicāz, His Excellency Ḥālet Paşa. . . .[18]

After six days, the steamer returned, and on Thursday 26 Ramażān at eight o'clock, we set out from Jidda and, on a sea as quiet as the Sweet Waters of Europe (*Kāğıdhāne denizi gibi*),[19] arrived at the Yanbū' harbor on Friday 27 Ramażān at six o'clock. In keeping with the orders of the Şeyh ül-Ḥarem, His Excellency 'Ādil Paşa,[20] to the chief district officer (*ḳā'im-maḳām*) of Yanbū', people came immediately from the chief district officer and the local military commanders to remove the candles from the ship and store them in a warehouse. They also showed us a pleasant caravansaray (*vekāle*) by the seaside. Since, on account of the approach of the noble festival (*'īd-i şerīf*, that is, the *'īd al-fiṭr* or *şeker bayram* at the end of Ramażān), the camel drivers had all gone to their villages and would return and set out in caravans (*ğafīle*, for *ḳafīle*) after the festival, it would be necessary to wait ten or fifteen days in Yanbū'. On that account, telling ourselves that it was obligatory (*vācib*) to go on, although it is always permissible to content oneself with what is decreed (*ḳażāya rıżā*), we decided to settle down in our seaside mansion. The secret reason for this period of residence became apparent two days later [515:] when I got sick. . . . [The doctor comes; one of A .D.'s friends despairs of his recovering, but he does.] Indeed, my friends, this was not something to call sickness; this was what they call purification of the spiritual apparatus (*taṭhīrāt-ı techīzāt-ı ma'nevīye*). . . .

Praise and thanks be to Him, on Tuesday, 8 Şevvāl, toward morning we set out in a caravan for Medina. As is known, they have what they call a *şatūf*,[21] which is a frame with a pair of seats (*bir çift māfedir*—for *maḥaffe*), that is, it is a seat about the size of an iron single bedstead, made of datepalm branches, and protected against the sun with fabric and oilcloth on top. Thank goodness, the person who became my companion was of our own kind. . . . That is, we found ourselves companions with Meḥmed Efendi, an old and faithful servant (*emekdār*) of the imperial supervisor of protocol (*teşrīfāt-ı hümāyūn nāẓırı*), Ḥāccī Maḥmūd Efendi, and also one of the dervishes of the late Ḥāccī Aḥmed Efendi of Gümüşhāne, may God sanctify his innermost heart. He would spend his evenings in *zikr*, and indeed, he kept quiet, never speaking with anyone; he was a good Nakşbendī, absorbed in his own spiritual state. . . .

With such a wonderful companion as Meḥmed Efendi, then, I mounted the camel-litter and with him on one side and my humble self on the other, we set out with the prayer that we might bow our shameful faces to the dust [at the tomb] of the Prophet of God, on whom be blessing and peace, and so make them clean and unsullied. We got about half the way, and came to a place in the wilderness known as the "Well of 'Abbās" (*Bīr 'Abbās*). [516:] There we remained one day and two nights. The reason for this was that the local *şeyh* wanted money to open the road.[22] They were not pleased about the caravan. Indeed, my heart grew weary with all the talk, and I could find no peace. At last, by the beneficence of God, we escaped from there.

The Ḥicāz road is a strange one. The stopping places (*konak*) are rather far apart; and one generally reaches the stopping places at night four or five hours after sundown. At that, what is called a stopping place will be a valley between two mountains. The camel drivers, helping people down from the camels, cry out that there are many thieves. In fact, there are not any thieves; they are the thieves. One had best not stray far from his camel-litter. One even relieves nature right beside it. If one goes five or ten paces, he gets hit with a stick and is deprived of whatever he has. We saw a lot of this kind of thing.[23] These places are not necessary to us (*buraları bize lāzım değildir*).

Praise be, with the aid of the saints, the point (literally "nose," *burun*) of our group entered Medina without getting bloodied, arriving safely at eleven o'clock on the night of Sunday, 13 Şevvāl (i.e., about an hour before dawn). Now, Şeyh 'Abbās Efendi had communicated with the chief guide of Medina, Dağestānīzāde Hāccī Meḥmed Efendi, and had also given us a letter; so they met us, and we went straight to their house. While we were there, we did not spend a *para*, everything being taken care of by the chief guide. Indeed, the fifty liras had lasted just that far, something over a hundred *kuruş* having remained. These were turned over to His Excellency's brother-in-law (*enişte*), Ebū Bekir Efendi; a register of income and expenditure was drawn up and presented to the corresponding secretary [Muhtār Efendi, Ebū Bekir being his brother-in-law].

The chief guide had a fine and rather large *selāmlık* with two or three rooms. Putting down anchor there, we struck up a friendship (*maḥabbet olduk* [sic]). We spent the night there, and the next morning early we went to the bath known as the bath of the Prophet, performed our ablutions (*ābdest ve ṭahāret edüb*), and donned the garments that are appropriate to the place.[24] That is, on our feet yellow outer boots (*yemenī*) and black slippers (*mes*, for *mest*), a woolen outer robe (*cübbe*) over a white inner robe (*entari*), and on the head a white turban wound (*sarık*) over a soft felt cap (*arakiye*).[25]

Thus, all together, we set out for the Prophet's tomb (*ḥarem-ı şerīf*). The house where we were staying being only sixty or seventy paces from the sacred enclosure, we immediately beheld the Gate of Peace (*Bāb-ı Selām*), at which point there appeared [among us] such a mystical state and such illumination as cannot be described by the pen but must be left to the apprehension of the enraptured (*'uşşāḳın vicdānına ḥavāle olunmuşdur*). We gave our shoes to the shoe-keeper. The threshold of the door was . . . of copper. . . . [517:] Kissing the threshold and rubbing our face and eyes on it, we entered the sacred enclosure.

With the chief guide in front and ourselves behind, reciting the appropriate prayers (*ed'īyeler ve ṣalavāt-ı şerīfeler*), we approached the grille (*şebeke-i sa'ādet*, surrounding the tomb of the Prophet). There we prayed for a long while. Then, going a few paces farther, we likewise recited prayers before [the tomb of] Abū Bakr, may God be pleased with him. After that, we went one or two steps farther and repeated special prayers before 'Umar, may God be pleased with him.[26] Going from there to the lower end of the Prophet's Garden (*ravża-i muṭahharanın aşağı ciheti*), we prayed similarly where the angels of the Divine Presence stood (*maḳām-ı melā'ike-i muḳarrebīn*).[27] Then, at the foot (*ayak ṭarafında*), we paid our respects to our mother Fāṭima, may God be pleased with her.[28] Then going a few steps farther, we recited prayers and the *ihlāṣ*[29] through the Door of Gabriel (*bāb-ı Cibrīl*) for the souls of the companions (of the Prophet, *aṣḥāb-ı kirām*), wives (*ezvāc-ı muṭahhara*), and children (*evlād-ı kirām*) buried in the perfumed earth of the Garden of Baḳī'a (*cennet-i Baḳī'e*, for Baḳī'), may God be pleased with all of them.[30] After that, passing before the special platform (*maḳṣūra*) for the *ağas* of the *Ḥarem-i Şerīf*,[31] facing toward 'Abbās, the uncle of the Prophet who is buried an hour away on Jabal Uḥud (over 'Uḥud crossed out), we again recited prayers and the *ihlāṣ*.[32] Then we again came before the presence of the Prophet, performed special prayers (*ed'īye ve ṣalavāt-ı mahṣūṣa*), withdrew one or two paces, faced the *ḳıbla*, gave praise and thanks to God, and rendered benedictions. From there, everyone went into his own spiritual state (*kendü ḥāliyle ḥallenur*). In this way, after we had performed the dawn (*ṣabāḥ*), noon (*öyle* [the more common orthography in Ottoman for *öğle*]), afternoon (*ikindi*), and night (*yatsı*) prayers, we did thus with the guide.[33]

As for kissing the threshold of the Gate of Peace and rubbing my face and eyes on it, during my stay there, I never placed my foot on the threshold as I entered the sacred enclosure, but stepped over it. On the day of departure, I kissed the threshold and rubbed my face and eyes on it as before and washed it completely (*ğusl*) with tears. For just as there was in the whole *umma* no sinner more guilty than myself, I had no title to acceptance but to revere the stones and earth of Medina the Radiant, to kiss them, and rub my face on them.

Since I had not been able to keep up the fast while traveling, we owed seventeen days. A week after entering Medina, we resolved to make up the fast (*ṣıyām-ı ḳażāya nīyet edüb*); and by the help of the saints, we fasted like sulṭāns. [518:] The chief guide, for the sake of our benefactor, the Trustee of the Treasure, showed us great respect and provided us with excellent meals morning and night, including *börek* and sweets and two or three cups (*kupa*) of tea apiece, for the duration of our stay. . . . Thus, while making up seventeen days of Ramażān, we busied ourselves from morning to night with worship in the sacred enclosure. After *ifṭār*, I would again go to the sacred enclosure and occupy myself thus until the night prayer.

Among the imāms of the *miḥrāb* of the Prophet was a Ḥāfız Tevfīḳ Efendi, whose father was one of the adepts of Şeyh Fehmī, may God sanctify his innermost heart, whom Tevfīḳ Efendi had also known, being shown much favor by him. This gentleman of exalted merit had the custom of reciting a few sections (*cüz'*) of the Qur'ān in the sacred enclosure between the sunset and night prayers (*beyn el-'işā'eyn ['işā'eyn]*). He also had an associate, and on Friday evenings they would do a *hatm [-i hvācegān]*. This poor soul fell into a spiritual infatuation with that gentleman (*'āşıḳ olub*) and in the evenings would take flight with love for him. Indeed, it seemed to me like hearing the Qur'ān from the very mouth of the Prophet. . . .[34]

[519:] When our fast was completed, we all set out in carriages to visit the exalted ʻAbbās, may God be pleased with him, who is buried in the perfumed earth on Jabal Uḥud.[35] The following day, we went on other visits, that is to the Mescid of Kubā'[36] and other *mescids* and places of visitation.

Since it was a fulfillment of duty, praise be, too, that the candles for the Tomb of the Prophet were accepted as free of breakage, compared to those of the year before. . . . They showed us the candles of the previous year. They were all in bits and completely broken. They had to be melted down and remade in Medina. That much breakage had not been seen. "What could we do? The *ḳā'im-maḳām* at Yanbūʻ got his hands on them; they wouldn't let us interfere. 'Turn them over to us, and we'll send them,' " they said. No doubt, the Arab camel-drivers, putting them onto and off their camels, had reduced them to this state. In any case, if it please God, our humble service was acceptable to His Messenger. For, showing this poor unworthy sinner a place near the Prophet, they accepted me. That is, according to the custom of the place, I turned over my *seccāde* to the water carrier (*saḳḳā*),[37] so that he might spread it at an appropriate place in the sacred enclosure for the five prayers. I would sit there whenever I went, and no one else would sit on it. Well, they spread my *seccāde* next to the sacred grille (*şebeke-i saʻādet*), so that there was no more than the space for eight or ten people between myself and the sacred window. They spread it beside the first pillar and in the first row, beyond which were the *miḥrāb* and the *minber*. Prayer performed between the blessed tomb and *minber* is like prayer performed in the highest heaven.

I found a worthy gentleman leaning against this pillar and reading the Qur'ān. I glanced at him. He was a holy scholar, whom the light of illumination surrounded from head to foot, and a manifestation of the perfect prophetic guide (*mürşid-i kāmil-i nebevī maẓharıdır*). After the prayer, I wanted to kiss his hand. Exactly as was the custom of Şeyh Fehmī, he too clasped my hands, and we kissed each other's hands in the Mevlevī fashion. He also uttered some *ṣūfī* expressions; from that I understood that he was a man of merit, as I had surmised. I concluded that in accordance with a spiritual sign to him from the Messenger of God, on whom be blessing and peace, he had given me to him as a guest. [520:] I therefore did all I could to honor him. And the exalted gentleman, too, showed extraordinary kindness to me, so much that other gentlemen asked him if he had known me for a long time. "Yes, I have known him for a very long time. He is my loyal and beloved friend (*eḥibbā-yı ṣādıḳımdır* [sic])," that is, he indicated [that he had known me] from the world of spirits.

I asked the guide who this worthy gentleman was. He said: "This gentleman is a Mağribī. They call him Mağribī Şeyh Tibbānī. He is of the Şāzilī order, a very great man whose blessing one should seek. Together with his disciples, he performs the *zikr* in the sacred enclosure every night. How did you encounter this gentleman? Have you known him for a long time?" I said: "No, sir. He deigned to accept us." He said: "He has been sitting there with his back against the pillar for a long time without speaking with anyone." Thus I received the good news.

Thereafter, I did not let go of the skirt of the master's robe, and we made the love of God flame up (*'işḳ ve maḥabbet şu'lelendirdik*). That is, during the forty-four days that we stayed in Medina, I only parted from him to sleep. Praise and thanks to Him, I took from him a blazing (lit. flourishing) light and its cover (*dört başı ma'mūr ābādān bir çirāğīyet berātı ve külāhı kapdım*),[38] and I became inflamed. Finally, an odor of prophecy and a soul-vivifying spirit of Oneness that came from the window of the tomb chamber (*ḥücre-i sa'ādet*), resembling neither musk nor ambergris, intoxicated both of us, until we stared at each other's faces like lifeless statues. The exalted *şeyh* only made signs with his eyebrows and eyes. Truly, the bliss of the moment could not be described and cannot be recaptured. It was like Solomon's throne, which, with a sigh, we cast to the wind, my friend.[39]

[To recite] the *hatm-i hvācegān* two days a week was my custom. Reciting it by turns at each of the four corners of the Prophet's Garden (*ravża-ı muṭahhara*), I thereby drank the delicious water of intercession and healing from the spiritual pool of prophecy (*ḥavuż-ı ma'nevī-['i] Cenāb-i Risāletpenāhīden āb-ı zülāl*). Still, contentment did not come, and my ardor was not satisfied. While I was seeking [some further] opportunity, on account of the approaching arrival of the Trustee of the Treasure, they raised the inner curtains of the Prophet's Tomb to sweep. Thus, it became possible to observe the interior completely. Immediately summoning all my boldness [521:] and saying "If you please, O Messenger of God!" (*Dakhīlaka yā Rasūl Allāh*), I drew near to the grille (*şebeke-i sa'ādet*). Kneeling down like a dog [i.e., in humility], I looked upward through the window.

The morning sun was just presenting its supplication through the tiny windows of the dome. The sides of the blessed tomb were veiled in satin, and the drapery was fastened with rings to iron and aloewood poles there.[40] Thus there was an interval where the part above the poles, that is, the upper part of the blessed tomb, could be seen. How that sacred place caught my eye! How it touched me! Mercy, o my God, how it touched me! My soul attained the Beloved! My soul attained its lord! My reason departed from my head, and I arrived at the wilderness of possession! Giving way at the knees, I collapsed there like a lifeless dog. After a while, I recovered my wits, and my ardor quietened. Truly, the spiritual light and the divine manifestations that I saw—praise be a hundred thousand times—remained imprinted on my poor heart (*naqş-u ṭabʿ*).[41] Whenever I look into my heart [I see them], but they cannot be described. . . .

On Thursday, 23 Zū 'l-Ḳaʿde, the imperial treasure arrived at Medina, and I went to wait on His Excellency Muhtār [Efendi]. Prayers and praises and great thanksgivings were rendered. He entered the Prophet's tomb chamber bearing the noble banner and came back out, no longer in possession of himself.[42] Truly, I saw [him] moving about without spirit or body. A moment later, he came to himself and went to the house where he was a guest. I remained at the chief guide's house with my group. Since our contacts were not all that frequent, one day in the mosque he took me and brought me with him to the house where he was staying. On the way, he said, "Since coming here, you have become different." Lightly, I answered: "Did we not come here to become different?"[43] He smiled. Thereafter, preparations to go to Mecca began, and they loaded our litters onto the great camels they had brought from Damascus. Loading up again with our companion, Meḥmed Efendi, we said "*Bismillāh*" and "By your leave, saints."

As a farewell, I had again rendered my homage in the presence of the Prophet. But here it could get long, my friend! A summary: I howled and moaned like a dog, washing my face and beard [522:] with my tears. Finally, I said: "If you please, o Messenger of God, and if you have taken this shameless Ibrāhīm into the circle of your intercession, let it be for the sake of your deputy and successor [Şeyh] Fehmī Efendi. [To show if you have done so], deign to move the jewel atop your tomb (*re's-i saʿādetinde olan cevher-i yektā ḥareket buyursun*), if you please, o Messenger of God."[44] Praise and thanks to Him, he deigned to move it. I repeated this three times. Three times it moved. Thus, in complete joy and peace of mind, moving like one without a soul [of his own], I came to the Gate of Peace. As in the past, I kissed the threshold and rubbed my face on it. May God bless [it] and grant his beneficence. . . .

On Sunday, 26 Zū 'l-Ḳaʿde, we left Medina in the retinue of the

Trustee of the Treasure and with our group at our side. We desired to go by the —rī road,[45] but that road had been blocked for five or six years. That is, since a great *şeyh* along that road had not been given his treasure (*sürresi*, for *ṣürresi*), he had not allowed any pilgrims by that route. But now it was desired to open that road in the name of His Excellency, the Corresponding Secretary [Muhtār Efendi], and to pass that way with the mediation (*delālet*) of some other *şeyhs*, and so we set out that way. Although that great *şeyh* sent a paper to the Trustee of the Treasure saying "I won't let you through here," it did not arrive until after we had left Medina, and so did not reach the Trustee of the Treasure. Consequently, we were going our way, relying on the mediation of the other *şeyhs*, when all of a sudden, one or two days out, we entered that *şeyh*'s frontiers. It got to be evening. Reaching the halting place and stopping, we set off a cannon. The *şeyh* heard the cannon's sound and asked "What is this cannon?" They told him it was the arrival of the treasure. "Strange; I wrote them a paper. They did not listen or pay attention." So saying, he flew into a rage.

The next day early, the caravan set out. Suddenly, I saw that the guard under its commander, 'Abd ül-Raḥmān Paşa, was advancing at full speed toward the front of the caravan. "What's this?" I said. They said, "We have come to the borders of that *şeyh*. They went to the front of the caravan to protect it." While my heart was somewhat afflicted at this, since there was no recourse but to place our trust in God, my companion Meḥmed Efendi and I occupied ourselves constantly with remembrance (of God) and spiritual concentration (*zikir ve rābıṭa*) as we descended from the mountain to the valley with the caravan. For an hour, everything around me was slippery stones, extending up to the sky. Now the camel drivers, too, became alarmed and drove their camels hard. In sum, the way was [523:] narrow, and the loads and camel-litters would knock together.

While we were in this state of dread, the sounds of weapons were heard from the soldiers in our front. In response, the soldiers at our sides sounded their bugles and shouted something with one voice. We supposed that the way before us was empty, that the soldiers in front were firing their weapons as a show of bravery, and that the soldiers at our sides were saluting back with their horns and crying "Long live the *Pādişāh*!" We went along this way for a while. I and Meḥmed Efendi became enraptured from the soldiers' shouting back and forth; weeping, we cried, "O God, grant triumph to the sulṭān!" and busied ourselves with prayer and remembrance of God.

At a certain point, we went beyond the frontiers of the man in question and fell upon the desert. At last, as everyone shared the good news, we reached safety and stopped at the halting place. We asked what had gone on and learned that, alas, it was not as we had supposed. For the *şeyh's* men had fired on the soldiers from those high rocks; the latter had returned fire, and the bugles and the soldiers' shouts signaled "For shame! For shame! For shame!" When it became clear that there were several killed and wounded on our side and also losses from the Arabs, we became very sad. In any case, the saints had made us understand things differently, so that our hearts would not be overwhelmed with fear and dread. Later, that *şeyh* came to the tent to meet with the Trustee of the Treasure. The latter reprimanded and chastised him and made certain threats. The *şeyh* said, "Since five or six years, they have not given me what is due me (*'ā'idātimi vermiyorlar*). I sent word to you not to go through here. I did this especially because you came relying on the other *şeyhs*." Then, praise God, His Excellency, after further admonitions, gratified the *şeyh* by promising him that he would get his back payments from His Excellency the *Şerīf* [of Mecca].[46]

The next day, we set out from there. With no more fear, we took to the road in security. With only two stops remaining to Mecca, we came to Rābiğ. The Mecca guide (*delīl*),[47] *Şeyh* 'Abbās Efendi, had come to Medina to meet us; having him with us, that night in Rābiğ we donned the pilgrim clothing (*iḥrāma girdik*).[48] Further, under the guide's leadership and by common consent, we declared our intention for the *ḥacc-ı kırān*[49] and adopted the *iḥrām* accordingly. . . . Praise be, this was a great success and a great favor from God, my friend. For as everyone [524:] knows, the *ḥacc-ı kırān* is superior and confers twice the recompense. In the state of ritual consecration from that point on, we set out like so many corpses wrapped in their shrouds. . . .[50]

On Wednesday, 6 Zū 'l-Ḥicce, God granted us an easy entry into Mecca the Venerated. After going straight to the Şeyh Maḥmūd quarter and setting up our tents there, we all came to the house of the guide, Şeyh 'Abbās Efendi. Following the meal after the evening (*akşam*) prayer, we performed the [525:] night prayer (*yatsu*) there; then about 2:30 [*à la turca*] with the guide in front of us and repeating the required prayers, we went straight to the Gate of Peace and through it into the mosque (*ḥarem-ı şerīf*) to the House of God. But how we went! I went like one who had been raised from the dead and was going to the place of judgment. The sacred enclosure was more awe-inspiring and dreadful and crowded than the place of judgment. With great difficulty, we went first to the Black Stone. Forced to push and shove people in order to touch the Black Stone, I thrust my head into the sacred opening as if with my last desperate effort. Rubbing my face and eyes and beard on it, and weeping the while, I made my black face clean and bright as I rubbed it on the Black Stone. Pulling from behind, they tugged my head from the opening like [that of] a lifeless corpse. I stood there a moment, and my wits returned to me.

I looked about, but not a soul from our group was there. At that, a confusion came over me that I could never describe. I stood dumbfounded, for humanity was swarming around me like a beehive, with a moaning and an uproar that filled one with dread. I did not know which way to go. While I was in this state of dread, a handsome youth (*maḥbūb-i ʻālem*) came to my side and, holding me tightly by the hand, led me to one side, toward the well of Zemzem, where our group was waiting for me. His Excellency the Corresponding Secretary had warned the guide not to leave this *dervīş* (*ʻāşıḳ*) to himself, or he would get lost; consequently, the guide had sent his son to get me and ordered him to lead me through the circumambulation without letting go of my hand. Thus, with this Ḥicāzī beloved holding my hand and me holding tightly to his, I circumambulated Mecca the Venerated [sic] seven times, repeating the required prayers; and then, leaving the mosque, we came and went between al-Ṣafā and al-Marwa seven times. But how I came and went. I was not in control of myself, but Şeyh ʻAbbās's son took me about. Praise be to Him . . ., everything being twofold because we had entered the consecrated state intending to perform the *ḥacc-ı kırān*, I had circumambulated the Noble House fourteen times and done the running (*saʻy*) fourteen.[51]

It was after seven o'clock, and I was exhausted. Since our benefactor Muhtār Efendi had not had his passion (*ʻişḳ*) inflamed [like mine], he had not been able to perform the circumambulation in this way, but, performing the circumambulation of arrival (*ṭavāf-ı ḳudūm*) and [526:] lacking endurance for the rest, had retired to his house, intending to fulfill the second part (here, *ikinci kere*; i.e., the running between Ṣafā and Marwa) after [the "standing" at] ʻArafāt. And I, having completed it, came to our place. But, while I remained oblivious to it through the joy of that night, the resulting pains in my knees and ankles gave me anguish for the next day or two.

Because the guide's house was small and not all of us could stay there, I, my companion Meḥmed Efendi, the corresponding secretary's brother-in-law Bekir Bey, and his companion, the director of the Sublime Porte Printing House, Muṣṭafà Efendi went to the cell of the corresponding secretary's mentor, Şeyh İsmāʿīl Efendi, adjoining the sacred enclosure. Our other companions remained at the guide's house. So, my friend, they say: "God builds a nest for the homeless bird"; it's true. The saints built a nest for this homeless Ibrāhīm, such that looking out from the window of the cell on the House of God and concentrating on it (*teveccüh ve rābıṭa*), I went to the sacred enclosure from prayer time to prayer time. And sometimes, I followed the prayer leader from the cell where I was. In other words, the cell was considered part of the Noble House (*beyt-i şerīf*). His Excellency the Corresponding Secretary also moved to stay at the house of the Corresponding Secretary of the Ḥicāz.[52] Coming from time to time to visit the *şeyh*, he would honor our cell and deign to say, "Brother, since you came here, I have lost you completely." And I would submit that I had become attached to the Great House like the Black Stone and could not break away for a minute.

Early on Thursday, the day after our arrival in Mecca, I rented two mounts and went with one of the guide's men to al-Muʿallā Cemetery[53] to pay my respects at the tomb of the *sulṭān-ı ʿulemā bi'llāh*, Fehmī Efendi, may God sanctify his innermost heart. And straightway, I paid my respects at the tomb of Hadīce (*Hadīce-'i Kübrā*), may God be pleased with her, then visited that of Āmina; then setting out according to the information I had previously received for the tomb of [Şeyh Fehmī], and searching devotedly among the tombstones with a haste and anxiety that almost blinded these eyes of mine, was unable to find it. Going about heartsick through the cemetery but finally [527:] remaining helpless, I went to the tomb-keeper of Our Mother Hadīce, Şeyh ʿAbdullāh Bārūm, and asked about the *şeyh*'s tomb. Immediately getting up from his place, he went a few steps, pointed it out, and returned. . . . Thus, my friend, the lover attained the beloved and the slave his master. But [it was] such a visitation as I cannot describe with the pen. I threw myself on his headstone and wept. . . . The guide's man stood astonished at all this. Consequently, so as not to detain him there a long time, I was forced to return, willing or not. I went back to ʿAbdullāh Bārūm Efendi, and entreating him to watch over the tomb of my master, I—though unworthy to do so—kissed his hand and presented him a recompense (*cā'izeleri*) [for doing so]; having gratified him, I returned.

The next day, Friday, following the midday prayer, mounting the camel with the litter together with my companion Meḥmed Efendi as before, we set out for ʿArafāt. But the crowding and the excitement along the way were indescribable. We were stuck within the city for an hour. . . . Later, by a different road, we reached the desert and, setting out on our way, reached the boundaries of ʿArafāt and the sacred mount that evening and set down at our tents. The next day, Saturday, was the eve of the festival. After the dawn prayer, we occupied ourselves with our own inner state in our tent (*kendi ḥālimizle ḥāllendik*). We prayed the afternoon prayer, mounted the camels, and set out for the Mount of Mercy. Praise be, through the assistance of the Trustee of the Treasure, we approached as close as the foot of that blessed mount. In other words, it was hectic, like the place of judgment. Until close to sunset, the preacher (*haṭīb efendi*) was reading a sermon on the mount. From time to time, everyone would wave handkerchiefs, and the cry "Here I am, O God, here I am; you are without partner; here I am"[54] truly made the sky ring.[55] The cries and lamentations and, in response, the mercy, forgiveness, and illumination granted there cannot be conveyed, my friend. [528:] That is, this convicted sinner, Aşçı Dede's sins were forgiven; plunging into the sea of mercy and forgiveness, he emerged again and saw with enraptured eye, amid the manifestation of divine grace, that he had become as undefiled as on the day of his birth. . . .

Now with the sunset call to prayer (*akşam ezāniyle*), the pilgrims set out. As if the sea of mercy had frothed over, and with the camels with their litters and soldiers on both sides, we set out for Muzdalifa in waves. Along the way, the joy was indescribable. Suddenly, too, it seemed to me that the sound of music [filled] both sides of the road and that torches made it like daylight, even that the smell of aloes wood filled the desert. This state brought me to ecstasy and, uncertain whether I was on earth or in heaven, I cast myself into the wilderness of the possessed. I asked my companion, "What's going on?" (*nedir bu ḥāl*). He said, "His Excellency the Şerīf is coming along behind us." I watched out for this eminence among descendants of the Prophet (*ḥazret-i seyyid-i sādāt*), and he passsed like a sulṭān in his carriage harnessed with four horses. Filled with excitement, I rendered prayers and praise. "God keep you! God bless you! March on, my sulṭān! The field is yours! It's for you! You are all joy, the soul and sulṭān of this world! Your music revives souls! From you they take pleasure and enjoyment!" And various [spiritually] secret things I said. The adept know them, my friend![56]

Arriving at Muzdalifa after the night prayer, we performed both the sundown and the night prayer (*akşam ve yatsu*). The next day we gathered small stones there, to be able to stone Satan at Minà [consistently written in this text as Mīna], and we performed the dawn prayer. We stood, as at 'Arafāt (*vaḳfeye durduk*).[57] Then we came to Minà. Immediately alighting at our tents, we went directly to the pillar (*nişān*) known as the last stone (*ḥacere-'i 'aḳabe*) and stoned Satan. One was to remain there three days. On the third day, Tuesday in the evening, we, that is, the Trustee of the Treasure and the people in his caravan, saying "Saints, by your leave," returned to Mecca.[58] That is . . . , we put on our own clothes and came [back] to our cell overlooking the sacred enclosure.

Now we began circumambulations (*ṭavāf*) by night and day and set about preparations for the [return] journey.[59] The *müftī* of the first regiment of the first brigade of the first division of the imperial guard, Meḥmed Şākir Efendi, [529:] being the foremost intimate, friend, and teacher of His Excellency Ḥāccī Muhtār Efendi, had come together [with him] to Damascus and from there to Medina and Mecca. I had met this gentleman of exalted worth at Medina and had the honor to become a part of his retinue. We were together night and day until my return from Mecca. There was much cordial conversation (*çok maḥabbetler*), and in the middle of the night we would go into the sacred enclosure to circumambulate and pray. Truly, the Zemzem [water] that we drank with this noble gentleman—let it not be exaggerated—was more than man could drink; that is, we drank immense amounts, and could not be blamed for it. He said: "My friend, I tell you that you are a true believer (*mu'min muvaḥḥidsiniz*), for the state of those whose faith is perfect is thus; those whose faith is imperfect, drink little of the noble Zemzem; and the hypocrites—I take refuge with God!—cannot drink it at all, or maybe swallow a drop with difficulty.[60] This gentleman, like myself, was an enraptured *dervīş* (*'āşıḳ*), with tears in his eyes and heart afire. He even went with us to the grave of our master [Şeyh Fehmī] to make our farewell. But while he was at the other places of visitaiton, I was clinging to the headstone of my master, wretchedly weeping and moaning. Everyone took some of the earth from the blessed tomb, put it in water, and drank it, so much that a good bit of earth was taken away. I also filled a little white pouch and took it with me. . . .

[After returning from the cemetery], I went to the government offices to present the letter of recommendation that 'Arif Paşa, commander of the Second Army, had drafted (*kırmış olduklan*—?) about me to the governor of the Ḥicāz, His Excellency Aḥmed Re'fet Paşa. . . .[61]

[530:] Since my traveling companion, Ḥāccī Meḥmed Efendi, had some connection with the Trustee of the Treasure's steward, Ḥüseyin Efendi, and on that account would wait to return with him, and since His Excellency, Muhtār Efendi's brother-in-law, Ḥāccī Bekir Efendi, would also do likewise, Bekir Efendi's traveling companion, Ḥāccī Muṣṭafà Efendi, now became mine. But my companions said: "God give you patience; this will be difficult for you." That is, this man's morals were something else (*ahlāḳı diğer bir ahlāḳ idi*). In any case, trusting in God, on Saturday, 16 Zū 'l-Ḥicce, hiring a camel and litter, we set out by caravan from Mecca for Jidda. Stopping for a night along the way, early the next day, Monday the eighteenth, we reached Jidda and, on the recommendation of Seyyid Aḥmed Efendi the guide, whose guest I had been before, we stayed at an adjoining house. We stayed at Jidda two nights.

There were many steamers waiting for the pilgrims. Since the first to depart would be the ship *Adana*, belonging to the Idare-i Mahṣūṣa [in Istanbul], and since tickets were being sold for six Ottoman liras a person, I immediately went with Muṣṭafà Efendi to get two tickets and we left Jidda on Wednesday, 20 Zū 'l-Ḥicce. Although Ḥāccī Muṣṭafà Efendi caused me much trouble along the way, the sickness on the day we boarded ship troubled me more. We endured it. Since there were many pilgrims, they put a lot of them in the hold. Thinking it might be comfortable, we too went down there. I quickly saw that with the crowding and the bad smells in the hold, there would be no comfort there; giving a lira and a half, as did others, I then moved alone to the stern deck. Muṣṭafà Efendi did not come. In fact, I had intended to part [from him], and it worked out so. . . . [Muṣṭafà Efendi took sick and had to be left for twelve days' quarantine at Ṭūr in Sinai (*Ṭūr-i Sīnā*)].[62] [531:] After parting from Muṣṭafà Efendi, I remained alone. For while our police officer Ḥāccī İsmā'īl was on the ship, our group had broken up at Mecca and everyone had remained on his own.

The day after we left Jidda, a gentleman named Ḥāccī Rif'at Efendi, telegraph officer of the İdāre-i Mahṣūṣa and a friend of Ḥāccī 'Alī Bey, who was a clerk in the correspondence office of our own

Edirne province [i.e., where A. D. then served] and had his bed on the deck next to mine, came along, sat on Ḥāccī ʿAlī Bey's bed, and got into a conversation. While talking of this and that to make him feel welcome, someone asked this Rifʿat Efendi where in Istanbul his house was. "We don't have a separate house," he said, "but rent [part of] a house in ʿİmāret Street in Şehzādebaşı. As soon as he had described certain features of the house, I said: "Saints alive! (*erenler*) That is a house that my family sold (*bizden satılmış*). Let me describe the inside of it for you." I described the inside of the house completely. I said: "My uncle Beşīr Ağa built that house. Then he fell into debt and sold it." Then I named the neighbors one by one.

Ḥāccī Rif ʿat Efendi was delighted and did not leave our side all day. Since he was the telegraph officer of the İdāre [to which the ship belonged], he had come to the Ḥicāz without money [cost], that is, he had paid nothing for the ship, and since he was staying in its main cabin (*baş kamara*), he said to me: "Obviously, since the ship is so crowded, you will have a lot of problems with the lavatories. If you will give a few *kuruş* to our steward, [the cabin] has ideal facilities, and you can always go there to do your ablutions, and then we can also sit there to talk. I reflected that this man must belong to one of the orders, and I asked. He was one of the *dervīş*es of the late Ḥāccī Aḥmed Efendi of Gümüşhāne, may God sanctify his innermost heart. I told him that I knew about the *şeyh* and recounted some things about him. I also talked about my own spiritual guide [Şeyh Fehmī], and I saw that the good Ḥāccī Rif ʿat took to me as if he had [again] found his late mentor. Saying "Mercy, sir! Let us stay together," he expressed his regard (*ʿalāḳa edercesine ʿarẓ-ı maḥabbetler etdi*). I accepted gladly, and he did not part from me, night or day. He waited on me like my own [532:] slave and expressed his affection. And, praise God, I realized that the saints had sent this gentleman of exalted worth to help this poor servant of theirs. And I, too, declaring my affection, took him as my spiritual son. I always went to the cabin. There I performed my ablutions; there I ate my meals; and he referred to me as his father. Since he did not part from me, the captain, Commander Ḥüseyin Bey, and the crew thought I really was his father. . . .[63]

We passed twelve days with great hardship [in the quarantine at Ṭūr] and then returned to the ship.[64] Our patron, His Excellency Ḥāccī Muhtār Efendi had taken sick en route in the Ḥicāz. . . . Since all those with him were relatives or dependents with no one from outside, and there was no one capable of resolving his problem [?], he—may God make him safe—fell into anxiety. Several times, he spoke as if God had intimated to him that I would return in health and soundness [533:] and he was comforted at that. . . . His Excellency's illness had been made known by the governor of the Ḥicāz to the palace secretariat, an imperial decree had been issued for him to come to Istanbul by sea, and he had returned to Jidda with his suite a week after I had. From there, boarding the Egyptian Company's steamer *Fayyūm*, he had reached Ṭūr in Sinai a week later. While at sea, they had bound Ḥāccī Yūnus's ship,[65] which had lost its rudder (*dümeni kırılub*)[66] and become disabled, to the *Fayyūm* and had brought it with them. And so their ship was vacated [for the quarantine] a week after ours. Instead of the quarantine, they went out to their own special place.

Here follows a copy of the letter that His Excellency Ḥāccī Muhtār Efendi wrote from the quarantine and sent to me by a guard.

> Dear El-Ḥācc İbrāhīm Efendi,
>
> May the harm to your head and eye be past, if it please God.[67] Since your haste in leaving Mecca resulted in your arriving in time to get a well-ordered Muslim ship like the *Adana*, it is worthy of pardon. Our haste served no purpose. For we ended up on an ill-managed and overcrowded ship like the *Fayyūm*. Having left Mecca quite sick, on the way to Jidda and at Jidda, we despaired of life. We got caught in a storm on the way to Ṭūr and were [still] sick. Yet we were fortunate that we were able to attach to our own ship Ḥāccī Yūnus's ship, which was in severe trouble on account of having lost its rudder (*dümeninin denize düşmesinden*) and having begun to take water with a thousand pilgrims on board. Since—praise God—your quarantine will, I believe, end in a day or two, you will reach Istanbul before us. Kindly convey our greetings to all friends and associates. Go by our house, too, and give them news of us. I send greetings to your companion Muṣṭafà Efendi and pray for him. . . . And finally may you remain in peace and health my friend.
>
> Muhtār[68]

. . . [535:] And so my friend, we returned from Ṭūr to the steamer. Rif'at Efendi met me and embraced me . . . [536:] and we withdrew to a corner. During the conversation, he said: "While you were at Ṭūr, I had a dream. Our mentor (*mürşid*) Ḥāccī Aḥmed appeared, but there was a worthy gentleman at his side. On his head a white turban, on his back a dervish cloak, he was the perfect spiritual guide, all radiant and smiling. . . . Aḥmed Efendi . . . said . . . to the other gentleman: 'According to your command, our Rif'at Efendi has been entrusted to me, your servant, and has been ordered to wait on you. . . .' As he said that, I awoke. I knew that the gentleman of exalted worth was my master's spiritual mentor. They had ordered me to serve you. I was very thankful for this and considered myself fortunate in this matter." So he concluded, and as for the service he rendered, it was truly indescribable. . . .[69]

Our ship left Ṭūr in Sinai at 8:30 on Monday, 9 Muḥarrem 1316, headed for Suez. We arrived at Suez on Tuesday the tenth, and stayed there one night on board. Departing the next day, Wednesday the eleventh, we entered the canal and passed the night there in the middle of the Sea of Pharaoh.[70] But we didn't see Pharaoh or Moses, my friend! We reached Port Said on Thursday the twelfth and, staying a night there also, we set out on Friday the thirteenth at nine.

On Monday, 16 Muḥarrem, at 5:30, we came to Urla, two or three hours from Izmir. This was the second quarantine, but compared to Ṭūr in Sinai it is a paradise. May the All High be pleased, fully equipped under the auspices of the *pādişāh* with buildings, [537:] fountains, water, grass, and trees, it is like a paradise. The quarantine officer came and announced on the ship that the stay here would be five days. And it was so permissively run that some of the more prominent *ḥāccīs* remained on the ship. We did not take most of the waterproof trunks (*sahāre*, presumably for *ṣaḥāre*) out [of the hold]. In sum, it was a superficial quarantine.

Yet, whatever the wisdom or the occult reason of it, fate found this much permissiveness too much for us. The doctor diagnosed the disease of an old woman who had taken sick at Ṭūr in Sinai . . . as contagious and, considering it a serious disease, notified Istanbul by telegraph. They sent the inspector (*müfettiş paşa*) who had examined us at Ṭūr, and who had gone on from there to Istanbul, to Urla posthaste; he came, examined her again, and concluded it was not the disease they thought. He reported to Istanbul, and by the time the answer had come, the time had amounted to ten days.

In that interval, His Excellency Muhtār Efendi's ship had caught up with us. He spent five days in the quarantine, then came on to Istanbul one day after us. And so the reason of it all became clear: as set forth earlier in this work, I had been one of the heralds (*çavuş*) who walked before [Şeyh Fehmī], and so now I went before Ḥāccī Muhtār Efendi to guard him.

In sum, on Tuesday, 24 Muḥarrem, we reboarded ship with difficulty. We spent the night on the ship, set off the next day at 9:30, and arrived at Izmir that day at 11:30. Staying there that night, the next day, Thursday the twenty-sixth, we departed at 8. The next day,

Friday the twenty-seventh early in the morning, at 11 [*à la turca*], we reached Ḳāle-'i Sulṭānīye [Çanakkale] and, without stopping there, on Friday evening, that is the night of Saturday, at 2:30, we came before Ḳāḍīköy and dropped anchor. Early in the morning, we entered past Palace Point [into the Golden Horn].

My son İsmā'īl Efendi came to the ship. From there, we went straight to our house at Taş Ḳaṣṣāb. After a rest, as His Excellency Muhtār Efendi had ordered, I immediately boarded the [local] steamer, set out for Anadolu Ḥiṣār, and from there went to his villa (*köşk*) at Küçük Su. [538:] Visiting his father-in-law Rıżā Bey Efendi, I made known that all of them were healthy and would arrive in Istanbul the next day, Sunday, in the morning. However, because they had not received the letter from his son-in-law Baṣrī Bey [?] and only had greetings from him, all of them were very worried and had decided [Muhtār Efendi] was dead. On seeing me, all of them had let out a cry. I said: "What's this?" Rıżā Bey explained. From the *ḥarem*, everybody came to the connecting door (*mābeyn kapusı*), and [Muhtār Efendi's wife] sent the housekeeper (*kethüdā hātūnı*) to my side. She asked and I [said]: "No. All of them are healthy, I swear." Then Rıżā Efendi went to the door and said: "My dear, this noble gentleman is trustworthy. He is a man of the pilgrimage (*ḥacc ül-ḥaremeyn bir ādamıdır*). He is swearing to you." He persuaded her, and that day they rejoiced exceedingly. They treated me with great consideration. She sent word from the harem: "Perhaps the gentleman will honor us today. A special soup has been prepared for him. Please let me send some for him to taste." And since it was mealtime, the food was brought out. I ate with Rıżā Bey and the imām and then, taking leave, came by rowboat (*kayık*) to Orta Köy.

From there, I went by tramway to the Imperial Artillery Foundry (*Tophāne-i 'Amire*), where I visited its auditor, our own Ḥüsnī Bey, and getting a month's leave for my son İsmā'īl Efendi, he has come with me to Edirne, my friend.[71]

The next day, Sunday, since His Excellency Ḥāccī Muhtār Efendi was to arrive on the *Fayyūm*, I went down to the quay early. I went to the customs office (*rüsūmāt dā'iresi*). His brother Rıżā Bey[72] and other relatives and dependents being there, we all went together to meet him in a small steamboat. They investigated out past the Yalı Köşk[73] and said "No steamer is in sight." We waited a moment; then it came to me that I had told the brethren (*ihvān*, i.e., everybody?) that they would get to Yalı Köşk at twelve. At a quarter of twelve, we set out [again?] from the quay. True enough, we encountered the *Fayyūm* off Ahur Kapu.[74] The brethren for whom we had been watching noticed us from the deck of the ship, and we went at their side past Palace Point [539:] into the inside [of the harbor]. Then going up onto the ship, we wept for joy and celebrated. In preparation for setting out to Edirne, I kissed His Excellency Muhtār's hand and made a fine farewell.

The next day, visiting Their Excellencies, the sulṭān's son-in-law, Hālid Paşa, and his brother, Aḥmed Paşa,[75] and some of the brethren, I presented gifts from the Ḥicāz. And especially, I visited and presented a gift to our director of the [Office of the] Corresponding Secretary of the Ministry of War, 'İzzet Efendi. In course of conversation, I mentioned having performed the *ḥacc* under the auspices, and with the protection, of His Excellency the Corresponding Secretary. 'İzzet Bey offered in response: "Yes, outwardly [*ẓāhir*] he protected you, but inwardly [*bāṭın*] you protected him." Indeed, high aspiration is part of the faith. Let the endeavor be an exalted one, my friend.

The following day, Friday, I had proclaimed [to be] for my brethren (*ihvān*, presumably meaning fellow *dervīşes*), and on that day, wearing the garments I had put on in the presence of the Refuge of Prophecy, I had a *ḥaccī* party (*ḥāccī cem'īyeti*) for them. That is, until evening, attired in that way, I gave according to custom, to all who came and went, Zemzem [water], oil, *lokum*, and *şerbet*. Thus we opened the door for a day. Afterward, we opened it likewise for a day to the ladies. Concluding thus happily (?—*hitāma misk diyerek*)—the old bath and the old bowl[76]—I again drew the mantle of seclusion (*'azlet hırḳası*) over my head and said: "Let us see what the mirror of existence (?—*āyīne-'i deverān*) shows, my friend!"

NOTES

1. The original manuscripts of the autobiography that contains this narrative are in the Istanbul University Library, MSS TY3222 (autograph of the first part of the work) and TY78–80 (fair copy with interpolations and continuation). See Marie Luise Bremer, *Die Memoiren des Türkischen Derwischs Aşçı Dede İbrāhīm* (Walldorf-Hessen, 1959), and Aşçidede Halil İbrahim, *Geçen Asrı Aydınlatan Kıymetli bir Eser: Hatıralar*, ed. Reşad Ekrem Koçu (Istanbul, 1960). Works calling attention to the manuscript: Osman Ergin, *İstanbul Mektepleri ve İlim, Terbiye ve San'at Müesseseleri dolayısile Türkiye Maarif Tarihi* (Istan-

bul, 1939–43), II, 325–30; Hellmut Ritter, *Das Meer der Seele* (Leiden, 1955), 491; Carter Vaughn Findley, "Social Dimensions of the Dervish Life, as Seen in the Memoirs of Aşçı Dede Halil İbrahim," in *Économie et Sociétés dans l'Empire Ottoman (fin du XVIIIe—début du XXe siècle)*, ed. Jean-Louis Bacqué-Grammont and Paul Dumont (Paris, 1982), 129–44. My efforts to understand these manuscripts have benefited from the inspired guidance of Annemarie Schimmel. Dona Straley has solved bibliographical and research problems with great expertise and good cheer. Steve Siebert of Dragonfly Software has contributed immeasurably to this and future projects by making it possible to combine the character set used here with the Nota Bene word processing program. Rick Cooper and Lynn Fauss have also played a major part in this respect. One source that should be mentioned in these notes has not been available to me. This is Eyyūb Ṣabrī Paşa, *Mir'āt ül-Ḥaremeyn* (Istanbul, 1301–6/1884–89), 3 vols. in 4.

2. William Ochsenwald, *Religion, Society, and the State in Arabia: The Hijaz Under Ottoman Control, 1840–1908* (Columbus, 1984), 15, 215; the railway never reached Mecca.

3. Cf. Annemarie Schimmel, *Mystical Dimensions of Islam* (Chapel Hill, 1975), 57, 137–38, 200, 237, 272–74, 280–82, 292.

4. On Şeyh Fehmī (d. 1880), leader of Nakşbendi-Hālidi *dervīşes* of Erzincan in eastern Anatolia, see M. L. van Ess-Bremer, art. "Fehmī," in *EI*², III, 878–79. As usual, Aşçı Dede refers to his spiritual mentor here not by name, but by a spiritual title: *sulṭān-ı 'ulemā bi'llāh efendimiz*. Instead of this title, frequently encountered in the passage translated here, we shall use Şeyh Fehmī's name.

5. A Nakşbendī rite, the *hatm-i hvācegān* consists of a number of *sūras* of the Qur'ān, recited in silent unison. See Hamid Algar, "Some Notes on the Naqshbandī Ṭarīqat in Bosnia," *Die Welt des Islams*, XIII (1971), 184.

6. The sending of a "treasure" with each year's pilgrimage caravan was a regular Ottoman practice from the conquest of the Arab lands under Selīm I to the last days of Ottoman control over the Ḥijāz. The Trusteeship of the Treasure was an important public function, entrusted each year to a prominent Ottoman official. The "treasure" consisted partly of grain and partly of money. Under Sulṭān 'Abd ül-Ḥamīd, the money amounted to some 3.5 million *kuruş* per year. Mehmet Zeki Pakalın, *Osmanlı Tarih Deyimleri ve Terimleri Sözlüğü* (Istanbul, 1946–53), III, 280–86; Charles M. Doughty, *Travels in Arabia Deserta* (London, 1923), I, 69. On the Ottoman pilgrimage caravans of an earlier period, see Karl K. Barbir, *Ottoman Rule in Damascus, 1708–1758* (Princeton, 1980), 108–77.

7. Identification from *Sālnāme-'i Devlet-i 'Alīye-i 'Osmānīye*, 1315, 154–55. The same as the Muhtār Efendi just mentioned as Trustee of the Treasure, this man was a disciple, like Aşçı Dede, of the Nakşbendī-Hālidī Şeyh Fehmī of Erzincan. Thence the special regard that A. D. displays for Muhtār Efendi; see Bremer, *Die Memoiren*, 122 and passim.

8. This presumably refers to a position in Muhtār Efendi's retinue as that year's trustee of the treasure (*ṣürre emīni*).

9. The "Prophet's Garden" is the part of the mosque at Medina between the Prophet's *minbar* and the chamber (*ḥujra*) enclosing his tomb; see Eldon Rutter, *The Holy Cities of Arabia* (London, 1928), II, 192, and plan opp. 232; R. B. Winder, art. "al-Madīna," *EI*², V, 1000.

10. The shrine of Abū Ayyūb Khālid ibn Zayd al-Anṣārī, outside the walls of Istanbul, adjoining the Golden Horn.

11. It is not clear whether this is the money that Muhtār Efendi said would be given him, his own money, or the sum of funds of both types. Of the eighty liras, some clearly went for familial purposes, some for expenses related to the transport of the candles. On p. 513 of the MS, A. D. does allude to having received fifty liras from Muhtār Efendi as travel expenses for himself and the ten sent to help with the candles.

12. This probably refers to the Ḳādirī Şeyh Ismā'īl of Erzurum, with whom A. D. himself had had contact; see Bremer, *Die Memoiren*. 66–70, 85. I have not found in A. D.'s memoirs any indication of a master-disciple relationship between "His Excellency," that is, Muhtār Efendi, and this *şeyh*, although there was such a relationship with Şeyh Fehmī.

13. Such expressions are common in what follows and will not always be translated here.

14. A. D.'s time reckoning is that of an Ottoman Islamic conservative. The day begins and ends at sundown. So in concept does the telling of the time (*alaturka [à la turca]* time, as opposed to *alafranga [à la franca*, European] time).

15. On these personages, see G. Vajda, art. "Dāniyāl," *EI*², II, 112–13; W. Montgomery Watt, art. "al-Iskandar," *EI*², IV, 127; B. Heller-[N. Stillman], art. "Luḳmān," *EI*², V, 811–13. On the sites, Sir Richard F. Burton, *Personal Narrative of a Pilgrimage to al-Madinah and Meccah* (New York, 1964), I, 12.

16. This is an extremely indirect route. Yanbū' is the port closest to Medina; Jidda is the port closest to Mecca; the first two are north of the second two. Suwākin is southeast from Jidda on the other side of the Red Sea, in the Sudan. Yanbū' is closer to Suez than either Jidda or Suwākin.

17. On this shrine, see Burton, *Narrative*, II, 273–75; Haji Khan and Wilfrid Sparroy, *With the Pilgrims to Mecca* (London, 1905), 105–6.

18. Ḥālet Paşa was another protégé of Aşçı Dede's spiritual mentor, Şeyh Fehmī of Erzincan, and an old friend of A. D.'s; Bremer, *Die Memoiren*, 54, 56, 58, 63, 79, 87, 89–90, 92, 93.

19. The reference is to the popular Istanbul outing spot at the head of the Golden Horn.

20. Meḥmed 'Ādil Paşa was *shaykh al-ḥaram al-sharīf* at Medina. The chief Ottoman official in the Ḥijāz was the governor general (*wālī*) at Mecca. There was also a *shaykh al-ḥaram al-sharīf* in Mecca; from 1891 to 1908, the post was held by the man who was also responsible for administration of the city (the *muḥāfız*), 'Osmān Paşa. In addition to the Ottoman governmental apparatus, there was also that of the local *amīr*, 'Awn al-Rafīḳ (1882–1905). *Sālnāme-'i Devlet-i 'Alīye-'i 'Osmānīye*, 1317, 376; Ochsenwald, *Religion, Society, and the State in Arabia*, 164–66, 209–10.

21. This is A. D.'s misunderstanding of the term *shuqdhuf*; cf. Ibrāhīm Rif'at Pasha, *Mir'āt al-Ḥaramayn* (Beirut, n.d.), I, 21; Burton, *Narrative*, I, 233–34, 270, 418, II, 69; C. Snouck Hurgronje, *Mekka in the Latter Part of the 19th Century* (Leiden, 1970), 26 ("litters of which one hangs on each side of the camel"); Rutter, *Holy Cities*, I, 151 ff., where he repeatedly mentions the "shugduf."

22. Cf. Burton, *Narrative*, I, 257–58, 265–66, 272–74.

23. Cf. episode en route from Mecca to Medina described in Muḥammad al-Sanūsī, *Al-Riḥla al-Ḥidjāziyya*, ed. 'Alī al-Shannūfī [Chenoufi] (Tunis, 1396–1402/1976–81), II, 204–5, also mentioning "al-shaḳādhif (ka-dhā)."

24. This is not to be confused with the special garb (*iḥrām*) that pilgrims are required to don as they approach Mecca. Other sources indicate no requirement of a specific costume at Medina, although the visitor to the mosque is supposed to go in best attire: Burton, *Narrative*, I, 309 n. 1.

25. See Reşad Ekrem Koçu, *Türk Giyim, Kuşam ve Süsleme Sözlüğü* (Ankara, 1967), 57–58 (*cübbe*), 102–5 (*entari*), 173 (*mest*, a kind of slipper, over which heavier shoes would be donned for outside wear), 246 (*yemeni*). The point of wearing both inner slippers and outer shoes appears to have been to keep the feet in a state of ritual cleanliness, so that after the initial ablution of the day, they would not have to be washed repeatedly; instead the slippers could be rubbed over (*mesḥ*, whence *mest* or *mes*). One would wear the slippers at home, at work, or at the mosque, and put on the heavier shoes over them to go outside. Cf. Burton, *Narrative*, I, 289–90; J. Schacht, art. "Wuḍū'," *EI*[1], IV, 1140–41; A. J. Wensinck, *The Muslim Creed* (London, 1965), 158–62.

26. The sites of the three tombs, all of which are in the same chamber behind the grille, are indicated to the worshiper by three circular openings in the grillwork; Burton, *Narrative*, I, 304–25; Rutter, *Holy Cities*, II, 193, and the plan of the Medina mosque opposite 232. For recent photographs of the grille, with the openings, and of the Prophet's *miḥrāb*, see Desmond Stewart, *Mecca* (New York, 1980), 52–53 (photographs by Mohamed Amin).

27. On the eastern side of the Prophet's tomb chamber (*ḥujra*) one comes to a spot where the Prophet received many of his revelations. Here worshipers recited a salutation to the angel Jibra'īl, God's messenger to the Prophet, and also the other three archangels, Mīkā'il, Isrāfīl, and 'Azrā'īl; Burton, *Narrative*, I, 326; Rutter, *Holy Cities*, II, 198; John Lewis Burckhardt, *Travels in Arabia* (London, 1829), 336. This site is known as the *Mahbaṭ Jibra'īl*. Among recent manuals for pilgrims, Hamza Kaïdi et al., *Mecca and Medinah Today* (Paris, 1980), 83, 214–20 (texts of prayers to recite at Medina) does not mention the archangels, but ends the visit at the tomb of 'Umar, while Anis Daud Matthews, *A Guide for Hajj and 'Umra* (Lahore, 1977), 184–206, does include the salutation to the archangels.

28. The tomb of the Prophet's daughter Fāṭima—or reputed tomb, as there is disagreement as to whether she is actually buried there—is not in the same tomb chamber with the Prophet's, but adjoins it to the north; see floorplan in Rutter, *Holy Cities*, II, opposite 232; Burton, *Narrative*, I, 327–28.

29. The 112th *sūra* of the Qur'ān.

30. In other words, they did not go out the Door of Gabriel, but from within it faced toward the cemetery of al-Baḳīʿ and prayed for the prominent members of the early Muslim community buried there. The Door of Gabriel is in the eastern side of the mosque, just opposite Fāṭima's tomb. Rutter, *Holy Cities*, II, 256–58, recounts visiting al-Baḳīʿ when the evidence of the Wahhābīs' destruction of the tombs was still fresh. Burckhardt had witnessed there a similar scene of Wahhābī tomb destruction a century earlier; Burckhardt, *Travels*, 346.

31. The *ağas* of the mosque at Medina were eunuchs, who formed much of the staff of the establishment, cleaning it and administering incomes assigned to it. A similar staff of eunuchs was attached to the Mosque in Mecca, one purported reason for this being that they could appropriately intervene in any disturbance involving women pilgrims in a way that male mosque attendants otherwise could not. See Burckhardt, *Travels*, 158–59, 342–44; Rutter, *Holy Cities*, I, 265–69, II, 235, 239–40. The employment of eunuchs in the two shrines corresponds to the important role, through the early nineteenth century, of the chief black eunuch (*kızlar ağası*) at the imperial palace in Istanbul in administering the revenues of *evḳāf* created to support the shrines: B. Lewis, art. "al-Ḥaramayn," *EI*², III, 175.

32. This refers to the same procedure of praying from within the mosque while facing toward a place outside, Jabal Uḥud, site of a battle between the still pagan Meccans and the Muslims in 625. The Prophet had a paternal uncle who was among the fallen at Uḥud and for whom pilgrims are instructed to pray, but it was Ḥamza ibn ʿAbd al-Muṭṭalib, not ʿAbbās ibn ʿAbd al-Muṭṭalib; see Burton, *Narrative*, I, 329; Rutter, *Holy Cities*, II, 204. ʿAbbās was also the Prophet's uncle, but is among those considered to be buried at *al-Baqīʿ*. Such slips of detail are frequent in A. D.'s account.

33. The meaning of this last sentence is not clear. Why does he name all of the five prayers except the sunset (*akşam*) prayer? At what time of day does he mean to say he performed the special rites of the visitation in Medina? The worshiper is supposed to complete them without delay upon arriving (Rutter, *Holy Cities*, II, 189), and A. D. should have arrived at the mosque in the morning. A. D. may mean that he completed the ritual visitations a number of times; all the ceremonies reportedly required only fifteen or twenty minutes: Burckhardt, *Travels*, 317, 339.

34. Here A. D. recounts a story about a *dervīş* and a Qur'ān reciter.

35. Again, the tomb is that of Ḥamza, not ʿAbbās; Burton, *Narrative*, I, 419–32; Rutter, *Holy Cities*, II, 244–48, visited it within a week after it was wrecked by the Wahhābīs (1925).

36. Burton, *Narrative*, I, 406–10; Rutter, *Holy Cities*, II, 250–54.

37. This reading is uncertain. It looks as if there is another letter between the *sīn* and the *qāf*, but it is not clear what it is. To judge from Burckhardt, *Travels*, 344–46, a mosque functionary who spread the carpets would more likely have been termed a *farrāsh*. However, Burton, *Narrative*, I, 331, speaks of "the Sakkā, or water-carrier of the mosque well," whose job was to give water from the well to mosque visitors.

38. The phrase *çırāğīyet berātı* repeats the same idea that we encountered on p. 505 of the MS, translating it as "the warrant of a small lamp." In both places, the idea of a burning light seems appropriate to the context and has been taken up in the translation. The exact intention of the word *berāt*, especially, is unclear. But the meaning of the phrase appears multileveled. The Persian word *çırāğ* means "lamp," or by extension "illuminator" or "teacher." From this word comes the Turkish *çırak*, meaning apprentice or novice, so that the phrase connotes the disciple's taking light from his spiritual master. The word *berāt* in Turkish usually means "warrant," which would almost surely be the first association in the mind of a bureaucrat like A. D. *Berāt* comes from the Arabic *barā'a*, meaning "notice" or "warning," "freedom from responsibility," or "innocence." The light taken from the master may thus carry with it a connotation of admonition or release from guilt. Quite possibly, the expression is a reference to some text, probably a mystical one; but I have not been able to determine what it is. The term *külāh* again may have multiple meanings. Literally, a cover or extinguisher for the lamp, it can also refer to headcoverings of a variety of types, including a fool's cap or that of a *dervīş*.

39. The reference appears to be to the Queen of Sheba's throne, magically transported before Solomon in response to his vizier Asaf's appeal to Divine Mercy. The story is an outgrowth of a Qur'ānic passage (27:15–44), elaborated in many later sources, including Rumī's *Mesnevī*, book iv (*The Mathnawí of Jalálu'ddín Rúmí*, ed and trans. Reynold A. Nicholson (London, 1977), 303 ff., especially 322–23, 329–30, where the point of the incident is to move the queen to give up her treasured throne and "Come and behold [God's] Kingdom!" See W. Montgomery Watt, "The Queen of Sheba in Islamic Tradition," in *Solomon and Sheba*, ed. James B. Pritchard (London, 1974), 85–103.

40. Cf. Rutter, *Holy Cities*, II, 192.

41. This idea evokes that from which the Nakşbendī order takes its name, i.e., that one's heart should be imprinted with the name of Allāh; see Algar, "Some Notes on the Naqshbandī Ṭarīqat in Bosnia," 183 n. 2.

42. On the *ağas'* opening the tomb chamber and admitting visitors to it, cf. Rutter, *Holy Cities*, II, 201–4.

43. Reading *Biz buraya başka türlü olmak için gelmedikmi dedim* (for . . . *gelmedik mi dedim*). My thanks to Robert Dankoff for advice on this and other passages.

44. On the jeweled ornaments of the tomb, cf. Burton, *Narrative*, I, 322; Rutter, *Holy Cities*, II, 195.

45. In the name of the road, the initial consonant is not fully legible. Otherwise, the word is legible and fully pointed. The reading would appear to be "Farī" or "Qarī." Comparing this with Burton's listing of the Mecca-Medina roads (*Narrative*, II, 58) suggests that what he calls the "Wady al-Kura" route is intended here.

46. On problems with the bedouin in this period, cf. Ibrāhīm Rif'at, *Mir'āt*, II, 70–75, 88–94, 121–24; Ochsenwald, *Religion, Society, and State in Arabia*, 32–34; Doughty, *Travels*, I, 55, 73–74; Burton, *Narrative*, II, 143–45.

47. The more common term for the guides at Mecca is *muṭawwif*. On these, see Snouck Hurgronje, *Mekka*, 24–26.

48. The reason for entering the state of consecration (*iḥrām*) at Rābigh was, of course, not the presence of the guide, but that this is the point (*mīqāt*) at which pilgrims coming from Syria, Egypt, or North Africa must do so. The *mawāqīt* of space and time are explained in pilgrimage manuals like Hamza Kaïdi et al., *Mecca and Medinah Today*, 46–47. Cf. also al-Sanūsī, *Al-Riḥla*, II, 157–58; Burton, *Narrative*, II, 138–41.

49. The term *qirān*, "conjunction," refers to the fact that the pilgrim who adopts the *iḥrām* with this intention performs both the lesser pilgrimage (*'umra*, which may otherwise be performed at any time of year) and the *ḥajj* (which can only be performed on set dates in the month of Dhū 'l-Ḥijja) without leaving the state of ritual consecration (*iḥrām*) outwardly symbolized, in the case of males, by the wearing of the two white seamless garments.

50. A. D. mentions passing through Wādī Fāṭima and an episode in which he wounded his head against the sharp branchwork at the top of his camel litter while trying to adjust his *iḥrām* garments.

51. This is a summary account of the *'umra* or "lesser pilgrimage." Between this initial sevenfold circumambulation of the Ka'ba (the *ṭawāf al-qudūm* or "of arrival") and the running (*sa'y*) between Ṣafā and Marwa, the pilgrim performs other rites, including praying two *rak'as* at the Station of Abraham (*Maqām Ibrāhīm*) and drinking water from the Zamzam well; J. Wensinck-J. Jomier-B. Lewis, art. "Ḥadjdj," *EI*², III, 35; al-Sanūsī, *Al-Riḥla*, 171–79. A. D.'s ecstasy at the Black Stone, his way of referring to the *şeyh*'s son, and the idea that anyone at the Black Stone—surrounded by a sea of humanity moving in the single direction of the *ṭawāf*—could become so disoriented as not to know which way to turn reveal deeply rooted traits of A. D.'s outlook as a Muslim, or more exactly as a *ṣūfī*.

52. Functionaries known as "corresponding secretaries" (*mektūbī*) were found throughout Ottoman administration and are perhaps best understood as something like an executive secretary to the senior official of a given agency. Provincial administrations and the ministries in Istanbul normally had a bureau headed by a functionary with this title.

53. Cf. Burton, *Narrative*, II, 248–50; Rutter, *Holy Cities*, I, 274–76; Ibrāhīm Rif'at, *Mir'āt*, I, 30–32 and ills. 28–31; Snouck Hurgronje, *Mekka*, 53–55. Among the most important figures buried in the cemetery according to tradition are the Prophet's mother, Āmina, and his wife, Khadīja, mentioned in the text.

54. Here A. D. quotes in Arabic, with a slight reordering of the words, the beginning of the *talbiya*, the prayer recited to complete assumption of the pilgrim's state of consecration and repeated frequently thereafter, up to the sacrifice on 10 Dhū 'l-Ḥijja: *Labbayka Allāhuma labbayka lā sharīka laka labbayka*.

55. This is A. D.'s account of the *wuqūf* ("standing") at 'Arafāt, the central event of the *ḥajj*, appointed for 9 Dhū 'l-Ḥijja. According to Rutter, *Holy Cities*, I, 162, the waving of the *ridā'* (the upper of the two *iḥrām* garments) served to let pilgrims too far away to hear the preacher on Jabal al-Raḥma

know when he called out *labbayk* so that they could take up the cry; see also Burton, *Narrative*, II, 178–99.

56. Cf. al-Sanūsī, *Al Riḥla*, II, 179–80.

57. This has to be an allusion to the "standing" (*wuqūf*) at Muzdalifa, appointed for 10 Dhū 'l-Ḥijja. Having spent the night at Muzdalifa, the pilgrims should "stand" before a monument called the *Mash'ar al-Ḥarām* before the dawn prayer. See Ibrāhīm Rif'at Pasha, *Mir'āt*, I, 47, 88–89, 332–33.

58. Here A. D. for some reason skips over the sacrificing of animals at Minà, coinciding with the *'īd al-aḍḥà* (10–12 Dhū 'l-Ḥijja), followed by the pilgrims' resumption of their normal attire and release from most of the *iḥrām* restrictions. A. D. should have sacrificed an animal, and many animals would certainly have been sacrificed around him. He also fails to mention the stoning of all three of the pillars at Minà, which each pilgrim is supposed to perform each day from 11 Dhū 'l-Ḥijja through the 13th. On the 10th, after stoning the *jamrat al-'aqaba*, making their sacrifice, and having their head shaved or their hair cut, pilgrims also commonly return to Mecca to perform the *ṭawāf al-ifāḍa*, then return to Minà for the 11th through the 13th. This *ṭawāf* can be postponed but, like the "standing" at 'Arafāt, is an indispensable obligation (*rukn*) of the pilgrimage. After the *ṭawāf al-ifāḍa*, the pilgrim emerges completely from the restrictions of *iḥrām*. A. D.'s failure to mention so many important and distinctive rites of the pilgrimage is perplexing. See A. J. Wensinck-J. Jomier-B. Lewis, art. "Ḥadjdj," *EI*², III, 36; Ibrāhīm Rif'at, *Mir'āt*, I, 75–142, with tables on 129–31, indicating the status of the various pilgrimage rites according to the four *madhāhib*; Burton, *Narrative*, II, 202–25.

59. These final circumambulations culminate in that of farewell (*ṭawāf al-wadā'*), which is considered obligatory (*wājib*) in the Ḥanafī *madhhab*.

60. On ideas and practices associated with Zamzam water, see Burckhardt, *Travels in Arabia*, 143–45; Snouck Hurgronje, *Mekka*, 21–22; Rutter, *Holy Cities*, I, 147–48, 261–62.

61. They exchange pleasantries. The Second Army was headquartered at Edirne, where A. D. served as a civil official in one of the offices of the army command.

62. This statement is out of chronological sequence and looks ahead. On p. 532, A. D. adds (in a passage not translated) that Muṣṭafà Efendi died in the hospital there.

63. A. D. continues about his *dervīş* contacts up to the time of the quarantine at Ṭūr in Sinai.

64. On the quarantines, cf. Ibrāhīm Rif'at, *Mir'āt*, II, 233–37; al-Sanūsī, *Al-Riḥla*, II, 281–85.

65. The wording actually says that it was "the rudderless and disabled Ḥaccī Yūnus's ship (*dümeni kırılub sakaṭlanmış olan Ḥāccī Yūnus'un vapurı*); but it seems more likely that A. D. meant "the disabled ship *Ḥāccī Yūnus*" and should have written . . . *Ḥāccī Yūnus vapurı*.

66. The phrase *dümen kırmak*, literally "to break a rudder," has the idiomatic meaning "to veer" or "to change directions." That the meaning here is the literal one is clear, however, from the reference further on in the text to "its rudder falling into the sea" (*dümeninin denize düşmesinden*).

67. This refers to the episode at Wādī Fāṭima on the way to Mecca, when A. D. hurt his head on the roof of his camel litter.

68. A. D. returned a suitably polite response, which he copied in full into his text. He went on to recount a dream he had and other correspondence exchanged among those in quarantine in Ṭūr. These passages add little and need not be translated here.

69. A. D. recounts an example of the trouble Rif'at Efendi went to trying to locate A. D.'s trunk in the hold of the ship.

70. The Great Bitter Lake? I have not been able to locate a "Sea of Pharaoh." Burton, *Narrative*, I, 195, 197, 201, mentions several places named after Moses and Pharaoh on the Red Sea near Suez.

71. A. D.'s shifting back and forth in time here creates an especially diarylike note in his additions to his memoirs. The shift in subject between successive clauses of a sentence probably indicates that this account is an unrevised first draft.

72. Is this "brother Rıżā Bey" different from the "father-in-law Rıżā," referred to variously as bey, efendi, or beyefendi, just above?

73. This is a place at Palace Point where the sultans once had a pavilion outside the walls of Topkapı Sarayı. Here, practically speaking, this is another way of referring to Palace Point.

74. A neighborhood of Istanbul near Topkapı Palace, on the shore of the Sea of Marmara, behind the Sulṭān Aḥmed mosque.

75. Sons of A. D.'s late patron, Dervīş Paşa, who was also a disciple of Şeyh Fehmī.

76. A. D. has already quoted this common Turkish proverb several times in the passage translated here. The point is that the old bath cannot be expected to have anything but an old bowl (which one uses to pour the water over oneself): having completed his pilgrimage, A. D. must return to his old familiar way of life.

34
Jews in the Ottoman Economy and Finances, 1450–1500

Halil Inalcik

THE PROMINENT ROLE played by the Jews in the Ottoman economic life of the fifteenth and sixteenth centuries was directly linked to two demographic events: the deportation of the Jews from the Balkan towns and their settlement in Istanbul after its conquest by Mehmed II in 1453, and the influx of the Iberian Jews, who had been expelled by the Spanish rulers in 1492, into the main cities of the empire. In fact, there was a sizable Jewish population in Istanbul before the Sephardic immigration in 1492. As the Ottoman survey of 1455[1] establishes, the Conqueror, keenly concerned with repopulating his new capital, subjected the Jews in the Balkan towns and cities to a forced immigration and settlement in Istanbul. In his efforts at repopulating and reconstructing his new capital, Mehmed the Conqueror deemed it necessary for people with large amounts of capital and business experience to settle in the city. The wealthy Muslims of the Ottoman cities, including Bursa, did not respond well to the order, and most of those who had come soon returned to their old homes. Using the age-old *sürgün*, or forced deportation and settlement method, the Conqueror brought into the city many Jewish families from the Balkan towns, including Edirne, Salonica, Zeitoon (Lamia), Filibe (Plovdiv), and Nicopolis. The extensive Jewish settlement which we find in the port area from Çifut-Kapı to Zindan-Kapı after the conquest is of particular interest, because this area was vital commercially to the city's economy, and because it had formerly been occupied by the Venetians, whom the sultan had forbidden to return after they were driven out during the conquest.[2] As loyal subjects, the Jews were regarded from an economic and political point of view as the ideal group for settlement in the area. They remained in the district until the construction of the Vālide (Yeni) Mosque began in 1597, when they were transferred to Hasköy on the other side of the Golden Horn.

The survey of 1455 also shows that just after the conquest, there were on the other side of the Golden Horn, in Pera, a group of about forty Jewish families, many of them quite wealthy. The Peran Jews apparently were already active in the Pera-Bursa-Caffa triangle during the Genoese period. Many of them were evidently immigrants from the Crimea or the Balkans (several in our list were from Castoria), and some of them had typical Turkish names (Aslan, Menteshe, and Khojabeg). Later on, the Jews of Galata must also have been transferred by the Conqueror to Istanbul, as no Jews are recorded in Galata in the survey of 1477. Our survey of 1477 records 1,647 Jewish households in Istanbul, which made up 11 percent of the total population at that time. During the following twelve years, 380 families were added to this figure. But starting in 1492, the arrival of the Sephardic Jews from Spain meant a real exodus which quadrupled the Jewish population of Istanbul.[3] According to the cautious estimate made by Loeb,[4] out of a total 165,000 Jews who emigrated from the Iberian peninsula after 1492, approximately 90,000 came to settle in the Ottoman dominions. Ottoman documents tell us that the immigrants were settled in the major Ottoman cities, Istanbul and other Balkan towns, as well as in Safed in Palestine. The same Ottoman sources give their total number as about 12,000 families; or if we use the coefficient of five souls per household, about 60,000 altogether. Later, when Istanbul became a thriving city, voluntary Jewish immigrants from Hungary and Germany, or from other parts of the Ottoman dominions, came to join the earlier settlers.

In the survey of 1535 we find 8,070 Jewish households in Istanbul. At the same time, Edirne, the second Ottoman capital, had a Jewish population of 201 households. In 1528 the eight Jewish communities of Edirne included those of *Alaman, Portugal, Katalan, Toledo, Gerush, Pulya, Ispanya,* and *Aragon.* In later times, those of Sicily (*Çiçilya*) and Italy were to join them.[5] At that time, 7 percent of the total population of Edirne was comprised of Jews, while Salonica was to become a real Jewish city after the settlement of the Sephardic immigrants. Whereas no single Jew was recorded in the survey of 1478, the city of Salonica had a Jewish population of 2,645 households in 1529, 1,229 Muslim, and only 989 Greek households.[6] Between 1529 and 1568, 162 new immigrant Jewish families further increased the Jewish population of Salonica.

Thus, in the period in which we are going to study the economic activities of the Jews, the principal Ottoman cities had quite large Jewish communities as a result of immigration from other Ottoman towns or from Europe.

A comparative study of Italian and Ottoman sources confirms the central role of the Jews as middlemen in the trade of European woolen cloth, Iranian silk, and Indian spices about 1500.

Jews in the Woolen Cloth Trade

From the twelfth century onward, the most important item of export from Europe to the East was fine quality woolen cloth. Fr. B. Pegolotti, writing about 1340, says that European woolen cloth was sold throughout the East as far afield as China.[7] By their dominant role in the trade in woolen cloth, the Jews controlled the most important and lucrative sector of East-West trade.

This trade required an extensive working capital, since the initial prices were high. According to the customs registers of Akkerman and Kilia dated 1504–7, Florentine (*Floridin*) varieties of cloth were the most expensive, priced between 35 and 40 *akça* per ell (68 cm) at these places (see Table VII). *Londra, Motun* (Mantua?), and Salonica cloth was about half this price, while Polish and Istanbul varieties representing inferior qualities sold at the modest price of 6 *akça*, almost the same price as that of felt. However, Salonica, Istanbul, and Polish cloth varied in quality and in price (see Table VII). Salonica woolen cloth manufactured by immigrant Jews included an inferior quality priced at 9 or 12, the average quality was at 20 or 23, and the superior quality at 45 *akça*. Salonica woolens manufactured by Jews included three main varieties, namely, *keçe* or felt, *beylik çuka*, or ordinary cloth for the Janissary uniform, and *sobraman* or *sopramani* for officers' uniforms. Florentine cloth, or *Floridin çuka* as it was called by the Ottomans, was reserved for the highest-ranked dignitaries in the army and the court. The price of Florentine cloth was considerably higher in 1501, perhaps as a result of the Ottoman-Venetian war (see Table I). The price of one *pastav* (ca. 34 m) of Florentine cloth fluctuated between 1,400 and 1,600 *akça* in the Istanbul and Bursa markets in 1501, while it was estimated at 1,200 *akça* at the customs of Akkerman in 1505 (see Tables III–VII).

Among the varieties of woolen textiles which Maringhi imported, the two most common types were *calisse* and *panni Fiorentini*. A Spanish, or perhaps originally Jewish product, *calisse*, or wool of Cadiz,[8] was imported from Spain. After being finished in Florence according to the Levantine taste, it was exported to Turkey, mostly via Ancona, Ragusa, and Edirne (Adrianople). Thence it was distributed to the Balkan cities and towns, or taken to Istanbul or Bursa to be re-exported to the Black Sea countries or Asia.

In his letters of 1501, Maringhi, the Florentine agent of Pera,[9] urged his patrons in Florence to increase their shipment of Spanish *calisse*. "Mellini," he said, "has undoubtedly bargained for two boatloads from Spain of 4000 pieces and probably there will be about 2000 pieces or more coming into the market from this source, and I think that these will not make the price go down." Maringhi assured that "they will have a good sale."

Apart from Jews, the other drapers mentioned in Maringhi's letters were Italians who had settled in Edirne, Istanbul, and Bursa.[10] On the other hand, Bursa court records inform us that there were also local Muslim cloth dealers who purchased woolen cloth directly from the Florentines.[11] Maringhi, following the price fluctuations in the local market, carefully measured and controlled the volume of goods to be imported and exported by the Florentine firms, and gave instructions to regulate their price and quality.

The principal distribution centers in Rumelia for European woolens were Ragusa (Dubrovnik) and Edirne. An Ottoman chronicle of the late fifteenth century (Paris, Bibliothèque Nationale, MS no. 1047, fol. 114b) informs us that in a fire which broke out in Edirne in July 1496, cloth stored by European merchants, and valued at one million *akça* (about 20,000 gold ducats) was destroyed.

Bursa became one of the centers of activity, serving an extensive hinterland in Anatolia and Syria, and involving merchants from Iran and Arab lands. The intensive commercial activity of the Jews in Bursa is by no means accidental.

Direct commercial relations of Bursa with Tabriz, Pera, and the Syrian emporiums of Damascus and Aleppo developed in the fourteenth and fifteenth centuries. The rise of Bursa as an international trade center was an extremely important development for the whole of the Levant trade, and it gave rise to an all-embracing reorganization of Near Eastern commerce and the trade routes. Apart from the major (Tabriz-Bursa) caravan route, another route was established from Ancona to Ragusa, and from there to Edirne, Bursa, and Istanbul. This became a cause of concern on the part of the Venetians.[12] In Bursa, as well as in other Ottoman cities, Jews assumed a dominant role in the cloth trade, and used an extensive network of traders in the Balkans and the Black Sea areas. Another setback for the Venetians occurred when Mehmed II pursued a policy of encouraging an increase in trade with Florence, Venice's principal rival in the cloth trade. Mehmed II hoped to break the role of the Venetians as intermediaries, by dealing directly with the Florentine cloth producers. Through the cooperation of the Florentines with the Jews, this policy was quite successful. It was particularly during the Venetian-Ottoman war of 1463–79 that the Florentines began to take the place formerly occupied by their rivals.[13] Florence's share in the Ottoman market began to expand through the foundation of commercial houses based in Pera. Bayezid II, needing the Medicis' friendship because of his brother Jem's presence in Italy, further encouraged the Florentine trade. It was only in the sixteenth century that Venice was finally able to establish a woolen cloth industry of its own, and thus became a successful rival of Florence in the Ottoman cloth market.[14]

Bursa court records concerning the transactions between Italians and Jews,[15] and the letters of Giovanni Maringhi,[16] an agent in Pera for the Medici, and four other Florentine woolen cloth manufacturers (the Galilei, Venturi, Neri, and Michelozzi), show various aspects of the commercial activity of the Jews during the period. Through Maringhi's letters we learn, for instance, that these Florentine firms were regularly selling their products to the Jewish drapers of Pera, Edirne, and Bursa (see Table I).

Istanbul was always the central marketplace and distribution point for textiles destined for the Black Sea region. According to a customs register for Caffa dated 1487,[17] the majority of the Jewish cloth merchants trading in the Crimea brought their goods from Istanbul (see Table III). It is to be remembered that following the Ottoman assumption of control over the ports of Caffa (1475), Kilia, and Akkerman (1484), the traffic with the northern countries grew considerably, as evidenced by the Ottoman customs records of these cities.

The register (dated 1487) of the unpaid customs dues at the port of Caffa[18] contains the names of eight Jewish merchants. These merchants fall into two groups (see Table III): those whoe exported native products of the area, chiefly hides of horses and cows, and those who imported costly silk and woolen cloth or spices in Caffa. Caffa in turn served as a center of distribution for northern markets in the Crimea, the Dasht, Muscovy, the Caucasus, and the Volga basin.

The data listing the Jewish merchants at the ports of Kilia and Akkerman presents the same pattern, as far as commodities traded were concerned (see Tables IV and V). There too, a particular category of merchants appears to have been exclusively engaged in the trade of woolen cloth and other fabrics; another group engaged in that of local products such as hides, leather, furs, horses, caviar, or goods of Tatar and *Rūs* origin (here *Rūs* or *Rūsī* means of Ukrainian or Ruthenian origin).

If we do not now find a clear reference to the once famous Tatar Route through Black Sea ports or the Moldavian Route, this does not mean that they disappeared in the Ottoman period as is usually assumed. Ottoman sources demonstrate the fact that this trade was quite active, with the sole difference being that Ottoman subjects and local merchants, including Jews, Greeks, and Armenians, encouraged by the Ottoman government through the application of lower customs rates and other inducements, replaced the Italians. Also, the Italians, whom we still find active in the Black Sea trade, were mostly coming from Ottoman Pera and Chios.

In Akkerman, while Moldavian (*Bogdānī*) and *Rūs* merchants were numerous, Muslim merchants from the south, chiefly from Istanbul and Edirne, still constituted the great majority of the merchants there, as in Caffa. There were also Muslim Tatars active in the northern Black Sea ports of Caffa, Akkerman, and Kilia.

Special mention should be made of woolen cloths and iron implements of the *Rūs* imported in quite sizable quantities into and through Akkerman. Jews such as Yehūda, Avraham, Mūsā, Ya'qūb, Ilyās, and Sha'bān (see Table V) belonged to the category of merchants who were engaged in the trade of such goods in Akkerman.

It should be added that along with Caffa and Kilia, Akkerman was an emporium for the export of hides by the Italians and Jews to Chios, and then to Italy and other European lands in this period. As for the volume of the European cloth trade in the Ottoman lands, Maringhi, who represented four Florentine firms in Pera, estimated in the year 1501 a marketing capacity for these firms between five and six hundred *panni* per annum, and noted that the market was undergoing continuous expansion. Naturally, these figures represented only a fraction of the cloth imports into the Levant. Upon Maringhi's death in 1506, his accounts were liquidated, and it was determined that the goods in his possession were worth a total of 127,000 ducats,[19] a vast sum for the period. Before the Salonica Jews started their production, Bayezid II had informed the Medici in 1483 that[20] he was ready to purchase 5,000 *panni* of cloth per annum. This amount was obviously designed only for the needs of the army and the court. Much earlier, in 1423, the Venetian Doge Tommaso Mocenigo stated[21] that Venice used to purchase 16,000 pieces of cloth per year from Florence, marketing them in North Africa, Egypt, Syria, Cyprus, the Balkan lands, and Byzantium, as well as in Crete, the Morea, and Istria.

What is of particular interest for us is that woolen cloth from Salonica and Istanbul was already traded in the northern Black Sea ports by 1500.

Ottoman Anatolia (Ankara and Tosya) exported to Italy and the northern countries a large amount of valuable mohair made from fine goat hair. In this lucrative trade with Italy, the Jews were particularly active. The Ottomans, however, showed no great interest in participating in or encouraging the trade in mohair, while the Florentine authorities were keenly concerned with the expansion of sales of Italian woolens in the Ottoman Empire. In this respect, we see the fundamental difference between the two economic systems. The Ottoman system was oriented toward limited production for the internal market, and remained closely bound to the limitations imposed by the guild system, protecting against the change in its structure and acting as both enforcer and supervisor of its regulations. At times the Ottoman government even imposed export restrictions, to stabilize the price of a product in the internal market at the desired level. The Ottomans did not fully understand the fundamental laws of the capitalist-mercantilist system until the nineteenth century.[22] It appears that one motive for encouraging the Jews to settle in the Ottoman Empire had been to establish and develop the woolen textiles industry to supply the internal market, evidently with no real mercantilistic intent.

While Jews played an important role in the distribution of imported fabrics within the Ottoman Empire, the Turkish Muslim merchants were, in general, in firm control of commercial activity. Their number far exceeded the non-Muslims. On the other hand, the Iranians and the Arabs from the East played a dominant role in supplying the Bursa market with Oriental textiles, silks, cottons, and spices. The Bursa *qāḍī* records of the period 1480–1500 provide ample evidence that the Jews were operating a lively business in Bursa with the merchants of Aleppo and Damascus, especially in the trade of spices, and with the Iranian merchants in the silk trade.

The Jewish merchants engaged in cloth trade were of different types. Ottoman regulations distinguished between the status of the wholesale import-merchant, the *tājir-i saffār*, who was an itinerant merchant bringing in goods either by caravan or by sea, and the resident merchant or *muqīm.*[23] Usually the traveling merchant was obliged to surrender his goods to an established local resident merchant. These local cloth merchants (*bezzāz*), who were also great merchants bearing the prestigious title of *khwāja* (hoca), could be either Muslims, Jews, or even locally resident Europeans. They pursued their trade usually from shops located in the *bezzāzistān*, or *bedestān,* which was a strongly protected trade mart for storing and selling precious imported textiles and jewelry. In the *bedestān* of Istanbul, for example,[24] we find five Jewish resident merchants in 1489, and eighteen in 1520, while in that same year there were 123 Muslims, thirteen Armenians, two Greeks, and one Italian. The increase in the number of Jewish merchants might be related to the arrival of Sephardic Jews in Istanbul after 1492. Every important city in the empire had its own *bedestān*. Among the fabrics stocked by the merchants in the *bedestān* were silks, fine woolens, fine cotton cloth, and linens. Usually we find that merchants specialized in one of these three types of cloth. The merchants in the *bedestān* would offer their imported cloth to the market in three ways. They sold the goods retail in their own shops in the *bedestān*, or wholesale to retailers at large, or to the caravan merchants, who took them to other Ottoman towns. The second group, also called *bezzāz*, purchased small consignments of cloth of various types for sale to the public in the neighborhood shops. The retailer *bezzāz* stocked a much greater variety (principally the cheaper cotton textiles) than did the merchants who specialized in luxury items. The larger *bezzāz* also sold their merchandise to the caravan merchants who traveled across the empire with their wares.[25] In our sources, we find Jews represented in each of these three categories (see Tables II and III). The Jewish merchants listed in Maringhi's records apparently all belonged to the categories of the prominent resident merchants, and caravan or roving merchants. At the same time, there were foreign Jewish merchants engaged in large-scale international export-import trade between Italy and Turkey, after the fashion of Maringhi. We find them mentioned in the Ottoman records under the distinctive title *Frenk yahūdīsi*.

Hājjī, a Muslim merchant of the woolen trade who died in Edirne in 1553, is an example of the typical wholesale cloth merchant operating on a large scale in the internal Ottoman textile market.[26] The stock of woolens in Hājjī's possession at the time of his death is enumerated in the following list:

Type of cloth	Amount	Price in *akça*
Florentine cloth	311 *pastav* (10,574 meters)	500 per *pastav*
Salonica cloth	30 meters	30 per *dhirā'*
London cloth from Salonica	19 meters	33 per *dhirā'*

60 *akça* = 1 gold ducat
1 *dhirā'* = 68 cm

From this list, we learn that the Jewish cloth manufacturers in Salonica were producing imitation kersey and broadcloth. However, the greatest part of Hājjī's stock consisted of imported Florentine cloth. Apart from these, his stock also included some other types of high-priced luxury textiles such as muslin (*dülbend*) and silken cloth. His customers belonged primarily to the Ottoman elite class. Among those listed are individuals bearing the titles *pasha, bey,* and *çelebi.* At the same time there were many Wallachians (*Eflak'lı*) among his customers. It may be supposed that he made shipments from Edirne to wholesale merchants in Wallachia. Two Jews, one named Manyas and the other Ya'qūb, are mentioned among those in debt for merchandise supplied. It appears that Hājjī made a great volume of sale on credit. Of a total estate valued at 858,953 *akça,* 530,000 *akça* were owed to him at the time of his death by various dealers, among them a Greek tailor by the name of Istamad.

Jewish Woolen Industries

Not only did the Jews play an important role in the East-West trade in fine woolens; they were also instrumental in founding an indigenous industry for the production of high-quality woolen cloth in Turkey. In the period after 1492, when Jews began to arrive in the Ottoman Empire from Spain, Salonica, and Safed emerged as important centers for a native woolen industry.[27] The most recent contribution to the subject is the publication of an Ottoman account book of Salonica cloth made for Janissaries, dated 1511.[28] According to this register, in 1511 the Ottoman government purchased 96,000 *dhirā'*, or 65,280 meters of cloth for the troops of Istanbul. There were 92,148 *dhirā'* provided by Salonica and 3,825 *dhirā'* from Istanbul. There was a total of 2,587,904 *akça*, or approximately 50,000 gold ducats, paid for this cloth. The following year, the amount paid for the cloth increased by fourteen percent. The cloth from Florence was purchased at much higher prices (see Tables VI, VII), but was designed to be distributed only among the commanding officers. Seventy years later, in 1584, government purchases of cloth from Salonica had reached 251,279 *dhirā'* (Sahillioğlu, p. 419, note 15), which showed an increase of more than one and a half times. We have already seen that there was great demand for Spanish *calisse* in Turkey. The Jewish weavers from Spain were now in Ottoman territory, and the woolens of Cadiz could be manufactured and sold at a lower price right in the sultan's lands. Thus, while the sultan was encouraging the Florentines in their woolen trade within his dominions, he was also welcoming Spanish Jews who would manufacture the woolen cloth which was much in demand in the Ottoman market. The court and the troops in Istanbul had been wearing this imported cloth for a long time, and the sultan was interested in supplying them with the best quality at the lowest price (for prices see Table VI).

As can be seen from the customs registers of the Black Sea ports (see Tables IV and V), the woolen cloth of Salonica and Istanbul appears to have been part of an established trade in the Ottoman market by 1500. The Ottoman-Venetian war of 1499–1502 must have contributed to its boom. We learn from the earliest available accounting lists of the Salonica cloth made for the Janissaries, dated 1511, of the variety, the amount, and the value of the cloth distributed among the *kuls,* or the servants of the sultan.

As for the woolen industry of Safed, it also reached an advanced level of development, with a capacity to supply the whole empire. According to the exaggerated account of Evliyā Çelebi,[29] who wrote in 1081/1670, there had formerly been a large "Jewish community of 70,000" living in Safed,[30] engaged in the woolen industry. But by the time of his visit they had mostly emigrated to Salonica. Among the famed products of Safed in former times, Evliyā Çelebi mentions felt, which at one time had presumably been manufactured "in workshops whose number was now, however, reduced to a mere 40." The felt of Safed, he claimed, was famous throughout the empire. Evliyā's report of 1670 notes that of the three *bedestāns* formerly existing in Safed, two had fallen into disuse, with only the Sinān Pasha *bedestān* remaining active. The building of these three *bedestāns* in Safed is a clear indication of the importance of the commercial activity there when the textile industry was at the peak of its production. "Textile industry," David de Ross writes in 1535, "is prospering every day [there in Safed]. It is said that this year alone 15,000 kerseys have been manufactured. . . . Some weavers make cloths of a quality as fine as those made in Venice." According to official surveys in 1539, the number of dye-houses (*boyahāne*) was only two, but by 1556 their number had doubled.[31] In the 1560s the stamp tax (*tamghā*) on the manufactured woolen cloth (*çuka*) and *qarziye* (*kersey*) gave a total yield of 12,000 *akça*. (The rate for the assessment of this tax was two *akça* per *pastav* for *karziye*, and about four *akça* per *pastav* for *çuka*.) From these figures we can estimate that at least 3,000, and perhaps as much as 6,000 *pastav* of cloth were produced each year in the Safed workshops about 1560.

The fact that *çuka* of Istanbul was frequently mentioned along with Salonica woolens in the customs registers indicates that there was in Istanbul a woolen cloth industry, again apparently established by Sephardic Jews.

Jews in the Silk and Spice Trades

By the time that Bursa had developed into the most important emporium for the silk trade between Iran and Europe,[32] the Jews had emerged as one of the most active groups engaged in this trade. Their rivals at this time were the Genoese and the Florentines. When a silk caravan from Iran arrived in Bursa, there was always intense competition between these three groups for the available merchandise. Maringhi, writing in 1501, comments on the Bursa market in one of his letters[33] in the following way:

> I think we shall make good profit in Bursa. There remains no *seta stravai* [of Astarabad, Iran] any other sort, since they weighed out the 20,000 pounds for the Genoese and Jews, which they sold at 66⅔ and 66¾ aspri the pound, cash. There is no news of a new lot appearing, so perhaps over there [in Italy] it will go up in price . . . so that we may expect to merit the grace of God in the sale of silk.

(For the Jewish merchants engaged in silk and silk cloth trade in general, see Tables II, III, IV, and VIII, and silk prices, Table VIII.)

In addition to the trade in woolen cloth and silk, the spice trade, for which Bursa again was the principal market, was another lucrative area of activity for the Jewish merchants. In Table II, numbers 1, 3, 4, 5, 6, and 7 are examples of Jewish merchants engaged in the wholesale trade of spices. Ya'qūb son of Samarīya from Balat (Istanbul) is of particular interest. In 1487, in one single transaction, we find him investing the huge sum of 225,000 *akça*, or about 4,500 gold ducats, in black pepper. A few months later, he made a new purchase of pepper and ginger, in the amount of 68,300 *akça*. According to our court records, he had been in the spice trade for more than a decade.

Among Jewish merchants engaged in the trade in spices and dyes at the Bursa market, Salamo, Salto,[34] Musa, and Mordehay were all immigrants from the Balkan cities of Castoria and Nicopolis, and appear to have settled in Istanbul. Usually they carried on their business from Istanbul through their agents in Bursa.

For the period under study, we have found no Jewish spice merchants going beyond the Bursa market toward the south for spices and dyes. It was Arab and Turkish merchants who were responsible for the spices imported in this market.[35] Before the Portuguese intervention in the Indian trade in 1501, quite a large proportion of the Indian imports coming into the Middle East appears to have been shipped to Bursa.[36]

In the 1470s, Benedetto Dei, a Florentine agent in the Levant, may not have been exaggerating when he claimed[37] that his citizens could buy spices at the Bursa market under more favorable conditions than could the Venetians in Alexandria. The Venetians, he said, were paying cash for spices, while the Florentines could simply exchange their home-manufactured woolen cloth for the Indian goods.

It appears that spice shipments taken to Istanbul were resold there to local retailers or traveling merchants, who took the precious wares to further markets in the Balkans and the Black Sea countries. In the customs registers we find many Jewish merchants who took spices to the Black Sea ports of Kilia, Akkerman, and Caffa (see Table V).

Jews in Tax Farming

Medieval manuals on commerce recommended the practice of dividing one's wealth into portions, and investing in various kinds of businesses. Along with the trade in precious commodities, the most profitable, if not the safest, way to invest capital in cash was to obtain tax farms of state revenues. Tax farming, extensively applied in the Ottoman Empire even at this early age, was a big business for those who had accumulated cash capital. Short of regular cash resources for its immediate needs, and lacking the expensive and complex tax collection system of a modern state, the Ottoman government encouraged commercial capitalists to take an interest in tax farming. Registers of tax farming, the so-called *muqāta'a defterleri* of the second half of the fifteenth century, contain many names of Turkish, Greek, and Jewish "capitalists" serving as tax farmers.[38]

We find Jews undertaking all kinds of tax farms everywhere in the empire, particularly in the big cities, important ports, and towns of Rumelia and Anatolia (see Table X). At the auctions of tax farms there was keen competition between bidders. For example, in 1483 a Jew, Sabbetay, son of Avraham, offered 1,200,000 *akça* and outbid all competitors for the tax farm of the saltworks of Thrace (Hrishna, Gömüldjine, and Karasu).[39]

In October 1477, offering an increase of 400,000 *akça*, a partnership of the Jew Altina, the Turk Seyyidī Küçük of Edirne, and an Italian by the name of Nikiroz undertook the collection of the customs dues of the ports in the Istanbul customs zone for 20,400,000 *akça* (45 *akça* was 1 gold ducat at this time). They thus outbid the previous offer made by a partnership of the Greek Palaiologos of Istanbul, Palaiologos Kassandros, and Lefteri Galyanos of Trebizond.[40] Anyone who engaged in tax farming had to find at least two sureties with assets large enough to meet the debt in case of default. In our records, the sureties designated by the Jewish bidders are all from the Jewish community, but as seen in the above example, Jews also joined partnerships with Muslim Turks. In this connection one should not forget that the latter group included many Jewish, Greek, or Italian converts.

In view of its incomparable importance for state finances, the customs house of Istanbul bestowed a very influential position upon its tax farmer, and during the fifteenth and sixteenth centuries this position was quite often held by a Jew. Jews also farmed other *muqāta'āt* of Istanbul. Besides rich merchants and money changers, there were also enterprising Jews who put together small savings or inherited money, and such people became quite prominent in tax farming operations. Whatever the initial source of their cash capital—trade, money changing, or usury—many of these tax farmers were to be found engaged in the business for a long time. We may call them professional tax farmers. They were assisted by Jewish scribes and financial experts.

Ya'qūb or Jacopo, an Italian Jew and court physician of Mehmed II, was once employed as *defterdār*, or finance minister of the sultan. The holder of this post was responsible for the completion of tax farm contracts for the state. The contemporary Ottoman chronicler 'Āshiq Pashazāde speaks[41] about him in the following words:

> He is responsible for all the unheard innovations in the Ottoman lands. The sultan's undertakings (*işler*) had not been entrusted to a Jew until he became a vizier in the imperial council, because they said Jews cause trouble. As soon as Ya'qūb the physician became a vizier, all of the greedy Jews came and interfered in the sultan's affairs. Also, previous to his arrival, it was not a custom to execute tax farmers. One day Ya'qūb went to pray in a Muslim congregational mosque. All the Jews of Istanbul became very disappointed and sad.

Traditionally, medicine and finances were two avenues for Jews to gain influence and power in medieval Muslim states. Under the Ottomans, the famous physician of Süleyman I, Joseph Hamon, was, like Ya'qūb, well known for using his influence for Jewish business and financial interests.[42] On the other hand, "the unheard innovations" of Ya'qūb might be a reference to the methods which he introduced in Ottoman finances from his experience in Italy. Mehmed the Conqueror's eagerness for expanding his financial resources and his open-mindedness toward profit innovations are well known.

'Āshiq Pashazāde's resentment against the favor which the Jewish tax farmers and financial experts were enjoying finds full confirmation in a petition[43] submitted to the sultan. The petitioner claimed,

> There are many Jews who, through the strength of money and wealth [bribery], hold positions within His Majesty the Sultan's government. At the same time, the Muslim subjects, who as professional scribes always pray for you, wander about in humiliation without food and clothing. . . . It is no secret to the sultan that the experts among the professional scribes of the Islamic faith wander in humiliation while the Jews, who are the enemy of the Islamic religion, enjoy positions in the high offices of the sultan and live in conceit and rancor.

In 1472, during Mehmed the Conqueror's reign, two tax farmers were hanged. They were Ya'qūb son of Isrā'īl, and Yehūda son of Solomon, who had obtained the tax farm of the state revenues of

Serres for a sum of 515,000 *akça*. They were in debt to the state for a sum of 390,024 *akça*. When their sureties, two Jews from Edirne named Isḥāq and Yehoshu'a, then residing in Istanbul, were unable to pay the debt at the end of a delay of five years, the sultan ordered their execution as well. All of this probably occurred when Ya'qūb Pasha, the Jewish vizier, was responsible for state finances. Thereupon, the Jewish community collected the money among themselves, each contributing five thousand *akça*, and thus paid the debt.[44] Jewish *responsa* literature provides us with many examples of such acts of collective solidarity on the part of the Ottoman Jewish communities.

NOTES

1. See *Dumbarton Oaks Papers*, XXIII–XXIV (1969–70), p. 24.

2. See T. Stoianovic, "Conquering Balkan Merchant," *JEH*, XX; the Jews living at *Judeca* in the port area of Constantinople were transferred to Pera sometime before 1061. The Jews again settled in this area as Venetian Jews in the fourteenth century (see D. Jacoby, "Les Quartiers juifs de Constantinople à l'époque byzantine," *Byzantion*, XXXVII [1967], p. 198; and idem, "Les Juifs vénitiens de Constantinople—leur communauté du XIIIe siècle jusqu'au milieu du XVe siècle," *Revue des études juives*, CXXXI [1972], pp. 397–472). During the Ottoman conquest in 1453, they seem to have shared in the fate of the Venetians, although some may have ransomed themselves and returned home. Immediately after the fall of the city, Venetian diplomacy made a great effort to reacquire their district, along with the commercial privileges which they had enjoyed under Byzantium (see F. Thiriet, *Regestes*, III, nos. 2934–76, in particular no. 2976 dated August 16, 1454). The Conqueror demanded that the Venetian government send back those Jews who had fled from Constantinople before or during the siege, and had taken refuge in Venice. The Venetian government agreed to this, with the proviso that they would continue to protect those Jews who preferred to stay in Venice (see document in F. Thiriet, III, no. 3046). For the Venetian Jews and the important role which they played in Ottoman-Venetian trade, see various publications by Benjamin Ravid, in particular, "The Establishment of the Ghetto Vecchio of Venice Dated 1541," *Proceedings of the Sixth World Congress of Jewish Studies* (Jerusalem, 1975), II, 153–67; "The Socio-Economic Background of the Venetian Expulsion and Readmission of the Venetian Jews, 1571–1573," *Essays in Modern Jewish History: A Tribute to Ben Halpern* (London and Toronto, 1982), pp. 28–54; "The First Charter of the Jewish Merchants of Venice, 1589," *Association of Jewish Studies Review* (Cambridge, Mass., 1976), I, 187–222; and *Economics and Toleration in Seventeenth-Century Venice* (Jerusalem, 1978), especially pp. 25–49. B. Ravid pointed out that "it was not until the sixteenth century that they [the Jews of Venice] appear to have assumed a significant role in Venetian commerce." The Sephardic Jews of the Ottoman Empire, "returning as Ottoman subjects to the ports of Christian Europe, including Venice, assumed a preponderant role in its [Venice's] over-

seas commerce" (*Economics and Toleration*, p. 26). The Ottoman government actively protected its Jewish subjects in Venice (see Tayyip Gökbilgin, "Venedik Devlet Arşivindeki Türkçe Belgeler," *Belgeler*, V–VIII [1968–1971], pp. 124–25, 139). The first document (pp. 124–25) mentions the Ottoman Jewish merchants taking the valuable mohair products of Ankara to Venice and Ancona.

3. I am preparing an independent study on the Jewish population in Istanbul; as part of the work, the unpublished sources will be reproduced and discussed; see now, Ö. L. Barkan, "Essai sur les données statistiques des registres de recensement, . . ." *JESHO*, I (1957), pp. 3–26; U. Heyd, "The Jewish Communities of Istanbul in the Seventeenth Century," *Oriens*, VI (1933), pp. 299–314; M. A. Epstein, *The Ottoman Jewish Communities and Their Role in the Fifteenth and Sixteenth Centuries* (Freiburg, 1980); and "Istanbul" (H. Inalcik), EI^2, pp. 238–42; for the Jews of Galata after 1492, see Epstein, op. cit., p. 178; Evliyā Çelebi, *Seyāhatnāme* (Istanbul, 1898), I, 431–32; R. Mantran, *Istanbul dans la seconde moitié du XVII*[e] *siècle* (Paris, 1962), pp. 57–63.

4. See W. Sombart, *The Jews and Modern Capitalism*, trans. M. Epstein (New York, 1962), p. 328 n. 1; cf. S. W. Baron, *A Social and Religious History of the Jews*, 2d ed. [New York, 1983), XI, chap. 50; XII, pp. 109 f. XVIII, pp. 36–37, 457 n. 42.

5. See documents reproduced in T. Gökbilgin, *Edirne ve Paşa Livası* (Istanbul Edebiyat Fakültesi Publication no. 508), p. 66; "Selānik" (T. Gökbilgin), *Islām Ansiklopedisi*, X, 337–49; see also *Sephardic and Oriental Jewish Heritage Studies*, ed. I. Ben-Ami (Jerusalem, 1982).

6. Cf. H. Lowry, "Portrait of a City: The Population and Topography of Ottoman Selanik (Thessaloniki) in the Year 1478," *Diptykha* (Athens, 1980–81), pp. 261–66, and Table XI; Epstein, op cit., pp. 263–64. While the *jizya* register for Rumeli dated 894/1488–89 records no Jews in Salonica, Castoria, Triccala, Gelibolu (Gallipoli), Joannina, and Galata (Ö. L. Barkan, "894 (1488–89) Yılı cizyesinin Tahsilātı, . . ." *Belgeler*, I [1964], pp. 39, 42, 49, 93, 94) the surveys subsequent to 1492 indicate Jewish communities in those cities. Epstein, op. cit., pp. 178–283; N. Beldiceanu, "Un acte sur le statut de la communauté juive de Trikkala," *REI*, XL (1972), pp. 129–38.

7. In general, see *The Cambridge Economic History of Europe*, ed. M. Postan and E. E. Rich (Cambridge, 1952), Chapter 6, "The Woolen Industry," and index s.v. "cloth trade"; M. Laurent, *Un Grand Commerce d'exportation au Moyen-Âge: La Draperie des Pays-Bas en France et dans les pays méditerranéens, XII*[e]*–XV*[e] *siècles* (Paris, 1935); J. B. Weckerlin, *Le Drap d'escarlate au Pegolotti* (Lyons, 1905); as a luxury fabric *skirlāt* or *iskirlāt* is mentioned in fourteenth-century Ilkhanid palace accounts, see Kiyā al-Māzandarānī, *Resāla-yë falakiyyä*, ed. W. Hinz (Wiesbaden, 1952), p. 173; cf. F. B. Pegolotti, *La Pratica della mercatura*, ed. A. Evans (Cambridge, Mass., 1936); index s.v. "Panni"; for a comprehensive study on this basic commodity of East-West trade, fifteenth-century Bursa court records provide a rich source of material.

8. G. R. B. Richards, *Florentine Merchants in the Age of the Medici* (Cambridge, Mass., 1932), see General Index: *calisse*.

9. Ibid., pp. 146–47, 160, 168.

10. Ibid., p. 184; F. Babinger, *Mehmed the Conqueror and His Time*, trans. R. Manheim (Princeton, 1978), index s.v. "Florence."

11. *Belgeler*, X, document no. 105.

12. See H. Inalcik, "Bursa," *Belleten*, XXI (1960), pp. 45–96; idem, "Bursa and the Commerce of the Levant," *JESHO*, III (1960), pp. 131–47, cf. E. Rivkin, op. cit.

13. For the Conqueror's favors to the Florentines see W. Heyd, op. cit., II, 336–47; F. Babinger, "Mehmed II der Eroberer und Italien," *Byzantion*, XXI (1951), pp. 127–70.

14. Domenico Sella, "The Rise and Fall of the Venetian Woolen Industry," *Crisis and Change in the Venetian Economy*, ed. Brian Pullan (London, 1968), pp. 88–105.

15. Some of these have been published in H. Inalcik, "Osmanlı Idare, sosyal ve Ekonomik Tarihile Ilgili Belgeler," *Belgeler*, X (1980–81), nos. 9, 46, 75, 89, 134, 148, 151, and 156; idem, "Bursa," *Belleten*, XXIV, 97–102.

16. Richards, op. cit., p. 184.

17. BVA, K. Kepeci, 5280. This register has been prepared for publication.

18. G. Veinstein, M. Berindei, and I are in the process of preparing the registers of Akkerman for publication.

19. Richards, op. cit., p. 186.

20. W. Heyd, *Histoire du commerce du Levant*, trans. F. Raynaud (Leipzig, 1936), II, 342.

21. W. Heyd, op. cit., II, 296.

22. See H. Inalcik, "Ottoman Economic Mind," *Social and Economic History of the Middle East*, ed. M. Cook (London, 1970), pp. 207–18; E. Rivkin, "Marrano-Jewish Entrepreneurship and the Ottoman Mercantilist Probe in the Sixteenth Century," *Proceedings of the Third International Conference of Economic History* (Munich, 1965); for comparison with the conditions of Jews in European countries, see Benjamin C. F. Ravid, *Economics and Toleration in Seventeenth-Century Venice* (Jerusalem, 1978); and Herbert S. Bloom, *The Economic Activities of the Jews of Amsterdam in the Seventeenth and Eighteenth Centuries* (London, 1937); for Ottoman Jewry in general, see now S. W. Baron, *A Social and Religious History of the Jews*, Vol. XVIII: *Late Middle Ages and Era of European Expansion (1200–1650), The Ottoman Empire, Persia, Ethiopia, India and China*, 2d ed. (New York, 1983), pp. 1–295 (full bibliography and comments, pp. 441–556).

23. See H. Inalcik, "Capital Formation in the Ottoman Empire," *JEH*, XXIX, p. 99.

24. H. Inalcik, "The Hub of the City: The Bedestan of Istanbul," *International Journal of Turkish Studies*, I (1979–80), pp. 1–9.

25. My classification of the *bezzāz* is based on the documents in Ö. L. Barkan, "Edirne Askerī Kassāmina Ait Tereke Defterleri (1545–1659)," *Belgeler*, III (1966), documents nos. 18, 22, 38, 49, 52, 60, 66, 68, 71, and 84.

26. Ö. L. Barkan, op. cit., pp. 120–23.

27. For a foreign observer on the Jews' freedom in trade within the empire, see H. Dernschwam, *Tagebuch (1553–1555)*, ed. F. Babinger (Munich, 1923), p. 109. I. S. Emmanuel, *Histoire de l'industrie des tissus des Israélites de Salonique* (Paris, 1935); J. Nehama, *Histoire des Israélites de Salonique* (Paris, 1936); S. Schwarzfuchs, "La Décadence de la Galilée juive du XVIe siècle et la crise du textile au Proche-Orient," *Revue des études juives*, CXXI (1962), pp. 169–70; Benjamin Braude, "Trading to the Levant Seas: Jews and English in Ottoman Commerce During the Sixteenth and Seventeenth Centuries," Ph.D. dissertation, Harvard University (History), 1975. Prior to the establishment of Jewish woolen industries in the empire, the coarse woolens manufactured in *Yanbolu* enjoyed wide distribution in the Ottoman market, particularly in the Rumeli and Black Sea regions. It seems that the origin of this industry is connected with production of the cloaks (*'abā*) worn by the local nomadic populations.

28. H. Sahillioğlu, "Yeniçeri Çuhası ve II. Bayezid'in son Yıllarında Yeniçeri Çuha Muhasebesi," *Güney Dogu Avrupa Araştırmaları Dergisi* (Istanbul, 1974), 2–3, pp. 414–19.

29. *Seyāhatnāme*, IX (Istanbul, 1935), 441.

30. Cf. B. Lewis, *Notes and Documents from the Turkish Archives* (Jerusalem, 1952), pp. 9–11, 28; A. Cohen and B. Lewis, *Population and Revenue in the Towns of Palestine in the Sixteenth Century* (Princeton, 1978), pp. 28–30, 155–69; Safed's Jewish population, consisting mostly of Sephardic Jews, grew by about 30 percent between 1525 and 1567. Population figures given in the archival documents belie Evliyā's figures, as the following table shows (Cohen and Lewis).

Population of Safed (households)

	1525–26	1555–56	1567–68
Muslims	693	1,093	986
Jews	233	719	945

A Breakdown of Country of Origin of the Jewish Population of Safed (households)

	1525–26	1555–56	1567–68
Musta'riba or native Jews	131	98	70
Spain (Cordova, Castile, Aragon, Seville)		243	485
Portugal		193	200
Morocco	33	38	52
Italy		74	80
France	48		
Germany		20	43
Hungary		12	15

31. See A. Cohen and B. Lewis, op. cit., p. 164.

32. See "Ḥarīr," *EI*², III, 209–18.

33. Richards, op. cit., p. 118.

34. A tax farmer engaged in various sectors of the economy, Salto (Shaltiel) was the most active in accumulating cash from small amounts of money left

idle in the hands of private individuals; see the charge brought against him in the document published by M. Epstein, op. cit., p. 289; for his role as the *ketkhuda* of the Jewish community see ibid., pp. 62–68. The reports in the Ottoman revenue (*muqāta'a*) books on the individual tax farmers provide interesting details on the careers of the Jewish tax farmers (ibid., pp. 101–49). Another example of an aggressive fortune-maker was Ben-Yamin, who started from scratch and became the supervisor of the Ottoman mint in Istanbul (see H. Sahillioğlu, "Bir Mültezim Zimem Defterine göre XV. Yüzyıl Sonunda Osmanlı Darphane Mukataaları," *IFM*, XXIII [1962–63], p. 200).

35. But there were Jews active in the commerce between Turkey and the Arab lands; one of them, "*dhimmī* Avraham," owned a ship which was active in the traffic between Antalya and Syria (Antalya Customs book dated 957/1558: BVA, Maliyeden Müd., no. 7387).

36. See H. Inalcik, "Bursa and the Commerce of the Levant," pp. 133–47.

37. See W. Heyd, op. cit., II, 345, 349–50.

38. The text published by H. Sahillioğlu, "Osmanlı Darphane Mukataaları," pp. 182–218.

39. T. Gökbilgin, *Edirne*, p. 131; the revenue of the village Hrishna was granted to the physician Ya'qūb about 1477 (ibid., p. 149).

40. BVA, Maliyeden Müdevver no. 7387, a register of the *muqāta'āt*.

41. *Tevārīkh-i Āl-i 'Osmān*, ed. Ç. N. Atsız (Istanbul, 1947), p. 244; for Ya'qūb's career, see F. Babinger, "Ja'qūb Pascha, Ein Leibarzt Mehmed's II. Leben und Schicksale des Maestro Jacopo aus Gaeta," *Rivista degli studi orientali*, XXVI (1951), pp. 87–113; cf. B. Lewis, "The Privilege Granted by Mehmed II to His Physician," *BSOAS*, XIV (1952), pp. 550–63.

42. Uriel Heyd, "Moses Hamon, Chief Jewish Physician to the Sultan Suleyman the Magnificent," *Oriens*, XV (1963), pp. 152–70; in a list of salaries of the Ottoman palace servants dated 920/1514 (TKP, archives, no. E. 5475, transcribed by Ö. L. Barkan, *IFM*, XV [1953–54], pp. 321–22). The palace physicians were classified into two distinct groups, the Muslims and the Jews; there were sixteen Muslim and six Jewish physicians. In the latter group were included Angelos, Ferhād, Hayim, Musa ben Hamon, Musa, and Shemuyil; in an edict of A.D. 908 the caliph al-Muqtadir admitted Jews and Christians into two state functions only, those of physicians and those of bankers (W. J. Fischel, *Jews in the Economic and Political Life of Medieval Islam* [London, 1968], p. 7).

43. TKP, Archives, no. 6176.

44. T. Gökbilgin, *Edirne*, p. 148; for the tax farmers imprisoned or executed under Mehmed II and Bayezid II, see ibid., pp. 92, 93, 95, 103, and 107; see also L. Fekete, *Die Siyāqat-Schrift* (Budapest, 1955), Table VI; the document is dated 904/1499; in this list of tax farmers released from prison are included three Jews, five Greeks, and eleven Muslims. Two of the latter were apparently converts. The tax farm of the salt works and ports of the Danube, farmed out for 4,200,000 *akça* for three years, was undertaken by the Jew Mordehay son of Sason (or Hamon?); see also Epstein, op. cit., index s.v. "tax farm."

TABLE I. Jewish merchants in business with Giovanni Maringhi, representative of four Florentine firms including Medici at Bursa, 1501-1502 (Source: G. R. B. Richards, *Florentine Merchants in the Age of the Medici* [Cambridge, Mass., 1932])

Name of Purchaser	Business Place	Amount of Goods Bought	Price in *akça*	Conditions	Date, Source
1. Bigliamino or Beniamino Alamano, Jewish draper	Istanbul	50 *pichi* of blue in 3 cuts through a broker (Uanno Lugo, Jew)		Tapiero sold them to another Jew. But *panni* were not satisfactory in quality. Since they were not turning out well the Jew delayed the payment	May 19, 1501, p. 99
2. Isaac Tapiero, broker	Bursa	8 *panni*	1,580 per *panno*	Over 4 months in 4 payments	May 22, 1501, p. 99
3. Beniamino Alamano, Jewish draper	Istanbul	33½ *pichi* of *panno bastardi* and 17½ *pichi* of pink	1,302 of total value		May 19, 1501, p. 100 great demand for *calisse*, a coarse Spanish cloth, and Florentine *panni*
4. Jusufio di Bacciaci, Jewish draper	Istanbul	3 *panni bastardi*, 19½ *pichi* of pink *panno* 4 *panni*	1,400 per *panno* 1,587 per *panno*		May 25, 1501, p. 102
5. Isaac Tapiero (see no. 2)	Bursa	12 *panni* 1 *panno bastardo*	1,596 per *panno* 1,404 per *panno*	crediting 10,000 *aspri* to Alamano	May 25, 1501, p. 102

TABLE I *(Continued)*

Name of Purchaser	Business Place	Amount of Goods Bought	Price in *akça*	Conditions	Date, Source
6. Federigo Spagniola, Jewish draper	Bursa	9 *panni* of high quality cloth 21 *panni*	1,600 per *panno*	250 ducats to be paid in one month and the rest on time	March 9, 1502, p. 178
7. Aaronne Rominati and Franco Mizitoni, a company of Jews	Istanbul	1 *panno*	1,595 *aspri* per *panno*		March 1502, p. 178
8. San Jacuda and Aaronne Lugo	Istanbul	22 *panni*	1,595 *aspri* per *panno*		March 1502, p. 178
9. Chiano, Jewish draper	Bursa	1 *panno*	1,600 *aspri* per *panno*		March 1502, p. 178
10. Abram Ruber (Jewish?) draper	Bursa	12 *panni*	1,600 *aspri* per *panno*		March 1502, p. 178

For the winter 1501–1502, more than 100 *panni* were sold in Edirne, 68 or 70 in Bursa (1,600 per *panno*), and 42 in Pera Instanbul. Maringhi considered it a success, and the prices excellent (Richards, 160–61). Another consignment at a value of 42,175 *aspri* (ca. 26 *panni* or pastav) was shipped to Caffa in the Crimea (ibid., p. 152). Maringhi said, "We should have to have every year 600 *panni*," and considered the market expanding (op. cit., p. 120). "I have," he added, "*panni* of both shops at an excellent price to Hebrew drapers." Most of the dealers of *Çuka* went bankrupt and their number fell from 35 to 10 by 1548 (F. Dalsar) *Bursa'da Ipekcilik*, p. 239).

Panno (panni): finely woven woolen cloth, or a measure of cloth equal to the Turkish *pastav* or 50 *dhirā'* or 34 m.
Panno bastardi: a coarse cloth made of native wool.
Aspri: Ottoman silver coin, *akça*, 52½ of which equaled one Hungarian gold coin in the winter of 1501 (Richards, p. 151).

TABLE II. Jewish merchants at the Bursa market according to the Bursa court records. (*Bursa Sicilleri*), 1479-1500

Name of Merchant	Origin	Goods Sold to	Goods Bought from	Price in *akça*	Credit Terms	Other Conditions	Date, Source
1. David son of Ilyās	born in Istanbul		Ṣadreddīn of Damascus: pepper, rosemary, etc.	46,040			August 1479, Bursa S.A. 3/3
2. ʻIvaḍ son of Ishaq and Yahshi son of Mūsā, Jews	both of Kastamoni, residing in Istanbul		Khoja Jemāleddīn, raw silk of Astarābād in the amount of 450 *lidre*	21,250	6 months	surety for each other	July 1480, Bursa S.A. 3/3
3. Yaʻqūb son of Samariyya	Istanbul (Balat)		Hoja ʻAlī, dyes (gum-lac, etc.)	16,700			December 1479, Bursa S.A. 3/3
4. Mūsā son of Süleymān, Jew	resident in Istanbul, born born in Nicopolis		Khoja Muslihiddīn, pepper	17,925			November 1480, Bursa S.A. 3/3
			Khoja Ibrāhīm, cloths (and credit)	28,000	1 year	through his agent in Bursa	June 1491, Bursa S.A. 8/8
5. Mordehay son of Süleymān	of Castoria residing in Balat, Istanbul		Ömer Çelebi, pepper, 12½ *qanṭār* and 4 *lodra*	10,900			August 1480, Bursa S.A. 3/3

TABLE II *(Continued)*

Name of Merchant	Origin	Goods Sold to	Goods Bought from	Price in *akça*	Credit Terms	Other Conditions	Date, Source
6. Ya'qūb son of Samariyya	of Castoria residing in Balat, Istanbul		Ömer Çelebi, pepper, cloves	1,070	6 months		December 1480, Bursa A.S. 3/3
7. Mūša son of Süleymān, Jew	of Nicopolis, residing in Azepler-Hamami, Istanbul		Khoja Muslihiddīn, pepper	7,925			December 1480, Bursa, S.A. 3/3
8. Arslan son of Sha'bān, Jew	of Castoria, residing in Balat, Istanbul		Khoja Muhyiddīn, cloth	17,000			1480, Bursa S.A. 3/3
9. Yahyā son of Mordehay	of Istanbul		Bernardo son of Bikhardo and Turvilo, Venetians	20,000		a loan	March 1491, Bursa S.A. 8/8
10. Suleyman son of Isrā'īl	of Istanbul merchant *(bezzāz)*		Ya'qūb, silk cloth called *vālā*	800			February 1491, Bursa S.A. 8/8
11. Arslan son of Ravi	of Balat, Istanbul		Muslihiddīn, raw silk	4,000		sued	February 1491, Bursa S.A. 8/8

TABLE II *(Continued)*

Name of Merchant	Origin	Goods Sold to	Goods Bought from	Price in *akça*	Credit Terms	Other Conditions	Date, Source
12. Natan son of Avraham		Mustafa, silk dealer *(qazzāz)*, raw silk		1,870	payment of 90 *akça* per month		February 1491, Bursa S.A. 8/8
13. Several Jewish merchants			Khoja Moḥammad of Lār, Iran raw silk	31,450			March 1491, Bursa S.A. 8/8
14. Ibrāhīm son of Yūsuf	of Istanbul		Agha son of Shaykh, of Iran, raw silk	3,572		paid through an agent	March 1491, Bursa S.A. 8/8
15. Ilyās son of Shemuyil	*Juhūdlar*, a quarter in Istanbul		Antonio son of Bartolemo, Genoese	1,853	1 year	transferred to Antonio's brother	April 1491, Bursa S.A. 8/8
16. Ilyakim son of Shemuyil	*Yahudi* quarter in Istanbul			2,750		died in Bursa	May 1491, Bursa S.A. 8/8
17. Paşabali son of Kru, Jew	of Tyre, western Anatolia		Piero son of Lonho, an Italian of Chios, 19 boxes of mastic			Paşabali sued Piero at the Porte	Sureties: European Jews in Bursa by the name of Zekeriya son of Mūsā, draper; Piero son of Domenico; Surarro son of Zoro; Yoro son of Agoston, July 1500, Bursa S.A. 18/17
18. David son of Ibrāhīm	European Jew		David son of Ishaq, a house in Bursa				July 1500, Bursa S.A. 18/17

TABLE III. Jewish merchants in register of customs of Caffa, 1487–1490

Merchant	Goods Imported			Goods Exported				
		Amount	Total Value			Total Value	Dues Paid	Sureties
1. Arslan, Jew (drowned)	Gold brocade (*Kemkhā*)	3 *kat*	3,000				239	
	Silk cloth *pushurī*	3 *kat*	900					
	Felt to make cloak	5 *kat*	1,000					
	Woolen cloth	1 *pastav* (73½ meter)	800					
2. Tuta, Jew	Silk cloth *pushurī*	3 *ṭaq*	3,800				693	
	Gold brocade	2 *ṭaq*	1,800					
	Plain brocade	3 *ṭaq*	1,500					
	Taffeta *yektā*	6 *top*	8,000					
	Silk cloth *dārāyī*	1 *ṭaq*	300					
	Apron of *Yazd*, black	18 *ṭaq*	700					
	Kerchief (of cotton)	56 *qaṭ*	400					
3. Yusuf, Jew	Rice and orpiment						84	Avram, Jew
4. Avram, son of Btir (?)				Horse hides	300	5,000	210	
5. Eliyado				Cow hides	101	5,000	30	
				Horse hides	60	1,800	80	
6. Tomarin	Wine	8 casks					160	
7. Khoja Bikesh, son of Kökgöz	Dye	13 qanṭar	5,000				210	
	Gold velvet	5 pieces	2,000				84	
8. Netil, Jew	Cloth *kisāī*	15 *kat*	12,000				504	his father
9. Eliyadon, Jew (the same as no. 5)				Horse hides	60	600	25	
10. Yusuf, Jew (the same as no. 3)				Horse hides	45			
				Clarified butter,	2 *tulum*	2,460	180	
				Leather of horsehair	30			
				Hair	2 *batman*			

TABLE IV. Jewish cloth merchants at the port of Kilia, 1504–1505

Name of Jewish Merchant	Origin	Goods bought	Price in *akça*	Date, Source
1. Lazari, Jew	Istanbul (?)	red dyed silk	200	March 1505, B.V.A., Maliyeden M. no. 6
2. Mūsā, Jew	Silistre	red dyed silk	1,900	*Ibid.*, 1505
		black silk	1,120	
		silk gold thread	400	
		dyed silk	80	
		Total	3,500	
		140	dues paid	
3. Sudjka, Jew	Istanbul	Florentine cloth (7 *pastav*)	8,740	*Ibid.*, July 1504
		"Londra" cloth (6 *pastav*)	6,434	
		Salonica cloth (300 *dhirā'*)	3,600	
		Istanbul cloth (37 pieces)	240	
		Brocade *dolābī* (3 pieces)	1,500	
		raw silk (7 *lidre*)	700	
		Other items	7,000	
		Total	28,214	
		848	dues paid	
4. Yūsuf, Jew	Istanbul	a variety of European cloths including English and Salonica with a total value of 17,600		*Ibid.*, July 1504
5. Hajjī Sujka, Jew (perhaps the same as no. 3)	Istanbul	Bursa brocade (4 pieces)	280	*Ibid.*, July 1504
		Bogasi of Borlu (32 pieces)	1,280	
		Pants of cotton (50 pieces)	150	
		Dyed linings (52 pieces)	936	
6. Ibrāhīm, Jew	Nicopolis	Florentine cloth (5 *pastav*)	6,000	*Ibid.*, January 1505
		Moton cloth (5 *pastav*)	4,500	
		Moton-Dubrovnik (6 *pastav*)	4,200	
		441	dues paid	

TABLE V. Jewish merchants at the port of Akkerman, 1505–1508.

Name	Origin	Goods Bought and Prices in *akça*	Date, Source
1. Istepan, Jew		Fox fur 700 (1 piece)	July 1505, B.V.A., Maliyeden M. no. 6
2. Arslan, Jew	Istanbul	Paid a sum of 744 *akça* to customs for the good unspecified in the register	August 1505, Ibid.
3. Ismā'īl, Jew	Istanbul	Customs dues paid: 129	September 1505, Ibid.
4. Avram	Istanbul	Customs dues paid: 131	October 1505, Ibid.
5. Sha'bān, Jew		Customs dues paid: 241	May 1505, Ibid.
6. Sha'bān, Jew		Customs dues paid: 30	July 1505, Ibid.
7. Baruh, Jew		Customs dues paid: 12	July 1505, Ibid.
8. Jew	Rusi	Customs dues paid: 108	April 1506, Ibid.
9. Mamsan, Jew		1 slave	April 1506, Ibid.
10. Eliya	Özü	Customs dues paid: 15	March 1506, Ibid.
11. Eliya, Jew		1 horse	April 1506, Ibid.
12. Yehuda son of Bogdan	Moldavia (Bogdan)	Russian bridles (49 *akça*) Russian purses (300) Russian knives (500) woolen cloth of Trske (9 bolts: 150 *akça*), Tatar fur hats (20 pieces: 100 *akça*), Tatar (Bulgārī) leather (48), a variety of furs (970)	February 1506, Ibid. Total of the goods imported was 2,157 *akça* and customs dues paid 108; goods transported in a cart
13. 'Abdī, Muslim draper	Edirne	A variety of Salonica cloths: 2,000 *akça* (2 *pastav*), cotton cloth 200 (100 *dhirā'*)	May 1505, Ibid.
14. Avraham	Özü	Cowhides, salted 60 pieces (1,000 *akça*) by sea	May 1505, Ibid.

TABLE V ***(Continued)***

Name	Origin	Goods Bought and Prices in *akça*	Date, Source
15. Ilyās, Muslim (see list of wares)	Belgrade	Textiles of cotton and linen imported by him; we find Salonica woolen cloth (*çuka*) 200 (1 *pastav*) and Istanbul woolen cloth 100 (½ *pastav*)	October 1506, Ibid.
16. Sha'bān, Jew	Istanbul	His imports included the following: black pepper 400 (10 *vukiyye*), kersey cloth 150 (6 *dhirā'*), coarse woolen 150 (5 pieces), cap of cloth 30, dyed raw silk 180 (3 *lidre*), soap 750 (5 boxes), nails and a variety of foodstuffs	August 1505, Ibid.
17. Sh'abān, Jew	Istanbul	Valonia 750 (25 *qanṭār*)	October 1505, Ibid.
18. Ya'qūb, Jew	Istanbul	Woolen cloth of Istanbul 200 (1 *pastav*), woolen cloths of various sorts 2000 (17 bolts), vinegar 500 (2 casks), customs dues paid: 108	September 1505, Ibid.
19. Ismā'īl, Jew	Istanbul	Clothings of woolen cloths 1,000 (10 bolts), cloths of Dubrovnik 1,000 (1 *pastav*), cloths of Mantua (*moton*) 400 (1 *pastav*), shoes for men 880 (40 pairs)	September 1505, Ibid., arrived by ship from Istanbul
20. Mūsā son of Ilyās, Jew		Woolen cloth 60 (1½ bolts), cloth of Dubrovnik, low quality 1,200 (3 *pastav*), cloth of Bergamishka (of Bergamo in Italy) for women 4,500 (4 bolts)	He arrived in the same ship as Ismā'īl, mentioned above
21. Mūsā, Jew	left Akkerman for Caffa by land	Bulgārī leather 9,000 (150 pairs), Rusi (Polish-Lithuanian) woolen cloth 2,400 *akça*, (2 *pastav*), customs dues paid: 570	August 1506, B.V.A., Maliye 15649
22. Eliya	Özü	Felt (*keçe*) 300 (2 pieces)	March 1506, Ibid., by sea

TABLE V *(Continued)*

Name	Origin	Goods Bought and Prices in *akça*	Date, Source
23. Isak, Jew	Rus	Fox skin 1,000 (50 pieces), lynx skin 50 (1 piece)	Ibid.
24. Ya'qūb, Jew	Rus	Fox skin 2,880, rabbit skin 100, and other kinds of skin 4,030, customs dues paid: 201½ *akça*	August 1506, Ibid., by sea
25. Ilyās, Jew		caviar 500 (2 *qanṭār*)	August 1506, Ibid., by sea
26. Yahaf, Jew	left Akkerman for Özü	Honey 910 (7 *qanṭār*), raisins 300 (6 *qanṭār*), apricot 100 (1 *qanṭār*) walnut	
27. Baruh, Jew		Kersey cloth 3,000 (6 *pastav*), cloth 3,000 (6 *pastav*), *vālā* silks 922	March 1508, Ibid., by sea
28. Sha'bān, Jew	left Akkerman for Istanbul	Bulgārī leather 460 (67 pairs)	August 1506, Ibid.
29. Sha'bān, Jew		Saddle 600, bow 280 (14 pieces), soap 2,400 (12 kāntār)	March 1508, Ibid.
30. Sha'bān, Jew	left Akkerman for Caffa	Honey 5,200 (40 *qanṭār*)	April 1508, Ibid., by sea
31. Ilyās, Jew	left Akkerman for Caffa	Honey 3,828 (30 *qanṭār*)	
32. Sinān, Jew	a ship coming from Istanbul	Hats of felt 720 (30 pieces)	May 1508, Ibid., by sea
33. Baruh, Jew	in the same ship	Clothings of woolen cloth 6,000 (24 pieces)	May 1508, Ibid., by sea
34. Baruh, Jew		Felt 960 (8 *pastav*), sugar 400 (1 *qanṭār*)	May 1508, Ibid., by sea

TABLE V *(Continued)*

Name	Origin	Goods Bought and Prices in *akça*	Date, Source
35. Muṣṭafā, Muslim (see list of wares)		Cloth of Salonica 1,200 (2 *pastav*) his load included soap, leather, cotton goods with a total value of 18,478 *akça*	June 1507, Ibid., by sea
36. Baba, Jew		Soap 1,800 (9 *qanṭār*)	June 1507, Ibid., by sea
37. Ya'qūb, Jew		Clothing (of woolen cloth) 3,200 (16 pieces), kersey cloth 2,000 (4 *pastav*), woolen cloth of Istanbul 100 (20 *dhirā'*), customs dues paid: 128 *akça*	June 1507, Ibid., by sea

TABLE VI. Annual governmental expenditures for the woolen cloth used for the Janissaries and other corps 916 (1510–1511) (Source: H. Sahillioğlu, "Yeniçeri Çuhası," *Güney-Doğu Araştırmaları Dergisi*, II–III, [1973-1974], 415-66)

Cloth	Amount Purchased in *Dhirā* (68 cm)	Price
Cloth of Salonica	92,148	15 *akça* 5 *fulus*
Cloth of Istanbul	3,825[1]	20½ *akça*
Cloth of Florence[2]	1,476	54 *akça*

[1]The editor gives it in another place (p. 425) as 3,852.

[2]The cloth of Florence included: *Kırmızı skarlat* (red *scarlatto*, price 185), *Fistiqī* (dark green, price 65), *Asumānī* (light blue, price 65), *Motun* (Mantua?, price 29).

TABLE VII. Prices of woolen cloth (*çuka*), 1504–1507

Merchandise	Price in *akça*	Market	Date	Source
1. *Floridin* (Florence)	40 per *dhirā'*	Akkerman	1507	B.V.A. Maliyeden M. 15649
2. *Floridin* (Florence)	1,200 per *pastav*	Kilia	1504–1505	Ibid.
3. *Floridin* (Florence)	1,200 per *pastav*	Akkerman	July 1505	Ibid.
4. *Karziya* (kersey)	500 per *pastav*	Akkerman	March 1507	Ibid.
5. *Londra* (London)	1,000 per *pastav*	Kilia	1504–1505	Ibid.
6. *Londra yarīsī* (half)	1,000	Akkerman	July 1504	B.V.A. Maliyeden M. 6
7. Venetian	833 per *pastav*	Bursa	October 1480	Bursa Sicil. A 3/3; sold by Zangiacomi
8. *Moton, Venedik* (Mantua?, Venice)	900 per *pastav*	Kilia	1504–1505	Maliyeden M. 15649
9. *Moton, Dubrovnik* (Mantua?, Ragusa)	700 per *pastav*	Kilia	1504–1505	Ibid.
10. *Trske* (Poland)	200 per *pastav*	Akkerman	April 1506	Ibid.
11. *Karlisa Rus*	323 per *pastav*	Akkerman	March 1506	Ibid.
12. *Karlisa Rus*	200 per *pastav*	Akkerman	September 1505	Ibid.
13. *Girlica (Karlisa)*	200 per *pastav*	Akkerman	July 1505	B.V.A. Maliyeden M. 6 (imported by moldovian merchants)
14. Raw wool *(yapaghī)*	½ *akça* per *'idād*			
15. Salonica	800 per *pastav*	Akkerman	July 1505	B.V.A. Maliye 6
16. Salonica	2 per *dhirā'*	Kilia	1504–1505	B.V.A., Maliye 15649
17. Salonica	400 per *pastav*	Kilia	1504–1505	Ibid.
18. Salonica	12 per *dhirā'*	Akkerman	July 1505	Ibid.

TABLE VII *(Continued)*

Merchandise	Price in *akça*	Market	Date	Source
19. Salonica	20 per *dhirā'*	Akkerman	April 1506	B.V.A. Maliye 15649
20. Salonica	45 per *dhirā'*	Akkerman	September 1506	Ibid.
21. Salonica	20 per *dhirā'*	Akkerman	September 1506	Ibid.
22. Salonica	300 per *pastav*	Akkerman	May 1507	Ibid.
23. Istanbul	6 per *dhirā'*	Akkerman	July 1505	Maliye 6
24. Istanbul	6 per *dhirā'*	Kilia	1504–1505	B.V.A. Maliye 15649
25. Istanbul	20 per *dhirā'*	Akkerman	May 1507	Ibid.
26. Istanbul colored	7 per *dhirā'*	Akkerman	September 1506	Ibid.
27. *Çuka* of orange color	1,100	Kilia	July 1505	Maliye 6
28. *Çuka* of red color	1,150	Kilia	July 1505	Ibid.
29. *Çuka* of sky blue color	900	Kilia	July 1505	Ibid.
30. *Çuka* of purple color	1,200	Kilia	July 1505	Ibid.
31. *Aba* (coarse felt cloak)	20 per piece	Caffa	1487	Caffa Customs, Kepeci 5280
32. *Keçe Kepenek* (felt cloak)	100	Akkerman	July 1505	Maliye 6
33. *Kebe* (coarse felt cloak)	23, 50	Akkerman	July 1505	Ibid.
34. Felt (*nemed*)	130 per *pastav*	Akkerman	April 1507	Ibid.
35. Felt (*nemed*)	120 per *pastav*	Akkerman	May 1507	Ibid.

1 *pastav* = 48.64 *dhirā'*; 1 *dhirā'* = 68 centimeters.

TABLE VIII. Price of raw silk per *lidre* (320.7 g) and silk cloth

Merchandise	Price in *akça*	Market	Date	Source
1. Red or green dyed	100	Bursa	June 1464	Bursa Sicil.
2. White	80	Bursa	June 1464	Bursa Sicil.
3. *Asterābādī*	50	Bursa	1467	Bursa Sicil.
4. *Asterābādī*	67	Bursa	1478	Bursa Sicil.
5. *Asterābādī*	68	Bursa	May 1478	*Belleten* XCIII, p. 67
6. *Asterābādī*	61	Bursa	February 1479	*Ibid.*, p. 74, sold to Sant of Galata
7. *Asterābādī*	48	Bursa	July 1480	*Belleten* XCIII, p. 67
8. *Asterābādī*	47	Bursa	August 1480	*Ibid.*, p. 88
9. *Asterābādī*	56	Bursa	1487	Bursa Sicil. A. 4/4
10. *Asterābādī*	70	Bursa	1488	Bursa Sicil. A. 4/4
11. Unspecified	67	Bursa	1486	Bursa Sicil. A. 4/4
12. *Tilānī*	50	Bursa	1487	Bursa Sicil. A. 4/4
13. *Tilānī*	44	Bursa	1487	Bursa Sicil. A. 4/4
14. Unspecified	125–150	Caffa	1487	Caffa customs, B.R. Kepeci 5280
15. Unspecified	82	Bursa	1494	Dalsar
16. *Gīlānī*	59–60	Bursa	May 1501	Florentine Mer. 67
17. *Asterābādī*	65	Bursa	July 1501	*Ibid.*, 106, 111
18. *Asterābādī*	69	Pera	July 1501	*Ibid.*, 115
19. *Asterābādī*	77	Bursa	1513	Dalsar
20. *Tilānī*	93	Bursa	1519	Dalsar
21. Albanian	72–80	Bursa	1519	Dalsar
22. Colored	100	Akkerman	July 1505	B.V.A., Maliye 6

TABLE VIII *(Continued)*

Merchandise	Price in *akça*	Market	Date	Source
23. Colored	90	Akkerman	March 1506	Maliye 15649
24. Colored	100	Akkerman	January 1506	Maliye 15649
25. White	80	Akkerman	August 1506	Maliye 15649
26. Red colored	90–95	Kilia		Maliye 15649
27. Black colored	70–80	Kilia		Maliye 15649
28. White colored	70	Kilia		Maliye 15649
29. "Seven-colored" (*Heft-renk*)	80	Kilia		Maliye 15649
30. Black	70	Akkerman	May 1507	Maliye 15649
31. Gold brocade	400–1,000 per *ṭāq*	Caffa	1487	Caffa customs, B.R. Kepeci 5280
32. *Kemkhā*, plain	500 per *ṭāq*	Caffa	1487	Caffa customs, B.R. Kepeci 5280
33. *Kemkhā, puşūrī*	300–350 per *ṭāq*	Caffa	1487	Caffa customs, B.R. Kepeci 5280
34. *Kemkhā* of Bursa	150 per *ṭāq*	Caffa	August 1506	Caffa customs, B.R. Kepeci 5280
35. *Kemkhā* of Gülistānī	50 per *qi'ṭā* (piece)	Caffa	May 1507	Caffa customs, B.R. Kepeci 5280
36. *Kemkhā, puşūrī*	200 per *qi'ṭā*	Akkerman	March 1506	B.V.A. Maliye 15649
37. *Vālā*	8 per *dhirā'*	Akkerman	March 1507	B.V.A. Maliye 15649
38. *Vālā* of Bursa	12 per *dhirā'*	Akkerman	August 1506	B.V.A. Maliye 15649
39. *Vālā*	25	Akkerman	April 1506	B.V.A. Maliye 15649
40. *Vālā al* (red)	13	Akkerman	April 1506	B.V.A. Maliye 15649

TABLE VIII *(Continued)*

Merchandise	Price in *akça*	Market	Date	Source
41. *Vālā al*	25		May 1507	B.V.A. Maliye 15649
42. Embroidered velvet (*kaṭīfe*)	1,400 per piece	Caffa	1487	Caffa customs, B.V.A. K. Kepeci 5280
43. Plain velvet	350–500 per *ṭāq*	Caffa	1487	Caffa customs, B.V.A. K. Kepeci 5280
44. Aṭlās (satin)	250, 400	Caffa	1487	Caffa customs, B.V.A. K. Kepeci 5280
45. *Tāfta* (taffeta)	1,250 per *top* or 17 per *dhirā'*	Caffa	1487	Caffa customs, B.V.A. K. Kepeci 5280
46. *Taftā dū Hezārī*	15 per *dhirā'*	Akkerman	April 1506	Caffa customs, B.V.A. K. Kepeci 5280
47. *Bürünjük*	20 per *dhirā'*	Akkerman	April 1506	B.V.A., Maliye M. 15649
48. *Bürünjük*	15 per *dhirā'*	Akkerman	January 1506	B.V.A., Maliye M. 15649
49. White *bürünjük*	40 per piece	Akkerman	August 1506	B.V.A., Maliye M. 15649

1 *dhirā'* = 68 cm.
1 *ṭāq* = fabric for one suit.

TABLE IX. Price of pepper, 1487–1508

Merchandise	Price in *akça*	Market	Date	Source
1. Black pepper *(fulful)*	26 per *vuqiyye*	Caffa	1487	Caffa customs, K. Kepeci 5280
2. Black pepper *(fulful)*	50 per *vuqiyye*	Akkerman	July 1505	B.V.A. Maliye 15649
3. Black pepper *(fulful)*	60 per *vuqiyye*	Akkerman	January 1506	B.V.A. Maliye 15649
4. Black pepper *(fulful)*	45 per *vuqiyye*	Akkerman	September 1507	B.V.A. Maliye 15649
5. Black pepper *(fulful)*	40 per *vuqiyye*	Akkerman	February 1508	B.V.A. Maliye 15649
6. Black pepper *(fulful)*	50 per *vuqiyye*	Akkerman	April 1507	B.V.A. Maliye 15649
7. Black pepper *(fulful)*	40 and 50 per *vuqiyye*	Akkerman	May 1507	B.V.A. Maliye 15649
8. Black pepper *(fulful)*	25 per *vuqiyye*	Akkerman	May 1507	B.V.A. Maliye 15649
9. Black pepper *(fulful)*	1,760 per *kantār*	Akkerman	May 1507	B.V.A. Maliye 15649
10. Black pepper *(fulful)*	50 or 60 per *vuqiyye*	Kilia	March 1505	B.V.A. Maliye 6

1 *vuqiyye* = 1.2828 g; 1 *qanṭār* = 44 vuqiyye (oqqa)

Ratio of gold ducat to Ottoman silver *akça*.

Dates	1 gold ducat in silver *akça*
1431	35
1436	36
1477	45
1479	45.5
1488	49
1500	53
1510	54
1526	55

TABLE X. Jewish tax farmers

Names, Partnerships	Subject of the tax farm	Amount of the farm in *akça*	Sureties	Other conditions	Date, Source
1. Altina, Jew, Seyyidī Küçük, Muslim from Edirne, and Nikiroz, "French" (Italian) in partnership	Customs dues of the ports within the customs of Istanbul	20,400,000, 4 years			October 1477, B.V.A., Maliyeden M. no. 7387
2. Anastas son of Eliya, of Nicopolis and Mūsā son of Ya'qūb	Customs dues at Bursa	70,000, 1 year			November 1471, Ibid.
3. Mūsā Küçük, Jew and Liazar son of Sha'bān	Customs dues at Bursa	360,000, 3 years			April 1475, Ibid.
4. Kara-Arslan son of Menahim	Customs dues at Bursa	370,000, 3 years			Sept. 1476, Ibid.
5. Abraham son of Mūsā of Trnovi, and Mardehay son of Eliya	Dues at the grain market and public scales of Bursa	400,000, 3 years	Mūsā son of Eliya and Mūsā son of Ya'qūb		Sept. 1488, Ibid.
6. Luvi	Customs dues on Salonica cloth at Iştip	2,200	Toviji, Jew	Since he disappeared the surety pays	August 1519, *Muqāṭa'āt defteri* (B.V.A. Maliyeden M. 149)
7. Danyal son of Ishaq of Istanbul and Proto son of 'Īsā	Brokerage at the markets of Istanbul and Pera	1,100,000			June 1479, B.V.A., no. 7387
8. Ismā'īl son of Abraham, and Yūsuf son of Abraham, immigrants from Europe (*Frengistān*)	Monopoly of candle making in Istanbul	160,533			1481, Ibid.
9. Ishaq son of Abraham	Monopoly of candle making in Istanbul	233,873			1481, Ibid.

TABLE X *(Continued)*

Names, Partnerships	Subject of the tax farm	Amount of the farm in *akça*	Sureties	Other conditions	Date, Source
10. Bruto son of Isaya and Arslan son of Süleymān	Mints of Istanbul, Edirne, and Gelibolu	18 million, 3 years	Yeshua son of David for Bruto, Bruto for Arslan		1481, Sahillioğlu, IFM, XXIII, 184
11. Azrāīl son of Eliya and Sha'bān son of Ishaq, and Andronikos son of Kantakuzenos	Mint of Istanbul				1481, Ibid.
12. Afsalom son of Eliya, Haskye son of Samariyya, David son of Yako, Sha'bān son of Ishaq, and Mūsā son of Ya'qūb	Mints of Novabri, Üsküb, and Serres	23,400,000, 3 years			1481, Ibid., 204

Jewish money exchangers in the service of the mints in 1481 (Sahillioğlu, *op. cit.*): Avram son of Ishaq (Filibe), Eliya (Nigbolu), Mūsā son of Eliya (Sofia), Sinān Jew (Trnovo), Mūsā known as Yasim, Yūsuf, Mūsā son of Eliya (Filibe), Avraham son of Ishaq, Benjamin, agent of the supervisor of the mints on behalf of Abdi Hoca, tax farmer of the mints.

35
Social Environment and Literature: The Reflection of the Young Turk Era (1908–1918) in the Literary Work of Ömer Seyfeddin (1884–1920)

Kemal H. Karpat

I. Introduction

MODERN SOCIAL LITERATURE of the Middle East, namely the short story, the novel, poetry, and, lately, the drama, is a rather faithful mirror of social and political transformations occurring in the society at large. Unlike other modes of intellectual expression, literature presents an internalized, psychological, and individualized interpretation of change and its effects. It appears, first, as a qualitative critique of transformation. Second, while remaining involved in the realm of values, it strives to justify the need for additional transformation. In some cases, it may well oppose and criticize certain moral and intellectual aspects of change.

The writer's personality and background often determine his views regarding the process of social change. The family is the basic institution in which the writer's early values are formed. In fact, it is the mother who may have the overwhelming formative impact upon the writer's personality and his basic viewpoint toward change. Consequently, some knowledge about the mother's background, experience, and personality would be valuable in understanding the Middle

Eastern writer. (We are not referring here to the mother's natural impact upon the child's personality, but to a series of special feminine qualities which might determine the writer's formation as an artist. Emotion, lyricism, tenderness, perception, empathy—that is, some of the basic qualities of an artist—may be attributed to the mother; whereas the model for courage, manliness, family responsibility, social position, etc., is provided by the father.)

We may divide (arbitrarily, merely for the sake of clarity) the system of values in a traditional society into two categories: personal and societal. Thus, one may say that the impact of the mother's personality and values is evident in an individual's intimate personal life, while fatherly values are dominant at a more general and impersonal societal level.

Modernization, notably the adoption of a written medium of communication and the translation of Western works (this a major source of intellectual influence hardly studied), coupled with a new social mobility, provided both the model and the avenue for gradually blending the more intimate and personal type of values rooted in the mother's psychology and personality into the generally manly societal system of values.

Education is another major variable in determining the writer's personality. This education received in schools must always be viewed in relation to the artist's family background, since such instruction, especially the value-oriented instruction, was molded, interpreted, and internalized through interaction with the basic family education. The education received from the modern types of schools had more often than not an ideological-political orientation. It strove to create idealized images of modern societies and states. Thus, the writer's view of modernization, as well as his opinion about his own role in this process was often shaped by the official view of what an ideal modern society ought to be. However, the writer's own personality, in which the motherly influence must be given due recognition, together with continuous exposure to ideas and certain standards of intellectual ethics, enabled the writer to adopt critical views, often in contradiction to the official dogma.

The third factor affecting the writer's personality and determining the tendencies of his literary work may be found in changes which occurred in his and his family's social status. Modernization in the Middle East disturbed, and continues to disturb, ancient social arrangements. Social dislocation and the ensuing accelerated mobility dealt a deadly blow to the idea of social immutability, a fundamental principle which had determined Middle Eastern philosophies and attitudes throughout centuries. Dislocation exposed the writer to new conditions of life. It dramatized the idea that values were relative, and brought the need for an explanation of all changes in order to facilitate social adjustment. Adjustment was possible only through a rational, cause-and-effect explanation based on the emerging secular and relativist view of the world, a view which conflicted with the ancient view that man's fate and the order in his society were preordained. Adjustment to a new mode of life through the acceptance of change was, above all, an intellectual and psychological problem demanding a broad range of emotional capabilities and a high level of perception and introspection, qualities which few ordinary people possessed. The writer thus played a vital role, not only in providing explanation and justification for social change, but also in establishing the criteria and standards for the acceptance of innovation and change. Moreover, the writer had to use a language or dialect easily understood by the majority of people, and had to express his ideas through familiar images and expressions.

The variables that are paramount, however, in ultimately determining the writers role as an agent of change and the force of his impact on society are talent, artistic sensibility, empathy (which need not be discussed), and commitment. Talent we may define as the inborn ability to turn a felicitous phrase, to express ideas or describe people, places, and events in such a way as to catch the attention of the reader despite his lack of prior interest in the topic. At this point, the degree of the author's own commitment, both to his art and to his cause, is crucial, for the reader's attention must be held and his mind engaged if the writer's words are to have a social impact. The work must, first, meet artistic criteria, and be writing of high literary quality. Then it must represent a synthesis between the writer as an individual, with his own needs and aspirations, and the society with its universal problems, feelings, and goals. Social problems give art a humanist, emotional dimension, while art offers society standards and perspective. A writer's commitment to a cause gives his work a sense of purpose and dynamism, but a prior commitment to literature—to the mastery of technique and to the spirit of art—is required. It is this kind of commitment which separates the artist from the politician, and gives force to his social comment.

Modern social writings in the Middle East (notably those in the

Ottoman Empire and modern Turkey, which we have studied extensively) appear in many instances as records of social events, of ideologies, of the clash of personalities, and the like. Events are often distorted; some individuals are ridiculed, others glorified, depending upon the writer's opinion. Thus, these works cannot be taken at face value as authentic documents. Yet, if social literature is read with a new understanding of its specific function and role in the process of modernization, these literary writings may provide new insights into and a new understanding of the entire history, and the social and political transformation, of the modern Middle East.

Current studies of so-called developing societies cover the factual, objective aspects of social transformation, but in most cases they fail to envisage the process in its human and psychological dimensions. We feel that a more complete understanding may be achieved through the acceptance and study of literature as a major source for historical, social, and political studies. In the Middle East, in particular, a series of additional reasons, such as changes in family structure, the expanded use of the vernacular, the passage from the old ideal of a universal community to the national state, and increased social differentiation augment the value of literature as a source for social research.

We shall attempt in the present paper to support the above hypotheses by analyzing some of the relevant short stories of Ömer Seyfeddin. We shall limit our treatment to three topics: (a) Ömer Seyfeddin's family background and formation as an artist; (b) the development of the idea of nationalism; and (c) the rise of intellectuals as a social group. The quotations in the text are taken almost exclusively from his short stories. The story titles are italicized. The footnotes provide, in addition to standard documentation, additional factual evidence supporting some of the points raised in the short stories. The reader is advised to pay special attention to the endnotes, which have been used extensively to identify the heroes in the stories with living personalities.

II. Ömer Seyfeddin's Background[1]

Ömer Seyfeddin was born in 1884 in Gönen, a small peaceful town in western Anatolia. His father, a Turk originally from the Caucasus region, was an officer in the army who rose to his rank of major not through school, but through a field commission in the army.[2] Seyfeddin's references to his father in his works are rare and not complimentary. The father appears as a cold, authoritarian man, determined to give a stern, traditional education to his children. The father's attitudes brought the child closer to his mother. Yet, the father's dogmatic attachment to his own view of family and education, coupled with his military profession, had a profound impact on Ömer. Throughout his life, Ömer had a powerful sense of ethics, loyalty, and attachment to country, as well as to other values he considered to be good.

The mother belonged to a relatively well-to-do intellectual family from Istanbul. "Intellectual" at this time meant pious and well-versed in Islamic religious teachings and practices. In his autobiographical stories *Kasagi, Ilk Namaz, Ant, Ilk Cinayet* ("Curry Comb," "First Prayer," "Pledge," "First Crime"), Ömer Seyfeddin repeatedly refers to his mother with a tenderness akin to religiosity. She was the most beloved person, whom he saw "surrounded by angels while she read the Koran" (*Kasagi*). Even if he went to Hell in the next world, the writer felt that the fire would not burn the corner of his face where she used to kiss him. Every morning as a child he "invented dreams in which a big bear carried him into the inn up in the forests," and she interpreted the dream for him to mean that he would become a great man, "a famous general whom nobody could hurt" (*Ant*). Much later, after he became a well-known writer, Ömer described most fully the impact of his mother on his career, as well as upon his role as an artist. In one of his most famous short stories, *Fon Sadriştayinin Oğlu* ("The Son of Von Sadristein"), he speaks through the mouth of his hero, a poet:

> Everything I learned comes from my mother. She raised me in a spirit of religious exaltation. The source of lyricism that you feel running through my poems is derived from the religious feeling [teaching] she gave me. My poems, stories, and tragedies were in her fairy tales. Her soul, which came from the people (*halk*), has grafted the love of the people onto my own soul. Because of this, the people's expressions are my rhyme, and the harmony of the people's language is my music.

The poet in Ömer Seyfeddin's story sets forth in a nutshell the basic literary-social problem of his time, namely, the need for a national language to bring together the masses and the elites.

> Before him [the poet], the poets and the learned insulted their own kin as being of low class [*avam*], and never shared their own feelings with them . . .

> but he [the poet] never looked upon his nation as divided into two groups, as *avam* and *havas*,[3] but instead [tried to unite] them together under a national ideal. . . . He generalized the usage of the Istanbul dialect[4] . . . which became the language of an entire nation. . . . He did not seek inspiration in French or Persian [literature], nor in the singing of dervishes[5] or folk poets,[6] but turned to his own soul. Thus he understood the Turkish feeling. He found his topics, stories, language, and bravery in the Turkish soul.

This description, in fact, fits perfectly Ömer's own literary-political accomplishments.

Ömer Seyfeddin spent his childhood mostly in Gönen, where he attended elementary school. His warm feeling for nature, his joy in living, his ability to establish intimate rapport with his subjects, as well as his realism, may be attributed in part to this early childhood spent in intimacy with the uninhibited natural environment of this town. The description in *Falaka* ("Wingle Tree") of his schoolhouse (ca. 1890) and of the teacher in Gönen is probably one of the best portraits of the educational system in the Ottoman Empire. Moreover, the origins of the legends and fairy tales which appear in various forms in his writing may easily be traced to the folklore of his native region.

Ömer eventually moved to Istanbul and enrolled in a military school, but seemed very happy to move later to a similar institution in Edirne, where class distinctions were less evident. Then he went back to Istanbul, where he finished his military education. Commissioned to teach in a military school in Izmir, he became acquainted with a small circle of men interested in literature. In Izmir he learned French, lest his literary tastes remain at the level of the *harabat* poets.[7] Later he translated *Illyada* (The *Iliad* of Homer, published in 1927) and *Kalavela*, both of which seem to have contributed to his understanding of the epic form. In Izmir he seems to have been influenced by Baha Tevfik, a rationalist-materialist Westernist and an apologist for the use of a simplified or vernacular Turkish, and Huseyin Hilmi (known as "the socialist"), who had published briefly the *Serbest Izmir* ("Free Izmir"), a literary review.

Later, from 1909 to 1911, Ömer served in the Balkans in the Monastir area with a unit fighting the nationalist guerilla bands. It is here that he acquired a first-hand knowledge of the Christian minorities, and especially of their nationalist aspirations. Indeed, Ömer's own nationalist ideas, as well as those of the entire revolutionary group in Salonica, which played a vital role in redefining the content of emerging Turkish nationalism in 1908–18, can properly be understood only in the light of their exposure to the ideas of the Balkan nationalists. Niyazi Bey, one of the leaders of the revolt in 1908, openly acknowledged that his nationalism was inspired by the Macedonian revolt of 1903.

Ömer eventually resigned from the army to become a contributor to *Genç Kalemler* ("Young Pens"), the major Turkish nationalist review defending the language reform. In Salonica he became acquainted with Ziya Gökalp, who had an overwhelming influence on his political ideas. Salonica, it must be noted, was the seat of the Union and Progress Committee, which organized the revolution of 1908, thus starting the chain of events which led to the establishment of the Republic. In fact, Salonica, a busy port with direct connections to the West, was for a while the *de facto* capital of the Ottoman Empire, as the seat of the ruling Union and Progress Committee.

During the Balkan war of 1912–13, Seyfeddin fought on the Greek front, and eventually, after defending his area almost to the last man, he was taken prisoner and spent about a year in a Greek prison. After the war he returned to Istanbul. He died of an unknown illness on March 6, 1920, at the age of thirty-six, just about the time he had reached intellectual and artistic maturity. That he planned to write a series of novels and plays is indicated by his unfinished works.

The literary career of Ömer Seyfeddin seems to have been intimately involved with the idea of using the vernacular as the language of Turkish literature. This idea was one of several that were basic to the projected language reform. Though language reform was one of the main principles of Ömer's own nationalist philosophy, he regarded the use of a simplified language not as an ideological weapon, but as an essential condition for mass communication and national education. In his letter offering to write for the review *Genç Kalemler*, he spoke about the adoption of the vernacular as a true "revolution in literature and language." Ömer's work consisted mostly of short stories. He wrote a total of 135 stories (found so far), most of which date from after 1917. Some of these deal with the same topic and have a common hero, and were therefore published together as a novel.

Some of Ömer's short stories were written very hurriedly, as publishing became his main source of livelihood.[8] Some stories appear merely as diary notes. Other stories lack organization, or even a plot, and contain profane allusions designed to interest the reader. Yet, each story has a literary quality, a power of suggestion and of communication, and a simplicity of feeling which leaves a moving and lasting impression. The artist always prevails, whether he discusses politics or a man's plight.

Ömer Seyfeddin was the Anton Chekhov of Turkey. He lived in anxiety in a society overwhelmed by internal change and threatened with extinction by outside powers, and he well expressed his own and his contemporaries' feelings. He used satire and humor to criticize the shortcomings of contemporary society and of the people around him. In 1918–20 he witnessed the defeat and occupation of the Ottoman Empire by the Allies and died without seeing the day of liberation.

The language used by Ömer Seyfeddin in his stories was his greatest contribution to modern Turkish literature. It was a simple but expressive language, as used in everyday life. Yet, it proved to be a powerful instrument of communication, conveying in crisp but natural expressions the thoughts and feelings shared by the overwhelming majority of the people. Unity through communication was thus achieved.

III. From Ottomanism to Turkish Nationalism: The Making of an Ideology

Turkish nationalism acquired its modern content during the Young Turk period. It developed together with the ideas of modernization, secularism, and reformism, to become the dominant ideology of the Turkish Republic after 1923. In Ömer Seyfeddin's writings, nationalism appears essentially as a search for a national consciousness through the adoption of the vernacular, the identification of the elite with the culture of the masses, and the achievement of progress within a national state. But Ömer also defended patriotism—that is, attachment to the land, to the people, and to the native culture—as an indispensable condition for unity and political-social integration. He was driven to this point of view, which was conditioned by his own background, and by the exigencies of the political order of which he became a part.

Ömer Seyfeddin's early idea of nationalism and patriotism seems to have been in the form of a natural attachment to one's place. He had been brought up to regard loyalty to the throne, maintenance of the status quo, and preservation of ancient values as part of a permanent social arrangement. But his apolitical attachment to the land began to change at the end of 1908, when he was transferred to a unit located around the village of Yakorit in the Monastir area of the

Balkans. There he met Bulgarian intellectuals, all nationalists, who claimed that Turks could not have political ideas, and consequently could not become nationalistic, because of their religious concept of state and society. The Bulgarians saw the Ottoman Empire not as a multinational state, but as a mere political order ruled by Turks who had no sense of national consciousness (see *Nakarat* ["The Refrain"]).[9] He discovered that the Balkan nationalists were firmly attached to their ideal of national liberation, and delighted in telling their national legends and in expressing their political ambitions. Even the young Bulgarian girl enamored of the Turkish officer sang "Nash, nash, Tzarigrad, nash." The officer thought that she sang love songs, only to be awakened to reality when an old man told him what the words meant: "Ours, ours, Istanbul is ours." The Balkan nationalists regarded the *Ilinden* (the revolt in Macedonia in 1903, which was rapidly quelled) as a symbol for the continuing struggle for independence, and as a reminder that sooner or later revenge had to be taken. (This, in fact, occurred later in the war of 1912–13, when most of the Ottoman possessions in the Balkans were lost to Bulgaria, Greece, and Serbia. The Bulgarian communist government completed this revenge by changing Turkish names to Christian ones in 1984–85, in effect achieving a forced conversion.)

The Balkan guerillas recruited men both by force and by persuasion. Some inhabitants wanted to emigrate to America and to lead their lives in this peaceful land, but could not get away. They had to stay and fight for the liberation of their native land. The heroine of one story, *Bomba* ("Bomb"), is a young woman, Magda, who is anxiously waiting for her husband to return home so that they can prepare to leave for America the next day. Instead, there comes the chief of the guerillas, to leave "a bomb" in the house. This turns out to be the head of Magda's husband. He had dared to defy the guerillas, and to try to avoid his "national responsibilities."

The nationalists in the Balkans won their struggle, often taking advantage of the Ottomans' goodwill, and forcing the Turks living in those areas to abandon their homes and lands (*Tuhaf bir Zülüm* ["A Strange Oppression"]). All this happened because the Turks' level of education was so low, and they were so deeply immersed in their religious, fatalistic concept of life, that they accepted everything as preordained. But the Ottoman intellectuals were not much better. Many joined the army merely to become staff officers in order to rise to positions of power and prestige, to live an easy life in Istanbul, and to go to the West as military attachés in order to enjoy life there (*Nakarat*).

Meanwhile, the nationalists among the Christian groups in the Balkans found support and understanding among their own kin. They had been molded together into a nation, helped by similarities of language and by the idea that they all had a common past. They spoke a simple, common language, in which class differences were not yet evident. Their songs and tales reflected so much of their daily life, their joys, and their aspirations, that they formed an integral part of their world and of themselves. Indeed, their lives had been remade and galvanized by a political ideal: nationalism.

The Young Turks' political impotence continued to manifest itself in military defeats and territorial losses, as indicated by the occupation of Tripolitania by the Italians in 1911. This occupation was labeled by Ömer Seyfeddin as a betrayal of the humanitarian ideals of brotherhood and the equality of men, and of the doctrines of freedom and independence which European nations preached to non-Europeans. The Italians, in the note addressed to the Ottoman government, claimed that Tripolitania was the only area left out of the European "civilizing" mission. Expressing Ömer's reaction to the West's betrayal of its own principles, Kenan bey, the hero of *Primo-Türk Çocuğu* ("Number One Turkish Son"), who had married an Italian girl and had become thoroughly Westernized, rejecting his own culture and identity, chose to return to his original cultural allegiance. His son, Primo, followed him.[10]

These developments could not fail to affect the old type of passive Turkish nationalism, which was oriented toward resistance and the preservation of the status quo. The Turkish intellectuals in Salonica experienced a growing desire to broaden the scope of their own nationalism in such a way as to achieve total national salvation, by creating the *Yeni Hayat* (New Life). This became, in fact, the ideal of the new generation. Ömer Seyfeddin moved with the new, active phase of nationalism, by defining the role of language and literature in the formation of national consciousness. In one story, *Ilk Düşen Ak* ("The First Gray Hair"), he declared through the mouth of his hero that people with a common religion and language should be considered as part of the same nation.[11]

Turkish nationalism, however, still lacked a dynamic, optimistic quality, and was thus unable to dispel the gloom generated by what was considered inevitable defeat (and even extinction) with the loss of Bosnia in 1908, the Italian War in 1911, and the disastrous Balkan War of 1913. This feeling was increased by a pathological inferiority complex toward Europe. Dr. A. Cevdet recommended a full imitation of everything European. A degree of self-confidence was restored only by the heroic resistance of the Turkish soldiers to the British invasion at the Dardanelles in 1915, known as the battle of Gallipoli in the Western literature. This was, in fact, the starting point of the political transformation of the Turkish Ottomans into Turks.[12] Indeed, the hero in *Çanakkaleden Sonra* ("After Gallipoli") used to believe fatalistically that his nation was doomed to perish, and that its people would become the slaves of the Russians, French, and English. But the incredible had happened: "The English and French battleships could not cross the Dardanelles . . . [consequently] his despair gradually disappeared, and he realized that he was part of a nation which had achieved self-realization, which had an ideal, and was alive."

Thus, the original literary nationalism/patriotism acquired distinctive activist political features. Gradually, this broader politically-oriented nationalism began to provide the basic viewpoint for judging people and events in society, including the national image of Turks. "The Turks were also a nation. But having lived in the *umma* (Muslim community), they ignored their own nationality and origin. One must modernize in order to become a nation, but many Turks started imitating the French, and therefore could not progress. In fact the Turks, similar to other nations, have a national personality of their own. They can advance if they can define their own nationality" (*Çanakkaleden Sonra*).[13]

Soon afterward, Seyfeddin began to treat the idea of nation and national personality as a focus of individual loyalty and cultural allegiance. This was evident in his bitter criticism of cultural alienation. He used with utmost mastery the genre of satire to ridicule those who denigrated their own country, culture, background, and national responsibility, seeking salvation in the blind acceptance and imitation of foreign models.[14]

The story *Fon Sadriştayinin Karisi* ("The Wife of Von Sadristein") is the best example of his criticism of cultural alienation. Sadrettin, who went to visit Germany, was so overwhelmed by the domestic qualities of modern German women that he divorced his Turkish wife in order to marry a German girl. He even adopted a new name, von Sadristein. His new wife was orderly, hard-working, economical, and so efficient that she gave birth to her child all by herself after delivering lunch to her husband, then returning to her feet to prepare his dinner. "Indeed," declared von Sadristein, "the entire wealth of Germany, the strength of her armies are the product of German womanhood . . . the German woman, who raised the population of Germany to sixty or seventy million people in a century, was able to lift my own weight from 125 to 200 pounds." However, later in life, when his son abandons him to go to America to seek adventure, and his wife remains insensitive to the country's spirit, von Sadristein realizes how lonely he is.

Criticism was also directed against the Ottomanists and Islamists who ignored nationalism. The former, many of whom became members of the opposition parties, regarded nationalism and Turkism as regressive currents opposed to the scientific humanitarian views of the West, and did not hesitate to cooperate with the occupying powers in Istanbul in 1918 (*Gayet Büyük Bir Adam* ["A Very Great Man"]).[15] The Islamists accused the nationalists of having destroyed Islamic unity, and thus inviting foreign occupation.

The war years (1914–18) brought about the addition of a new historical dimension to Seyfeddin's concept of Turkish nationalism. "If the artist cannot find the [necessary] exaltation in a contemporary ideal, he should turn to the romantic past, for in the past thousands of heroes live in legends" (*Kaç Yerinden* ["Many Places"]). It was evident that if the nation could become aware of its past achievements and glories, its will to fight would be enhanced.[16] Discipline, loyalty, and obedience to the commander (*Ferman* ["Decree"]), the wit to outdo the enemy (*Kütük* ["Log"] and *Vire* ["Surrender"]), a belief in predestined glory (*Kizilelma Neresi* ["The Site of Red Apple"]), and an unshaken belief in ultimate victory were characteristics of the victorious ancestors of the Turks, according to Ömer, and he brought these characteristics to public attention in his stories.

The First World War was nearing its end; the defeat of Ottoman armies seemed inevitable, as did the doom of the Union and Progress Party and its policies. Ömer Seyfeddin had supported the Union and Progress chiefly because he believed that its policies would rejuvenate and modernize the country. In a short story he wrote:

> When the constitution was reinstated [in 1908] we used to dream that all our [intellectual] resources would stream forward like hidden springs, and we would reach the level of Europe in ten or fifteen years. We returned to our birthplaces, to our farms and occupations. We believed in everything written

in the Istanbul newspapers . . . but here [in Anatolia] there is just one idea: reaction. Indeed, this is a most persistent ideal. (*Memlekete Mektup* ["Letter Home"])

Eventually, his disillusion with the party grew, and his contributions to the *Yeni Mecmua* (New Review), in which he published many of his stories, became rare. Like many other nationalists, Ömer began to be preoccupied with the policy to be followed in case of foreign occupation.[17] He voiced the general idea that the salvation of the country lay in the leadership of great men with exceptional qualities, who had total dedication to government service and the country, as in the glory days of the Ottoman Empire (*Köse Vezir* ["Beardless Vizier"]). The desire for a charismatic leader had become a practical necessity, but this was not enough: the struggle for liberation was to begin in the Anatolian homeland among the masses, with the firm conviction that the Turks would always survive. The hero of this story writes to his friend:

We Turks went through many disasters in history. Our state was left without a government and without a ruler. Brothers became each others' enemies. But at the end we still managed to get together. We didn't perish. . . . I shall not stay here [in Istanbul]. At the first occasion, I shall start on my journey. . . . Istanbul needs guidance from the countryside. From now onward we must listen to the heartbeat of our beloved nation, wherever we are; in our homes, up in the high mountains, in our mud-covered, white-walled hamlets by the foaming wells. . . . Yes, we have endless problems and unbearable misery. But we have a soul which death cannot ever [dare] to approach. Even when this soul is deemed to have died, it is not dead. At the most unexpected time, it suddenly revives. (*Memlekete Mektup*)

Indeed, even as Ömer Seyfeddin was writing these lines, the struggle for liberation, and the painful process of national formation, had already begun in Anatolia and was ready for its leader, Mustafa Kemal.[18]

Seyfeddin passed away on March 6, 1920, without having seen the fulfillment of his national dream. He had lived step by step through the disintegration of the multinational empire and the failure of Pan-Turkism. He did not see the rise of the Turkish national state, but he did witness its beginnings: the burgeoning idea of a nation united by a common language, and aware of its political existence. His literary writings had contributed greatly toward the achievement of this vital step in the process of nation formation.

IV. The Intellectual: Social Status and Political Role

The Young Turk Revolution of 1908 aimed at reinstating the constitutional régime of 1876, which had been abrogated by Sultan Abdulhamid II (1876–1909). In practice, however, this political revolution proved merely the starting point of a series of profound social and cultural changes. The rise of intellectuals to positions of power in the government, press, and education, and the rapid politicization of all major spheres of public life, were the most significant outcomes of change. The schools established after 1869 and the economic activity, stimulated chiefly by trade, of the second half of the nineteenth century had given the process of change a content and direction different from that of the Tanzimat era.

The Union and Progress era (1908–18) may be considered a transitional phase, in which the old bureaucratic aristocracy and the religious elites, as well as the upper-class groups created in the nineteenth century, were replaced by a small property-owning, and an especially large intellectual class which used the expanded power of the central government to establish its own social and political hegemony, to become in fact a ruling class. The rise of this class to political power and social preeminence created a series of conflicts: first, it challenged the older bureaucrats, who strove to preserve their positions at all cost; second, it found itself at odds with the entrepreneurial groups that were expanding rapidly due to the government's economic policy of "division of labor." The aim of this policy was to create a national economy based on a native Turkish middle class of entrepreneurs and property owners. (The war years greatly stimulated the growth of this class.) The intellectuals' rise to power also raised other problems. First, there was a need to define the function of the intellectual within the framework of an emerging national state and its goal of modernization. Second, there was the problem of adapting society to the new pattern of social stratification, and of defining the new social strata as well as the criteria for status assignment. Third, there was the question of creating the symbols, the images, and the attitudes necessary for recognition, acceptance, and respect for the intelligentsia in society.

These problems were far more complicated than they appeared at first sight. In both theory and practice, Ottoman society was pervaded by a strong system of social ranking and class function that was rooted in centuries-old tradition. Moreover, the intelligentsia, as a new social and political group, was called upon to undertake political functions (political socialization, indoctrination, integration, creation of a national identity) for which it could find only limited precedent in its own culture. In addition, it was expected to perform differentiated, specialized technical tasks for which it had only limited professional preparation. Thus, the intellectuals' rise to power was a multidimensional process of social differentiation and adaptation.

The problems outlined above manifested themselves in everyday life in the form of personal failure, frustration, or achievement. Irony and drama, the comedy of man and the tragedy of society, were blended together in concrete human situations. Only an artist with deep sensitivity, but also with a sense of humor, could have grasped the infinite aspects of these events. Ömer Seyfeddin's stature as a writer derives essentially from his ability to grasp and to describe the most intimate effects of change, as reflected in individuals' attitudes. The stories dealing with nationalist themes, though important for the study of ideology, are often rhetorical, didactic, and repetitious. But the stories relating to social change, and notably those dealing with the intelligentsia, are outstanding in every respect. The writer becomes personally and directly involved, for the story he tells is often that of a group to which he himself belonged.[19]

A series of stories, such as *Yuf Borusu Seni Bekliyor* ("Damnation Awaits You"), describe the passing of the old-time aristocracy; others, such as *Niçin Zengin Olmamiş* ("Why Did Not He Become Rich?"), dealing with the black market profiteers, *Türkçe Reçete* ("Turkish Prescription"), *Yemin* ("Oath"), *Namus* ("Honor"), *Kesik Biyik* ("Cut Mustache"), provide insights into social conflicts and the clash of values. Four stories, known as the Cabi Efendi series, *Mermer Tezgan* ("Marble Bench"), *Dama Taşlari* ("Draughts Pawns"), *Makul Bir Dönüş* ("Reasonable Return"), and *Acaba Ne Idi?* ("What Was It?"), analyze the gradual adaptation of a fatalistic, traditional-minded man to the economic-minded new society, and the rise of a new type of bourgeoisie. We shall not analyze the aforementioned stories, but concentrate instead on the novel known as *Asilzadeler* ("Nobles"), or *Efruz bey*.[20]

The hero in all of the seven stories making up the novel is one and the same Efruz bey.[21] It would seem impossible one man could have so many different roles and carry out so many different functions which would normally require prolonged specialization, but this was possible in the early days of the Young Turk Revolution. The old standards had broken down. The new regime created a number of new political positions in order to consolidate its own power, but it still had no objective criteria to distinguish the opportunist from the honest man, the skilled person from the ignoramus. Each story criticizes some shortcoming of contemporary intellectuals: their lack of political education and failure to understand modern national ideals; their reaction to social mobility; their historical romanticism and ignorance of the country's true situation; their abuse of power and their frivolousness, which they justified in terms of nationalism, modernity, and language reform; and finally, their search for superficial amusement, and their uselessness to society. As a symbol of this rootlessness, Seyfeddin chooses one single hero, Efruz bey, who plays several often contradictory roles.

The career of Efruz bey begins amid the following circumstances. Ahmet bey, a petty official, had succeeded during the regime of Abdulhamit II in giving everybody the impression that he was on the sultan's side. And, of course, like all status seekers, he had to be *comme il faut* and *distingué*, so he falsely implied that he had studied at Galatasaray, the French *lycée*, where one became "modern" and "Europeanized." One morning, Ahmet was quick to notice a small official note in the newspaper, to the effect that the constitution had been reinstated.[22] He made his way to the Foreign Ministry, where everybody strove to speak French, and shouted "Long live freedom!" There he engaged in an abusive criticism of Abdulhamit, and described how he, Ahmet bey, had single-handedly forced the sultan at pistol point to reinstate freedom. Recounting in public his fantastic exploits as an underground activist, Ahmet bey soon became a freedom hero. Since secrecy was the virtue of all revolutionaries (Union and Progress was a secret organization, and remained one even years after it had assumed power), Ahmet claimed that he had kept his real name so secret that even his own mother did not know it. Then he invented a "real name," *Efruz* ("the illuminator"). The credulous mob, carrying him on its shoulders, quickly converted the name to *Afaroz* ("the excommunicated"). Efruz bey then provided a definition of freedom: "It means the Constitution. The Constitution means without difference of sex and sect . . . which means there is no sex and sect . . . a free man becomes equal, and equality means brotherhood, and thus there remain no differences of religion and nationality" (*Hürriyete Laik Bir Kahraman* ["A Hero Deserving Freedom"]).[23]

Soon, however, Efruz bey is unmasked by the real revolutionaries, the Union and Progress Society; but, still undaunted, he seizes other opportunities, which are plentiful. The breakdown of the old order had enabled commoners to break the social mold, and to attempt to lead an upper-class life. Men who felt that they were socially superior to others, in particular the intellectuals, sought avidly for arguments to create superior positions and status for themselves. They were the new class, the nobles of the new order, and they especially sought to prove their nobility by not dealing in "unbecoming" occupations, such as regular work and politics. And since achievement had not yet become the criterion for status assignment, they sought stature in prescriptive claims. Their affiliation with the Ottoman bureaucratic aristocracy, temporarily downgraded by the revolution, being of no use, they turned to race and ancient history. Efruz bey and his friends, who were all supposedly graduates of the Galatasaray, became convinced that "without nobility this country would sink" (*Asiller Klübü* ["The Nobles' Club"]). They reinterpreted history to prove their own noble origin, which they preferred to find somewhere outside Turkey. Ömer Seyfeddin satirized their alienation and ignorance. One claimed that he was the descendant of Lord Johnson Sgovat, who came as British ambassador to Sultan Orhan (1326–59). The sultan married him to his "stepsister" (*süt kiz kardeş* in the text, that is, "nurtured by the same nurse"), and kept him in the Empire. Another claimed that he was the Eternal Prince of Kara Tanburin, and proved that his family was of divine origin.[24] The third, Kaysussujufuzzrtaf, traced his origin to the romantic era of desert life, when his ancestors carried out the *ghazwa* and had their name mentioned in the *Mu'allaqāt*. Efruz bey himself "felt" the entire history of his noble family in the depths of his heart, as clearly indicated by his father's journey to Kastamonu, the land of Kizil Ahmet. He therefore became "Prince Efruz of Kizil." Soon these "nobles" met to establish an organization for the purpose of locating other nobles, of giving them back their "proper" titles, and of fighting for their rights. The meeting was broken up by the police, since the meeting place was an illegal gambling house. But Efruz bey, sensing that the police *razzia* was a commoners' plot against the nobility, confessed to the gambling charge in a Don Quixote-style gesture, and went serenely to jail, convinced that the "nobles" had succeeded in keeping their worthy endeavor a secret.

Efruz bey eventually became convinced that one had to cultivate oneself in order to become useful to the nation. His basic motives were, however, still personal: namely, to build a reputation as a learned man. In fact, he had actually become, in a very short time, an expert in every branch of learning, including national history.[25] Like many of his intellectual friends, he believed that the villager remained uncorrupted by the cosmopolitan, materialistic life dominant in the cities. The villager, in his view, was the "true" Turk, who had preserved all the virtues of the Turkish soul, such as friendliness and honesty, in their primitive beauty. But on a visit to rural areas, Efruz bey and his friends are treated rudely by the villagers, who even charge him five times the normal price for food. He is disappointed, but still hopeful that his image of the Turkish peasant was correct. Indeed, one boy in the village had shown them utmost friendliness and even refused to take the money offered for his services; so Efruz bey pointed out the boy to the villagers as the model of the rural Turkish peasant. But the peasants laughingly tell him: "He is not a villager . . . but a gypsy" (*Tam Bir Görüş* ["A Complete View"]).

Soon afterward, like many intellectuals interested in nationalism, Efruz bey became a prodigious lecturer on the subject. He delivered his lectures to audiences gathered in various branches of the Türk Ocaklari.[26] In each lecture, he managed to mention as many as twenty book titles, although he had not read the books. In one lecture he claimed that knowledge was to be sought everywhere, "from the time of the cradle to the grave," and that one had to go even "to China in order to get it."[27] With quick and formal logic, Efruz bey demolished all other theories, all accepted ideas, and established his own views. The chairman of the Türk Ocagi, jealous of Efruz bey's success, dared to challenge his statements on "scientific" grounds. Indeed, in repeating the *ḥadīth* about knowledge in Arabic, Efruz bey had mistakenly said from the "grave to the cradle," and thus had violated the foundations of scientific causality. However, the audience, composed mostly of Turks from Russia, was very friendly to Efruz bey. They called him "our Tolstoi," for he had told them, "You are the real Turks. The Turks of Turkey are not Turks. They are degenerates. We shall get civilization from you, and we all shall become Tatars" (*Bilgi Bucaginda* ["In the Land of Knowledge"]).[28] In his talks, Efruz bey covered every branch of knowledge, for instance: "The science of social events is called sociology and is part of the natural sciences, because it uses induction [*sic*], that is to say, it starts from a conclusion and goes to the premise." Actually, when he said "from the grave to the cradle," Efruz claimed that he had conformed to this basic method of reasoning.

Efruz bey's views on the question of language reform, a most vital topic during the Young Turk era, outdid all the proposals put forth by the apologists for a purified Turkish. The existing grammar rules are to be reversed, and all "Arabic, Persian, and French words in the language, including the spoken language, are to be left out. Words without a Turkish counterpart are to be taken from Tatar and Mongolian, with Turkish suffixes added."[29] Some of his followers pointed out the practical difficulties involved in so drastic a language reform, but Efruz bey had the solution: faith. (In fact, the language thus invented became in the Republic the distinguishing mark of a small ruling minority of intellectuals, and thus separated them from the masses.)

This linguistic interest led Efruz bey to another major problem which indeed preoccupied the nationalists at that time, namely, the historical origin and the achievements of Turks. Efruz bey's most original finding, rivaling that of the greatest minds of his time, was that Americans were Turks. He also became involved in discussions concerning alphabet reform, and voiced immediate support for the alphabet proposed by Dr. Ismail Hakki of Milas.[30] Finally, the serious-minded leaders of the nationalist movement asked Efruz bey to submit his talks in writing before delivery. Unable to do so, Efruz decided, under the pretext that morality was corrupted, to retire and live in the geographic fountainhead of Turkish nationalism, that is, in Turan.

Efruz bey soon reappeared in the role of an educator. But this time, he decided to seek the advice of another well-known educator, Mufat bey.[31] The latter did not believe in a Turkish national educational system, but rather in a practical one oriented toward the individual and his needs. Claiming that he had studied pedagogy in Europe, Efruz bey attacked his mentor, Mufat bey. He became an ardent supporter of "natural" education, going to the extreme to defend the state of nature. Efruz agreed with those educators who considered even school furniture a luxury, for luxury incited the poor against the rich. This was, in fact, proof that he was not a theorist. In order to realize his ideas on education, he decided to establish an open-air school at Hayirsizada (Useless Island, located in the Sea of Marmara); hence the title of the story *Açik Hava Mektebi*. This school was eventually to become self-supporting, like the Anglo-Saxon schools.[32] It was to be a school without books, paper, or pencils, and to involve no homework. He put his ideas before the schoolchildren, who agreed enthusiastically to all his proposals, including the idea of addressing their principal by his first name—which, being too long, was shortened to *Mistik*, a derogatory nickname.[33] But instead of reaching the island, the place where he intended to establish his school, Efruz ended up in Yalova, a resort town. Finally, at the peak of his intellectual prowess, Efruz bey, convinced that he was "an oral writer," "a famous poet without poems," and "a genius without any works," criticized everything and everyone, including the writer, and established his own literary school (*Inat* ["Stubborness"]).[34] Surrounded by his disciples, he had the last word on any intellectual, philosophical, or literary problem. Even when proved wrong, he would not change his opinion or position. He thought that he was at the pinnacle of intellectual achievement. Closed in his own shell, he had become a self-satisfied, escapist egomaniac.

V. Conclusion

The short stories of Ömer Seyfeddin appear to reflect the social and political events of his time. It is rather easy to draw a parallel between them and actual events, ideas, and personalities which shaped the Young Turk era. Whatever their shortcomings, these short stories do enable the reader to look at the process of modernization from inside, and thus to gain a new insight into the individual's adjustment to social change. This is vital, because in the ultimate analysis, it is the individual who bears the impact of change. Thus, a more complete and refined evaluation of the function played by literature, as well as the transformation of the literature itself within the framework of the general process of change, should greatly broaden our understanding of change. Moreover, such a retrospective approach would add a much-needed historical perspective to studies on modernization.

NOTES

1. The best study of Ömer Seyfeddin's life and of contemporary events is by Tahir Alangu, *Ömer Seyfeddin Ülkücü Bir Yazarin Romani* [The Novel of a Patriot Writer] (Istanbul, 1968). Intimate and basic information about the writer is provided by his friend and supporter, the publisher of *Genç Kalemler*, the nationalist review of Salonica, Ali Canip (*Yontem*), in *Ömer Seyfettin, Hayat ve Eserleri* (Istanbul, 1935); a new, enlarged version of this work was published in Istanbul in 1947. Other useful works are Hilmi Yücebaş, *Ömer Seyfettin, Hayati, Hatiralari, Şiirleri* (Istanbul, 1960); Hikmet Dizdaroğlu, *Ömer Seyfettin* (Ankara, 1964); Yaşar Nabi, *Ömer Seyfettin* (Istanbul, 1961). A good survey is

in Otto Spies's *Die türkische Prosaliteratur der Gegenwart* (Leipzig, 1943), pp. 16–26. There is also a useful series of dissertations prepared by the Turkish Literature School of Istanbul University. A short analysis is in H. B. Paksoy, "Nationality and Religion: Three Observations from Ömer Seyfettin," *Central Asia Survey* III, iii (1984), pp. 109–15. Other sources are indicated below.

2. The *alay zabit* and *mektepli zabit* were two categories of officers. The first rose from the rank and file, and represented the unbending, loyal, military spirit of the old army. The troops were greatly attached to these officers. Their modest origin and constant service in the army brought them close to their men. These officers could not advance beyond a given rank. The *mektepli*, or "schooled" officers, represented the elite who could reach the highest positions in the army. The level of schooling was the social and professional barrier which divided the two groups. After the revolution of 1908, the *alayli* officers were retired; this was one of the factors contributing to the army's support of "reactionary" upheaval during that year.

3. This expression is important in understanding criteria of social differentiation in Ottoman society. It can be translated as "mass" and "elite." Actually, the true meaning of *havas* was "those who possess high feelings and ideas, and live in such a world," and of *avam*, "those who live in the low world of sensations."

4. The idea of using a Turkish dialect, namely the dialect spoken in Istanbul, was put forth by Ziya Gökalp, the nationalist ideologue of the period. The purpose was to achieve national unity, and a common language was considered an essential condition for this.

5. The reference is to a group of poets in the nineteenth century who, inspired by the school of the mystical poet Şeyh Galip, strove to maintain the religious (*Ṣūfī*) type of poetry. In the eighteenth and nineteenth centuries, this poetry was often recited in the *tekke*, or living quarters, of the mystical dervishes. These latter-day hedonist mystics, however, had little relation to the old mystics.

6. *Saz Şairleri*, or folk poets, became important as the representatives of folklore during the rise of Turkish nationalism after 1908. In reality, these were poets in their own right, often dealing with local themes, but using the vernacular. Some writers, in part inspired by Fuat Köprülü, the historian who studied the folk poets, began to imitate their style.

7. This was a group of bohemian poets of the nineteenth century, whose social pessimism and escapism was reflected in their poems exalting the material pleasure derived from wine drinking.

8. Ömer Seyfeddin's complete literary works were first published, beginning in 1938, by Muallim Ahmet Halit Yaşaroğlu, a publishing house in Istanbul, in nine volumes: I. *Ilk Düşen Ak.* II. *Yüksek Okçeler.* III. *Bomba.* IV. *Gizli Mabet.* V. *Asilzadeler.* VI. *Bahar ve Kelebekler.* VII. *Beyaz Lale.* VIII. *Mahcupluk Imtihani.* IX. *Tarih Ezeli Bir Tekerrürdür.* These were reprinted, in a revised, annotated edition, by the same house under the direction of Şerif Hulusi after 1958. In fact, the edition of 1958 was the sixth printing, but with the

addition of a tenth volume, entitled *Nokta*. The best edition, including some newly discovered stories, is that undertaken by Tahir Alangu; the new set was published by the Rafet Zaimler publishing house in Istanbul, beginning in 1962. This last series is the most comprehensive one, though not the best organized. It bears the following titles: I. *Bomba* [Bomb]. II. *Beyaz Lale* [White Tulip]. III. *Ilk Düşen Ak* [The First Gray Hair]. IV. *Yüksek Okçeler* [High Heels]. V. *Eski Kahramanlar* [Ancient Heroes]. VI. *Gizli Mabet* [Secret Temple]. VII. *Bahar ve Kelebekler* [Spring and Butterflies]. VIII. *Efruz bey* [Mr. Efruz]. IX. *Falaka* [Swingle Tree]. X. *Mahcupluk Imtihani* [Trial of Shyness]; and XI. *Aşk Dalgasi* [Love Wave].

In addition, Seyfeddin has a sociopolitical story, originally written in 1913, *Ashab-i Kehfimiz* [Nobles] (1918), which is often described as a novel; a Turanist pamphlet *Yarinki Turan Devlet* [Tomorrow's State of Turan] (1914), reprinted by N. Sencer in 1958; and a series of unfinished works. See the Alangu edition of his works, pp. 535–44, and the Dizdaroğlu biography, pp. 32–36.

Seyfeddin continues to be widely read in Turkey. New editions of his works have been reprinted, but so far none has equaled Alangu's edition, which was reissued in 1982. The Bilgi publishing house published the same works in 1970.

9. This story has a subtitle: "From the Diary of an Old Officer Who Spent His Youth in Macedonia."

10. Another story, *Piç* [Bastard], describes a Turk who is happy to discover that he was illicitly conceived by a Frenchman and his adulterous Turkish mother.

11. There is no precise information about the date of publication of this biographical story. Many of the ideas expressed in it may be found in Ziya Gökalp's nationalist writings. It must be noted that Ömer Seyfeddin's early ideas on nationalism were influenced by Turanism, and by the idea that kinship and blood relations are unity-forming bonds. After 1914, these views were gradually discarded. As early as 1911, Seyfeddin published an article on the "New Language" in *Genç Kalemler*. Here he called on young people to save the nation through "strong and serious progress." "Progress is possible," he wrote, "through the development of science, technology, and literature among us. In order to publicize [generalize] these, we need a common national language . . . without a natural and national language, science, technology, and literature will remain as they are today, an enigma. Let us abandon the language of the yesterdays. Let us write spoken Turkish, as it lives with all its rules and principles" (reproduced in the Alangu edition, p. 170, and in Dizdaroğlu, op. cit., pp.48–50).

12. In 1915, Ömer Seyfeddin, together with a group of other writers, visited the Gallipoli battlefield. For the Gallipoli campaign, Alan Moorehead's *Gallipoli* (New York, 1956) is still the best-known popular account, although other, more recent works give far better insights. See Robert R. James, *Gallipoli* (New York, 1965).

13. The ideas expressed in this story also appear elsewhere. "The nation has essentially one single language. The *umma* has one common religion but different languages, such as the language of the Turkish and Arab nations, which form the Muslim *umma*. The language of one is Arabic, of the other Turkish. Ottomanism is a state and not a nationality (nation). Since Ottomanism is not nationalism, there cannot be a language called Ottoman" (see Yöntem, 1947 ed., p. 138).

14. This theme is repeated in various forms in the stories of Ömer Seyfeddin. It comes out usually as a contrast between the modes of life, of *alafranga*, "à la française," versus *alaturca*, "à la turque," or "modern" versus "traditional." Ömer Seyfeddin envisaged this conflict as disruptive to family harmony, and as creating unhappiness (see *Nadan*). One personal reason for this extreme attitude toward cultural alienation may have been caused by Ömer Seyfeddin's divorce. His wife seems to have had an excessive liking for modern forms of life, while Ömer was interested in its essence. *Nadan* is an excellent story, portraying conflicts between husband and wife caused by differing concepts of modernity.

15. The hero in this story is easily identified as Riza Tevfik, known also as "the philosopher." He was one of the chief opponents of the Union and Progress Party, and then opposed the nationalists during the struggle for national liberation. He was eventually exiled, but returned to Turkey toward the end of his life. See his memoirs, *Serabi Ömürüm* [My Illusory Life] (Istanbul, 1949).

16. Actually, in 1915, and then again in 1917, the ruling Union and Progress Party found it necessary to resuscitate the patriotic zeal of officers and soldiers through literary epic writings. The progovernment newspaper, *Tanin*, pointed out that the French and the Germans were making extensive use of literature to stimulate their citizens' bravery and sacrifice. The Turkish writers, *Tanin* complained, were not sufficiently nationalistic to produce a similar literature. See the article, reproduced in the Alangu edition, pp. 350–51. Ömer Seyfeddin answered the call by writing more than twenty stories whose subjects were taken from Ottoman history. He used as sources for some of his stories the *Chronicle of Naima* (1655–1718), and especially, the *Chronicle of Ibrahim Peçevi* (1574–1651), whose ideological views of Ottoman history suited his views. In fact, one story, *Baş Vermeyen Şehit* [The Martyr Who Wouldn't Give His Head], is taken almost intact from *Peçevi's Chronicle* (Istanbul, 1847), I, 356–67, 358–63. This chronicle, which describes events of the sixteenth century, includes a series of legends. Ömer's stories with historical subjects are usually collected in a volume entitled *Eski Kahramanlar* [Ancient Heroes].

17. In 1917 several intellectuals, including Yusuf Akçura, were already holding meetings at the headquarters of the *Türk Yurdu* [Turkish Homeland], the principal nationalist ideological review, in an attempt to define the essential characteristics of Turkish nationalism. The idea was to stress those features, language and religion, which had wide popular appeal, in order to mobilize

the population for resistance if the country should be occupied by the Allies. Halide Edip Adivar, *Mor Salkimli Ev* (Istanbul, 1936), pp. 189 f.

18. The movement of national resistance began in the latter part of 1918. The story itself was published in *Büyük Mecmua* on March 13, 1919.

19. In fact, in the introduction to the novel *Efruz bey*, the author apologizes to his hero for exposing him, by saying: "My dear Efruz, everybody knows you as much as he knows himself. Today nobody is a stranger to you, for even if you are not 'all' of us, you are a part of us."

20. We have used for this study the series edited by Şerif Hulusi, *Asilzadeler Efruz bey* [The Nobles-Efruz bey] (Istanbul, 1956–57). Pertev N. Boratav was the first to call attention to the continuity existing in the six stories which form the Efruz bey cycle. The author himself, in his original announcement, mentioned only five stories. See P. N. Boratav, *Ömer Seyfeddin, Folklor ve Edebiyat* (Ankara, 1945), II, 171–81. See also *Yurt ve Dünya* (March-April 1942), pp. 68–75. The first story appeared in the newspaper *Vakit* in 1919 and the rest in 1926, well after the writer's death.

21. The seventh story, *Sivrisinek* [The Mosquito], was added by the last editor, Alangu. It contains the author's final explicit judgment of Efruz bey. His opinion is, however, implicitly evident in the previous six stories, and consequently *Sivrisinek*, being more didactic, has less value than the others.

22. This is exactly how the sultan announced the reinstatement of the constitution of 1876, thus accepting the demands of the officers and intellectuals, who had rebelled in Salonica in the summer of 1908.

23. The eyewitnesses to the revolution agree that "freedom" meant whatever one wanted it to be: a white-clad nun, the right to do whatever one wished to do, the members of the Union and Progress Central Committee, etc.

24. Many heroes in these stories are easily identifiable as Ömer Seyfeddin's contemporaries. Eternal Prince, for instance, was the nationalist thinker Yusuf Akçora (later Akçoraoğlu), born in the Kazan region of Russia, who did, in fact, claim that his family tree could be historically traced for some fifteen hundred years. Akçora was the representative of the "pure Turkish" school. This school was accused of implying that the Ottoman Turks had become mixed with other races, whereas the nordic Turks, or Tatars, had preserved their racial purity. In the Republic, Yusuf Akçora was one of the guiding forces during the first historical and linguistic conventions which established Government policy in these fields.

25. The hero in this story, according to Ali Canip Yöntem, the closest friend of Ömer Seyfeddin, was Haşim Nahit ("Erbil"); see Hulusi (ed.), *Asilzadeler*, II, 147.

26. *Türk Ocaklari* ("Turkish Hearths") were cultural organizations established in 1911. These became centers of nationalist education and indoctrination, as well as stepping stones for intellectuals seeking power and status.

27. These are two well-known *ḥadīths* which emphasize the value of science and learning. The fact that *ḥadīth* could be made the object of satire is an indication of the level of irreligiosity reached during the Young Turk era.

28. See n. 24.

29. It is extremely difficult to translate this wordplay ridiculing various linguistic theories discussed by intellectuals of the Young Turk era. These discussions continued in the Republic, and are still as void of essence as they were during Ömer Seyfeddin's time. The writer mentions the actual names of many intellectuals involved in these discussions, and ridicules many poets whose art had hitherto been considered unassailable: "Hamid [Abdullah] is considered a genius because nobody knows his works." Hamid was the idol of the romantics at the turn of the century.

30. This was a proposal for language reform. It envisaged the use of Arabic letters separated from each other as in the Latin printed alphabet. Apparently, it was briefly used in 1911. See Hulusi (ed.), *Asilzadeler*, II, 149, n. 17.

31. Mufat bey was the well-known Arab nationalist writer Sāṭi' al-Ḥuṣri, who was in Istanbul as an official in the Ministry of Education, and became involved in the educational polemics of the period. Ismail Hakki Baltacioğlu, the well-known Turkish educator, is also mentioned in the story. See Hulusi (ed.), *Asilzadeler*, II, 150.

32. This is probably an allusion to Robert College in Istanbul, which was seeking ways to become self-supporting, and which until recently had operated a pig farm.

33. The humor of these speeches can be grasped only when viewed in the light of Turkish fondness for titles and the traditional respect for old age and rank.

34. In *Inat* [Stubbornness], Efruz bey personifies the poet Yahya Kemal Beyatli, and also answers one critic who had chided him on the awkward use of a verb tense.

36
A Forgotten Ottoman Romance

G. M. Meredith-Owens

THIS IS A preliminary description of a probably unique prose romance, of which the only known copy is a sumptuously illustrated manuscript in the collection of His Highness Prince Sadruddin Aga Khan, first identified by the present writer in 1977. Up to now the sixty-nine fine and spirited miniatures,[1] made at the Palace Studio when the manuscript was transcribed for Murād III (1574–95) in 1002/1593–94, have received most attention, but little has been done to trace the origins of the work. The author, 'Alī ibn Naqīb Ḥamza, says in the preface, "I wanted to translate a goodly tale from the books of annals. I searched and discovered a wonderful adventure story of which every word gives comfort to the soul and bestows joy upon the heart, making manifest pleasure, enjoyment, and delight." From the title *Tuhfet ül-leṭā'if* it would seem that we have here a composite work, but it is more likely to be a free adaptation of a lost Persian or Turkish original. The fact that it is not a mere translation is suggested by the Turkish *ghazals* scattered throughout the romance which indicate that Naqīboghlu,[2] as he calls himself several times in the text, was a poet of some talent. In general the romance is more original than had been anticipated, and there has been a great deal of imagination shown in selecting the names of some of the characters, for not all of them are part of the stock-in-trade of romancers. Naqīboghlu mentions more than once that the *Tuhfet ül-leṭā'if* was written for Murād II (1421–51), but a more precise indication is provided by a reference to the Battle of Varna (November 1444) and a eulogy of Sulṭānzādeh Meḥemmed who succeeded his father for some months in 1444. He relinquished the throne to Murād in view of the impending crisis which culminated in the victory at Varna, and in 1446 Murād was finally reinstated as sultan, thanks to the influence of Čandarlı Khalīl Pasha.

The basic theme of the romance is the love story of Shāh Rāmīn, son of King Ardeshīr of Ghaznī in the region of Zāvul, for Māh-Pervīn, daughter of the king's vizier Shehrūz. The latter is the villain of the piece, and threw Māh-Pervīn into the sea in a chest when he found his honor compromised by her association with Shāh Rāmīn. King Ardeshīr was poisoned by the treacherous and ambitious minister who cast the rightful successor Shāh Rāmīn into prison. A faithful jailer released the young prince, who then set forth in search of Māh-Pervīn. In answer to her fervent prayers, Māh-Pervīn was saved from drowning, and her chest was wafted by gentle breezes to the shore of an island held by Jārūs, castellan of Pūrābād. She was forced to escape from him when she found him becoming too amorous, by plying him with wine. Shāh Rāmīn fell in with a caravan led by a merchant named Ṣāliḥ. He accompanied them, and saved the travelers from a bear the size of an elephant, and when they were taken by a band of robbers, Shāh Rāmīn evaded capture and rescued them all from the clutches of Hūr, the chief of the band. The cloth merchants went on until they reached the city of Sīmāb on the sea coast. Here the ruler Ṣuhrāb received them all hospitably, recognizing that Shāh Rāmīn was of royal blood, treating him like a younger brother and keeping him behind while Ṣāliḥ and the others resumed their journey by sea. They stopped to provision and water at an island inhabited by monstrous beings, and made their way to the ship pursued by these horrors. Off the next island they encountered Māh-Pervīn in a small boat, and took her aboard. On the return voyage to Sīmāb, an adverse wind blew the ship to Hind, where the king was named Kīmān Shāh. When they arrived there, the customs officials discovered Māh-Pervīn, and reported this to Kīmān Shāh at his capital 'Arqānūyah. He persisted in believing that she was a slave girl, fell in love with her, and Ṣāliḥ had to sell her to the king for 20,000 dinars. Jārūs, finding that the bird had flown, led an army toward Ghaznī in pursuit of Māh-Pervīn. On the way he met Ṣāliḥ's ship, and was told about her fate. Jārūs, of course, presented his own version of the incident with Māh-Pervīn in a favorable light. The ship sailed to Sīmāb where Jārūs met Shāh Rāmīn, begged his pardon, and was permitted to join him and his faithful friend Ṣuhrāb on the quest for Māh-Pervīn. When a certain Lūṭbā refused to help them and closed his gates against them, Jārūs reduced Lūṭbā's fortress Aqlāb in a brilliant feat of arms. Continuing their journey by sea, they put in at islands where creatures such as Hog-heads, Wild Men (a kind of demon or ghoul), and some monsters with eyes instead of heads on their shoulders and mouths on their breasts attacked them. When these androphages had put his army to flight, Shāh Rāmīn prayed, and God sent the Lion-Birds to his aid. The Divine Creator had vouchsafed them speech and had commanded them to fly from the island of Famgush. On their departure, they left him feathers, so that when faced with danger, Shāh Rāmīn should burn a small piece and the smell would bring them to the rescue.

The travelers next reached the vast city of 'Arqānūyah, standing in the middle of a plain, where Māh-Pervīn was being held by Kīmān Shāh. She had resisted his advances, threatening to commit suicide with a dagger. The king had tried to starve her into submission, so she had pretended to comply. Shāh Rāmīn had lodged with an old woman who went begging to the palace and contrived to make her way inside and tell Māh-Pervīn that Shāh Rāmīn was in the city. After an exchange of messages, the old woman proposed to smuggle Shāh Rāmīn into the palace disguised as her daughter. This plan was completely successful and the lovers were soon united. Both collapsed into each other's arms, insensible with emotion, and the old woman revived them with some water she found. Māh-Pervīn rewarded the old woman liberally and enjoined her to keep the secret that Shāh Rāmīn was inside dressed as a woman. His faithful companions were anxious at his absence, and decided to write a letter asking for the return of Māh-Pervīn, which Jārūs could take to Kīmān Shāh. On the way Jārūs intercepted two of Kīmān's spies, but he let them go and tell Kīmān about Shāh Rāmīn. Kīmān informed Jārūs that he was enraged at what he thought was Shāh Rāmīn's presumption, refused the request, and defied anyone to take Māh-Pervīn from him. She was, he said, a fitting mate for a king of India.

At this news, the combined forces of Jārūs and Ṣuhrāb moved on 'Arqānūyah. His friends thought that perhaps Shāh Rāmīn had gone mad with love and wandered into the mountains. The two armies faced one another, and the fighting began with a challenge to single combat made by an Indian champion mounted on a war-elephant to Ītgīn[3]. Like Rustam, Ītgīn felled the elephant with a blow on its forehead, and slew the Indian together with ten other Indian warriors who followed. Another paladin from India named Tārūy, a veritable Goliath, was overthrown and captured by Ītgīn. The army of Kīmān Shāh was routed, and retreated at nightfall. Although the captive Tārūy was interrogated, not without threats, he could say nothing of the whereabouts of Shāh Rāmīn, so Ṣuhrāb released him. A further defiant message came from Kīmān Shāh and was answered by Ṣuhrāb. Kīmān, having made his vizier Shuhūr read out the letter, decided to go to his private apartments. Māh-Pervīn, hearing the commotion, induced Shāh Rāmīn to put on his woman's dress at once. Kīmān told Māh-Pervīn how he had been to war over her, and that the question was now whether he should give her up. Feminine cunning prompted her to declare that a dream had made her fall in love with Kīmān. Why therefore should the king give her up? Unfortunately, Shāh Rāmīn in the guise of a slave girl so much attracted Kīmān that he desired the beautiful "girl," and Māh-Pervīn was obliged to relinquish "her" to be lodged among the royal concubines.

Next day the battle between the two armies was resumed, with an Indian champion named Pāpūr confronting a number of heroes, including Ītgīn, who captured him with the support of Yāghān, a Georgian slave of Ṣāliḥ the merchant. Both armies were now becoming concerned about their losses, and Kīmān asked for a respite which was granted by Ṣuhrāb and the others. A concubine of Kīmān named Gülchīn helped Māh-Pervīn and Shāh Rāmīn to escape, after administering a stupefying draught or philter to Kīmān, so that he became unconscious. Shāh Rāmīn soon made his way back to his followers. Kīmān quarreled with Pāpūr, who fled to Shāh Rāmīn pursued by Kīmān on an elephant. The Indian vizier ordered up troops to support their king, and a sharp fight took place between pro-Kīmān and pro-Pāpūr factions which enabled Shāh Rāmīn to win a victory. Shāh Rāmīn entered the palace of Kīmān dressed as a page, and served the king in this capacity, hearing everything going on. After an interlude raiding the city of Ṣinghūn, they reduced Kīmān's capital and Shāh Rāmīn sat upon Kīmān's throne. His first action was to order the release of Gülchīn's mother Sulṭān Bakht[4] from the prison into which Kīmān had cast her as a reprisal for her daughter's perfidy. Kīmān was imprisoned in a cistern after Shāh Rāmīn's companions had interceded for his life.

The next portion of the romance tells of the rebellion of the five brothers of Pāpūr against the authority of Shāh Rāmīn as sovereign of Hind. After some fighting and parleying, to which much space is devoted, the brothers became reconciled to the new ruler. During the absence of Shāh Rāmīn on campaign, Kīmān Shāh escaped from prison, having bribed Zengī, the guard placed over him. He had promised to grant anything Zengī desired. Kīmān ordered Zengī to take Māh-Pervīn away to his brother Jem who ruled in the city of

Dādyān, and from whom he required support. Māh-Pervīn, however, was able to elude Zengī when he went to recover his horse which had been stampeded by a lion. Kīmān was overpowered by Gülchīn, who followed Māh-Pervīn and eventually caught up with her. A Jew came wandering by, and saw Māh-Pervīn asleep by a spring. He fell deeply in love with her, but she ran off in such a panic that she soon found herself in thraldom to a repulsive witch named Gandūsah, who made Māh-Pervīn obey and serve her as apprentice through the power of magic. Both the Jew and Zengī trailed Māh-Pervīn to the witch's cave, and were changed into an ass and a bear, respectively. Eventually, Māh-Pervīn learned enough of the black art to turn the witch into a mule. She discovered behind the witch's cave a young prince Rūzbih, son of the ruler of Berber, who had fallen under the power of sorcery with his beloved Ḥüsn-i Qamer, a king's daughter. The Jinns had rescued her from the witch, but Rūzbih never saw her again, and was distressed. Both Rūzbih and Māh-Pervīn traveled on together, taking the metamorphosed Jew with them. When they reached the seashore, they met servants sent by the king of Berber to find Rūzbih. Māh-Pervīn was persuaded to go with them, and found Ḥüsn-i Qamer on a remote island.

Gülchīn, searching for Māh-Pervīn, came upon Demsāz, the young castellan of Qaylaya. She offered to undertake a mission to Bīdād, the ruler of Qirāṭ, with whom Demsāz was on bad terms, but her pretended role, as a present from Demsāz to Bīdād, was taken so seriously by Bīdād that she had to make him drunk, tie him up, and make her escape. All this was witnessed by Khujastah, the body-servant of Bīdād, who recognized Gülchīn as being of royal blood and aided her disappearance. It was possible for Demsāz to overcome Bīdād with the assistance of Khujastah, and to succeed him as ruler. Gülchīn sailed away with Demsāz, while she and Khujastah escaped from the hideous Black Pirates who had captured her by admitting Demsāz into the pirate stronghold.[5] Shāh Rāmīn released Kīmān Shāh from the cistern and learned that he had entrusted Māh-Pervīn to Zengī. The young prince wandered off alone in search of Māh-Pervīn, followed by his army.

The episode which follows introduces another paladin, Parr u bāl, son of the sultan of Khitāy, who told Shāh Rāmīn how he had heard from a dervish of a marvelous city seven miles in circumference, built by Shedīd, brother of Sheddād, one of the sons of ʿĀd. It contained an immense citadel guarded by four towers, each bearing a potent talisman consisting of a mounted figure carrying a weapon. With the help of the old man Akmā'īl, who had been associated with the Prophet Ilyās, Shāh Rāmīn and his troops entered the citadel. Although the main gate was locked, they found the key in the hand of yet another talisman in the form of an automaton mounted on an ox. When they took it away, the figures emitted a flood of water from their mouths, which almost overwhelmed them until it finally drained away into the moat. The wonders of this city of Dār ül-Bekām (the place of fulfilled desire) left them speechless. While wandering around, they were attacked by a monster with elephant's ears, tusks like a boar's, and a voice like thunder. This monster was overcome by the two Lion-Birds. In answer to his request, they flew Shāh Rāmīn, together with Akmā'īl and Parr u bāl, around the four automata. They read the riddles of these talismans, not without difficulty and contrivance, since all were provided with booby-traps. These four figures were all devised by Shedīd ibn 'Ād, whose tomb the three were able to visit. First they slew the demon 'Arṣūn, whose body came to life once more as soon as it was buried. The adventurers were then attacked by a further strange beast, the *'uqāb-i zehrnāk* (poison-eagle), which emerged from behind the tomb of Shedīd. It combined the characteristics of several animals, but had two rotary disks for wings. In the center of each was an eye surrounded by an immense ring spouting fire which dazzled the eye and tore human bodies asunder. After a bitter fight, Shāh Rāmīn was able to kill the brute with a well-aimed arrow, but at the cost of one of the Lion-Birds, which was besprinkled with the burning urine of the animal. More battles with monstrosities followed, and an encounter with a sorcerer named Ma'rkavūs, who held Shāh Rāmīn in captivity for a while.

In the meantime Ḥüsn-i Qamer, searching for Shāh Rāmīn, went off in one direction while Rūzbih and Māh-Pervīn went in another. It was hoped that she would join them with Shāh Rāmīn. Rūzbih and Māh-Pervīn made their way to the seashore, where they were captured by the Elephant-heads. At length, they broke out of the chamber in the palace in which they were confined, and released forty men and forty maidens whom they found imprisoned there. These sailed away with them and joined Ḥüsn-i Qamer at the rendezvous.

Gülchīn, Demsāz, and their supporters stayed for a time in the castle of the Black Pirates, but for diversion camped on the seashore. The usual Mer-folk came out led by the King of the Sea, including a band of ox-headed men who attacked them. An army of fairies led by their King Emlāḥ came to help Gülchīn and Demsāz, capturing the King of the Sea who was released, and returned to his uncharted depths. Later he came back with more half-animal, half-human creatures, and offered Gülchīn, Demsāz, and Emlāḥ costly gifts which they would not accept. After resting for several days, Gülchīn and Demsāz went on their way accompanied by Emlāḥ and his host of fairies. On their journey inland they found Māh-Pervīn and Rūzbih encamped by a spring and a joyful reunion took place.

Shāh Rāmīn remained in the power of the sorcerer until one night the Prophet Ilyās appeared to him in a dream, and taught him a prayer, by reciting which he would be safe from all harm including black magic. With his blessed hand, Ilyās freed Shāh Rāmīn from his bonds, and he overcame the sorcerer's spells and killed him. Finding a horse grazing, he rode off to join his friends. The same spell helped him to escape from the Lion-heads, and he smoked out the Half-Men from their lair. Kīmān Shāh managed to break out of prison and, meeting a stranger on his flight, killed him to preserve his own anonymity. He took the man's saddlebag, walking to the next village, as both his horses had been devoured by lions. Unfortunately for him, the saddlebag was soon recognized as the property of the murdered man, and Kīmān was arrested. He soon escaped from custody and fled. On his flight he joined some riders from Ghaznī going to Baghdad, bearing dispatches from the usurper Shehrūz, asking the ruler of Iraq to search for Shāh Rāmīn and Māh-Pervīn. When he arrived at Baghdad, Kīmān was befriended by Sarūyah, King of Iraq.

Eventually Ḥüsn-i Qamer found Shāh Rāmīn, and gave him news of Māh-Pervīn. By the aid of the Fairies, she conveyed him to the island of Khurremābād where Shāh Rāmīn and Māh-Pervīn sat in state on a golden throne with Rūzbih and Demsāz on the right hand, and Ḥüsn-i Qamer and Gülchīn on the left. A vast army, which comprised the Fairies and the hosts of the King of the Sea, was mustered to recover the throne at Ghaznī for Shāh Rāmīn, but it was decided first to deal with Sarūyah, who now supported with armed force the cause of Kīmān. While marching on Baghdad, Shāh Rāmīn intercepted a letter from Qabar[6] Khān, King of the Magians, to Sarūyah stating that his son Qayter[7] Khān was coming to marry Sarūyah's daughter, and promising him every possible support. Shāh Rāmīn entered Baghdad in disguise, and saw how Kīmān Shāh had become the evil genius of the Iraqi court. The letter written by Shāh Rāmīn, cautioning Sarūyah about the real character of Kīmān, only angered

Sarūyah and stirred him up against Shāh Rāmīn. When the army of Shāh Rāmīn and his companions drew up in array outside the city, a series of single combats between noted champions took place, while Shāh Rāmīn passed in and out of the enemy camp in disguise. He became an agent in the service of Sarūyah, and in this capacity was sent to Qabar Khān, to whom he revealed his true identity. The king of Iraq had a chamberlain named Ṭahmās with a brother called Pesheng. These two advised Sarūyah to send his daughter Semenzār for safety to Hamadan, where there was a strong castle, and this was done forthwith. More fighting took place, in which the supernatural auxiliaries such as the Fairies and Mer-folk played an important part, and rolled back the Iraqis. Kīmān urged Sarūyah to continue the battle, and Kīmān penetrated Shāh Rāmīn's camp in disguise. He also wrote to Shehrūz at Ghaznī, informing him about the situation. Here there is a break in the narrative, owing to the loss of a few folios, but it seems clear that Shāh Rāmīn had made his way to Semenzār at Hamadan, and had planned her escape to Qayter Khān. The princess drugged Shāh Rāmīn and packed him into a chest to be taken back to Baghdad by Ṭahmās. In the course of the journey, Ṭahmās fell asleep by a stream, and both his horse and camel, as well as his chests, fell into the hands of a robber named 'Ujāf. Ṭahmās, awakening, finding that everything had gone, made his way off on foot and ran into Shāh Rāmīn and 'Ujāf. Shāh Rāmīn returned to Hamadan, and Semenzār was drugged and conveyed in a chest to Qabar Khān, who had now summoned his son Qayter. When they heard that Semenzār had gone, Kīmān offered to recover her for Sarūyah, who in gratitude promised Kīmān her hand. The vizier of Iraq, however, strongly advised his master against giving his daughter to Kīmān, since the latter was thoroughly unscrupulous and might one day dethrone Sarūyah.

Kīmān and Shāh Rāmīn began to intrigue against each other in the Iraqi camp, both in disguise. Shāh Rāmīn on his return to his own lines encountered Kīmān engaged in espionage, and soon detected that he was an Indian, guessing his true identity. He was able to capture him by guile, pretending that he himself was an enemy to Shāh Rāmīn. Sarūyah was filled with fury when he heard of this, and vowed to release Kīmān and recover his daughter. He set the Iraqi army in motion, but to forestall any attempt at rescue, Shāh Rāmīn erected a gallows and hanged Kīmān Shāh in the ground between the two armies. The arrival of Qayter Khān with the Magian army ended the fighting. Sarūyah Shāh took counsel with his minister Fakhr-i Dānā who advised him to make peace with Shāh Rāmīn, and thus the two were reconciled. Gifts were exchanged between them, and with the death of Kīmān, there was now no obstacle to the marriage of Semenzār and Qayter Khān. At Baghdad, Shāh Rāmīn found the jailer who had released him from prison at Ghaznī and had then fled to Iraq for safety. He and his wife, once Māh-Pervīn's nurse, were liberally rewarded.

After this, the vassals of Shāh Rāmīn clamored for action against Shehrūz, so the entire army marched toward Zāvulistān, resting for several days by the Hirmand (Helmand) River. Here they found the army of Shehrūz encamped on the river bank. An attempt made by Shāh Rāmīn to call Shehrūz to order, by means of a letter carried by Jārūs, ended in complete failure. In the ensuing battle, Shehrūz was worsted, and retreated. Several single combats took place between renowned champions, and Sarūyah brought up the Iraqi army to support Shāh Rāmīn. The veteran warrior Merd-efkan was captured by Shāh Rāmīn and then offered to go and parley with Shehrūz, asking him to resume his office as vizier and accept Shāh Rāmīn as his rightful sovereign. An example had already been made of three captured Zāvulī notables who had abused Shāh Rāmīn to his face, even though he had spared their lives; and it was hoped that the hangings, witnessed by the relatives of the condemned, would provide a valuable lesson of the price of rebellion. Shehrūz, enraged, spurned this advice to submit, and threatened to kill Merd-efkan who fought his way out. After being rescued by a timely sortie led by Shāh Rāmīn himself, Merd-efkan, with his army of five thousand men, abandoned the cause of Shehrūz, and persuaded his brother Shīr-efkan to do the same. Together they made an early dawn attack on Shehrūz, whose army was dwindling every day through desertions to Shāh Rāmīn. The newcomers were treated with consideration, and forbearance was shown to them after they had changed sides.

After a few days of rest, it was decided to move on the Zāvul region to settle conclusions with Shehrūz, now preparing to withstand a siege of the city of Zāvul,[8] reinforced with contingents from as far afield as Sīstān and Kūhistān. Many of his followers were now unwilling to serve a usurper, and advised Shehrūz to make terms with Shāh Rāmīn. He would not be moved, and tried to ambush Shāh Rāmīn in a mountain defile. There is here another lacuna in the text, and next we read of panic among the retainers of Shehrūz on the approach of the loyalist forces under Shāh Rāmīn to invest the city. The besiegers wasted a month in fruitless atacks, but one day an arrow brought a message from Māh-Pervīn's old nurse, now in the city, offering to open the Kūhistān Gate. This she arranged, but Shehrūz heard what was afoot, and looked over the ramparts to see the battle going against him. After this comes a considerable break in the narrative, and there is only half of a double-page miniature, the missing part of which must show the vizier looking down on the attackers and preparing to repel them. Shehrūz hid in a disused oven awaiting a suitable moment to slip away in the confusion following the fall of the city to Shāh Rāmīn. There he was safe, until it was decided to use the oven in preparations for a feast, and then he was caught and imprisoned. Shāh Rāmīn at last sat upon his father's throne in state surrounded by his paladins. His wedding to Māh-Pervīn took place in the spring, attended by Bihrūz Shāh of Berber and his son Rūzbih, who was married at the same time to Ḥüsn-i Qamer. The hand of Gülchīn was bestowed on Jārūs, and the nuptials of Semenzār and Qayter Khān were also celebrated. While all were rejoicing, Shehrūz escaped from confinement, killed his guards, and made his way to the Oxus. Shāh Rāmīn sent a force to bring him in, but they could not find him until the surviving Lion-Bird suddenly appeared, and told them where Shehrūz was to be found. By the time they arrived, Shehrūz had discovered a boat, and was making his way across the river. He paid no heed when they called on him to return, promising that no harm would befall him, so some of Shāh Rāmīn's followers made rafts and tried to overtake him. Rather than surrender, Shehrūz jumped into the water and perished. The slaves recovered his body, and Māh-Pervīn ordered that it should receive decent burial. Shāh Rāmīn and Māh-Pervīn lived happily ever after with their two sons and two daughters.

It will be seen that much of the material is familiar from such romances as the *Dārābnāmah*, where one encounters the episode of the woman locked up in a chest and cast into the sea, as well as in the Persian prose *Iskandarnāmah* and the *Tale of Shahryār and Shāh Zamān*, to quote only one example. What distinguishes the *Tuḥfet ül-leṭā'if* from other works in this category is the impression of refinement it leaves. This is because it was certainly written for reading aloud in the Palace, and the author reveals himself here and there as something of a courtier. Despite the stereotyped clichés and situations, its very artlessness lends the romance a charm of its own, with its heroes larger than life, its underlying sense of justice, and strong religious feeling; and even in its imperfect state, the terse and vivid style of some parts of the narrative, with a wealth of archaic vocabulary and phraseology, make the *Tuhfet ül-leṭā'if* well worth further investigation, whether we are dealing with an adaptation of a Persian or an original Turkish tale.

In conclusion I should like to express my thanks to Prince Sadruddin Aga Khan for allowing me to study his manuscript.

NOTES

1. A further study of the miniatures is in preparation. They are remarkable for their minute attention to details of dress and architecture, and are related to those in the following manuscripts: The prose romance *Qiṣṣah-ı Ferrukhrūz* and the *Shāhnāmah* translation (respectively Or. 3298 and Or. 7204 in the British Library), as well as a *Shāhnāmah* version in the collection of Edwin Binney III, who also possesses a detached double-page illustration from this identical copy belonging to Prince Sadruddin, depicting Shehrūz in flight to the city of Zāvul. (See *Turkish Treaures from the Collection of Edwin Binney, 3rd* [Portland, 1979], pp. 78–79, and *Turkish Miniature Paintings and Manuscripts* [Los Angeles, 1973], p. 58.) There is also a close connection with the large bold illustrations of the *Siyer ül-Nebi* in the Spencer Collection at New York. (See Ernst J. Grube, "The *Siyar-i Nabī* of the Spencer Collection in the New York Public Library," in *Atti del Secondo Congresso Internazionale di Arte Turca* [Naples, 1965], pp. 149–76.)

2. Neither of the two poets recorded as bearing this name can be identified with the author of the romance in point of date.

3. With the meaning of "host" or "master of the house," but perhaps this is a Turkish name to be read as "Etkin" ("Ay-tegin"?).

4. Or Bakht-i Sulṭān in another context. She was the daughter of the king of Khwārizm.

5. Called Ākhirjān or Āghirjān.

6. Perhaps to be read as Quber (lark).

7. Possibly from Qaydhār.

8. In the latter half of the romance, the city of Ghaznī is always referred to as Zāvul.

37

On Suleiman's *Sabīls* in Jerusalem

Myriam Rosen-Ayalon

THE OTTOMAN IMPACT on the architecture of Jerusalem can be ascribed to a great extent to the reign of a single sultan, Suleiman the Magnificent. Three major chapters in the history of the architecture of Jerusalem during this period can be discerned: the restoration of the exterior of the Dome of the Rock; the rebuilding of the city walls and gates; and the construction of several public water fountains (*sabīls*) scattered about the city.[1] Of these three ensembles, only the series of *sabīls* seems to have been an original initiative, and not merely a restoration of existing monuments.

The *sabīls* provide the basis for this preliminary study. Actually, these public water fountains were an integral part of a much larger project undertaken in the days of Suleiman: the restoration and expansion of the entire water supply system for the city. The literary sources reveal much in great detail, but here we shall concentrate on the analysis of the *sabīls* alone.[2] The subject of our study thus comprises a group of six *sabīls* erected within a few months of each other (29 June 1536 to 13 February 1537), in various parts of Jerusalem (fig. 37.1).[3]

A pioneering study of these monuments, largely concerning the related problem of water supply to Jerusalem in medieval times, up to the Ottoman period, was carried out by Max van Berchem.[4] In his study, van Berchem even laid the groundwork for the study of the architecture of these *sabīls*: the present contribution, however, goes somewhat farther, providing plans and measurements of these monuments—data so far not published—and seeks the specific artistic and architectural formula of these structures.

It thus becomes evident—as van Berchem believed—that all six

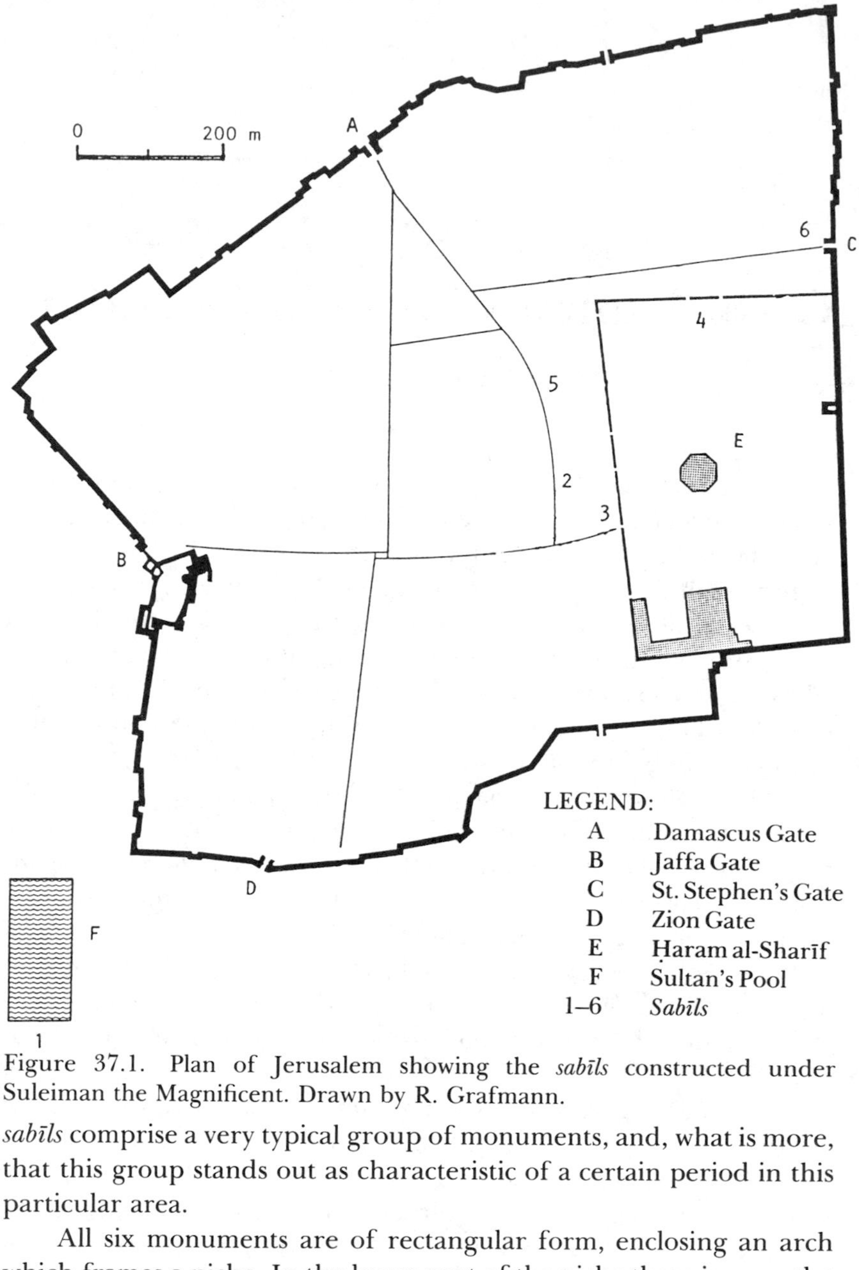

Figure 37.1. Plan of Jerusalem showing the *sabīls* constructed under Suleiman the Magnificent. Drawn by R. Grafmann.

sabīls comprise a very typical group of monuments, and, what is more, that this group stands out as characteristic of a certain period in this particular area.

All six monuments are of rectangular form, enclosing an arch which frames a niche. In the lower part of the niche there is an outlet (no longer operative in any of the six fountains), the water having flowed into a trough at the bottom of the niche. Each monument differs slightly in size and details of decoration, despite the fact that all of them are built on a generally uniform pattern.

In proceeding with our study, we shall follow their chronological order, as successfully established by van Berchem, briefly repeating parts of his description where necessary. *Sabīl* No. 1 (figs. 37.2, 37.3) stands on the road to Bethlehem, just beyond the city walls. It measures 3.62 m wide, with a niche 1.86 m wide and sunk to a depth of 0.71 m. The flanking pillars are 0.88 m wide each. As we shall see, this width of the flanking pillars repeats itself in several of the *sabīls*.

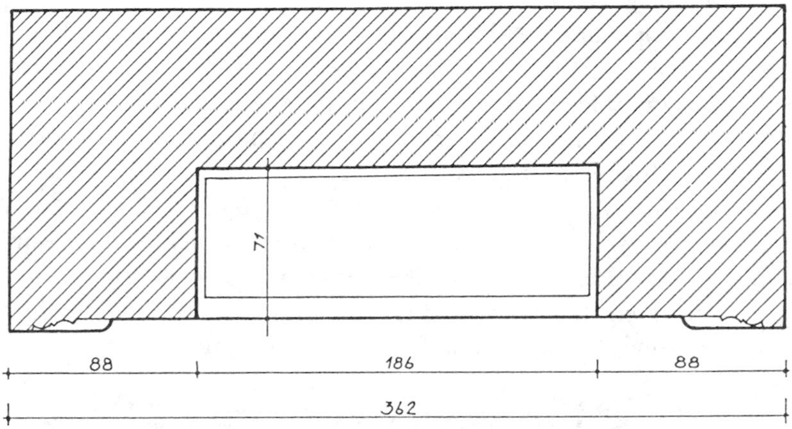

Figure 37.2. Plan of *Sabīl* No. 1. Drawn by G. Solar.

Figure 37.3. *Sabīl* No. 1. Photo: Garo.

An inscribed slab of marble, set at the center of the niche, gives the date of 10 Muḥarram 943 (29 June 1536).[5]

All three edges of the *sabīl* facade have a molding described by van Berchem as "composée d'une gorge et d'un boudin séparés par un filet."[6] The pointed arch of the niche is lined by a zig-zag "ribbon" arch, enclosing a remarkable series of stalactite niches, emphasized by a dome-shaped central niche within the vault. There is a flat, decorative disc or medallion spandrel flanking the arch.

The proportions of this *sabīl* are today somewhat misleading, for the roadway is at a considerably higher level than in the days of Suleiman, or indeed even in the mid-nineteenth century. Van Berchem already comments on the change of the road level, and when comparing his photograph with our Fig. 37.3, a considerable difference can clearly be seen.[7] A photograph taken in 1856 by Auguste Salzmann shows three features, now hidden, which also appear on some of our other *sabīls*: a small shallow niche for the water outlet; a trough to catch the water; and an "inverted volute" terminating the lower molding on each of the flanking pillars (fig. 37.4).[8]

Figure 37.4. *Sabīl* No. 1, as it was in 1856.
Photo: Auguste Salzmann.

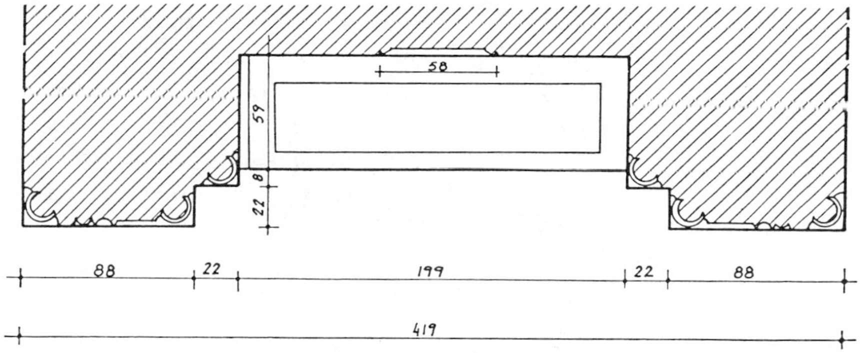

Figure 37.5. Plan of *Sabīl* No. 2. Drawn by G. Solar.

Figure 37.6. *Sabīl* No. 2. Photo: Garo.

Sabīl No. 2 (figs. 37.5, 37.6) is situated on al-Wād Street, somewhat south of the entrance to Sūq al-qaṭṭānīn. Its facade is 4.9 m wide, considerably larger than that of *Sabīl* No. 1; the flanking pillars are each also 0.88 m wide, with an additional inner molding on each side 0.22 m wide, framing the actual niche. The niche is 1.99 m wide and 0.59 m deep. Here the small, shallow niche in the lower part, with the outlet, can clearly be seen, with its peculiar patterned arch, crowned by a square prolongation at the top.

The inscription is dated less than half a year later than that of Sabīl No. 1: 1 Rajab 943 (14 December 1536).[9]

The decoration generally resembles that of *Sabīl* No. 1, though it is not identical. At either side, the pointed arch bends out horizontally, forming a sort of "label-stop." Further, this outer arch encloses two additional arches resting on slender columns, which are crowned by capitals, and which stand on pedestals. The series of stalactite niches is surmounted here by a scalloped half-rosette motif. In the flanking spandrels are raised triangles, which had originally contained rosette medallion insets. One of the latter can still be seen in van Berchem's photograph (fig. 37.7).[10] Three similar roundels had been set into the stalactite motif, but only one is extant. (A large roundel of this sort is set above the *sabīl*, against a background of carved floral motifs.) On either flanking pillar there is a molding running down the middle, terminating below in an inverted volute. At the outer edge of each flanking pillar is a pair of slender columns, one set above the other, with a cornice between them (a continuation of the cornice of the arches). Atop the entire frame is a billet molding.

Sabīl No. 3 (figs. 37.8, 37.9) faces the entrance of Bāb al-silsila onto the Ḥaram al-sharīf. It is 3.86 m wide, of which the niche is 2.36 m wide and 0.62 m deep. The small, shallow niche for the water outlet is identical in pattern and size (0.55 m wide) with that of *Sabīl* No. 2.[11]

The inscribed slab reveals that the construction of this *sabīl* terminated exactly three weeks after the date of *Sabīl* No. 2: 22 Rajab 943 (4 January 1537).[12]

The pointed arch framing the inner zig-zag arch is very similar to that of *Sabīl* No. 1. However, instead of the stalactite niches of *Sabīls* Nos. 1 and 2, a beautifully carved rosette fills the upper part of the niche. In the spandrels are triangles of carved stone. The restored roundels under either end of the arch, as seen in Fig. 37.9, replace round medallions, one of which can be seen in the old photograph. The other one was clearly missing even in earlier photographs.[13]

Figure 37.7. *Sabīl* No. 2, as it was in 1923. Photo from Max van Berchem, *Matériaux pour un Corpus Inscriptionum Arabicarum* (Cairo, 1923).

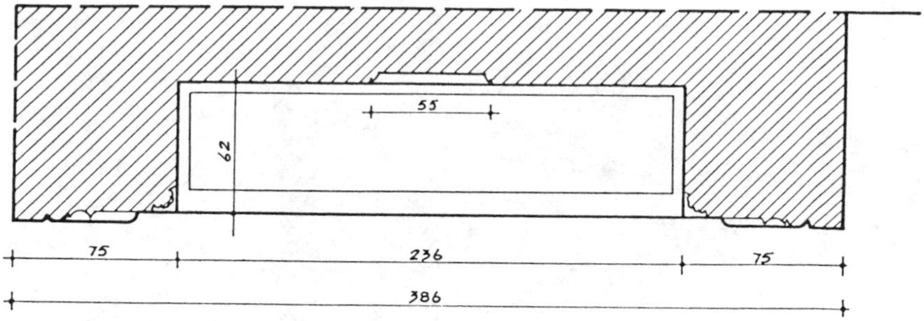

Figure 37.8. Plan of *Sabīl* No. 3. Drawn by G. Solar.

Figure 37.9. *Sabīl* No. 3. Photo: Garo.

The original roundels here may well have matched the small carved rosette at the peak of the arch. (The restored roundels bear modern *waqf* inscriptions.) Here again, as on *Sabīl* No. 2, the molding on the flanking pillars terminates below in an inverted volute, while the uppermost molding is again of billet pattern.

Another interesting feature which can be seen here is the clustered columns, plaited at the middle, flanking the niche and crowned by capitals, repeated higher within the niche, somewhat reminiscent of the stalactite niche motif. The trough is an ancient sarcophagus, as was the erstwhile trough of *Sabīl* No. 2, visible on early photographs.

Sabīl No. 4 (figs. 37.10, 37.11) is the only one of the group built within the Ḥaram, at its northern edge. It is also the largest of the group, 4.94 m wide, with a niche 2.78 m wide and 1.34 m deep.[14]

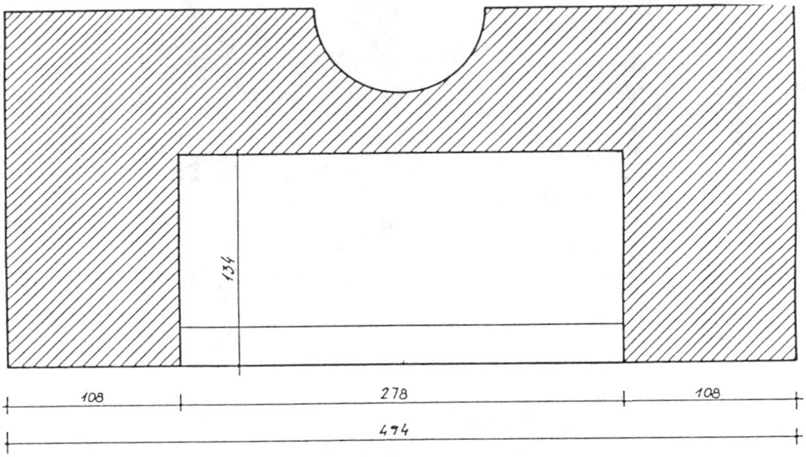

Figure 37.10. Plan of *Sabīl* No. 4. Drawn by G. Solar.

The inscription gives the date, a few days later than that of *Sabīl* No. 3, early in Sha'bān 943 (mid-January 1537).[15]

Here again there is a pointed arch framing a zig-zag band, as on *Sabīls* Nos. 1 and 3. In the spandrels, flat triangles resemble those of *Sabīls* Nos. 2 and 3, but are plain. Within the niche are small stalactite niches, as in *Sabīls* Nos. 1 and 2 (though slightly different). Two further features here are characteristic of the entire architectural group: the molding on the flanking pillars, terminating below in inverted volutes; and the clustered columns flanking the niche, plaited at the middle, as on *Sabīl* No. 3.

Figure 37.11. *Sabīl* No. 4. Photo: Garo.

The small, shallow niche in the lower part of the main niche resembles those in *Sabīls* Nos. 1–3. At the bottom there is a trough.

Sabīl No. 5 (figs. 37.12, 37.13) is located at the corner of al-Wād Street and 'Alā' al-Dīn Street, which leads to the Ḥaram through Bāb al-naẓīr. This is the smallest of the six *sabīls,* with a total width of 3.55 m; the side pillars measure 0.87 m wide, very close to the 0.88 m of *Sabīls* Nos. 1 and 2 (and 6, as we shall see below). The shallow niche here also resembles most of the others (0.56 m wide).

The inscribed slab gives a date of completion less than a month after that of *Sabīl* No. 4: 2 Ramaḍān 943 (12 February 1537).[16]

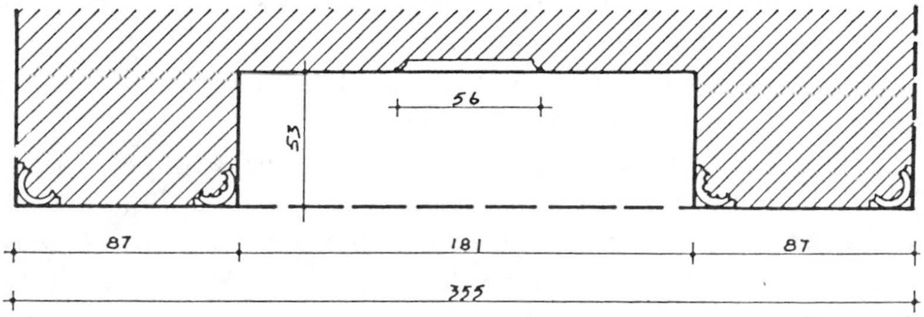

Figure 37.12. Plan of *Sabīl* No. 5. Drawn by G. Solar.

The main arch frames a double series of carved arches. At the center is a carved rosette. At both ends are round columns, as can be seen on the drawing of the plan (fig. 37.12). In the spandrels

Figure 37.13. *Sabīl* No. 5. Photo: Garo.

are flat triangles, and clustered, plaited columns flank the niche. Atop is a billet molding, once again. Though the small, shallow niche is now seen at street level, it is clear that the street used to be much lower, as can be seen in earlier photographs.[17]

Sabīl No. 6 (figs. 37.14, 37.15) is located just within St. Stephen's Gate. The poorest preserved of all the *sabīls*, its total width is 3.73 m; the side pillars measure 0.88 m wide, as on *Sabīls* No. 1 and 3 (and close to the 0.87 m width on *Sabīl* No. 5). The main niche is 0.52 m deep; the small, shallow niche, recently exposed, is 0.59 m wide. This is the only one of the *sabīls* lacking its original inscription, which was missing already at the beginning of this century.[18] On an old photograph, one can also see a trough, now missing.[19] Despite these missing features, in all probability this *sabīl* does belong to our group, from the days of Suleiman, as has already been convincingly argued by van Berchem.[20]

In the spandrels, there used to be flat triangles, as can be seen in old photographs, similar to those of *Sabīls* Nos. 4 and 5. The molding framing the niche here, terminating below in inverted volutes, is also similar to that seen on other of our *sabīls* (e.g., Nos. 3 and 4).

Of these six *sabīls*, at least three have some older element or elements incorporated into their fabric, in secondary use; these elements are probably Crusader in origin (though the troughs/sarcophagi may, of course, be older). Thus, in *Sabīl* No. 2 the inner arches and the two pairs of columns on which they rest; in *Sabīl* No. 3 the main rosette and the two carved triangles in the spandrels; and in *Sabīl* No. 5, the inner series of floral arches and the pair of clustered columns, plaited in their middle, together with their capitals (the central rosette is seemingly medieval Islamic). All of these reused elements are what van Berchem has termed "Latin."[21] But the question remains: what was the actual tradition of these Crusader carvings?[22]

These "borrowed" fragments, which were well integrated within the *sabīls*, do not basically alter the architectural formula of this group. Thus, of the six *sabīls*, the one containing the most characteristic elements seems to be *Sabīl* No. 4, the one on the Ḥaram—and it is this one which we can consider as the exemplar of this episode of Ottoman architecture.

A most interesting feature of this group of *sabīls* is that almost all of the elements contributing to its scheme can be traced back to traditions in this region prior to the Ottoman period. The main motif of the zig-zag arch (as on *Sabīls* Nos. 1, 3, and 4) can be seen in many

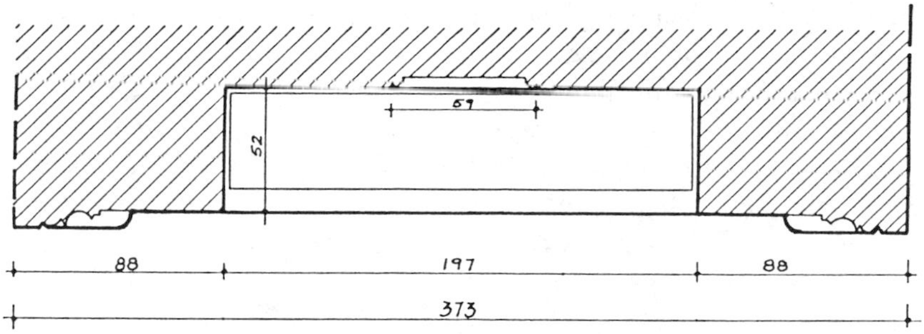

Figure 37.14. Plan of *Sabīl* No. 6. Drawn by G. Solar.

Figure 37.15. *Sabīl* No. 6. Photo: Garo.

Mamlūk buildings in Syro-Palestine,[23] and doubtless a long tradition could be traced for this element. The concept of two medallions in the spandrels flanking the main arch (*Sabīls* Nos. 1 and 2, and, to some extent, No. 3) is a very traditional pattern for Islamic gates (e.g., Bāb al-naṣr in Cairo, and later, in North Africa, the gates of Marrakesh, al-Manṣūra, and others), and very commonly, for *miḥrābs* throughout the Islamic world in various periods.[24]

The very concept of stalactite niches filling the area within or beneath an arch or vault, as on *Sabīls* Nos. 1, 2, and 4, is a basic feature of Mamlūk architecture. Again, it would be pointless to enumerate the many examples scattered throughout Syria, Palestine, and Egypt. Among the varied examples, however, a resemblance can be traced even in such a detail as the small, flat arches seen in the lower row of stalactites in *Sabīl* No. 1, in the very similar decoration in Jāmiʿ al-ʿAṭṭār in Tripoli.[25]

Similarly, *Sabīl* No. 2 offers a comparison with another detail of Mamlūk architecture. Above the stalactite niche motif there is a half rosette, a combination closely resembling that in the doorway vault of the Mausoleum of Sitt Tunshuq in Jerusalem, as well as in the *miḥrāb* of the Madrasa Muẓahirīya.[26]

One of the most frequently repeated elements of decoration in most of our *sabīls* of this group (Nos. 2, 3, 4, and 6; and most probably also originally in No. 1) is the molding framing the *sabīl* and terminating below in an inverted volute. Mamlūk architecture again provides a source for this motif, in Jerusalem itself: in the doorway of the mausoleum of the Tashtamurīya, where the inverted volute creates a space for a lovely glazed ceramic inlay (fig. 37.16).[27]

Concerning the upper billet molding, which can be seen on *Sabīls* Nos. 2, 3, and 5, van Berchem suggested that it was a reused Crusader element,[28] which though the motif could be traced to Crusader origins (as seen, e.g., similarly on St. John's baptistery in Byblos, among many other examples[29]), was used afterward in various buildings in the city.[30]

One of the most interesting motifs among those connected with our *sabīls* is surely the clustered, plaited columns flanking the main niches, as on *Sabīls* Nos. 3, 4, and 5. This seems to be a case of local interpretation of an earlier architectural motif. Indeed, Jerusalem has preserved a considerable number of Crusader twisted or plaited columns in secondary use (e.g., fig. 37.17). Such elements can be seen in various Islamic monuments in Jerusalem;[31] and they can be considered as having inspired this new version, decorating Suleiman's *sabīls*

Figure 37.16. Detail of the mausoleum of the Tashtamurīya, showing the inverted volute with ceramic inlay. Photo Garo.

in the city; all the more since such a pair of a reused cluster of columns does, in fact, decorate our *Sabīl* No. 5.

Finally, it is interesting to note that this particular feature present in all six *sabīls*—namely, the shallow niche at the bottom—is precisely a Turkish motif. Indeed, this type of profile of the arch can be seen on a number of Turkish monuments.[32]

This brief survey indicates that the six *sabīls* dating to the days of Suleiman display characteristics which bind them into a single type of monument, despite their diversity in details. Furthermore, they

Figure 37.17. Facade of the Nahawīya, showing Crusader plaited columns in secondary use. Photo: Z. Radovan.

seem to belong to a distinct type of *sabīl* apparently not found in other periods or at other places.

In Jerusalem itself, the earlier *sabīls* (of the Ayyubid and Mamlūk periods) are of distinct, different types.[33] Thus, at the beginning of the Ottoman period we find this new type of *sabīl* in Jerusalem which differs not only from pre-Ottoman *sabīls*, but also from contemporaneous *sabīls* elsewhere, as well.

In Cairo, the published Ottoman *sabīls* are described as *Sebil-Kuttab*, of typical Ottoman-Egyptian style.[34] This is a completely different type of structure, often two-storied. In Syria, published *sabīls* also illustrate something quite different:[35] in Aleppo, we find a *sabīl* which has been dated to the days of Suleiman, for there does not seem to exist sufficient information on its style.[36]

Even if we turn to the very center of Ottoman architecture, Turkey itself, we find that none of the several types of *sabīls* which present themselves, ranging over various periods, resembles the group distinguished in Jerusalem.[37]

Here, in these very *sabīls* in Jerusalem, we have the beginnings of research on a subject which has so far not enjoyed the systematic study it deserves.[38] The prerequisite of preexisting available Crusader elements, in combination with earlier Crusader and Mamlūk architectural traditions, apparently did not exist in Turkey, Egypt, or Syria in the same way, and we may conclude that this is one of the interesting local chapters in Islamic architecture, illustrating a little-known aspect of Mamlūk influence on Ottoman architecture in Jerusalem as interpreted under Suleiman the Magnificent.[39]

NOTES

1. On public works in Jerusalem during the Ottoman period, see Amnon Cohen, "Local Trade, International Trade and Government Involvement in Jerusalem During the Early Ottoman Period," *Asian and African Studies*, XII (March 1978), pp. 5–12.

2. An interesting study [in Hebrew] has recently been made by an advanced student at the Hebrew University of Jerusalem, I. Salama; I wish to thank him for allowing me to peruse it.

3. Max van Berchem, *Matériaux pour un Corpus Inscriptionum Arabicarum*, Jérusalem, "Ville" (Cairo, 1923) [henceforth *CIA*], pp. 413–17. There may have been three further *sabīls* built in the early Ottoman period which are lost today, see Amnon Cohen, op. cit., pp. 6–7.

4. *CIA*, pp. 418–27.

5. *CIA*, p. 413.

6. *CIA*, p. 423.

7. *CIA*, p. 423, and Pl. XCII, No. 110.

8. Ely Schiller, ed., *The First Photographs of Jerusalem* (Jerusalem, 1978), p. 197.

9. *CIA*, p. 414.

10. *CIA*, Pl. XCIV, No. 111.

11. This part, again recently exposed, cannot be seen on the early twentieth-century photograph, as in *CIA*, Pl. XCII, No. 112.

12. *CIA*, p. 415.

13. *CIA*, Pl. XCII, No. 112.

14. On its back is a *miḥrāb*. A special study on *miḥrābs* on the Temple Mount is in preparation by the author of this article.

15. *CIA*, p. 416.

16. *CIA*, p. 417.

17. *CIA*, Pl. XCV, No. 114.

18. *CIA*, Pl. XCVI, No. 113.

19. Ibid.

20. *CIA*, pp. 417–18.

21. *CIA*, pp. 424–25.

22. Helmut Buchhausen, *Die Süditalienische Bauplastik im Königreich Jerusalem* (Vienna, 1978), attributing all the material discussed to the south of Italy. Surprisingly, this very rich collection of reused Crusader elements overlooks the arches, columns, and capitals of our *Sabīl* No. 2. Against this view, see Zehava Jacoby, "The Workshop of the Temple Area in Jerusalem in the Twelfth Century: Its Origin, Evolution and Impact," in *Zeitschrift für Kunstgeschichte* XLV (1982), pp. 325–94; and more recently, by the same author, the book review of Buchhausen, in *Zeitschrift für Kunstgeschichte*, III (1984), pp. 400–403.

23. There is little point in listing the various monuments which use this motif, as can be found in *CIA*, p. 425.

24. K. A. C. Creswell, *Muslim Architecture in Egypt* (Oxford, 1959), fig. 119; idem, *Early Muslim Architecture* (Oxford, 1969), I, fig. 374, to name a few.

25. Hayat Salam-Liebich, *The Architecture of the Mamluk City of Tripoli* (Cambridge, Mass., 1983), fig. 60.

26. M. H. Burgoyne, "Some Mameluke Doorways in the Old City of Jerusalem," *Levant*, III (1971), Pl. XIV, a; idem, "A Mamluke Street in the Old City of Jerusalem," *Levant* V (1973), Pl. XXIV, B. It is amusing to note that Salam-Liebich compares this element on our *Sabīl* No. 3 with the same feature in the Mamlūk Madrasa Qādirīya in Tripoli—but uses a false argument. There, the *sabīl* is attributed to Qāyet Bāy, and dated to 1455! The comparison per se is, of course, valid—but rather again, illustrates the Mamlūk impact on the architecture of our Ottoman *sabīls*.

27. Salam-Liebich, op. cit., p. 166, figs. 150, 151.

28. *CIA*, p. 425.

29. Salam-Liebich, op. cit., fig. 193.

30. Indeed, this motif can be seen on a Mamlūk wall: Burgoyne, "A Mamluke Street," Pl. XXI, a.

31. Buchhausen, op. cit., figs. 75, 77, 81, 90, 113, 115, 119, 120, are among the most obvious examples.

32. Sedad Hakki Eldem, *Works of Turkish Architecture* (Istanbul), Plates 142, 290, 291, 289.

33. *CIA*, Pl. LXI, No. 164, the Ayyubid *sabīl* Sha'lān, and Pl. LXXXVII, No. 188, the Mamlūk *sabīl* of Qāyet Bāy.

34. *CIA*, *Egypte*, pp. 611–12.

35. See Sabīl 'ayn al-tinah, in Tripoli from the Mamlūk period, Salam-Liebich, op. cit., fig. 182.

36. Unfortunately, there is no photograph of this Aleppo *sabīl*, but only a reference: Ernst Herzfeld, *CIA*, *Syrie du Nord, Inscriptions et monuments d'Alep* (Cairo, 1955), p. 43. However, there are some *sabīls* in Aleppo from the Mamlūk period which seem to contain architectural features which may be considered forerunners of our *sabīls*, Herzfeld, *CIA*, pp. 396–97, Pl. CLXVIII, and maybe more so, Pl. CLXV, b.

37. For the diversity of Ottoman *sabīls* in Turkey, see Albert Gabriel, *Une Capitale turque Brousse Bursa* (Paris, 1958), pp. 197–99, Plates XCI, 1–4; XCII, 1–6. Oktay Aslanapa, *Turkish Art and Architecture* (London, 1971), pp. 257–59 and Pl. 204.

38. In the article "Sabīl" in *EI*[1], there is no reference whatsoever to the architecture of these monuments.

39. Another interesting analysis will illustrate the many features discussed in this group of *sabīls* that are relevant to the study of the contemporaneous Gates of Jerusalem.

38
Zur Wiederempfindung der osmanischen Reimprosa

Andreas Tietze

ÜBER REIM an sich ist viel gedacht und geschrieben worden. Dass er mehr ist als Schnörkel, äusserliches Beiwerk, ästhetische Spielerei mit höchstens mnemotechnischer Funktion, ist uns längst klar geworden. Wie die Symmetrie in der Architektur zum Beispiel, hat auch er Aussagewert. Der Reim drückt der Aussage den Stempel der Endgültigkeit auf.

Schon in der vorislamischen Periode kannte die türkische Literatur den rhythmischen Aufbau der Rede, deren Unterteilung durch den Parallelismus der grammatischen Formen festes Gefüge und auch schon Reimklang erhielt. An dem islamischen—das heisst persischen—Vorbild lernte man dann ein wohlausgebildetes System kennen, dem nachzueifern man sich bemühte, das einzuholen aber lange Zeit als ein unerreichbar fernes Ziel erscheinen musste.

Nicht nur in der Poesie, auch in der Prosa haben Reim und Rhythmus ihre Funktion, auch sie kann "Dichtung" sein. Für uns ist diese Form der "Dichtung" heute schwer verständlich. Unser Begriff der Prosa ist funktionell. In allem, was nicht zur Aussage selbst gehört, was nur "Verzierung," nur Beiwerk ist, sehen wir eine Abschweifung vom Thema, ein überflüssiges, retardierendes, ja störendes Element.

Ohne ein Verständnis für die Reimprosa aufzubringen, können wir dieser Kunstform der klassischen osmanischen Literatur nicht gerecht werden; sie muss uns dann schwülstig, gekünstelt, verspielt vorkommen. Ausserdem werden wir sie verwirrend finden und Mühe haben, aus dem Wortgestrüpp den Sinn herauszuschälen.

Um dem abzuhelfen, habe ich in meinen Publikationen der letzten

Jahre verschiedene Versuche gemacht, die Feinheiten der osmanischen Kunstprosa dem Verständnis des Lesers näherzubringen. Meine anfänglichen Bemühungen, alle Komponenten der Kunstprosa durch graphische Mittel anschaulich zu machen, gab ich aber bald auf und beschränkte mich auf die Anschaulichmachung der Reimprosa als ihres wichtigsten Elementes. Mein Ziel war dabei ein zweifaches: erstens sollte auf diese Weise ein wichtiges stilistisch-ästhetisches Element dem Leser vor Augen geführt werden, und zweitens sollte ihm das Verständnis der stets langen Perioden durch die Sichtbarmachung der sie aufbauenden, parallel angeordneten Elemente erleichtert werden. Anders als im Gedicht der klassischen Periode sind nämlich die reimenden Teile der Prosa syntaktische Parallelismen. Die Auflösung einer längeren Periode in ihre reimenden Komponenten erleichtert daher dem Leser die Übersicht über die gesamte Satzstruktur.

Dies mag hier an einem Beispiel gezeigt werden. In einem Sammelwerk (UCLA Research Library, Special Collections 898 T 19) findet sich der hier folgende Brief des Dichters Nevʿī-zāde (1583–1635):

Nevʿī-zāde efendi aḥbābdan birine göndermişdür.

Hevā-yı ʿālem muʿtedil olduqca hevā-yı dil müteġayyir ü mütebeddil olub sevdā-yı maḥabbet-i aḥbāb sebeb-i ḥareket ü ıżṭırāb olmaġa başladı. Bu ḥīnde sükūt ʿinde l-ʿuqelā ṭavr-ı mecnūn ve muṭāleʿa-ı fünūn qażīyetü l-fütūn-ı cünūn olmaq fehm olunub eger bār-ı xāṭır olmazsaq yarın ʿale s-seher āfitāb zīr-i ufqdan ser ve cenāb-ı şerīf hicāb-ı cāme-xōbdan peyker göstermedin ẕerre-misāl qapudan duxūle mecāl olmazsa bacadan nüzūl muqarrerdür.

Mine l-muxliṣ,

Nevʿī

Das kurze Billet, das zuerst den Wunsch des Dichters, seinen Freund zu sehen, ausdrückt und dann seinen Besuch am nächsten Morgen ankündigt, ist in Nevʿī-zādes elegantem Reimprosastil abgefasst. Es lässt sich—mit zwei unwesentlichen Vereinfachungen von Tautologien—wie folgt übersetzen:

Von Herrn Nevʿī-zāde an einen seiner Freunde geschickt:

Während das Wetter in der [Aussen]welt "gemässigt" (temperiert) ist, ist das Wetter des Herzens "veränderlich." Die Sehnsucht nach einer gemütlichen Unterhaltung mit Freunden hat begonnen [innere] Unruhe zu erzeugen. In solchen Augenblicken an Ruhe zu denken, wäre—nach der Ansicht kluger Leute–das Betragen eines Irren, und sich mit dem Studium der Wissenschaften zu beschäftigen liesse sich als ein Fall von Ränken böser Geister verstehen. Wenn wir also keine Unannehmlichkeit bereiten (wörtlich: keine Belastung des Gemüts sind), werden wir morgen in aller Frühe, bevor die Sonne ihr Haupt über den Horizont erhebt und bevor Eure Hoheit hinter dem Bettvorhang hervorgetreten (wörtlich: das Antlitz gezeigt)—sollte es uns nicht glücken, wie ein Sonnenstäubchen durch die Türe einzudringen—durch den Kamin [das Rauchloch] [zu Euch] heruntersteigen.

Von [Eurem] aufrichtig ergebenen

Nev'ī

Die Aussage des Briefleins kann einfach und klar genannt werden. Sie ist höflich, etwa in dem Bescheidenheitsplural (*pluralis modestatis*) der ersten Person, der hier als "Eure Hoheit" übersetzten Anredeform *cenāb-ı şerīf* ("ehrenwerte Gegenwart") der zweiten Person, sowie in der Vermeidung aller possessiven Hinweise auf die erste und zweite Person, die nur mit-verstanden (*sous-entendu*) sind, wodurch die Aussage einen herben, gleichsam verallgemeinernden Klang erhält. Die Aussage ist ausserdem witzig, indem sie in ihrem letzten Satz das Bild des Eindringens durch das Rauchloch, wenn die Türe versperrt ist, heraufbeschwört, wie es in volkstümlichen Redensarten wie *kapıdan kovsan bacadan düşer* "wirft man ihn bei der Türe hinaus, so kommt er durch das Rauchloch wieder herein" vorgebildet ist. Nicht ausgedrückt in der Übersetzung ist der "poetische" Bau des Briefes, der vor allem durch die Reimprosa bestimmt ist. Er lässt sich wie folgt graphisch zum Ausdruck bringen:

Nev'ī-zāde efendi aḥbābdan birine göndermişdür

Hevā-yı 'ālem mu'tedil

olduqca

hevā-yı dil müteġayyir ü mütebeddil
olub
sevdā-yı maḥabbet-i aḥbāb
sebeb-i ḥareket ü ıżṭırāb
olmağa başladı.
Bu ḥīnde sükūn
'inde l-'uqelā ṭavr-ı mecnūn
ve muṭāle'a-ı fünūn
qażīyetü l-fütūn-ı cünūn
olmaq fehm olunub
eger bār-ı xāṭır olmazsaq yarın 'ale s-seher
āfitāb zīr-i ufqdan ser
ve cenāb-ı şerīf hicāb-ı cāme-xōbdan peyker
göstermedin
ẕerre-misẕāl
qapudan
duxūl-
e mecāl
olmazsa bacadan
nüzūl
muqarrer-
dür.

Mine l-muxliṣ
Nev'ī

Bei der Anordnung des Textes auf Grund der Reimprosa kommen nicht alle "poetischen" Komponenten zum Ausdruck. So etwa wird die Gegenüberstellung von *hevā-yı 'ālem* und *hevā-yı dil* in den Anfängen der beiden ersten Zeilen nicht besonders betont, ebenso die Alliteration der Wortanfänge *sevdā-yı* und *sebeb-i* in der dritten und vierten Zeile sowie von *'inde* und *'uqelā*. Die Parallelität der Wortbildung von *müteġayyir* und *mütebeddil* müsste eigentlich hervorgehoben werden, wie auch die *figura etymologica* von *maḥabbet-i aḥbāb* oder in der Gegenüberstellung von *mecnūn* und *cünūn.* Auch die Binnenreime *dil* ~ *mütebeddil, fütūn* ~ *cünūn, afitāb* ~ *cenāb* ~ *hicāb* ~ *cāme-xōb* könnten dem unaufmerksamen Leser leicht entgehen. Sie sind aber weniger wichtig als das System der syntaktisch gleichgestellten reimenden Elemente, deren deutliche Trennung den Bau der Perioden klarlegt und damit ihr Verständnis beachtlich erleichtert.

Eine Wiedergabe in deutscher Übertragung unter Berücksichtigung des poetischen Charakters ist nur in der Form einer Nachdichtung möglich. Eine solche habe ich an dem Beispiel dieses Briefes versucht und mir dabei nicht allzu viele dichterische Freiheiten erlaubt. Ihr Abdruck sei mir hier gestattet als ein Stück in der Beweisführung, dass einer vollwertigen Wiedergabe der klassischen osmanischen Kunstprosa nur in Gedichtform entsprochen werden kann.

Brieflein an einen Freund:

So milde auch das Wetter in der Welt,
Des Herzens Barometer ist auf Sturm gestellt.
Den Freund zu sehen ist mein banges Sehnen,
Das mich durchzieht und lässt in Qual mich stöhnen.

In solcher Zeit an stilles Ruh'n zu denken
Nach Worten Weiser wäre wider die Natur;
Sich in das Studium der Wissenschaft versenken,
Versuchung böser Geister wär' es nur.

Drum, falls als Störung dieses nicht empfunden,
Will morgen früh ich in den ersten Stunden,
Noch eh' die Sonn' ihr Haupt am Horizont erhoben,
Noch eh' Ihr, werter Freund, des Schlafgemaches Vorhang
fortgeschoben,
Gleich einem Sonnenstäubchen durch den Türritz dringen
Oder, so das nicht geht, mich durch den Rauchfang zu Euch
niederschwingen.

Euer ergebener

Nev'ī

39
Güldeste-i Eş'ār: A Birthday Garland for Professor Bernard Lewis*

John R. Walsh

Mahāfil-i sudakādan du'āla geldi nidā
Eserlerin gibi

1406/1986

KADI BURHĀNEDDİN

(İz, p. 146; 8th beyt omitted)

Āh baḫuñ ışqa vu ḥālātına

This is love, behold, and these the states of it,
These absurdities which frenzied hearts commit.

Having burned with longing in his absence, now
Can I bear our hours of union? Am I fit?

I proclaim his edict making me his slave,
Gladly I bear witness to his beauty's writ.

He who sees that face and still retains his heart
Can we hope the other wonders would admit?

When the zephyr told the story of his locks,
We believed all it reported, every bit.

With his beauty for a mount my love rides forth;
Where his horse treads there my heart lies opposite.

---

*All the verses here translated were selected from Fahir İz, *Eski Türk Edebiyatında Nazım* (Istanbul, 1966), Vol. I.

Dearest, if in beauty's Egypt they should sell
Joseph of Ken'ān for you, how apposite!

So you'd learn of your beloved's true intent?
Climb the seven tiers of heaven, none omit.

What's the need of ailing hearts for drugs and such?
To the glances of his eye all ills submit.

Ah, that stature! my one Resurrection Day!
At its portents I stand consternation-hit.

I am thirsting for his lips, he for my blood.
May the Lord all creatures of their needs acquit!

NESĪMĪ

(İz, p. 160m)

Firqat içinde yüregüm gör nice yara yaradur

Behold how from desire my heart is wounded, and to what extent,
And how my breast with all this grieving has been scored and sorely rent!
Although your heart, my Idol, is as cold as marble, hard as stone,
Some kindness show to those who love you, all their lives in longing spent.
I drank the poisons of distress and now I'm ailing painfully.
How can you leave your lover thus? Devise some cure for his ailment.
Could I by any means or manner ever tire of this abuse?
For my Beloved's heartlessness is only for his lover meant.
Though painful his coy ways and sharp rebukes, their absence pains me, too.
With such a state must anyone prepared to love him be content.
Upon the boundless sea of love I set my fragile bark adrift;
Come, guide it to the shore of your embrace, for such is its intent.
In what respect can I compare the sun and moon to your fair face?
They both are feeble stars, whereas your bright cheek lights a firmament.
To anyone whose taste is for the wine from which no rue ensues,
How valueless is piety and all its specious ornament!
Nesīmī, soul and body, being from the dust of His locks born,
To dust he will return, and thus regain his proper element.

AHMEDĪ

(İz, p. 169g)

Gel gel ki senden ayru bu ʿayşuñ ṣafāsı yoḫ

Come, come, for joy is so much less whenever you're not here!
Let's make the best of this short life, for fortune's fickle, Dear.

For once let's live life to the full and unrestrainedly,
While still we're able; for this world is doomed to disappear.

One simple devotee of love, without deceit or guile,
Is better than a thousand mummers, wool-clad and austere.

Forever will I keep on seeking union with my Love;
And this is all my heart's desiring in this earthly sphere.

Be patient and enduring if you wish to cure love's ills;
For only patience works; of other cures I've yet to hear.

Can anyone attain the goal to which love's highway leads,
Who's not prepared to suffer gladly hardship and ill-cheer?

But he who sacrifices his existence to this quest
Should find eternal life wherein there is no death to fear.

Who seeks the arms of his Beloved must endure disdain;
What ease is granted by this world to which woes are not near?

Those witching eyes can claim their heart-sore victims by the score,
But there is no one stricken quite as Ahmedī, that's clear!

ŞEYHĪ

(İz, p. 177)

İy ṣabā peyk-i revānsın ḫaberüm cāna irür

You're my envoy, gentle breeze, so tell my loved one how I fare;
Let my Lord know of the heartbreak I, his servant, have to bear.

Make the dust around his doorway cool refreshment to the heart;
As to life-restoring waters, lead the sick and thirsting there.

When you scent horizons distant, musk-redolent from his locks,
Let a whiff of the aroma perfume, too, this sad heart's air.

Have the hoopoe's cries of bravo greet the ears of his vizir,
But to Solomon himself the moanings of the ant declare.

"There's no way," I told the wind, "will lead you to that Moon's retreat.
Kiss his footprints; you'll reach Venus, yea and Saturn, by that stair."

By eternal compact is my life committed to that glance;
Boy, I might as well be drunk, so fetch the wine nor any spare!

Wind of morning, take a deep breath, then to Persia straightway speed,
There convey to Husrev Şeyhī's offering of plaint and prayer.

AHMED PAŞA

(İz, p. 196°)

Ser-nāme-i maḥabbeti cānāna yazmışam

With fond avowals to my lover as a dedication,
I wrote upon my parchment heart a treatise on frustration.

I noted down the laments of the hapless nightingale,
And by the zephyr's hand I gave the garden information.

The tale of your wild tresses, in the heart preserved, became
The model for the plaints I wrote on scrolls of conturbation.

I fixed your image on my eye, and 'twas as if I'd etched
Upon a coral wine-cup lines of joyous inspiration.

In writing of the fervor felt by Ahmed for your cheek,
I all but was ablaze myself, so great was my elation.

DĀ'Ī

(İz, p. 213h)

Sebeb nedür ki bizi qodı gitdi yār dirīġ

Why has the Beloved gone and left us on our own? alas!
Can it be that he'd forsake his lover unbeknown? alas!

We did not appreciate his favors when we had them, so
It is fitting that we now should weep and sorely moan, alas!

Ah, I sigh that life has passed this wise in longing and regret.
Yea, a thousand sighs a minute, not just one alone, alas!

Maybe it's because we were not thankful for its gifts enough
That a vengeful Fortune so besets us that we groan, alas!

If you're wise at all you'll take the time to ponder well on this:
In the world's good faith there can no confidence be shown, alas!

He'll end up embarrassed, who so vaunts his rank and dignity.
Where's the gain if finally it's into shame he's thrown? alas!

Hopefully some portion of God's mercy will befall, Dā'ī;
Otherwise expectancy will past control have grown, alas!

FUZŪLĪ

1

(İz, p. 255[n])

Benı zikr itmez il efsane-i Mecnūna mā'ildür

The people never mention me, it's only of Mecnûn they'd tell.
But how can he with me compare, whose grief the written word
can spell?

Don't ask that desert-denizen, Mecnūn, what heartbreaks I endure!
How can they know about the sea who only on the seashore dwell?

Mecnūn could never be, as I, the talk of misadventure's town:
Compared to me he's sane, and would a sane man welcome such
a hell?

No matter what the lover's trouble, his Beloved sets it right.
But if that Darling's not aware that something's wrong—
then nothing's well!

He does not read the portents of my flood of tears when we're apart;
How heedless is that Brute of what will be when sounds this world's
death knell!

Don't blame the poor scholastic if he can't perceive the Truth of Love;
Of this he's ignorant, although in other fields he may excel.

The people say, Fuzūlī, that your sufferings exceed Mecnūn's;
And even Mecnūn says so—an admission which the facts compel!

2

(İz, p. 265[o1])

Meni cāndan uṣandurdı cefādan yār uṣanmaz mı

My lover's made me tired of living; does he never tire of spite?
Forever must my lamp of love be dark, my sighs set skies alight?

All ailing lovers have their pains assuaged by the Beloved's grace.
Why is the cure withheld from me? Does he believe that I'm all right?

They told me to reveal to him this grief I'm hiding. If I do,
That miscreant might not believe a word—but then again he might.

Throughout the nights of longing fiercely burns my heart,
my eyes shed blood;
My moans arouse the neighbors—would they'd rouse my dormant
luck a mite!

Beholding your rose cheek, my eyes discharge a stream opaque
with blood.
When roses are in season, Dear, are not most rivers muddied quite?

I really wasn't drawn to you; but you deprived me of my will.
Did once they see you, wouldn't those who blame me now become
contrite?

Fuzūlī's such a love-crazed scamp that folk recoil from him with shock.
But ask what is this love he bears, and wants to bear without respite.

HAYĀLĪ

1

(İz, p. 272[b])

Ol gün qanı ki gün gibi sūzān idüm saña

Ah, where has that day gone when I, like a sun, burned with longing
for you?
Wherever you went, an obsequious shadow, along I went too.

Eternity still held creation a secret enclosed in its breast,
When in love's retreat I succumbed to your beauty, your loveliness
knew.

The rose had no color and neither aroma, the breeze no élan,
When I was the sad nightingale in your garden, and you I did woo.

When you, like Medine, were teasing your pilgrims, withdrawn
and afar,
Already was I like the Ka'be amidst you, my veils rent in two.

My Lord, I'm Hayālī who, even before there was place for the world,
Enjoyed place of honor as guest whom you showed hospitality to.

2

(İz, p. 279[z])

Harāb olubdur o ābād gördügün göñlüm

It lies in ruins now that heart you knew in better days;
A surfeit of despair that heart—you met is happy phase.

Although it strode the world, a law unto itself, my Dear,
It's now your slave, that heart you thought so carefree in its ways.
Familiar with unkindness, now it begs for cruelty,
That heart you took for granted in your kind or harsh displays.

It saw your mole, a bait inside the net your locks devise;
That heart you thought a hunter was ensnared, and thus it stays.

Resourceful as Ferhād you deemed it, ah Hayālī, now
In mountains of distress that heart's a clay among the clays.

NEV'Ī

(İz, p. 299)[1])

Ṭāli' bu vech ile dūn serkeş nigār böyle

Lowly so's the state of fortune, thus the wayward beauties go.
Such is fate, and such are sweethearts. Lo, the wretched lover, lo!

When together dread of parting, when apart it's grief that's felt.
Such the anguish born of longing; moments of fulfillment so.

What's the chance I'll ever win that graceful Cypress for my own?
Such is his elusiveness, and such the bashfulness I show.

Testy is my sweetheart, proud too; cruel are my rivals all.
Such is the rose and such the thorns; and hence the nightingale
heart's woe!

Cast not forth the body's frail bark on the whirlpools of chagrin.
Patience, heart! the winds of fortune will not always this way blow.

Will poor Nev'ī ever find the strength to bear this load of cares,
With a body so worn out, a heart that's so with grief laid low?

NEF'Ī

(İz, p. 344j)

Biz rind-i harābātī vü mestān-ī elestez

God's inebriates are we, and have been since the world was new;
Reeling from the wine of love, we'll greet the Day of Judgment, too.

We are not beholden to the tavern keeper for our drink,
Being hand-in-hand with one whose wines attest God's grandeur true.

Does it matter if the rosy wine-cup never leaves our hands?
We'll not be lapsed penitents, nor do things we swore not to do.

Is it strange our nature should be thought a sea of hidden truths?
Like a wine we're all elation, like a draught we're sunk from view.

What is, like Nef'ī here and hereafter we, too, be reviled?
We are lovers, we are poets, we are topers through and through.

ŞEYHÜLİSLĀM YAHYĀ

(İz, p. 357)

'Işquñ odına ey gül yanarsa cān-ı şeydā

If in the fierce fire of your love this frantic soul should burn,
My Rose, each pile of ash will breed a nightingale in turn.
Indeed, the kingdom of the heart is wary of that lip;
From such a spark the world could well take flame from stem to stern.

Love's tavern now is crowded with a drunken clientele;
The cups are full, so don't, my friend, these boon companions spurn.

The heart is purged of gloom, but still there lacks a cheerful face;
With aught but loveliness should such bright mirrors have concern?

Yahyā, my eye's black pupil on her cheek's black mole attends,
The while my heart's dark recesses for her dark tresses yearn.

BAHĀYĪ

(İz, p. 370ᵇ)

Ṭaġıtduñ ḫvāb-ı nāz-ı yārı ey feryād n' eylersin

Moans, what are you up to? You've disturbed the feigned sleep of
my Sweet!
Your alarums have left the world in ruins that was once so neat.

Pity my poor wounded heart and let it stay snared in your locks;
Why release a crippled bird, its broken wings in vain to beat?

Good Physician, though you have a remedy for all complaints,
Can you cure the lover born to madness by some healing feat?

Wind—just look!—you've blown my Sweetheart's plaits and ringlets
all awry,
Causing once again confusion by behavior indiscreet.

Everyone's been martyred by the sword of love the Darling wields;
Why do you, o killing glance, still draw your saber to compete?

Though, Bihzād, you sketch with skill the moles and down on Beauties'
cheeks,
When these are intent on mischief will they not your skills defeat?

No more than Bahāyī can you know the blessing of repose;
So, my stricken heart, whence comes this carefree manner and conceit?

VECDĪ

(Iz, 372[d])

Şebistān-ı ġamam bezmümde şem'-i enverüm yoqdur

No candle burns where I hold tryst. How like a night of grief
I've grown!
Which is to say, in this false world there's not a Sweetheart mine alone.

All turbaned heads display this day their dew-kissed rosebuds
jauntily,
Yet in the garden of the world no single petal do I own.

I've not been smitten by a glancc, nor taken captive by dark locks,
So in the ranks of love's campaigners my position's quite unknown.

By love's reagents has my heart been assayed as of purest gold;
And still no silver-breasted Darling has the slightest interest shown.

Past joys forgotten, I've become a love-flamed candle, waxen grief;
Nocturnal to the core, there's nothing left to do when night has flown.

A tavern boy with rosy cheeks, a glass of wine—I've neither one.
Why should I not then tear my clothes and cry on pleading cry intone?

So great, o Vecdī, is the love of Istanbul within me, that
If I had wings I'd fly there; but, of course, I haven't—hence this moan.

NĀ'İLĪ

(İz, p. 379[j])

Hevā-yı ʿışqa uyub kūy-ı yāra dek giderez

To where my Sweetheart dwells I'll go, following love's star;
Companion to the morning breeze, to where spring holds bazaar.

In tattered dervish cloak, I'll take a begging bowl and go
To regions where they give one alms in wine, however far.

With God's name on my lips I'll face the gallows like Mansūr,
Creating tumult such as shall the Throne of Heaven jar.

And should my taste remember how they were, your candy lips,
I'd leave at once for Egypt, nay, for distant Kandahar!

I'll venture with Senā'ī on the road of poverty
And travel to where anchorites such as Külhanī are.

O fickle Sphere, if Nā'ilī could set his hands on you,
He'd have you up for judgment at the Primal Mover's bar.

NĀBĪ

(Iz, p. 388)

Va'de-i ḫāṭır-firībüñ düzd-i ḫvāb itdüñ bu şeb

You have made seductive pledges pilfer me of sleep tonight,
Through my nightgown's warp and woof made fire and fever creep tonight.

While my sighs turned dark night darker, over what gay company
Did your lovely face, aglow, like beams of moonlight sweep tonight?

Possibly I've been remiss in serving you as is your due;
I have sinned; but, in forgiving, you have sown to reap tonight.

Not your haughty airs nor yet your coyness kept you from the feast;
No, I think, ashamed to face me, to your house you keep tonight.

I'm the one who has the headache, but the red glow of your cheek
Turns my rival's eyes to phials of cordial while I weep tonight.

All the night till morning with your vision I discoursed at length;
Whom did you deem meet to hold in conversation deep tonight?

Ah, poor Nābī, wracked with longing, sinks up to his neck in tears,
Presaging that Judgment Day when waves shall wildly leap, tonight.

NAHĪFĪ

(İz, p. 412f)

Göz gördi göñül sevdi seni ey yüzi māhum

To see you was to love you, ah my moon-faced Beauty, straightaway!
For you I'd sacrifice my life—what's wrong in that, inform me, pray?

Do not my sad demeanor and my look of sheer bewilderment
Attest the fact that I'm in love, in terms too telling to gainsay?

Keep faith with me and make me glad; come, let my wretched fortune be
Consumed in fires of envy when it sees the favors you display.

Ah cruel one, how can that stone you call a heart resist for long
These fiery sighs of mine which render granite down to ashes gray?

A very troubled lover is Nahīfī, anguish sears his breast;
So don't, my Lord, torment your slave, provoking tears this cruel way.

NEDĪM

(İz, p. 454)

Gülzāra ṣalın mevsimidür geşt-ü-güẕāruñ

Come, hips swaying, to the garden; now the time for strolling's nigh.
Strutting Cypress, come and tell us how you found the spring gone by.
Loose your locks and let your cheek in sable garments meet the eye.
Strutting Cypress, come and tell us how you found the spring gone by.
Come, you with the rosebud mouth, your nightingales are calling you!
Grace the garden so we'll not regret the rose that once there grew.
Tread the grassy places now, for winter soon will tread them, too.
Strutting Cypress, come and tell us how you found the spring gone by.
Let your dark pretense of beard grow on that glowing cheek,
my Dear—
Make a stuff of crimson trimmed with sable all the rage this year.
If the tulip's out of season, bring the vintner's bouquet here.
Strutting Cypress, come and tell us how you found the spring gone by.
Full of fruits of every sort, the world's a heaven here below;
Will you not the fruit of your companionship likewise bestow,
Of your bounty, to your lovers each your secret kisses blow?
Strutting Cypress, come and tell us how found the spring gone by.
O my heart-enchanting rascal, there's a line of verse I find
Rather charming, though its meaning's somewhat vague and
ill-defined.
Yet, I think Nedım composed it with a clear intent in mind:
"Strutting Cypress, come and tell us how you found the spring
gone by."

III
THE MODERN MIDDLE EAST

40
Shiblī Shumayyil: Medical Philosopher and Scientist

Georges C. Anawati

IN THE NINETEENTH century, there took place in the Middle East, and particularly in Lebanon and Egypt, a movement of rebirth called the *Nahḍa*, whose principal causes were Bonaparte's expedition in Egypt, the work of the missionaries, and the foundation of two universities in Beirut, the American University founded in 1866, and the French one founded in 1874.[1]

People in the Middle East became aware of their identity as Arabs, while at the same time they appreciated Western culture, in its economic, industrial, political, scientific, and philosophical aspects. Among the leaders of this *Nahḍa*, there were several preeminent personalities such as Ṭahṭāwi, Bustāni, Afghānī, Muḥammad ʻAbduh, Faraḥ Anṭūn, Yāzijī, Ṣarrūf, Qāsim Amīn, Jurjī Zaydān, and Rīḥāni. Dr. Shiblī Shumayyil was one of these personalities, and I shall discuss him as follows: first, his biography; second, his publications; third, his philosophical attitude; and finally, his activity as a physician.

Shiblī Shumayyil was born in 1850 in the village of Kafr Shima, to the south of Beirut. His family, which was Greek Catholic, was an accomplished one, devoted to science, literature, jurisprudence, and the Arabic language. His father Ibrāhīm, his two brothers Malḥam and Amīn, his cousins Qayṣar and Rashid were, like the Bustānī dynasty, zealous in the service of the Arabic language and literature, as were the Yāzijīs and the Taqlās, who also originated from Kafr Shima.

After his early schooling at home and in the village school, he entered the Syrian Protestant College which had been founded in 1866 in Beirut by American missionaries. Shiblī Shumayyil, Faris Nimr, and Ya'qūb Ṣarrūf were among the earliest graduates of the college. The first organized effort in the Arab national movement has been traced to a group whose members were all educated at the Syrian Protestant college.

Discussions arose between liberals and conservatives about the basic question of the part which Protestant Christian doctrines should play in the education provided by the college. A conflict arose between students and the directors of the college occasioned by the teaching of Edwin Lewis, a professor in the Medical School, who gave a commencement speech in which he accorded mild praise to Darwin and his theory. Edwin Lewis was dismissed, and students went on strike in response to his dismissal. Eventually, Cornelius Van Dyk and some liberal colleagues resigned. Finally, most of the expelled students refused to return to the college, and tried to complete their studies independently.[2]

Dr. Ya'qūb Ṣarrūf, later the founder of *al-Muqtaṭaf*, and a fellow student of Shiblī Shumayyil gave a vivid description of his behavior during his studies.[3] He writes:

> The School of Medicine was founded in 1866, in a small building near the National School which had been founded previously by the immortal Butrus al-Bustānī. The author of these lines [it is Ya'qūb Ṣarrūf who is speaking] was among the first-year students. We immediately began to study higher mathematics and natural sciences, together with literary and linguistic subjects.
>
> In the autumn of the following year, a section was founded for instruction in the medical sciences. Students who had taken first-year courses in the college, together with others from other schools, joined the college. Among them was a young man of about seventeen, small in stature with a brown complexion, and a rapid mind, and whose face showed signs of excellence and intelligence. He was wearing European clothing, which at that time was unusual among the local people. This was the person whose biography is given here. But most of these students who come from other schools were day students: They attended the lectures and then went home. So we did not see this young man often during that year.
>
> In the third year, the college moved to another place which had been rented, with a large hall for general teaching and for lectures, and where the students had desks, one for every two students. Chance put us together, Shumayyil and myself, and we sat as neighbors for two years; we helped each other in subjects which we had in common, such as in botany, chemistry, and physiology, and in those to which we were naturally inclined, such as poetry and the art of writing.

By a curious coincidence, we had been born in neighboring villages. From his village came the Shaykh Naṣīf al-Yāzijī, our master and the master of the Arabic language at this time in Syria. From our village came Fāris al-Shidyāq, the director of the review *al-Jawā'ib*, one of the greatest experts in the Arabic language, in poetry and in the art of writing. Each of us was eager to imitate his compatriot and to follow in his footsteps.

I finished my scientific training in the summer of 1870 and left the school. Shumayyil completed his medical courses in the summer of 1871. I came back to teach in the college, in the summer of 1873. With Dr. Fāris Nimr, I founded *al-Muqtaṭaf*.

After that, I happened to publish a little article in which I spoke of Professor Tyndall's experiments which showed the impossibility of spontaneous generation, which [at that time] was the opinion of a great number of scientists: that is, the generation of living beings from matter which does not contain their seed.

By then, Dr. Shumayyil had moved to Egypt and traveled to Europe. He had become acquainted with some biological research by specialists in this field. He had become convinced by what he thought was proof, of the truth of the theory of evolution and of the generation of one species from another, and also of the theory of spontaneous generation. He wrote a letter to me objecting to my article, and a discussion arose between us.

Here we have the end of the first period of Dr. Shumayyil's life and the beginning of his scientific and literary activity. We have no information concerning his stay in Europe, which was decisive for the orientation of his mind: from this time onward, he became a radical materialist. It is interesting to note that he was not a partisan of evolutionism when he left the university; but is it not strange that he chose as a subject for his doctoral dissertation, "The Variations of Animals and Man According to Climate, Food, and Education"? Dr. Ṣarrūf declares that it was very unfortunate that the university at that time did not offer him a chair for teaching scientific subjects, but left him instead to turn his mind to sociological and philosophical problems.

Shiblī Shumayyil came to Egypt when he was twenty-five years old, and it became his second fatherland. For ten years he remained in Tantah practicing medicine. Then, in 1885 he moved to Cairo, and in 1886 he began to publish the medical review *al-Shifā'* of which I shall speak later on.

In the introduction of his book, *Falsafat al-nushū' wa'l-irtiqā'*, published in 1910, Dr. Shumayyil says that his education was exclusively scientific, so that his mind was not spoiled by literature. He is probably exaggerating, because at that time he felt a strong aversion to literature and men of letters, an attitude for which Miss Mayy, Mary Ziyadah, reproached him mildly in an article devoted to his own poetry. Perhaps Shumayyil was reacting against the traditional education of the time. He was devout in his youth, but fell with undue rapidity under the impact of evolution, and became a fervent partisan of transformism in its worst aspect, denying the spirituality and the immortality of the human soul, and of any kind of afterlife.

Dr. Shumayyil suffered from asthma, and said to his friend Ṣarrūf that one day it would prove fatal to him. And indeed, he died in 1917 after a severe attack of this ailment. His funeral was a kind of triumph: many admirers attended the religious ceremony at the Greek Catholic church in Cairo, and the great poets Khalil Muṭrān and Ḥāfiz Ibrāhīm celebrated him in brilliant poems.

In the biography which Dr. Ṣarrūf published of his friend just after his death, the director of the *Muqtaṭaf* pointed out the main characteristics of his old friend's personality: he was a scientist and a social man, with a penetrating mind, prompt to grasp certain ideas but also too prompt to expound what he thought was true, even if it was unusual and contrary to the generally held opinion. He had not received sufficient training in rigorous mathematical method, and was unable to give apodeictic reasons for his first intuitions. He himself confessed this cast of mind, in an article of the newspaper *al-Mu'ayyad*, saying, "My misfortune—if this may be called a misfortune—is that as soon as a truth appears to me, it attracts me to such an extent that I cannot refrain from expressing it."[4]

Despite this uncontrolled enthusiasm in his scientific philosophy, which made him pass from pure hypothesis to indisputable certitude, he was careful and prudent in his medical practice, following classical medicine, not prone to use treatments or new medicines which had not yet been thoroughly verified. He did not, for instance, use salvarsan or seawater, which were recommended at that period. But he did have a rare power of intuition in diagnosis, "as if," says Ṣarrūf, "he were inspired. He was so clever in diagnosis that he found that the cause of many events was 'auto-suggestion.' "[5]

Dr. Shumayyil had a wonderful memory. Dr. Ṣarrūf assures us that it was not rare to see him saying, when a question was mentioned:"I wrote an article on this subject thirty years ago, in which I said so and so"; and he would be able to recite one or several pages of the article from memory. Or else,"I composed a poem in which I said," and he would recite twenty or more verses, to the point, adds Ṣarrūf, that "he knew by heart things which I had written, and which had completely disappeared from my memory.

He was affable, a good speaker, and witty in conversation. When he reached his sixties, his asthma grew worse, but he remained cheerful and jovial. He was much cherished by his friends and by all who used to visit him, because they found in him good faith, true love, a sense of fairness and, most of all, a great moral courage. He did not fear to tell an unjust man that he was unjust, even if he was a king. On the other hand, together with this pride toward the unjust and arrogant, he was the most gentle-hearted man with the weak and the miserable. Continues Ṣaffūf,

> Concerning his religious attitude, when you read his writings you think that he is an extreme materialist; but in reality he belongs to the extreme spiritualists, going to the point of believing in good and bad fortune and trying to discover a law of chance. Because he abstained from material things and because of his prodigal generosity, he did not know how to draw material profit from his work. If he had added to his skill in medicine some money-making skill, he would have lived in great comfort, and would have died leaving a fortune. But he was much more eager to collect his writings than to collect money.

His Works

Shiblī Shumayyil was a prolific writer. He mastered his mother tongue, and was able to coin many scientific neologisms in order to expound new ideas, particularly those imported from the West. We are told that he knew also French very well, but we have not been able to see his French articles. In any case, he often quoted scientific texts from French reviews.

Since he studied medicine at the American University of Beirut, he was surely able to read English, and so had direct access to the works of Spencer and Darwin. But we doubt if he knew German, and his translation of Büchner's book must have been done from an English or a French translation. He did not mention in his Introduction from what text he had made his translation. And he pointed out in the title of the book that the translation had been made *ma'a ba'ḍ taṣarruf fīh*, "with a certain liberty with the text," so that he does not tell us that he added to or subtracted from the original German text.

The publications of Dr. Shumayyil are as follows:

I. Some new editions of classical medical texts, already existing in Arabic; they were reproduced in his review *Al-Shifā'*: (1) *Kitāb al-ahwiya wa'l-miyāh wa'l-buldān li-Ibuqrāt al-ṭabīb* (Cairo, 1885), containing twenty-four questions, with an introduction and a biography of Hippocrates; (2) *Kitāb al-fuṣūl* of Hippocrates; and (3) the *Urjūza* (*Canticum*) of Avicenna.

II. Many articles concerning medicine and the history of Arab medicine in his medical review.

III. A great number of his articles were devoted to expounding and interpreting Darwinism in the line of Büchner, and were published in the review *al-Muqtaṭaf*. He collected these articles in two volumes in 1910 and published them under the title *Kitāb falsafat al-nushū' wa'l-irtiqā'*. The first volume, which is subtitled *majmū'at al-duktūr Shiblī Shumayyil*, contains the following: (a) A preliminary note (*dībāja*) indicating the contents of the book. (b) The translation and commentary of the book of Büchner (*Sharḥ Büchner 'alā madhhab Darwin*), in five chapters. This text had been previously edited by Dr. Shumayyil in 1884 at al-Muqtaṭaf Press, but in small type. The new edition is much more elegant and easier to read. (c) *The Truth (al-ḥaqīqa)*, a dissertation containing responses to the objections made against Darwin's theory. This text has also been published before, in 1885, in a separate book. (d) An appendix (*mulḥaq*) containing fourteen essays on the subject of life, in order to prove the materialist concept of life.[6]

The second volume of the ideas of Dr. Shumayyil contains articles which had been published in various newspapers, discussing some problems of the day, attacking governmental decisions, or replying to opponents. Dr. Shumayyil was outspoken, and could not resist making sharp comments when he felt that his correspondents were not at the level of his evolutionism. He himself calls this collection of articles "topics of civilization, natural science, history, literature, politics, criticism, and humoristic matters."

IV. *Risālat al-ma'ātis*, a little treatise imitating the *Risālat al-ghufrān* of al-Ma'arrī.

V. *Shakwa wa-amal* (*Complaint and hope*), a small book in which he summed up his view of what was wrong with the Ottoman Empire: the lack of science, justice, and liberty.

VI. Finally, three years of the medical review *al-Shifā'*, which I shall present in a moment.

His Scientific Philosophy

Dr. Shumayyil had no esteem for philosophers, and considered all their works irrelevant and useless. To read them is a waste of time.

His unique creed was "Science," and he firmly believed that it is science which is able to solve the great problems of life in all its aspects, social, economic, political, and so on. He was a victim of his time, a period in which recent, marvelous scientific discoveries were exciting the minds of those who had no true humanistic culture and who were blind to religious experience. Science became the new religion for them, "the key to the secret of the universe, even a mode of worship," as stated by Professor Albert Hourani.

We have seen before that Dr. Shumayyil, with fervor, enthusiasm, and some naïve credulity, had embraced Darwinism, but as it was constructed by Huxley and Spencer in England and Haeckel and Büchner in Germany, out of the cautious hypothesis of Darwin himself. Shumayyil affirmed the unity of force and matter and the unity of all being. Matter has existed from eternity, and will exist forever; all things, even what is called soul, are formed by a spontaneous process from it, passing by stages from the mineral to the human; each stage arises from the past without a break, by the operation of forces inherent in matter itself. At the summit of the process, man is formed. He is the first being who is able to control nature and its laws, inserting himself into the process and replacing the struggle for existence with cooperation and the division of labor.

But man's soul is neither spiritual nor immortal. Shumayyil says, for instance:

> The soul of an animal is a result of material operations, such as the functioning of the nerves; and the brain resembles the operations of the stomach, and of florescence in plants. Soul is a mode of the force inherent in matter, as brain is a mode of the matter connected with force. Matter is in movement, and movement is eternal. Its immobility is only apparent; in itself, matter is in a constant attraction which disintegrates its contents, and also in a repulsion which disperses its parts. Love and antipathy are not in man's heart only, but also in the heart of minerals, and in it is their principle and the principle of all life. Life and death are no more than change in matter and in form.[7]

This unity of the universe at its different levels arouses Dr. Shumayyil's enthusiasm, and he dares to apply to it the term reserved in Islamic theology for the Unity of God, *tawḥīd*. With such a premise, what becomes of religion? A pure creation of man, Dr. Shumayyil assures us; it is man's imagination which created different religions fighting one another, when man was rude and ignorant. He grew accustomed to these ideas. But when he became aware of the reality of things, as discovered by science, he abandoned every kind of religion. The more men go astray from religion, the more society grows up, because religion restrains the mind's liberty and is a source of division in mankind.

In a strict sense, Dr. Shumayyil would not have said that he was against religion, for he respected all beliefs, but he surely was against the men of religion who desired domination and who exploited their brothers in humanity.

This new vision of things had vast social and political implications. Sound laws could only be derived from valid human sciences. Theocracy and despotism are unnatural and false. A true system must give rein to the universal process of development which permits man to "live in accordance with himself," but also in cooperation with others. Laws and institutions could not be regarded as infallible and unchanging; they must change together with the conditions of welfare. This change should be gradual, but in some circumstances, violent revolution is indeed unavoidable.

What must unite men is not religion, because it divides human society; not even national fanaticism, which is as bad as religion. Loyalty must sooner or later be given to the world.

Shumayyil was the first to spread the concept of socialism, even if he did not forge the term itself (*ishtirākīya*). But for the Egypt of his time, he was concerned much more with the liberal problems of the limits of the State. He wanted government to interfere positively in order to bring about cooperation in pursuit of the general welfare, for instance, in finding work for all, in insuring that wages were equal, and in improving public health. And in 1908, he suggested a program for a Socialist Party in Egypt some parts of which are perfectly utopian.[8]

In any case, despite the utopian character of his proposals, there are some good hints of help to intellectuals and politicians in Egypt and the Ottoman Empire in their quest for constitutional government. And from this point of view, Dr. Shumayyil contributed to introducing the secular movement into the Middle East.

Shiblī Shumayyil the Physician

It remains for us to consider Shiblī Shumayyil's role in the field of medicine, and to see how effectively he contributed to making Western medicine known in the Arab countries, especially in Egypt. He was perfectly aware of the tremendous lead of the West in this field, and was convinced that what his compatriots needed above all was to know, without delay, the recent achievements of medicine, so as to put them at the service of their patients. He confessed, with some melancholy, that so far scientists in the Middle East had had no opportunity to undertake scientific research, because of a lack of well-equipped laboratories. This is why he thought that it would be helpful to his compatriots for him to present to them, in a periodical, the latest results of medical research in Europe and the United States.

It was in this spirit that in February 1886 he started his Arabic review, which he called *al-Shifā'* (*Healing*), printed by the Muqtaṭaf Press, and in the same format as the already famous review.[9] In the first issue, in several preliminary pages he explained the aim and the limits of his publication. He recognized that there were Arabic medical reviews before *al-Shifā'*: *al-Ya'sūb* and *al-Muntakhab* in Cairo, and *al-Ṭabīb* in Syria. These were all excellent, but unfortunately they had been obliged to cease publication. He hoped that his review would fare better.

The subjects to be dealt with in the review were medicine and surgery and all that is connected with them, without going beyond these fields. Anatomy, physiology, chemistry, and the natural sciences would be mentioned only when they involved a medical question. A section of the review would be devoted to pharmacology, giving new practical preparations whose usefulness had been proved. Interest would also be shown in "administrative health" (*al-ṣiḥḥa al-idārīya*), that is, reports concerning health, reform projects, information on births and deaths (including the causes of death), and meteorological data in order to learn the relation of diseases with seasonal and weather variations. Medical advice would also be provided.

A part of the review would be devoted to presenting European or Arabic books received, in which, says Dr. Shumayyil, "the European custom" (*ṭarīqat al-Afranj*) would be applied, that means an objective and critical analysis of the book, and not a mere compliment to the author.

Dr. Shumayyil was fortunate from the beginning in having the voluntary collaboration of Dr. Herbert Milton, Director of Qaṣr al-'Aynī Hospital. A group of distinguished physicians soon made contributions: Salem Pasha, Hassan Pasha Mahmoud, Abati Pasha, Grant Bey, Ahmad Pasha Hamdi, Muhammad Bey 'Alwi, Ibrahim Soussa.

Al-Shifā' was issued monthly at first, in the hope that it would become fortnightly. The first issue was thirty-two pages long, printed at the press of *al-Muqtaṭaf*, with the same dimensions as the already renowned review. Dr. Shumayyil was able to maintain the review for three years, 1887–89 (and not five, as said by many biographers). It ceased publication at the end of 1889, for different reasons: the Ministry of Health suspended its financial aid, instruction at the Faculty of Medicine changed to English, and, alas, some intrigues aroused by envy. At the end of the last issue Dr. Shumayyil explained, with stoic sadness, why he was obliged to stop publication.

I have been able to consult the collection of the three volumes of the review, which are in the National Library in Cairo (*Dār al-Kutub*). Volumes I and III still have their alphabetical indexes, which were carefully prepared. I obtained photocopies of these two indexes. In order to give an idea of the preoccupations of Arab medicine at the end of the nineteenth century, I have tried to classify roughly the subjects of the journal's first year. I obtained the following data:

DISEASES

acne of youth *1*, 222
amaebia *1*, 137
ankylostoma *1*, 352
Basedow disease *1*, 353
bilharzia *1*, 149
blennorragy *1*, 381
chorea, treatment
  by arsenic *1*, 272
  by bromhydric acid *1*, 158
cold abcesses *1*, 384
diabetes
  connection with malaria toxines (*'alāqatuhu bilsumūm al-ijamīya*)
  treatment by boric acid *1*, 158
diphtheria
  real treatment *1*, 379
  treatment by mercury chloride *1*, 294, 334, 357
  treatment by vinegar *1*, 277
dysentery *1*, 377
elephantiasis (*dā' al-fīl*) *1*, 339
erysipela (*ḥumra*)
  treatment by sodium benzoate, *1*, 392
glycosuria *1*, 267
gonorrhea (*sayalān majra al-būl*)
  treatment with lime juice (*al-laymūn al-ḥāmid*), *1*, 382
hernia
  treatment by ether *1*, 60
hiccups (*al-shahaqa*) *1*, 250, 271
leprosy
  treatment by electricity *1*, 50
liver
  cirrhosis of *1*, 321
lupus *1*, 286
measles *1*, 352
nasal polyps *1*, 313
puerperal eclampsy *1*, 251
pustula *1*, 311
rabies
  its microbe *1*, 110
  its treatment 1, 320, 351
  preservation *1*, 65, 177
stomach atrophy *1*, 276
syphilis *1*, 178
  external treatment by mercury chloride *1*, 96
  of children *1*, 287
tetanus *1*, 282
tuberculosis *1*, 298
  contagion *1*, 103, 353
tumor of the ovary *1*, 118
  cancerous tumors *1*, 73
  fatty tumors (*awrām shaḥmīya*)
  malignant tumors *1*, 319
  tumor of the neck *1*, 161
typhoid *1*, 352
  artificial anus during its treatment *1*, 352

typhoid (continued)
microbe of *1*, 339
relapse of *1*, 63
treatment by tepid water *1*, 12
uterus
cancer *1*, 273
its widening *1*, 61
vomiting of pregnant women (*qay' al-ḥabāla*) *1*, 129

SURGERY

bursting of intestines (*inbithāq al-ma'y*) *1*, 235
hysterectomy *1*, 155
osteomalicia (softening of the bones) (*layn al-'iẓām*) *1*, 129
rachitis (*al-kusāḥa*), *1*, 129
removal by surgery of a part of the intestine *1*, 114
seclusion of placenta *1*, 52

TEETH, NOSE, EYES

hiccups (*al-fuwāq*)
treatment by sneezing *1*, 253
mouth
how to keep it healthy *1*, 56
nasal polyps *1*, 313
nervous diseases: their relation to the nose *1*, 249
nosebleed (*al-ru'āf*)
ringing of the ear (*ṭanīn al-udhun*) *1*, 37, 106, 295
teeth caries *1*, 285
tongue *1*, 377
trachoma *1*, 374

NATURAL CHEMICAL REMEDIES

arbutine *1*, 63
atropine *1*, 382
cocaine *1*, 93
cocainomania *1*, 220
madness provoked by *1*, 220
used to pulverize calculus (stones) *1*, 221
ergot *1*, 63
hamamelis *1*, 93
quinine
for treatment of malignant pustules *1*, 319
turpentine
treatment of malignant tumors *1*, 319

CHEMICAL REMEDIES

amyl nitrite *1*, 93
antipyrine *1*, 92, 278, 290
arsenic *1*, 63
boric acid *1*, 158
bromhydric acid *1*, 158
calomel *1*, 351
chlorodyne *1*, 222
ethyl iodide *1*, 255
hydroquinone *1*, 280
iodine in treatment of intermittent fever (*al-ḥumma al-mutaqaṭṭi'a*) *1*, 45, 382
mercury chloride (*sulaymānī*)
provoking stomach diseases *1*, 251
treatment of syphilis *1*, 86
for washing uterus *1*, 253
methyl chloride *1*, 218
osmic acid *1*, 64
phenic acid
for treatment of dyspepsia *1*, 33
pilocarpine in dental treatment *1*, 220
potassium iodide *1*, 320
ptomaines *1*, 42
resorcine *1*, 253, 280
saccharine *1*, 220
sparteine *1*, 93, 279
thalline *1*, 280

LABORATORY

Bacillus of Erlich
how to discover it *1*, 80
Urine
method of finding sugar in it *1*, 378
method of finding albumin *1*, 381

MISCELLANEA

Arab medicine *1*, 174, 214
Arabic words *1*, 191
asphyxia by lavatory fumes *1*, 31
baths of Helwan *1*, 366
bitter substances
influence on digestion *1*, 281
death
signs of *1*, 124

fraud in medicine *1*, 380
hemoglobin *1*, 286
Hippocrates
  K. al-fuṣūl *1*, 316
laudanum
  provoking poisoning *1*, 227
madness
  treatment by suggestion (*bil-istiḥwā'*) *1*, 97
  marriage between relatives *1*, 380
patients
  how to examine them *1*, 291, 329
physiognomy of the nervous system *1*, 214
protoplasma *1*, 206
public health *1*, 28, 58, 94, 126, 157, 197, 219, 256, 288
spleen
  its connection with thyroid gland *1*, 59
syrups *1*, 267
water of Cairo *1*, 125
yawning
  its utility *1*, 125

Conclusion

In conclusion to this modest essay on Dr. Shiblī Shumayyil, I would say that what remains of interest from his work is the historical medical data contained in the collection of *al-Shifā'*. If some industrious Arabist is interested in the history of medicine at the end of the nineteenth century in the Arab world, he will find in this collection useful details concerning this period.

In addition, anyone who is interested in the medical and scientific vocabulary of Arabic will find in the same collection, and also in his two volumes of *Opera omnia*, a large quantity of useful linguistic material.

Finally, concerning his religious attitude, the Lord "who alone sounds hearts and minds" has asked us not to judge, in order not to be judged. I shall end my paper with the testimony of one of Dr. Shumayyil's friends, Amīn al-Riḥānī, who was influenced by him: "For me, there is no doubt that he will be near God—if we believe in the Sacred Books—because he always fought against injustice."

NOTES

1. The best introduction for the background of Shibī Shumayyil and his connection with the *Nahḍa* is: Albert Hourani, *Arabic Thought in the Liberal Age 1798–1939* (Oxford, 1962), which contains a good bibliography on the subject up to 1962. For Shumayyil, see pp. 248–53. More recent books: Donald M. Reid, *The Odyssey of Farah Antun: A Syrian Christian's Quest for Secularism* (Minneapolis and Chicago, 1975); for Shumayyil see pp. 75–77, 116–17, and

passim; Thomas Philipp, *Ǧurgi Zaidan: His Life and Thought* (Beirut, 1979); Louis Gardet, *Les Hommes de l'Islam.*

2. Cf. Nabīh Fāris, "Al-madrasa al-kullīya," *al-Abḥāth*, XX (1967), pp. 323 ff.; "Ṣaff 1883 fī 'l-madrasa al-kullīya," *al-Abḥāth* XXI (1968), pp. 39–55; Nadia Farag, "The Lewis Affair and the Fortunes of *al-Muqtaṭaf*," *Middle Eastern Studies*, VIII (1972), pp. 72–83; A. L. Tibawi, "History of the Syrian Protestant College" in Fu'ād Ṣarrūf, ed., *AUB Festival Book* (Beirut, 1967).

3. See *al-Muqtaṭaf*, L (1917), pp. 105–12, 225–31, 266–69. See also Ismā'īl Maẓhar, who was his fervent admirer but did not follow his materialist philosophy: "Shiblī Shumayyil wa-fikrat al-taṭawwur fī'l-sharq al-'arabī, 1860–1917," in *Majallat al-kitāb*, pp. 126–35.

4. *al-Muqtaṭaf* (February 1917), p. 108. The transliteration is: Ammā anā fa-āfatī—idhā kāna dhālika yu'addu āfatan—annahu matā badat lī ḥaqīqatun, tastahwīnī ḥattā lā a'ūda aḥfaẓu nafsī 'an ibdā'ihā.

5. Ibid. The transliteration is: wa-balaghat minhu 'l-firāsatu an 'allala ḥawāditha kathīratan bi'l-istihwā'i 'l-dhātī qabla an shā'a hādhā 'l-ta'līlu fī Urūbā.

6. The titles of the articles are: (1) *Istifhām* ("Inquiry"); (2) *Al-Ḥīra 'illat al-baḥth* ("Perplexity is the cause of research"); (3) *Al-Ḥiss wa anwā'uhu al-mukhtalifa* ("Sensory perception and its various types"); (4) *Kull al-sirr fī 'l mādda* ("The entire secret is in matter"); (5) *Al-Mādda dhāt ḥiss* ("Matter which has sensation"); (6) *Al-Ḥayāt khāṣṣa min khaṣā'iṣ al-mādda* ("Life is one of the properties of matter"); (7) *Al-Ḥayāt* ("Life"); (8) *Al-Ḥayāt wa'-l-jādhibīya* ("Life and attraction"); (9) *Mulāḥaẓāt fī 'l-ḥayāt* ("Some observations on life"); (10) *Al-Ḥayāt fī a'māq al-miyāh* ("Life is in profound waters"); (11) *Al-Ḥayāt wa-aṣl al-ajsām al-ḥayya* ("Life and the principle of living bodies"); (12) *Ḥayāt al-jamād* ("The life of minerals"); (13) *Aṣl al-ḥayat* ("The origin of life"); (14) *Khulāṣat mā taqaddama* ("Summary of the preceding articles").

7. In *Falsafat al-nushū'*, I, 50.

8. Hourani, *Arabic Thought*, p. 253: "In a more ambitious programme for a socialist party in Egypt, written in 1908, he suggested that the party should have both a negative and a positive policy. It should aim at destroying all useless books, the School of Law, the new university which was in process of being established, the Mixed Courts, indeed all courts as now established, companies which monopolized the water supply, and newspapers which spread dissension by talking about 'Muslim and Copt and immigrant' (*dakhil*—this was a reference to Egyptian attacks on the Lebanese immigrants in Egypt). Having thus destroyed almost all existing institutions, it should then establish a real university where the sciences were studied, a technical college in place of the School of Law, very simple local law courts, public institutions for the distribution of water, elementary schools in every village and quarter, and proper newspapers."

9. Cf. Phillippe de Tarrazi, *Ta'rīkh al-ṣaḥāfa al-'arabīya* (Beirut).

SELECTED BIBLIOGRAPHY

For the biography of Shiblī Shumayyil and his personality and his works, see *GAL*, S III, pp. 212–13; Daghir, *Maṣādir al-dirāsa al-adabīya* (Beirut, 1956), II, 497–500, with abundant bibliography, especially Arabic books and articles; Kaḥḥāla, *Mu'jam al-mu'allifīn* (Damascus, 1957–61), IV, 294; Sarkīs, *Mu'jam al-maṭbū'āt* (Cairo, 1928); Shaykhō, *Al-Adab al-'arabīya fī-'l-qarn al-'ishrīn* (Beirut, 1926), p. 78; Marūn 'Abbūd, *Ruwwād al-nahḍa al-ḥadītha* (Beirut, 1952), pp. 198–99. Ziriklī *Al-A'lām*, III, 7; Jean Lecerf, "Shibli Shuymayyil, Métaphysicien et moraliste contemporain," in *Bulletin d'études orientales*, I (1931), pp. 153–86.

Jean Fontaine, *Le Désaveu chez les écrivains libanais chrétiens de 1825 à 1940*, dissertation, Paris (Sorbonne) 1970. Excellent section (pp. 153–60), and good bibliography (pp. 233–59).

We have not had access to the dissertation of Georges Hārūn, in French, entitled *Shibli Shumayyel*, and published at the Lebanese University in 1984 or 1985.

41
Councils and Community: Minorities and the *Majlis* in *Tanẓimat* Jerusalem

Benjamin Braude

...whereas in former times in the Ottoman state, the communities were ranked with the Muslims first, then the Greeks, then the Armenians, then the Jews, now all of them were put on the same level. Some Greeks objected to this saying: "The government has put us together with the Jews. We were content with the supremacy of Islam."

Cevdet Pasha, *Tezakir*, commenting on the Reform Decree of 1856[1]

THE PARTICIPATION OF non-Muslims in the official councils of government was one of the distinctive features of the *Tanẓimat*.[2] In the 1840s Reshid Pasha first instituted a system of urban councils in the Ottoman Empire. For Syria and Palestine at least, this reform had ample precedent. In the eighteenth century a *walī* from time to time would convene a provincial council, *dīwān*, composed of the senior local Ottoman officials, as well as the leading *'ulāmā*, and, on occasion, the Muslim notables. During the Egyptian occupation, Ibrāhīm Pasha and Muḥammad 'Alī regularized this system, replacing it with a more comprehensive and representative urban council in every town over 2,000 inhabitants.[3] This council, called the *majlis al-shūrā*, included not only the local Muslim leaders, but also representatives from the Christian and Jewish communities.

It was in fact this *majlis* which formed the model and for a time the actual institution when Ottoman rule returned to the Levant in 1840–41. Indeed the Ottomans ordered local councils in Palestine to continue their activities "as in the time of the Egyptian government."[4] Ottoman acceptance of the reforms of a rival is not surprising since even during the time of the occupation Istanbul maintained the legal fiction that it remained the ultimate sovereign power, the region being under a kind of joint Ottoman–Muḥammad ʻAlī rule: "Ottoman in theory, Egyptian in practice."[5] Significantly Muḥammad ʻAlī and his family accepted and acted upon this same legal fiction, for they recognized that only Ottoman recognition would give their claims of succession legitimacy. Their insecurity is also apparent in the curious fact that they never propagated a name for their dynasty.

On 10 November 1840/15 Ramaḍān 1256 as the Ottoman forces were returning to Palestine and Muḥammad ʻAlī's army was being evacuated—just a week earlier Acre had fallen—an order was issued in Jerusalem naming the members of the local *majlis.* It consisted of the following: nine Muslims—Muḥammad Abū al-Suʻūd, who was, among other titles, the *naqīb al-ashrāf,* Muḥammad ʻAlī al-Husaynī, Khalil al-Khālidī, ʻUthmān Abū Suʻūd, Muḥammad Darwīsh ʻAlīzāde, Shakir al-Mūwaqqat, Najm al-Dīn al-Jamāʻī, Ibrāhīm al-Muḥtadī, and Muḥammad al-Ramlī; one representative of the Jewish community, Khūwāja Rūne (? Aaron); and two representatives of the Armenians, Yūsuf and Yāqūb Jāsir. In addition two other Muslims served the council, the clerk Jārāllah and his assistant, Wafa.[6] This must have been the first urban council in Jerusalem during direct Ottoman rule and it may very well have been the first in the Empire.[7] Considering the circumstances under which it was formed—the transition from Egyptian to Ottoman rule—its composition, and perhaps its prerogatives as well as its very members, reflected Egyptian more than Ottoman policy and practice.

The purview of the council system under Egyptian rule had been quite broad. It was to be the arm of the state which dealt with all the affairs of the town and its inhabitants, charged with judicial, administrative, economic, and legislative tasks. However, its decisions were generally of only an advisory nature and it was kept subservient to the local governor.[8] Although the local council had the right of appeal, according to one European observer, it never dared to do so.[9] Nonetheless the practice of the council was not completely at variance with its theoretical responsibilities. In Aleppo, for example, the British consul reported that it was the council that fixed the price of goods supplied to the army. The post of council member had gained sufficient recognition that at least some were paid regular salaries. It was drawn from the town's leading families, but it also included merchants, "who examine mercantile affairs." In Damascus and Beirut, as well as Jerusalem, Christians and Jews were appointed to the council.[10]

Moshe Ma'oz has suggested that although similar in framework to the Egyptian, the "substance and character" of the Ottoman *majlis* developed in a completely different fashion. Specifically he claimed that the Ottoman council was less representative of the population as a whole and more under the control of the traditional Muslim leaders (*'ulāmā'* and *'a'yān*).[11]

Although the Ottomans may have lessened the influence of the middle class merchants, who under the Egyptians had formed, in Ma'oz's words, "the backbone" of the council, they continued Christian and Jewish representation. This is clear not only from their presence in the 1840 Jerusalem *majlis*, but also from the *majlis* of 1851, which was described in an extensive report by the Prussian Vice-Consul in Jerusalem, Gustav E. Schultz.[12] The composition of the council had changed somewhat in eleven years, but some original members remained. There were now four regular Muslim members, Muḥammad Darwīsh (who may be the same as Muḥammad Darwīsh 'Alīzāde), Shaykh 'Uthmān (who may be identical with 'Uthmān Abū al-Su'ūd), Asad Efendi, Sayyid Infuf [?] al-Nusayba, in addition to four others ex officio, the mufti, Mustafa Efendi, Muḥammad Efendi al-Khālidī, who was now the *naqīb al-ashrāf*, his brother, and the *qāḍī*, who was not named. The Latin representative was Ya'qūb al-Ardī; the Greek, Shammas Juluf; the Armenian, Jiryes al-Khayyat; and the Jew, Ḥayim el-Serish. At its full complement the council then had eight Muslims, and four non-Muslims, a slightly more favorable non-Muslim presence than that of 1840, but still out of proportion to the actual population which was at the time roughly 5,000 Muslims, 4,000 Christians, and 6,000 Jews. However, since many of the non-Muslims, particularly the Jews, were not Ottoman subjects, their low representation is not surpising. Indeed according to reports based on an 1851 local census there were only 970 Jews registered with the Jerusalem authorities as Ottoman subjects.[13] According to Shultz the regular Muslim members were chosen by lot from the five hundred Jerusalem notables, while the non-Muslims were selected by their communities. The *majlis* met in regular session under the chairmanship of the pasha.

Schultz took an extremely critical view of the functioning of this institution. He believed that it failed to check the pasha's power, as he felt it should, since none of the local notables were prepared to oppose any of the government's wishes. Furthermore he chastised the people of Jerusalem and their representatives for lacking "moral courage, integrity, and unselfishness, love of justice, and other virtues of citizens."[14] James Finn, the British consul in Jerusalem, held an opposing view. He attributed considerable authority to the Muslim members, particularly the "close corporation of Arab families, not recognized by law, but influenced by position." According to Finn, they had

> usurped all the municipal offices among them. These men were mostly descended from the original conquerors of the country. . . . Some of them hold hereditary posts . . . such as Mohammed Danef in the Hharam, Mohammed Durweesh at the Sepulchre of David. . . . Then there are the Khaldi [? Khalidi], the Wafa . . . all enjoying the title of Efendi . . . or in their own phraseology " 'ayan.". . . [By contrast] the few transient Turkish officials . . . are helpless in effective administration against or without the local knowledge and corporate union of these 'ayan, of whom indeed several pashas have had to stand in awe.[15]

Finn's view in all likelihood is more accurate, based as it was on nearly two decades of service in Jerusalem. By contrast Schultz witnessed the *majlis* in action for a very short period. His experience was limited to the 1851 session which he described in September of that year, just two weeks before his death. In all likelihood the initial workings of the new council—it seems it had been reestablished after a hiatus of a few years—might indeed have awed its members until familiarity bred its customary contempt and allowed them to reassert their traditional power and authority.

By contrast both Schultz and Finn agreed about the lowly position of the non-Muslims on the council. The Prussian was particularly indignant about the servile behavior of the Christian and Jewish members who had been raised to fear the Muslims. Hayim al-Serish, for example, did nothing but kiss the hands of the Muslim notables whenever he could. Finn echoed these complaints. He dismissed the Jewish representative as "an insignificant person, who dared not open his mouth."[16] The native Christian members "suffer themselves to be bullied down into consent of unrighteous verdicts at the dictation of the Muslim members."[17]

This picture of humble and limited non-Muslim representation in the *majlis* is consistent with later accounts, both Christian and Jewish. John P. Newman, an American Methodist minister who traveled through Palestine in the spring of 1861, wrote of the municipal council on which non-Muslims "are members by sufferance."[18] Even in the last decades of Ottoman rule, Jewish participation in *meclis idare*, which now replaced *majlis al-shūrā*, was sporadic and ineffective.[19]

However, it would be a mistake to conclude from this account that non-Muslim representation had little or no significance. Even if the immediate practical result was limited, the mere presence of Christians and Jews on Ottoman governmental bodies had a symbolic effect, suggesting the beginning of a change in social attitudes on the part of Muslims. As Finn himself said, "considerable benefits have already resulted to them [the non-Muslims] from this new form of government."[20] This transformation of attitudes was even more significant with regard to relations between Christians and Jews, for the power and prestige of *majlis* membership was a useful tool in determining precedence and influence within and between these communities.

It played a particularly important role in the increasingly sharp conflicts which developed between the Jews and the newly established Protestant church in Jerusalem, whose prime mission was the conversion of that community. The importance of the council in the struggle between these groups emerges from a series of disputes which erupted from 1850 onward. In that year the Ottoman government extended official recognition to the Protestant community within the Empire.[21] They were now considered a *millet*, with privileges and rights like the other recognized non-Muslim communities. Emboldened by their new status the Protestant mission in Jerusalem became involved in a number of incidents. The first of these occurred in 1851, the very year of the council's reestablishment and involved none other than Hayim al-Serish or perhaps, Seresli.[22] His behavior on the occasion of this dispute was in marked contrast to the humble and deferential character he had assumed toward his Muslim colleagues on the *majlis*. Bishop Samuel Gobat, Anglican Primate of Jerusalem, provided a detailed account of the incident:

> On the 19th day of June 1851, a Jew named Daood Rahhmon presented himself crying, to Mr. Nicolayson an English Clergyman, who is also Wakeel of the Protestant Community, and declared that on the Saturday about 3 o'clock in the afternoon being in the Jewish Quarter, he was desired by Mustafa Basheeti to go to speak with the Chief Rabbi [Jacob Covo]—accordingly he went, and on his arrival at the said house he found an assembly of Jews, who immediately placed him in a place until the end of Sabbath and then brought him before Chief Rabbi—All the Assembly rose up against him and beat him much with sticks, also pipe sticks, without enquiring anything

of him. And amongst those who were present were Hhaiim es Sizily [i.e., Hayim Seresli] the Dragoman, Abraham Ashkenazi, Judah Passo, Joseph Karbon, and Ephraim Naon, with others of the assembly who then imprisoned him and called for the Tufenkchi Bashi Khaleel Aga er Risras, who was accompanied by four Janissaries, Khaleel Karajuni, Khaleel Kidamani, the slave of Khaleel Aga and Ahhmad en Nickari—these took him to the Seraglio and imprisoned him there till Sunday when the Dragoman came and fetched him out of prison and brought him to the house of the Chief Rabbi—After this he was taken back to prison the second time and was there till the afternoon of Tuesday when Hhaiim es Sizily the Dragoman, and one of the number of the Medjlis brought him into the Medjlis to declare his repentance, that is to say in presence of Mohammed Durwish Effendi, and Sheikh Abu Saood Effendi, with the said Hhaiim—He kissed their hands and went without a word being mentioned of his being guilty of anything.—He believes that his only crime is that of having sent his children to the Protestant school to learn to read.

Then Mr. Nicolayson seeing the marks of the blows on his body, inquired who could witness to it. . . . At that time Daood Rahhmon asked of the said Wakeel to receive him as a Christian Protestant of the Subjects of the Sublime Porte—he promised him to do so, after examination, and finding him in a state of fear, banished out of his own home, he took him as a servant and delivered him to the doorkeeper of the Church premises, to remain with him until he could examine him.

After that the said Wakeel went to Jaffa for a few days.

And yesterday, being Wednesday the 2nd of July, the Janissaries of the government seized him near the Castle-gate, about 3 o'clock in the afternoon, took him openly to the Seraglio, and there imprisoned him.

Then we heard that at night he was taken to the Makhkameh and brought back to prison not knowing any reason. . . . [23]

On 12 August Consul Finn forwarded Gobat's statement to the British ambassador in Constantinople, Sir Stratford Canning, with the additional note that "the Jewish official Dragoman Hhaiim es Sirzily is the same person of whom I have previously complained, as having excited the rioters of Silwan in February 1850 to resist the funeral of an English Jewish Subject—He still retains his seat in the Council."[24]

Clearly Hayim Seresli had used his position as council member to bring the weight of Ottoman authority against David Rahman, the would-be convert. Lacking similar status themselves, the Protestants were hard-pressed to respond. On their behalf consul Finn did protest to the Ottoman governor, Adhem Pasha (who served 1849–51), but he was unable to gain satisfaction and the case dragged on for years.[25] Recognizing their weakness vis-à-vis the Jews they sought the same advantage their rivals had. The Protestant community was still trying to establish itself. First the status of their bishop had to be raised. On 21 March 1854 Finn sent his dragoman to Yakub Pasha Karaosmanoğlu, the newly installed governor—he had arrived just five days earlier, with the request that he treat "our Bishop on official visits on the same level with the Latin Patriarch." Finn's diary entry suggests the difficulty encountered; his dragoman "went twice during the day but found him [the Pasha] too much occupied."[26] Complicating the Protestant position were the disputes and rivalries which had repeatedly erupted between Finn and his Anglican bishop.[27] Thus it was in a somewhat jaundiced fashion that he noted in his diary on 25 August of that same year, "His LP [Lordship] the Bishop informed me that he had of late made application to the Pasha to have native Protestant Members introduced into the Town Councils of Jerusalem & Nablus—but that H.E. [His Excellency] had refused, on the ground that no such provision was made in the Firman received about 2 months ago—"[28] When Yakub Pasha died in October no further action could be taken on Gobat's proposal until a new governor was installed. Sometime after the arrival of Yakub's replacement, Kāmal Pasha, in February 1855, the Protestants finally did gain a seat for themselves on the *majlis*. Kāmal was regarded as sympathetic to the Christians and a consistent Anglophile. Indeed he once even attended an Anglican church service in Jerusalem.[29]

Despite the new governor, the Protestants did not maintain their presence for very long, as the following private and confidential letter dated 30 November 1855 reveals:

Although my object was never to make proselytes from other Christians, yet we have a good number of native protestants here and elsewhere. We had much difficulty in introducing their Khodji Bash [sic] (or chosen head) into the Medjlis. We however succeeded last winter [probably late winter since Kāmal Pasha did not arrive until 15 February], and his seat was given him between the Khodji Bashas of other christian [sic] Churches and that of the Jews. With this arrangement I was perfectly satisfied. But when Sir Moses Montefiore was here [July-August] he requested the Pasha to put the protestant Khodji Bashe [sic] under the Jewish. The Pasha wished to please him, but he felt it to be somewhat incongruous to put the Jews over the co-religionists of the Queen of England, till Mr. Consul Finn stepped in to support Sir Moses' request (being led to it by his enthusiastic admiration of the superiority of the Jewish character). Then the Pasha yielded; and when since requested to replace the protestant Khodji Bashe [sic] in his place, he expressed his willingness to do it if Mr. Finn was not in the way. Now since the protestant Khodji Bashe has refused to put his seat under the Jewish, he is no longer admitted into the Medjlis. I think if the protestant had been placed under the Jew at first, I should not have objected, but so it is a degradation and giving an official occasion to people to say that the protestants are no christians. But I cannot interfere without coming into collision with Mr. Finn, & this I must avoid. Wherefore I should be exceedingly thankful, if you would help in any way, though I should be sorry to cast unnecessary trouble upon you.[30]

The letter was written by Samuel Gobat to the British Consul in Damascus, Richard Wood. Since there is no evidence that Protestants served on the *majlis* at any subsequent time it is not likely that Wood ever intervened in the matter or, if he did so, it was without success.[31] While Gobat's letter had little practical result it does serve a number of historiographical purposes. It demonstrates once again the tensions which had arisen between him and Finn over proselytism among the Arabs, who were the "other Christians" of the letter, versus proselytism among the Jews, which the consul had favored. In all likelihood, Finn feared that too aggressive a Protestant presence on the *majlis* would only increase Jewish antagonism to his mission. Gobat by contrast had lost hope in it. Indeed after some initial success among the Jews, the rising number of converts were coming from the Arab population.[32] The unidentified Khawaja Başı must have come from that new element. The ultimately negative outcome of the struggle illustrates the central argument of this essay, that non-Muslim membership in the *majlis* was more important for relations within the non-Muslim community than it was for relations between Muslims and non-Muslims. Since the prime Protestant purpose in joining the *majlis* was to gain precedence within the non-Muslim community it was better for them to have no position at all, than to have the lowest position of all.

NOTES

I thank Dr. Israel Bartal and Prof. Bernard Wasserstein for their many helpful suggestions. I thank as well Mr. Patrick Plunkett for permission to quote from the Richard Wood Papers, Middle East Library, St. Antony's College, Oxford.

1. Quoted in Benjamin Braude and Bernard Lewis, "Introduction," *Christians and Jews in the Ottoman Empire, the Functioning of a Plural Society*, Vol. I: *The Central Lands*, ed. B. Braude and B. Lewis (New York, 1982), p. 30.

2. Moshe Ma'oz, "Syrian Urban Politics in the Tanzimat Period Between 1840 and 1861," *Bulletin of the School of Oriental and African Studies*, XXIX (1966), 277–301.

3. Yitzhak Hofman, "The Administration of Syria and Palestine Under Egyptian Rule (1831–1840)," *Studies on Palestine During the Ottoman Period*, ed. Moshe Ma'oz (Jerusalem, 1975), p. 331.

4. Ma'oz, "Urban Politics," p. 282, based on British diplomatic dispatches from Jerusalem, 28 October 1840, 28 June 1841, and a *sijill* from Jaffa, 22 November 1840/27 Ramaḍān 1256.

5. Hoffman, p. 318.

6. 'Ārif al-'Ārif, *al-Mufaṣṣal fī Tārikh al-Quds* (Jerusalem, 1961), p. 315, and Aref al-Aref [sic], "The Closing Phase of Ottoman Rule in Jerusalem," *Studies on Palestine*, p. 337. Please note that there are errors of transcription in both versions. I have tried to present the most likely readings when the two are in contradiction. Al-'Arif gives no archival source for the document, except to say that he stumbled upon it.

7. This contradicts the claim that the first Ottoman *majlis* in Jerusalem was instituted in 1851. For that assertion see Yair Hirschfeld, "Some Findings on Prussian and Ottoman Policies During the 1840s Based on the Writings of Dr. Gustav E. Schultz, the First Prussian Vice-Consul to Jerusalem, 1842–1851," *Palestine in the Late Ottoman Period, Political, Social, and Economic Transformations*, ed. David Kushner (Jerusalem, 1986), pp. 271–72.

8. Ma'oz, "Urban Politics," p. 281.

9. M. F. Perrier, *La Syrie sous le gouvernement de Mehemet-Ali* (Paris, 1842), quoted in Hofman, pp. 332–33.

10. British diplomatic dispatches from Aleppo (30 January 1832), Beirut (20 July 1832), and *Mudhakkirat Tārikhiyya*, ed. Qusṭanṭīn al-Bāshā, quoted in Hofman, p. 331.

11. Ma'oz, "Urban Politics," p. 283.

12. Hirschfeld, pp. 271–72.

13. Since this figure was supposed to include all males, not just heads of households, it should not be subject to the normal multiplier of four or five. Jehoshua Ben-Arieh, *Jerusalem in the 19th Century, the Old City* (Jerusalem, 1984), pp. 131, 191, 273. For the problems for municipal reform caused by non-Muslims who avoided the status of Ottoman subject, see Steven Rosenthal, "Minorities and Municipal Reform in Istanbul, 1850–1870," *Christians and Jews in the Ottoman Empire*, I, pp. 369–85.

14. Quoted in Hirschfeld, p. 272.

15. James Finn, *Stirring Times, or Records from Jerusalem Consular Chronicles of 1853 to 1856*, ed. Elizabeth Anne Finn (London, 1878), I, 180–81.

16. Dispatch of 11 August 1853, *The British Consulate in Jerusalem in Relation to the Jews of Palestine, 1838–1914*, ed. Albert M. Hyamson (London, 1939), part I, 215.

17. *Stirring Times*, I, 179.

18. John P. Newman, *"From Dan to Beersheba" or, the Land of Promise as It Now Appears* (New York, 1868), p. 161.

19. See, for example, the comments of David Yellin, from 1896 in his

Yerushalayim shel Tmol (Jerusalem, 1972), pp. 11–12, and of Gad Frumkin from a few years later in his *Derekh Shofet bi-Yerushalayim* (Tel-Aviv, 1954), p. 110; also Haim Gerber, *Ottoman Rule in Jerusalem, 1890–1914*, pp. 131–32, which discusses these accounts. For a different approach see Moshe Ma'oz, "Changes in the Position of the Jewish Communities of Palestine and Syria in Mid-Nineteenth Century," *Studies on Palestine*, p. 156.

20. Dispatch of 4 January 1860 in Hyamson, part I, 268.

21. For text of Firman see *Stirring Times*, I, 156–58.

22. It is likely that he came from one of the most active and distinguished Jewish families in Jerusalem. In the next generation they produced Shelomo Israel Seresli, editor, publisher, and prolific author. The family itself originated in Serres, a small town close to Salonica. They migrated to Palestine in 1806–7. Moshe David Gaon, *Yehude ha-Mizraḥ be-Erez Yisrael* (Jerusalem, 1937), part II, 298–99, 682; and Pinhas Grayevsky, *Zikhhron le-Ḥovavim Rishonim*, pamphlet 4, 34 (not seen).

23. "Translation of a Document received by Mr. Consul Finn from his Lordship the Anglican Bishop," Hyamson, part I, 173–74.

24. Hyamson, part I, 173.

25. Dispatch of 15 December 1852 in Hyamson, part I, 212; entries for 1852 and 1853 in *A View from Jerusalem, 1849–1858: The Consular Diary of James and Elizabeth Anne Finn*, ed. Arnold Blumberg (Cranbury, N.J., 1980), pp. 113, 130–31; Arnold Blumberg, *Zion Before Zionism, 1838–1880* (Syracuse, 1985), p. 163.

26. *Diary of . . . Finn*, p. 161; *Stirring Times*, I, 450, 452.

27. Robert Buchanan, *Notes of a Clerical Furlough Spent Chiefly in the Holy Land* (London, 1859), pp. 204–9 and Abdul-Latif Tibawi, *British Interests in Palestine, 1800–1901* (London, 1961), pp. 122–42.

28. *Diary of . . . Finn*, p. 170.

29. Elizabeth Anne Finn, *Reminiscences of Mrs. Finn* (London, 1929), p. 123, 128; *Diary of . . . Finn*, pp. 187, 207–8; Blumberg, *Zion*, p. 73.

30. S. Angl. Hierosol. [Samuel Gobat], Jerusalem, to Richard Wood, Damascus, 30 November 1855, Richard Wood Papers, Private Papers Collection, Middle East Library, St. Antony's College, Oxford; for Montefiore's dates, see *Diaries of Sir Moses and Lady Montefiore*, ed. Louis Loewe, with introduction by Raphael Loewe, and new index (London, 1983), II, 45 and *Diary of . . . Finn*, pp. 197–200. Significantly in none of these diaries nor in *Stirring Times* or *Reminiscences of Mrs. Finn* is there any reference to this controversy.

31. The Finns never mention him nor is a Protestant cited in later lists of *majlis* members, see *inter alia*, Gerber, pp. 131–32.

32. *Stirring Times*, I, 154–55 and Tibawi, *British Interests*, pp. 89, 93, 111, 117.

42
The Expansion of the First Saudi State: The Case of Washm

Michael Cook

I. Introduction

THE CREATION OF the first Saudi state is an instance of a classic pattern of state formation in Arabian history. One takes a religious doctrine of a politically activist kind; one mobilizes a tribal population, which may or may not be nomadic; and one fuses them into a state—of sorts. Yet seen in this perspective, at least two features of the Saudi case are surprising. One relates to the doctrine. The dogmatic background to the Saudi expansion was not some heretical activism, Shīʿite or Khārijite, but the notoriously quietist Ḥanbalite brand of Sunnism. The issue this raises is the exact nature of the doctrinal innovation—or renovation—effected by Muḥammad ibn ʿAbd al-Wahhāb; and it is not the subject of this paper. The other surprising feature relates to the tribes, or more precisely to their location: Najd.

A glance at the history of Arabia between the rise of Islam and modern times is enough to show that the normal distribution of such states as are found in Arabia is around the edges of the peninsula—in the Ḥijāz, the Yemen, Oman, and more shakily the northeast. It is no great mystery why this should be so. One cannot make ropes out of sand, and it is around the edges of the peninsula that the resources of Arabia are concentrated—the best agricultural land, the commercial revenues that go with frontage on the Indian Ocean, and the call on the wealth of the outside world made by the sanctuaries of the Ḥijāz.

Najd, by contrast, is a relatively unpromising area. It lacks the rainfall and commercial revenues of the Yemen or Oman, and has nothing to compare with the sanctity of the Ḥijāz. It does indeed contain oases in large numbers; but they are too widely scattered, and too much on a level, to provide a plausible material basis for a state. The previous record of state formation in Najd had accordingly been a rather poor one. Between the Yamāma of the time of the Prophet and the first Saudi state, we encounter only the Banū 'l-Ukhayḍir of the third to fifth centuries of the Hijra—a minor dynasty of ʿAlid *sharīfs* of bad reputation who ruled in southern Najd.[1] Neither of these phenomena seems to have been comparable in scale to the Saudi state. It is thus a legitimate question why and how this state should have appeared in so unexpected a quarter.

This paper is not an answer to this question, legitimate or otherwise. But it does attempt to examine the Saudi expansion into one small part of Najd with this issue in mind.

II. Background

Washm is a region some eighty miles west-northwest of Riyāḍ.[2] It consists essentially of a long, thin depression which runs from the northwest to the southeast. In or near this depression lies a string of settlements; there are seven of them,[3] strung out over a distance of some twenty-five miles. In our period, as in the early days of the third Saudi state, their economy doubtless rested on a combination of agriculture—dates and cereals[4]—and pastoralism.[5] At the end of the first Saudi state the combined population of the settlements was estimated to be about 12,400 souls.[6] The region is almost surrounded by long, thin tongues of sand desert; these tongues run parallel to the depression, and in places encroached on the settlements themselves.[7] These sand deserts may have contributed to the relative isolation of the region.[8]

The diagram given below shows the relative positions of the seven settlements. I have also indicated (in brackets) the tribal affiliation of their populations, where the sources reveal this.[9] Several settlements were inhabited in our period by subtribes of Tamīm: Marāt[10] and Tharmadā'[11] by the ʿAnāqir, Farʿa by the Nawāṣir,[12] and Ushayqir by the Wuhaba.[13] Shaqrā' seems already to have been inhabited by the non-Tamīmī Banū Zayd.[14] I do not have adequate data for Uthayfiya[15] and Qarā'in,[16] though the former at least is likely to have had a Tamīmī population.

- Ushayqir (Wuhaba)
- Far'a (Nawāṣir)
- Shaqrā' (Banū Zayd)
- Qarā'in (?)
- Uthayfiya (?)
- Tharmadā' ('Anāqir)
- Marāt ('Anāqir)

The area has shown a striking continuity of settlement in historical times. This is apparent in terms of the names of the settlements. All of them reappear in Philby's account of his journey through Washm at the end of the First World War.[17] Going back to the fourth century, four of the seven appear by name in the geography of Hamdānī[18]—and they were hardly new in his day. For example, the vituperative Umayyad poet Jarīr ibn al-Khaṭafī had close links with Uthayfiya.[19] A measure of continuity is likewise apparent in terms of the tribal composition of the population. Hamdānī records the presence of Tamīm in the settlements of Washm,[20] and this again was nothing new in his day.[21] In the twelfth century, Tamīm was still the dominant element in the population; the subtribes, of course, were new. Between the twelfth century and the time of Philby's visit, the tribal affiliation of one settlement (Marāt) seems to have changed; but in at least three cases (Tharmadā', Far'a, and Ushayqir), the populations still belonged to the same subtribes of Tamīm.

We are perhaps lucky to have any sources at all with which to write the history of an inner Arabian region as small and remote as Washm.[22] For the pre-Saudi period, there is a local Najdi historical tradition going back to the first half of the eleventh century;[23] this tradition is associated in part with the scholars of Ushayqir,[24] a town which was by Najdi standards a major center of learning. The material is annalistic and fragmentary in the extreme[25]—on Schachtian criteria we should have to date it well before the time of Khalīfa ibn Khayyāṭ. From the same milieu stems some useful genealogical material,[26] and there is a biographical literature relating to the scholars of Ushayqir and other centers of learning.[27] For the period of the Saudi expansion, the Saudi chronicles are rather fuller and more continuous in their coverage of events.[28] But the materials they offer would still strike any reader of Ṭabarī as jumbled and threadbare. There are also some epistles from Ibn ʻAbd al-Wahhāb to persons in Washm, though they tend to be allusive and hard to date.[29] The sources are thinnest of all for the period following the annexation of Washm.[30] There are no archival sources, and the outside world begins to provide direct accounts of Washm only with the collapse of the first Saudi state.[31]

These sources have already been used to a greater or lesser extent by modern scholars concerned with the history of Najd at large in our period.[32]

III. Pre-Saudi Politics: External

The most striking feature of the politics of pre-Saudi Washm is the very local character of its political horizons.[33]

In the first place, it is unusual for its settlements to have political relations with areas or populations outside Washm. On the west, Washm is occasionally exposed to the unwelcome attentions of the Sharīfs of Mecca in their more expansionist moods; thus there was a Meccan attack on Ushayqir in 1107.[34] On the east, there are occasional, and less one-sided, relations between settlements in Washm and other settlements in Najd. Thus in 1088, Tharmadā' raided Ḥuraymilā'; in 1095, Ḥuraymilā' returned the compliment.[35] In 1125, the people of Thādiq were involved in an attack on Tharmadā'.[36] In 1147, some men of Julājil played a part in the internal quarrels of Ushayqir.[37] There seems also to have been a clash between Tharmadā' and Raghba.[38] But such relations are subject to two noteworthy limitations. First, within Washm only the two largest settlements are involved—Tharmadā' and Ushayqir. Second, the Najdi settlements which have recorded relations with Washm are all located in the neighboring regions of Sudayr and Miḥmal. (The horizons of emigration from Washm seem to have been somewhat wider.[39])

In the second place, there is very little attestation of political (or other) relations between the settlements of Washm and the bedouin tribes of Najd. The only clear case is a report of the cooperation of a subtribe of Ẓafīr with Tharmadā' in an attack on the neighboring settlement of Uthayfiya in 1119;[40] Ẓafīr was one of the major bedouin tribes of Najd.[41] A doubtful case concerns Ushayqir and the Fuḍūl in 1103 or 1104.[42]

In the third place, political horizons are strikingly restricted within Washm itself. For the purposes of this analysis we can divide the region into three zones: the north (Ushayqir and Far'a), the center (Shaqrā' and Qarā'in), and the south (Uthayfiya, Tharmadā', Marāt). For the center, the historical tradition offers only an obscure reference to an attack by Shaqrā' on Qarā'in in 1099.[43] I shall take up a testimony from outside the tradition in due course.[44] For the north and south, however, the information is relatively abundant. The immediately striking point is that we hear nothing of any mutual relations between north and south;[45] the far north and the deep south seem to be different political worlds. Let us look at each in turn.

In the south, the pattern of intersettlement relations is reasonably clear. Tharmadā' is the local bully, while Uthayfiya and Marāt are its victims—Uthayfiya in 1119,[46] Marāt in 1136.[47] But I know no historical evidence that Tharmadā' at any stage *ruled* over either of its neighbors[48] (though we might well not know if it had done). Thus in 1116 a political refugee from Tharmadā' is able to find asylum in Uthayfiya.[49] In the north, there is attestation of relations between Ushayqir and Far'a. Here, as in the south, one party is bigger, namely Ushayqir. But as we shall see, Ushayqir (unlike Tharmadā') was wracked by domestic discord, and so in no condition to act with any consistency as the local bully. The pattern of relations is accordingly less one-sided: Far'a attacked Ushayqir unsuccessfully in 1111;[50] Ushayqir attacked Far'a with more success in 1135,[51] but suffered a reverse in 1139;[52] and peace was made in 1149.[53] During the years 1135–39, it seems likely that Far'a was actually ruled from Ushayqir.[54] The conduct of these hostilities can hardly have imposed great logistic strain on either of the parties, inasmuch as the two settlements are separated only by about half a mile.[55] What is remarkable is that two settlements a few minutes walk from each other should in general have been mutually independent.[56]

Two questions are worth asking at this point. One is whether this whole picture has been painted too negatively by virtue of the poverty of the sources. And indeed, my picture is more than likely to be incomplete. Thus a recent study, using sources unavailable to me, refers to relations between Tharmadā' and one of the hamlets of Qarā'in,[57] and even between Tharmadā' and Ushayqir.[58] Another case in point is the stray item of information from outside the historical tradition alluded to above. In one of his epistles, Ibn 'Abd al-Wahhāb taunts the people of Shaqrā' (by now within the Wahhābī fold) with their sluggishness in making war on Tharmadā'; after all, he remarks, they used in former times to go to war with the ruler of Tharmadā' over something as trifling as an insult or a donkey.[59] If these reports are exact, they attest a considerably wider range of relations within Washm than was suggested above. But even this hardly transforms our vision of the external relations of the settlements of pre-Saudi Washm. My analysis will be *substantially* misleading only if the annalists made a habit of recording trivial events and ignoring significant ones—though such perversity is not beyond them.[60]

The other question worth asking is whether such extreme fragmentation had always prevailed in Washm, or whether it was something new and hence, arguably, problematic. Certainly the local historical tradition preserves no memory of a more unified Washm. There is, however, a report by the sixth-century geographer Yāqūt, quoting a bedouin informant, to the effect that five towns of Washm share a common defensive wall.[61] This amenity has no parallel in our period, or in modern times,[62] and points to a certain community of purpose. If this more unified Washm had a center, it must have been Tharmadā', since Yāqūt describes it as the chief place of Washm.[63]

IV. Pre-Saudi Politics: Internal

What sort of civil order and disorder prevailed within the settlements of Washm? The general pattern is simple enough:[64] each settlement has its boss,[65] and the alternative to an effective local boss is chaos. Thus we do not encounter any kind of nonmonarchic polity, be it democratic or oligarchic; nor, as we have seen, do we find one settlement ruling another for any length of time. It can be assumed, and sometimes shown, that the boss belongs to a ruling lineage.

Almost the only thing we learn about the nature of the power of the boss is that it is open to challenge.[66] Indeed much of our historical material is a record of such challenges. It is also clear from this material that there are significant variations in the stability of regimes in different settlements, though in many cases the information is scanty. As before, the historical tradition is at its worst on the politics of central Washm, and what it tells us of Far'a[67] in the north and Uthayfiya[68] in the south is scarcely worth discussing. For Marāt, in the far south, we have a little more. Four bosses are named, all belonging to the local 'Anāqir subtribe of Tamīm. All recorded successions are violent: on three occasions the incumbent ruler is killed, while in another case he flees the settlement.[69] But it is only for the big two—Tharmadā' and Ushayqir—that the information is relatively plentiful. The contrast it reveals is striking.

In the case of Tharmadā', our sources are uniquely rich. We are privileged to know the names and dates of all rulers between 1081 and 1184, together with their genealogical relationships and the manner in which their reigns ended. This information is presented in the diagram.[70] The picture that emerges is of a town that had got itself together. Four long reigns span a period of a century. Throughout this period, power is retained within a single lineage, the Āl Khunayfir; and the succession is relatively peaceful, with three of the four rulers dying natural deaths. But even Tharmadā' is not immune to civil strife, and two cases of this are recorded.[71] In 1116, there is a bloody succession in which the incumbent ruler is killed, his sons flee,[72] and power shifts to a different sublineage within the Āl Khunayfir. In 1151, blood is again shed within the ruling lineage, but without a change of ruler.[73]

THE RULERS OF THARMADĀ'

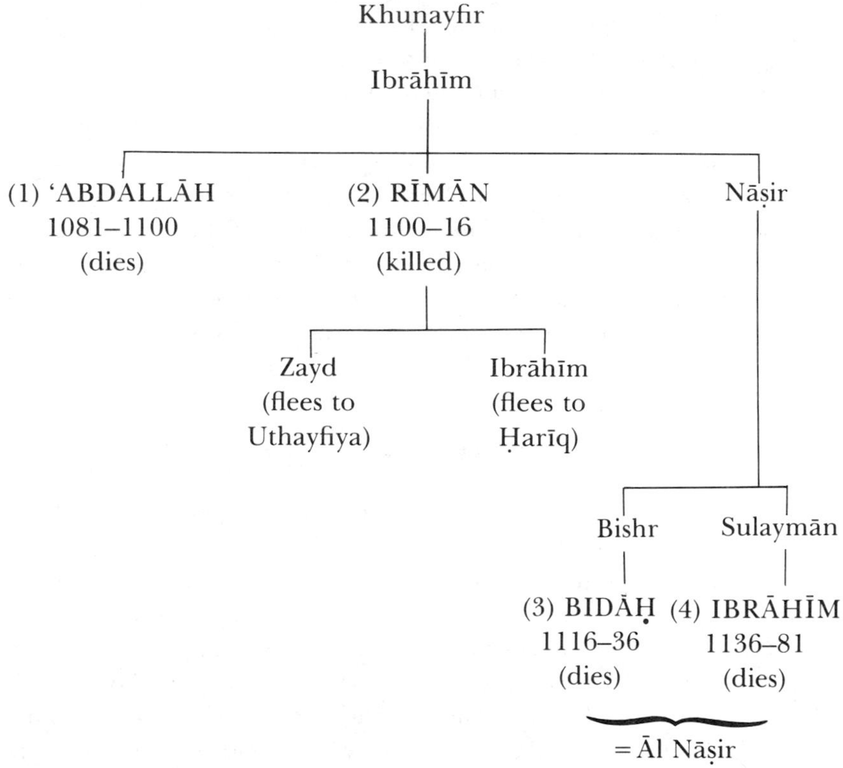

Ushayqir, by contrast, seems to be the least cohesive of all the settlements of Washm,[74] despite the fact that its population belonged to a single subtribe of Tamīm, the Wuhaba.[75] Only one boss of Ushayqir is mentioned by name, a certain Raqrāq who at his death in 1155 was apparently ruler of the settlement as a whole.[76] Only eight years previously, in 1147, he had been no more than the boss of a single quarter,[77] a position he may have attained as early as 1135.[78] Against this isolated identification of a single boss, we have a good many references to ruling lineages (*ru'asā'*). The lineages in question are the Āl Bassām ibn Munīf[79] and the Āl Muḥammad[80] (to which Raqrāq belonged); they may have enjoyed their status as ruling lineages simultaneously.[81] At the same time, there are frequent references to civil conflict. Sometimes this seems to be a matter of sporadic outbursts—as in 1084–85,[82] 1109,[83] and 1135.[84] But at other times there is recurrent mention of hostilities over several years, giving the impression of periods of more or less continuing civil war;[85] there is such a period in 1114–19,[86] and another in 1144–49.[87]

What is all this fighting about? As usual, the sources do not tell us much.[88] As might be expected, the struggles are between rival lineages, some half-dozen of which are involved at one time or another,[89] sometimes leaving town or returning according to their fortunes.[90] The lineages in turn are associated with particular quarters and markets. There is more than one market, and probably three;[91] a market may be the scene of fighting, and may be destroyed or rebuilt in the course of events.[92] Whatever the sources of these conflicts, it is clear that they run deep. On two occasions, we find that periods of sustained conflict issued in some kind of partition of the town: in 1119, each side built its own public buildings, and in 1147, separate emirates were established in different parts of the town.

V. The Conquest

In 1157, the ruler of Dir'īya in the 'Āriḍ pledged his support to Ibn 'Abd al-Wahhāb and his controversial doctrine. The expansion of the Saudi state under its new Wahhābī aegis began shortly afterward. As early as 1161, this activity was impinging on Washm.[93]

It may be best to begin by stressing what the Saudi conquest was not. It was not the work of a massive army moving slowly but surely through Washm, picking off one settlement after another and bringing them under its alien yoke. Not that Washm had any immunity to conquest by overwhelming force—it was to experience it a few decades later at the hands of the Egyptians.[94] But a conquest that took the Egyptians a matter of weeks was for the Saudis the work of a generation. Why this should have been so is not hard to see.[95] The resources of the early Saudi state were on the same low level as those of its enemies in Washm and elsewhere; and partly as a result, its military efforts were extensive rather than intensive in character. The Saudis had no professional army, and lacked the equipment for siege warfare. Their characteristic mode of warfare was the sweeping, but transient raid mounted by a part-time "citizen" army.

The Saudi war effort in Washm[96] was thus notably light in touch. The Saudi raiders appeared repeatedly in Washm, seized booty, and fought minor battles.[97] But their style of warfare, though in no way soft-hearted, was by the standards of the outside world neither atrocious nor heavy. This can be seen from the casualty figures which the Saudi chroniclers regularly report. According to these figures, Saudi attacks cost Washm some 350 men in a total of fourteen engagements spread over two decades, more than half of the losses being suffered by Tharmadā'.[98] Equally telling is the fact that, over the whole course of the struggle, the Saudis only once laid siege to any of the settlements of Washm,[99] and never captured one.[100] The pressure they exerted on Washm was perhaps as much as anything economic.[101] The most positive feature of their war effort, and one quite alien to pre-Saudi Najd, was its sheer persistence. Washm was never in any real sense conquered; but at the end of twenty years of intermittent hostilities, a consensus seems to have emerged that the resistance was not worth continuing. Significantly, there is no indication that a Saudi army was operating in Washm at the time when this decision was taken.[102]

In the course of the twenty-year conflict, from 1161 to 1181, the settlements of Washm responded to the Saudi threat in different ways. The larger settlements, Tharmadā' and Ushayqir, kept up their resistance to the end. Tharmadā', as the casualty figures already cited suggest, was a major center of opposition to the Saudi expansion.[103] It was raided seven times by the Saudis.[104] Within Washm it appears as the leader of a kind of southern block;[105] at the same time, it engaged in active relations with other parts of Najd,[106] and renewed its link with the Ẓafīr bedouin.[107] Its role was thus appropriate to its size and domestic cohesion. Ushayqir, as might be expected, played no such active role in the struggle. It was raided by the Saudis in 1170, 1173, and perhaps 1175,[108] and harassed by local pro-Saudi forces from

1175 until its eventual submission,[109] presumably in 1181.[110] What is surprising, given its history of disunity, is that none of the lineages of Ushayqir seems to have espoused the obvious tactic of a Saudi alliance against its enemies; but we know virtually nothing of the internal politics of Ushayqir in this period.[111] It may be added that the reaction of Ushayqir to the Saudi expansion may not have been free of a certain academic pique toward the pretensions of Ibn ʻAbd al-Wahhāb.

We can turn now to the responses of the small fry. Marāt, which had encounters with the Saudis in 1163 and 1175,[112] shows the same diehard hostility as Tharmadā': in describing the general submission of Washm in 1181, a Saudi chronicler remarks that "even" Marāt converted.[113] This may reflect a degree of solidarity with Tharmadā'. Bully though the latter may have been, both settlements were inhabited by the same subtribe of Tamīm.[114] Uthayfiya, the northern neighbor of Tharmadā', has a more checkered history. It remained in the anti-Saudi camp until at least 1167;[115] but by 1175 it had gone over to the Saudis,[116] perhaps to spite Tharmadā'. Then, in 1176, the people of Uthayfiya went back on their Saudi allegiance with the help of Tharmadā', with which they then made common cause.[117] In central Washm, Qarā'in likewise seems to have changed sides in the middle years of the war: whereas in 1170 it served as a base and refuge for anti-Saudi forces operating against Shaqrā',[118] in 1175 it is associated with an attack on a caravan in the Saudi interest.[119] In the north, Farʻa would seem to resemble Uthayfiya in taking advantage of the Saudi expansion to play games with a larger neighbor, here Ushayqir. Farʻa joined the Saudi camp during a Saudi raid in 1175,[120] and spent the rest of the war being unpleasant to Ushayqir, capturing its southern towers.[121]

This leaves us with the most adventurous response of all, that of Shaqrā'. Shaqrā' was an ancient settlement—it is mentioned by Hamdānī,[122] and figures in a document the original of which was written in 747.[123] But as we have seen, the Najdi historical tradition has almost nothing to say about the role of Shaqrā' in the politics of pre-Saudi Washm. It is a reasonable inference that the settlement was then a political nonentity. Yet in 1168 Shaqrā' joined the Saudis,[124] the first of the settlements of Washm to do so.[125] Thereafter Shaqrā' was doggedly, if not always energetically, loyal to the Saudi cause.[126] It sustained a major attack by an anti-Saudi coalition in 1170,[127] and it seems to have remained the only Saudi outpost in Washm in 1171.[128] But by 1175 it had company, for in this year it was joined by the people of Qarā'in and Uthayfiya to the south in an attack on a caravan,[129] while to the north it was in the same year that Far'a converted, perhaps at the hands of the people of Shaqrā'.[130] But Shaqrā' remained the bastion of the Saudi position in Washm, and stuck by its Saudi allegiance even during the second invasion of Najd by the Banū Khālid of Aḥsā' in 1178.[131] At the end of the first Saudi state, it was the only settlement in Washm to resist the Egyptian conquest in 1233.[132] Why the people of Shaqrā' should have chosen to throw in their lot with the Saudis in this way we do not know. The fact that they belonged to the Banū Zayd may have done something to set them apart from the Tamīmī population of Washm as a whole.[133]

From this discussion it will be obvious that the integration of Washm into the Saudi state was not a victory of overwhelming force. If it had been, the process would not have taken twenty years. But equally, the outcome was far from being a spontaneous local response to the charms of Wahhābī doctrine or of the Saudi political order. Not a single settlement in Washm chose to see the light prior to the first Saudi attack, and even then seven years had to pass before the conversion of Shaqrā'. Nothing, in short, suggests that Washm accepted the new order because it either wanted or needed it.[134] Yet on balance, it is the relative autonomy of local responses to Saudi pressure that deserves underlining. Two points are worth adding in this connection.

The first is the restricted role of Saudi—as opposed to local—troops in Washm. Saudi troops were, as we have seen, of crucial importance as raiders. But they play little part as an army of occupation. Shaqrā' joined the Saudis in 1168, but it was not until 1175 that the Saudis put a garrison of their own into Shaqrā'.[135] Even then, it seems to have been local forces from Shaqrā' and Far'a that played the main part in the hostilities against Ushayqir.[136]

The second point is the degree to which the ruling lineages of pre-Saudi times appear to have survived the Saudi expansion. As usual the documentation is fragmentary, and it is a pity that we do not seem to know the provenance of any of the early emirs of Shaqrā' under Saudi rule.[137] But in Washm as a whole, there is no attested case of a local boss being replaced by a Saudi nominee from outside.[138] At the same time, there are three cases in which continuity can be demonstrated. The first is Uthayfiya, where the boss had been captured by the Saudis in 1167 or 1168;[139] he must have converted in captivity and been sent back to rule Uthayfiya in the Saudi interest, since he was killed when the people of Uthayfiya abandoned the Saudi allegiance in 1176.[140] The second case is Far'a, where the emir converted with his people in 1175, after which he and his subjects made war on Ushayqir; he was still in power in 1196.[141] Finally, in the case of Tharmadā', the emir converted with the end of resistance in Washm at large; he remained in power, but died later in the year.[142] We know nothing of the succession.[143]

It would be wrong, however, to suggest that the political life of pre-Saudi Washm simply continued under a Saudi veneer. There had been at least one dramatic change: the old local horizons had widened. The immediate effect of Saudi pressure on the settlements of Washm was, as we have seen, to enhance the role of Tharmadā'. This development was, of course, abortive. It was under Saudi rule, not against it, that Washm was to be united; and the way in which this came about meant that Tharmadā' forfeited its primacy to the upstart people of Shaqrā'.[144] When the Saudi chroniclers mention "the people of Washm" among the armies which continued the expansion of the Saudi state after 1181, it is the emirs of Shaqrā' who are their leaders.[145]

VI. The Conversion

Pre-Saudi Washm was a remote region of the Islamic world, but it was neither geographically nor culturally marginal. Since at least the tenth century it had belonged to the Ḥanbalite school of Sunni Islam,[146] of which Ushayqir was the Najdi metropolis.[147] The Ḥanbalite scholars of Najd were in written contact with their fellow-Ḥanbalites outside Arabia,[148] and many of them had studied in Syria or Egypt.[149] Within Washm, the position of Ushayqir as a center of scholarship was of course exceptional. Elsewhere in the region scholars were undoubtedly much thinner on the ground. In the sources available to me, we hear only of one, who died in Qarā'in in 1099.[150] But in the context of the Saudi expansion, we shall encounter three *maṭāwi'a*, one in Marāt and two in Tharmadā'.[151] The *muṭawwa'* of a town was, it seems, the *imām* of its mosque,[152] and at the same time the local scholar and religious leader.[153] It is likely enough that other settlements in Washm also had their *maṭāwi'a*.

We have no comparable information regarding popular religion in Washm. We need not concern ourselves with the bedouin, except to note that Ibn 'Abd al-Wahhāb, in his strictures on their religious life, makes specific reference to Ẓafīr.[154] Turning to the settled population, we are perhaps entitled to balk at the general characterization of Najdi Islam (or the lack of it) purveyed by the Wahhābī sources.[155] In any case, none of the local cults which are stigmatized in these sources[156] seems to have been located in Washm; nor have I encountered any reference to Ṣūfism in the area.[157] As always, this may reflect the poverty of our sources. But given the strength of the Ḥanbalite scholarly presence in Ushayqir, it is hard to imagine Washm as a land of ebullient polytheism.

What little we learn of the spiritual conquest of Washm fits well enough with this analysis. The Saudi chronicles, while abounding in religious jargon,[158] are strangely lacking in specifically religious events in their coverage of Washm. At no point do they record a confrontation between the new doctrine and any form of popular religion. No cultic trees are felled, no tombs are demolished, there are no clashes with saints or Ṣūfīs. Again, this may be the fault of our sources. But it may also bear out the striking observation of Ibn 'Abd al-Wahhāb himself that the opposition he had met came not from the laity (*'āmma*) but from the scholars (*khāṣṣa*).[159] He did, of course, insist that questions of monotheist doctrine (*tawḥīd*) were not matters for scholars alone.[160] But it was to the scholars of Washm, not its laity, that he devoted the lion's share of his propagandist attention.[161]

Three epistles written by Ibn 'Abd al-Wahhāb to *maṭāwi'a* of Washm are preserved by Ibn Ghannām.[162] The first is a reply to a letter from Muḥammad ibn 'Abbād, *muṭawwa'* of Tharmadā'.[163] This Ibn 'Abbād, who died in 1175,[164] is also known to us as a chronicler.[165] Ibn 'Abd al-Wahhāb refers to him twice in other epistles, once to include him in what is effectively a list of his scholarly enemies,[166] and once to present him as a temporizer who claims to acknowledge the truth, but to be unable to get it across to the 'Anāqir (i.e., the ruler of Tharmadā').[167] In the epistle in question, Ibn 'Abd al-Wahhāb addresses him as a Muslim,[168] complimenting him on some of the views he has expressed in his letter, and correcting him on others. What bothers Ibn 'Abd al-Wahhāb is a lack of deeds to accompany these (on the whole) exemplary words. He details three occasions when anti-Wahhābī tracts had been brought to Tharmadā';[169] on each of them Ibn 'Abbād unaccountably failed to speak out. He may indeed have temporized on occasion, but he was clearly not in fact a supporter of Ibn 'Abd al-Wahhāb.

The second epistle is addressed to Muḥammad ibn 'Īd, also a *muṭawwa'* of Tharmadā'.[170] Ibn 'Abd al-Wahhāb elsewhere presents him as a temporizer in the same style as Ibn 'Abbād.[171] The chroniclers, however, tell us that he was killed in battle with the Saudis in 1180.[172] In the epistle in question, which deals with the key doctrinal issue dividing Ibn 'Abd al-Wahhāb from his enemies,[173] Ibn 'Īd is ranged among the latter.[174]

The third epistle is a reply to a letter from Aḥmad ibn Ibrāhīm, *muṭawwa'* of Marāt.[175] We can probably think of him as a small-time *muṭawwa'*, since unlike Ibn 'Abbād and Ibn 'Īd he seems not to crop up in other sources. As befits the record of Marāt, he is treated as an enemy,[176] though invited to visit Dir'īya under safe-conduct.[177] However, it is suggested that he too is something of a temporizer, since he had written that he wished to take counsel with the ruler of Tharmadā'.[178]

In the meantime, Washm was being deluged with anti-Wahhābī epistles and tracts. The ruler of Ushayqir could supply copies of such epistles from the scholars of the Ḥijāz.[179] He was also peddling a tract by a Baṣran. The ruler of Tharmadā' received letters from the scholars of Sudayr. A tract by a scholar of Aḥsā' was likewise propagated in Tharmadā'.[180] But the most prominent anti-Wahhābī figure in the war of propaganda, and the *bête noire* of Ibn 'Abd al-Wahhāb, was without doubt 'Abdallāh ibn 'Īsā al-Muways (d. 1175), *qāḍī* of Ḥarma in Sudayr.[181] Ibn 'Abd al-Wahhāb's epistles bristle with references to this man and his proceedings.[182] Unforgivably, Muways had had the advantage of a Syrian education, and seems not to have been unduly modest about it.[183] Not that it was anything to be proud of—one of the teachers of his Syrian teachers was the unspeakable 'Abd al-Ghanī al-Nābulsī (d. 1143), a follower of the infidel Ibn 'Arabī.[184] In the course of his anti-Wahhābī activities, Muways paid conspicuous visits to polytheistic sanctuaries, making speeches alerting their devotees to the Wahhābī menace.[185] What concerns us directly is the fact that Muways had also addressed a polemical epistle to the people of Washm.[186] The unflattering tone of this composition is suggested by its allegation that Ibn 'Abd al-Wahhāb's doctrine was an innovation from Khurāsān.[187]

As might be expected, Ibn 'Abd al-Wahhāb also had some friends among the scholars of Washm. An epistle to a *muṭawwa'* of Sudayr reveals the course of a controversy over an abstruse theological issue. An anti-Wahhābī preacher (*khaṭīb*) had taken a stand on the question, and had then been condemned by two Wahhābīs of Washm.[188] A process of polemical escalation then ensued: Muways condemned the two Wahhābīs, whereupon Ibn 'Abd al-Wahhāb came to their rescue.[189]

We cannot locate either the preacher or his Wahhābī critics, though the chances are that the latter were in Shaqrā'.

The unsteady military expansion of the Saudi state was thus accompanied by the literary raids and skirmishes of the scholars. The scene was a lively one, and its protagonists contrived to involve both local rulers and foreign scholars in the fray.

We have little idea how much upheaval the religious life of Washm underwent with the integration of the area into the Saudi state. As already indicated, we have no evidence of drastic discontinuity at a popular level, which is not to say that there was none. Among the scholarly community, the coming of Saudi rule no doubt contributed to the circulation of elites. Thus in Marāt we hear in 1194 of the death of a *qāḍī* whose connections with Ibn 'Abd al-Wahhāb were so close that he is likely to have been a Saudi intruder.[190] But did the Saudis significantly alter the structure of religious authority in Washm? And if so, how well did the local scholars adapt? We remain in the dark.[191] At a guess, the conversion of Washm may have been marked by something of the same lightness of touch as its conquest.[192]

VII. Conclusion

It may be worth returning at this point to the issue raised in the introduction to this paper.[193] We can best begin with a couple of points about the early expansion of the Saudi state in Najd which follow on from the discussion of Washm.

The first point is that this expansion was almost everywhere slow and unsteady. We have seen this in detail in the case of Washm; and more or less the same is true, with regional variations, for Miḥmal, Sudayr, Kharj, and Qaṣīm—not to mention the 'Āriḍ itself.[194] In other words, the creation of a pan-Najdi state from a starting point within Najd was very much an uphill struggle.

The second point concerns the resource endowments of the Saudis and their enemies. Najd, says a local proverb, goes to the man with the long lance.[195] But no one's lance was in fact that much longer in pre-Saudi Najd than anyone else's. It is at least arguable that in the early years of their expansion, the one thing the Saudis had more of than their enemies was quite simply persistence.[196] Not that the latter were faint-hearted—men like Dahhām ibn Dawwās in Riyāḍ, Ibrāhīm ibn Sulaymān in Tharmadā', and Zayd ibn Zāmil in Kharj, were tough and able rulers who had no intention of being pushed around. Yet the Saudi state proved to have the edge on them: all three at one time or another submitted to the Saudi yoke, and in one way or another all three lost out in the end.[197] If we ask what gave the Saudis the edge on them, it is hard to divorce persistence from faith. Dahhām and his likes fought for immediate human goals; they were liable to get exhausted and pack it in. The Saudis fought for God.[198]

In short, the forces for and against the creation of a Najdi state were very evenly balanced; and the factor which eventually tipped the balance in favor of the Saudis may well have been faith.

In a wider perspective, there are two alternative frames of reference with which one might approach the question why the Saudi state appeared when and where it did.

The first might be dubbed the steady state model, were not statelessness a more appropriate term; it could be outlined as follows. For reasons indicated in the introduction, Najd was not state-friendly territory. Admittedly, state formation was *possible* in Najd; so it did occasionally happen—witness Yamāma, the Banū 'l-Ukhayḍir, and the Saudis (the latter indeed being recidivists). But equally, state formation was *unlikely* in Najd; so it did not happen often, and when it did, it was not usually on a large scale. The mere fact that history had lurched into the twelfth century did nothing to alter this. On such a view, then, the formation of the Saudi state is simply an unusually large fluctuation, to be attributed (if at all) to adventitious factors. It so happened that Ibn 'Abd al-Wahhāb possessed in exceptional measure the sublime obstinacy of faith, a quality which, suitably mixed with charisma and cunning, enabled him to pit himself against the refractoriness of Najdi society and win. No one had really tried to play the religious card since Musaylima. Who, then, is to say that such a venture would have had any less chance of success in the fourth century or the tenth? And who is to deny that the venture could in fact have failed at any number of points in the twelfth?

The alternative approach might be termed the expanding society model. Here we look, not for a combination of unchanging structure and random lurch, but for the steady march of history. Our task is then to scan the history of pre-Saudi Najd for a suitable developmental process, one that could have altered the balance of forces by increasing the potential for state formation. In this perspective Ibn 'Abd al-Wahhāb may be seen as the unwitting instrument, or alternatively the brilliant exponent, of the logic of history; but his role is to nudge history in a certain direction, not to make it.

There are two species of opinion to contend with here. The first seeks a developmental process endogenous to Najdi society. A theory of this kind has been presented with considerable vigor by Juhany in a study frequently cited above. His thesis is that the period from the tenth century (and perhaps before) to the twelfth was one of remarkable growth in Najd.[199] The population was on the increase, among both nomads[200] and sedentaries,[201] to the point of giving rise to acute pressure of men on resources.[202] The scale of political organization was increasing, with the emergence of such settlements as Tharmadā' in the role of regional powers.[203] Learning was likewise blossoming, with a phenomenal growth in the numbers of scholars.[204] The result was that the denizens of this expanding society "needed peace and order for the protection of their lives and economic gains."[205] The emergence of the Wahhābī movement, and the formation of the Saudi state, were thus a "natural outcome" of this development.[206]

My own reaction to this thesis is somewhat skeptical. To demonstrate that processes of such a kind have taken place in a society can be a delicate matter for researchers with access to substantial archival evidence; here it is probably impossible. There is no way in which the scrappy and disjointed material available for pre-Saudi Najd could be made to add up to a column of figures. Juhany is, of course, well aware of the limitations of his sources.[207] What this means is that, to elicit evidence of a developmental process, Juhany is forced into a considerable measure of eisegesis. This is easily seen in the case of population growth. Mostly what the sources tell us about is *movements* of population, and it is mainly on these that Juhany fixes. If people move into Najd, they thereby increase the population.[208] If, on the other hand, they move out of Najd, they do so because the population has already increased, thereby creating pressure on resources.[209] Either way, movement is read as evidence of growth. The case for the emergence of regional powers seems equally doubtful. With regard to the case of Tharmadā', enough has been said above;[210] the general point is the difficulty of showing, with the source material available to us, that a given center possessed in the twelfth century a power it had not had before. Turning to the rising numbers of scholars, we encounter a classic issue in source interpretation. All the biographical compilations are late.[211] Is an increasing number of biographies per century then to be taken as evidence that more scholars were active? Or simply that more of those active have made it into the sources? Finally, it has to be said that if the Saudi state represented the peace and order of which the population of Najd was in need, then a large part of the population seems to have been unduly slow to appreciate this. None of this criticism precludes the possibility that something along the lines of Juhany's thesis is substantially correct. But if so, it is hard to see how we could come to *know* this.

The alternative to an endogenous process is an exogenous one; and here we have at least the advantage that we know a lot more about what was going on outside Najd than we do about processes within it. Was the outside world beginning to impinge on Najd in a way in which it had not done before?

Politically, the answer is almost certainly negative. Najd was being subjected to intermittent bullying on the part of the Sharīfs of Mecca and the Banū Khālid of Aḥsā'.[212] But this pressure was hardly enough to have elicited the Saudi state as an apparatus of Najdi self-defense. Still less is there reason to think in terms of political pressures from states outside Arabia, Ottoman, Iranian, or European. In this respect Najd was far less subject to outside influence than it had been in Sasanian, Umayyad, or early 'Abbasid times.

Economic relationships are a different matter. It is perhaps time to remind ourselves that the twelfth Muslim century was also the eighteenth Christian one, and that the world's trade was by now a great deal larger and more extensive than it had ever been before. Could the increasing pull of the world market have made itself felt in Najd, tipping the local balance in favor of state formation?[213]

In the first instance, we might look for a call on local production for a European market comparable to that which facilitated the formation of a state in northern Palestine in the same period. But here we shall undoubtedly be disappointed. There was no cash-crop produced by the settled population of Najd for a European market; if there had been, the whole character of the Saudi expansion might have been very different.[214]

But more modest commercial links between Najd and the international trade of the Persian Gulf undoubtedly existed,[215] and the Najdi population at the end of the first Saudi state is described as a highly mercantile one.[216] An increase in the volume of such trade, though trivial by the standards of the outside world, could well have been crucial in Najd. What can we say of the hypothesis that such an increase lies behind the formation of the Saudi state?

This hypothesis might be advanced in either a stronger or a weaker form. In the strong form, the Saudi state would be seen as an organization whose *raison d'être* was to serve the needs of commerce.

To my knowledge, neither the history of the Saudi state, nor the content of Wahhābī doctrine, provides positive support for such a view.[217] At the same time, it is striking that when the Saudis eventually reached the shores of the Persian Gulf, Wahhābism proceeded to entrench itself as the faith, not of the mercantile 'Utūb, but of the Qāsimī pirates.[218] The suggestion that the Saudi state existed for the protection of trade would have carried little conviction for the survivors of their depredations.

This leaves the possibility of advancing the commercial hypothesis in a weaker form. An increase in the trade of Najd with the outside world could still have played a crucial part in making available the resources which rendered the emergence of the Saudi state a real possibility. Did such an increase in fact take place? And if so, did it have the desired effect? The questions are good ones, but it is hard to see how they could be answered with the scanty materials at our disposal.

The hypothesis that long-term historical change lies behind the emergence of the first Saudi state is accordingly not to be dismissed.[219] But we are perhaps on solider ground in regarding the event as an act of God.[220]

NOTES

1. On the Banū 'l-Ukhayḍir, see Ḥamad al-Jāsir, *Madīnat al-Riyāḍ 'abr aṭwār al-ta'rīkh* (Riyāḍ, 1966), 69–76; also U. M. Al-Juhany, "The History of Najd Prior to the Wahhābīs; A Study of Social, Political and Religious Conditions in Najd During Three Centuries Preceding the Wahhābī Reform Movement" (University of Washington Ph.D., 1983), 79–81.

2. The best description of Washm known to me is that given by Philby on the basis of his visit at the end of the First World War (H. S. B. Philby, *Arabia of the Wahhabis* [London, 1977], 86–126). See also Juhany, *History*, 53.

3. The number rises to eight if Qarā'in is divided into its two component hamlets, Ghisla and Waqf (see Philby, *Arabia*, 96f., where the vocalization "Ghusla" seems, however, to be incorrect). I exclude the outlying settlements of Ḥurayyiq and Qaṣab, which are sometimes included in Washm.

4. See Philby, *Arabia*, 86f., and the further details to be found in his accounts of the individual settlements. As might be expected, this agricultural economy is occasionally attested in the sources for our period. For the planting of new palm-groves in Ushayqir in the twelfth century of the Hijra, see Juhany, *History*, 235 n. 145; for palm-groves in the story of the expulsion of the Banū Wā'il from Ushayqir about the year 700, see Ibn 'Īsā, *Ta'rīkh ba'ḍ al-ḥawādith*

al-wāqi'a fī Najd, ed. Ḥ. al-Jāsir (Riyāḍ, 1966), 29.2, 29.3 (hereafter this source will be cited as "I."); for a mention of a palm-grove of Tharmadā' in the course of military operations in 1171, see Ibn Ghannām, *Rawḍat al-afkār* (Bombay, 1337), 2:60.24, 61.1 (hereafter "G."); Ibn Bishr, *'Unwān al-majd fī ta'rīkh Najd* (Mecca, 1349), 1:40.6 (hereafter "B."). Grain farming is likewise mentioned in the story of the expulsion of the Banū Wā'il from Ushayqir (I.29.1, 29.3). There is a stray reference to the harvest at Ushayqir in 1107 (Ibn Bishr, in the *sawābiq* to his *'Unwān al-majd*, conveniently brought together in the edition of Beirut *ca.* 1968, 412.18 [the *sawābiq* are here at 1:387–424, hereafter "Bs."]; and see Juhany, *History*, 291 n. 19). We hear of the millet (*dhura*) of Ushayqir in 1139 (Bs.424.1; compare Philby, *Arabia*, 122 and n. 4). The crops of Tharmadā' are mentioned in 1161 (G.2:15.14; B.1:22.6). (On the story of the expulsion of the Banū Wā'il, see Juhany, *History*, 135f.)

5. For the pastoral economy of what Philby refers to as the "home tribes," *sc.* the settled population, see his *Arabia*, 86; also 95, 116. The practice described by Philby of taking the flocks out to pasture in the morning and bringing them home in the evening is familiar to our sources. It appears in the story of the expulsion of the Banū Wā'il, wherein the latter and the Wuhaba take their flocks out to pasture on alternate days (I.28.8, 29.2); and in 1180, Saudi forces seized the flocks of Tharmadā' as they were being taken out to pasture in the morning (G.2:86.24; also F. Mengin, *Histoire de l'Egypte* [Paris, 1823], 2:467).

6. So Mengin, *Histoire*, 2:163. Of these, 2,400 are said to be fit to bear arms. A century later we have a range of estimates of the population of Washm: 6,000 to 7,000 (J. G. Lorimer, *Gazetteer of the Persian Gulf* [Calcutta, 1908–15], 2:1928); 12,000 (Admiralty War Staff, Intelligence Division, *A Handbook of Arabia*, vol. 1 [1916], 366): 15,500 (the total yielded by adding up Philby's figures for the individual settlements).

7. Shaqrā' and Tharmadā' were both said to be affected in this way in a source of the early thirteenth century (see the text as reproduced in Ḥ. al-Jāsir, "Mu'arrikhū Najd," *al-'Arab*, 5 [1971], 796.1).

8. Cf. Philby, *Arabia*, 86.

9. As will appear in individual cases, it is often impossible to be sure whether a given subtribe is the sole or merely the dominant element in the population of a settlement in our period. But with two marginal exceptions (see below, notes 13f.), there is no indication in the sources available to me that any of the settlements was populated by more than one tribal group. It is also impossible to be certain whether there was any significant nontribal population in Washm, but again I find no mention of such a population in the sources. (On such populations in Najd in general, see Juhany, *History*, 174.)

10. All known rulers of the politically unstable settlement of Marāt are 'Anāqir in the period 1084–1136 (see below, note 69, in particular the references to Ibn 'Īsā). Philby records the population as mainly Dawāsir and Qaḥṭān (*Arabia*, 89 n. 2; see also *Handbook of Arabia*, 604; Lorimer, *Gazetteer*, 2:1929; M. Freiherr von Oppenheim, *Die Beduinen* [Leipzig and Wiesbaden, 1939–68], 3:110). A change of population could well have taken place in Marāt during

a period of depopulation at the end of the first Saudi state, if the ruined village referred to by Sadlier in 1819 as "Miriah" is Marāt (G. F. Sadlier, *Diary of a Journey Across Arabia* [Bombay, 1866], 68).

11. The ruling Āl Khunayfir of Tharmadā' belonged to the 'Anāqir (for this lineage, see below, note 70). In 1119 we find the suggestive, though not conclusive, equation *al-'Anāqir ahl (balad) Tharmadā'* (I.87.2; Bs.417.12). Philby records the population as 'Anāqir (*Arabia*, 92; see also von Oppenheim, *Beduinen*, 3:170).

12. In the politics of Far'a we hear only of Nawāṣir (for references see below, notes 50–54, 67). In 1149, we have the equation *al-Nawāṣir ahl al-Far'a* (I.104.3). See also Juhany, *History*, 203. Philby likewise records the population as Nawāṣir (*Arabia*, 120; see also von Oppenheim, *Beduinen*, 3:170).

13. All lineages that figure in the political life of Ushayqir in our period (see below, note 89, for the major ones) belong to the Wuhaba subtribe. The story of the expulsion of the Banū Wā'il leaves the Wuhaba in exclusive possession of the town (I.28–30), and identifies them as *ahl Ushayqir* (I.28.5). Philby likewise records the population as Wuhaba (*Arabia*, 121; see also von Oppenheim, *Beduinen*, 3:170). The only element in the population which the sources indicate to belong to a different tribal group is the scholarly lineage of the Āl Bakr, of the tribe of Subay' (see I.59.2 and Bs. 402.13 [1059]; I.78.5 and Bs.413.13 [1109]; I.79.8 [1111]). (We need not concern ourselves with the scholastic disagreement as to whether the Wuhaba belong to Tamīm proper or to the closely related Ribāb, see for example the genealogy at I.206.9, 207.7.)

14. See Juhany, *History*, 212f. Juhany implies that the Banū Zayd were already in Shaqrā' in the eleventh century, though it is not clear whether there is hard evidence for this. They are mentioned in a passage (the sense of which is not clear to me) in a letter of Ibn 'Abd al-Wahhāb to the people of Shaqrā' exhorting them to make war on Tharmadā' (*Majmū'at al-rasā'il wa'l-masā'il al-Najdīya* [Cairo, 1346–49], 1:6.18; the letter is not earlier than 1168, when the people of Shaqrā' converted, nor later than 1181, when Tharmadā' did so). Philby fails to record the tribal affiliation of the people of Shaqrā', though he mentions that the governor belonged to the Banū Zayd (*Arabia*, 106); but Lorimer specifies that the population is mostly Banū Zayd (*Gazetteer*, 2:1755; and see von Oppenheim, *Beduinen*, 3:163, describing the population as entirely Banū Zayd, and noting their presence also in Ushayqir). In the same letter, Ibn 'Abd al-Wahhāb refers to the category of the *jār* in Shaqrā' (*Majmū'a*, 1:7.1), and this, on Juhany's analysis, would point to the existence of later settlers who might be of different tribal background (*History*, 176, 178f.); but no such group is attested elsewhere in the sources available to me for Shaqrā'.

15. We hear of a seizure of Uthayfiya by the 'Azā'īz in 1115 (I.85.6) or 1116 (Bs.416.14); whether this represents a change of population or simply of rulers is unclear. A modern scholar describes the 'Azā'īz in our period as emirs of Uthayfiya, adding that they were Tamīmīs (A. M. Ibn Khamīs, *al-Majāz bayn al-Yamāma wa'l-Ḥijāz* [Riyāḍ, 1970], 55, and cf. the verses of

Ḥumaydān al-Shuway'ir there quoted). In 1286 the 'Azā'īz are referred to as *ahl balad Uthayfiya* (I.179.4). The ruling lineage at the time of the Saudi expansion is the Āl Zāmil (see below, note 139); in Philby's time the Zāmil subsection of Tamīm were one part of the population, the other part being the Sa'd subsection of the same tribe (*Arabia*, 95; so also von Oppenheim, *Beduinen*, 3:170, whereas Lorimer has the population as Subay', *Gazetteer*; 2:1930).

16. I have no data for Qarā'in. Philby assigns Waqf to a "Luhaba" subtribe of Tamīm, and Ghisla to the 'Anāqir (*Arabia*, 97; and see von Oppenheim, *Beduinen*, 3:170, 171 n. 5).

17. Philby, *Arabia*, 89, 92, 93, 96, 97, 120, 121.

18. Hamdānī, *Ṣifat jazīrat al-'Arab*, ed. D. H. Müller (Leiden, 1884), 163.24, 164.1 (citing a certain Jarmī, and mentioning Tharmadā', Uthayfiya, Ushayqir, and Shaqrā'; his Dhāt Ghisl may be Ghisla). For a list in what seems to be an older source in which Marāt also appears, see Juhany, *History*, 73.

19. See Yāqūt, *Mu'jam al-buldān*, ed. F. Wüstenfeld (Leipzig, 1866–73), 1:121.6, according to which most of the settlement belonged to his descendants, and he himself had been in Uthayfiya and owned property there.

20. Hamdānī, *Ṣifa*, 164.1.

21. See Juhany, *History*, 73, 172.

22. For helpful surveys of sources on the history of Najd at large in our period, see Jāsir, "Mu'arrikhū Najd," and Juhany, *History*, 8–38. Both authors have access to a good deal more material than I do.

23. See Jāsir, "Mu'arrikhū Najd," 788–92; Juhany, *History*, 9–16. Of the works in question, only that of Manqūr (d. 1125), a well-known scholar of Sudayr, is available to me (Manqūr, *Ta'rīkh*, ed. 'A. al-Khuwayṭir [Riyāḍ, 1970]). For the rest, I am using the material mainly as transmitted in the works of two later scholars, Ibn Bishr (d. 1290) ("Bs.," see above, note 4) and Ibn 'Īsā (d. 1343) ("I.," see above, note 4); on these works, see Jāsir, "Mu'arrikhū Najd," 881–84, 885–88; Juhany, *History*, 19, 20f. The annotation and indexing of Jāsir's edition of Ibn 'Īsā are very helpful. Juhany makes extensive use of a manuscript containing five chronicles of the twelfth to early thirteenth century, three of them not known to Jāsir (see Juhany, *History*, 9–12). Both Jāsir and Juhany also refer to works dating from the Saudi period which contain pre-Saudi materials and are not available to me, notably those of Fākhirī (d. 1277) and Bassām (d. 1346) (see Jāsir, "Mu'arrikhū Najd," 797, 888–92; Juhany, *History*, 20, 21). My impression is that the transmission of pre-Saudi materials in historical works of the Saudi period is pretty conservative, and that such elaboration as is found (notably in the work of Ibn 'Īsā) is well-informed (on this point, see Juhany, *History*, 22f.). I am in no position to sketch the transmission history of these materials.

Addendum: Fākhirī's chronicle has now been published (*al-Akhbār al-Najdīya*, ed. 'A. Y. Shibl [Riyāḍ, n.d.]). With a few exceptions, I have added references to his work only where his information differs from that found in the sources I already cite.

24. See Jāsir, "Mu'arrikhū Najd," 788–91; Juhany, *History*, 38 n. 13.

25. See Juhany, *History*, 12f., and the apt illustration of the point, ibid., 14–16. We have to do with history written to remind those who know, not to inform those who don't.

26. See Juhany, *History*, 23–25. I have used the genealogical texts relating to the Wuhaba of Ushayqir appended by Jāsir to his edition of Ibn 'Īsā (I.205–31); a closely related text was abstracted by Philby (*Arabia*, 383–92).

27. See Juhany, *History*, 26–28. None of this material is available to me directly.

28. The two major chronicles are those of Ibn Ghannām (d. 1225) and Ibn Bishr ("G." and "B." respectively, see above, note 4). As pointed out by A. M. Vasil'iev in his monograph on the first Saudi state (*Puritane Islama? Vakhkhabizm i pervoye gosudarstvo Saudidov v Aravii, 1744/45–1818* [Moscow, 1967], 7), a closely related early Saudi account must underlie the chronicle of Saudi history given by Mengin (*Histoire*, 2:449–544; cf. ibid., 1:vi).

29. See above, note 14, and below, notes 163, 170, 175.

30. For the purposes of this paper I have checked the chronicles of Ibn Ghannām and Ibn Bishr down to 1209.

31. The earliest European to pass through Washm seems to have been Sadlier in 1819; for his perfunctory account, see above, note 10.

32. See particularly 'A. al-'Uthaymīn, "Najd mundh al-qarn al-'āshir al-hijrī," *al-Dāra*, 1, no. 4 (1975), 3, no. 3 (1977), 4, nos. 1, 3 (1978) *bis*; Juhany, *History*; H. S. Philby, *Sa'udi Arabia* [London, 1955], 8–146 (a useful account of the background and history of the first Saudi state, but without references); G. S. Rentz, "Muhammad ibn 'Abd al-Wahhâb (1703/04–1792) and the Beginnings of Unitarian Empire in Arabia" (University of California Ph.D., 1948) (a well-researched narrative of Saudi history to 1206); Vasil'iev, *Puritane Islama?* The studies I have most benefited from are those of Rentz and Juhany.

33. This is in marked contrast to the horizons of scholarship in the area (see below, notes 148f.).

34. Bs.412.15 (and cf. Manqūr, *Ta'rīkh*, 72.1, and I.77.6, without mention of Ushayqir). For a survey of Sharīfian pressure on Najd at large in the tenth to twelfth centuries, see Juhany, *History*, 261–67.

35. Bs.406.17; I.69.3.

36. Bs.419.9.

37. I.103.11.

38. Juhany, *History*, 199, 277. This does not seem to be supported by the references given ibid., 277 n. 51; it may be supported by the reference to Ibn Yūsuf given ibid., 233 n. 110, if it refers to Raghba.

39. Emigrations from Washm often have destinations in Sudayr or Miḥmal, as in the story of the settlement of the expelled Banū Wā'il of Ushayqir in Tuwaym (I.28.3, and cf. above, notes 4, 13); compare the Āl Ibn Ḥasan which migrated from Ushayqir to Ḥarma (I.66.5), or the Āl Ṣuqayh which migrated from the same town to settle Qarīna in 1101 (I.75.2). Much further information on emigrations from Washm is given by Juhany, with reference

to the 'Anāqir of Tharmadā' (*History*, 190–99), the Nawāṣir of Far'a (ibid., 203–7), the Wuhaba of Ushayqir (ibid., 207–11), and the Banū Zayd of Shaqrā' (ibid., 213). Though it is not easy to isolate instances of emigration from Washm in our period, it is worth noting that the range of destinations includes not just Sudayr and Miḥmal (as ibid., 191, 197f., 199, 209) but also extends to the northwest into the Qaṣīm (ibid., 194 f., 204f., 209, 210f.), to the southeast (ibid., 199), and to the southwest (ibid., 213).

40. Bs.417.12. Ibn Bishr specifies that the subtribe involved was the Ṣumada, for whom see von Oppenheim, *Beduinen*, 3:60. Ibn 'Īsā does not mention the role of Ẓafīr in the incident (I.87.2). Cf. also Juhany, *History*, 270 and 291 n. 28.

41. See von Oppenheim, *Beduinen*, 3:54; Juhany, *History*, 114–16. The tribe had a powerful paramount chieftaincy in the lineage of the Āl Ṣuwayṭ/Suwayṭ (see von Oppenheim, *Beduinen*, 3:54, 61 n. 2; thus for one such chief, see I.66.12 [1086] and I.82.9 [1113]; for a second, I.101.13 [1142] and I.102.13 [1144]; for a third, G.2:16.22 [1163] and B.1:25.17 [1165]). Presumably the authority of these chiefs extended to the Ṣumada. On relations between nomads and sedentaries in Najd in general in our period, see Juhany, *History*, 269–72.

42. See Bs.411.21; Manqūr, *Ta'rīkh*, 69.6, and the editor's note 6 thereto; Fākhirī, *Akhbār*, 85.10. The Fuḍūl are described by von Oppenheim as wholly settled (*Beduinen*, 3:163), but in our period there were clearly nomadic Fuḍūl (I.58.13 [1057]; I.66.1 [1085]; and see Juhany, *History*, 128 f.).

43. Manqūr, *Ta'rīkh*, 65.4 (referring to the hamlet of Ghisla). This notice is not taken up by Ibn Bishr or Ibn 'Īsā.

44. See below, note 59.

45. According to Juhany, however, the Āl Nāṣir of Tharmadā' (who ruled from 1116, cf. below, note 70) clashed with Ushayqir (*History*, 199, 277). This statement is not supported by the references given ibid., 293 n. 51; it may be supported by the reference to Ibn Yūsuf given ibid., 233 n. 110, if this concerns Ushayqir.

46. I.87.2; Bs.417.12.

47. I.96.11 (and cf. Bs.422.7). There was also a clash between the two towns in 1124 (Bs.419.7).

48. Contrast the view advanced by Juhany that Marāt and Uthayfiya were "old dependent settlements" of Tharmadā' over which the Āl Nāṣir of Tharmadā' "continued to expand and consolidate their authority" (*History*, 276). In the case of Marāt, Juhany adduces (*a*) the fact that the ruling lineage were 'Anāqir (and had been so since at least 1084, cf. below, note 69) (*History*, 198 f.), and (*b*) the conflict between the Āl Nāṣir and "the chiefs of Marāt" (*History*, 276 f.), *sc.* in 1124 and 1136 (see above, note 47). The first point is hardly evidence that Marāt was controlled by the 'Anāqir of *Tharmadā'*. The second point is in itself no more persuasive. The accounts of the events in question that are available to me carry no implication that either clash issued in the subjection of Marāt to the rule of Tharmadā'; indeed in the case of the clash

of 1124, we are told that the man who came to power in that year was a previous ruler of the town who had fled in 1121 (see below, note 69). But it may be that Juhany has other sources with different or fuller information (at *History*, 292 n. 48, it is not clear whether the references to Ibn ʿAbbād and Ibn Yūsuf pertain to Marāt or Uthayfiya). In the case of Uthayfiya, Juhany states that it was "controlled by the ʿAnāqir" (*History*, 199), and that the Āl Nāṣir of Tharmadāʾ "regained influence" over it following a rebellion stirred up by the poet Ḥumaydān al-Shuwayʿir (*History*, 277). As far as the historical sources are concerned, the statements of Fākhirī (*Akhbār*, 93.2) and Ibn Bishr (to which might be added that of Ibn ʿĪsā) regarding the events of 1119 (see above, note 46) give no indication that the outcome was the hegemony of Tharmadāʾ over Uthayfiya; the other historical sources cited by Juhany (*History*, 292 n. 48) are not available to me. Turning to the story of the role of Ḥumaydān al-Shuwayʿir (ibid., 277 and 292 n. 49), it should be noted that we have to do with a richly embroidered popular narrative quite different in style from the annals of the Najdi historians. It is available to me only in relatively modern versions (as Ibn Khamīs, *Majāz*, 55 f.; also Philby, *Arabia*, 93 f., from the oral tradition of Uthayfiya at the end of the First World War); I have no means of judging the historical accuracy of its reminiscence. If the details were reliable, it would tell us that Uthayfiya had at some stage in the lifetime of Ḥumaydān (around the early twelfth century, cf. Bs.414.13 [1111]) paid tribute to Tharmadāʾ, though retaining sufficient independence to grant asylum to the fleeing poet and his son; and that Uthayfiya was victorious in the conflict which ensued.

49. See the genealogy at I.216.1.

50. I.81.3 (and cf. Bs.414.6 and Manqūr, *Taʾrīkh*, 75.3).

51. I.95.4; Bs.421.16 (mentioning a previous peace). Both authorities state that the Nawāṣir were expelled from Farʿa and their castle (*qaṣr*) destroyed.

52. I.100.5; Bs.424.1. Both record the recovery of Farʿa by the Nawāṣir.

53. I.104.3.

54. See above, notes 51f. This is also the implication of the rather different account of the events given by Juhany on the authority of Ibn Yūsuf (*History*, 205 and 235 n. 136). Here it is the boss and his cousin who are expelled in 1135, and in turn expel the invaders in 1139.

55. Philby, *Arabia*, 121.

56. Juhany, by contrast, takes the view that the "repeated attempts by the inhabitants of Ushayqir to capture al-Farʿah . . . suggest that al-Farʿah was owned or controlled by the inhabitants of the larger town of Ushayqir" (*History*, 203). I do not have access to his source for these attempts (Ibn Yūsuf, see ibid., 234 n. 128); but repeated attempts are scarcely evidence of success.

57. Juhany, *History*, 277. Juhany states that the Āl Nāṣir of Tharmadāʾ "extended their authority" over Waqf, citing Ibn Yūsuf (*History*, 292 n. 50).

58. See above, note 45.

59. *Majmūʿa*, 1:6f., especially 7.1 (and cf. above, note 14). Juhany cites this epistle as evidence of the expanding power of Tharmadāʾ (*History*, 277

and 293 n. 51); but it hardly attests this. Incidentally, the paraphrase of a further passage from this epistle given by Ibn Khamīs (*Majāz*, 55) is misleading.

60. To anticipate somewhat, it is instructive to compare the treatment of the Saudi conquest of Washm given by Ibn ʿĪsā, who continues in the old historiographical tradition, with the accounts given by the chroniclers of the Saudi state, Ibn Ghannām and Ibn Bishr. For the period 1161–81, Ibn ʿĪsā has only three relevant entries: the Saudi raid on Tharmadā'of 1161 (I.108.9), that of 1164 (I.109.7), and the death of the ruler of Tharmadā' in 1181 (I.112.11). If this material is compared to that presented in section v below, it will be seen that Ibn ʿĪsā (*a*) confines his entries to the single settlement of Tharmadā', (*b*) reports only two out of eight Saudi raids on that settlement, and (*c*) gives no indication that as of 1181 Washm had been converted to Wahhābism and incorporated into the Saudi state. It should, however, be noted that Fākhirī gives a much fuller account, amounting to ten relevant entries (*Akhbār*, 106–14).

61. Yāqūt, *Muʿjam*, 4:930.22. The point of such a wall would be to keep out nomadic pastoralists, not armies.

62. Philby in his accounts of the settlements mentions four of them as being individually walled (*Arabia*, 89, 92, 114, 120); such was doubtless the situation in our period.

63. Yāqūt, *Muʿjam*, 4:930.23.

64. As Niebuhr says of Najd, the region "is parcelled out among so many petty Sovereigns, that almost every little town has its own Schiech" ([C.] Niebuhr, *Travels Through Arabia and Other Countries in the East* [Edinburgh, 1792], 2:128).

65. The sources use a variety of terms for this figure with no great consistency: *shaykh*, *amīr*, *ra'īs*, *rāʿī*, *ṣāḥib* (followed by the name of the settlement).

66. Juhany gives a far richer account of the power of the Najdi bosses (*History*, 175–82, particularly his remarks on retainers and taxation). This account may well apply to the settlements of Washm, but it is not possible to document this from the sources available to me.

67. We know the names of two bosses of Farʿa in the pre-Saudi period: Dabbūs ibn Dukhayyil, killed in the attack on Ushayqir in 1111 (see above, note 50); and Ibrāhīm ibn Ḥusayn, who was expelled in 1135 but returned in 1139 (see above, note 54; for the rule of his grandson in Saudi times, see below, note 141). We hear of an episode of civil strife among the Nawāṣir in 1121 (Bs.418.9; and see Manqūr, *Ta'rīkh*, 81.3). (There seems to be no reason to connect this episode with the colonization of Midhnab by Nawāṣir, cf. Juhany, *History*, 204 and 234 n. 130.)

68. Here we have nothing to go on except the obscure reference to the seizure of the settlement by the ʿAzāʾīz in 1115 or 1116 (see above, note 15) and the rule of the Āl Zāmil at the time of the Saudi expansion (see below, notes 139 f.). Did the Āl Zāmil then belong to the ʿAzāʾīz?

69. In 1084 Rāshid ibn Ibrāhīm takes power (Bs.405.12); in 1093 he is killed, and ʿUbayka ibn Jār Allāh takes over (I.68.6; Bs.407.18); in 1096 he

in turn is killed (I.70.3; Bs.409.1). We then hear nothing till 1115, when Ibrāhīm ibn Jār Allāh (presumably a brother of 'Ubayka) takes power (I.85.6; Bs.416.3; but cf. Manqūr, *Ta'rīkh*, 79.2, recording the accession of one "Ibn Raṣī'," who might or might not be the same person, in 1116). In 1121 Ibrāhīm fled, and Māni' ibn Dhibāḥ took over (I.88.5; Bs. 418.13); in 1124 [Ibrāhīm] ibn Jār Allāh took power for the second time, following a clash with Tharmadā' (Bs.419.8); and in 1136 Ibrāhīm ibn Jār Allāh, together with three relatives of a previous ruler, was killed in another conflict with Tharmadā' (I.96.12; Bs.422.7). All these bosses may belong to a single ruling lineage, but this cannot be ascertained. Fākhirī's reference to 'Ubayka ibn Jār Allāh as ruler of Tharmadā' is presumably an error (*Akhbār*, 80.7). The significance of his reference to the affairs of Marāt in 1122 (ibid., 94.2) is obscure to me.

70. The references are as follows: (1) 'Abdallāh ibn Ibrāhīm became boss in 1081 (Bs.405.9); in 1100 he died and was succeeded by his brother (2) Rīmān (I.74.10; Bs.411.1; Manqūr, *Ta'rīkh*, 66.8; and the genealogy at I.215.6); in 1116 the Āl Nāṣir killed him and seized power (I.85.15; Bs.416.11; Manqūr, *Ta'rīkh*, 78.8; and the genealogy at I.215.9). Although the ruler as of 1116 is not named, it was presumably (3) Bidāḥ ibn Bishr, since he was ruler in 1119 (Bs.417.13); he died in 1136, and was succeeded by his cousin (4) Ibrāhīm ibn Sulaymān (I.96.8; Bs.422.7). Ibrāhīm ruled till his death in 1181, three of his sons having predeceased him (see below, note 143). The sources refer to these rulers as *shaykh*, *ra'īs*, or *ṣāḥib Tharmadā'*; the Saudi chroniclers also use the term *amīr* (see for example G.2:11.22; B.1:52.2).

71. Juhany speaks of *four* incidents (*History*, 275, without reference to the sources); but this seems likely to result from a conflation of events in Tharmadā' and Marāt (compare ibid., 198).

72. See above, note 70, and, for the flight of the sons of Rīmān, the genealogy at I.216.1.

73. The ruler kills the family of his cousin and predecessor (I.105.5).

74. The large number of incidents of civil strife in Ushayqir, and the consequent division of the town, are noted by Juhany (*History*, 208, 275).

75. See above, note 13.

76. "Raqrāq" is in fact the nickname of Muḥammad ibn 'Abdallāh ibn Shabāna of the Āl Muḥammad (I.95.5), who is described at his death as *amīr balad Ushayqir* (I.106.9). (The *ṣāḥib Ushayqir* whose death is reported by Ibn Bishr in 1139 [Bs.423.26] is a scholar [see I.100.7], rather than a boss.)

77. I.103.9.

78. Ibn 'Īsā ascribes the attack on Far'a in that year to Raqrāq and "the people of Ushayqir," which suggests that he led the attack. On the other hand, the account of this attack given by Juhany on the authority of Ibn Yūsuf (see above, note 54; also *History*, 34 and 42 nn. 71f.) ascribes it to the Āl Musharraf, a lineage quite distinct from the Āl Muḥammad to which Raqrāq belonged. (On the genealogy of the Āl Musharraf, see I.223.6.)

79. Or more particularly the Āl Ibn Ḥasan (see I.66.4 [1085]; I.88.1 [1119]; I.95.2 [1135]); and compare the role of the Āl Bassām ibn Munīf as

emirs of their own southern quarter of the town as of 1147 (I.103.13). For the genealogy of the Āl Bassām ibn Munīf, see I.220.3.

80. See I.78.9 (1109); I.95.5 (1135). For the genealogy of the Āl Muḥammad, see I.225.4.

81. Compare the dates of the attestations in notes 79f. above. Although all but a few of the Āl Muḥammad are said to have left Ushayqir for good in 1109 (I.78.11; Bs.413.11), Raqrāq belonged to this lineage, and Ibn ʿĪsā notes many families of the Āl Muḥammad in Ushayqir (see the genealogy at I.225–27; the descendants of Raqrāq himself turn up in Shaqrā', I.225.12).

82. I.65.7, 66.2.

83. I.78.8; Bs.413.11. Manqūr refers to fighting in 1112 (*Ta'rīkh*, 75.11).

84. I.95.1.

85. In addition to the data which follow, there is mention of a peace ending unspecified domestic discord in 1104 or 1105 (Manqūr, *Ta'rīkh*, 69.9, and the editor's footnote 9 thereto); this may have marked the end of another such period. It is not clear to me whether the incident of 1103 or 1104 recorded by Manqūr (ibid., 69.6) and Ibn Bishr (Bs.411.21) was one of domestic strife.

86. For the events of 1114, including an abortive peace, see I.83.2; and cf. Manqūr, *Ta'rīkh*, 77.2, and the editor's footnote 3 thereto; also Bs.415.11 (speaking rather of the Āl Bassām taking power). For 1115, see I.84.7, 84.11; Bs.416.2 (second item); Manqūr, *Ta'rīkh*, 78.1. For 1116, see Bs.417.14 (= Ibn ʿĪsā's first item for 1115). There are no entries for 1117, but for 1118, see I.86.5; for the peace of 1119, see I.87.3; and for a subsequent killing in that year, I.88.1.

87. For 1144, see I.103.1; for 1145, I.103.3; there is no entry for 1146, but for 1147 see I.103.9; there is none for 1148, but for 1149 see I.104.5.

88. Juhany states that the disputes in Ushayqir were sometimes about agricultural and pastoral resources, but without giving specific examples (*History*, 208, and cf. 235 n. 146). This may be true, but it is not supported by the sources available to me.

89. These are the Āl Bassām ibn Munīf (cf. above, note 79), including the Āl Ibn Ḥasan and Āl al-Qāḍī (for the appurtenance of the Āl Ibn Ḥasan to the Āl Bassām ibn Munīf, see I.66.4, 95.2; the Āl al-Qāḍī are their "cousins," I.95.1); the Āl Bassām *tout court* (the descendants of which Bassām?); the Āl ʿAsākir (see the genealogy at I.221.6); the Āl Rājiḥ (I.222.3); the Āl Muḥammad (cf. above, note 80); and the Āl Khirfān (I.227.8). See also the genealogical summary at I.213.11, 214.8.

90. In 1109, the Āl Khirfān, Āl Rājiḥ, and Āl Muḥammad leave town, but the first two return shortly after, whereas the last for the most part does not (Bs.413.11; I.78.11; Juhany, *History*, 208 and 235 n. 148, citing also Ibn Yūsuf and Fākhirī, *Akhbār*, 88.7; but cf. above, note 81). In 1115, the Āl Khirfān and Āl Rājiḥ again depart (I.84.9); but the Āl Khirfān recover their quarter later in the year (I.84.11; Bs.416.2; Manqūr, *Ta'rīkh*, 78.1; Juhany, *History*, 209 and 235 n. 149, citing also Fākhirī, *Akhbār*, 91.5), and the Āl Rājiḥ are back by 1119 (I.87.4).

91. Viz. the *sūq al-shimāl* (mentioned in 1115 and 1147), the *sūq al-madīna* (mentioned in 1114, 1115, 1119, and 1149), and *al-sūq al-janūbī* (mentioned in 1147).

92. The *sūq al-madīna* is destroyed when the Al Rājiḥ leave in 1115 (I.84.8), and rebuilt by them in 1119 (I.87.4). Compare the destruction of "the 'Aqdat al-Munayyikh and Ghazya" in 1109 (I.78.10), and the building of the 'Aqdat al-Masjid in 1119 (I.87.5). The word *'aqda* normally refers to a walled town, or to the wall itself (see Jāsir's explanation in his glossary to Ibn 'Īsā, I.250; also C. M. Doughty, *Travels in Arabia Deserta* [London, 1936], 2:582, *s.n.* "Âj-jidát").

93. G.2:14.11; B.1:21.20. These events were already in the making in 1160 (G.2:11.21, 12.1, 12.25). At this stage, the Saudis had already attacked Riyāḍ (1159), but had not yet turned against Sudayr (1164) or Kharj (1165), let alone the Qaṣīm (1182).

94. See Philby, *Sa'udi Arabia*, 135 f.

95. For an analysis of Saudi warfare, see M. S. M. el-Shaafy, "The Military Organisation of the First Sa'udi State," *The Annual of Leeds University Oriental Society*, 7 (1969–73).

96. The events in Washm are chronicled by Ibn Ghannām (G.2:14–88), Ibn Bishr (B.1:21–51), and Mengin (*Histoire*, 455–68). Modern accounts include those of Philby (*Sa'udi Arabia*, 44–63) and Rentz (*Muhammad ibn 'Abd al-Wahhâb*, 63–149).

97. See the details given below for the individual settlements. Note also the abortive raid on Washm led by the emir of Ḍurmā in 1170 (G.2:58.23; B.1:34.17), and a raid of 1173 (the third of that year) which likewise seems not to have reached Washm proper (G.2:67.1; B.1:43.21; Mengin, *Histoire*, 2:457f.).

98. In 1161, Tharmadā' lost about seventy men (G.2:14.19; B.1:22.2; I.108.12). In 1163, Tharmadā', Marāt, and Uthayfiya together lost twenty-five men (G.2:18.9; B.1:24.12). In 1165, thirty men of Sudayr and Washm were killed in action against Ḍurmā (B.1:26.20; cf. G.2:19.12). In 1167 or 1168, nearly sixty (B.1:29.8) or nearly seventy (G.2:52.15) were lost in a further intervention by the ruler of Tharmadā' in Ḍurmā. In 1168, a coalition which included Washm lost sixty men in an attack on Ḥuraymilā' (G.2:55.13; B.1:30.17). In 1170, another coalition lost about fifteen (G.2:58.2) or seventeen (B.1:34.6) men in an attack on Shaqrā'; and in the same year four men of Ushayqir were killed by a Saudi raid (G.2:59.5; B.1:34.20). In 1171, Tharmadā' lost twelve men (G.2:61.8; B.1:40.12) to a Saudi attack, and in 1173 another four (G.2:66.3; B.1:43.9); in the same year Ushayqir lost twenty (B.1:43.13) or about thirty (G.2:66.13) men in a Saudi raid (Mengin, *Histoire*, 2:457, has the same figure as Ibn Bishr—which counts against the suggestion of Rentz that Mengin was using Ibn Ghannām, see *Muhammad ibn 'Abd al-Wahhâb*, 310). In 1175, Marāt lost nearly twenty men to a Saudi attack (G.2:69.23; B.1:45.6 is vague). In the same year Far'a lost seven men (G.2:70.2; B.1:45.7 is again vague); while in a further raid on some destination in Washm, which Ibn Bishr thinks was Ushayqir, twenty-five men were killed, *sc.* on the anti-Saudi side (B.1:45.14). In 1180, Tharmadā' lost about twenty men in

what seems to have been the last Saudi raid on the town (G.2:87.2; B.1:50.22; Mengin, *Histoire*, 2:467). (All these figures are for casualties on the anti-Saudi side. Figures for Saudi casualties are rarely given. In the raid on Tharmadā' in 1171, Saudi losses are given as nearly twenty by Ibn Ghannām, and about thirty by Ibn Bishr; in the raid on Marāt in 1175, they are given by Ibn Ghannām as two; in the raid on Far'a in the same year, Ibn Ghannām specifies that there were no Saudi casualties; in the raid on Tharmadā' of 1180, Ibn Bishr implies that the Saudis lost about twenty men.) The accuracy and comprehensiveness of these figures invite question; but at least there is no reason to expect the Saudi chroniclers deliberately to understate the losses suffered by their enemies.

99. For the twenty-day siege of Qarā'in in 1170, see G.2:58.3; Mengin, *Histoire*, 2:455.

100. They missed an opportunity to take Tharmadā' in 1161, when the defenders had made an unsuccessful sortie and taken refuge in a castle (*qaṣr*) (G.2:14.20; B.1:22.1).

101. There is, however, little attestation of this in the sources for Washm. The Saudis are reported to have destroyed the crops of the people of Tharmadā' in the raid of 1161 (G.2:15.14; B.1:22.6), and to have seized their flocks in that of 1180 (G.2:86.24; Mengin, *Histoire*, 2:467). There is no mention of the cutting down of palms and fruit trees in Washm, though this is amply attested elsewhere in the annals of the Saudi expansion (see, for example, G.2:59.8 [Thādiq, 1170]; G.2:91.19 [Ḥā'ir, 1184]; G.2:103.3 [Kharj, 1189]).

102. For the submission of Washm in 1181, see G.2:88.10; B.1:51.22; Mengin, *Histoire*, 2:468 (stressing the easy terms on which this submission was accepted). Mengin mentions an earlier submission of Washm together with Miḥmal (*Histoire*, 2:456, under 1757); but the parallel passages in the Saudi chronicles for 1172 speak only of Miḥmal (G.2:65.6; B.1:42.22).

103. The prominence of the ruler of Tharmadā' in the resistance to the Saudis is noted by Juhany (*History*, 199, 277).

104. The Saudis raided Tharmadā' in (1) 1161 (G.2:14.14; B.1:21.22; I.108.9); (2) again in 1161 (G.2:15.12; B.1:22.5); (3) 1163 (G.2:18.5; B.1:24.8; I.109.7 under 1164); (4) 1171 (G.2:60.18, B.1:40.6); (5) 1173 (G.2:65.24; B.1:43.9; Mengin, *Histoire*, 2:457); (6) 1175 (G.2:70.5; Mengin, *Histoire*, 2:459); (7) 1180 (G.2:86.23; B.1:50.20; Mengin, *Histoire*, 2:467). Fākhirī's chronology differs slightly: he places the raid of 1171 in 1170 (*Akhbār*, 110.8), and that of 1180 in 1179 (ibid., 114.6).

105. In 1163, forces from Marāt, Uthayfiya, and Tharmadā' joined to resist a Saudi attack (G.2:18.6; B.1:24.10). In 1167 or 1168, forces sent by the emir of Tharmadā' to Ḍurmā included a contingent from Marāt (B.1:29.3)—and presumably also one from Uthayfiya, since it was on this occasion that the boss of Uthayfiya was taken prisoner by the Saudis (see below, note 139). In 1176, when the people of Uthayfiya went back on their Saudi allegiance, they did so with the help of the ruler of Tharmadā', throwing in their lot with him (see below, note 117).

106. In 1160, ʻUthmān ibn Muʻammar—the pro-Saudi but suspect ruler of ʻUyayna—was intriguing with the rulers of Riyāḍ and Tharmadāʼ (G.2:11.22, 12.1); according to Ibn Ghannām, it was after this that the ruler of Tharmadāʼ prepared for war (G.2:13.1). In 1163, Ibn Muʻammar was again intriguing with the ruler of Tharmadāʼ (G.2:16.22). In 1167 or 1168, the latter intervened against the Saudis in Ḍurmā (G.2:52.5; B.1:29.2). In 1168, he led the people of Washm as part of a wider alliance which attacked Ḥuraymilāʼ (B.1:30.9; cf. G.2:54.24, where the ruler of Tharmadāʼ is not mentioned). In 1171, he and others of the people of Washm again joined a coalition against Ḥuraymilāʼ (B.1:41.16; cf. G.2:63.15, where again the ruler of Tharmadāʼ is not mentioned). Other incidents in which "the people of Washm" appear in anti-Saudi coalitions are also likely to have involved the leadership of Tharmadāʼ (see, for example, G.2:56.11 [1169]; G.2:57.14, B.1:34.1 and Mengin, *Histoire*, 2:455 [1170]; G.2:64.6, B.1:42.16 and Mengin, *Histoire*, 2:456 [1172]; also below, note 107).

107. For the incident of 1119, see above, note 40. The link reappears in 1163 (G.2:16.22, referring to Ibn Suwayṭ, i.e., Fayṣal ibn Ṣuwayṭ, chief of Ẓafīr, see B.1:25.17 [1165], and cf. above, note 41). In other reports, we find Ẓafīr similarly associated with the people of Washm in opposition to the Saudis, but without specific reference to Tharmadāʼ; this happens twice in 1165 (G.2:19.7 and B.1:25.17; G.2:19.14, but cf. B.1:26.19); twice in 1170 (G.2:58.5 and Mengin, *Histoire*, 2:455 (but cf. B.1:34.8); G.2:58.23 and B.1:34.17). In the last instance, as in 1119, the subtribe involved is the Ṣumada (read so in the printed text of Ibn Ghannām, as in the manuscript British Library, Add. 23,345, fol. 27b.17). Ibn ʻAbd al-Wahhāb makes unflattering reference to the "Āl Ẓafīr" in a letter to an addressee in Tharmadāʼ (G.1:137.24). In the context of Najdi politics at large, Ẓafīr are among the most prominent enemies of the Saudi state (see von Oppenheim, *Beduinen*, 3:54f.); they begin to appear in this role in 1159 (not 1163, as there stated, see G.2:7.22; B.1:17.18), and are found on the Saudi side only from 1200 (G.2:140.8).

108. See G.2:59.1 and B.1:34.20 (1170); G.2:66.9, B.1:43.12 and Mengin, *Histoire*, 2:457 (1173); B.1:45.14 (1175).

109. Ibn Bishr states that the people of Farʻa made war on Ushayqir for seven years till the latter submitted, in the course of which they occupied the southern towers (*burūj*) of Ushayqir (B.1:45.9; for the *burūj* of Ushayqir, cf. I.29.7). More specifically, he states that the ruling lineage of Farʻa and the people of Shaqrāʼ built a fort over against Ushayqir (B.1:45.16); Ibn Ghannām, however, presents this castle as a Saudi initiative (G.2:70.8; similarly Mengin, *Histoire*, 2:459). The contradiction is noted by Rentz (*Muhammad ibn ʻAbd al-Wahhâb*, 115 n. 3).

110. Cf. above, note 102. Ibn Bishr does not redeem his promise to return to the conversion of Ushayqir (B.1:45.11).

111. I have only two *testimonia*, both doubtful. (*a*) According to Philby, his genealogical source (see above, note 26) stated that the founder of the Āl

Bassām in 'Unayza arrived there in 1173 (or 1174) from *Ushayqir*, which he had left because of "local disturbances" (*Arabia*, 281 f., and cf. 386). But Ibn 'Īsā, who places the move about 1179, has him migrate from *Ḥarma*, not Ushayqir (I.112.4). (*b*) In letters to addressees in Tharmadā' and Marāt, Ibn 'Abd al-Wahhāb mentions the "son (*walad*) of Muḥammad ibn Sulaymān." In one passage, he is said to be in Uthayfiya (G.1:135.4; as often, the popular form "Wuthaythiya" is used, and the pointing is somewhat distorted, but the reading is assured by that of the manuscript British Library, Add. 23,344, fol. 64a.13). In the other passage, however, he is said to be in Ushayqir (G.1:209.6; as often, the popular form "Wushayqir" is used, but the reading is clear and has the support of the same manuscript, fol. 95a.23). In the first reference, he is described as the boss (*rā'ī*) of the town. If, as I tend to assume, the town is in fact Ushayqir, we have here a reference to one of its rulers at the time of the Saudi expansion.

112. See G.2:18.4 and B.1:24.10 (1163); G.2:69.1, B.1:45.5 and Mengin, *Histoire*, 2:459 (1175).

113. G.2:88.12. Mengin has it that Marāt submitted during the raid of 1175 (*Histoire*, 2:459).

114. See above, notes 10 f.

115. Uthayfiya appears on the Saudi side in 1163 (G.2:18.6; B.1:24.10), and again in 1167 or 1168 (see below, note 139).

116. For this terminus, see below, note 119.

117. G.2:73.3 (and cf. B.1:46.16).

118. G.2:57.15, 57.24; B.1:34.6; Mengin, *Histoire*, 2:455.

119. B.1:45.21. The caravan was attacked by the people of Shaqrā', Uthayfiya, and Qarā'in.

120. For the raid, see G.2:69.25; B.1:45.6; for the submission, see G.2:70.3; B.1:45.7. As noted by Rentz (*Muhammad ibn 'Abd al-Wahhâb*, 115 n. 1), the two sources differ as to whether Far'a converted at the hands of Shaqrā' (so Ibn Ghannām) or Dir'īya (so Ibn Bishr). (Under the year 1179, Ibn Bishr makes an obscure reference to the killing of three Nawāṣir [*sc.* of Far'a] by the people of Shaqrā' [B.1:49.20].)

121. See above, note 109.

122. Hamdānī, *Ṣifa*, 164.1.

123. 'A. F. al-Mubārak, "Wathā'iq al-aḥwāl al-shakhṣīya min al-nāḥiya al-ta'rīkhīya," *al-'Arab*, 2 (1967), 58.2, and cf. 55, no. 5.

124. Under 1168, Ibn Ghannām reports the conversion of most of the people of Shaqrā' (*'āmmat ahl Shaqrā'*), at the same time rather suggesting that there had been dispute over the issue in the town (G.2:53.19). (Mengin has it that Shaqrā' converted as late as 1175; see *Histoire*, 2:459.)

125. Ibn Bishr describes the people of Shaqrā' as the first to join the Saudi state (B.1:33.22), presumably meaning that they were the first in Washm to do so.

126. A lack of energy at some point is indicated by the rebuke administered

by Ibn ʿAbd al-Wahhāb in his letter to the people of Shaqrāʾ (see above, note 59).

127. G.2:57.14; B.1:34.1; Mengin, *Histoire*, 2:455. This coalition was mobilized in response to the activity of Shaqrāʾ on the Saudi side (B.1:33.23).

128. Under this year Ibn Bishr refers to anti-Saudi forces drawn from the people of Washm "other than Shaqrāʾ " (B.1:41.17).

129. See above, note 119.

130. See above, note 120.

131. B.1:48.18; cf. G.2:81.20, and Mengin, *Histoire*, 2:464.

132. Philby, *Saʿudi Arabia*, 135 f.; B.1:189.19, 190.21.

133. See above, note 14.

134. If desperate political straits had provided an effective motive for joining the Saudis, one might have expected Ushayqir to jump at the opportunity.

135. G.2:70.12.

136. See above, note 109.

137. The following emirs are named in the first thirty years of Saudi rule: (1) Muḥammad ibn Jammāz is referred to as emir of Shaqrāʾ and of Washm at large in 1188 (B.1:62.12; cf. G.2:107.8 [1189]). (2) ʿAbdallāh ibn Sadḥān, who died in battle in 1194, was at the time emir of the troops of Washm (*amīr ghazw ahl al-Washm*, B.1:72.21; at G.2:120.3, he is described as *min kibār ahl Shaqrāʾ*). (3) Muḥammad ibn Muʿayqil appears as a Saudi commander from 1205 (G.2:170.1 [1205]; 191.2, 191.17 [1208], associating him with the forces of Washm). In 1208, Ibn Bishr supplies the information that he was *ṣāḥib balad Shaqrāʾ* (B.1:101.8, naming him *ʿAbdallāh ibn* Muḥammad ibn Muʿayqil, presumably in error); and a later entry for the same year implies that he was emir of the people of Washm (B.1:101.20; and see Mengin, *Histoire*, 2:508).

138. Contrast the general statement on this aspect of Saudi policy made by the anonymous author of the *Lamʿ al-shihāb fī sīrat Muḥammad ibn ʿAbd al-Wahhāb* (ed. A. M. Abū Ḥākima [Beirut, 1967], 106; I cite this work according to the pagination of the manuscript, which is indicated in the printed text).

139. Under 1168, Ibn Bishr records the capture of ʿAbd al-Karīm ibn Zāmil, *raʾīs* of Uthayfiya (B.1:29.9; and see G.2:52.16, under 1167). He seems to have belonged to an already established lineage, since in 1163 we hear of the death in battle of ʿAlī ibn Zāmil, emir of Uthayfiya, and of others of the Āl Zāmil (G.2:18.10; B.1:24.13).

140. More precisely, we are told of the killing of ʿAbd al-Karīm ibn Zāmil (G.2:73.7; B.1:46.16), and left to infer that he was the ruler at the time.

141. For the conversion, see B.1:45.6. (Ibn Ghannām does not mention the role of the ruler, G.2:70.3.) Ibn Bishr names the ruler as Manṣūr ibn Ḥamad ibn Ibrāhīm ibn Ḥusayn, which identifies him as a grandson of the boss of the 1130s (see above, note 67). Soon after he refers to the Āl Manṣūr as the bosses (*ruʾasāʾ*) of Farʿa (B.1:45.16). For the same Manṣūr as *raʾīs* of Farʿa in 1196, see B.1:77.10.

142. B.1:52.1. Again Ibn Ghannām makes no mention of the role of the

ruler (G.2:88.10); while Ibn ʿĪsā mentions the death of the ruler (I.112.11), but not the conversion. Juhany states that the conversion *followed* the death of the ruler (*History*, 277 and 293 n. 53); however, his source has the same relative chronology as Ibn Bishr (Fākhirī, *Akhbār*, 114.10).

143. One son of Ibrāhīm ibn Sulaymān, named ʿAbd al-Muḥsin, had been killed in battle against the Saudis in 1171 (G.2:61.8; cf. B.1:40.12, where for *Ibrāhīm wa-* read *al-amīr*, as in the manuscript British Library, Or. 7718, fol. 25b.3). Two further sons of his died in battle in 1180, namely Rāshid and Ḥamad (B.1:50.22; cf. G.2:87.2, where the text should clearly read *Ḥamad wa-Rāshid*, and Mengin, *Histoire*, 2:467, referring to one son only). Whether Ibrāhīm had other sons is not recorded.

144. The relative position of the two towns has changed more than once with the ups and downs of Saudi power in Washm. Already in 1234 a reversal is apparent in the arrangements made by Ibrāhīm Pasha (I.147.2); and for later developments, see Philby, *Arabia*, 92, 117. The author of the *Lamʿ al-shihāb* describes Shaqrāʾ as the *dār al-imāra* of Washm at the end of the first Saudi state (397).

145. See above, note 137. (For further references to the role of the people of Washm in the wars of the first Saudi state, see for example G.2:119.24, ranging the people of Washm alongside those of the ʿĀriḍ and Sudayr in 1194; Philby, *Saʿudi Arabia*, 92, 108, 121.

146. Useful surveys of the religious life of pre-Saudi Najd are given by ʿUthaymīn ("Najd," final installment) and Juhany (*History*, 240–59). For a survey of the Najdi contribution to Ḥanbalite legal literature, see M. ʿA. al-Rashīd, "Quḍāt Najd athnāʾ al-ʿahd al-Saʿūdī," *al-Dāra*, 4, nos. 2, 3, 4 (1978), and 5, no. 1 (1979), second installment, 110–20. (Despite its title, Rashīd's study deals mainly with the pre-Saudi period.)

147. For the prominence of the scholars of Ushayqir in the biographical sources, see ʿUthaymīn, "Najd," final installment, 34, and the more detailed figures given in Juhany, *History*, 248f. Incidentally, the density of scholars in Ushayqir may have meant that the personnel of *dīn* and *dawla* were less distinct than elsewhere. Thus in 1115 a *qāḍī* of the Āl Bassām was killed in the course of civil conflict (I.85.1), an unusual event by Najdi standards.

148. See Juhany, *History*, 248, with a celebrated example pertaining to Ushayqir.

149. See the figures given in Juhany, *History*, 246 (with two examples from Ushayqir, ibid., 242f.); also Rashīd, "Quḍāt Najd," first installment, 26f.

150. I.74.7. Rashīd states that he was the *qāḍī* of Qarāʾin ("Quḍāt Najd," first installment, 24). It may be added that a scholar of Ushayqir who died in 1059 (see I.59.2) had a grandson who was *qāḍī* of Qarāʾin (B.1:233.9); according to Rashīd, he moved there from Ushayqir, and was *qāḍī* there till his death in 1185 ("Quḍāt Najd," second installment, 106).

151. See below, notes 163, 170, 175.

152. For the vocalization and sense of the term, see Jāsir's entry in his glossary to Ibn ʿĪsā (I.250.16). His explanation is supported by the case of Ibn ʿĪd (see below, note 172). The *muṭawwaʿ* may also have been the *qāḍī*:

Rashīd states that the *qāḍīs* of Najd acted as *imāms* ("Quḍāt Najd," first installment, 18); and cf. below, notes 164, 170.

153. Witness the preeminence of the *maṭāwiʿa* in the polemical correspondence of Ibn ʿAbd al-Wahhāb.

154. G.1:137.24 (cf. above, note 107); see also G.1:187.3, 188.14. For bedouin religion in Najd at large, see Juhany, *History*, 281.

155. Such reserve finds respectful expression in the work of ʿUthaymīn ("Najd," final installment, 40–43) and Juhany (*History*, 281f.).

156. See particularly the somewhat barrel-scraping list compiled by Ibn Ghannām (G.1:7.9–8.14). For a discussion of these and other attestations of dubious religious practices, see G. R. Puin, "Aspekte der wahhabitischen Reform, auf Grundlage von Ibn Ġannāms 'Rauḍat al-afkār'," in T. Nagel *et al.*, *Studien zum Minderheitenproblem im Islam 1* (Bonn, 1973), 54–58; also Juhany, *History*, 282f.

157. Such references are scarce enough anywhere in Najd; I have encountered only two. (1) A *responsum* of the reformer's father, ʿAbd al-Wahhāb ibn Sulaymān (d. 1154), attests the presence of Qādirīs of the exotic variety in Ḥarma (*Majmūʿa*, 1:523–25; this text is misleadingly described by H. Laoust as a tract "against the cult of saints," see *EI*², *s.v.* "Ibn ʿAbd al-Wahhāb," col. 678a). (2) Ibn ʿAbd al-Wahhāb himself refers to Ṣūfīs (*mutaṣawwifa*) in Miʿkāl (in the ʿĀriḍ) who followed the teachings of Ibn ʿArabī (d. 638) and Ibn al-Fāriḍ (d. 632) (G.1:191.19).

158. This aspect of the language of Ibn Ghannām is well brought out by Puin ("Aspekte," 87–96).

159. G.1:223.4 (in an epistle to the *muṭawwaʿ* of Raghba).

160. G.1:191.11. The term I render as "scholars" is *maṭāwiʿa*.

161. His letter to the people of Shaqrāʾ exhorting them to make war on Tharmadāʾ (*Majmūʿa*, 1:6f., see above, note 14) does not discuss questions of doctrine or cult.

162. I leave aside a short dogmatic epistle addressed to nine named persons whom Ibn Ghannām states to be *maṭāwiʿa* of Sudayr, Washm, and Qaṣīm (G.1:120–22); none of the nine are to my knowledge *maṭāwiʿa* of Washm. Equally, I make no attempt in what follows to analyze the dogmatic issues discussed in the epistles.

163. G.1:131–36.

164. I.111.7. According to Rashīd, he was the *qāḍī* of Tharmadāʾ ("Quḍāt Najd," second installment, 104).

165. He is the author of one of the unpublished chronicles used by Juhany (see above, note 23). Juhany states that he spent the last twenty years of his life in Tharmadāʾ (*History*, 38 n. 13).

166. G.1:138.15. He appears here in the company of Muways and others (for Muways, see below, note 181).

167. G.1:210.6. That the reference is primarily to Ibrāhīm ibn Sulaymān, the ruler of Tharmadāʾ, is clear from the context.

168. He is addressed as *al-akh Muḥammad ibn ʿAbbād*, and properly greeted

(G.1:132.1); at the same time, Ibn 'Abd al-Wahhāb stresses that his criticisms of Ibn 'Abbād's conduct are the counsels of a friend (*naṣīḥa*) (G.1:135.21). But a certain polemical irony seems to lurk between the lines.

169. The instances given are the following. (1) The scholars of Sudayr wrote to the ruler of Tharmadā', who passed on what they had written to Ibn 'Abd al-Wahhāb (G.1:134.20). (2) The ruler of Ushayqir (or Uthayfiya, see above, note 111) brought to Tharmadā' a tract composed by a Baṣran; he read it out there, and used it to confute Ibn 'Abd al-Wahhāb's supporters (*jamā'atanā*—implying the existence of a Wahhābī group in Tharmadā'?) (G.1:135.1). Ibn 'Abd al-Wahhāb adds that this tract is much used by his Najdi opponents against him; Ibn Ismā'īl likewise has a copy. Elsewhere Ibn 'Abd al-Wahhāb speaks of a tract by a certain Qabbānī which had been copied in Aḥsā' and Najd (G.1:209.9). Both passages presumably refer to the same work, that of Aḥmad ibn 'Alī al-Baṣrī al-Qabbānī (C. Brockelmann, *Geschichte der Arabischen Litteratur* [Weimar etc., 1898–1949], supplementary volumes, 2:532, no. 7, with a reference to a manuscript in Hyderabad). The Ibn Ismā'īl who had a copy is frequently named by Ibn 'Abd al-Wahhāb among his scholarly enemies, but I am unable to identify him. (3) A tract by Ibn 'Afāliq was sent by Muways to Ibn Ismā'īl, who brought it to Tharmadā' and read it out there (G.1:135.15). The reference is doubtless to the work of Muḥammad ibn 'Afāliq al-Aḥsā'ī (see Brockelman, *Geschichte*, supplementary volumes, 2:532, no. 8, where the number of the Berlin manuscript should read "2158").

170. G.1:136–42. Ibn Ghannām describes him as *min maṭāwi'at Tharmadā'* (G.1:136.14). Tharmadā' may thus have had more than one *muṭawwa'*; alternatively, Ibn 'Īd (d. 1180) may have succeeded Ibn 'Abbād (d. 1175). According to Rashīd, they were successive *qāḍīs* of Tharmadā' ("Quḍāt Najd," second installment, 104).

171. G.1:210.5. This passage, like a good many others in these epistles, is not clear to me.

172. G.2:87.2; B.1:50.23. Ibn Bishr here describes him as *imām ahl al-balad*.

173. Viz. *takfīr* and *qitāl*.

174. In place of a proper greeting, we find *waffaqanā 'llāhu wa-iyyāhu* (G.1:136.15).

175. G.1:207–12. This epistle is not earlier than 1170, since it mentions the (involuntary) visit of three well-known *maṭāwi'a* of Sudayr to Dir'īya (G.1:210.23), an event known to have occurred in that year (G.2:59.22).

176. In place of a greeting, we have *hadānā 'llāhu wa-iyyāhu* (G.1:207.20); and later he is described as an opponent (*mukhālif*) (G.1:210.22).

177. G.1:210.22, 211.1.

178. G.1:205.5.

179. G.1:209.5 (unless Uthayfiya is meant, see above, note 111). Surprisingly, I cannot document the involvement of scholars of Ushayqir in these polemics.

180. For these writings, see above, note 169.

181. For this scholar, see I.111.6; B.1:45.19. When Saudi forces suppressed

the apostasy of Ḥarma nearly twenty years after his death, they made a point of cutting down "the palm-grove of Muways" entire (G.2:118.9 [1193]).

182. Thus he appears in each of the three epistles discussed above (see for example G.1:135.5, 138.15, 208.14). Ibn 'Abd al-Wahhāb refers to him as "al-Muways," except in one passage where we find "Walad al-Muways" (G.1:148.14; I assume this to be the same man).

183. Ibn 'Abd al-Wahhāb refers to him as "your Syrian" (*Shāmīyukum*, G.1:156.9), "a man with claims to learning who has come from Syria with a load of books" (G.1:128.2), and the like (see also G.1:126.18, 153.3). Ibn 'Abd al-Wahhāb had been only too anxious to study in Syria, but had not been able to afford it (B.1:8.10).

184. G.1:154.5, referring contemptuously to this "man called 'Abd al-Ghanī." For a more sympathetic account of relations between this versatile Ṣūfī and his Ḥanbalite pupils, see J. Voll, "The Non-Wahhābī Ḥanbalīs of Eighteenth Century Syria," *Der Islam*, 49 (1972), 286f.

185. G.1:139.3, 208.22. The sanctuaries in question include the Qubbat al-Kawwāz and the Qubbat Abī Ṭālib; the former is associated in another passage with the Qubbat al-Zubayr (G.1:208.8), and the latter was apparently the tomb of a rapacious *sharīf* in the Ḥijāz (G.1:9.5).

186. For this epistle, see G.1:148.14; cf. also the references to *khuṭūṭ* of Muways and others at G.1:214.6, 223.15, and below, note 189.

187. G.1:148.12; see also G.1:129.10, 129.24. This, incidentally, seems to be the earliest attestation of the motif of Ibn 'Abd al-Wahhāb's Iranian connection.

188. One was a certain Ibn 'Īdān (see for example G.1:123.7); he may or may not be identical with the Ḥasan ibn 'Abdallāh ibn 'Īdān who died as *qāḍī* of Ḥuraymilā' in 1202 (B.1:84.1; I.124.5; according to Rashīd, he had been *qāḍī* there since 1171, "Quḍāt Najd," second installment, 104). The other is not named.

189. G.1:122–31. The letter of Muways to the people of Washm here in question may be distinct from that referred to above (see particularly G.1:122.23).

190. Ḥamad (or Aḥmad) ibn Ibrāhīm was the pupil and son-in-law of Ibn 'Abd al-Wahhāb, as well as a distant kinsman, and had settled with him in Dir'īya (see B.1:73.5; I.211.7). One of his sons was likewise *qāḍī* of Marāt, perhaps in his lifetime (Rashīd, "Quḍāt Najd," second installment, 106; third installment, 77).

191. Ibn Bishr describes 'Abd al-'Azīz ibn 'Abdallāh al-Ḥuṣayn al-Nāṣirī as *qāḍī* of Washm under the rule of 'Abd al-'Azīz (B.1:129.15, 232.16). Did his jurisdiction then extend over all Washm, and if so, what was the status of the *qāḍīs* of Marāt (see above, note 190) or Qarā'in (see B.1:234.2)?

192. A characteristic figure is perhaps the *qāḍī* of Washm just mentioned (note 191). He was clearly a local, since he had studied at a very young age under a *qāḍī* of Qarā'in (cf. above, note 150). But he had also studied for several years with Ibn 'Abd al-Wahhāb, to whom he owed his appointment as *qāḍī* of Washm (B.1:233.8).

193. What follows has no claim to be founded in my research; the questions discussed are in any case probably unanswerable.

194. The selection of terminal dates for the Saudi conquest of these areas is a somewhat arbitrary decision (this in itself being an indication of the messiness of the process), but the following data give a rough indication of the duration of the conflict. In Miḥmal, where Ibn ʻAbd al-Wahhāb had support from a very early date, submission too came early, in 1172. In Sudayr, where hostilities had begun in 1164, the struggle continued into the 1190s. In Kharj it lasted from 1165 to 1199. In the Qaṣīm, where it began only in 1182, it continued intermittently till around the turn of the century. In the ʻĀriḍ, the war with Riyāḍ began in 1159 and was concluded only in 1187. Subsequent conquests outside Najd tended to be far more rapid. I am indebted to my graduate students at Princeton in 1984 for most of what I know of the Saudi conquest outside Washm, and in this instance to Mona Zaki, Michael Bonner, Dina LeGall, and Noha Aboulmagd.

195. *Najd li-man ṭālat qanātuh* (see ʻUthaymīn, "Najd," third installment, 27).

196. By the twelfth century, of course, power in Najd grew more from the barrel of a gun than the tip of a lance, and in this field Ibn ʻAbd al-Wahhāb had the reputation of a considerable innovator (for his contribution to Arabian military technology, see *Lamʻ al-shihāb*, 67, 503–7). Shaafy, by contrast, lays emphasis on the generally poor quality of Saudi arms ("Military Organisation," 70f.).

197. For the submission and death of Ibrāhīm ibn Sulaymān, see above, note 142. Dahhām submitted twice for short periods; in 1187, he abandoned his town through a personal loss of nerve rather than any military or political exigency. Both Ibrāhīm and Dahhām had lost more than one son in the conflict. Zayd ibn Zāmil submitted briefly in 1189–90, and was killed in 1197.

198. The spiritual resources which this made available to them are caught in the Koranic text with which Ibn ʻAbd al-Wahhāb met his followers after they had suffered a catastrophic defeat at the hands of the Najrānī invaders of 1178: "And be not dismayed, neither be ye grieved; for ye shall be superior *to the unbelievers* if ye believe. If a wound hath happened unto you *in war*, a like wound hath already happened unto the *unbelieving* people: and we cause these days *of different success* interchangeably to succeed each other among men; that God may know those who believe, and may have martyrs from among you (God loveth not the workers of iniquity); and that God might prove those who believe, and destroy the infidels" (Q.3:139–41, trans. Sale; see B.1:48.10). The passage forms part of the battery of verses revealed following the defeat of the Muslims at Uḥud in the year 3 (see Ibn Hishām, *al-Sīra al-nabawiyya* [Cairo, 1955], 2:110.8; and cf. Ibn ʻAbd al-Wahhāb, *Mukhtaṣar sīrat al-rasūl* [Damascus, 1958], 179.12). It can also be argued that faith in one way made it easier for the enemies of the Saudi state to submit when the struggle went against them: the brute fact of submission to superior human force could be glossed as an acknowledgment of divine truth.

199. For a general statement of his thesis, see Juhany, *History*, 2–5.

200. Ibid., 124, 152.

201. See particularly ibid., 225–57.

202. See for example his picture of conditions in Ushayqir (ibid., 208).

203. Ibid., 275–80, 285; for Tharmadā', see also ibid., 198 f.

204. Ibid., 240–57, 284, 298.

205. Ibid., 286.

206. Ibid., 289; and see 286 f., 301.

207. See for example ibid., 36, 240.

208. See ibid., 3, 226.

209. See ibid., 4, 219, 226 f., 298. (For Washm, see ibid., 199, 208, 211.)

210. See above, note 48 (and cf. note 56 on Ushayqir).

211. None of those used by Juhany is older than the second Saudi state (ibid., 26 f.).

212. For these pressures, see ibid., 261–69; A. M. Abu Hakima, *History of Eastern Arabia, 1750–1800* (Beirut, 1965), 128.

213. What follows represents a reaction to some unpublished suggestions of Nikki Keddie regarding the impact of eighteenth-century European trade on Islamic societies.

214. Note the key feature of the French connection as exploited by Aḥmad Jazzār Pasha: the sale of cotton to a European market provided the resources which made it possible for him to create and pay for a *professional* army such as earlier local rulers in the same region had not possessed.

215. For this trade, see Abu Hakima, *History*, 40; *Lam' al-shihāb*, 514. Cf. also Juhany, *History*, 222.

216. *Lam' al-shihāb*, 510–12.

217. The only exception I know of is a statement that Muḥammad ibn Sa'ūd gave foreign merchants a protection they would not otherwise have enjoyed from his mischievous subjects (*Lam' al-shihāb*, 99).

218. This contrast is noted by Abu Hakima (*History*, 143).

219. Such a hypothesis would obviously be correct for the third Saudi state; I suspend judgment on the second.

220. This paper was presented at a conference on "Eighteenth century renewal and reform movements in Islam," held in Jerusalem in 1985; I would like to thank the organizer, Nehemia Levtzion, and the participants for their comments. I am also indebted to Michael Lecker for a rich commentary on an earlier draft.

43

Jeux sans frontières: Philby's Travels in Southern Arabia

J. B. Kelly

VERY LITTLE WAS known in the early decades of this century about that portion of Arabia which lies between longitudes 46° and 56°E and latitudes 18° and 24°N, that is to say, between al-ʻĀriḍ and Jabal Ṭuwaiq in the west and the Oman steppes in the east, and between the steppes of Dhufār and the Ḥaḍramaut in the south and the hinterland of the Gulf coast in the north. Over most of this region stretched the vast sand sea known to the tribesmen of central and northern Arabia as the *Rubʻ al-Khālī*, or "Empty Quarter," and to the tribesmen along its southern and eastern limits simply as *al-rimāl*, "the sands." Only two Europeans had ventured to the outskirts of the sands before 1930: Major R. E. Cheesman, who in 1921 explored the Jibān tract at the base of the Qatar peninsula and the adjoining Jāfūra desert (itself a northern extension of the Rubʻ al-Khālī) as far as the oasis of Jabrīn; and Bertram Thomas, vizier to the sultan of Oman, who in the winter of 1929–30 journeyed from Salāla, on the coast of Dhufār, across the Qāra Mountains and along the edge of the sands to the Ramlat al-Mughshin.

Thomas had his heart set on becoming the first European to cross the Rubʻ al-Khālī. So, too, did Harry St. John Bridger Philby, who in 1930 was living in Jidda, where he divided his time between running a trading and transport company and courting the favor of King Ibn Saʻūd. Throughout the summer and autumn of 1930 Philby fretted over the possibility that Thomas, whose reconnaissance of the southern approaches of the Rub‘ al-Khālī the previous winter had been reported by the Royal Geographical Society, might be planning an imminent attempt upon the great desert. The thought that Thomas might snatch the laurel before he, Philby, could reach for it was almost more than Philby could bear—especially after he had, that very summer, converted to Islam, the better to advance his various causes with Ibn Sa‘ūd, not least of which was the crossing of the Empty Quarter. So corrosive and intemperately expressed were Philby's feelings of jealousy toward Thomas that they became a matter of public record, inspiring the novelist Josephine Tey to write a fictional account of the one-sided feud, later to be published under the title of *The Singing Sands*. In it the character of Philby, thinly disguised under another name, appears in a decidedly unattractive, though far from inaccurate, light.

As fate would have it, the race was won by Thomas, who, in the winter of 1930–31, made the crossing from Dhufār in the south to Qatar in the north. When the news reached Philby, he was beside himself with fury and despair. According to Daan van der Meulen, the Netherlands consul at Jidda, he poured contumely and derision upon Thomas's achievement. "Of what value was a journey performed in a straight line and so fast that it amounted to a race with death?" he asked scornfully. Unlike Thomas, he boasted to van der Meulen, he would explore the Rub‘ al-Khālī thoroughly. "I am going now and you will not see me for a year, perhaps two years, or you will never see me again."[1] Again, as fate would have it, Philby's journey, when he undertook it a year later, lasted not much longer than Thomas's. A good portion of it, moreover, traversed the same, or nearly the same ground, and in its later stages it was, if anything, even more of a race with death than Thomas's had been. Where Philby's journey differed essentially from that of Thomas was in having a hidden purpose, one which Philby never revealed at the time but which was later to surface obliquely in his narrative of his journey, *The Empty Quarter*, published in 1933. That purpose, which was directly linked to the territorial ambitions of his patron, Ibn Sa‘ūd, can be discerned by a comparison between Philby's personal log of his travels and what he later wrote in *The Empty Quarter*, as well as by an examination of the circumstances surrounding a later expedition which he made in 1936 along the western and southern fringes of the Rub‘ al-Khālī. But before engaging in this comparison and examination, it is necessary to take some brief note of where matters stood in 1930 with respect to the limits of Ibn Sa'ūd's territories north of the Rub' al-Khālī.

At the end of the First World War, Ibn Sa'ūd had embarked upon a series of conquests which in the next decade and a half were to extend his sway over all of central and northern Arabia. The boundaries of the sultanate of Najd with the kingdom of Iraq and the sheikhdom of Kuwait were laid down in the Treaty of Muḥammara (5 May 1922) and the Protocol and Convention of 'Uqair (2 December 1922), while those with the emirate of Transjordan were defined a few years later. All three boundary settlements had been negotiated with Ibn Sa'ūd by Great Britain, acting in her capacity as the mandatory power in Iraq and Transjordan, and as the protecting power in Kuwait. No attempt was made in these years to delimit Ibn Sa'ūd's territories in the east or south of the peninsula, simply because there was no compelling reason to do so. At the time of the signing of the Convention of 'Uqair, however, Sir Percy Cox, the High Commissioner in Iraq, who had negotiated the convention on behalf of the British government, had indicated to Ibn Sa'ūd where he considered the eastern boundary of the sultanate of Najd to lie.

Cox found it necessary to make this notification to Ibn Sa'ūd because he had discovered, on arrival at 'Uqair, that the Saudi ruler was engaged in negotiation with a representative of the Eastern and General Trading Syndicate, Major Frank Holmes, for the award of an oil concession for the province of al-Ḥasā. At Cox's request, Ibn Sa'ūd produced a copy of the draft concessionary agreement, together with its accompanying map, which depicted the southern boundary of the proposed concessionary area as a straight line running due east, well south of the Qatar peninsula, to meet the lower Gulf coast at Khawr al-Dhuwaihin.

Cox immediately challenged this casual and cavalier annexation of Qatar to Ibn Sa'ūd's dominions. The status of Qatar had been the subject of a convention concluded between the British and Ottoman governments in July 1913, when the eastern limits of the Ottoman *sanjaq* of Najd (as it then was) were defined by a straight line running from a point on the Gulf coast, directly opposite the island of Zakhnūniya, due south (more or less down longitude 50°25′E) to the Rub' al-Khālī. Thereafter the line was generally known, from the color in which it was drawn on the map attached to the convention, as the "Blue Line." A second Anglo-Ottoman convention in March

1914 defined the limits of Ottoman jurisdiction in southwestern Arabia as a straight line (the "Violet Line") running from a named point on the eastern marches of the Yemen northeastward into the Rub' al-Khālī to meet the Blue Line on latitude 20°N. When Ibn Sa'ūd accepted appointment as Ottoman *walī* of Najd, in a written agreement which he concluded with the Porte in May 1914 (an agreement which, *inter alia*, required him to respect all treaties entered into by the Ottoman Empire), he also assumed an obligation to respect the Blue Line as his eastern frontier. As it happened, the Blue Line corresponded closely with the eastern limits of his authority at the time. The obligation continued to exist after his independence of the Porte and his dependence upon the British government were separately and simultaneously recognized in a treaty which he concluded with Cox in December 1915.

It was these considerations which led Cox at 'Uqair in December 1922 to take issue with the definition of Ibn Sa'ūd's southeastern frontier in the concessionary agreement which Ibn Sa'ūd was negotiating with Holmes. According to Major H. R. P. Dickson, the acting British political agent in Bahrain, who was present when Cox discussed the agreement with Ibn Sa'ūd and Holmes, the High Commissioner took a red pencil and drew a line on the concessionary map from the head of the Dawḥat al-Salwa, at the western foot of Qatar, across the Jāfūra desert to the Jaw al-Dukhan, about one hundred miles to the southwest. "That," he told Ibn Sa'ūd, "is the line." Cox then crossed out the southern sector of the concessionary boundary marked on the map, expressing as he did so, Dickson records, "considerable annoyance at this barefaced attempt on the part of both Major Holmes and Bin Saud to bluff him."[2] Later in the month, Cox amended the course of the line which he had drawn to take account of the fact that an *ikhwān* settlement (or *hijra*) lay to its east. The amended line, which ran due south from the head of the Dawḥat al-Salwa (more or less down longitude 50°40′E), was incorporated in the revised concessionary agreement signed by Ibn Sa'ūd and Holmes early in 1923. The southern boundary of the concessionary area was defined in the agreement as a line running along latitude 24°15′N from its intersection with Cox's Salwa line in the east to its intersection with the southern end of the Wādī Fārūq in the west (at approximately longitude 49°15′E).[3]

Ibn Sa'ūd accepted both Cox's original definition of his southeastern frontier, and the subsequent amendment, without protest. Nor did he see fit to challenge the definition (indeed, the subject was never raised in his exchanges with the British political authorities in the Gulf) for another decade, that is, until after he had granted the Standard Oil Company of California (SOCAL) an oil concession covering the eastern half of his dominions, a concession which St. John Philby was partly instrumental in securing for SOCAL in the twelve months following his crossing of the Rub' al-Khālī.

To understand the political, as opposed to the personal, motives behind Philby's exploration of the Rub' al-Khālī in the winter of 1931–32, some notice must first be taken of Bertram Thomas's crossing a year earlier; for the data that Philby was to gather about the location of wells, the tribes which frequented them, and the extent of their respective *diyār* (grazing grounds) were to constitute the basis of a claim which he was later to put forward in *The Empty Quarter* for wide dominion on the part of Ibn Sa'ūd. This was particularly the case with the Murra, a tribe which ranged into the central sands and most of whose sections had by the early 1930s submitted to Riyāḍ. What Philby and Thomas individually had to say about the Murra, therefore, is of central importance to our story.

Thomas began the first leg of his historic journey at Salāla, on the coast of Dhufār, on 10 December 1930. After crossing the mountain divide and the *najd*, the broken inner slope of the Qāra range, he set out across the steppe for Shiṣar well. With him, as guides, went a group of Rāshid, the most far-ranging of the Badu tribes who roamed the sands, and an assortment of Karab, 'Awāmir, and Bayt Kathīr to serve as *rabī'as* (or *rafīqs*) should they encounter any of their fellow tribesmen *en route*. From Shiṣar well, Thomas made his way to the Ramlat Shu'ayt, beyond which rose the mountainous dunes of the 'Urūq al-Dhaḥiya, the first and most formidable of the dune ranges which Thomas would have to traverse. Once across the 'Urūq al-Dhaḥiya he found the going somewhat easier, especially when he reached the Dakāka, a tract of rolling sand downs which was the favorite pasturage of the Rāshid.

Here his chief Rāshidī guide, Sheikh Ṣāliḥ ibn Kalut, who had gone ahead of him by a few days, brought in a small party of Murra, led by Ḥamad ibn Hādī, a minor sheikh of the Hathalayn, a subsection of the Al Ghufrān division of the Murra. "The plan," Thomas relates, "was that they would bear me westwards through these sands of Dakāka to the waterhole of Shanna."[4] Plentiful rains had fallen the

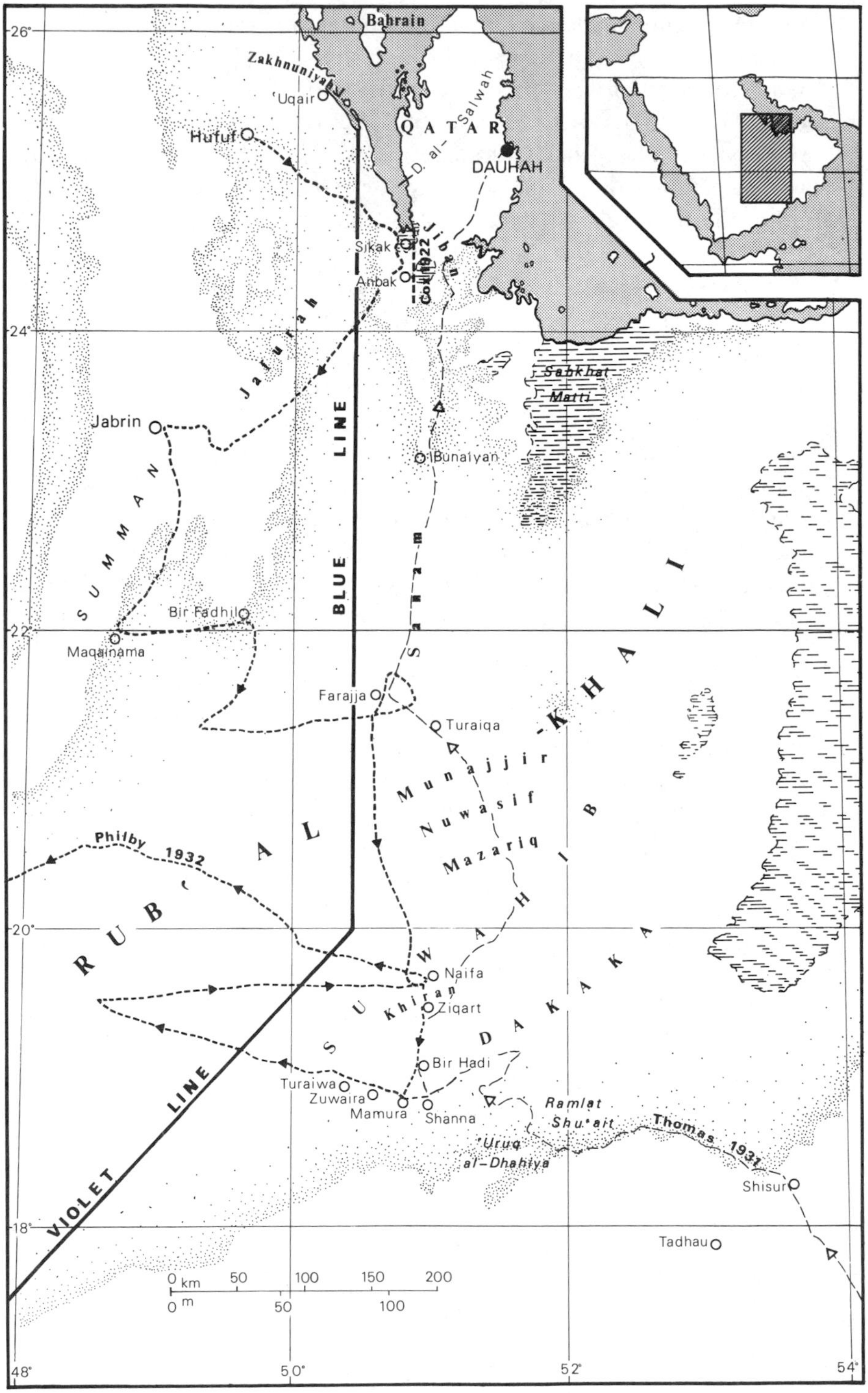
Bahrain
Zakhnuniyah I.
'Uqair
Hufuf
QATAR
D. al-Salwah
DAUHAH
Sikak
Anbak
Cox 1922
Jiban
Jafurah
Jabrin
SUMMAN
BLUE LINE
Bunaiyan
Sabkhat Matti
Sahmah
Bir Fadhil
Maqainama
Farajja
Turaiqa
Munajjir
Nuwasif
Mazariq
Philby 1932
RUB' AL KHALI
BIL HA
SUWAHIB
Naifa
Khiran
Ziqart
DAKAKA
Bir Hadi
Turaiwa
Zuwaira
Mamura
Shanna
Ramlat Shu'ait
'Uruq al-Dhahiya
Thomas 1931
Shisur
Tadhau
VIOLET LINE
0 km 50 100 150 200
0 m 50 100
26°
24°
22°
20°
18°
48°
50°
52°
54°

MAP 43.1

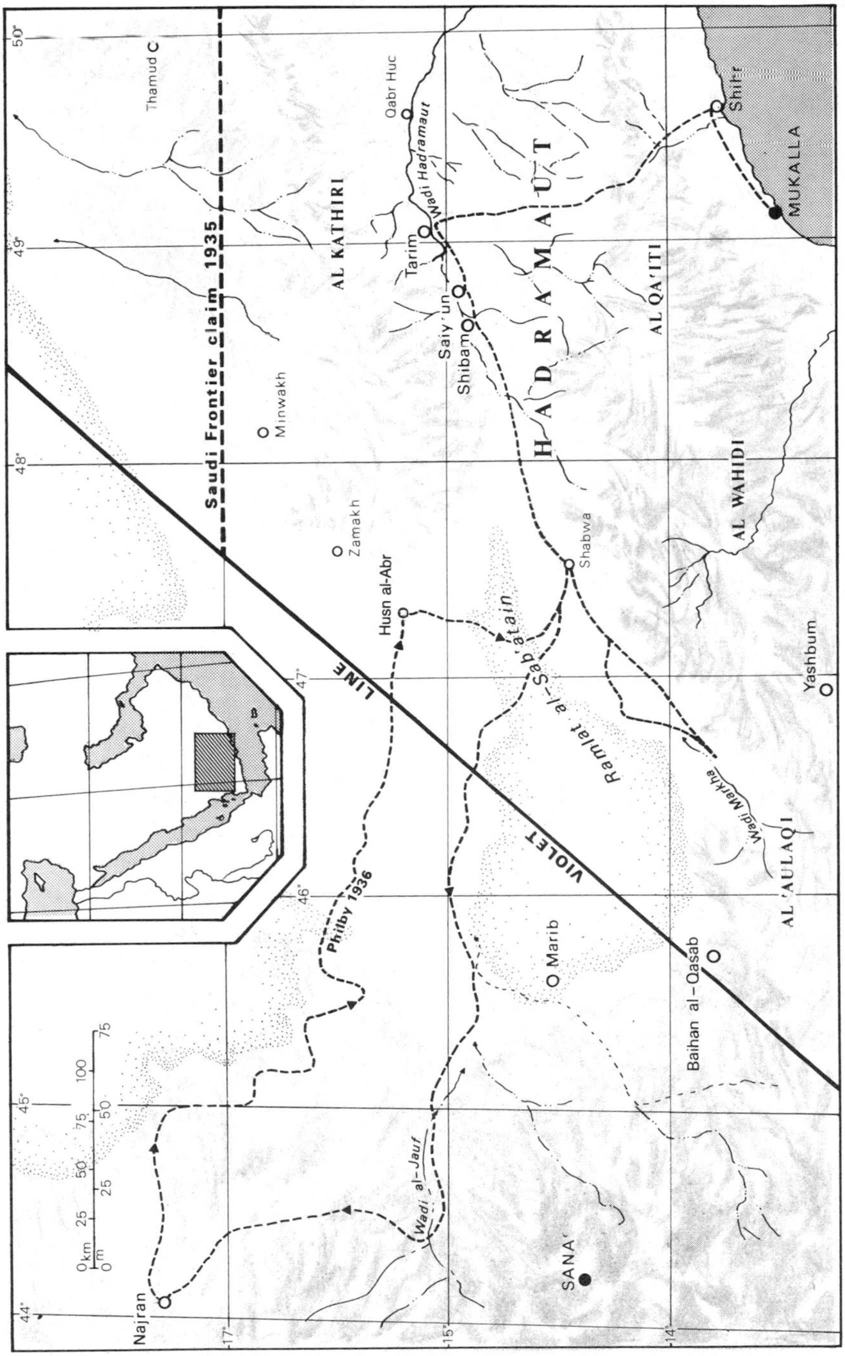
Saudi Frontier claim 1935
VIOLET LINE
Philby 1936
HADRAMAUT
AL KATHIRI
AL QA'ITI
AL WAHIDI
AL 'AULAQI
MUKALLA
Shihr
Qabr Huc
Wadi Hadramaut
Tarim
Saiy'un
Shibam
Thamud
Minwakh
Zamakh
Husn al-Abr
Shabwa
Ramlat al-Sab'atain
Wadi Markha
Yashbum
Marib
Baihan al-Qasab
Wadi al-Jauf
SANA'
Najran

MAP 43.2

previous season, so the grazing in the Dakāka was exceptionally good and the Rāshid were much in evidence. The Dakāka, Thomas was told, was mainly frequented, year in and year out, by the Rāshid, although "parties of Murra are said to come from time to time and spend the summer in Dakāka on account of its comparatively sweet water."[5]

On 4 January 1931 Thomas and his escort reached Shanna, one of a group of wells (the others included Māmūra, Turaywa, and Zuwayra) on the western edge of the Dakāka. Shanna's location Thomas reckoned to be longitude 50°45′E, latitude 19°N. Raiders from the sands, making for the Ḥaḍramaut, had no choice but to travel by way of these wells; so, too, had raiding parties from the Ḥaḍramaut steppes bent on forays to the distant north. (At Shanna Thomas encountered a party of Karab and Manāhil making their way homeward to the Ḥaḍramaut steppes from Abu Dhabī territory.) The Dakāka, consequently, was the scene of frequent tribal clashes, and Thomas's *rabī'a* from the Murra, Sheikh Ḥamad, was constantly on the lookout as they traveled for Sa'ār (who dwelled along the western steppes of the Ḥaḍramaut), with whom he was at blood feud.

On 10 January Thomas and his party, now reduced to thirteen men, set out northward from Shanna, traveling roughly along longitude 51°30′E. In the central sands of Mazāriq, Nuwasif, and Munajjar (about latitude 21°N) their line of march veered to the northwest, so as to take them through the Sanām tract, where the Murra guides knew the location of sweet-water wells like Turayqa and Farajja—the latter reputedly dug by a Murri named Faraj who, so the local folklore had it, had also dug Shanna well. Thomas reached Farajja on 21 January. On the march the next day (somewhere in the latitude of 21°40′N) he sighted the only sizable herd of Murra camels he had encountered on his travels. His route now lay due north, slightly to the east of longitude 51°E. On 24 January he left the sands of the Sanām behind, and a day later he reached the much frequented well of Bunaiyan, at the northern limit of the sands in this longitude. The sea was only eighty miles or so away.

North of Bunaiyan Thomas and his escort moved warily, for report had it that there were *ikhwān* raiding parties in the region. Sometime in the early 1920s Ibn Sa'ūd had established two small *ikhwān* colonies at Sikak and Anbāk near the southwestern foot of Qatar. Although the two settlements had subsequently been virtually deserted by their Murri inhabitants, it was not beyond the bounds of possibility that some Murra might still roam the Jibān, the low-lying series of saltflats, gravel plains, and sandhills running south-southeastward across the base of Qatar from the head of the Dawḥat al-Salwa. In the event, Thomas's party met no one on its route, except for a few Manāṣīr. On 6 February, Thomas reached Dawḥa and the end of his great journey.

While Thomas's crossing of the Rub' al-Khālī was of the nature of a lone enterprise (he traveled without the knowledge, let alone the support, of the British political authorities in the Gulf, the only assistance afforded him being that provided by the sultan of Oman, Taimūr ibn Faiṣal, from whose territory he launched his assault on the central sands), Philby's crossing was of another order, though one would be hard put to realize it from the account given by his official biographer, Elizabeth Monroe. Her attention focuses primarily, to the exclusion of other considerations, upon Philby's constant fretting during the latter half of 1931 over the absence of any sign from Ibn Sa'ūd that permission to attempt the crossing might be forthcoming, even though he hung about the court at Riyāḍ for weeks on end, "practising desert conditions and going for long periods without water." Then, so his biographer relates, "in mid-December, without warning and, as it were, on impulse, the King spoke the longed-for words. He could set out."[6]

A somewhat different version of the circumstances surrounding Philby's departure for the Rub' al-Khālī is to be found in two lengthy articles published in the official Saudi gazette, *Umm al-Qura*, on 13 and 20 May 1932. It appears that in the spring and early summer of 1931 the emir of al-Ḥasa, Ibn Jiluwi, had dispatched a punitive expedition into the Rub' al-Khālī to hunt down some camel raiders. The expedition had not been wholly successful, so a second expedition was organized toward the close of 1931 to complete the work. When Philby learned of the imminent departure of this expedition he glimpsed his chance to attain his ambition, and petitioned Ibn Sa'ūd to be allowed to accompany it. *Umm al-Qura*'s issue of 13 May printed Philby's letter to Ibn Sa'ūd, which was dated 8 Sha'bān 1351/18 December 1931 and began:

> As I have learnt that you intend to send some of your officials to the Rub' al-Khālī, I beg Your Majesty to allow me to proceed with them and in return for such permission being granted me I hereby depose as follows: I declare that the journey is made willingly and of my own accord and desire.

Despite this disclaimer, and despite a further declaration in his letter which absolved Ibn Sa'ūd from any responsibility for his safety, Philby went on to make another sweeping deposition.

> I undertake to furnish Your Majesty's Government with all information I may collect during that journey; such information will be the property of Your Majesty's Government and I will not publish any of it before asking permission from Your Government.
>
> I declare that my Government [i.e., the British Government] have no right to claim anything as a result of the discoveries I may make. All territories I may discover and information I may obtain are the property of Your Majesty and no one has the right to claim any of them. I undertake to place your flags of victory, with your servants, over every high place we may pass by.[7]

The British minister at Jidda, Sir Andrew Ryan, interpreted the undertakings in Philby's letter as being "of interest in connection with possible territorial claims."[8] If this surmise is correct, then it makes Philby's linking up with the punitive expedition something more than a fortuitous occurrence. Substance is lent to Ryan's surmise by an earlier article which appeared in *Umm al-Qura* on 19 February 1932, announcing the recent dispatch of an expedition, on the express orders of Ibn Sa'ūd, to traverse the Rub' al-Khālī and "to investigate that part of his country." "All members of the expedition, technical or otherwise," the *Umm al-Qura* article stated, "have been taken into the service of the Government on contract and have promised not to publish any information on their own account, but to submit it to the Government, who will select what is necessary for publication. The Government have reserved to themselves the publication of information regarding that section of their territory."

In forwarding extracts from the article to the Foreign Office at the end of February, the British chargé d'affaires at Jidda commented that the *Umm al-Qura* statement that all members of the expedition had been taken into the service of the Saudi government presumably included Philby as the "technical member." The rest of the party, as the article elsewhere made clear, was made up exclusively of tribesmen. The chargé d'affaires added: "It is also significant that the paper refers more than once to the regions to be penetrated by the expedition as being 'within Ibn Sa'ūd's territory.' "[9] A month later *Umm al-Qura* ran a further article about the expedition, describing its proposed route and reiterating that its purpose was to collect information about "that part of the dominions of His Majesty the King, about which people have for a long time been talking and expressing unfounded ideas." In somewhat enigmatic vein the article continued: "Our friend Mr. Philby, about whose movements we have read many false rumours concerning which, however, we have preferred to keep silent until the work of the mission has been crowned with success, has accompanied that mission."[10]

Philby's expedition left Hufūf in the Ḥasā Oasis at the end of the first week of January 1932 and headed southeastward across the Jāfūra desert to Qaṣr al-Salwa, at the western foot of Qatar. Besides Philby, the party consisted of eighteen sheikhs or members of sheikhly families from sections of the Murra, 'Ajmān, Bani Hājir, and Manāṣīr tribes, riding on thirty-two Omaniya camels. At Salwa the party turned southward to traverse the Jibān by way of the deserted *ikhwān* settlements of Anbāk and Sikak. Recrossing the Jāfūra in its lower reaches, the party traveled southwestward toward the Jabrīn Oasis, where it arrived in the third week of January. Leaving Jabrīn on 21 January, Philby headed southward, skirting the edge of the Summān plateau, his destination being Maqainama well, some seventy miles away. From Maqainama Philby struck eastward to Bīr Fādhil well, midway between longitudes 49°30′ and 50°E and a little to the north of latitude 22°N. There, on 29 January, he entered the great sands.[11]

His route from Bīr Fādhil took him southward and eastward to the well of Farajja, in the Sanām tract, where Thomas had watered a year earlier. From Farajja Philby's line of march southward veered to the west of Thomas's ("I was naturally anxious to keep as far from his route as possible . . ."[12]), running roughly down longitude 50°48′E to just below latitude 20°N, by which stage he was in the vicinity of longitude 51°E, the furthermost eastern point that he was to reach in his travels. He was now in the southern reaches of the Suwahib region, near the well of Nayfa in the Khirān tract, north of the Dakāka sands. Philby was a little apprehensive about venturing into the Dakāka even though his chief guide, 'Alī ibn Ṣālih ibn Jahmān, was of the Ghufrān section of the Murra which frequented Al Khirān and Shanna well (the same section to which Thomas's Murri guide, Ḥamad ibn Hādī, belonged). At Jabrīn Philby had been told by a Murri who had come up from the Shanna area that

> the rumour of our coming had already preceded us by the mouth of Saif ibn Tannāf, sheikh of the Manāhil, who had actually been at Hufūf when preparations were being made for our expedition and had promptly gone off to warn the desert of our coming. He [i.e., the Murri informant] therefore prophesied, and rightly prophesied, that we should find the desert deserted

by all humanity, as all the grazing tribes had, when he came north, been making preparations for an immediate withdrawal to the safe shelter of the southern mountains.[13]

The reason for the tribes' nervousness, so Philby reported later, was that they thought his party was on a punitive mission for Emir Ibn Jiluwi.

The southern tribes . . . had retired to the southern mountains, while such Murra elements as had remained in the south with the Rāshid relatives-in-law of Ḥamad ibn Ṣultān ibn Hādī—Bertram Thomas's guide of the previous year and a near cousin of 'Alī Jahmān—similarly preferred to keep at a safe distance from our path lest our purpose might be to collect the taxes which for the moment they were not bothering to pay into the King's treasury.[14]

A rather different impression of Philby's thoughts, lacking all these bold suggestions about the length of Ibn Sa'ūd's reach and the fear instilled in the southern tribes by the approach of the expedition, is gained from reading what Philby set down in his actual travel log, as he hesitated before venturing into the Dakāka tract.

On the 11th [February] I stayed behind at AIN SALA while the camels went down to water at NAIFA (about three or four hours to eastward of us) and with them went ZAYID and ALI [ibn Jahmān] en route for the Arab camps about SHANNA or thereabouts in search of Sûlūm [plural of SILM = *rafiq*]. From NAIFA Ibn Humaiyid accompanied these two as far as the watering of ZIQART where we are in due course to await their coming. They are thus allowing themselves some six or seven days to complete the task of collecting the necessary rafiqs to take us into the "enemy" territory. I had a long talk with them the night before they left and, after much pressure and with apparent unwillingness, Ali suggested that 100 Riyals apiece (i.e., his top figure) would be required to buy the services of HAMAD IBN SULTAN IBN HADI (Al Murra, but living with the RASHID to one of whose Shaikhs his daughter is married), SAIF IBN TANNAF of the MANAHIL and HASAN IBN KALUT of the RASHID, while a similar sum might be required for a representative of the SA'AR. . . . I gave them the choice of three objectives, namely (1) the sea, (2) QABR HUD and (3) SHIBAM or some other town or settlement of the HADHRAMAUT valley. Of these the second would seem to be the nearest as my traverse and Polaris observation which coincide very nicely give me a Latitude here of 19°57′N while my Longitude must be somewhere between 50° and 51° East and Qabr Hud Lies on Long. 50° and Lat. 16°.[15]

Philby's two guides returned within the appointed time to report that they had come upon no one at Shanna well or on the way there. So on 18 February Philby left Ziqirt, where he had rendezvoused with the guides, for Shanna, which he reached two days later. What is notable about the pages of his log covering the journey to Shanna and his two-day sojourn there is that, whereas up to this time Philby had been in the habit of writing a fairly full narrative of the successive stages of his journey at each halting place, these pages are blank, aside from a few jottings about topographical features and geographical coordinates set down on the march. It is a singular omission, for his arrival at Shanna, one would have thought, should have been the high-water mark of his journey, marking, as it did, the successful completion of his crossing of the Rub' al-Khālī. As such, it surely called for the expression of the same kind of exuberant self-congratulation he customarily indulged in elsewhere in his travel logs and published writings.

Little, if any, further light is thrown upon the circumstances of Philby's halt at Shanna in the chapter devoted to it in his book, *The Empty Quarter*, published the following year. Virtually the entire chapter is taken up with matters which make no appearance in his travel log, the greatest number of pages being devoted to an account of his arguments with his companions who were anxious to be away from Shanna as quickly as possible and who stubbornly refused to venture one step further southward. Here, at least, Philby was accurately reflecting the impression conveyed by his entries in his travel notes and log about his hesitation in approaching Shanna, especially when in one passage of his book he reports that his guide Zāyid (who had scouted to Shanna ahead of Philby) urged him not to go beyond Shanna. "Before us lies the land of the enemy, the land of fear. We cannot venture into it without peacemakers. We are frightened. We are in danger. We must not linger here. We must go back."[16]

Yet only a few pages before Philby had written about his arrival at Shanna: "Some days earlier Zāyid and 'Alī Jahmān, having scoured the countryside in vain for signs of grazing Arabs, had visited Shanna and scored the King's brand-mark in the moist sand by the well's mouth by way of declaring our identity—a precaution calculated to warn off all but those who might be strong enough and willing to provoke the King's wrath."[17]

Since there is not a word in Philby's travel notes or log about the two guides' scoring Ibn Sa'ūd's *wasm* (camel brand) in the sand at Shanna well, it is difficult to resist the conclusion that this detail is pure invention on Philby's part. As such, it is at one with other similar flourishes scattered throughout the chapter headed "Shanna" in *The Empty Quarter*, all of which were designed to prove (a) that the land around Shanna was part of the *dīrah*, or range, of the Murra, (b) that the Murra were to a man loyal subjects of Ibn Sa'ūd, and (c) that the king's authority stretched as far south as this point. Thus, in his book Philby has the Murri sheikh, 'Alī ibn Jahmān, pointing out to him, on their arrival at Shanna, "all the familiar landmarks of what he regarded as the home pastures of his own folk" (p. 222); whereas in his route notes he merely records: "Ali's points from camp: 204 Shanna 1, 204 Zuwaira 4, 216 Turaiwa 1, 203 Mamura 5, 204 Bir Ibn Suwailim, 204 Arfaqa 2, 38 Bir Hadi."[18] The entry in his travel log is equally terse: "Ali pointed out sandridge beyond Shanna with Zuwaira watering at its R extremity."[19]

The same motive presumably prompted the further claims made by Philby in *The Empty Quarter* (pp. 224–25) that Shanna well itself was dug by 'Alī ibn Jahmān only two years earlier, in the winter of 1929–30, when the Ghufrān section of the Murra sought refuge in the Shanna district from the depredations of the *ikhwān*, then in revolt against Ibn Sa'ūd, who were marauding in northern Ḥasā, where the Ghufrān were normally accustomed to spend the winter months. "From that day to this," Philby writes (p. 225), "Shanna has been the cynosure of grazing or raiding tribesmen, a fount of life in the southern sands and equally for that reason a source of death and danger." Whether or not 'Alī ibn Jahmān was the first to dig Shanna well no one can now say; but it is worth noting that Philby himself writes of Bīr Fādhil well (to the northward), where he had camped in the last week of January: "By further enquiry, however, I elicited the fact that the actual shafts have existed since time immemorial, while the 'digging' of our well, for instance, by the Ghafrān meant no more than its rediscovery and clearing."[20] His travel notes (under the date 28 January 1932) say of Bīr Fādhil: "Main well 2 K from ours at 213 from it and its covering removed by a Sa'ar ghazi of last April which drank of it and left it open so it has since been buried by sand."[21]

It is, in any case, of no great consequence whether a Murri actually dug Shanna well or, as seems more likely, simply cleared it, in the winter of 1929–30. For, as Thomas had observed when he halted there the following winter, and Philby himself also conceded, Shanna was but one of numerous wells in the western Dakāka sands to which a number of tribes—Rāshid, Murra, Manāhil, 'Awāmir, Sa'ar, and Karab being the most prominent—resorted year in and year out. If

Shanna was a Murra well, and the western Dakāka was part of the Murra range, as Philby seemed to be claiming, why did he refer to it in his travel log as "enemy territory," and why did he and his party go in such fear while watering there? And is it likely, for all his bold words about "the King's wrath," "the King's men," and "the King's brand-mark," that Ibn Sa'ūd's reach would have extended so far in 1930–32, when he had barely been able to suppress the *ikhwān* revolt in the north a mere year or two earlier, and only then with the aid of the British authorities in the Gulf and Iraq?

From Shanna, which he left on 22 February 1932, Philby struck west by northwest across the sands in a bid to cross the western sector of the Rub' al-Khālī to Sulaiyil and the Wādī Dawāsir. On the first day he passed by Māmūrā well, then Zuwayra ("tracks here of fifteen men who watered here fairly recently, a raiding party") and Turaywa ("recently visited by Arabs who watered here").[22] In the Qa'amiyyāt tract he came across "the tracks of the men who frightened us at Shanna and of rest of party of 7 or 8 Sa'ar."[23] For the next five days Philby and his escort plodded westward, over increasingly difficult sand terrain, devoid of waterholes. At the end of the fifth day, with the tribesmen growing mutinous (Philby later learned that they had plotted to kill him) and the camels nearly worn out, he was forced to turn back to Nayfa well, which he reached in another five days. Here he divided his party, sending one group northward while he set out westward from Nayfa with the remainder on 5 March to make the crossing to the Wādī Dawāsir. Ten days later, again without coming upon any water or decent grazing, he and his escort reached Sulaiyil. From there Philby made his way by easy stages to Mecca, where he arrived on 5 April.[24]

The publication of *The Empty Quarter* in 1933 left little room for doubt that Philby's purpose in crossing the Rub' al-Khālī had been not only to win renown for himself but also to extend the bounds of Ibn Sa'ūd's kingdom—or at least to prepare the ground for an attempt to extend them. The occasion for such an attempt arose not long afterward, following Ibn Sa'ūd's award of an oil concession for the eastern half of his kingdom to the Standard Oil Company of California in May 1933. Although the concessionary agreement did not stipulate where the eastern and southern boundaries of the concessionary area ran, it soon became apparent that Ibn Sa'ūd took a very enlarged view of where they were, which was a long way beyond the line he had claimed and Sir Percy Cox had corrected at ʻUqair in 1922. In negotiations with the British government between the spring of 1934 and the summer of 1935, Ibn Saʻūd advanced a claim to the entire Rubʻ al-Khālī and a good slice of the Oman, Dhufār, and Ḥaḍramaut steppes as well. His claim, he asserted, was based upon the allegiance paid him by all the nomadic tribes frequenting the border sands and central sands of the Rubʻ al-Khālī. On closer examination, however, the claim appeared to be based, so far as the southern reaches of the Rubʻ al-Khālī were concerned, solely upon the *dīrah* of the Murra. At one stage in the negotiations, the deputy Saudi foreign minister produced a list of 160 supposedly Murra wells, which included Māmūrā, Zuwayra, and Turaywa in the Dakāka, but not, interestingly enough, Shanna. Also on the list were the wells of Shiṣar, Tadhau, Sanau, and Thāmūd.[25] Since the first two wells were on the steppes of Dhufār, and the latter pair on the Ḥaḍramaut steppes, the alleged *dīrah* of the Murra seemed to be of indeterminate, not to say inordinate, extent.

Ibn Saʻūd's frontier claim was formally embodied in a note handed to the British minister at Jidda on 3 April 1935. The southern frontier he claimed for his dominions began in the east at the intersection of longitude 56°E with latitude 19°N, namely, in the Jiddat al-Harāsīs district of Oman, from which point it ran in a straight line across the Dhufār *saiḥ*, or steppe, about fifty miles distant from the Qara Mountains, to the intersection of longitude 52°E with latitude 17°N, deep in the heart of the Mahra country. From there the line continued westward along parallel 17°N, north of the Ḥaḍramaut, to its junction with the Violet Line of the 1914 Anglo-Ottoman Convention.[26]

The entire claim, not to put too fine a point on it, was preposterous. The line proposed by Ibn Saʻūd cut through the *diyār* of the Harāsīs tribe of Oman, of the Bayt Kathīr of Dhufār, of the Haraizi section of the Mahra, of the Manāhil and ʻAwāmir of the northern Ḥaḍramaut, and of the Saʻar and Karab farther west. Not only did none of these tribes owe allegiance to Ibn Saʻūd, but he himself made only a half-hearted and short-lived attempt to claim them as his subjects. Moreover, since the Murra, as Bertram Thomas had discovered in his travels, did not range farther eastward than longitude 51°E or farther southward than the Dakāka, it was difficult to see how Ibn Saʻūd could base a claim to territory beyond these limits on their *dīrah*. As for the tribes whose *diyār* Ibn Saʻūd was claiming as Saudi territory, Thomas told a senior official of the India Office in October 1934:

Ibn Saud had sent emissaries to the Saar, Manahil, etc. But these tribes, together with the El Kathiri and the Mahra tribes of the southern steppe, did not pay *Zakat* to Ibn Saud, and had rejected overtures made to them by emissaries sent to them by the King. The tribes which used the sands did pay *Zakat* to Ibn Saud in a loose sort of way, but it would be dangerous to base too much on this. An occasional section of the Al Kathiri, e.g., the Rashid, living in the sands and exposed to depredations of the Al Murra, will at intervals pay *Zakat* particularly when pastures are to the northward. The fact that he [Thomas], with a Rashidi escort, was in the later stage of his journey across the Rub al-Khali (from Bunaiyan Northwards) endeavouring to avoid the Wahabi elements in the North, while Mr Philby, even with a Saudi escort provided by Ibn Jiluwi, could not move south of Shanna, helped to illuminate the position.[27]

The British government rejected Ibn Sa'ūd's frontier claim of 3 April 1935 as unrealistic. Nor were the British prepared to accept tribal *diyār* as the sole criterion for the determination of territorial sovereignty. "There was a wide difference," Fuad Bey Hamza, the Saudi deputy foreign minister, was told during discussions held in London in July 1935, "between the extreme limits within which a tribe might wander (and which would inevitably overlap with the limits of other tribes) and the actual territory within which a tribe was predominant."[28]

The following November the British made a counter-offer to Ibn Sa'ūd of a southern frontier which began in the east at the intersection of longitude 55°E with latitude 20°N, ran westward in a straight line to the intersection of longitude 52°E with latitude 19°N, and from there, again in a straight line, to the intersection of latitude 18°N with the Violet Line.[29] Ibn Sa'ūd rejected the offer within twenty-four hours of its being made to him. There, for all practical purposes, the Anglo-Saudi frontier negotiations ceased. Ibn Sa'ūd, however, had by no means abandoned, or even shelved, his territorial ambitions in the direction of southern Arabia; and to further them he would seem once again to have enlisted the help of St. John Philby.

"The politics of the southern steppe is completely free from Bin Sa'ud's influence," wrote Bertram Thomas in *Arabia Felix* in 1932, "and the great tribes of Sa'ar, Manahil, Kathir and Mahra, and the lesser ones of Karab, Yam, Nahad and Nisiyin are laws unto themselves. The most powerful single element is the Sa'ar. . . . The Sa'ar tribe and its allies are today the serious menace to peace in the southern sands. Numerically powerful—perhaps two thousand rifles—they derive strength from their remoteness, and have hitherto refused to receive an embassy from Bin Sa'ud."[30]

In December 1935, barely a fortnight after he had rejected the British frontier offer, Ibn Sa'ūd summoned Philby to his court at Riyāḍ. Writing in *The Times* a little more than a year later, Philby recorded of their meeting:

> King Ibn Saud asked me whether I would like to undertake an expedition towards the south to map the extremities of his dominions in that direction. Having just arrived from the Mediterranean the fantastic idea of reaching the Indian Ocean by land flashed across my brain. Najran and Shabwa wove themselves into the dream. Abha had never before been reached by a European. Hadhramaut had never been reached from the north. The Rub' al Khali had never been crossed by motor-car. . . . The Asir mountains and the recently demarcated frontier between the Yemen and Saudi Arabia demanded to be placed on the map. My brain jumbled all these objectives together without thinking too minutely of their details or the difficulties involved. I accepted the King's invitation.[31]

Whether the conclave at Riyāḍ had been as simple and innocent as Philby's ingenuously enthusiastic report made it out to be is open to question—to say the least. Ibn Sa'ūd had a way of "creating facts" to advance his territorial designs, the most recent example of which had been the Wahhābī infiltration of Najrān in the preceding half-dozen years, which had resulted in the transfer of that place to Saudi Arabian sovereignty in the frontier settlement which Ibn Sa'ūd forced upon the imām of Yemen by the Treaty of Ṭā'if in 1934.

Philby set out from Ibn Sa'ūd's camp at 'Ushaira, near Mecca, in late May 1936. Traveling with three motor vehicles, he made his way *via* Khurma and Bisha to Abhā, the capital of the 'Asīr. From there he crossed the broken country at the head of the Wādī Tathlīth to Najrān, where he arrived at the end of June. After waiting a month for petrol supplies to reach him from Mecca, he left Najrān at the end of July with two motor vehicles and an escort of eight Saudi soldiers and a dozen camel riders provided by the governor of Najrān. Instead of proceeding with the mapping of the Saudi-Yemeni frontier, which had been his stated purpose in going to Najrān, Philby headed southeastward, skirting the western edge of the Rub' al-Khālī and making for the wells of Ḥuṣn al-Abr on the southern steppes. From al-Abr he and his escort crossed the heavy sands of the Ramlat al-Sab'atain to Shabwa, once the capital of the Ḥimyarite kingdom, and now a pile of ruins. After spending a few days examining the ruined city Philby crossed the watershed to the southeastward and descended into the Wadī Ḥaḍramaut. With him went half a dozen Saudi guards and some thirty camel riders, his original complement of a dozen riders having been reinforced on his route south from Najrān by *rabī'as* from the Yām, Daham, Karab, and Sa'ar tribes. The Yām were, in the main, a recognizably Saudi tribe, the Daham reputedly Yemeni in allegiance, the Karab (whose paramount sheikh resided at Shabwa) nominally subjects of the Upper 'Aulāqi sultan, and the Sa'ar, in whose territory lay al-Abr wells, dependents in name at least of the Kathīrī sultan of Saiy'ūn and Tarīm. Philby's journey along the Wādī Ḥaḍramaut took him eastward through Shibām and Saiy'ūn as far as Tarīm, where he thought it best to turn back. Halfway to Shibām one of his vehicles broke an axle. As a replacement could not be procured locally, Philby decided to send most of his escort back to Shabwa, while he himself retraced his steps to Tarīm and from there made his way down to Mukallā on the coast, where he hoped to procure a spare axle. His decision was also influenced, he later confessed modestly, by the thought "of being the first human being in all probability to have crossed Arabia from north to south; certainly the first of whom such a feat can be recorded."[32] On 29 August he reached the coast at Shiḥr, and two days later he arrived in Mukallā. From there he telegraphed to Aden to ask for a new axle and other items to be sent to him.

Philby's progress through the Ḥaḍramaut had been viewed by the British authorities in Aden with a certain disquiet, not only because his failure to apprise the Aden authorities beforehand of his intentions, or even of his presence in the Protectorate, was, in the words of the acting Resident, Colonel M. C. Lake, "an impolite and discourteous act," but also because he was accompanied by a sizable escort of Saudi soldiers and tribesmen.[33] When Lake received Philby's request for spare parts on 31 August he telegraphed back the same day:

> I shall be glad to know of the future movements of yourself and Sa'udi party in the Aden Protectorate. I wish to remind you that Shabwa and the Hadhramaut are in the Aden Protectorate which is not administered by His Majesty's Government but whose interests are governed by His Majesty's Government. It is therefore advisable for intending travellers to obtain the permission of this Residency before visiting places in the interior. This is all the more important when the traveller is accompanied by a party from a Foreign Government.[34]

Lake's telegram went on to ask whether there was any truth in the report that Philby intended on his return journey to visit the Upper 'Aulāqi sultanate. If there were, Lake said, he would be obliged if Philby would confirm it so that advance notice might be given to the sultan.[35] Philby replied two days later in characteristic vein:

My visit Hadhramaut itself entirely due necessity reprovision, purchase petrol *et cetera* and visit coast due breakage shaft locally irreplaceable. First opportunity communicate you duly utilised here owing defective communication remainder Protectorate area. Apart Hadhramaut whole journey lay in unexplored, undemarcated territory whose political status am not competent discuss. Respectfully deprecate such discussions. My party has no official character whatever though inevitably organised at Najran. It awaits my return Shabwa resume unfortunately interrupted journey. Vaguely plan making towards Beihan and working north through sandbelt to Najran. Do not contemplate visiting Aulaqi territory but many thanks offer assistance in that direction.[36]

Lake had meanwhile been in touch with the Colonial Office which authorized him, if Philby's Saudi guards were still with him, to require their prompt withdrawal from Protectorate territory. The receipt of Philby's evasive telegram of 2 September, which was couched in such a way as to give the impression that none of his escort had moved beyond Shabwa, while at the same time it sought to deny the existence of British authority north of the Ḥaḍramaut, determined the Resident to give him his marching orders. On 2 September he telegraphed to Philby, asking him to withdraw his Saudi armed escort from the Protectorate as soon as possible, and reproving him for not having informed the Aden authorities in advance of his intention to travel in the Protectorate. As for the explanation and assertions contained in Philby's telegram of 2 September, Lake commented:

I appreciate that necessity took you into the Hadhramaut but as far as I am aware necessity did not take you and your armed party to Shabwa which is definitely within the Aden Protectorate. Further the Ahl Karab who roam the vicinity of Shabwa and whose Chief lives there are nominally vassals of the Upper Aulaqi Sultan. The recognised Northern boundary of the Aden Protectorate from near Dhala north-eastwards is indicated by a N.E. line [i.e., the Violet Line] and is as you state undemarcated and to a great extent unexplored, and the political status of the territory south of this line, which includes Shabwa, is not a matter for discussion as it is *de facto* under the protection of His Majesty's Government. The BAL HARITH tribe N.E. of BEIHAN AL QASAB are under the Sharif of Beihan, who is a Treaty Chief, and I must request you with your Sa'udi armed party not to enter Beihan territory including that of the BAL HARITH unless traverse across a portion of the latter is necessary for topographical reasons, and, should you desire to visit Beihan yourself unaccompanied by armed Sa'udis, to inform me before you leave Mukalla.[37]

A few days after the dispatch of this telegram the spare parts for Philby's vehicle arrived at Mukallā and he left immediately for the Wādī Ḥaḍramaut and Shabwa. A week later Lake flew up to Mukallā, and then to Shibām and Tarīm, to find out exactly what Philby had been up to. From the Quʻiṭī sultan of Mukallā, who had had several conversations with Philby, Lake learned that Philby had endeavored to impress upon everyone he talked to the benefits of living under Ibn Saʻūd's rule. The king, he said, was anxious to extend these benefits to the people of the Ḥaḍramaut, in token of which he intended to build a road for motor vehicles from Najrān to the Ḥaḍramaut so that the Ḥaḍramis might make the pilgrimage more easily. At Shibām and Tarīm Lake heard much the same thing from the Kathīrī sultan and the head of the prominent Al Kāff family. At Shibām, as at Mukallā, Philby had claimed that all the tribes living between Ḥuṣn al-Abr and Najrān had agreed to be under Saudi protection, and he had urged the Ḥaḍramis to follow suit, suggesting that they might appoint a delegation to travel back with him to the Hijaz.[38]

There is a strong possibility—though solid evidence to substantiate it is difficult to come by—that Philby's visit to the Ḥaḍramaut was in some way connected with the activities in the Ḥaḍrami sultanates of adherents of the Irshādī movement, based in the Netherlands East Indies. The *jamʻiyyat al-irshād*, or "Religious and Guidance Association," had been founded in Batavia in 1914 by expatriate Ḥaḍramis with the express aim of challenging the ascendancy of the *saiyid* class in the Ḥaḍrami community in the East Indies. Although the Irshādī movement initially was purely religious in character, it assumed with the passage of the years more of a secular aspect, its ultimate aim being to end the social and economic, as well as religious, dominance of the *sāda* in Ḥaḍrami society. Inevitably the doctrines of the movement, which by the 1930s were becoming tinged with Arab nationalist sentiment, spread to the Ḥaḍramaut itself, where they caused a certain amount of apprehension among the *sāda*.

The Quʻiṭī sultan, Ṣāliḥ ibn Ghālib, told Lake that he suspected a connection between Philby's arrival in the Ḥaḍramaut and the distribution during his stay of a seditious pamphlet calling for radical social, economic, and political reform. The pamphlet was circulated in the name of the Kathīrī Irshādiya and was dated 27 July 1936 (8 Jumada I, 1355). One of its demands could be construed as a call to Ḥaḍramis to place themselves under Saudi rule.

> The Arabian Peninsula is today in a state of striving for the unity of the Arab nations. It is incumbent on us as a keen and an intelligent nation which continues to maintain its freedom to reform ourselves first and then to be in readiness to participate and join the Arab Union under the leadership of the Lion of the Peninsula and its master, His Majesty the King of Sa'udi Arabia.[39]

A number of Irshādī adherents were at this time reported to be living at Riyāḍ, where they were said to have become Wahhābīs. It is not beyond the bounds of probability that Philby may have made contact with some of them during his visit to Riyāḍ in December 1935, when, by his own admission, he discerned in the mission of demarcating the Saudi-Yemeni frontier, with which Ibn Sa'ūd charged him at that time, an opportunity to penetrate as far as the Ḥaḍramaut.

While Lake had been making his inquiries in the Ḥaḍramaut, Philby had been making his presence felt elsewhere in the Protectorate. Stung by the acting Resident's peremptory order to remove his Saudi escort from the country, he had, after returning to Shabwa, taken off for the Upper 'Aulaqī country with his Saudi guards in tow. They were stopped in the Wādī Hammām by Nasiyīn tribesmen, who prevented them from continuing on to Markha. The Upper 'Aulaqī sultan subsequently wrote to the authorities at Aden protesting against the intrusion of Saudi soldiers into his territory and asking to be informed "whether the Sa'udi Government have been given any authority over the Hadhrami interior." "As far as we 'Aulaqis are concerned," the sultan added, "we do not wish them to enter our country at all."[40] The receipt of the sultan's protest led Lake to issue a notification in the Protectorate gazette in late October stating that Philby had not traveled under the auspices of the British government, nor had his entry into the protectorate in company with his Saudi guards been authorized by the Aden authorities.

Although Lake had no direct evidence to link Philby's journey with Ibn Sa'ūd's territorial ambitions, he was not prepared to dismiss the possible existence of such a link out of hand. He was willing to concede that Philby's journey might have had its origin in the latter's urge to explore a corner of Arabia which he had not traversed before and few if any Europeans had seen. It was also possible, Lake admitted, that, "being such an ardent admirer of Ibn Sa'ud, he could not resist the temptation to proclaim aloud the virtues of his hero" to the tribal sheikhs he encountered. "But," Lake cautioned his superiors in London, "in view of the conversations now being conducted by His Majesty's Government with the Sa'udi Government over the boundaries of Sa'udi Arabia, and of Ibn Sa'ud's tendency to claim more than His Majesty's Government is willing to concede, it is quite likely that Mr Philby's intrigue may have had the unofficial, if not the official, support of the King, and that it was financed by the latter."[41]

Sir Reader Bullard, the British minister at Jidda, was not so sure that Ibn Sa'ūd had given Philby any instructions or even encouragement to say what he had said in the Ḥaḍramaut, especially his repeated assertions that all the tribes between there and Najrān were under Saudi authority. "I cannot believe," Bullard wrote to the Foreign Office in late October, "that Ibn Saud, while in the middle of negotiations on this point would even desire still less authorise Mr Philby to make the wild statements that are now attributed to him." The most likely explanation of Philby's conduct, Bullard believed, was that he would use any occasion "to engage in log-rolling on behalf of the ruler to whom he has paid many rather sycophantic tributes in his writings on Saudi Arabia." It was equally likely, Bullard thought, that in making such extravagant territorial claims for Ibn Sa'ūd as he had, Philby was unaware of the location of the frontier with the Aden Protectorate which the king himself had formally claimed only eighteen months previously.[42] This frontier, it may be recalled, ran along parallel 17°N from its junction with longitude 52°E in the east to its intersection with the Violet Line in the west, some 60 miles north of Ḥuṣn al-Abr in the Sa'ar country and 120 miles north of Shabwa in Karab territory.

The object of all this speculation had meanwhile made his way back to Najrān by way of the Yemen foothills, traversing the Jauf district and penetrating to within sight of Mārib. The imām of Yemen, Yaḥya ibn Muḥammad Ḥamīd ud-Dīn, was incensed by Philby's boldness, more particularly as the Yemeni-Saudi frontier in the area through which Philby had passed had not been defined. The imām had also been told that Philby had engaged among the local inhabitants in both pro-Saudi and anti-Yemeni propaganda. Writing to the Resident at Aden, Sir Bernard Reilly (who had lately returned to his post) to protest against Philby's activities, the imām informed Reilly that while in his territory Philby had passed himself off as a British official representative, demanding to be recognized as such and accorded the appropriate privileges and immunities.[43]

Reilly took the protest seriously, since Philby's activities could be construed as a challenge to Yemeni sovereignty over al-Jauf and Mārib, just as his proselytizing on behalf of Ibn Sa'ūd among the tribes of the Aden Protectorate could be regarded as a challenge to Britain's treaty authority over them. The Colonial Office shared Reilly's concern, and in late November asked the Foreign Office to deliver a strong protest to Ibn Sa'ūd against Philby's incursion into the Protectorate. Initially the Foreign Office was inclined to agree with the Colonial Office's view. "Strong reaction on our part is necessary," commented one member of Eastern Department, "both from the point of view of our hold over the tribes and in order to prevent Ibn Saud from thinking that he can again employ Mr Philby in the same way, with impunity."[44] George Rendel, the head of Eastern Department, concurred. "However friendly we may be with Ibn Saud," he observed, "and however little Ibn Saud may be directly responsible for Mr Philby's anti-British activities, the fact remains that, if we do not protest at this gross violation of our frontier, Ibn Saud himself will be likely to think the less of us and be tempted to embark in this area on the same process of peaceful penetration as that which he has so successfully carried out in the hinterland of Qatar and Abu Dhabi."[45]

At the same time, however, the Foreign Office was reluctant to antagonize Ibn Sa'ūd at this juncture, when it was trying both to reconcile him to British policy in Palestine and to counter the infiltration of Italian influence along the Arabian littoral of the Red Sea. While Rendel and his colleagues were still trying to decide whether or not to protest to Ibn Sa'ūd, word arrived from Bullard at Jidda that he had demanded an explanation of Philby's behavior from the Saudi deputy foreign minister, Faud Bey Ḥamza. After consulting Ibn Sa'ūd, Fuad Bey told Bullard in the first week of December that Philby had been instructed to demarcate the Saudi-Yemeni frontier in the Najrān area, for which purpose he had been supplied with guides and an escort. He had not been authorized to go beyond the borders of Saudi Arabia, nor was the Saudi Government aware that he had ventured south of Najrān until a complaint was received from the imām of Yemen about Philby's traverse of al-Jauf and detour to the environs of Mārib.[46]

The explanation left a number of questions unanswered, not least the critical one of Philby's passage through the Aden Protectorate with an armed Saudi escort. The Colonial Office, as already indicated, had been particularly concerned that Ibn Sa'ūd should be left in no doubt that the British Government maintained its position regarding the Protectorate frontier and would not tolerate any Saudi encroachments, especially in the Shabwa area. (Bullard had pointed out Shabwa on a map to Fuad Bey, who agreed that it lay within the confines of the Protectorate, well south of the line claimed by Ibn Sa'ūd as his frontier in this region.[47]) Nevertheless the Foreign Office saw in Fuad Bey's explanation an opportunity to soft-pedal over the whole affair. Accordingly Bullard was instructed to use his own judgment whether or not to lodge a formal protest with the Saudi government. Bullard chose to deal with the matter not by way of a protest but by writing a personal letter to the Saudi foreign minister, Emir Faiṣal ibn 'Abdul 'Azīz. The letter, after acknowledging the receipt of the Saudi government's assurance, conveyed by Fuad Bey, that Philby had not been authorized to go beyond Najrān, went on to point out that Philby's unexpected arrival in the Aden Protectorate with an armed Saudi escort could have provoked an incident with the Protectorate tribes, especially if they had assumed that he had come on a mission for the Saudi government. Bullard concluded by expressing the hope that the Saudi government might see fit to take some suitable action to impress upon Philby the irresponsible nature of his conduct, which could well have had a harmful effect upon Anglo-Saudi relations.[48]

Emir Faiṣal's reply to Bullard bordered on the insolent. The whole question of Philby's wanderings, he wrote back in late December, had been endowed with an importance it did not possess.

> In remote deserts it is very difficult to distinguish the actual frontiers if they are not fixed and known, just as it is difficult to comply with the special arrangements concerning the crossing of the frontiers particularly when there are not special officials for such purpose. . . . The Government of H. M. the King had no knowledge of the intention of Mr Philby to go to the Hadramaut. It was therefore impossible for the necessary application to be made for permission for him to go there. . . . When Mr Philby was asked by the responsible authorities in the Hadhramaut why he had gone there in such manner he replied that he held a British passport and that he was prepared to produce it to the frontier officials had there been any. . . . He was not entrusted with any mission by the Government of H. M. the King and he only went into the Hadhramaut because he had to get his cars repaired. . . . As to the armed persons said to have accompanied Mr Philby, they were merely such guides, guards and servants as escort everyone who travels in the desert.

If Philby had transgressed in any way, Faiṣal concluded, it was up to the British government to deal with him since he was, after all, a British subject.[49]

There was no doubt in Bullard's mind that Faiṣal's reply had been concocted with the aid of information supplied by Philby. The allusion to the vagueness of frontiers in the desert, and the jibe about his readiness to produce his British passport had there been any frontier official to whom to show it, bore Philby's unmistakable imprint. Bullard's suspicions were confirmed by Fuad Bey at the end of December when he returned to Jidda from Riyāḍ, where he had gone to help draw up Faiṣal's reply to Bullard's letter. The deputy foreign minister again tried to justify Philby's excursion to the Ḥaḍramaut by saying that it was necessitated by the breakdown of one of his vehicles. Bullard disposed of this argument by pointing out that Philby's original penetration south to Shabwa was not occasioned by any breakdown or the need for spare parts, and the excursion to Shabwa was just as much a violation of Protectorate territory as that to the Ḥaḍramaut had been. (Bullard might also have pointed out that the breakdown only occurred between Shibām and Tarīm, that is to say, well inside the Ḥaḍramaut.)[50]

Fuad Bey also admitted in the course of conversation that Philby had been acting as an employee of the Saudi government. Three weeks later Philby himself confirmed the fact in the first of two articles on Shabwa which he published in *The Times* on 18 and 19 January 1937. In a passage which has been quoted earlier he made it crystal clear that he had been asked by Ibn Sa'ūd "to undertake an expedition towards the south to map the extremities of his dominions in that direction." He also made it clear in the same passage that he intended to take advantage of this commission to penetrate to Shabwa, traverse the Ḥaḍramaut, and reach the Indian Ocean.[51]

In another passage Philby gave a strong indication of what he perceived to be the proper limits of his royal patron's dominions.

> For all the unpleasant reputation of the Shabwa people, I never imagined for a moment that they would refuse admission to men travelling under the auspices of Ibn Saud. In that confidence I was fully justified, and it was indeed a revelation throughout this southern section of my journey how completely the magic name of the Arab King dominates the desert scene to the farthest limits of the Empty Quarter and even beyond.

Since the previous October, when he had returned to Najrān, Philby had been in the 'Asīr mapping the Saudi-Yemeni frontier. He was expected back in Jidda in February 1937 in time for the pilgrimage, and Bullard awaited his return with interest—although, as he warned the Foreign Office, he did not expect to get much from Philby in the way of a straightforward explanation of his more questionable exploits.

I foresee that he will dramatise himself as a Prometheus, bringing the fire of archaeological knowledge from Shabwa, with His Majesty's Government in the part of Zeus and H. M. Minister as the vulture with no other business in life but to peck at Mr Philby's long-suffering liver, already deeply pitted from similar heroic experiences in India and Iraq and Trans-Jordan.[52]

Philby reached Jidda in mid-February. He called on Bullard on 18 February before leaving the same day for Mecca. Bullard reported afterward,

As I anticipated, Mr Philby was in his most heroic Prometheus mood. Indeed he was even more difficult than I had expected, for to his desire to bring the light of science to mankind is now added a quite ferocious intention to expose the alleged duplicity of His Majesty's Government towards the Arabs of the Peninsula. He asserts that the second part of this programme was added only under the provocation which he considers he received from the Aden authorities.

Questioned by Bullard, Philby denied that his expedition had been financed by Ibn Sa'ūd, or that it had any object other than scientific investigation. He was unapologetic about his visit to Shabwa which, he claimed, lay in "unexplored, undemarcated territory." His journey to that place, therefore, could properly be regarded as "on all fours with that of Bertram Thomas across the Rub' al-Khālī" in 1930–31. It was "fantastic," he said, for the Aden authorities to claim that Shabwa lay within the Protectorate. It did not; and for the British government to try to exert its authority over the region was a violation of the promises of independence made to the Arabs during the late war. Philby also affected to know all about the respective Saudi and British proposals for the delimitation of the southern frontier of Saudi Arabia. For his part, he added gratuitously, he would be inclined to seek more territory for Ibn Sa'ūd than the king himself was claiming.[53]

Bullard had little difficulty in exposing the flaws in Philby's argument. The promises of Arab independence made in the McMahon correspondence, he told him, excluded Aden and the Arabian principalities in treaty relationship with the British government. Though Philby might argue "that His Majesty's Government had no treaty then and have none now with the Arab chief of Shabwa, and regard this as the last word on a subject of great practical and legal complexity," the fact remained that Shabwa lay well beyond the limits of the southern frontier claimed by Ibn Sa'ūd—as Philby should know, if he really was familiar, as he asserted he was, with the nature of this claim. His further assertion that his expedition had been identical with that of Bertram Thomas across the Rub' al-Khālī was equally false. "It is true that Mr Thomas was at the time in the employ of the Sultan of Muscat," Bullard observed, "but he had no official escort, and the Sultan had never given reason to anyone to suppose that he wished to increase his territory." What was more, the whole of Thomas's route lay to the east of the Blue and Violet Lines, which at that time represented the legal boundary of Ibn Sa'ūd's dominions in the east and south of the Peninsula.[54]

Reporting the details of the conversation to the Foreign Office, Bullard observed that Philby's latest travels had produced no factual evidence that would be of use to Ibn Sa'ūd in pressing his frontier claims. He had not ventured into the steppe country to the east of al-Abr wells, although he may have picked up some information about it. According to Bertram Thomas, the principal wells along the steppe, Sanau and Thāmūd in the Ḥaḍramaut. Shiṣar and Tadhau in Dhufār, were almost exclusively frequented by tribes to whose allegiance Ibn Sa'ūd laid no claim, even though the four wells themselves lay within the frontier line he had proposed.[55] "It is unlikely," Bullard concluded, "that Mr Philby has collected any better information on this point than Bertram Thomas, who passed through the territory in question and halted at Shisur; but he may make it more difficult for Ibn Saud to renounce his claim, by representing the tribes hereabouts as entirely beyond the control of the authorities in the coastal states, but ready and willing to submit to Ibn Saud."[56]

Perhaps the most instructive comment upon Philby's travels in southwestern Arabia in the summer of 1936 was provided by an incident which occurred the following July when Philby was back in England, harvesting the plaudits to which he believed he was entitled for his daring and enterprise. In the course of delivering what one witness described as "a long and tiresome account of his recent journey" to the Central Asian Society, Philby broke off to launch into a virulent attack upon the late acting Resident at Aden, Colonel Lake, for allegedly endangering his life when he was traveling in the Protectorate. The reason for Philby's rage, apparently, was the note which Lake had issued in the Protectorate gazette dissociating the British government from Philby's activities. Although Philby charged that the notification practically amounted to an invitation, if not an incitement, to the tribes to murder him, one member of his audience suspected that the real cause of his anger was the description of him in the Aden gazette as traveling "disguised as an Arab."[57]

The charge, needless to say, was groundless. It was not until Philby, contrary to the assurance he had given while at Mukallā, ventured into the Upper 'Aulaqī sultanate that Lake considered the notification to be necessary. By the time it was published in late October 1936 Philby was back at Najrān. His life, in any case, had never been in any imminent danger while he was in the 'Aulaqī country, thanks to the presence nearby, of which Philby remained and continued to remain unaware, of a British political officer. The officer in question, R. A. B. Hamilton (Lord Belhaven) had been at Yashbum, in 'Aulaqī territory, when word reached him of the arrival at Shabwa of a party of Saudi tribesmen and soldiers, led by a European. Guessing at once that this must be Philby, Hamilton sent the chief *qāḍī* of Baihān, who was visiting Yashbum, to Markha in Upper 'Aulaqī country, to restrain the tribes from attacking Philby's party should it appear in their territory. A year later, when Hamilton learned of Philby's accusation against Lake, he commented laconically: "Had a Political Officer not been close to him Mr Philby and his party would have been in considerable danger. The presence of a Political Officer in W/T communication with Aden may have saved his life."[58]

British authority, it would seem, rather than the magic of Ibn Sa'ūd's name, had safeguarded Philby's passage across the northern marches of the Aden Protectorate.

NOTES

1. Quoted in Elizabeth Monroe, *Philby of Arabia* (London, 1973), p. 176.

2. [India Office Records, London] Political External Collections (L/P and S/12), vol. 2130, Collection 6/62, Dickson no. 143 to Political Resident, Persian Gulf, 4 July 1933.

3. [Public Record Office, London] Colonial Office Records (C.O.) 730/37, file 53899, Cox to Secretary of State for the Colonies, 4 January 1923, enclosing copy of the revised concessionary agreement.

4. *Arabia Felix* (London, 1932), p. 188.

5. Ibid., p. 200, n. 2.

6. Monroe, *Philby*, p. 177.

7. [P.R.O.] Foreign Office Records (F.O.) 371/16023, E4175/946/25 Sir Andrew Ryan (H.B.M. Minister, Jidda) no. 312 to Secretary of State for Foreign Affairs, 23 July 1932, enclosing copy of letter.

8. Ibid.

9. F.O. 371/16023, E1343/946/25, C. G. Hope Hill no. 109 to S/S Foreign Affairs, 27 February 1932.

10. F.O. 371/16023, E2047/946/25, Hope Gill no. 165 to S/S Foreign Affairs, 6 April 1932, enclosing extract from *Umm al-Qura*, 25 March 1932.

11. The punitive section of the expedition, having apprehended the wanted tribal raiders, had meanwhile started back for Hufuf, to deliver its captives to the mercy of Ibn Jiluwi. According to *Umm al-Qura*, the miscreants subsequently "had their arms and legs cut off." (See Ryan's dispatch 312 of 23 July 1932, above, enclosing extract from *Umm al-Qura* of 13 May 1932).

12. Philby, *The Empty Quarter* (London, 1933), p. 13.

13. Philby, "Rub' al-Khali: An Account of Exploration in the Great South Desert of Arabia," *Geographical Journal*, LXXXI, no. 1 (Jan. 1933).

14. Philby, *Empty Quarter*, p. 226.

15. [St. Antony's College, Oxford] Philby Papers, Box XII, file 2, "Diary of a Journey Across the Rub' al-Khali, 1932," fol. 204. Qabr Hud was in Manahil territory, north of the Ḥaḍramaut.

16. *Empty Quarter*, p. 230.

17. *Empty Quarter*, p. 225.

18. [Royal Geographical Society] Philby Mss., Notebook 2/G, entry dated 20 February 1932.

19. [St. Antony's, Oxford] Philby Papers, Box XII, file 2, "Diary of a Journey. . ." fol. 223.

20. *Empty Quarter*, p. 136.

21. [R.G.S.] Philby MSS, Notebook 2/F *addendum*.

22. [St. Antony's, Oxford] Philby Papers, Box XII, file 2: "Diary of a Journey . . ." fols. 225/22.

23. [R.G.S.] Philby MSS Notebook 2/G, entry dated 23 February 1932.

24. See *Empty Quarter*, passim. Philby gave a verbal account of his journey a few days after its end to the British chargé d'affaires at Jidda. See F.O. 371/16023, E2055/946/25, Hope Gill to C. E. A. Warner (F.O.), 8 April 1932.

25. See F.O. 371/18907, E4314/77/91, Statement by Fuad Bey Hamza, 8 July 1935.

26. F.O. 371/18906, E2700/77/91, Note from Fuad Bey Hamza, 3 April 1935 enclosed in Ryan's no. 109 of April 1935.

27. F.O. 371/17815, E6769/279/91, Note of discussion with J. G. Laithwaite (I.O.), 19 October 1934.

28. F.O. 371/18907, E4126/77/91, Record of third discussion, 2 July 1935.

29. See F.O. 371/18908, E7574/77/91, Note dated 25 November 1935, enclosed in Ryan's no. 351 of 10 December 1935.

30. *Arabia Felix*, pp. 271, 273.

31. "Shabwa, the Lost Arabian City: Part 1—A Mission for a King," *The Times*, 18 January 1937.

32. "Shabwa . . ." *The Times*, 18 January 1937.

33. See C.O. 725/39/16, File 78150, Lake tel. 62 to Secretary of State for the Colonies, 24 August 1936.

34. Ibid., Lake tel. 2504 to Philby, 31 August 1936.

35. Ibid.

36. C.O. 725/39/16, File 78150, Philby tel. to Lake, 2 September 1936.

37. Ibid., Lake tel. C/1447 to Philby, 7 September 1936.

38. C.O. 725/39/16, File 78150, Lake dispatch no. 492 to S/S, Colonies, 30 September 1936, enclosing R.A.F. intelligence report, 26 September 1936, and letter from sultan of Shihr and Mukalla, n.d.

39. C.O. 725/39/16, File 78150, Proclamation by the Kathiri Society Office, Batavia, enclosed in Lake dispatch no. 494 to S/S Colonies, 7 October 1936. See also Aden Political Intelligence Summary no. 506, 7 October 1936, enclosed in Lake despatch no. 538 to S/S Colonies, 28 October 1936.

40. C.O. 725/39/16, File 78150, letter to Political Secretary, Aden, dated 23 Rajab 1355/9 October 1936.

41. Ibid., Lake no. 492 to S/S Colonies, 30 September 1936.

42. F.O. 371/19979, E7172/5404/91, Bullard no. 289 to S/S Foreign Affairs, 25 October 1936.

43. C.O. 725/39/16, File 78150, Reilly no. 544 to S/S Colonies, 4 November 1936, enclosing letter from imām dated 2 Sha'bān 1355/21 October 1936.

44. F.O. 371/19979, E7271/5404/91, Minute by J. C. Sterndale Bennett, 28 November 1936.

45. Ibid., Minute by Rendel, 2 December 1936.

46. F.O. 371/19979, E7546/5404/91, Bullard tel. 122 to F.O., 3 December 1936.

47. Ibid.

48. F.O. 371/19979, E8006/5404/91, Bullard no. 2101/316/55 to Faisal, 8 December 1936. See also E7546/5404/91, F.O. tel. 135 to Bullard, 5 December 1936.

49. F.O. 371/20776, E206/206/91, Faisal no. 2/9/6 to Bullard, 7 Shawwal 1355/21 December 1936.

50. F.O. 371/20776, E376/206/91, Bullard no. 330 to S/S Foreign Affairs, 29 December 1936.

51. See above, at note 31.

52. F.O. 371/20776, E376/206/91, Bullard no. 330 to S/S Foreign Affairs, 29 December 1936.

53. F.O. 371/20776, E1633/206/91, Bullard no. 27 to S/S Foreign Affairs, 28 February 1937, enclosing summary of Philby's statement.

54. Ibid.

55. See above, at note 25.

56. Bullard no. 27 of 28 February 1937, above.

57. C.O. 725/46/6 File 78150, H. R. Cowell (C.O.) to Sir Bernard Reilly (Aden) 19 July 1937.

58. Ibid. Note by Hamilton, 5 August 1937, enclosed in Reilly no. C/1044 to Cowell, 7 August 1937.

44

The Rise of King ‘Abd al-‘Azīz ibn Sa‘ūd During the Era of Ottoman Sultan ‘Abd al-Ḥamīd II (1876–1909)

C. Max Kortepeter

I. Introduction

AS IN A fog slowly lifting over Istanbul, we are nowadays in a position to peer through the mist and perceive the main outlines of the policies of the imperial powers and of the Ottoman Empire during the formative years of the third Saudi state at the beginning of the twentieth century. Popular ideas in Istanbul and Riyāḍ have often fed upon notions that the Arabs were ever inimical to Ottoman interests and conversely, that the Ottomans had singled out the Saudi family for special persecution.

In actuality, the Ottomans, in the first years of the nineteenth century, were forced to deal with the crisis caused by the landing of Napoleon in Egypt in 1798. Meanwhile, the rising Saudi power in Arabia struck two audacious blows at the Ottoman Empire shortly thereafter: Karbalā in Iraq, one of the most sacred Shi‘ī shrines, was sacked and desecrated in 1801, and two years later in 1803, the Saudis seized Mecca and Medina. The sons of Muḥammad ‘Alī, the Albanian governor of Egypt, acting at the behest of Sultan Maḥmūd II (1808–39), retook the Holy Cities in 1812 and 1813, thus permitting the sacred annual pilgrimage to proceed again. As a further act of retaliation, Ibrāhīm Pasha, son of Muḥammad ‘Alī, led his Egyptians to a sack of al-Dir‘īya, the Saudi capital, in 1818. The Ottomans executed

'Abdallāh ibn Sa'ūd, the Saudi leader and imām, shortly thereafter in Istanbul.

Obviously, the splendor and the problem of a new purifying faith is that its followers bring ecstasy to themselves but sometimes hardship to others. The Saudis carried the new faith to every community in their orbit which did not practice Islam in accordance with the *dīn al-tawḥīd*, the unitary faith known as Wahhābism in western Europe. This new version of Islam, which sought to observe strictly the various precepts of the faith as set forth in the sacred Qur'ān, was instigated by Muḥammad ibn 'Abd al-Wahhāb (1703–92) and accepted as the official faith of the Saudis of Dir'īya in 1744–45.[1]

In like manner, however, an imperial Islamic power such as the Ottoman Empire, to maintain its own claims to legitimate rule, was bound to pursue its own version of warfare (the *ghazwa*) against infidels, while at the same time protecting Muslims and non-Muslims in the *Dār al-Islām* and preserving the Holy Law. Moreover, the Ottoman rulers further asserted their legitimacy by becoming the servitors and protectors of the sacred Muslim cities of Mecca and Medina (*khādim al-ḥaramayn*) and sheltering the worshipers who performed the prescribed annual pilgrimage.

Herein lies the basic conflict between the Saudi/Wahhābī state of the eighteenth and nineteenth centuries and the Ottoman imperial government: zealous, reforming believers versus an imperial system sustained by Islamic beliefs defined to fit the needs of a vast multinational empire in a rapidly changing external political environment—one which was indeed quite hostile to any Muslim state. By the third quarter of the nineteenth century, as we approach the era of Sultan 'Abd al-Ḥamīd II (1876–1909), the major question facing the Ottoman Empire had ceased to be who would control the marches of Arabia, with the exception of course of Mecca and Medina, but rather: "Who would control the Islamic heartlands, Muslims or Europeans?" In this study, we shall indicate how the Saudi state emerged in this complex era from the ruins of the Saudi civil war of the 1870s and 1880s, and made a reluctant peace with the Ottomans prior to World War I.

II. Three Phases of British Imperial Advance in Arabia

The continuation of the Saudi emirate at the beginning of the twentieth century took place in a climate of major European penetration of the Ottoman Empire, the growth and development of advanced technology which imperial powers tried to monopolize, and the failure of the Ottoman leadership to formulate an ideology to which the Muslim community, in all its diversity, could give its undivided loyalty. British imperial policy in the nineteenth century passed through three phases: an initial shift away from imperial Russia in support of the Ottoman Empire; a second shift away from France and its coziness with the regime of Muḥammad ʻAlī; and finally, a reconciliation with Russia and France at the beginning of the twentieth century, to safeguard her position against the rise of imperial Germany.

Because of the threat imperial Russia posed to the eastern Mediterranean and ultimately to India, Britain had abandoned her support of Russia after the Russo-Turkish War of 1828–29, which had enabled Greece to gain her independence. (Greece, being Orthodox like Russia, was considered to belong to the Russian sphere of influence.) Shortly thereafter, in the 1830s, Lord Palmerston, the British foreign secretary, formulated the principle that various routes, the lifelines to India through the Mediterranean, must be kept within the British orbit. The decision was thus taken in Whitehall to "beef up" the Ottoman Empire by helping to modernize its political and administrative system and its armed forces, so that it could withstand any further Russian encroachments to the south.[2] Independent of the British, the Ottomans had imported a German military mission headed by young Captain Helmut von Moltke in 1834, the same officer who would lead the defeat of France in 1870 with a new kind of German rifle. The sultan also signed a treaty with the United States in 1830, with the initial objective of gaining the latest U.S. technology in naval shipbuilding. The British tacitly approved these moves, because a strengthened Ottoman military establishment meant that Britain would not have to garrison its lines of communication across the Middle East to India.

The British, for two reasons, were less pleased with the rise of Muḥammad ʻAlī as a possible defender of their "lifelines." Muḥammad ʻAlī and his sons, especially Ibrāhīm Pasha, rapidly carved out their own spheres of influence and conquest, into the Sudan, Syria, and the Arabian Peninsula; moreover, all of this was accomplished with the close assistance of Britain's rival, Restoration France, particularly in the sphere of military modernization and technology. Ibrāhīm Pasha had also begun to recruit native Egyptians into his army and staff positions, thus acquiring the potential for large fighting forces. We have already noted how Sultan Maḥmūd used the forces of

Muḥammad 'Alī to destroy the first Saudi state and regain control of the Holy Cities of Mecca and Medina. When Ibrāhīm Pasha swept into Najd in 1817–18 to end forever the Saudi state, the British, who had suffered from the Qawāsim pirates in the Gulf, were so pleased that Captain G. F. Sadleir was sent from Bombay to congratulate him, a mission which ended on a sour note when Ibrāhīm failed to address Lord Hastings properly in a letter. Later, Ibrāhīm's invasion of Anatolia forced Britain's hand. Muḥammad 'Alī, under the threat of British gunboats, renounced his conquests of Syria (including Lebanon) in 1840, and withdrew his troops. Meanwhile, in 1839 Britain had occupied Aden.[3] This move against Muḥammad 'Alī was, of course, an indirect rebuff of France, which had helped train the Egyptian army, and was currently training Egyptians in French schools.

While the Ottomans were glad to have the overt threat of Muḥammad 'Alī's expansion northward, which had even penetrated into Anatolia in 1832, stopped decisively by Britain, the Ottomans had already paid a heavy price in the treaty of Balta Liman of 1838, which gave Britain unheard-of privileges to trade freely in the Empire, while paying only customs of 3 percent *ad valorem*. Cheap British goods flooding Ottoman markets began to wreak havoc with local crafts, guilds, and merchants and, incidentally, began to put a lot of money in the pockets of the non-Muslim *millets* which served as agents, with *berath* (extra-territorial privileges) of foreign trading companies.[4]

Another price the Ottomans paid was that of turning a blind eye to creeping British imperialism in the Perso-Arabian Gulf. The British residents in the Gulf not only took a hand in exports and imports as far north as Baghdad and Basra, fostering mail service (giving up the Baghdad route in 1837 for the Red Sea) and the quarantine system adopted by the Ottomans in the early 1830s; they also interfered with the slave trade and watched Ottoman troop movements. Thus, for the time being, the British left the garrisoning of the Middle East to the Ottomans, knowing full well that the British navy and the newly-developed river gunboats could bring further British interference into the Gulf, if need be.

As a case in point with regard to "creeping" British imperialism in the Gulf, one may note that shortly before the era of the well-remembered Saudi ruler, Fayṣal ibn Turkī (1834–38, 1843–65), the British, taking advantage of the vicissitudes of the first Saudi period of eclipse, consolidated their hold on certain of the emirates and sultanates within the Gulf. The British, since the mid-seventeenth century, had maintained a factory (after the fall of Portuguese Hormuz) on Persian soil at Jask, then Bandar 'Abbās, and finally at Bushehr. Diplomatic relations with Persia were secured in 1809 and 1814 by General Malcolm and Sir H. Jones, after Napoleon's threat to the region had subsided. It was from Bushehr thus that Britain first began its surveillance of Russia's moves against the Qajars in the Caucasus. As may be recalled, there was for a time one of those classic squabbles between Whitehall and Calcutta about which British representative should dominate in Tehran. According to the *Gazetteer*, at the beginning of the nineteenth century there was a British residency in Baghdad (1798) and in Muscat (1798, confirmed in 1800), both subordinate to Bushehr. The residency in Iraq actually shifted between Baghdad and Basra, with Kuwait used as a backup position when the Ottomans became really hostile. The Basra residency was on occasion termed the "Residency for Turkish Arabia." The final British move in the Gulf in the early phase was associated with the suppression of piracy and the slave trade. The maritime truce and arrangements for the so-called Trucial Oman came in 1835.[5]

The second phase of British imperial actions in the Middle East took place against the background of the Crimean War and the Sepoy Rebellion in India. The Palmerston system had not worked effectively because the Ottomans were initially unsuccessful in making the*Tanẓimat* or western reforms work; hence, Russia continued to put pressure on the Ottoman government. The pressure for concessions in Jerusalem and the right of Russian intervention on behalf of the Christian Orthodox in the empire led to the Crimean War and the collapse of the Russian military establishment. But the absence of British regiments from India during the war also exposed British India. The Sepoy rebellion of 1857 started allegedly over the use of pig fat lubricants on British cartridges. The real cause of Muslim revolt was much more serious: the British, since the Battle of Plassey in 1757, had rapidly taken over the perquisites, the status, and much of the trade income which the Indian Muslims had enjoyed since late medieval times. The rebellion signaled the British government that the East India Company could no longer manage its huge Indian trust. It also indicated that the British, if they were to remain in India, must do more to appease the Indian Muslim elite. Queen Victoria's government took direct control in 1858.

The collapse of the Russian imperial forces in the Crimea in 1855, and the decisive defeat of the French by Prussian forces in 1870 using rapid-fire, breech-loading rifles, made possible the second phase of British empire-building in the Middle East. Only as long as France and Russia were *perceived* as strong rivals to the British in the Mediterranean area did the Palmerston system of coddling the Turks make sense. With both France and Russia neutralized, in spite of DeLesseps's completion of the Suez Canal in 1869, Britain could now consolidate her position in Africa and the Middle East. This process was made easier after the death of Fayṣal ibn Turkī in 1865 and the subsequent development of the Saudi civil war between the emırs 'Abdullāh and Sa'ūd.

Britain was particularly interested in Egypt, which was still strongly in the French orbit of affairs. The Khedive Ismā'īl had studied and lived in France and had got himself deeply in debt to French bankers.[6] In 1875 Britain's prime minister, Benjamin Disraeli, picked up the Khedive's shares of the Suez Canal Company, thus involving Britain in the khedival government. Later, in 1879, Khedive Ismā'īl was forced out of office by Britain and France, a move which sparked an Egyptian national reaction led by Colonel 'Urābī, later minister of war, who placed Egypt in a confrontation with Britain. Neither France nor Sultan 'Abd al-Ḥamīd wanted any part in a move for occupation and pacification by Britain. Thus began Britain's long occupation of Egypt in 1882. Only two years previously, the Tory government of Disraeli had fallen. His place was taken by the outspoken Gladstone of the Liberals, who had gained great popularity by attacking the Ottoman suppression of rebellion in Bulgaria. The Russians had intervened and had advanced to the walls of Istanbul in another Russo-Ottoman war, that of 1877–78. After the war in 1878, Britain had gained control of Cyprus in the Treaty of Berlin, and France, having lost Alsace-Lorraine in 1870 to Prussia, was given the go-ahead by Prussia's Bismarck to take control of Tunisia (1881), in accordance with the current diplomatic practice of "compensation."

Clearly Britain had, with the occupation of Egypt, completely abandoned the Palmerston policy of propping up the Ottoman Empire, just at a time when the Ottomans were making significant headway in their *Tanẓimat* with impressive European-style schools, a modern army and navy, a more equitable (though less Islamic) legal system, and an attempt at liberal parliamentary government in 1876–77.

The British proconsuls in India had their hands full in providing a new political system for India after the Sepoy Rebellion, and hence, apart from monitoring the slave trade and piracy in the Gulf, were content to follow affairs in central Arabia through already established residencies in the Gulf. In the 1860s and 1870s, the Russian occupation of Central Asia and her shadow-boxing into Afghanistan also preoccupied the British government in India. Word had been sent out to the Gulf residencies not to involve themselves in any manner with affairs in central Arabia, which was considered Ottoman territory. These restrictions did not apply to W. G. Palgrave, a reputed agent of Napoleon III of France, who journeyed, as he claimed, to the portals of Riyāḍ in 1862. As if not to be outdone, the British resident at Bushehr, Colonel Lewis Pelly, matched the visit with a trip to Riyāḍ in 1865, shortly before Fayṣal ibn Turkī died. Fayṣal was well aware of the implications for his own possessions of the British lording it over the emirates of the Gulf. The suspicion lingered in Arabia that the British were really feathering their own nest while checking piracy and the slave trade.[7]

But the days of the romantic visitors to the interior of Arabia soon gave way to the realism of the 1880s and 1890s, when British advance and Ottoman checkmating became quite serious. Pelly had wanted to move out of Persia to a more "civilized" location, and had suggested Ras Masandam jutting out into the Straits of Hormuz in Oman. After the sudden thrust of the Ottomans into al-Ḥasā in 1871 and the subsequent garrisoning of Doha, Al-Qatīf, and Kuwait, there were cries of alarm from a number of British residents that something must be done to protect British interests.[8]

Clearly, after the rupture of the former good relations between the Porte and Britain as the British turned their show of force in Egypt into a permanent occupation, one cannot be surprised that the Ottomans now took a different view of the British presence in the Perso-Arabian Gulf. The Ottomans forced the British to clarify the ambiguity of their presence by laying claim to Bahrain and the Trucial States in the late 1880s. In 1890 Britain placed her protective umbrella, meaning gunboats, over Bahrain and the Trucial States. The Turks also began to make life difficult for the British navigating on the Shaṭṭ al-'Arab in the mid-1890s. Thus, they aroused British suspicions that the Ottomans were wishing to extend their claims to Muḥammara in Persia.

But for an agreement with France dating back to 1862, the British, in the 1890s, would have made Oman a protectorate. As a compromise, the British got the sultan of Oman to sign an agreement in 1891 that he would alienate none of his territory to a foreign power without

British consent. This agreement did not stop the French from setting up a consulate in Oman in 1893, causing much nervousness for the British resident thereafter.

One of the really interesting side-shows in the Gulf in this period was the appearance of serious Russian moves to set up a base on Persian territory: a coaling station, possibly a naval base, and a railroad from Tabriz to the Gulf. By the turn of the century, a Russian shipping company was making irregular calls at Aden, Oman, some Gulf ports, and points eastward to India. The drive for a Russian presence in the Gulf would probably have taken permanent shape or led to strife with the Indian government, had not these plans been rather upset by the Russian defeat at the hands of the Japanese in 1904, an event certainly helped to fruition by the British.[9] The termination of British-Russian rivalry in Persia came in 1907 with the Anglo-Russian Agreement which basically divided Persia into spheres of operation, the British in the south and the Russians in the north, with a neutral zone between.

To round out the British scene in the Gulf prior to World War I, one must note the British settlement with Kuwait. This came about with the accession of Mubārak Āl Ṣabāḥ in 1896, a tough leader with a deep suspicion of Ottoman moves in the area. While still pursuing their policy of nonintervention, the British, fearing a move for annexation by either the Turkish governor in Basra or the Āl Rāshid from Ḥayl, took steps to guarantee the security of Kuwait in 1899. This arrangement was followed by the setting up of British agencies in Kuwait and Bahrain in 1904. ʻAbd al-Raḥmān ibn Fayṣal had taken refuge with his family in Kuwait after the routing of his forces in Burayda in 1891. And it was from Kuwait that the young ʻAbd al-ʻAzīz ibn Saʻūd would start the reconquest of the Arabian Peninsula for his family in 1901.

To end this section on a note of symmetry, it seems appropriate to mention briefly the coincidence of a certain William Knox d'Arcy, an Englishman who had struck it rich in the Australian gold fields, arriving on the Gulf scene in 1901. D'Arcy gained the first oil concession from the shah of Persia, and discovered oil in 1908 in Masjid al-Sulayman. His discovery seemed to confirm the correctness of the British interest in the Gulf which had developed in the nineteenth century.[10]

III. The Ottoman Crisis: European Technology and Ideology

The longevity of a political system deeply reflects the attitude of that system's leaders toward innovation, both in technology and in ideology. The period 1683 to 1829 for the Ottoman Empire must be characterized as an era of political decentralization and defeat, with heavy losses of Ottoman territory in Europe, primarily to Austria and Russia. The Ottoman social system passed through a time of major challenge in this same period, apparently losing its unity, self-confidence, and will to create or adopt innovations.

In the eighteenth century, a printing press had come into operation and had been closed down repeatedly, and there were also attempts to modernize the army and navy with the aid of renegade European officers such as the Comte de Bonneval, or hired specialists such as the Baron de Tott.[11] But it was the sudden jolts rendered to Ottoman society by the Russian defeats of 1774 and 1791, and the French Revolution of 1789 which had finally caused the provincial and central elites of the Empire to rouse themselves from complacency. This sense of alarm gave to Sultan Selīm III (1789–1807) and a handful of far-sighted viziers the chance to introduce a successful program for military modernization and to open Ottoman embassies in Europe's leading capitals.[12] With the rise of imperial France, led by Napoleon, a conservative coalition of provincial and urban elites, supported by the Russian ambassador, engineered the death of the sultan and a reversal of military innovation. These elite elements had coalesced behind a religious facade to ensure the continuity of their status, privileges, and traditional sources of income.[13]

Ottoman society, after more than a century of internal disintegration and laxness of discipline, had lost touch with its own processes of regeneration. Only a vibrant empire, not petty warring factions, could generate the bureaucratic, military, and intellectual strength to introduce innovation. Most eighteenth-century Ottoman leaders had not been in a position to grasp the degree of change which had taken place beyond *Dār al-Islām*. As the Ottoman poet Nedīm mourned: "I traveled in the lands of the infidels and viewed mansions; but when I visited the lands of Islam, I saw ruins."[14] Only the men defending Islam in the frequent wars had experienced the new technology of Europe, but where had gone the administrative systems to which the *mujāhid* could report? Nor were the Ottomans prepared intellectually to grasp the significance of European scientific and ideological changes in the eighteenth century. These changes had accelerated technological innovation by removing the Church from its interference in scientific and technological matters. Conversely, men of science were reluctant to meddle in affairs of the spirit. Sir Isaac Newton never did reveal his skepticism about the Trinity. But as we know, Voltaire openly made fun of *l'infâme*, the reactionary Church of France.

The Ottoman elite had barely grasped what had taken place in France (through the new ambassadorial reports) when they began to see the results of further European innovations. J. C. Hurewitz in his study *Middle East Politics: The Military Dimension*, comments specifically on this Ottoman dilemma of always trying to catch up with new European innovations. Professor Hurewitz calls attention to the important difference between imitating and borrowing technology, and the development of technology out of indigenous institutions.

The intellectual and technological challenges which became apparent to the Ottoman elite in the 1820s and 1830s, as they mastered Western languages, were at the time threatening the very existence of Islam and the State. Moreover, as we have noted, within the gates of the Empire, the sultan's vassal, Muḥammad 'Alī, the *wālī* of Egypt (1805–48), had so effectively built upon the earlier reforms of Sultan Selīm III and had trained a native Egyptian army with French officers so well, that his forces had defeated the Saudi/Wahhābī state in the first decades of the century, the Greeks in the 1820s, and the sultan's own forces in the 1830s, much to the consternation of Istanbul and the European powers. In short, the Middle Eastern states, given the right leadership, could quickly master Western technology! Reluctantly, the reactionary wing of the Ottoman elite realized that they must close ranks with Sultan Maḥmūd II (1808–39) and with the reforming viziers to eliminate those social groups retarding technological innovation. Otherwise, the Empire would be annexed out of existence. The Janissary corps, which had once defended the Empire, now became, because of its reactionary attitudes, the chief scapegoat, and was eliminated in 1826 along with its supporting elites.

In Egypt, France held the dominant position, and imperial Russia, having just promoted the independence of Greece, was laying the groundwork in the 1830s to make Ottoman Turkey a Russian satellite. As we have already observed, both France and Russia had failed to consider the rise to prominence in Britain of Viscount Palmerston in the 1830s. For the crucial thirty years of Ottoman history, 1840 to 1870, including the dangerous Crimean War (1853–55), the Palmerston system proved a stroke of genius. It bought time and protection for the Ottomans while they learned the latest techniques of artillery, acquired better military equipment, refurbished their navy and its training, laid telegraph lines, built modern schools, and improved civil administration and public health. Istanbul and some provincial cities began to look almost modern, with new roads, gas lights, and a developing municipal government. In the nick of time, it seemed, the Ottomans had grasped the need to change, not just the military, but the society at large, to survive against ideological and technological, as well as political challenges from Western Europe. By the 1870s, when Europe was poised to acquire vast new territories which would soon encompass 84 percent of the world's surface, the Ottomans had put in place an innovative system which would make it costly for European powers to take additional Ottoman territory. Yet the Empire, with continual nationalist revolts, steadily lost territory. Thus, we are faced with one final question: what, then, was still pulling the Empire apart? The answer, now to be examined, possibly lies in the area of overwhelming European encirclement, new stages of technology, or perhaps most important of all, the lack of a cohesive ideology.

Groping for an Ottoman Ideology

In the initial attempts to stop the encroachments of European powers into *Dār al-Islām*, considerations of ideology did not enter the picture. In the eighteenth century, there had been much platitudinal reference to the "need to return to the good old days of Sultan Sulaymān in the sixteenth century." But on the eve of the nineteenth century, it was clear that the Ottoman Empire could go the way of Moghul India if major changes in the Empire did not take place. The occupation of Mecca by the Wahhābī-Saudi warriors was a sharp reminder that even Muslims were not happy with current developments.

Sultan Maḥmūd II had seen his predecessor, Sultan Selīm III, killed by armed reactionaries in 1807. As long as the reactionary *'ulāmā'*—and many members of that class were quite enlightened—and the Janissary corps controlled the capital, the state could not even take measures to modernize the armed forces. The irony of this situation was that throughout Islamic history, Muslims had been in the forefront as innovators and modernizers in technical fields. Thus, when the Janissaries were eliminated in 1826, partly because of cowardice during the Greek war, this became known in Ottoman annals as the *vaqʿat-i khayrīya*, or "auspicious event." Thereafter, as we have noted above, advances in technology and the study of science, though slow in starting, presented no major ideological problem. It is true, however, as during the regime of Muḥammad ʿAlī, the funds for military modernization, already in the sultanate of Maḥmūd II, were partially derived from plucking the coffers of the Waqf, to the consternation of *ʿulāma'*. But without the Janissaries or, as in the case of Egypt, without the Mamlūks, state power began to override the power of the *ʿulāma'* in the 1820s and 1830s.[15]

The real challenge to Ottoman leaders and to Ottoman intellectuals in the mid-decades of the nineteenth century came from a different source: how could a multi-ethnic, multi-religious Islamic empire, operating on the basis of Islamic law, come to terms with new European political concepts, such as liberalism and nationalism, which were becoming attractive to non-Muslims and Muslims alike? In particular, nationalism would cause problems, as had been demonstrated by the Greek and Serbian revolts, because nationalism encouraged solidarity groups to organize separatist movements and to seek the support of the all-too-willing imperial powers to intervene on their behalf.

With respect to liberalism, the question of a proper mixture of popular sovereignty, a constitution, and parliaments to legislate in the place of a sultan has challenged Muslim leaders ever since. But as Ottoman society was traditionally very mobile in its class structure, each generation cast up men deriving from practical, down-to-earth peasant, lower middle class, or provincial bureaucratic family backgrounds, who put forth new solutions to old problems. After the death of Sultan Maḥmūd in 1839, the solution proposed by Muṣṭafā Reshīd Pasha (1800–58), formerly ambassador to both France and England in the crucial thirties, and the scion of a notable family from Kastamonu,[16] was to produce a general reform of the state known as the *Tanẓimat*. The first generation of *Tanẓimat* reformers typically had learned French or English in the *Terjuman Odası*, the Government translation school, or through private tutors. Many of them also had first-hand experience in Europe serving in diplomatic posts. They were later criticized by literary figures in Young Ottoman circles for accepting the superficial and missing the substance of European culture.[17]

But the first phase of the *Tanẓimat* attempted to address the liberal position that non-Muslims were treated as second class citizens. In actuality, the Muslim and non-Muslim elites had for generations lorded it over the other elements of Ottoman society. The Khaṭṭ-i Sherīf of 1839 had called for the security of life, honor, and property of all subjects, an orderly tax system, and the regulation of military conscription, reducing service to five years instead of for life. And indeed, some reform became evident as Muslim and non-Muslim sat together in mixed tribunals and in police courts. Also, some secular primary and secondary schools were opened which paralleled the *maktabs* and *madrasas* run by the *'ulāmā'*. In principle, conscription would now apply to non-Muslims also, but the *bedel*, or payment for exemption, continued in force, because the Muslim community was still not ready to accept non-Muslims as officers. To each governor was also attached a council consisting of Muslims and some non-Muslims, but such councils proved initially unable to escape the power of local notables. Thus, there had been a beginning, but the vast majority of the Muslims were suspicious of what they saw as the alienation of the Holy Law. Most non-Muslims were not satisfied either, because the changes came too slowly for groups who were being offered shortcuts to an El Dorado by nationalists, or through the propaganda of foreign powers. As Americans and others opened mission schools, initially attended mostly by members of minority communities, the instructors too tended to be critical of the meager results of the government, and sometimes openly encouraged separatism.[18]

The results of the second phase of the *Tanẓimat* after the Crimean War and up to the accession of Sultan 'Abd al-Ḥamīd in 1876 were more impressive in all areas pertaining to administrative, educational, and legal reforms. Indeed, there developed a parallel trend in the Ottoman state to the liberal ideas of Europe. Instead of dismissing liberalism outright, Muslim writers sought to show that many elements of science and liberal government had been derived from previous Islamic societies. This line of reasoning had some merit with regard to science, but one sees little of the liberal tradition in previous Islamic governments.

Ottoman reform produced, of course, its own problems. The *millet* religious leaders resented having their powers restricted by the lay councils created by the *Tanẓimat*. In fact, the more the Ottoman government made important concessions to the *millets*, the more the *millet* leaders, fearing absorption and loss of power, tended to accentuate communal differences and urge the revival of national languages. When Ottoman leaders tried to develop a real Ottoman citizenship, such as they admired in Europe, they met with opposition from both Muslims and non-Muslims. The less-privileged Muslims understandably did not wish to give up whatever advantage they might have had vis-à-vis non-Muslims, because their position was already difficult. And had they not always borne the brunt of the fighting against foreign invasion? The *millets* obviously would try to avoid absorption, at a time when western governments were intriguing with their leaders to create separatist movements.

If the first phase of the *Tanẓimat* sought to answer criticisms of national and religious inequalities, the second phase tried to adjust to the demands of liberalism, by promoting a constitution and a parliament. While the Young Ottoman literary movement appeared more protective of what they saw as old Muslim values than did the leaders of the *Tanẓimat*, their writings supported the development of an Islamic means, such as a constitution, to insure a broad consensus for the Ottoman government.[19] The reformers, such as Fu'ād Pasha and 'Alī Pasha, the protégés of Muṣṭafā Reshīd, had set up a high court, a council for reform, and a *shura-yi devlet* or Council of Ministers, and in the 1870s, with the guidance of the Young Ottomans and the support of the rising liberal star, Midḥat Pasha (his image was that of a conqueror in Arabia), a constitution and a parliament were instituted in 1876 as a part of the accession agreement, reluctantly accepted by Sultan 'Abd al-Ḥamīd. Also, older Islamic institutions and schools continued to exist alongside the new secular institutions, making the formulation of a state ideology and an Ottoman allegiance difficult. One of the determining factors for a conservative policy during the sultanate of 'Abd al-Ḥamīd would be the removal from Ottoman control and responsibility by the imperial powers of most of the non-Muslim areas of the Empire when the Treaty of Berlin came into force in 1878.[20]

IV. Sultan 'Abd al-Ḥamīd II (1876–1909): Technology and Pan-Islam

By the accession of Prince Ḥamīd in 1876, the ambitions of the imperial powers to pick up colonies as marketplaces for their manufacturing and as supply sources for raw materials all over the world were quite apparent. Moreover, the imperial powers had taken such a lead in technological development that traditional societies could no longer compete without a complete revamping of their social structures. As a result, most of Asia and Africa came under European tutelage.[21]

A major exception was the Arab and Turkish heartlands of the Ottoman Empire. There are a number of reasons why the Ottomans were able to hold the Europeans at bay. Perhaps the most important factor was the deep rivalry between Britain and Russia over Persian and Ottoman territories. There were also forbidding deserts and mountains in the Ottoman interior, and a people prepared to fight to their deaths. At mid-century, as we have noted, Russia's advances into the Balkans had been slowed, as they came up against large Muslim populations and the threat of British intervention. Indeed, France and Britain had become so alarmed at the prospect of a Russian presence on the Mediterranean that they joined with the Ottomans to fight the Crimean War, 1853–55. This abrupt halt to Russia's advance had given the Ottomans a chance to modernize their armed forces, largely through German and British help.

In the Arabian peninsula, however, Ḥamīd had to face another reality of politics. The British, before the Crimean War, had steadily strengthened their hold over Aden, the Ḥijāz, and the Perso-Arabian Gulf. They had also interceded decisively in Egypt in the 1870s. The Ottoman government had recognized this "creeping imperialism," and had taken some measures to thwart British activities.

It is, of course, stylish in the historiography of some Arab countries to consider, in hindsight, that the Ottoman presence in previous centuries was somehow a mistake or illegitimate. But one may easily fall into an anachronism here. In the eyes of many Sunni Muslims in the Arab heartlands, right up to the era of Sultan 'Abd al-Ḥamīd, Ottoman rule was viewed as the most legitimate government available.[22] In every emirate and district there were strong pro-Ottoman factions. We therefore must view as legitimate the actions and the attempts of Sultan 'Abd al-Ḥamīd to maintain a position of his own in the Yemen, the Ḥijāz, Najd, and the Perso-Arabian Gulf. Otherwise, we are forced logically to say that Christian governments, the Portuguese, the Dutch, the French, and finally the British had the *real* legitimacy to rule over and acquire the wealth of Arab lands, which is an absurdity. One may, of course, argue that the British permitted local emirates to blossom into maturity more readily than the Ottomans would have done, but one would also have to conjecture how rapidly the Ottoman state, including the Arabs, might have flourished had they benefited from the wealth which Western powers subsequently gained from the Middle East!

As a case in point, the thrust of Midḥat Pasha's forces down the western coast of Arabia to occupy al-Ḥasā and Qatar in 1871 and subsequent years, with the assistance of the then friendly emirate of Sheikh 'Abdallāh ibn Sabāḥ (r. 1866–92) of Kuwait, must be considered a legitimate attempt by the Ottoman government to slow the British advance in that quarter.[23] The Ottomans, of course, welcomed the advances made to them by 'Abdallāh ibn Fayṣal, the rival claimant to the Saudi leadership, because this overture increased the legitimacy of their thrust into al-Ḥasā and their claim to suzerainty over Najd.[24]

Moreover, it is rather interesting to observe the quaintly genteel Middle Eastern way the Ottoman governor of Basra dealt with Sheikh Mubārak ibn Ṣabāḥ after he murdered his rival and gained the accession in 1896. In the first instance, the Ottomans gently reminded Sheikh Mubārak that he was a part of *their* system, by sending a health officer to enforce quarantine regulations in 1897. At the time, the British recognized Ottoman rights there, and gave no succor to Shaykh Mubārak. It is almost amusing to see how quickly Lord Curzon and the entire Indian service responded in 1898 and 1899, when it was rumored that both Germany and Russia were planning railroads to the Gulf. Another Ottoman soft touch came in the following year, when a dispute arose, over Mubārak's accession, between Mubārak and Jawsim ibn Muḥammad al-Thānī of Qatar, who was defending the rights of the children of the murdered Sheikh of Kuwait. The Ottomans sent the *naqīb al-ashrāf* of Basra for an unsuccessful negotiation.[25] There were no such genteel actions practiced by the British one year later, when four gunboats took up moorings in front of the Sheikh's palace. Obviously this sudden reversal of British policy, just like the sudden thrust of the Ottomans into al-Ḥasā and Qatar, had little to do with local politics or piracy, as the British had claimed. Rather, by having Mubārak sign the exclusion agreement in January 1899, the British had acted to block the possibility that either Russia or Germany might obtain a concession to build a railroad which would terminate on or near Kuwait territory.

After Britain occupied Egypt in 1882, she could exercise control at the Suez Canal over all transport between the Indian Ocean and the Mediterranean. Neither the Ottomans, the Germans, nor the Russians were happy with such a control, and hence each, in their own way, sought to circumvent its effects through various railroad schemes.

The Ottomans, before building the Ḥijāz Railroad, with a spur line to 'Aqaba, had to fight bitterly with Britain (i.e., Lord Cromer) over who "owned" 'Aqaba and the littoral of the Arabian coast, Egypt or the Ottomans. Obviously, the desire of Britain to control all accesses to India would boost their interest in the Ḥijāz. Also, the Ḥijāz, as the chief shrine of the Muslims, and the Yemen, because of its coffee production, were both sources of considerable income for the British. Regular steamship service between the Red Sea and India had already begun in 1836.[26]

Clearly the only hope which the Ottomans had of checking British interests in the Arabian Peninsula would be to build railroads both to the Gulf and down the inner coast of the Ḥijāz. Such railroads would not only break the British monopoly over trade at Suez, it would also give the Ottomans a more rapid means of maintaining order in the farther reaches of their Empire. It is important to remember that before the British closed off the railroad option in the Gulf, there had been important opportunities for the Gulf region to become a part of expanding Ottoman and world economies, and at a much earlier date. The Persian side of the Gulf and Bahrain's economy matured fairly early because of oil discoveries, but the blossoming of the Gulf economy never really got under way until after World War II.

Sultan 'Abd al-Ḥamīd II came to power in 1876 after a series of complex events. His uncle, 'Abd al-'Azīz, had taken his own life in 1876 and his half-brother, Murād V, the heir apparent, had lost his mental balance. Although it was against his own personal views of Ottoman needs, he was forced to follow the dictates of Midḥat Pasha's liberal faction, which at the time controlled the capital, and to authorize the promulgation of a constitution and a parliamentary election. But shortly thereafter, under the guise of giving full attention to winning the war, after the Russian invasion of 1877–78, Ḥamīd closed parliament and suspended the constitution. Thereafter he ruled by decree in the tradition of his ancestors.

No integrated study of the era of Sultan 'Abd al-Ḥamīd exists, but one may extrapolate Ḥamīd's policies from his actions and his meager writings.[27] Hardly since the seventeen-century had the House of Osmān placed on the throne a ruler who was so well-versed in politics and economics. The fact that a number of his policies ended in failure, or indeed were poorly conceived, does not detract from this observation. He first stopped the erosion of his own power by locking up, executing, or exiling the liberal faction. Second, he ended the bleeding of his troops in the Balkans by reluctantly signing the Treaty of Berlin. Finally, he had to come to terms with the British occupation of Egypt in 1882. The British, the French, the Russians, and the Austrians, as a result of the Treaty of Berlin, had all obtained Ottoman territory; thus, Ḥamīd knew that he must seek out a new ally in Europe. Prussia had, since 1834, supplied officers to train Ottoman forces in standard European drill and weaponry. Not long after Ḥamīd's accession, General von der Goltz began the reorganization of the army. A number of young Turkish officers were also sent to Germany for advanced training. These amicable contacts eventually led to the visit of Kaiser Wilhelm II in 1889, and the beginning of a close friendship with Germany resulting in the World War I alliance. The sultan gained from his alliance with Germany much of the technology he sought from Western Europe: new siege guns for the Dardanelles, new rifles and machine guns for the army, and other military equipment. Ottoman medical services were also upgraded. In turn, the German-owned Anatolian railroad gained approval in 1899 for the extension of its tracks from Konya to Bahgdad and the Persian Gulf.[28] Lord Curzon knew of the move before the signing; hence, his memo of 19 November 1898 to secure Kuwait for Britain.

When the British and Germans eventually negotiated an agreement to terminate the railroad at Basra, the intentions of the Ottoman government, to thwart British imperialism in the Gulf, had been gravely set back. Sir Reader Bullard, almost as an afterthought, admits that the British occupation of Cyprus and of Egypt gave the death blow to former cordial relations between the two powers, but he fails to note the impact on Ottoman affairs of Britain's encirclement of Arabia.[29]

As these events were taking place, Ḥamīd and his Grand Vizier Küçük Sa'īd Pasha, whose detailed memoirs are important for the period, were taking steps to preempt the Ottoman young men, so that their energies might be channeled into the service of the state. Millions of liras were poured into upgrading the Western-style lycées in the Empire.[30] Moreover, the elite government schools for civil servants (*mülkiye*), for medical personnel (*ṭibbiye*), and for army officers (*ḥarbiye*) received generous subsidies. Sultan 'Abd al-'Azīz had also lavished much of the public and private purse on the purchase of naval vessels and the training of officers. But Ḥamīd had made a serious tactical error in dealing with this rising elite. He had suppressed the Young

Ottomans, the supporters of a modest liberalism and constitution. But the Young Ottomans were prolific writers, and their works now circulated, like Russian *samizdat*, among the young men in the official academies. As a result, these young men were destined to form (in 1889) the new constitutional movement, the *ittihad ve terakki jemiyeti*, which became known simply as the Young Turk Movement.[31] It was this group which destroyed the sultan's power in 1908.

The Pan-Islamic Movement

Another major policy switch took place under Ḥamīd. Previous Ottoman governments of the *Tanẓimat* era had bent over backward trying to please their Christian *millets* and European governments by instituting liberal reforms and tightening up administrative procedures. Obviously, such measures had not been popular with the majority of the sultan's Muslim subjects. But also young Ḥamīd had found the results disturbing. Christian *millets* continued to revolt and to plot with imperial powers for their interference in the internal affairs of the Empire. The net result was that more Ottoman territory fell into the hands of Christian governments. Ḥamīd increasingly followed policies which he believed would favor Muslims and halt the loss of territory. Such policies became easier each year, as most of the provinces with large numbers of Christians were torn away. Thus, while many of the purely educational and technological aspects of the *Tanẓimat* continued during the Ḥamīd era, the ideology of the Ḥamīd regime became strongly anti-*Tanẓimat* with regard to its liberal tendencies and ideology. Even the prominent literary movements of the era, obviously coached by palace trends, turned their interests to scientific and conservative themes.

Professor Niyazi Berkes has written most incisively on the intellectual history of the Ḥamīdian period. He views the spread and the great increase in members of the mystical lodges (*ṭarīqāt*) or dervish orders throughout the realm as a part of the Ḥamīdian policy of feeding religious reaction and obscurantism to the masses, instead of liberal jargon and ideas. In fact, all discussion of liberal activities or even political developments in Western Europe was now censured out of the newspapers and journals. Thus, the popular religious traditions—even magic, sorcery, and saint worship—among the masses were simply the popular side of the Pan-Islamic movement, which was designed to influence the more sophisticated members of the Islamic community.[32]

As we have already noted, the 1850s and 1860s marked an important turning point throughout the Islamic world because the major European powers began acquiring control over vast new territories where before they had been content to maintain coaling stations or trading posts along the shorelines of Asia, Africa, and the Middle East. This new scramble for colonies was made possible by the discovery of drugs, such as quinine to fight malaria, as well as the development of the telegraph, river gunboats with which to penetrate interiors, and rapid fire rifles and machine guns (1890s), made of high quality steel which native blacksmiths could not forge.[33]

It became stylish for European scholars to account for the "fanatic and irrational" reaction of Muslims to the annexation of their homelands by referring to the writings of Ibn Khaldūn, the fourteenth-century Arab historian and social observer. Ibn Khaldūn had observed that Arab regimes were periodically overthrown by tribal and popular elements which swept into the oases and cities to establish their own version of a just government closely attuned to the precepts of the Holy Qur'ān.

As noted previously, Islamic writers, such as Namik Kemāl and Jamāl al-Dīn al-Afghānī, had made liberal ideas more palatable to the Islamic community by noting many parallels to liberalism in previous Islamic practice. But in contrast to the intellectual discourses, the Sepoy Rebellion of 1857 had been an overt, bloody, and dangerous reaction to the steady onslaught of British imperial expansion at Muslim expense. So also would be the movement of the Mahdī in the Sudan in the 1880s and 1890s, a movement which closely paralleled the observations of Ibn Khaldūn about grass-roots Muslim politics. The Mahdī would also doubtless have been successful, but his troops at Omdurman (1898) had antique muzzle-loading weapons with which to face General Kitchener's modern breech-loading rifles, Maxim machine guns, and heavy guns mounted on river sloops. It was a slaughter similar to a clash between the Zulus and a South African police patrol, where thirty policemen with four Maxims wiped out 10,000 Zulus armed with spears. Such was the heroism of nineteenth-century imperialists.[34]

The advocacy of Pan-Slavism by Russia in the 1860s and 1870s also struck a sympathetic note among Muslim intellectuals: if Pan-Slavism worked for the Russians, why should not Pan-Islam work for the Ottomans? The ultimate answer for the Ottomans came in World War I, and parallels an old Turkish proverb: "One does not stretch one's feet beyond the length of one's quilt."

The Career of Jamāl al-Dīn al-Afghānī

The threads of the Pan-Islamic movement in the last decades of the nineteenth century can be followed effectively by outlining the activities of Jamāl al-Dīn al-Afghānī (1838–97), one of its most fervent advocates. Sayyid Jamāl al-Dīn was reared in the rational, religio-political ferment of mid-century Iran, but as he sought to influence western Muslim leaders, most of whom were Sunni, he claimed Afghan origins. His biographer, Nikki Keddie, believes that Afghānī may have been in India at the time of the Great Mutiny, but certainly, in any case, right afterward. After his stay in India, he spoke of the Sepoy Rebellion as "Holy War," and all his life he held a strong hatred of British imperialism. He attacked the ideas of Sayyid Aḥmad Khān (1817–98), the great Indian Muslim modernist thinker, because of his apparent subservience to the British. Yet Aḥmad Khān doubtless influenced Jamāl al-Dīn with his insistence on the acquisition by Muslims of a Western education and a mastery of Western science. His imbibing of Western science in India may have given Afghānī his early skepticism about some aspects of formal religion.[35] After spending 1866 to 1868 in Kabul, Afghānī resided in Istanbul for a couple of years, coming into close contact with the men of the *Tanẓimat*, especially Munīf, president of the Council of Education, and Taḥsīn, head of the newly founded University of Istanbul. In a series of lectures at the university, Afghānī shocked the *'ulāmā'* by describing prophecy as a kind of "craft." Hoja Taḥsīn, of Albanian origin, performed a simple physics experiment in which he placed a pigeon inside a closed lamp, indicating what happened as the pigeon exhausted the oxygen. Afghānī was deported and the university was closed! Moving to Egypt in 1870, Afghānī received a small stipend to teach within the orbit of Al-Azhar. He quickly gained popularity among the students with his lectures on the medieval Islamic philosophers, a timely topic because young Egyptians were seeking a national ideology with which to strengthen their society. Afghānī strongly supported a rational interpretation of puzzling religious issues. He also indicated how the sacred Qur'ān and the traditions (*ḥadīth*) presented no barriers to the acquisiton of modern science, parliaments, and strong national armies.

He also joined the freemasons and made speeches chastizing Khedive Ismāʿīl and the British. Finally, he encouraged his young followers to found newspapers and journals.

Ordered out of Eygpt in 1879 with some possible British pressure in the background, he appeared in Hyderabad as a guest of the *niẓām* (prince). He worked and studied in India from 1879 to 1882, keeping company mostly with the Westernizers, the followers of Sir Sayyid Aḥmad Khān. But suddenly at the end of his stay, he made a complete turnabout in his political and ideological positions. Did he see an opportunity to serve a new role in the conservative Ḥamīd government in Istanbul if he adopted a Pan-Islamic stance? Or did he simply feel the noose of imperialism rapidly strangling the independent action of all Muslims? Afghānī had often sought out prominent individuals so that his ideas might have a maximum impact. His parting shot at his Indian hosts was the book attacking the modernists: *The Truth about the Neicheri Sect* (Neicheris being followers of nature or natural law instead of revealed law), later translated into Arabic as *The Refutation of the Materialists*. The annexation of large tracts of Muslim territory in Russian Central Asia, North Africa, the Middle East, and India had turned many influential Muslims away from Western models of self-renewal.[36]

Thereafter, Afghānī settled in Paris for about three years (1883–86), where he and Muḥammad ʿAbduh, the latter his most avid disciple from Egypt, produced a journal, *Al-ʿUrwat al-wuthqā* ("The Strongest Link," i.e., the Qur'ān) supporting Pan-Islamic views, but also suggesting that Muslims must master science. This period corresponded to the rise of the Mahdī, Muḥammad Aḥmad (1881), the Chosen One, the type of charismatic leader predicted by Ibn Khaldūn. Afghānī worked with Wilfred Blunt, a wealthy British supporter of an independent Egypt, who hoped that he and Afghānī could negotiate the British withdrawal from Egypt and an amicable settlement with the Mahdī. The effort failed, and General Gordon died in January 1885, when the Mahdī's troops stormed Khartoum. About this time, Afghānī came into contact with Sultan ʿAbd al-Ḥamīd.[37]

But the sultan and his entourage saw little need at the time to summon this well-known agitator, opportunist and political activist to Istanbul. The sultan already had Muslim activists, in particular, Abū 'l-Hudā, an Arab from Aleppo, who served as chief religious adviser to the sultan, and ʿIzzet ʿAbed, another Syrian, who served as second secretary of the *Mabeyn* or palace administration. Ḥamīd gave much credit in his memoirs to 'Izzet as a prime mover in the Ḥijāz railroad project.[38] In keeping with his policy of tilting in favor of Muslims, Ḥamīd promoted a number of Arabs and Albanians to important posts in the army and administration. The most prominent general of the Young Turk revolution was the Arab, Maḥmūd Shevket. Ismā'īl Kemāl Bey, the Muslim Albanian nationalist, served as governor of Tripoli until 1901, and his compatriot, Meḥmet Ferīd Pasha Vlora, served the sultan as grand vizier. The presence of influential Arabs in the palace and the Army was not overlooked by Arab leaders. The British were aware that Sheikh Mubārak of Kuwait regularly sent "gifts" to 'Izzet Pasha. Emir 'Abd al-Raḥmān ibn Fayṣal, while living in exile in Kuwait, also received a small pension from the Ottoman court.[39]

In the very unsettled conditions of the Arab world at the beginning of the twentieth century, the government of 'Abd al-Ḥamīd was very sensitive to Arab interests. Moreover, if we look at the platforms of the Arab political parties at the time of the Young Turk revolution, there is a broad spectrum of political goals, from desiring full independence, to federation, to the status quo.[40] There was a tendency for all parties to cover all bases.

As Keddie has pointed out, Afghānī was like many other Muslim idealists, agitators, conservatives, and revolutionaries in the last decades of the century. They were appalled by the ease with which imperial powers were taking control everywhere; they thus looked to the Ottoman Empire as a last hope. The concept of Pan-Islam was beginning to serve in the Empire as a serious rallying point, a substitute for nationalism.[41]

But Afghānī was not an ordinary politician. Rebuffed by the sultan, he had been invited to visit Russia by the well-known liberal, turned conservative journalist and publisher of the *Moscow Journal*, Michael Katkov. Afghānī had sailed to Bushehr from England, and then journeyed to Tehran in 1887. Receiving a cool reception at the court of Naṣr al-Dīn Shāh, he proceeded to Russia where he spent two years. His sponsor, Katkov, had died, but Afghānī ingratiated himself with Nikolai Pobedonostsev, the ultra-conservative, anti-liberal bureaucratic head of the Russian Orthodox Church, and with Zinoviev, head of the Division of Asian Affairs in the Foreign Ministry. His anti-British attitudes found ready listeners, but Russia was in no position to challenge Britain in the Middle East. Russia, however, was alert to the British concessions in Persia, such as that of the national bank, and demanded equal treatment from the shah. When the shah made a third trip to Europe via St. Petersburg in 1889, Afghānī attached himself to the shah's entourage on the return trip to Tehran.

At this point, Afghānī played an important catalytic role in the boycott of the tobacco concession in 1891. Rudely evacuated from Persia into Ottoman Iraq, Afghānī helped to engineer a totally new tactic. Formerly, Afghānī and other reformers had pressured government officials to make reforms, but in 1891 an alliance of *'ulāmā'*, merchants, modernizers, and the city population joined together to block the concession. Tehran was paralyzed. This tactic worked so well that it would not be forgotten by future reformers and power brokers, including Khomeinī.[42]

Back in London in 1892, Afghānī was summoned to Istanbul by Abū 'l-Hudā. At first he was reluctant to go because they had learned in Istanbul that he had given some support to Wilfred Blunt's scheme for an Arab caliphate.[43]

Initially, Afghānī maintained close relations with the sultan when he arrived in Istanbul, but in time he was denounced by Abū 'l-Hudā for making intrigues against the sultan among the *softas* in the *madrasas*. Especially troubling had been his secret meeting with the Khedive, 'Abbās Ḥilmī, in 1895 because 'Abbās Ḥilmī had been mentioned as a candidate for an Arab caliphate. Henceforth, Afghānī was out of favor at court and, particularly after the assassination of the shah in 1896, in which he had a hand, he was kept virtually under house arrest. He died of chin cancer in 1897. Jamāl al-Dīn's life had virtually touched all aspects of the Pan-Islamic movement and, for this reason, he is a fascinating figure for students of that critical period.

V. The Rise of King 'Abd al-'Azīz and the Last Years of Sultan 'Abd al-Ḥamīd

In the eighteenth and nineteenth centuries, the Ottoman Empire had grown relatively weaker in relation to a handful of European imperial powers. In a broad sense, the Islamic-Ottoman state had become a pawn of the British in its competition with imperial Russia.

If a tally of former leading Islamic states were taken in 1900, one would note that the Moghul Empire of India had fallen to the British; the Muslim East Indies to the Dutch; Muslim North Africa to the French; Muslim Central Asia to Russia; and Persia to Russia and

Britain. By 1900, even the rivalry between Cairo and Istanbul had ended with Egypt's occupation by Britain in 1882.

Within the borders of the Ottoman Empire, we have found a number of contending groups with divergent interests, particularly among those *millet* factions seeking foreign sponsors. But, just as in Russia, where a struggle continued between "Westernizers" and "Slavophils," so also in the Ottoman Empire, the dominant ideological struggle took place in Istanbul between former "men of the *Tanẓimat*," now styled "Constitutionalists" (liberals supporting a western-style parliament, a constitution, and limits to autocratic power), and the Pan-Islamists who believed in maintaining a strong centralized Islamic government protected by an elite army and bureaucracy, seeking to be well-versed in modern science and technology. Much less attention was given to integrating the peasantry, the urban workers, and the nomadic tribes into the Ottoman system, except through taxation and conscription, but the Ottoman government, mindful of a British threat to its Arab territories, made a major effort to hold on to the Arabian Peninsula, the wellspring of Ottoman legitimacy in the Islamic world. The *millets* were by and large attracted by the liberal reformers, but by 1900 their numbers had been so drastically reduced by emigration and separatist movements that their welfare no longer seriously concerned the state. Herein lay the basic contention between the Ottomans and the Armenian, Greek, Slav, Jewish, and Albanian nationalists. The maintenance of the boundaries of the Empire and the protection of Muslims and of the Holy Places remained a first priority. The greatest importance was placed on railroad building and the modernization of the armed forces. Thus, a major policy of Sultan 'Abd al-Ḥamīd's government was to foster the building of the Ḥijāz railroad with largely Muslim capital and engineers, and to complete the Baghdad railroad with foreign, mainly German and British, capital and contractors. The railroads were symbolic of the sultan's decision to fight creeping British imperialism in Arabia. To Arabs, other than those tribes immediately benefiting from the new subsidies,[44] the railroads seemed a threat to their local autonomy, a means for Ottoman taxation, recruitment, and the requisitioning of camels, horses, and sheep in wartime.

Thus, the forging of better relationships between the Ottoman government and the nomadic and seminomadic tribes of Iraq, Syria, and Arabia presented a serious challenge to the Ottoman government in the first decade of the twentieth century. In the past, the desert and steppe areas were generally left to their own devices, as long as the pilgrimage and trade routes remained open. To insure the safety of vital routes, a delicate relationship between the sultan's officials and tribal leaders had long been in effect.[45] On the western, or Ḥijāz, side of the Arabian Peninsula, some tribes connected closely to the Holy Cities received regular food and cash subsidies from the Ottomans through the offices of the *sharīf* of Mecca, who was appointed from among the better-known *ashrāf* by the sultan. Tribes living along the chief pilgrim and trade routes regularly conducted trade and escort services for pilgrims and merchants. They also sold or leased horses and camels, and fed pilgrims from their flocks of sheep. On the official pilgrimage routes from Egypt, Damascus, or Baghdad, special trade fairs to arrange mounts, food, and escorts were a regular part of the pilgrimage. Also the *amīr al-ḥajj* was expected to present "gifts" and purses (*kise*) to the tribal sheikhs through whose territory they passed. In addition, the tribal sheikhs sent gifts and some thoroughbred horses to the sultan's stables as a token of their submission. The exchange of purses of silver and gold coin and of thoroughbreds was also the general practice when dealing with the sheikhs in Najd. Often, the relationship would also be recognized by a ceremony awarding robes of honor (*khil'a*) and a document of appointment from the sultan to a sheikh by the closest Ottoman governor or the *amīr al-ḥajj*.

While the Ottomans had taken their claims of suzerainty over the desert Arabs seriously and had expended much blood and treasure to maintain a modicum of control, the Arabs of the interior of Arabia had often marched to a different drummer. In the Ḥijāz, the Ottomans appointed the *sharīf* of Mecca as their deputy, but the *sharīf* always had considerable independent power to raise troops, to tax the tribes, or to take a portion of the customs duties at Jidda. The Ottomans exercised their leverage through *waqf* for *madrasas* and mosques, subsidies of treasure and grain, and through their garrisons in all major towns. As a case in point, Sharīf Ḥusayn, prior to World War I, was able to extend his influence and tax collecting as far as Hayl and Qāsim, thus challenging both the Ibn Sa'ūd and the Ibn Rashid. In the Yemen, the Ottomans after the mid-nineteenth century exercised control over the Tihāma along the shores of the Red Sea and, by agreement, shared the rule of the highlands with the Shī'i Zaydī imām in the north. The imām claimed direct descent from Ḥasan ibn 'Alī, and therefore inherited the legitimacy and charisma of the Prophet himself. In terms of basic military capacity, the opening of the Suez Canal (1869) and of the Ḥijāz railroad (1908), together with increased Ottoman naval capacity, made it possible for the Ottomans to reestablish their presence in the Yemen and al-'Asīr.

On the Iraqi side of the great Syrian desert, the mixed population of Jews, Christians, Sunnis and Shī'is, and important minorities of Persians and Kurds, made it easier for the Ottomans to make a case for their presence, because of the danger of unrest and massacre if the imperial presence were removed.

As regards the Ottoman Pan-Islamic policies, sophisticated Arabs viewed them askance because they knew that a legitimate caliph must be an Arab, in accordance with the medieval jurists. Many Arab leaders were pragmatic enough to go along with the policy until they could determine whether or not the Ottomans could protect their interests in the twentieth century as well as the British could. The question of Islam seemed to play a secondary role. Of course, after the Young Turk revolution, which was not very popular among the conservative Arabs, there developed in Syria a third alternative, the move for an Arab union. This was later supported by Sharīf Ḥusayn and his sons, to gain a permanent position of eminence for the family. This alternative developed into the British-inspired Arab revolt in 1917.[46]

The dramatic story of how the emir 'Abd al-'Azīz ibn Sa'ūd retook the Saudi capital in January 1902, and gradually reestablished Saudi power over much of the Arabian Peninsula, has often been told. A passage from the *Persian Gulf Gazetteer* describes briefly, while missing the drama, some events of that first year:

> At this juncture the cause of Ibn Sa'ūd suddenly began to make progress in the south. About the 15th of January 1902, 'Abd al-'Aziz bin 'Abd ur-Rahman made a sudden dash from the side of Hasa . . . and recovered Riyadh for his father. . . . With this force he surprised and slew the Shammar governor and took possession of Riyadh, to the general satisfaction of the inhabitants. Ibn Rashid's garrisons were then expelled from the neighboring districts of Kharj and Hariq; and it was represented to the Porte by Ibn Sa'ūd that the country would be ruled by him as a loyal subject of the Sultan.[47]

While every book deals with the bravery and audacity of Emir 'Abd al-'Azīz, most histories do not further analyze the relations between the rising Saudi state, the declining star of the Al Rashid, and the serious attempt of the Ottomans to keep the Arab tribes from falling into the British lap like ripe apples.

We have, in short, a clear-cut case, in political science parlance, of a center-periphery conflict: the Ottomans attempting at the center to devise an ideology and to modernize the state apparatus to hold the state together, while on the periphery, the power of the Ottoman minions, the Al Rāshid, had deteriorated to such a point that a number of tribes no longer felt secure remaining in their orbit. In the 1870s, the Ottomans had sought out a leader in Najd who could establish the stability which Fayṣal ibn Turkī Al Sa'ūd had maintained until his death. They had found such a leader in Muḥammad ibn 'Abdallāh Al Rashid (r. 1871–97), head of the Shammar, and a sheikh capable of exerting his influence over a number of tribes in north-central and eastern Arabia without being too heavy-handed.

The Saudis had dominated the tribes and oases of Najd and eastern Arabia for almost 150 years. Even though the Saudis lost out to the Al Rashid in the 70s and 80s, and decisively in the Battle of Mulayda in 1891 (basically because of internal dynastic feuds since Fayṣal's death in 1865), they were still regarded as the imāms of the austere Wahhābī faith, a charisma which they would not shed very quickly. Not unlike the Al Rashid under Muḥammad, the Saudis required a just and wise leader, first to reinstate himself among their closest followers, the 'Utayba, the Mutayr, and the 'Ujmān, and the oases of Qāsim, Subay', and Sudayr, then they could exert their influence on a wider range of tribes such as Qaḥtān (in al-Ḥasā) and others. The Ottomans made a shrewd choice in backing the Al Rashid when Rashid leadership was strong, but they lacked the flexibility to shift their support in treasure and weapons to the Saudis when the latter's star began to rise.

As the Ottomans struggled with a Pan-Islamic ideology, the future king of Arabia had other challenges on his mind. Doubtless his father, who had been held captive in Baghdad, had warned him of the new technologies. If not, he could have seen with his own eyes the power of the British fleet in the Gulf and the importance of the telegraph while he lay in exile in Kuwait. Only a few years hence, control of the deserts and oases would be determined by machine guns mounted on aircraft and motor vehicles, and the region would be attached more closely than ever to imperial politics. But in 1902 the desert still presented a formidable barrier to outsiders, thus providing a resourceful desert leader many opportunities to manipulate local forces. In the skills of the desert, young 'Abd al-'Azīz was a master.

Once the citadel in Riyāḍ was in Saudi hands, the emir knew that he first could count on his ideological brothers, the Wahhābīs and the Ḥanbalī Sunnis. Basically, these were, apart from the settled oasis people of Banū Tamīm, the 'Ujmān (Ḥanbalī), the Al Murra, the Dawāsir, the Subay', and the Mutayr. Muḥammad ibn Hindī of the eastern 'Utayba initially had close personal ties with Ibn Sa'ūd, but later was drawn into the orbit of Sharīf Ḥusayn of Mecca. While Saudi strength had always been concentrated in southern Najd, the power of the Al Rashid was always more diffuse, being spread out over northern Arabia from the pilgrim road in the Ḥijāz to the Euphrates and the region of Kuwait. Thus Saudi tactics were always better served by sudden attacks rather than prolonged warfare. Indeed, it was the Al Rashid interest in taking Kuwait in 1902, at Ottoman urging, that had deflected Rāshidī attention from Riyāḍ. The Ottomans, blocked by the British in 1899, had put pressure on Kuwait by garrisoning Safwān, Umm Qaṣr, and Babiyan Island in 1902 to secure the outlet of the Shaṭṭ al-'Arab to the Gulf. Even the *walī* of Basra had visited Sheikh Mubārak in 1901, urging him to come back into the Ottoman fold.[48]

The Ottoman strategy to maintain a hold on the Arab lands is apparent. They planned to use the Al Rashid as the centerpiece of a great northern Arabian consolidation stretching from the Ḥijāz railroad to Kuwait and al-Ḥasā.[49] Each major tribe along the railroad would receive a subsidy for protecting it, similar to what they had traditionally received for guarding the pilgrim caravans, the major difference being that the demand for camels and horses would now disappear, a terrible financial blow to the breeders, the rank and file nomads. The Banū Ṣakhr, who held territory from the Jabal Druze to Ma'an, were given the responsibility for the railroad from Jizak to Kerak. Their leader, Fawwaz, was made an Ottoman official in Jizak, and he did not hesitate to use Ottoman troops, led by the Damascus governor, Bagdātlı Samī Pasha, against the Rwala (sub 'Anaza) in 1911. This action is said to have turned Sheikh Nawwaf and his son, Nūrī al-Sha'lān, into Unionists (Arab Unionist movement in Damascus). Undaunted, the Rwala, distant kin of the Saudis, took Jawf from the Al Rāshid in 1911.[50] The Banū 'Aṭiya, kinsmen of the 'Anaza (and hence the Saudis) and rivals of Huwayta to the west, took responsibility for the railroad from Ma'an to Dār al-Ḥamrā' (they were traditional enemies of the Shammar). The Fuqarā' and the Banū Wahhāb protected the railroad from Dār al-Ḥamra' to Madā'in Ṣālih (tributary to the Ibn Rāshid and enemies of the Huwayta). The relationship of the

Ibn Rashid with the Fuqarā' was strategically important because the Ottomans supplied their ally at Qal'at Mu'adhdham just north of Madā'in Ṣālih. The Aydu protected a stretch to the south of Madā'in Ṣālih. The Hutaym, settled Arabs living in Khaybar and Medina, paid taxes to the Ottomans (or the *sharīf*), while their members living in Jabal Shammar paid the Rashidīs. The Ḥarb were supposed to protect the railroad from Khaybar to Medina, together with the Juhayna and the Billī, but the Ḥarb were also known to be the chief highwaymen fleecing the pilgrims on the camel route from Medina to Mecca.[51]

Thus, with garrisons and annual subsidies, payable during the pilgrimage, the Ottomans tried to keep the western tribes within their orbit. One can only imagine the tremendous dislocations of persons when this whole system, dating back hundreds of years, collapsed in World War I. The Ottomans had not counted, of course, on the revolt of Sharīf Ḥusayn, who was able to draw into the Unionist movement the powerful tribes of the west, the 'Anaza, the Huwayta, the Ḥarb, and the 'Utayba, who were largely the enemies of the Rāshidīs and the Ottomans. (Actually one way to view the Arab Revolt is to observe that British subsidies in 1917 merely took the place of Ottoman arrears in payments to the tribes; thus, not surprisingly, bread came before Islamic ideology!)

In truth, the Ottomans had counted on the Ibn Rashid, partly as a matter of habit, but also because of the strategic location of the Shammar, straddling the key routes of northern Arabia. From the railroad, Hayl could be reached in four days. Over this route came money, rifles, ammunition, and some machine guns, later even motor cars.[52] Also military units could be moved in rapidly from Basra. Conversely, the Ibn Rashid supplied the Ottomans with camels, as in the Egyptian campaign of World War I.

It is noteworthy that the Al Rashid received their supplies traditionally from Baghdad via Najaf and the general region of the Shaṭṭ al-'Arab. In the past, the Al Rashid had received about a third of their revenues from the Baghdad pilgrim *maḥmal*, the so-called Shī'i pilgrimage, passing through Hayl.[53] When the Al Rashid grew weaker, this route was cut by the Dhāfir to the harm of both tribes. It is little wonder that the oasis dwellers welcomed strong rulers and paid taxes to keep such depredations at a low level! When the Al Rashid sought help against the Saudis in the struggle for al-Qāsim in 1904–5, the Ottoman forces and the Munāfiq were sent by the *walī* of Basra, dispatched from Istanbul by telegraph. As is well known, this particular clash ended with an agreement that the Al Sa'ūd and the Al Rashid would live in their respective districts of north and south Najd, while the Ottomans garrisoned the towns of al-Qāsim.

While these political relationships provide important background, there still remains the question of what factors tipped the balance in favor of the Ibn Sa'ūd when all the cards seemed to be in the hands of the Ibn Rashid. Three or four final points deserve our consideration: leadership, weapons supply, British subsidies, knowledge of horses and camels, and the new turn of events in Istanbul after the Young Turk Revolution in 1908. It is clear that all Arab sheikhs, in an ideal situation, wanted their independence, including the Al Rashid, both from the Ottomans and from the British. Many, however, did not foresee the price such an individualistic policy would demand. Even the Prophet Muḥammad had warned of the dangers of individualism![54] The Ottoman intentions had become quite clear: to keep the British out of Ottoman territories. Many of the older sheikhs sympathized with the tradition-minded sultan, but the young sheikhs wanted to take their chances with the British and the Arab Unionists, in hindsight a naïve proposition. But the Young Turk Revolution had introduced new, unknown elements, and were not many of the Young Turkish army officers very unsympathetic to Arab ways? Clearly, the rulers of Hayl found it difficult to adjust to the Young Turks even when Arab officers held prominent posts. The observations of Elie Kedourie about the lack of enthusiasm in Arab provincial cities for the Revolution would apply even more to the lords of the desert.[55]

The crucial factor in the Rashidī-Saudi struggle was leadership, and not Wahhābism, because the Al Rashid also supported the *dīn al-tawḥīd*, though they lacked the charisma of being imāms like the Saudis. After the death of 'Abd al-'Azīz ibn Mut'ib in 1906, a blood bath lasting two years took place in Hayl over who would be his successor. Had it not been for the cool head of Majid, the son of Ḥamūd ibn Subḥān, the old vizier of Muḥammad ibn 'Abdallāh, the entire state would have collapsed.[56] After protecting the ten-year-old Sa'ūd ibn 'Abdallāh, Majid ibn Ḥamūd made him emir in 1908. When Majid died in 1909, he was succeeded by another able vizier, Zāmil ibn Subḥān. When the latter was murdered in 1914, the end was in sight for the Al Rashid because the young Sa'ūd Al Rashid never developed a strong sense of leadership.[57]

In the matter of arms supply, we have some interesting British statistics from the Gulf on breech-loading (new-type) rifles:

Years:	1895–96	1896–97
Place received:		
Muscat	4,350	20,900
Bushehr	——	30,000

We also have information from Musil regarding how arms were being shipped to al-Qāsim from Kuwait.[58] We may thus conclude that Ibn Sa'ūd had access to the best weapons available and British subsidies to purchase them. In the absence of full proof, we may conjecture that the Rāshid forces depended on the Ottomans to supply them with weapons, but one wonders if they were able to send their best quality pieces. Wilfred Blunt in his *Diaries* mentions that Martini rifles and some cannon were sent to 'Abd al-'Azīz Al Rāshid at his accession in 1903.[59]

As we are essentially dealing with a case of traditional desert warfare, we must also ask the question of which force, the Rāshidī or the Saudi, enjoyed the advantage in terms of quality horse and camel mounts. We may gain some idea of this matter from the comments of the Blunts, experts on horses, in their book, *A Pilgrimage to Nejd*, a trip made in 1879.[60] Anne Blunt, in discussing the "Najdi thoroughbred," cautioned that the best horses were bred in the Nafūd, where abundant pasturage was available. This expert horsewoman named her favorite breeds found in the stables of Muḥammad Al Rāshid, but stated that they were all really "ponies" (i.e., short of stature) as compared to the fine horses she had seen among the 'Anaza. She condemned the poor care given by the emir of Hayl to his horses, and noted that, because the Saudi lineage was 'Anaza, they still probably had the best breeding mares and stallions, even though many had been lost recently. The Mutayr, the Banū Khālid, the Dhafir, and the Shammar were the principal horse breeders. The best camel breeders were the 'Utayba, the Qaḥṭān, the Dawāsir, the Shammar, and the Mutayr.[61] In 1902 the 'Utayba, the Dawasīr, and the Mutayr declared for the Saudis, but later the 'Utayba sided with the *sharīf* of Mecca. Only the Qaḥṭān and the Shammar camels were available to the Ibn Rashid, and the Qaḥṭān of al-Ḥasā submitted to the Saudis in 1913.

This final excursus into the tactical and strategic roles of the camel and horse in desert warfare should not be taken amiss. It is clear that the key factor in the reestablishment of the Saudis as the preeminent family in Saudi Arabia was the leadership qualities of King 'Abd al-'Azīz ibn Sa'ūd and the courage of his close followers. By reviewing the unequal struggle for Arabia of the British and the Ottomans, we have seen how vital this apparently remote region was to Ottoman legitimacy and survival. Both Britain and the Ottomans committed first-rate military leaders and administrators to deal with Arab affairs. Sir Percy Cox was the principal resident in the Gulf at Bushehr, and he was ably assisted by Captain Shakespear, the resident in Kuwait, who met an untimely death as technical adviser (for new weapons?) in a skirmish with the Al Rāshid. The proconsul of India at the beginning of the twentieth century was of course the formidable, intolerant Lord Curzon. Apart from the tremendous effort put forth by the Ottomans to manage the steppe and the desert with the Ḥijāz railroad, a point frequently overlooked, the Ottomans also practiced a mixture of *tawfīq*, *mudāra*, and *al-sayf* in their diplomacy, "the carrot and the stick," as we say today. But one need only mention also top-notch Ottoman leaders: Midḥat Pasha; Bagdātlı Samī Pasha, former minister of the gendarmerie, who quelled the Druze, the Rwala, and the Banū Jazi of the Huwayṭa as governor of Syria in 1910–11; and Naẓīm Pasha, the last minister of war of Sultan Ḥamīd, who as governor of Baghdad dealt a heavy blow to the Dulaym in 1910. With the help of the Al Subḥān viziers and Ottoman supplies and detachments, the Al Rāshid were able to weather the terrible fratricide of 1906–8, but by World War I they had lost most of their tribal allies through mismanagement and injustice. Emir 'Abd al-'Azīz ibn Sa'ūd had driven the Ottomans out of al-Ḥasā in 1913 during the Balkan wars, but continued the fiction that he would rule in the name of the sultan, that is, the Young Turks. Al-Ḥasā was Banū Khālid territory, and the Ottomans had appealed to their ancient lineage and prowess. A number of Shī'is also lived there; hence, both groups had their reasons for giving their support previously to the Ottomans. But as King 'Abd al-'Azīz once observed, it is bad policy in the desert to support tribes who were "once renowned" (i.e., has-beens). Of course, British support for Emir 'Abd al-'Azīz was decisive.

It is not enough to conclude, however, that the Ottomans simply backed the wrong horse in Arabia. From the outset, the Saudi-Wahhābī ideology virtually ruled out the cooperation of the Saudis with the Ottomans, particularly with the Ottoman need to control the Ḥijāz and to support what might be termed "liberal Islam." The British in that era (like the Americans today) were accepted as tutors in Arabia because they were viewed as neutral to Islam, technologically useful, and free spenders.

The Ottoman conception of forming a new, strong, and united Middle Eastern state, a meritocracy and a technocracy, within the framework of an Islamic commonwealth, might have sufficed to hold the empire together, if Sultan ʿAbd al-Ḥamīd had maintained at least some tolerance of liberalism, for he had generally maintained the stance of a concerned Islamic ruler. By contrast, the Young Turks had posed as liberals, but their Pan-Turkic, nationalist, and irreverent views assured that they would lose the support of many Arabs and other nationalities. Finally, the alliance with Germany, a state which had challenged British world hegemony, militarily and economically, reawakened in so-called European liberal, imperialist, economic circles, the long-standing desire to eliminate the Turkish Empire altogether. (It is, after all, easier to deal with dependent statelets than a prickly empire.) The proven oil wealth of the Middle East also made the elimination of the Empire desirable. In many respects, the ideal of the Ḥamīdian era, combining an aggressive Pan-Islam with a technocracy—now fueled by the black gold of the desert—has lived on in the modern Saudi state.

NOTES

1. See R. B. Winder, *Saudi Arabia in the Nineteenth Century* (New York, 1965) for a definitive study of the Saudi state in the previous century.

2. D. Holden and R. Jones, *The House of Saud* (London, 1981), pp. 19 f. The papers of Palmerston are available to the researcher of this important era: see the popular Kingsley Martin, *The Triumph of Lord Palmerston* (London, 1963). For the standard work on the diplomacy of the era, see M. S. Anderson, *The Eastern Question 1774–1923* (New York, 1966), 88–148.

3. Anderson, loc. cit.; Winder, pp. 40–46; H. V. F. Winstone, *Captain Shakespear, a Portrait* (London, 1976), *passim.* On Aden, see J. Kirkman and Brian Doe, eds., "The First Days of British Aden," *Arabian Studies*, II, pp. 179–202.

4. H. Inalcik, article "Imtiyāzāt," *EI*², III, 1179–89.

5. J. G. Lorimer, *Gazetteer of the Persian Gulf, Oman, and Central Arabia* (Calcutta, 1915), I, 172–88.

6. D. R. Headrick, *The Tools of Empire* (New York, 1981), pp. 96–104; David Landes, *Bankers and Pashas* (Cambridge, 1958), *passim.*

7. Lorimer, I, 244–46; Winder, pp. 217–28.

8. Lorimer, I, 247, 255.

9. Lorimer, I, 301, 304–12; R. Lockhart, *Reilly Ace of Spies* (London, 1967).

10. Sir Reader Bullard, *Britain and the Middle East* (London, 1951), pp. 55–58.

11. Carlo Cipolla, *Guns, Sails and Empire* (New York, 1965), pp. 90–155; A. Adnan-Adivar, *Osmanli Türklerinde Ilim* [Science among the Ottoman Turks], rev. ed. (Istanbul, 1963).

12. See B. Lewis, *The Emergence of Modern Turkey* (London, 1963), *passim*; Baron de Tott, *Memoirs*, 3 vols. (London, 1786), especially Volume II, where the baron discusses the devastating influence of Russian artillery on the Ottoman forces.

13. Niyazi Berkes, *The Development of Secularism in Turkey* (Montreal, 1964), pp. 71–135.

14. "Gezdim diyar-i kuffar, kashaneler gördüm; gezdim diyar-ı Islam, viraneler gördüm."

15. Sherif Mardin, *The Genesis of Young Ottoman Thought* (Princeton, 1963), pp. 81–132. There are a number of books on the era of Muḥammad 'Alī. One may readily consult Helen A. B. Rivlin, *The Agricultural Policy of Muhammad Ali in Egypt* (Cambridge, 1961) and the new study by Afaf Lutfi al-Sayyid Marsot, *Egypt in the Reign of Muhammad Ali* (Cambridge, 1984).

16. See the article, "Mustafa Reşid Pasa," *Islam Ansiklopedisi*, IX, 107.

17. Mardin, pp. 107–32.

18. Roderic Davison, *Reform in the Ottoman Empire, 1856–1876* (Princeton, 1963), pp. 3–51.

19. Mardin, pp. 259–83.

20. Berkes, pp. 173–222.

21. Headrick, pp. 3–14, 204–10.

22. M. Morsay Abdullah, "Changes in the Economy and Political Attitudes, and the Development in Culture on the Coast of Oman Between 1900 and 1940," *Arabian Studies*, II, 167–78.

23. Lorimer, pp. 1014–16.

24. Ibid., p. 243.

25. Ibid., pp. 1020–22.

26. Saleh M. Al-Amr, *The Hijaz Under Ottoman Rule, 1869–1914* (Riyāḍ, 1978), pp. 169–235 and the article "Ḳahwa," EI^2, IV, 453.

27. See Berkes, especially the "Portrait of the Hamidian Regime," pp. 256–65, and also Sultan 'Abd al-Ḥamīd's own memoir, *Siyasi Hatiratim* (Istanbul, 1974).

28. Bullard, 51 and E. M. Earle, *Turkey, the Great Powers and the Baghdad Railway* (New York, 1923) and Maybelle K. Chapman, *Great Britain and the Baghdad Railway*, Smith College Studies in History XXXI (Northhampton, 1948).

29. Muhammad R. Harraz, *Al-Dawla al-'uthmanīya wa-shubat jazīrat al-'Arab, 1840–1909* (Cairo, 1970), pp. 184–99.

30. See Stanford and Ezel Shaw, *History of the Ottoman Empire*, II, 172–272, and the important bibliography on the era of ʿAbd al-Ḥamīd, II, 453–56. For documents and budgets, see *Said Pasha Hatiratı*, 3 vols. (Istanbul, 1912) and Joan Haslip, *The Sultan* (London, 1958), a popular biography of Sultan ʿAbd al-Ḥamīd.

31. Three recent studies throw much light on the Young Turk era: Lewis, pp. 206–33; Feroz Ahmad, *The Young Turks* (Oxford, 1969); and Elie Kedourie, *Arab Political Memoirs and Other Studies* (London, 1974).

32. Berkes, pp. 256–65.

33. Headrick, pp. 96–126.

34. Ibid.; Headrick quotes Winston Churchill, who took part in the slaughter at Omdurman and described it in *The River War: An Account of the Reconquest of the Soudan* (New York, 1933), pp. 274, 279, 300.

35. Nikki Keddie, *An Islamic Response to Imperialism* (Berkeley, 1968), pp. 10–14; note also Keddie's full-length biography of Al-Afghānī, *Sayyid Jamāl ad-Dīn al-Afghānī, a Political Biography* (Berkeley and Los Angeles, 1972).

36. Keddie, *Islamic Response*, pp. 14–25; *Sayyid Jamal*, pp. 143–81.

37. *Sayyid Jamal*, p. 374.

38. ʿAbd al-Ḥamīd, *Siyasi Hatiratim*, pp. 107–8; William Ochsenwald has done an excellent study in his *The Hijaz Railroad* (Charlottesville, 1980).

39. Winder, p. 278.

40. See C. Ernest Dawn, *From Ottomanism to Arabism* (Urbana, 1973) and Zeine N. Zeine, *The Emergence of Arab Nationalism* (Beirut, 1966).

41. Keddie, *Islamic Response*, pp. 25–26.

42. Keddie, *Sayyid Jamal*, pp. 370–71.

43. Ibid., p. 374.

44. Ochsenwald, *passim*; there are a number of document records collected by British civil servants which are extremely useful for the Ḥijāz and Gulf researcher, e.g., J. A. Saldana, *Persian Gulf Gazetteer* (Précis of Nejd Affairs, 1804–1904) (Byculla, 1904), and Admiralty War Staff, Intelligence Division, *A Handbook of Arabia* (London, 1916). The collection by Lorimer has been cited above. The study by Jacob Landau, *The Hejaz Railway and the Muslim Pilgrimage: A Case of Ottoman Political Propaganda* (Detroit, 1971) was not available for this paper, nor were the studies of Robin Bidwell: *Travelers in Arabia* (New York, 1976) and his edition of Great Britain Foreign Office Records, *The Affairs of Arabia, 1905–1906* (London, 1971). Ibrahim al-Rashid is editing a series entitled *Documents on the History of Saudi Arabia* (Salisbury, NC, 1976), Vol. I, which are gleaned from the U.S. Archives. For the period under study, the report of July 1908 of G. B. Ravndal, U.S. consul general in Beirut, is of interest, pp. 1–30.

45. C. M. Kortepeter, "The Rebellion of Saʿd ibn Zayd Against the Ottomans (1671–1672)" in A. R. Al-Ansary, *Sources for the History of the Arabian Peninsula* (Riyāḍ, 1979).

46. Lorimer, I, 324.

47. Lorimer, I, 1143–44.

48. Lorimer, I, 359–60.

49. Admiralty, *Handbook*, p. 381.

50. The Czech writer Alois Musil, in his book, *Arabia Deserta* (New York, 1927) describes his sojourn among the Rwala in 1908–9; already the relentless war for dominance among the tribes had begun. Musil takes sides with the Saudis, and urges Prince Nūrī of the Rwala to aid them by taking Jawf from the Al Rashid. He also reports that merchants of the 'Anaza are selling guns in al-Qāsim which they had purchased in Kuwait. Walls are knocked down, palm trees destroyed, and any Shammar warriors captured were left to die in the desert without mounts and nourishment. "The sandy desert of the Wefud wants her sacrifices, therefore we must render these unto her," states a sheikh quoted by Musil (pp. 282–86).

51. Admiralty, *Handbook*, pp. 45 f.

52. Winstone, p. 61; as reported in the *Said Pasha Hatiratı*, 75,000 T.L. were sent to the Al Rashid in 1907. Justin McCarthy in his *The Arab World, Turkey and the Balkans: A Handbook of Historical Statistics* (Boston, 1982) has provided us with some interesting insights into the Ottoman administration in Arab areas (p. 188):

Provincial Divisions:
1885 Provincial Capital: Baghdad—claims also Najd and Qatif
1899 Basra becomes the capital—claims Najd, Qatif, Qatar
1916 Basra. . . .—claims Qatar and Kuwait (Qatif fell to Saudis)

Salary and Expenses (1910–11)		Taxes Collected
Medina:	12,570,107 *kurush*	
Yemen:	4,702,380 *kurush*	9,063,894
Ḥijāz:	21,864,651 *kurush*	27,717
Basra:	18,910,480 *kurush*	11,288,806

53. Lady Anne Blunt, *A Pilgrimage to Nejd* (London, 1881). See her estimates of Muḥammad Al Rashid's income (II, 287).

54. Qur'ān, Sūra 33.

55. Kedourie, pp. 124 f.

56. For a description of Ḥamūd and Majid, see Anne Blunt, I, 228.

57. There is a small error in either Winder or the Admiralty *Handbook* regarding the father of Sa'ūd Al Rashid.

58. Musil, pp. 282–86.

59. In Wilfred Blunt, *My Diaries* (New York, 1923); see II, 39.

60. Anne Blunt, II, 2–17.

61. For a description of the tribes, see Admiralty, *Handbook*, pp. 45–95.

45
Pen and Purse: Ṣābūnjī and Blunt

Martin Kramer

IN THE ANNALS of early Arab nationalism, John Louis Ṣābūnjī occupies a position of minor eminence. A former priest of the Syrian Catholic Rite, Ṣābūnjī entered a turbulent career in journalism, publishing several Arabic newspapers in London, and openly calling into question the Ottoman sultan's right to the caliphate. His newspaper *Al-Naḥla*, which he published in London from 1877, was one of the most influential of the early Arabic political journals, and one of the boldest.

Yet it is well known that the early Arabic newspapers, particularly those published by émigrés, could not bear their own weight financially. They were subsidized, usually in a secret way, by interested parties. Far from constituting open and sincere platforms of opinion, newspapers often amplified the views of silent benefactors, who were prepared to pay to see their political notions in print. Ṣābūnjī himself must have been a heavily subsidized journalist, as was suggested in another study.[1] But the identity of his patrons was necessarily inferred, since it was not possible to document Ṣābūnjī's relationship with any one of his benefactors. Now a packet of Ṣābūnjī's letters sheds new light on his reluctant dependence upon one of his most important clients: the English Arabophile, Wilfrid Scawen Blunt.[2]

I

Ṣābūnjī's first employment in Blunt's service was not as a journalist, but as a tutor in Arabic to Lady Anne Blunt, in 1880. In this capacity, Ṣābūnjī did more than instruct Lady Anne in the intricacies of the language: together they translated Blunt's radical *Fortnightly*

Review articles into Arabic.[3] These strongly Turcophobe writings, which were later published together under the title *The Future of Islam*, proposed the severing of the Arabs from Turkish rule, and the establishment of an Arab caliphate. As Blunt himself later wrote, his *Fortnightly Review* pieces "found their way, to some extent, in translation to Egypt,"[4] so that even in Ṣābūnjī's limited capacity as Lady Anne's tutor, he became swept up in Blunt's anti-Ottoman agitation. Early in 1881, while the Blunts were away in Arabia, Ṣābūnjī began his own campaign, in a newspaper appropriately called *Al-Khilāfa*. According to Ṣābūnjī, this newspaper consisted of "very strong articles against the Turks, their bad administration, and their claim to the title of 'El-Khelaphat.' "[5]

There is no evidence that Blunt subsidized this newspaper, although it echoed an indictment of the Ottoman caliphate made by Blunt himself. But after Blunt's return from Arabia, he did propose that Ṣābūnjī accompany him on his forthcoming trip to the Ḥijāz and the Yemen. Blunt would need the help of an interpreter, were he to get in touch with the "future leaders of reform and liberty in Islam" whom he hoped to identify.[6] Ṣābūnjī seemed the very best choice.

Although the two men apparently did not enter into a formal contract, Ṣābūnjī did set down terms in a letter to Blunt. Ṣābūnjī would not be Blunt's servant, but his "attaché interpreter," cooperating with Blunt "in your plan as much as it is in my power," in return for payment and a generous application of patronage. Blunt would cover Ṣābūnjī's traveling expenses, and provide him with £100 "so that I may settle some of my little affairs, before starting." He also asked Blunt "to procure for me an English passport, if it be possible; and I shall try my best to procure a Persian one, if the Ambassador [Malkūm Khān] be in London before I leave." On their return to England, Blunt would provide Ṣābūnjī with a remuneration left "entirely to your sound judgement, and well-known generosity. You and Lady Anne have always treated me kindly and with princely generosity." Finally, Ṣābūnjī asked that Blunt seek to "procure for me some appointment in the British Service, through your good recommendation and influence. . . . I am perfectly convinced, that there will be no lack of energy, or will in this matter on your part, if there will be any hope for success."[7]

A deal was struck. Blunt set out for Arabia in November 1881, in his quest for men who might refashion Islam. But during a stopover in Egypt, he became fascinated by Aḥmad 'Urābī, whose movement quickly won his sympathy and support. And at Blunt's side was Ṣābūnjī, his "attaché interpreter," who had a dual role. According to Blunt, Ṣābūnjī "had a real genius" for collecting information: on arrival in Cairo, he "was presently busy all the city over seeking out news for me, so that in a very few days we knew between us pretty nearly everything that was going on."[8] Ṣābūnjī also accompanied Blunt to his meetings with Egyptians, where Ṣābūnjī's role was that of translator, and he was at Blunt's side when 'Urābī first received this odd Englishman who so wholeheartedly embraced the Egyptian cause.

Indeed, so adeptly did Ṣābūnjī fulfill his mission that in June 1882, Blunt sent Ṣābūnjī to Egypt in his stead, to conduct private diplomacy on Blunt's behalf. "Sabunji is to go instead of me, and will do just as well." For his trouble, Ṣābūnjī would receive £30 a month plus expenses, and left for Alexandria with a £100 advance and Blunt's explicit instructions.[9] Blunt's *Secret History of the English Occupation of Egypt* reproduces Ṣābūnjī's dispatches to Blunt, written during the crucial months of June and July 1882, and culminating in the bombardment of Alexandria. Ṣābūnjī, dining at 'Urābī's table and sitting up late with the Nationalist leaders, kept Blunt appraised of the mood in the Nationalist camp, and supposedly transmitted Blunt's detailed advice to 'Urābī. In his book, Blunt expressed his great satisfaction with Ṣābūnjī's performance of his mission as "my representative":

> I could hardly have used more influence personally with Arabi and the other leaders that I succeeded in exercising through Sabunji. Sabunji was an admirable agent in a mission of this kind, and it is impossible I could have been better served. His position as ex-editor of the "Nahleh," a paper which, whether subsidized or not by Ismaïl, had always advocated the most enlightened views of humanitarian progress and Mohammedan reform, gave him a position with the Azhar reformers of considerable influence, and he was, besides, heart and soul with them in the National movement. As my representative he was everywhere received by the Nationalists with open arms, and they gave him their completest confidence. Nor was he unworthy of their trust or mine. The letters I sent him for them he communicated to them faithfully, and he faithfully reported to me all that they told him.[10]

It is striking, then, to read a rather disparaging comment on Ṣābūnjī's service in Edith Finch's biography of Blunt. Without providing details, she contradicts Blunt's clear testament to Ṣābūnjī's reliability: "Although not able wholly to trust [Ṣābūnjī], Blunt used him for what he was worth, first as his teacher in Mohammedan thought, afterward as secretary and finally, in the time of the Nationalist uprising in Egypt, as his emissary." Indeed, according to Finch, Ṣābūnjī "turned out later to be something of an Oriental scallywag," although she accepts Blunt's testament to Ṣābūnjī's trustworthiness during the crisis of 1882.[11]

From what seed did this distrust spring, from what time did it date? The answers to both questions are to be found in a revealing letter from Ṣābūnjī to Blunt. Ṣābūnjī arrived back in London in late July or early August 1882. There he found his patron Blunt busily writing about the Egyptian drama, with a considerable emphasis upon his own mediation attempts during the crisis. Blunt's piece, entitled "The Egyptian Revolution: A Personal Narrative," was to appear in *The Nineteenth Century*, a leading journal of opinion. Inevitably, Ṣābūnjī figured in the draft of this account, and Blunt was surprised to discover that this did not please Ṣābūnjī at all. True, Ṣābūnjī voiced no opposition when Blunt first mentioned the references to Ṣābūnjī in his narrative; but there soon followed a letter from Ṣābūnjī, seething with resentment at the possibility that his employment might become a matter of record:

Since I left you, I have been thinking, whether it would be expedient or not, to have my name mentioned in the paper you are about to publish. After due consideration I came to conclusion that that portion of the narrative concerning myself, not only would not add any valuable strength to your argument, but it would weaken also [a] great deal my relations with my friends. Since you represent me in your narrative as a *hired* agent, to carry out your designs, you put me just in that same light in which my bitter enemies attempted to expose me with regard to Ismail. The difference in the eye of the public would consist only in the change of the name of the hirer. You know, however, that our agreement was a confidential one, and it was never me[a]nt to be published in the papers. Now, by your putting me before the public in such an unfavourable light of a *hired agent*, or of a *tool*, as your narrative suggests, you simply confirm my enemies['] former calumnies and pain my friends['] hearts. What excellent recompense for my earnest and honest work! In a time like this, frothing with prejudices, and while the nation's passions have reached the apex of their efferves[c]ence, the most logical reasons and the most convencing proves [*sic*] will produce no effect whatever. They would rather irritate than sooth. As to myself not being a British subject, nor an Egyptian, I need not give reason to anyone of my political doings, and nobody has any right to question me about my political views; hence, it would be useless to take upon yourself the responsibility of my political career. By doing so, you as an Englishman inconvenience yourself without doing any good to me as a stranger to both belliger[e]nt parties. But if you intend

> presenting the public with a complete and too naive narrative of your eastern politics, you might do so without mentioning the names of those who assisted you. The simple saying that you had carried on your political transactions with the leaders of the National party through the help of trustworthy Mohammedan & Christian friends would do just as well.[12]

This twisted logic for the suppression of the truth could not conceal what must have been Ṣābūnjī's reason for fearing its publication. Despite the fact that Blunt footed the entire bill for Ṣābūnjī's Egyptian adventures, and regarded Ṣābūnjī as his exclusive "agent," Ṣābūnjī must have presented himself in Egypt as an independent actor, working not in Blunt's employ but in his own. Indeed, nowhere in Ṣābūnjī's dispatches from Egypt did he give any indication that he had informed the Nationalists of his mission and its sponsor. 'Urābī once introduced him as "a friend of Mr. Blunt,"[13] but Ṣābūnjī obviously sat amidst the Nationalists as his own man, never making a clean breast of the fact of his employment. Blunt was indeed "too naive" to have assumed that Ṣābūnjī would have presented himself in Egypt as acting in Blunt's private service—a naïveté matched only by Ṣābūnjī's, for assuming that the notoriously indiscreet Blunt would not wish to publish his version of the Egyptian saga in full. It is Ṣābūnjī's prospect of being found out in a lie which gives his letter of protest a certain vulnerable poignancy.

Did Ṣābūnjī's failure to represent his position frankly to the Egyptians shake Blunt's confidence in his "emissary"? Blunt not only kept Ṣābūnjī but obliged him, omitting all reference to Ṣābūnjī from the article. Yet if Ṣābūnjī's Egyptian friends had not even known that he was in Blunt's service, then Blunt's own initiatives might well have been lost in transmission. If this likelihood occurred to Blunt, it remained an inner doubt. When he did write his *Secret History*, many years later, he made no allusion to Ṣābūnjī's self-misrepresentation. Indeed, Blunt's overwrought testimony to Ṣābūnjī's trustworthiness (on a page titled "Sabunji's Good Qualities") must have come to dispel any doubt as to Blunt's own influence upon 'Urābī, and the significance of Blunt's mediation. Ṣābūnjī's letter now casts a shadow upon both.

II

Judith Lady Wentworth, in her embittered portrait of her father, averred that Blunt squandered a great part of her mother's fortune "in subsidies to the charlatans who besieged his door."[14] In addition to providing services of questionable value, Ṣābūnjī also sought outright subsidies from Blunt for his Arabic newspapers. Ṭarāzī, in his *Ta'rīkh al-ṣiḥāfa al-'arabīya,* lists Ṣābūnjī's numerous patrons, who financed his no less numerous journals, but Blunt does not figure among them.[15] A begging letter from Ṣābūnjī to Blunt is therefore of great interest, not only for the light which it sheds upon their relationship, but for its detailed revelation of what it cost to publish an Arabic newspaper in exile. The letter was written in May 1882, at the height of Blunt's confidence in Ṣābūnjī, after their trip to Egypt but before Ṣābūnjī had been sent as Blunt's "emissary" to 'Urābī:

Last, year, you were kind enough to promise me, that you will, for this year, subsidize my paper by £ 100—. You see now, that I did all I could to make the paper attractive & interesting to the Arabs. This number has cost me £ 24–6–0, for 1000 copies. Here are the details.

Front page	£ 6– 7–0
Five cuts	4– 7–0
To the compositers of the Arabic types	4–15–0
To the printer & paper	5– 2–0
Postage	3–15–0
	24– 6–0

The next number, of course, will not come to that much; It still will not cost less than £ 15—. So the expenses exceed my scanty means. Hence, I shall be very much obliged to you if you would grant me the favour of £ 150— as a subsidy to my paper, which is, in some sense, your's too. I have been spending a great deal of money lately, & I feel in want of some help to be able to carry on this hard work.[16]

While the letter does not specify which of Ṣābūnjī's newspapers was in such dire need of a subsidy, information in the letter allows an accurate inference. Ṣābūnjī's *Al-Naḥla* ceased to appear in late 1880. As we have seen, it was succeeded by *Al-Khilāfa* in early 1881, but Ṭarāzī states that this was soon succeeded, also in 1881, by a newspaper entitled *Al-Ittiḥād al-'arabī,* of which only three issues appeared. As Blunt pledged his subsidy sometime in 1881, and was asked to make good his promise in 1882, it seems certain that Ṣābūnjī's begging letter refers to *Al-Ittiḥād al-'arabī.* This is supported by Ṣābūnjī's claim that he had done all that he could to make the paper "interesting to the Arabs."

Of this obscure newspaper, all that Ṭarāzī has to say is that it appealed to speakers of Arabic "to form one league against the Turks in all the Arab lands." When Ṣābūnjī saw that there was really no hope for such unity, he closed the newspaper after only three issues.[17] In content, then, *Al-Ittiḥād al-'arabī* must have echoed Blunt's own ideas about the corruption of the Turks and the virtues of Arab independence from Turkish misrule. Ṣābūnjī's letter makes it clear that Blunt had indeed intended to support an Arabic newspaper meant to subvert Ottoman authority in Arab lands. But less than a month after Ṣābūnjī's appeal, Blunt sent him to Egypt on a more important mission. The growing preoccupation of both Blunt and Ṣābūnjī with the affairs of Egypt must have been the real reason for the newspaper's closure: both set aside their anti-Ottoman agitation, in order to expound upon freedom for Egypt and the failings of British policy. Blunt's revised position after the occupation of Egypt was that "the restoration of a more legitimate [i.e., Arab] Caliphate is deferred for the day when its fate shall have overtaken the Ottoman Empire. This is as it should be. Schism would only weaken the cause of religion, already threatened by a thousand enemies."[18] After the fall of Egypt, Blunt would not have supported a newspaper meant to aggravate precisely that schism.

Yet this did not end Ṣābūnjī's association with Blunt. "Sabunji remained in my employment till the end of 1883,"[19] in a capacity defined by Blunt as "my Oriental secretary."[20] Ṣābūnjī undoubtedly handled much of the Arabic correspondence and translations involved in Blunt's support for 'Urābī's defense. But Blunt may have backed one of Ṣābūnjī's other pursuits: there is indirect evidence for the irregular appearance of *Al-Naḥla* in 1883, and for the inclusion in it of a laudatory biography of Blunt.[21] It seems not unlikely that Blunt would have subsidized the newspaper of his secretary, along the very lines suggested in Ṣābūnjī's begging letter. *Al-Naḥla* of 1883 would have differed from *Al-Ittiḥād al-'arabī* of 1881–82 in criticizing British imperial policy rather than Turkish oppression of the Arabs. (Likewise *Al-Naḥla* when it began to reappear regularly in April 1884.) Thus ended the anti-Ottoman and Arab separatist phase of Ṣābūnjī's journalistic career, a phase which coincided almost precisely with Blunt's own preoccupation with the same ideas. It seems likely that this embarrassing coincidence disqualified Ṣābūnjī and his newspapers from mention by George Antonius in *The Arab Awakening*, where early Arab nationalism is not allowed to spring from any but the purest of sources.

III

Ṣābūnjī's last mission in Blunt's service was to accompany Blunt on a visit to Egypt and Ceylon, beginning in September 1883. Blunt had discovered that Ṣābūnjī's activities had created "so much suspicion" in the Foreign Office, and so resolved not to take him. After all, Ṣābūnjī had conducted himself a year earlier as a leading participant in 'Urābī's movement. But Blunt's arrangements for other assistance in Egypt fell through, "and I have consequently determined to take Sabunjī. The fact is I should be very helpless without him, and if it should so happen that I could be of any good it would be as well to have him at hand." But Blunt made this assurance to Gladstone's private secretary: "I shall caution Sabunji to get into no mischief, and he has always acted as far as I am aware squarely in his service with me."[22] This utter dependence upon Ṣābūnjī had led Blunt to overlook Ṣābūnjī's deceit of the previous year. But Blunt's vouching for Ṣābūnjī in this letter of assurance carried an important rider. Ṣābūnjī had served him squarely only "as far as I am aware," for Blunt could not dismiss the likelihood that the Foreign Office had solid evidence to the contrary. During the fruitless Egyptian stopover, Blunt confined Ṣābūnjī to Port Said (although he "sent Sabunji like a raven from the Ark to get intelligence" in the town), and was happy to quit Egypt for Ceylon without Ṣābūnjī's getting arrested.[23]

Blunt had failed in his attempt to have the Nationalist leaders repatriated, and he brought no good news to the Egyptian exiles in Ceylon. Still, once in Colombo, "Sabunji went forth like the raven from the Ark, and did not any more return!"[24] Ṣābūnjī's stint in Blunt's service had come to an end. He would now tie his fate to 'Urābī's, in anticipation of an inevitable and triumphal return to Egypt. As it happened, Ṣābūnjī quarreled with 'Urābī over the bill for Blunt's stay in Colombo, 'Urābī not agreeing to pay his share, or Ṣābūnjī having falsified the account of expenses, or both. Blunt had largely judged 'Urābī through Ṣābūnjī's interpretations, yet now Ṣābūnjī charged that 'Urābī had "cunningly managed to deceive his best friends." Ṣābūnjī, in another agitated letter to Blunt, called 'Urābī "a pseudo-patriot," a "degraded & ambitious ignoramus," "a bigamist and adulterer," and the "biggest lier [*sic*] I ever saw in my life."[25] It was an indictment of 'Urābī which Blunt, as 'Urābī's greatest defender, could never have accepted. "In spite of ['Urābī's] faults and failings, there is something great about him which compels one's respect. His faults are all the faults of his race, his virtues are his own."[26] Ṣābūnjī returned to London, where he was of much more value to 'Urābī's enemies than to Blunt. His revived *Al-Naḥla* of 1884 began a violent campaign against 'Urābī,[27] of which Blunt would not have approved. It also set Ṣābūnjī at odds with his former ally Ya'qūb Ṣanū', and probably earned him the patronage of the ex-Khedive Ismā'īl.[28]

Ṣābūnjī's subsequent career warrants separate study, but it may be characterized as a quest for the perfect patron. He had hoped that Blunt could get him "some appointment in the British Service," but this had become quite impossible. Eventually he fixed his gaze upon Sultan 'Abd al-Ḥamīd II. When Blunt found Ṣābūnjī in Istanbul in 1893, his old friend was "in fine feather, having a permanent post as translator to the Sultan." The terms were enviable: "He gets £ 40 a month and a house at Prinkipo, and so is in clover."[29] Ṣābūnjī could not have found steadier employment, and he served his former nemesis from 1891 until a revolution cleared Yıldız Palace in 1909. By that time, Ṣābūnjī had lost even the appearance of a revolutionary, just as he had once shed his priest's cassock. Blunt dined with him in London in 1909, discovering that Ṣābūnjī "has become the type of what he doubtless was till the other day, a Yıldız Palace spy, a little furtive old man dressed in black with a black skull cap on his head, a jewel in his shirt front and another jewel on his finger."[30]

NOTES

1. See L. Zolondek, "Sabunji in England 1876–91: His Role in Arabic Journalism," *Middle Eastern Studies*, XIV, i (January 1978), pp. 102–15.

2. The letters are preserved in the West Sussex County and Diocesan Record Office, Chichester, Acc. 5306, file 53 (hereafter: Blunt-Chichester). These are a portion of Blunt's recently opened papers, the bulk of which are in the Fitzwilliam Museum in Cambridge. I wish to thank the Right Hon. the Viscount Knebworth, for permission to examine the Chichester collection.

3. Elizabeth Longford, *A Pilgrimage of Passion: The Life of Wilfrid Scawen Blunt* (New York, 1979), p. 163.

4. Wilfrid Scawen Blunt, *Secret History of the English Occupation of Egypt* (London, 1907), p. 122. Elsewhere Blunt wrote: "My articles in the *Fortnightly* were translated while I was in Cairo [in 1881] and read and approved by my friends and by the Nationalist press." Wilfrid Scawen Blunt, "The Egyptian Revolution: A Personal Narrative," *The Nineteenth Century*, XII (1882), p. 332.

5. Ṣābūnjī to Lady Anne Blunt, May 25, 1881, Blunt-Chichester.

6. Blunt, "The Egyptian Revolution," p. 328.

7. Ṣābūnjī to Blunt, October 22, 1881, Blunt-Chichester.

8. Blunt, *Secret History*, p. 163.

9. Blunt, *Secret History*, pp. 296, 298.

10. Blunt, *Secret History*, p. 299.

11. Edith Finch, *Wilfrid Scawen Blunt 1840–1922* (London, 1938), pp. 122, 156.

12. Ṣābūnjī to Blunt, August 9, 1882, Blunt-Chichester.

13. Ṣābūnjī to Blunt, June 18, 1882, in Blunt, *Secret History*, p. 342.

14. Lady Wentworth, *The Authentic Arabian Horse and His Descendents* (3d ed.; Canaan, NY, 1979), p. 74.

15. Phillipe de Ṭarāzī, *Ta'rīkh al-ṣiḥāfa al-'arabīya* (4 vols; Beirut, 1913–33), II, 250–53.

16. Ṣābūnjī to Blunt, May 12, 1882, Blunt-Chichester.

17. Ṭarāzī, *Ta'rīkh al-ṣiḥāfa*, II, 252–53.

18. Wilfrid Scawen Blunt, *The Future of Islam* (London, 1882), p. viii.

19. Blunt, *Secret History*, p. 299.

20. Wilfrid Scawen Blunt, *Gordon at Khartoum* (London, 1911), p. 45.

21. Zolondek, p. 108.

22. Blunt to Edward Hamilton, September 14, 1883, in Blunt, *Gordon at Khartoum*, p. 572.

23. Blunt, *Gordon at Khartoum*, p. 51.

24. Wilfrid Scawen Blunt, *India under Ripon* (London, 1909), p. 19.

25. Ṣābūnjī (Umballa) to Blunt (Allahabad), January 6, 1884, Blunt-Chichester.

26. Blunt, *India under Ripon*, p. 25.

27. *Al-Naḥla*, May 16, 1884. Angry reference to this number of the paper is made by 'Urābī in a letter to Blunt, June 23, 1884, in file 2 of the Chichester collection.

28. Zolondek, p. 109.

29. Wilfrid Scawen Blunt, *My Diaries 1888–1914* (London, 1932), pp. 102, 105. Ṭarāzī speaks of £ 50 a month, and a well-furnished house in one of the capital's best suburbs; Ṭarāzī, *Ta'rīkh al-ṣiḥāfa*, II, 74.

30. Blunt, *My Diaries*, p. 664.

46
Safety in Numbers: Reflections on the Middle Eastern Balance of Power

Dankwart A. Rustow

THE MIDDLE EASTERN international scene in recent decades has offered a strange spectacle of contradictions. More than any other part of the world, the region bristles with weapons, seethes with conflict and discontent, and erupts into wars and terrorism. And since the late 1940s, the Middle East has been a major arena of the Cold War between Russia and the United States.

Despite such endemic turmoil, the Middle Eastern state system has proved durable, and political boundaries have undergone no major change in more than half a century. Russia's Turkish and Iranian frontiers are the one direction in which Communist power remains confined within the original 1921 borders of the Soviet Union. The Iranian upheaval of 1978–79 has been the only full-fledged revolution in the region. Elsewhere, a vast variety of domestic regimes have consolidated, and traditional monarchs continue to rule half the countries of the Middle East.

I shall propose in the present essay that this remarkable stability amidst unrest is the result of a balance of power both within the Middle East and beyond. However precarious that equilibrium may seem, a historical comparison will suggest that, with its regional and global elements, it is more solid than was the play of forces that preserved the Ottoman Empire in earlier centuries. After detailing some of the specific patterns that help preserve the present balance, I shall seek to derive a number of lessons for the conduct of United States policy toward the Middle East.[1]

The flow of arms into the Middle East has been heavier than into any comparable world region. The United States, under Truman's containment doctrine, began arming Greece and Turkey in 1947, and after 1967 became Israel's principal supplier. The Soviet Union's dramatic agreement with 'Abd al-Nāṣir's Egypt in 1955 was followed by a growing export of Soviet arms to Egypt, Iraq, Syria, Libya, South Yemen, and other countries. The French entered the field in the 1950s, providing arms first to Israel, then to Iraq, Libya, the Sudan, and others. By the 1970s, Israel itself had become a major arms producer; and vast oil revenues in Saudi Arabia, Iran, Iraq, Libya, and other countries dramatically increased their appetite for arms—and international competition to supply them.[2]

More than half of the Third World's arms imports have gone to the Arab countries, Israel, and Iran; and their value has increased more than tenfold since the 1960s.[3] In the Middle Eastern countries themselves, military expenditures (calculated in constant prices) rose more than 25-fold between 1950 and 1979. By the 1980s, Israel, seven Arab countries, and Iran were devoting more of their economic resources to military purposes than were any other countries in the world.[4]

The arms that have been accumulating in the Middle East are of ever more sophisticated design; indeed, some of the regional confrontations from the Sinai war of 1956 to the Syrian-Israeli aerial battles over Lebanon in 1982 and the April 1986 U.S. raid on Libya have provided military planners in Washington and Moscow with the most accurate estimates of the comparative prowess of their latest arsenals. No atomic weapons have been used or even tested by Middle Eastern countries; yet Israel is known to have the capacity for developing such arms at short notice—and its 1981 raid on Iraq's nuclear reactor showed its determination to prevent Arab countries from reaching that same stage.

Conventional weapons accumulate in the Middle East at a faster rate than anywhere else outside NATO and the Warsaw Pact—and nowhere are they as likely to be used. Israelis and Arabs have fought more wars in four decades than did Germans and French in a century, and the war aims have escalated over the years. The 1948 war was fought, in effect, to repartition the Palestine Mandate after Britain's departure. But since the days of Egypt's Jamāl 'Abd al-Nāṣir, Arab leaders have proclaimed their intention of "throwing Israel into the sea." The wars of 1956 and 1967 were launched by Israel as preemptive strikes but resulted in temporary or permanent territorial gains. By the time of Israel's 1982 invasion of Lebanon, Prime Minister Menachem Begin was extolling the virtues of aggressive "wars of choice" over defensive "wars of necessity";[5] and Defense Minister Ariel Sharon made little secret of his hopes to impose a new political order on Lebanon and, later, Jordan.

The Iraq-Iran War already has lasted longer than World War II. Other protracted wars have been fought on the fringes of the Middle East between South Yemen and Oman, in the southern Sudan, in the western Sahara, and between Somalia and Ethiopia in the Horn of Africa; and the Turkish intervention of 1974 has left the island of Cyprus divided between two armed camps.

The Cold War has focused on the Middle East, on and off, from the Soviet threat to Greece, Turkey, and Iran in 1945–47 to the invasion of Afghanistan in 1980. Ever since the initial Soviet weapons deal with Egypt and the 1956 war, moreover, the superpower and regional conflicts have tended to intertwine. Rarely have the superpowers come as close to nuclear confrontation as they did in the Arab-Israeli War of 1973. As President Richard M. Nixon later recalled, the messages exchanged at the time between Washington and Moscow "left little to the imagination."

Even short of war, the Middle East is riddled with lesser disputes: Syria still has not conceded the loss of the *sanjaq* of Alexandretta (Hatay) to Turkey in 1938, or indeed officially recognized the separation of Syria and Lebanon in 1920. Iraq, before its 1980 attack on Iran, had announced territorial claims on all of Kuwait. Nor has there been any shortage of movements aimed at radically redrawing the Middle Eastern map—from Jamāl 'Abd al-Nāṣir's Pan-Arabism in the 1950s and 1960s to the periodic plans of Libya's Mu'ammar al-Qadhdhāfī to merge with one or another of his near or distant Arab neighbors, to Ayatollah Khomeini's Islamic fundamentalism which rejects the very rationale and legitimacy of the region's state system.

Within the Middle Eastern countries themselves, violent overthrow became the prevalent form of political change. Syria experienced as many as three military coups in 1949 alone. The coups that overthrew the monarchy in Egypt in 1952 and in Iraq in 1958 radically changed those countries' political courses. In Lebanon in the mid-1970s, the central government dissolved into a congeries of armed camps representing the major denominational factions. In Iran, the revolution of 1978 replaced a conservative hereditary monarchy with a radical clerical regime.

What, then, has been the net effect of this increasing militarization? In the Middle East as in other parts of the world, military establishments are commonly called "defense forces" or "departments of defense"[6]—yet, obviously, if no one thought of doing any aggression, no defense would be required. Thus, we may assume that expansion of frontiers is the initial motive behind the accumulation of arms and the launching of wars, and we may assess the results by a look at the map.

A first look at the historical map indicates that the number of separate political units in the Middle East has remained constant since 1926, when Najd and Ḥijāz were unified into Saudi Arabia. Political changes have not been regionwide. Rather they have occurred within, or at the margins of, the political entities that emerged after the First World War: former mandates and protectorates have become independent; what was Palestine has been transformed into Israel and its occupied territories; and Lebanon (as we noted) has dissolved into separate and shifting armed camps. Also, many countries have changed their official names: notably, the Trucial Sheikhdoms have become the United Arab Emirates; and the Aden Crown Colony and Protectorate is now the People's Democratic Republic of Yemen.

An even closer look reveals only two significant changes of frontiers since the 1920s: the cession (by peaceful negotiation!) of Alexandretta from Syria to Turkey in 1938–39; and the Golan Heights, conquered from Syria in 1967 and incorporated into Israel in 1981. Other boundary changes either have turned out to be temporary, such as Jordan's annexation of the West Bank (1950–67) and Israel's occupation of the Sinai peninsula (1967–82); or they have involved agreed minor rectifications of frontiers, mostly in uninhabited deserts. In sum, if the question is about armaments changing frontiers, the empirical answer from the Middle East is "Much Ado About Nothing."

Within such stable boundaries, there have been major changes of regime. One side effect of the heavy flow of arms into the region has been the increasing prominence of the military in the domestic politics of Middle Eastern countries. The heads of state or government in nearly all Arab republics since the 1950s have been military men. So have all but one president of the Turkish Republic where, since the 1950s, a broad movement toward democracy has been interrupted by military interventions, notably in 1960–61, 1971–73, and 1980–83.[7] In Israel, too, men of military background form an integral part of the top political leadership. Even traditional monarchs, in strengthening their own rule, have placed increasing reliance on their armed forces.

Nonetheless, aside from the dramatic events of the Iranian Revolution, the number of violent overthrows of governments has declined from decade to decade since the 1950s; conversely, several Middle Eastern rulers have set new records of continuity in office. Egypt since the military coups of 1952–54 has managed two peaceful successions after the death of ʻAbd al-Nāṣir in 1970 and the assassination of Sādāt in 1981. Muʻammar al-Qadhdhāfī has been in power in Libya since 1969, Ḥāfiẓ al-Asad in Syria since 1970, and Saddām Ḥusayn in Iraq since 1979. Jordan, upon cutting its links with Britain in the 1950s, appeared to be one of the weakest and most artificial Middle Eastern political entities—yet its monarch, King Ḥusayn, has set a record of political tenure since his accession in 1953. (Among the runners-up, Habib Bourguiba has been president of Tunisia since 1956, and in Morocco King Ḥasan II succeeded in 1961.) Similarly, assassinations of heads of state did not topple regimes (Jordan, 1951; Saudi Arabia, 1975; Egypt, 1981).

In retrospect, the high number of political upheavals in the 1950s and 1960s would seem to represent a testing of political alternatives after the thirty- to sixty-year interlude of European imperial rule. One such alternative was the constitutional monarchies left behind by the British, which adapted and survived in Jordan and along the Gulf; and another the military regimes that took their place in Egypt, Iraq, and Libya. Meanwhile, a more subtle and durable form of imperial-local collaboration developed between international (mostly American) oil companies and the various monarchical regimes—which adapted and survived on the Arabian peninsula, and collapsed (in 1953 and again in 1978) in Iran.

A similar testing of alternatives occurred among Middle Eastern states. Boundaries drawn by European imperialists commanded little respect, and unification schemes such as "Greater Syria," or the "Fertile Crescent," or, most grandiosely, ʻAbd al-Nāṣir's dream of "Arab Unity" from Morocco to Oman, enjoyed a brief rash of popularity. But when it came to implementation, the political structures left behind by the imperialists proved more durable than expected, and rival ambitions of leaders in the several states helped consolidate the divisions. 'Abd al-Nāṣir himself achieved no more than a temporary union (1958–61) with Syria, which collapsed just as it was to be economically implemented; and a looser "federation" with North Yemen.

The growing strength of the military in domestic politics was promoted by this successive crumbling of such bases of legitimacy as Ottoman-Islamic tradition, European imperial rule, and parliamentary government and linguistic nationalism as adapted from Europe. As Thomas Hobbes long ago suggested, political "authority is to trump in card-playing, save that in matter of government, when nothing else is turned up, clubs are trumps."[8]

By the 1960s, the short-lived union of Syria with Egypt had dissolved, and the British were completing their withdrawal from the Middle East, leaving full play to the more permanent factors of the post-colonial situation, all of which tended toward stable balance.

One obvious factor was geography. The Middle East is indeed in the middle: it joins the three continents of the Old World and is deeply penetrated by branches of two oceans. More lines of communication criss-cross here than anywhere else in the world; and long-distance trade has always passed through the region, whether by sailboat and camel caravan in bygone days or by steamship, tanker, and airplane in our own. Would-be world conquerors from Alexander to Napoleon started their ventures in the Middle East; and the region has been *en route* for Russia's quest for warm-water ports, Britain's imperial "lifeline" to India, Germany's *Drang nach Osten*, and Harry Truman's policy of containment of Soviet expansionism. Even secondary or remote powers have tested their wider ambitions in the Middle East, such as Italy in establishing its short-lived colonial empire in Libya, the Dodecanese, and Ethiopia; the French Fourth and Fifth Republics in exporting arms successively to Israel, Iraq, and Libya; Japan in obtaining oil concessions in the Gulf; and Mao's China in supplying foreign aid to North Yemen. In sum, the Middle East marks the intersection of more outside political interest and ambition than does any other part of the world.

The region itself is sparsely populated, and, aside from oil, poor in resources. The combined population of the seventeen states from Libya to Iran and from Turkey to the Sudan is smaller than that of the United States; and it is concentrated along the coasts and river valleys, with uninhabitable, arid stretches marking most of the divisions. Since petroleum abounds in the least populous countries, oil and population have provided alternative stakes in the regional gamble for power.

History has made a crucial contribution to the Middle Eastern equipoise. The present boundaries, we noted, were drawn mostly during the European imperial interlude (ca. 1880–1920). Earlier, most of the region was under the single rule of the Ottoman Empire, the largest and most durable realm west of China since the fall of Rome. The massive defeats of 1683–99 and 1768–74, however, showed the Ottomans clearly inferior to European innovations in military technology and organization. And the Ottomans' efforts to update their military and administrative structures at first compounded the weakness.

Among the reformist sultans, Selīm III was deposed by the Janissaries (1807), once the empire's military elite; and they in turn were destroyed by Maḥmūd II (1826). ʿAbdülʿazīz, Murād V (1876), and ʿAbdülḥamīd II (1909) were deposed by officers of the newly Westernized army. Maḥmūd's Prussian adviser, Helmuth von Moltke, strikingly observed that the sultan had "to raze to the ground any other authority" and "clear the site before setting up his own building. The first part of his great task the Sultan carried through . . . ; in the second he failed."[9] One reason for this failure was the sultans' indecision in choosing a European model for their new army. As von Moltke noted, "The unfortunate result was an army on the European model with Russian jackets, French *règlements*, Belgian rifles, Turkish caps, Hungarian saddles, English sabres, and instructors from all nations."[10]

Earlier, the sultans throughout their far-flung realms had established a system of religious tolerance among Muslims, Greek and Armenian Christians, and Jews; and of "ethnic division of labor"[11] among Turks, Arabs, Greeks, Armenians, Serbs, and many others. Such a pattern of peaceful coexistence had contrasted sharply with the petty political divisions and bitter religious wars of Europe from the time of the Albigeois and Bogomils to the Peace of Westphalia (1209–1648). But, now, in the days of decline of the Ottomans, this multiple coexistence became an added liability as nationalism spread to Balkan Christians and later to Arabs, Armenians, and Turks. Thus in 1873, Nāmık Kemāl's drama *The Fatherland (Vatan)*, celebrating soldierly heroism in resisting the siege of a frontier fortress during the latest war with Russia, "aroused such dangerous enthusiasms"[12] that the authorities felt the need to ban the play and banish the playwright.

"In the multitude of counselors there is safety," counsels the book of Proverbs (11:14); but for the late Ottomans, plurality had ambiguous effects: there was danger as well as safety in numbers. There was security in ruling over a variety of nationalities within a prosperous ethnic division of labor; there was peril in a polyglot multitude of subjects liable to being carried away by nationalist aspirations. There were risks in having a miscellany of sources of military training and equipment, with the results that von Moltke so vividly described. There was danger in confronting numbers of European enemies when they were united, and some safety whenever these fell to quarreling among themselves. There was profit in drawing on multiple sources of foreign aid, and safety in choosing among a variety of potential allies.

Rivalry and conflict among Westerners enabled the Ottomans to diversify their sources of educational assistance. American missionaries established colleges in Beirut, Istanbul, and Cairo that were to play a lively role in the Westernization of Arab and Turkish intellectual life. In 1859 Napoleon III donated to the sultan the elitist Lycée de Galatasaray. By the 1880s, German officers were put fully in charge of military training in the Ottoman army. Two generations later, the exodus of German intellectuals from Hitler's Reich enabled Kemal Atatürk to build up the new Turkish university system according to European standards.[13]

Above all, in the shifting alignments of power politics in the eighteenth and nineteenth centuries, the sultans were fortunate to be facing not one united Europe, but half a dozen rival powers—first Austria and Russia, and then France and Britain, and later also Germany and Italy. Bonaparte's thrust into Egypt, deep in the Ottoman Empire (1798), was foiled by the intervention of the British fleet. When the Russians were in reach of Istanbul (1829), British, French, and Austrian diplomats joined to halt their advance; and soon afterward (1854), a grand coalition of Europeans invited the Ottomans to join the counterattack on Russia's Crimea. Eager as each power might be to benefit from the demise of the "Sick Man of Europe,"[14] it was even more determined to forestall its rivals.

The only answer to the "Eastern Question" on which the European powers could occasionally agree was to partition the Ottoman Empire at its edges, creating weak nation-states in the Balkans (1804–78); balancing Russia's acquisition of Kars-Ardahan (1878) with British occupation of Cyprus; dividing North Africa (1881–1912) into separate British, French, and Italian colonies—and, meanwhile, taking the Empire's revenues into joint receivership (1881).

Were it not for the fact that the Ottomans, in an uncharacteristic lapse of judgment, "stumbled into a major European war"[15] in the autumn of 1914, the final collapse of their empire might well have come much later. As it turned out, the Ottoman defeat of 1918 allowed the Europeans to partition the Arab Fertile Crescent into British and French mandates (1920). In the Turkish rump of the Ottoman Empire, an even bolder partition scheme was foiled as Mustafā Kemāl, the later Atatürk, rallied the defeated Turkish armies to their victorious War of Independence (1919–22). In that process, incidentally, Kemāl made good use of the old balance-of-power tactic of concluding separate diplomatic agreements with the Italians, Bolshevik Russians, and French (March–October 1921), thus leaving Britain as the last, reluctant supporter of the Greek invasion of Anatolia.

Wherever the Europeans took over from the Ottomans, the principle of "divide and rule" was carried further. The British encouraged Zionist settlement in Palestine in hopes, partly, of locating a friendly population near the strategically important Suez Canal; and later (1921) partitioned Transjordan from the remainder of Palestine. Religious minorities, such as Egypt's Coptic Christians, Syria's Alawite Muslims, and Iraq's Assyrians became the favorite recruits for the imperialists' administrative cadres or military forces. In Syria, the French created autonomous areas for Lebanese Christians, Alawites, and Druze. On Cyprus, the British encouraged a deeper division between Greeks and Turks than had ever prevailed under Ottoman rule.

In sum, a united Europe might have advanced into the Middle East after 1683 or 1774 as rapidly as the Ottomans had marched from Istanbul to Vienna (1453–1529), and thereby brought about a complete takeover. Instead, a politically divided Europe delayed the Ottoman demise by one or two centuries and decisively contributed to the present political division in the Balkans and the Middle East. As a result, the territories that in 1683 formed a single Ottoman Empire today are divided among no fewer than twenty-seven countries: six nations in southeastern Europe (Hungary, Yugoslavia, Albania, Greece, Bulgaria, Romania), Turkey, Cyprus, Israel, and thirteen Arab states (Syria, Lebanon, Jordan, Iraq, Kuwait, Bahrain, Qatar, South Yemen, North Yemen, Egypt, Libya, Tunisia, and Algeria)—as well as parts of the Soviet Union, Czechoslovakia, Iran, the Sudan, and Saudi Arabia.

Exhausted by their conflicts of 1914–18 and 1939–45, the European powers soon abandoned all Middle Eastern outposts in a performance that turned out to be an act of divide-rule-and-depart. Still, their twenty-fold partition of the Middle East has survived into the era of regional conflict and Cold War; and the recent balance among a score of regional states and two outside superpowers has proved far safer than was the death dance of half a dozen powers around one "Sick Man of Europe."

The net effect of geography and history on the post-1945 Middle East has been a spell of stable boundaries and political independence unprecedented since the eighteenth century. With a modicum of skillful interplay in the region itself and of clearheaded policy from Washington, they may last well into the twenty-first century.

The mechanics of the Middle Eastern balance of power may be reduced to a few simple principles.[16]

1. CHECKERBOARD: *Most Middle Eastern states are* (a) *at odds with their neighbors;* and hence (b) *inclined to be more friendly toward their neighbors once removed*—a twofold tendency that we might term the "neighborly enmity" and "checkerboard" principles. Territorial claims, historic grudges, ethnography, sectarianism, or ideology can readily be invoked to justify neighborly enmity, of which relations between Syria and Iraq, Syria and Turkey, Iraq and Iran, Greece and Turkey, Libya and Egypt, Egypt and Sudan, North and South Yemen, South Yemen and Oman, and Ethiopia and Somalia provide good illustrations. Note, for example, that the rivalry between Syria and Iraq has persisted through numerous changes of regime, and acquired particular intensity when both countries in the 1960s were ruled by the local branches of the same Ba'th Party. The neighborly enmity principle also explains the difficulty of keeping both Greece and Turkey in NATO's military structure once the Cyprus dispute flared up in the 1970s.

Conversely, the checkerboard principle accounts for Iran's close relations with Israel in the shah's day, and with Syria since then. It similarly explains why the only schemes of Arab unity that briefly worked in al-Nāṣir's day were those between noncontiguous states: Egypt, Syria, and (more loosely) North Yemen.

2. COUNTERBALANCE: *Middle Eastern states will try to counterbalance any shifts in power* (a) *by turning away from a country that is becoming more powerful or is expanding* and (b) *rallying to the weaker side in a given conflict.* A recent illustration is the Gulf Cooperation Council formed by Saudi Arabia and the Gulf Emirates to support Iraq against Iran—but only after 1981, when Iraq seemed in danger of losing the war that it had so frivolously started the year before. The same reversal in fortunes secured for Iraq the active support of Jordan (at odds with Iraq ever since the bloody 1958 coup that overthrew King Ḥusayn's cousin) and Egypt (Iraq's chief rival for Arab leadership since the 1940s). By mid-1986, even Iraq and Syria were exploring a resumption of diplomatic relations.

In relations with outside powers, the checkerboard and balance principles have made Middle Easterners encourage the presence of the far-away foreigner as a counterweight to foreigners at hand. Thus the Ottomans welcomed the involvement of the British in 1798, the Germans after 1870, and the Americans in 1918. Similarly, the Arabs encouraged the Soviet Union in the 1950s so as to help speed the departure of the British.

The effects of the checkerboard principle are readily apparent in the recent geopolitical map of the region. The strongest resistance to Soviet intrusion into the Middle East has come from what John Foster Dulles used to call the "Northern Tier" of countries. Turkey has been America's closest Middle Eastern ally for more than four decades. Revolutionary Iran, soon after its bitter quarrel with the United States in the hostage crisis of 1979–81, turned impartially against the "devil in Moscow" as well—closing the Communist Tudeh party and supporting anti-Soviet rebels in Afghanistan. Conversely, the Soviets over the years have had their closest relations with countries on the far side of the Middle East (South Yemen; Somalia, then Ethiopia; and Libya) and with Syria. Syria's close relations with Moscow are largely a consequence of its location between Israel and Turkey, the two countries with the closest relations with the United States—and, conversely, Washington has been fortunate that its two best friends are two squares apart on the checkerboard.

3. CHANGING SIDES: A specific implication of the balance principle might be termed the "switch in time." Egypt, having welcomed close relations with the Soviet Union in the 1950s, shifted to the United States when Soviet assistance teams had become so numerous and intrusive as to be perceived as an "occupation." A double switch occur-

red in the Horn of Africa in 1977, when Soviets and Cubans, after years of supporting Somalia in its protracted war with Ethiopia, were faced with expulsion—and shifted their support to Ethiopia instead.

Of course, the outside power itself may initiate the switch. Thus the Soviet Union supported the 1947 partition of Palestine and recognized Israel *de jure* within days after the United States did so—its motive presumably being a desire to confirm this first major instance of colonialist departure from the region. Soon, however, Moscow shifted support to the Arabs, who offered the wider arena for anti-Westernism and potential influence.

In sum, the most aggressive or expansionist players in the Middle East power game will face the largest number of antagonists. Allies will shift from the stronger to the weaker side in a conflict. Weapons will flow by preference to those who have the least—and since arms sales can be switched even more readily than can alliances, newcomers to the arms export and import games will readily find one another. In these and other ways the balance-of-power game as played in the Middle East has become a potent stabilizing force that tends toward stalemate and helps preserve existing frontiers.

The game, of course, becomes more predictable when played among the same cast of players. We noted that the average tenure of Middle Eastern rulers has substantially increased in recent decades, and the surfeit of weapons and the military deadlock have indirectly contributed to this result. Soldiers too weak to defeat the armies of neighboring states may well prefer to do a timely switch from the foreign to the home "fronts"—and prove strong enough to depose unarmed civilian governments.[17] Once the soldiers have seized power, or become an active partner in the government, they can use their growing military budgets as patronage for potential followers and as a deterrent for unarmed opponents, with oil revenues and military aid from the superpowers adding further to the available resources. In the mid-1960s, "public consumption" (that is, government expenditure) in Middle East countries typically ranged from 13 to 25 percent of GNP; 20 years later the proportion had doubled.[18]

The preponderance of the military in Middle Eastern politics shows no sign of abating; yet in the contest across frontiers, there is some indication that the futility of violence is becoming more widely recognized. Middle Eastern leaders have freely indulged in grand political visions such as Enver Pasha's Pan-Turkism, 'Abd al-Nāṣir's Pan-Arabism, the Greater Israel proposed by "revisionist" Zionists from Vladimir Jabotisky to Ariel Sharon, or the regionwide Islamic revolution envisaged by the Muslim Brethren and the followers of Ayatollah Khomeini—only to find that their organizational and military means were totally inadequate to the imaginary task.[19] The disparity of means and ends, over time, has caused the more visionary leaders to become isolated, or to be replaced by others ready to scale down their aspirations.

In 1922, Enver Pasha perished in the pursuit of his Central Asian dreams, while the grimly realistic Muṣṭafā Kemāl (Atatürk) rebuilt the Anatolian remnant of the Ottoman Empire into a Turkish nation-state. In Egypt, after the failure of 'Abd al-Nāṣir's Pan-Arab plans, and defeat in three wars against Israel, Anwar al-Sādāt performed his radical shift toward Egyptian nationalism, peace with Israel, and close relations with Washington.

Israel since 1948 has faced a twofold dilemma. First, no matter how many wars its armies may win on the battlefront, there will always be more Arabs beyond the armistice lines—and more embittered for having been defeated. If Israel is ever to live in peace, it is with Arabs that peace will have to be made. Second, the Arab population in Israel's post-1967 *de facto* boundaries already constitutes two-fifths of the total and (at present population growth rates) will become a majority before long. This has led many Israelis to conclude that the problem of the occupied territories must be resolved for Israel's own sake: if the country is to become the Jewish and egalitarian community envisaged by the founding fathers of Zionism, the Gaza Strip and the populated parts of the West Bank must be returned to some form of Arab rule. Hence Israel in the 1970s developed the Allon Plan, and Shimon Peres, in his prime ministership of 1984–86, proved eager to explore the possibility of peace with Jordan.

The opposite solution, of security through further expansion and perhaps expulsion of Arabs, also has its advocates; but it spectacularly failed its first practical test. Begin's "war of choice" in Lebanon was the first war that Israel lost, and cost more Israeli lives than had terrorism and four earlier wars combined. Hence, the outcome, on balance, strengthened the moderate elements in the political spectrum—and caused Prime Minister Begin to end his fifty-year political career in a state of deep personal depression.

Among the Arab countries, Qadhdhāfī's Libya has been the region's most aggressive country and holds the all-time record for mergers or federations (including with Egypt, Sudan, Syria, Tunisia, Malta, Chad, and Morocco) that remain unimplemented. Iraq's Ṣaddām Ḥusayn has long since repented of his aggression against Iran, but the war continues as a result of the Khomeini regime's stubborn refusal to negotiate while Ṣaddām is in office.

The most dramatic failure has been that of Yāsir 'Arafāt's PLO, which from its inception espoused as its single-minded aim the violent ejection of the Zionists from the Palestinian homeland. Far from posing any major threat to Israel, 'Arafāt's PLO instead attempted, but failed, to overthrow King Ḥusayn's regime in Jordan (in the "Black September" of 1970); settled in Lebanon, where it materially contributed to the country's political decay; and was eventually driven out by separate military actions by Israel (1982) and Syria (1983), to find refuge in far-away Tunisia. With his military and political base shattered, 'Arafāt proved equally inept at shifting to the diplomatic game, as is indicated by the protracted (and in the end futile) preliminary negotiations with King Ḥusayn in the "peace process" of 1984–86.

The United States, as the superpower that has helped to constrain Russian expansionist designs on the region, has been a major factor in the regional balance of the recent Middle East. In the eyes of Middle Easterners, the United States at the time of the Truman Doctrine could count on two major assets: it had emerged as the strongest victor from World War II, but had never attempted to establish any colonial empire in the Middle East. Its colonial ambitions at the turn of the century had been directed toward the Pacific and Caribbean regions, whereas the Middle East had attracted American missionaries, educators, and businessmen.

Woodrow Wilson's "Fourteen Points" of 1917 thus were nowhere as enthusiastically received as in the Middle East. When Wilson sent the King-Crane mission to the Levant to ascertain local sentiment about the possibility of postwar British or French mandates, the report was that the Syrians would rather have an independent state, but if there must be a mandate, they preferred one by the United States. In occupied Istanbul, a Society for Wilson's Principles (*Vilson Prensipleri Cemiyeti*) was formed, counting among its founders Hālide Edīb, the first Turkish woman graduate of Robert College; and Muṣṭafā Kemāl (Atatürk) had some difficulty, within the nascent Turkish nationalist movement in Anatolia, in squelching sentiment in favor of an American mandate over the rump of the Ottoman Empire.[20] The fact that the United States soon withdrew from the world scene into isolationism—leaving it to others to demonstrate the colonialist realities of the mandate system—tended to enhance its good reputation in the interwar years.

The specific foundations for the post-1945 Middle East balance were laid when Turkey, under the leadership of Atatürk's successor, Ismet Inönü, avoided stumbling into World War II, indeed, resisted strong German and Allied pressures to join. The result was that, after the war, the Middle East did not fall prey to Soviet occupation (as did Eastern Europe) or partition (as did Germany and Korea). When the Soviets in 1945 put massive diplomatic pressure behind their demands for territorial concessions in northeastern Turkey and "joint defense" of the Turkish Straits, the Ankara government showed itself determined to "fight to the last Turk."[21]

By 1947, the Truman Doctrine and the American program of aid to Greece and Turkey gave American endorsement to Turkey's policy; and the U.S.-Turkish alliance was confirmed with the dispatch of Turkish troops to Korea (1950) and Turkey's admission to NATO (1952). It is only behind this firm barrier of Turkey as a Western ally that governments in Cairo or Baghdad have been able to play their "switch-in-time" game of leaning to Moscow one year and Washington the next without incurring the fate of their colleagues in Prague, Budapest—or Kabul.

The United States under Truman and Eisenhower was determined not only to keep the Soviets out of the Middle East; it also encouraged the departure of the British by backing the formation of Israel and, above all, by its strong stand in 1956 against the British-French landings at Suez. Most remarkably, in the light of previous Middle Eastern experience with outside powers, Washington had no intention of filling the political vacuum it was thus helping to create; an act of self-abnegation that, perhaps, became most evident with the rapid departure of the U.S. Marines that President Eisenhower dispatched to Lebanon (July–October 1958).

Meanwhile, the United States had established close relations with Israel, based on such factors as the common nature of their societies as immigrant democracies, the New England pilgrims' myth of America as the New Zion, and the strong sympathies among U.S. Jewish organizations for modern Zionism.[22] In the Middle Eastern context, American relations with Israel tended to strengthen the multistate balance, by reinforcing the political separation of the surrounding Arab states.

Henry Kissinger formulated more explicitly the desirability, from Washington's point of view, of a stand-off in the Arab-Israeli conflict. Thus the United States airlifted military supplies to Israel only when the first round of the 1973 war had gone against it, and then interrupted those supplies until Israel had agreed to a cease-fire with Egypt. In dealing with Israel's antagonists, Kissinger rightly anticipated that the Arabs having gone to Moscow for weapons of war, would come to Washington to gain territory and peace.[23] The so-called oil embargo, proclaimed by Saudi Arabia and others in sympathy with Egypt, caused some needless panic. Nonetheless, it is clear that the embargo was little more than a public relations gesture and that even the oil price increase of 1973–74 primarily hurt America's competitors in Europe and Japan; and hence it is not fanciful to suggest that it was the United States itself that "won the Yom Kippur and oil wars."[24]

By the 1970s, the United States had thus well established its policies of close ties with Turkey to keep out the Soviets, and encouraging a military balance and, where possible, peace between Arabs and Israelis. To these were added in the early 1980s a policy of responding to Middle Eastern requests for specific military help against aggressive neighbors, as when the Reagan administration dispatched AWACS radar planes to help ward off Iranian raids on Saudi oil installations, or to Egypt to prevent Libyan air raids; or, when at joint Saudi-Egyptian request, the Americans helped clear the Red Sea of Libyan-laid mines. These policies have been successful largely because they have reinforced the existing tendencies toward integrity of Middle Eastern states and balance among them. Unfortunately, these successes have attracted far less public attention than have our Middle Eastern failures.

The most blatant of those failures resulted from policies that ignored the principles of state integrity, and hence of interstate balance. One of these was the crucial support given by the CIA to the coup that restored the shah in 1953, at the price of undermining his popularity ever after, and shifting the leadership of the subsequent revolution to the most anti-Western and anti-American elements. A similar mistake was the encouragement given to the military coup in Greece in 1967, which has caused needless difficulty with subsequent democratic regimes in Athens, including the present government of Andreas Papandreou. A mistake even more blatant (if more quickly remedied) was the dispatch of U.S. Marines to intervene in the Lebanese war in 1982–84. Since the United States has no intention of establishing its colonial rule in any part of the Middle East, we should refrain from interference in the domestic affairs of any of the countries of the region.

Rather, our policy should be based on the principle of "peaceful pluralism," that is, of "live and let live."[25] The record shows that we can get along with countries that range from genuine democracies (such as Israel) to democracies struggling with intermittent military intervention (Turkey), to single-party regimes (Egypt, Algeria, Iraq), to constitutional or traditional monarchies (Jordan and the Arab countries of the Gulf). Even the presence of a "Democratic People's Republic" in South Yemen or an internal war spluttering along in Ethiopia or the Sudan do not immediately threaten American interests. And if Libya, or Syria, can indeed be identified as the masterminds of anti-Western terrorism in recent years, it seems clear that metal detectors and baggage inspection at airports will be safer remedies than air raids such as that of April 1986 against Libya. In sum, we can live with a wide variety of Middle Eastern regimes—and with the balance of power implicit in that multitude of states.

To keep that Middle East pluralism peaceful, we should be ready to do our utmost to help negotiate peace when the parties themselves show their readiness to do so, as did Begin and Sādāt in 1977–79, and as Ḥusayn and 'Arafāt did not do in 1982–86. And we should respond positively when our friends in the region call on us for help against aggression from their neighbors, as we did in the dispatch of AWACs to Egypt and Saudi Arabia.

Meanwhile, we should remember that Turkey's presence as a bridge to the Middle East and as a barrier to Russian incursion is a crucial condition for such a policy of peaceful pluralism. Just as our containment policy, as formulated in the Truman Doctrine, in effect endorsed Turkey's previous determination to resist Soviet encroachment "to the last Turk," so our policy of encouraging peaceful pluralism can take as a convenient precedent Turkey's neutrality between Iraq and Iran—and its thriving commercial relations with both.

NOTES

1. My analysis converges broadly with that of L. Carl Brown in his path-breaking book *International Politics in the Middle East: Old Rules, Dangerous Game*

(Princeton, 1984). Where Brown stresses the continuity of diplomatic attitudes and techniques since the days of the Eastern Question, my own approach starts from the mounting flow of arms and the resulting deadlocks in recent decades. I fully agree with Brown that a games theory approach combined with some depth of historical perspective "offers a way to greater objectivity" (p. 14) and hence to sounder policy formulation (see his suggestive concluding section: "Present Policy Options in the Light of the Eastern Question Experience," pp. 268–77).

2. On the impact of oil income on arms purchases, see the tabulations in my book *Oil and Turmoil: America Faces OPEC and the Middle East* (New York, 1982), pp. 278 f., 282 f.

3. If we define the Middle East narrowly as Egypt, the Arab countries of Asia, Israel, and Iran, we find that its share of Third World major weapons imports rose from 36.1% in 1961–68 to 46.7% (1969–73), and 48.8% (1974–78), and declined fractionally to 48.3% for 1979–83. If Libya, Algeria, and Morocco are added, the share of the Middle East in this last period rises to as much as 61.9%—nine of the twelve leading importers being Middle Eastern states. See Stockholm International Peace Research Institute, *World Armaments and Disarmaments: SIPRI Yearbook 1984* (London and Philadelphia, 1984), pp. 178, 180. The value of those imports to the Middle East more narrowly defined rose from less than 400 million in constant 1975 dollars in 1964 to as much as 5 billion in 1982 and 1983: ibid., pp. 212 f. On the twenty-five-fold rise since 1950, see ibid., 1979, pp. 20 ff.

4. The countries leading the world in military expenditures as a share of their gross national (or gross domestic) product are Iraq (33.7%), Israel (29.8%), Oman, Saudi Arabia, North Yemen, Syria, South Yemen, Jordan, Iran, and Lebanon (13.3%)—in that order. See International Institute for Strategic Studies, *The Military Balance 1985–1986* (London, 1986), p. 171 (the South Yemen figure being for 1980, the remainder for 1983). By comparison, the corresponding U.S. percentage in the first three years of the Reagan administration only went up from 5.6% (1980) to 7.4% (1983). For earlier data (1965, 1978) cf. Charles A. Taylor and D. A. Jodice, eds., *World Handbook of Political and Social Indicators* (New Haven, 1983), pp. 24 ff.

5. See his speech before the Israel National Defense College, *Jerusalem Post Weekly*, August 22–28, 1982, p.14 f.

6. Even some of the sources cited earlier perpetuate this mythology. Thus, where SIPRI speaks forthrightly of "military expenditures," IISS speaks of "defence expenditure and military manpower."

7. For earlier appraisals of the role of the military in the Middle East see my articles "The Military in Middle Eastern Society and Politics" in Sydney N. Fisher, ed., *The Military in the Middle East* (Columbus, Ohio, 1965), pp. 3–20; and "Political Ends and Military Means in the Late Ottoman and Post-Ottoman Middle East," in V. J. Parry and Malcolm Yapp, eds., *War, Technology and Society in the Middle East* (London, 1975, pp. 386–99); and my book *A World of Nations* (Washington, DC, 1967), chap. vi. On the role of the military

and the growth of democracy in Turkey, cf. my book *Turkey: America's Forgotten Ally* (New York: Council on Foreign Relations, 1987), chap. 4.

8. Thomas Hobbes, "A Dialogue of the Common Laws," *English Works*, ed. W. Molesworth (London, 1839–45), VI, 122.

9. Helmuth von Moltke, *Briefe* (5th ed., Berlin, 1891), pp. 409 f., as translated by Bernard Lewis, *The Emergence of Modern Turkey* (2d ed., London, 1968), p. 126.

10. Von Moltke, p. 418, my translation.

11. For that term, see Carleton S. Coon, *Caravan: The Story of the Middle East* (New York, 1951), p. 27.

12. Lewis, op. cit., p. 141.

13. Cf. Fritz Neumark, *Zuflucht am Bosporus* (Frankfurt, 1980).

14. The phrase goes back to a remark by Czar Nicholas I in 1853: "We have a sick man—a seriously sick man on our hands."

15. Lewis, op. cit., p. 237.

16. My five principles (1 a, b; 2 a, b; and 3) may be compared with the more detailed catalog of twelve rules (1 to 6 and 7 a–f) furnished by L. Carl Brown (op. cit., pp. 16–18). Specifically, compare his rule 2 of comprehensive "realignments" with my "switch in time" (rule 3, above), and his rule 6 of "homeostasis" with my rules of "counterbalance" (2 a–b).

17. Jamāl 'Abd al-Nāṣir's *Egypt's Liberation: Philosophy of the Revolution* (New York, 1955), p. 23 and passim, uses a variant of the "stab-in-the-back" motif familiar from post-1918 Weimar Germany to justify this particular switch: Egypt's defeat in the 1948 Palestine War was the fault not of the army, but of the government in Cairo with which the army squared accounts by its coup four years later.

18. Michael Adam, ed., *The Middle East: A Handbook* (New York, 1971), p. 11. For later figures see World Bank, *World Tables* (Baltimore: Johns Hopkins University Press, annual).

19. On the failure of earlier reorganization schemes, see D. A. Rustow, "Political Ends and Military Means," loc. cit. On Enver, see my article "Enwer Pasha," *EI*², *II*, 698–702. It is interesting to note that the senseless loss of lives in distant Yemen, by Ottoman Turks in 1910–12, and by Egyptians in the 1960s, provided powerful arguments to both Kemāl and Sādāt in scaling down their predecessors' ambitions.

20. Cf. D. A. Rustow, "Atatürk as Founder of a State," in *Philosophers and Kings,* ed. Rustow (New York, 1971).

21. See Rustow, *Turkey: America's Forgotten Ally*, p. 88.

22. On all of these see the excellent study of Peter Grose, *Israel on the Mind of America* (New York, 1983).

23. Henry Kissinger, *White House Years* (Boston, 1979), p. 559 and *Years of Upheaval* (Boston, 1982), p. 632.

24. D. A. Rustow, "Who Won the Yom Kippur and Oil Wars?" *Foreign Policy* XVII (Winter 1974–75), pp. 166–75.

25. On "peaceful pluralism," see Rustow, *Oil and Turmoil*, pp. 259 ff.; for a more detailed critique of the intervention in Lebanon see my article "Realignments in the Middle East," *Foreign Affairs*, LXIII, iii (February 1985), esp. pp. 582–85. This essay was written in 1985 and revised early in 1987, before the reinforced U.S. naval presence in the Persian Gulf.

47

Between Nationalists and "Moderates": France and Syria in the 1930s

Itamar Rabinovich

IN NOVEMBER 1934 the new French High Commissioner, Comte de Martel, tried to have the draft French-Syrian treaty, prepared under his predecessor and signed by the Syrian Government, approved by the Syrian parliament. The treaty was to replace the League of Nations mandate as the basis of France's paramountcy in Syria, and to place French-Syrian relations on a footing similar to the apparently successful British-Iraqi relationship. The effort failed, and the Mandatory authorities were forced to withdraw the proposed treaty and to suspend the uncooperative Chamber. The standard histories of the period ascribe the French failure to the effective opposition of the nationalists who, though a numerical minority in the Parliament, drew on their political skills, moral conviction, and popular support in order to defeat a text regarded as inadequate.[1]

A similar explanation was offered at the time by French diplomats and practitioners baffled by their inability to overcome the opposition of what they viewed as a manipulative urban minority: "Elections thus regularly send to a Syrian parliament a majority of moderate rural notables, inclined to cooperate with the Mandatory Power, and an active minority of cultivated intellectuals who, in moments of political crisis, easily impose their maneuvers on a so-called moderate majority, amorphous and lacking a political tradition. This is the underlying reason for the Mandatory Power's failure so far to resolve the Syrian question on a contractual basis."[2]

But in a note prepared by the Levant Department of the Quai d'Orsay in March 1934, in which President Doumergue and Foreign Minister Herriot were warned against Ṣubḥī Bey Barakāt, the Speaker of the Syrian Parliament, a rather more complex explanation was offered for the debacle which had occurred some four months earlier. According to that version, the Speaker, who in 1932 had been elected to Parliament and to his position as a pro-French "moderate," played an important role in aborting the High Commissioner's policy in November 1933. Ṣubḥī Bey was at the time a powerful and influential politician. He commanded a bloc of twenty-eight deputies in a Chamber of seventy, and was reelected in October for a second term by forty-six deputies. But the Speaker, for reasons that will be explained below, harbored a grudge against the High Commissioner, and took his revenge. He signed the nationalist manifesto that denounced the draft treaty and its Syrian signatories, and mobilized "moderate" deputies to oppose it in Parliament. He further clashed with the Mandatory authorities when the latter made a point of suspending the Chamber before it had the opportunity to reject the treaty formally. The speaker, the Quai d'Orsay charged subsequently, tried to "falsify" the record of the meeting, so as to include in it the nationalist manifesto, and to create the impression that a majority of the delegates had adopted it and rejected the draft treaty.[3]

This fuller and, in all likelihood, correct[4] version of France's failure to obtain a satisfactory Syrian treaty in 1933 reveals a missing dimension in the traditional view of her policies toward mandatory Syria. That view has assigned much of the blame for the failure of these policies to France's inability to come to terms with Syrian Arab nationalism and its representatives, and to the inherent weakness of the more cooperative "moderate" politicians through whom she chose or was forced to govern. It should be supplemented and nuanced by a recognition of the flaws and errors with which France's relationship with her Syrian supporters abounded. From this wider perspective, a less deterministic view of France's ultimate failure can be taken.[5]

France and the Syrian Arab Nationalists

During the first decade of her rule in Syria, France's attitude toward and relationship with the Syrian Arab nationalist politicians went through three phases.

The first began with the destruction of Fayṣal's Arab government in Damascus in July 1920, and lasted until 1925. It was shaped primarily by the mutual hostility between the French authorities and Syrian Arab nationalism whose roots can be traced to well before World War I. A small but influential colonial lobby in France had been promoting a French claim to a sphere of influence in (an ill-defined) Syria.[6] To the nascent Arab nationalist movement the French claim, particularly its "civilizing" dimension and the historic connection with the region's Christian communities, appeared threatening. The advocates of French hegemony in "La Syrie Intégrale," in turn, did not envisage an Arab-Muslim Syria, but a particular Syrian entity shaped by its distinctive history and cultural tradition.[7]

The antagonism was exacerbated by the circumstances of World War I and the ensuing peace settlement. France's claim to hegemony and influence in part of geographic Syria was recognized and endorsed by her wartime allies. But an overlapping (not to say contradictory) commitment was given by the British to the Arab nationalist claim over inland Syria, and an Arab nationalist government under the Hashimite prince Fayṣal was installed in Damascus with British support. To the Arab nationalists, the French now appeared as an enemy bent on destroying their achievements and dispossessing them. The French, in turn, viewed the Arab nationalists not only as obstacles to their influence, but also as the instrument of an inimical British policy. All efforts to effect an accommodation between France and Fayṣal having failed, the French dislodged him by force and established their rule on the ruins of his state.[8]

It was against this background that the French authorities organized their mandatory government in Syria. Syrian Arab nationalism was a hostile force to be combated and weakened. Robert de Caix, the chief architect of French policy in Syria and a leader of the colonial movement in France, was far from underestimating the challenge of Arab nationalism. To him it was a dangerous idea, whose influence could undermine France's position in her far more crucial North African possessions. But it could be checked through an alliance with the forces of particularism and traditionalism. A divided Syria controlled by the French through cooperative conservative local forces and leaders was the formula he advocated and subsequently applied together with General Gouraud, the first High Commissioner.[9]

This policy began to change, and then collapsed in 1925. The third High Commissioner, General Sarrail, in an effort to liberalize France's policy, allowed a nationalist opposition, the People's Party, to form and operate. But far more significant was his unwitting contribution to the outbreak of the Druze Revolt, which developed into a general rebellion that the French authorities were hard put to quell. Sarrail was recalled and his successor, Henri de Jouvenel, sought a political solution to the crisis. He dismissed the unpopular president Ṣubḥī Bey Barakāt, and tried to replace him with Sheikh Tāj al-Dīn al-Ḥasanī, who was considered a moderate nationalist. However, the latter's conditions for taking office were unacceptable to the French and the choice finally fell on Damād Aḥmad Nāmī Bey, whose Cabinet initially included nationalist ministers in its ranks. In 1926 de Jouvenel was replaced by a professional diplomat, Henri Ponsot, whose main task was to establish a constitutional and parliamentary framework in Syria, and to have a Syrian government, enjoying parliamentary support, sign a treaty with France. Ponsot's strategy was clearly inspired by Britain's apparent success in Iraq, where its control was exercised through a cooperative local elite with sound Arab nationalist credentials. He was also operating under the other pressures that had constrained French policy in Syria from the outset: the asymmetry between her real interests and the investment required to sustain them, the need to meet France's obligations to the League of Nations, and the hostility of part of the French political spectrum to France's presence and policies in the Levant.

In any event, Ponsot's efforts to find a compromise solution failed. Elections were conducted by Tāj al-Dīn al-Ḥasanī, and they produced a constituent assembly with a large majority of "moderate" rural notables. Still, the nationalist minority, now organized into a National Bloc, dominated the proceedings, and it introduced into the text of the proposed constitution several articles that the High Commissioner found absolutely unacceptable. The situation was deadlocked, the assembly was suspended, and Tāj al-Dīn al-Ḥasanī continued to govern Syria on behalf of the French, as an unsatisfactory but workable intermediate solution.

France and the "Moderate" Politicians

Unwilling or unable to govern Syria through the nationalist politicians, the French mandatory authorities had to rely on a group of cooperative and pragmatic politicians who came to be known as moderates. Their function was defined succinctly by de Martel in 1935 in the following terms:

A government sufficiently strong to undertake responsibility for the conduct of affairs to provide together with the French *délégués* and *conseillers* effective control that will be sufficiently discreet so that the men in power do not appear before public opinion as mere instruments in our hands.[10]

Three of the politicians mentioned above (Ṣubḥī Bey Barakāt, Damād Aḥmad Nāmī Bey, and Sheikh Tāj al-Dīn al-Ḥasanī), together with Ḥaqqī Bey al-'Aẓm, were the chief instruments of this policy. An attempt to identify the underlying differences between the group of Syrian politicians who chose to cooperate with the mandatory authorities and those who, as Syrian Arab nationalists, chose to oppose them, would fall outside the scope of this essay,[11] but an outline of the political careers of France's principal local allies should illuminate an important aspect of France's Syrian policy.

Ḥaqqī Bey al-'Aẓm, a scion of one of Syria's most distinguished families, had been a member of the pre-World War I "Ottoman Party for Decentralized Administration," a rather moderate group that advocated Arab autonomy within the Ottoman framework. In 1922 he was appointed governor of the State of Damascus, and in 1924 to the first cabinet of the newly created Syrian state. In 1929 he was one of the founders of the Syrian Reform Party—a small group of traditional politicians without real membership or popular support.

In terms of both personality and career, Ṣubḥī Bey Barakāt presents an interesting contrast with Ḥaqqī Bey al-'Aẓm. A landed notable from the region of Antakya, he was ethnically more Turkish than Arab, and his command of Arabic was and remained imperfect. His leadership style was shaped by his powerful personality, but its effectiveness was compromised by the vindictive and violent streaks in his character. Nor was Ṣubḥī Bey very consistent: by the end of the 1920s he had gone through three changes of course and orientation. He began by fighting against the French in northern Syria, but subsequently made his peace with the new authorities and was willing to cooperate wih them. In 1922, when the mandatory authorities decided to form a Syrian federation, they placed Ṣubḥī Bey at its head. His forceful personality, anti-French past, and north-Syrian orientation seemed to qualify him for the conduct of a policy seeking to demonstrate that a Syrian state was not necessarily identified with the Arab nationalism of the Damascene notables. When a Syrian state was established in January 1925, he was made its first head. Despite charges of nepotism and corruption, Ṣubḥī Bey was considered by the French a successful administrator. But the outbreak of the 1925 revolt marked the end of his success. His high-handed methods were in tune as long as the military effort to quash the rebellion continued, but once the new High Commissioner, de Jouvenel, decided to seek an accommodation with the nationalists, their Syrian foe had to be sacrificed.[12]

Ṣubḥī Bey did not go down gracefully. Before parting, he published a statement endorsing the nationalist platform. This was not forgotten by the High Commission's staff, and during the 1928 elections the French authorities and Sheikh Tāj al-Dīn al-Ḥasanī joined forces to keep him out of the constituent assembly.

Ṣubḥī Bey's successor as Syria's head of state in 1926 was Aḥmad Nāmī Bey, who as a former son-in-law to a former Ottoman sultan was known as Damād. He was of Circassian extraction, grandson of the Ottoman governor of Tripoli whose family had settled in the Beirut area. He accepted the post only on the basis of a program that the nationalists were also willing to endorse by joining his first cabinet.[13]

The Damād remained in office for twenty months. In early 1928 the High Commissioner, Ponsot, decided to hold elections for a constituent assembly and to appoint another head of government to conduct them. For one thing, the Damād had become too ambitious for the French—he actually exerted pressure on them to appoint him King of Syria. He seemed also to have completed a familiar cycle, and to have made too many enemies among both the nationalists and the other moderte politicians.[14]

The conduct of the 1928 elections was entrusted, instead, to Sheikh Tāj al-Dīn al-Ḥasanī, who had been the mandatory authorities' original choice in 1926. His platform and list of demands were too close to the nationalist position, and he was not willing then to accept the High Commission's terms. This added a mild nationalist aura to his other asset: he was the son of Sheikh Badr al-Dīn al-Ḥasanī, a venerated and popular *'ālim* in Damascus. Once in office, he proved to be a very shrewd politician who managed very well with the local French authorities, and excelled in cultivating an effective lobby in metropolitan France.[15]

The Reassessment of 1930

Effective as Sheikh Tāj al-Dīn may have been as a political instrument, he and his government could not solve France's fundamental dilemma. The constituent assembly remained suspended, and a course of evolution leading through the passing of a constitution, parliamentary elections, the signing of a treaty with an elected government, and its approval by the Syrian parliament, did not seem feasible. The negotiations which preceded the Anglo-Iraqi treaty of 1930 and its eventual signing only served to underline the difference between Britain's apparent success and France's failure, and to aggravate the latter's predicament.

Against this background, Henri Ponsot and his High Commission's staff held in late 1929 and early 1930 a long series of meetings and consultations, with a view to devising a new political strategy. The process was completed in February 1930, and the conclusions drawn by the High Commission were summed up in an unusually revealing note penned by its staff.[16]

As the High Commission saw it, a fundamental choice had to be made in the first place between the nationalists and "the so-called moderates." The option of a deal with the nationalist mainstream, as represented by the National Bloc, was ruled out at the outset. The platform presented by Hāshim al-Atāsī persuaded the High Commission that the gap between "their interests and our prestige remained unbridgeable."[17]

But an intermediate option could be considered. In their negotiations with the authorities, the nationalists had intimated that they were willing to settle on a practical compromise. Let the French force their hands by imposing the amended text of the constitution unilaterally, and proceed with the formation of a cabinet composed of "second echelon" nationalists whose task it would be to negotiate a Franco-Syrian treaty. Despite its apparent attractiveness this option, too, was discarded by the High Commission. Its memorandum cited two principal reasons which militated against such a compromise. It would, the High Commission argued, constitute too abrupt a change in a policy that should carefully prepare the transition from a *régime d'autorité* to a *régime de conseil*. A hasty transfer of power could produce a situation in which force would have to be employed. Nor was there, it continued, a sufficient measure of confidence or community of views that could enable France to overcome the residues of the past. Did this pessimistic view mean, as it seemed to imply, that France could never come to terms with the nationalists? Not necessarily, was the answer:

> We can hope that some day, when the normal working of the constitutional institutions brings the nationalists to power, it will also produce between us and them, between the positions we keep and the ones they acquire, a certain

balance . . . but we cannot rely on the nationalists to create this balance, or to help us in good faith to prepare the conditions for it. Handing power more or less directly into their hands, through the promulgation of the constitution, would be tantamount to deliberately providing them with all the opportunities, and to entering immediately into battle on a terrain which we will have no time to prepare.[18]

Having thus rejected the idea of a compromise with the nationalists, the High Commission was left to choose a "moderate" politician to govern Syria on its behalf. It saw four possibilities:

(A) A combination of the Hashimite Prince Ḥaydar as King of Syria and Rashīd Riḍā al-Rikābī as his Prime Minister. Both men were very attractive to the French, but their hour seemed to have passed. A Syrian monarchy was no longer feasible, and the authoritarian approach associated with al-Rikābī was out of tune with a French policy committed to a *programme sagement libéral.*[19]

(B) Ṣubḥī Bey Barakāt. The High Commission's rancor seemed to have dissipated when it described his qualifications: "He enjoys the advantage . . . of having provided proof of his governing ability, his loyalty and even disinterestedness. He rests in northern Syria on a clientele that is still vigorous and devoted." But the countervailing considerations were more powerful. Ṣubḥī Bey was bound to unite against him both the "nationalists" and all the other moderates. The mandatory authorities could in theory "carry him on their arms" to electoral victory, but they felt that they did not "presently possess the organization . . . necessary for undertaking such an adventure . . . it is too late or too early, the old structure of the authoritarian regime having been weakened morally and materially, and the future structure of a consultative regime being still too rudimentary."[20]

(C) The group of politicians and factions led by Ḥaqqī Bey al-'Aẓm and the Damād Aḥmad Nāmī Bey, and loosely federated under the title of "The United Parties." The High Commission had little esteem for either their effectiveness or their program. Al-'Aẓm was described rather uncharitably as "of mediocre intelligence and weak character." The Damād was described as "a courteous and nonchalant gentleman, devoid of administrative experience and breadth of political views." As a group, their governing capacity had been tested twice and found to be deficient. They were "strong in speech and feeble in action, and history has taught us that they were the first sinkers of the destinies entrusted to them."[21]

(D) Having discarded these three alternatives, the High Commission was bound to settle on the fourth. The process of consultation and search departed from the assumption that the government of Sheikh Tāj al-Dīn had to be replaced; it ended with the conclusion that under the circumstances the French would be best served by retaining it. The High Commission was far from starry-eyed about either the character or the political capacity of the incumbent, but it failed to discover a better choice. It tended to ascribe his bad reputation and lack of popularity to his competitors' jealousy rather than to a genuine popular sentiment. He had shown that he could run the country reasonably well without requiring a particular effort on the part of the mandatory authorities to sustain him. Given a facelift, his government should be able to proceed with the promulgation of the constitution and with the holding of elections.[22]

The 1931–32 Elections

The High Commission's plan was indeed carried out in stages. Tāj al-Dīn al-Ḥasanī was retained and his government, following the promulgation of the amended constitution, supervised the parliamentary elections that were held in stages from November 1931 to January 1932. The new parliament was to meet in June 1932 to elect the president, the prime minister and its own speaker. The new administration's principal task would be the negotiation and signing of a Franco-Syrian treaty.

In retrospect, it becomes clear that in this sequence the elections of 1931–32, more specifically the elections in Aleppo, were of particular importance. Ironically, it transpired that the unexpected extent of the mandatory authorities' success in these elections was counterproductive to their own purposes.

As the 1928 elections to the Constituent Assembly had shown, it was difficult, despite the efforts of the French authorities and their Syrian partners, to reduce the nationalist representation beyond a certain point. Leaders like Hāshim al-Atāsī in Ḥimṣ, Sa'dallāh al-Jābirī in Aleppo, and Jamīl Mardam in Damascus commanded clienteles and networks that practically guaranteed electoral success. France's problem, as mentioned above, derived from the fact that the nationalist minority, once in Parliament, easily dominated the inchoate "moderate" majority.

But in the 1931–32 elections the nationalists were totally defeated in Aleppo, and northern Syria dispatched to Parliament a solid bloc of twenty-eight deputies led by Ṣubḥī Bey Barakāt. Some of the factors which explain this surprising outcome were inherent in the special circumstances in Aleppo: the large number of Christian and Jewish voters, particularly in the electoral college (224 Christians and Jews as against 280 Muslims), a primacy given to economic over political considerations, and a sense of local patriotism reinforced by a familiar resentment of Damascene hegemony. The availability of a powerful local leader and his (uncharacteristic) success in overcoming rivalries with other "moderate" leaders and in reassuring the Christian communities of his own tolerance were crucial in channeling this political potential in one direction. Still more crucial were the efforts and pressures exerted by the French authorities. The *Délégué Adjoint* referred to these rather euphemistically when he subsequently congratulated himself and his colleagues:

> But it was necessary to allow that [silent] majority to liberate itself and become selfconscious, as well as to instill in it enough self-confidence in order to express itself.[23]

Another report by the same *Délégué Adjoint* was more specific in describing his contribution to this outcome. In the first round of the elections on 20 December, he wrote: "Twelve voting stations in the popular Muslim quarters were invaded by a throng of nationalist voters." Determined to prevent "a repetition of the situation which favored the nationalist party in 1928," and in view of the ineffectiveness of the Syrian police and gendarmerie, the *Délégué Adjoint* brought in Algerian and Senegalese units of the French army. Several nationalist candidates, among them the lawyer and writer Edmond Rabbath, were arrested. The others made the mistake of withdrawing their candidacies and resubmitting them on the next day, thus confounding their supporters. It was hardly surprising that when the votes were counted on 21 December, not a single nationalist candidate was chosen to the college of electors.[24]

This outcome led to protests and demonstrations both in Damascus and Aleppo. But the protest and violence were not purely the work of the nationalists. In Aleppo the French authorities traced them to the Syrian director of police and to the director of *Waqf*. Both were considered underlings of Sheikh Tāj al-Dīn al-Ḥasanī. The Sheikh, it was suggested, understood very well that the election results in

Aleppo had turned Ṣubḥī Bey Barakāt into a leading candidate for the presidency of the state, and was seeking to have the elections in Aleppo repeated. After all, commented the *Délégué Adjoint* in Aleppo:

> There have always existed among the moderates rivalries based on ambition, and no one can ignore the fact that during his incumbency Sheikh Tāj al-Dīn invested a far greater effort against his moderate than against his nationalist rivals.[25]

Ṣubḥī Bey Barakāt and the Syrian Presidency

We do not know how the High Commissioner and his staff reacted to their supporters' overwhelming success in Aleppo. Their representatives' satisfaction, however, clearly betrayed no sense of the disruptive effect it was to have on France's policy in Syria during the next few years.

In fact it did not require Tāj al-Dīn's astuteness to understand that the election results were bound to inflate Ṣubḥī Bey's ambitions and to enhance his claim on the presidency of the state. He commanded an impressive bloc of twenty-eight in a chamber of seventy and, furthermore, interpreted the results as a moral victory and a vindication of his earlier policies. The High Commission, in turn, maintained the position it had taken in 1930: that the man was not suitable for leading Syria into a contractual relationship with France. On April 17, in the aftermath of an attempt on Ṣubḥī Bey's life, Henri Ponsot painted an uncharitable portrait of a politician who was "Yesterday the leader of a band and today the leader of a party. His manner is to force things, and his name remains closely associated in Damascus with the events of 1925. He embodies the North's animosity to the South, and conciliation is alien to his character."[26]

The High Commissioner was clearly impressed by a memorandum submitted earlier that month by Ḥaqqī Bey al-'Aẓm, who minced no words in denigrating Ṣubḥī Bey's character and record.[27] Ṣubḥī Bey himself had already discovered that the High Commission was determined to deny him the presidency, and came to argue his case. The record of his discussions with M. Chauvel and M. Reclus of the High Commission's staff is most interesting.

To M. Reclus he explained that he deserved the presidency in return for the many services he had rendered, particularly during the 1925 revolt. Furthermore, he had been invited by the mandatory authorities prior to the recent elections "to rally the moderate elements of Northern Syria." Having accomplished this task as well, he should be made president, and would not settle on the speakership of Parliament with which the French wanted to console him. If the French failed him, he threatened, he would resign together with his supporters, and confront them with a situation like that of 1928.

In M. Chauvel's ears, Ṣubḥī Bey developed other arguments, some of them rather ingenuous, in order to explain why he wanted to be president and did not want to be elected speaker. But more significant was his poignant allusion to the ambivalence which he had correctly detected in a French policy that could not come to terms with the nationalists, and yet would not commit itself fully to the "moderate" collaborators with the Mandate. In his own words:

> He could not fail to notice among the mandatory officers two distinct tendencies; that a similar state of affairs had been the true and underlying cause of the events of 1925 and 1928, and that he must reach the conclusion that the same cause would lead once again to the same results.[28]

In April, it thus became clear to the High Commission that the conflict with Ṣubḥī Bey Barakāt could have serious repercussions on its policies. It was also causing tensions between M. Lavastre, the *délégué* in Aleppo, who took Ṣubḥī Bey's side, and his colleagues in Damascus and Beirut. In an effort to resolve these problems, the High Commissioner dispatched one of his aides, M. Solomiac, to Aleppo and the North, and then held, in the course of May 1932, three staff meetings in his office. The notes taken during these meetings on 14, 19, and 30 May provide a rare glimpse into the inner workings of the High Commission.[29]

Most of the first session was taken up by M. Solomiac's report on his northern tour. He heard from Ṣubḥī Bey Barakāt yet another rendition of his familiar positions, and established in his conversations with other politicians that Ṣubḥī Bey indeed had the solid support of twenty-eight delegates. Ṣubḥī Bey outlined to M. Solomiac an interesting strategy for neutralizing the nationalists' opposition to his presidency. He was willing to let them head the cabinet, and even to have two of his supporters resign their seats, so that nationalist candidates could win them in by elections. With regard to the treaty he was willing to accommodate all of France's wishes.

The session held on 19 May consisted mostly of a debate between M. Lavastre and M. Solomiac, the first promoting Ṣubḥī Bey's candidacy for the presidency, and the latter opposing it. There was an obvious personal antagonism between the two administrators, but it is curious to observe to what an extent the traditional competition between Aleppo and Damascus was transformed into a French bureaucratic feud. M. Solomiac, in any event, reported that the nationalists in Damascus remained vehemently opposed to Ṣubḥī Bey Barakāt. They were in a conciliatory mood, willing to accept moderate candidates for the three senior positions (president, prime minister and speaker) and to send their representatives to the new Cabinet, but all this on the condition that Ṣubḥī Bey did not become president. The disagreement was not resolved, and it was decided to hold another, final, session.

That session was held on 30 May. With the High Commissioner's support, M. Solomiac defeated M. Lavastre, and a decision was made to have Ṣubḥī Bey elected speaker. Two other candidates for the presidency, the nationalist Hāshim al-Atāsī and the moderate Muḥammad 'Alī Bey al-'Ābid were disqualified, and Ḥaqqī Bey al-'Aẓm was chosen as the High Commissioner's candidate for the presidency. The assembled forum was aware of its candidate's "weakness of character and lack of energy," but saw several advantages in him:

> Francophile since the first hour, who has never changed his attitude . . . with regard to Syrian opinion he appears as a neutral personality. No serious hostility can be turned against him. He appeared together with nationalist candidates on the mixed list that had been formed in Damascus before the last elections. His election will be equally satisfying for the minorities, with regard to whom he had loyally followed our directions.[30]

But when the new parliament met on 6 June, Ḥaqqī Bey was not elected president, and had to settle on the premiership. Ṣubḥī Bey was indeed elected speaker, and it was Muḥammad 'Alī Bey al-'Ābid who was elected president. Al-'Ābid was the son of Ahmad 'Izzat Pasha al-'Ābid, who had played a cardinal role in conducting Sultan 'Abd al-Ḥamīd's Arab policy. His son (born in 1874) had not played an important role before his election to the presidency.[31] It is not known exactly what happened between 30 May and 6 June which led to Ḥaqqī Bey's losing the presidency and Muḥammad 'Alī Bey al-'Ābid's winning it. The version offered by Khālid al-'Aẓm, that the latter succeeded in building a coalition of Damascene "moderates" and nationalists to support him, may very well be true. It is also likely that the High Commission was anxious that Ṣubḥī Bey might seek the presidency after all, and might have tacitly supported al-ʿĀbid's deal with the nationalists.

France, Ṣubḥī Bey, and the Abortive Treaty

For nearly a year and a half the arrangements completed in June 1932 seemed to function well. Ḥaqqī Bey al-ʿAẓm was made prime minister, and as they had promised earlier, the nationalists endorsed his cabinet by taking two of the portfolios.

Ṣubḥī Bey also seemed to have made his peace with the mandatory authorities. In October 1932 he was reelected speaker by a sweeping majority of forty-six out of fifty (he was originally elected by thirty out of sixty-eight in the second round of voting). In July 1933 the speaker planned a trip to Paris, in the course of which he wanted to present his own ideas on the question of the Franco-Syrian treaty to the Quai d'Orsay. Some Syrian politicians excelled in maneuvering between the politicians and bureaucrats of Paris and the Beirut High Commission, but if Ṣubḥī Bey tried to follow this strategy, he was not successful.

Thus on 25 July the Quai d'Orsay Levant Department, in coordination with the High Commission in Beirut, submitted to the minister of foreign affairs a background note on Ṣubḥī Bey, who had asked for an audience with the minister. The note provided a lengthy account of the speaker's political career that was somewhat critical, but on the whole fair-minded. After reviewing the disagreement over the presidency in 1932, the note stated that "since his election he gave active support to the mandatory power, but has not relinquished his ambition, namely to become—due to a political crisis—president of the Syrian Republic."[32] The Department and the High Commissioner were in agreement on the political program that Ṣubḥī Bey wanted to present in Paris:

> On certain points the speaker appears to be more demanding than the extremist circles. One cannot be surprised by a spirit so devoid of any political finesse, and who certainly lacks any sense of what can be nuanced political action.

But since, in the Department's view, Ṣubḥī Bey had given France devoted service on several occasions, and since he did represent in Syria "an undeniable force," his request for an audience should be granted. The minister and his aides were warned, however, to treat their guest with caution, and to avoid giving him the impression that his program was acceptable to them. The cold shoulder given him in the Quai d'Orsay had no soothing effect on Ṣubḥī Bey. After returning to Syria in autumn, he drew closer to the nationalists, and it took the High Commissioner's intervention to foil his efforts to organize a joint delegation with the nationalists that would go to Paris to present to the authorities there the wishes of the Syrian population.[33]

His rapprochement with the nationalists culminated in the cooperation, described above, which led on 19 November, 1933 to the failure in Parliament of the draft treaty signed by the government. From that point on, it was open warfare between Ṣubḥī Bey and the French authorities, the High Commission in Beirut and the Levant Department in Paris. One of his attempts to get over their heads to the president of the Republic and to the minister of foreign affairs, by sending them in March 1934 a telegram complaining of the High Commissioner and the Syrian government, gave the Levant Department another opportunity of reviewing the speaker's career and his latest activities.[34]

The slight reserve and criticism of the July 1933 memorandum were replaced by acrimony. The speaker was now painted as an unusually ambitious and unprincipled authoritarian politician. It was now argued that he had been cooperating with the nationalists since June 1932, and his role in the debacle of November 1933 was described in great detail.

The telegram sent to Paris was seen by the Department as yet another piece of trouble-making. It strongly recommended that the president and the minister of foreign affairs not respond to it, and refrain even from acknowledging its receipt, because

> the mere acknowledgment of the arrival of his telegram, banal as it is, addressed to the speaker is bound to be interpreted and presented by him as an encouragement to persevere in his nefarious ways. . . . In the present delicate circumstances of Syrian politics local opinion will be further confounded—which we have every interest to prevent.[35]

Compared to the damage he caused French policy in Syria in November 1933, these were irksome but minor incidents. The mandatory authorities had to contend for the duration of the Chamber's term with a hostile speaker, but in the larger scheme of things this was not one of their principal problems. In 1936 they finally decided to come to terms with the nationalists, and a new Chamber dominated by the National Bloc was elected. Subsequently, however, it transpired that ambivalence toward the Syrian Arab nationalists was inherent in French policy. France signed a treaty with the National Bloc, but did not ratify it. After some two years of government by the National Bloc, a "moderate" team was called in 1939 to administer Syria on behalf of the French.[36]

Conclusion

The explanations generally offered for the failure of France's Mandate in Syria tend to emphasize French underestimation of Syrian Arab nationalism as the single most important flaw in France's Syrian policy. Closer examination of France's conduct in Syria in the 1930s, of the choices it could and did make, of its relations with rivals and supporters, and of the discourse used among the French officials and between them and their Syrian interlocutors, calls for a modification of that view.

The original concept of France's mandatory government in Syria had indeed been formulated by Robert de Caix with a view to combating Syrian Arab nationalism. But while he believed that it could be defeated, he was far from belittling it. De Caix's policy was relinquished in 1925, but the ambiguity toward Syrian Arab nationalism that was inherent in it lingered. By the end of the 1920s, France's policy makers had come to believe that Syrian Arab nationalism could not be defeated, and yet they could not devise a way of coming to terms with it. It is true, as André Raymond writes, that many of the French officials tended to see nationalism as an urban phenomenon whose hold was limited to Western-educated intellectuals, and which had no roots in the larger rural population.[37] That very language, as we saw, was still used with regard to Syria in 1935. But by then it was tempered by the realization that the small minority of nationalist intellectuals had the urban masses spellbound, and completely dominated the rural notables in any parliamentary setting.

If this was indeed the case, then it followed that the nationalist politicians represented the wave of the future, that they were bound to win, and that any policy not based on cooperation with them amounted to little more than playing for time. The *note confidentielle* of February 1930 came very close to saying as much. It also followed that there was something wrong and artificial about France's cooperation with the "moderates." The French knew that they could find a Syrian Ismā'īl Ṣidqī: Ṣubḥī Bey Barakāt and Rīḍā al-Rikābī could have played the role. But France did not possess the will, the resources, or even the true interests that such a policy required in the 1930s. The French preferred to rule through weaker politicians, some of whom they actually despised, and to pursue a policy clearly lacking in conviction. They were not the last European power to do so in the Middle East.

NOTES

1. A. H. Hourani, *Syria and Lebanon* (London, 1946), pp. 194–96 and S. H. Longrigg, *Syria and Lebanon Under French Mandate* (London, 1958), pp. 195–97.

2. M.A.E. (Ministère des Affaires Etrangères) Levant, 1918–1940, Syrie-Liban, Vol. 490, pp. 125–33, note written apparently at the Quai d'Orsay. Unless otherwise indicated, all documents from the French archives quoted below are from this series, and they will be identified by volume number alone.

3. M.A.E., Vol. 488, pp. 101–6, note written on 9.3.1934 by the Levant Department with regard to Ṣubḥī Bey Barakāt.

4. The description in the Quai d'Orsay's note is matched by Khālid al-'Aẓm's version in his memoirs. *Mudhakkirāt Khālid al-'Aẓm* (Beirut, 1973), I, 173–75. Curiously, the incident was overlooked by the usually observant British Consul, who failed to devote much attention to the mandatory authorities' relationship with Ṣubḥī Bey.

5. French policy in the Levant in the interwar period has, until recently, been a neglected subject, certainly when compared to the study of British policy in the Middle East. Soon after World War II, Pierre Rondot published a perceptive study of France's failure in the Levant, "L'Experience du Mandat Français en Syrie et au Liban (1918–1945)," *Revue générale du droit international public* (1948), pp. 1–23. Albert Hourani's book is a study of Syria and Lebanon rather than of France's policies, and Longrigg's book is very thorough but not the work of a historian. After a long hiatus, several studies have appeared which mark the beginning of a change in this picture: E. Burke III, "A Comparative View of French Native Policy in Morocco and Syria," *Middle Eastern Studies* (1973); C. Andrew and A. S. Kanya Forstner, *France Overseas* (London, 1981); A. Raymond, "La Syrie du Royaume Arabe à l'indépendance (1914–1946)," in A. Raymond, ed., *La Syrie d'aujourd'hui* (Paris, 1980), and several recent essays by Philip S. Khoury.

6. For a rich and incisive study of the French colonial movement and its influence on French policy in the Levant up to 1920 see Andrew and Kanya Forstner, op. cit., passim.

7. See K. Salibi, "Islam and Syria in the Writings of Henri Lammens," in B. Lewis and P. M. Holt, eds., *Historians of the Middle East* (London, 1962), pp. 330–42.

8. Andrew and Kanya Forstner, op. cit., passim.

9. De Caix's views and plan were laid out in a seminal memorandum entitled "Note sur la politique de l'accord avec Feysal" (26.1.1920). I am grateful to Prof. Elie Kedourie, who has made this document available to me. A comparison of de Caix's note with the policy implemented after July 1920 will immediately establish his profound influence on the actual course of events. See also Burke's article mentioned in n. 5.

10. Note by de Martel, 12.3.1935, M.A.E., Vol. 490, pp. 102–8.

11. This subject will probably be dealt with by Philip S. Khoury in his forthcoming book on Syrian politics in the interwar period.

12. In retrospect the Quai d'Orsay came to believe, or at least argue, that Ṣubḥī Bey's conduct and mistakes contributed to the transformation of the Druze rebellion into a Syrian revolt. It thus argued that he had persecuted the leaders of the People's Party and pushed them into the arms of the Druze, that he had weakened the police and gendarmerie, etc. See the notes on Ṣubḥī Bey Barakāt of July 1933 and March 1934, M.A.E., Vol. 486, pp. 1–4 and Vol. 488, pp. 101–6.

13. The composition and history of the Damād's cabinet are analyzed in an unusual document authored by Pierre 'Alyye, the *délégué* in Damascus, under the title "Rapport sur le gouvernement national provisoire" (8.6.1926). The report is available in the Henri de Jouvenel Papers in the departmental archive of La Corrèze.

14. "Note confidentielle sur la situation politique en Syrie," 20.2.1930, M.A.E., Vol. 477, pp. 232–59.

15. For a biographical note on Sheikh Tāj al-Dīn see "Note pour le service du protocole," 11.7.1935, M.A.E., Vol. 491, pp. 39–43.

16. See the "Note confidentielle" cited in n. 14.

17. Ibid., pp. 3–4, 11–15.

18. Ibid.

19. Ibid., pp. 16–19.

20. Ibid., pp. 19–21.

21. Ibid., pp. 21–23.

22. Ibid., pp. 23–26.

23. On the 1931–32 elections in Aleppo, see the *Délégué Adjoint*'s two reports of 9 January, M.A.E., Vol. 480, pp. 245–56, and the account by M. Gennardi of the High Commission's "Contrôle de Wakf," ibid.

24. Ṣubḥī Bey sorted out his differences with his local rival, Shākir al-Ni'mat, on the very eve of the elections, ibid.

25. The *Délégué Adjoint's* report of 13.2.1932, M.A.E., Vol. 481, pp. 27–30.

26. Henri Ponsot's telegram of 17.2.32, M.A.E., Vol. 481, pp. 90–92.

27. "Note confidentielle remise par Hakki Bey al-Azem au sujet de la Candidature de Soubhy Bey Barakat à la Présidence de la République," M.A.E., Vol. 481, pp. 112–18.

28. "Résumé d'un Entretien entre Soubhy Bey Barakat et M. Reclus," 14.4.1932; "Résumé des déclarations faites par Soubhy Bey Barakat à M. Chauvel," 14.4.32, M.A.E., Vol. 491, pp. 107–11.

29. "Conférence Politique du 14 Mai 1932 Procès-Verbal sommaire," "Entretien du 19 Mai 1932 sur la situation politique en Syrie et les prévisions concernant la réunion de la Chambre et les désignations aux differents postes à pouvoir"; "memorandum d'un entretien au sujet de la Présidence de la République de Syrie," 30.5.1932, M.A.E., Vol. 481, pp. 119–27, 128–34, and 148–60.

30. Memorandum of 30.5.1932, cited in n. 29.

31. See "Notice biographique sur . . . Muhammad 'Ali Bey Abed," M.A.E., Vol. 481, pp. 242–43.

32. Departmental note on Ṣubḥī Bey Barakāt, 25.7.1933, M.A.E., Vol. 486, pp. 1–4.

33. Departmental note on Ṣubḥī Bey Barakat, March 1934.

34. Ibid.

35. Ibid.

36. Rondot, op. cit., compares France's success in working through Charles Debbas in Lebanon to its failure to find an equally effective local prop in Syria.

37. A. Raymond, op. cit., pp. 67–68.

48
Islam and Democracy: The Case of the Islamic Republic of Iran

Roger M. Savory

THERE HAS BEEN much debate on the question, does the Islamic tradition carry within itself the seeds of democracy or not? This paper will discuss this general question, and will then address the specific case of the system of government currently in place in the Islamic Republic of Iran. This system, called by Imām Khumaynī *wilāyat-i faqīh*, or "the governance of the jurisprudent,"[1] is the product of a particular form of Islam, namely, the Ithnā 'asharī form of Shī'i Islam. First, some general remarks regarding the views on government held by members of the "majoritarian"[2] sect in Islam, namely, Sunni Muslims.

I. Sunni Views on Government

From the time of the Prophet, Islam has been concerned with political power.

> For Muslim statesmen and administrators, political power was the very essence of Islam. They could not conceive of Islam or themselves outside the framework of a political system.[3]

Muḥammad was not only a prophet,[4] but the political leader and lawgiver of the first Muslim community at Medina. Under his successors, a long line of caliphs (Arabic: *khalīfa*) who were the titular heads of the Islamic state for more than six hundred years, the state was seen primarily as "the frame within which Islam with its demands on the 'community of believers' (the *umma*) and on the individual Muslim must be lived."[5] The classic formulation of the functions of the caliph by al-Māwardī (d. A.D. 1058) includes the defense and maintenance of religion, the protection of the territory of Islam, and the waging of *jihād* ("holy war") against those who refused to accept Islam or submit to Muslim rule.[6] Ibn Khaldūn, writing in the fourteenth century, reiterates the same theme: "his functions are the protection of religion and the government of the world."[7]

By the time al-Māwardī wrote, however, his theoretical formulation of Islamic government was already out of date. From the middle of the tenth century onward, heads of state calling themselves variously *amīr* and *sulṭān*, and basing their claim to power simply on *force majeure*, had usurped most of the caliph's political, military, and administrative authority. Was the pious Muslim to recognize the legitimacy of such rulers? The opinion of the overwhelming majority of Muslim jurists from the tenth until the fourteenth centuries was that the paramount consideration was the unity and security of the *umma*, the Muslim community or state. Any alternative was preferable to allowing any part of *Dār al-Islām*, the Islamic world, to fall into the hands of infidels. This could best be prevented if Muslims gave their allegiance to *de facto* Muslim rulers, even if the latter had seized power by force (as was usually the case). It therefore followed logically that juridical and political theory had to be amended to legitimize this "emirate by seizure" (*imārat al-istīlā'*). The key Qur'ānic text used by the jurists to justify the wresting of power by force from the hands of the successors of the Prophet of God was:

> O ye who believe! Obey God, and obey His Messenger, and those who are in authority among you. [4:59]

The interpretation of this text begged many questions. How were "those in authority among you" to be identified? What if there were not agreement among Muslims on the identity of "those in authority"? Were Muslims to give the same unquestioning obedience to usurping emirs and sultans as they had been enjoined to give the caliph? Muslim tradition had always insisted that the caliph must receive unhesitating obedience, for "whosoever rebels against the Khalifa, rebels against God."[8] What if the *de facto* ruler were a tyrant? Were Muslims still to be loyal to him? "Yes," said a majority of jurists, because tyranny was preferable to anarchy. The overriding consideration was *maṣlaḥa*, the interests of the state.

Two points deserve notice at this juncture: first, although by the fourteenth century an accommodation had been reached among Sunnis between the theory and practice of government, no such accommodation had been reached in *Ithnā 'asharī* political theory; second, because of the nature of the Islamic tradition, debates on the sort of questions posed above were not the arid arguments of jurists, but the very stuff of Realpolitik.

II. Is the Sunni Tradition Democratic?

Prima facie, the Qur'ānic verse quoted above would appear to militate against the establishment of democratic forms of government in Islamic states, unless the source of authority to which obedience is enjoined by the Qur'ān is located in the people. Since the first dawning of democracy at Athens in the sixth century B.C., it has been impracticable for all eligible citizens to assemble in one place at the same time in order to express their will through the ballot, and those countries which are democracies today are "indirect" democracies, that is, states in which the citizens express their will through their elected representatives. Possession of a national assembly is not, in itself, a guarantee of democracy. The Islamic Republic of Iran has a national assembly, but is not a democracy. Certain other criteria have to be satisfied: elections must be free, and must be held frequently and periodically. All citizens must have the right to vote. Campaigning by political parties must be free. Citizens must not be subjected to intimidation when they cast their vote. The state must not be a single-party state; the voter must have a genuine choice of political parties. The elected body must have genuine legislative power. It must control the budget. Elected representatives must be able "publicly to question, discuss, criticize and oppose government measures without being subject to threats of interference or arrest."[9]

Since the end of World War II, Islam has affirmed in the strongest possible terms that, in an Islamic state, sovereignty is *not* vested in the people. Pakistan, which came into being in 1947 as a result of the termination of the British raj in India, possessed an advantage not vouchsafed to other Muslim states, namely a *tabula rasa* on which it could write a new constitution without the encumbrance of institutional baggage from the past. In 1951 a panel of thirty-three accredited *'ulāmā'*, representing all the various schools of religious thought in Pakistan, enunciated what were, in its opinion, the fundamental principles of an Islamic state. The two primary principles were:

> 1. Ultimate Sovereignty over all Nature and all Law shall be affirmed in Allah, the Lord of the Universe alone;
>
> 2. The Law of the land shall be based on the Qur'an and the Sunnah, and no law shall be passed nor any administrative order issued in contravention of the Qur'an and the Sunnah.[10]

Pakistan thus "embodies the Muslim assurance that Islam is a religio-political entity, unique, separate, distinctive."[11] But in no way is it a democracy. Sovereignty belongs to God, and not to the people; and the law of the land is the *sharī'a*, the religious law of Islam. The latter condition automatically means that a concept enshrined in most Western democratic constitutions, namely, that all citizens are equal before the law, cannot obtain in Pakistan.

If democracy in the Western sense is not part of the Islamic tradition, why do Muslims exercise themselves about it? The answer, I think, lies partly in the pressure exerted on Muslim countries by such Western ideas as nationalism and secularism, and partly in the initial desire of Muslims to emulate the West. No idea could have been more disruptive of the Muslim concept of the indivisibility of the *umma* than the Western idea of nationalism and its concrete manifestation, the modern nation-state. "Nationalism is the very antithesis of Islam."[12] No doctrine could have been more destructive of the Islamic dogma of the inseparability of religion and politics than the Western post-Reformation doctrine of the separation of Church and State. No wonder that a modern Iranian theologian has declared that "the thesis that religion and politics are separate is a fabrication of the colonial powers."[13] Nevertheless, many Muslim leaders—Arabs, Turks, and Persians—initially rushed to embrace the former, and many Muslim intellectuals, correctly perceiving that their objective of a liberal democratic constitution could not be attained without the latter, adopted it and continue to proclaim it.

Since the end of the eighteenth century, following the Napoleonic invasion of Egypt in 1798, there has been a massive intrusion of Western ideologies into the Middle East. As Bernard Lewis has pointed out, "liberalism and fascism, patriotism and nationalism, communism and socialism, are all European in origin";[14] and I would add secularism to this list. The Muslim intellectuals who went to Europe during the nineteenth century for their university education became conscious that their own countries had fallen behind the West, not simply in the arts of war and technological development in general, but in political development—in the development of less autocratic and more democratic forms of government; in education; and in social development—in regard to the enfranchisement and emancipation of women, the abolition of slavery, and so on. Their initial reaction was that there must be some key to this progress on the part of the West; if only they could discover this key, the Muslim world could share in this progress. The exclamation by Sayyid Ḥasan Taqīzāda, a prominent leader of the 1905–9 Constitutionalist Movement in Iran, that "We must Westernize ourselves, body and soul!" was echoed by Muslim intellectuals in many other countries. In many Muslim countries, nationalism served its purpose as an ideology which united Arabs, Persians, or Turks, first to resist and then to repulse European influence. However, the leaders of those Muslim countries which had been the colonies, mandated territories, protectorates or quasi-colonies (like Iran) of European powers, once their use of the ideology of nationalism had enabled them to achieve their independence, discovered that the necessary concomitant of nationalism, namely secularism, sooner or later brought them into conflict with those elements of the population which had not accepted the "colonialist" proposition that religion and politics should be separate. Even in Turkey, which under the leadership of Kemāl Atatürk went farther than any other Muslim country on the path to secularization, and which is still officially a secular state, Islam has shown a notable revival since the death of Atatürk. The result has been the rise, in almost all Muslim countries, of "fundamentalist"[15] groups and parties which have in common, among other ideological trappings, a militant anti-Westernism. Increased popular support for such groups has led to the eclipse of the "Islamic modernists," those Muslim intellectuals who, beginning in the nineteenth century, advocated the "Herodian" response to the impact of the West, to use Toynbee's term. The Islamic modernists shared the view that some modification of the normative tradition of Islam was required if the Islamic world were to be able to adapt itself successfully to the exigencies of the twentieth century. Today, however, the proponents of such views in the Muslim world are rare, and, if they voice them, they are almost inevitably branded as being un-

Islamic and traitors to Islam. On this point, Toynbee's words, written in 1948, are prophetic:

> The "Zealot" [*sc.* "fundamentalist"] tries to take cover in the past, like an ostrich burying its head in the sand. . . . the "Herodian" courageously faces the present and explores the future.[16]

According to Toynbee, the "Zealot" faces certain death when, armed with spear and shield, he charges a machine gun, but the "Herodian," by changing horses in midstream, may fall into the river and be swept away by the current.[17] The eclipse of the "Herodians" in the Muslim world has naturally been accompanied by the rejection, either in part or *in toto*, of their ideas.

III. Reaffirmation of the Incompatibility of Islam and Democracy

The fact that we all live in Marshall McLuhan's "global village" has necessarily brought the Islamic world (*Dār al-Islām*) and the non-Muslim world (*Dār al-Ḥarb*) into closer contact with each other. As W. M. Watt has noted, "one of the great facts about the later twentieth century is that the world has become an 'inter-religious' world."[18] Regrettably, closer contact has not always resulted in a greater measure of mutual understanding. On the contrary, it has sharpened the rivalry between the two great faiths, Christianity and Islam, each of which has always been convinced of its own superiority and self-sufficiency. This sharpening of the rivalry has led to the strengthening of "Zealot" groups within the Muslim world, such as the Jamā'at-i Islāmī in Pakistan and the Ikhwān al-Muslimīn in Egypt, and to the creation of new, even more extreme, groups such as Egypt's Jamā'at al-Takfīr wa'l-Hijra and Lebanon's "Islamic Jihād." The militancy of the Ikhwān al-Muslimīn may be judged by its redefinition of *Dār al-Islām*, which in classical Islamic terminology meant "territory under Muslim rule," to include "any stretch of land where there is a Muslim."[19] In Iran, the same militant trend culminated in the Islamic Revolution of 1979. The World of Islam Festival organized in Great Britain in 1976 marked the high point in post-World War II rapprochement between *Dār al-Islām* and *Dār al-Ḥarb*, but already represented an attempt to swim against a tide which was flowing strongly against it.

The revival of "Zealotism" was greatly reinforced in the years following 1973 by the newly found economic power of the OPEC cartel, and the strong strain of utopianism in many of the "zealot" movements was reflected in an even greater degree of rejection of Western ideologies. A notable casualty of this process has been the idea of democracy in the Muslim world. No longer do Muslim intellectuals attempt to construct theories of "Islamic democracy" based on such key texts as Qur'ān 42:38:

Their affair being counsel between them (*amruhum shūrā baynahum*) [Arberry's translation].

Nor do they any longer attempt to reconcile Western liberal constitutional democracy with Islam as had the "Herodians." On the contrary, contemporary Muslim writers assert that they reject the Western ideology of democracy because it is a flawed and corrupt system of government. What is seen in the West as the freedom of the individual is regarded by modern Muslim "zealots" as license. This attitude is particularly noticeable, in a culture in which male honor is based on female chastity, in regard to the emancipation of women. This attitude has always, of course, been present in the Muslim perception of the West, and is an important part of what I have called the "standard *'ulāmā'* perception"[20] of the West. Alternatively, contemporary Muslim writers assert, for example, that "the alluring idea of democracy" has never been put into practice, and that the "pompous slogan" of "government of the people by the people" is an unrealizable dream.[21]

IV. The Ithnā 'Asharī Shī'i View of Governance

It was noted above that the accommodation eventually reached among Sunnis between the theory and practice of government in medieval Islam was never reached, or even attempted, in the *Ithnā 'asharī* Shī'i tradition.[22] The fundamental problem is that, in *Ithnā 'asharī* Shī'i theory,[23] ever since the commencement of the period of the "greater occultation" of the Hidden Imām, a period which began in A.D. 940–41, the *mujtahids* have claimed to be the representatives on earth of the Hidden Imām. This would not in itself constitute a "problem" but for the fact that, in *Ithnā 'asharī* Shī'i belief, the only legitimate ruler of an *Ithnā 'asharī* Shī'i state is the Hidden Imām. In his continuing absence, legitimacy is vested in his representatives on earth, namely, the *mujtahids*. In other words, the *mujtahids* exercise the "general agency" (*niyābat-i 'āmma*) on behalf of the Hidden Imām.

Since 1501, therefore, when Shāh Ismā'īl declared that *Ithnā 'asharī* Shī'ism was to be the official religion of the newly established Ṣafavid state, the potential has existed for tension and conflict between the *mujtahids*, claiming to be the only legitimate rulers of the state, and the shahs, representing the nontheocratic, Iranian as opposed to Islamic, strand in Persian culture, and being, in the eyes of the *mujtahids*, usurpers. For some two hundred years, the Ṣafavid shahs, by dint of pragmatic policies of considerable ingenuity, managed to persuade the mass of the people that they had at least as good a claim to legitimacy as had the *mujtahids*. Toward the end of the seventeenth century, however, the shahs lost control of the religious institution, and the eighteenth and nineteenth centuries saw a steady growth in the power of the *'ulāmā'* vis-à-vis the shah. In 1890, there occurred the first significant trial of strength between the *'ulāmā'* and the shah, in the matter of the Tobacco Concession, and the shah was defeated. As a result of their brief flirtation with the idea of a liberal democratic constitution in 1906–7, and their subsequent disillusionment with the idea, *'ulāmā'* suspicion of anything smacking of secularism was reinforced. Consequently, when in 1924 Riḍā Khān proposed to establish a republic, with himself as president, the *'ulāmā'* mounted a massive campaign of opposition to the idea, and once again the shah had to concede defeat. There is little doubt that the *'ulāmā'* looked across the border at what Atatürk was doing in Turkey, and were not reassured by what they saw. The modernizing and secularizing policies of the Pahlavi shahs over a period of half a century eventually gave the *'ulāmā'* the opportunity to mobilize the masses against a shah whom they characterized as an "enemy of Islam," and in February 1979 they were swept to power by the Islamic Revolutionary Movement led by Imām Khumaynī. The slogan of the Revolution, *Shāh raft, Imām āmad* ("the Shah has gone; the Imām has come"), is surely one of history's tersest phrases to describe such a cataclysmic event.

V. The Nature of Khumaynī's "Governance of the Jurisprudent"

On assuming supreme power in Iran in February 1979, Khumaynī set about the establishment of an Islamic Republic. It should be noted at the outset that, in Khumaynī's ideology, "Islamic Republic" simply means "Islamic state." The term "Republic," as used by Khumaynī, has nothing whatever to do with the Western concept of a republic based on constitutional democracy.

The Islamic Republic of Iran is, by virtue of its own internal dynamics, a totalitarian state. By "totalitarian state" I mean a "political system dominated by a single party and ideology, in which all political, economic and social activities are absorbed and subsumed and all dissidence suppressed by police terrorism." The "total monopoly of the ordinary flow of information and public argument is essential to such a system."[24] As was noted earlier, one of the key Qur'ānic texts on the subject of government is:

> O ye who believe! Obey God, and obey His Messenger, and those who are in authority among you. [4:59].

In the Islamic Republic of Iran, the *mujtahids* (sc. *āyatullāh*s)[25] have declared themselves to be "those who are in authority." As the representatives on earth of the only legitimate ruler in an *Ithnā 'asharī* Shī'i state, namely, the Hidden Imām, they have over the centuries arrogated to themselves the characteristics and attributes of the Hidden Imām. The most important of these, in terms of its political implications, is the dogma of the personal and doctrinal infallibility or sinlessness (*'iṣma*) of the imāms. The *mujtahids* are also the custodians and only authorized interpeters of the *sharī'a*, the religious law of Islam, which has been restored by the Khumaynī government[26] and has replaced the legal system, based on Western models, which was in force under the Pahlavi regime. The *sharī'a*, based in the last analysis on the Qur'ān, has itself the force of divine authority. The authority of the *mujtahids* in the Islamic Republic of Iran is therefore absolute.

Put in the simplest terms, obedience to the *faqīh* equals obedience to the Hidden Imām equals obedience to God. Conversely, disobedience to the *faqīh* equals disobedience to the Hidden Imām equals disobedience to God. Consequently, disobedience to the *faqīh* constitutes both a crime against the state and a sin against God, and the normal penalty for such disobedience is death. Since 1979, the leaders of the Islamic Republican Party, which is the only political party in the state, have used their absolute power to deny civil and human rights in Iran, and spokesmen for the regime have asserted that the very concept of human rights is of Western provenance, and therefore by definition un-Islamic. In such a system, what is the answer to the classic question *quis custodiet ipsos custodes*?

The view of Imām Khumaynī himself is that "Islamic government does not correspond to any of the existing forms of government." Islamic government is not a tyranny; it is not absolute; it is constitutional, he says. It is not constitutional in the sense of being

> based on the approval of laws in accordance with the opinion of the majority. It is constitutional in the sense that the rulers are subject to a certain set of

> conditions . . . that are set forth in the Noble Qur'ān and the Sunna of the Most Noble Messenger. . . . Islamic government may . . . be defined as the rule of divine law over men.[27]

In other words, sovereignty belongs to God, and not to the people. How, then, can Imām Khumaynī claim, as he does, that he is merely carrying out the will of the people? His answer is that an Islamic government implements the *sharī'a*, which all Muslims have "recognized . . . as worthy of obedience," and therefore, by inference, reflects the will of the people.[28] Clearly there is no opportunity here for non-Muslim citizens of the state to express *their* will. In Imām Khumaynī's view, a government which implements the divine will through the medium of the *sharī'a* is far preferable to the Western democratic system, in which those "claiming to be representatives of the majority of the people approve anything they wish as law and then impose it on the entire population."[29] Of course, liberal constitutional democracy rests upon, among other presuppositions, the willingness of the minority to accept the rule of the majority. It seems likely, therefore, that Imām Khumaynī's answer to the question, *quis custodiet ipsos custodes*? would be "the *sharī'a*." As he puts it, "the law of Islam . . . has absolute authority over all individuals *and the Islamic government*."[30] However, since the *fuqahā'* are the only legitimate interpreters of the sharī'a, and since the *fuqahā'* in the *Ithnā 'asharī* Shī'i tradition are said to be infallible, one is brought back to my original proposition that the Islamic Republic of Iran, by virtue of its own internal dynamics, is a totalitarian state.

It was noted above that one of the characteristics of a totalitarian state is that the views of dissidents are not tolerated. According to Imām Khumaynī, "individual opinion, even if it be that of the Prophet himself, cannot intervene in matters of government or divine law; here, all are subject to the will of God."[31] All non-Islamic governments are said to be "systems of *kufr* ("unbelief") by definition, and all traces of *kufr* must be removed from Muslim society and destroyed.[32] It follows that all Iranians who advocate any form of secular government, be it constitutional monarchy, a republic, or any form of nontheocratic government, are at risk, and the members of groups advocating any form of secular government have been severely purged by the regime. These groups include many former supporters of Dr. Musaddiq's National Front coalition and of its more revolutionary successor, the National Freedom Movement; many members of the *soi-disant* "Islamic socialists," the Mujāhidīn-i Khalq (literally, "People's Crusaders for the Faith"); of the Fidā'īyīn (Marxist-Leninists); and of the Tudeh Party, the Communist Party of Iran. All these groups initially supported Khumaynī's Islamic Revolutionary Movement and assisted in the overthrow of the shah. This constituted *une trahison des clercs*, and stemmed from the refusal of the intellectuals to believe that Imām Khumaynī meant what he said. One recalls the similar disbelief on the part of many intellectuals in Britain and Western Europe that Hitler intended to implement the plan of action set forth by him in *Mein Kampf*.

One often hears in Iranian émigré circles, from the lips of members of the Iranian intelligentsia, the indignant protest that Khumaynī has "hijacked" the Revolution. Those who thought either that an accommodation could be reached with Khumaynī, or that they would be able "to send the mullas back to their mosques" after the Revolution and put in place a Western-style liberal democratic constitution, displayed a lamentable ignorance of Iranian history and of the *Ithnā 'asharī* Shī'i tradition. One also frequently hears the complaint from such circles that Imām Khumaynī's system of government, *wilāyat-i faqīh*, constitutes an innovation (*bid'a*) in the *Ithnā 'asharī* Shī'i tradition, and is an unjustifiable invention of Imām Khumaynī. The latter, not surprisingly, rejects this argument. "The subject of the governance of the *faqīh*," he says, "is not something new that I have invented; since the very beginning, it has been mentioned continually."[33] On this point, I agree with Imām Khumaynī, to the extent that, in my view, the *potential* for the doctrine of *wilāyat-i faqīh* was always latent within the *Ithnā 'asharī* Shī'i tradition.[34] That Imām Khumaynī saw the possibility of developing this potential into a revolutionary ideology is a tribute to his political acumen, which many people, both in Iran and in the West, underestimated.

VI. An Analysis of the 1979 Constitution of the Islamic Republic of Iran

(i) *Rights and freedoms of the individual*

A stipulation of most Western constitutional instruments is that all citizens shall enjoy equal rights before the law. Article 8 of the Supplementary Fundamental Laws of 7 October 1907, the second of two documents which together embody the first Iranian Constitution of 1906–7, enunciates this principle:

The people of the Persian Empire are to enjoy equal rights before the law.[35]

Article 3 (n) of the 1979 Constitution of the Islamic Republic of Iran appears to guarantee similar rights. The preamble to Article 3 states that the government has the duty of directing all its resources to the following goals, including (3n):

securing the comprehensive rights of all citizens, both women and men, and the establishment of judicial security for all, *as well as the equality of all before the law.*[36]

This provision must however be read in conjunction with Article 4, which reads:

All civil, penal, financial, economic, administrative, cultural, military, political and other laws and regulations must be based on Islamic criteria. This principle applies absolutely and generally to all articles of the Constitution as well as to all laws and regulations, and the *fuqaha* on the Council of Guardians have the duty of supervising its implementation.[37]

In other words, "equality before the law" means only "equality before the *sharī'a*," and is therefore subject to the limitations of that law. For example, under the *sharī'a* there is no equality between Muslims and non-Muslims, or between male Muslims and female Muslims. In this regard, it is significant that, in 1907, only one of the three leading *mujtahids* of that time was prepared to support Article 8 quoted above.[38] By 1907, it had become clear that the majority of the *'ulāmā'* understood constitutional freedoms to mean only "freedoms within the framework of Islamic law."

The same restriction limits various rights granted by the 1979 Constitution which at first sight might be assumed to be of universal application. For example, Article 20 reads:

All citizens of the nation, both women and men, equally enjoy the protection of the law and enjoy all human, political, economic, social, and cultural rights, in conformity with Islamic criteria.[39]

The rights which are theoretically to be enjoyed by "all citizens" are in fact only to be enjoyed *in toto* by Muslim citizens. For example, the Constitution (Article 64) does not grant political representation in the *Majlis* (Parliament) to Bahā'īs.[40] Some articles of the 1979 Constitution purport to grant the individual immunity against arbitrary arrest; to forbid "affronts to the dignity and honor" of persons arrested; to assert the presumption of innocence until guilt has been determined by a competent court; to forbid the use of torture; and to guarantee the inviolability of property.[41] Since the accession to power of the Khumaynī regime, however, these constitutional rights have been violated, and these guarantees have been shown to be worthless by the actions of the state. The individual Muslim has never weighed very heavily in the balance whenever the interests (*maṣlaḥa*) of the state are at stake. The Khumaynī regime has invoked the charge of *fasād fī 'l-arḍ* ("causing corruption in the land") to set aside the protections theoretically afforded by the Constitution. The great advantage of the charge "causing corruption in the land," from the point of view of the state prosecutor, is that it is a moral charge, invoking a general ethical principle, and not a legal charge in the Western sense. It is the prosecutor who defines what is meant by "causing corruption in the land," and consequently no defense against such a charge is possible. As I have noted elsewhere, the soteriological and millennial theories which form part of Khumaynī's ideology have led to the suspension of all moral judgment on the part of the regime, and have found expression, as is usually the case with salvationist utopianism, in tyrannical political practice.[42]

The only article which appears to bear on freedom of speech is No. 23, which reads:

> The interrogation of persons concerning their opinions is forbidden, and no one may be molested or taken to task simply for holding a certain opinion.[43]

The press, and the media in general, are subject to very definite control by the state. Article 24 states:

> Publications and the press are free to present all matters *except those that are detrimental to the fundamental principles of Islam or the rights of the public.* The details of this exception will be specified by the law.[44]

In other words, what the press may discuss is defined by the *sharī'a*, and the only authoritative interpreters of the *sharī'a* are the *fuqahā'*, who are by definition infallible. This Article of the Constitution has led to a rather paradoxical situation in which journalists do not ask the authorities to tell them what they may *not* discuss, but ask them to tell them what they *may* discuss—in other words, to provide them with "safe" information. The mass media (radio and television) are totally subject to state control. Article 175 reads:

The free diffusion of information and views, in *accordance with Islamic criteria*, must be assured in the mass media (radio and television). The media are to be administered *under the joint supervision of the three powers*—the judiciary (Supreme Judicial Council), the legislative, and the executive—in a manner to be determined by law.[45]

Since university students were skillfully exploited by the Islamic Republican Movement prior to the 1979 Revolution, and constituted a powerful center of antiShah sentiment and activism, it is not surprising that the Khumaynī regime was quick to recognize that the universities might also become centers of dissent against itself. For nearly four years, all Iranian universities were closed, and during this period they were purged of all faculty deemed not to be in sympathy with the regime. At the same time, the curriculum was revised to conform to the ideology of the Islamic Revolution. Imām Khumaynī criticized the universities for failing to provide students with "an Islamic education." He called for a fundamental revision of the curriculum. The universities, he said, "must be reconstructed in such a way that our young people will receive a correct Islamic education side-by-side with their acquisition of formal learning, *not a Western education*."[46] A blunt warning was delivered by the imām to students who might think of trying to obstruct the process of ideological purification: "I request that all of our young people not resist or try to sabotage the reform of the universities; if any of them do so, I will instruct the nation as to how to respond."[47]

The fact that, in an Islamic state governed by the *sharī'a*, non-Muslims are second-class citizens, of course raises interesting questions regarding the degree to which such a state is entitled to assume the loyalty to the state of its non-Muslim citizens. It has been argued, for instance, on the basis of Qur'ān 2:256 ("No compulsion is there in religion" [Arberry's translation]), that non-Muslim citizens could not be compelled to fight in defense of a Muslim state. Non-Muslim citizens in an Islamic state are also discriminated against by the fact that the head of such a state would necessarily be a Muslim. Other articles of the 1979 Constitution which bear on the status of non-*Ithnā 'asharī* Shī'is and of non-Muslims are Articles 12 and 13. Article 12 stipulates that adherents of the four Sunni schools— Ḥanafīs, Shāfi'īs, Ḥanbalīs, and Mālikīs—are "to be accorded full respect," as are members of the Zaydī Shī'i sect;[48] Ismā'īlī Shī'is, however, are significantly ignored. Article 13 prescribes that the only recognized religious minorities are Zoroastrians, Jews, and Christians; Bahā'īs are not accorded recognition.[49]

(ii) *The powers of the state and of its leader*

The principle that "sovereignty belongs to God," which was noted earlier as a fundamental principle of an Islamic state, and which at one stroke rules out of court the possibility of a democratic state in the Western sense in which sovereignty is vested in the people, is clearly restated in the 1979 Constitution (Article 56).[50] The key concept, which defines and limits the powers of the executive and legislative branches, is the doctrine of *wilāyat-i faqīh*. The right of the jurisprudents to constitute the only source of legitimate power in an *Ithnā 'asharī* Shī'i state is reiterated time and time again, as is the doctrine of the infallibility of the *fuqahā'*. Among these *fuqahā'* there is one preeminent *faqīh* who is entrusted by the people with the office of *walī* ("leader"). At the present time this office is entrusted to Imām Khumaynī. In pre-1979 *Ithnā 'asharī* Shī'i theory, one of the *mujtahids* was designated the *marja' al-taqlīd*, "a *mujtahid* whose authoritative guidance is followed in matters of Islamic practice and law,"[51] who was considered to be *primus inter pares*. Since the promulgation of the 1979 Constitution, however, and the precise definition of the powers of the Leader therein, the fine distinction of being primus inter pares seems to have widened into a gulf. There are no theoretical or constitutional limits to the power of the leader. Imām Khumaynī is the *marja' al-taqlīd*, and "is to exercise governance and all the responsibilities arising therefrom" (Article 107). He appoints the supreme judicial authority of the country, and is the supreme commander of the armed forces, with power to appoint and dismiss the chief of the general staff; to appoint and dismiss the commander-in-chief of the Corps of Guards of the Islamic Revolution (*pāsdārān*); to appoint the supreme commanders of the three branches of the armed forces; to declare war and peace and to mobilize the armed forces.[52] When these powers are reinforced by *Ithnā 'asharī* messianism and the doctrine of the infallibility of the *mujtahids* as the representatives on earth of the Hidden Imām, the resulting polity is a totalitarian state of a degree which must evoke the reluctant admiration even of the leaders of the Soviet Union.

Articles 110 and 113 of the 1979 Constitution make it clear that the president of the Islamic Republic of Iran is subordinate to the leader. Candidates may stand for election to the office of president only with the approval of the leader, and the president may be dismissed from office "after the issue of a judgement by the Supreme Court convicting him of failure to fulfill his legal duties, or a vote of the National Consultative Assembly (the Majlis) testifying to his political incompetence."[53] The existence of a judiciary which is independent of the executive power is a moot case, since the head of the Supreme Court and the prosecutor-general are both nominated by the leader (Article 162), and these two officials constitute two of the five members of the Supreme Judicial Council (Article 158).[54] The prime minister is clearly a person of little political importance (except as an additional support to the president and the leader), since he is a nominee of the president (Article 124).[55]

In the 1906–7 Constitution, an unsatisfactory instrument which satisfied neither of the principal groups in the Constitutional Movement, the Westernized intellectuals and the *'ulāmā'*, but merely institutionalized their diametrically opposed views, there was an all-important article which, if implemented, would have given the *mujtahids* veto power over all legislation submitted to the *Majlis*. This article called for the establishment of a "Committee composed of not less than five *mujtahids* or other devout theologians," who would "carefully discuss and consider all matters proposed in the Assembly [sc. *Majlis*], and reject and repudiate, wholly or in part, any such proposal which is at variance with the Sacred Laws of Islam, so that it shall not obtain the title of legality."[56] Not surprisingly, this committee of *mujtahids* remained a dead letter under the Pahlavi shahs, and not surprisingly, the idea of a supervisory body composed of *mujtahids* which would control the whole legislative process resurfaced in the 1979 Constitution. The difference is that the new body, called the Council of Guardians, has far more sweeping powers than were envisaged for the abortive committee of *mujtahids*.

The Council of Guardians consists of twelve jurisprudents (*fuqahā'*), six to be selected by the leader, and six to be elected by the *Majlis* from names submitted to it by the Supreme Judicial Council.[57] As noted above, the leader nominates two of the five members of the Supreme Judicial Council. The leader is therefore assured of a controlling majority (eight out of twelve) on the Council of Guardians. Legislation submitted to the Council of Guardians requires a majority vote of all members (Article 96), so only seven votes are actually needed to prevent the passage of any particular piece of legislation. Not only does the Council of Guardians have the duty of "ensuring that legislation passed by the Majlis does not conflict with the *sharī'a*,"[58] but the *Majlis* itself has no legal status in the absence of a Council of Guardians:

> The National Consultative Assembly does not have legal validity if there is no Council of Guardians in existence other than to approve the credentials

of its members and select six jurists who are to sit on the Council of Guardians [see above].[59]

"The interpretation of the Constitution" is the responsibility of the Council of Guardians (Article 98),[60] and this role is important in preventing any deviation from the "imām's line," the official ideology of the Islamic Republican Party. It is Article 99, however, which gives the Council of Guardians total control of various aspects of the electoral process and the ability to manipulate public opinion:

> The Council of Guardians has the responsibility of supervising the election of the President of the Republic, the elections for the National Consultative Assembly, and the direct consultation of popular opinion and referenda.[61]

VII. The Social and Political Implications of the Doctrine of *Tawḥīd*

Imām Khumaynī, in formulating the ideology which gained him mass support and swept him to power in February 1979, skillfully blended together a number of disparate traditional and revolutionary ideas.[62] Among the most potent of these ideas is messianism, but Imām Khumaynī has gone beyond traditional *Ithnā 'asharī* messianism and has developed an apocalyptic world view which, when transferred to the political plane, sees the world in terms of an apocalyptic struggle between the forces of good and evil. An interesting part of this development has been the new interpretation placed on the doctrine of *tawḥīd*.

In the normative Islamic tradition, the term *tawḥīd* (which, curiously enough, does not occur in the Qur'ān),[63] means the "unity" or "unicity" of God. The ideologues of the Islamic Revolution in Iran, however, have developed the doctrine of *tawḥīd* into a world view with far-reaching social and political implications. According to these ideologues, *tawḥīd* signifies a world view which regards the whole universe as a unity, a unity in which there is no contradiction or disharmony. *Tawḥīd* cannot accept "legal, class, social, political, racial, national, territorial, genetic or even economic contradictions."[64] All contradictions which do exist in these areas constitute *shirk*.[65] Sharī'atī's thought, as always, is diffuse and lacking in logical development, but the present president of the Islamic Republic of Iran, Sayyid 'Alī Khāmana'ī, has defined the concept of *tawḥīd* as a world view in much more precise terms.[66] After reiterating that *tawḥīd* is not just an intellectual and philosophical theory, but a social, economic and political doctrine as well,[67] Khāmana'ī proceeds to elaborate the social and political implications of *tawḥīd*. It is the "natural right" of God, as the Creator, to determine "man's social and legal systems."[68]

> Any intervention on the part of others in determining the course of human action, is equivalent to infringement on Divine prerogatives, which in turn amounts to a claim of being equal to God, and hence is tantamount to *shirk* or polytheism.[69]

In the political sphere, the principle of *tawḥīd* excludes "any right of sovereignty and guardianship of anyone over human society except God."[70] "It is only when the affairs of society are entrusted by a Power Transcendental to an individual or a council of rulers, with *a power commensurate with their responsibilities*" [my emphasis] that society can "be expected to be free from all deviations and excesses."[71] In other words, the primary aim of the state is not to confer freedoms on the individual citizen, but to prevent "deviations." According to Khāmana'ī, "the divinely-appointed ruler, unlike a 'majority' or a 'nation,' is not susceptible to deception and domination, nor is he like a 'party' which can be turned into a tool of dictatorship and repression."[72] After reiterating that sovereignty and authority rest solely with God, Khāmana'ī declares that this sovereignty has to be exercised by those appointed by God. Through such persons "the Divine laws and ideals can be implemented, resulting in the realization of a Divine social order."[73] In this way, since "those appointed by God" are synonymous with the *ūlū 'l-amr* of Qur'ān 4:59, and since the *ūlū 'l-amr* in *Ithnā 'asharī* Shī'i theory are the infallible *fuqahā'*, one is led once more, this time by the new interpretation of the doctrine of *tawḥīd*, to the concept of the ideal state as a totalitarian state governed by the *fuqahā'*. Sharī'atī even goes so far as to interpret the cardinal *Ithnā 'asharī* Shī'i doctrine of the imāmate in similar terms:

> The political philosophy and the form of regime of the *umma* is not the democracy of heads, not irresponsible and directionless liberalism which is the plaything of contesting social forces, not putrid aristocracy, not anti-popular dictatorship, not a self-imposing oligarchy. It consists rather of "purity of leadership" (not the leader, for that would be fascism), committed and revolutionary leadership, responsible for the movement and growth of society on the basis of its world-view and ideology, and for the realization of the divine destiny of many in the plan of creation. This is the true meaning of imamate![74]

By "leadership" Sharī'atī is presumably alluding to the *fuqahā'*, and "purity of leadership" is presumably a reference to the arrogation to themselves by the *fuqahā'* of the *'iṣma* (infallibility) of the imāms. The disparaging remarks about democracy and liberalism merely reflect the standard view of these Western ideas held by many Muslims. The words in parentheses are intriguing. Is Sharī'atī saying that he is willing to accord *'iṣma* to the *fuqahā* as constituting a leadership, in other words, as exercising the general agency (*niyābat-i 'āmma*) on behalf of the Hidden Imām, but not to a single leader, because that would lead to totalitarianism? If this is a correct interpretation of his words, it would suggest that, were he alive today, Sharī'atī would be forced to consider the doctrine of *wilāyat-i faqīh* a heresy.

VIII. Conclusion

This study seems to support the following propositions: first, there is no possibility of an Islamic state's evolving into a democrtic polity, because it is prevented from doing so by the two essential postulates of an Islamic state: (1) that sovereignty belongs to God, and not to the people; (2) that the *sharī'a* is the law of the land. As many Islamic modernists have seen, the separation of religion and politics, and the replacement of the *sharī'a* by manmade codes of law, are prerequisites for the establishment in Islamic states of democracy in the Western sense.

> Islamic rule, then, is not "democratic" in the Western technical sense. To hope that it might become democratic is equally far beside the point as claiming—no doubt apologetically—that it is. Such verbal acrobatics can only lead to confusion. Its basis is not the implementation of the popular will duly aggregated, but of the divine norm duly applied.[75]

Second, the Islamic Republic of Iran is a totalitarian state, whether one bases this judgment on the traditional *Ithnā 'asharī* Shī'i view of theocratic government, or on the more recent reinterpretation of the doctrine of *tawḥīd* by *Ithnā 'asharī* jurisprudents and ideologues as a world view. *Tawḥīd*, thus reinterpreted, not only defines the nature of society and the political structure of the state, but metamorphoses the concept of the unicity of God into an apocalyptic struggle between good and evil.

NOTES

1. See "Islamic Government," in *Islam and Revolution: Writings and Declarations of Imam Khomeini*, Hamid Algar, ed. and trans. (Berkeley, 1981) [hereafter Algar I], pp. 27–166.

2. An ugly neologism which has the sole merit of avoiding the use of value-laden terms such as "orthodox" and "heterodox" to denote the Sunni and Shī'i traditions respectively.

3. Kalim Siddiqui, *Beyond the Muslim Nation-states* (London, 1980), p. 5.

4. According to Muslim tradition, he was the last, the "seal," of the prophets.

5. E. I. J. Rosenthal, "The Role of the State in Islam: Theory and Medieval Practice," a paper presented to the Colloquium on Tradition and Change in the Middle East (Harvard University, 1968), p. 1.

6. *EI*[1], II, 884.

7. *EI*[1], II, 885.

8. *EI*[1], II, 884.

9. A summary of the entry "Democracy," from which this quotation is also taken, in *The Fontana Dictionary of Modern Thought*, ed. Alan Bullock and Oliver Stallybrass (London, 1977) [hereafter Bullock and Stallybrass], p. 161.

10. *An Analysis of the Munir Report*, ed. and trans. Khurshid Ahmad (Karachi, 1956), pp. 12–16.

11. Kenneth Cragg, *Counsels in Contemporary Islam*, Islamic Surveys 3 (Edinburgh, 1965), p. 15.

12. Kalim Siddiqui, *Beyond the Muslim Nation-states*, p. 10.

13. Introduction by 'Alī Davani to *Mahdī-yi Maw'ūd*, his translation of Vol. XIII of the *Bihār al-Anwar* of 'Allāma Majlisī (Tehran, 1345/1966), p. 111.

14. Bernard Lewis, *The Middle East and the West* (London, 1963–64), p. 114.

15. An unsatisfactory term. Anyone who calls for a return to the "fundamentals" of his faith is in a sense a "fundamentalist." For a discussion of this issue, see Roger M. Savory, "Ex Oriente Nebula: An Inquiry into the Nature of Khomeini's Ideology," in *Ideology and Power in the Middle East:* Studies in honor of George Lenczowski, ed. Peter J. Chelkowski and Robert J. Pranger (Durham and London, 1988), pp. 339–62 [hereafter Savory I]. Perhaps the term "zealots," as used by Arnold J. Toynbee in his chapter "Civilisation on Trial," Chapter 10 of *Islam, the West and the Future* (1948), would be preferable.

16. Toynbee, op. cit., pp. 194–95.

17. Toynbee , op. cit., p. 195. Toynbee was writing before the advent of present-day sophisticated terrorism. He doubtless had in mind such events as the attack on the zeriba at Omdurman by Mahdist forces in 1898.

18. W. M. Watt, *Islamic Revelation in the Modern World* (Edinburgh, 1969), p. 1.

19. I. M. Husaini, quoted in Gustave von Grunebaum, "Some Recent Constructions and Reconstructions of Islam," in *The Conflict of Traditionalism and Modernism in the Muslim Middle East*, ed. Carl Leiden (Austin, 1966), p. 146.

20. See Roger Savory, "Muslim Perceptions of the West: Iran," in Bernard Lewis, Edmund Leites, and Margaret Case, editors, *As Others See Us: Muslim Perceptions, East and West* (New York, 1985–86).

21. Muhammad Taqi Ja'fari, "Theocracy and Democracy," in *Al-Tawḥīd* (Islamic Propaganda Organization, International Relations Department, Islamic Republic of Iran, Tehran) I, i (Muḥarram 1404/October 1983), p. 132.

22. Said Amir Arjomand, in his book *The Shadow of God and the Hidden Imam: Religion, Political Order and Societal Change in Shi'ite Iran from the Beginning to 1890* [hereafter Arjomand] (Chicago, 1984), claims that an accommodation *was* made in Qājār times, and cites the *Tuḥfat al-mulūk* of Āqā Sayyid Ja'far ibn 'Alī Isḥāq Kashfī (died 1850–51), in support of his view (pp. 226 f.). But "one swallow does not make a summer," and I would contend that, in default of further evidence, Kashfī's theory was not accepted by the majority of Qājār *'ulāmā'*. Arjomand's claim (p. 229) that "Kashfī's political theory can be taken to represent the unified normative order that governed the relations of authority in the Qājār body politic" is contradicted by his allusions to the high state of tension between the hierocracy and the shah during the reign of Nāṣir al-Dīn Shāh (1848–96).

23. For a detailed discussion of this theory, see Roger M. Savory, "The Problem of Sovereignty in an Ithna 'Ashari ("Twelver") Shi'i State" in *Middle East Review*, XI, iv (Summer 1979), pp. 5–11; reprinted in Michael Curtis, ed., *Religion and Politics in the Middle East*, Westview Special Studies on the Middle East (Boulder, 1981), pp. 129–38 [hereafter Savory II]; and "Religion and Government in an Itnā 'Ašarī Šī'ī State," in *Israel Oriental Studies*, X (1983), pp. 195–210 [hereafter Savory III]. See also Hamid Algar, *Religion and State in Iran 1785–1906: The Role of the Ulama in the Qajar Period* (Berkeley and Los Angeles, 1969), pp. 1–44.

24. Bullock and Stallybrass, p. 640.

25. In recent times, there has been a proliferation of *mujtahids*, and an escalation of hierarchical ranks and titles resulting from the debasement of the rank of *mujtahid*. The date of the first use by some *mujtahids* of the title *āyatullāh* [lit.: "miraculous sign of God's power"; in Qur'ānic usage, *āyāt* are the *vestigia Dei*], is disputed, but the title was probably coined about the time of the 1905–9 Constitutional Revolution. Because the term *āyatullāh* has in turn become devalued, it has been necessary to create a new category of *āyatullāhhā-yi 'uẓmā*, or "Grand *Āyatullāhs*."

26. *Constitution of the Islamic Republic of Iran*, trans. Hamid Algar (Berkeley, 1980), Article 4, p. 29 [hereafter Algar II].

27. Both quotations from Algar I, p. 55.

28. Algar I, p. 56.

29. Algar I, p. 56.

30. Algar I, p. 56 (my emphasis added).

31. Algar I, p. 57.

32. Algar I, p. 48.

33. Algar I, p. 124. One infers from this that *wilāyat-i faqīh* was in place even during the period of the Lesser Occultation (A.D. 873–940), when it was, of course, not needed.

34. On this point I disagree with Said Amir Arjomand. On his position, see, for example Arjomand p. 269.

35. E. G. Browne, *The Persian Revolution of 1905–1909* (London, 1966), p. 374.

36. Algar II, p. 29.

37. Algar II, p. 29.

38. 'Abdul Hadi Ha'iri, *Shi'ism and Constitutionalism in Iran* (Leiden, 1977), p. 232.

39. Algar II, p. 36.

40. Algar II, pp. 51–52.

41. Articles 32; 39; 37 and 38. See Algar II, pp. 39–41.

42. See Savory I. See also Amnesty International, *Law and Human Rights in the Islamic Republic of Iran: A Report Covering Events Within the Seven Month Period Following the Revolution of February 1979* (February, 1980), p. 7; and list of post-revolutionary executions till 12 August 1979 (pp. 136–88).

43. Algar II, p. 37.

44. Algar II, p. 37 (my emphasis added).

45. Algar II, p. 91 (my emphasis added).

46. Algar I, p. 297 (my emphasis added). See also Savory I.

47. Algar I, p. 298.

48. Algar II, p. 32.

49. Algar II, p. 32.

50. Algar II, p. 49.

51. Algar II, p. 93.

52. Algar II, pp. 67–68.

53. Algar II, pp. 67–68; 70.

54. See Algar II, pp. 85–86.

55. Algar II, pp. 73–74.

56. Article 2 of the Supplementary Fundamental Law of 1907; for the full text, see Savory III, pp. 202–3.

57. Article 91; Algar II, p. 60.

58. Ibid.

59. Article 93; Algar II, pp. 60–61.

60. Algar II, p. 62.

61. Algar II, p. 62.

62. For a full discussion of this ideology, see Savory I.

63. See *EI*[1], article "Tawḥīd" by D. B. Macdonald.

64. Alī Sharī'atī, "The World-View of Tauḥid," in *On the Sociology of Islam*, trans. Hamid Algar (Berkeley, 1979), pp. 82, 86 [hereafter Sharī'atī].

65. Sharī'atī, p. 86.

66. Sayyid 'Alī Khamene'i, "Al-Tawḥīd (Qur'ānic Monotheism) and Its Social Implications," in *Al-Tawḥīd*, I, iii (Rajab 1404/April 1984), pp. 55–77 [hereafter Khāmana'ī].

67. Khāmana'ī, p. 56.

68. Khāmana'ī, p. 63.

69. Ibid.

70. Ibid.

71. Khāmana'ī, p. 64.

72. Ibid.

73. Ibid.

74. Alī Sharī'atī, "The Ideal Society—the *Umma*," in *On the Sociology of Islam*, trans. Hamid Algar (Berkeley, 1979), pp. 119–20.

75. C. A. O. van Nieuwenhuijze, *The Lifestyles of Islam* (Leiden, 1985), p. 145.

49
The Jewish Courtier Class in Late Eighteenth-Century Morocco as Seen Through the Eyes of Samuel Romanelli

Norman A. Stillman and Yedida K. Stillman

MUCH HAS BEEN written about individual court Jews in the history of the Islamic world. A great deal of recent scholarly writing in particular has been devoted to the Jewish courtiers and their class ethos in medieval Muslim Spain.[1] Bernard Lewis has himself made a number of valuable contributions to the literature on Jewish courtiers from various lands and various periods of Islamic history.[2] There is as yet, however, no definitive study of the phenomenon comparable to Selma Stern's monograph on the *Hofjude* in seventeenth- and eighteenth-century Central Europe,[3] and such a work remains a major desideratum.

Most of the depictions of Jewish courtiers in the Islamic world tend to be fairly positive, if not even laudatory. This is due in no small measure to the official, "establishment" nature of many of the Jewish sources. It is also due to the fact that some of the best known Jewish courtiers were indeed extremely talented administrators, financiers, or diplomats, as well as men of piety and learning who were deeply devoted to the welfare of their coreligionists. Among these may be included men such as Neṭīra and his sons in ʿAbbasid Baghdad, Ḥasday ben Shaprūṭ in Umayyad Córdoba, Samuel ben Naghrēla in Zirid Granada, and Don Joseph Nasi in Ottoman Constantinople.

This generally complimentary image of Jewish courtiers from Muslim lands is, understandably, not always found in the Islamic sources, which usually have relatively little to say about the *ahl al-dhimma* at all, and about Jews even less. When they do make mention of any non-Muslim government officials, they frequently exhibit a marked hostility toward them. In fact, Lewis has observed that "probably the commonest single form of complaint" registered against *dhimmīs* in Islamic sources is their serving in high office.[4] The very existence of unbelievers in government positions was considered by many Muslims to be a violation of the theoretical contract of protection between the *dhimmīs* and the Islamic state.[5] However, since there was often a wide gap in Islamic history between the ideal and the actual, Islamic jurists did make some allowances for *dhimmī* participation in government service within certain carefully prescribed boundaries, although the issue remained one of continuous debate.[6]

The present paper examines another important source on the subject of court Jews in Islamic lands—in this instance, Morocco of the late eighteenth century. This intimate and, on the whole, damning portrait comes from the pen of the early Haskala writer Samuel Romanelli, an Italian Jew, who during the years 1786–90 was stranded due to the loss of his passport in the Sherīfan Empire of Morocco. Romanelli has left us a gripping account of his sojourn there entitled *Massā' Ba'rāv* (Travail in an Arab Land).[7] The book was first published in Berlin in 1792 and has enjoyed considerable popularity with Hebrew readers ever since, appearing in no less than nine editions. Aside from some excerpts and brief summaries, no full translation of the work has been made into any European language.[8]

While in Morocco, the resourceful Romanelli, who in addition to his literary talents was an accomplished linguist fluent in ten languages, was compelled to live by his wits. During the first year of his stay in Morocco, Romanelli found his livelihood in such varied occupations as preaching in the synagogue, teaching Spanish, translating for foreign sea captains in the port of Tangier, and acting as secretary for European consuls, among them the Habsburg representative and pioneer Orientalist Franz von Dombay.[9]

In January 1788,[10] Romanelli began his intimate acquaintance with the Jewish courtier class of Morocco when he entered the service of Elijah Levi, one of the most powerful Jewish secretaries of Sultan Sīdī Muḥammad ibn 'Abdallāh (1757–90). Like most of the Moroccan

Jewish courtiers of the period, Elijah Levi acted as an intermediary for the sultan with foreign merchants and consuls, and his name appears in the correspondence of several European consulates.[11] Like other members of the Sephardi elite in Morocco, he was useful to the Makhzen (the Moroccan government) because of his knowledge of at least one European language—Spanish[12]—and because of his contacts with the international network of Sephardi merchants in Gibraltar, Europe, and the Near East.[13]

Concerning Elijah Levi's outward appearance, Romanelli tells us relatively little, saying that he was a man well on in years and that his face was pitted with pock marks. The only other physical feature he notes is Levi's beard which had only recently grown in again after having been cut off by order of the sultan when the Jewish official had fallen into temporary disgrace.[14] Levi's personality, however, is given a much more ample description. He was, according to Romanelli, "craftier than any serpent or than all the beasts of the field. He was secretive in everything he did; not a thought would pass from his lips. He would reward profusely all who publicized his glory, while depriving anyone who darkened his good name or brought disgrace upon him."[15]

Such behavior was, of course, not unusual among courtiers and other members of the elite of power in Islamic countries. In traditional Middle Eastern and North African societies, rank and distinction were—and in many cases still are—considered to be divinely ordained. Modesty was not a virtue for the powerful, since station was to be recognized, not glossed over.

As a general rule, however, Jews holding high office had to show some prudence in their conduct because of their anomalous and precarious situation. Elijah Levi did not exhibit any such caution. "He was," according to Romanelli, "king of the arrogant and would walk proudly erect, speaking as though his words were a mighty wind. He would even dare to pass an Arab mosque without removing his shoes in a display of his power at court so that all would come to fear him."[16] Elijah Levi even dared to ride his mule directly into a Berber market, openly flouting the provision of the Pact of 'Umar in its Moroccan form which forbade Jews from riding except on the open road outside of Muslim settlements. The people in the market, not knowing who the Jew was, fell upon him and would have killed him. Romanelli informs us that Elijah did not lose his nerve, but began to shout and haughtily informed them that he was a royal servant. "When he mentioned the king, they trembled at his words and were stunned by his approach."[17]

According to Romanelli, it was fear more than anything else that courtiers like Elijah Levi inspired. He portrays them as a group—Muslims and Jews alike—to be with rare exceptions vicious, venal abusers of power who themselves lived continually on the brink of destruction. As Romanelli describes them:

> Such people, whether Jew or Gentile, are merely instruments of the Sultan. As long as the Sultan needs their services, they are valuable instruments. But if they lose the Sultan's favor for even a moment, they are lost forever like their own excrement, and those that knew them will ask, "Where are they?"[18] They are feared, not loved. Capable only of evildoing, they know nothing of benevolence. They thrive on the destructions of others. They would disown their fathers and mothers, seeing nothing of them. They would not recognize their brothers, nor would they even know their own children. Such a man would befriend another in word and win his heart, present him with a gift, and then return to plot his murder. They draw the mighty with false hopes and drag the young in their terror. But as they stand upon their heights of greatness, the abyss widens under their feet.[19] One word from the Sultan's mouth and they vanish. A nation will groan under their rule; a town will rejoice at their death. The majority of them will not die as most men do, nor will they be judged like other men—"whether by sentence of death, or corporal punishment, by confiscation of property, or imprisonment."[20] Their bodies might be cut up, and their homes turned into dunghills.[21] I have found only one in a thousand who graced others with his goodness. Not a single one of them has come to a natural end.[22]

This general indictment of the courtier class, or *ṣḥāb al-sulṭān* ("the intimates of the ruler") as they were known in eighteenth-century Morocco,[23] is not merely a rhetorical flourish of hyperbole. Romanelli amply backs up his sweeping general condemnation of courtiers such as Elijah Levi with numerous reports of corruption, deceit, and intrigue. In one episode, for example, Levi is told that he has been cheated by a business associate.[24] In another episode, Jacob Attal, a Tunisian Jew and one of the sultan's favorites, describes a rare clock in the home of another Jewish courtier just to arouse the sultan's cupidity so that he will confiscate it.[25]

Of all the accounts of intrigue, the most terrifying is that of the Cardozo brothers from Gibraltar. One settled in London, while the other two came to Morocco and entered the sultan's service. For a while they associated with Elijah Levi, but eventually there was a falling out, and the latter plotted revenge. He brought a letter to Sīdī Muḥammad which he had taken from the Cardozos' business file. The letter was from the brother in London, who in reply to an invitation by his brothers in Morocco, wrote that he preferred to remain where he was rather than expose himself to danger in a country where "both the king and the people are untrustworthy, and there is only destruction in their midst." Elijah Levi tore off the first half of the letter and brought the offending part to the sultan alleging that it was the Cardozo in Morocco who had written the insulting passage. Levi's rival was immediately seized, tortured, and killed. The youngest Cardozo was put into prison, where he had been languishing for two years when Romanelli met him.[26] Romanelli's account of the Cardozo affair is fully corroborated by the Venetian consular correspondence of the period.[27]

Although denouncing a fellow Jew to the Gentile authorities has always been regarded as an extremely serious offense in Jewish law,[28] the practice was not unknown among the Jewish courtiers of eighteenth-century Morocco as a means of punishing or eliminating rivals and enemies. Elijah Levi's behavior in the Cardozo affair was not without parallels. Earlier in the century, the well-known Jewish courtier Moses ben ʿAṭṭār, who served under Mūlāy Ismāʿīl, denounced two Jewish brothers to the sultan for having struck a Muslim, as a result of which they were tortured severely. When a Jewish court found Ben ʿAṭṭār guilty of maliciously informing upon fellow Jews and ordered him to make restitution, he publicly tore up the court order.[29] Powerful courtiers such as Moses ben ʿAṭṭār and Elijah Levi were simply above Jewish communal jurisdiction—a fact admitted with regret by Jewish legal authorities of the period, such as Rabbi Jacob Abenṣūr.[30]

Romanelli does not depict Elijah Levi as having much interaction with the Jewish community. He never mentions him in any role of confessional leadership or patronage of institutions or scholars. Neither does he ever speak of him attending study sessions in the yeshiva, even though such sessions are mentioned several times throughout the narrative, with Romanelli giving the names of important people in attendance. He only notes that when Levi did show up in the synagogue on the Sabbath following his reinstatement in office, he expected a *piyyūṭ* (a liturgical poem) to be sung in his honor when he was called up to the Torah. This was a particularly important propaganda gesture for Levi after his temporary disgrace, in order to "renew his glory in the eyes of the Jews."[31]

Elijah Levi's personal lifestyle was more in keeping with that of a Muslim grandee than a Jew. Romanelli informs us that he had three wives, all of whom could be found—at least some of the time—under the same roof and were constantly feuding over conjugal rights.[32] Now although bigamy was not unknown among Moroccan Jews, especially among the *Tōshāvīm* (Jews of native North African ancestry, as opposed to the *Megorāshīm*, or Jews of Iberian origin), polygamy was extremely rare.[33] Romanelli mentions one or two wealthy Jews as having two wives, but only Levi as having three.[34] He also mentions his having houses in several of the imperial cities—again, something only possible for a member of the courtier elite.

One of the rare Jewish courtiers described by Romanelli who seems to have been a glowing exception to the unpleasant rule was R. Mordechai de la Mar (or, al-Baḥḥār in Arabic) of Mazagan. He is portrayed as the very antithesis of the sinister Elijah Levi: "wise, honest, and God-fearing."[35] According to Romanelli, the difference between the two men "was the superiority of light over darkness."[36] While traveling, he shared his own tent, his food, and even his bedding with Romanelli. "He spoke kindly and gave orders as if requesting a favor."[37] Such a gentle and humble demeanor for a courtier was most unusual to say the least. For even R. Mordechai al-Ḥazzān Bekkā of Meknes, the only other powerful Jewish courtier to be described as "learned and honest gentleman" who genuinely "looked after his people's interest," is also reported to have gone beyond all bounds in his hubris, being the only Jew to "ride through the marketplace and the streets while smoking."[38]

Unlike Elijah Levi, R. Mordechai de la Mar was loved by his people. When he came to Marrakesh, all the Jewish women came out to greet him with music and dancing, and the rabbinical council and communal leaders came to inquire after his welfare. When he was summoned to appear before the sultan, "the Jews prayed and fasted on his behalf so that he would be treated mercifully."[39]

R. Mordechai is the only Jewish courtier in the book whom Romanelli shows having Muslim friends. In fact, when he is betrayed by the malicious Jacob Attal, it is R. Mordechai's friend, the pasha of Dukkala, who warns him of the danger and helps him to escape.[40]

Most of the Jewish courtiers whom Romanelli knew met a violent end when Mūlāy Yazīd succeeded his father in 1790. The new sultan harbored a grudge not only against his father's former advisers in general, but against the Jewish community in particular, and his relatively short but bloody reign began with a famous series of anti-Jewish persecutions.[41] Elijah Levi was seized and severely beaten. When condemned to death, he embraced Islam and was spared—although he died shortly thereafter.[42] Jacob Attal tried to convert to Islam, but was not allowed to , and his mouth was gagged with an iron collar. According to Romanelli, he was torn apart.[43] R. Mordechai al-Ḥazzān Bekkā was given the choice of death or apostasy, but chose to die a Jew.[44] As for R. Mordechai de la Mar, the only courtier to be positively depicted in the book, Romanelli reports that he had no word of him and expresses the hope that perhaps Divine Providence and R. Mordechai's own personal righteousness would somehow protect him and that he would survive the disaster.[45] Since Romanelli finally succeeds in escaping from Morocco just at this time, he can offer no further details.

The fate of the Moroccan Jewish courtiers described by Romanelli in his eye-witness account accords well with Bernard Lewis' general observation regarding Jewish (and, of course, Christian as well) court figures in the Islamic world:

> But this kind of power, like the authority from which it derived, was always precarious. It could be ended abruptly and painfully by the death or ousting of the ruler, by the loss of favor of the favorite, or by a simple change in political circumstances. Such a fall, after such a rise, could often be disastrous for the family and the community of the incumbent, who rose and fell with him.[46]

NOTES

1. For court Jews in the Muslim East, see Walter J. Fischel, *Jews in the Economic and Political Life of Mediaeval Islam*, 2d ed. (New York, 1969); and S. D. Goitein, *A Mediterranean Society II: The Community* (Berkeley and Los Angeles, 1971), especially pp. 374–80. For court Jews in Islamic Spain, see Joseph Weiss, "Tarbūt ḥaṣrānīt ve-shīra ḥaṣrānīt: berūrīm le-havḥānat shīrat Sefārād ha-'Ivrīt," *World Congress of Jewish Studies*, I (Jerusalem, 1952); Eliyahu Ashtor, *The Jews of Moslem Spain* (Philadelphia, 1973–84), 3 vols.; Norman A. Stillman, "Aspects of Jewish Life in Islamic Spain," in *Aspects of Jewish Culture in the Middle Ages*, ed. Paul E. Szarmach (Albany, 1979), pp. 51–84; and especially Gerson D. Cohen's essays and notes to his edition and translation of Abraham Ibn Daud, *Sefer ha-Qabbalah* (Philadelphia, 1967).

2. Bernard Lewis, "The Privilege Granted by Mehmed II to His Physician," *BSOAS* XIV (1952), pp. 550–663; idem, "Paltiel: A Note," *BSOAS* XXX

(1967), pp. 177–81. See also his translation of the chapter dealing with Joseph ben Naghrēla's downfall, from Sultan 'Abdallāh's *Kitāb al-tibyān* in Lewis (ed. and trans.), *Islam from the Prophet Muhammad to the Capture of Constantinople* (New York, 1974), I, 123–34.

3. Selma Stern, *The Court Jew: A Contribution to the History of Absolutism in Europe*, with a new introduction by Egon Mayer (New Brunswick, 1985).

4. Bernard Lewis, *The Jews of Islam* (Princeton, 1984), pp. 28–29.

5. See A. S. Tritton, *The Caliphs and Their Non-Muslim Subjects: A Critical Study of the Covenant of 'Umar* (Oxford, 1930), pp. 18–36.

6. According to al-Māwardī, the great theoretician of Islamic government, a *dhimmī* could hold an "executive vizierate" (*wizārat al-tanfīdh*), but not one with genuine authority to command (*wizārat al-tafwīḍ*). See al-Māwardī, *al-Aḥkām al-sulṭānīya wa'l-wilāyāt al-dīnīya* (Cairo, 1960), p. 27.

7. The most complete biography of Romanelli and survey of his works is Ḥayyim (Jefim) Schirmann, *Shemū'ēl Rōmānēllī: ha-Meshōrēr veha-Nōdēd* (Jerusalem, 1968). The fullest account in English is Norman A. Stillman and Yedida K. Stillman, "Samuel Romanelli and his *Massā' Ba'rāb*," *Hebrew Annual Review* IX (1985).

8. The editions are enumerated and described in Schirmann, *Shemū'ēl Rōmānēllī*, App. A, pp. 73–74. The present writers are in the final stages of preparing a complete, annotated English translation of the *Massā' Ba'rāv*. Many articles and bibliographies cite an English translation by Solomon Schiller-Szinessy, the Hungarian-born British scholar. The latter had planned such a translation as the Second Part of his Hebrew edition (Cambridge, 1886), and its scheduled publication for 1887 was even announced. However, it never appeared.

9. Concerning Dombay, whose many contributions to Oriental Studies include the first grammar of colloquial Moroccan Arabic, see Norman A. Stillman, "A New Source for Eighteenth-Century Moroccan History in the John Rylands University Library of Manchester: The Dombay Papers," *Bulletin of the John Rylands University Library of Manchester*, LVII (1975), pp. 463–86. Romanelli had a very high regard for Dombay whom he refers to only as "the Viennese gentleman." See Romanelli, *Massā' Ba'rāv*, pp. 39, 46–47.

10. Not December 1787, as in Schirmann, *Shemū'ēl Rōmānēllī*, p. 23. Romanelli, *Massā' Ba'rāv*, p. 76 tells us that it was in the Hebrew month of Shevat, which with the exception of 1785, always began during January in the eighteenth century. See Eduard Mahler, *Handbuch der jüdischen Chronologie* (Leipzig, 1916), Table, p. 586.

11. See e.g., Pierre Grillon, *Un Chargé d'affaires au Maroc: La Correspondance du consul Louis Chenier, 1767–1782* (Paris, 1970), I, 175–76; Enrico de Leone, "Mohammed Ben 'Abdallâh e le Repubbliche Marinare," *Il Veltro* VII (1963), p. 677; Haus-, Hof- und Staatsarchiv, Vienna, Marokko Karton 3.

12. Romanelli, *Massa' Ba'rav*, p. 77 makes a point of saying that Levi spoke to him "in pure Spanish." That is, not in Haketia, the Judeo-Spanish vernacular of the Sephardi Jews of northern Morocco.

13. Ibid.

14. Ibid., pp. 76 and 77.

15. Ibid., p. 77.

16. Ibid.

17. Ibid., p. 87.

18. Paraphrasing Job 20:7.

19. See Isaiah 5:14.

20. Ezra 7:26.

21. Daniel 2:5.

22. Romanelli, *Massā' Ba'rāv*, p. 78.

23. Ibid. For the use of *ṣḥāb* (Classical Arabic *aṣḥāb*) in Moroccan Arabic, see Louis Brunot, *Textes arabes de Rabat II: Glossaire* (Paris, 1952), p. 423–24.

24. Romanelli, *Massā' Ba'rāv*, p. 86.

25. Ibid., p. 111.

26. Ibid., pp. 79–83.

27. See Enrico de Leone, "Mohammed Ben 'Abdallâh e le repubbliche marinare," p. 677.

28. Haim Hermann Cohen, "Informers in Jewish Law," *Encyclopaedia Judaica*, VIII, cols. 1370–73.

29. Shalom Bar-Asher, "The Jewish Community in Morocco in the 18th Century: Studies in [*sic!*] History of the Social Status and Self-Government of the Jews of Fes, Meknes, and Sefrou." Ph.D. diss. (Jerusalem, 1981), p. 45 (Heb.). Ben 'Aṭṭār also seems to have been responsible for the death of three innocent Jews (ibid., pp. 44 and 138, n. 22). By contrast, David Corcos, a modern Jewish historian, describes Moses ben 'Aṭṭār as "pious, generous, and learned," and notes that "he built and maintained many schools for poor children." See D. Corcos, "Atar," *Encyclopaedia Judaica*, III, col. 812. This, of course, is entirely consistent with the idealizing tendency which we noted at the beginning of this paper.

30. Shlomo Deshen, *Individuals and the Community: Social Life in 18th–19th Century Moroccan Jewry* (Tel Aviv, 1983), p. 47 [Heb.]; also Bar-Asher, *The Jewish Community in Morocco*, p. 45 [Heb.].

31. Romanelli, *Massā' Ba'rāv*, p. 84. (Even today, it is not uncommon to have such poems recited—and often composed extemporaneously—when an important personage is called to the Torah.)

32. Ibid., pp. 98–99.

33. See Haïm Zafrani, *Études et recherches sur la vie intellectuelle juive au Maroc de la fin du 15ᵉ au début du 20ᵉ siècle. Première Partie: Pensée juridique et environnement social, économique et religieux* (Paris, 1972), pp. 90–94; also Jane S. Gerber, *Jewish Society in Fez, 1450–1700: Studies in Communal and Economic Life* (Leiden, 1980), pp. 62–63.

34. Romanelli, *Massā' Ba'rāv*, pp. 42 and 110.

35. Ibid., p. 105.

36. Ibid., p. 108.

37. Ibid.

38. Ibid., pp. 110–11.

39. Ibid., p. 109.

40. Ibid., p. 111.

41. Concerning these incidents, see H. Z. (J. W.) Hirschberg, *A History of the Jews in North Africa* (Leiden, 1981), II, 292–301; and Norman A. Stillman, "Two Accounts of the Persecution of the Jews of Tetouan in 1790," *Michael* V (1978), pp. 130–42.

42. Romanelli, *Massā' Ba'rāv*, pp. 136–37.

43. Ibid., p. 136. The English physician William Lempriere, who was also in Morocco at this time, describes Attal's fate slightly differently. According to him, Attal's hands were cut off, and after being allowed to linger in this state for three days, he was beheaded. See William Lempriere, *A Tour from Gibraltar to Tangier, Sallee, Mogodore, Santa Cruz, Tarudant; and Thence Over Mount Atlas, to Morocco: Including a Particular Account of the Royal Harem, &c.*, 2d ed. (London, 1793), p. 466. (This account is not included in the first edition of Lempriere's book.)

44. Romanelli, *Massā' Ba'rāv*, p. 138.

45. Ibid., p. 140.

46. Lewis, *The Jews of Islam*, p. 91.

50
Oriental Studies as an Instrument of Intercultural Communication

C. A. O. van Nieuwenhuijze

Introduction

ORIENTAL AND AFRICAN studies, like Islamic and other religious studies, are increasingly being recognized as belonging to the encompassing genus of cross-cultural studies. Another such instance is anthropology.

In these studies, the self-effacing role of the scholar has, since the Enlightenment, been taken to be axiomatic. The established historical-philosophical methodology is explicitly subservient to this ideal.

In the context of decolonization this image has, of late, been rudely challenged. The claim to objectivity has been exposed as a fraudulent device to disguise, and indeed to bolster, ethnocentrism, not merely as a natural posture, but as a ruthless practice. That is carrying the matter rather far.

It is not the purpose of this paper to deny the inherently instrumental nature of cross-cultural studies. The belief that they are strictly a case of *l'art pour l'art* is certainly charming, yet hard to substantiate. There is also room for a more utilitarian, less idealistic appreciation. However, if this, in turn, is to be credible, it should not set out from misrepresentation of the setting in which such studies play their role, namely, intercultural transactions or intercultural communication. Given the multiple occurrence of sociocultural collectivities (tribes, nations, etc.), this phenomenon is inherent in the existence of mankind.

To single out, for the purpose of challenging the idealistic vision of cross-cultural studies, one specific manifestation of this setting as the point of departure for one's challenge is bound to entail a short-circuiting in the argument. This, in turn, can but jeopardize its validity. Thus, if it be true that, wittingly or inadvertently, certain instances of Oriental and similar studies have played the role of handmaiden to colonialism, this could, nonetheless, not be read as meaning that the inherent ethnocentrism of such studies will invariably cause them to be colonialist. For proof, it suffices to recall that they were in full swing prior to the advent of colonialism.

It is perhaps typical of the mood of decolonization that these studies should now be accused of being such. Still, decolonization is at least as much future-oriented as it is retrospective. Rather than a backward-looking approach, one may elect to adopt a more prospective manner in elaborating a thesis regarding the instrumental nature of cross-cultural studies. Besides, there must be ways of avoiding the contamination of general considerations (such as the issue of ethnocentrism) and the specifics of one time-and-place-conditioned situation (such as the phenomenon of colonialism).

This paper is devoted to a description and discussion of two early attempts to come to grips with this alternative kind of exercise. It sets out from two considerations, one referring to the general, not to say basic, problem, and the other to the forward-looking aspect of contemporary concerns. The basic consideration is that as an instrument of intercultural transactions, cross-cultural studies have an inherent problem of ethnocentrism. Their methodologies are accordingly bound to reflect a systematic effort to "control for it," as the sociologists say, or, if you prefer, to domesticate it. The specifically forward-looking approach, under contemporary circumstances, sets out from the realization that, given a global prospect of collective interaction or interdependence, intercultural transactions and their instrument, cross-cultural studies are bound to acquire increasingly vital significance for the survival of mankind.

The occasion is provided by the interactions of the European Common Market (EEC = European Economic Community) with some of its partners abroad.

In the Lomé-III convention of 8 December 1984, the EEC has added a second dimension to the intercultural dialogue in which it has, notwithstanding the limitations of its formal aims, found it proper to engage. The first of these is the Euro-Arab Dialogue. The second concerns the so-called APC countries: countries in Africa, the Pacific, and the Caribbean which, on the strength of former colonial ties to what is now an EEC member state, stand in a special relationship to the European community as a whole.

In both cases, cultural concerns have been recognized as afterthoughts, so to speak. They have not been part of the initial considerations informing the decision to engage upon regular cooperation. Thus, when they entered the picture, the fact that they did so was noteworthy in itself.

It is now proposed, first, to review quickly how the cultural dimension came into view in each case, and then to consider the inevitably experimental way in which it has been handled thus far. In so doing, it will be possible to tease out the instrumental role of Oriental and African studies.

Culture in the Euro-Arab Dialogue

"Euro-Arab Dialogue" is the official name of a formal engagement of the EEC and the League of Arab States (for short, the Arab League) first launched by President Pompidou at the European summit in Copenhagen in December 1973, just after the eruption of the oil crisis. Disrespectful of solemn statements of purpose, some skeptics hold that it began and then continued endlessly as a deaf men's dialogue. What prompted the European initiative was an acute need to safeguard access to oil. The Arabs instantly saw and seized their opportunity to seek support for their handling of the Palestine problem in international forums. In the backdrop remains, hazy yet compelling, the feeling that, since both regions lie under the threat of fallout from superpower competition, they should be able to build protective strength through joint effort.

Both sides have stubbornly persisted in working at cross purposes. In the intial motives, there was no mutuality of interest. Of course, they have identified and pursued other purposes, of more clearly mutual significance, as they have gone along; but somehow these remain in the shadow of the uneven match of primary motives.

The aims effectively pursued have proliferated and eventually been assorted under a number of headings. Each of these is attended to by a joint committee at ministerial level. Thus, Committee no. 7 deals with social and cultural affairs. In committee work, the representatives of ministries of member countries on both sides are more conspicuous, in all their diversity, than the common institutions of each. There is, moreover, a glaring absence of permanent and adequate liaison, for lack of a duly equipped clearing house. The price paid for jealously guarded national sovereignty is high indeed.

Committee 7, mostly entangled in thankless nitty-gritty about migrant labor and incidental activities in the recondite realm which bureaucrats refer to as culture, decided, some seven years ago, in favor of a conspicuous and symbolic event, namely a cultural symposium. For once culture—however defined—was chosen as the arena in which the Euro-Arab Dialogue should prove meaningful and effective.

A "specialized group," not so much representative as competent, was created for the purpose. Crossing countless hurdles, including the fallout from the Camp David accords, this group eventually convened a successful colloquium, organized in Hamburg by the Deutsches Orient Institut. The proceedings have meanwhile been published in Arabic, English, and French editions. (English version: D. Hopwood, ed., *Euro-Arab Dialogue: The Relations Between the Two Cultures, Acts of the Hamburg Symposium, April 11th to 15th 1983* [London: Croom Helm, 1985].) I shall have more to say about the substance of this symposium.

Budding Cultural Dialogue Between EEC and APC

EEC-APC contacts are a different matter at root. They represent the aftermath of the colonial bond in such a way as to enlarge, on both sides, the definition of the entities concerned. The reference is to Europe instead of, say, Britain or France, and to the APC countries instead of, say, Senegal or Jamaica. The object of the relationship is the natural sequel to enlightened colonialism, namely, the uplift of recently independent states to a condition of material well-being loosely described as advancement. The privileged means are access to the European Common Market and development assistance. Here again, mutuality of interest is more a matter of intent than of actual realities.

Apparently, there is in this case little risk of a deaf men's dialogue. Actually, as those concerned begin reluctantly to realize, rather more commonality of views and purposes has been assumed to exist than was effectively operational. There are now disenchanted minds ready to concede that the audible consensus about aims and means of development has been to a large extent a matter of one closed circuit of teachers and their pupils. (The Institute of Social Studies in The Hague, to mention one example, has, on the strength of a faculty of just over 50, built, in just over 30 years, a body of well over 3,000 alumni spread over all countries of the Third World. Calculated on the strength of the number of development training facilities, with and without the name, in the "advanced" countries, the size of the resulting network, invertebrate yet holding closely together in terms of ideas, must be staggering.) But once the pupils have had to fend for themselves in performing development tasks, their world has invariably proved less amenable to their ready recipes than they had been led to believe it would be, what with development theory being claimed to be "general." As if this problem of the relevance of the established development paradigm were not enough trouble, the props are at the same time falling from underneath it, as the Western *philosophie vécue* from which it derives falls upon hard times. Under such conditions, there is clearly more to the stalemate in the North-South dialogue than the unbridgeable demands of selfishness on both sides. This state of affairs in turn is bound to reflect in goings-on between EEC and APC.

In comparison with the Euro-Arab Dialogue, it could appear as an advantage that in this case, the procedural elements pivot upon accords each of which was concluded for a limited period. This makes for built-in updating of implementation on the strength of feedback from recent experience, and should make for enduring clarity and adequacy of aims and purposes; all the more so if it becomes reflected in appropriate joint institutionalization.

It is thanks to the latitude of movement provided by the renewal of conventions that cultural considerations have been introduced, clearly in line with current rethinking of development theory and practice. The Lomé-III convention is innovative, precisely in that it contains a significant number of quite specific references to culture, and creates room for appropriate provisions. The catchwords are "cultural dimension and social implications" of development cooperation (Title I, chap. 2, art. 10).

On 13–15 June 1985, a private colloquium, jointly organized by French and Belgian agencies (JFT: Joint Task Force on Development Issues, Brussels: Institut Robert Schuman pour l'Europe, Paris: Centre Culturel "Les Fontaines," Chantilly), was devoted to a first reconnoitering of implications and possibilities. Concerning this meeting I shall also have more to say.

Culture: An Afterthought?

The skeptic will observe that in both cases, the resort to a cultural approach or focus—singling out the cultural dimension, as it is often called—is an evasion rather than an authentic strategy. Were it not for acute problems with the practice of the standing development paradigm, few would be ready to adopt this course, leading into what they insist on considering as nonessentials. Support for it is, on the part of many, as yet a matter of the benefit of the doubt. All this is no valid reason to write it off in advance. Necessity is, after all, one of the few forces capable of prompting new beginnings, ventures into the unknown.

How are such ventures initiated? It is in search of an answer to this question that I propose to take a closer look at the two meetings just mentioned.

In so doing, it is to be kept in mind that both have inevitably been double-barreled propositions, even though perhaps not intended as such. They were at once initial exercises in intercultural dialogue and joint efforts to envisage the aims and modalities of such dialogue. Altogether a typically human situation.

The Hamburg Symposium

To the organizers of the Hamburg symposium, certain potential stumbling blocks were readily predictable.

There was, for example, the possibility, not to say probability, that some European Arabist would hold up a mirror to the Arabs present in such a manner that these would turn away in dismay, leaving the instigator of the mishap to guess the reason. On the Arab site there exists the inclination, urgent on account of ongoing sociocultural change, toward idealizing self-presentation. This is made in hope of a response in terms of empathic recognition, yet at the peril, seldom taken into account, of sterile admiration. On both sides, the monologue of ethnocentric preoccupation threatens to nip dialogue in the bud.

There is also a matter of imbalance, on several counts. For example, in Europe it customarily requires an Arabist, or a person who passes for one, to address matters Arab. Anyone else is a noninitiate, not supposed to have the information on which to base an opinion. Among modern-educated Arabs, virtually anyone can claim a measure of familiarity with things European and, by consequence, the entitlement to an opinion. It is no doubt for this same reason that the average

Arab intellectual sees no need for Occidental studies as a special scholarly concern.

Besides, there is imbalance in the modality of self-presentation. Europeans tend to present themselves in terms of problematic issues, Arabs in terms of self-respect, occasionally verging on apologetics (not just religious apologetics).

Then there is imbalance regarding the underlying conception of culture. The European perception wavers between two unreconciled notions, one narrow and segmentary, the other broad and comprehensive. The Arab notion, until recently less expressive of a vital concern, tends to appear as a congeries of incidental interests, many of them variously named and several of a somewhat academic, not to say esoteric nature. Matters of actual interest, that by Western terminology would belong in the cultural bracket, may be known under different, more specific names. One of these, nowadays, is "religion." What both sides have in common is a certain reticence about culture as a categorical notion, no doubt under the impact of felt sociocultural change. Cultural identity, or something to that effect, is sensed to be at stake. Notwithstanding all the talk about cultural activities (in the bureaucratic sense of the term), certain inhibitions or distortions are at play where culture is at issue in intercultural encounters.

Under such circumstances, a joint exercise in considering cultural backgrounds (it was felt that nothing less would do) was bound to be a daunting, indeed hazardous venture. This is where methodology enters the scene. The obvious need was for a procedure fostering true dialogue, a real and effective meeting of minds. Listening would have to be recognized as the precondition to self-expression.

Two devices have mainly been adopted for the purpose. One is to limit initial presentations to self-presentation, in such a manner as to be accessible to the other side. The other is convergence of interest on topics, or preferably issues, designed to be readily accessible to both sides, whether in one phrasing geared to the perceptions of both, or in two optimally symmetrical phrasings each attuned to the specific perception of one side. The combination of these two devices paves the way for effective exchanges. Participants from one side are induced to address those of the other side with questions rather than with statements.

Here are some illustrations of topics designed for convergent treatment, phrased as paired titles: "Literature, theater, and film in the Arab world as symptoms of cultural change: a general discussion of present trends," linked to "Western-European literature, theater and art: cultural change in public debate"; "The post-modern Western civilization of Western Europe: the significance of transition for the Euro-Arab Dialogue," in conjunction with "Arab civilization in contemporary times: the internal and external dimensions of a phase of transition and its significance for the cultural dialogue with Western Europe." With such topics, and granted a degree of symmetry in the approach employed by each of the two speakers, the path toward dialogue is wide open.

Practice has made it clear that the assumption of an adequate degree of symmetry of treatment has its limitations. In fact there is every reason to be cautious in one's expectations in this regard, precisely in view of the fact that participants are present in their capacities as bearers of different civilizations. The redeeming factor, curious to see, is nothing other than that which the current preoccupation with cultural identity will soft-pedal or indeed ignore, namely, shared background of modern training in advanced scholarship. Consciously or unawares, the academics who gather in international scholarly meetings do speak a common language of discourse. It depends, to an extent, on the topic whether this language will be sensed to be adequate, and hence prove applicable.

The Hamburg program featured one topic on which two speakers turned out to speak different languages. It was phrased, for the Arab speaker, as "Religion and the modern spiritual revival in the Arab countries: its meaning for the cultural dialogue with Western Europe —withdrawal or rapprochement?" and for the European as "Religion and secularization in Western Europe: their significance for the cultural dialogue with the Arab world." The European presentation was descriptive-analytic; the Arab one was in terms of conviction. Each was excellent by its proper yardstick. Between them, the discussion failed to achieve its focus.

In retrospect it is easy to see that more briefing of the speakers, at the peril of seeming overbearing or indeed unacceptable, might have been in order. This, however, does not take care of the basic issue, of culture-conditioned difference in style of treatment of a given subject. To this problem I propose to return in a while.

The Chantilly Colloquium

The colloquium on the cultural provisions of Lomé-III started by doing what the Hamburg symposium had avoided, namely, addressing the notion of culture in its categorical sense. The Hamburg topics had been either a matter of specific issues in specific civilizations at a given time or, at a maximum admissible level of generality, the condition and prospects of a given civilization at a given juncture.

Ambassador Raymond Chasle, of Mauritius, credited with most of the effort toward the introduction of "culture" into Lomé-III, introduced the theme of the colloquium by asking attention for the meaning of the term, in a presentation that could well serve as an updating of the noted work by A. L. Kroeber and Clyde Kluckhohn, "Culture, a Critical Review of Concepts and Definitions" (Harvard University, *Peabody Museum Papers* XLVII, i [1953]). Such an exercise is necessarily inconclusive, but somehow it helped to give the audience some common ground or shared mood for the discussions to come.

These were anchored in two further topics. One was a double-entry topic of roughly the same kind as used in Hamburg. For the European side it was entitled (in my translation) "Cultural identity crisis, technical progress, and economic transformation in Europe," and for the APC side it read "The relationships between the promotion of cultural identities and economic and social development in the APC countries." If mutuality of perspective was intended, it had not been made explicit. The other topic was "The social and cultural implications of economic, financial, and technical cooperation."

On paper, an EEC-APC encounter on topics like these appears an immensely complicated proposition. In practice, this complexity was trimmed down to more workable proportions by the actual composition of the body of participants. On the European side the French-speaking element, both French and Belgian, was predominant, and on the APC side French-speaking Africans made up the large majority. This togetherness has its established pattern of discourse, and it was this which facilitated—and characterized—the proceedings to a considerable extent.

Whether on this account, or simply due to the nature of the succession of Lomé accords, the centerpiece of the discussions has been the accentuation of culture, in the categorical sense, as a crucial consideration in development cooperation. There has been hardly any addressing of issues of common interest within the cultural context of the two sides, as in Hamburg. The reference was steadfastly to culture, or African culture, categorically.

This had intriguing implications. For the purposes of the debate it proved necessary, time and again, to set out from the existence of one African culture, not by way of a working hypothesis or, for that matter, as an ideal or a deeper essence, but simply as an effective datum. It is this culture—so it was repeatedly maintained—that has to be referred to as the proper frame of reference for development thinking and action. Almost in the same breath, however, demands were made for the resuscitation or revitalization of this civilization, in what could sound like a replay of the earlier mood of *négritude*. Certainly to the non-Africanist, this coincidence raises fascinating questions.

For one, to what extent is the reference to one effective African culture a statement of fact? Or is it rather an expression of the ongoing struggle to achieve an up-to-date cultural identity, standing above pernicious tribalism, and capable of responding to the challenges emerging on all sides? It could appear as if those setting out from one African culture as an effective datum were anticipating, whether constructively or merely in a mood of wishful thinking, the prospective outcome of efforts under way. No doubt such efforts (for example Alassane Ndaw, *La Pensée africaine: Recherches sur les fondements de la pensée négro-africaine* [Dakar: Les Nouvelles Editions Africaines, 1983]) in turn are symptomatic of the struggle for cultural identity, which is far from being just a matter of scholarly exercises.

Another question refers to the implications of the implicit reification of a culture in the act of assuming it to be effectively given and, as such, serviceable first as the frame of reference for both the conception and the practice of development, and second, as the guideline for development cooperation. One is instantly reminded of the adverse consequences such reasoning may have. Think of the Iranian situation since the Khumaynī revolution. There, a given cultural norm, labeled "religion," is being literalistically employed as a Procrustean bed by means of which to manage public affairs, including development. A scary prospect indeed. Fortunately, there was no evidence that anyone invoking the idea that culture is somehow the frame of reference for development was ready for this kind of consequence; perhaps because such an idea would hardly be African.

A more important stricture refers to the consistent categorical use of the notion "culture." True, the established development paradigm ignores culture, to the extent of ignoring its own basically cultural nature. But the belated introduction of a cultural aspect or dimension cannot remedy this, because the straw that breaks the camel's back is something else. Due to the combination of an economistic-mechanistic bias and of a claim to universality, there is no way of ascertaining the effective relevance of the development paradigm to the specific conditions under which it is being put to work. We have adopted an inevitably clumsy mode of speech in trying to express the resulting embarrassment. We say that it ignores the cultural reality and misses the boat as a result. But "cultural" here means nothing but the full specificity of reality which eludes the restrictive focusing of economism. The crux of the matter is relevance; the role of the notion "culture" is no more than to serve as a ready reference to that which eludes the grasp of the development profession. Culture is, so to speak, their blind spot.

This conclusion will, however, remain inconsequential unless and until one is ready to be specific, by referring not to culture categorically but to its live specificity of a given time and place. All that can be hoped to result from categorical talk is some initial sensitization of one's audience. During the preparations for the July 1985 world conference of the Society of International Development, the largest development lobby in the world, a good deal of ink and effort was spent on introducing a cultural perspective. In the actual proceedings, lip service was paid to culture, in such a way as to prevent it from rocking the boat. It remained, for all practical purposes, a supererogatory consideration, tolerated in order not to displease its advocates. The problem is, clearly, that in order to render justice to the kind of considerations of which the reference to "culture" is symptomatic, one has to change one's discourse altogether. "Rethinking development" has to do with fundamentals of outlook, not just modalities of procedure.

This having been said, it remains to admit that initial sensitization may have its uses. Events in Chantilly provided the jumping board for a move into a discussion of desirable institutionalization of the cultural concern as a newly identified cause in need of promotion. There is nothing against this. The state of the Euro-Arab Dialogue is proof of the lamentable consequences of inadequate institutionalization. Still, there is no skipping essentials. The task left unattended to by the colloquium will have to be tackled. Institutions of the kind envisaged will readily shape up as promotional lobbies, if only for reasons of self-maintenance. As such, they will have to bank on the outcomes of fundamental work done, rather than undertaking it.

The Rules of the Game

In the course of the argument thus far, a few loose ends have been left unresolved. It is time to assemble them, in an attempt to clarify matters a little further, if possible. Once this is done, cross-cultural studies may be taken into consideration. The emerging issues come under four headings: actors, roles, script, and scene.

ACTORS. Those participating in intercultural exchanges, whether consciously or—more often—unwittingly, are rarely expert in intercultural transactions. The same holds true, shocking to say, of those whose profession or avocation is cross-cultural studies. "The other" is the object of their study, on which they report to their own kind. (This goes to the extent that the expatriate Arab teaching in an American or European university will pose as a Western Orientalist with added facility of language and perhaps access to sources, and address his writing about the alien Arab world to a Western public with which he is bound to identify for the purpose.) Interaction with "the other," not always considered indispensable, is mostly a mere tool of observation.

The imminent conclusion, that "ne'er the twain shall meet," is kept under cover by procedural means. One of these is that findings about "the other" are not supposed to concern him, or indeed to be noticed by him. I recall how a study on an Egyptian topic that at the time was mildly sensitive politically was published in a European language generally unknown in the Arab world, in order, as the author volunteered to explain, to avoid unnecessary trouble. This was certainly shrewd, but was it wise? Another device, already mentioned, is that intercultural communication is conducted in a nominally common language which, upon closer consideration, is derived from the language of one side as acquired by the other. In Euro-Arab encounters where, say, Arabic, English, and French are in use, the common mode of expression, regardless of language used, is of a kind holding the middle between the French and British modes, and of the three, Arabic is adapted the most. The net result is that the actual problem of cross-cultural exchange shifts from the demarcation line between participants belonging each to his or her own civilization, toward and, indeed, into the minds of those who, regardless of their cultural roots, have partaken of the other civilization. The common language serves, then, as a mask suggesting workable resemblance as a common trait between parties concerned. This type of situation is far too obvious to be overlooked. Indeed it is regularly and at times incisively discussed. (An excellent example is Abdallah Laroui, *La Crise des intellectuels arabes: Traditionalisme ou historicisme?* [Paris: Maspéro, 1974]. Another one is Moncef Chelli, *La Parole arabe: Une Théorie de la relativité des cultures* [Paris: Sindbad, 1980]). Still its implications are rarely spelled out in a measured way.

The upshot is that, while intercultural communication is steadily increasing and increasingly crucial to the survival of mankind, those in positions to engage upon it are and remain ill-equipped to do their job. Ethnocentrism distorts their perception and blocks their way. The extreme illustration is, of course, the contemporary politician in charge of foreign affairs, whose every move is closely checked for conformity to the preoccupations of home politics, as informed by the stereotype images of the world abroad prevailing among the electorate and reinforced by the media. It is no doubt superfluous to add, concerning this situation, that institutional provisions, such as a New International Information Order to be decreed by governments, are to no avail, doomed as they are to substitute one, possibly more virulent, ethnocentrism for another.

ROLES. The division of roles concomitant to the natural posture of participants in intercultural transactions is conducive to nothing so much as a deaf men's dialogue. The case of Malinowski's Trobrianders (*Argonauts of the Western Pacific* [London 1922, repr. New York: Dutton, 1961]), who exchanged goods by a system dispensing with actual encounters, is an extreme institutionalization, but nonetheless an accurate illustration of the normal wariness about mutual involvement resulting from natural ethnocentrism on both sides. Where encounters are unavoidable, "the other" will inevitably feature as a mirror reflecting "self." The perception of the other thus gained will invariably be manipulated in search of the most pleasing, that is, self-reinforcing, reflection. Idealizing self-presentation, indeed vindication of self, are inherently part of the act.

As discussed, there exist certain procedural devices for avoiding extreme consequences. At intercultural meetings, one can ask each side to initiate the exchanges by means of a self-presentation purposively geared to being accessible to the other with his different premises and concomitant approach. The image one has of the other, being an integral part of one's own self-perception, could, and perhaps should, be included in such self-presentation. To the extent that this requirement anticipates a perception of the other not entirely conditioned by one's own ethnocentrism, it could appear to be asking for the impossible. This difficulty stands to be lessened, however, given the reciprocity marking the entire exercise. As stated, listening is a precondition to self-expression. The image of the other is relevant only insofar as it is part of the makeup of self. It is in this, and only in this, quality that it has to be explicated.

SCRIPT. International and intercultural transactions are seldom prompted by manifest common interest inducing joint effort. More frequently, not to say normally, it is a matter of coincidence of different, perhaps competing or, indeed, conflicting interests forcing an encounter. This may be in terms of negotiation and conciliation, or of antagonism and hostility. The prompting motives of the Euro-Arab Dialogue are by no means exceptional. Nor should it be difficult to discern an equally discordant configuration of interests at the cradle of EEC-APC intercourse.

Upon closer inspection, the nexus of development problems is a significant case in point. The relationship between "developed" and "developing" parts of mankind, apart from being, to a considerable extent, the result of reified definitions of an overly categorical nature, has all the ambiguities of intercultural exchange. This goes to the extent of implying dependency on both sides, rather than on one, as is still too often said to be the case. Besides, it illustrates how the complexities of interaction between cultures will be at once obfuscated and hampered by a smokescreen of allegedly common perception and procedure: the case of the shared technical language discussed before. Seen in this light, the current demand for "rethinking development" proves to have far-reaching implications of a most fundamental nature. It inquires into the nature of intercultural interaction in the context of, first, sociocultural identities going through sociocultural change on each side, and, on top of that, global change as it affects the several sociocultural components of mankind. At the same time, it exposes the veil of common language and understanding (in this case, the established development paradigm) employed hitherto as being wide open to challenge, and outdated to boot.

Given this state of affairs, it would be unrealistic to demand or expect that in meetings such as those described, significant results might be achieved by a random assortment of persons, however expert each may be in his own way, who have never worked together before. It is already something if some of the right questions begin to be adumbrated. This applies to the Chantilly meeting. It also applied to an earlier seminar of the Konrad Adenauer Stiftung, in which development features as one out of a range of topics identified as significant in the perspective of the budding Euro-Arab dialogue (H. Dobers and U. Haarmann, eds., *The Euro-Arab Dialogue* [Sankt Augustin bei Bonn:

Konrad Adenauer Stiftung, 1983]). Such realistic consideration is, however, no reason for desisting. On the contrary, it shows the need to persevere.

In persevering, the search for topics of discussion designed to make for convergence of interests stands out as a promising device. In organizing a second Euro-Arab dialogue seminar, this time on technology, the Konrad Adenauer Foundation has adhered to this idea, with encouraging results. (Publication, edited by H. Dobers, forthcoming.) It has also been adopted for the annual Euro-Arab Dialogue Lecture sponsored by the Luftiya Rabbani Foundation in The Hague, Holland.

Besides, and perhaps even more importantly, there is cause to recall a largely forgotten approach initiated by Hans Leisegang (*Denkformen*, 2d ed. [Berlin: Walter de Gruyter, 1951]) and also implied by Karl Jaspers (*Psychologie der Weltanschauungen*, 4th ed. [Berlin: Springer, 1954]). Given the plurality of world views and concomitant thought patterns and lifestyles, one has two options. One of these is the search for metalanguage; the other is the laborious and painstaking effort of direct comparison on the strength of incidental comparabilities identified, with transposition as an ultimate prospect. The former runs the risk of leading into endless and fruitless regression, of the kind illustrated, with regard to time, by another forgotten author, J. W. Dunne (*An Experiment with Time* [London: Faber & Faber, 1958]). The latter is currently attracting some attention in circles of computer experts such as Joseph Weiszenbaum (*Computer Power and Human Reason: From Judgment to Calculation* [New York: Freeman, 1976]). The experience being gained and the ideas being developed in this field do appear to have a bearing on the topic of present concern.

SCENE. The setting of intercultural transactions is not to be taken as a given. Of course, it is to a significant extent a determinant of what can and will be enacted. But upon closer consideration, the relationship between actors and setting is one of reciprocity: if not in the short term (as the great delusion of development thinking would have it), then certainly in the longer term.

The actual condition of a culture or civilization, once identified as a matter of concern in itself, is inherently ambiguous. It is, beyond doubt, a given reality, apparently reifiable to a tantalizing degree (and this not just to the inventorizing anthropologist). On the other hand, it is an elusive context in which individuals and collectivities are immersed in a manner and to a degree for which it is extremely difficult to account. This involvement is to an extent a matter of effort necessarily spent; in another respect, it is an encompassing process undergone. To complicate things further, cultures are inherently open systems. This is the face of the coin countervailing that of ethnocentrism. Contrary to what would seem to be the consequence of ethnocentrism, intercultural transactions, whether manifest or latent, whether dramatic or insignificant, are normal. If it might appear that the open system pattern is the exception to the rule of ethnocentrism, the obverse is equally the case.

Most of these considerations are lost upon the day-to-day self-identification of the actors: more so, strange to observe, when their actual significance is greater. To be conscientious in regard to these is a matter of deciding to pay attention to what in the daily run of affairs tends to remain below the horizon—a specific task to be identified and attended to.

The Role of Cross-Cultural Studies

This remark at last leads the argument back to its chosen topic, the use or function of cross-cultural studies. My proposition is that the considerations just briefly presented add up to a challenge addressed to cross-cultural studies. A market demand that is being reinforced as it changes. A new opportunity.

That this implies a need for reorientation seems beyond doubt. Both the image of "the other," and the interaction with him to which it is instrumental, are subject to an irreversible change of the perspective in which they feature. Self-realization, rather than remaining a virtually autonomous act, will increasingly appear as one element of interaction, which in turn is conditioned by interdependence. Self-vindication to the point of domination, even exploitation, of the other is currently being exposed as eventual self-destruction.

Images of "the other" will continue to be formed and upheld. But henceforth, they will increasingly prove to have a double destination, namely the one—individual or, more probably, collectivity—producing and using it, and the one portrayed. Image as vehicle of interaction. A new criterion is added for the purpose of assessing its validity, namely, whether those portrayed will consider it fair.

Accepting this need for reorientation, what about practical implications? I propose to envisage these taking Oriental, more specifically Arab and Islamic studies as a case in point. Emergent issues can be assorted under four headings, namely addressing, matching, mediation, and method. These are, of course, less cryptic than I make them sound.

ADDRESSING. The matter of the double address of Arabist or Islamicist information released has far-reaching consequences for the demands made upon the person engaged in Arab or Islamic studies. He or she must be able to anticipate the *optique* not of one, but of two kinds of readership. This poses two sets of problems.

The audience or readership in his own culture area has changed. Depending upon the topic chosen, it may nowadays be much wider than the circle of fellow Arabists and Islamicists. If in the past a somewhat esoteric appearance of work published could rate as acceptable, or indeed proper, there is now a broadening public waiting to be informed—at once an obligation and a temptation. If apparently esoteric work remains indispensable for certain purposes such as, say, making classical texts accessible, one has to count with the emergence of a parallel *Literaturgattung* alongside. On the other hand, there is a budding and growing Arab-Islamic audience, or rather, readership. They claim perfect competence on their own terms, and are increasingly critical.

The further implication is that the Arabist-Islamicist can no longer limit himself to total immersion in Arab-Islamic civilization as the sole precondition for his work. Once the public is wider than the circuit of peers, Western civilization and religion, having inevitably featured all the time as the tacitly yet quite effectively presupposed frame of reference for the scholarly work being done, will have to be accounted for explicitly. A backstopping by systematically acquired knowledge, on the part of the Orientalist, of his Occidental civilization is henceforth indispensable. On it depends the feasibility of the comparison that is more and more required toward reciprocal clarification. Henceforth, it will not do for the Orientalist to disclaim competence concerning his own civilization. The practical question is, then, what constitutes the appropriate level of such competence.

MATCHING. A situation where Oriental and similar studies conducted by Westerners are unmatched by reciprocal and countervailing studies by "the others" is anomalous. It is typical of colonialism, a phase of both Western and world history that begins more and more to resemble an interlude, marked as it has been by the predominance of one culture area, not just over another one, but virtually over all others. That most of us continue to consider it to be normal is simply due to the fact that we have grown up in a world constellation of which colonialism was a significant feature.

A normal situation, certainly in a world of increasing collective interaction in ever more intensive interdependence, would be the matching of Oriental by Occidental studies, and a concomitant enrichment by cross-cultural studies worldwide, conducted between any one culture area and another. The result would be a network of reciprocal cross-cultural studies covering the civilizations into which mankind happens to be divided.

The relative simplicity of this prospect is somewhat disturbed by existing conditions.

One, already mentioned, is the circumstance that Arab-Islamic studies nowadays are conducted by a scholarly community consisting not only of Westerners, but also of a growing number of expatriate Arabs, many of them Muslims. It would be a mistake to think that this makes for the reciprocity just meant. To all of these scholars, the Arab world and Islam are the subject-matter of investigation, and all of them use the same sources and methods. The main practical requirement the Arab/Muslim Orientalist has to face is that he meet the same career criteria as his Western colleagues and competitors. Their natural *optique* is consequently reversed to a considerable extent. The resulting unease will occasionally flare up and cause further confusion.

The other cause of trouble, also mentioned before, is the reliance, for purposes of cross-cultural communication, upon a technical language with which one party identifies, and which the other adopts for the purpose. This shifts the locus of the encounter away from the actual cultural divide, toward the inner workings of one side. The net effect there is the problem, sometimes accentuated and on other occasions hushed up, of cultural identity as envisaged and indeed, experienced by a spearhead group such as the "modern" Arab intellectuals. It is occasionally alleged that traditional Arab/Islamic scholarship is unaffected by such complexities and perplexities. This contention ignores the way the several types of Arab scholarship are necessarily interwoven. The most salient illustration is al-Azhar (comp. A. Chris Eccel, *Egypt, Islam and Social Change: Al-Azhar in Conflict and Accommodation* [Berlin: Schwarz, 1984]).

A further difficulty, affecting the emergence of Occidental studies, is that they have to take form in a time of decolonization. The overtones of self-assertion induced by this circumstance are inevitably more ambiguous than might have been the case under different conditions. If, as a result, mistakes are made such as Westerners used to make during the successive stages of colonialism, those making them now can feel excused or even justified. But mistakes they remain.

As regards Occidental studies there exist, then, three attitudes. Some will engage in them, while giving free rein to pent-up reactions. Others will desist, out of concern lest they commit the errors to which this leads. Yet others are too preoccupied with things at home to bother. Suspended among these three orientations hangs the prospect of Occidental studies, for the time being. It is hardly improved by redeeming factors. There is, as yet, scanty academic reward for scholars venturing into them. Exercises in cultural identity, reflecting an isolationism that may or may not have use for ethnocentric reference to the West, take precedence. And those international agencies charged with the task of fostering effective intercultural exchanges tend to be remiss any time the need for initiatives announces itself. Still, the need is there.

One may perhaps speculate on whether, pending the development of Occidental studies (and not only in the Arab world), cross-cultural work among non-Western civilizations stands to be hampered. The question is, which is the better way of toning down the fascination with the West to healthy proportions: studying the West, or studying something else. I propose to leave it unanswered, as it carries us too far beyond our present scope.

MEDIATION. The new aspect of the role of cross-cultural studies, currently being added to the preexistent ones, is mediation and facilitation, not for one, but for both sides to given intercultural encounters (many of these not identified as such). The Arabist and the Islamicist—to limit the argument to these cases again—have, so to speak, a role of outreach in addition to their traditional one of feedback. No doubt, the most felicitous manner of playing it will be in conjunction and in cooperation with their counterparts, the Occidentalists on the other side. Awaiting the effective appearance of the latter, they will have to stand in as best they can, anticipating the necessary completion of the equipment for intercultural transactions. Anticipation, in a situation like this, may have the welcome side effect of prompting.

Let me illustrate the prospective result, by suggesting a clarification in the division of roles employed in meetings such as the Cultural Symposium of the Euro-Arab Dialogue and the Euro-Arab Seminar on Technology of the Konrad Adenauer Foundation. In both events, the primary need was for Europeans and Arabs thoroughly familiar with the subject matter on the agenda, as featuring in the context of their respective civilizations. In certain cases, this meant active involvement in the culture concerned. This requirement has precedence over the desirability that those invited on each side should be sufficiently conversant with the other civilization to get their message across. Indeed, were one to add this as a second requirement of equal importance, one would risk limiting the number of eligible persons so much that no meeting could be convened. Nonetheless, the need is for presentations fully accessible to the other side, and prepared with this aim in mind. It is in helping to resolve the problem arising at this point that cross-cultural expertise has a crucial role to fulfill. It is the function of facilitating, indeed making possible, the transfer of information from (and typical of) one cultural orbit into a different one. This function is bound to have various manifestations, ranging from program design to clarification, spontaneous or upon request, during the proceedings. It is by no means unlikely that out of experience gained in this very practical role a new Orientalist/Occidentalist *Literaturgattung* might eventually emerge.

METHOD. One can readily envisage a number of difficulties that will emerge and have to be surmounted before the reorientation envisaged can take effect successfully. The central one, by no means novel, is the need to account for ethnocentrism in a more effective way than hitherto, so as not to jeopardize or indeed preclude intercultural communication.

Available methodologies, notably the historical-philological one, and that of the social sciences, are felt to be inadequate, each for reasons having to do with its own characteristics. Whereas the former has a problem of comparison for lack of a capability to identify comparables, the latter suffers from a spurious claim at universality inspired by rampant ethnocentrism. On the other hand, they seem to be too similar at the level of basic conceptualization for their competition to trigger an effective, eventually creative *Methodenstreit*.

It may perhaps help if, instead of looking for method in the framework of the classical subject-object relationship presupposed in objectifying scholarship (common to both methods just mentioned), one were to concentrate on intersubjectivity, not just as the procedure of exchanges, but as the cement which holds reality together. The occasion could not be more propitious. It appears, however, that the fascinating vista opening up here is beyond our present scope.

51
State and Class in Egypt: A Review Essay

P. J. Vatikiotis

EGYPT HAS ATTRACTED students of history, economic and political affairs since time immemorial. Herodotus in antiquity, Islamic writers in the Middle Ages, European travelers in the seventeenth, eighteenth- and nineteenth centuries have all left records of their impressions of that country. Scientists and scholars recruited by Napoleon Bonaparte accompanied him on his expedition of conquest to Egypt in 1798. They produced a massive, multivolume encyclopedic work about the country.[1] After the British occupation of Egypt a century later, British administrators wrote prolifically about it. Developments in the nineteenth century and the involvement of European powers in the affairs of Egypt gave rise to a massive literature about the country, especially in English, French, and Italian.[2]

At the turn of the century, writers on Egypt concerned themselves with its agricultural and financial problems, and its relations with Britain. After the Second World War, they considered its new Arab-Islamic role in the Middle East, its leadership of radical nationalist movements, its confrontation with the new state of Israel, and its role in the rivalry between the superpowers. Events after 1952 reclaimed the attention of even a wider community of students and authors, fascinated perhaps by that country's intractable economic and social problems on the one hand, and by its tenacious continuity and survival on the other. Egypt simply seemed to be there with its teeming millions, eternal Nile, and its long-suffering and patient, albeit changing, fellah. For the last half-century, Egypt has held a prominent position and played a leading role in the affairs of a proliferating number of neighboring independent states, exhibiting a capacity for innovation, leadership, economic and political experimentation, literary flair, and cultural primacy in the Arab world. Now students are once again examining Egypt's economic, social, and political problems generated by its rapidly increasing population, its dwindling resources, and its somewhat changed relations with its neighbors and the superpowers.

Until, say, 1952, writers on public and international affairs focused their studies of Egypt on the domestic political struggle among the monarch, the party politicians, and the British who were still occupying the Suez Canal. They also noted the country's efforts to rid itself of the British presence—and connection—and the impact of this policy on the region's security and its relations with external powers. After 1952 students were attracted by the new military regime in Egypt, its wars with Israel, its radical Arab policy, and its new state capitalist economy with its radical measures of agrarian reform, nationalization of commercial and industrial concerns, sequestrations of property and other assets, the abolition of political parties, and experimentation with single-party political arrangements. Dominated as the new regime was for nearly two decades by the charismatic Gamāl 'Abd al-Nāṣir, the attraction of Egypt to students of contemporary history and politics was that much greater. When after 1955 Nāṣir forged a close alliance with—and became dependent on—the Soviet Union, the interest of students of strategy and international relations was aroused further.

There were attempts to consider the "new" Egypt as representing a breakthrough in the political and economic development of states in the Middle East and Africa, and as constituting a model of the non-European national socialist experiment and an example of a non-aligned neutralist country able to exploit to its advantage the rivalry between the superpowers, the United States of America and the Soviet Union. The interpretations offered ranged from the ideological to the pragmatic. After the death of Nāṣir in 1970 his successor, Sādāt, embarked upon unexpectedly radical policies, when he reversed the direction of his country's domestic economic policies and, to some extent, political arrangements, as well as its external orientation. Thus, the link with the Soviet Union was abruptly severed in 1972 in favor of a restoration of relations with the United States and the West. The radical Arab policy of the recent past was abandoned in favor of a rapprochement with the more conservative, but significantly oil-rich Arab states in the region. At home, a systematic whittling down of the near total state control of the economy was undertaken in conjunction with the abolition of the single-party political organization in favor of a more diffuse, albeit centrally controlled, pluralist or multiparty system. Most arresting was the dramatic ending of the state of war with Israel and the signing of a peace treaty with that country in March 1979. This one act alone had immediate repercussions in the Arab Middle East and among the great powers.

Books assessing the record of the Nāṣir regime appeared both during his tenure of office and after his death.[3] A great deal of writing was also occasioned by President Sādāt's new policies.[4] The fact that ex-soldiers ruled Egypt since 1952, that is, for more than three decades, whatever the variations in style and differences of policy orientation between one chief of state and another, still raises the same questions. How have they dealt or how are they dealing with certain perennial problems of domestic policy: the economy, political arrangements, and institutions and social matters.

These questions are being raised at a time when essentially the same elite is in control of the country's affairs and when militant Islamic perceptions are on the ascendant, challenging the legitimacy of this elite, whose perceptions, incidentally, are not all that different. The governing elite and the religious militants share the same reverence for the classical Arab tradition, the tradition of the "Muslim Fathers," of the language of their revealed scriptures. In short, they partake of the same romanticism regarding the tradition and the past. They pay the same lip service to Arab unity, despite the reality of the Arab world's fragmentation. The governing elite is on the whole reticent and meek in criticizing the social and political condition of their country. The Islamic militants, on the other hand, are vociferous, violent, but unoriginal in their proposals to remedy it. The real difference between them perhaps is to be found in the governing elite's willingness to modernize the economy and society by borrowing money, ideas, and skills from abroad, while at the same time clinging to their romantic view of the tradition. In this way, they avoid the discomfort and trauma of a reinterpretation of, or even a break with, that tradition. In this way too, their handling of vital problems remains opportunistic, mechanical, and voluntary, but as yet never seemingly original, or drastically new. They continue to succumb to the pressure of a vision of society and this world held by a completely different civilization and culture—that of the West—that is, modernity, which at the same time they wish to oppose and reject because of different perceived interests and in order to preserve their own cultural heritage and identity. Westernization, they fear, will alienate them from this heritage. Yet their insistence on an identification with a great tradition and past culture causes them to succumb to an even more debilitating kind of alienation. The religious militants on the other hand reject this approach as being un-Islamic.

The books considered here address themselves to the recurrent problems of Egyptian domestic policy, namely, the economy, political arrangements and institutions, administrative and social matters. They also neatly divide themselves into an examination of the political economy and public policy of Eygpt, the administrative and bureaucratic aspects of Egypt's development programs and aspirations, and the structure of political power. They all concentrate on the post-1952 period. The one exception which deals with the interwar period is nonetheless critically relevant to any discussion of the economic and political features of post-1952 Egypt.

John Waterbury's *Egypt: Burdens of the Past, Options for the Future*[5] is a collection of essays and reports written for the American Universities Field Staff (AUFS) over a period of five years. It is a passionate exposition of the enormity of the economic and political problems faced by Egypt, and the hard choices that must be made by Egyptians if they are not to starve by the end of the century. To this extent, Waterbury's presentation of the problem is aimed at the illumination of public policy and vice versa. He formulates the problem in stark, realistic—even desperate—terms:

> The fact is that the triangular relationship between land, man and water in Egypt has become so strained that any and all solutions must be considered regardless of their cost. Ultimately, the final solution may be the relegation of the agricultural sector to a role of minimal significance in Egypt's economy, and that, in turn will depend on the success of the industrialization effort. But the conundrum remains: the agricultural factor must carry the economy by providing surplus value, domestic buying power, and foreign export earnings, at the same time that its masters plan its demise. It is a moot question whether or not Egypt will be able to make the transition without trials even more severe than those of the last twenty years;[6]

and suggests that in the struggle between right and left, the recent move to the right is

> in essence marginal to the more fundamental question of economic policy, investment programme, supplying needed public services and even more

importantly essential consumer goods to a growing population buffetted by inflation and relative fixed wages.[7]

He comes to the conclusion that if Egypt is to continue to feed its population and remain economically viable, it requires no less than a technological revolution "for the country simply to hold even." Along with Egyptian experts, Waterbury can see no ideal plan for land use and crop allocation that will meet Egypt's food needs. In this connection, he asserts that Arab unity and/or economic integration is an economic necessity for Egypt, not a political choice. He is not too sanguine, however, about its prospects, given the fact of inter-Arab political rivalries and the conflict with Israel.

In the second volume of his trilogy on Egypt, *Hydropolitics of the Nile Valley*, published a year later,[8] Waterbury takes up the more complex, wider issue of regional resource planning and its vital importance, not only for Egypt, but for all the Nile riparian states in Africa. Here he throws into sharp relief the stark lunacy of sovereign national economic planning in the face of a hopelessly interdependent major common resource, the waters of the Nile. He challenges the concept of state sovereignty and national self-interest in the face of dwindling scarce resources in the world. For Egypt, the availability of ever greater amounts of Nile water forces her to be embroiled in the politics of the Sudan in particular, and of Africa in general. He recognizes the early steps toward hydrological integration that were taken under British control as of the 1890s, and considers the so far unsuccessful attempts at the economic integration of the Nile Valley, that is, Egypt and the Sudan, as well as the problems posed by political unity should it ever be achieved. Professor Waterbury emphasizes the importance of regional and international resource management if countries like Egypt and the Sudan are to survive economically, let alone prosper, in the future, for they remain vulnerable and their security is at stake.

Having surveyed Egypt's economic requirements and considered the kind of national, regional, and international policies needed for the well-being of the Nile Valley, Waterbury proceeds to an evaluation and assessment of the political economy of the Nāṣir and Sādāt regimes, covering the thirty-year period from 1952 to 1982.[9] He correctly, in my view, rejects the contention of enthusiastic social scientists that a "bourgeoisie" or rural "middle class" sired the regime of soldiers in Egypt in 1952. In fact, he is dubious about the superimposition of European or Western notions of state and class on the Egyptian case in order to support the argument that one social class or another gives rise to a particular state or even controls it. Whatever incipient classes there may be, rural or urban, these are, according to Waterbury, "subordinate to the state bourgeoisie."

Despite the author's correct instinct—prompted by his feeling about a country he lived in for several years—that there is an "official class" which constitutes the "ruling class," some parts of his analysis remain weak, essentially because he is anxious to observe the social science idiom. Such an "official class" (or state bourgeoisie) has always existed in Egypt. The state in Egypt creates "classes," rather than the other way around. Muḥammad ʻAlī founded first a state and then the official class to help him govern it. His grandson, the Khedive Ismāʻīl, accelerated and expanded this process further. A recent monograph, *Egypt Under the Khedives, 1805–1879, From Household Government to Modern Bureaucracy*, by F. Robert Hunter,[10] supports this thesis. A detailed study of the formation, composition, and evolution of the bureaucratic elite from Muḥammad ʻAlī's household government, and especially under the Khedive Ismāʻīl, based on such sources as Amīn Sāmī, *Taqwīm al-Nīl*, and pension files of officials, the monograph depicts a new centralized bureaucracy as the greatest influence upon Egyptian political life in nineteenth-century Egypt, to the extent that this new bureaucratic elite was the main vehicle for Egypt's entry into the modern age. Its two components and mainstays of state power—the army and the civil bureaucracy—have allowed for a continuity in the exercise of state power that belies the proliferation of social forces in this century. Significantly, it is for this reason that those aspiring to power—as well as influence that may depend on economic power—seek to take over the state, the machinery of power. Achieving control of the state automatically grants one the use of the official class in its service. Only a free and open civil society can produce social classes that are interested in and can influence the nature of political arrangements and the control of the state, without necessarily having actually to administer the state, but having only to choose those who will do so.

A major attempt to argue the existence of a rural middle class, consisting of middle-size landowners and their importance to the maintenance of the Nāṣir regime, is made by Professor Leonard Binder in his *In a Moment of Enthusiasm: Political Power and the Second Stratum in Egypt* (Chicago, 1978). Borrowing from Gaetano Mosca's *The Ruling Class*,[11] and anxious to emphasize social structure rather than cultural influence in relation to the political process, Binder proceeds on the premise that a ruling elite in Egypt was formed from the rural bourgeoisie; that this bourgeoisie or middle class constituted not the ruling class, but the second stratum whose support was crucial to Nāṣir's rule. Binder, that is, assumes there are close links between the military-bureaucratic elite of the state and this rural middle class.

To be sure, during the interwar period, and particularly in the Wafd Party, a close link between the Wafd and influential Egyptians in the countryside—village *'umdas*, landowning notables—was the basis of that party's countrywide electoral success. Earlier in the century, a whole new political elite, which later became the governing class of the independent Egyptian state, had its roots in the landowning groups of the countryside. It acquired political influence and power in the Wafd. Binder, however, seems to argue that after 1952 his rural middle class suppressed both the large landowners and the interwar urban elite, to become the representatives of the Egyptian people. Nāṣir therefore had no alternative but to base his power on their support. This was the purpose of his Agrarian Reform and his other revolutionary economic measures. "In a moment of enthusiasm," this rural middle class supported the regime of soldiers.

The author then proceeds to document the existence of this rural middle class that was independently supporting the military regime, by elaborate empirical-statistical studies of the National Union and its successor, the Arab Socialist Union. Underlying this empirical exercise is the elementary notion that the development of rural capitalism nurtures a rural middle class. Needless to say, even if this is true, a sizable portion of this rural middle class quickly moves to the city to join a geographically urban, but not quite sociologically or culturally urbanite, "middle class."

If the National Union was the political organization that embodied this "second stratum," one wonders why an autocratic regime's single-state political organization for national mobilization was created by decree, that is, the fiat of the ruler in 1957 (even though ostensibly on the basis of the 1956 Constitution), and abolished by decree after the adoption of the National Charter in 1962–63 which, in turn, created the Arab Socialist Union to replace it. These changes in the fundamental political representation of the Egyptian public, and these new institutions for the legislative function of the state, reflected neither the expressed wishes of the rural middle class, nor those of any other civilian group. Nor were they the consequence of open, peaceful conflict, competition, and political debate among classes and social groups. In fact, they represented the decisions of the state/ruler, made at its convenience and on the basis of its needs.

As of 1956–57, state involvement in the direction of the national economy heralded the further development of state capitalism, the expansion of the public sector, and the greater control of the national economy by the state. Land reform, the Egyptianization of capital, and nationalization between 1952 and 1963 all implied the expansion of national state power. These measures implied, in turn, the rapid expansion of a *state bourgeoisie*, of an official "middle class" that was largely embodied in a vast military-technocratic bureaucracy. In fact, this state bourgeoisie was if anything as much of an official class created by a regime of soldiers as was the old one created by Muḥammad 'Alī's new state, or Khedive Ismā'īl's Europeanization programs. John Waterbury is closer to the mark when he rejects both the petit bourgeois and rural middle-class interests in the Nāṣir regime. In fact, he rejects a real class basis for the regime. In less sociological jargon, this simply means that the military regime took over the state official class of the country and enlarged it, so as to constitute a state bourgeoisie which it used for its own purposes.

Thus, it is unlikely that the presumed rural middle class, or any other broad social class, had a vested interest in the regime's socialist policies of the 1960s. Only the newly expanded state bureaucracy of soldiers, administrators, and technocrats did. They were the architects of the so-called socialist transformation, as well as the main cause of its failure. Neither the National Union nor the Arab Socialist Union really came close to representing the interests—corporate or otherwise—of the rural middle class or the urban petite bourgeoisie. In the end, both political institutions were shown to be the administrative-control structures of the state.

Leading members of rural and provincial society in Egypt have always been influential in local affairs, as well as crucial either as agents of or mediators with central power and authority. Their influence in an agrarian society clearly rested on their landholdings or their control over landed property and water resources. This much Professor Binder can justifiably contend. What he cannot and fails to show is that in its extensive representation in the National Union and the Arab Socialist Union, a rural middle class either influenced central power appreciably, limited it, or made it accountable, or that it was indispensable to central power's survival.

To be sure, "in a moment of enthusiasm," the military oligarchy of 1952 may have been considered by the rural—but very much so by the deprived urban—masses as reflecting, if not actually representing, their hopes and aspirations. The subsequent behavior of a vastly expanded and strengthened national state bourgeoisie, or "official governing class," suggests that its links with a rural middle class were more romantic and propagandistic, and less real or functional in social structural terms.

If one considers two other recent studies of Egypt, Professor Binder's thesis erodes even further. One of these, *Family, Power and Politics in Egypt* by Robert Springborg (University of Pennsylvania Press, 1982), is really a study of the life and career of Sayed Marei and his family. An agronomist by training and the son of a relatively wealthy provincial landowning family, Marei in his career combined politics with agriculture. In discussing his political career as a young Sa'dist deputy after 1942, Springborg highlights his dexterous use of family landed wealth and professional qualifications in pursuit of political status after 1952. The elite political culture of Egypt, however, does not lend itself to economically-based class analysis. It is very much determined and defined by the state. Thus, the state and political elite of Egypt are autonomous, that is, not dependent on a class structure. Its leading members and other recruits may often come from distinct strata of society, such as Sayed Marei's typical rural notability, but this only highlights the economic and political importance of large family and kinship groups that constitute a network from which the state political elite recruits its members.

> Families and alliances of families clearly continue to take precedence over commitment to larger and impersonal social, economic, and political organizations that have grown up in modern Egypt.[12]

To be sure, since 1952—and even earlier—aspiring members of such rural/provincial kinship groups must offer something beyond their comfortable origins or wealthy rural background. And this is usually technical-professional, military, or bureaucratic: all qualifications based on modern, secular, European-style education or training. This is not qualitatively that much different from the common route of political elite or state official class membership in the nineteenth century, if one recalls particularly the careers of 'Alī Pasha Mubārak, Rifā'a al-Ṭahtāwī, Muḥammad 'Abduh, Sa'd Zaghlūl, Aḥmad Luṭfī al-Sayyid, Taha Ḥusayn, Muṣṭafā Naḥḥās, and others of their generation or cohorts.

If one is to consider a "middle class" in Egypt at all, then its main component, according to another recent study by Nazih N. M. Ayubi,[13] is the bureaucracy, that is, the "state official class." The author argues that the stratification of society is linked to bureaucratic functions, and that there is a close relationship between the power structure and bureaucratic formations. To this extent, Egypt appears as an administrative polity, since most of the components of the political system are comprehensively bureaucratized. And because of the peculiarly long agricultural-political culture of the country, with its feature of highly centralized power, the dominant class is political rather than economic, and the top classes or strata are bureaucratic rather than socioeconomic. The last characterization is corroborated by Robert Tignor's recent study, *State, Private Enterprise and Economic Change, 1918–1952* (Princeton University Press, 1984), about which more below.

What Ayubi suggests is that the control of public bureaucracy leads to the control of the sources of wealth in Egypt. To illustrate this he uses as a case study the "developmental nationalism" of the 1952 regime. Its operational framework was that of "hydraulic politics," such as the harnessing of the Nile waters and their use for agriculture and industry, and the concentration of political power for the achievement of national goals. With such a concept, the whole developmental strategy of the regime, Ayubi argues, was technical, not ideological; organizational, not sociopolitical. In contrast to Binder's study of the National Union and the Arab Socialist Union, Ayubi puts forward the thesis that these political structures or institutions "emerged from within the existing bureaucracy and [their] internal development was more in the direction of bureaucratization than politicization."[14] Similarly, all steps toward improving the local government system were administrative in nature, since they were initiated by central authority.

Ayubi asserts that the fundamental weakness of the 1952 regime's reform and development programs was the "organizational engineering" approach to them. No attention was paid to ideas, values, attitudes, and political participation. The state control of the economy then produced excessive hierarchy. The proliferation of public organizations and central agencies to direct this command economy created a new bureaucracy; in fact, several layers of it. Within it, the connection between formal education and bureaucratic advance was promoted further, when under state socialism the new expanded state bureaucracy offered great privileges. The expanded bureaucratic elite, consisting of university-educated sons of the relatively well-to-do (whether landlords, businessmen, professionals, or soldiers) became a new privileged class of salaried state officials. These replaced the old groups of absentee landowners, the liberal professions, and the cosmopolitan financier-entrepreneurs. This "new elite," according to Ayubi,

> is not basically different from the old one, either in social background or in professional experience. . . . The only outstanding change in the characteristics of the bureaucratic leadership is that concerning education.[15]

Moreover, the country's civil service became a general—and the largest—employment agency, employing 60 percent of its graduates, and engaging nearly 35 percent of its labor force in the service sector. "The rate of bureaucratic growth," Ayubi concludes, "has thus exceeded the rate of growth in population, employment and/or production."[16]

It is the officers, technocrats, and administrators in this expanded bureaucracy, or state official class, who now constituted the middle and upper income strata of society. They became the "technicians" of development, and the implementors of the "developmental nationalism" strategy of the rulers. But to them, and according to their ethos as the core official class of a bureaucratic polity, development was not a matter of political institutions, nor of ideological prefferences. Rather, technology replaced ideology, and organization obviated the need for politics. Soldiers, engineers, agronomists, applied scientists, doctors, and lawyers working for the state viewed the problems of development as mainly ones of applied technology. They did not ponder, let alone consider, the need to transform attitudes and institutions if they were to induce and introduce the kind of radical and sustained change that was required. Or, as Ayubi concluded his study of the post-1952 period, "technology and organization cannot replace politics. . . ."[17] This was a basic flaw in Egypt's revolution and developmental nationalism.

Most of the authors considered here emphasize the central role of the state in the national economy as well as all other aspects of national life in Egypt. Where does that leave the matter of classes and their role in the attempted economic, social, and political transformation of Egypt after 1952? Where, in particular, does it leave Professor Binder's rural middle class? The simple answer could be that in Egypt it was only after 1935–36—others might argue after 1945—that social forces and national groups appeared expressing views about society, power, and the state that differed radically from those of the political elite and bureaucratic official class. But they were hardly allowed to develop. In 1952, the soldiers simply overwhelmed them and dispensed with them forcefully and quickly. Whether or not they constituted a class, or classes, was irrelevant and meaningless to the control of the state, and, with it, the state official class, or as some would prefer, the state bourgeoisie. The latter expanded or contracted according to the state's policy and needs.

The trouble with much of the social science writing about Egypt—and Professor Binder's work is a good example—is that despite its furious diligence and pious—almost puritanical—desire for a better preformance from the Egyptians, it suffers from not having consciously experienced pre-1952 Egypt—and not even pre-1962 Egypt. It also exhibits an unfamiliarity with the 1930s and 1940s, when politicized Egyptians, and especially those who came to power in 1952, were not conscious of class, but rather of moral, sectarian, and national indignation. But they all, sooner or later, joined the state official class; in fact, they struggled and scrambled to do so, some of them harboring a vague desire to control it one day. There is a kind of "research student"-contrived enthusiasm (and frustration) about much of this, especially when social scientists discover to their Western surprise that what they (or at least their theories) most desire does not lend itself, or respond, to their rational ministrations. One searches in vain for an *arresting* statement in all of this writing that depicts pithily, or encapsulates and captures, both the agony and the ecstasy of Egypt, the country and the people. One fears that reflection has been sacrificed to a highly mechanical and methodical dissection of highly rationalized economic requisites for Egypt's political evolution and survival. To this extent, there is, alas, no lasting quality to the written records—or exercises—themselves. They are not classic documents, but rather, only the recipes of one technician or another. Professor Waterbury's conclusions support this critique.

It is in Robert Tignor's much-needed economic history of the interwar period in Egypt that one meets the problem of a bourgeoisie in the proper sense of the term. Like Waterbury and Ayubi, Tignor emphasizes the important role of the state in economic development, when "all elements of the ruling elite looked to the state to further their interests."[18] The same can be said of the native bourgeoisie, consisting of native Egyptians and long-term resident foreigners. For

Tignor, the incipient "middle class," in the sense of a bourgeoisie, of the interwar period comprised local entrepreneurs headed by such men as Ṭal'at Ḥarb (Pasha), founder of the Bank Miṣr group of enterprises, and Aḥmad 'Abūd, the engineer-industrialist who founded a mini-industrial empire in Egypt, and the resident foreign businessmen and industrialists. Even though the modernization efforts of that period were dominated by the state, it was this nascent mixed native-foreign Egyptian bourgeoisie which tried to transform the economy during the interwar period, and to lay the foundations of the industrialization programs that were carried out later by the Nāṣir regime.

Tignor identifies three dominant groups before the Great War. These were the British political and military establishment, metropolitan (mainly European) capital, and the Egyptian landed oligarchy. He is, however, careful to emphasize that the British political establishment in Egypt were not simply the agents of metropolitan capital, since Egypt was of great strategic importance and value to British imperial interests. Then, by 1920, Egypt enjoyed the advantages of a relatively high standard of living and income from a lucrative cash export crop, cotton. It still lagged behind, however, in education, entrepreneurial, and managerial skills. Yet a few Egyptian nationalists like Ṭal'at Ḥarb and his cohorts, together with resident foreign entrepreneurs, in the interwar period, "articulated a vision of a transformed Egypt economically." The difficulty was that the foreigners among them never acquired the political status needed to realize their vision.

What Tignor suggests is the existence of a nascent local Egyptian bourgeoisie composed of natives and foreigners who were not committed to maintaining the status quo. They wished to diversify the economy by making it less dependent on cotton exports, and more autonomous by strengthening Egyptian control over it, in order to bring about structural change as well as economic growth. They failed, in part because they never achieved political power, which was retained largely, if not exclusively, by the "landed magnates." Despite the abolition of the Capitulations, taxation reform, and the creation of a central bank, as well as all the efforts for modernization of the private sector, and Ismā'īl Sidqī's Tariff Reform in 1930–31, which attempted to "forge an alliance of industrialists and landowners," the achievements of this native bourgeoisie were limited. There was ultimately development, but little growth, if any. There was no improvement in the standard of living. The growth of population, the inequitable distribution of income, and massive urbanization militated against these efforts. Above all, like all other segments of the country's elite, this native bourgeoisie also looked to the state to further its interests, but lacked the political power with which to influence the government's control over the economy. As for the resident foreign wing of this bourgeoisie, its commitment to European values in the face of rising Egyptian nationalism

> doomed them to being cast out of the country. Yet their contributions to Egypt's economic change were impressive. As a social group they were an alien enclave; as an economic force, they were dynamic and farsighted.[19]

Thus, the best survey of the economic history of Egypt in the interwar period—a very good complement to Charles Issawi's classic survey *Egypt in Revolution*,[20] which covered a longer historical period—emphasizes the predominance of the state over social classes, in the sense that the latter are still unable to mitigate, or reduce, its overwhelming power.

NOTES

1. *Description de l'Égypte* (Paris, 1809–12).

2. See Bibliography in P. J. Vatikiotis, *The History of Egypt*, 3d ed. (London, 1985).

3. For example, Ahmad Abul Fath, *L'Affaire Nasser* (Paris, 1962); Patrick K. O'Brien, *The Revolution in Egypt's Economic System* (London, 1966); Anouar Abdel Malek, *Egypt, Military Society* (New York, 1968); P. J. Vatikiotis, ed., *Egypt Since the Revolution* (London, 1968); Jean Lacouture, *Nasser* (Paris, 1971); Robert Stephens, *Nasser: A Political Biography* (London, 1971); Anthony Nutting, *Nasser* (London, 1972); Mohamed Heikal, *Nasser: The Cairo Documents* (London, 1972); Hrair R. Dekmejian, *Egypt Under Nasser* (London, 1972); Robert Mabro, *The Egyptian Economy, 1952–1972* (London, 1974); Raymond Baker, *Egypt's Uncertain Revolution Under Nasser and Sadat* (Cambridge, Mass., 1978).

4. See, for instance, David Hirst and Irene Beeson, *Sadat* (London, 1981); Mark Cooper, *Transformation of Egypt* (London, 1982); Mohamed Heikal, *Autumn of Fury* (London, 1983); Raphael Israeli, *Man of Defiance: A Political Biography of Anwar Sadat* (London, 1985).

5. Bloomington, Indiana, 1978.

6. Page 107.

7. Page 11.

8. Syracuse, 1979.

9. *The Egypt of Nasser and Sadat* (Princeton, 1983).

10. Pittsburgh, 1984.

11. One English edition of the Mosca classic is a translation by Hannah D. Kahn, edited by Arthur Livingston (New York, 1939).

12. Page 83.

13. *Bureaucracy and Politics in Contemporary Egypt* (London, 1980).

14. Page 185.

15. Pages 369, 370.

16. Page 252.

17. Page 501.

18. Pages 13–14.

19. Page 252.

20. London, 1963.

52
The Euphrates Expedition

M. E. Yapp

THE EUPHRATES EXPEDITION was an investigation of the suitability for steam navigation of the River Euphrates, and was carried on between 1835 and 1837. Full-length accounts of the Expedition were written by its leader, Colonel F. R. Chesney, and by another member, William Ainsworth; other members of the expedition wrote shorter pieces on particular aspects of the investigation.[1] To most readers, however, the expedition is best known through the well-known book by Halford L. Hoskins, entitled *British Routes to India.*[2] In that book Hoskins essayed two purposes. First, he offered an account of several attempts to develop communications between Britain and India, notably those routes which ran through the Middle East; and second, he suggested that these attempts constituted elements in a British design of improving and safeguarding the routes to India as well as evidence for the existence of that design; and further, that the protection of the routes to India was the major British interest in the Middle East and was at the heart of British concern with the Eastern Question. The fundamental interest of Britain in the Eastern Question, he claims, was to safeguard all the lines leading to India and to make them, if possible, into British routes.

According to Hoskins it was during the 1820s and 1830s that the protection of the routes to India came to predominate over older European concerns in British Eastern policy; like C. W. Crawley, Hoskins saw the Greek Revolt as a significant episode in this change of emphasis, and he linked with that event Muḥammad ʻAlī's invasion of Syria.[3] More than any other factor, argued Hoskins, it was the Egyptian occupation of Syria that created a political situation which originated a British interest in the reopening and development of the

Persian Gulf and Mediterranean routes after 1830. The strategic advantages of the route through Syria and Iraq to the Persian Gulf, especially when considered in relation to a possible threat to India from Russia, made that route of greater importance than the Red Sea route, which was subject to the control of Muḥammad ʻAlī. Hence Britain chose to support Ottoman claims rather than the rival pretensions of Muḥammad ʻAlī.

With Dwight E. Lee's *Great Britain and the Cyprus Convention Policy of 1878*, Hoskins' book has been quoted extensively by those many subsequent writers who have asserted that the protection of the routes to India was the leading factor in British policy in the Eastern Question.[4] Those who dispute this proposition, and assert either the preeminence of trade or the centrality of European politics, may follow two lines of argument: to demonstrate that statesmen were more concerned with these other factors; and/or to reexamine the episodes described by Hoskins (and Lee) and endeavor to show that the routes' interpretation does not fit the facts. The Euphrates Expedition, which forms an important element in the assemblage of episodes by which Hoskins supports his theory, provides a useful test of the possibilities of the second line of argument. The purpose of this article, which does not pretend to supply a complete account of the Expedition, is to consider the extent to which the Euphrates Expedition fits into a British concern for the routes to India. The principal new source used is the papers of the cabinet minister who was responsible to Parliament for the Expedition, the president of the Board of Control for the Affairs of India, Sir John Cam Hobhouse.

The Euphrates Expedition must be seen in the context of five developments: the technological breakthrough in steam navigation and the hopes held out for that new mode of transport; the new interest in the trade to India and in communications with the subcontinent; the development of Russophobia in Britain; the Eastern crisis caused by the activities of Muḥammad ʻAlī; and the evolution of British relations with Iraq. It will be helpful to begin with a brief review of each of these phenomena.

Steamboats were pioneered in France in the late eighteenth century, and their possibilities were much enhanced by the development of the paddle wheel in 1802 and of iron ships from 1821. To many men in the 1820s a commercial revolution was presaged by these advances, for not only could the new ships be used to improve transport in Europe, but they seemed peculiarly adapted to use on the great rivers of the Americas, Asia, and Africa, where they could open up whole continents for trade. One enthusiast was Macgregor Laird (1808–61) who took two small steamers up the Niger in 1832, although he was compelled to abandon the expedition when thirty-nine of the forty-eight Europeans died of fever or wounds. A more sedentary supporter of steam navigation was the novelist, Thomas Love Peacock (1785–1866), who was also a servant of the East India Company. In September 1829 Peacock prepared a lengthy paper on the application of steam to the internal and external commerce of India, in which he described the possibilities of the use of steamboats on the rivers of Asia.[5] Laird and Peacock were alike not only in their optimism about the use of steam for commerce, but also in their belief that steam could serve a still greater purpose. Trade was the agent of civilization; technological and material progress were indissolubly linked to the growth of mental and spiritual powers. As that other child of the Enlightenment, Lord William Bentinck, Governor General of India 1828–35, expressed the matter, steam would bring about a moral revolution in Asia.[6]

Peacock's paper also summarized progress in the development of steam communications with India. The great bulk of traffic with India was via the Cape of Good Hope and, although there were experiments with steam on this route, the cheapness of sail meant that, where time was of little consequence, goods would still be moved for many years by traditional means on this route. Where time was important, as with mails and passengers, the advantages of the use of steamboats on routes which ran through the Middle East were apparent. These routes were already well established; although the Red Sea route was first used in 1760, it was the route through Syria and Iraq which was the principal route for overland communication between Britain and India from the middle of the eighteenth century onward, and the servicing of the route was an important part of the duties of the East India Company's representatives in Basra, Baghdad, and Aleppo.[7] The journey across the desert from Basra to Aleppo was long, arduous, and occasionally dangerous, however; if the time taken for the sea journey from Bombay to Suez could be substantially reduced and the hazards of navigation in the Red Sea overcome, then the shorter land journey from Suez to the Mediterranean looked much more attractive, particularly after Muḥammad ʻAlī made the journey safer. Steam navigation supplied the key, and early experiments with rapid communications with India focused on the use of steam on the

Bombay-Suez route, linked to Mediterranean steam packets. In the early 1830s it seemed possible that the Syria-Iraq route would fall into disuse and British officials in the area lose one of their functions, just at the time when the end of the monopoly of trade by the East India Company and the Levant Company had removed another of their principal raisons d'être.

The rise of hostility to Russia in Britain has been chronicled in detail by J. H. Gleeson, and it will be sufficient here to note that there were three elements in that hostility.[8] The first was the image of Russia as the principal threat to the liberties of Europe, an impression greatly strengthened by Russia's suppression of the Polish revolt in 1830. The second was a picture of Russia as a threat to the peace of Europe by virtue of her ambitions in southeast Europe and her rivalry in that region with Austria, seen in Britain as the major element of stability in the East. The third element was the view of Russia as a threat to British interests in India, a view which drew popular strength from the writings of Colonel G. de Lacy Evans (1787–1870) who described the alleged ease with which Russia might march an army across Turkestan to attack India.[9] Experts derided Evans' speculations concerning a direct Russian invasion but asserted that a threat to India was in prospect through the establishment of Russian control over Iran, the gradual approximation of Russian power to the frontiers of India and the consequent unrest which would develop within India. During the 1830s projects designed to ward off this danger informed British policy in Central Asia.[10]

The fourth development was the rise of Muḥammad 'Alī of Egypt and his challenge to the authority of his sovereign, the Ottoman sultan, by his seizure of Syria in 1830 and his defeat of the Ottoman armies sent against him. For a moment it seemed possible that Muḥammad 'Alī might march on Istanbul and either overthrow the sultan or impose his control over the Empire. The Ottoman Empire appealed for help but the only response came from Russia. By the Treaty of Unkiar Skelessi (Hünkâr Iskelesi) Russia agreed to assist the Ottomans. Muḥammad 'Alī halted the Egyptian advance. To Britons, however, the Russo-Ottoman treaty appeared to allow Russia a dangerous degree of influence over Ottoman affairs and, during the following years, the foreign secretary, Lord Palmerston, bent his efforts toward the reduction of Russian influence and the confirmation of the independence and integrity of the Ottoman Empire. In his turn Muḥammad 'Alī sought legitimization of his position in Syria from the sultan and, subsequently, when that attempt appeared unavailing, looked to obtain from Europe recognition of his own independence. To Palmerston a bid for Egyptian independence was especially obnoxious because he foresaw that such a development was likely to precipitate a partition of the Ottoman Empire and, possibly, a general European war. Throughout the remainder of the 1830s, he endeavored to hold Muḥammad ʻAlī in check and, when the opportunity presented itself in 1840, he built a European coalition which administered a decisive check to Muḥammad ʻAlī's ambitions.[11] In these Palmerstonian schemes the Euphrates Expedition could play a useful minor role, for a British flag on the rivers of Iraq could deter Muḥammad ʻAlī from prosecuting, in an easterly direction, any further ambitions which he might entertain; and it could also demonstrate British support for Ottoman sovereignty.

The final necessary background element is British policy in Iraq, or Turkish Arabia, as it was known at the time. During the eighteenth century Britain, through the East India Company, had a modest and declining interest in trade with Iraq, and maintained an agent at Basra to supervise commercial dealings. In 1798, as a consequence of Bonaparte's invasion of Egypt, Britain acquired a brief political interest in Iraq which was given substance by the establishment of a political agent at Baghdad.[12] The agent represented the East India Company, although it is true to say that the Company and its Governments in India had no political interest in Iraq. There followed a long period during which the British agents in Iraq attempted to show that they served a useful purpose, whether from the point of view of trade, communications, politics, or strategy, and the Company tried, in a desultory fashion, to get rid of them. In 1806 the acting governor general, Sir George Barlow, stated that "the real and necessary duties of these Residencies (Baghdad and Basra) are in the opinion of the Governor General very limited," and recommended the closure of the Baghdad agency.[13] The renewed French scare of 1807–8 came to the rescue of the Baghdad agency, however, and it survived, aided by the circumstance that it was placed under the control of the Bombay Government which found the post a useful outlet for patronage. In 1821, however, the Baghdad Residency was abolished and British representation in Iraq reduced to an assistant Resident at Basra, Lieutenant Robert Taylor, who was placed under the authority of the Resident at Bushir. The decision reflected the continuing British Indian conviction that Iraq was of little or no interest.

It was during the early 1830s that Britons came to discover a new, political interest in Iraq deriving from the apprehension of a Russian threat to India through that country. The inspiration of this fear was Taylor, who, like his predecessors, endeavored to find some plausible reason for his official existence. During the Russo-Iranian war of 1826–28, it seemed possible that Russia might occupy the town of Sulaymanīya in Kurdish Iraq, and Taylor promptly gave voice to fears, similar to those expressed in the early years of the century, of a Russian threat to India. In January 1828 this alleged threat was used by him as the principal argument to support a proposal to assist Dā'ūd Pasha, the last of the semi-independent Mamlūk Pashas of Baghdad, to modernize his armed forces, and to move the Residency back from Basra to Baghdad.[14]

Taylor's proposals were received sympathetically at Bombay by the governor, Sir John Malcolm, who had put forward similar proposals in 1807 with reference to France. Malcolm, an altogether more subtle thinker than the Basra agent, gave Taylor's crude version of the Russian threat a more sophisticated polish. He discounted the possibility of a direct Russian invasion of India and argued, instead, that the spread of Russian influence in Iraq would lead to intrigue and unrest in India, obliging Britain to spend much more on defense.[15] In fact, Malcolm placed Iraq in exactly the same position as he had long set Iran, and advocated substantially the same policy in both countries.

Malcolm's arguments failed to persuade his own Council in Bombay and were coolly received in Calcutta, where the acting governor general, William Butterworth Bayley, declared that the danger from Russia was remote and in any case should be met not by expensive arrangements in Iraq, but by developing the resources of India. He rejected Dā'ūd's proposals and ordered Taylor to remain at Basra.[16] In London, however, Malcolm's proposals met a different reception. Although the Court of Directors of the East India Company supported Bayley, the new president of the Board of Control, Lord Ellenborough, who was strongly influenced by apprehensions of Russian menaces to British interests, welcomed Dā'ūd's proposals as likely to contribute to the strengthening of the Ottoman Empire against Russia. Taylor should go to Iraq to reorganize the pasha's troops with the aid of British officers, and he should develop river navigation. "Pray, jump at any offer of the Pasha of Baghdad if he comes to us again," he wrote to Malcolm.[17]

In the event, nothing came of the new initiative. Taylor had omitted from his arguments a decisive factor: Dā'ūd did not want a new army to resist Russia, but rather to oppose the attempts of his lawful Ottoman sovereign to establish control over Baghdad. Plainly, Britain could take no hand in this conflict. In 1831 Ottoman control was reestablished in Baghdad, and the opportunity to turn Iraq into a British buffer state had gone. Malcolm and Ellenborough also left their posts and the new president, Charles Grant, told Taylor to stay out of politics.[18]

Taylor was undeterred by this setback and in 1832 brought forward proposals on behalf of the new Ottoman governor of Baghdad which were almost identical with his earlier project launched on behalf of Dā'ūd. Curiously enough, Grant completely reversed the policy which he had proclaimed in 1831, and instructed Taylor to go to Baghdad and assist in training Iraqi troops and developing river navigation.[19] Why Grant should have changed his mind is unclear, although the phenomenon was not uncommon. In any case, nothing, apart from Taylor's move, came of his interest because it soon became apparent, even to Taylor, that the only use for British-trained Iraqi troops would be to fight British-trained Iranian troops, given the bad relations which subsisted between the two countries. Since Britain set the Iranian alliance above that with Iraq, Taylor was told to subordinate his actions to those of the minister in Tehran. Taylor tried to salvage something from the disaster, unconvincingly blaming Russia for the troubles between the Ottomans and Iran, and even suggesting that Britain should remove 'Alī Riḍā Pasha, the governor, on the grounds of his alleged sympathy for Russia, and occupy Iraq.[20] Grant squashed this proposal and instructed Taylor to preserve absolute neutrality and limit his activities to the collection of information.[21] His Middle East expert at the Board of Control, Henry Ellis, wrote of Taylor at this time:

> Like all persons employed in the countries that belong partly to Europe and partly to India, he is very anxious to bring himself within the sphere of European diplomacy and there is certainly something peculiar in the atmosphere of Baghdad and Bussora that diplomatizes the heads of all the Company's Residents there.[22]

Ellis believed that Taylor should revert to commercial duties alone. This, however, was impossible, for it was too difficult to defend a post on the scale of a Residency on commercial grounds alone, and

Taylor needed a political purpose to survive. Threats from Russia and Egypt were his lifeblood, and steam navigation and the Euphrates Expedition an answer to his prayers.

It is now time to introduce the leading figure in the Euphrates Expedition. Francis Rawdon Chesney (1789–1872) was an interesting and complicated man. Like many another son of a humble Ulster Scots family, he went into the army, and he was commissioned in the Royal Artillery in 1805. He saw no active service, however, and seemed content to pass his life in home garrisons. The pattern of his life changed markedly after the death of his first wife in 1825. He sought a position with the canceled Niger expedition and, in 1827–28, went on a long, lonely walking tour of Europe to study the battlefields of Napoleon. Returning from his journey, he was once more rejected by the great love of his life, Everilda Fraser, and was plunged into deep depression. In similar circumstances Arthur Conolly set off for Central Asia and Henry Lugard for East Africa. Chesney went to Istanbul to take part in the war against Russia. He had had no previous interest in the Middle East, and his decision seems to have been inspired wholly by the rebuff he had suffered.[23]

Chesney arrived in Istanbul with a cargo of Congreve rockets to sell to the Ottoman army, ideas of forming a rocket troop and defending the passes against the Russian invaders, and a plan for steamships on the Black Sea.[24] But the fighting was over, and Chesney was left to kick his heels in Istanbul for the winter. Being an excellent whist player, his company was in demand among the British community, and it seems likely that it was at the dinner and card tables of the British Embassy that Chesney first encountered the political and strategic notions which formed his stock in trade during the following years.[25] His new friends, who included the well-known Russophobe and friend of David Urquhart, Ross of Bladenburg, as well as the ambassador, Sir Robert Gordon, believed that Britain should have come to the aid of the Ottomans against Russia, and were full of speculations about the dangers from Russia to British interests, including possible threats to India. Chesney adopted these views and was soon given an opportunity to play an active part in promoting modes of counteraction.

Chesney accepted an invitation from Gordon to examine proposals for communications with India through Egypt. While still in Egypt carrying out this mission, he received a further commission to compare the merits of the Egyptian route with that through Syria and Iraq.

As it happened, this second request coincided with news of the death of his brother, and his own growing desire to accomplish some great enterprise which would secure for himself distinction and rewards was enhanced by the need to provide for his brother's family.[26] Ambition burned the more brightly in Chesney because it had to make up for lost time.

Having examined the route through Egypt, Chesney set off for Syria and Iraq, descending the Euphrates to the Persian Gulf (pausing to exchange views with the hospitable Taylor) before journeying through Iran, where he dabbled in plans for an Ottoman-Iranian alliance against Russia, and caused some diplomatic embarrassment. From Iran he went through Asia Minor to Istanbul to write up his reports, before returning to London on 26 September 1832. By now he had seen his opportunity as the architect of the Euphrates route, and he radically modified his earlier unfavorable view of the possibilities of navigation on the river and elaborated new strategic advantages for the route.

In London Chesney became a very active lobbyist for the Euphrates route. His biographers tell us that he inherited from his father "an implicit belief in the principle of working the sources of influence, and seldom left any great man unbesieged if his word were likely to affect the matter in hand."[27] Chesney had already met Stratford Canning in Istanbul and had enlisted his aid in winning over Palmerston. Also from Istanbul was Gordon, who was also employed in the cause. Chesney now cultivated certain prominent East India Company directors, including Sir Robert Campbell, whose son he had met in Iran, together with another ally, John McNeill, Sir Robert Inglis, and the aged John Sullivan, through whom he gained access to Sir Herbert Taylor and thence to William IV, who was also attracted to Chesney's schemes. Another denizen of Leadenhall Street, Thomas Love Peacock, sympathized with Chesney's aims. Among ministers, Lansdowne and Ripon showed interest, but the one man whom Chesney most wanted to secure, Palmerston, refused to meet Chesney. However, Charles Grant, the president of the Board of Control, a man notorious for his inability to resist the arguments of others, did lend his uncertain support to the project.

Chesney maintained his lobbying throughout 1833 and had his report printed at his own expense.[28] He was assisted in his campaign by the progress of the Eastern crisis consequent upon Muḥammad 'Alī's seizure of Syria; the resourceful Chesney devised plans for a steam expedition to penetrate the Dardanelles if Russia attempted to capture Istanbul.[29] However, it is noticeable that when the Eastern problem was raised in Parliament no connection was made with the navigation of the Euphrates; although Chesney's campaign had made some progress, his ideas were very far from general approval. Indeed, they were put before Parliament on only one occasion in 1833, when Inglis intervened in the debate on the third reading of the East India Company Charter Bill. "It was necessary," he said,

> that the Government should pay attention to the influence of Russia along the line of the Euphrates. We had greatly neglected the frontier policy on that side of our Indian Empire. . . . Whatever . . . was a great object with France, or with any other power, hostile to us, ought to have been equally a great object with ourselves: and we ought not to forget how frequently this line of attacking the English possessions in India had been in the contemplation of other powers. Whatever, then, pre-occupied and secured a direct and rapid communication between England and India was most important for the maintenance of our empire in Asia.[30]

In the debate, no one took up the point.

As time went on, Chesney concentrated his efforts on securing the appointment of a committee to look at the problem of steam navigation, a matter which certainly engaged the attention of the public. Hoskins claims, on the alleged authority of Chesney's *Narrative*, that the matter was considered at this time in Cabinet and that, although no agreement was reached, it was decided to take the matter to Parliament.[31] In fact the *Narrative* merely states that the matter was considered by some Cabinet ministers, and the biography mentions no Cabinet meeting, only a committee which met on 30 January 1834 and considered political problems, the advance of Russia, steam, and the Euphrates route.[32] Chesney believed that the committee had been assembled through the influence of the king. At all events, there is evidence of ministerial interest in the project from March 1834. Consideration was given to government financing of an experiment and in April, William Cabell, one of the permanent officials at the Board of Control, who was going over the papers to brief Grant, inquired if Chesney would be prepared to lead an expedition to the Euphrates.[33] On 3 June, Grant moved for the appointment of a select committee to inquire into the best means of promoting steam communication with India; the motion was agreed, and the committee commenced its inquiries on 9 June. It was a triumph for Chesney.

The report of the committee was also eminently satisfactory, for it recommended that Parliament should vote £ 20,000 to pay the costs of an expedition to test the suitability of the Euphrates for steam navigation. The committee examined twenty-five witnesses, of whom some gave purely technical evidence about steam or navigation, and others concentrated on the problems of the Red Sea, the Cape route, and the Mediterranean. But twelve witnesses gave evidence about Iraq and the Persian Gulf, a circumstance which reflected both Chesney's propaganda and the presupposition of the committee that the merits of the Red Sea route were already established and that the unknown element was the Euphrates route. In its report, the committee argued that a regular line of steam communication should be established via the Red Sea, but that it was desirable that there should be an alternative route available during the months of June to September, when the southwest monsoon made the westbound route through the Red Sea difficult. The Euphrates route was untried, but the committee believed navigation was possible through the whole year, any doubts relating only to the period November to February when the river was at its lowest. It concluded that the Euphrates route offered many advantages, physical, commercial, political, and financial.

The committee's decision to try the Euphrates route was based upon technical and commercial grounds; only the brief reference to political advantages suggests that there could have been strategic factors in its decision. Whether the committee's reticence on politics was due to lack of conviction, doubts whether Parliament would respond to such arguments, or concern that to give publicity to political interests might have diplomatic repercussions is unclear. Certainly, it received ample evidence on strategic and political questions affecting the route.

Judging from questions directed to witnesses, the political factor which most agitated the minds of committee members was the attitude of the Arab tribes which inhabited the banks of the Euphrates. There was no evidence that the committee was interested in the possibility that Britain might cultivate support among the Arabs which might under some circumstances be turned to political advantage; rather, there were fears that Arab hostility might endanger the security of the route. But from Chesney and Peacock the committee received detailed testimony concerning the Russian danger.

Peacock argued that it was important to prevent Russia from occupying the Euphrates and excluding Britain from the river. The establishment of a British steamship service would give Britain a right to object to Russian interference. Peacock also put in evidence his 1829 memorandum in which he was more explicit about the possibility that Russia might establish control over the Euphrates and form a position on the Gulf from which she could menace India. The 1829 paper had been written under the dual influence of the Russian successes against the Ottomans, which culminated in the Treaty of Adrianople, and of the theories of Lieutenant Colonel G. de Lacy Evans. At that time, Peacock had accepted Evans' argument to the effect that a Russian invasion of India was most likely to follow the Turkestan route. Although subsequent discussion had demolished that view, Peacock cherished some lingering affection for it and was later, in 1839, to advocate using British steamboats on the Oxus to obstruct the Russian advance in the same way that in 1834 he wished to employ them on the Euphrates. Peacock was strongly supported by Chesney, who claimed that the Euphrates afforded the easiest Russian approach toward India; Russia could plant a fully equipped force at Basra six or seven weeks after setting off from her existing position in Transcaucasia, and two or three weeks later be in control of Cape Jask at the mouth of the Gulf. From Jask, Russia could either move to a direct invasion of India or, which was more likely, adopt a threatening posture "which would of itself shake our moral power over the natives," and oblige Britain to undertake a large expenditure on ships and troops. Chesney claimed that the political advantages of the Euphrates route, by establishing a barrier against Russia, exceeded the value of the route for communications. He also threw in, for good measure, some other merits including commerce, the reinvigoration of the Ottoman Empire by the revival of the overland trade, and the conversion of Arabia to Christianity. But Chesney staked his main case on the strategic argument, and wisely so, for the communications arguments pointed strongly toward concentration on Egypt. It is interesting, however, that he did not use the argument that the Euphrates route could be useful in checking the ambitions of Muḥammad ʿAlī; again, the omission may have been tactical, because the testimony of other witnesses was very strongly in favor of Muḥammad ʿAlī, who was depicted as a farsighted, modernizing ruler, with whom Britain would do well to cooperate.

Chesney's strategic arguments received some support from other witnesses (Lieutenant Colonel W. M. G. Colebrooke, James Bird, and W. J. Bankes, M.P.), but it is interesting to note that his views failed to appeal to those who knew the region best. The greatest disappointment to Chesney came from Sir Harford Brydges-Jones who, while he was Resident at Baghdad at the beginning of the century, had been among the first to point to the Russian danger. In 1834, however, Jones ridiculed the threat. True, Russia might easily descend the river, but she could derive no advantage from the possession of Basra; no Russian force could advance on India by land or sea. Gideon Colquhoun, who had served many years in Basra, claimed that Russia had no interest in the area, and Colonel E. G. Stannus, a former Resident in the Persian Gulf, who preferred the Red Sea route, maintained that there were no political or commercial advantages in the Euphrates route. In the circumstances, it is unsurprising that the committee placed no emphasis on the political advantages of the route, and while it is evident that some members found the arguments attractive, there was no consensus that the route could serve strategic ends.

Curiously enough, after Parliament had accepted the report and voted the money, Chesney hesitated to accept the leadership of the Expedition for which he had campaigned so long. Not until 20 August did he agree to go, after other candidates had refused the job or had been deemed unsuitable. Without more information it is difficult to understand his reluctance. It may be that ministers had doubts about his fitness for the task, or it may be that Chesney himself was beginning to think that the Expedition, the advantages of which he had oversold and the difficulties of which he had underplayed, might fail and the failure rebound upon the head of its leader and chief promoter. Or it may be that he was dissatisfied with the conditions of his appointment, in particular that he should not have the authority of martial law.

Once he had accepted the job, Chesney threw himself into the work with his familiar energy. He took great care in choosing the members of the expedition and in supervising the collection of its stores and equipment. His interference in the design of the two steamboats being built by Laird appears to have been unfortunate; they were certainly underpowered, and one was subsequently condemned by the naval officers as wholly unsuitable for the work.[34] But it may be that Chesney was already too conscious of the problems of the shortage of money. The East India Company topped up the Parliamentary grant with another £ 5,000, but it was plain that it was going to be exceedingly difficult to keep within the budget.

At one point the Expedition was almost canceled. The Whig ministry fell, and the president of the Board of Control in the new Tory ministry, Lord Ellenborough, appeared to Chesney to be less than enthusiastic. Ellenborough had grave doubts, later justified, about Chesney's fitness to lead the expedition. Chesney was told by his friend Inglis that Ellenborough thought Chesney "a red-hot Irishman, likely to lead others to serious danger."[35] But for the fact that preparations were already well advanced, and the circumstance that the king was still a strong supporter, Chesney thought it might have been canceled and at one time, when the Ottoman government hesitated to grant the necessary permission, Ellenborough almost did stop it.

Ellenborough also had doubts about Chesney's chosen route. One of Chesney's most controversial decisions was that the expedition should land at the Syrian coast and the vessels be transported in sections to the Euphrates, where they would be assembled prior to descending the river to Basra. Leaving aside the physical problems of the land transport and the possible political problems (with Muḥammad 'Alī in occupation of Syria), the logical starting point was in any case Basra, because the main doubts about the navigability of the river concerned its ascent, not the descent. Ellenborough wanted the Expedition to proceed via Basra although, with some help from the Admiralty, Chesney eventually won the argument and got his way. Chesney's insistence on the Syrian route requires some explanation, however. It may be that he quite underestimated the difficulties of the overland journey, although they should have been obvious enough, and had no idea that there might be problems with Muḥammad 'Alī. Another possible explanation is that he feared that if he chose the Basra route he would come immediately under the orders of the government of India, which did not want the Expedition. There is yet another explanation, however, which seems possible in the light of future events: namely, that Chesney feared that a Basra starting point would immediately expose the difficulties of the ascent of the Euphrates, which he had obscured during his campaign. A Syrian starting point might give the Expedition an opportunity to demonstrate some merits before its fundamental weakness was exposed.

The Expedition set sail from Liverpool in February 1835 and arrived at the mouth of the Orontes (modern Suveydiye) on 3 April. Landing began on 6 April; Chesney did not wait for permission, believing the Egyptian authorities would be opposed. He was to blame Egypt for serious delays to the expedition, principally through the failure of the local authorities to provide transport. There seems little doubt that Chesney was seeking a scapegoat. He was a poor organizer, and there was a real shortage of labor and animals for transport in

Syria; when Chesney agreed to pay the market price he obtained what he wanted quickly enough, and he later conceded that he would have been better advised to buy transport rather than hire it.[36] Chesney's reluctance to buy was due to his worries about money and time. The expedition was due to terminate on 31 July 1836 and Chesney's case for an extension would be strengthened if he could show the delays were not his fault. In fact, it was his decision to assemble the *Tigris* steamer to try the navigation of the Orontes, and his mistaken decision, when the vessel failed miserably to overcome the current, not to disassemble it but to divide it into large sections, which accounted for some of the loss of time; and it was his original decision to choose the Syrian route which was the principal culprit, because, instead of the few weeks that he had estimated, it took almost a year to transport the vessels to the Euphrates and assemble them there. And this feat was achieved only by the exercise of the most remarkable ingenuity by the officers (mainly Royal Navy) whom he had chosen.

The Egyptian attitude, however, requires some explanation. Chesney asserted that Egyptian hostility was inspired by Russia, and similar reports came from Cairo and Istanbul, where the ambassador, Lord Ponsonby, as diligently anti-Russian as Chesney, supported the commander's complaints.[37] But it is difficult to believe these stories of Russian hostility for which hard evidence is lacking. If Russia did not welcome the expedition, she had too little interest in the matter to do much to oppose it. More probably it was the Ottoman authorities who encouraged Ponsonby to believe in the threat of a Russo-Egyptian alliance directed against Britain. The Ottomans did not want to accede to the British request that they should issue a direct order to Muḥammad ʻAlī to assist the expedition, because this would constitute a degree of recognition of the pasha's position in Syria.

A second possible explanation for Egyptian opposition is that Muḥammad ʻAlī wanted Iraq and thought that the presence of the Euphrates Expedition would make the realization of this goal more difficult. It was suggested that the Ottoman attitude was dictated by a wish for the Expedition to proceed via Basra, so that it might convey supplies to fortify Basra and Baghdad against an Egyptian attack. Certainly, in 1837–38 there were fears that Muḥammad ʻAlī might turn against Iraq.[38] But such alleged designs do not seem relevant to Muḥammad ʻAlī's attitude in 1835.

In 1835 Muḥammad ʻAlī was still primarily concerned with obtaining recognition of his position in Syria. It so happened that in September 1834 Palmerston's letter asking for Muḥammad 'Alī's assistance with the expedition crossed a letter from Muḥammad 'Alī asking for British consent to the pasha's proposal to make himself independent of the Porte. Inevitably, the two questions became linked. When Muḥammad 'Alī received Palmerston's uncompromising rejection of his own proposal, it may well be (there is no direct evidence) that he thought he could obtain some recognition of his control of Syria by refusing to cooperate with the Expedition until ordered to do so by the Porte. And if the Porte refused, he could hope that Britain would have to deal with him directly, thereby strengthening his claim to independence. The gambit, if such it was, failed; Muḥammad 'Alī quickly abandoned it and, on 25 May, issued orders to give the expedition full support. The delay was not considerable and Muḥammad 'Alī did not bow to British threats. At the end of June, Palmerston prepared a dispatch to Campbell, the consul in Egypt, threatening naval action against Muḥammad 'Alī, but this ultimatum was not sent. Palmerston substituted for it a modest warning which was itself unnecessary; the foreign secretary's comment that "Mohamad Ali has knocked under" is misleading.[39]

Although there is little evidence for any of the three explanations of Egyptian hesitation offered above, the first two seem quite improbable. Russia had little to gain from support for Muḥammad 'Alī; her policy was to support Ottoman integrity. Muḥammad 'Alī's subsequent cooperation with the expedition argues against the second explanation and, in any case, such ambitions as he cherished toward Iraq could be secured only with British support. The logic of Muḥammad 'Alī's position points to the third explanation and also accounts for Palmerston's strong reaction to the pasha's initial failure to cooperate. There is no evidence that Palmerston took any other interest in the Expedition at this time, and his willingness to threaten violent action against Muḥammad 'Alī is both a sign that he did not think Russia would support the pasha and evidence of his determination to support Ottoman integrity. The Expedition provided an opportunity to administer a cheap and strong rebuke to Muḥammad 'Alī as a warning against talk of independence.

The Euphrates Expedition failed in its principal object of proving the suitability of the Euphrates route for the rapid transit of mails. Not until March 1836 did the Expedition leave Bir after the assembly of the vessels was completed. Descending the river the steamboats frequently ran aground, and on 21 May the *Tigris* was lost at Iskarīya, between Raqqa and 'Ana, with the loss of twenty men. With his usual courage, Chesney persisted with the Expedition and continued his descent to Basra in the remaining vessel, the *Euphrates*. The *Euphrates* then required a complete refit before it could attempt the ascent of the river, and Chesney bravely took it across the Gulf to Bushir. By this time, many of the members of the Expedition had lost heart and Chesney was almost inclined to abandon the venture. However, he persuaded his officers to stay on, and replaced those of his crewmen who took their discharge with volunteers from Indian Navy ships. By 1 September 1836, the *Euphrates* was back at Muhammara. At this point, the appropriate course would have been to have attempted the ascent of the Euphrates, but instead Chesney explored the Karun on the grounds that the Indian mails had not arrived, and then ascended the Tigris to Baghdad, where he received news that the time limit for the Expedition had been extended to 31 January 1837. Returning to Qurna, the *Euphrates* encountered the *Hugh Lindsay* which had been waiting for two weeks with the Indian mails. Chesney could avoid the crucial test no longer, and on 24 October began the ascent of the Euphrates. He anticipated, he declared optimistically, no difficulties. The fears of his naval officers, however, were amply vindicated when the *Euphrates* came to grief in the Lamlum Marshes when the cross head of the air pump of the larboard engine fractured. Chesney could have tried a repair, but he seized the excuse to abandon a hopeless venture, took the vessel back to Basra, and set off for India, leaving the Expedition under the command of his friend, Major J. B. B. Estcourt, to investigate the Karun further. Estcourt broke up the Expedition on 31 January 1837 and its members returned overland to England.

Chesney remained in India five months. He had lost nothing of his persuasiveness and secured the support of the governor of Bombay, Sir Robert Grant. Grant issued orders to keep the Expedition in being, although these orders arrived too late to prevent Estcourt from terminating the business. If the Expedition were abandoned, wrote Grant, Russia would seize control of the route through Iraq and it "will cost us millions in the sequel."[40] "Grant has been bitten by Chesney and is gone a little crazy," was the comment of the president of the Board of Control, Sir John Hobhouse, when he read this letter.[41] Chesney also made an effort to see the governor general, Lord Auckland, but Auckland had already made up his mind to abandon the Euphrates route. Defeated, Chesney returned to England, via the Gulf and the desert, and arrived in London on 8 August 1837.

For the failure of the Expedition Chesney blamed Russian intrigue, Muḥammad ʻAlī, local officials, and France. Without any evidence the French vice consul at Basra, Victor Fontanier, was accused of inciting the local Arabs to oppose the Expedition. While it is true that Fontanier harbored deep suspicions of British designs in Iraq, it is also plain that he made no attempt to interfere with the Expedition. Chesney also blamed some of his colleagues and claimed that he was placed at a disadvantage by the refusal of martial law powers. It is true that there was friction among the officers, and on one occasion the second in command of the Expedition, Henry Blosse Lynch, imprisoned two of his colleagues aboard the *Tigris* because they quarreled with his brother who was a passenger aboard the vessel.[42] But it would be more true to say that Chesney received from his subordinates a commitment far beyond anything that might have been expected. The main cause of the failure was the unsuitability of the steamers for the work they had to accomplish, and for this and for other matters Chesney must accept a major share of the blame. He made a series of bad decisions, continually disobeyed orders, and diverted the Expedition from its main object. Hobhouse came to distrust him. "He is not a safe man," he wrote.[43] If the Expedition were to be continued in any form, Hobhouse intended that it should be under the command of Lynch.

In fact the Expedition was continued under a different name (the Euphrates flotilla of the Indian Navy), and under the command of Lynch. For practical purposes Lynch came under the authority of the Board of Control in London and received his instructions from the president, Hobhouse. His first instructions were simple and modest. Lynch was to show the British flag on the rivers of Iraq. Nothing was to be attempted which might fail.[44]

Why did Hobhouse continue the Euphrates experiment? The answer is clear: a British presence in Iraq would assist British policy in the Eastern crisis. In June 1838 Muḥammad ʻAlī had indicated his intention to declare his independence. Failing a united European response and in the absence of agreement in Cabinet or full support for vigorous British action from Parliament, Palmerston and Hobhouse were obliged to employ Indian resources to make a unilateral demonstration of British power in the Middle East. This demonstration was accomplished through the annexation of Aden and the maintenance of a presence in Iraq. At one time, Hobhouse contemplated the dispatch of troops from India to support the Flotilla and even thought wistfully of the annexation of Iraq, an action proposed once more by Taylor, who was never the man to pass by such an opportunity.[45] The importance of Iraq, Hobhouse informed Taylor, was real and recognized in London, "but I cannot say that you have furnished us with any pretext for occupying or taking possession of that portion of the Turkish Empire; and I do not see how we could, with common decency, undertake any such exploit."[46]

As the crisis of summer 1838 subsided so also did Hobhouse's heady enthusiasms. In October he informed Taylor that the government had no wish to interfere in the concerns of the Pashalik, and Taylor should not suggest the contrary to anyone.[47] And he urged Lynch to make better arrangements for the safe conveyance of mails "which is of a great deal more importance than the politics of Turkish Arabia."[48] In December 1838 he again warned Lynch and Taylor against direct political interference and against promising "assistance which we might afterwards be unable to afford."

> The navigation of the Tigris and Euphrates is a legitimate object which we have a fair pretext for attempting and by the accomplishment of which, we may silently obtain that influence with the Arab tribes which will more than half ensure our permanent predominance.[49]

Hobhouse reproved Taylor for suggesting the establishment of a British protectorate over Baghdad. Such things were easy to propose, he wrote, "but it is not easy to change a whole course of policy [support for Ottoman integrity], and assume an attitude totally different from that which has been hitherto maintained." He had been amused, he remarked, by Taylor's recommendations at a time when the great European powers were at peace. Not, Hobhouse said, that he would be sorry if the matter could be accomplished, "but such developments are not made upon paper." As for Muḥammad 'Alī, Taylor should not worry what he would do, because the pasha would do only what Britain told him to do.[50]

During the following months, Taylor and Lynch continued to put forward proposals for extending British commitments in Iraq. Should we, asked Lynch in May 1839, continue to prop up an effete Turkish power or should we support the Arab tribes who would make wonderful soldiers and provide a permanent defense for India?[51] But Hobhouse offered no encouragement. During the Eastern Crisis he was content to show the flag. And this Lynch achieved with some success. In the summer of 1838 Lynch succeeded in passing the Lamlum marshes in the *Euphrates* and reaching Hīt; and in 1840, reinforced with three new steamers ordered by Hobhouse during his 1838 enthusiasms, he extended his survey work. In 1841 the flotilla was at Beles, where the ships provided a diversion during the operations in Syria against Ibrāhīm.[52] But with the ending of the Eastern Crisis, the last reason for maintaining the Flotilla departed, and in 1842 all but one of the steamers were transferred to the Indus. Only the little *Nitocris* continued to show the flag on the rivers of Iraq under the command of Felix Jones. Indeed, under Jones the *Nitocris* even performed the service originally expected of the steamers, namely of carrying some mails up the Euphrates, a service which was continued until the Iraq overland mail was finally abolished in 1862, and all overland mails transferred to the dominant Red Sea route. Even after the abolition of the Indian Navy in 1863, steamers continued to ply the rivers; the last steamer and stores were acquired by Lynch's brother, Thomas Kerr Lynch, who founded the Euphrates and Tigris Steam Navigation Company.

In conclusion, it will be useful to review the Euphrates Expedition in the light of the objectives assigned to it. The first and ostensible object was to improve the service for passengers and mails between Britain and India. By 1837 it was clear that the Red Sea route was established as the preferred all-year-round route for communications, and the Euphrates route was unnecessary.[53] A second object was trade. There is no evidence of any pressure by British or Indian merchants for the opening of the rivers for trade, and no evidence of any notable increase in trade as a result of the Expedition.[54] The Euphrates Expedition must therefore be judged in relation to its political objectives.

The political objectives were varied. One purpose was the old one of building an influence among the Arab tribes which could be used to reinforce British representations in Istanbul, or to secure British interests in the event of the disintegration of the Pashalik of Baghdad, or to raise a force to oppose an invasion by destroying the enemy's subsistence.[55] These goals were unattainable, because the Arabs wanted protection against Ottoman authority, and this Britain would not supply.[56] A second purpose was the establishment of British influence in Iraq so as to ward off any threat from Russia to India or any threat from Muḥammad ʻAlī to Baghdad. It was the Russian threat which had figured in the original schemes of Chesney and Taylor: the Egyptian element was added in the mid-1830s.

The predominance of political objectives in the conception of the Euphrates Expedition receives apparent confirmation in a letter written by Hobhouse to the East India Company chairmen in December 1835. In the light of the possibility that the Pashalik of Baghdad might break up, the Expedition, argued Hobhouse, could be an important factor in establishing such a British influence in Iraq

> as would prevent that important province from falling sacrifice to the ambitious designs of Mehemet Ali in the first instance, and finally of the Russian Emperor . . . the masters of India cannot be indifferent to the chances that may fix the standard of Russia on the shore of their own seas. That the political sight of the British Flag on the Euphrates and Tigris might long retard, if not altogether prevent, such a catastrophe no one can deny; and as the Gulf into which these great rivers discharge themselves is now under the protection of your own marine force, the extension of your influence in that part of Asia seems required by a due regard to your own security.[57]

But Hobhouse's argument cannot be accepted at face value. The purpose of his letter was to persuade the East India Company to take financial responsibility for the Expedition, the funds voted by Parliament being exhausted and the Treasury refusing to find more.[58] Hence his choice of arguments was intended to demonstrate that the Expedition was an Indian interest. In fact, the chairs were wholly unconvinced; they saw no interest but that of communications, and for that purpose they were well satisfied with the Red Sea. They wanted nothing to do with the Euphrates Expedition.

The doubts about the honesty of Hobhouse's use of the political argument are strengthened by the evidence of his correspondence with Lord Auckland, the governor general of India. To Auckland, Hobhouse used only communications arguments, because Auckland would accept no political arguments. The governor general had no notion of quarreling with Muḥammad ʻAlī; in September 1838 he wrote, "I would rather quarrel with Turkey than with Egypt and would earnestly wish to remain friends with both."[59] Nor did Auckland respond to the communications argument: the Red Sea was good enough for mails, and India had no other interests. He regarded the Euphrates Expedition as a waste of time.

The almost universal hostility toward the Expedition on the part of those who bore responsibility for India must raise serious questions about the political arguments connected with the security of India and of the routes to India. In fact, political arguments did have their importance, but that importance derived from Europe, not from India. Hobhouse, throughout the period, followed the lead of Palmerston. As we have seen, Palmerston had no apparent interest in the Expedition, as long as it was justified by reference to Indian interests. His interest derived from his view that it was necessary to contain the ambitions of Muḥammad 'Alī, not because they threatened India but because they threatened the Ottoman Empire, and through that state the peace of Europe. Once the 1838 crisis, caused by Muḥammad 'Alī's independence project, was over, Palmerston's interest in the Expedition diminished, and so also did that of Hobhouse. Thereafter, Hobhouse returned to political matters only briefly in response to the alleged threat that the Arabian campaign of Khurshid Pasha might be turned against Basra.[60] His response, however, was much less vigorous than it had been in 1838. Once Palmerston came to believe that a European coalition to check Muḥammad 'Alī could be formed, the motive for unilateral British action departed; such action could, indeed, be an obstacle to European agreement.

The true origin of the Euphrates Expedition is to be found not in strategy, but in personal ambition. To Chesney, Taylor, and Lynch, an active British policy in Iraq was a means of securing their jobs and advancing their personal interests. They were able propagandists, and readily exploited the possibilities presented by contemporary political transactions. It was the weakness of the commercial and communications case for the Euphrates which drove them to place their reliance upon politics and strategy. They had some success in persuading their fellows and they were helped by the fortune of the Eastern crisis. But in the end they failed, partly for technological reasons, but ultimately because they could not persuade the people who mattered most that their arguments had real substance. So Chesney went back to the army, Lynch to retirement in Paris, and Taylor was replaced in Baghdad in 1843. He was, wrote the then president of the Board of Control, Lord Fitzgerald, "the most unsatiable Gibemouche that has ever been diplomatically employed. What he sends as collected information is absolute nonsense."[61]

NOTES

1. F. R. Chesney, *The Expedition for the Survey of the Rivers Euphrates and Tigris*, 2 vols. (London, 1850), and *Narrative of the Euphrates Expedition* (London,

1868); W. F. Ainsworth, *Personal Narrative of the Euphrates Expedition*, 2 vols. (London, 1888). Other members wrote accounts in contemporary periodicals or included descriptions in their memoirs. Extracts from some of these are in S. Lane-Poole, ed., *Life of General F. R. Chesney* (London, 1885).

2. Halford L. Hoskins, *British Routes to India* (New York, 1928; repr. London, 1966).

3. C. W. Crawley, "Anglo-Russian Relations, 1815–40," *Cambridge Historical Journal*, III (1929), pp. 47–73.

4. Dwight E. Lee, *Great Britain and the Cyprus Convention Policy of 1878* (Cambridge, Mass., 1934).

5. T. L. Peacock, Memorandum on the application of steam to the internal and external commerce of India, September 1829, in Parliamentary Papers, House of Commons, *Report of the Select Committee on Steam Navigation to India*, 14 July 1834, Appendix.

6. Parliamentary Papers, House of Commons. *Report of the Select Committee on the Best Means of Establishing a Steam Communication with India by Way of the Red Sea*, 9 June 1837. Evidence (Q 1954).

7. Holden Furber, "The Overland Route to India in the Seventeenth and Eighteenth Centuries," *Journal of Indian History*, XXIX (1951), which, however, seriously underestimates the use of the route through Syria and Iraq.

8. J. H. Gleason, *The Genesis of Russophobia in Great Britain* (Cambridge, Mass., 1950).

9. G. de Lacy Evans, *The Designs of Russia* (London, 1828), and *On the Practicability of a Russian Invasion of British India* (London, 1829).

10. See M. E. Yapp, *Strategies of British India: Britain, Iran and Afghanistan, 1798–1850* (Oxford, 1980), Part II.

11. The best account of Palmerston's Eastern policy is in Sir Charles Webster, *The Foreign Policy of Palmerston, 1830–1841*, 2 vols. (London, 1951).

12. See M. E. Yapp, "The Establishment of the East India Company's Residency at Baghdad, 1798–1806," *Bulletin of the School of Oriental and African Studies*, XXX (1967), pp. 323–36.

13. Edmonstone to Bombay 21 January 1806, in Osbourne, Memo., n.d. Bengal Political and Secret Proceedings 382. Consultation 20 May 1806, No. 4236. India Office Records.

14. Taylor to Bombay 13 January 1828, cited in M. G. Khan, "British Policy in Iraq, 1828–43," Ph.D. diss., London 1967, pp. 379–80. This unpublished thesis contains the most comprehensive account of British policy in Iraq during the period with which it is concerned and the fullest description of the Euphrates Expedition.

15. Malcolm, Minute 23 March 1828, in Khan, op. cit., 381–85.

16. Governor General in Council (GGC) to Bombay 2 May 1828, ibid.

17. Ellenborough to Malcolm (pte) 27 October 1829, Public Records Office (PRO) 30/9/4 Part 5/2.

18. Secret Committee (SC) to GGC No. 237 of 1 July 1831, Boards Drafts of Secret Letters to India (BDSLI) 8. India Office Records.

19. SC to GGC No. 257 of 28 April 1832, BDSLI 8.

20. Khan, op. cit., p. 207.

21. SC to GGC No. 292 of 18 April 1834, BDSLI 8.

22. Ellis to Grant 13 September 1833, Factory Records Persia (FRP) 48. India Office Records.

23. Lane-Poole, op. cit., p. 169.

24. Colonel Chesney, *The Russo-Turkish Campaigns of 1828 and 1829*, 2d ed. (London, 1854), pp. xxvi–xxviii.

25. Lane-Poole, op. cit., pp. 187–88.

26. Ibid., p. 194.

27. Ibid., p. xi.

28. *Reports on the Navigation of the Euphrates, Submitted to Government by Captain Chesney, R.A.* (London, 1833).

29. Lane-Poole, op. cit., p. 271.

30. Hansard Series III, 20, col. 19, 26 July 1833.

31. Hoskins, op. cit., p. 156.

32. Chesney, *Narrative*, p. 146; Lane-Poole, op. cit., p. 269.

33. Lane-Poole, op. cit., p. 33.

34. Ibid., p. 306.

35. Ibid., p. 282.

36. Chesney to Hobhouse (pte) 1 December 1835, Home Miscellaneous Series (HM) 838, 338. India Office Records. See also Estcourt to Hobhouse (pte) 16 December 1835, HM 833, 121; Chesney to Hobhouse (pte) 27 February 1836, ibid., 128; Cameron to Hobhouse (pte) 12 October 1836, HM 837, 133; Ainsworth, op. cit., i, 198; Chesney, *Narrative*, p. 205; Khan, op. cit., pp. 204–6.

37. Chesney to Hobhouse (pte) 22 September 1835, HM 838, 338.

38. Cp. Lynch to Hobhouse (pte) 11 August 1837, HM 838, 215; Hobhouse to Lynch (pte) 28 October 1837, HM 838, 218.

39. Palmerston to Hobhouse (pte) 30 June 1835, Add. MS 46915 fol. 11, British Library.

40. Grant to Hobhouse (pte) 18 January 1837, HM 841, 2.

41. Hobhouse to Auckland (pte) 29 March 1837, HM 838, 11.

42. Chesney to Hobhouse (pte) 5 May 1837, HM 838, 79.

43. Hobhouse to Auckland (pte) 26 January 1837, HM 837, 171.

44. Hobhouse to Grant (pte) 9 June 1838, HM 838, 388; see also p. 433.

45. Taylor to Hobhouse (pte) 9 July 1838, HM 841, 168.

46. Hobhouse to Taylor (pte) 28 August 1838, HM 838, 435.

47. Hobhouse to Taylor (pte) 24 October 1838, HM 838, 463.

48. Hobhouse to Lynch (pte) 24 October 1838, HM 838, 461.

49. Hobhouse to Lynch (pte) 26 December 1838, HM 839, 63.

50. Hobhouse to Taylor (pte) 26 December 1838, HM 839, 61.

51. Lynch to Hobhouse (pte) 28 May 1839, HM 841, 369.

52. C. R. Low, *History of the Indian Navy*, 2 vols. (London, 1877), II, 47.

53. Hobhouse to Auckland (pte) 1 June 1837, HM 838, 49.

54. Both Chesney (Chesney to Hobhouse [pte] 9 June 1836, HM 837, 4) and Lynch (Lynch to Hobhouse [pte] 15 October 1838, HM 841, 230).

55. Chesney to Hobhouse (pte) 20 April 1836, HM 833, 160.

56. Lynch to Hobhouse (pte) 11 August 1837, HM 838, 215. Lynch continued to press the Arab policy.

57. Hobhouse to Chairs 20 December 1835, HM 833, 57.

58. Spring-Rice to Hobhouse (pte) 4 August 1836, HM 837, 36.

59. Auckland to Lushington (pte) 17 September 1838, Add. MS 37694 fol. 47, British Library.

60. Hobhouse to Lynch (pte) 4 March 1840, HM 839, 293. Hobhouse had abandoned his earlier ideas of sending Indian troops to Basra, and in September 1839 informed Sir James Carnac, the governor of Bombay, that Muḥammad ʻAlī could be stopped only by European action. (Hobhouse to Carnac [pte] 16 September 1839, HM 839, 193.)

61. Fitzgerald to Ellenborough (pte) 9 April 1843, PRO 30/12/42.